MARKETING

MARKETING

Concepts and Strategies

SEVENTH EDITION

WILLIAM M. PRIDE
Texas A & M University

O. C. FERRELL
Memphis State University

HOUGHTON MIFFLIN COMPANY   BOSTON

DALLAS   GENEVA, ILLINOIS   PALO ALTO   PRINCETON, NEW JERSEY

To Nancy, Michael, and Allen Pride

To Linda Ferrell

PART OPENING IMAGES: Part I, Guido Alberti Rossi/The Image Bank; Part II, Dawson Jones/Stock, Boston; Part III, Wayne Eastep Inc.; Park IV, photo courtesy of Media General; Part V, Terry Heffernan; Part VI, Hing/Norton; Part VII, Brett Froomer/The Image Bank.

Figure on page 319 adapted from *Strategic Marketing* by D.J. Kollat, R.D. Blackwell, J.E. Robeson, copyright © 1972 by Holt, Rinehart and Winston, Inc., reprinted by permission of the publisher.

Printed in the U.S.A.

Library of Congress Catalog Number: 90–83026

ISBN: 0–395–43358–4

ABCDEFGHIJ–D–9543210

BRIEF CONTENTS

CONTENTS

PREFACE

There is no question that we live in an increasingly complex and changing world. Recent political and economic upheavals have shaken established systems to their foundations; ease of communication and commercial exchange has transformed us into a global society; and environmental concerns have become a number-one priority for many people in the world. To provide insight into marketing in this changing environment, *Marketing: Concepts and Strategies* presents a comprehensive framework that integrates traditional concepts with the realities of today.

The study of marketing has always been relevant because it is a key element in the functioning of society. Our economy, our lifestyles, and our physical well-being are directly or indirectly influenced by marketing activities. *Marketing: Concepts and Strategies* is widely used because it provides comprehensive coverage and stimulates student interest with its readable style and extensive use of interesting, real-life examples. The depth of coverage in this text provides students with a full understanding of the marketing discipline.

CHANGES IN THE SEVENTH EDITION

Marketing: Concepts and Strategies has always focused on the concepts most relevant to the development and implementation of marketing strategies. To keep pace with new developments in the teaching and practice of marketing, the Seventh Edition provides the most comprehensive and up-to-date coverage of international marketing and of marketing ethics and social responsibility.

- In including a new chapter entitled "Marketing Ethics and Social Responsibility," we have provided a new approach to one of the most important yet misunderstood topics in marketing. We offer a framework for understanding ethical decision making and delineate ethical issues that students will confront in the real world of marketing. We also emphasize the need for social responsibility in organizations and provide approaches for making socially responsible decisions to be effective and successful in the business community.
- The international chapter has been completely revised to include a section on regional trade alliances and markets. Topics include the U.S. and Canada Free Trade Agreement, Mexico trade and the Maquiladora industries, Europe 1992, Pacific Rim Nations, and changing relations with eastern Europe and the Soviet Union.

The overall design and basic features of the text were carefully reviewed and revised to make the material as fresh and appealing as possible.

■ We have created a new attractive visual presentation of the content to stimulate readers' interest. In addition, we have made the writing more lively, readable, and concise.
■ We have also included many new examples of challenges facing real organizations as they market products and attempt to take advantage of unexpected opportunities in this changing world.
■ Marketing Updates integrate fundamental marketing issues and concepts with the real-world practice of marketing. These inserts are generally about well-known companies and focus on issues that students will be able to relate to easily.
■ Each chapter continues to include two cases, half of which are completely new and the other half updated for the 1990s.

In addition, text coverage has been completely revised and updated to include major changes and additions such as the following:

■ A greater emphasis on environmental issues and the protection of our environment (see especially Chapters 2 and 3).
■ New coverage on VALS lifestyles and recent research findings in the area of segmentation (see Chapter 4).
■ The latest research and new developments in our understanding of consumer buying behavior (see Chapter 5).
■ Material on recent developments and issues related to conducting marketing research studies (see Chapter 7).
■ More in-depth discussion of environmentally safe packaging (see Chapter 8).
■ Expanded coverage of the merger trend among wholesalers (see Chapter 11).
■ A new section on retail positioning and expanded coverage on retail locations (see Chapter 12).
■ An updated section on recent findings related to information processing and communication in marketing (see Chapter 14).
■ A more concise and strategic approach to understanding the nature and impact of advertising and publicity (see Chapter 15).
■ A completely revised and updated section on sales promotion (see Chapter 16).
■ A total reorganization of the chapter on strategic market planning, including more concise coverage of portfolio analysis and a new section outlining the marketing plan (see Chapter 19).
■ A new section on internal marketing (see Chapter 20).
■ Updated and increased depth of coverage on industrial marketing (see Chapter 21).
■ More in-depth coverage of services marketing incorporating the latest research in this area and increased emphasis of nonbusiness marketing as a subset of services marketing (see Chapter 22).

Despite these changes, we believe that users of earlier editions will find the seventh edition to have the same strengths that have made previous editions so popular. This edition, like its predecessors, explores the depth and breadth of the field, combining detailed real examples with comprehensive coverage of marketing concepts and strategies used widely outside of the business world as well as in it. By focusing on the universal concerns of marketing decision makers, we demonstrate that marketing is a vital and challenging field of study—and a part of our world that influences almost everything we do.

FEATURES OF THE SEVENTH EDITION

As always, our goal is to provide a comprehensive and practical introduction to marketing, easy both to teach and to read. The entire book is structured to excite students about marketing and to make learning comprehensive and efficient.

- *Learning objectives* open each chapter, providing students an overview of new concepts.
- A *vignette* introduces each chapter's marketing issues.
- *Examples* of familiar products and organizations make concrete and specific the generalizations of marketing theory.
- Two *Marketing Updates* in each chapter, focusing on recognizable firms and products, extend the discussion of marketing topics and decisions.
- Numerous *figures, tables, and photographs* augment the text and increase comprehension.
- A complete chapter *summary* reviews the major topics discussed.
- A *list of important terms* (highlighted in the text) provides a study aid, helping students expand their marketing vocabulary.
- *Discussion and review questions* encourage further study and exploration of chapter material.
- Two concise, stimulating *cases* provoke discussion at the end of each chapter.
- A *diagram of the text's organization* at the beginning of each part shows students how material in the upcoming part relates to the rest of the book.
- A *strategic case* at the end of each part helps students integrate concepts from throughout that part.
- A *glossary* at the end of the text defines more than 625 important marketing terms.
- *Appendices* discuss career opportunities in marketing and provide additional insights into financial analysis in marketing.
- A *name index* and a *subject index* enable students to find topics of interest quickly.

TEXT ORGANIZATION

We have organized the seven parts of *Marketing: Concepts and Strategies* to give students a theoretical and practical understanding of marketing decision making. Part I presents an overview of marketing, discusses general marketing concepts, and considers the marketing environment, ethics and social responsibility, types of markets, target market analysis, buyer behavior, and marketing research. Part II focuses on the conceptualization, development, and management of products. Part III examines marketing channels, institutions, and physical distribution. Part IV covers promotion decisions and methods, including advertising, personal selling, sales promotion, and publicity. Part V is devoted to pricing decisions and Part VI to marketing management and discussions of strategic market planning, organization, implementation, and control. Part VII explores strategic decisions in industrial, service, nonbusiness, and international marketing.

STUDENT SUPPLEMENTS

In addition to numerous instructor support materials (discussed in the front of the Instructor's Manual), the package for this text includes aids to both teaching and learning:

- A Study Guide helps students to review and integrate chapter content.
- *Marketing Cases,* Fourth Edition, supplements the cases in the text with 42 others that demonstrate how marketing decisions are made.
- *Marketing: A Simulation,* Second Edition, gives student teams working on micro-computers valuable experience in making marketing decisions.
- *Microstudy Plus,* a self-instructional program for microcomputers, reinforces learning of key concepts.
- *Micromarket: Computer Applications,* a Lotus-based disk, includes exercises that provide hands-on experience in making marketing decisions.

Through the years, professors and students have sent us many helpful suggestions for improving the text and ancillary components. We invite your comments, questions, or criticisms. We want to do our best to provide materials that enhance the teaching and learning of marketing concepts and strategies. Your suggestions will be sincerely appreciated.

William M. Pride
O. C. Ferrell

ACKNOWLEDGMENTS

Like most textbooks, this one reflects the ideas of a multitude of academicians and practitioners who have contributed to the development of the marketing discipline. We appreciate the opportunity to present their ideas in this book.

A number of individuals have made many helpful comments and recommendations in their reviews of this or earlier editions. We appreciate the generous help of these reviewers.

Joe F. Alexander
Abilene Christian University

Mark I. Alpert
University of Texas at Austin

Linda K. Anglin
Mankato State University

George Avellano
Central State University

Emin Babakus
Memphis State University

Siva Balasabramanian
University of Iowa

Joseph Ballinger
Stephen F. Austin State University

Guy Banville
Creighton University

Thomas E. Barry
Southern Methodist University

Charles A Bearchell
California State University—Northridge

Richard C. Becherer
Wayne State University

Russell Belk
University of Utah

W. R. Berdine
California State Polytechnic Institute

Stewart W. Bither
Pennsylvania State University

Roger Blackwell
Ohio State University

Peter Bloch
Louisiana State University

Wanda Blockhus
San Jose State University

Paul N. Bloom
University of North Carolina

James Brock
Montana State University

John R. Brooks, Jr.
Houston Baptist University

Jackie Brown
University of San Diego

William Brown
University of Nebraska at Omaha

William G. Browne
Oregon State University

John Buckley
Orange County Community College

Karen Burger
Pace University

Pat J. Calabro
University of Texas at Arlington

Linda Calderone
*State University of New York
College of Technology at Farmingdale*

Joseph Cangelosi
East Tennessee State University

James C. Carroll
University of Southwestern Louisiana

Terry M. Chambers
Appalachian State University

Larry Chonko
Baylor University

Barbara Coe
North Texas State University

Ernest F. Cooke
Memphis State University

Robert Copley
University of Louisville

John I. Coppett
University of Houston—Clear Lake

Melvin R. Crask
University of Georgia

William L. Cron
Southern Methodist University

Benjamin J. Cutler
Bronx Community College

Norman E. Daniel
Arizona State University

Lloyd M. DeBoer
George Mason University

Ralph DiPietro
Montclair State College

Lee R. Duffus
University of Tennessee

Robert F. Dwyer
University of Cincinnati

Thomas Falcone
Indiana University of Pennsylvania

Gwen Fontenot
University of Northern Colorado

David J. Fritzsche
University of Portland

Robert Grafton-Small
University of Strathclyde

Harrison Grathwohl
California State University—Chico

Alan A. Greco
University of N. Carolina—Charlotte

Blaine S. Greenfield
Bucks County Community College

Shanna Greenwalt
Southern Illinois University

Thomas V. Greer
University of Maryland

Jim L. Grimm
Illinois State University

Charles Gross
University of New Hampshire

Roy R. Grundy
College of DuPage

Joseph Guiltinan
University of Notre Dame

Joseph Hair
Louisiana State University

Timothy Hartman
Ohio University

Salah S. Hassan
George Washington University

Del I. Hawkins
University of Oregon

Merlin Henry
Rancho Santiago College

Charles L. Hilton
Eastern Kentucky University

Elizabeth C. Hirschman
Rutgers, State University of New Jersey

Robert D. Hisrich
University of Tulsa

George C. Hozier
University of New Mexico

John R. Huser
Illinois Central College

Donald L. James
Fort Lewis College

Ken Jensen
Bradley University

Yvonne Karsten
Mankato State University

Jerome Katrichis
Temple University

Philip Kemp
DePaul University

William M. Kincaid, Jr.
Oklahoma State University

Roy Klages
State University of New York at Albany

Douglas Kornemann
Milwaukee Area Technical College

Priscilla LaBarbara
New York University

Patricia Laidler
Massasoit Community College

Bernard LaLonde
Ohio State University

Richard A. Lancioni
Temple University

David M. Landrum
Central State University

Irene Lange
California State University—Fullerton

Charles L. Lapp
University of Dallas

Virginia Larson
San Jose State University

John Lavin
Waukesha County Technical Institute

Hugh E. Law
East Tennessee University

Ron Lennon
Barry University

Jay D. Lindquist
Western Michigan University

David H. Lindsay
University of Maryland

Paul Londrigan
Mott Community College

Anthony Lucas
Community College of Allegheny County

William Lundstrom
Old Dominion University

Stan Madden
Baylor University

Gerald L. Manning
Des Moines Area Community College

Gail Marco
Robert Morris College

James McAlexander
Iowa State University

John McFall
San Diego State University

Jack McNiff
State University of New York College of Technology at Farmingdale

Lee Meadow
Bentley College

Brian Meyer
Mankato State University

Stephen J. Miller
Oklahoma State University

William Moller
University of Michigan

Kent B. Monroe
Virginia Polytechnic Institute

Carlos W. Moore
Baylor University

Hal Teer
James Madison University

Dillard Tinsley
Stephen F. Austin State University

Hale Tongren
George Mason University

James Underwood
University of S.W. Louisiana

Barbara Unger
Western Washington University

Tinus Van Drunen
Universiteit Twente (Netherlands)

Poondi Varadarajan
Texas A & M University

Dale Varble
Indiana State University

Charles Vitaska
Metropolitan State College

James F. Wenthe
University of Georgia

Sumner M. White
Massachusetts Bay Community College

Alan R. Wiman
Rider College

Ken Wright
West Australia College of Advanced Education—Churchland Campus

George Wynn
James Madison University

Our special thanks go to Gwyneth M. Vaughn for her extreme diligence in editing and improving the manuscript. Gwyn assisted with many aspects of the project, and we are grateful. We deeply appreciate the assistance of Barbara Gilmer and Diane Dowdell for providing editorial suggestions, technical assistance, and support. For assistance in completing numerous tasks associated with the text and ancillary items, we express appreciation to Marty Butler, Amy Flanagan, Mike Hartline, Neil Herndun, Keith Jones, Emily Kays, Linda Lindbaugh, Wendy Reed, Marissa Salinas, and Debbie Thorne.

We are grateful to Mary Gilly, University of California at Irvine, for developing the casebook, *Marketing Cases,* Fourth Edition. Our special thanks go to Sundar A. Bharadwaj and Anandhi S. Bharadwaj for creating and developing the exercises in the *Micromarket: Computer Applications* program. For creating *Marketer: A Simulation,* Second Edition, we wish to thank Jerald R. Smith, University of Louisville. We express our sincere thanks to George H. Lucas, Jr. for writing numerous new items for the Test Bank. A great deal of thanks also go to Edwin C. Hackleman for developing the computerized test preparation program and for creating *Microstudy Plus.* We appreciate the efforts of Margaret Cunningham, Queens University, in developing the *Marketing Strategy* computer disk. We especially thank Jim L. Grimm, Illinois State University, for drafting the financial analysis appendix.

We express appreciation for the support and encouragement given us by our colleagues at Texas A & M University and Memphis State University. We also appreciate the efforts of the 36 marketing educators who contributed guest lectures for the *Lecture Enrichment Series, Volume 2* and whose names are included in the Preface of that ancillary. This teaching aid would not have been possible without their willingness to share their knowledge and ideas.

MARKETING

PART I AN ANALYSIS OF MARKETING OPPORTUNITIES

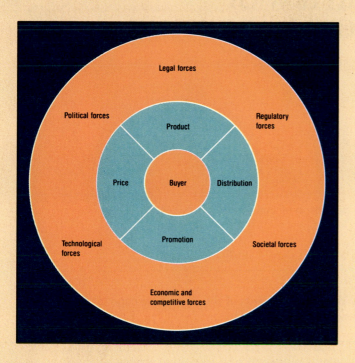

In Part I we introduce the field of marketing and provide a broad perspective from which to explore and analyze various components of the marketing discipline. In the first chapter we define marketing and discuss why an understanding of it is useful in many aspects of everyday life, including one's career. We provide an overview of general strategic marketing issues such as market opportunity analysis, target markets, and marketing mix development. Marketers should understand how environmental forces can affect customers and their responses to marketing strategies. In Chapter 2 we discuss political, legal, regulatory, societal, economic and competitive, and technological forces in the environment. Chapter 3 deals with the role of ethics and social responsibility in marketing decisions and activities. Chapter 4 focuses on one of the major steps in the development of a marketing strategy: selecting and analyzing target markets. Understanding elements that affect buying decisions enables marketers to better analyze customers' needs and evaluate how specific marketing strategies can satisfy those needs. In Chapter 5 we examine consumer buying decision processes and factors that influence buying decisions. We stress organizational markets, organizational buyers, the buying center, and the organizational buying decision process in Chapter 6. Chapter 7 includes a discussion of the role of a marketing information system and the basic steps in the marketing research process. ◆

1 AN OVERVIEW OF STRATEGIC MARKETING

Objectives

To understand the definition of marketing

To understand why a person should study marketing

To gain insight into the basic elements of the marketing concept and its implementation

To understand the major components of a marketing strategy

To gain a sense of general strategic marketing issues, such as market opportunity analysis, target market selection, and marketing mix development

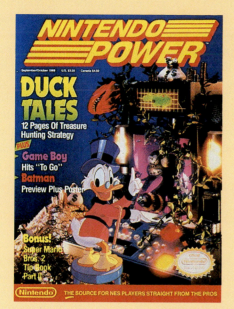

Just as established video game companies were suffering from severe, worldwide sales decline, Nintendo of Japan introduced its Nintendo Entertainment System in the United States. Nintendo took the devastated video game industry by storm, realizing that the depressed market was due to frustrated, rather than fickle, customers.

Nintendo officials recognized that overproduction and poor product quality caused the industry's crash. Nintendo's strategy was to offer the consumer more sophisticated, arcade-quality games while keeping a strict guard over product quality and availability. Nintendo now has $2.6 billion in sales of the $3 billion video game market.

Nintendo's basic system costs around $100, with individual game cartridges selling from about $35 to $50. The company's video game success generated a variety of other ventures: a Saturday morning cartoon program, a cereal, a magazine with a total of more than one million paid subscription households, and an assortment of T-shirts, lunch boxes, posters, and school supplies. Nintendo marketers are eager to make the company name synonymous with video games.

The primary goal of Nintendo's marketing effort is to maintain high product quality. Nintendo strictly controls the supply and number of licensed game titles. It provides each game licensee with a shrink-wrapped package bearing the official Nintendo Seal of Approval. It also carefully monitors the total volume of systems and cartridges shipped to retailers, irritating some retailers, as they are unable to meet customer demands. ◆

Photo © 1990 Nintendo. Nintendo Poser® is a registered trademark of Nintendo.

Based on information from James Cox, "Nintendo Keeps the Frenzy High," USA Today, Nov. 21, 1989, pp. 1B–2B; Joe Mandese, "Power Plays," Marketing & Media Decisions, March 1989, pp. 101–103, 106; Stewart Wolpin, "How Nintendo Revived a Dying Industry," Marketing Communications, May 1989, pp. 36–38, 40.

Why is Nintendo successful in an industry that some analysts view as declining? The company is using effective marketing efforts. Nintendo has determined what customers want: high quality, arcadelike video games. Its marketing effectiveness is reflected in the fact that it has achieved a large share of the video game market in just a few years.

This first chapter is an overview of the concepts and decisions covered in the text. In this chapter we first develop a definition of marketing and explain each element of the definition. Then we look at some of the reasons why people should study marketing. We introduce the marketing concept and consider several issues associated with implementing it. Next we define and discuss the major tasks associated with marketing strategy: market opportunity analysis, target market selection, marketing mix development, and management of marketing activities. We conclude by discussing the organization of this text.

MARKETING DEFINED

If you ask several people what *marketing* is, they will respond with a variety of descriptions. Marketing encompasses many more activities than most people realize. Since it is practiced and studied for many different reasons, it has been, and continues to be, defined in many ways, for academic, research, or applied business purposes. According to one definition,

> Marketing is the process of planning and executing the conception, pricing, promotion, and distribution of ideas, goods, and services to create exchanges that satisfy individual and organizational goals.[1]

This definition, developed by the American Marketing Association (AMA), is widely accepted by academics and marketing managers.[2] It emphasizes that marketing focuses on planning and executing activities to satisfy customers' demands. Whereas earlier definitions restricted marketing as a business activity, this definition is broad enough to indicate that marketing can occur in nonbusiness organizations.

Although the AMA definition is certainly acceptable, we believe that marketing should be defined still more broadly. A definition of marketing should indicate that marketing consists of activities performed by individuals and organizations. In addition, it should acknowledge that marketing activities occur in a dynamic environment. Thus we define marketing as follows:

> **Marketing** consists of individual and organizational activities that facilitate and expedite satisfying exchange relationships in a dynamic environment through the creation, distribution, promotion, and pricing of goods, services, and ideas.

In this definition, an **exchange** is the provision or transfer of goods, services, and ideas in return for something of value. Any product may be involved in a marketing

1. Reprinted from *Dictionary of Marketing Terms,* Peter D. Bennett, Ed., 1988, p. 54, published by the American Marketing Association. Used by permission.

2. O. C. Ferrell and George Lucas, "An Evaluation of Progress in the Development of a Definition of Marketing," *Journal of the Academy of Marketing Science,* Fall 1987, p. 17.

TABLE 1.1 *Possible decisions and activities associated with marketing mix variables*

MARKETING MIX VARIABLES	POSSIBLE DECISIONS AND ACTIVITIES
PRODUCT	Develop and test-market new products; modify existing products; eliminate products that do not satisfy customers' desires; formulate brand names and branding policies; create product warranties and establish procedures for fulfilling warranties; plan packages, including materials, sizes, shapes, colors, and designs
DISTRIBUTION	Analyze various types of distribution channels; design appropriate distribution channels; design an effective program for dealer relations; establish distribution centers; formulate and implement procedures for efficient product handling; set up inventory controls; analyze transportation methods; minimize total distribution costs; analyze possible locations for plants and wholesale or retail outlets
PROMOTION	Set promotional objectives; determine major types of promotion to be used; select and schedule advertising media; develop advertising messages; measure the effectiveness of advertisements; recruit and train salespersons; formulate compensation programs for sales personnel; establish sales territories; plan and implement sales promotion efforts such as free samples, coupons, displays, sweepstakes, sales contests, and cooperative advertising programs; prepare and disseminate publicity releases
PRICE	Analyze competitors' prices; formulate pricing policies; determine method or methods used to set prices; set prices; determine discounts for various types of buyers; establish conditions and terms of sales

exchange. We assume only that individuals and organizations expect to gain a reward in excess of the costs incurred. So that our definition will be fully understood, we now examine each component more closely.

■ Marketing Consists of Activities

Marketing products effectively requires many activities. Some are performed by producers; some are accomplished by intermediaries, who buy products from producers or from other intermediaries and resell them; and some are even performed by purchasers. Marketing does not include all human and organizational activities, but only those aimed at facilitating and expediting exchanges. Table 1.1 lists several major categories and examples of marketing activities. Note that this list is not all-inclusive. Each activity could be subdivided into more specific activities.

■ Marketing Is Performed by Individuals and Organizations

All organizations perform marketing activities to facilitate exchanges. Businesses as well as nonbusiness organizations, such as colleges and universities, charitable organizations, community theaters, and hospitals, perform marketing activities. For example, colleges and universities and their students engage in exchanges. To receive instruction, knowledge, entertainment, a degree, the use of facilities, and sometimes room and board, students give up time, money, and perhaps services in the form of labor; they may also give up opportunities to do other things. Likewise,

FIGURE 1.1
Exchange between buyer and seller

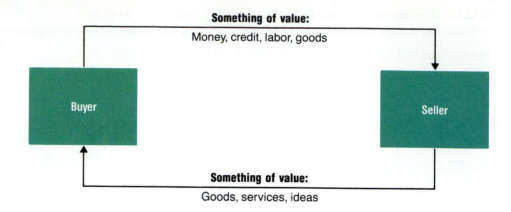

Something of value:
Money, credit, labor, goods

Buyer

Seller

Something of value:
Goods, services, ideas

many religious institutions engage in marketing activities to satisfy their "customers." For example, Willow Creek Community Church in South Barrington, Illinois conducted a survey to determine why some of the residents did not attend any church in the community. The church used the survey results to develop programs to satisfy the religious needs of these residents.[3] Even the sole owner and operator of a small neighborhood store decides which products will sell, arranges deliveries to the store, prices and displays products, advertises, and assists customers.

■ **Marketing Facilitates Satisfying Exchange Relationships**

For an exchange to take place, four conditions must exist. First, two or more individuals, groups, or organizations must participate. Second, each party must possess something of value that the other party desires. Third, each party must be willing to give up its "something of value" to receive the "something of value" held by the other party. The objective of a marketing exchange is to receive something that is desired more than what is given up to get it, that is, a reward in excess of costs. Fourth, the parties to the exchange must be able to communicate with each other to make their somethings of value available.[4]

Figure 1.1 illustrates the process of exchange. The arrows indicate that the parties communicate that each has something of value available to exchange. Note, though, that an exchange will not necessarily take place just because these four conditions exist. Nevertheless, even if there is no exchange, marketing activities still have occurred. The somethings of value held by the two parties are most often products and/or financial resources, such as money or credit. When an exchange occurs, products are traded for other products or for financial resources.

An exchange should be *satisfying* to both the buyer and the seller. In fact, in a study of marketing managers, 32 percent indicated that creating customer satisfaction was the most important concept in a definition of marketing.[5] Marketing activities, then, should be oriented toward creating and maintaining satisfying exchange relationships. Marketing Update 1.1 focuses on how companies build strong relationships with customers. To maintain an exchange relationship, the buyer must be

3. Thomas A. Stewart, "Turning Around the Lord's Business," *Fortune,* Sept. 25, 1989, pp. 116–28.

4. Philip Kotler, *Marketing Management: Analysis, Planning, Implementation, and Control,* 6th ed. (Englewood Cliffs, N.J.: Prentice-Hall, 1988), p. 6.

5. Ferrell and Lucas, p. 20.

COMPANIES THAT CUSTOMERS LOVE

There are some companies that customers just seem to love; for whatever reason, these relatively few firms have the advantage of a devoted clientele. Usually, clients are attracted to certain businesses because of product or service quality, or both. Since competitors of these popular companies are eager to capture the customers who consistently return to their favorites, the beloved firms must keep striving to maintain their reputations as superior businesses.

According to a customer-service consulting firm, to keep a customer a business typically spends one-fifth of the amount that it spends on acquiring a new one. It makes sound financial sense for business owners to invest in training employees to focus on customers' desires and listen attentively to customers' complaints and suggestions. A handful of disgruntled customers each telling numerous relatives and friends about even minor dissatisfactions might significantly harm the reputation of a business.

Practices as minor as ensuring that the hood of a car is free from black fingerprints after an oil change or that there are plenty of napkins to accompany a home-delivered piping-hot pizza can sometimes make the difference when a customer is deciding which firm to call on. Companies with large and loyal followings tend to pay close attention to details, realizing that the details are what normally differentiates firms.

Seattle-based Nordstrom Inc., a department store chain, has built its sparkling reputation on customer service and attention to detail. Customers obviously love Nordstrom: it is number one in sales per square foot among all the department stores in the United States. As customers walk through the doors of a Nordstrom store, their coats are checked courteously at the door. Live piano music creates a distinct atmosphere for the shopping experience. Nordstrom stores even provide parents of infants with tables for changing diapers. The 90-year-old company recently expanded to the East Coast after years of exclusively serving the western United States. The primary concern of Nordstrom executives is that their new stores live up to the status and service quality of their established locations.

Victor Alhadeff, founder of Egghead Software, took what he learned as an employee of Nordstrom and applied it to the computer software industry. Alhadeff allows his customers to try out software before they purchase it—a practice almost unheard of among software sellers. He offers a wide selection of merchandise and has a very liberal merchandise-return policy. Judging by Alhadeff's success, his commitment to pleasing customers will make Egghead Software a strong competitor and another of the small number of companies that customers love.

SOURCES: Ripley Hotch, "Treat Customers with Respect," *Nation's Business,* Nov. 1988, p. 30; Tom Peters, "Know How to Profit in Your Own Time? Service Pays," *Houston Chronicle,* Jan. 4, 1988, p. IV-2; and Francine Schwadel, "Courting Shoppers," *Wall Street Journal,* Aug. 1, 1989, pp. A1, A9.

FIGURE 1.2 *Customer satisfaction.*
Lands' End tries to build strong customer relationships through a guarantee of satisfaction.

SOURCE: Courtesy of Lands' End

satisfied with the good, service, or idea obtained in the exchange; the seller must be satisfied with the financial reward or something else of value received in the exchange. For instance, to encourage satisfying exchange relationships with its customers, Lands' End, which markets clothing through catalogs (see Figure 1.2), does not sell anything that its employees would not be comfortable wearing themselves. Furthermore, the telephone operators, who answer the firm's toll-free order number within three rings, are knowledgeable about Lands' End merchandise and can make suggestions about styles, sizes, and colors. These and other activities ensure that Lands' End customers are not only satisfied with the exchange, but that they keep calling back to order more merchandise. Ensuring customer satisfaction boosted Lands' End's sales by 65 percent in three years.[6]

Maintaining a positive relationship with buyers is an important goal for a seller, regardless of whether the seller is marketing cereal, financial services, or an electric generating plant. Through buyer-seller interaction, the buyer develops expectations about the seller's future behavior. To fulfill these expectations, the seller must deliver on promises made. Over time, a healthy buyer-seller relationship results in

6. Susan Caminiti, "A Mail-Order Performance: Lands' End Courts Unseen Customers," *Fortune*, Mar. 13, 1989, pp. 44–45.

FIGURE 1.3
Building satisfying customer relationships. In this advertisement, Toyota is promoting the idea that it desires to build long-term customer relationships by providing high quality service.

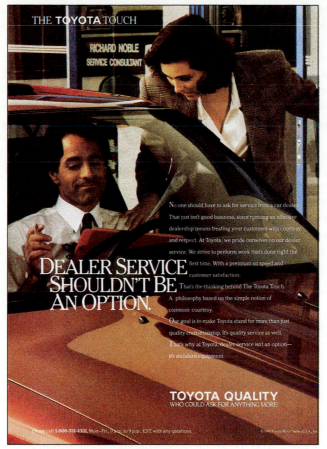

SOURCE: Courtesy of Toyota Motor Sales, U.S.A., Inc.

interdependencies between the two parties. The buyer depends on the seller to furnish information, parts, and service; to be available; and to provide satisfying products in the future. For example, car buyers depend on Toyota and other car makers to provide quality automobiles, as well as service, warranties, information about various car models, fair prices, and convenient dealer locations. The Toyota advertisement in Figure 1.3 emphasizes the firm's commitment to high quality service. The seller depends on the buyer to continue purchasing from the seller. Toyota depends on buyers to purchase its automobiles to supply it with the funds needed to meet its organizational objectives.

■ Marketing Occurs in a Dynamic Environment

The marketing environment consists of many changing forces: laws, regulations, political activities, societal pressures, changing economic conditions, and technological advances. Each of these dynamic forces has an impact on how effectively marketing activities can facilitate and expedite exchanges. For example, the development and acceptance of facsimile (FAX) machines has given businesses another vehicle through which to promote their products. Some office supply sellers and restaurants send advertisements about their goods and services to businesses and individuals through their FAX machines.

■ Marketing Involves Products, Distribution, Promotion, and Pricing

Marketing means more than simply advertising or selling a product; it involves developing and managing a product that will satisfy certain needs. It focuses on making the product available at the right place, at the right time, and at a price that is acceptable to customers. It also requires transmitting the kind of information that will help customers determine if the product will in fact be able to satisfy their needs.

■ Marketing Focuses on Goods, Services, and Ideas

We already have used the word *product* a number of times in this chapter. For purposes of discussion in this text, a *product* is viewed as being a good, a service, or an idea. A *good* is a physical entity one can touch. A Mazda Miata, a compact disc player, Kellogg's Frosted Flakes, a bar of soap, and a kitten in a pet store are examples of goods. A *service* is the application of human and mechanical efforts to people or objects in order to provide intangible benefits to customers. Services such as airplane travel, dry cleaning, hair styling, banking, medical care, and day care are just as real as goods, but an individual cannot actually touch them. *Ideas* include concepts, philosophies, images, and issues. For instance, a marriage counselor, for a fee, gives spouses ideas to help improve their relationships. Other marketers of ideas include political parties, churches, and schools.

WHY STUDY MARKETING?

After considering the definition of marketing, one can understand some of the obvious reasons why the study of marketing is relevant. In this section we discuss several perhaps less obvious reasons why one should study marketing.

■ Marketing Activities Are Used in Many Organizations

From 25 to 33 percent of all civilian workers in the United States perform marketing activities. The marketing field offers a variety of interesting and challenging career opportunities, such as personal selling, advertising, packaging, transportation, storage, marketing research, product development, wholesaling, and retailing. In addition, many individuals who work for nonbusiness organizations engage in marketing activities. Marketing skills are used to promote political, cultural, church, civic, and charitable activities. The advertisement in Figure 1.4 encourages support of the World Wildlife Fund, a not-for-profit organization. Whether a person earns a living through marketing activities or performs them without compensation in nonbusiness settings, marketing knowledge and skills are valuable assets.

■ Marketing Activities Are Important to Businesses and the Economy

A business organization must sell products to survive and to grow. Directly or indirectly, marketing activities help sell an organization's products. By doing so, they generate financial resources that can be used to develop innovative products. New products allow a firm to better satisfy customers' changing needs, which in turn enables the firm to generate more profits. For example, each year *Fortune* publishes a list of what its staff considers the top products. Recently, among these products of the year were the Sony Video Walkman, NEC Ultralite Laptop computer, Ricoh Mirai camera, Max Factor's No Color Mascara, Wilson Profile tennis racket, erasable optical computer disks, and Herman Miller's Ergon 2 chair.[7] All these products produce considerable profit for the firms that introduced them.

7. Edward C. Baig, "Products of the Year," *Fortune,* Dec. 5, 1988, pp. 89–98.

FIGURE 1.4

Promotion of a not-for-profit organization. The World Wildlife Fund uses marketing efforts to obtain contributions.

SOURCE: World Wildlife Fund/The Conservation Fund

Our highly complex economy depends heavily on marketing activities. They help produce the profits that are essential not only to the survival of individual businesses, but also to the health and ultimate survival of the economy as a whole. Profits are essential to economic growth because without them businesses find it difficult, if not impossible, to buy more raw materials, hire more employees, attract more capital, and create the additional products that in turn make more profits.

■ Marketing Knowledge Enhances Consumer Awareness

Besides contributing to the well-being of our nation, marketing activities permeate our lives. In fact, they help us improve the quality of our lives. Studying marketing activities allows us to weigh costs, benefits, and flaws more effectively. We can see where they need to be improved and how to accomplish that goal. For example, if you have had an unsatisfactory experience with a warranty, you may have wished that laws were enforced more strictly to make sellers fulfill their promises. Similarly, you may have wished that you had more information about a product—or more accurate information—before you purchased it. Understanding marketing enables

TABLE 1.2 *National survey results regarding marketing myths*

MYTHS	STRONGLY AGREE	SOMEWHAT AGREE	NEITHER AGREE NOR DISAGREE	SOMEWHAT DISAGREE	STRONGLY DISAGREE
Marketing and selling are about the same thing	12.1% (245)	31.8% (645)	23.4% (476)	21.2% (431)	11.5% (234)
A grocery store owner takes home at least $3 for every $10 bag of groceries sold	19.5% (400)	23.9% (486)	30.4% (619)	15.0% (305)	11.1% (226)
Products that are advertised a great deal cost more	30.7% (625)	36.4% (741)	13.9% (282)	13.3% (270)	5.7% (117)
Wholesalers make high profits that significantly increase prices consumers pay	35.6% (725)	37.9% (771)	16.0% (326)	8.1% (164)	2.4% (49)
Marketing is the same thing as advertising	13.1% (265)	36.2% (734)	22.9% (465)	20.0% (406)	7.7% (157)

SOURCE: William M. Pride and O. C. Ferrell; a national survey of U.S. households, 1985.

us to evaluate the corrective measures (such as laws, regulations, and industry guidelines) that may be required to stop unfair, misleading, or unethical marketing practices. The results of a national survey presented in Table 1.2 indicate that there is a considerable lack of knowledge about marketing activities, as reflected by the sizable proportion of respondents who agree with the myths in the table.

■ **Marketing Costs Consume a Sizable Portion of Buyers' Dollars**

The study of marketing will make you aware that many marketing activities are necessary to provide people with satisfying goods and services. Obviously, these marketing activities cost money. In fact, about one-half of a buyer's dollar goes for marketing costs. A family with a monthly income of $2,000 that allocates $400 to taxes and savings spends about $1,600 for goods and services. Of this amount, $800 goes for marketing activities. Clearly, if marketing expenses consume that much of your dollar, you should know how this money is used.

THE MARKETING CONCEPT

Some organizations have tried to be successful by buying land, building a factory, equipping it with people and machines, and then making a product that they believe consumers need. However, these organizations frequently fail to attract buyers with what they have to offer because they defined their business as "making a product" rather than as "helping potential customers satisfy their needs and wants." Such organizations have failed to implement the marketing concept.

FIGURE 1.5

Using the marketing concept.

Reader's Digest is sending a clear message that its people are making a difference by finding out what customers want and then fulfilling those customers' desires.

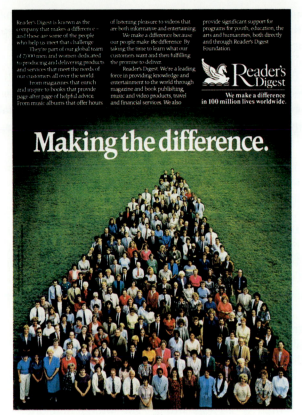

Reader's Digest is known as the company that makes a difference – and these are some of the people who help us meet that challenge.

They're part of our global team of 7,000 men and women dedicated to producing and delivering products and services that meet the needs of our customers all over the world.

From magazines that enrich and inspire to books that provide page after page of helpful advice. From music albums that offer hours of listening pleasure to videos that are both informative and entertaining.

We make a difference because our people make *the* difference. By taking the time to learn what our customers want and then fulfilling the promise to deliver.

Reader's Digest. We're a leading force in providing knowledge and entertainment to the world through magazine and book publishing, music and video products, travel and financial services. We also provide significant support for programs for youth, education, the arts and humanities, both directly and through Reader's Digest Foundation.

Reader's Digest

We make a difference in 100 million lives worldwide.

Making the difference.

SOURCE: Reprinted with permission from the Reader's Digest Association, Inc., 1990.

According to the **marketing concept**, an organization should try to provide products that satisfy customers' needs through a coordinated set of activities that also allows the organization to achieve its goals. Customer satisfaction is the major aim of the marketing concept. First an organization must find out what will satisfy customers. With this information, it then attempts to create satisfying products. But the process does not end there. The organization must continue to alter, adapt, and develop products to keep pace with customers' changing desires and preferences. For example, as indicated in the advertisement in Figure 1.5, Reader's Digest tries to learn what customers want and to provide products that satisfy those desires. The marketing concept stresses the importance of customers and emphasizes that marketing activities begin and end with them.

In attempting to satisfy customers, businesses must consider not only short-run, immediate needs but also broad, long-term desires. Trying to satisfy customers' current needs by sacrificing their long-term desires will only create future dissatisfaction. For instance, people want efficient, low-cost energy to power their homes and automobiles, yet they react adversely to energy producers who pollute the air and water, kill wildlife, or cause disease or birth defects. To meet these short- and long-run needs and desires, a firm must coordinate all its activities. Production, finance, accounting, personnel, and marketing departments must work together.

The marketing concept is not a second definition of marketing. It is a way of thinking—a management philosophy guiding an organization's overall activities. This philosophy affects all efforts of the organization, not just marketing activities. However, the marketing concept is by no means a philanthropic philosophy aimed at helping customers at the expense of the organization. A firm that adopts the marketing concept must not only satisfy its customers' objectives but also achieve its own goals, or it will not stay in business long. The overall goals of a business might be directed toward increasing profits, share of the market, sales, or a combination of all three goals. The marketing concept stresses that an organization can best achieve its goals by providing customer satisfaction. Thus, implementing the marketing concept should benefit the organization as well as its customers.

■ Evolution of the Marketing Concept

The marketing concept may seem like an obvious and sensible approach to running a business. However, businesspeople have not always believed that the best way to make sales and profits is to satisfy customers. A famous example is Henry Ford's marketing philosophy for cars in the early 1900s: "The customers can have any color car they want as long as it is black." The philosophy of the marketing concept emerged in the third major era in the history of U.S. business, preceded by the production and the sales eras. Surprisingly, nearly forty years after the marketing era began, many businesses still have not adopted the marketing concept.

The Production Era.   During the second half of the nineteenth century, the Industrial Revolution was in full force in the United States. Electricity, rail transportation, the division of labor, the assembly line, and mass production made it possible to manufacture products more efficiently. With new technology and new ways of using labor, products poured into the marketplace, where consumer demand for manufactured goods was strong. This production orientation continued into the early part of this century, encouraged by the scientific management movement that championed rigidly structured jobs and pay based on output.

The Sales Era.   In the 1920s, the strong consumer demand for products subsided. Businesses realized that products, which by this time could be made quite efficiently, would have to be "sold" to consumers. From the mid-1920s to the early 1950s, businesses viewed sales as the major means of increasing profits. As a result, this period came to have a sales orientation. Businesspeople believed that the most important marketing activities were personal selling and advertising.

The Marketing Era.   By the early 1950s, some businesspeople began to recognize that efficient production and extensive promotion of products did not guarantee that customers would buy them. These businesses, and many others since then, found that they must first determine what customers want and then produce it, rather than simply make products and try to change customers' needs to fit what is produced. As more organizations have realized the importance of knowing customers' needs, U.S. businesses have entered into the marketing era, one of customer orientation.

■ Implementing the Marketing Concept

A philosophy may sound reasonable and look good on paper, but that does not mean it can be put into practice easily. The marketing concept is a case in point. To implement it, an organization must focus on some general conditions and recognize several problems. Because of these conditions and problems, the marketing concept has yet to be fully accepted by American businesses.

Because the marketing concept affects all types of business activities, and not just marketing activities, the top management of an organization must adopt it whole-heartedly. High-level executives must incorporate the marketing concept into their philosophies of business management so completely that it becomes the basis for all the goals and decisions that they set for their firms. They must also convince other members of the organization to accept the changes in policies and operations that flow from their acceptance of the marketing concept.

As the first step, management must establish an information system that enables it to discover customers' real needs and to use the information to create satisfying products. Because such a system is usually expensive, management must be willing to commit money and time for development and maintenance. Without an adequate information system, an organization cannot be customer oriented.

Management's second major task is to restructure the organization. We pointed out that if a company is to satisfy customers' objectives as well as its own, it must coordinate all activities. To achieve this, the internal operations and the overall objectives of one or more departments may need restructuring. If the head of the marketing unit is not a member of the organization's top-level management, he or she should be. Some departments may have to be abolished and new ones created. Implementing the marketing concept demands the support not only of top manage-ment, but also of managers and staff at all levels within the organization.

Even when the basic conditions of establishing an information system and reor-ganizing the company are met, the firm's new marketing approach may not work perfectly. First, there is a limit to a firm's ability to satisfy customers' needs for a particular product. In a mass production economy, most business organizations cannot tailor products to fit the exact needs of each customer. Second, although a company may try to learn what customers want, it may be unable to do so, and when it does correctly identify customers' needs, it often has a hard time developing a product that satisfies those needs. Many companies spend considerable time and money to research customers' needs and yet still create some products that do not sell well. Third, by striving to satisfy one segment of society, a firm sometimes dissatisfies other segments. Government and nonbusiness organizations also experi-ence this problem. Fourth, a company may have trouble maintaining employee morale during any restructuring needed to coordinate the activities of various de-partments. Management must clearly explain the reasons for the changes and com-municate its own enthusiasm for the marketing concept.

MARKETING STRATEGY

To achieve the broad goal of expediting desirable exchanges, an organization's mar-keting managers are responsible for developing and managing marketing strategies. Specifically, a **marketing strategy** encompasses selecting and analyzing a target market (the group of people whom the organization wants to reach) and creating and maintaining an appropriate **marketing mix** (product, distribution, promotion, and price) that will satisfy those people. A marketing strategy articulates a plan for the best use of the organization's resources and tactics to meet its objectives.

When marketing managers attempt to develop and manage marketing activities, they must deal with two broad sets of variables: those relating to the marketing mix and those that make up the marketing environment. The marketing mix decision

FIGURE 1.6
Components of the marketing mix and marketing environment

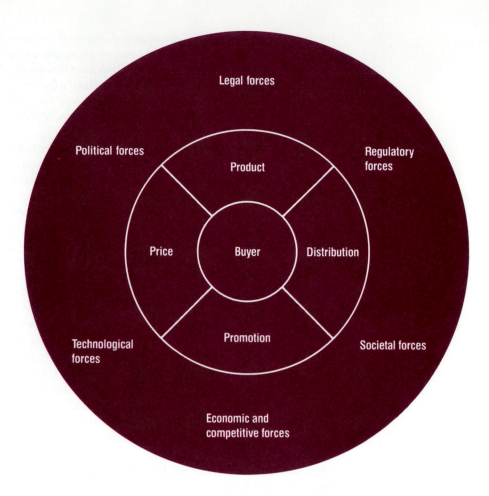

variables—product, distribution, promotion, and price—are factors over which an organization has control. As Figure 1.6 shows, these variables are constructed around the buyer. The marketing environment variables are political, legal, regulatory, societal, economic and competitive, and technological forces. These factors are subject to less control by an organization, but they affect buyers' needs as well as marketing managers' decisions regarding marketing mix variables.

To develop and manage marketing strategies, marketers must focus on several marketing tasks: marketing opportunity analysis, target market selection, marketing mix development, and effective marketing management. Figure 1.7 lists these tasks, along with the chapters of this book in which they are discussed.

Marketing Opportunity Analysis

A *marketing opportunity* exists when circumstances allow an organization to take action toward reaching a particular group of customers. An opportunity provides a favorable chance or opening for the firm to generate sales from identifiable markets. For example, after an early snowstorm, marketers of snow shovels have a marketing opportunity—an opportunity to reach customers who need snow shovels.

Marketers should be capable of recognizing and analyzing marketing opportunities. An organization's long-term survival depends on developing products that satisfy its customers. Few organizations can assume that products popular today will

FIGURE 1.7
Marketing strategy tasks

Generic marketing management tasks

Marketing opportunity analysis and target market selection

- The marketing environment (Chapter 2)
- Marketing ethics and social responsibility (Chapter 3)
- Target market evaluation (Chapter 4)
- Consumer markets and buying behavior (Chapter 5)
- Organizational markets and buying behavior (Chapter 6)
- Marketing research and information systems (Chapter 7)

Marketing mix development

- Product decisions (Chapters 8 and 9)
- Distribution decisions (Chapters 10, 11, 12, and 13)
- Promotion decisions (Chapters 14, 15, and 16)
- Price decisions (Chapters 17 and 18)

Marketing management

- Strategic market planning (Chapter 19)
- Implementing strategies and measuring performance (Chapter 20)

interest buyers ten years from now. A marketing organization can choose among several alternatives for continued product development through which it can achieve its objectives and satisfy buyers. It can modify existing products (for example, Citrus Hill and Minute Maid have added calcium to their orange juice products to address increasing health consciousness among customers), introduce new products (such as J.R. Simplot's MicroMagic microwavable fast foods that go from the freezer to the table in two minutes), and delete some that customers no longer want (such as disk cameras). A company may also try to market its products to a greater number of customers, convince current customers to use more of a product, or perhaps expand marketing activities into additional states or countries. Diversification into new product offerings through internal efforts or through acquisitions of other organizations may be viable options for a firm. For example, BSN Groupe, a French consumer goods marketer of pasta, bakery goods, and other products, bought RJR Nabisco's European consumer goods division, gaining the rights to market a number of highly successful Nabisco products in Europe. An organization's ability to pursue any of these alternatives successfully depends on its internal characteristics and the forces within the marketing environment.

Internal Organizational Factors. The primary factors inside an organization that should be considered when analyzing marketing opportunities are organizational objectives, financial resources, managerial skills, organizational strengths and weaknesses, and cost structures. Most organizations have overall organizational objectives. Some marketing opportunities may be consistent with these objectives; others are not, and to pursue them is hazardous. Frequently, the pursuit of such opportunities ends in failure or forces the company to alter its long-term objectives.

Obviously, a firm's financial resources constrain the type of marketing opportunities it can pursue. Typically, an organization does not develop projects that can bring economic catastrophe. In some situations, however, a firm must invest in a high-risk opportunity, because the costs of not pursuing the project are so high. Thus a computer manufacturer, such as IBM, must conduct product research and development and produce computers featuring cutting-edge technology, such as the IBM PS/2 80, if it wants to remain competitive with other computer makers.

The skills and experience of its management also limit the types of opportunities that an organization can pursue. A company must be particularly cautious when exploring the possibility of entering unfamiliar markets with new products. If it lacks appropriate managerial skills and experience, the firm can sometimes acquire them by hiring additional managerial personnel.

Like people, most organizations have strengths and weaknesses. Because of the types of operations in which a firm is engaged, it normally has employees with specialized skills and technological information. Such characteristics are a strength when launching marketing strategies that require them. However, they may be a weakness if the company tries to compete in new, unrelated product areas.

An organization's cost structure may be an advantage if the company pursues certain marketing opportunities and a disadvantage if it pursues others. Such factors as geographic location, employee skills, access to raw materials, and type of equipment and facilities all can affect the cost structure.

Marketing Environment Forces.   The *marketing environment,* which consists of political, legal, regulatory, societal, economic and competitive, and technological forces, surrounds the buyer and the marketing mix (see Figure 1.6). We explore each major environmental force in considerable depth in Chapter 2. Marketers know that they cannot predict changes in the marketing environment with certainty. Even so, over the years, marketers have become more systematic in taking these forces into account when planning their competitive actions.[8]

Marketing environment forces affect a marketer's ability to facilitate and expedite exchanges in three general ways. First, they influence customers by affecting their lifestyles, standards of living, and preferences and needs for products. Because a marketing manager tries to develop and adjust the marketing mix to satisfy consumers, the effects of environmental forces on customers also have an indirect impact on the marketing mix components. Second, marketing environment forces help determine whether and how a marketing manager can perform certain marketing activities. Third, the environmental forces may affect a marketing manager's decisions and actions by influencing buyers' reactions to the firm's marketing mix.

Although forces in the marketing environment sometimes are viewed as "uncontrollables," a marketing manager may be able to influence one or more of them. However, marketing environment forces fluctuate quickly and dramatically, which is one reason why marketing is so interesting and challenging. Because these forces are highly interrelated, a change in one may cause others to change. For example, after four major oil spills within three months in 1989 (in Alaska, Delaware, Rhode

8. Gene R. Laczniak and Robert F. Lusch, "Environment and Strategy in 1995: A Survey of High-Level Executives," *Journal of Consumer Marketing,* Spring 1986, p. 28.

Island, and Texas), people's feelings toward the shipping of petroleum products and toward oil companies in general became less positive. As outrage over the damage increased, the federal government took legal action against the companies and individuals responsible for the accidents. Congress considered legislation to regulate the shipping of petroleum products and to halt exploration for oil in some particularly sensitive areas. The oil companies then began to seek new technology to prevent spills and to clean them up quickly and safely. In addition, the world's top oil companies formed the Petroleum Industry Response Organization (PIRO) and established a $250 million fund for research and activities designed to quicken the response to accidents and make transporting petroleum safer.[9]

Even though changes in the marketing environment produce uncertainty for marketers and, at times, hurt marketing efforts, they can also create opportunities. After the 1989 oil spills, for example, more companies began developing and marketing products designed to contain or dissipate spilled oil. Thus a marketer must be aware of changes in environmental forces not only to adjust to and influence them but to capitalize on the opportunities they provide.

■ Marketing Strategy: Target Market Selection

A **target market** is a group of persons for whom a firm creates and maintains a marketing mix that specifically fits the needs and preferences of that group. When choosing a target market, marketing managers try to evaluate possible markets to see how entering them would affect the company's sales, costs, and profits. Marketers also attempt to determine if the organization has the resources to produce a marketing mix that meets the needs of a particular target market and if satisfying those needs is consistent with the firm's overall objectives. The size and number of competitors already marketing products in possible target markets is also of concern.

Marketing managers may define a target market as a vast number of people or as a relatively small group. For example, Royal Crown Cola Co., the maker of RC and Diet Rite colas, is focusing its marketing efforts on adults aged 18 to 34. Because The Coca-Cola Company, PepsiCo, and other soft drink companies primarily target other age groups, Royal Crown believes that it can compete more effectively by focusing on an adult target market.[10] Although a business may concentrate its efforts on one target market through a single marketing mix, businesses often focus on several target markets by developing and employing multiple marketing mixes. Reebok, for example, has different marketing mixes for several target markets. It markets different types of shoes to meet the specific needs of joggers, walkers, aerobics enthusiasts, and other groups.

Target market selection is crucial to generating productive marketing efforts. At times, products and organizations fail because marketers do not identify the appropriate customer groups at which to aim their efforts. Organizations that try to be all things to all people typically end up not satisfying the needs of any customer group very well. It is important for an organization's management to designate which customer groups the firm is trying to serve and to have adequate information about these customers. The identification and analysis of a target market provide a foundation on which a marketing mix can be developed.

9. Ken Wells, "Credibility Gap: Oil Industry's Inability To Contain Spills at Sea Poses Political Trouble," *Wall Street Journal,* June 26, 1989, pp. A1, A4.

10. Michael J. McCarthy, "Royal Crown Cola Shifts Focus of Ads, Aiming for Adults Rather Than Teens," *Wall Street Journal,* June 5, 1989, p. B5.

■ Marketing Strategy: Marketing Mix Development

As mentioned earlier, the marketing mix consists of four major components: product, distribution, promotion, and price. These components are called marketing mix decision variables because a marketing manager decides what type of each component to use and in what amounts. A primary goal of a marketing manager is to create and maintain a marketing mix that satisfies consumers' needs for a general product type. Notice in Figure 1.6 that the marketing mix is built around the buyer (as is stressed by the marketing concept). Bear in mind, too, that the forces of the marketing environment affect the marketing mix variables in many ways.

Marketing mix variables often are viewed as controllable variables because they can be changed. However, there are limits to how much these variables can be altered. For example, because of economic conditions or government regulations, a manager may not be free to adjust prices daily. Changes in sizes, colors, shapes, and designs of most tangible goods are expensive; therefore, such product features cannot be altered very often. In addition, promotional campaigns and the methods used to distribute products ordinarily cannot be changed overnight.

Marketing managers must develop a marketing mix that precisely matches the needs of the people in the target market. Before they can do so, they have to collect in-depth, up-to-date information about those needs. The information might include data about the age, income, race, sex, and educational level of people in the target market; their preferences for product features; their attitudes toward competitors' products; and the frequency and intensity with which they use the product. Armed with these kinds of data, marketing managers are better able to develop a product, distribution system, promotion program, and price that satisfy the people in the target market.

Let us look more closely at the decisions and activities related to each marketing mix variable (product, distribution, promotion, and price). Table 1.1 is a partial list of the decisions and activities associated with each marketing mix variable.

The Product Variable.   As noted earlier, a product can be a good, a service, or an idea. The **product variable** is the aspect of the marketing mix that deals with researching consumers' product wants and designing a product with the desired characteristics. It also involves the creation or alteration of packages and brand names and may include decisions regarding warranty and repair services. The actual production of products is not a marketing activity.

Product variable decisions and related activities are important because they are involved directly with creating products that satisfy consumers' needs and wants. Marketing Update 1.2 focuses on J. M. Smucker Company's approach to providing satisfying products. To maintain a satisfying set of products that will help an organization achieve its goals, a marketer must be able to develop new products, modify existing ones, and eliminate those that no longer satisfy buyers or yield acceptable profits. For example, after realizing that competitors were capturing large shares of the frozen breakfast market, Heinz introduced thirteen new low-calorie breakfast items under its Weight Watchers name.[11]

The Distribution Variable.   To satisfy consumers, products must be available at the right time and in a convenient location. In dealing with the **distribution variable**, a marketing manager seeks to make products available in the quantities

---

11. Judann Dagnoli and Julie Liesse Erickson, "New Niches for Breakfast," *Advertising Age,* June 26, 1989, p. 4.

J.M. SMUCKER COMPANY STRIVES TO PROVIDE SATISFYING PRODUCTS

The J.M. Smucker Company, a family-run firm based in Orrville, Ohio, has surpassed Kraft's and Welch's to become the giant of the $1 billion-a-year jam, jelly, preserves, and marmalade industry. Since its founding in 1897, the Smucker family has taken a personal interest not only in business operations, but also in fostering high quality products. Smucker's rise to prominence is largely due to its attention to detail and its deep sense of obligation to its customers. Smucker's executives want to live up to their advertising slogan: "With a name like Smucker's, it has to be good."

Quality, integrity, and customer relations make up the foundation of Smucker's company philosophy. Every person visiting the Orrville plant receives a card on which is printed a short discourse on the importance of quality to Smucker's employees, products, manufacturing methods, and marketing efforts. Family executives personally meet every one of the company's 1,500 employees; and chief executive Paul Smucker personally writes thank-you notes to all new shareholders.

Smucker's will not purchase advertising time during television programs that contain violence or sexually oriented scenes. Smucker's wants to maintain its wholesome, old-fashioned image. Anxious to keep this treasured image, Smucker's also pays for full-time federal government inspectors who monitor the entire jam and jelly manufacturing process. Because of this, Smucker's is the only company to carry the Agriculture Department's top U.S. Grade A designation on all its products.

Paul Smucker (grandson of the founder) and his sons Tim (chairman) and Richard (president) are not comfortably resting on their laurels. The Smuckers know they must fend off foreign jam companies, as well as a variety of domestic competitors. Smucker's must also capitalize on the new wave of health awareness and calorie-consciousness in the United States, in addition to consumers' interests in new tastes.

SOURCES: "The Corporate Elite," *Business Week,* Oct. 21, 1988, p. 276; Robert McMath, "Jelly Companies Unveil Preserves at Jam Session," *Adweek's Marketing Week,* July 25, 1988, p. 8; Andrew N. Malcolm, "Of Jams and a Family," *The New York Times Magazine,* Nov. 15, 1987, pp. 83, 88, 108–109; and Julianne Slovak, "J.M. Smucker Co.," *Fortune,* Jan. 16, 1989, p. 80.

desired to as many customers as possible and to keep the total inventory, transportation, and storage costs as low as possible. A marketing manager may become involved in selecting and motivating intermediaries (wholesalers and retailers), establishing and maintaining inventory control procedures, and developing and managing transportation and storage systems.

The Promotion Variable.   The **promotion variable** relates to activities used to inform one or more groups of people about an organization and its products. Promotion can be aimed at increasing public awareness of an organization and of new or existing products. In addition, promotion can serve to educate consumers about product features or to urge people to take a particular stance on a political or social issue. It may also be used to keep interest strong in an established product that has been available for decades. The advertisement in Figure 1.8 is an example.

The Price Variable.   The **price variable** relates to activities associated with establishing pricing policies and determining product prices. Price is a critical component of the marketing mix because consumers are concerned about the value obtained in an exchange. Price often is used as a competitive tool; in fact, extremely intense price competition sometimes leads to price wars. For example, AT&T, MCI, and Sprint are engaged in long-distance telephone service rate wars to gain new business. Because MCI and Sprint now offer long-distance service comparable in quality to that traditionally offered by AT&T, price has become the main competitive element in the long-distance telephone service market.[12] Price can also help to establish a product's image. For instance, if the makers of Calvin Klein's Obsession tried to sell that perfume in a one-gallon jug for $3.95, consumers probably would not buy it because the price would destroy the prestigious image of Obsession.

Developing and maintaining an effective marketing mix is a major requirement for a strong marketing strategy. Thus, as indicated in Figure 1.7, a large portion of this text (Chapters 8 through 18) focuses on the concepts, decisions, and activities associated with the components of the marketing mix.

■ Marketing Management

Marketing management is a process of planning, organizing, implementing, and controlling marketing activities to facilitate and expedite exchanges effectively and efficiently. Effectiveness and efficiency are important dimensions of this definition. *Effectiveness* is the degree to which an exchange helps achieve an organization's objectives. *Efficiency* is the minimization of resources an organization must spend to achieve a specific level of desired exchanges. Thus the overall goal of marketing management is to facilitate highly desirable exchanges and to minimize as much as possible the costs of doing so.

Planning is a systematic process of assessing opportunities and resources, determining marketing objectives, developing a marketing strategy, and developing plans for implementation and control. Planning determines when and how marketing activities will be performed and who is to perform them. It forces marketing managers to think ahead, to establish objectives, and to consider future marketing activities. Effective planning also reduces or eliminates daily crises.

Organizing marketing activities refers to developing the internal structure of the marketing unit. The structure is the key to directing marketing activities. The

---

12. Janet Guyon, "Stung by Rivals, AT&T Is Fighting Back," *Wall Street Journal,* June 30, 1989, p. B1.

SOURCE: Levi Strauss and Co.

marketing unit can be organized by functions, products, regions, types of customers, or a combination of all four.

Proper implementation of marketing plans hinges on coordination of marketing activities, motivation of marketing personnel, and effective communication within the unit. Marketing managers must motivate marketing personnel, coordinate their activities, and integrate their activities both with those in other areas of the company and with the marketing efforts of personnel in external organizations, such as advertising agencies and research firms. An organization's communication system must allow the marketing manager to stay in contact with high-level management, with managers of other functional areas within the firm, and with personnel involved in marketing activities both inside and outside the organization.

The marketing control process consists of establishing performance standards, evaluating actual performance by comparing it with established standards, and reducing the difference between desired and actual performance. An effective control process has four requirements. It should ensure a rate of information flow that allows the marketing manager to quickly detect differences between actual and planned levels of performance. It must accurately monitor different kinds of activities and be flexible enough to accommodate changes. The control process must be economical so that its costs are low relative to the costs that would arise if there were no controls. Finally, the control process should be designed so that both managers and subordinates can understand it. To maintain effective marketing control, an organization needs to develop a comprehensive control process that evaluates marketing operations at regular intervals. In Chapters 19 and 20 we examine the planning, organizing, implementing, and controlling of marketing activities in greater detail.

THE ORGANIZATION OF THIS BOOK

Figure 1.6 is a map of the overall organization of this book. Chapter 2 discusses the marketing environment variables listed in the outer portion of Figure 1.6, and Chapter 3 explores marketing ethics and social responsibility. Then we move to the center of the figure, analyzing markets, buyers, and marketing research in Chapters 4, 5, 6, and 7, respectively. Chapters 8 through 18 explore the marketing mix variables, starting with the product variable and moving clockwise around Figure 1.6. Chapters 19 and 20 discuss strategic market planning, organization, implementation, and control. Chapters 21, 22, and 23 scrutinize decisions and activities that are unique to industrial marketing, international marketing, and services marketing. If, as you study, you wonder where the text is leading, look again at Figure 1.6.

SUMMARY

Marketing consists of individual and organizational activities that facilitate and expedite satisfying exchange relationships in a dynamic environment through the creation, distribution, promotion, and pricing of goods, services, and ideas. An exchange is the provision or transfer of goods, services, and ideas in return for something of value. Four conditions must exist for an exchange to occur: (1) two or more individuals, groups, or organizations must participate; (2) each party must have something of value desired by the other; (3) each party must be willing to give up what it has in order to receive the value held by the other; and (4) the parties to the exchange must be able to communicate with each other to make their somethings of value available. In an exchange, products are traded either for other products or for financial resources, such as cash or credit. Products can be goods, services, or ideas.

It is important to study marketing because it permeates our lives. Marketing activities are performed in both business and nonbusiness organizations. Moreover, marketing activities help business organizations generate profits, the lifeblood of a capitalist economy. The study of marketing enhances consumer awareness. Finally, marketing costs absorb about half of each consumer dollar.

The marketing concept is a management philosophy prompting a business organization to try to satisfy customers' needs through a coordinated set of activities that also allows the organization to achieve its goals. Customer satisfaction is the major objective of the marketing concept. The philosophy of the marketing concept emerged in the United States during the 1950s, after the production and the sales eras. To make the marketing concept work, top management must accept it as an overall management philosophy. Implementing the marketing concept requires an efficient information system and sometimes the restructuring of the organization.

Marketing strategy involves selecting and analyzing a target market (the group of people whom the organization wants to reach) and creating and maintaining an appropriate marketing mix (product, distribution, promotion, and price) to satisfy this market. Marketing strategy requires that managers focus on four tasks to achieve set objectives: (1) marketing opportunity analysis, (2) target market selection, (3) marketing mix development, and (4) marketing management.

Marketers should be able to recognize and analyze marketing opportunities, which are circumstances that allow an organization to take action toward reaching a particular group of customers. Marketing opportunity analysis involves reviewing both internal factors (organizational objectives, financial resources, managerial skills, organizational strengths, organizational weaknesses, and cost structures) and external ones (the political, legal, regulatory, societal, economic and competitive, and technological forces of the marketing environment).

A target market is a group of persons for whom a firm creates and maintains a marketing mix that specifically fits the needs and preferences of that group. It is important for an organization's management to designate which customer groups the firm is trying to serve and to have some information about these customers. The identification and analysis of a target market provide a foundation on which a marketing mix can be developed.

The four variables that make up the marketing mix are product, price, promotion, and distribution. The product variable is the aspect of the marketing mix that deals with researching consumers' wants and designing a product with the desired characteristics. A marketing manager tries to make products available in the quantities desired to as many customers as possible and to keep the total inventory, transportation, and storage costs as low as possible—the distribution variable. The promotion variable relates to activities used to inform one or more groups of people about an organization and its products. The price variable refers to establishing pricing policies and determining product prices.

Marketing management is a process of planning, organizing, implementing, and controlling marketing activities to facilitate and expedite exchanges effectively and efficiently. Planning is a systematic process of assessing opportunities and resources, determining marketing objectives, developing a marketing strategy, and developing plans for implementation and control. Organizing marketing activities refers to developing the internal structure of the marketing unit. Properly implementing marketing plans depends on coordinating marketing activities, motivating marketing personnel, and effectively communicating within the unit. The marketing control process consists of establishing performance standards, evaluating actual performance by comparing it with established standards, and reducing the difference between desired and actual performance.

IMPORTANT TERMS

Marketing	Product variable
Exchange	Distribution variable
Marketing concept	Promotion variable
Marketing strategy	Price variable
Marketing mix	Marketing management
Target market	

Discussion and Review Questions

1. What is marketing? How did you define marketing before you read this chapter?
2. Why should someone study marketing?
3. Discuss the basic elements of the marketing concept. Which businesses in your area use this concept? In your opinion, have these businesses adopted the marketing concept? Explain.
4. Identify several business organizations in your area that obviously have not adopted the marketing concept. What characteristics of these organizations indicate nonacceptance of the marketing concept?
5. Describe the major components of a marketing strategy. How are the components related?
6. Identify the tasks involved in developing a marketing strategy.
7. What are the primary issues that marketing managers consider when conducting a market opportunity analysis?
8. What are the variables in the marketing environment? How much control does a marketing manager have over environmental variables?
9. Why is the selection of a target market such an important issue?
10. Why are the elements of the marketing mix known as variables?
11. What types of management activities are involved in the marketing management process?

■ Cases

1.1 Simplot's MicroMagic Foods

The executives at J.R. Simplot Co. believed there was a mass market for microwavable fast food and, despite some early setbacks, they were right. The Boise, Idaho–based potato processor, whose initial claim to fame was supplying McDonald's and other restaurants with French fries, has been producing such strong sales numbers that competitors like Kraft, Quaker Oats, ConAgra, and Campbell have been prompted to develop their own varieties of microwavable snacks. Simplot's Micro-Magic line includes several types of French fries, potato sticks, burgers, milkshakes, a chicken sandwich, and a ham-and-cheese sandwich that looks and feels grilled. Simplot is currently test marketing a MicroMagic pizza line in several Midwestern cities. MicroMagic is clearly the dominant competitor in the $180 million segment that it created, controlling about 50 percent of all sales volume.

In the early 1980s, Simplot managers decided to enter the retail food business. Simplot purchased Okrays, a line of frozen potato products in 1984. Later that year, Simplot launched microwavable French fries under the name "Zap-ums" specifically designed for sale in convenience stores. Despite extensive research and development, Zap-ums failed miserably. Simplot then repackaged the French fries for supermarkets. In tests, the product (still under the Zap-ums name) flopped. Simplot finally experimented with different names and decided to go with MicroMagic.

In 1985, under the MicroMagic name, the fries were introduced to 35 percent of the overall U.S. market. The fries were the first product ever to be designed exclusively for microwave ovens. Simplot was taking a huge risk: at that time only about 30 percent of U.S. households owned a microwave.

In addition to introducing the first microwavable French fries, Simplot also originated the first microwavable hamburger, and the first (and still only) microwavable milkshake on the national market. Simplot officials place primary importance on being the first to introduce a product. By letting other companies "pursue" them, they believe they will be able to allocate more money to marketing efforts and reap other benefits as well, such as brand recognition and an established following. Simplot executives are proud that they can bring a product from conception to supermarket shelves in 18 months, which is half the time it takes their competitors. After they introduce a product, Simplot executives "fine tune" it through minor changes in pricing, advertising, packaging, or by making other alterations.

Simplot discovered that a primary factor for a new product's success is to first get the product on supermarket shelves and then keep it there. Before MicroMagic emerged as a thriving product, Simplot concentrated on building distribution. With the surge in competition, though, Simplot has had to shift much of its attention to consumer requirements. Simplot officials realize that they cannot neglect retailers' needs or those of ultimate consumers.

When it first introduced its MicroMagic line, Simplot took the risky approach of letting the product sell itself—it had a meager budget for advertising. In its first two years, Simplot spent only $3.1 million on MicroMagic's advertising, which is quite small in comparison to competitors' advertising expenditures. It currently spends over $23 million annually on advertising. Simplot officials are confident that microwavables will soon become established as quality—as well as convenience—foods.

Simplot executives are striving for advertising efficiency. A new MicroMagic television commercial went from concept to airtime in six weeks. They also rotate MicroMagic commercials during high-usage periods. For instance, advertisements for MicroMagic French fries, which are generally not considered a late-night food item, are shown during the day. Sandwiches are advertised in spots that complement their appeal as desirable lunches and dinners. Milkshakes, perceived as late-night snacks, are advertised at night. Simplot also spends heavily on radio time, especially in markets such as Los Angeles and Chicago where commuters spend a large amount of time listening to their car radios.

With its MicroMagic line, Simplot is attempting to capitalize on the growing trend toward food that is quickly and easily prepared. The theme line in Micro-Magic advertisements is "Give 'em MicroMagic right now." Using a detailed nation-wide study conducted by an Indianapolis-based market research company, Simplot officials found that their target market is families with very active lifestyles. These families want good-tasting food that does not take long to prepare. Simplot executives are hoping that MicroMagic will satisfy these needs.

SOURCES: Julie Liesse Erickson, "Simplot Bites Back in Micro Snack War," *Advertising Age,* Feb. 27, 1989, p. 4; Julie Liesse Erickson, "Simplot Wizardry Zaps Snack Market," *Advertising Age,* May 8, 1989, pp. S-6, S-10; and David Kalish, "Prestoburgers," *Marketing & Media Decisions,* March 1989, pp. 47–49.

Questions for Discussion

1. Is Simplot basing its decisions on the marketing concept? Explain.
2. Evaluate Simplot's philosophy that it is better to be first to introduce a product than to pursue the one that was first.
3. What environmental changes have occurred that have led to a marketing opportunity for Simplot's microwavable foods?

1.2 RJR Nabisco Focuses on Strategic Marketing

Most of us are familiar with the red triangle trademark on packages of Nabisco cookies and crackers. This instant recognition is due to RJR Nabisco's understanding of the marketing concept. The company realizes that it must carefully coordinate its activities both to satisfy customer needs and to achieve its own objectives. Marketing was the key to success for the many different companies that made up R.J. Reynolds Industries and Nabisco Brands, Inc., before they were united under the name RJR Nabisco in 1985. Strategic marketing planning is crucial to the success of this huge company, which has annual sales of more than $17 billion.

R.J. Reynolds bought Nabisco to take advantage of Nabisco's strengths and to minimize its own organizational weaknesses. After purchasing Nabisco, officials at R.J. Reynolds developed numerous marketing strategies to accommodate an assortment of many different brands. Now the marketing department must devote itself to such disparate products as Winston, Salem, and Camel cigarettes; Oreo cookies; Planters peanuts; Ritz crackers; and Del Monte pineapples, all of which are sold throughout the world.

The directors of RJR Nabisco restructured and streamlined the organization, trying to increase productivity and reduce waste. For example, they moved the Planters (peanuts) and Life Savers (candy) units into the tobacco division. The action led to more efficient distribution of these products because they are frequently sold in the same outlets. Company executives sold the Heublein Inc. liquor division and Kentucky Fried Chicken.

Tobacco is still the primary moneymaker for RJR Nabisco, accounting for 60 percent of the corporation's earnings. The company's profit margin on tobacco products is 29 percent. It costs the company a mere 17 cents to produce a pack of cigarettes, which it then sells to distributors for about 80 cents. RJR Nabisco's share of the tobacco market is about 32.5 percent; however, there has been an overall decline in the domestic consumption of tobacco products. To meet the goal of being the low-cost cigarette producer, RJR Nabisco built Tobaccoville, a $1 billion super-modern production facility in North Carolina. Tobaccoville allowed the company to cut its tobacco work force by nearly 20 percent, saving the company at least $60 million per year. Now operating at full capacity, the plant manufactures 110 billion cigarettes per year, one-fifth of the entire industry's production.

RJR Nabisco is a leader in many of the nation's food markets as well. Oreo cookies have been the number-one seller in the cookie market for more than seventy years. The company's crackers are still on top after several decades, and its nutritious cereals are rapidly gaining market share as consumers become more health conscious. RJR Nabisco officials plan to continue restructuring in this area, trimming operations and selling those units that do not fit in.

RJR Nabisco management constantly analyzes and adjust its marketing mix to maintain and increase its profit margin. The corporate leadership is strongly committed to research and development and is creating new products and improving older ones.

Distribution and promotion are also important to RJR Nabisco. The company tries to make its products available to distributors at low prices to pass on the savings to consumers. New facilities have opened so that adequate supplies of products may be readily obtainable. RJR Nabisco vigorously promotes its products and plans to increase promotional expenditures. In the past, Nabisco promotions have been some of the most innovative and memorable within the industry. RJR Nabisco faces the challenge of targeting many diverse products at equally diverse target markets.

Obviously, marketing is very important to RJR Nabisco and its continuing success. The company's officials recognize the significance of the marketing concept and employ strategic market planning both to accomplish company goals and to meet consumer needs. With effective marketing, RJR Nabisco is able to make its products available to consumers, to make consumers aware of new products, and to establish a reasonable pricing policy. Perhaps marketing is as essential to RJR Nabisco as the cream filling is to an Oreo.

SOURCES: Melvin J. Grayson, *27 Million Daily: The Story of Nabisco Brands* (Parsippany, N.J.: Nabisco Brands, 1984); Kevin Maney, "Move Shows It's Not Giving Up Tobacco," *USA Today,* June 22, 1987, pp. 1, 2B; Bob Messenger, "The Leading 50 Prepared Food and Beverage Processors," *Prepared Foods,* July 1986, pp. 40–46; *The RJR Nabisco 1986 Annual Report;* and Bill Saporito, "The Tough Cookie at RJR Nabisco," *Fortune,* July 18, 1988, pp. 32–46.

Questions for Discussion

1. What is the purpose or role of marketing strategies used by RJR Nabisco?
2. Does RJR Nabisco attempt to follow the marketing concept? Explain.
3. What types of environmental forces are most likely to influence the marketing of RJR Nabisco's tobacco brands?

2 THE MARKETING ENVIRONMENT

Objectives

To understand the concept of the marketing environment and the importance of environmental scanning and analysis

To identify the types of political forces in the marketing environment

To understand how laws and their interpretation influence marketing practices

To determine how government regulations and self-regulatory agencies affect marketing activities

To identify societal issues that marketers must deal with as they make decisions

To understand how economic and competitive factors affect organizations' ability to compete and customers' willingness and ability to buy products

To explore the effects of new technology on society and on marketing activities

*I*n an effort to capitalize on the rising interest in environmental matters and to ease the increasing concern over the shrinking number of available landfills, several companies have introduced products made of "degradable plastics." Discarded plastics are a serious environmental problem because they take about 500 years to fully decompose. Because of consumers' heightened concern for the environment, some analysts predict that the demand for degradable plastics will grow at a rapid pace for the next several years.

In the $1 billion-a-year market for trash bags, plastics manufacturers are eager to improve their image among the expanding number of environmentally conscious consumers. Any firm that markets products that can ease the pressure on landfills stands to gain a competitive advantage over rival companies. Several firms have started selling degradable plastic trash bags.

Environmental groups and the Federal Trade Commission are investigating the biodegradability and photodegradability assertions of the marketers of the plastic trash bags. So far, seven states have established a multistate task force to investigate such claims. These groups want to be certain that the plastics truly are degradable. Some researchers claim that the "biodegradable" bags only break down into smaller pieces of plastic that still do not readily decompose. Other environmental advocates question the photodegradability claims made by some companies. When plastic bags are buried in landfills, they are not exposed to light and therefore cannot photodegrade. Executives at a firm that sells "degradable" trash bags assert that they have adequate substantiation for their claims. They do emphasize that labels on the bags' packaging and print advertisements for the bags state that the product has "limited degradability." Currently, no standards of degradability have been set. ◆

Photo by Dan Helms/Compix.

Based on information from Brian Bremner, "A New Sales Pitch: The Environment," *Business Week,* July 24, 1989, p. 50; Jennifer Lawrence, "FTC Investigates Degradability Claims," *Advertising Age,* Jan. 1, 1990, p. 2; Pamela Sherrid, "A Bag Pits Big Oil vs. Big Ag," *U.S. News & World Report,* Apr. 24, 1989, p. 52; and Robert V. Wilder, "'Disappearing' Package: Pipe Dream or Savior?" *Modern Plastics,* Aug. 1989, pp. 40–45.

As you can see from this example, various forces can have a tremendous impact on the decisions and activities of marketers. This chapter explores the political, legal, regulatory, societal, economic and competitive, and technological forces that make up the marketing environment. First we define the marketing environment and consider why it is critical to scan and analyze it. Then we discuss the political forces that generate government actions affecting marketing activities. We examine the effects of laws and regulatory agencies on these activities and describe the desires and expectations of society. Next we consider the effects of general economic conditions: prosperity, recession, depression, and recovery. We also examine several types of economic forces that influence companies' ability to compete and consumers' willingness and ability to buy. Finally, we analyze the major dimensions of the technological forces in the environment.

EXAMINING AND RESPONDING TO THE MARKETING ENVIRONMENT

The **marketing environment** consists of external forces that directly or indirectly influence an organization's acquisition of inputs and generation of outputs. Inputs might include personnel, financial resources, raw materials, and information. Outputs could be information (such as advertisements), packages, goods, services, or ideas. As indicated in Chapter 1 and as shown in Figure 1.6, we view the marketing environment as consisting of six categories of forces: political, legal, regulatory, societal, economic and competitive, and technological. Although there are numerous environmental factors, most fall into one of these six categories.

Whether they fluctuate rapidly or slowly, environmental forces are always dynamic. Changes in the marketing environment create uncertainty, threats, and opportunities for marketers. Although the future is not very predictable, marketers can estimate what will happen. We can say with certainty that marketers will continue to modify their marketing strategies in response to the dynamic environment. Marketing managers who fail to recognize changes in environmental forces leave their firms unprepared to capitalize on marketing opportunities or to cope with threats created by changes in the environment. If an organization cannot deal with an unfavorable environment, it may go under. For example, many savings and loan associations in the Southwest could not cope with depressed oil and real estate markets in the mid-1980s. When their customers, who depended on income from oil and real estate investments, defaulted on their loans and mortgages, these S & Ls went out of business. Thus monitoring the environment is crucial to an organization's survival and to the long-term achievement of its goals.

■ **Environmental Scanning and Analysis**

To monitor changes in the marketing environment effectively, marketers must engage in environmental scanning and analysis. **Environmental scanning** is the process of collecting information about the forces in the marketing environment. Scanning involves observation; perusal of secondary sources, such as business, trade, government, and general-interest publications; and marketing research. However, managers must be careful not to gather so much information that sheer volume makes analysis impossible.

Environmental analysis is the process of assessing and interpreting the information gathered through environmental scanning. A manager evaluates the information for accuracy, tries to resolve inconsistencies in the data, and, if warranted assigns significance to the findings. Through analysis, a marketing manager seeks to describe current environmental changes and to predict future changes. By evaluating these changes, the manager should be able to determine possible threats and opportunities linked to environmental fluctuations. Understanding the current state of the marketing environment and recognizing the threats and opportunities arising from changes within it help marketing managers assess the performance of current marketing efforts and develop marketing strategies for the future.

■ Responding to Environmental Forces

In responding to environmental forces, marketing managers can take two general approaches: to accept environmental forces as uncontrollable or to confront and mold them. If environmental forces are viewed as uncontrollable, the organization remains passive and reactive toward the environment. Instead of trying to influence forces in the environment, its marketing managers tend to adjust current marketing strategies to environmental changes. They approach market opportunities discovered through environmental scanning and analysis with caution. On the other hand, marketing managers who believe that environmental forces can be shaped adopt a proactive approach. For example, if a market is blocked by traditional environmental constraints, they may apply economic, psychological, political, and promotional skills to gain access to it or operate within it. Once they identify what blocks a market opportunity, marketers can assess the power of the various parties involved and develop strategies to try to overcome environmental forces.[1] For example, AIG, an insurance and financial services marketer, promotes the reform of the U.S. liability system by legislative and judicial bodies, as shown in Figure 2.1. AIG indicates that the current liability system increases prices, discourages new product development, and makes U.S. companies less competitive in overseas markets.

In trying to influence environmental forces, marketing management may seek to create market opportunities or to extract greater benefits relative to costs from existing market opportunities. For instance, a firm losing sales to competitors with lower-priced products may strive to develop technology that would make its production processes more efficient; greater efficiency would allow it to lower the prices of its own products. Political action is another way of affecting environmental forces. Thus the Daylight-Saving Time Coalition—a group of candy, sporting goods, and barbecue products manufacturers; convenience stores; fast-food chains; and greenhouses—successfully lobbied Congress to switch the date for the start of daylight-saving time from the last Sunday to the first Sunday in April. The coalition argued that the extra daylight would boost its members' sales by millions of dollars. A proactive approach, then, can be constructive and bring desired results. However, managers must recognize that there are limits on how much an environmental force can be shaped and that these limits vary across environmental forces. Although an organization may be able to influence the enactment of laws through lobbying, it is unlikely that a single organization can significantly increase the national birthrate or move the economy from recession to prosperity.

We cannot generalize and say that either of these approaches to environmental response is better than the other. For some organizations, the passive, reactive approach is most appropriate, but for other firms, the aggressive approach leads to

1. Philip Kotler, "Megamarketing," *Harvard Business Review,* March-April 1986, pp. 117–24.

FIGURE 2.1   *Responding to environmental forces.*
AIG, an insurance and financial services marketer, promotes the reform of the U.S. liability system, indicating that this will make U.S. companies more competitive in overseas markets.

SOURCE: Courtesy AIG

better performance. The selection of a particular approach depends on an organization's managerial philosophies, objectives, financial resources, customers, and human skills and on the composition of the set of environmental forces within which the organization operates.

The rest of this chapter explores in detail each of the six environmental forces—political, legal, regulatory, societal, economic and competitive, and technological.

POLITICAL FORCES

The political, legal, and regulatory forces of the marketing environment are closely interrelated. Legislation is enacted, legal decisions are interpreted by the courts, and regulatory agencies are created and operated, for the most part, by persons elected or appointed to political offices. Legislation and regulations (or their lack) reflect the current political outlook. Consequently, the political force of the marketing environment has the potential to influence marketing decisions and strategies.

Marketing organizations need to maintain good relations with elected political officials for several reasons. When political officials are well disposed toward particular firms or industries, they are less likely to create or enforce laws and regulations unfavorable to these companies. For example, political officials who believe that oil companies are making honest efforts to control pollution are unlikely to create and enforce highly restrictive pollution control laws. In addition, governments are big buyers, and political officials can influence how much a government agency purchases and from whom. Finally, political officials can play key roles in helping organizations secure foreign markets.

Many marketers view political forces as beyond their control; they simply try to adjust to conditions that arise from those forces. Some firms, however, seek to influence political events by helping to elect to political offices individuals who regard them positively. Much of this help is in the form of campaign contributions. Although laws restrict direct corporate contributions to campaign funds, corporate money may be channeled into campaign funds as personal contributions of corporate executives or stockholders. Not only do such actions violate the spirit of the corporate campaign contribution laws; they are also unethical. A sizable contribution to a campaign fund may carry with it an implicit understanding that the elected official will perform political favors for the contributing firm. A corporation may even contribute to the campaign funds of several candidates who seek the same office. Occasionally, some businesses find it so important to ensure favorable treatment that they make direct illegal corporate contributions to campaign funds. Some businesses have even bypassed campaign funds in favor of more direct contributions. One Texas poultry producer handed out $10,000 checks to several Texas state senators who were considering legislation that would reform the state's workers' compensation laws. Most of the senators returned the checks to avoid the appearance of any breach of ethics.[2]

LEGAL FORCES

A number of laws influence marketing decisions and activities. Our discussion will focus on procompetitive and consumer protection laws and their interpretation.

■ **Procompetitive Legislation**

Procompetitive legislation is enacted to preserve competition. Table 2.1 briefly describes several major procompetitive laws, most of which were enacted to end various practices deemed unacceptable by society. We describe the most important of these in greater detail next.

The Sherman Antitrust Act. The **Sherman Antitrust Act** was passed in 1890 to prevent businesses from restraining trade and monopolizing markets. The act condemns "every contract, combination, or conspiracy in restraint of trade." It also prohibits monopolies or attempts by businesses to monopolize a particular market or industry. Enforced by the Antitrust Division of the Department of Justice, the Sherman Antitrust Act applies to firms operating in interstate commerce and to U.S. firms operating in foreign commerce.

The Clayton Act. Because the Sherman Antitrust Act was written in rather vague terms, the courts have not always interpreted it as its creators intended. Consequently, the Clayton Act was passed in 1914 to limit specific activities that tend to reduce competition. The **Clayton Act** specifically prohibits price discrimination, tying and exclusive agreements, and the acquisition of stock in another corporation "where the effect may be to substantially lessen competition or tend to create a

2. R.G. Ratcliffe and Robert Cullick, "Wrongdoing Denied by 9 Senators," *Houston Chronicle,* July 8, 1989, pp. 1A, 8A.

TABLE 2.1
Major federal procom-
petitive laws affecting
marketing decisions

ACT	PURPOSES
Sherman Antitrust Act (1890)	Prohibits contracts, combinations, or conspiracies to restrain trade; establishes as a misdemeanor monopolizing or attempting to monopolize
Clayton Act (1914)	Prohibits specific practices such as price discrimination, exclusive dealer arrangements, and stock acquisitions in which the effect may notably lessen competition or tend to create a monopoly
Federal Trade Commission Act (1914)	Created the Federal Trade Commission; also gives the FTC investigatory powers to be used in preventing unfair methods of competition
Robinson-Patman Act (1936)	Prohibits price discrimination that lessens competition among wholesalers or retailers; prohibits producers from giving disproportionate services or facilities to large buyers
Wheeler-Lea Act (1938)	Prohibits unfair and deceptive acts and practices regardless of whether competition is injured; places advertising of foods and drugs under the jurisdiction of the FTC
Celler-Kefauver Act (1950)	Prohibits any corporation engaged in commerce from acquiring the whole or any part of the stock or other share of the capital or assets of another corporation when the effect substantially lessens competition or tends to create a monopoly
Consumer Goods Pricing Act (1975)	Prohibits the use of price maintenance agreements among manufacturers and resellers in interstate commerce
Trademark Counterfeiting Act (1980)	Provides civil and criminal penalties against those who deal in counterfeit consumer goods or any counterfeit goods that can threaten health or safety

SOURCE: Adapted from Joseph Plummer, "The Concept and Application of Life Style Segmentation," *Journal of Marketing,* January 1974, p. 34.

monopoly." In addition, the act prohibits members of one company's board of directors from holding seats on the boards of competing corporations. The Clayton Act also exempts farm cooperatives and labor organizations from antitrust laws.

The Federal Trade Commission Act and the Wheeler-Lea Act.   Also passed in 1914, the **Federal Trade Commission Act** created the Federal Trade Commission (FTC), which today regulates the greatest number of marketing practices. Like the Clayton Act, the Federal Trade Commission Act was written to strengthen antimonopoly provisions of the Sherman Antitrust Act. Whereas the Clayton Act prohibits specific practices, the Federal Trade Commission Act more broadly prohibits unfair methods of competition. This act also empowers the FTC to work with the Department of Justice to enforce the provisions of the Clayton Act. Later sections of this chapter discuss the FTC's regulatory activities.

The creators of the Federal Trade Commission Act, like those of the Sherman Antitrust Act, found that the courts did not always interpret the act as they had intended. For instance, in the 1931 Raladam case, the Supreme Court ruled that a producer's misrepresentation of an obesity cure was not an unfair method of competition because the firm's action did not injure competition.[3] This ruling—among others—spurred Congress in 1938 to pass the **Wheeler-Lea Act**, which essentially makes unfair and deceptive acts or practices unlawful, regardless of whether they injure competition. It specifically prohibits false and misleading advertising of foods, drugs, therapeutic devices, and cosmetics; it also provides penalties for violations and procedures for enforcement.

The Robinson-Patman Act.   During the early 1930s, when the Depression was at its peak, the Federal Trade Commission found that many of the low prices that suppliers offered to chain stores could not be justified on the basis of cost savings arising from quantity purchases. Eventually, in 1936, after several years of economic hardship, pressure from the FTC and popular political support for further legislation led to the passage of the Robinson-Patman Act.

The **Robinson-Patman Act** is significant because it directly influences pricing policies. Its most important provision prohibits price discrimination among different purchasers of goods of similar grade and quality where the effect of such discrimination tends to reduce competition among the purchasers or gives one purchaser a competitive edge. The Robinson-Patman Act did *not* outlaw price differentials— price differentials are legal if they can be justified as cost savings or as meeting competition in good faith. The act also makes it unlawful to knowingly influence the setting of prices or to receive discriminatory prices when they are prohibited by the Robinson-Patman Act. Finally, it outlaws providing services or facilities to purchasers on terms not offered to all purchasers on more or less equal terms.

Thus the pricing provisions of the Robinson-Patman Act deal only with discriminatory price differentials. Price differentials become discriminatory when one purchaser (usually a retailer) can acquire similar quantities of goods of like grade and quality at lower prices than competing purchasers dealing with the same supplier. Such price differentials give that purchaser an unfair advantage in the market and ultimately reduce consumers' opportunities to choose from among a number of products, stores, and prices.

■ Consumer Protection Legislation

The second category of regulatory laws, **consumer protection legislation**, is not a recent development. During the mid-1800s, lawmakers in many states passed laws to prohibit the adulteration of food and drugs. However, consumer protection laws at the federal level mushroomed in the mid-1960s and early 1970s. A number of them deal with consumer safety—such as the food and drug acts, designed to protect people from actual and potential physical harm caused by adulteration or mislabeling of foods and drugs. Other laws prohibit the sale of various hazardous products, such as flammable fabrics and toys that may injure children.

To help consumers become better informed, Congress has passed several laws concerning the disclosure of information. Some laws require that information about specific products, such as textiles, furs, cigarettes, and automobiles, be provided on labels. Other laws focus on particular marketing activities—product development and testing, packaging, labeling, advertising, and consumer financing.

3. *Federal Trade Commission v. Raladam Company,* 283 U.S. 643, 1931.

■ Interpreting Laws   Laws certainly have the potential to influence marketing activities, but the actual effects of the laws are determined by how marketers and the courts interpret the laws. Laws seem to be quite specific because they contain many complex clauses and subclauses. In reality, however, many laws and regulations are stated in vague terms that force marketers to rely on legal advice rather than their own understanding and common sense. Because of this vagueness, some organizations attempt to gauge the limits of certain laws by operating in a legally questionable way to see how far they can get with certain practices before being prosecuted. Other marketers, however, interpret regulations and statutes very conservatively and strictly to avoid violating a vague law.

Although court rulings directly affect businesses accused of specific violations, they also have a broader, less direct impact on other businesses. When marketers try to interpret laws in relation to specific marketing practices, they often analyze recent court decisions, both to understand better what the law is intended to do and to gain a clearer sense of how the courts are likely to interpret it in the future.

REGULATORY FORCES

Interpretation alone does not determine the effectiveness of laws and regulations; the level of enforcement by regulatory agencies is also significant. Some regulatory agencies are created and administered by government units; others are sponsored by nongovernmental sources. In our discussion, we first turn to federal, state, and local government regulatory units and then examine self-regulatory forces.

■ Federal Regulatory Agencies   Federal regulatory agencies influence many marketing activities, including product development, pricing, packaging, advertising, personal selling, and distribution. Usually, they have the power to enforce specific laws, such as the Federal Trade Commission Act, as well as some discretion in establishing operating rules and drawing up regulations to guide certain types of industry practices. Because of this discretion and overlapping areas of responsibility, confusion or conflict as to which agencies have jurisdiction over specific types of marketing activities is common.

The Federal Trade Commission.   Of all the federal regulatory units, the **Federal Trade Commission (FTC)** has the broadest powers to influence marketing activities. The agency consists of five commissioners, each appointed for a term of seven years by the president of the United States with Senate approval. Not more than three commissioners may be members of the same political party, and their terms of office are staggered to ensure continuity of experience in the judgment of cases. The FTC has many administrative duties under existing laws, but the policy underlying them all is the same: "To prevent the free enterprise system from being stifled or fettered by monopoly or anti-competitive practices and to provide the direct protection of consumers from unfair or deceptive trade practices."[4]

One major function of the FTC is to enforce laws and regulatory guidelines falling under its jurisdiction. When it receives a complaint or otherwise has reason to believe that a firm is violating a law, the commission issues a complaint stating that the business is in violation. If the company continues the questionable practice, the FTC can issue a cease and desist order, which is simply an order for the business

4. "Your Federal Trade Commission" (Washington, D.C.: Federal Trade Commission, 1977), pp. 8–9.

to stop doing whatever caused the complaint in the first place. The firm can appeal to the federal courts to have the FTC order rescinded. However, the FTC can seek civil penalties in the courts, with a maximum penalty of $10,000 a day for each violation if a cease-and-desist order is violated.

The FTC also provides assistance and information to businesses so that they will know how to comply with laws. New marketing methods are evaluated every year. When general sets of guidelines are needed to improve business practices in a particular industry, the FTC sometimes encourages firms within that industry to establish a set of trade practices voluntarily. The FTC may sponsor a conference to bring together industry leaders and consumers for this purpose. Although the FTC regulates a variety of business practices, it allocates a large portion of its resources to curbing false advertising, misleading pricing, and deceptive packaging and labeling. For example, the FTC challenged a Campbell Soup Company's advertisement in which the company claimed that its soups are low in fat and cholesterol and therefore help to reduce the risk of heart disease. The FTC's complaint against Campbell said that the advertisement was misleading because it failed to disclose that the soups have a high sodium content, which might actually increase the risk of heart disease.[5]

The activities and policies of the Federal Trade Commission and other regulatory agencies are heavily influenced by the political environment, and specifically by the policies and agendas of the political administration in power at the time. During the administration of President Jimmy Carter, for example, the FTC actively regulated trade practices and strictly enforced FTC regulations. The administration of President Ronald Reagan, however, adopted a policy of laissez-faire (allowing business basically to regulate itself), and the FTC did not strictly enforce laws and regulations on advertising, pricing, and other business practices. In fact, the Reagan administration deregulated some industries, as we discuss later in this section. When George Bush succeeded Reagan as president in 1989, the FTC once again became more vigorous in enforcing business trade regulations. The FTC of Bush's administration is expected to be especially aggressive in enforcing regulations on advertising that includes health claims or promotes alcohol and tobacco products.[6] Thus it is very important for marketers to monitor the marketing environment to detect possible changes in policy resulting from changes in government administration.

Other Federal Regulatory Units.   Unlike the Federal Trade Commission, other regulatory units are limited to dealing with specific products, services, or business activities. For example, the Food and Drug Administration (FDA) enforces regulations that prohibit the sale and distribution of adulterated, misbranded, or hazardous food and drug products. Thus, the FDA outlawed the sale and distribution of most over-the-counter baldness remedies after research indicated that few of the products were effective in restoring hair growth. Table 2.2 outlines the major areas of responsibility of seven federal agencies.

As marketing activities become more complex, some of the responsibilities of federal units overlap. When authority over a specific product or marketing practice cannot be assigned to a single federal unit, marketers must try to comply with many different regulations and regulatory agencies.

---

5. Steven W. Colford and Judann Dagnoli, "FTC Attacks Campbell Ad Health Claim," *Advertising Age,* Jan. 30, 1989, pp. 2, 89.

6. Steven W. Colford, "Bush FTC May Clamp Down on Ads," *Advertising Age,* Apr. 17, 1989, p. 63.

TABLE 2.2
Major federal regulatory agencies

AGENCY	MAJOR AREAS OF RESPONSIBILITY
Federal Trade Commission (FTC)	Enforces laws and guidelines regarding business practices; takes action to stop false and deceptive advertising and labeling
Food and Drug Administration (FDA)	Enforces laws and regulations to prevent distribution of adulterated or misbranded foods, drugs, medical devices, cosmetics, veterinary products, and particularly hazardous consumer products
Consumer Product Safety Commission	Ensures compliance with the Consumer Product Safety Act; protects the public from unreasonable risk of injury from any consumer product not covered by other regulatory agencies
Interstate Commerce Commission (ICC)	Regulates franchises, rates, and finances of interstate rail, bus, truck, and water carriers
Federal Communications Commission (FCC)	Regulates communication by wire, radio, and television in interstate and foreign commerce
Environmental Protection Agency (EPA)	Develops and enforces environmental protection standards and conducts research into the adverse effects of pollution
Federal Power Commission (FPC)	Regulates rates and sales of natural gas producers, thereby affecting the supply and price of gas available to consumers; also regulates wholesale rates for electricity and gas, pipeline construction, and U.S. imports and exports of natural gas and electricity

SOURCE: Adapted from Joseph Plummer, "The Concept and Application of Life Style Segmentation," *Journal of Marketing,* January 1974, p. 34.

■ State and Local Regulatory Agencies

All states—as well as many cities and towns—have regulatory agencies that enforce laws and regulations regarding marketing practices within their states or municipalities. The case discussed in Marketing Update 2.1 illustrates how agencies in Florida are taking action against fraudulent marketing practices. State and local regulatory agencies try not to establish and enforce regulations that conflict with those of national regulatory agencies. Instead, they generally enforce laws dealing with the production and sale of particular goods and services. Utilities, insurance, financial, and liquor industries are among those commonly regulated by state agencies.

■ Nongovernmental Regulatory Forces

In the absence of governmental regulatory forces and in an attempt to prevent government intervention, some businesses try to regulate themselves. For example, several U.S. newspapers have voluntarily banned advertisements for tobacco products from their pages.[7] Trade associations in a number of industries have developed self-regulatory programs. Even though these programs are not a direct outgrowth of laws, many were established to stop or stall the development of laws and governmental regulatory groups that would regulate the associations' marketing practices.

7. Patrick Reilly, "Ad Bans Go Local; City Official Asks Paper to Drop Tobacco," *Advertising Age,* Jan. 9, 1989, p. 42.

Sometimes trade associations establish codes of ethics by which their members must abide or risk censure by other members, or even exclusion from the program. For example, many cigarette manufacturers have agreed, through a code of ethics, not to advertise their products to children and teen-agers.

Self-regulatory programs have several advantages over governmental laws and regulatory agencies. They are usually less expensive to establish and implement, and their guidelines are generally more realistic and operational. In addition, effective industry self-regulatory programs reduce the need to expand government bureaucracy. However, these programs also have several limitations. When a trade association creates a set of industry guidelines for its members, nonmember firms do not have to abide by them. In addition, many self-regulatory programs lack the tools or the authority to enforce guidelines. Finally, guidelines in self-regulatory programs are often less strict than those established by government agencies.

Better Business Bureaus.   Perhaps the best-known nongovernmental regulatory group, the **Better Business Bureau** is a local regulatory agency supported by local businesses. Today more than 140 bureaus help settle problems between consumers and specific business firms. Each bureau also acts to preserve good business practices in a locality, although it usually does not have strong enforcement tools for dealing with firms that employ questionable practices. When a firm continues to violate what the Better Business Bureau believes to be good business practices, the bureau warns consumers through local newspapers or broadcast media that a particular business is operating unfairly.

The Council of Better Business Bureaus is a national organization comprising all the local Better Business Bureaus. The National Advertising Division (NAD) of the Council of Better Business Bureaus operates a self-regulatory program that investigates claims regarding alleged deceptive advertising. For example, after NAD reviewed a commercial for a Nintendo video game, it complained that the advertisement implied that Nintendo was the sole marketer of ice hockey video games, when in fact two other ice hockey games were on the market. Nintendo disagreed with the complaint, but agreed to consider NAD's concerns in future advertising campaigns.[8]

National Advertising Review Board.   The Council of Better Business Bureaus and three advertising trade organizations have created a self-regulatory unit. Called the **National Advertising Review Board (NARB)**, it considers cases in which an advertiser challenges issues raised by the National Advertising Division about an advertisement. Cases are reviewed by panels drawn from NARB members, who represent advertisers, agencies, and the public. The following example describes a typical case handled by the panels:

> NAD claimed that Featherspring International's advertisements for flexible foot supports include therapeutic claims that could not be substantiated by "scientifically planned studies," and therefore were misleading. Featherspring countered that medical, professional, and consumer testimonials and endorsements, as well as pages copied from technical and scientific publications on foot and lower back problems, were adequate backing for its therapeutic claims and took the case to the NARB for a final decision.[9]

8. "NAD Polishes Off Cleaners' Dispute," *Advertising Age,* Jan. 16, 1989, p. 49.

9. "Two Marketers Challenge NAD on Ad Decisions," *Advertising Age,* June 19, 1989, p. 66.

DEWKIST SELLS NONEXISTENT PLANTS

Recently, the Florida State Comptroller's office ordered Dewkist Plants, Inc., to stop selling unregistered securities in orchid and palm plants. State officials charged that the company was selling ownership interests in more plants than it actually had and that it was essentially operating a fraudulent scheme. Dewkist had orchestrated a fraudulent investment program in which early investors receive returns from funds obtained from newer investors, who often get nothing.

In 1984 George K. Bissell and F. Charles Donohue acquired some assets of John's Inc. and formed Dewkist Plants, Inc. Dewkist developed a business plan designed to generate large amounts of funds. Through the Dewkist Plant Growers Program, Dewkist offered to sell ownership interests in plants that the company hoped to sell to wholesalers and retailers for resale as houseplants. Dewkist claimed that investors who bought the plant-growing securities could realize as much as a 30 percent return on their investments when the mature plants were sold to wholesalers and retailers.

In exchange for a $50,000 investment, Dewkist agreed to care for and market the investors' plants. Upon maturation, Dewkist would sell the plants to wholesalers and retailers. The prospectus claimed that Dewkist had an established customer base, which consisted of supermarkets, home centers, flower shops, and mass-marketing stores and such well-known names as Kroger, K mart and Wal-Mart.

According to a cease and desist order issued by the State of Florida, 203 investors put up a total of $13.5 million into the Dewkist Plant Growers Program between February 1987 and November 1988. As of November 18, 1988, however, the company had little or no money in its bank accounts. Florida state investigators found that the company had far fewer plants and seeds on inventory than it claimed.

Dewkist filed for bankruptcy in federal court on December 29, 1988. On June 20, 1989, Donohue and Bissell were arrested on fifty-three criminal charges, which included racketeering, organized fraud, sale of unregistered securities, and securities fraud. Both denied any wrongdoing. The case is still pending.

SOURCES: "2 Executives Accused of Plant Scam," *Orlando Sentinel,* Jan. 1, 1989, p. B3; Suzy Hagstrom, "2 Charged in Nursery Scheme: Investors May Have Lost $13.5 Million," *Orlando Sentinel,* June 21, 1989, pp. B1–B2; Emergency Cease and Desist Order Issued by the Division of Securities of the State of Florida Department of Banking and Finance to Dewkist Plants, Inc., and Charles Donohue and George K. Bissell, Dec. 22, 1988; telephone conversation with William G. Reeves, chief trial counsel, Florida State Comptroller's Office, Jan. 11, 1989; company profile and other sales materials from Dewkist Plants, Inc.; and the Council of Better Business Bureaus and the North American Securities Administration, "Ponzis and Pyramids," in *Investor Alert! How to Protect Your Money from Schemes, Scams, and Frauds* (New York: The Benjamin Co., 1988), pp. 106–17.

The NARB has no official enforcement powers. However, if a firm refuses to comply with its decision, the NARB may publicize the questionable practice and file a complaint with the FTC.

■ Deregulation

As mentioned earlier, the federal government attempted in the 1980s to deregulate some industries in an effort to reduce the costs and paperwork associated with enforcing regulations and maintaining regulatory agencies. Although deregulation of the airline, railroad, trucking, and banking industries has stirred controversy, most members of these industries continue to act responsibly without the enforcement of regulatory agencies and laws. Nevertheless, society's reaction to deregulation is still mixed. Although consumers enjoyed the low fares resulting from the airfare wars waged throughout the airline industry after deregulation, they are unhappy with the level of service quality provided by the airlines and are especially concerned about increasing accident rates. Similarly, in the banking industry, competition is more intense, and banks can offer new products because they are no longer restricted to traditional checking and savings accounts. On the negative side, the number of bank and savings and loan association failures has risen since deregulation, and some of those failures were attributed to unethical or illegal practices. Future administrations may seek to reregulate these industries in the future.

SOCIETAL FORCES

Societal forces comprise the structure and dynamics of individuals and groups and the issues that engage them. Society becomes concerned about marketers' activities when those activities have questionable or negative consequences. For example, in recent times publicized incidents of unethical behavior by marketers and others have perturbed and even angered consumers. Chapter 3 therefore takes a detailed look at marketing ethics and social responsibility. When marketers do a good job of satisfying society, praise or positive evaluation rarely follows. Society expects marketers to provide a high standard of living and to protect the general quality of life. In this section we examine some of society's expectations, the vehicles used to express those expectations, and the problems and opportunities that marketers experience as they try to deal with society's often contradictory wishes.

■ Living Standards and Quality of Life

In our society, we want more than just the bare necessities; we want to achieve the highest standard of living possible. For example, we want not only protection from the elements, but also comfort and a satisfactory lifestyle. We want food that is safe and readily available, in many varieties and in easily prepared forms. We use our clothing to protect our bodies, but most of us want a variety of clothing for adornment and to project an "image" to others. We want vehicles that provide rapid, safe, and efficient transportation. We desire communication systems that give us information from around the globe—a desire apparent in the popularity of products such as facsimile machines and the twenty-four-hour news coverage provided by the Cable News Network. In addition, we want sophisticated medical services that prolong our life and improve our physical appearance. We also expect our education to equip us both to acquire and to enjoy a higher standard of living.

Our society's high material standard of living is not enough. We also desire a high degree of quality in our lives. Since we do not want to spend all our waking hours working, we seek leisure time for hobbies, recreation, and relaxation. The quality of

FIGURE 2.2

Environmentally concerned. Union Carbide expresses its commitment to cleaner air, purer water, less waste, and fewer carcinogens.

ENVIRONMENTAL EXCELLENCE

It's not an impossible dream.
We're committed to achieving it.
And we're making progress.

Our commitment: Cleaner air. Purer water. Less waste.
Among our goals, as we continue to improve our technology and
operating techniques: We will ultimately eliminate releases of
known and suspect carcinogens to the environment.

For a summary of some of our recent accomplishments and future
plans, send for Toward Environmental Excellence: A Progress Report,
available free on request from:

Union Carbide Corporation
Corporate Communications Department, Section C-2
39 Old Ridgebury Road   Danbury, CT 06817-0001

UNION CARBIDE

"We must be measured not by words, but by deeds."
Robert D. Kennedy
Chairman

SOURCE: Courtesy Union Carbide Corporation

life is enhanced by leisure time, clean air and water, an unlittered earth, conservation of wildlife and natural resources, and security from radiation and poisonous substances. A number of companies are expressing concerns about the quality of life. Union Carbide, for example, sends a clear message in Figure 2.2 that it is committed to environmental excellence.

Because of these desires, consumers have become increasingly concerned about environmental issues such as pollution, waste disposal, and the so-called greenhouse effect. Society's concerns have created both threats and opportunities for marketers. For example, one of society's biggest environmental problems is lack of space for garbage disposal, especially of plastic materials such as disposable diapers and Styrofoam packaging, which are not biodegradable. Companies like Penton Publications (see Figure 2.3) are expressing concerns about the garbage problem. Several cities have passed laws banning the use of all plastic packaging in stores and restaurants, and federal and local governments around the world are considering similar legislation. This trend has created problems for McDonald's and other fast food restaurants, which will have to develop packaging alternatives. Other firms, however, see such environmental problems as opportunities. Procter & Gamble, for example, markets its Spic & Span cleaner in bottles made of recycled plastic.[10] Environmentally responsible, or "green," marketing is even more extensive outside the United States. For example, West German companies Audi, Volkswagen, and BMW are

10. Brian Bremner, "A New Sales Pitch: The Environment," *Business Week,* July 24, 1989, p. 50.

FIGURE 2.3
Environmental concern—garbage. Penton Publications expresses concern about our 100 million ton garbage problem.

THERE'S ONE THING WE AMERICANS STILL PRODUCE BETTER THAN ANYBODY.

Last year we produced 160 million tons of it. More than half a ton from each of us. Plastic, aluminum, lawnmowings, rubber, glass, paper, and opportunity.

Your garbage is fast becoming somebody's bread and butter.

That's because trash is so troublesome. New York City alone throws away 27,750 tons of garbage every day. The problem: where to throw it.

Up till now, 80% of American garbage was dumped into landfills. But nobody wants to live next door to one. And in the last ten years, 70% of the landfill sites in the U.S. have closed.

That means for recyclers and incinerators, opportunity has opened.

Entrepreneurs with energy are improving waste-to-energy technologies, generating electricity at the same time they reduce the volume of landfill garbage by up to 90%. Already aluminum smelters are recycling 50% of the cans that are produced, and many communities are looking for new ways to recover the value of discarded iron, steel, glass, and paper.

One of the places they are looking is in publications like ours.

Penton believes that its thirty-two business, industry, and professional magazines have a responsibility to help people in business understand the new and react to it. Anticipate and exploit it.

To those who say opportunity is getting hard to find in America today, we say "Garbage."

We believe that a strong American business press helps make strong American business. And we appreciate your advertising support.

Penton Publications
Our issues address the tough issues.

Air Transport World, American Machinist, Automation, Chemical Engineering Catalog, Computer Aided Engineering, Contracting Business, The Foodservice Distributor, Foundry Management & Technology, Government Product News, Heating/Piping/Air Conditioning, Hydraulics & Pneumatics, Industry Week, Lodging Hospitality, Machine Design, Material Handling Engineering, Materials Engineering, Millimeter, Modern Office Technology, New Equipment Digest, Occupational Hazards, The PT Distributor, Penton Executive Network, Power Transmission Design, Precision Metal, Progressive Architecture, Restaurant Hospitality, School & College, 33 Metal Producing, Transportation & Distribution, Used Equipment Directory, Welding Design & Fabrication, Welding Distributor.

SOURCE: Reprinted with permission of Penton Publishing Inc.

manufacturing "cleaner" automobiles, which do not pollute the atmosphere as much as traditional automobiles. Italian chemical companies are investing billions to reduce toxic wastes from their plants, and British industry is investing equally large sums to scrub acid emissions from power stations and to treat sewage more effectively.[11] Marketing Update 2.2 provides additional details on how Wal-Mart Stores, Inc., and other firms are using "green" marketing to satisfy customers' concerns about the environment.

As these examples illustrate, changes in the forces of the marketing environment require careful monitoring and often demand a clear and effective response. Since marketing activities are a vital part of the total business structure, marketers have a responsibility to help provide what members of society want and to minimize what they do not want.

Consumer Movement Forces

The **consumer movement** is a diverse group of independent individuals, groups, and organizations that seeks to protect the rights of consumers. The main issues pursued by the consumer movement fall into three categories: environmental protection, product performance and safety, and information disclosure. The movement's major forces are individual consumer advocates, consumer organizations and other interest groups, consumer education, and consumer laws.

11. Robin Knight, with Eleni Dimmler, "The Greening of Europe's Industries," *U.S. News & World Report,* June 5, 1989, pp. 45–46.

WAL-MART FOCUSES ON "GREEN" MARKETING

With a new ecological awareness, consumers today want their environment protected from pollutants, toxins, and exploitation. Environmental, or "green," marketing is a way for marketers to appeal to consumers' environmental concerns. "Green" products are safer for the environment and include items such as biodegradable garbage bags and diapers, tissues made from recycled paper, and detergent that is free of phosphates. By effectively marketing such products, a company can improve its bottom line as well as the biosphere.

The media have bombarded the public with information on the desperate state of America's landfills, the medical refuse that washed ashore on northeastern beaches, and the damage done to Alaskan waters by the eleven million gallons of oil spilled by the *Exxon Valdez*. Taking note of the crises and disasters, consumers have shown an interest in products that do not endanger the environment in any way.

Sam Walton, chief executive officer of Wal-Mart Stores, Inc., was among the first business executives to embrace the notion of green marketing. Wal-Mart, the fastest growing retailer in the United States and an influential leader in the retail industry, wants to offer shoppers the option of purchasing environmentally safe products instead of ones that contribute to pollution and landfill problems. Wal-Mart executives want to stock merchandise with packaging that is better for the environment in three respects—manufacturing, use, and disposal.

Through advertisements, Walton announced that he is seeking "safe" products to sell in Wal-Mart stores. The headline for one full-page advertisement in the *Wall Street Journal* and *USA Today* confirmed Walton's search for products that do not harm the environment. As part of special advertising to promote "green" items, Walton plans to place signs next to environmentally safe products so that customers will be drawn to them.

A survey of one thousand adults found that 77 percent were willing to pay extra for a product packaged with recyclable or biodegradable materials. More than 53 percent stated that they had not bought a particular product in the last year because they worried about that product's effect on the environment. As Wal-Mart executives see it, environmental concerns may loom so large for consumers that they will affect everyday decisions. One Wal-Mart executive said that customers are concerned about the quality of land, air, and water, and would like the opportunity to do something positive.

SOURCES: Christy Fisher and Judith Graham, "Wal-Mart Throws 'Green' Gauntlet," *Advertising Age,* Aug. 21, 1989, pp. 1, 66; Jeremy Main, "Here Comes the Big New Cleanup," *Fortune,* Nov. 21, 1988, pp. 102–103, 106, 110, 112, 114, 118; and Kevin Maney, "Companies Make Products Nicer to Nature," *USA Today,* Aug. 23, 1989, pp. 1B–2B.

Consumer advocates, such as Ralph Nader, take it upon themselves to protect the rights of consumers. They band together into consumer organizations, either voluntarily or under government sponsorship. Some organizations, such as the National Consumers' League and the Consumer Federation of America, operate nationally, whereas others are active at state and local levels. They inform and organize other consumers, raise issues, help businesses develop consumer-oriented programs, and pressure lawmakers to enact consumer protection laws. Some consumer advocates and organizations encourage consumers to boycott products and businesses to which they have objections. The American Family Association and Christian Leaders for Responsible TV have organized consumer boycotts against advertisers on television programs that feature sex, violence, or profanity. The boycotts prompted a few advertisers, including Kimberly-Clark and Tambrands, to drop advertising during some controversial programs, such as "Married . . . With Children."[12]

Educating consumers to make wiser purchasing decisions is perhaps one of the most far-reaching aspects of the consumer movement. Increasingly, consumer education is becoming a part of high school and college curricula and adult education programs. These programs cover many topics—for instance, what major factors should be considered when buying specific products, such as insurance, real estate, automobiles, appliances and furniture, clothes, and food; the provisions of certain consumer protection laws; and the sources of information that can help individuals become knowledgeable consumers.

ECONOMIC AND COMPETITIVE FORCES

The economic and competitive forces in the marketing environment influence both marketers' and customers' decisions and activities. In this section, we first examine the effects of general economic conditions. We also focus on buying power, willingness to spend, spending patterns, and competition. Then we look at competitive forces, including types of competitive structures, competitive tools, and methods for monitoring competitive behavior.

■ **General Economic Conditions**

The overall state of the economy fluctuates in all countries. These changes in general economic conditions affect (and are affected by) the forces of supply and demand, buying power, willingness to spend, consumer expenditure levels, and the intensity of competitive behavior. Therefore, current economic conditions and changes in the economy have a broad impact on the success of organizations' marketing strategies. Fluctuations in the U.S. economy follow a general pattern often referred to as the business cycle. In the traditional view, the business cycle consists of four stages: prosperity, recession, depression, and recovery.

During **prosperity**, unemployment is low and total income is relatively high. Assuming a low inflation rate, this combination causes buying power to be high. To the extent that the economic outlook remains prosperous, consumers generally are willing to buy. In the prosperity stage, marketers often expand their product mixes (product, distribution, promotion, and price) to take advantage of the increased buying power. They sometimes capture a larger market share by intensifying distribution and promotion efforts.

12. Wayne Walley, "Decency Debate; Angered by 'Lewd' TV Programs, Groups Threaten Sponsor Boycotts," *Advertising Age*, Mar. 6, 1989, pp. 1, 74.

Because unemployment rises during a **recession**, total buying power declines. The pessimism that accompanies a recession often stifles both consumer and business spending. As buying power decreases, many consumers become more price- and value-conscious; they look for products that are basic and functional. For instance, people ordinarily reduce their consumption of the more expensive convenience foods and strive to save money by growing and preparing more of their own victuals. Individuals buy fewer durable goods and more repair and do-it-yourself products. During a recession, some firms make the mistake of drastically reducing their marketing efforts and thus damage their ability to survive. Obviously, marketers should consider some revision of their marketing activities during a recessionary period. Because consumers are more concerned about the functional value of products, a company must focus its marketing research on determining precisely what product functions buyers want and then make sure that these functions become part of its products. Promotional efforts should emphasize value and utility.

A **depression** is a period in which unemployment is extremely high, wages are very low, total disposable income is at a minimum, and consumers lack confidence in the economy. The federal government has used both monetary and fiscal policies to offset the effects of recession and depression. Monetary policies are employed to control the money supply, which in turn affects spending, saving, and investment by both individuals and businesses. Through fiscal policies, the government can influence the amount of savings and expenditures by altering the tax structure and by changing the levels of government spending. Some experts believe that effective use of monetary and fiscal policies can eliminate depressions from the business cycle.

Recovery is the stage of the business cycle in which the economy moves from depression or recession to prosperity. During this period, the high unemployment rate begins to decline, total disposable income increases, and the economic gloom that lessened consumers' willingness to buy subsides. Both the ability and the willingness to buy rise. Marketers face some problems during recovery—for example, the difficulty of ascertaining how quickly prosperity will return and of forecasting the level of prosperity that will be attained. In this stage, marketers should maintain as much flexibility in their marketing strategies as possible to be able to make the needed adjustments as the economy moves from recession to prosperity.

■ Consumer Demand and Spending Behavior

Marketers must understand the factors that determine whether, what, where, and when people buy. In Chapters 5 and 6 we look at behavioral factors underlying these choices, but here we focus on the economic components: buying power, willingness to purchase, and spending patterns.

Buying Power. The strength of a person's **buying power** depends on the size of the resources that enable the individual to purchase and on the state of the economy. The resources that make up buying power are goods, services, and financial holdings. Fluctuations of the business cycle affect buying power because they influence price levels and interest rates. For example, during inflationary periods, when prices are rising, buying power decreases because more dollars are required to buy products. Table 2.3 compares 1980 and 1990 prices for selected products.

The major financial sources of buying power are income, credit, and wealth. From an individual's viewpoint, **income** is the amount of money received through wages, rents, investments, pensions, and subsidy payments for a given period, such as a month or a year. Normally, this money is allocated among taxes, spending for

TABLE 2.3 *A comparison of 1980 and 1990 prices for selected products*

PRODUCT	1980	1990	PERCENT CHANGE
Roll of Kodak Color Film: 35 mm, 24 exp., 100-speed	$3.08	$4.60	+49%
Lionel Electric Train Set	$63	$75	+19%
Monthly Electric Bill: 500 Kilowatt-hours from Union Electric Company, St. Louis	$23.86	$36.90	+55%
Single-Family Home: Median price of an existing home	$62,200	$93,000	+50%
One-Day Admission to Walt Disney World: Adult, child	$13, $11	$29, $23	+123%, +109%
Fast Food Meal: McDonald's hamburger, regular fries and small soft drink	$1.21	$1.93	+60%
Plumbing Service Call: Idaho Pump & Plumbing Company, Boise	$21	$32	+52%
Grand Ole Opry: Nashville, adult admission	$8	$14	+75%
Movie Tickets: Average price for 2 adults and 2 children	$10.76	$16.64	+55%
Super Bowl Ticket: Super Bowl XIV & Super Bowl XXIV	$30	$125	+317%
Chevrolet Caprice Classic Wagon: 8 cylinders	$7,158	$15,725	+120%
Armani Man's Suit: Medium weight, wool, 2-piece navy blue at Boyd's in Philadelphia	$550	$950	+73%
Omaha (Neb.) World-Herald: Daily newspaper	$.10	$.25	+150%
L.L. Bean Country Corduroy Pants	$30.50	$39	+28%
Stieff Sterling Silver: Golden Winslow style flatware, service for eight	$3,476	$4,464	+28%
Haircut, Styling and Blow Dry: Plaza Hotel, New York City	$26	$33	+27%
Haircut: Rims Barber Shop, Billings, Montana	$6	$7	+17%
Athletic Shoes: Pair of Converse All-Stars	$20	$30	+50%
Round-Trip Flight: Full fare, NY-LA on American Airlines	$570	$1,234	+117%
Oscar Mayer Hot Dogs: One pound, all-beef franks	$1.94	$2.52	+30%
Loaf of Bread: Home Pride Buttertop 20 oz., Shopwell, New York City	$.71	$1.95	+124%
Quart of Milk: Shopwell, New York City	$.45	$.87	+93%
Webster's New World Dictionary: 2nd college ed., 3rd college ed.	$11.95	$17.95	+50%
People Weekly: Cover Price	$.75	$1.95	+160%
One Year of a College Education: Undergraduate tuition, room and board, Ohio State University, Columbus	$3,192	$5,550	+74%
One Day in the Hospital: Semi-private room at Saint Mary's Hospital, Mayo Foundation, Rochester, Minn.	$109	$265	+143%
Doctor's Appointment: First visit to general practitioner, South Atlantic region	$30.94	$58.29	+88%
Pack of Camel Cigarettes	$.65	$1.57	+142%
Broadway Show Orchestra Seat: At Winter Garden Theater, NYC Then: "Comin' Uptown" Now: "Cats"	$25	$55	+120%
Cable Car Ride: San Francisco	$.25	$2	+700%
La-Z-Boy Recliner Chair: Model 817	$299	$450	+51%
Monopoly Game	$6.99	$10	+43%

SOURCE: Copyright 1990, USA TODAY. Reprinted with permission.

goods and services, and savings. The average annual family income in the United States is approximately $25,986.[13] However, because of the differences in people's educational levels, abilities, occupations, and wealth, income is not equally distributed in this country (or in other countries).

Marketers are most interested in the amount of money that is left after payment of taxes. After-tax income is called **disposable income** and is used for spending or saving. Because disposable income is a ready source of buying power, the total amount available in a nation is important to marketers. Several factors affect the size of total disposable income. One, of course, is the total amount of income. Total national income is affected by wage levels, rate of unemployment, interest rates, and dividend rates. These factors in turn affect the size of disposable income. Because disposable income is the income left after taxes are paid, the number of taxes and their amount directly affect the size of total disposable income. When taxes rise, disposable income declines; when taxes fall, disposable income increases.

Disposable income that is available for spending and saving after an individual has purchased the basic necessities of food, clothing, and shelter is called **discretionary income**. People use discretionary income to purchase entertainment, vacations, automobiles, education, pets and pet supplies, furniture, appliances, and so on. Changes in total discretionary income affect the sales of these products—especially automobiles, furniture, large appliances, and other costly durable goods.

Credit enables people to spend future income now or in the near future. However, credit increases current buying power at the expense of future buying power. Several factors determine whether consumers use or forego credit. First, credit must be available to consumers. Interest rates, too, affect consumers' decisions to use credit, especially for expensive purchases such as homes, appliances, and automobiles. When credit charges are high, consumers are more likely to delay buying expensive items. Use of credit is also affected by credit terms, such as the size of the down payment and the amount and number of monthly payments.

A person can have a high income and very little wealth. It is also possible, but not likely, for a person to have great wealth but not much income. **Wealth** is the accumulation of past income, natural resources, and financial resources. It may exist in many forms, including cash, securities, savings accounts, jewelry, antiques, and real estate. Like income, wealth is unevenly distributed. The significance of wealth to marketers is that as people become wealthier they gain buying power in three ways: they can use their wealth to make current purchases, to generate income, and to acquire large amounts of credit.

Buying power information is available from government sources, trade associations, and research agencies. One of the most current and comprehensive sources of buying power data is the *Sales & Marketing Management Survey of Buying Power*, published annually by *Sales & Marketing Management* magazine. As Table 2.4 shows, the *Survey of Buying Power* presents effective buying income data and the buying power index for specific geographic areas, including states, counties, and most cities with populations exceeding forty thousand. The *Survey of Buying Power* also contains population and retail sales data for the same geographic areas (not shown in Table 2.4).

The most direct indicators of buying power in the *Survey of Buying Power* are effective buying income and buying power index. **Effective buying income (EBI)** is similar to what we call disposable income; it includes salaries, wages, dividends,

13. Judith Waldrop, "Inside America's Households," *American Demographics,* Mar. 1989, pp. 22–23.

TABLE 2.4 Sales & Marketing Management's *U.S. metropolitan area projections*

METRO AREA County City	Total EBI ($000)	Median Hsld. EBI	% of Hslds. by EBI Group (A) $10,000–$19,999 (B) $20,000–$34,999 (C) $35,000–$49,999 (D) $50,000 & Over				Buying Power Index
			A	B	C	D	
SUBURBAN TOTAL	17,435,081	39,533	13.6	21.6	18.9	37.6	.5019
SAN FRANCISCO–OAKLAND–SAN JOSE CONSOLIDATED AREA	**106,804,389**	**35,227**	**15.7**	**22.0**	**18.3**	**32.0**	**3.1130**
SAN JOSE	**26,185,653**	**41,717**	**12.3**	**20.3**	**19.3**	**40.2**	**.7518**
Santa Clara	26,185,653	41,717	12.3	20.3	19.3	40.2	.7518
Mountain View	1,319,203	35,676	14.1	26.4	21.2	30.0	.0398
Palo Alto	1,341,521	44,012	12.1	19.6	16.4	44.4	.0411
San Jose	12,097,651	40,894	12.8	20.0	20.2	38.4	.3488
Santa Clara	1,650,887	39,478	13.0	22.9	19.4	36.9	.0531
Sunnyvale	2,349,000	41,807	11.6	22.3	19.9	40.3	.0657
SUBURBAN TOTAL	12,746,481	42,460	11.9	20.7	18.3	41.8	.3619
SANTA BARBARA–SANTA MARIA–LOMPOC	**5,269,900**	**29,021**	**20.5**	**24.5**	**17.2**	**23.9**	**.1707**
Santa Barbara	5,269,900	29,021	20.5	24.5	17.2	23.9	.1707
Lompoc	419,915	27,269	21.9	23.8	20.2	17.8	.0135
Santa Barbara	1,349,235	24,823	23.4	26.0	14.1	20.0	.0479
Santa Maria	672,705	26,583	21.6	27.1	19.8	16.1	.0310
SUBURBAN TOTAL	2,828,045	33,246	18.2	23.1	17.6	29.9	.0783
SANTA CRUZ	**3,514,362**	**28,956**	**20.1**	**23.2**	**16.8**	**24.9**	**.1019**
Santa Cruz	3,514,362	28,956	20.1	23.2	16.8	24.9	.1019
Santa Cruz	682,328	24,315	22.5	22.4	15.3	20.0	.0250
SUBURBAN TOTAL	2,832,034	30,326	19.5	23.4	17.2	26.2	.0769

SOURCE: Reprinted by permission of *Sales & Marketing Management.* Copyright 1989, *Sales & Marketing Management. Survey of Buying Power,* 1989.

interest, profits, and rents, less federal, state, and local taxes. The **buying power index (BPI)** is a weighted index, consisting of population, effective buying income, and retail sales data.[14] The higher the index number, the greater the buying power. Like other indexes, the buying power index is most useful for comparative purposes. Marketers can use buying power indexes for a particular year to compare the buying power of one area with the buying power of another, or they can analyze trends for a particular area by comparing the area's buying power indexes for several years.

14. *Sales & Marketing Management 1989 Survey of Buying Power,* Aug. 7, 1989.

Income, wealth, and credit equip consumers to purchase goods and services. Marketing managers should be aware of current levels and expected changes in buying power in their own markets because buying power directly affects the types and quantities of goods and services that consumers purchase, as we see later in our discussion of spending patterns. Just because consumers have buying power, however, does not mean that they will buy. Consumers must also be willing to use their buying power.

Consumers' Willingness to Spend.   People's **willingness to spend** is, to some degree, related to their ability to buy. That is, people are sometimes more willing to buy if they have the buying power. However, a number of other elements also influence willingness to spend. Some elements affect specific products; others influence spending in general. A product's absolute price and its price relative to the price of substitute products influence almost all of us. The amount of satisfaction currently received or expected in the future from a product already owned may also influence consumers' desire to buy other products. Satisfaction depends not only on the quality of the functional performance of the currently owned product, but also on numerous psychological and social forces.

Factors that affect consumers' general willingness to spend are expectations about future employment, income levels, prices, family size, and general economic conditions. If people are unsure whether or how long they will be employed, willingness to buy ordinarily declines. Willingness to spend may increase if people are reasonably certain of higher incomes in the future. Expectations of rising prices in the near future may also increase the willingness to spend in the present. For a given level of buying power, the larger the family, the greater the willingness to buy. One of the reasons for this relationship is that as the size of a family increases, a greater number of dollars must be spent to provide the basic necessities of life to sustain the family members. Finally, perceptions of future economic conditions influence willingness to buy. For example, in the late 1980s, rising short-term interest rates and changes in the tax laws that phased out deductions for interest paid on loans and credit cards made credit card purchases more expensive and cooled consumers' willingness to spend.[15]

Consumer Spending Patterns.   Marketers must be aware of the factors that influence consumers' ability and willingness to spend, but they should also analyze how consumers actually spend their disposable incomes. Marketers obtain this information by studying consumer spending patterns. **Consumer spending patterns** indicate the relative proportions of annual family expenditures or the actual amount of money spent on certain kinds of goods and services. Families are usually categorized by one of several characteristics, including family income, age of the household head, geographic area, and family life cycle. There are two types of spending patterns: comprehensive and product-specific.

The percentages of family income allotted to annual expenditures for general classes of goods and services constitute **comprehensive spending patterns**. Comprehensive spending patterns or the data to develop them are available in government publications and in reports of the Conference Board—a national trade organization for businesses. In Table 2.5, comprehensive spending patterns are classified

15. Mark Memmott, "Consumers Are Spent, Saving More," *USA Today*, Aug. 31, 1989, pp. 1, 2B.

TABLE 2.5 *Spending Based on Family Life Cycle*

ITEM	All Consumer Units	Total Husband and Wife Consumer Units	Husband and Wife Only	Husband and Wife with Children			Other Husband and Wife Consumer Units	One Parent at Least One Child Under 18	Single Person and Other Consumer Units
				Oldest Child Under 6	Oldest Child 6–17	Oldest Child 18 or Over			
Total Expenditures	$21,788	$27,024	$23,071	$24,024	$29,865	$32,869	$27,987	$16,916	$14,910
Food	15.6%	15.6%	14.6%	14.2%	16.5%	16.4%	16.8%	17.3%	15.0%
Alcoholic Beverages	1.4%	1.1%	1.3%	1.1%	1.0%	1.1%	1.1%	0.8%	2.1%
Housing	30.4%	29.6%	30.2%	35.8%	30.8%	24.3%	27.1%	34.2%	31.9%
Utilities, Fuels, and Public Services	7.7%	7.6%	7.6%	7.1%	7.5%	7.6%	8.4%	8.8%	7.9%
Housefurnishings and Equipment	4.0%	4.2%	4.5%	4.3%	4.4%	3.6%	3.5%	3.4%	3.5%
Apparel and Services	5.5%	5.4%	4.7%	5.4%	6.0%	5.6%	5.3%	6.6%	5.5%
Transportation	20.1%	20.7%	20.4%	18.8%	19.2%	23.3%	23.4%	16.9%	19.3%
Health Care	4.1%	4.2%	5.5%	3.7%	3.2%	3.8%	4.4%	2.8%	4.2%
Entertainment	4.8%	5.0%	4.4%	5.0%	6.0%	4.6%	4.2%	4.3%	4.3%
Personal Care	9.4%	9.5%	1.1%	0.7%	0.9%	1.0%	1.0%	0.9%	0.9%
Reading	0.6%	0.6%	0.7%	0.6%	0.6%	0.6%	0.5%	0.5%	0.7%
Education	1.4%	1.3%	1.0%	0.4%	1.3%	2.7%	1.0%	1.7%	1.6%
Tobacco and Smoking Supplies	1.0%	1.0%	1.0%	0.9%	0.9%	0.8%	1.3%	1.1%	1.1%
Miscellaneous	1.4%	1.1%	1.1%	1.1%	1.1%	1.1%	1.3%	1.5%	2.2%
Cash Contributions	3.4%	3.3%	4.0%	2.2%	2.6%	3.9%	2.8%	5.3%	3.4%
Personal Insurance and Pensions	9.3%	10.1%	10.0%	9.9%	10.0%	10.6%	9.9%	6.0%	7.7%

SOURCE: U.S. Department of Labor, Bureau of Labor Statistics, "Consumer Expenditure Survey: Interview Survey," August 1986, pp. 31–32.

TABLE 2.6 *Annual dollar expenditures for nonfrozen bakery products by various household incomes*

	Total	Under $5,000	$5,000–$10,000	$10,000–$15,000	$15,000–$20,000	$20,000–$25,000	$25,000–$35,000	$35,000–$50,000	$50,000 and Above
HOUSEHOLDS (MILLIONS)	70.0	12.5	12.5	10.2	8.7	8.0	10.7	5.4	2.1
DISTRIBUTION OF HOUSEHOLDS	100.0%	17.9	17.9	14.5	12.4	11.4	15.3	7.7	3.1
AVERAGE HOUSEHOLD SIZE	2.6	1.9	2.1	2.4	2.8	3.0	3.1	3.4	3.3
DISTRIBUTION OF PERSONS	100.0%	13.0	14.7	13.4	13.5	13.0	18.6	10.0	3.9
DISTRIBUTION OF INCOME	100.0%	2.5	7.4	10.2	12.2	14.3	25.4	17.8	10.2
EXPENDITURES OF DOLLARS	*Average*								
Nonfrozen bakery products	144.79	98.01	112.89	117.98	151.22	165.77	192.42	215.82	210.64
White bread	40.64	31.68	33.81	37.66	41.99	48.22	49.42	50.62	44.26
Bread other than white	16.98	11.91	14.52	15.45	17.27	17.67	21.14	23.00	28.60
Fresh biscuits, rolls, etc.	17.55	9.51	11.37	13.14	19.13	20.57	24.43	33.40	29.55
Cakes and cupcakes	16.29	9.57	14.10	11.50	18.23	17.44	22.44	25.38	25.21
Cookies	19.52	12.31	13.62	14.95	19.87	22.71	29.16	29.99	29.78
Crackers	11.23	7.79	8.59	9.66	10.70	13.03	14.50	16.65	19.74
Bread and cracker products	2.11	1.06	1.25	1.70	2.19	2.51	2.42	5.16	4.14
Doughnuts, sweetrolls, etc.	15.81	11.46	11.58	10.59	15.76	18.48	22.78	24.72	23.62
Fresh pies and tarts	4.67	2.72	4.05	3.32	6.09	5.16	6.12	6.90	5.73

HOUSEHOLD INCOME

SOURCE: Consumer Research Center, *How Consumers Spend Their Money* (New York: Conference Board, 1984), pp. 20, 44. Used by permission.

by the life cycle of the family. Note the variation in expenditures between two-parent families and single-parent families.

Product-specific spending patterns indicate the annual dollar amounts families spend for specific products within a general product class. Information sources used to construct product-specific spending patterns include government publications, the Conference Board, trade publications, and consumer surveys. Table 2.6 illustrates a product-specific spending pattern. Notice the differences between this type of spending pattern and the comprehensive ones. The products listed fall into one general product category, and the figures are stated in dollar amounts.

A marketer uses spending patterns to analyze general trends in the ways that families spend their incomes for various kinds of products. For example, a person who is considering opening a bakery might use the data in Table 2.5 to estimate the demand for various categories of bakery products. Analyses of spending patterns yield information that a marketer can use to gain perspective and background for decision making. However, spending patterns reflect only general trends and thus should not be used as the sole basis for making specific decisions.

■ Assessment of Competitive Forces

Few firms, if any, operate free of competition. Broadly speaking, all firms compete with each other for consumers' dollars. From a more practical viewpoint, however, a business generally defines **competition** as those firms that market products that are similar to, or can be substituted for, its products in the same geographic area. For example, a local A & P supermarket manager views all grocery stores in town as competitors but almost never thinks of other types of local or out-of-town stores as competitors. In this section, we consider the types of competitive structures and the importance of monitoring competitors.

Types of Competitive Structures.   The number of firms that control the supply of a product may affect the strength of competition. When only one or a few firms control supply, competitive factors will exert a different sort of influence on marketing activities than when there are many competitors. Table 2.7 presents four general types of competitive structures: monopoly, oligopoly, monopolistic competition, and perfect competition.

A **monopoly** exists when a firm turns out a product that has no close substitutes. Because the organization has no competitors, it completely controls the supply of the product and, as a single seller, can erect barriers to potential competitors. In actuality, most monopolies that survive today are local utilities, such as telephone, electricity, and cable companies, which are heavily regulated by local, state, or federal agencies. These monopolies are tolerated because of the tremendous financial resources needed to develop and operate them; few organizations can obtain the resources to mount any competition against a local electricity producer, for example.

An **oligopoly** exists when a few sellers control the supply of a large proportion of a product. In this case, each seller must consider the reactions of other sellers to changes in marketing activities. Products facing oligopolistic competition may be homogeneous, such as aluminum, or differentiated, such as cigarettes and automobiles. Usually, barriers of some sort make it difficult to enter the market and compete with oligopolies. For example, because of the enormous financial outlay required, few companies or individuals could afford to enter the oil-refining or steel-producing industries. Moreover, some industries demand special technical or marketing skills that block the entry of many potential competitors.

TABLE 2.7 *Selected characteristics of competitive structures*

TYPE OF STRUCTURE	NUMBER OF COMPETITORS	EASE OF ENTRY INTO MARKET	PRODUCT	KNOWLEDGE OF MARKET	EXAMPLE
Monopoly	One	Many barriers	Almost no substitutes	Perfect	Dayton (Ohio) Power and Light (gas and electricity service)
Oligopoly	Few	Some barriers	Homogeneous or differentiated (real or perceived differences) products	Imperfect	Philip Morris (cigarettes)
Monopolistic competition	Many	Few barriers	Product differentiation with many substitutes	More knowledge than oligopoly; less than monopoly	Levi Strauss (jeans)
Perfect competition	Unlimited	No barriers	Homogeneous products	Perfect	Vegetable farm (sweet corn)

Monopolistic competition exists when a firm with many potential competitors attempts to develop a differential marketing strategy to establish its own market share. For example, Levi's has established a differential advantage for its blue jeans through a well-known trademark, design, advertising, and a quality image. Although many competing brands of blue jeans are available, this firm has carved out its market share through use of a differential marketing strategy.

Perfect competition, if it existed at all, would entail a large number of sellers, not one of which could significantly influence price or supply. Products would be homogeneous, and there would be full knowledge of the market and easy entry into it. The closest thing to an example of perfect competition would be an unregulated agricultural market.

Few, if any, marketers operate in a structure of perfect competition. Perfect competition is an ideal at one end of the continuum, with monopoly at the other end. Most marketers function in a competitive environment that falls somewhere between these two extremes.

Competitive Tools.   Another set of factors that influences the level of competition is the number and types of competitive tools used by competitors. To survive, a firm uses one or several available competitive tools to deal with competitive economic forces. Once a company has analyzed its particular competitive environment and decided which factors in that environment it can or must adapt to or influence, it can choose among the variables that it can control to strengthen its competitive position in the overall marketplace.

Probably the first competitive tool that most organizations grasp is price. Bic Corp., for example, markets disposable pens and lighters that are similar to competing products but less expensive. However, there is one major problem with using price as a competitive tool: competitors will often match or beat the price. This threat is one of the primary reasons for employing nonprice competitive tools that are based on the differentiation of market segments, product offering, promotion, distribution, or enterprise.[16]

By focusing on a specific market segment, a marketer sometimes gains a competitive advantage. For instance, Apple Computer, Inc., and International Business Machines Corp. (IBM) have each tried to gain a competitive edge by incorporating product features that make their brands distinctive to some extent. Firms use distinguishing promotional methods to compete, such as advertising and personal selling. Competing producers sometimes use different distribution channels to prevail over each other. Merchants may compete by placing their outlets in locations that are convenient for a large number of shoppers.

Monitoring Competition.   Marketers in an organization need to be aware of the actions of major competitors. They should monitor what competitors are currently doing and assess the changes occurring in the competitive environment. Monitoring allows firms to determine what specific strategies competitors are following and how those strategies affect their own. It can also guide marketers as they try to develop competitive advantages and aid them in adjusting current marketing strategies, as well as in planning new ones. Information may come from direct observation or from sources such as salespeople, customers, trade publications, syndicated marketing research services, distributors, and marketing studies.

An organization needs information about competitors that will allow its marketing managers to assess the performance of its own marketing efforts. Comparing their company's performance with that of competitors helps marketing managers recognize strengths and weaknesses in their own marketing strategies. Data about market shares, product movement, sales volume, and expenditure levels can be useful. However, accurate information on these matters is often difficult to obtain.

TECHNOLOGICAL FORCES

The word *technology* brings to mind creations of progress such as computers, superconductors, lasers, and heart transplants. Even though such items are outgrowths of technology, none of them is technology. **Technology** has been defined as the knowledge of how to accomplish tasks and goals.[17] Often this knowledge comes from scientific research. The effects of technology are broad in scope and today exert a tremendous influence on our lives.

Technology grows out of research performed by businesses, universities, and nonprofit organizations. More than half of this research is paid for by the federal government, which supports investigations in a variety of areas, including health, defense, agriculture, energy, and pollution. Because much federally funded research

16. Wroe Alderson, *Dynamic Marketing Behavior* (Homewood, Ill.: Irwin, 1965), pp. 195–97.

17. Herbert Simon, "Technology and Environment," *Management Science,* June 1973, p. 1110.

requires the use of specialized machinery, personnel, and facilities, a sizable proportion of this research is conducted by large business organizations that already possess the necessary specialized equipment and people.

The rapid technological growth of the last several decades is expected to continue through the 1990s. Areas that hold great technological promise include digital electronics, artificial intelligence, superconductors, materials research, and biotechnology. Current research is investigating new forms of memory chips and computers that are a hundred times faster and smaller than current models. Because these and other technological developments will clearly have an impact on buyers' and marketers' decisions, we now turn, in our discussion, to the effects of technology on society and marketers. We then consider several factors that influence the adoption and use of technology.

■ The Impact of Technology

Marketers must be aware of new developments in technology and their possible effects because technology can and does affect marketing activities in many different ways. Consumers' technological knowledge influences their desires for goods and services. To provide marketing mixes that satisfy consumers, marketers must be aware of these influences.

The various ways in which technology affects marketing activities fall into two broad categories. It affects consumers and society in general, and it influences what, how, when, and where products are marketed.

Effects of Technology on Society. Technology determines how we, as members of society, satisfy our physiological needs. In various ways and to varying degrees, eating and drinking habits, sleeping patterns, sexual activities, and health care are all influenced by both existing technology and changes in technology. Technological developments have improved our standard of living, thus giving us more leisure time; they have also enhanced information, entertainment, and education. As indicated in Figure 2.4, General Dynamics supports a program in which robotics is used to stimulate students and enhance their education.

Nevertheless, technology can detract from the quality of life through undesirable side effects, such as unemployment, polluted air and water, and other health hazards. Some people believe that further applications of technology can soften or eliminate these undesirable side effects; others argue that the best way to improve the quality of our lives is to decrease the use of technology.

Effects of Technology on Marketing. Technology also affects the types of products that marketers can offer. The introduction and general acceptance of cassette tapes and compact discs drove manufacturers of vinyl long-playing (LP) albums out of business or forced them to invest in new technology. Yet this technology provided new marketing opportunities for recording artists and producers, record companies, retailers, and those in related industries. The following items are only a few of the many thousands of existing products that were not available to consumers twenty years ago: home plaque-removal systems, disposable 35mm cameras, cellular telephones, ultralight laptop computers, and high-resolution television.

Computer technology helps make warehouse storage and keeping track of stored products more efficient, and therefore, less expensive. Often these savings can be passed on to consumers in the form of lower prices. Because of technological changes in communications, marketers now can reach large masses of people through a variety of media more efficiently. The development and widespread use of

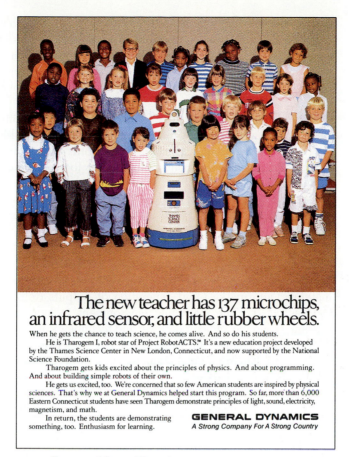

The new teacher has 137 microchips, an infrared sensor, and little rubber wheels.

When he gets the chance to teach science, he comes alive. And so do his students.

He is Tharogem I, robot star of Project RobotACTS.™ It's a new education project developed by the Thames Science Center in New London, Connecticut, and now supported by the National Science Foundation.

Tharogem gets kids excited about the principles of physics. And about programming. And about building simple robots of their own.

He gets us excited, too. We're concerned that so few American students are inspired by physical sciences. That's why we at General Dynamics helped start this program. So far, more than 6,000 Eastern Connecticut students have seen Tharogem demonstrate principles of light, sound, electricity, magnetism, and math.

In return, the students are demonstrating something, too. Enthusiasm for learning.

GENERAL DYNAMICS
A Strong Company For A Strong Country

SOURCE: Courtesy of General Dynamics

facsimile machines and services, for example, allows marketers to send their advertisements directly to selected groups of customers who want their products.

Technological advances in transportation enable consumers to travel farther and more often to shop at a larger number of stores. Changes in transportation also have affected the producers' ability to get products to retailers and wholesalers. The ability of present-day manufacturers of relatively lightweight products to reach any of their dealers within twenty-four hours (via overnight express delivery services, such as Federal Express) would astound their counterparts of fifty years ago.

Adoption and Use of Technology

Through a procedure known as **technology assessment**, managers try to foresee the effects of new products and processes on their firm's operation, on other business organizations, and on society in general. With the information gained through a technology assessment, management tries to estimate whether the benefits of using a specific kind of technology outweigh the costs to the firm and to society at large. The degree to which a business is technologically based will also influence how its management responds to technology. Firms whose products and product changes grow out of recent technology strive to gather and use technological information.

Although available technology could radically improve their products (or other parts of the marketing mix), some companies may put off applying this technology as long as their competitors do not try to use it. The extent to which a firm can protect inventions stemming from research also influences its use of technology. How secure a product is from imitation depends on how easily it can be copied by others without violating its patent. If new products and processes cannot be protected through patents, a company is less likely to market them and make the benefits of its research available to competitors.

How a company uses (or does not use) technology is important for its long-run survival. A firm that makes the wrong decisions may well lose out to the competition. Poor decisions may also affect its profits by requiring expensive corrective actions. Poor decisions about technological forces may even drive a firm out of business.

SUMMARY

The marketing environment consists of external forces that directly or indirectly influence an organization's acquisition of inputs (personnel, financial resources, raw materials, information) and generation of outputs (information, packages, goods, services, ideas). The marketing environment includes political, legal, regulatory, societal, economic and competitive, and technological forces.

To monitor changes in these forces, marketers practice environmental scanning and analysis. Environmental scanning is the process of collecting information about the forces in the marketing environment; environmental analysis is the process of assessing and interpreting the information obtained in scanning. This information helps marketing managers predict opportunities and threats associated with environmental fluctuation. Marketing management may assume either a passive, reactive approach or an active, aggressive approach in responding to these environmental fluctuations. The choice depends on an organization's structure and needs and on the composition of the environmental forces that affect it.

The political, legal, and regulatory forces of the marketing environment are closely interrelated. The current political outlook is reflected in legislation and regulations or the lack of them. The political environment may determine what laws and regulations affecting specific marketers are enacted and how much the government purchases and from which suppliers; it can also be important in helping organizations secure foreign markets.

Federal legislation affecting marketing activities can be divided into procompetitive legislation—laws designed to preserve and encourage competition—and consumer protection laws. The Sherman Antitrust Act sought to prevent monopolies and activities that limit competition; subsequent legislation, such as the Clayton Act, the Federal Trade Commission Act, the Wheeler-Lea Act, and the Robinson-Patman Act, were directed toward more specific practices. Consumer protection laws generally relate to product safety and information disclosure. The actual effects of legislation are determined by how marketers and the courts interpret the laws.

Federal regulatory agencies influence most marketing activities. Federal, state, and local regulatory units usually have the power to enforce specific laws and some discretion in establishing operating rules and drawing up regulations to guide certain types of industry practices. Self-regulation by industry represents another regulatory force; marketers view this type of regulation more favorably than government action because they have more opportunity to take part in creating the guidelines. Self-regulation may be less expensive than government regulation, and its guidelines are generally more realistic. However, such regulation generally cannot assure compliance as effectively as government agencies.

Societal forces refer to the structure and dynamics of individuals and groups and the issues that concern them. Members of our society want a high standard of living and a high quality of life, and they expect business to help them achieve these goals. The consumer movement is a diverse group of independent individuals, groups, and organizations that attempts to protect the rights of consumers. The major issues taken up by the consumer movement fall into three categories: environmental protection, product performance and safety, and information disclosure. Consumer rights organizations inform and organize other consumers, raise issues, help businesses develop consumer-oriented programs, and pressure lawmakers to enact consumer protection laws.

The economic factors that can strongly influence marketing decisions and activities are general economic conditions, buying power, willingness to spend, spending patterns, and competitive forces. The overall state of the economy fluctuates in a general pattern known as a business cycle. The stages of the business cycle are prosperity, recession, depression, and recovery.

Consumers' goods, services, and financial holdings make up their buying power—that is, their ability to purchase. The financial sources of buying power are income, credit, and wealth. After-tax income used for spending or saving is called disposable income. Disposable income left after an individual has purchased the basic necessities of food, clothing, and shelter is called discretionary income. Two measures of buying power are effective buying income (which includes salaries, wages, dividends, interest, profits, and rents, less federal, state, and local taxes) and the buying power index (a weighted index consisting of population, effective buying income, and retail sales data). The factors that affect consumers' willingness to spend are product price, the level of satisfaction obtained from currently used products, family size, and expectations about future employment, income, prices, and general economic conditions. Consumer spending patterns indicate the relative proportions of annual family expenditures or the actual amount of money spent on certain kinds of goods and services. Comprehensive spending patterns specify the percentages of family income allotted to annual expenditures for general classes of goods and services. Product-specific spending patterns indicate the annual dollar amounts families spend for specific products within a general product class.

Although all businesses compete for consumers' dollars, a company's direct competitors are usually the businesses in its geographic area that market products that resemble its own or can be substituted for them. The number of firms that control the supply of a product may affect the strength of competition. There are four general types of competitive structures: monopoly, oligopoly, monopolistic competition, and perfect competition. Marketers should monitor what competitors are currently doing and assess the changes occurring in the competitive environment.

Technology is the knowledge of how to accomplish tasks and goals. Product development, packaging, promotion, prices, and distribution systems are all influenced directly by technology. Several factors determine how much and in what way a particular business will make use of technology; these factors include the firm's ability to use technology, consumers' ability and willingness to buy technologically improved products, the firm's perception of the long-run effects of applying technology, the extent to which the firm is technologically based, the degree to which technology is used as a competitive tool, and the extent to which the business can protect technological applications through patents.

IMPORTANT TERMS

Marketing environment
Environmental scanning
Environmental analysis
Procompetitive legislation
Sherman Antitrust Act
Clayton Act
Federal Trade Commission Act
Wheeler-Lea Act
Robinson-Patman Act
Consumer protection legislation
Federal Trade Commission (FTC)
Better Business Bureau
National Advertising Review Board
  (NARB)
Societal forces
Consumer movement
Prosperity
Recession
Depression

Recovery
Buying power
Income
Disposable income
Discretionary income
Wealth
Effective buying income (EBI)
Buying power index (BPI)
Willingness to spend
Consumer spending patterns
Comprehensive spending patterns
Product-specific spending patterns
Competition
Monopoly
Oligopoly
Monopolistic competition
Perfect competition
Technology
Technology assessment

DISCUSSION AND REVIEW QUESTIONS

1. Why are environmental scanning and analysis so important?
2. How are political forces related to legal and governmental regulatory forces?
3. Describe marketers' attempts to influence political forces.
4. What types of procompetitive legislation directly affect marketing practices?
5. What was the major objective of most procompetitive laws? Do the laws generally accomplish this objective? Why or why not?
6. What are the major provisions of the Robinson-Patman Act? Which marketing mix decisions are influenced directly by this act?
7. What types of problems do marketers experience as they interpret legislation?
8. What are the goals of the Federal Trade Commission? List the ways in which the FTC affects marketing activities. Do you think a single regulatory agency should have such broad jurisdiction over so many marketing practices? Why or why not?
9. Name several nongovernmental regulatory forces. Do you believe that self-regulation is more or less effective than governmental regulatory agencies? Why?
10. Describe the consumer movement. Analyze some active consumer forces in your area.
11. In what ways can each of the business cycle stages affect consumers' reactions to marketing strategies?
12. What business cycle stage are we experiencing currently? How is this stage affecting business firms in your area?
13. Define income, disposable income, and discretionary income. How does each type of income affect consumer buying power?

14. How is consumer buying power affected by wealth and consumer credit?
15. How is buying power measured? Why should it be evaluated?
16. What factors influence a consumer's willingness to spend?
17. What does the term *technology* mean to you?
18. How does technology affect you as a member of society? Do the benefits of technology outweigh its costs and dangers?
19. Discuss the impact of technology on marketing activities.
20. What factors determine whether a business organization adopts and uses technology?

■ CASES

2.1   Suzuki Samurai Copes with Safety Controversy

Officials of the Japanese Suzuki Motor Corp. and its American subsidiary, Suzuki of America Automotive Corp., were extremely pleased with the sales figures of the Suzuki Samurai after it was introduced in the United States in late 1985. The Samurai, a four-wheel-drive sport/utility vehicle, appealed to a wide range of consumers. College students, off-road enthusiasts, and urban professionals all seemed to love the sporty look and fun image of the Samurai. Its low price tag also helped sales immensely. The popularity of the Samurai might have turned it into a target, though, as more and more attention was focused on it. Today, Suzuki Samurai sales are at a low point as dealers try to cope with questions about the Samurai's safety.

Suzuki's troubles with the Samurai began when NBC reported on the Samurai's tendency to roll over. Soon afterward, Consumer Union, publishers of *Consumer Reports*, gave the Samurai a "not acceptable" rating in its magazine, the first such rating the magazine handed out in ten years. Automobile researchers for *Consumer Reports* claim that during common evasive maneuvers—for example, if a driver were to swerve back and forth on the road to avoid an accident—the Samurai is likely to roll over. Consumer Union was so concerned about the safety of the Samurai that it demanded that Suzuki recall the 150,000 Samurais then on the road, refund owners' purchase price, and remove the vehicle from the market.

One of several class-action lawsuits has been filed against Suzuki by a Pennsylvania physician on behalf of all Samurai owners. The doctor believes that Suzuki purposely attempted to conceal knowledge of the Samurai's instability. Another class-action suit charges that Suzuki promoted the safety of the Samurai even though the company knew the vehicle was unsafe. The suit maintains that Suzuki and the firm that handles its public relations and advertising continuously committed mail and wire fraud and conspiracy to screen the Samurai's design flaws. The lawsuit refers to the National Traffic Highway Safety Administration's figures that show forty-four Samurai rollover incidents resulting in at least twenty-five deaths and more than sixty injuries.

Suzuki officials maintain that the Samurai is as safe as any other four-wheel-drive vehicle. A high-ranking Suzuki executive called *Consumer Reports'* rollover accounts "defamatory." Suzuki executives charge that *Consumer Reports'* researchers changed their rollover test methodology when they were testing the Samurai. Furthermore, regarding the twenty-five deaths linked to Samurai rollovers, Suzuki directors assert that more than 50 percent of the accidents in which these deaths occurred can be attributed to drunk drivers.

Unlike West German Audi AG officials, who initially did not respond to consumer complaints of sudden acceleration in their Audi 5000, Suzuki executives are aggressively battling the allegations against the Samurai. Suzuki officials have increased their advertising budget to publicly address safety issues. Suzuki has placed more than $1.5 million into its television media schedule to respond to the *Consumer Reports* indictment. A few months after the *Consumer Reports* article became public, Suzuki began an extensive buyer and dealer incentive program, and sales of Samurais rocketed. Suzuki managers saw this as a sign of declining public concern over the rollover issue. Suzuki was mistaken, however. Once it removed the generous incentives, Samurai sales began to sink again.

Suzuki officials are determined to fight their way out of this controversy, even though the fight is very expensive. Suzuki stands to lose public credibility if it cannot successfully prove the Samurai's roadworthiness. Many Suzuki officials are worried that the controversy surrounding the Samurai will spread to other Suzuki products and that sales figures of its other automobiles and even motorcycles will be adversely affected.

Meanwhile, Suzuki continues to sell Samurais, even though the figures are not as high as anticipated before the controversy. Suzuki managers were pleased when the Center for Auto Safety's petition to the federal government for the recall of Samurais was refused. Suzuki will have to work hard to restore the reputation of its Samurai. The Japanese automobile company may have a difficult time keeping the sporty little four-wheel-drive on the road.

SOURCES: Cleveland Horton and Raymond Serafin, "Wounded by Samurai?" *Advertising Age*, June 20, 1988, p. 101; " 'Samurai Rollover Rap Is Bum,' Suzuki Says," *Ward's AutoWorld*, July 1988, p. 34; "Samurai Sales Hit Record," *Chicago Sun Times*, Sept. 6, 1988; Janice Steinberg, "Suzuki Acts to Right Slipping Samurai Sales," *Advertising Age*, July 25, 1988, p. S-10; "Suit Charges Safety Fraud by Suzuki," *Star-Ledger* (Newark, N.J.), June 15, 1988; "Suzuki Calls Consumer Group's Safety Tests on Samurai 'Flawed,' " *Los Angeles Times*, June 10, 1988; "Suzuki Revamps Ads to Combat Safety Charges," *Detroit News*, Mar. 4, 1988; and "Ten Products That Made News in 1988," *Advertising Age*, Jan. 2, 1989, p. 12.

Questions for Discussion

1. What kinds of environmental forces is Suzuki facing regarding the safety issue?
2. Evaluate Suzuki's way of dealing with the safety controversy.
3. What improvements could be made in Suzuki's approach to coping with the safety issue?

2.2   The *Wall Street Journal* Faces a Challenging Environment

For more than a hundred years the writers, editors, and reporters of the *Wall Street Journal* have provided readers with important information on the business environment of the United States and the world. The paper started when Charles H. Dow, Edward D. Jones, and their silent partner, Charles M. Bergstresser, began printing a four-page afternoon business newspaper that sold for 2 cents a copy. In 1902, the publisher C. W. Barron purchased the paper and turned over its control to his wife. Today Barron's descendants still own a controlling interest in the paper.

Published by Dow Jones & Co., the *Wall Street Journal* is among the country's most prestigious papers. Its experienced staff and ultramodern printing facilities make the *Wall Street Journal* a lofty model for other newspapers. Businesspeople in many parts of the world read it almost religiously. Its reliability and relatively traditional format make the *Journal* a comfortable cornerstone of American business, and its nearly two million subscribers are clear evidence of the paper's success. However, recent developments have made many at the *Journal* uneasy about the future.

They worry that today's extremely busy businessperson simply does not have the forty minutes to an hour needed to peruse the paper every morning. Present-day businesspeople, especially high-ranking company executives, must make decisions quickly and so want a more immediate, up-to-the-minute medium of information. Electronic information systems, with their instantaneous data retrieval capabilities, might soon make the *Wall Street Journal* obsolete.

Moreover, the *Journal's* subscription list is shrinking and advertising sales are down. Largely because of the bull market in the 1980s, business news has become very popular. Daily newspapers across the nation have extended their coverage of business, investments, and the economy; business programs on network and cable television now draw large audiences; and more people than ever are reading business magazines. As readers seek business information from these media, they are less likely to rely on the *Wall Street Journal*. Advertisers have diverted their funds as well, to cover the extended business press. The *Wall Street Journal* now has ten localized editions that its directors hope will lure new advertisers.

The *Journal's* staff attributes its problems to three major events: (1) the October 1987 stock market crash that reduced the number of investors; (2) the large number of layoffs that occurred because of mergers and streamlining efforts in corporate America; and (3) new competition, especially from electronic information transmittal. However, the paper's officials expect it to survive all challenges.

Ironically, another part of the Dow Jones & Co. family poses perhaps the greatest competitive threat to the *Wall Street Journal*. The Dow Jones Information Services Group is growing rapidly. Its new DowVision information system is on the cutting edge of electronic business information. By using Dow Jones News/Retrieval, subscribers can call up *Journal* stories on their personal computers early on publication day and also receive up-to-the-minute accounts of financial developments in London and Tokyo. One investment banker has indicated that the *Journal's* circulation problems during the last five years can be traced to Information Services.

Management at the *Journal* hopes that busy executives will continue to take time to spend reading their newspaper. But as time becomes more valuable and crucial to businesspeople and investors, many may opt to get their business news directly from their personal computers. The staff at the *Wall Street Journal* believes that accurate, timely, important, and fair news coverage will be enough to hold their readers' attention and loyalty, whether it appears on a printed page or on a computer screen.

SOURCES: Dennis Farney, "One Newspaper's Century: The Inside Story," *Wall Street Journal,* June 23, 1989, pp. C1, C3–C4, C12; Patrick Reilly, "Expanding Its Horizons," *Advertising Age,* June 19, 1989, pp. 43–44; and Alex Taylor III, "A Tale Dow Jones Won't Tell," *Fortune,* July 3, 1989, pp. 100–102, 106, 108–109.

Questions for Discussion

1. Which environmental forces are influencing the performance of the *Wall Street Journal* the most? Explain.
2. Could some of the environmental forces that are adversely affecting the *Journal* be treated as opportunities instead of threats?
3. Has the *Wall Street Journal's* management employed a passive approach or an active approach in dealing with environmental forces? Explain.

3 MARKETING ETHICS AND SOCIAL RESPONSIBILITY

Objectives

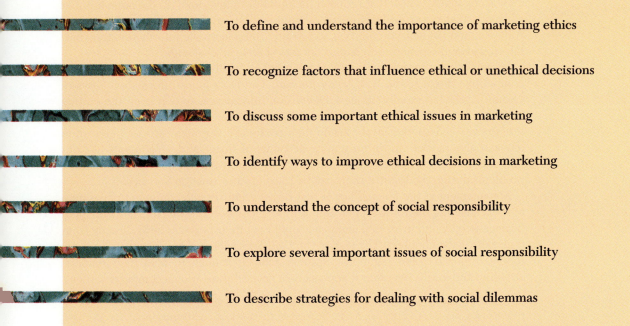

To define and understand the importance of marketing ethics

To recognize factors that influence ethical or unethical decisions

To discuss some important ethical issues in marketing

To identify ways to improve ethical decisions in marketing

To understand the concept of social responsibility

To explore several important issues of social responsibility

To describe strategies for dealing with social dilemmas

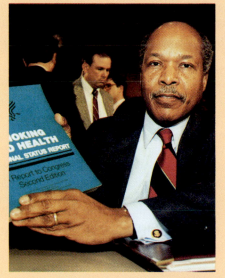

In 1990 Louis Sullivan, U.S. Secretary of Health and Human Services, asked advertising agencies to "demonstrate their ethics" by forsaking all tobacco advertising. Sullivan believes it is "morally wrong to promote a product, which when used as intended, causes death." More specifically, Sullivan wants tobacco companies to stop targeting tobacco advertisements at women, youths, and minorities.

RJR Nabisco, the number-two cigarette marketer, is under fire for a plan to target a new brand of cigarettes, called Dakota, at young, poorly educated, blue-collar women. The outcry arose after RJR's confidential marketing documents on the brand, code-named "Project Virile Female," were publicized in *The Wall Street Journal, Advertising Age,* and *The Washington Post.* In late 1989, RJR was forced to abandon test marketing of another brand called Uptown, which would have been targeted at blacks, after protests from health groups, anti-smoking forces, and Louis Sullivan. Although many people may be opposed to smoking, Thomas Lauria of the Tobacco Institute has spoken out in favor of preserving the freedom to advertise a legal product. He feels that the anti-smoking forces may be a threat to any company that wishes to promote its product in the United States.

The tobacco-advertising controversy relates to both ethics and social responsibility. The ethics issues relate to marketers that make decisions to target specific groups of customers and influence them to purchase cigarettes. Social responsibility issues develop as advocacy groups to try to curtail the advertising and sales of products that are legal but possibly dangerous, unsafe, or unhealthy: cigarettes, sugared cereals targeted at children, and malt liquor and fortified wine targeted at the poor, inner-city blacks and Hispanics. ◆

Photo by Timothy A. Murphy.

Based on information from Tom Squitieri, "Health Chief: Show 'Ethics,' Put End to Ads," *USA Today,* Feb. 21, 1990, p. A1; David Craig, "Health Issues Fuel Strikes," *USA Today,* Feb. 20, 1990, p. B1; Stuart Elliot and James Cox, "Advocacy Groups Attack Ad Tactics," *USA Today,* Feb. 20, 1990, pp. B1, B2; Alix M. Freedman and Michael J. McCarthy, "New Smoke from RJR Under Fire," *Wall Street Journal,* Feb. 20, 1990, pp. B1, B6; Michael Specter, "RJR Targets 'Partying' Women for Cigarette," *(Memphis) Commercial Appeal,* Feb. 17, 1990, p. A1.

I ssues such as the tobacco-advertising controversy illustrate that all marketing activities can be judged as morally right or wrong by society, consumers, interest groups, competitors, and others. Although most marketers operate within the limits of the law, some marketers do engage in activities that are not considered acceptable by other marketers, consumers, and society in general. A number of recently publicized incidents in marketing, such as deceptive or objectionable advertising, misleading packaging, questionable selling practices, manipulation, corruption, and pollution, have raised questions as to whether specific marketing practices are acceptable and beneficial to society. The issues of what is acceptable in marketing practices and what obligations marketers have to society are issues of marketing ethics and social responsibility.

This chapter gives an overview of the role of ethics and social responsibility in marketing decision making. We first define marketing ethics and discuss the factors that influence ethical decision making in marketing. We also outline some specific ethical issues in marketing and discuss ways to improve ethics in marketing decisions. Then we address the issue of social responsibility and consider the impact of marketing decisions on society. Some strategies for dealing with social responsibility dilemmas are also developed. We close the chapter by comparing and contrasting the concepts of marketing ethics and social responsibility.

THE NATURE OF MARKETING ETHICS

Though a very important concern in marketing decisions, ethics may be one of the most misunderstood and controversial concepts in marketing. No one has yet discovered a universally accepted approach to dealing with marketing ethics. However, this concept and its application need to be examined to foster marketing decisions that are acceptable and beneficial to society. In this section we consider the meaning of marketing ethics.

■ **Marketing Ethics Defined**

Ethics relate to moral evaluations of decisions and actions as right or wrong on the basis of commonly accepted principles of behavior. For our purposes, then, **marketing ethics** are moral principles that define right and wrong behavior in marketing. The most basic ethical issues have been formalized through laws and regulations to provide conformity to the standards of society. At a minimum, marketers are expected to conform to these laws and regulations. However, it is important to realize that marketing ethics go beyond legal issues; ethical marketing decisions foster mutual trust among individuals and in marketing relationships.

Ethics are individually defined and may vary from one person to another. Although individual marketers often act in their own self-interest, there must be standards of acceptable behavior to guide all marketing decisions. Marketers need to operate in accordance with sound moral principles based on ideals such as fairness, justice, and trust.[1] Consumers generally regard unethical marketing activities—for instance, deceptive advertising, misleading selling tactics, price collusion,

1. Donald P. Robin and R. Eric Reidenbach, "Social Responsibility, Ethics in Marketing Strategy, Closing the Gap Between Concept and Application," *Journal of Marketing,* January 1987, pp. 44–58.

and the willful marketing of harmful products—as unacceptable and often refuse to do business with marketers that engage in such practices. Thus when marketers deviate from accepted moral principles to further their own interests at the expense of others, continued marketing exchanges become difficult, if not impossible.[2]

■ **Marketing Ethics Are Controversial**

Few topics in marketing are more controversial than ethics. Most marketing decisions can be judged as right or wrong, ethical or unethical. But everyone has different ideas as to what is ethical or unethical depending on personal values, the nature of the organization, and their experiences in life. Many marketers have such strong convictions about what is morally right or wrong that they deeply resent discussions of alternative ways to make ethical decisions.

Regardless of how a person or an organization views the acceptability of a particular activity, if society judges that activity to be wrong or unethical, then this view directly affects the organization's ability to achieve its goals. Although not all activities deemed unethical by society may be illegal, consumer protests against a particular activity may result in legislation that restricts or bans it. When an organization engages in unethical marketing activities, it may not only lose sales as dissatisfied consumers refuse to deal with it, but it may also face lawsuits, fines, and even jail for its executives. Sara Lee Corp., for example, faces a lawsuit brought by Oscar Mayer Foods Corp. for patent, trademark, and copyright infringement. Oscar Mayer executives sued because they believe that Sara Lee's Bryan brand Lunch & Munch product duplicates its own Lunchables—a line of lunch products containing sliced meats, cheeses, and crackers separately packaged in a compartment tray with a napkin. The resemblances include the tray, package size, display of contents, language, layout, graphics, and product positioning.[3] If Sara Lee loses the suit, it will be forced to drop its Lunch & Munch product and pay heavy fines for infringement. Such examples illustrate the importance of understanding marketing ethics and recognizing ethical issues.

Because marketing ethics are so controversial, it is important to state that it is not the purpose of this chapter to question anyone's personal/ethical beliefs and convictions. Nor is it the purpose of this chapter to examine the behavior of consumers, although consumers, too, may be unethical (engaging, for instance, in coupon fraud, shoplifting, and other abuses). Instead, its goal is to underscore the importance of ethical issues and help you learn about ethical decision making in marketing. Understanding the impact of ethical decisions in marketing can help you recognize and resolve ethical issues within an organization.

UNDERSTANDING THE ETHICAL DECISION-MAKING PROCESS

To grasp the significance of ethics in marketing decision making, one must first examine the factors that influence the ethical decision-making process. Personal moral philosophies, organizational relationships, and opportunity are three factors that interact to determine ethical decisions in marketing (see Figure 3.1).

2. Vernon R. Loucks, Jr., "A CEO Looks at Ethics," *Business Horizons,* March-April 1987, p. 4.
3. Charles Conner, "Oscar Mayer Aims Lawsuit at Sara Lee," *Commercial Appeal,* Jan. 24, 1990, p. B9.

FIGURE 3.1
Factors that influence the ethical decision-making process

■ Moral Philosophies

Moral philosophies are principles or rules that individuals use to determine the right way to behave. They provide guidelines for resolving conflicts and ensuring mutual benefit for all members of society.[4] People learn these principles and rules through socialization by family members, social groups, religion, and formal education. Figure 3.2 highlights one example of personal ethical decision making by an employee while on the job. Each moral philosophy has its own concept of rightness or ethicalness and rules for behavior. We discuss here two distinct moral philosophies: utilitarianism and ethical formalism.

Utilitarianism.   Utilitarian moral philosophies are concerned with maximizing the greatest good for the greatest number of people. Utilitarians judge an action on the basis of the consequences for all the people affected by the action. In other words, in a situation with an ethical component, utilitarians compare all possible options and select the one that promises the best results. Under utilitarianism, then, it would be unethical to act in a way that leads to personal gain at the expense of society in general. Consider the following example of an organization adopting a utilitarian philosophy. In 1990, the offices of Delta Airlines in Ireland received a telephone threat from terrorists that one of its transatlantic flights would be bombed. Delta decided to publicize the threat and announced that it would allow customers holding tickets on its transatlantic flights to transfer their tickets to other airlines without penalty.[5] When Pan Am Airlines received a bomb threat in 1988, it did not notify the public; the loss of more than two hundred lives in the terrorist bombing of Pan Am flight 103 and the negative publicity directed at Pan Am damaged the firm. Thus, after weighing the possible loss of life and the negative publicity surrounding a terrorist bombing or crash against the loss of revenues and profits, Delta executives probably concluded that publicizing the bomb threat and letting passengers decide whether to fly on Delta would be best.

Ethical Formalism.   Other moral philosophies focus on the intentions associated with a particular behavior and on the rights of the individual. Ethical formalism develops specific rules for behavior by determining whether an action can be taken consistently as a general rule without concern for alternative results.[6] Behavior is

---

4. James R. Rest, *Moral Development Advances in Research and Theory* (New York: Praeger, 1986), p. 1.

5. "CNN Worldday," Cable News Network (TV), Jan. 5, 1990.

6. F. Neil Brady, *Ethical Managing: Rules and Results* (New York: Macmillan, 1990), pp. 4–6.

FIGURE 3.2
Ethical decision making.
Domino Pizza driver
Darryl Kosanovich's personal ethical concerns
influenced his decision to
stop and rescue a small
boy riding a bike in the
street between two
parked cars.

IN WESTMONT, PA, ONE OF OUR DRIVERS DELIVERED
A HEALTHY 3-YEAR-OLD BOY.

On August 12, 1989, Domino's Pizza® driver Darryl Kosanovich was making a delivery when he noticed a little boy on a bike riding into the street between two parked cars. ☐ Sensing danger, Kosanovich, himself the father of two small children, acted quickly. Just as a car sped around the corner, he pulled the boy off the bike and to safety. ☐ "I never saw anything like that," said a witness. "He would have been hit. He pulled him away just in time." ☐ Whether it's in Westmont, or in any of the thousands of other locales served by Domino's Pizza, folks like Darryl are giving their best to the community.

AND YOU THOUGHT WE ONLY DELIVERED PIZZAS.   © 1989 Domino's Pizza, Inc.

SOURCE: Courtesy of Domino's Pizza Inc.

judged on the basis of whether it infringes on individual rights or universal rules. The Golden Rule—do unto others as you would have them do unto you—exemplifies ethical formalism. So does Immanuel Kant's categorical imperative: that every action should be based on reasons that everyone could act on, at least in principle, and that action must be based on reasons that the decision maker would be willing to have others use.[7] In marketing, ethical formalism is consistent with the idea of consumer choice. For example, consumers have a right to know about possible defects in an automobile or other products that relate to safety.[8]

Applying Moral Philosophies to Marketing Decision Making.   Traditionally, it has been assumed that personal moral philosophies remain constant in both work and nonwork situations. However, research has shown that most business persons use one moral philosophy at work and a completely different one outside of work.[9]

7. O.C. Ferrell and Larry G. Gresham, "A Contingency Framework for Understanding Ethical Decision Making in Marketing," *Journal of Marketing,* Summer 1985, p. 90.

8. Ibid.

9. John Fraedrich, "Philosophy Type Interaction in the Ethical Decision Making Process of Retailers" (Ph.D. diss., Texas A&M University, 1988).

Another study found that although personal moral philosophies and values enter into ethical decisions in business, they are not the central component that guides the decisions, actions, and policies of an organization.[10] This finding may explain why individuals switch moral philosophies between home and work and why personal values make up only one part of an organization's total value system.

Some marketers use the logic that anything is fair that defeats the competition and increases profits. They have used warfare concepts such as "guerrilla warfare," "pre-emptive first strikes," and "counterattacks" to justify questionable and possibly unethical actions. A distinction should be made between competitors and enemies. Competitors are rivals that compete for customers and markets according to socially accepted rules. Central to the science of warfare is total conquest and elimination, in some cases, of the enemy. Therefore the marketing as warfare comparison raises ethical concerns given the destructive nature of the history of warfare.[11]

Others view marketing as a game such as football or boxing, in which ordinary rules and morality do not apply. For example, what if a boxer decided it was wrong to try to injure another person or a football player was afraid of hurting another player if he made contact? Sports have rules and referees to regulate the game to provide safety and equality. However, because customers in marketing exchanges are not economically self-sufficient, they cannot choose to withdraw from the "game of marketing." Given this condition, marketing ethics must make clear what rules do and should apply in the "game of marketing." Even more important, the rules developed must be appropriate to the nonvoluntary character of participation in the game. Most members of society hold that moral principles and standards of acceptable behavior should guide decisions related to the welfare of customers.[12]

Ethical behavior may be a function of two different dimensions of an organization's value structure: the organization's values and traditions, or corporate culture, and the personal moral philosophies of the organization's individual members. An employee assumes some measure of moral responsibility by agreeing to abide by an organization's rules and standard operating procedures. When a marketer decides to behave unethically or even illegally, it may be that competitive pressures and organizational rewards provided the incentive.

■ Organizational Relationships

People learn personal moral philosophies, and therefore ethical behavior, not only from society in general, but also from members of their social groups and their organizational environment. Relationships with one's employees, coworkers, or superiors create ethical problems, such as maintaining confidentiality in personal relations; meeting obligations, responsibilities and mutual agreements; and avoiding undue pressure that may force others to behave unethically. Employees may have to deal with assignments that they perceive as creating ethical dilemmas. For example, a salesperson may be asked to lie to a customer over the phone. Likewise, an employee who sees another employee cheating a customer must decide whether to report the incident.

10. William C. Frederick and James Weber, "The Value of Corporate Managers and Their Critics: An Empirical Description and Normative Implications," in *Research in Corporate Social Performance and Social Responsibility,* ed. William C. Frederick and Lee E. Preston (Greenwich, Conn.: JAI Press, 1987), pp. 149–150.

11. Charles L. Tomkovick, "Time for a Cease-Fire with Strategic Marketing Warfare," in *Advances in Marketing,* Peter J. Gordon and Bert J. Kellerman, eds. (Southwest Marketing Association, 1990), p. 212.

12. Eric H. Beversluis, "Is There 'No Such Thing as Business Ethics'?" *Journal of Business Ethics,* No. 6, 1987, pp. 81–88.

Marketing managers must carefully balance their duties to the owners or stockholders who hired them to carry out the organization's objectives and to the employees who look to them for guidance and direction. In addition, managers must also comply with society's wishes and ethical evaluations. Striking an ethical balance among these areas, then, is a difficult task for today's marketing decision makers.

The role of top management is extremely important in developing the culture of an organization. Most experts agree that the chief executive officer or the vice president of marketing sets the ethical tone for the entire marketing organization. Lower-level managers obtain their cues from top management, yet they, too, impose some of their personal values on the company. This interaction between corporate culture and executive leadership helps determine the ethical value system of the firm.

Powerful superiors can affect employees' activities and directly influence behavior by putting into practice the company's standards of ethics. Young marketers in particular indicate that they often go along with their superiors to demonstrate loyalty in matters related to judgments of morality. The status and power of significant others is directly related to the amount of pressure they can exert on others to conform to their expectations. A manager in a position of authority can exert strong pressure to assure compliance on ethically related issues. In organizations where ethical standards are vague and supervision by superiors is limited, peers may provide guidance in an ethical decision.

The role of peers (significant others) in the decision-making process depends on the person's ratio of exposure to unethical behavior to exposure to ethical behavior. The more a person is exposed to unethical activity in the organizational environment, the more likely it is that he or she will behave unethically.[13] Employees experience conflict between what is expected of them as workers and managers and what they expect of themselves based on their own personal ethical standards.

■ Opportunity

Opportunity provides another pressure that may determine whether a person will behave ethically. Opportunity is a favorable set of conditions that limit barriers or provide rewards. Rewards may be internal or external. Internal rewards are the feelings of goodness and worth one experiences after an altruistic action. External rewards are what people expect to receive from others in terms of values generated and provided on an exchange basis. External rewards are often received from peers and top management in the form of praise, promotions, and raises.

If a marketer takes advantage of an opportunity to act unethically and is rewarded or suffers no penalty, he or she may repeat such acts as other opportunities arise. For example, a salesperson who receives a raise after using a deceptive sales presentation to increase sales is being rewarded for this behavior and so will probably continue the behavior. Indeed, opportunity to engage in unethical conduct is often a better predictor of unethical activities than personal values.[14]

Besides rewards and the absence of punishment, other elements in the business environment help to create opportunities. Professional codes of ethics and ethics-related corporate policy also influence opportunity by prescribing what behaviors are acceptable. The larger the rewards and the lesser the punishment for unethical behavior, the greater is the probability that unethical behavior will be practiced.

13. O.C. Ferrell, Larry G. Gresham, and John Fraedrich, "A Synthesis of Ethical Decision Models for Marketing," *Journal of Macromarketing*, (Fall 1989), pp. 58–59.

14. Ferrell and Gresham, p. 92.

ETHICAL ISSUES IN MARKETING

A person will not make an ethical decision unless he or she recognizes that a particular issue or situation has an ethical or moral component. Thus developing awareness of ethical issues is important in understanding marketing ethics. An **ethical issue** is an identifiable problem, situation, or opportunity requiring an individual or organization to choose from among several actions that must be evaluated as right or wrong, ethical or unethical. Any time an activity causes consumers to feel deceived, manipulated, or cheated, a marketing ethical issue exists, regardless of the legality of that activity.

Ethical issues typically arise because of conflicts among individuals' personal moral philosophies and the marketing strategies, policies, and the organizational environment in which they work. Ethical issues may stem from conflicts between a marketer's attempts to achieve organizational objectives and customers' desires for safe and reliable products. For example, the Ford Pinto automobile became highly controversial in the 1970s after consumer advocates claimed that Ford had saved money in the design of the car's gas tank and that Pintos involved in accidents were subject to explosions and fires. Similarly, organizational objectives that call for increased profits or market share may pressure marketers to steal competitors' secrets, knowingly bring an unsafe product to market, or engage in some other questionable activity. For example, in South Korea, Lucky Goldstar Group markets a laundry detergent packaged in an orange box with a whirlpool design just like Procter & Gamble's Tide brand. The product is called Tie, and Procter & Gamble does not make it or license it to Goldstar.[15] Obviously, the attempt to develop a Tide look-alike without Procter & Gamble's permission creates an ethical issue.

Regardless of the reasons behind specific ethical issues, once the issues are identified, marketers and organizations must decide how to deal with them. Thus it is essential to become familiar with many of the ethical issues that may arise in marketing so that they can be identified and resolved when they occur. We cannot, of course, discuss every possible issue that could develop in the different marketing mix elements. But our examination of a few issues can provide some direction and lead to an understanding of the ethical problems that marketers must confront.

■ **Product Issues**

In general, product-related ethical issues arise when marketers fail to disclose risks associated with the product or information regarding the function, value, or use of the product. Figure 3.3 illustrates that N.L. Chemicals, Inc. provides specialty chemicals used in printing, adhesives, and cosmetics that protect the health and safety of consumers and minimize environmental pollution. Competitive pressures can also create product-related ethical issues. As competition intensifies and profit margins diminish, pressures can build to substitute inferior materials or product components to reduce costs. An ethical issue arises when marketers fail to inform customers about changes in product quality; this failure is a form of dishonesty about the nature of the product. Consider the following example. In the face of increasing financial difficulties and declining market share, Beech-Nut Nutrition Corporation changed the composition of its apple juice, one of its best-selling products. Instead of selling juice made from apples, the company substituted a chemical concoction that had the taste, smell, and look of apple juice. However, the

---

15. Damon Darlin, "Where Trademarks Are Up for Grabs," *Wall Street Journal,* Dec. 5, 1989, p. B1.

Making the world white, clean and bright.

From the coating on a golf ball to the ink and paper of this page, NL Chemicals' products are in many of the everyday items that surround you. Our titanium pigment products are used worldwide to provide whiteness, brightness and opacity to paint, paper, plastics and ceramics. In addition, our broad line of specialty chemicals is found in inks, coatings, adhesives, cosmetics and more.

Ranked among the FORTUNE 500, we have earned our success by producing innovative, quality products using state-of-the-art processes that are protective of our environment and the health and safety of our neighbors, employees and those who use our products. At NL Chemicals, we believe a clean world means a bright future.

NL
Chemicals, Inc.
P.O. Box 700
Hightstown, NJ 08520
(609) 443-2000

Circle 125 on Reader Service Card

SOURCE: Courtesy of Kronos, Inc.

company did not inform consumers of the change, and in fact, continued to label and promote its product as being 100 percent apple juice.[16] When marketers do not inform customers that product components are not of the same quality as promoted, ethical issues arise because consumers are being deceived. In this case, Beech-Nut not only lost millions of dollars in fines, but also lost sales after the scheme was publicized. Moreover, its executives were indicted for being dishonest about the true nature of the product.

A similar ethical problem arose when the chairman of Chrysler Corporation, Lee Iacocca, learned that several Chrysler executives had driven new Chryslers with the odometers disconnected and then sold the cars as new, without disclosing that the cars had been driven. Some of the cars had been involved in accidents and repaired. In this case, however, Iacocca apologized for the company's unethical behavior in a national press conference and developed a program to compensate customers who had bought the predriven cars. Iacocca took out two-page advertisements in *USA Today*, *The Wall Street Journal*, and *The New York Times* to apologize for the unethical mistake and added that "the only thing we're recalling here is our integrity." Such messages send a signal to all employees in the organization, as well as to customers, concerning a firm's ethical standards.[17]

16. Mini Hall, "O.J. Wasn't 100% Pure," *USA Today*, July 26, 1989, p. A1.

17. Jacob Scheslinger, "Chrysler Finds a Way to Settle Odometer Issue," *Wall Street Journal*, Dec. 10, 1987, p. 7.

■ Promotion Issues

The communication process provides a variety of situations that can create ethical issues: for instance, false and misleading advertising and manipulative or deceptive sales promotions, tactics, or publicity efforts. In this section we consider some ethical issues linked to advertising and personal selling. We also examine the use of bribery in personal selling situations.

Advertising.   Unethical actions in advertising can destroy the trust customers have in an organization. Sometimes ads are questioned because they are unfair to a competitor. For example, after McDonald's introduced a chicken product in some regions, Kentucky Fried Chicken aired commercials featuring a clown named Mr. R. McDonald being questioned by a congressional committee. In one spot, when asked what McDonald's has that Kentucky Fried Chicken does not, Mr. McDonald replies, "Toys. . . . Lots of toys." CBS refused to air the spot, saying, "We felt the commercial was unfairly denigrating to the corporate image of McDonald's." Although both NBC and ABC aired the commercials, CBS considered the ads to be ethically questionable.[18]

Abuses in advertising can range from exaggerated claims and concealed facts to outright lying. Exaggerated claims cannot be substantiated; for example, commercial claims that a certain pain reliever or cough syrup is superior to any other on the market often cannot be verified by consumers or experts. Concealed facts are material facts deliberately omitted from a message. For example, the front of the package of Tyson Chicken Quick patties states that the product is "ideal for microwaves." On the back of the package, however, the instructions recommend using a conventional oven for best results. When consumers learn that promotion messages are untrue, they may feel cheated and refuse to buy the product again; they may also complain to government or other regulatory agencies. Consequently, marketers should take care to provide all important facts and to avoid making claims that cannot be supported. Otherwise they risk alienating their customers.

Another form of advertising abuse involves ambiguous statements—statements using words so weak that the viewer, reader, or listener must infer advertisers' intended messages. These "weasel" words are inherently vague and enable the advertiser to deny any intent to deceive. For example, *help* is a common "weasel" word, as in, "helps prevent, helps fight, or helps make you feel."[19] Such advertising practices are questionable if they deceive the consumer outright. Although some marketers view such statements as acceptable, others do not. Thus vague messages remain an ethical issue in advertising.

Personal Selling.   A common problem in selling activities is judging what types of sales activities are acceptable. Consumers sometimes perceive salespeople as unethical because of the common belief that sales personnel often pressure customers to purchase products they neither need nor want. Nevertheless, the sales forces of most firms, such as IBM and Procter & Gamble, are well educated, well trained, and professional, and they know that they must act ethically or risk losing valuable

18. Scott Hume, "Squawk over KFC Ads—Company Challenges Y&R with New Strategy," *Advertising Age,* Jan. 15, 1990, p. 16.

19. Archie B. Carroll, *Business and Society: Ethics and Stakeholder Management* (Cincinnati: South-Western Publishing, 1989), pp. 228–230.

TABLE 3.1

Which of these gifts could be considered a bribe?

Pen and pencil set (with company logo)
Five-year supply of scratch pads (with company logo)
Dinner at a four-star French restaurant
Box of grapefruit shipped to your house each Christmas
Box of groceries delivered to your door each week
Season tickets to sport of your choice
Weekend cruise of the New England coast
Three-day, all-expenses-paid golfing vacation
Retreat to a Canadian fishing camp, via chartered jet
Lavish trip to an exotic foreign locale
$500 in cash

SOURCE: Adapted from E.J. Muller, "Traffigraft; Is Accepting a Gift from a Vendor a Breach of Ethics? To Some People, It's Just a Perk. To Others, It's Poison." *Distribution*, January 1990, p. 38. © 1990 Distribution Magazine. Reprinted with permission.

customers and sales. Although most salespersons are ethical, some do engage in questionable actions. For example, some salespersons have used very aggressive and manipulative tactics to sell almost worthless securities, gemstones, vacations, or other products over the phone. Marketing Update 3.1 describes how some of these "boiler room" salespersons have defrauded customers. Even though these salespeople may be fined and jailed for their activities, their unethical and often illegal actions contribute to consumers' mistrust of telephone selling and of personal selling in general.

At one time or another, most salespeople face an ethical conflict in their jobs. For example, a salesperson may have to decide whether to tell a customer the truth and risk losing the customer's business, or somehow mislead the customer to appease him or her and ensure a sale. Failure to adequately train salespeople in how to deal with such situations leaves them unprepared to cope with ethical issues when they arise. Furthermore, sales personnel who are untrained and confused about what action to take when facing an ethical dilemma often experience high levels of job frustration, anxiety, and stress.

Frequently, the problem of ethics has a snowball effect. Once a salesperson has deceived a customer, it becomes increasingly difficult to tell the truth later. If the customer learns of the deception, the sales representative will lose all credibility in the eyes of the customer, as well as that customer's associates and friends. Thus the manner in which a salesperson deals with an ethical issue can have far-reaching consequences for both the individual and the firm.

Bribery in Selling Situations.   When payments, gifts, or special favors are granted to obtain a sale or for some other reason, there is always some question of bribery. A bribe is anything given to improperly influence the outcome of a decision. Even when a bribe is offered to benefit the organization, it is usually considered unethical, and it hurts the organization in the long run for it jeopardizes trust and fairness. Table 3.1 lists some possible gifts that could be offered by a salesperson in an attempt to gain sales. As you can see, defining a bribe is often a matter of personal values and judgment.

BOILER ROOMS USE
QUESTIONABLE TELEPHONE SALES TACTICS

The term *boiler room* is used to describe small organizations in which salespersons, or brokers, use aggressive and often questionable telephone sales tactics to sell usually worthless precious metals, land, art, vacations, vitamins, and stocks. Penny stocks, a favorite of many boiler room operations, are securities that cost less than $1 and often trade "over the counter" rather than through an organized exchange, making them difficult to regulate. Boiler room operators have little trouble pushing penny stocks to eager investors because they are priced so cheap and because former legitimate penny stock companies, such as Apple Computer, have netted huge returns for investors.

The scam typically begins with an aggressive broker calling a potential customer to tout penny stock investments, often using a scripted presentation. Some brokers, including those at the now-defunct Investors Center, Inc., in Hauppauge, New York, use a "six-call approach" to persuade investors to purchase penny stocks, the value of which has often been inflated several times. The first few calls help build the investor's confidence. The sales pitch is made in the third and fourth calls, often bolstered with promises that the penny stock company has grand plans to acquire successful companies in the future. The brokers fail to mention, however, that the touted investments are often shell companies, with no assets or sales, and that the "acquisitions" generally are companies in which the boiler room owners hold a controlling interest.

The broker typically hypes the stock as the "absolute deal of a lifetime," and the customer may be warned that if he or she takes time to think about it or consult an adviser, the chance will be lost forever. ICI's sales scripts also included "excuses," or additional phrases that helped brokers close sales or refute clients' doubts or objections. The boiler room salespersons are aggressive, persuasive, and persistent, and before long, the investor, eager to get rich quickly, has purchased the stocks. However, when the customer wants to cash out of his or her investment (or the investment goes bad), the salesperson steers the customer into another investment, usually another worthless stock. Many investors never get their money back.

SOURCES: Martha Brannigan, "Victims of Investment Scams Seem Condemned to Repeat Past Errors," *Wall Street Journal,* Mar. 24, 1988, p. 29; Council of Better Business Bureaus and the North American Securities Administrators Association, *Investor Alert! How to Protect Your Money from Schemes, Scams, and Frauds* (New York: Benjamin, 1988), pp. 142–155; "The Penny Stock Scandal," *Business Week,* Jan. 23, 1989, pp. 74–80; and David Zigas, "The Final Frenzy of a Penny Stock Shop," *Business Week,* Mar. 13, 1989, p. 128.

Bribes have led to the downfall of many marketers, legislators, and government officials. One bribery and kickback scandal involved a top civilian official at a U.S. Defense Department procurement agency that bought and distributed clothing and gear used by the armed forces. Deputy Director Frank Coccia was fired after investigators learned that he had accepted huge kickbacks (a form of bribery) from clothing manufacturer salespersons that wanted lucrative government contracts. The scandal came to light when one of the contractors, who was caught fixing false payment claims with the Pentagon, agreed to cooperate with investigators to expose Coccia and others who accepted bribes and kickbacks and engaged in fraudulent practices.[20] Such practices are pernicious, for they stifle fair competition among businesses and limit consumer choice.

■ **Pricing Issues**

Price fixing, predatory pricing, and failure to disclose the full price associated with a purchase are typical ethical issues. The emotional and subjective nature of price creates many situations in which misunderstandings between the seller and buyer cause ethical problems. Marketers have the right to price their products so that they earn a reasonable profit, but ethical issues may crop up when a company seeks to earn high profits at the expense of its customers. For example, the Federal Communications Commission found that Nynex, which owns the New York and New England Telephone companies, has been inflating the prices it charged its subsidiaries for goods and services in order to boost its own profits. There is some concern that the practice may have resulted in higher telephone rates for Nynex customers.[21]

As discussed in Chapter 2, a number of laws address pricing issues. Both the Federal Trade Commission Act and the Wheeler-Lea Act prohibit deceptive pricing. For various reasons, marketers may wish to sell the same type of product at different prices. Provisions of the Robinson-Patman Act, as well as those of the Clayton Act, limit the use of such price differentials. Not all price differentials are illegal, but differentials can be questioned from an ethical perspective. For example, Nintendo, the videogame marketer, is under investigation for allegedly raising its prices by 20 to 30 percent during the Christmas buying season and manipulating the supply of games available at that time.[22] Note that this may be as much a legal issue as an ethical one if federal regulators decide that Nintendo has taken advantage of consumers. If price differentials tend to lessen or injure competition, they are considered discriminatory and are prohibited.

■ **Distribution Issues**

Ethical issues in distribution involve relationships among producers and marketing middlemen. Marketing middlemen, or intermediaries (wholesalers and retailers), facilitate the flow of products from the producer to the ultimate consumer. Each intermediary performs a different role and agrees to certain rights, responsibilities, and rewards associated with that role. For example, producers can expect retailers to honor payment agreements and keep them informed of inventory needs. Failure to make payments in a timely manner may be considered an ethical issue.

20. Edward D. Pound, "Pentagon Payoffs: Honored Employee Is a Key in Huge Fraud in Defense Purchasing," *Wall Street Journal*, Mar. 2, 1988, p. 1.

21. John R. Wilke and Mary Lu Carnevale, "Wrong Numbers: Nynex Overcharged Phone Units for Years, An FCC Audit Finds," *Wall Street Journal,* Jan. 9, 1990, pp. A1, A10.

22. Paul M. Barrett, "Nintendo-Atari Zapping Contest Goes to Washington," *Wall Street Journal,* Dec. 8, 1989, p. B1, B4.

The numerous relationships among marketing intermediaries present many opportunities for conflicts and disputes, including judgments about right or wrong, ethical or unethical behavior. Manipulating a product's availability for purposes of exploitation and using coercion to force intermediaries to behave in a specific manner are particularly serious ethical issues in the distribution sphere. For example, a powerful manufacturer can exert undue influence over an intermediary's choice whether to handle a product or how to handle it.

Other ethical issues in distribution relate to some stores' refusal to deal with some types of middlemen. A number of conflicts are developing in the distribution of microcomputer software. Many software-only stores are bypassing wholesalers and establishing direct relationships with software producers. Some dishonest stores are "hacking," or making unauthorized copies of software, preventing the producers from getting their due compensation. These occurrences have spawned suspicion and general ethical conflict in the distribution of software.[23]

Much controversy also surrounds retailers such as Wal-Mart Stores, Inc., which often insists on doing business only with a producer rather than going through an intermediary. Wal-Mart has been accused of threatening to buy from other producers if firms refuse to sell directly to it. Similar buy-direct policies are in effect at Lowe's Companies, Inc., the nation's largest retailer of do-it-yourself building supplies, and at Builder's Square, a home improvement chain owned by K mart. These retailers, which emphasize low prices, maintain that the no-middleman approach cuts costs and does not involve any ethical issues.[24] However, some small companies cannot afford to maintain their own sales forces and must rely on intermediaries to sell their products to retailers. The refusal of Wal-Mart and others to deal with intermediaries effectively shuts these smaller companies out of the market because they cannot compete with companies that have their own sales forces.

IMPROVING ETHICAL DECISIONS IN MARKETING

Conflicts between personal moral philosophies and corporate values, organizational pressures, and opportunity interact to create situations that may cause unethical behavior. It is possible to improve ethical behavior in an organization by eliminating unethical persons and improving the organization's ethical standards.

One way to approach improvement of an organization's ethical standards is by considering a "bad apple-bad barrel" analogy. Some people always do things in their own self-interest regardless of organizational goals or accepted moral standards; they are sometimes called "bad apples." To eliminate unethical behavior, an organization must rid itself of the bad apples, or unethical persons. It can attain this goal through screening techniques and through the enforcement of ethics codes.[25] How-

23. Lanny J. Ryan, Gay C. Dawson and Thomas Galek, "New Distribution Channels for Microcomputer Software," *Business*, October-December 1985, pp. 21–22.

24. Karen Blumenthal, "A Few Big Retailers Rebuff Middlemen," *Wall Street Journal*, Oct. 21, 1986, p. 6; Arthur Bragg, "Wal-Mart's War on Reps," *Sales & Marketing Management*, March 1987, pp. 41–43; and "Reps Riled Over Wal-Mart Ban," *DM*, January 1987, p. 12.

25. Linda K. Trevino and Stuart Youngblood, "Bad Apples in Bad Barrels: A Causal Analysis of Ethical Decision Making Behavior," *Journal of Applied Psychology*, 1990.

ever, organizations too sometimes become "bad barrels"—not because the individuals within them are bad, but because the pressures to survive and succeed create conditions that reward unethical behavior. A way of resolving the problem of the bad barrel is to redesign the organization's image and culture so that it conforms to industry and societal norms of ethical behavior.[26]

By sensitizing marketers to ethical issues and potential areas of conflict, it is possible to eliminate or defuse some of the ethical pressures that occur in daily marketing activities. Awareness and sensitivity toward ethical issues can eliminate the risk of making unethical decisions. Ethical values must be built into the organizational culture and marketing strategy.[27] This can be achieved by establishing codes of ethics and by controlling unethical behavior when it occurs.

■ Codes of Ethics

It is hard for employees to determine what is acceptable behavior within a company if the company does not have uniform policies and standards. Without standards of behavior, employees will generally make decisions based on their observations of how their peers and managers behave. **Codes of ethics** are formalized rules and standards that describe what the company expects of its employees. Codes of ethics encourage ethical behavior by eliminating opportunities for unethical behavior because employees know both what is expected of them and the punishment for violating the rules. They also help marketers deal with ethical issues or dilemmas that develop in daily operations by prescribing or limiting certain activities. Codes of ethics do not have to be so detailed they take into account every situation, but they should provide general guidelines for achieving organizational goals and objectives in a morally acceptable manner. Top management should provide leadership in implementing the codes.

Table 3.2 is the American Marketing Association Code of Ethics. The code does not cover every ethical issue, but it is a useful overview of what marketers believe are sound moral principles for guiding marketing activities. This code could be used to help structure an organization's code of ethics.

■ Controlling Unethical Behavior

Ethical behavior in marketing must be based on a strong moral foundation, including personal moral development and an organizational structure that encourages and rewards desired ethical action. The pressures of competition must be understood and coped with to improve ethical behavior. The idea that marketing ethics is learned at home, at school and in family relationships does not recognize the impact of opportunity and the organization on ethical decision makers.

If a company is to maintain ethical behavior, its policies, rules, and standards must be worked into its control system. If the number of employees making ethical decisions on a regular basis is not satisfactory, then the company needs to determine why and take corrective action through enforcement. Enforcement of standards is what makes codes of ethics effective. If codes are window dressing and do not relate to what is expected or what is rewarded in the corporate culture, then the codes serve no purpose except to give an illusion of concern about ethical behavior.

26. Ibid.
27. Robin and Reidenbach, pp. 44–58.

TABLE 3.2 *Code of Ethics, American Marketing Association*

Members of the American Marketing Association (AMA) are committed to ethical professional conduct. They have joined together in subscribing to this Code of Ethics embracing the following topics:

Responsibilities of the Marketer

Marketers must accept responsibility for the consequences of their activities and make every effort to ensure that their decisions, recommendations, and actions function to identify, serve, and satisfy all relevant publics: consumers, organizations and society. Marketers' professional conduct must be guided by:

1. The basic rule of professional ethics: not knowingly to do harm;
2. The adherence to all applicable laws and regulations;
3. The accurate representation of their education, training and experience; and
4. The active support, practice and promotion of this Code of Ethics.

Honesty and Fairness

Marketers shall uphold and advance the integrity, honor, and dignity of the marketing profession by:

1. Being honest in serving consumers, clients, employees, suppliers, distributors and the public;
2. Not knowingly participating in conflict of interest without prior notice to all parties involved; and

3. Establishing equitable fee schedules including the payment or receipt of usual, customary and/or legal compensation for marketing exchanges

Rights and Duties of Parties

Participants in the marketing exchange process should be able to expect that:

1. Products and services offered are safe and fit for their intended uses;
2. Communications about offered products and services are not deceptive;
3. All parties intend to discharge their obligations, financial and otherwise, in good faith; and
4. Appropriate internal methods exist for equitable adjustment and/or redress of grievances concerning purchases.

It is understood that the above would include, *but is not limited to,* the following responsibilities of the marketer:

In the area of product development management:

Disclosure of all substantial risks associated with product or service usage

Identification of any product component substitution that might materially change the product or impact on the buyer's purchase decision

Identification of extra-cost added features

THE NATURE OF SOCIAL RESPONSIBILITY

The concepts of ethics and social responsibility are often used interchangeably, although each has a distinct meaning. **Social responsibility** in marketing refers to an organization's obligation to maximize its positive impact and minimize its negative impact on society. Whereas ethics relate to individual decisions, social responsibility concerns the impact of an organization's decisions on society. Figure 3.4 illustrates the concept of maximizing a positive impact on society through advertising. Here Russell Corporation provides a campaign to encourage student athletes to take their education seriously and to graduate.

For example, years ago Anheuser-Busch test-marketed a new adult beverage called Chelsea. Because the beverage contained less than one-half percent alcohol—about the same as apple cider—consumer groups labeled the beverage "kiddie beer" and protested that the company was being socially irresponsible by making an alcoholic drink available to minors. Anheuser-Busch's first reaction was defensive;

TABLE 3.2   *continued*

In the area of promotions:

Avoidance of false and misleading advertising

Rejection of high pressure manipulations, or misleading sales tactics

Avoidance of sales promotions that use deception or manipulation

In the area of distribution:

Not manipulating the availability of a product for purpose of exploitation

Not using coercion in the marketing channel

Not exerting undue influence over the resellers' choice to handle a product

In the area of pricing:

Not engaging in price fixing

Not practicing predatory pricing

Disclosing the full price associated with any purchase

In the area of marketing research:

Prohibiting selling or fund raising under the guise of conducting research

Maintaining research integrity by avoiding misrepresentation and omission of pertinent research data

Treating outside clients and suppliers fairly

Organizational Relationships

Marketers should be aware of how their behavior may influence or impact on the behavior of others in organizational relationships. They should not encourage or apply coercion to obtain unethical behavior in their relationships with others, such as employees, suppliers or customers.

1. Apply confidentiality and anonymity in professional relationships with regard to privileged information.

2. Meet their obligations and responsibilities in contracts and mutual agreements in a timely manner.

3. Avoid taking the work of others, in whole, or in part, and represent this work as their own or directly benefit from it without compensation or consent of the originator or owner.

4. Avoid manipulation to take advantage of situations to maximize personal welfare in a way that unfairly deprives or damages the organization or others.

Any AMA members found to be in violation of any provision of this Code of Ethics may have his or her Association membership suspended or revoked.

SOURCE: Reprinted by permission of the American Marketing Association.

it tried to claim that the beverage was not dangerous and would not lead children to stronger drink. However, the company later decided to withdraw the beverage from the marketplace and reformulate it so that it would be viewed as more acceptable by society.[28] Social responsibility, then, can be viewed as a contract with society, whereas ethics relate to carefully thought out rules of moral values that guide individual and group decision making.

■ **Impact of Social Responsibility on Marketing**

Marketing managers try to determine what accepted relationships, obligations, and duties exist between the marketing organization and society. Recognition is growing that for a firm's survival and competitive advantage, the long-term value of conducting business in a socially responsible manner far outweighs short-terms costs.[29] To

28. Carroll, *Business and Society,* p. 45.

29. Margaret A. Stroup, Ralph L. Newbert, and Jerry W. Anderson, Jr., "Doing Good, Doing Better: Two Views of Social Responsibility," *Business Horizons,* March-April 1987, p. 23.

FIGURE 3.4

Social responsibility. This organization is trying to make a positive impact on society by trying to impress on young people the importance of completing their education.

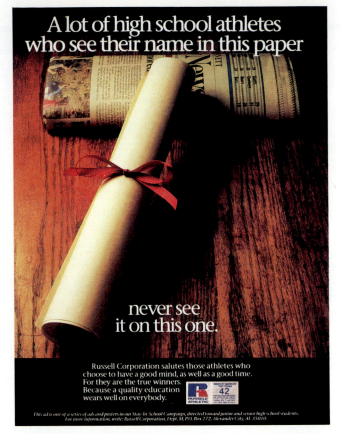

SOURCE: The Russell Corporation

preserve socially responsible behavior while achieving organizational goals, organizations must monitor changes and trends in society's values. For example, companies around the world are developing and marketing more nutritional and healthier products in response to increasing public concerns about cancer and heart disease. Furthermore, marketers must develop control procedures to ensure that daily decisions do not damage their company's relations with the public. An organization's top management must assume some responsibility for the employees' conduct by establishing and enforcing policies.

Being socially responsible may be a noble and necessary endeavor, but it is not a simple one. To be socially responsible, marketers must confront certain major issues. When PepsiCo promoted its Fritos corn chips with the Frito-Bandito character, it offended American Hispanics, who put such pressure on the company that the advertising campaign was dropped. PepsiCo certainly did not run the Frito-Bandito campaign with the idea of perpetuating a stereotype; however, it may have failed to consider the social consequences of its promotional campaign.[30] Marketers therefore must determine what society wants and then predict the long-run effects of their decisions, often by turning to specialists such as lawyers, doctors, and scientists.

30. Archie B. Carroll, "In Search of Moral Managers," *Business Horizons,* March-April 1987, p. 11.

The eagle has landed.

In Oklahoma and Mississippi. Georgia and Alabama. Where few bald eagle nests have produced young in the last 50 years. Using precious eggs and dedicated effort, the Sutton Avian Research Center is successfully raising eaglets from fuzzy to fierce. And releasing them into the habitats bald eagles used to call home. Phillips Petroleum supports this unique program to re-establish our endangered national symbol.

After all, if Man can land an Eagle on the moon, he can surely keep them landing on the earth.

For more information, contact the George Miksch Sutton Avian Research Center, Inc., P.O. Box 2007, Bartlesville, OK 74005, (918) 336-7778.

SOURCE: Courtesy Phillips Petroleum Company

However, specialists do not necessarily agree with each other, and the fields in which they work can yield findings that undermine previously acceptable marketing decisions.

Forty years ago, for example, tobacco marketers promoted cigarettes as being good for one's health. Now, years after the discovery that cigarette smoking is linked to cancer and other medical problems, society's attitude toward smoking is changing, and marketers are confronted with new social responsibilities, such as providing a smoke-free atmosphere for customers. Most major hotel chains allocate at least some of their rooms for nonsmokers, and most other businesses within the food, travel, and entertainment industries provide smoke-free environments or sections.

Because society is made up of many diverse groups, finding out what society as a whole wants is difficult, if not impossible. In trying to satisfy the desires of one group, marketers may dissatisfy others. For example, in the smoking debate, marketers must balance smokers' desires to continue to smoke cigarettes against nonsmokers' desires for a smoke-free environment.

Moreover, there are costs associated with many of society's demands. For example, society wants a cleaner environment and the preservation of wildlife and habitats, but it also wants low-priced gasoline and heating oil. Figure 3.5 illustrates how Phillips Petroleum is trying to improve the habitats for eagles as well as provide gasoline. Thus, companies that market these products must carefully balance the costs of providing low-priced products against the costs of manufacturing and packaging their products in an environmentally responsible manner. Such a balance is difficult, if not impossible, to achieve to the satisfaction of all members of society. Marketers must also evaluate the extent to which members of society are willing to pay for what they want. For instance, consumers may want more information about a product yet be unwilling to pay the costs the firm incurs in providing the data. Thus marketers who want to make socially responsible decisions may find the task difficult.

■ Social Responsibility Issues

Although social responsibility may seem to be an abstract ideal, managers make decisions related to social responsibility on a daily basis. To be successful, a business must determine what customers, government regulators, and competitors, as well as society in general, want or expect in terms of social responsibility. Table 3.3 summarizes several major categories of social responsibility issues, which include the consumer movement, community relations, and green marketing.

Consumer Issues.   One of the most significant social responsibility issues in marketing is the consumer movement, which Chapter 2 defines as the efforts of independent individuals, groups, and organizations to protect the rights of consumers. A number of interest groups and individuals have taken actions such as lobbying government officials and agencies, letter-writing campaigns, public service announcements, and boycotts of companies they consider are irresponsible.

Ralph Nader, one of the best-known consumer activists, continues to crusade for consumer rights. Consumer activism on the part of Nader and others has resulted in legislation requiring various safety features in cars: seat belts, padded dashboards, stronger door latches, head restraints, shatter-proof windshields, and collapsible steering columns. Activists' efforts have helped facilitate the passage of several consumer protection laws, such as the Wholesome Meat Act of 1967, the Radiation Control for Health and Safety Act of 1968, the Clean Water Act of 1972, and the Toxic Substance Act of 1976.

Also of great importance to the consumer movement are four basic rights spelled out in a consumer "bill of rights" drafted by President John F. Kennedy. These rights include the right to safety, the right to be informed, the right to choose, and the right to be heard.

Ensuring consumers' right to safety means that marketers have an obligation not to market knowingly a product that could harm consumers. This right can be extended to the idea that all products must be safe for their intended use, must include thorough and explicit instructions for proper and safe use, and must have been tested to ensure reliability and quality.

Consumers' right to be informed means that consumers should have access to and the opportunity to review all relevant information about a product before buying it. Many laws have been passed that require specific labeling on product packaging to satisfy this right. Congress is considering legislation that would limit marketers' use of terms such as "light," "diet," "no-salt," and "natural" on product labeling without providing detailed nutritional information on the labels to substantiate those claims. The current use of the terms has resulted in consumer confusion about health

TABLE 3.3
Social Responsibility Issues

ISSUE	DESCRIPTION	MAJOR SOCIETAL CONCERNS
Consumer Movement	Activities undertaken by independent individuals, groups, and organizations to protect their rights as consumers	The right to safety The right to be informed The right to choose The right to be heard
Community Relations	Society anxious to have marketers contribute to its well-being, wishing to know what businesses do to help solve social problems Communities demanding that firms listen to their grievances and ideas	Equality issues Disadvantaged members of society Safety and health Education and general welfare
Green Products	Consumers insisting not only on the quality of life but also on a healthful environment so that they can maintain a high standard of living during their lifetimes	Conservation Water pollution Air pollution Land pollution

claims. For instance, Sara Lee Corp. was forced to drop a line of "Light" products that had the same number of calories as its regular products because of the resulting confusion and lawsuits.[31] In addition, labels on alcoholic and tobacco products inform consumers that these products may cause illness and other problems.

The right to choose means that consumers must also have access to a variety of products and services at competitive prices. This means that they should be assured of satisfactory quality and service at a fair price. Activities that reduce competition among businesses in an industry jeopardize this right of consumers.

The right to be heard assures consumers that their interests will receive full and sympathetic consideration in the formulation of government policy. For example, when the Federal Communications Commission (FCC) was considering alternatives, including reregulation, to improve competition within the cable television industry, it invited comments from interest groups and the public.[32] The right to be heard also promises consumers fair treatment when they complain to marketers about their products. This right benefits marketers, too, because when consumers complain to manufacturers about a product, this information can help them modify the product to make it more satisfying.

31. Stephen Barlas, "Congress Mulls Strict Nutrition Labeling Law," *Marketing News,* Jan. 22, 1990, pp. 1, 11.

32. Mary Lu Carnevale, "FCC Votes to Examine Cable-TV Rules, With an Eye on Beefing Up Competition," *Wall Street Journal,* Jan. 12, 1990, p. A3.

Community Relations.   Social responsibility also extends to marketers' roles as community members. Individual communities expect marketers to contribute to the satisfaction and growth of their communities. Thus many marketers view social responsibility as including contributions of resources (money, products, time) to community causes such as education, the arts, recreation, disadvantaged members of the community, and others. Philip Morris, for example, sponsors several programs that focus on art and music. Shearson Lehman Hutton, a division of American Express, founded Project Access to Computer Training (PACT), a program that prepares qualified physically handicapped persons for computer-related jobs. The company also has a policy of hiring some of these individuals.[33] Honeywell, Shell Oil, Ogilvy & Mather, Aetna Life and Casualty, and Hewlett-Packard all have programs that contribute funds, equipment, and personnel to educational reform. Shell, for example, sponsors adopt-a-school programs in Houston and Washington, D.C., through which it channels money and employee volunteers to assist local schools.[34] Similarly, IBM donates or reduces the price of computer equipment to educational institutions. All these efforts, of course, have a positive impact on local communities, but they also indirectly help the organizations in the form of good will, publicity, and exposure to potential future customers. Thus, although social responsibility is certainly a positive concept, most organizations do not embrace it without the expectation of some indirect long-term benefit.

Green Marketing.   **Green marketing** refers to the specific development, pricing, promotion, and distribution of products that do not harm the environment. The Alliance for Social Responsibility, an independent coalition of environmentalists, scientists, ethicists, and marketers is one group involved in evaluating products to determine their environmental impact and marketers' commitment to the environment. Several environmental groups have also joined together to create a seal of approval to distinguish products that are environmentally safe. Companies receiving the green seal will be able to use it in advertising and public information campaigns and on packaging.[35]

Developing a green marketing program is not easy, however. Procter & Gamble's experience in marketing its new Downy fabric softener refill product is a case in point. Although the Downy refill package does not carry a green label designation, it manifests the company's environmentally responsible approach: The product has 75 percent less packaging materials (which does not waste resources and takes up less space in land-fills). However, the Consumer Product Safety Commission has questioned the safety of the new Downy refill package because it is pint-sized and resembles a milk carton. The commission deems it inappropriate to package a household chemical in a container that children might confuse with a milk carton. Procter & Gamble claims that Downy is not hazardous and may cause only mild nausea if ingested.[36] This example illustrates the difficulty of being environmentally

33. "American Express Public Responsibility; A Report of Recent Activities," Office of Public Responsibility, American Express Company, 1987, p. 8.

34. Patricia A. Galagan, "Joining Forces: Business and Education Take on Competitiveness," *Training and Development Journal,* July 1988, p. 28.

35. Christy Fisher, "Seal of Green Planned: Environmental Group to Give Product Approvals," *Advertising Age,* Nov. 20, 1989, p. 3.

36. Laurie Freeman, "Gov't Questions Downy Refill," *Advertising Age,* Nov. 20, 1989, p. 40.

responsible in packaging and satisfying all members of society with the new package design. Marketing Update 3.2 describes an environmentally responsible decision by Du Pont.

■ Strategies for Dealing with Social Responsibility Issues

There are four basic strategies for systematically dealing with social responsibility issues: reaction, defense, accommodation, and proaction.

Reaction Strategy.   A business adopting a **reaction strategy** allows a condition or potential problem to go unresolved until the public learns about it. The situation may be known to management (as were one car maker's problems with gas-tank combustibility) or it may be unknown (as was the sudden acceleration of the Audi 5000 without direct action from the driver). In either case, the business denies responsibility but tries to resolve the problem, deal with its consequences, and continue doing business as usual to minimize the negative impact.

Defense Strategy.   A business using a **defense strategy** tries to minimize or avoid additional obligations linked to a problem or problems. Commonly used defense tactics include legal maneuvering and seeking the support of trade unions that embrace the company's way of doing business and support the industry. Businesses often lobby to avoid government action or regulation. For example, Advo, a direct mail firm, lobbied against an increase in bulk postal rates because it knew it would have to pass on these increases to its clients, advertisers, and advertising agencies. The company realized that sizable increases in postal rates could put it at a competitive disadvantage in relation to print media, such as newspaper inserts, which do not use the U.S. Postal Service. Thus Advo took a defensive position to protect its own and its clients' interests.

Accommodation Strategy.   A business using an **accommodation strategy** assumes responsibility for its actions. A business might adopt the accommodation strategy when special-interest groups are encouraging a particular action or when the business perceives that if it fails to react Congress will pass a law to ensure compliance. Figure 3.6 illustrates how ICI is developing cooling systems that use ozone-friendly fluorocarbons.

For example, McDonald's developed a nutrition-oriented advertising campaign to appease dietitians and nutritionists who had urged legal action in several states to require that accurate nutritional information be provided on all fast-food products. However, McDonald's campaign, instead of soothing the interest groups, riled them up. The groups claim that McDonald's portrayal of its food as healthful was inaccurate. A McDLT, fries, and shake contain 1,283 calories, approximately 60 percent of the entire recommended daily calorie intake for an adult woman. In addition, that meal contains 15 teaspoons of fat, 10 teaspoons of sugar, no fiber, and approximately 70 percent of the daily allowance of sodium. Dietitians and nutritionists petitioned the U.S. Food and Drug Administration in the hope that it would require product nutritional labeling to alert consumers to the high levels of fat, sodium, and sugar and low levels of starch and fiber.[37] McDonald's chose to take an accommodation

37. "McD Ads Draw Protests From Nutritional Experts," *Nation's Restaurant News,* June 22, 1987, p. 26.

DU PONT STOPS MAKING
ENVIRONMENTALLY HARMFUL PRODUCT

Scientists have long contended that chlorofluorocarbons (CFCs) are destroying the ozone layer in the upper atmosphere—the layer that shields the earth from the sun's harmful ultraviolet rays. Chlorofluorocarbons are inert substances used in refrigeration and foam packaging. Their use as propellants in aerosol containers was banned in the 1970s, when researchers first learned that CFCs were destroying the ozone. In March 1988, an international study reported that the ozone layer over the Northern Hemisphere was being rapidly and seriously depleted. Scientists had already discovered a hole in it over Antarctica the year before. Du Pont & Co., which holds 25 percent of the CFC market with its product Freon, realized that it had to act responsibly to protect the environment.

After the results of the international study were publicized, the company announced that it would phase out production of Freon, which contributes $600 million to Du Pont's sales, as soon as it had substitutes ready for the market. The company expects to reduce production by 95 percent by the year 2003. Du Pont has been spending $10 million a year trying to develop a substitute for CFCs and already has two in production.

Du Pont has also asked other nations and companies that produce chlorofluorocarbons to abide by a 1987 treaty that calls for at least a 50 percent reduction in the production of CFCs by 1999. Scientists, however, say the treaty is too little and too late to stop the problem of the deteriorating ozone. They believe that the decay of the ozone layer will result in an increase in skin cancer, damaged crops, and harm to marine life.

Environmental groups praised Du Pont's decision to stop making the harmful chemical as an example of corporate social responsibility. These groups hope that the company's action will encourage other companies to stop producing chlorofluorocarbons. Although Du Pont stands to lose millions of dollars in sales by discontinuing the production of Freon, the company realized that it had an obligation to stop making the product because of the damage it has done, and is yet to do, to the environment.

SOURCES: Mary Lu Carnevale, "Du Pont Plans to Phase Out CFC Output," *Wall Street Journal,* Mar. 25, 1988, pp. 2, 4; "Ozone: Du Pont Does Good," *U.S. News & World Report,* Apr. 4, 1988, p. 13; Tim Smart, with Joseph Weber, "An Ozone Hole over Capitol Hill," *Business Week,* Apr. 4, 1988, p. 35.

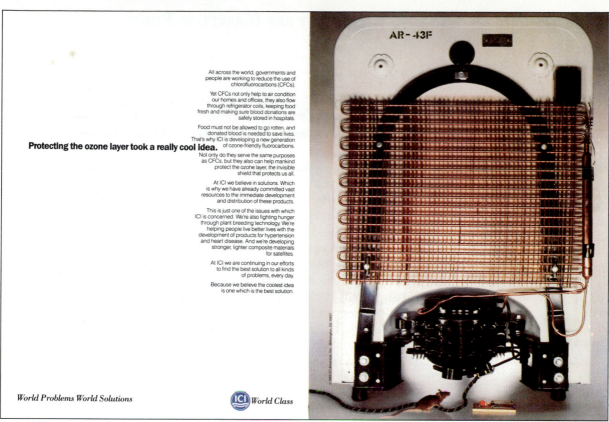

All across the world, governments and people are working to reduce the use of chlorofluorocarbons (CFCs).

Yet CFCs not only help to air condition our homes and offices, they also flow through refrigerator coils, keeping food fresh and making sure blood donations are safely stored in hospitals.

Food must not be allowed to go rotten, and donated blood is needed to save lives. That's why ICI is developing a new generation of ozone-friendly fluorocarbons.

Protecting the ozone layer took a really cool idea.

Not only do they serve the same purposes as CFCs, but they also can help mankind protect the ozone layer, the invisible shield that protects us all.

At ICI we believe in solutions. Which is why we have already committed vast resources to the immediate development and distribution of these products.

This is just one of the issues with which ICI is concerned. We're also fighting hunger through plant breeding technology. We're helping people live better lives with the development of products for hypertension and heart disease. And we're developing stronger, lighter composite materials for satellites.

At ICI we are continuing in our efforts to find the best solution to all kinds of problems, every day.

Because we believe the coolest idea is one which is the best solution.

World Problems World Solutions   **ICI** *World Class*

FIGURE 3.6   *Developing products that solve ecological problems.*
ICI shows its concern about protecting the ozone layer by developing products that do not contain chlorofluorocarbons.

SOURCE: Courtesy of ICI Americas Inc. Created by Saatchi and Saatchi

strategy to curtail lobbying against nutritional information disclosure when it probably should have adopted a proactive strategy.

Proactive Strategy.   A business that uses a **proactive strategy** assumes responsibility for its actions and responds to accusations made against it without outside pressure or the threat of government intervention. A proactive strategy requires management, of its own free will, to support an action or cause. For example, Toyota Motor Corp. decided to recall its popular 1990 model Lexus LS 400 automobile to repair several defects. Although none of the defects had caused any accidents or injuries, Toyota has a reputation for quality and excellence, which it promotes heavily in advertising. Consequently, its executives probably concluded that the most responsible action to take was to fix the defects before any injuries or deaths occurred.[38] Even if the recall should temporarily harm the Lexus image, Toyota's prompt and responsible action will probably draw a positive response from consumers in the long run.

38. Gregory A. Patterson, "Lexus to Recall All Its LS 400 Luxury Models," *Wall Street Journal,* Dec. 5, 1989, pp. B1, B11.

SOCIAL RESPONSIBILITY AND MARKETING ETHICS

Although the concepts of marketing ethics and social responsibility are often used interchangeably, it is important to remember that ethics relate to individual moral evaluations—judgments about what is right or wrong in a particular decision-making situation. Social responsibility is the obligation of an organization to maximize its positive impact and minimize its negative impact on society. Thus social responsibility deals with the total effect of marketing decisions on society. These two concepts work together because a company that supports both socially acceptable moral philosophies and individuals who act ethically is likely to make decisions that have a positive impact on society.

One way to evaluate whether a specific behavior is ethical and socially responsible is to ask other persons in an organization if they approve of a specific behavior. For social responsibility issues, contact with concerned consumer groups and industry or government regulatory groups may be helpful. Also a check to see if there is a specific company policy about the activity may resolve the issue. If other persons in the organization approve of the activity and it is legal and customary within the industry, chances are the activity is acceptable from both an ethical and social responsibility perspective.

A rule of thumb for ethical and social responsibility issues is that if they can withstand open discussion and result in agreements or limited debate, then an acceptable solution may exist. Nevertheless, even after a final decision is reached, different viewpoints on the issue may remain. Openness is not the end-all solution to the ethics problem. However, it does create trust and facilitates learning relationships.[39]

SUMMARY

Marketing ethics are moral principles that define right and wrong behavior in marketing. Most marketing decisions can be judged as ethical or unethical. Ethics are a very important concern in marketing decisions, yet ethics may be one of the most misunderstood and controversial concepts in marketing.

Personal moral philosophies, organizational factors, and opportunity are three important components of ethical decision making. Moral philosophies are principles or rules that individuals use to determine the right way to behave. They provide guidelines for resolving conflicts and ensuring mutual benefit for all members of society. Utilitarian moral philosophies are concerned with maximizing the greatest good for the greatest number of people. Ethical formalism philosophies, on the other hand, focus on general rules for guiding behavior and on the rights of the individual. Organizational relationships with one's employees or superiors create ethical problems such as maintaining confidentiality in personal relations; meeting obligations, responsibilities, and mutual agreements; and avoiding undue pressure

39. Sir Adrian Cadbury, "Ethical Managers Make Their Own Rules," *Harvard Business Review*, September-October 1987, p. 33.

that may force others to behave unethically. Opportunity—a favorable set of conditions that limit barriers or provide internal or external rewards—to engage in unethical behavior provides another pressure that may determine whether a person behaves ethically. If an individual uses an opportunity afforded him or her to act unethically and escapes punishment or even gains a reward, that person is more likely to repeat such acts when circumstances favor them.

An ethical issue is an identifiable problem, situation, or opportunity requiring an individual or organization to choose from among alternatives that must be evaluated as right or wrong. Ethical issues typically arise because of conflicts among individuals' personal moral philosophies and the marketing strategies, policies, and the organizational environment in which they work. Product-related ethical issues may develop when marketers fail to disclose risks associated with the product or information that relates to understanding the function, value, or use of the product. Competitive pressures can also create product-related ethical issues. The promotion process provides situations that can result in ethical issues, such as false and misleading advertising and deceptive sales tactics. Sales promotions and publicity that use deception or manipulation also create significant ethical issues. Bribery may be an ethical issue in some selling situations. The emotional and subjective nature of price creates conditions where misunderstandings between the seller and buyer lead to ethical problems. Ethical issues in distribution relate to relationships and conflicts among producers and marketing middlemen.

Codes of ethics, which formalize what an organization expects of its employees, eliminate the opportunity for unethical behavior because they provide rules to guide conduct and punishments for violating the rules. If the number of employees making ethical decisions on a regular basis is not satisfactory, the company needs to determine why and take corrective action through enforcement. Enforcement of standards is what makes codes of ethics effective.

Social responsibility in marketing refers to an organization's obligation to maximize its positive impact and minimize its negative impact on society. Marketing managers try to determine what accepted relationships, obligations, and duties exist between the business organization and society.

To be successful, a business must determine what customers, government regulators, and competitors, as well as society in general, want or expect in terms of social responsibility. Major categories of social responsibility issues include the consumer movement, community relations, and green marketing. The consumer movement refers to the activities of independent individuals, groups, and organizations in trying to protect the rights of consumers. Communities expect marketers to contribute to the satisfaction and growth of their communities. Green marketing refers to the specific development, pricing, promotion, and distribution of products that do not harm the environment.

Four basic strategies for dealing with social responsibility issues are reaction, defense, accommodation, and proaction. A business adopting a reaction strategy allows a condition or potential problem to go unresolved until the public learns about it. A business using the defense strategy tries to minimize or avoid additional obligations associated with a problem or problems. In the accommodation strategy, a business assumes responsibility for its actions. A business that uses the proactive strategy assumes responsibility for its actions and responds to accusations made against it without outside pressure or the threat of government intervention.

The concepts marketing ethics and social responsibility work together because a company that has a corporate culture built on socially acceptable moral philosophies with individuals who have good personal values will generally make decisions that have a positive impact on society. If other persons in the organization approve of an activity and it is legal and customary within the industry, chances are the activity is acceptable from both an ethical and social responsibility perspective.

IMPORTANT TERMS

Marketing ethics	Green marketing
Moral philosophies	Reaction strategy
Ethical issue	Defense strategy
Codes of ethics	Accommodation strategy
Social responsibility	Proactive strategy

DISCUSSION AND REVIEW QUESTIONS

1. Why is ethics an important consideration in marketing decisions?
2. How do the factors that influence ethical or unethical decisions interact?
3. Are there ethical concerns in approaching marketing as warfare with the view that competitors are the enemy?
4. What are some of the areas that result in major ethical issues in marketing?
5. How can ethical decisions in marketing be improved?
6. How can people with different personal values join together to make ethical decisions in an organization?
7. What is the difference between ethics and social responsibility?
8. What are major social responsibility issues?
9. Describe strategies for dealing with social responsibility issues.
10. How do you determine when a gift or payment is a bribe in marketing?

◼ CASES

3.1 Philip Morris Tobacco Advertising Creates Controversy

One of the more controversial issues in marketing today is the promotion of tobacco products. Television and radio advertisements for tobacco products were banned in 1971 in response to pressure by interest groups; all other tobacco advertising is regulated by the federal government, with some self-regulation by the tobacco industry. The government requires that a health-hazard warning be placed on all cigarette packs and prohibits advertising targeted at children, schools, and universities. Nonetheless, tobacco companies are still among the top five advertisers nationally in newspapers, on billboards, and in magazines, spending $2 billion annually.

Many members of the federal government, consumer groups, religious groups, and the medical profession want *all* advertising of tobacco products banned as a means of reducing consumption of cigarettes. They believe that even print advertisements encourage smoking, especially among certain segments of society. Their efforts to curtail tobacco advertisements have been fueled by increasing public concern over diseases caused by smoking, as well as the health of the nation in general. Antismoking interest groups, such as the Citizens Against Tobacco Smoke, Action on Smoking and Health, and the Group Against Smoking Pollution, believe that present tobacco advertising campaigns do not adequately inform consumers about the dangers associated with smoking cigarettes and see a total ban on such advertising as the only solution.

The antitobacco advertising controversy took on a new twist in late 1989 after Philip Morris, the nation's leading cigarette manufacturer, introduced a television advertising campaign designed to boost consumers' awareness of the Philip Morris name and its many products. Besides cigarettes, its products include those made by Kraft, General Foods, and Miller Brewing. Philip Morris planned to spend $60 million over two years on the campaign, which celebrated the 200th anniversary of the U.S. Bill of Rights. The advertisements focused on themes of liberty and freedom of speech and featured the words of John F. Kennedy, Franklin D. Roosevelt, Harry Truman, and Martin Luther King, Jr. Each advertisement provided an address or phone number for consumers to obtain a copy of the Bill of Rights. None mentioned cigarettes or smoking themes.

Nevertheless, antismoking groups charged that the advertisements violated the ban on advertising tobacco products on television and were really promoting smoking because they included the company's logo. The groups further charged that the company used the "rights" campaign to distract smokers from the adverse health effects of smoking. Others believe that it is wrong for any company to use something as "sacred" as the Bill of Rights to promote itself, much less a controversial product that causes disease and death. There was also some speculation that Philip Morris, which has long touted smokers' rights under the Bill of Rights, may have developed the campaign as a defense against the possibility of further antismoking legislation. Congress held a hearing in November 1989 to consider the issues raised by the Philip Morris advertisements. Legislation that would address such issues may be eventually enacted.

The response to the campaign surprised and angered Philip Morris executives. They said that the campaign celebrated America's Bill of Rights and the freedoms it guarantees and had nothing to do with cigarettes or smoking. They maintained that the advertisements were developed to inform consumers about the company's changing identity after it acquired Kraft and General Foods. Philip Morris continued to run the advertisements despite the debate they generated.

None of the tobacco marketers like the prospect of a total advertising ban, and they are monitoring the Philip Morris case carefully. In addition, they are aggressively lobbying Congress, appearing at congressional hearings on the subject, and running advertisements to combat negative publicity about cigarette smoking. One weapon that the marketers have seized upon is the results of studies conducted after cigarette advertisements were banned from television in 1971. Those studies showed that cigarette smoking actually increased after the ban went into effect. Cigarette marketers have argued, therefore, that further bans on tobacco product advertising will have little effect.

Tobacco producers also point out that they are concerned and responsible advertisers. The industry has spent portions of its advertising budgets running advertisements advocating safety and moderation. For example, RJR Nabisco has run advertisements aimed at teen-agers asking, "Does smoking really make you look more grown up?" Other tobacco product marketers are following suit, at least in part to stave off federal legislation.

The tobacco advertising controversy is a particularly touchy issue because the First Amendment to the Constitution guarantees free speech without prior censorship, a fact probably not lost on Philip Morris in the development of its "rights" advertising campaign. Cigarette marketers do not want their right to free commercial speech restricted, and they do not believe that the government can constitutionally ban their First Amendment rights. They believe that it is wrong to take away any industry's right to free speech just because certain groups do not like the products the industry manufactures. Many of those who are against an advertising ban on tobacco products are also concerned that such a ban would set a dangerous precedent. They fear that it could lead to bans even on products that have not been shown to cause harm.

There is no obvious solution to this debate. Compromise does not seem to be a possibility because neither side seems willing to concede anything at this time. If the consumer groups involved are not immediately successful in getting their desired ban on tobacco advertising, they will not give up because they believe that the health of the nation is threatened. But the producers will not give up either. Part of the complexity of this issue lies in the constitutionality of such a ban: whether the government has the authority to prohibit the right to commercial free speech, weighed against the necessity of protecting its citizens against products that may be harmful. This controversy will continue to be in the news during the next few years and the outcome will certainly affect the way products are advertised in this country.

SOURCES: Joe Agnew, "Alcohol, Tobacco Marketers Battle New Ad Restraints," *Marketing News,* Jan. 30, 1987, pp. 1, 12; "Antismoking Groups Fuming over Philip Morris TV Ads," *Marketing News,* Dec. 4, 1989, p. 5; Steven W. Colford, "Congress Eyes PM's 'Rights,'" *Advertising Age,* Nov. 13, 1989, pp. 1, 94; Steven W. Colford, "Tobacco Ad Foes Press Fight," *Advertising Age,* Feb. 23, 1987, p. 12; Alix M. Freedman, "Philip Morris to Launch Image Ads," *Wall Street Journal,* Nov. 1, 1989, p. B1; Robyn Griggs, "Philip Morris Hearings: Smoke, No Fire; Observers Say Outcry Relates Mostly to Issue of Tobacco Ads," *Adweek,* Nov. 20, 1989, pp. 1, 10; and Camille P. Schuster and Christine Pacelli Powell, "Comparison of Cigarette and Alcohol Advertising Controversies," *Journal of Advertising,* 1987, pp. 26–33.

Questions for Discussion

1. Which of the four strategies discussed in the text are Philip Morris and other tobacco marketers following in their response to environmental forces?
2. In view of the results of research on expenditures for tobacco advertisements, what would you logically conclude about your advertising budget if you wanted to increase sales of tobacco products?
3. Do you think that the manufacturers and advertisers of tobacco products are acting in an ethical, socially responsible manner?

3.2 The Wreck of the *Exxon Valdez*

In 1989, Exxon Corporation and Alyeska Pipeline Service Company—a consortium, owned by Exxon and seven other oil companies, that operates the Trans-Alaska pipeline and the shipping terminal in Valdez, Alaska—faced much criticism over their handling of a major oil spill from an Exxon tanker. The *Exxon Valdez* ran aground near Valdez, Alaska, spilling 240,000 barrels—11 million gallons—of crude oil that eventually covered 2,600 square miles of Prince William Sound and the Gulf of Alaska.

The *Exxon Valdez* ran aground atop Bligh Reef, rupturing its hull, soon after midnight on March 24, 1989, while the helmsman was attempting to maneuver the nearly 1,000-foot ship around some floating ice. Captain Joseph Hazelwood had left the ship's third mate, who was not licensed to pilot the vessel through the treacherous waters of Prince William Sound, at the helm while he slept below deck. The spill spread rapidly during the next few days, killing thousands of sea birds, sea otters, and other wildlife; covering the pristine coastline with oil; and curtailing the fishing season in the sound.

The events following the spill reveal that neither Exxon nor Alyeska was prepared to handle a spill the size of that leaked by the *Exxon Valdez,* despite repeated assurances to the contrary. To relieve public concern about the safety of the Alaskan environment, Alyeska Pipeline Service, its eight oil company owners, and federal officials promised in 1972 that the tanker fleet operating out of Valdez would incorporate safety features such as double hulls and protective ballast tanks to minimize the possibility of spills. By 1977, however, Alyeska had convinced the Coast Guard that the safety features were unnecessary, and few ships in the Valdez fleet incorporated them. The *Exxon Valdez* did not.

Alyeska had also filed a comprehensive contingency plan detailing how it would handle spills from the pipeline or the Valdez terminal. The contingency plan provided that in the event of an oil spill from a tanker, emergency crews would encircle the spill with containment booms within five hours. But it took them thirty-six hours to fully encircle the *Exxon Valdez.* Alyeska's contingency plan further specified that an emergency crew would be on hand at all times. For a time, Alyeska did have an emergency team on location to respond to a spill but disbanded most of it by 1981 to cut costs. Exxon's staff of oil spill experts had also been reduced because of personnel cutbacks. An Exxon spokesman said that he was not aware that the cutbacks affected Alyeska's initial readiness to combat a spill.

A state audit of the equipment Alyeska should have had on hand at the time of the spill demonstrated that the company was unprepared. The company had only two of the three tugboats and seven of the thirteen oil skimmers that were supposed to be available. The company also had only 14,000 feet of boom for containing spills; the contingency plan specified 21,000 feet. The barge that carried the booms and stored skimmed oil was also out of service because it had been damaged in a storm before the spill. In any case, the required equipment would not have been enough because a tanker such as the *Exxon Valdez* is almost 1,000 feet long and holds 1.2 million barrels of oil. The booms available barely encircled the giant ship, much less a sizable slick. Moreover, Alyeska was in violation of its own contingency plans when it failed to notify state officials that the barge was out of service. The damaged barge was pressed into service for cleanup operations anyway.

Furthermore, Alyeska and Exxon did not have enough chemical dispersants to fight the spill. They were not ready to test the effectiveness of the dispersants until eighteen hours after the spill, and then they conducted the test by tossing buckets of chemicals out of the door of a helicopter. The helicopter's rotor wash dispersed the chemicals, and they missed their target altogether. Exxon eventually applied tens of thousands of gallons of dispersants, but by then the oil had become too emulsified for dispersants to work properly. Moreover, the skimmer boats used to scoop oil out of the sea were so old that they kept breaking down and clogging. The skimmers filled rapidly and had to be emptied into nearby barges, requiring long periods of downtime. Cleanup efforts were further hampered by communication breakdowns between coordinators on shore and crews at the scene because of technical problems and limited range. Despite pleas from fishermen, Exxon and Alyeska also failed to mobilize the fleet of private fishing boats standing by. Exxon admitted that the early efforts were chaotic, but no more so than the response to any major disaster.

Nine hours after the wreck, Captain Hazelwood was tested for alcohol. The test showed that his blood alcohol content exceeded that allowed by Coast Guard regulations for a person operating a ship. Four other crewmen, including the third mate, tested negative for alcohol. Exxon officials later admitted that they knew that the captain had gone through an alcohol detoxification program, yet they still gave him command of the *Exxon Valdez,* Exxon's largest tanker.

The public was outraged by the spill itself and highly critical of Exxon's and Alyeska's cleanup efforts. Exxon's chairman, Lawrence Rawl, apologized to the public and accepted liability for the spill and responsibility for its cleanup. By summer, the company had 11,000 people, 1,400 vessels, 38 oil skimmers, and 72 aircraft working to clean up beaches and save wildlife. Nonetheless, many felt that Exxon and Alyeska's cleanup efforts were inadequate and too slow, and they did not believe that Exxon's idea of "clean" was clean enough. There were also disputes as to how much oil had actually been cleaned up. Several thousand Exxon credit card holders returned their cards to the company (some in oil-filled sandwich bags); others boycotted Exxon service stations and products.

Exxon also came under fire for a number of public relations snafus during the crisis. Chairman Rawl did not comment on the spill for nearly six days, and then he did so from New York. Crisis management experts believe that Rawl's delayed response and failure to appear on the scene angered consumers, despite Exxon's efforts to clean up the spill. Consumers also became angry over some of Exxon's public statements. For example, one Exxon executive told reporters that consumers would pay for the costs of the cleanup in higher gas prices. Exxon's attempts to blame the cleanup delays on the Coast Guard and Alaskan officials were also damaging. Furthermore, Exxon insisted in a July memorandum that it would stop all cleanup operations on September 15, 1989, regardless of how much shoreline remained to be cleaned. However, when the memo was revealed, it generated so much public and government protest that Exxon officials promised to resume the cleanup in the spring of 1990 if the Coast Guard determined a need for it.

Exxon's response to the crisis certainly hurt its reputation and credibility with the public. Exxon claims that it had saved $22 million by not building the *Exxon Valdez* with a second hull. But some experts believe that the cost of the cleanup effort may exceed $2 billion, of which insurance companies would pay only $400 million. In addition, more than 150 lawsuits had been filed against Exxon as a result of the spill; more are expected. On August 15, 1989, the state of Alaska also filed suit against Exxon, as well as subsidiaries of Amerada Hess Corp., Atlantic Richfield Co., British Petroleum Co., Mobil Corp., Phillips Petroleum Co., and Unocal Corp.—the largest owners of Alyeska Pipeline Services Co.—for mismanaging the response to the oil spill. The suit demands both compensatory and punitive damages that may exceed $1 billion. However, although Captain Hazelwood was indicted for his actions in the incident, he was acquitted on all the charges except negligent discharge of oil. He was fined and sentenced to clean Alaskan beaches for 1,000 hours. Exxon may have to pay billions more to settle lawsuits and claims from fishermen and Alaskan businesses, as well as any civil and criminal penalties levied by the Alaskan and federal governments.

SOURCES: Stuart Elliot, "Public Angry at Slow Action on Oil Spill," *USA Today*, Apr. 21, 1989, pp. B1, B2; William Glasgall and Vicky Cahan, "Questions That Keep Surfacing After the Spill," *Business Week*, Apr. 17, 1989, p. 18; "In Ten Years You'll See 'Nothing,'" *Fortune*, May 8, 1989, pp. 50–54; Charles McCoy and Ken Wells, "Alaska, U.S. Knew of Flaws in Oil-Spill Response Plans," *Wall Street Journal*, Apr. 7, 1989, p. A3; Bill Nichols, "State Fears Exxon Will 'Walk Away,'" *USA Today*, Sept. 13, 1989, pp. 1A, 2A; Lawrence G. Rawl, Letter to Exxon Shareholders, Apr. 14, 1989; Richard B. Schmitt, "Exxon, Alyeska May Be Exposed on Damages," *Wall Street Journal*, Apr. 10, 1989, p. A8; Allanna Sullivan, "Alaska Sues Exxon Corp., 6 Other Firms," *Wall Street Journal*, Aug. 16, 1989, pp. A3, A4; Ken Wells, "Alaska Begins Criminal Inquiry of Valdez Spill," *Wall Street Journal*, Mar. 30, 1989, p. A4; and Ken Wells and Charles McCoy, "How Unpreparedness Turned the Alaska Spill into Ecological Debacle," *Wall Street Journal*, Apr. 3, 1989, pp. A1, A4; Cable News Network, March 22, 1990.

Questions for Discussion

1. Ethics relates to individual decisions. What were the ethical issues in this case?
2. What were the social responsibility issues in this case?
3. What effect did the wreck of the Exxon Valdez have on Exxon's marketing strategy for consumer products such as gasoline?

4 TARGET MARKETS: SEGMENTATION AND EVALUATION

Objectives

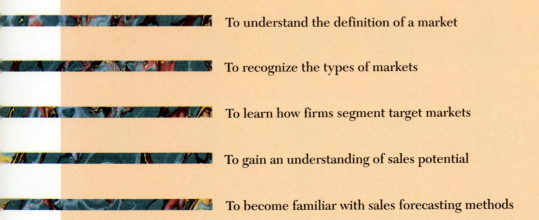

To understand the definition of a market

To recognize the types of markets

To learn how firms segment target markets

To gain an understanding of sales potential

To become familiar with sales forecasting methods

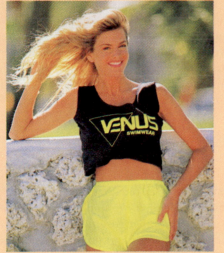

Seizing a market opportunity to capitalize on the popularity of competition body building and the lack of appropriate fashions for such competition, Daryle Scott began Titan Bodybuilding, Inc., supplying competition body builders' wear from a spare room in his home in 1982. However, Scott soon recognized that the group of people wanting to purchase Titan's products was small; he therefore decided to form a new venture, Venus Swimwear Ltd., to sell women's swimwear through mail-order catalogs.

Venus Swimwear aims its products at college-age women who lead active lives—its target market. The design, manufacture, and marketing of Venus products is handled in-house. Scott attributes the company's success to good swimsuit design that appeals to young, active women. The firm produces more than 100,000 bathing suits in 125 designs per year, with an average selling price of $45. Venus also permits customers to mix sizes when ordering two-piece suits. To reach the target market, Venus advertises in magazines such as *Cosmopolitan, Glamour,* and *Shape and New Body* and publishes several catalogs each year. The company sends out more than 3 million catalogs annually and generates 90 percent of its business through mail order. Venus also sponsored the first annual "Miss Venus Swimwear" contest, which was held in 1989 in Clearwater Beach, Florida, to increase awareness of the firm's products.

After achieving success by selling through catalogs, Venus expanded its market through 1,200 retail stores around the country. It has also started exporting to Canada, Australia, Taiwan, and Europe. In 1989, Titan Bodybuilding and its subsidiary, Venus Swimwear, expected to gross $4.5 million. Venus contributes about 80 percent of the firm's annual gross sales, with the remainder coming from Titan. ◆

Photo courtesy of Venus Swimwear.

Based on information from Dawn White, "Swimwear Company Makes a Splash in Market," *Jacksonville Business Journal,* Sept. 25, 1989, p. 3; *American Swimwear,* March 1990, p. 27; and correspondence from Daryle V. Scott, President, Venus Swimwear, Jacksonville, Fl., Jan. 19, 1990.

A marketer such as Venus Swimwear identifies or singles out groups of customers for its products and directs some or all of its marketing activities at those groups. It develops and maintains a marketing mix (a product, a distribution system, promotion, and price) that effectively satisfies the needs of customers in those groups.

In this chapter we explore markets and market segmentation. We first define the term *market* and describe the major types of markets. Then we examine the approaches and strategies typically used to select target markets, and the numerous variables commonly used to segment markets. Next we discuss market measurement and evaluation. Finally, we describe the primary sales forecasting techniques.

WHAT ARE MARKETS?

The word *market* has a number of meanings. People sometimes use it to refer to a specific location where products are bought and sold, for example, a flea market. A large geographic area may also be called a market. Sometimes the word refers to the relationship between the supply and demand of a specific product, as in the question, "How is the market for oat bran products?" At times, "market" is used to mean the act of selling something.

In this book, a **market** denotes an aggregate of people who, as individuals or as organizations, have needs for products in a product class and who have the ability, willingness, and authority to purchase such products. In general use, the term *market* sometimes refers to the total population—or mass market—that buys products. However, our definition is more specific; it refers to persons seeking products in a specific product category. For example, students are part of the market for textbooks, as well as markets for calculators, pens and pencils, paper, food, music, and other products. Obviously, there are many different markets in our complex economy. In this section we discuss the requirements for a market and the general types of markets.

■ **Requirements for a Market**

For a group of people to be a market, it must meet the following four requirements.

1. The people must need or want a particular product. If they do not, then that group is not a market.
2. The people in the group must have the ability to purchase the product. Ability to purchase is a function of their buying power, which consists of resources such as money, goods, and services that can be traded in an exchange situation.
3. The people in the group must be willing to use their buying power.
4. The people in the group must have the authority to buy the specific products.

Individuals can have the desire, the buying power, and the willingness to purchase certain products but may not be authorized to do so. For example, high school students may have the desire, the money, and the willingness to buy alcoholic beverages, but a liquor producer does not consider them a market because until students are 21 years old (in most states), they are prohibited by law from buying alcoholic beverages. An aggregate of people that lacks any one of the four requirements thus does not constitute a market.

■ Types of Markets

Markets can be divided into two categories: consumer markets and organizational or industrial markets. These categories are based on the characteristics of the individuals and groups that make up a specific market and the purposes for which they buy products. A **consumer market** consists of purchasers and/or individuals in their households who intend to consume or benefit from the purchased products and who do not buy products for the main purpose of making a profit. Each of us belongs to numerous consumer markets for such products as housing, food, clothing, vehicles, personal services, appliances, furniture, and recreational equipment. Consumer markets are discussed in more detail in Chapter 5.

An **organizational**, or **industrial**, **market** consists of individuals or groups that purchase a specific kind of product for one of three purposes: resale, direct use in producing other products, or use in general daily operations. The four categories of organizational, or industrial, markets—producer, reseller, government, and institutional—are discussed in Chapter 6.

SELECTING TARGET MARKETS

In Chapter 1 we say that a marketing strategy has two components: (1) the selection of the organization's target market and (2) the creation and maintenance of a marketing mix that satisfies that market's needs for a specific product. Regardless of the general types of markets on which a firm focuses, marketing management must select the firm's target markets. The next section examines two general approaches to identifying target markets: the total market approach and market segmentation.

■ Total Market, or Undifferentiated, Approach

An organization sometimes defines the entire market for a particular product as its target market. When a company designs a single marketing mix and directs it at the entire market for a particular product, it is using a **total market** (or **undifferentiated**) **approach**, shown in Figure 4.1. This approach assumes that all customers in the target market for a specific kind of product have similar needs and, therefore, that the organization can satisfy most customers with a single marketing mix. This single marketing mix consists of one type of product with little or no variation, one price, one promotional program aimed at everybody, and one distribution system to reach all customers in the total market. Products that can be marketed successfully through the total market approach include staple food items, such as sugar and salt, and certain kinds of farm produce.

The total market approach can be effective under two conditions. First, a large proportion of customers in the total market must have similar needs for the product.

FIGURE 4.1
Total market, or undifferentiated, approach

Organization   Single marketing mix   Target market

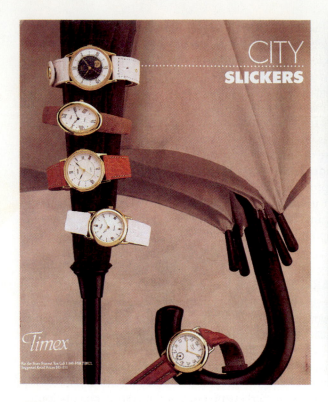

FIGURE 4.2 *Supplying a heterogeneous market.*
The watch market is heterogeneous, as indicated by the need for inexpensive, functional watches such as Timex and more costly, prestigious and glamorous watches such as Christian Dior.

SOURCE: Timex ad: Permission granted by Timex Corporation; Christian Dior ad: Courtesy of Christian Dior—New York Inc.

A marketer using a single marketing mix for a total market of customers with a variety of needs will find that the marketing mix satisfies very few people. Anyone could predict that a "universal car," meant to satisfy everyone, would satisfy very few customers' needs for cars because it would not provide the specific attributes that a specific person wants. Second, the organization must be able to develop and maintain a single marketing mix that satisfies customers' needs. The company must be able to identify a set of product needs that are common to most customers in a total market, and it must have the resources and managerial skills to reach a sizable portion of that market. If customers' needs are dissimilar or if the organization is unable to develop and maintain a satisfying marketing mix, then a total market approach is likely to fail.

Although customers may have similar needs for a few products, in the case of most products these needs are decidedly different. In such instances, a company should use the market segmentation approach.

■ **Market Segmentation Approach**

Markets made up of individuals with diverse product needs are called **heterogeneous markets**. Not everyone wants the same type of car, furniture, or clothes. For example, some individuals want an economical car, others desire a status symbol, and still others seek an automobile that is roomy and comfortable for travel. The automobile market, then, is an example of a heterogeneous market. For such hetero-

FIGURE 4.3
Market segmentation approach

Organization   Single marketing mix   Market

geneous markets, the market segmentation approach is appropriate. As shown in Figure 4.2, the market for watches is quite diverse. Timex provides a watch for $45 to $50 whereas Christian Dior's market seeks a more upscale, exclusive watch.

As Figure 4.3 shows, **market segmentation** is the process of dividing a total market into market groups consisting of people who have relatively similar product needs. The purpose is to design a marketing mix (or mixes) that more precisely matches the needs of individuals in a selected market segment (or segments). A **market segment** consists of individuals, groups, or organizations with one or more similar characteristics that cause them to have relatively similar product needs. For instance, the soft drink market can be divided into segments consisting of cola drinkers, non-cola drinkers, and drinkers of diet drinks.

The principal rationale for segmenting markets is that an organization is better able to develop a marketing mix in a diverse market that satisfies a relatively small portion of a total market than it is to develop a mix that meets the needs of all people. The segmentation approach differs from the total approach because it aims one marketing mix at one segment of a total market rather than directing a single marketing mix at a total market.

The market segmentation approach is widely used. In the next sections we analyze several of its main features, including the types of market segmentation strategies and the conditions required for effective segmentation.

■ Market Segmentation Strategies

There are two major segmentation strategies: the concentration strategy and the multisegment strategy.

Concentration Strategy.　When an organization directs its marketing efforts toward a single market segment by creating and maintaining one marketing mix, it is employing a **concentration strategy**. Lamborghini, for example, focuses on the luxury sports car segment and directs all its marketing efforts toward high-income individuals who want to own high-performance luxury cars. The chief advantage of the concentration strategy is that it allows a firm to specialize. The firm can analyze the characteristics and needs of a distinct customer group and then focus all its energies on satisfying that group's needs. A firm can generate a large sales volume by reaching a single segment. In addition, concentrating on a single segment permits a firm with limited resources to compete with much larger organizations, which may have overlooked some smaller segments.

Specialization, however, means that a company puts all its eggs in one basket—clearly a disadvantage. If a company's sales depend on a single segment and

FIGURE 4.4
Multisegment strategy

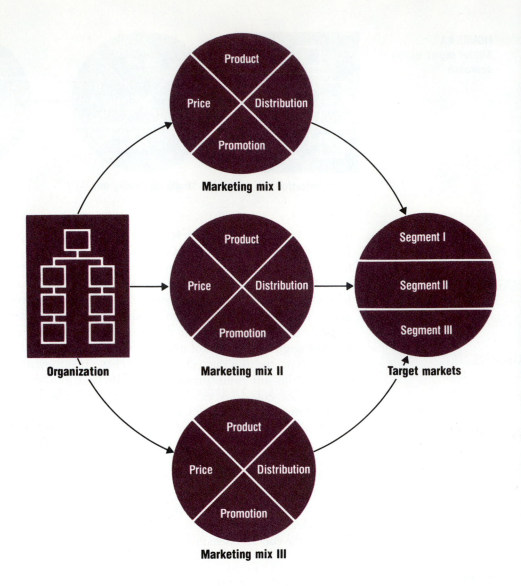

Marketing mix I

Product

Price · Distribution

Promotion

Organization

Marketing mix II

Product

Price · Distribution

Promotion

Segment I

Segment II

Segment III

Target markets

Marketing mix III

Product

Price · Distribution

Promotion

the segment's demand for the product declines, the company's financial strength also declines. Moreover, when a firm penetrates one segment and becomes well entrenched, its popularity may keep it from moving into other segments. For example, in the automobile market, Ferrari would have trouble moving into the economy car segment, whereas Hyundai would find it difficult to enter the luxury car segment. Marketing Update 4.1 discusses Polaroid's marketing of a product using a total-market approach rather than its traditional concentration strategy.

Multisegment Strategy.   With a **multisegment strategy** (see Figure 4.4), an organization directs its marketing efforts at two or more segments by developing a marketing mix for each selected segment. After a firm uses a concentration strategy successfully in one market segment, it sometimes expands its efforts to additional segments. For example, Jockey underwear has traditionally been aimed at one segment: men. However, the company now markets underwear for women and

POLAROID USES THE TOTAL-MARKET APPROACH FOR A NEW FILM PRODUCT

The Polaroid Corporation's marketing of instant photography cameras and films was a classic example of the concentration strategy; it targeted products at only one segment of the photography market, a segment that belonged solely to Polaroid. Even when the Eastman Kodak Corporation attempted to move into the instant photography market, Polaroid sued for patent infringement and won. However, the king of instant photography found itself in an uneasy predicament in the late 1980s: the popularity of instant photography had seriously waned.

Because more than half of Polaroid's annual revenues came from sales of instant cameras, the company's future seemed to be in doubt. The demand for instant cameras and film peaked in 1978 and had since been declining steadily. Despite Polaroid's attempts to boost demand with such products as the Spectra system in 1986, other forces that Polaroid could not control slowly changed the marketplace. The advent of one-hour photo-processing labs made regular photography faster and more convenient. The camcorder and VCR allowed for the instant development of moving pictures. In addition, the push to electronic cameras, which use magnetic disks rather than film to record images, created instant filmless photography. Thus, changing technology made Polaroid the sole owner of an ever-shrinking market.

It was not surprising, then, that Polaroid decided to adopt a different strategy for a new film product. Polaroid's strength had long been those consumers who preferred no-fuss, point-and-shoot photography. So, in 1989 Polaroid introduced OneFilm, a 35mm film that can be used in any lighting situation. OneFilm was targeted at those consumers who found the process of matching 35mm film to different light situations confusing.

However, Polaroid's new strategy did not solve its problems. Many photographers believe that, although OneFilm is designed for every use, it isn't precisely right for many photographic situations. Thus, during its first Christmas, the biggest film-selling period, only 30 to 35 percent of the major retail chains sold OneFilm, although Polaroid had expected it to be carried by at least twice that. Polaroid, therefore, may reevaluate its segmentation strategy.

SOURCES: Suzanne Alexander, "Polaroid Trims Profit Projections for 1989 and 1990," *Wall Street Journal,* Nov. 29, 1989, p. B2; Alex Beam, "Is Polaroid Playing to a Market That Just Isn't There?," *Business Week (Industrial/Technology Edition),* Apr. 7, 1986, pp. 82–83; Brian Dumaine, "How Polaroid Flashed Back," *Fortune,* Feb. 16, 1987, pp. 72–76; Keith H. Hammonds, "A New Focus for Polaroid: Conventional Film," *Business Week (Industrial/Technology Edition),* July 25, 1988, p. 36; Peter Pae, "For Makers of Photo Film, Holidays Are War Days," *Wall Street Journal,* Dec. 13, 1989, p. B1.

FIGURE 4.5
Jif's multisegment strategy.
Jif's application of the multisegment strategy resulted in their supporting education, therefore giving consumers a "non-taste" point-of-difference to discriminate among peanut butters.

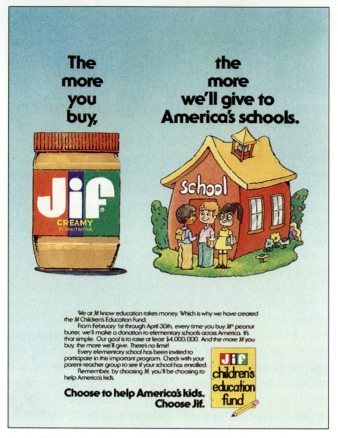

SOURCE: Reprinted with permission of Campbell Soup Company

children as well. The marketing mixes used for a multisegment strategy may vary as to product differences, distribution methods, promotion methods, and prices.

A business can usually increase its sales in the aggregate market through a multisegment strategy because the firm's mixes are being aimed at more people. In Figure 4.5, Jif supports the Children's Education Fund by making donations to elementary schools across the country. The goal is to motivate buyers who do not have a strong brand commitment to choose Jif. A company with excess production capacity may find a multisegment strategy advantageous because the sale of products to additional segments may absorb this excess capacity. On the other hand, multisegment strategy often demands a greater number of production processes, materials, and people; thus production costs may be higher than with concentration strategy. Keep in mind also that a firm using a multisegment strategy ordinarily experiences higher marketing costs. Because this strategy usually requires more research and several different promotion plans and distribution methods, the costs of planning, organizing, implementing, and controlling marketing activities increase.

■ **Conditions for Effective Segmentation**

Whether a firm uses the concentration or the multisegment strategy, five conditions must exist for market segmentation to be effective. First, consumers' needs for the product must be heterogeneous. If they are not, there is little need to segment the market. Second, the segments must be identifiable and divisible. The company must find some basis for effectively separating individuals in a total market into groups, each of which has a relatively uniform need for the product. Third, the total market should be divided in such a way that the segments can be compared with respect to estimated sales potential, costs, and profits. Fourth, at least one segment must have enough profit potential to justify developing and maintaining a special marketing mix. Finally, the company must be able to reach the chosen segment with a particular marketing mix. Some market segments may be difficult or impossible to reach because of legal, social, or distribution constraints. For instance, marketers of Cuban rum and cigars are not permitted to sell to the U.S. market because of political and trade restrictions.

CHOOSING SEGMENTATION VARIABLES

Segmentation variables are the characteristics of individuals, groups, or organizations that are used for dividing a total market into segments. For example, location, age, sex, or rate of product usage can all be a means of segmenting.

Several factors are considered in selecting a segmentation variable. The segmentation variable should be related to customers' needs for, uses of, or behavior toward the product. Stereo marketers might segment the stereo market on the basis of income and age—but not on the basis of religion, because one person's music-listening needs do not differ much from those of persons of other religions. Furthermore, if individuals or organizations in a total market are to be classified accurately, the segmentation variable must be measurable. For example, age, location, and sex are measurable because such information can be obtained through observation or questioning. But segmenting a market on the basis of intelligence is extremely difficult because this attribute is harder to measure accurately.

A company's resources and capabilities affect the number and size of segment variables used. The type of product and the degree of variation in consumers' needs also dictate the number and size of segments targeted by a particular firm. In short, there is no best way to segment markets. For example, the number and size of the segments J.C. Penney's uses to divide the clothing market may not be appropriate for Borden to use in dividing the market for dairy products.

Choosing a segmentation variable or variables is a critical step in segmenting a market. Selecting an inappropriate variable limits the chances of developing a successful strategy. To help you understand better the possible segmentation variables, we now look closely at three aspects of the topic: the major types of variables used to segment consumer markets; the types used to segment organizational markets; and single-variable versus multivariable segmentation.

■ **Variables for Segmenting Consumer Markets**

A marketer shaping a segmentation strategy to reach a consumer market can choose one or several variables from a broad assortment of possible ones. As shown in Figure 4.6, segmentation variables can be grouped into four categories: (1) demographic, (2) geographic, (3) psychographic, and (4) behavioristic.

Demographic Variables. A demographer studies aggregate population characteristics such as the distribution of age and sex, fertility rates, migration patterns, and mortality rates. The demographic characteristics that marketers commonly turn to in segmenting markets include age, sex, race, ethnicity, income, education, occupa-

FIGURE 4.6
*Segmentation variables
for consumer markets*

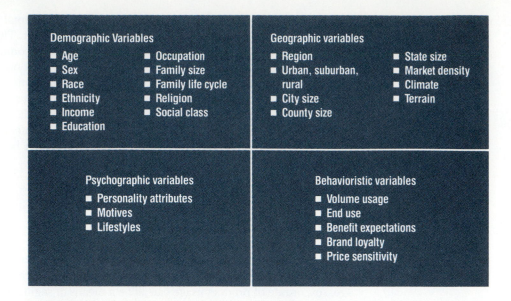

Demographic Variables
- Age
- Sex
- Race
- Ethnicity
- Income
- Education
- Occupation
- Family size
- Family life cycle
- Religion
- Social class

Geographic variables
- Region
- Urban, suburban, rural
- City size
- County size
- State size
- Market density
- Climate
- Terrain

Psychographic variables
- Personality attributes
- Motives
- Lifestyles

Behavioristic variables
- Volume usage
- End use
- Benefit expectations
- Brand loyalty
- Price sensitivity

tion, family size, family life cycle, religion, and social class. Marketers rely on these demographic characteristics both because they are often closely linked to customers' product needs and purchasing behavior and because they can be readily measured.

Age is a commonly used variable for segmentation purposes, but marketers need to be aware of the distribution of age and how that distribution is changing. Figure 4.7 shows the proportion of the U.S. population in various age groups for 1985 and projections for the year 2000. All age groups (except the 5 to 13 group) that include persons now 34 years old or younger are expected to decrease, and all other age categories are expected to increase. In 1970, the average age of a U.S. citizen was 27.9; currently, it is about 32. According to projections, the average age in the year 2000 will be 35.5. Mars, the second leading candy marketer, introduced Sussânde —a line of chocolates aimed at adults (see Figure 4.8).

Marketers are increasingly aiming their marketing efforts at children. There are 28 million in the 12 to 19 demographic age group, and in 1988 they spent $55 billion, received from allowances and gifts. These teen-agers spent another $33.5 billion on family grocery shopping, for in households with only one parent or where both parents work children have to take on additional responsibilities such as cooking, cleaning, and grocery shopping. Moreover, the 42 million children under the age of 12 have about $6.2 billion to spend on their own. Marketers are beginning to recognize the buying power of today's children and are targeting more products at them. Polaroid, for example, designed its Cool Cam video camera for the 9 to 14 age group, and Delta Air Lines created a frequent flier program for children aged 2 to 12. When H.J. Heinz learned that children eat one-third more ketchup than adults and often choose the family brand, the company created a youth-oriented ad campaign to appeal to them.[1]

Gender is another demographic variable commonly used to segment a number of markets, including clothes, soft drinks, nonprescription medications, toiletries, magazines, and even cigarettes. The U.S. Census Bureau reports that girls and women

1. Patricia Sellers, "The ABC's of Marketing to Kids," *Fortune,* May 8, 1989, pp. 114–120.

FIGURE 4.7

U.S. age distribution and projected changes

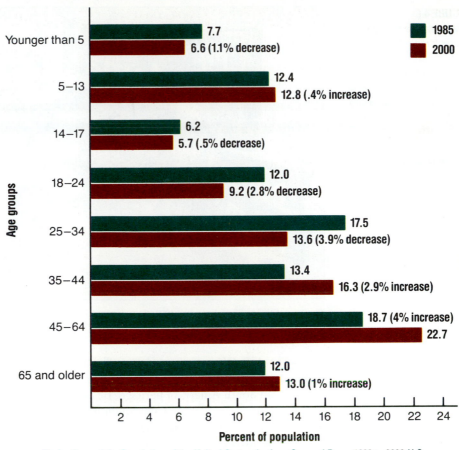

Age groups / Percent of population

- **1985**
- **2000**

Younger than 5	7.7 / 6.6 (1.1% decrease)
5–13	12.4 / 12.8 (.4% increase)
14–17	6.2 / 5.7 (.5% decrease)
18–24	12.0 / 9.2 (2.8% decrease)
25–34	17.5 / 13.6 (3.9% decrease)
35–44	13.4 / 16.3 (2.9% increase)
45–64	18.7 (4% increase) / 22.7
65 and older	12.0 / 13.0 (1% increase)

SOURCE: *Projections of the Population of the United States, by Age, Sex and Race, 1983 to 2080,* U.S. Department of Commerce, Bureau of the Census, May 1984, p. 8.

account for 51.2 percent and that boys and men represent 48.8 percent of the total U.S. population.[2] The deodorant market is a primary example of gender segmentation—Secret deodorant is marketed specifically to women whereas Old Spice deodorant is directed toward men.

Because it strongly influences people's product needs, income often provides a way of dividing markets. It affects the ability to buy (discussed in Chapter 2) and the aspirations for a certain style of living. Product markets segmented by income range from housing, furniture, clothing, and food to automobiles and certain kinds of sporting goods. Lanvin jewelry, shown in Figure 4.9, is targeted to upper income consumers. Income is not distributed evenly across all American households. Although in 1988 the median household income was $25,986, the median income for married couples with children was $36,206, and the median income for single-person households was only $12,512.[3] Figure 4.10 shows the distributions of annual family income for 1975, 1980, and 1985.

Marketers have also turned to ethnicity as a means of segmenting markets for goods such as food, music, and clothing and for services such as banking and insur

2. "How USA Has Changed in the '80s," *USA Today,* Oct. 17, 1989, p. 13A.

3. Judith Waldrop, "Inside America's Households," *American Demographics,* March 1989, p. 23.

Mars targets the adult market.
SUSSÂNDE® Fine Chocolates, a new line of adult premium candies, is designed to compete with foreign brands such as Ferraro, Callard and Bowser, and Lindt. The products are priced higher than the SNICKERS® Bar yet lower than gourmet brands such as Godiva.

SOURCE: © Ethel M Chocolates, Inc. 1989

ance. The U.S. Hispanic population illustrates the importance of ethnicity as a segmentation variable. Made up of people of Mexican, Cuban, Puerto Rican, and Central and South American heritage, this ethnic group is growing five times faster than the general population. Consequently, Campbell Soup Co., Procter & Gamble, and other companies are targeting U.S. Hispanic consumers. They view the Hispanic segment as attractive because of its size and growth potential. However, targeting Hispanic customers is not an easy task. For example, although marketers have long believed that Hispanic consumers are exceptionally brand loyal and prefer Spanish-language broadcast media, recent research has failed to support this notion. Not only do advertisers disagree about the merits of Spanish-language media; they also question whether it is suitable to advertise to Mexicans, Puerto Ricans, and Cubans using a common Spanish language.[4] Each culture has its own unique language—thus, to lump Hispanic groups together does not allow the message to effectively reach each segment. These findings suggest that marketers should carefully research the Hispanic market segment before developing marketing mixes for it.

Among the factors shaping the product needs of a household are marital status and the presence and age of children. These characteristics can be combined into a single variable, sometimes called the *family life cycle.* Housing, appliances, food, automobiles, and boats are a few of the numerous product markets sometimes segmented by family life cycle stages. The family life cycle has been broken down in several different ways, including the following:

1. Young
   a. Single without children
   b. Married without children
   c. Single with children
   d. Married with children

4. Joseph G. Albonetti and Luis V. Dominguez, "Major Influences on Consumer-Goods Marketers' Decision to Target U.S. Hispanics," *Journal of Advertising Research,* February-March 1989, pp. 9–11.

SOURCE: Ad for Dahne and Weinstein by Oscar Heyman and Sons, N.Y.

2. Middle-aged
   a. Single without children
   b. Married without children
   c. Single with children
   d. Married with children
   e. Single without dependent children
   f. Married without dependent children

3. Older
   a. Single
   b. Married.[5]

However, the composition of American households is changing. The number of single-person households has increased from 17 percent in 1970 to about 25 percent in the late 1980s. The "typical" American family of two adults (with one being the breadwinner) and two children makes up only 6 percent of all U.S. households. In fact, in 1988, nonfamily households—that is, households in which one person lives alone or with unrelated people—outnumbered married couples with children.[6] Almost 60 percent of all adult women work outside the home. Of these women, 40 percent have children below the age of 6. More than two-thirds of all adults are married, but people are waiting longer to get married and are having fewer children. About half of all families do not have children younger than 18.

5. Adapted with permission from Patrick E. Murphy and William A. Staples, "A Modernized Family Life Cycle," *Journal of Consumer Research*, June 1979, Table 2, p. 16.

6. Waldrop, p. 22.

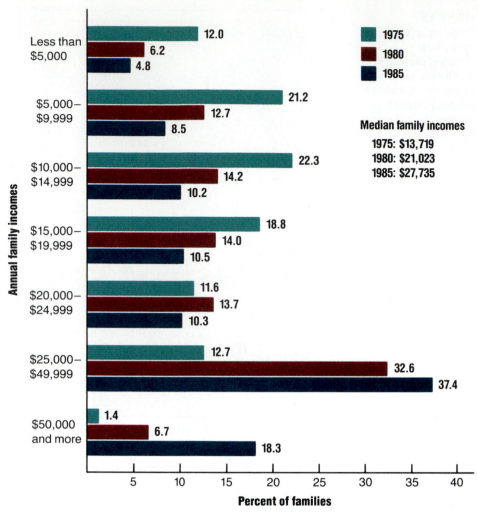

FIGURE 4.10
Distribution of annual family income for 1975, 1980, and 1985 (in unadjusted dollars)

■ 1975
■ 1980
■ 1985

Median family incomes
1975: $13,719
1980: $21,023
1985: $27,735

Annual family incomes

Less than $5,000
- 12.0
- 6.2
- 4.8

$5,000– $9,999
- 21.2
- 12.7
- 8.5

$10,000– $14,999
- 22.3
- 14.2
- 10.2

$15,000– $19,999
- 18.8
- 14.0
- 10.5

$20,000– $24,999
- 11.6
- 13.7
- 10.3

$25,000– $49,999
- 12.7
- 32.6
- 37.4

$50,000 and more
- 1.4
- 6.7
- 18.3

Percent of families

SOURCE: "Money Income and Poverty Status of Families and Persons in the United States: 1986," *Current Population Reports,* U.S. Department of Commerce, Bureau of the Census, July 1987, p. 11.

People of the same age may have diverse product needs because they are in different stages of the family life cycle. Persons in a particular life cycle stage may have very specific needs that can be satisfied by precisely designed marketing mixes. Young, educated single adults may desire small but well-appointed apartments or condominiums; many can afford expensive clothing, stereo systems, and appliances such as microwave ovens. Divorced women with children may be seeking life insurance. A middle-aged couple with children no longer at home has more discretionary income for entertainment, expensive restaurants, and travel. Victoria's Secret lingerie, advertised in Figure 4.11, appeals to young, female consumers.

There are many more demographic variables. For instance, publishers of encyclopedias and dictionaries segment markets by education level; brewers sometimes aim their products at broad occupational categories; and producers of cosmetics and hair-care supplies may segment markets according to race. Certain types of foods and clothing are directed toward people of specific religious sects.

FIGURE 4.11
How marketers address the age variable.
The appeal of Victoria's Secret to a younger target market is evident in their advertising.

SOURCE: Victoria's Secret Stores, 10 Margaret St., London, Division of The Limited, Inc.

Geographic Variables.   Geographic variables—climate, terrain, natural resources, population density, and subcultural values—also influence consumer product needs. Markets may be divided into regions because one or more geographic variables cause customers to differ from one region to another. A company that sells products to a national market might divide the United States into the following regions: Pacific, Southwest, Central, Midwest, Southeast, Middle Atlantic, and New England. A firm operating in one or several states might regionalize its market by counties, cities, zip code areas, or other units.

Marketers sometimes segment on the basis of state populations, and they use population figures in estimating demand. Between 1980 and 1988, the U.S. population grew by 13 percent,[7] but the population in all regions did not grow proportionally. While the South and the West registered significant increases, the Midwest and East experienced only minor gains. Some areas—New York, Rhode Island, and the District of Columbia—lost population. The map in Figure 4.12 shows the projected population growth (or loss) of each state between 1980 and 2000. Note that the

7. Waldrop, p. 20.

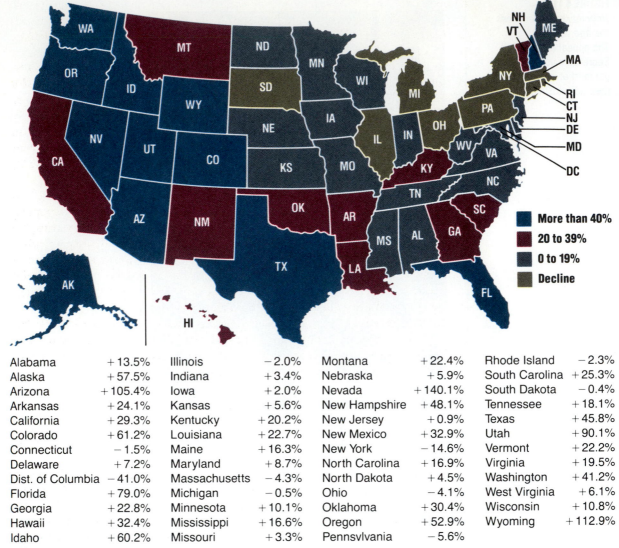

Alabama	+13.5%	Illinois	−2.0%	Montana	+22.4%	Rhode Island	−2.3%
Alaska	+57.5%	Indiana	+3.4%	Nebraska	+5.9%	South Carolina	+25.3%
Arizona	+105.4%	Iowa	+2.0%	Nevada	+140.1%	South Dakota	−0.4%
Arkansas	+24.1%	Kansas	+5.6%	New Hampshire	+48.1%	Tennessee	+18.1%
California	+29.3%	Kentucky	+20.2%	New Jersey	+0.9%	Texas	+45.8%
Colorado	+61.2%	Louisiana	+22.7%	New Mexico	+32.9%	Utah	+90.1%
Connecticut	−1.5%	Maine	+16.3%	New York	−14.6%	Vermont	+22.2%
Delaware	+7.2%	Maryland	+8.7%	North Carolina	+16.9%	Virginia	+19.5%
Dist. of Columbia	−41.0%	Massachusetts	−4.3%	North Dakota	+4.5%	Washington	+41.2%
Florida	+79.0%	Michigan	−0.5%	Ohio	−4.1%	West Virginia	+6.1%
Georgia	+22.8%	Minnesota	+10.1%	Oklahoma	+30.4%	Wisconsin	+10.8%
Hawaii	+32.4%	Mississippi	+16.6%	Oregon	+52.9%	Wyoming	+112.9%
Idaho	+60.2%	Missouri	+3.3%	Pennsylvania	−5.6%		

FIGURE 4.12 *Projected U.S. population growth in 1980–2000 (percent)*

SOURCE: U.S. Census Bureau.

heaviest growth is predicted for Florida and the western states. Nine states and the District of Columbia are expected to decline in population. To analyze the market accurately and segment it properly, marketers must be aware of both current population patterns and projected changes in these patterns.

City size can be an important segmentation variable. Some marketers want to focus their efforts on cities of a certain size. For example, one franchised restaurant organization will not locate in cities of less than 200,000 people. It has concluded that a smaller population base would not result in adequate profits. Other firms, however, seek opportunities in smaller towns.

Because cities often cut across political boundaries, the U.S. Census Bureau developed a system to classify metropolitan areas (any area with a city of at least fifty thousand or with an urbanized area of at least fifty thousand and a total metropolitan population of at least a hundred thousand). Metropolitan areas are categorized as one of the following: a metropolitan statistical area (MSA), a primary metropolitan statistical area (PMSA), or a consolidated metropolitan statistical area (CMSA). An MSA is an urbanized area encircled by nonmetropolitan counties and is neither socially nor economically dependent on any other metropolitan area. A metropolitan area within a complex of at least one million inhabitants can elect to be named a PMSA. A CMSA is a metropolitan area of at least one million consisting of two or more PMSAs. There are 21 CMSAs, including one in Puerto Rico (see Figure 4.13). The five largest CMSAs—New York, Los Angeles, Chicago, Philadelphia, and San Francisco—account for 20 percent of the U.S. population. The federal government provides a considerable amount of socioeconomic information about MSAs, PMSAs, and CMSAs that can aid market analysis and segmentation.

Market density refers to the number of potential customers within a unit of land area, such as a square mile. Although market density is related generally to population density, the correlation is not exact. For example, in two different geographic markets of approximately equal size and population, the market density for office supplies might be much higher in one area than in another if one area contains a much greater proportion of business customers. Market density may be a useful segmentation variable because low-density markets often require different sales, advertising, and distribution activities than high-density markets.

Climate is commonly used as a geographic segmentation variable because it has such a broad impact on people's behavior and product needs. The many product markets affected by climate include air-conditioning and heating equipment, clothing, gardening equipment, recreational products, and building materials.

Psychographic Variables.   Marketers sometimes use psychographic variables, such as personality characteristics, motives, and lifestyles, to segment markets. A psychographic dimension can be used by itself to segment a market, or it can be combined with other types of segmentation variables.

Personality characteristics are helpful when a product resembles many competing products and consumers' needs are not greatly affected by other segmentation variables. However, segmenting a market according to personality traits can be risky. Although marketing practitioners have long believed that consumer choice and product use vary with personality and lifestyle, until recently, marketing research had indicated only weak relationships. It is, of course, hard to gauge personality traits accurately—especially since most personality tests were developed for clinical use, and not for segmentation purposes. New, more reliable measurements devised for personality characteristics have indicated a stronger association between personality and consumer behavior.[8]

When appealing to a personality characteristic, a marketer almost always selects one that many people value positively. Individuals with this characteristic, as well as those who would like to have it, may be influenced to buy that marketer's brand. For example, the soft drink Dr Pepper has been promoted as "not for everyone," "the unusual," for those who are "independent," "strong-minded," or "outgoing." Marketers who take this approach do not worry about measuring how many people have the positively valued characteristic because they assume that a sizable proportion of people in the target market either have it or want to have it.

8. John L. Lastovicka and Erich A. Joachimsthaler, "Improving the Detection of Personality-Behavior Relationships in Consumer Research," *Journal of Consumer Research,* March 1988, pp. 583–587.

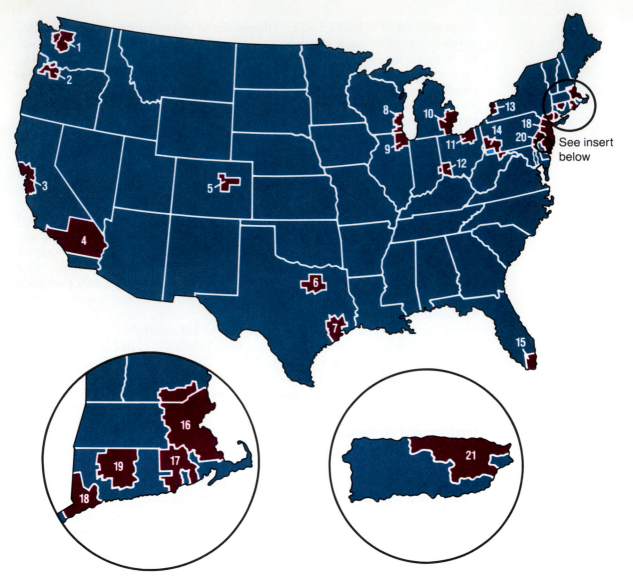

Consolidated Metropolitan Statistical Area (CMSA)

1 Seattle—Tacoma
2 Portland—Vancouver
3 San Francisco—Oakland—San Jose
4 Los Angeles—Anaheim—Riverside
5 Denver—Boulder
6 Dallas—Fort Worth
7 Houston—Galveston—Brazoria
8 Milwaukee—Racine
9 Chicago—Gary—Lake County
10 Detroit—Ann Arbor
11 Cleveland—Akron—Lorain

12 Cincinnati—Hamilton
13 Buffalo—Niagara Falls
14 Pittsburgh—Beaver Valley
15 Miami—Fort Lauderdale
16 Boston—Lawrence—Salem
17 Providence—Pawtucket—Fall River
18 New York—Northern New Jersey—
    Long Island (Part)
19 Hartford—New Britain—Middletown
20 Philadelphia—Wilmington—Trenton
21 San Juan — Caguas

FIGURE 4.13 *Consolidated metropolitan statistical areas and projected growth*

SOURCE: U.S. Census Bureau.

TABLE 4.1
Lifestyle dimensions

ACTIVITIES	INTERESTS	OPINIONS
Work	Family	Themselves
Hobbies	Home	Social issues
Social events	Job	Politics
Vacation	Community	Business
Entertainment	Recreation	Economics
Club membership	Fashion	Education
Community	Food	Products
Shopping	Media	Future
Sports	Achievements	Culture

SOURCE: Reprinted, adapted, from Joseph Plummer, "The Concept and Application of Life Style Segmentation," *Journal of Marketing*, January 1974, p. 34, published by the American Marketing Association. Used by permission.

Motives are another means of segmenting markets. In such cases, a market is divided according to consumers' reasons for making a purchase. Product durability, economy, convenience, and status are motives that affect the types of product purchased and the choice of stores in which they are bought. For example, one motive for the purchase of soft drinks in two-liter bottles or six-packs is economy.

Lifestyle segmentation groups individuals according to how they spend their time, the importance of things in their surroundings (their homes or their jobs, for example), their beliefs about themselves and broad issues, and some socioeconomic characteristics such as income and education.[9] Lifestyle analysis provides a broad view of buyers because it encompasses numerous characteristics related to people's activities, interests, and opinions. Table 4.1 illustrates factors that are a part of the major dimensions of lifestyle.

One of the more popular studies of lifestyle is conducted by the Value and Lifestyle Program (VALS) of the Stanford Research Institute. This program surveys American consumers to select groups with identifiable values and lifestyles. The program has identified three broad consumer groups: Outer-Directed, Inner-Directed, and Need-Driven consumers. In 1989 a VALS 2 classification was introduced that categorized consumers into five basic lifestyle groups: Strugglers, Action-Oriented, Status-Oriented, Principle-Oriented, and Actualizers. The VALS studies have been used to create products as well as to segment markets. VALS characteristics can also be used to select advertising media and determine advertising content. While the VALS studies are the most widely used basis for segmenting consumers by lifestyle, many other lifestyle classification systems do exist.

For example, one study divided supermarket shoppers into six segments based on their lifestyle activities. Avid Shoppers (about 25 percent of all shoppers) are the traditional supermarket shoppers who cook most of their meals, shop frequently, and look for bargains. Kitchen Strangers (20 percent) are usually childless men or women who seldom cook and eat take-out and restaurant food instead. Low-income families and individuals who usually buy only basic food products are classified as Constrained Shoppers. Hurried Shoppers are busy consumers who eat mostly at

9. Joseph T. Plummer, "The Concept and Application of Life Style Segmentation," *Journal of Marketing*, January 1974, p. 33.

home but look for shopping and cooking short cuts. Older working people whose children have left home, leaving them more money to spend on groceries, are known as Unfettered Shoppers. Finally, Kitchen Birds, primarily the elderly, are very light eaters.[10] By segmenting markets in this way, supermarket chains can try to create marketing mixes that satisfy the needs of each segment. The Kroger and Safeway chains, for example, now offer full salad bars and take-out food to appeal to the Kitchen Stranger segment.

Even though psychographic variables can effectively divide a market, they are not used very much. For one thing, they are harder to measure accurately than other types of segmentation variables, and their links to consumers' needs are sometimes obscure and unproven. For another, segments based on psychographic variables may not be reachable. Thus a marketer may determine that highly compulsive individuals want a certain type of clothing, but no specific stores or specific media vehicles—such as television or radio programs, newspapers, or magazines—appeal precisely to this group and this group alone.

Behavioristic Variables.   Firms can divide a market on the basis of some feature of consumer behavior toward a product, commonly involving some aspect of product use. For example, a total market may be separated into users and nonusers. Users may then be classified as heavy, moderate, or light. To satisfy a specific group, such as heavy users, a marketer may have to create a distinctive product, set special prices, or initiate special promotion and distribution activities. Thus airlines such as Delta offer frequent flier programs, which reward customers who regularly fly on their planes with free trips and discounts on rental cars and lodging.

How customers use or apply the product may also determine segmentation. To satisfy customers who use a product in a certain way, some feature—say, packaging, size, texture, or color—may have to be designed precisely to make the product easier to use, safer, or more convenient. For instance, Crest, Colgate, and other brands of toothpaste are now packaged with pump dispensers because consumers wanted easier-to-use dispensers. In addition, special distribution, promotion, or pricing activities may have to be created.

Benefit segmentation is the division of a market according to the benefits that consumers want from the product. Although most types of market segmentation are based on the assumption that there is a relationship between the variable and customers' needs, benefit segmentation is different in that the benefits the customers seek *are* their product needs. Thus individuals are segmented directly according to their needs. By determining the benefits desired, marketers may be able to divide people into groups that are seeking certain sets of benefits. For example, marketers of mouthwashes target many consumer group concerns: plaque, gingivitis, fresh breath, and fighting germs. Another example can be found in Marketing Update 4.2, which describes some coffee makers' efforts to target consumers who want high quality coffees with superior taste.

The effectiveness of benefit segmentation depends on several conditions. First, the benefits sought must be identifiable. Second, using these benefits, marketers must be able to divide people into recognizable segments. Finally, one or more of the resulting segments must be accessible to the firm's marketing efforts. Marie's, as shown in Figure 4.14, determined that the market segment for reduced-calorie dressing merited the development of this new product.

10. "Supermarket Shoppers Fall Into Six Groups," *Wall Street Journal,* June 13, 1989, p. B1.

GOURMET COFFEE SHOPS TARGET COFFEE CONNOISSEURS

The percentage of American coffee drinkers has declined from 74.7 percent in 1962 to 52.5 percent in 1989, and they consume only 1.67 cups per day, down from 3.12 cups in 1962. Large coffee marketers blame the decline on caffeine concerns, a growing preference for soft drinks, and a general trend toward specialty foods, but many consultants and gourmet coffee producers blame the big producers' use of cheaper, inferior beans when the price of good quality beans rose. Many small gourmet coffee marketers are now targeting dissatisfied coffee drinkers who want a better tasting cup of coffee. Sales of these small specialty stores are steadily growing—totaling $675 million in 1989, nearly 10 percent of total coffee sales—while their corporate competitors are struggling to enter the gourmet market.

Sales at the Coffee Connection, a gourmet coffee chain, have risen 30 percent annually in recent years. The New Orleans–based P.J's Coffee and Tea Co., which sells flavored coffees like chocolate raspberries and cream, has seen sales quadruple to $1.5 million since 1984. It has added a toll-free number for its heavy mail-order business and plans to open three new stores. Likewise, the Starbucks Coffee Co. roasted more than two million pounds of coffee in 1988 and expected to double that in 1989. Starbucks offers more than 30 varieties of coffee beans, priced from $7.45 to $25 per pound. To keep its coffee flavors pure, the company uses specially treated paper bags and cups and prohibits store employees from smoking or wearing perfume.

The leading regular coffee brands—Folgers, Maxwell House, and Chock Full O'Nuts—are now introducing "premium" or "gourmet" coffees, targeting consumers who want better tasting coffee with less-than-gourmet-shop prices ($3 to $5 for 13 ounces versus $5 to $40 per pound in gourmet shops). Nonetheless, small gourmet coffee marketers say they are not worried about the corporate giants eroding their market because they believe that consumers associate the large companies with mediocre coffee. They know that many coffee lovers are willing to pay more for better taste and selection and the typical atmosphere and knowledgeable clerks found in most gourmet coffee shops.

SOURCES: Judann Dagnoli, "Maxwell House Gets Reheated," *Advertising Age,* Nov. 27, 1989, pp. 1, 116; Martin Friedman, "Coffee Marketers Hope to Enliven a Slumbering Market," *Adweek,* Oct. 9, 1989, p. 40; and Mark Robichaux, "Boom in Fancy Coffee Pits Big Marketers, Little Firms," *Wall Street Journal,* Nov. 6, 1989, pp. B1, B2.

FIGURE 4.14
Benefit segmentation.
Marie's recognized there
was an accessible mar-
ket for reduced-calorie
dressings.

As this brief discussion shows, consumer markets can be divided according to numerous characteristics. Some of these variables, however, are not particularly helpful for segmenting industrial or organizational markets.

■ Variables for Segmenting Organizational Markets

Like consumer markets, industrial or organizational markets are sometimes segmented, but the marketers' aim is to satisfy the needs of organizations for products. Marketers may segment organizational markets according to geographic location, type of organization, customer size, and product use.

Geographic Location.   We noted that the demand for some consumer products can vary considerably among geographic areas because of differences in climate, terrain, customer preferences, or similar factors. Demand for organizational products also varies according to geographic location. For example, the producers of certain types of lumber divide their markets geographically because their customers' needs vary regionally. Geographic segmentation may be especially appropriate for reaching industries that are concentrated in certain locations. Furniture producers, for example, are concentrated in the Southeast, whereas most iron and steel producers are located in the Great Lakes area.

Type of Organization.   A company sometimes segments a market by the types of organizations within that market. Different types of organizations often require

FIGURE 4.15
*Single-variable
segmentation*

| Less than $10,000 | $10,000– $19,999 | $20,000– $40,000 | More than $40,000 |

Annual income

different product features, distribution systems, price structures, and selling strategies. Given these variations, a firm either may concentrate on a single segment with one marketing mix (concentration strategy) or focus on several groups with multiple mixes (multisegment strategy). A carpet producer could segment potential customers into several groups, such as automobile makers, commercial carpet contractors (firms that carpet large commercial buildings), apartment complex developers, carpet wholesalers, and large retail carpet outlets.

Customer Size.   An organization's size may affect its purchasing procedures and the types and quantities of products it wants. Size can thus be an effective variable for segmenting an organizational market. To reach a segment of a particular size, marketers may have to adjust one or more marketing mix components. For example, customers who buy in extremely large quantities are sometimes offered discounts. In addition, marketers often have to expand personal selling efforts to serve larger organizational buyers properly. Because the needs of larger and smaller buyers tend to be quite distinct, marketers frequently use different marketing practices to reach various customer groups.

Use of Product.   Certain products, especially basic raw materials such as steel, petroleum, plastics, and lumber, are used in numerous ways. How a company uses products affects the types and amounts of the products purchased, as well as the method of making the purchase. For example, computers are used for engineering purposes, basic scientific research, and business operations, such as word processing, bookkeeping, and telephone service. A computer producer may segment the computer market by types of use because organizations' needs for computer hardware and software depend on the purpose for which the products are purchased.

■ Single-Variable or Multivariable Segmentation

Selecting the appropriate variable for market segmentation is an important marketing management decision because the variable is the primary factor in defining the target market. So far, we have discussed segmentation by one variable. In fact, more than one variable can be used, and marketers must decide the number of variables to include.

Single-variable segmentation is achieved by using only one variable. The segmentation shown in Figure 4.15 is based on income alone. (Although the areas on the graph are the same size, this does not mean that the segments are the same size or equal in sales potential.) Single-variable segmentation, the simplest form of segmentation, is the easiest to perform. However, a single characteristic gives marketers only moderate precision in designing a marketing mix to satisfy individuals in a specific segment.

FIGURE 4.16
*Multivariable
segmentation*

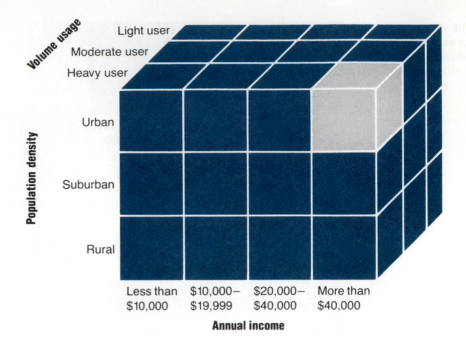

To achieve **multivariable segmentation**, more than one characteristic is used to divide a total market (see Figure 4.16). Notice in the figure that the market is segmented by three variables: income, population density, and volume usage. The people in the highlighted segment earn more than $40,000, are urban dwellers, and are heavy users. Multivariable segmentation provides more information about the individuals in each segment than does single-variable segmentation. More is known about the people in each segment of Figure 4.16 than about those in the segments of Figure 4.15. This additional information may allow a company to develop a marketing mix that will satisfy customers in a given segment more precisely.

The major disadvantage of multivariable segmentation is that the larger the number of variables used, the greater the number of resulting segments. This proliferation reduces the sales potential of many of the segments. Compare, for example, the number and size of the segments in Figure 4.15 with the number and size of those in Figure 4.16.

The use of additional variables can help create and maintain a more exact and satisfying marketing mix. However, when deciding on single-variable or multivariable segmentation, a marketing manager must consider whether additional variables will actually help improve the firm's marketing mix. If using a second or third variable does not provide information that ensures greater precision, there is little reason to spend more money to gain information about the extra variables.

Evaluating Markets and Forecasting Sales

Whether taking a total market approach or opting for segmentation, a marketer must be able to measure the sales potential of its chosen target market or markets. Moreover, a marketing manager must determine the portion or share of the selected market that the firm can capture relative to its objectives, resources, and managerial

Marketing potential
- Based on economic, social, and other environmental variables underlying the total demand for a product

Sales potential
- Appraisal of past performance, resources, and future efforts of a firm and projection of the firm's share of sales in the industry

Sales forecast
- Expected sales for future time periods based on a specified level of marketing effort

skills, as well as to those of its competitors. Developing and maintaining a marketing mix consume a considerable amount of a company's resources. Thus the target market or markets selected must have enough sales potential to justify the cost of developing and maintaining one or more marketing mixes.

The potential for sales can be measured along several dimensions, including product, geographic area, time, and level of competition.[11] With respect to product, potential sales can be estimated for a specific product item (for example, diet Coke) or an entire product line (for example, Coca-Cola, Coca-Cola classic, diet Coke, diet caffeine-free Coke, and cherry Coca-Cola are one product line). A manager must also determine the geographic area to be included in the estimate. In relation to time, sales potential estimates can be short range (one year or less), medium range (one to five years), or long range (longer than five years). The competitive level specifies whether sales are being estimated for a single firm or for an entire industry. Thus marketers measure sales potential for both the entire market and for their own firms and then develop a sales forecast (Figure 4.17).

■ Market and Sales Potentials

Market potential is the total amount of a product that customers will purchase within a specified period at a specific level of industrywide marketing activity. Market potential can be stated in terms of dollars or units and can refer to a total market or to a market segment. As shown in Figure 4.17, market potential depends on economic, social, and other marketing environment factors. When analyzing market potential, it is important to specify a time frame and to indicate the relevant level of industry marketing activities. Pan Am determined that in one year 3,300,000 customers traveled to Europe on its planes—more customers than any other airline had (see Figure 4.18). Based on these findings, Pan Am marketers are able to estimate the market potential for European travel in the following year, taking into account other environmental factors.

11. Philip Kotler, *Marketing Management: Analysis, Planning, and Control,* 6th ed. (Englewood Cliffs, N.J.: Prentice-Hall, 1988), p. 257.

FIGURE 4.18

Determining market potential.
Pan Am determined that 3,300,000 people used its airline to travel to Europe in one year—more customers than any other airline. Based on these statistics, and accounting for any changes in environmental factors, Pan Am marketers can estimate market potential for the next year.

SOURCE: Courtesy of Pan American World Airways, Inc.

Note that marketers have to assume a certain general level of marketing effort in the industry when they estimate market potential. The specific level of marketing effort certainly varies from one firm to another, but the sum of all firms' marketing activities equals industry marketing efforts. A marketing manager also must consider whether and to what extent industry marketing efforts will change. For instance, in estimating the market potential for the spreadsheet software industry, Microsoft Corp. must consider changes in marketing efforts by Lotus and other software producers. If marketing managers at Microsoft know that Lotus is planning to introduce a new version of the Lotus 1-2-3 Spreadsheet product with a new advertising campaign, this fact will contribute to Microsoft's estimate of the market potential for computer software.

Sales potential is the maximum percentage of market potential that an individual firm within an industry can expect to obtain for a specific product. Several general factors influence a company's sales potential. First, the market potential places absolute limits on the size of the company's sales potential. Second, the magnitude of industrywide marketing activities has an indirect but definite impact on the company's sales potential. Those activities have a direct bearing on the size of the market potential. When Domino's Pizza advertises home-delivered pizza, for example, it indirectly promotes pizza in general; its commercials may, in fact, help sell Pizza Hut's and other competitors' home-delivered pizza. Third, the intensity and effectiveness of a company's marketing activities relative to those of its competitors affect the size of the company's sales potential. If a company is spending twice as much as any of its competitors on marketing efforts and if each dollar spent is more effective in generating sales, the firm's sales potential will be quite high compared with that of its competitors.

There are two general approaches to measuring sales potential: breakdown and buildup. In the **breakdown approach**, the marketing manager first develops a general economic forecast for a specific time period. Next, market potential is estimated on the basis of this economic forecast. The company's sales potential is then derived from the general economic forecast and the estimate of market potential.

In the **buildup approach**, an analyst begins by estimating how much of a product a potential buyer in a specific geographic area, such as a sales territory, will purchase in a given period. Then the analyst multiplies that amount by the total number of potential buyers in that area. The analyst performs the same calculation for each geographic area in which the firm sells products and then adds the totals for each area to calculate the market potential. To determine the sales potential, the analyst must estimate, by specific levels of marketing activities, the proportion of the total market potential that the company can obtain.

For example, the marketing manager of a regional paper company with three competitors might estimate the company's sales potential for bulk gift-wrapping paper using the buildup approach. The manager might determine that each of the sixty-six paper buyers in a single sales territory purchases an average of 10 rolls annually. For that sales territory, then, the market potential is 660 rolls annually. The analyst follows the same procedure in each of the firm's other nine sales territories and then totals the sales potential for each sales territory (see Table 4.2). Assume that this total market potential is 18,255 rolls of paper (the quantity expected to be sold by all four paper companies). Then the marketing manager would estimate the company's sales potential by ascertaining that it could sell about 33 percent of the estimated 18,255 rolls at a certain level of marketing effort. The marketing manager might develop several sales potentials, based on several levels of marketing effort.

Whether marketers use the breakdown or the buildup approach, they depend heavily on sales estimates. To get a clearer idea of how these estimates are derived, let us explore sales forecasting.

■ Developing Sales Forecasts

A **sales forecast** is the amount of a product that the company actually expects to sell during a specific period at a specified level of marketing activities. The sales forecast differs from the sales potential: It concentrates on what the actual sales will be at a certain level of marketing effort, whereas the sales potential assesses what sales are possible at various levels of marketing activities, assuming that certain environmental conditions will exist. Businesses use the sales forecast for planning, organizing, implementing, and controlling their activities. The success of numerous activities depends on the accuracy of this forecast.

A sales forecast must be time specific. Sales projections can be short (one year or less), medium (one to five years), or long (longer than five years). The length of time chosen for the sales forecast depends on the purpose and uses of the forecast, the stability of the market, and the firm's objectives and resources.

TERRITORY	NUMBER OF POTENTIAL CUSTOMERS	ESTIMATED PURCHASES	TOTAL
1	66	10 rolls	660 rolls
2	62	10	620
3	55	5	275
4	28	25	700
5	119	5	595
6	50	20	1000
7	46	10	460
8	34	15	510
9	63	10	630
10	55	10	550
		Total company sales potential	6,000 rolls

To forecast sales, a marketer can choose from a number of forecasting methods. Some of them are arbitrary; others are more scientific, complex, and time consuming. A firm's choice of method or methods depends on the costs involved, the type of product, the characteristics of the market, the time span of the forecast, the purposes of the forecast, the stability of the historical sales data, the availability of required information, and the forecasters' expertise and experience.[12] The common forecasting techniques fall into five categories: executive judgment, surveys, time series analysis, correlation methods, and market tests.

Executive Judgment.   At times, a company forecasts sales chiefly on the basis of **executive judgment**, which is the intuition of one or more executives. This approach is highly unscientific but expedient and inexpensive. Executive judgment may work reasonably well when product demand is relatively stable and the forecaster has years of market-related experience. However, because intuition is swayed most heavily by recent experience, the forecast may be overly optimistic or overly pessimistic. Another drawback to intuition is that the forecaster has only past experience as a guide for deciding where to go in the future.

Surveys.   A second way to forecast sales is to question customers, sales personnel, or experts regarding their expectations about future purchases.

Through a **customer forecasting survey**, marketers can ask customers what types and quantities of products they intend to buy during a specific period. This approach may be useful to a business that has relatively few customers. For example, a computer chip producer that markets to less than a hundred computer manufac-

12. David Hurwood, Elliot S. Grossman, and Earl Bailey, *Sales Forecasting* (New York: Conference Board, 1978), p. 2.

turers could conduct a customer survey. PepsiCo, though, has millions of customers and cannot feasibly use a customer survey to forecast future sales.

Customer surveys have several drawbacks. Customers must be able and willing to make accurate estimates of future product requirements. Although industrial buyers can sometimes estimate their anticipated purchases accurately from historical buying data and their own sales forecasts, many cannot make such estimates. In addition, for a variety of reasons, customers may not want to take part in a survey. Occasionally, a few respondents give answers that they know are incorrect, making survey results inaccurate. Moreover, customer surveys reflect buying intentions, not actual purchases. Customers' intentions may not be well formulated, and even when potential purchasers have definite buying intentions, they do not necessarily follow through on them. Finally, customer surveys consume much time and money.

In a **sales-force forecasting survey**, members of the firm's sales force are asked to estimate the anticipated sales in their territories for a specified period of time. The forecaster combines these territorial estimates to arrive at a tentative forecast.

A marketer may survey the sales staff for several reasons. The most important one is that the sales staff is closer to customers on a daily basis than other company personnel; therefore it should know more about customers' future product needs. Moreover, when sales representatives assist in developing the forecast, they are more likely to work toward its achievement. Another advantage of this method is that forecasts can be prepared for single territories, for divisions consisting of several territories, for regions made up of multiple divisions, and then for the total geographic market. Thus the method readily provides sales forecasts from the smallest geographic sales unit to the largest.

Despite these benefits, a sales-force survey has certain limitations. Salespeople can be too optimistic or pessimistic because of recent experiences. In addition, salespeople tend to underestimate the sales potential in their territories when they believe that their sales goals will be determined by their forecasts. They also dislike paperwork because it takes up the time that could be spent selling. If the preparation of a territorial sales forecast is time consuming, the sales staff may not do the job adequately.

Nonetheless, sales-force surveys can be effective under certain conditions. If, for instance, the salespeople as a group are accurate—or at least consistent—estimators, the overestimates and underestimates should counterbalance each other. If the aggregate forecast is consistently over or under actual sales, then the marketer who develops the final forecast can make the necessary adjustments. Assuming that the survey is well administered, the sales force can have the satisfaction of helping to establish reasonable sales goals. It can also be assured that its forecasts are not being used to set sales quotas.

When a company wants an **expert forecasting survey**, it hires experts to help prepare the sales forecast. These experts are usually economists, management consultants, advertising executives, college professors, or other persons outside the firm who have solid experience in a specific market. Drawing on this experience and their analyses of available information about the company and the market, the experts prepare and present their forecasts or answer questions regarding a forecast. Using experts is expedient and relatively inexpensive. However, because they work outside the firm, experts may not be as motivated as company personnel to do an effective job.

Time Series Analysis. The technique by which the forecaster, using the firm's historical sales data, tries to discover a pattern or patterns in the firm's sales over time is called **time series analysis**. If a pattern is found, it can be used to forecast sales. This forecasting method assumes that the past sales pattern will continue in the future. The accuracy, and thus the usefulness, of time series analysis hinges on the validity of this assumption.

In a time series analysis, a forecaster usually performs four types of analysis: trend, cycle, seasonal, and random factor.[13] **Trend analysis** focuses on aggregate sales data, such as a company's annual sales figures, from a period of many years to determine whether annual sales are generally rising, falling, or staying about the same. Through **cycle analysis**, a forecaster analyzes sales figures (often monthly sales data) over a period of three to five years to ascertain whether sales fluctuate in a consistent, periodic manner. When performing **seasonal analysis**, the analyst studies daily, weekly, or monthly sales figures to evaluate the degree to which seasonal factors, such as climate and holiday activities, influence the firm's sales. **Random factor analysis** is an attempt to attribute erratic sales variations to random, nonrecurrent events, such as a regional power failure, a natural disaster, or political unrest in a foreign market. After performing each of these analyses, the forecaster combines the results to develop the sales forecast.

Time series analysis is an effective forecasting method for products with reasonably stable demand, but it is not useful for products with highly erratic demand. Joseph E. Seagram & Sons, Inc., an importer and producer of liquor and wines, uses several types of time series analyses for forecasting and has found them quite accurate. For example, Seagram's forecasts of industry sales volume have proved correct within ± 1.5 percent, and the firm's sales forecasts have been accurate within ± 2 percent.[14] Time series analysis is not always so dependable.

Correlation Methods. Like time series analysis, correlation methods are based on historical sales data. When using **correlation methods**, the forecaster attempts to find a relationship between past sales and one or more variables such as population, per capita income, or gross national product. To determine whether a correlation exists, the forecaster analyzes the statistical relationships among changes in past sales and changes in one or more variables—a technique known as regression analysis. The objective of regression analysis is a mathematical formula that accurately describes a relationship between the firm's sales and one or more variables; however, the formula indicates only an association, not a causal relationship. Once an accurate formula has been established, the analyst plugs the necessary information into the formula to derive the sales forecast.

Correlation methods are useful when a precise relationship can be established. However, a forecaster seldom finds a perfect correlation. Furthermore, this method can be used only when the available historical sales data are extensive. Ordinarily, then, correlation techniques are futile for forecasting the sales of new products.

Market Tests. Conducting a **market test** involves making a product available to buyers in one or more test areas and measuring purchases and consumer responses

---

13. Kenneth E. Marino, *Forecasting Sales and Planning Profits* (Chicago: Probus Publishing, 1986), p. 155.

14. Hurwood, Grossman, and Bailey, p. 61.

to distribution, promotion, and price. Even though test areas are often cities with populations of 200,000 to 500,000, test sites can be larger metropolitan areas or towns with populations of 50,000 to 200,000. A market test provides information about consumers' actual purchases rather than about their intended purchases. In addition, purchase volume can be evaluated in relation to the intensity of other marketing activities—advertising, in-store promotions, pricing, packaging, distribution, and the like. On the basis of customer response in test areas, forecasters can estimate product sales for larger geographic units. For example, the Smith Collins Co., a publishing company, test-markets its business trade books in a few cities in Texas and Illinois so that managers can estimate how many books the company can sell in the whole nation.

Because it does not require historical sales data, a market test is an effective tool for forecasting the sales of new products or the sales of existing products in new geographic areas. The test gives the forecaster information about customers' real actions rather than intended or estimated behavior. A market test also gives a marketer an opportunity to test various elements of the marketing mix. But these tests are often time consuming and expensive. In addition, a marketer cannot be certain that the consumer response during a market test represents the total market response or that such a response will continue in the future.

■ Using Multiple Forecasting Methods

Although some businesses depend on a single sales forecasting method, most firms use several techniques. A company is sometimes forced to use several methods when it markets diverse product lines, but even for a single product line several forecasts may be needed, especially when the product is sold in different market segments. Thus a producer of automobile tires may rely on one technique to forecast tire sales for new cars and on another to forecast the sales of replacement tires. Variation in the length of the needed forecasts may call for several forecast methods. A firm that employs one method for a short-range forecast may find it inappropriate for long-range forecasting. Sometimes a marketer verifies the results of one method by using one or several other methods and comparing results.

SUMMARY

A market is an aggregate of people who, as individuals or as organizations, have needs for products in a product class and who have the ability, willingness, and authority to purchase such products. A consumer market consists of purchasers and/or individuals in their households who intend to consume or benefit from the purchased products and who do not buy products for the main purpose of making a profit. An organizational or industrial market consists of persons and groups who purchase a specific kind of product for resale, direct use in producing other products, or use in day-to-day operations. Because products are classified according to use, the same product may be classified as both a consumer product and an organizational product.

Marketers use two general approaches to identify their target markets: the total market and the market segmentation approaches. A firm using a total market approach designs a single marketing mix and directs it at an entire market for a particular product. The total market approach can be effective when a large proportion of individuals in the total market have similar needs for the product and the organization can develop and maintain a single marketing mix to satisfy those needs.

Markets made up of individuals with diverse product needs are called heterogeneous markets. The market segmentation approach divides the total market into groups consisting of people who have similar product needs. The purpose is to design a marketing mix (or mixes) that more precisely matches the needs of persons in a selected segment (or segments). A market segment is a group of individuals, groups, or organizations sharing one or more similar characteristics that cause them to have relatively similar product needs. There are two major types of market segmentation strategies. In the concentration strategy, the organization directs its marketing efforts toward a single market segment through one marketing mix. In the multisegment strategy, the organization develops different marketing mixes for two or more segments.

Certain conditions must exist for market segmentation to be effective. First, consumers' needs for the product should be heterogeneous. Second, the segments of the market should be identifiable and divisible. Third, the total market should be divided so that the segments can be compared with respect to estimated sales potential, costs, and profits. Fourth, at least one segment must have enough profit potential to justify developing and maintaining a special marketing mix for that segment. Fifth, the firm must be able to reach the chosen segment with a particular marketing mix.

Segmentation variables are the dimensions or characteristics of individuals, groups, or organizations that are used for dividing a total market into segments. The segmentation variable should be related to customers' needs for, uses of, or behavior toward the product. Segmentation variables for consumer markets can be grouped into four categories: demographic (age, gender, income, ethnicity, family life cycle), geographic (population, market density, climate), psychographic (personality traits, motives, and lifestyle), and behavioristic (use). Segmentation variables for organizational markets include geographic factors, type of organization, customer size, and product use. Besides selecting the appropriate segmentation variable, a marketer must also decide how many variables to use. Single-variable segmentation involves only one variable, but in multivariable segmentation, more than one characteristic is used to divide a total market.

Whether using a total market or a market segmentation approach, a marketer must be able to measure the sales potential of the target market or markets. Market potential is the total amount of a product that customers will purchase within a specified period at a specific level of industrywide marketing activity. Sales potential is the maximum percentage of market potential that an individual firm within an industry can expect to obtain for a specific product. There are two general approaches to measuring sales potential: breakdown and buildup. A sales forecast is the amount of a product that the company actually expects to sell during a specific period of time and at a specified level of marketing activities. Several methods are used to forecast sales: executive judgment, surveys (customer, sales force, and executive surveys), time series analysis (trend analysis, cycle analysis, seasonal analysis, random factor analysis), correlation methods, and market tests. Although some businesses may rely on a single sales forecasting method, most organizations employ several different techniques.

IMPORTANT TERMS

Market
Consumer market
Organizational, or industrial, market
Total market (or undifferentiated) approach
Heterogeneous markets
Market segmentation
Market segment
Concentration strategy
Multisegment strategy
Segmentation variables
Market density
Benefit segmentation
Single-variable segmentation
Multivariable segmentation
Market potential

Sales potential
Breakdown approach
Buildup approach
Sales forecast
Executive judgment
Customer forecasting survey
Sales-force forecasting survey
Expert forecasting survey
Time series analysis
Trend analysis
Cycle analysis
Seasonal analysis
Random factor analysis
Correlation methods
Market test

DISCUSSION AND REVIEW QUESTIONS

1. What is a market? What are the requirements for a market?
2. In your local area, is there a group of people with unsatisfied product needs who represent a market? Could this market be reached by a business organization? Why or why not?
3. Identify and describe the two major types of markets. Give examples of each.
4. What is the total market approach? Under what conditions is it most useful? Describe a present market situation in which a company is using a total market approach. Is the business successful? Why or why not?
5. What is the market segmentation approach? Describe the basic conditions required for effective segmentation. Identify several firms that use the segmentation approach.
6. List the differences between the concentration and the multisegment strategies. Describe the advantages and disadvantages of each strategy.
7. Identify and describe four major categories of variables that can be used to segment consumer markets. Give examples of product markets that are segmented by variables in each category.
8. What dimensions are used to segment industrial or organizational markets?
9. How do marketers decide whether to use single-variable or multivariable segmentation? Give examples of product markets that are divided through multivariable segmentation.
10. Why is a marketer concerned about sales potential when trying to find a target market?
11. What is a sales forecast and why is it important?
12. Under what conditions are market tests useful for sales forecasting? Discuss the advantages and disadvantages of market tests.

■ CASES

Case 4.1 The *St. Louis Sun*

The *St. Louis Sun,* the nation's newest metropolitan daily newspaper, was going head-to-head against a 111-year old competitor, the *St. Louis Post-Dispatch.* Founded by Ralph Ingersoll II, head of Ingersoll Publications Co., which operates a chain of 193 newspapers, the *Sun* planned to appeal to St. Louis households that did not read the *Post-Dispatch.* The *Post-Dispatch,* with a daily circulation of about 378,000 and Sunday circulation of around 561,000, was the premier St. Louis newspaper. However, Ingersoll believed that the *Post-Dispatch* failed to serve two-thirds of the 2.4 million residents of the St. Louis area. That market segment was the *Sun's* target market.

Local columnist Kevin Horrigan, who left the *Post-Dispatch* for a position at the *Sun,* said the *Post-Dispatch* was for serious news consumers whereas the *Sun* was for people who didn't have time to read a serious daily paper. The *Sun,* he said, would offer more "fun stuff." To interest those consumers who don't read newspapers, the *Sun* management took a "warm and fuzzy approach." A brochure entitled "An Open Letter to the People of Greater St. Louis" promised the *Sun* would "rekindle the American dream" and be a "kindly" newspaper.

To reach its target market, Ingersoll designed a colorful tabloid-format newspaper for today's video-oriented world. Publications such as *USA Today* have changed the public's expectations of what a newspaper should provide. Thus, the *Sun* made use of full color. The stories in each edition began and ended on the same page and took no longer than ten minutes to read. The top of each page had a headline indicating the topic on that page, for example, baseball, movies, etc. There were no stories on county budgets, robberies, or other such news. Instead, political, religious, and sports-oriented opinion columns abounded. According to some experts, the *Sun's* coverage of sports would be a key factor in its promotion. The first edition contained some 30 pages of sports news.

The *Sun* was published seven days a week, but Ingersoll had come up with a new twist. The week's big edition came out on Saturday instead of Sunday when the *Post-Dispatch* and most other newspapers distributed their big editions. The *Sun's* Saturday morning edition contained a colorful comics and activity section, as well as a TV programming guide. Prices were the same as the competition's—25 cents for regular editions and $1 for the larger one.

The *Sun* was launched with a $2.2 million advertising and marketing campaign. Television advertisements included the sounds of Handel's *Messiah* as background music. Six hundred thousand inserts introducing the *Sun* were placed in Ingersoll's Business Journals of Greater St. Louis publications. On its first day of publication, Ingersoll distributed coffee, donuts, and free copies of the *Sun's* inaugural edition to passersby in front of the *Sun's* offices, accompanied by a Dixieland band. Although original plans for the inaugural edition called for 100,000 copies, 200,000 copies were printed and sold quickly. The largest newsstand in the St. Louis area sold its 700 copies in just two hours, compared to only 350 copies of the *Post-Dispatch.* First-day readers expressed hope that competition would improve the quality of newspapers available in St. Louis. Some readers indicated that the *Sun's* tabloid size made the newspaper easy to read and they felt the paper was more polished than they had expected.

Ingersoll spent $20 million on the paper's printing plant, facsimile equipment, and 5,000 red vending machines, but spent relatively little on the reporting staff. He believed that other newspapers gave reporters too much leeway in pursuing investigative stories he considered of limited interest. The *Sun's* emphasis was not on finding the news but rather on packaging it for the target market as entertainment, not education or information.

No metropolitan newspapers have been launched successfully since 1940. Ingersoll conceded that there were some financial risks in launching the *St. Louis Sun,* but felt potential pretax profits of $30 million were worth the risks. Two months after the first edition rolled off the presses, the *Sun* achieved an average circulation of 100,000, including 65,000 subscriptions, which was double the paper's projections. The newspaper industry was certainly watching to determine whether the *Sun's* strategy of targeting an untapped segment of the St. Louis market would pay off and whether other new metropolitan newspapers could be successfully launched in the 1990s. However, the *St. Louis Sun* folded at the end of April 1990, after seven months and $40 million in losses.

SOURCES: Laura Coleman, "Many Wonder If *Sun* Holds Fire to Survive," *(Memphis) Commercial Appeal,* Sept. 24, 1989, pp. C1, C2; Pat Guy, "*St. Louis Sun* Proves to Be Hot Item," *USA Today,* Sept. 26, 1989, p. 4B; William A. Henry, III, "Sun-Rise in St. Louis," *Time,* Sept. 25, 1989, p. 60; Ira Teinowitz, "Big 'Sun' Set for Saturday," *Advertising Age,* Aug. 14, 1989, p. 38; Ira Teinowitz, "Re-emergence of a Two-Paper City," *Advertising Age,* Nov. 6, 1989, pp. S9, S10, S11; "Why Daily Papers Are Hard Pressed," *U.S. News & World Report,* May 7, 1990, p. 13.

Questions for Discussion

1. Did the *Sun* understand and properly define its target market?
2. What techniques could have been used to forecast sales of the *Sun?*
3. Evaluate why, after seven months and $40 million in losses, Ingersoll Publications decided to terminate publication of the *St. Louis Sun?*

Case 4.2   American Firms Increase Marketing Efforts to Hispanic Market

American marketers, from Anheuser Busch to Coca-Cola and from Campbell Soup to Procter & Gamble, spent $600 million in 1989 advertising their products to Hispanics in the United States, up from less than $300 million in 1983. Why has the Hispanic market segment suddenly become so attractive to marketers? The U.S. Hispanic population is growing at five times the rate of the total population because of high birth rates and immigration from Latin America. The Hispanic market is also fairly concentrated, with approximately 90 percent of the Hispanic population found in eight states: California, Texas, New York, Florida, New Mexico, Arizona, New Jersey, and Colorado. By some estimates, Hispanics will represent 10 percent of the U.S. population by the year 2000.

But, the Hispanic market is appealing not only because of its rapid growth, but also for its significant buying power—more than $171 billion worth in 1989. The national average income for Hispanic households in 1989 was $30,243, and although this figure is one-third lower than the U.S. average, Hispanics tend to have larger families and to spend a larger percentage of their income on goods and services than do other segments of the U.S. market. Marketers have long believed that Hispanic customers are also extremely brand loyal and often willing to pay extra for familiar name brands, though recent research has called this into question.

Marketers also have more advertising vehicles than ever to reach the American Hispanic population. The most widely used media is the nearly 200 Spanish-language radio stations in the United States. Three Spanish-language television networks—Univision, Telemundo, and Galavision—and 28 television stations across the nation also provide forums for marketers targeting U.S. Hispanics. In addition, there are more than 1,500 Hispanic magazines, journals, and newspapers.

One of the most popular advertising vehicles to reach Hispanics is the television program "Sabado Gigante," a popular game/talk/variety/advertisement show viewed by 4 million Hispanics on Saturday nights on the Univision network. The show, which reaches 37 percent of all U.S. Hispanic households, includes personal product endorsements from the host, promotional tie-ins, and audience sing-alongs of product jingles for common products such as Hamburger Helper, Mazola oil, and Coors beer. After being featured on "Sabado Gigante," sales to Hispanics of Reese's peanut butter cups tripled.

Despite the buying power and concentrated nature of the Hispanic market, Hispanics are not easy for marketers to reach. Educational achievement is lower for Hispanics than for non-Hispanics. Compared to an 11 percent high-school drop-out rate for non-Hispanics, 40 percent of Hispanics fail to graduate from high school. Marketers also find it difficult to reach Hispanics effectively because the Hispanic market is actually three different market segments. Mexican-Americans comprise 60 percent of the U.S. Hispanic population; Central and South American Hispanics, 21 percent; and Caribbean Hispanics, the remaining 19 percent. Although there are many similarities among these three groups, there are subtle and important differences that complicate marketing activities directed at Hispanics. For example, when Borden advertised its ice cream under the Mexican slang term *nieve*, which literally means "snow," it successfully marketed ice cream to Hispanics from Texas to California. In the east, however, Cubans, Central Americans, and Puerto Ricans believed that the product actually *was* snow!

Because of these subtle but important differences among Hispanic market segments, the Campbell Soup Company decided to use different advertisements on Spanish-language television when it launched a major Hispanic marketing campaign for its soups. One commercial was targeted at Mexican-Americans, another at Hispanics of Caribbean origin. The Mexican-American advertisement showed a young woman preparing food in a southwestern-style kitchen while pop music played in the background. By contrast, the Caribbean ad had a grandmother cooking in a plant-filled kitchen with traditional Caribbean music in the background. By using these subtle differences in advertising, Campbell avoided targeting all Hispanics at once, a mistake frequently made by companies attempting to market to Hispanics for the first time.

In addition to marketing its soups to Hispanics, in 1988, the company introduced a line of Caribbean-style foods under the Casera label. Casera competes directly with Goya foods, the market leader. Campbell also tested some Mexican food items in California under the Casera label to see if there was a demand for these products. Campbell's management is realizing the importance of the Hispanic market, which is now the second fastest-growing population group in the United States. The company was one of the first to actively target this market, and it hopes that the

Hispanic market will become one of Campbell's most profitable specialty markets in the future.

Many other companies are pursuing sales from the Hispanic market. Coca-Cola has featured such Hispanic celebrities as Fernando Valenzuela in its commercials; Pepsi put the Miami Sound Machine on stage with the "Taste of a New Generation." American Express plans to feature well-known Hispanics in its award-winning "Portraits" campaign. Best Foods, the manufacturer of Mazola cooking oil, is particularly interested in the Hispanic segment because Hispanics use three to four times as much cooking oil as the general public. Approximately 20 percent of Mazola's sales come from Hispanics. Thus, although targeting the U.S. Hispanic market is not easy, for marketers willing to make the extra effort, increased sales and brand loyalty from Hispanic customers are the reward.

SOURCES: José de Cordoba, "More Firms Court Hispanic Consumers—But Find Them a Tough Target Market," *Wall Street Journal,* Feb. 18, 1988, p. 25; Christine Dugas, Mark N. Vamos, Jonathan B. Levine, and Matt Rothman, "Marketing's New Look," *Business Week,* Jan. 26, 1987, pp. 64–69; Carlos E. Garcia, "Hispanic Market Is Accessible, If Reseach Is Designed Correctly," *Marketing News,* Jan. 4, 1988, pp. 46–47; Shelly Garcia, "New Study Targets Changing Hispanic Markets," *Adweek,* Apr. 24, 1989, p. 59; Rick Marin, "3 1/2 Hours of 'Gigante' Advertising," *Insight,* July 17, 1989, pp. 60–61; Eva Pomice and Anne Moncreiff Arrarte, "It's a Whole *Nuevo Mundo* Out There," *U.S. News & World Report,* May 15, 1989, pp. 45–46; Howard Schlossberg, "Hispanic Market Strong, But Often Ignored," *Marketing News,* Feb. 19, 1990, pp. 1, 12; U.S. Population Reference Bureau, U.S. Department of Commerce, 1989; Mary Westerman, "Death of the Frito Bandito," *American Demographics,* March 1989, pp. 28–32.

Questions for Discussion

1. Is there one U.S. Hispanic market or can the market be divided into additional segments?
2. Could understanding the U.S. Hispanic market help a company in targeting a market in Latin America?

5 CONSUMER BUYING BEHAVIOR

Objectives

To understand the types of consumer buying behavior and stages in the consumer buying decision process

To recognize the stages of the consumer buying decision process

To explore how personal factors may affect the consumer buying decision process

To learn about the psychological factors that may affect the consumer buying decision process

To examine the social factors that influence the consumer buying decision process

To understand why it is important that marketers attempt to understand consumer buying behavior

T-shirts illustrate some of the factors that influence consumers' purchasing decisions. At times, people want to express their membership in a particular group and T-shirts provide a vehicle for this expression. For example, a high school senior may purchase a "class of" T-shirt to tell others that he or she is a member of the graduating class of a particular high school. Florida State University alumni may wear "Seminoles" T-shirts to football games to indicate group membership. Likewise at election time, supporters from different camps may declare themselves Democrats or Republicans by the T-shirts they wear.

People buy T-shirts that communicate something about their personality. A T-shirt that says "I Am A UFO" may express a sense of humor whereas one that says "All this and brains too!" may express a sense of confidence (or conceit). An owner (or wishful owner) of a BMW may express personal status from product ownership by displaying the car's logo on a T-shirt.

T-shirts can also be used as ritual artifacts to commemorate beverage consumption, rock music concerts, or even a specific athletic contest. For some young people, identifying with these events may even commemorate or symbolize adolescent initiation into adulthood.

Consumers' desires to express their personality in a comic way led to the development of Lin-Tex Marketing. Lin-Tex began putting comic strip characters, like those from "Bloom County" and "Mother Goose and Grimm," on T-shirts. The company now has 15 nationally known comic strips under exclusive license, and this year's sales are estimated at $7 million. The success of Lin-Tex Marketing is evidence that a good understanding of the forces that shape consumer behavior is helpful in reaching profitable market segments. ◆

Photo © Ken Kerbs Photography, 1990.

Based on information from T. Bettina Cornwell, "T-Shirts as Wearable Diary: An Examination of Artifact Consumption and Garnering Related to Life Events," *Advances in Consumer Research*, Vol. 17, 1990; Al Ebbers, "Shirt Tales," *Nation's Business*, Jan. 1990, p. 17.

A symbolic communication is expressed through the clothes that consumers buy and wear. T-shirts are a good example of this symbolic communication. **Buying behavior** is the decision processes and acts of people involved in buying and using products.[1] **Consumer buying behavior** refers to the buying behavior of ultimate consumers, those persons who purchase products for personal or household use, not for business purposes. Marketers should analyze consumer buying behavior for several reasons. First, buyers' reactions to a firm's marketing strategy have a great impact on the firm's success. Second, as indicated in Chapter 1, the marketing concept stresses that a firm should create a marketing mix that satisfies customers. To find out what satisfies customers, marketers must examine the main influences on what, where, when, and how consumers buy. Third, by gaining a better understanding of the factors that affect buying behavior, marketers can better predict how consumers will respond to marketing strategies.

Although marketers may try to understand and influence consumer buying behavior, they cannot control it. Some critics credit them with the ability to manipulate buyers, but marketers have neither the power nor the knowledge to do so. Their knowledge of behavior comes from what psychologists, social psychologists, and sociologists know about human behavior in general. Even if marketers wanted to manipulate buyers, the lack of laws and principles in the behavioral sciences would prevent them from doing so.

In this chapter we begin by examining the types of decision making that consumers engage in. Then we analyze the major stages of the consumer buying decision process and consider the personal, psychological, and social factors that influence it. We conclude by assessing the importance of understanding consumer buying behavior.

TYPES OF CONSUMER BUYING BEHAVIOR

Consumers usually want to create and maintain a collection of products that satisfy their needs and wants in both the present and future. To achieve this objective, consumers make many purchasing decisions. For example, people must make several decisions daily regarding food, clothing, shelter, medical care, education, recreation, or transportation. As they make these decisions, they engage in different decision-making behaviors. The amount of effort, both mental and physical, that buyers expend in decision making varies considerably from situation to situation. Consumer decisions can thus be classified into one of three broad categories: routine response behavior, limited decision making, and extensive decision making.[2]

A consumer practices **routine response behavior** when buying frequently purchased, low-cost items that need very little search and decision effort. When buying such items, a consumer may prefer a particular brand, but he or she is familiar with several brands in the product class and views more than one as being acceptable. The products that are bought through routine response behavior are purchased

---

1. James F. Engel, Roger D. Blackwell, and Paul W. Miniard, *Consumer Behavior,* 5th ed. (Hinsdale, Ill.: Dryden Press, 1986), p. 5.

2. John A. Howard and Jagdish N. Sheth, *The Theory of Buyer Behavior* (New York: Wiley, 1969), pp. 27–28.

almost automatically. Most buyers, for example, do not spend much time or mental effort selecting a soft drink or a snack food. If the nearest soft-drink machine does not offer Sprite, they will quite likely choose a 7-Up or Slice instead.

Buyers engage in **limited decision making** when they buy products occasionally and when they need to obtain information about an unfamiliar brand in a familiar product category. This type of decision making requires a moderate amount of time for information gathering and deliberation. For example, if Procter & Gamble introduces an improved Tide laundry detergent, buyers will seek additional information about the new product, perhaps by asking a friend who has used the product or watching a commercial, before they make a trial purchase.

The most complex decision-making behavior, **extensive decision making**, comes into play when a purchase involves unfamiliar, expensive, or infrequently bought products—for instance, cars, homes, or an education in a college or university. The buyer uses many criteria to evaluate alternative brands or choices and spends much time seeking information and deciding on the purchase.

By contrast, **impulse buying** involves no conscious planning but rather a powerful, persistent urge to buy something immediately. For some individuals, impulse buying may be the dominant buying behavior. Impulse buying, however, often provokes emotional conflicts. For example, a man may want to have the new golf bag he just saw right away and so purchases it on the spot, but he also feels guilty because he knows his budget is limited that month.

The purchase of a particular product does not always elicit the same type of decision-making behavior. In some instances, we engage in extensive decision making the first time we buy a certain kind of product but find that limited decision making suffices when we buy the product again. If a routinely purchased, formerly satisfying brand no longer pleases us, we may use limited or extensive decision processes to switch to a new brand. For example, if we notice that the gasoline brand we normally buy is making our automobile's engine knock, we may seek out a higher octane brand through limited or extensive decision making.

THE CONSUMER BUYING DECISION PROCESS

As defined earlier, a major part of buying behavior is the decision process used in making purchases. The **consumer buying decision process**, shown in Figure 5.1, includes five stages: (1) problem recognition, (2) information search, (3) evaluation of alternatives, (4) purchase, and (5) postpurchase evaluation. Before we examine each stage, consider these important points. First, the actual act of purchasing is only one stage in the process; the process is begun several stages before the actual purchase. Second, even though, for discussion purposes, we indicate that a purchase occurs, not all decision processes lead to a purchase; the individual may end the process at any stage. Finally, all consumer decisions do not always include all five stages. Persons engaged in extensive decision making usually go through all stages of this decision process, whereas those engaged in limited decision making and routine response behavior may omit some stages.

■ **Problem Recognition**

Problem recognition occurs when a buyer becomes aware that there is a difference between a desired state and an actual condition. For example, consider a marketing student who wants a reliable, advanced calculator for use in a finance course. When

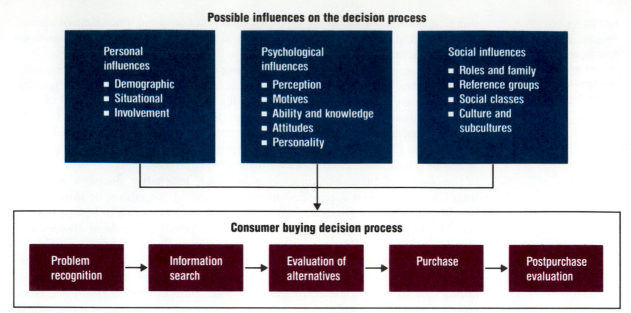

FIGURE 5.1 *Consumer buying decision process and possible influences on the process*

her old calculator stops working, she recognizes that a difference exists between the desired state—a reliable calculator—and the actual condition—a nonworking calculator. She therefore decides to buy a new calculator.

Sometimes a person has a problem or need but is unaware of it. As shown in Figure 5.2, some consumers might not be aware of the advantages of using a bath gel. Neutrogena has attributes not available in regular soap bars. Marketers use sales personnel, advertising, and packaging to help trigger recognition of such needs or problems. For example, a university bookstore may advertise business and scientific calculators in the university newspaper at the beginning of the term. Students who see the advertisement may recognize that they need calculators for their course work. The speed of consumer problem recognition can be rather slow or quite rapid.

Information Search

After recognizing the problem or need, the buyer (if continuing the decision process) searches for information about products that will help resolve the problem or satisfy the need. For example, the above-mentioned student, after recognizing the need for a calculator, may search for information about different types and brands of calculators. Information is acquired over time from the consumer's surroundings. However, we must remember that the impact of the information depends on how the consumer interprets it.

There are two aspects to an information search. In the **internal search**, buyers first search their memory for information about products that might solve the problem. If they cannot retrieve enough information from their memory for a decision, they seek additional information in an **external search**. The external search may focus on communication with friends or relatives, comparison of available brands and prices, marketer-dominated sources, and/or public sources. An individual's personal contacts—friends, relatives, associates—often are credible

FIGURE 5.2
Problem recognition. Neutrogena makes consumers aware of the advantages of a shower and bath gel.

SOURCE: Neutrogena Corporation, Los Angeles, CA.

sources of information because the consumer trusts and respects these sources. Utilizing marketer-dominated sources of information, which include salespersons, advertising, package labeling, and in-store demonstrations and displays, typically does not require much effort on the consumer's part. Buyers can also obtain information from public sources—for instance, government reports, news presentations, publications such as *Consumer Reports,* and reports from product-testing organizations. Consumers frequently view information from public sources as highly credible because of its factual and unbiased nature.

Consumer groups are increasingly demanding access to all relevant product information. However, the greater the quantity of information available to buyers, the more the buyer may be overloaded with information. Research indicates that consumers make poorer choices when faced with large amounts of information.[3] Improving the quality of information and stressing features important to buyers in the decision process may help buyers make better purchase decisions.

How consumers use and process the information obtained in their search depends on a number of features of the information itself, namely, availability, quantity, quality, repetition, and format. If all the necessary information for a decision is available in the store, consumers may have no need to conduct an internal

3. Kevin L. Keller and Richard Staelin, "Effects of Quality and Quantity of Information on Decision Effectiveness," *Journal of Consumer Research,* September 1987, pp. 200–213.

information search. Having all information externally available makes the consumer's decision process easier,[4] increases utilization of the information, and may thus facilitate a purchase.

Repetition, a technique well known to advertisers, increases consumer learning of information. When seeing or hearing an advertising message for the first time, the recipient may not grasp all its important details but learns more details as the message is repeated. Nevertheless, even when commercials are initially effective, repetition eventually causes the phenomenon of "wearout": consumers pay less attention to the commercial and respond to it less favorably than they did at first.[5]

The format in which information is transmitted to the buyer may also determine its use. Information can be presented verbally, numerically, or visually. For a wide variety of consumer tasks, pictures are remembered better than words, and the combination of pictures and words further enhances learning.[6] Consequently, marketers pay great attention to the creation of the visual components of their advertising materials.

A successful information search yields a group of brands that a buyer views as possible alternatives. This group of products is sometimes called the buyer's *evoked set*. For example, an evoked set of calculators might include those made by Texas Instruments, Hewlett-Packard, Tandy, Sharp, and Casio.

■ Evaluation of Alternatives

To evaluate the products in the evoked set, a buyer establishes criteria for comparing the products. These criteria are the characteristics or features that the buyer wants (or does not want). For example, one calculator buyer may want a solar-powered calculator with a large display and large buttons, whereas another may have no preference as to the size of features but happens to dislike solar-powered calculators. The buyer also assigns a certain level of importance to each criterion; some features and characteristics carry more weight than others. Using the criteria, a buyer rates and eventually ranks the brands in the evoked set. The evaluation stage may yield no brand that the buyer is willing to purchase; in that case, a further information search may be necessary.

Marketers can influence consumers' evaluation by *framing* the alternatives—that is, by the manner in which the marketer describes the alternative and its attributes. Framing can make a characteristic seem more important to a consumer and can facilitate its recall from memory. For example, by stressing a car's superior gasoline mileage over that of a competitor's, a car maker can direct consumers' attention toward this point of superiority. Framing affects the decision processes of inexperienced buyers more than those of experienced ones.[7] If the evaluation of alternatives yields one or more brands that the consumer is willing to buy, the consumer is ready to move on to the next stage of the decision process—the purchase.

4. Gabriel Biehal and Dipankar Chakravarti, "Consumers' Use of Memory and External Information in Choice: Macro and Micro Perspectives," *Journal of Consumer Research*, March 1986, pp. 382–405.

5. Bobby J. Calder and Brian Sternthal, "Television Commercial Wearout: An Information Processing View," *Journal of Marketing Research*, May 1980, pp. 173–186.

6. Michael J. Houston, Terry L. Childers, and Susan E. Heckler, "Picture-Word Consistency and the Elaborative Processing of Advertisements," *Journal of Marketing Research*, November 1987, pp. 359–369.

7. James R. Bettman and Mita Sujan, "Effects of Framing on Evaluation of Comparable and Noncomparable Alternatives by Expert and Novice Consumers," *Journal of Consumer Research*, September 1987, pp. 141–154.

■ Purchase

In the purchase stage, the consumer chooses the product or brand to be bought. The selection is based on the outcome of the previous evaluation stage and on other dimensions. Product availability may influence which brand is purchased. For example, if the brand ranked the highest in evaluation is not available, the buyer may purchase the brand that is ranked second.

During this stage, the buyer also picks the seller from whom he or she will buy the product. The choice of the seller may affect the final product selection—and so may the terms of sale, which, if negotiable, are determined during the purchase decision stage. Other issues such as price, delivery, warranties, maintenance agreements, installation, and credit arrangements are discussed and settled. Finally, the actual purchase takes place during this stage, unless, of course, the consumer terminates the buying decision process before reaching that point.

■ Postpurchase Evaluation

After the purchase, the buyer begins evaluating the product to ascertain if its actual performance meets expected levels. Many of the criteria used in evaluating alternatives are applied again during the postpurchase evaluation. The outcome of this stage is either satisfaction or dissatisfaction. These feelings strongly influence consumers' motivation and information processing. Consumers' satisfaction or dissatisfaction determines whether they make a complaint, communicate with other possible buyers, and purchase the product again.[8]

Shortly after a purchase of an expensive product, the postpurchase evaluation may result in **cognitive dissonance**—doubts that occur because the buyer questions whether the right decision was made in purchasing the product. For example, after buying an expensive calculator, the marketing student may feel guilty about the purchase or have doubts about whether she purchased the right brand and quality. A buyer who experiences cognitive dissonance may attempt to return the product or may seek positive information about it to justify that choice.

As shown in Figure 5.1, there are three major categories of influences that are believed to affect the consumer buying decision process: personal, psychological, and social factors. The remainder of this chapter focuses on these factors. Although we discuss each major factor separately, keep in mind that their effects on the consumer decision process are interrelated.

PERSONAL FACTORS INFLUENCING THE BUYING DECISION PROCESS

A **personal factor** is one that is unique to a particular person. Numerous personal factors can influence purchasing decisions. In this section we consider three categories of them: demographic factors, situational factors, and level of involvement.

■ Demographic Factors

Demographic factors are individual characteristics such as age, sex, race, ethnicity, income, family life cycle, and occupation. (These and other characteristics were discussed in Chapter 4 as possible variables for segmentation purposes.) Demographic factors have a bearing on who is involved in family decision making. For

---

8. Robert A. Westbrook, "Product/Consumption-Based Affective Responses and Postpurchase Processes," *Journal of Marketing Research,* August 1987, pp. 258–270.

example, children aged 6 to 17 have more influence in the buying decision process for breakfast cereals, ice cream, soft drinks, and even the family car than ever before.[9] Demographic factors may also partially govern behavior during a specific stage of the decision process. During the information stage, for example, a person's age and income may affect the number and types of information sources used and the amount of time devoted to seeking information. Marketing Update 5.1 describes how pet food marketers are capitalizing on changing demographic trends.

Demographic factors also affect the extent to which a person uses products in a specific product category. Consumers in the 15 to 24 age group often purchase furniture, appliances, and other household basics as they establish their own households. On the other hand, those in the 45 to 54 age group spend more money on luxury and leisure products after their children have left home.[10] Brand preferences, store choice, and timing of purchases are other areas on which demographic factors have some impact. Consider, for example, how differences in occupation result in variations in product needs. A college professor may earn almost as much annually as a plumber does. Yet the professor and the plumber spend their incomes differently because the product needs that arise from these two occupations vary considerably. Although both occupations require the purchase of work clothes, the professor purchases suits and the plumber buys jeans and work shirts. The types of vehicles they drive also vary to some extent. What and where they eat for lunch are likely to be different. Finally, the "tools" that they purchase and use in their work are not the same. Thus occupation clearly affects consumer buying behavior.

■ Situational Factors

Situational factors are the external circumstances or conditions that exist when a consumer is making a purchase decision. Sometimes a consumer engages in buying decision making as a result of an unexpected situation. For example, a person may hurriedly buy an airline ticket to spend the last few days with a dying relative. Or a situation may arise that causes a person to lengthen or terminate the buying decision process. For instance, a consumer who is considering the purchase of a personal computer and is laid off from work during the stage of evaluating alternatives may decide to reject the purchase entirely.

Situational factors can influence a consumer's actions during any stage of the buying decision process, and in a variety of ways. Uncertainty about future marital status may sway a consumer against making a purchase. On the other hand, a conviction that the supply of necessary products is sharply limited may impel people to buy them. For example, consumers have purchased and hoarded gasoline and various food products when these products were believed to be in short supply. Even the weather may affect buying behavior. A hurricane warning usually sends coastal residents rushing to stock up on bottled water, batteries, and emergency food supplies and to fill up their cars' gas tanks. These and other situational factors can change rapidly; their influence on purchase decisions can be sudden and can also subside quickly.

The time available to make a decision is a situational factor that strongly influences consumer buying decisions. If there is little time for selecting and purchasing a product, a person may make a quick choice and purchase a readily available

9. Patricia Sellers, "The ABC's of Marketing to Kids," *Fortune,* May 8, 1989, p. 115.

10. Judith Waldrop, "Inside America's Households," *American Demographics,* March 1989, pp. 20–27.

PET-FOOD MARKETERS PROFIT FROM TRENDS

The nation's more than 100 million dogs and cats are eating better than ever. Today, American dogs can dine on meatloaf made from lamb and brown rice and finish off the meal with ice cream. Cats can feast on Pacific mackerel in crab jelly or sardines and chicken. In 1987, Americans spent $3.1 billion on dog food, $2.1 billion on cat food, but only $757 million on baby food.

Why are Americans lavishing such attention on their pets? Experts suggest that people are forming closer bonds with their pets, in part because there are more single people living alone and more couples without children. Both groups have chosen to adopt pets to serve as companions and substitute children. In addition, the human trend toward better nutrition and fitness has been extended to pets, who are often considered family members.

Because of these trends, higher-priced, more nutritious premium pet foods are taking a larger percentage out of the nearly $6 billion pet-food market. Although total pet-food sales have been flat in recent years, sales of premium foods are growing. Sales of canned gourmet cat food rose 16.8 percent in 1988, and sales at specialty pet-food stores that sell the premium pet foods rose 18 percent in the same year.

Pet-food marketers have recognized that consumers want healthier food for their pets and are developing new products to satisfy them. The nation's leading pet-food marketer, Ralston Purina, offers O.N.E., a premium dry dog food made from corn, rice, and whole chicken; Fit & Trim, a low-calorie food for overweight dogs; and Unique, a line of gourmet canned cat foods. Carnation, another leading pet-food marketer, sells a gourmet cat food line under the name Fancy Feast. Many premium pet-food products, such as Iams dog and cat foods and Hills Science Diets for dogs and cats, are distributed through veterinarians and pet stores rather than traditional supermarkets. Premium pet snacks are also becoming more popular. Lick Your Chops, a Connecticut firm, markets a line of all-natural veterinarian-tested dog foods and snacks in consultation with a French baker. Finally there is Frosty Paws, an ice-cream specially formulated for dogs, which contains less milk and sugar than ice cream made for humans.

SOURCES: Sam Gugino, "Haute Dog: Market for Canine, Kitty Cusine Going Upscale," *Bryan-College Station (Texas) Eagle,* June 14, 1989, p. 4C; Michelle Manges, "For Today's Pampered Pets, It's a Dog-Eat-Steak World," *Wall Street Journal,* May 18, 1989, p. B1; John C. Maxwell, Jr., "Cats Trigger Pet-Food Gains," *Advertising Age,* Aug. 12, 1985, p. 31; Marcia Staimer, "Food for Thought," *USA Today,* Oct. 12, 1989, p. 1A.

brand. The amount of available time also affects the way consumers process the information contained in advertisements[11] and the length of the stages within the decision process. For example, if a family is planning to buy a washing machine for a new home, its members may gather and consider a great deal of information. They may read *Consumer Reports,* talk to friends and salespersons, look at a number of advertisements, and spend a good deal of time on comparative shopping in a number of stores. However, if the family's 20-year-old Kenmore washing machine suddenly breaks down and cannot be repaired, the extent of the information search, the number of alternatives considered, and the amount of comparative shopping may be much more restricted. Indeed, given the limited-time factor, if these family members were reasonably satisfied with the performance of the old machine, they may buy another Kenmore because they know the brand.

■ Level of Involvement

Many aspects of consumer buying decisions are affected by the individual's **level of involvement**—the importance and intensity of interest in a product in a particular situation. A buyer's level of involvement determines why he or she is motivated to seek information about certain products and brands but virtually ignores others. The extensiveness of the buying decision process varies greatly with the consumer's level of involvement. The sequence of the steps in this process may also be altered. Low-involvement buyers may form an attitude about a product and evaluate its features after purchasing it rather than before.[12] Conversely, high-involvement buyers spend much time and effort researching their purchase beforehand. In Figure 5.3, IBM provides an 800 number which buyers may use to gain additional information on its office equipment. Computers are products that undergo a great deal of investigation before they are chosen.

A consumer's level of involvement depends on a number of factors. Consumers tend to be more involved in the purchase of high-priced goods and of products that are visible to others, such as clothing, furniture, or automobiles. As levels of perceived risk increase, involvement levels are likely to rise. Furthermore, individuals may experience enduring involvement with a product class. *Enduring involvement* is an ongoing interest in a product class because of personal relevance. For example, people often have enduring involvement with products associated with their leisure activities. Their search and information-gathering processes for these products occur over extensive periods of time. Photography enthusiasts enjoy reading about and examining new types of cameras and films; snow skiers frequent sports stores even during the summer months.

Buyers may also experience *situational involvement* resulting from the particular circumstance or environment in which they find themselves. This type of involvement is temporary because the conditions that triggered the high degree of involvement may change.[13] If a person is searching for a silver serving tray to buy for a wedding gift, for example, he or she may experience a high level of involvement in the purchase decision. The person's information search and evaluation of alternatives may be extensive. However, once the selection has been made, he or she no longer sees a silver serving tray as being personally relevant.

11. Houston, Childers, and Heckler, pp. 359–369.

12. Thomas S. Robertson and Hubert Gatignon, "Competitive Effects on Technology Diffusion," *Journal of Marketing,* July 1986, pp. 1–12.

13. Ibid.

FIGURE 5.3   *Reaching consumers who have a high level of involvement.*
IBM provides a strong service policy supporting both its office equipment and others'. An 800 number is also provided for high-involvement buyers who may want additional information.

SOURCE: Courtesy of International Business Machines Corporation

Many purchase decisions do not generate great involvement on the consumer's part. When the involvement level is low, as with routine response purchases, the buying is almost automatic, and the information search and evaluation of alternatives are extremely limited. For example, grocery shopping represents low-involvement purchase decisions for many consumers; products are chosen out of habit and with minimal effort.

PSYCHOLOGICAL FACTORS INFLUENCING THE BUYING DECISION PROCESS

Psychological factors operating within individuals partly determine people's general behavior and thus influence their behavior as consumers. The primary psychological influences on consumer behavior are (1) perception, (2) motives, (3) ability and knowledge, (4) attitudes, and (5) personality. Even though these psychological factors operate internally, later in this chapter we will see that they are very much affected by social forces outside the individual.

FIGURE 5.4
Are the horsemen riding to the left or to the right?

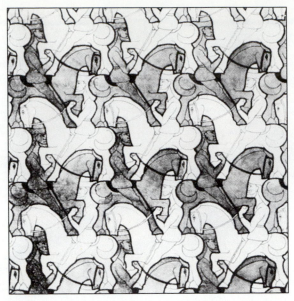

SOURCE: © 1988 M.C. Escher c/o Cordon Art—Baarn—Holland.

■ Perception

Are the horsemen in Figure 5.4 riding to the left or to the right? It could be either way depending on how you perceive the riders. Different people perceive the same thing at the same time in different ways. Similarly, the same individual at different times may perceive the same item in a number of ways. **Perception** is the process of selecting, organizing, and interpreting information inputs to produce meaning. **Information inputs** are the sensations received through sight, taste, hearing, smell, and touch. When we hear an advertisement, see a friend, smell polluted air or water, or touch a product, we receive information inputs.

As the definition indicates, perception is a three-step process. Although we receive numerous pieces of information at once, only a few of them reach awareness. We select some inputs and ignore many others because we do not have the ability to be conscious of all inputs at one time. This phenomenon is sometimes called **selective exposure** because we select inputs that are to be exposed to our awareness. If you are concentrating on this paragraph, you probably are not aware that cars are outside making noise, that the light is on, or that you are touching this book. Even though you are receiving these inputs, you ignore them until they are mentioned.

There are several reasons why some types of information reach awareness while others do not. An input is more likely to reach awareness if it relates to an anticipated event. For example, a person hoping to attend an upcoming concert is likely to listen to a radio advertisement containing ticket information for the concert. An input is likely to reach consciousness if the information helps satisfy current needs. Thus you are more likely to notice a commercial for Kentucky Fried Chicken if you are hungry. Finally, if the intensity of an input changes significantly, the input is more likely to reach awareness. When a store manager reduces a price slightly, we may not notice because the change is not significant, but if the manager cuts the price in half, we are much more likely to recognize the reduction.

The selective nature of perception leads to two other conditions: selective distortion and selective retention. **Selective distortion** is changing or twisting currently received information. This condition can occur when a person receives information that is inconsistent with personal feelings or beliefs. For example, on seeing an advertisement promoting a brand that he or she dislikes, a person may distort the information to make it more consistent with prior views. This distortion substantially lessens the effect of the advertisement on the individual. In the **selective retention** phenomenon, a person remembers information inputs that support personal feelings and beliefs and forgets inputs that do not. After hearing a sales presentation and leaving the store, a customer may forget many of the selling points if they contradict prior beliefs.

The information inputs that do reach awareness are not received in an organized form. To produce meaning, an individual must enter the second step of the perceptual process—organize and integrate the new information with that already stored in memory. Ordinarily, this organizing is done rapidly.

Interpretation—the third step in the perceptual process—is the assignment of meaning to what has been organized. A person bases interpretation on what is familiar, on knowledge already stored in memory. For this reason, a manufacturer that changes a package design faces a major problem. Since people look for the product in the old, familiar package, they might not recognize it in the new one. Unless a package change is accompanied by a promotional program that makes people aware of the change, a firm may lose sales.

Although marketers cannot control people's perceptions, they often try to influence them. Several problems may arise from such attempts, however. First, a consumer's perceptual process may operate in such a way that a seller's information never reaches that person. For example, a buyer may block out a store clerk's sales presentation. Second, a buyer may receive a seller's information but perceive it differently than was intended. For example, when a toothpaste producer advertises that "35 percent of the people who use this toothpaste have fewer cavities," a customer could infer that 65 percent of the people who use the product have more cavities. Third, a buyer who perceives information inputs that are inconsistent with prior beliefs is likely to forget the information quickly. Thus if a salesperson tells a prospective car buyer that a particular model is highly reliable and requires few repairs but the customer does not believe it, the customer probably will not retain the information very long.

In addition to perceptions of packages, products, brands, and organizations, individuals also have self-perceptions. That perception is called the person's **self-concept** or self-image. It is reasonable to believe that a person's self-concept affects purchase decisions and consumption behavior. The results of some studies suggest that buyers purchase products that reflect and enhance their self-concepts. For instance, a person might purchase Levi's jeans and rugby shirts to project a casual, relaxed self-concept.

■ Motives

A **motive** is an internal energizing force that orients a person's activities toward satisfying a need or achieving a goal. Motivation is the set of mechanisms for controlling movement toward goals.[14] A buyer's actions at any time are affected by a set of motives rather than by just one motive. At a single point in time, some motives in the set have priority, but the priorities of motives vary from one time to another.

14. James R. Bettman, *An Information Processing Theory of Consumer Choice* (Reading, Mass.: Addison-Wesley, 1979), pp. 18–24.

FIGURE 5.5
Identifying consumer motives.
Trident identifies oral hygiene as a motive to purchase its product.

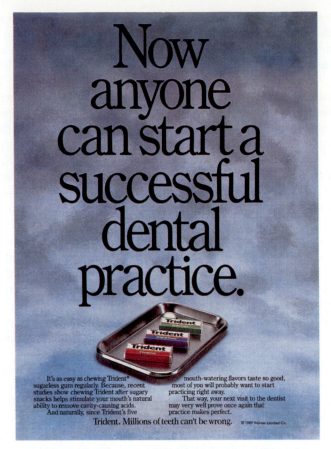

It's as easy as chewing Trident® sugarless gum regularly. Because, recent studies show chewing Trident after sugary snacks helps stimulate your mouth's natural ability to remove cavity-causing acids. And naturally, since Trident's five mouth-watering flavors taste so good, most of you will probably want to start practicing right away.

That way, your next visit to the dentist may very well prove once again that practice makes perfect.

Trident. Millions of teeth can't be wrong. © 1989 Warner-Lambert Co.

SOURCE: Courtesy of Warner-Lambert Company—American Chicle Group

For example, a person's motives for having a cup of coffee are much stronger right after waking up than just before going to bed. Motivation also affects the direction and intensity of behavior. Individuals must choose which goals to pursue at a particular time.

Motives that influence where a person purchases products on a regular basis are called **patronage motives**. A buyer may shop at a specific store because of such patronage motives as price, service, location, honesty, product variety, or friendliness of salespeople. For example, Tianguis, a chain of southern California grocery stores, stocks a wide variety of Hispanic products, such as empanadas and tortilla mixes, with Spanish labels and has Spanish-speaking check-out clerks, as well as mariachi bands, to encourage the area's large Hispanic population to frequent its stores.[15] To capitalize on patronage motives, a marketer should try to determine why regular customers patronize a store and then emphasize these characteristics in the store's marketing mix.

Marketers conduct motivation research to analyze the major motives that influence consumers to buy or not buy their products. In Figure 5.5, it is easy to

15. Alfredo Corchado, "Hispanic Supermarkets Are Blossoming," *Wall Street Journal,* Jan. 23, 1989, p. B1.

determine that Trident is marketing its gum to those concerned with dental health and cavity prevention. Motives, which often operate at a subconscious level, are difficult to measure. Because people ordinarily do not know what motivates them, marketers cannot simply ask them about their motives. Most motivation research relies on interviews or projective techniques.

When researchers study motives through interviews, they may use depth interviews, group interviews, or a combination of the two. In a **depth interview**, the researcher tries to get the subject to talk freely about anything to create an informal atmosphere. The researcher may ask general, nondirected questions and then probe the subject's answers by asking for clarification. A depth interview may last for several hours. In a **group interview**, the interviewer—through leadership that is not highly structured—tries to generate discussion about one or several topics among a group of six to twelve people. Through what is said in the discussion, the interviewer attempts to discover people's motives relating to some issue such as the use of a product. The researcher usually cannot probe as far in a group interview as in a depth interview. To determine the subconscious motives reflected in the interviews, motivation researchers must be extremely well trained in clinical psychology. Their skill in uncovering subconscious motives from what is said in an interview determines the effectiveness of their research. Both depth and group interview techniques can yield a variety of information. For example, they might help marketers discover why customers continue to buy high-calorie fried foods even though most say they are trying to reduce their intake of cholesterol and calories.

Projective techniques are tests in which subjects are asked to perform specific tasks for particular purposes while in fact they are being evaluated for other purposes. Such tests are based on the assumption that subjects unconsciously will "project" their motives as they perform the required tasks. However, subjects should always be informed that the test is an unstructured evaluation. Researchers trained in projective techniques can analyze the materials a subject produces and can make predictions about the subject's subconscious motives. Some common types of projective techniques are word-association tests and sentence-completion tests.

Motivation research techniques can be reasonably effective but are far from perfect. Marketers who want to research people's motives should obtain the services of professional psychologists skilled in the methods of motivation research.

■ Ability and Knowledge

Individuals vary in their **ability**—their competence and efficiency in performing tasks. One ability of interest to marketers is an individual's capacity to learn. **Learning** refers to changes in a person's behavior caused by information and experience. The consequences of behavior strongly influence the learning process. Behaviors that result in satisfying consequences tend to be repeated. For example, when a consumer buys a Snickers candy bar and likes it, he or she is more likely to buy a Snickers the next time. In fact, the individual will probably continue to purchase that brand until it no longer provides satisfaction. But when the effects of the behavior are no longer satisfying, the person will switch to a different brand, perhaps, or stop eating candy bars altogether.

When making purchasing decisions, buyers have to process information. Individuals have differing abilities in this regard. For example, when purchasing a home computer, a well-educated potential buyer who has experience with computer systems may be able to read, comprehend, and synthesize the considerable quantities of information found in the technical brochures for various competing brands. On

SOURCE: Nike Inc.

the other hand, another buyer with more limited abilities may be incapable of performing this task and will have to rely on information obtained from advertisements or from a sales representative of a particular brand.

Another aspect of an individual's ability is knowledge. **Knowledge** is made up of two components: familiarity with the product and expertise, which is the individual's ability to apply the product.[16] The duration and intensity of the buying decision process depends on the buyer's familiarity or prior experience in purchasing and using the product. For example, in Figure 5.6, Nike, a well-known manufacturer of adult and children athletic shoes, builds awareness that its product is also available in infant sizes. The individual's knowledge influences his or her search for, recall, and use of information.[17]

When making purchase decisions, inexperienced buyers may use different types of information than more experienced shoppers who are familiar with the product and purchase situation. Inexperienced buyers use price as an indicator of quality

16. Joseph W. Alba and J. Wesley Hutchinson, "Dimensions of Consumer Expertise," *Journal of Consumer Research,* March 1987, pp. 411–454.

17. Akshay R. Rao and Kent B. Monroe, "The Moderating Effect of Prior Knowledge on Cue Utilization in Product Evaluations," *Journal of Consumer Research,* September 1988, pp. 253–264.

more frequently than buyers who have some knowledge of a particular product category.[18] Thus two potential purchasers of an antique desk may use quite different types of information in making their purchase decision. The inexperienced buyer is likely to judge the desk's value by the price, whereas the more experienced buyer may seek information about the craftsman, time period, and place of origin to judge the desk's quality and value.

Consumers who lack expertise may seek the advice of others when making a purchase or take along a "purchase pal." More experienced buyers have greater confidence; they also have more knowledge about the product or service and can tell which product features are reliable cues to product quality. For example, consider two young students who want reliable cars for travel back and forth to college. One has no expertise with regard to automobiles and is unsure about what features to use to judge a car. He finds the information given in the automobile brochures confusing and feels intimidated by the salesperson. Therefore he goes for advice to his father, who has purchased many cars, and takes him along to the car dealership when making the purchase. The other student has been interested in cars all her life and has worked in a large car dealership for several summers. Even though this is her first car purchase, she is an expert with regard to cars and knows what features are important. She is confident and knowledgeable and makes her purchase decision unassisted.

Marketers sometimes help customers to learn about their products and to gain experience with them. Free samples encourage trial and reduce purchase risk. In-store demonstrations aid consumers in acquiring knowledge of product uses. Test drives give new car purchasers some experience with an automobile's features. Consumers also learn when they experience products indirectly, by way of information from salespersons, advertisements, friends, and relatives. Through sales personnel and advertisements, marketers offer information before (and sometimes after) purchases to influence what consumers learn and to create a more favorable attitude toward the products.

Although marketers seek to influence what a consumer learns, their attempts are seldom fully successful. Marketers encounter problems in attracting and holding consumers' attention, providing consumers with the kinds of information that are important for making purchase decisions, and convincing them to try the product.

Attitude

Attitude refers to knowledge and positive or negative feelings about an object or activity. The objects or acts toward which we have attitudes may be tangible or intangible, living or nonliving. For example, we have attitudes toward sex, religion, politics, and music, just as we do toward cars, football, and pizza.

An individual learns attitudes through experience and interaction with other people. Just as attitudes are learned, they can also be changed. Nevertheless, an individual's attitudes remain generally stable and do not change from moment to moment. Likewise, at any one time, a person's attitudes do not all have equal impact; some are stronger than others.

Consumer attitudes toward a firm and its products greatly influence the success or failure of the firm's marketing strategy. When consumers have strong negative attitudes toward one or more aspects of a firm's marketing practices, they may not only stop using the firm's product but also urge their relatives and friends to do

18. Ibid.

likewise. For example, when an oil spill from the supertanker *Exxon Valdez* fouled beaches and killed wildlife in Alaska's Prince William Sound, the public judged Exxon's response to cleaning up the spill as inadequate and cosmetic. As a result, many consumers boycotted Exxon products. Nearly twenty thousand Exxon credit card holders cut up their cards and sent them back to Exxon, exhorting their friends to do the same.

Since attitudes can play such an important part in determining consumer behavior, marketers should measure consumer attitudes toward prices, package designs, brand names, advertisements, salespeople, repair services, store locations, features of existing or proposed products, and social responsibility activities. Several methods can help marketers gauge these attitudes. One of the simplest ways is to question people directly. An attitude researcher for Keytronics, a computer-keyboard manufacturer, for example, might ask respondents what they think about the style and design of Keytronics' newest keyboard. Projective techniques used in motivation research can also be employed to measure attitudes. Sometimes marketers evaluate attitudes through attitude scales. An **attitude scale** usually consists of a series of adjectives, phrases, or sentences about an object. Subjects are asked to indicate the intensity of their feelings toward the object by reacting to the adjectives, phrases, or sentences in a certain way. For example, if a marketer were measuring people's attitudes toward oil companies, respondents might be asked to state the degree to which they agree or disagree with a number of statements, such as "Oil companies engage in environmentally sound drilling and exploration activities."

When marketers determine that a significant number of consumers have strong negative attitudes toward an aspect of a marketing mix, they may try to change consumer attitudes to make them more favorable. This task is generally long, expensive, and difficult and may require extensive promotional efforts. For example, the Beef Industry Council, an organization of beef producers, has attempted to use advertising to change consumers' attitudes toward beef by presenting it as a nutritious food. Some of the advertisements contain information about the caloric content, fat, cholesterol, sodium, and protein levels. In the same vein, both business and nonbusiness organizations try to change people's attitudes about many things, from health and safety to product prices and features.

■ Personality

Personality is all the internal traits and behaviors that make a person unique. Each person's unique personality arises from heredity and personal experiences. Personalities typically are described as having one or more characteristics, such as compulsiveness, ambitiousness, gregariousness, dogmatism, authoritarianism, introversion, extroversion, aggressiveness, competitiveness. Marketing researchers attempt to find relationships among such characteristics and buying behavior. Even though a few links among several personality characteristics and buyer behavior have been determined, the results of many studies have been inconclusive. Some researchers see the apparently weak association between personality and buying behavior as due to unreliable measures rather than a lack of relationship.[19] A number of marketers are convinced that a consumer's personality does influence the types and brands of products purchased. For example, the type of clothing, jewelry, or automobile that a person buys may reflect one or more personality characteristics. Figure 5.7 provides examples of the type of persons who wear Tony Lama boots.

19. John L. Lastovika and Erich A. Joachimsthaler, "Improving the Detection of Personality-Behavior Relationships in Consumer Research," *Journal of Consumer Research,* March 1988, pp. 583–587.

FIGURE 5.7 *Appealing personalities.*

Tony Lama boots are worn by such diverse personalities as retired sheriff Dalton Hogg and musician Richard Marx.

SOURCE: Courtesy of Tony Lama Company

At times, marketers aim advertising campaigns at general types of personalities. In doing so, they use positively valued personality characteristics, such as gregariousness, independence, or competitiveness. Products promoted this way include beverages, automobiles, cigarettes, and clothing.

SOCIAL FACTORS INFLUENCING THE BUYING DECISION PROCESS

The forces that other people exert on buying behavior are called **social factors**. As shown in Figure 5.1, they can be grouped into four major areas: (1) roles and family influences, (2) reference groups, (3) social classes, and (4) culture and subcultures.

■ **Roles and Family Influences**

All of us occupy positions within groups, organizations, and institutions. Associated with each position is a **role**—a set of actions and activities that a person in a particular position is supposed to perform, based on the expectations of both the individual and surrounding persons. Because people occupy numerous positions, they also have many roles. For example a man may perform the roles of son, husband, father, employee or employer, church member, civic organization member, and student in an evening college class. Thus there are several sets of expectations placed on each person's behavior.

An individual's roles influence both general behavior and buying behavior. The demands of a person's many roles may be inconsistent and confusing. To illustrate, assume that the man mentioned above is thinking about buying a boat. While he wants a boat for fishing, his children want one suitable for water skiing. His wife wants him to delay the boat purchase until next year. A coworker insists that he should buy a particular brand, known for high performance. Thus an individual's buying behavior is partially affected by the input and opinions of family and friends.

Family roles relate directly to purchase decisions. The male head of household is likely to be involved heavily in the purchase of products such as liquor and tobacco. Although female roles have changed, women still make buying decisions related to many household items, including health-care products, laundry supplies, paper products, and foods. Husbands and wives participate jointly in the purchase of a variety of products, especially durable goods. Some students aged 16 to 24 may be rebellious; their brand loyalty can be quite changeable. Marketers frequently promote their products during spring break to catch this hard-to-reach group at a time when they are more receptive to a promotional message.[20] Children are making many purchase decisions and influencing numerous household purchase decisions that traditionally were made only by husbands and wives. When two or more family members participate in a purchase, their roles may dictate that each is responsible for performing certain tasks: initiating the idea, gathering information, deciding whether to buy the product, or selecting the specific brand. The particular tasks performed depend on the types of products being considered.

Marketers need to be aware of how roles affect buying behavior. To develop a marketing mix that precisely meets the needs of the target market, marketers must know not only who does the actual buying, but also what other roles influence the purchase. Because sex roles are changing so rapidly in our country, marketers must ensure that their information is current and accurate.

■ Reference Groups

A group becomes a **reference group** when an individual identifies with it so much that he or she takes on many of the values, attitudes, or behaviors of group members. The person who views a group as a reference group may or may not know the actual size of the group. Most people have several reference groups, such as families, friends, fraternities and sororities, and civic and professional organizations.

A group can be a negative reference group for an individual. Someone may have been a part of a specific group at one time but later rejected the group's values and members. One can also specifically take action to avoid a particular group.[21] However, in this discussion we refer to reference groups as those that the individual involved views positively.

A reference group may serve as a point of comparison and a source of information for an individual. A customer's behavior may change to be more in line with the actions and beliefs of group members. For example, a person might stop buying one brand of audiocassettes and switch to another on the advice of members of the reference group. Generally, the more conspicuous a product, the more likely it is

20. Martha T. Moore, "Spring Break: Brand Names Chase Sales," *USA Today,* Mar. 17, 1989, p. B1.

21. Henry Assael, *Consumer Behavior and Marketing Action* (Boston: Kent Publishing, 1987), p. 369.

that the brand decision will be influenced by reference groups. An individual may also seek information from the reference group about other factors regarding a prospective purchase, such as where to buy a certain product. The degree to which a reference group will affect a purchase decision depends on an individual's susceptibility to reference-group influence and the strength of his or her involvement with the group.

A marketer sometimes tries to use reference-group influence in advertisements by suggesting that people in a specific group buy a product and are highly satisfied with it. In this type of appeal, the advertiser hopes that many people will accept the suggested group as a reference group and buy (or react more favorably to) the product. Whether this kind of advertising succeeds depends on three factors: how effectively the advertisement communicates the message, the type of product, and the individual's susceptibility to reference-group influence.

■ Social Classes

Within all societies, people rank others into higher or lower positions of respect. This ranking results in social classes. A **social class** is an open group of individuals who have similar social rank. A class is referred to as "open" because people can move into and out of it. The criteria for grouping people into classes vary from one society to another. In the United States, we take into account many factors, including occupation, education, income, wealth, race, ethnic group, and possessions. In the Soviet Union, wealth and income are less important than education and occupation in determining social class: although Russian doctors and scientists do not make a great deal of money, they are highly valued in Russian society. A person who is ranking someone does not necessarily apply all of a society's criteria. The number and the importance of the factors chosen depend on the characteristics of the individual being ranked and the values of the person who is doing the ranking.

To some degree, persons within social classes develop and assume common patterns of behavior. They may have similar attitudes, values, language patterns, and possessions. Social class influences many aspects of our lives. For example, it affects our chances of having children and their chances of surviving infancy. It influences our childhood training, choice of religion, selection of occupation, and how we spend our time. Because social class has a bearing on so many aspects of a person's life, it also affects buying decisions. For example, upper-class Americans seem to prefer luxury automobiles such as the BMW and Mercedes Benz, which symbolize their status, income, and financial comfort. Marketing Update 5.2 describes how Nissan and Toyota attempted to market automobiles that compete in this same market.

The analyses of social class commonly divide people in the United States into three to seven categories. Social scientists Richard Coleman and Lee Rainwater developed the Coleman-Rainwater classification, which comprises seven categories. They are as follows:

1. Upper Americans
   a. *Upper-upper class* (0.3 percent): high society; includes those of inherited wealth, aristocratic names
   b. *Lower-upper class* (1.2 percent): the newer social elite, drawn from current professional, corporate leadership
   c. *Upper-middle class* (12.5 percent): the rest of college graduate managers and professionals; lifestyle centers on private clubs, causes, and the arts

LEXUS AND INFINITI TARGET AFFLUENT CONSUMERS

For many years, two European cars ruled the luxury market—Mercedes Benz and BMW. Now, Nissan and Toyota, successful Japanese car marketers with quality reputations, are vying for a share of the market with new luxury models. However, Nissan and Toyota have discovered that their names will not guarantee instant success in the luxury car market.

The problem faced by Nissan and Toyota was how to crack the European luxury car images of Mercedes and BMW. In general, affluent car buyers regard these European models as the ultimate in luxury. Nissan and Toyota, then, had to find ways to convince affluent consumers that the Nissan Infiniti and the Toyota Lexus luxury models were equal to the European models. Interestingly, each company set about this task in different ways.

Nissan chose to market the Infiniti with an unusual advertising campaign aimed at increasing awareness for the brand. The ads did not show the Infiniti but instead showed nature scenes built around philosophical copy. The ads created very high brand awareness and stimulated heavy traffic in Infiniti showrooms, but did not bring about the spectacular sales anticipated. In fact, low sales prompted Infiniti dealers to call for a new advertising strategy.

Toyota achieved somewhat different results with its approach for the Lexus. Advertisements for the Lexus were more traditional. They showed the car and emphasized luxury, performance, and safety. Toyota also mailed promotional literature on the Lexus to 800,000 prospective buyers, receiving more than 65,000 responses. Of those, 23,000 were considered "hot prospects" because they provided phone numbers and indicated willingness to test drive the Lexus. Initial sales figures for the top-of-the-line Lexus LS 400 were very brisk; however, sales for the less expensive ES 250 were very slow.

Nissan and Toyota had believed their reputations were strong enough to establish themselves in the luxury-car market, but they had not counted on consumers failure to equate Japanese cars with the Mercedes or the BMW. Thus, they discovered that many consumers were unwilling to alter their perceptions of product images.

SOURCES: Larry Armstrong, "No Joyride for Japan," *Business Week,* Jan. 15, 1990, pp. 20–21; Larry Armstrong, "Two Ways to Say BMW in Japanese," *Business Week,* Dec. 18, 1989, p. 155; "Infiniti Ads Trigger Auto Debate," *Advertising Age,* Jan. 22, 1990, p. 49; Raymond Serafin, "Lexus Ads Sidestep Japanese Heritage," *Advertising Age,* Aug. 7, 1989, p. 59.

2. Middle Americans
    a. *Middle class* (32 percent): average-pay white-collar workers and their blue-collar friends; live on "the better side of town," try to "do the proper things"
    b. *Working class* (38 percent): average-pay blue-collar workers; lead "working class" lifestyle whatever the income, school background, and job
3. Lower Americans
    a. *Lower class* (9 percent): working, not on welfare; living standard is just above poverty
    b. *Lower-lower class* (7 percent): on welfare, visibly poverty stricken; often have no steady employment.[22]

Coleman suggests that for purposes of consumer analysis and mass marketing the consuming public should be divided into the four major status groups shown in Table 5.1, but he cautions marketers to remember that there is considerable diversity in people's life situations within each status group.

Social class determines to some extent the type, quality, and quantity of products that a person buys and uses. Social class also affects an individual's shopping patterns and the types of stores patronized. Advertisements are sometimes based on an appeal to a specific social class.

■ Culture and Subculture

Culture is everything in our surroundings that is made by human beings. It consists of tangible items, such as foods, furniture, buildings, clothing, and tools, and intangible concepts, such as education, welfare, and laws. Culture also includes the values and wide range of behaviors that are acceptable within a specific society. The concepts, values, and behaviors that make up a culture are learned and passed on from one generation to the next.

Culture influences buying behavior because it permeates our daily lives. Our culture determines what we wear and eat, where we reside and travel. Certainly, society's interest in the healthfulness of food has affected companies' approaches to developing and promoting their products. It also influences how we buy and use products and our satisfaction from them. For example, in Figure 5.8, Good Seasons promotes its product as an easy way to prepare the freshest and most delicious salads at home. Good Seasons is meeting cultural standards as to the type of food we like to eat and ease of preparation. In American culture, time scarcity is a growing problem because of the rise in the number of women who work and the current emphasis we place on physical and mental self-development. Many people do time-saving shopping and buy time-saving products to cope with this scarcity.[23]

Because culture, to some degree, determines how products are purchased and used, it in turn affects the development, promotion, distribution, and pricing of products. Food marketers, for example, have had to make a multitude of changes in their marketing efforts. Thirty years ago most families in our culture ate at least two meals a day together, and the mother devoted four to six hours a day to preparing those meals. Now more than 60 percent of the women in the 25 to 54 age group are employed outside the home, and average family incomes have risen considerably.

22. Richard P. Coleman, "The Continuing Significance of Social Class in Marketing," *Journal of Consumer Research,* December 1983, p. 267. Copyright © The Journal of Consumer Research, Inc., 1983. Reprinted by permission of the University of Chicago Press.

23. Leonard L. Berry, "The Time-Sharing Consumer," *Journal of Retailing,* Winter 1979, p. 69.

TABLE 5.1 *Social class behavioral and purchasing characteristics*

CLASS (% OF POPULATION)	BEHAVIORAL TRAITS	BUYING CHARACTERISTICS
Upper (14); includes upper-upper, lower-upper, upper-middle	Income varies among the groups, but goals are the same Various lifestyles: preppy, conventional, intellectual, etc. Neighborhood and prestigious schooling important	Prize quality merchandise Favor prestigious brands Products purchased must reflect good taste Invest in art Spend money on travel, theater, books, and tennis, golf, and swimming clubs
Middle (32)	Often in management Considered white collar Prize good schools Desire an attractive home in a nice, well-maintained neighborhood Often emulate the upper class Enjoy travel and physical activity Often very involved in children's school and sports activities	Like fashionable items Consult experts via books, articles, etc., before purchasing Will spend for experiences they consider worthwhile for their children (e.g., ski trips, college education) Tour packages; weekend trips Attractive home furnishings
Working (38)	Emphasis on family, especially for economic and emotional supports (e.g., job opportunity tips, help in times of trouble) Blue collar Earn good incomes Enjoy mechanical items and recreational activities Enjoy leisure time after working hard	Buy vehicles and equipment related to recreation, camping, and selected sports Strong sense of value Shop for best bargains at off-price and discount stores Purchases automotive equipment for making repairs Enjoy local travel; recreational parks
Lower (16)	Often down and out through no fault of their own (e.g., layoffs, company takeovers) Can include individuals on welfare; the homeless Often have strong religious beliefs May be forced to live in less desirable neighborhoods In spite of their problems, often goodhearted toward others	Most products purchased are for survival Ability to convert good discards into usable items Enjoyment of everyday activities when possible

SOURCE: Adapted with permission from Richard P. Coleman, "The Continuing Significance of Social Class to Marketing," *Journal of Consumer Research,* pp. 265–280, 1983, 10 (December), with data from J. Paul Peter and Jerry C. Olson, *Consumer Behavior: Marketing Strategy Perspective* (Homewood, Ill.: Irwin, 1987), p. 433.

SOURCE: GOOD SEASONS is a registered trademark of Kraft General Foods, Inc. Reproduced with permission.

These shifts, along with the problem of time scarcity, have resulted in dramatic changes in the national per capita consumption of certain foods: frozen dinners, shelf-stable foods, such as Lunch Bucket and Top Shelf, and take-out foods.[24]

When U.S. marketers sell products in other countries, they often see the tremendous impact that culture has on the purchase and use of products. International marketers find that people in other regions of the world have different attitudes, values, and needs, which in turn call for different methods of doing business, as well as different types of marketing mixes. Some international marketers fail because they do not or cannot adjust to cultural differences. The effect of culture on international marketing programs is discussed in greater detail in Chapter 23.

A culture can be divided into **subcultures** according to geographic regions or human characteristics, such as age or ethnic background. In our country, we have a

24. Mona Doyle, "The Metamorphosis of the Consumer," *Marketing Communications,* April 1989, pp. 18–22.

number of different subcultures: West Coast, teen-age, and Asian-American, for example. Within subcultures, there are even greater similarities in people's attitudes, values, and actions than within the broader culture. Relative to other subcultures, individuals in a certain subculture may have stronger preferences for specific types of clothing, furniture, or foods. For example, there is a greater per capita consumption of rice among southerners than among New Englanders or midwesterners. American teen-agers want to wear the latest fashions—for example, the surfwear and sports clothing made by Quiksilver, Inc.

Marketers must recognize that even though their operations are confined to the United States, to one state, or even to one city, subcultural differences may dictate considerable variations in what products people buy. There will also be differences in how people make purchases—and variations in when they make them as well. To deal effectively with these differences, marketers may have to alter their product, promotion, distribution systems, or price to satisfy members of particular subcultures.

Understanding Consumer Behavior

Marketers try to understand consumer buying behavior so that they can offer consumers greater satisfaction. Yet a certain amount of customer dissatisfaction remains. Some marketers have not adopted the marketing concept and so are not consumer oriented and do not regard customer satisfaction as a primary objective. Moreover, because the tools for analyzing consumer behavior are imprecise, marketers may not be able to determine accurately what is highly satisfying to buyers. Finally, even if marketers know what increases consumer satisfaction, they may not be able to provide it.

Understanding consumer behavior is an important task for marketers. Even though research on consumer buying behavior has not supplied all the knowledge that marketers need, progress has been made during the last twenty years and is likely to continue in the next twenty. Not only will refinements in research methods yield more information about consumer behavior, but the pressures of an increasingly competitive business environment will make such information much more urgent for marketers.

Summary

Buying behavior is the decision processes and acts of people involved in buying and using products. Consumer buying behavior refers to the buying behavior of ultimate consumers, those who purchase products for personal or household use, not for business purposes. Analyzing consumer buying behavior is important to marketers; if they are able to determine what satisfies customers, they can implement the marketing concept and better predict how consumers will respond to different marketing strategies.

Consumer decisions can be classified into three categories: routine response behavior, limited decision making, and extensive decision making. A consumer uses routine response behavior when buying frequently purchased, low-cost items that require very little search and decision effort. Limited decision making is used for products that are purchased occasionally and when a buyer needs to acquire information about an unfamiliar brand in a familiar product category. Extensive decision making is used when purchasing an unfamiliar, expensive or infrequently bought product. Impulse buying is not a consciously planned buying behavior but involves a powerful, persistent urge to buy something immediately. The purchase of a certain product does not always elicit the same type of decision-making behavior.

The consumer buying decision process includes five stages: problem recognition, information search, evaluation of alternatives, purchase, and postpurchase evaluation. All decision processes do not always culminate in a purchase, and all consumer decisions do not always include all five stages. Problem recognition occurs when a buyer becomes aware that there is a difference between a desired state and an actual condition. After recognizing the problem or need, the buyer searches for information about products that will help resolve the problem or satisfy the need. In the internal search, buyers search their memories for information about products that might solve the problem. If they are unable to retrieve from memory sufficient information to make a decision, they seek additional information through an external search. A successful search will yield a group of brands, called an evoked set, that a buyer views as possible alternatives. To evaluate the products in the evoked set, a buyer establishes certain criteria by which to compare, rate, and rank the different products. Marketers can influence consumers' evaluation by framing the alternatives.

In the purchase stage, the consumer selects the product or brand on the basis of results from the evaluation stage and on other dimensions. The buyer also chooses the seller from whom he or she will buy the product. After the purchase, the buyer evaluates the product to determine if its actual performance meets expected levels. Shortly after the purchase of an expensive product, for example, the postpurchase evaluation may provoke cognitive dissonance, which is dissatisfaction brought on by the consumer's doubts as to whether he or she should have bought the product in the first place or would have been better off buying another brand that had also ranked high in the evaluation.

Three major categories of influences are believed to affect the consumer buying decision process: personal, psychological, and social factors. A personal factor is one that is unique to a particular person. Personal factors include demographic factors, situational factors, and level of involvement. Demographic factors are individual characteristics such as age, sex, race, ethnicity, income, family life cycle, and occupation. Situational factors are the external circumstances or conditions that exist when a consumer is making a purchase decision. The time available to make a decision is a situational factor that strongly influences consumer buying decisions. An individual's level of involvement—the importance and intensity of interest in a product in a particular situation—also affects the buying decision process. Enduring involvement is an ongoing interest in a product class because of personal relevance. Situational involvement is a temporary interest resulting from the particular circumstance or environment in which buyers find themselves.

Psychological factors operating within individuals partly determine people's general behavior and thus influence their behavior as consumers. The primary psychological influences on consumer behavior are perception, motives, ability and knowledge, attitudes, and personality. Perception is the process of selecting, organizing, and interpreting information inputs (the sensations received through sight, taste, hearing, smell, and touch) to produce meaning. Selective exposure is the phenomenon of people selecting the inputs that are to be exposed to their awareness; selective distortion is changing or twisting currently received information. When a person remembers information inputs that support personal feelings and beliefs and forgets inputs that do not, the phenomenon is called selective retention. The second step of the perceptual process requires organizing and integrating the new information with that already stored in memory. Interpretation—the third step in the perceptual process—is the assignment of meaning to what has been organized. In addition to perceptions of packages, products, brands, and organizations, individuals also have a self-concept, or self-image.

A motive is an internal energizing force that orients a person's activities toward satisfying a need or achieving a goal. Patronage motives influence where a person purchases products on a regular basis. To analyze the major motives that influence consumers to buy or not buy their products, marketers conduct motivation research, using depth interviews, group interviews, or projective techniques.

Individuals vary in their ability—their competency and efficiency in performing tasks. Ability includes both learning and knowledge. Learning refers to changes in a person's behavior caused by information and experience. Knowledge is made up of two components: familiarity with the product and expertise—the individual's ability to apply the product.

Attitude refers to knowledge and positive or negative feelings about an object or activity. Consumer attitudes toward a firm and its products greatly influence the success or failure of the firm's marketing strategy. Marketers measure consumers' attitudes with projective techniques and attitude scales.

Personality comprises all the internal traits and behaviors that make a person unique. Some marketers believe that a person's personality does influence the types and brands of products purchased.

The forces that other people exert on buying behavior are called social factors. Social factors include the influence of roles and family, reference groups, social classes, and culture and subcultures. All of us occupy positions within groups, organizations, and institutions, and each position has a role—a set of actions and activities that a person in a particular position is supposed to perform, based on the expectations of both the individual and surrounding persons. A group is a reference group when an individual identifies with the group so much that he or she takes on many of the values, attitudes, or behaviors of group members. A social class is an open group of individuals who have similar social rank. Culture is everything in our surroundings that is made by human beings. A culture can be divided into subcultures on the basis of geographic regions or human characteristics, such as age or ethnic background.

Marketers try to understand consumer buying behavior so that they can offer consumers greater satisfaction. Refinements in research methods will yield more information about consumer behavior, and the pressure of an increasingly competitive business environment will spur marketers to seek fuller understanding of consumer decision processes.

IMPORTANT TERMS

Buying behavior
Consumer buying behavior
Routine response behavior
Limited decision making
Extensive decision making
Impulse buying
Consumer buying
  decision process
Internal search
External search
Cognitive dissonance
Personal factor
Demographic factors
Situational factors
Level of involvement
Psychological factors
Perception
Information inputs
Selective exposure
Selective distortion

Selective retention
Self-concept
Motive
Patronage motives
Depth interview
Group interview
Projective techniques
Ability
Learning
Knowledge
Attitude
Attitude scale
Personality
Social factors
Role
Reference group
Social class
Culture
Subcultures

DISCUSSION AND REVIEW QUESTIONS

1. Name the types of buying behavior consumers use. List some products that you have bought using each type of behavior. Have you ever bought a product on impulse?
2. What are the major stages in the consumer buying decision process? Are all these stages used in all consumer purchase decisions?
3. What are the personal factors that affect the consumer buying decision process? How do they affect the process?
4. How does a consumer's level of involvement affect his or her purchase behavior?
5. What is the function of time in a consumer's purchasing decision process?
6. What is selective exposure? Why do humans engage in it?
7. How do marketers attempt to shape consumers' learning?
8. Why are marketers concerned about consumer attitudes?
9. How do roles affect a person's buying behavior?
10. Describe reference groups. How do they influence buying behavior? Name some of your own reference groups.
11. In what ways does social class affect a person's purchase decisions?
12. What is culture? How does it affect a person's buying behavior?
13. Describe the subcultures to which you belong. Identify buying behavior that is unique to your subculture.

■ CASES

5.1 Burger King Revamps Its Image

After years of declining market share, unsuccessful advertising campaigns, management upheaval, and finally, a takeover by British-owned Grand Metropolitan, P.L.C., Burger King Corp. wanted to change consumers' perceptions of the company and their attitudes toward it. Under a new chief executive officer, Barry Gibbons, Burger King altered its marketing mix to stem its declining market share (17 percent of the $60 billion fast-food market) and to change its image by relating the Burger King experience to consumers' self-concepts. In a break from fast-food marketers' traditional focus on price and treatment of their products as "commodities," Burger King developed a new advertising campaign, designed to set it apart from competitors and its own troubled past.

A random survey showed that the consumers who already patronized Burger King restaurants were overwhelmingly positive about the chain. Such satisfied patrons help boost sales by positive word-of-mouth advertising. But to push up sales and lure competitors' customers, Burger King had to develop a new promotional campaign—a campaign that would enhance consumers' perceptions of the second-largest hamburger chain. Using "attitude advertising," Burger King is now trying to establish a positive relationship with consumers and create a different image with its daring "sometimes you've gotta break the rules" advertising campaign. The campaign itself breaks a few of the fast-food industry's advertising rules.

The $150 million campaign focuses on getting both consumers and Burger King management to think differently about the company. The resulting advertisements downplay traditional product shots and jingles and focus instead on entertainment, humor, and a spirit of independence. Although most fast-food advertisements usually have mouth-watering shots of food, the Burger King ads include only occasional glimpses of Burger King signs or products and avoid the traditional Burger King flame-broiling action shot. They attempt instead to provide an image of a Burger King experience that is fun and entertaining.

The campaign includes six "hip" television advertisements showing people "breaking the rules" to get Burger King food. In one, an aircraft-carrier crew awaiting its "orders" receives Burger King food by helicopter. In another, a teen-age boy uses his dad's Mercedes to deliver a salad to a pretty girl. The intent is to position Burger King in the hearts of potential customers rather than trying to show the superiority of a specific product.

Another rule breaker is the radio advertising campaign. Officials say that during two weeks of unprecedented saturation two-thirds of America will have heard ten Burger King radio commercials. The series of radio spots feature original Burger King songs from a variety of stars, including Mel Torme, John Lee Hooker, the Fabulous Thunderbirds, and Tone-Loc.

In an unusual (and appropriately rule-breaking) collaboration, Burger King hired two advertising agencies to handle the new advertising campaign. Rather than dividing responsibilities, the two agencies developed a team concept, with the idea that both would have equal creative input opportunities.

CEO Gibbons has changed more than just Burger King's promotion. To support the advertising and to contribute to the new Burger King image, he also made changes in product and price. Now there are daily 99 cent specials and Burger King doubles—double-decker burgers with different toppings.

Other changes affect the operation of individual franchisees' operations. By laying off 550 employees in the headquarters and company field offices, Burger King pared down its management hierarchy. Gibbons has insisted that all Burger King restaurants focus on uniformity, cleanliness, and teamwork. He has also sent the message that Burger King will purge franchisees with sloppy, unprofitable restaurants by closing them or, if necessary, buying them. In addition, Burger King is remodeling many company-owned outlets and lowering the rent for new franchisees who lease their buildings from the company. Franchisees have been told to prepare for new menu boards and to clear space for more in-store displays.

All these actions have been taken to support the theme of entertainment, humor, and a fun experience. The changes in Burger King's marketing mix should help alter consumers' views of the company and make the Burger King image more consistent with consumer self-concept, leading to a more positive attitude toward the firm.

SOURCES: Based on information from James Cox, "Bold Campaign Aims to Beef up Market Share," *USA Today,* Sept. 28, 1989, pp. 1B, 2B; Bob Garfield, "Burger King Breaks from Indecisive Past," *Advertising Age,* Oct. 2, 1989, pp. 1, 68; Scott Hume, "A New 'Personality'," *Advertising Age,* Oct. 2, 1989, pp. 1, 66; Scott Hume, "Burger King Ads Will Count," *Advertising Age,* Oct. 2, 1989, p. 66; and Jane Weaver, "Getting Attitude: Creatives Scrutinize Ads Without Products," *Adweek,* Oct. 23, 1989. p. 27.

Questions for Discussion

1. How difficult will it be to change consumer perceptions about Burger King?
2. Burger King claims to use "attitude advertising." Based on the text discussion on attitudes, what should this advertising accomplish?
3. If the Burger King image is more consistent with the consumer's self-concept, what will be the result?

5.2   Beef Industry Council Tries to Change Attitudes

Once a staple in the American diet, beef has lost favor with many health-conscious consumers in recent years. The American Meat Institute reported that per capita consumption of beef fell to 72.7 pounds in 1988, down 7.3 percent from 1986. But the beef industry is fighting back, spending $29 million dollars to persuade consumers that red meat, trimmed of excess fat, can be just as lean and nutritious as white meat. The goal is to improve consumers' overall attitude toward beef and increase their willingness to buy it.

Administered by the Beef Industry Council, the current promotional effort follows the successful "Beef Gives Strength" point-of-purchase campaign, which helped raise beef sales by 16 percent in participating stores several years ago. The new campaign, "Real Food for Real People," which previously featured celebrities James Garner and others in television, radio, and print advertisements, now will spotlight noncelebrities from four small U.S. towns with famous names. Each fifteen- or thirty-second spot features a narrator describing how local consumers enjoy beef. A spot filmed in Manhattan, Montana, for example, opens with a skyline shot and features a New York strip steak. The narrator discusses Manhattan's reputation for great restaurants: "Try all three," he says. Additional commercials with the same theme were made for Luck, Wisconsin; Yale, Washington; and Utopia, Texas. This campaign also marks the first time that the council has included nutrition and calorie information in its television advertisements. For instance, one commercial shows that three ounces of sirloin has 172 calories.

The beef industry is aiming most of its current marketing efforts toward two market segments in particular: consumers who have active lifestyles and those who consider themselves health-conscious. A recent survey found that together these two groups make up 50 percent of the market and are the consumers least likely to eat beef. Consumers who seldom or never buy beef are usually between the ages of 25 and 54; have above-average levels of education; earn at least $30,000 annually; and are likely to hold professional, technical, or managerial positions. Because other groups observe and sometimes try to imitate these consumers, the beef industry hopes that the campaign will improve their attitudes toward beef and is therefore directing much of the campaign's budget at them.

The Beef Industry Council is also working on the concept of cooperative advertising with retailers. Its promotional ideas include the following:

1. Sharing the cost of installing in-store videos
2. Developing a scoring system to reward retailers for featuring beef at or above a certain level
3. Finding ways to encourage retailers to buy more pretrimmed beef, thereby sending a message to producers that leaner beef is preferred

To boost demand for beef in individual stores, retailers are supplementing the industrywide promotion with marketing efforts of their own. For example, during the past few years, most major retailers have successfully reduced the fat trim on beef cuts from one-half to one-quarter inch. Some meat experts believe that eventually a one-eighth inch trim will be standard. The ninety-store P&C Food Market chain, based in Syracuse, New York, sells convenience to its shoppers via smaller beef packages for smaller households, precut beef for stir-fry cooking, and pre-stuffed meats and peppers. In its meat departments, P&C also has tested informational videos, which are accompanied by beef recipes and other printed materials for shoppers to take home. The company reports that beef sales remain stable.

The industry also is counting on technology to help meet the demand for new tastes. In the category of light beef—which is at least 25 percent leaner than standard cuts and can be advertised by brand name—several new beef products have been brought to market. One of the first, Key Lite, produced by Texas-based Chianina Lite Beef, Inc., is said to taste as good as choice grade beef, with 36 percent fewer calories. Ranchers in several western states are experimenting with low-cholesterol beef, produced without chemicals. Colorado rancher Mel Coleman has shipped twenty thousand head of "all-natural" cattle raised on pesticide-free corn and alfalfa. Marketed as Coleman Natural Beef, the meat is produced without hormones, growth stimulants, or antibiotics and is available in New York, California, Texas, Colorado, and Massachusetts.

Although meat retailers acknowledge that brand-name and natural beef products may reassure skeptical consumers, resulting in consumer brand loyalty and higher sales for packers, they also point out that the new cuts are usually more expensive than standard beef, which may drive other consumers away. Some retailers believe that the prices of branded beef will drop as sales build.

SOURCES: Cathy Cohn, John Morse, and Patrick Geoghegan, "More Cash, More Pizzazz Could Spell Relief for Beef," *Supermarket News,* Jan. 19, 1987, pp. 12–13; Julie Liesse Erickson, "Beef Council Trims Out Celebrities," *Advertising Age,* Aug. 14, 1989, p. 47; Patrick Geoghegan, "$21 Million Earmarked to End Beef Sales Slump," *Supermarket News,* Nov. 17, 1986, p. 1; Joanne Lipman, "Beefing Up Beef's Allure," *Wall Street Journal,* Oct. 6, 1989, p. B4; Barbara Lippert, "The Beef Council's Celeb-Kabob As Blue Plate Special," *Adweek's Marketing Week,* Sept. 26, 1988, p. 73; Annetta Miller, "And Now, Designer Beef," *Newsweek,* Mar. 10, 1986, p. 57, and "A Sizzling Food Fight," *Newsweek,* Apr. 20, 1987, p. 56; Patricia Natschke, "Ads' Role: Changing Consumer Attitudes," *Supermarket News,* Feb. 15, 1988, p. 25; and Eileen Norris, "Beef Council Leans on Point-of-Purchase," *Advertising Age,* Aug. 15, 1985, p. 32.

Questions for Discussion

1. An attitude refers to knowledge and positive or negative feelings about an object or activity. How have attitudes toward beef changed over the last ten years?
2. How might the American Beef Industry Council change attitudes toward beef?
3. How can culture and subculture explain beef consumption? How might the American Beef Industry Council use this information in developing a marketing strategy for the consumption of beef?

6 ORGANIZATIONAL MARKETS AND BUYING BEHAVIOR

Objectives

To become familiar with the various types of organizational markets

To identify the major characteristics of organizational buyers and transactions

To understand several attributes of organizational demand

To become familiar with the major components of a buying center

To understand the stages of the organizational buying decision process and the factors that affect this process

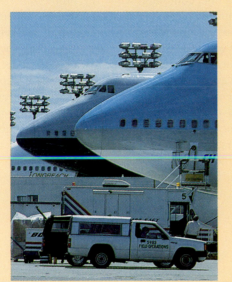

Orders for commercial airplanes are booming as loudly as the jumbo jets themselves. Seattle-based Boeing Co. has recently been bombarded with requests from airlines for its 737s, 747s, 757s, and 767s. As an organizational marketer, Boeing has been immensely successful. Today Boeing holds 55 percent of the orders for commercial jet airliners in the world.

After convincing Northwest, KLM, United Lufthansa, Cathay Pacific, and other airlines to buy its jets, Boeing now faces harsh criticism from these customers for falling several months behind the delivery schedule. These airlines, which had to adjust their flight schedules to compensate for a shortage of aircraft, have requested that Boeing give them cash discounts, complimentary spare parts, and other concessions because it did not fulfill its delivery promises.

Boeing has responded to the rush of orders by increasing its work force to more than 155,000 employees, up 83 percent since 1983. Boeing is also enrolling workers in special training and quality control programs. The company's executives are trying to force its suppliers to speed up delivery of airplane components, but many of Boeing's 1,500 suppliers require long product lead times. For example, landing gears for individual planes need to be ordered at least two years in advance.

With the public's growing concern for airplane safety and the high cost of hiring and training new workers, many analysts predict that Boeing will face tough times in the future, in spite of the currently expanding market due to replacement of old fleets. As Boeing speeds up its production, declining quality may become a major problem. Already two of Boeing's major customers, Japan Air Lines and British Airways, have complained about poor quality.

To maintain its impressive market share, Boeing needs to carefully modernize and expand its plants, as well as use marketing to better serve present customers and attract new ones. ◆

Photo by Rich Frishman.

Based on information from Doug Carroll, "But Boon in Orders Proves to be a Bane," *USA Today,* May 25, 1989, pp. B1–B2; Maria Shao, "Trying Times at Boeing," *Business Week,* Mar. 13, 1989, pp. 34–36; and "Taking the Strain," *The Economist,* Jan. 28, 1989, p. 68.

Although Boeing is struggling with a problem—too many orders—its effective marketing efforts, as well as other factors, led to the problem. Boeing must now employ marketing efforts to keep customers contented while the problem is being resolved. Boeing's customers come from organizational markets; it does not serve ultimate customers directly. We define an organizational or industrial market in Chapter 4 as consisting of individuals or groups that purchase a specific type of product for resale, for use in making other products, or for use in daily operations.

In this chapter we look more closely at organizational markets and organizational buying decision processes. We first discuss the various kinds of organizational markets and the types of buyers that make up these markets. Next we explore several dimensions of organizational buying, such as the characteristics of the transactions, the attributes and concerns of the buyers, the methods of buying, and the distinctive features of the demand for products sold to organizational purchasers. Finally, we examine organizational buying decisions by considering how they are arrived at and who makes the purchases.

TYPES OF ORGANIZATIONAL MARKETS

In Chapter 4 we identify four kinds of organizational, or industrial, markets: producer, reseller, government, and institutional. The following section describes the characteristics of the customers that make up these markets.

■ Producer Markets

Individuals and business organizations that purchase products for the purpose of making a profit by using them to produce other products or by using them in their operations are classified as **producer markets**. Producer markets include buyers of raw materials, as well as purchasers of semifinished and finished items used to produce other products. For example, a manufacturer buys raw materials and component parts to use directly in the production of products. Grocery stores and supermarkets are part of the producer markets for numerous support products, such as paper and plastic bags, counters, scanners, and floor-care products. Farmers are part of the producer markets for farm machinery, fertilizer, seed, and livestock. A broad array of industries make up producer markets; the industries range from agriculture, forestry, fisheries, and mining to construction, transportation, communications, and utilities. As the data in Table 6.1 indicate, the number of business units in national producer markets is enormous.

Manufacturers are geographically concentrated. More than half are located in only seven states: New York, California, Pennsylvania, Illinois, Ohio, New Jersey, and Michigan. This concentration sometimes enables an industrial marketer to serve customers more efficiently. Within certain states, production in just a few industries may account for a sizable proportion of total industrial output.

■ Reseller Markets

Reseller markets consist of intermediaries, such as wholesalers and retailers, who buy finished goods and resell them to make a profit. (Wholesalers and retailers are discussed in Chapters 11 and 12.) Other than making minor alterations, resellers do not change the physical characteristics of the products they handle. With the excep-

TABLE 6.1
Number of firms in industry groups

INDUSTRY	NUMBER OF FIRMS
Agriculture, forestry, fishing	558,000
Mining	279,000
Construction	1,829,000
Manufacturing	633,000
Transportation, public utilities	709,000
Finance, insurance, real estate	2,376,000
Services	6,812,000

SOURCE: *Statistical Abstract of the United States,* 1989, p. 517.

tion of items that producers sell directly to consumers, all products sold to consumer markets are first sold to reseller markets.

Wholesalers purchase products for resale to retailers, to other wholesalers, and to producers, governments, and institutions. Of the 415,829 wholesalers in the United States, a large percentage are located in New York, California, Illinois, Texas, Ohio, Pennsylvania, and New Jersey.[1] Although some highly technical products are sold directly to end users, many products are sold through wholesalers who, in turn, sell products to other firms in the distribution system. Thus wholesalers are very important in helping to get a producer's product to customers. Wholesalers often carry many products, perhaps as many as 250,000 items. When inventories are vast, the reordering of products normally is automated and the wholesaler's initial purchase decisions are made by professional buyers and buying committees.

Retailers purchase products and resell them to final consumers. There are approximately 1.44 million retailers in the United States. They employ about 16 million people and generate close to $1 trillion in annual sales.[2] Some retailers carry a large number of items. Drugstores, for example, may stock up to 12,000 items, and some supermarkets may handle as many as 20,000 different products. In small, family-owned retail stores, the owner frequently makes purchasing decisions. Large department stores have one or more employees in each department who are responsible for buying products for that department. As for chain stores, a buyer or buying committee in the central office frequently decides whether a product will be made available for selection by store managers. For most products, however, local store management makes the actual buying decisions for a particular store.

When making purchase decisions, resellers consider several factors. They evaluate the level of demand for a product to determine in what quantity and at what prices the product can be resold. They assess the amount of space required to handle a product relative to its potential profit. In Figure 6.1, Nabisco's message to resellers, specifically grocery stores, deals with the profitability of the six featured brands. Retailers, for example, sometimes evaluate products on the basis of sales per square foot of selling area. Since customers often depend on a reseller to have a product when they need it, a reseller typically evaluates a supplier's ability to

1. *Statistical Abstract of the United States,* 1989, p. 763.

2. Ibid., p. 753.

FIGURE 6.1

Focusing on reseller markets.

Nabisco's message to resellers emphasizes the profitability of stocking these brands.

SOURCE: Nabisco Biscuit Company.

provide adequate quantities when and where wanted. Resellers also take into account the ease of placing orders and the availability of technical assistance and training programs from the producer. More broadly, when resellers consider buying a product not previously carried, they try to determine whether the product competes with or complements products the firm is currently handling. These types of concerns distinguish reseller markets from other markets. Marketers dealing with reseller markets must recognize these needs and be able to serve them.

■ **Government Markets**

Federal, state, county, and local governments make up **government markets**. They spend billions of dollars annually for a variety of goods and services to support their internal operations and to provide citizens with such products as highways, education, water, energy, and national defense. For example, in 1987, the U.S. federal government spent more than $280 billion on defense.[3] Governmental expenditures annually account for about 20 percent of the U.S. gross national product.

Besides the federal government, there are 50 state governments, 3,042 county governments, and 83,166 other local governments.[4] The amount spent by federal,

3. *Statistical Abstract of the United States,* 1989, p. 326.

4. Ibid., p. 266.

TABLE 6.2

Annual expenditures by government units for selected years (in billions of dollars)

YEAR	TOTAL GOVERNMENT EXPENDITURES	FEDERAL GOVERNMENT EXPENDITURES	STATE AND LOCAL EXPENDITURES
1960	151	90	61
1970	333	185	148
1975	560	292	268
1980	959	526	432
1981	1,110	625	485
1983	1,351	786	565
1986	1,696	844	852

SOURCE: *Statistical Abstract of the United States*, 1989, p. 268.

state, and local units during the last thirty years has increased rapidly because the total number of government units and the services they provide have both increased. In addition, the costs of providing these services have increased. In Table 6.2, notice that the federal government spends just under half of the total amount spent by all governments.

The types and quantities of products bought by government markets reflect societal demands on various government agencies. As citizens' needs for government services change, so does the demand for products by government markets. Because government agencies spend public funds to buy the products needed to provide services, they are accountable to the public. This accountability explains their relatively complex set of buying procedures. Some firms do not even try to sell to government buyers because they do not want to deal with so much red tape. However, many marketers have learned to deal efficiently with government procedures and do not find them to be a stumbling block. For certain products, such as defense-related items, the government may be the only customer. The U.S. Government Printing Office publishes and distributes several documents explaining buying procedures and describing the types of products various federal agencies purchase.

The government makes its purchases through bids or negotiated contracts. To make a sale under the bid system, a firm must apply for and be approved in order to be placed on a list of qualified bidders. When a government unit wants to buy, it sends out a detailed description of the products to qualified bidders. Businesses that wish to sell such products submit bids. The government unit usually is required to accept the lowest bid. When buying nonstandard or highly complex products, a government unit often uses a negotiated contract. Under this procedure, the government unit selects only a few firms and then negotiates specifications and terms; it eventually awards the contract to one of the negotiating firms. Most large defense-related contracts held by such companies as McDonnell Douglas, General Dynamics, Northrop, and others are made through negotiated contracts.

Although government markets can have complicated requirements, they can also be very lucrative. When the Postal Service or other government agencies modernize obsolete computer systems, successful bidders can gain a billion dollars during the life of a contract, which is usually five years or more. Some firms have established separate departments to facilitate marketing to government units.

■ Institutional Markets

Organizations that seek to achieve charitable, educational, community, or other nonbusiness goals constitute **institutional markets**. Members of institutional markets include churches, some hospitals, civic clubs, fraternities and sororities, colleges, and charitable organizations. Institutions purchase millions of dollars' worth of products annually to provide goods, services, and ideas to congregations, students, patients, club members, and others. Because institutions often have different goals and fewer resources than other types of organizations, marketers may use special marketing activities to serve these markets.

DIMENSIONS OF ORGANIZATIONAL BUYING

Having gained an understanding of the different types of organizational customers, we now need to consider the dimensions of organizational buying. First we examine several characteristics of organizational transactions. Then we discuss several attributes of organizational buyers and some of their primary concerns when making purchase decisions. Next we consider methods of organizational buying and the major types of purchases. We conclude the section with a discussion of how the demand for industrial products differs from the demand for consumer products.

■ Characteristics of Organizational Transactions

Organizational (or industrial) transactions differ from consumer sales in several ways. Orders by organizational buyers tend to be much larger than individual consumer sales. Suppliers often must sell their products in large quantities to make profits; consequently, they prefer not to sell to customers who place small orders.

Generally, organizational purchases are negotiated less frequently than consumer sales. Some purchases involve expensive items, such as machinery, that are used for a number of years. Other products, such as raw materials and component items, are used continuously in production and may have to be supplied frequently. However, the contract regarding the terms of sale of these items is likely to be a long-term agreement, requiring negotiations, for example, every third year.

Although negotiations in organizational sales are less frequent than in consumer sales, they may take much longer. Purchasing decisions are often made by a committee; orders are frequently large and expensive; and products may be custom-built. There is a good chance that several people or departments in the purchasing organization will be involved. One department might express a need for a product; a second department might develop its specifications; a third might stipulate the maximum amount to be spent; and a fourth might actually place the order.

One practice unique to organizational sales is **reciprocity**, an arrangement in which two organizations agree to buy from each other. Reciprocal agreements that threaten competition are illegal. The Federal Trade Commission and the Justice Department take action to stop anticompetitive reciprocal practices. Nonetheless, it is reasonable to believe that a certain amount of reciprocal dealing occurs among small businesses and, to a lesser extent, among larger companies as well. Because reciprocity influences purchasing agents to deal only with certain suppliers, it can lower morale among agents and lead to less-than-optimal purchases.

■ Attributes of Organizational Buyers

We usually think of organizational buyers as being different from consumer buyers in their purchasing behavior because they are better informed than consumer buyers about the products they purchase. To make purchasing decisions that fulfill an organization's needs, organizational buyers demand detailed information about products' functional features and technical specifications.

Organizational buyers, however, also have personal goals that may influence their buying behavior. Most organizational purchasing agents seek the psychological satisfaction that comes with organizational advancement and financial rewards. Agents who consistently exhibit rational organizational buying behavior are likely to achieve these personal goals because they are performing their jobs in ways that help their firms achieve organizational objectives. Suppose, though, that an organizational buyer develops a close friendship with a certain supplier. If the buyer values friendship more than organizational promotion or financial rewards, he or she may behave irrationally from the firm's point of view. Dealing exclusively with that supplier regardless of better prices, product qualities, or services from competitors may indicate an unhealthy or unethical alliance between the buyer and seller.

■ Primary Concerns of Organizational Buyers

When they make purchasing decisions, organizational customers take into account a variety of factors. Among their chief considerations are quality, service, and price.

Most organizational customers try to achieve and maintain a specific level of quality in the products they offer to their target markets. To accomplish this goal, they often buy their products on the basis of a set of expressed characteristics, commonly called *specifications*. Thus an organizational buyer evaluates the quality of the products being considered to determine whether they meet specifications.

Meeting specifications is extremely important to organizational customers. If a product fails to meet specifications and malfunctions for the ultimate consumer, the organizational customer may drop that product's supplier and switch to a different one. On the other hand, organizational customers are ordinarily cautious about buying products that exceed specifications because such products often cost more and thus increase an organization's production costs.

Organizational buyers also value service. The services offered by suppliers influence directly and indirectly organizational customers' costs, sales, and profits. When tangible goods are the same or quite similar—as is true in the case of most raw materials—the goods may be sold at the same price in the same kind of containers and may have the same specifications. Under such conditions, the mix of services provided to customers is likely to be the major way that an organizational marketer gains a competitive advantage. As shown in Figure 6.2, the industrial chemicals division of Procter & Gamble, for example, promotes a specific mix of services.

Specific services vary in importance. Among those commonly desired are market information, inventory maintenance, on-time delivery, repair services, and credit. Organizational buyers are likely to need technical product information, data regarding demand, information about general economic conditions, or supply and delivery information. Maintaining an adequate inventory is critical because it helps make products accessible when an organizational buyer needs them and reduces the buyer's inventory requirements and costs. Since organizational buyers are usually responsible for ensuring that the products are on hand and ready for use when needed, on-time delivery is crucial. Furthermore, reliable, on-time delivery saves the organizational customers money, enabling them to carry less inventory. Organizational purchasers of machinery are especially concerned about obtaining repair services and replacement parts quickly because inoperable equipment is costly. Caterpillar Inc., a manufacturer of earth-moving, construction, and materials-handling machinery, has built an international reputation, as well as high profits, by providing prompt service and replacement parts for its products around the world.

FIGURE 6.2

Services mix.
Procter & Gamble's
industrial chemicals division indicates that
it sells satisfaction
through an extensive mix
of customer services.

SOURCE: The Procter & Gamble Company

Suppliers can also give extra value to organizational buyers by offering credit. Credit helps improve an organizational customer's cash flow and reduce the peaks and valleys of capital requirements, thus lowering the firm's cost of capital. Although a single supplier cannot provide every possible service to its organizational customers, a marketing-oriented supplier creates a service mix that satisfies the target market.

Providing service has become even more critical for organizational marketers because customer expectations about service have broadened. Now, for instance, communication channels that allow customers to ask questions, complain, submit orders, and trace shipments are indispensable aspects of service. Organizational marketers also need to strive for uniformity of service, simplicity, truthfulness, and accuracy; develop customer service objectives; and monitor or audit their customer service programs. Firms can monitor their service by formally surveying customers or informally calling on customers and asking questions about the service they received. Marketers with a strong customer service program reap a reward: their customers keep coming back long after the first sale.[5] To succeed with their program, however, they must conduct research to determine customers' expectations in regard to product quality and service.[6]

5. John I. Coppett, "Auditing Your Customer Service Activities," *Industrial Marketing Management*, November 1988, pp. 277–284.

6. Thomas L. Powers, "Identify and Fulfill Customer Service Expectations," *Industrial Marketing Management*, November 1988, pp. 273–276.

Price matters greatly to an organizational customer because it influences operating costs and costs of goods sold, and these costs affect the customer's selling price and profit margin. When purchasing major equipment, an industrial buyer views the price as the amount of investment necessary to obtain a certain level of return or savings. Thus an organizational purchaser is likely to compare the price of a machine with the value of the benefits that the machine will yield. Caterpillar lost market share to foreign competitors because its prices were too high (see Marketing Update 6.1). An organizational buyer does not compare alternative products strictly by price; other factors, such as product quality and supplier services, are also major elements in the purchase decision. For example, one study found that in the buying decision process for mainframe computer software operating systems, buyers indicated that intangible attributes, such as the seller's credibility and understanding of the buyer's needs, were very important in the decision process.[7]

Methods of Organizational Buying

Although no two organizational buyers go about their jobs in the same way, most use one or more of the following purchase methods: *description, inspection, sampling,* or *negotiation.* When the products being purchased are commonly standardized according to certain characteristics (such as size, shape, weight, and color) and are normally graded using such standards, an organizational buyer may be able to purchase simply by describing or specifying quantity, grade, and other attributes. Agricultural produce often fall into this category. In some cases, a buyer may specify a particular brand or its equivalent when describing the desired product. Purchases on the basis of description are especially common between a buyer and seller who have established an ongoing relationship built on trust.

Certain products, such as large industrial equipment, used vehicles, and buildings, have unique characteristics and may vary regarding their condition. For example, a particular used truck might have a bad transmission. Consequently, organizational buyers of such products must base their purchase decisions on inspection.

In buying based on sampling, a sample of the product is taken from the lot and evaluated. It is assumed that the characteristics of this sample represent the entire lot. This method is appropriate when the product is homogeneous—for instance, grain—and examination of the entire lot is not physically or economically feasible.

Some industrial purchasing relies on negotiated contracts. In certain instances, an organizational buyer describes exactly what is needed and then asks sellers to submit bids. The buyer may take the most attractive bids and negotiate with those suppliers. In other cases, the buyer may not be able to identify specifically what is to be purchased but can provide only a general description—as might be the case for a special piece of custom-made equipment. A buyer and seller might negotiate a contract that specifies a base price and contains provisions for the payment of additional costs and fees. These contracts are most likely to be used for one-time projects, such as buildings and capital equipment.

Types of Organizational Purchases

Most organizational purchases are one of three types: new-task purchase, modified rebuy purchase, or straight rebuy purchase. In a **new-task purchase**, an organization makes an initial purchase of an item to be used to perform a new job or to solve a new problem. A new-task purchase may require the development of product specifications, vendor specifications, and procedures for future purchases of that

---

7. Jim Shaw, Joe Giglierano, and Jeff Kallis, "Marketing Complex Technical Products: The Importance of Intangible Attributes," *Industrial Marketing Management,* 18 (1989), pp. 45–53.

CATERPILLAR CUTS COSTS TO BECOME MORE COMPETITIVE

Caterpillar Inc., manufacturer of construction, materials-handling, and earth-moving machinery, has had to change—and change quickly—to successfully compete with foreign competitors. After Japanese and European competitors acquired huge chunks of market share in the United States and in Europe, Caterpillar executives turned their undivided attention toward revitalizing their production plants. Caterpillar officials knew that they had to become more flexible and respond to market demands more quickly.

Caterpillar installed its System 100 dynamic-simulation computer to reduce product development times. The computerized modeling system has worked tremendously well. The System 100 is a real-time simulation system that tests new control systems for earth-moving vehicles and diesel engines. By using this system, workers can now run the equivalent of 30 instrumented tests in one day.

Caterpillar officials have also integrated machines and processors and have altered the physical locations of factory machinery to speed manufacturing. Fewer machine tools and the reduction of material handling have led to greater efficiency. Plant automation has also brought Caterpillar reduced labor costs and improved product quality. Its "Plant With a Future" (PWAF) program has cost the company over one billion dollars but has turned Caterpillar into one of the world's most efficient builders of equipment.

As Caterpillar employees continue to simplify product designs, rearrange plant floors, and further employ their "common sense" approach to manufacturing, Caterpillar executives feel confident that they will continue to successfully compete with foreign rivals. Caterpillar's improved plants and shorter product development times have allowed it to enter new markets with new machines faster than other companies. Caterpillar may face increased competition in the future, though, as rivals begin to copy Caterpillar's methods and strategy.

SOURCES: "Computerized Modeling for Faster Product Development," *Diesel Progress,* November 1988, pp. 60, 62; Dave Fusaro, "Caterpillar, Deere, Case Do Big Things in Small Cells," *Metalworking News,* April 18, 1988, p. 17; and Lauri Giesen, "Caterpillar Reveals Billion Dollar PWAF Program," *Metalworking News,* June 6, 1988, pp. 4, 29.

product. To make the initial purchase, the organizational buyer usually needs much information. A new-task purchase is important to a supplier, for if the organizational buyer is satisfied with the product, the supplier may be able to sell the buyer large quantities of the product for a period of years.

In a **modified rebuy purchase**, a new-task purchase is changed the second or third time it is ordered or the requirements associated with a straight rebuy purchase are modified. For example, an organizational buyer might seek faster delivery, lower prices, or a different quality level of product specifications. A modified rebuy situation may cause regular suppliers to become more competitive to keep the account. Competing suppliers may have the opportunity to obtain the business.

A **straight rebuy purchase** occurs when a buyer purchases the same products routinely under approximately the same terms of sale. Buyers require little information for these routine purchase decisions. The buyer tends to use familiar suppliers that have provided satisfactory service and products in the past. These suppliers try to set up automatic reordering systems to make reordering easy and convenient for organizational buyers. A supplier may even monitor the organizational buyer's inventory and indicate to the buyer what needs to be ordered.

■ Demand for Industrial Products

Products sold to organizational customers are called industrial products, and consequently, the demand for these products is called industrial demand. Unlike consumer demand, industrial demand is (1) derived, (2) inelastic, (3) joint, and (4) more fluctuating. As we discuss each of these characteristics, remember that the demand for different types of industrial products varies.

Derived Demand.   Because organizational customers, especially producers, buy products to be used directly or indirectly in the production of goods and services to satisfy consumers' needs, the demand for industrial products derives from the demand for consumer products; therefore it is called **derived demand**. For example, the demand for certain types of computer chips derives from consumers' demands for faster and smaller personal computers. In the long run, no industrial demand is totally unrelated to the demand for consumer goods.

The derived nature of industrial demand is usually multilevel. Industrial sellers at different levels are affected by a change in consumer demand for a particular product. For instance, consumers today are more concerned with health and good nutrition than ever before, and as a result are purchasing more products with less cholesterol and salt. When consumers stopped buying high-cholesterol shortenings and margarine, the demand for equipment used in manufacturing these products also dropped. Thus factors influencing consumer buying of various food products affected food processors, equipment manufacturers, suppliers of raw materials, and even fast-food restaurants, which have had to switch to vegetable oils for frying. Changes in derived demand result from a chain reaction. When consumer demand for a product changes, a wave is set in motion that affects demand for all firms involved in the production of that consumer product.

Inelastic Demand.   The demand for many industrial products at the industry level is inelastic, which simply means that a price increase or decrease will not significantly alter demand for the item. (The concept of price elasticity of demand is discussed further in Chapter 18.) Because many industrial products contain a number of parts, price increases that affect only one or two parts of the product may yield only a slightly higher per-unit production cost. Of course, when a sizable price increase for a component represents a large proportion of the product's cost, then demand may become more elastic because the price increase in the component causes the price at the consumer level to rise sharply. For example, if manufacturers of aircraft engines substantially increase the price of these engines, forcing Boeing to raise the prices of the aircraft it manufactures, the demand for airliners may become more elastic as airlines reconsider whether they can afford to buy new aircraft. An increase in the price of windshields, however, is unlikely to greatly affect the price of the airliners or the demand for them.

The characteristic of inelasticity applies only to industry demand for the industrial product, not to the demand curve faced by an individual firm. Suppose that a spark plug producer increases the price of spark plugs sold to manufacturers of small engines but its competitors continue to maintain their lower prices. The spark plug company would probably experience reduced unit sales because most small-engine producers would switch to the lower-priced brands. A specific firm is vulnerable to elastic demand, even though industry demand for a particular product is inelastic.

Joint Demand.   The demand for certain industrial products, especially raw materials and components, is subject to joint demand. **Joint demand** occurs when two or more items are used in combination to produce a product. For example, a firm that manufactures axes needs the same number of ax handles as it does ax blades; these two products are demanded jointly. If there is a shortage of ax handles, then the producer will buy fewer ax blades.

Understanding the effects of joint demand is particularly important for a marketer selling multiple jointly demanded items. Such a marketer must realize that when a customer begins purchasing one of the jointly demanded items, a good opportunity exists for selling related products. Similarly, when customers purchase a number of jointly demanded products, the producer must exercise extreme caution to avoid shortages of any one of them because such shortages jeopardize the marketer's sales of all the jointly demanded products.

Demand Fluctuations.   As already mentioned, the demand for industrial products may fluctuate enormously because it is derived from consumer demand. In general, when particular consumer products are in high demand, their producers buy large quantities of raw materials and components to ensure that they can meet long-run production requirements. In addition, these producers may expand their production capacity, which entails the acquisition of new equipment and machinery, more workers, and more raw materials and component parts.

Conversely, a decline in the demand for certain consumer goods significantly reduces the demand for industrial products used to produce those goods. In fact, under such conditions, a marketer's sales of certain products may come to a temporary standstill. When consumer demand is low, industrial customers cut their purchases of raw materials and components and stop buying equipment and machinery, even for replacement purposes.

A marketer of industrial products may notice changes in demand when its customers change their inventory policies, perhaps because of expectations about future demand. For example, if several dishwasher manufacturers who buy timers from one producer increase their inventory of timers from a two-week to a one-month supply, the timer producer will have a significant immediate increase in demand.

Sometimes price changes can lead to surprising temporary changes in demand. A price increase for an industrial item may initially cause organizational customers to buy more of the item because they expect the price to rise further. Similarly, demand for an industrial product may be significantly lower following a price cut because buyers are waiting for further price reductions. Fluctuations in demand can be significant in industries in which price changes occur frequently.

ORGANIZATIONAL BUYING DECISIONS

Organizational (or **industrial**) **buying behavior** refers to the purchase behavior of producers, resellers, government units, and institutions. Although several of the same factors that affect consumer buying behavior (discussed in Chapter 5) also influence organizational buying behavior, a number of factors are unique to the latter. In this section we first analyze the buying center to learn who participates in making organizational purchase decisions. Then we focus on the stages of the buying decision process and the factors that affect it.

■ **The Buying Center**

Relatively few organizational purchase decisions are made by just one person; mostly, they are made through a buying center. The **buying center** refers to the group of people within an organization who are involved in making organizational purchase decisions. These individuals include users, influencers, buyers, deciders, and gatekeepers.[8] One person may perform several of these roles. These participants share some goals and risks associated with their decisions.

Users are the organization members who actually use the product being acquired. They frequently initiate the purchase process and/or generate the specifications for the purchase. After the purchase, they also evaluate the product's performance relative to the specifications. Influencers are often technical personnel, such as engineers, who help develop the specifications and evaluate alternative products. Technical personnel are especially important influencers when the products being considered involve new, advanced technology.

Buyers are responsible for selecting suppliers and actually negotiating the terms of purchase. They may also become involved in developing specifications. Buyers are sometimes called purchasing agents or purchasing managers. Their choices of vendors and products, especially for new-task purchases, are heavily influenced by persons occupying other roles in the buying center. For straight rebuy purchases, the buyer plays a major role in the selection of vendors and in negotiations with them. Deciders actually choose the products and vendors. Although buyers may be the deciders, it is not unusual for different people to occupy these roles. For routinely purchased items, buyers are commonly the deciders. However, a buyer may not be authorized to make purchases that exceed a certain dollar limit, in which case higher-level management personnel are the deciders. Gatekeepers, such as secretaries and technical personnel, control the flow of information to and among the persons who occupy the other roles in the buying center. Buyers who deal directly with vendors also may be gatekeepers because they can control the flow of information. The flow of information from supplier sales representatives to users and influencers often is controlled by personnel in the purchasing department.

The number and structure of an organization's buying centers are affected by the organization's size and market position, by the volume and types of products being

---

8. Frederick E. Webster, Jr., and Yoram Wind, *Organizational Buying Behavior* (Englewood Cliffs, N.J.: Prentice-Hall, 1972), pp. 78–80.

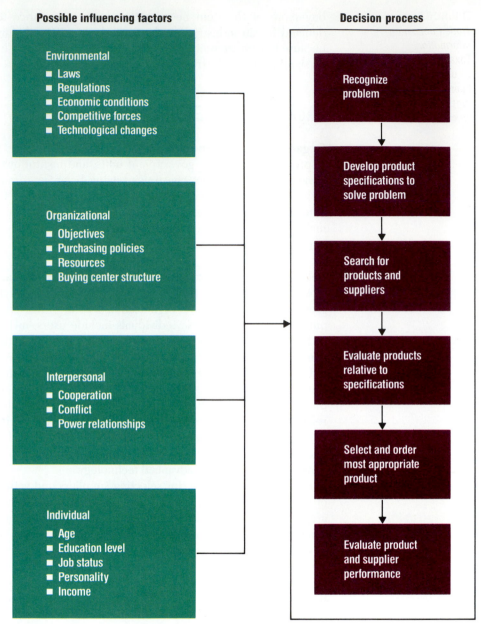

FIGURE 6.3
Organizational buying decision process and factors that may influence it

Possible influencing factors

Environmental
- Laws
- Regulations
- Economic conditions
- Competitive forces
- Technological changes

Organizational
- Objectives
- Purchasing policies
- Resources
- Buying center structure

Interpersonal
- Cooperation
- Conflict
- Power relationships

Individual
- Age
- Education level
- Job status
- Personality
- Income

Decision process

- Recognize problem
- Develop product specifications to solve problem
- Search for products and suppliers
- Evaluate products relative to specifications
- Select and order most appropriate product
- Evaluate product and supplier performance

SOURCE: Adapted from Frederick E. Webster, Jr., and Yoram Wind, *Organizational Buying Behavior*, 1972, pp. 33–37. Adapted by permission of Prentice-Hall, Englewood Cliffs, N.J.

purchased, and by the firm's overall managerial philosophy regarding exactly who should be involved in purchase decisions. A marketer attempting to sell to an organizational customer should determine who is in the buying center, the types of decisions each individual makes, and which individuals are the most influential in the decision process. Because in some instances many people make up the buying center, marketers cannot contact all participants; instead, they must be certain to contact a few of the most influential.

SOURCE: Courtesy of Texaco Chemical Company

■ Stages of the Organizational Buying Decision Process

Like consumers, organizations follow a buying decision process. It is summarized on the right side of Figure 6.3. In the first stage, one or more individuals recognize that a problem or need exists. Problem recognition may arise under a variety of circumstances, for instance, when a machine malfunctions or a firm is modifying an existing product or introducing a new one. Individuals in the buying center, such as users, influencers, or buyers, may be involved in problem recognition, but it may be stimulated by external sources, such as sales representatives.

The second stage of the process—development of product specifications—requires organizational participants to assess the problem or need and determine what will be necessary to resolve or satisfy it. During this stage, users and influencers, such as technical personnel and engineers, often provide information and advice for developing product specifications. By assessing and describing needs, the organization should be able to establish product specifications.

Searching for possible products to solve the problem and locating suppliers is the third stage in the decision process. Search activities may involve looking in company files and trade directories, contacting suppliers for information, soliciting proposals from known vendors, and examining catalogs and trade publications. The industrial advertisement in Figure 6.4 is an example of information available in trade publi-

SOURCE: Shuford Mills Inc. Special Products Division

cations. Some vendors may not be viewed as acceptable because they are not large enough to supply the needed quantities, and others may have poor records of delivery and service. In some instances the product is not available from any existing vendor and the buyer must find a company that can design and build the product. Innovative companies, like 3M (see Marketing Update 6.2), are sought.

If all goes well, the search stage will result in a list of several alternative products and suppliers. The fourth stage is evaluating the products on the list to determine which ones (if any) meet the product specifications developed in the second stage. The advertisement in Figure 6.5 stresses the product performance characteristics of Shurtuff Envelopes and helps potential customers determine if the product meets their specifications. At this point, too, various suppliers are evaluated according to multiple criteria, such as price, service, and ability to deliver.

The results of the deliberations and assessments in the fourth stage are used during the fifth stage to select the product to be purchased and the supplier from whom to buy it. In some cases, the buyer may decide to choose several suppliers. In others, only one supplier is selected—a situation known as sole sourcing. Sole sourcing has traditionally been discouraged except when a product is available from only one company; firms that have contracts with the federal government are still required to have several sources for an item. Sole sourcing is becoming more popular today, partly because such an arrangement means better communications

3M COMPANY: AN INNOVATIVE SOURCE

Since its early days, Minnesota Mining & Manufacturing, the St. Paul, Minnesota–based 3M Company, has had a reputation for innovation and creativity. Having developed over 60,000 products ranging from the popular Post-it note and familiar Scotch tape to a synthetic ligament for injured knees and translucent dental braces, 3M is a virtual new-product machine.

3M encourages employees to develop new products. Employees are allowed to spend 15 percent of their time at work on their own projects. They can apply for special 3M Genesis grants that provide researchers with up to $50,000 for individual projects. They can actually manage the new product if it proves to be successful. And management is as tolerant of experimental failures as they are supportive of potential blockbusters. 3M even ties employee promotions and bonuses to new product development.

Employees at 3M use their entrepreneurial spirit to pursue organizational markets as well. One 3M chemist created a special filter to clean lubricants in metalworking shops. The market for such a filter, even though it worked extremely well, was worth only one million dollars. Management was so impressed, however, that it allowed the employee to continue to tinker with the filter. Eventually, the worker entered into a joint venture with a 3M customer, PPG Industries Inc., which sells paint-primer systems to car manufacturers. Apparently, the filters PPG employees were using to strain out impurities were not very effective, and the 3M chemist's filters turned out to work much better. It was later discovered that the filters were also efficient strainers for machine oil, paint, edible oils, water, and beer. Now, the filters serve a $20 million market.

Employees at 3M are constantly trying to discover products that will fill industrial and organizational niches. The creative spirit at 3M gives employees the flexibility and encouragement they need to keep producing technological breakthroughs. It is no wonder that some business analysts consider 3M to be the most innovative company in the world.

SOURCES: Russell Mitchell, "Masters of Innovation," *Business Week,* April 10, 1989, pp. 58–63; Margaret Nelson, "Top Priority at 3M Is Communications," *Purchasing,* March 10, 1988, pp. 104–105, 109; and Thomas Osborn, "How 3M Manages for Innovation," *Marketing Communications,* November/ December 1988, pp. 17–22.

between buyer and supplier, stability and higher profits for the supplier, and often lower prices for the buyer. However, most organizations still prefer to purchase goods and services from several suppliers because this approach lessens the possibility of disruption caused by strikes, shortages, or bankruptcy. The actual product is ordered in this fifth stage and specific details regarding terms, credit arrangements, delivery dates and methods, and technical assistance are worked out.

During the sixth stage, the product's performance is evaluated by comparing it with specifications. Sometimes, even though the product meets the specifications, its performance does not adequately solve the problem or satisfy the need recognized in the first stage. In that case, the product specifications must be adjusted. The supplier's performance is also evaluated during this stage, and if it is found wanting, the organizational purchaser seeks corrective action from the supplier or searches for a new supplier. The results of the evaluation become feedback for the other stages and influence future organizational purchase decisions.

This organizational buying decision process is used in its entirety primarily for new-task purchases. Several of the stages, but not necessarily all, are used for modified rebuy and straight rebuy situations.

■ Influences on Organizational Buying

Figure 6.3 also lists the four major categories of factors that influence organizational buying decisions: environmental, organizational, interpersonal, and individual.

You may remember from Chapter 2 that environmental factors are uncontrollable forces such as politics, laws, regulations and regulatory agencies, activities of interest groups, changes in the economy, competitors' actions, and technological changes. These forces generate a considerable amount of uncertainty for an organization, and the uncertainty can make individuals in the buying center apprehensive about certain types of purchases. Changes in one or more environmental forces can create new purchasing opportunities and make yesterday's purchase decisions look terrible. For example, rapid developments in computer and communications technology sometimes render newly purchased computer or telephone systems obsolete, or at least less desirable, in only a few years. For this reason, organizations approach the buying decision process for such products with special caution.

Organizational factors influencing the organizational buying decision process include the buyer's objectives, purchasing policies, and resources, as well as the size and composition of its buying center. An organization may have certain buying policies to which buying center participants must conform. For instance, a firm's policies may mandate long-term contracts, perhaps longer than most sellers desire. The nature of an organization's financial resources may require special credit arrangements. Any of these conditions could affect purchase decision processes.

The interpersonal factors are the relationships among the people in the buying center. The use of power and the level of conflict among buying center participants influence organizational buying decisions. Certain persons in the buying center may be better communicators than others and may be more convincing. Often these interpersonal dynamics are hidden, making them difficult for marketers to assess.

Individual factors are the personal characteristics of individuals in the buying center, such as age, education, personality, and position in the organization. For example, a 55-year-old manager who has been in the organization for twenty-five years may affect the decisions made by the buying center differently than a 30-year-old person who has been employed only two years. How influential these factors are depends on the buying situation, the type of product being purchased, and whether the purchase is new-task, modified rebuy, or straight rebuy. The negotiating styles of people vary within an organization and from one organization to another. To be effective, a marketer must know customers well enough to be aware of these individual factors and the effects they may have on purchase decisions.

SUMMARY

Organizational markets consist of individuals and groups that purchase a specific kind of product for resale, for direct use in producing other products, or for use in day-to-day operations. Producer markets include those individuals and business organizations that purchase products for the purpose of making a profit by using them to produce other products or by using them in their operations. Intermediaries who buy finished products and resell them for the purpose of making a profit are classified as reseller markets. Government markets consist of federal, state, and local governments, which spend billions of dollars annually for goods and services to support their internal operations and provide citizens with needed services. Organizations that seek to achieve charity, education, community, or other not-for-profit goals constitute institutional markets.

Organizational transactions differ from consumer transactions in several ways. The transactions tend to be larger, and negotiations occur less frequently, though they are often lengthy. Organizational transactions sometimes involve more than one person or one department in the purchasing organization. They may also involve reciprocity, an arrangement in which two organizations agree to buy from each other. Organizational customers are usually viewed as more rational than ultimate consumers and as more likely to seek information about a product's features and technical specifications.

When purchasing products, organizational customers are particularly concerned about quality, service, and price. Quality is important because it directly affects the quality of products the buyer's firm produces. To achieve an exact level of quality, organizations often buy their products on the basis of a set of expressed characteristics, called specifications. Because services can have such a direct influence on a firm's costs, sales, and profits, such matters as market information, on-time delivery, and availability of parts can be crucial to an organizational buyer. Although an organizational customer does not depend solely on price to decide which products to buy, price is of prime concern because it directly influences a firm's profitability.

Organizational buyers use several purchasing methods, including description, inspection, sampling, and negotiation. Most organizational purchases are new task, modified rebuy, or straight rebuy. In a new-task purchase, an organization makes an initial purchase of an item to be used to perform a new job or to solve a problem. In a modified rebuy purchase, a new-task purchase is changed the second or third time it is ordered or the requirements associated with a straight rebuy purchase are modified. A straight rebuy purchase occurs when a buyer purchases the same products routinely under approximately the same terms of sale.

Industrial demand differs from consumer demand along several dimensions. Industrial demand derives from the demand for consumer products. At the industry level, industrial demand is inelastic. If the price of an industrial item changes, demand for the product will not change as much proportionally. Some industrial products are subject to joint demand, which occurs when two or more items are used in combination to make a product. Finally, because industrial demand derives from consumer demand, the demand for industrial products can fluctuate widely.

Organizational, or industrial, buying behavior refers to the purchase behavior of producers, resellers, government units, and institutions. Organizational purchase decisions are made through a buying center—the group of people who are involved in making organizational purchase decisions. Users are those in the organization who actually use the product. Influencers help develop the specifications and evaluate alternative products for possible use. Buyers are responsible for selecting the suppliers and negotiating the terms of the purchases. Deciders choose the products and vendors. Gatekeepers control the flow of information to and among persons who occupy the other roles in the buying center.

The stages of the organizational buying decision process are problem recognition, the development of product specifications to solve the problem, the search for products and suppliers, evaluation of products relative to specifications, selection and ordering of the most appropriate product, and evaluation of the product's and the supplier's performance.

Four categories of factors influence organizational buying decisions: environmental, organizational, interpersonal, and individual. The environmental factors include laws and regulations, economic conditions, competitive forces, and technological changes. Organizational factors influencing the organizational buying decision process include the buyer's objectives, purchasing policies, and resources, as well as the size and composition of its buying center. The interpersonal factors are the relationships among the people in the buying center. Individual factors are the personal characteristics of individuals in the buying center, such as age, education, personality, position in the organization, and income.

Important Terms

Producer markets
Reseller markets
Government markets
Institutional markets
Reciprocity
New-task purchase
Modified rebuy purchase

Straight rebuy purchase
Derived demand
Joint demand
Organizational (or industrial) buying
  behavior
Buying center

Discussion and Review Questions

1. Identify, describe, and give examples of four major types of organizational markets.
2. Regarding purchasing behavior, why are organizational buyers generally considered more rational than ultimate consumers?
3. What are the primary concerns of organizational buyers?
4. List several characteristics that differentiate organizational transactions from consumer ones.
5. What are the commonly used methods of organizational buying?

6. Why do buyers involved in a straight rebuy purchase require less information than those making a new-task purchase?
7. How does industrial demand differ from consumer demand?
8. What are the major components of a buying center?
9. Identify the stages of the organizational buying decision process. How is this decision process used when making straight rebuys?
10. How do environmental, organizational, interpersonal, and individual factors affect organizational purchases?

◼ CASES

6.1 Faber-Castell Markets Low-Tech Products to Organizational Markets

When Faber-Castell Corp. finalized its acquisition of Eberhard Faber Inc., the rejoining of two major writing instrument companies was complete. Both firms trace their ancestry to Kaspar Faber, the inventor of pencil lead as we know it. In the late nineteenth century, the Faber pencil business split into three separate companies: German-based A.W. Faber-Castell Corp., Faber-Castell Corp., and Eberhard Faber.

Eberhard Faber, the originator of the familiar yellow pencil, had been producing wood-cased pencils since 1849, maintaining a 10 percent share of the $100 million pencil market. The company's sales of pencils, pens, erasers, and rubber bands had been increasing in Third World countries, but recent U.S. sales had been essentially static. As a result, Eberhard Faber's U.S. pencil sales accounted for less than 20 percent of its worldwide sales, and earnings had declined during recent years.

When the pencil market became particularly competitive in the early 1980s, Eberhard Faber's top management concluded that the key to greater domestic profitability was marketing. At first the firm made some mistakes. For example, after producing yellow pencils for nearly a century, the company decided to introduce a natural-looking pencil: bare cedar wood covered with a coat of clear lacquer. Eberhard Faber projected a 15 percent market share for the new product, thinking that the current trend toward naturalness would carry over into the pencil market. But pencil dealers avoided the new product, preferring to stick with a proven seller.

Another strategic miscalculation involved the company's redoubled efforts in art supplies, a market that yields greater profit margins than the highly competitive office products market. Because Eberhard Faber's Design markers were already successful, the company acquired several art supply firms, such as NSM, maker of leather portfolios. At the same time, however, the company began to neglect the commercial office products field that accounted for two-thirds of its total sales. In this market, which includes sales to corporations under private labels as well as the Eberhard Faber name, the firm found itself gaining a reputation for noncompetitive pricing and sluggish new-product development, despite the consistently good quality and service it offered.

New executives tried to revamp every aspect of the company's ineffective marketing operation. To build sales among office product wholesalers, they increased the advertising budget, created new promotional programs, and redesigned the company's catalogs and order sheets. They developed new products, such as five-sided erasers in stylish colors. With commodity products such as rubber bands, they marketed quality and price. Nearly every product package was updated. Office products distributors say such moves definitely improved the company's image.

Continuing to struggle despite its efforts, Eberhard Faber began seeking a buyer. Faber-Castell, seeing an opportunity to increase market share and protect the Faber trade name, bought Eberhard Faber. Now, there seems to be one clear pencil giant. Industry analysts are not quite sure about the direction and the strategies that Faber-Castell will adopt, but, despite all the high-tech developments of the recent years, there will probably always be a place for the familiar yellow pencil.

SOURCES: James Braham, "Ho-Hum: How Do You Peddle a Low-Tech Product?" *Industry Week*, June 9, 1986, pp. 53–56; "Faber-Castell Acquires Eberhard Faber," *Office Systems*, February 1988, p. 12; Alix M. Freedman, "The Next Thing You Know, They'll Change the Coke Formula," *Wall Street Journal*, June 27, 1985, p. E33; Martha E. Mangelsdorf, "I'm My Own Grandpa," *Inc.*, May 1988, p. 13; and Al Urbanski, "Eberhard Faber," *Sales & Marketing Management*, November 1986, pp. 44–47.

Questions for Discussion

1. What types of organizational markets (as classified in this chapter) purchase the products Faber-Castell makes?
2. Most purchases of Faber-Castell's office products would be of what type: new task, modified rebuy, or straight rebuy? Why?
3. Why were the "natural-looking" pencils less than successful?
4. Evaluate changes made in this firm's marketing efforts.

6.2 Intel Serves Organizational Markets

A company in Santa Clara, California, has a kind of monopoly that the old-time capitalists of the early 1900s would be proud to control. More than 70 percent of all personal computers (PCs) rely on Intel technology. Intel supplied the "brain" to IBM's first personal computer and to every IBM PC assembled since then. IBM compatibles also rely on Intel's chips. Even Japanese computer companies consume massive numbers of Intel's chips. Now, however, faster and more sophisticated computer work stations are giving PCs a strong challenge as *the* technological tool for scientists, engineers, and businesspeople. Work stations are becoming more powerful and less expensive—and more popular. Intel's current and very challenging goal is to maintain its PC "monopoly" while dominating the market for the new RISC (reduced instruction set computing) chip that will likely revolutionize the computer work stations of the future.

Some computer analysts think that Intel may eventually control the RISC market, though smaller companies like Sun and MIPS are eager to give Intel a strong fight. Because Intel is so devoted to its PC market and the development of the RISC, it has in the past missed opportunities to enter some other lucrative markets. It seems that the market for "handmaiden" chips (chips that enhance performance and provide additional functions, such as graphics) could have easily been controlled by Intel. But Intel executives did not aggressively pursue this product area, and now other computer technology companies are reaping large financial gains.

Because of these and similar events, Intel executives have modified their company strategy somewhat. They are now committed to strengthening their other products, such as semiconductors, memory chips, and personal computers. Intel has devoted more funds to research and development, investing huge amounts in leading-edge CAD (computer-aided design) equipment to reduce product development time. The Intel management is excited by a new technology invented by RCA, then sold to GE, then finally purchased by Intel (for an estimated, and surprisingly low, price of $20 million). Digital video interactive, DVI, will bring a full-motion color picture and stereo sound to PCs. Computer users having access to DVI capabilities will be able to extensively manipulate the images on their computer screens.

Believing that their company was becoming bloated and outdated, the Intel management has closed eight obsolete plants since 1984. It has also reduced the work force by six thousand employees and made a new commitment to customer service, trying to remedy its reputation as an unresponsive and sometimes arrogant supplier.

Andrew S. Grove, Intel's chief executive officer, has said that his primary hope for the future is to position Intel as the heart, spine, and framework of the entire computer industry. Because much of today's software has been written for the IBM PCs, this software is designed to work with Intel's chips and will likely guarantee continued success for Intel at least for the short term.

Intel recently received a grant from the federal Defense Advanced Research Projects Agency to develop a special supercomputer prototype that will utilize two thousand "processors," with each processor having the power of a traditional supercomputer. By using multiple processors and microchips, the prototype to be developed will be able to solve very complicated multipart problems.

Called "the Touchstone project," the prototypes and later commercial models will probably be used for engineering simulations, molecular models, and aerodynamic studies. The Touchstone program revolves around Intel's i860 microchip—a chip containing one million transistors. Because of the low price of the i860 (about $750), Intel can produce the Touchstone prototype for about one tenth the price of a comparable system using today's technology. When commercially available, Touchstone computers will sell for an estimated $10 million to $20 million. Intel officials predict that Touchstone prototypes will be operating by the end of 1991.

Employee turnover, especially among management, is extremely low at Intel, which is unusual for a computer company. This and Intel's reputation as a leading innovator make it an attractive firm for young and talented engineers, designers, programmers, and managers. Armed with ingenuity and an improved marketing strategy, Intel is not afraid of the probable new wave of work station wars. However, it is not overconfident either. A group of 128 Japanese companies have been trying to perfect a technology called TRON that could compete head to head with Intel's PC microprocessors. Grove, Intel's CEO, takes this still hypothetical confrontation seriously. He has remarked that he never laughs at anything Japanese because the Japanese never give up. It does not appear that Intel will give up either.

SOURCES: Richard Brandt and Otis Port, "Intel: The Next Revolution," *Business Week*, Sept. 26, 1988, pp. 74–78, 80; Stuart Gannes, "IBM and DEC Take on the Little Guys," *Fortune*, Oct. 10, 1988, pp. 108–109, 112, 114; Carrie Gottlieb, "Intel's Plan for Staying on Top," *Fortune*, Mar. 27, 1989, pp. 98–100; and Dan McMillan, "Intel Grant Paves Way for Accessible Supercomputers," *Daily Journal of Commerce*, (Portland, OR) Apr. 5, 1989.

Questions for Discussion

1. What types of organizational markets does Intel serve?
2. When purchasing Intel computer chips, what type of organizational buying method or methods would a personal computer manufacturer use?
3. What are the characteristics of the demand for Intel computer chips?

7

MARKETING RESEARCH AND INFORMATION SYSTEMS

Objectives

To understand the importance of and relationship between research and information systems in marketing decision making

To distinguish between research and intuition in solving marketing problems

To learn the five basic steps for conducting a marketing research project

To understand the fundamental methods of gathering data for marketing research

Not long ago, the role of the male in family purchases was well defined. Because males were the major income provider, they usually made the final decisions about important household purchases. In the 1990s, however, men are becoming more involved in purchasing decisions for a wider variety of products. In today's market, male roles and buying behaviors are more diverse and fragmented. As a result, marketing researchers today have a more difficult task in defining male target markets and designing ways to reach them.

One role that more men have taken on is grocery shopping. A mid-1980s report by the Campbell Soup Company and *People* magazine indicated that male shoppers accounted for 40 percent of all food purchases. About 37 percent of the men surveyed said they shopped for food more often than they did a few years ago. A 1989 study conducted for *Men's Health* also indicated that the number of men performing a larger share of the grocery shopping had increased to about 43 percent.

Marketing research has pinpointed several factors behind evolving male purchasing patterns: higher divorce rates, delayed marriages, changing sex roles within the family, and increasing numbers of working women. Men have often been stereotyped as inexperienced, impulsive, and disorganized shoppers. Although research has found that men are less likely than women to use lists, coupons, or to comparison shop, their buying habits appear to be linked more to age and marital status than to gender.

Because marketing research has identified these changes in men's purchasing patterns, astute food marketers are now targeting food and food-related items to men and women. To attract more male shoppers, grocery stores are using product demonstrations during evening hours, purchasing guides, and newspaper ads that emphasize shopping ease and convenience. ◆

Photo by Miro Vintoniv/Stock, Boston.

Based on information in Eileen B. Brill, "Super Marketers Pursue the New Consumers," *Advertising Age*, Oct. 13, 1986, p. S4; Scott Donaton, "Study Boosts Men's Buying Role," *Advertising Age*, Dec. 4, 1989, p. 48; Priscilla Donegan, "The Myth of the Male Shopper," *Progressive Grocer*, May 1986, pp. 36–38; Ronald D. Michman, "The Male Queue at the Checkout Counter," *Business Horizons*, May-June 1986, pp. 51–55; Eileen Prescott, "New Men," *American Demographics*, Aug. 1983, p. 16.

T|o implement the marketing concept, marketers require information about the characteristics, needs and wants of their target markets. Given the intense competition in today's marketplace, it is unwise to develop a product and then look for a market where it can be profitably sold. Marketing research and information systems that provide practical, unbiased information help firms avoid the assumptions and misunderstandings that could result in poor marketing performance.

In this chapter we focus on the ways of gathering information needed to make marketing decisions. We first distinguish between managing information within an organization (a marketing information system) and conducting marketing research. Then we discuss the role of marketing research in decision making and problem solving, compare it with intuition, and examine the individual steps of the marketing research process. We also take a close look at experimentation and various methods of collecting data. In the final section, we consider the importance of marketing research and marketing information systems.

Defining Marketing Research and Marketing Information Systems

Marketing research is the systematic design, collection, interpretation, and reporting of information to help marketers solve specific marketing problems or take advantage of marketing opportunities. It is a process for gathering information not currently available to decision makers. Marketing research is conducted on a special-project basis, with the research methods adapted to the problems being studied and to changes in the environment. The American Marketing Association defines marketing research as follows:

> Marketing research is the function which links the consumer, customer, and public to the marketer through information—information used to identify and define marketing opportunities and problems; generate, refine, and evaluate marketing actions; monitor marketing performance; and improve understanding of marketing as a process. Marketing research specifies the information required to address these issues; designs the method for collecting information; manages and implements the data collection process; analyzes the results; and communicates the findings and their implications.[1]

A **marketing information system (MIS)** is the framework for the day-to-day management and structuring of information gathered regularly from sources both inside and outside an organization. As such, an MIS provides a continuous flow of information about prices, advertising expenditures, sales, competition, and distribution expenses. When information systems are strategically created and then institutionalized throughout an organization, their value is enhanced.[2] Figure 7.1 illustrates the chief components of an MIS.

1. Reprinted from *Dictionary of Marketing Terms,* Peter D. Bennett, Ed., 1988, pp. 117–118, published by the American Marketing Association. Used by permission.

2. Andrea Dunham, "Information Systems Are the Key to Managing Future Business Needs," *Marketing News,* May 23, 1986, p. 11.

FIGURE 7.1

An organization's marketing information system

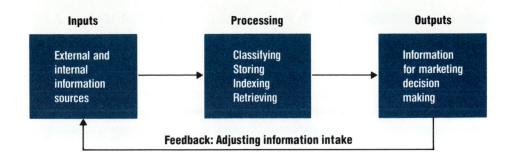

The inputs into a marketing information system include the information sources inside and outside the firm assumed to be useful for future decision making. Processing information involves classifying it and developing categories for meaningful storage and retrieval. Marketing decision makers then determine which information—the output—is useful for making decisions. Finally, feedback enables those who are responsible for gathering internal and external data to adjust the information inputs systematically.

Regular reports of sales by product or market categories, data on inventory levels, and records of salespersons' activities are all examples of information that is useful in making decisions. In the MIS, the means of gathering data receive less attention than do the procedures for expediting the flow of information. For example, as shown in Figure 7.2, TEC register systems provide complete inventory information to control waste and increase profitability. The main focus of the marketing information system is on data storage and retrieval, as well as on computer capabilities and management's information requirements. RJR Nabisco, for example, handles hundreds of thousands of consumer contacts each year, usually inquiries about product usage, nutrition, and ingredients. This consumer feedback is computerized and made available on demand throughout the company's operating divisions. Marketing Update 7.1 describes how more and more companies are using toll-free telephone services to gather important data for their marketing information systems and marketing research.

The main difference between marketing research and marketing information systems is that marketing research is an information-gathering process for specific situations, whereas an MIS provides continuous data input for an organization. Nonrecurring decisions that deal with the dynamics of the marketing environment often call for a data search structured according to the problem and decision. Marketing research is usually characterized by in-depth analyses of major problems or issues. Often the information needed is available only from sources outside an organization's formal channels of information. For instance, an organization may want to know something about its competitors or to gain an unbiased understanding of its own customers. Such information needs may require an independent investigation by a marketing research firm.

Data brought into the organization through marketing research become part of its **marketing databank**, a file of data collected through both the MIS and marketing research projects. The marketing databank allows researchers to retrieve information that is useful for addressing problems quite different from those that prompted the original data collection. Often a research study developed for one purpose proves valuable for developing a research method or indicating problems in re-

1-800 PHONE NUMBERS: NOT JUST FOR COMPLAINTS ANYMORE

Many U.S. companies have made toll-free 800 numbers an integral part of their ongoing customer service programs. Originally, toll-free numbers were used as a way to satisfy consumer complaints. Persistent complaints often provide an early glimpse at changing consumer tastes, allowing a company to alter its marketing strategy accordingly. However, though hearing consumer complaints remains the top priority of 800 phone lines, other uses for the service are on the rise.

Companies today are increasingly using 800 numbers to solicit consumer opinions on a variety of matters, such as package colors, product taste, and advertising. Toll-free phone lines also help in spotting new fads and fashions, test-marketing new products, and finding and solving consumer problems before they get out of hand. In many cases, callers are asked to take part in focus groups or to test a new product. Information obtained in this manner can be added to a firm's marketing information system for later use.

Consumer attitudes toward 800 numbers are also changing. When the numbers were first introduced, consumers saw them as a privilege given to them by business. Today consumers tend to regard 800 numbers as a right, and they react negatively to companies that do not provide toll-free numbers. As a result, the use of toll-free numbers by consumers is rising. AT&T reported that the total number of calls on its toll-free lines in 1989 was roughly seven billion, up from about two billion in 1984. By 1992, the toll-free market is expected to grow to $6.8 billion, and consumer use of 800 lines is expected to keep increasing well into the next century.

Although 800 numbers provide many benefits to both consumers and companies, they are not cheap. It is estimated that starting an 800 program in a medium-sized firm would cost at least $250,000. Yearly staffing and maintenance costs raise this figure substantially. General Electric's GE Answer Center, considered the largest and the best of all 800 programs, costs the company about $10 million per year. Still, companies that provide 800 numbers find them to be well worth the investment.

SOURCES: Brent Bowers, "Companies Draw More on 800 Lines," *Wall Street Journal,* Nov. 6, 1989, pp. B1, B8; Daniel Briere, "Toll-Free Services Market Set for Explosive Growth," *Network World,* July 3, 1989, pp. 1, 20–37; Carol Dixon, "Eight Tips for 800 Success," *Marketing Communications,* March 1989, pp. 50–51; "How to Use 800 Numbers Effectively," *Agency Sales Magazine,* May 1988, pp. 12–14; Ruth Podems, "What's in Store for the 1990's?" *Target Marketing,* Oct. 1988, pp. 22–23; Bristol Voss, "Telemarketing: A 10-Letter Word for 800 Numbers?" *Sales & Marketing Management,* Sept. 1988, pp. 97–98.

FIGURE 7.2
Gathering information.
TEC POS Systems track units sold by product group, by time frame, and number of customers, to allow control of inventory and product mix.

SOURCE: Courtesy TEC America, Inc. Gardena, CA

searching a particular topic. For instance, data obtained from a study by Ford Motor Co. on the buying behavior of purchasers of its Mustang model may be used in planning a new two-seat sports car to be introduced in the future. Consequently, marketers should classify and store in the databank all data from marketing research and the MIS to facilitate use of the information in future marketing decisions.

Databanks vary widely from one organization to another. In a small organization, the databank may simply be a large notebook, but many organizations employ a computer storage and retrieval system to handle the large volume of data. Figure 7.3 illustrates how marketing decision makers combine research findings with data from an MIS to develop a databank. Although many organizations do not use the term *databank*, they still have some system for storing information. Smaller organizations may not use the terms *MIS* and *marketing research*, but they normally do perform these marketing activities.

After a marketing information system—of whatever size and complexity—has been established, information should be related to marketing planning. The following section discusses how marketers use marketing information, intuition, and judgment in making decisions.

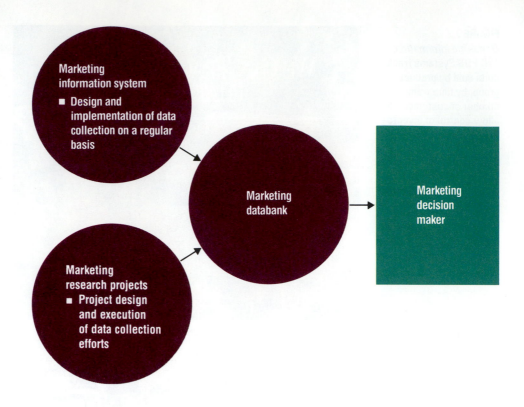

FIGURE 7.3
Combining marketing research and the marketing information system

Marketing information system
■ Design and implementation of data collection on a regular basis

Marketing research projects
■ Project design and execution of data collection efforts

Marketing databank

Marketing decision maker

INFORMATION NEEDS AND DECISION MAKING

The real value of marketing research and marketing information systems is measured by improvements in a marketer's ability to make decisions. Marketers should treat information in the same manner as other resources utilized by the firm, and they must weigh the costs of obtaining information against the benefits derived. Information is worthwhile if it results in marketing mixes that better satisfy the needs of the firm's target markets, leads to increased sales and profits, or helps the firm achieve some other goal.

Marketing research and marketing information systems provide the organization with customer feedback, without which a marketer cannot understand the dynamics of the marketplace. As managers recognize its benefits, they assign marketing research a much larger role in decision making. For example, Japanese managers, who put much more faith in information they get directly from wholesalers and retailers, are beginning to grasp the importance of consumer surveys and scientific methods of marketing research as they seek ways to diversify their companies.[3]

The increase in marketing research activities represents a transition from intuitive to scientific problem solving. In relying on *intuition,* marketing managers base decisions on personal knowledge and past experience. However, in *scientific decision making,* managers take an orderly and logical approach to gathering information. They seek facts on a systematic basis, and they apply methods other than trial and error or generalization from experience.

3. Johny K. Johansson and Ikujiro Nonaha, "Market Research the Japanese Way," *Harvard Business Review,* May-June 1987, pp. 16–22.

	RESEARCH	**INTUITION**
NATURE	Formal planning, predicting based on scientific approach	Preference based on personal feelings
METHODS	Logic, systematic methods, statistical inference	Experience and demonstration
CONTRIBUTIONS	General hypotheses for making predictions, classifying relevant variables, carrying out systematic description and classification	Minor problems solved quickly through consideration of experience, practical consequences

Despite the obvious value of formal research, marketing decisions are often made without it. Certainly, minor problems that must be dealt with at once can and should be handled on the basis of personal judgment and common sense. If good decisions can be made with the help of currently available information, then costly formal research may be superfluous. However, as the financial, social, or ethical risks increase or the number of courses of action multiplies, full-scale research as a prerequisite for marketing decision making becomes both desirable and rewarding.

We are not suggesting here that intuition has no value in marketing decision making. Successful decisions blend both research and intuition. Statistics, mathematics, and logic are powerful tools in problem solving, and the information they provide can reduce the uncertainty of predictions based on limited experience. But these tools do not necessarily bring out the right answers. Consider an extreme example. A marketing research study conducted for Xerox Corporation in the late 1950s indicated a very limited market for an automatic photocopier. Xerox management judged that the researchers had drawn the wrong conclusions from the study and decided to launch the product anyway. That product, the Xerox 914 copier, was an instant success. An immediate backlog of orders developed, and the rest is history. Though the Xerox example is an extreme one, by and large a proper blend of research and intuition offers the best formula for a correct decision. Table 7.1 distinguishes between the roles of research and intuition in decision making.

THE MARKETING RESEARCH PROCESS

To maintain the control needed for obtaining accurate information, marketers approach marketing research in logical steps. The difference between good and bad research depends on the quality of the input, which includes effective control over the entire marketing research process. Figure 7.4 illustrates the five steps of the marketing research process: (1) defining and locating problems, (2) developing

FIGURE 7.4 *The five steps of the marketing research process*

hypotheses, (3) collecting data, (4) interpreting research findings, and (5) reporting research findings. These five steps should be viewed as an overall approach to conducting research rather than as a rigid set of rules to be followed in each project. In planning research projects, marketers must think about each of the steps and how they can best be adjusted for each particular problem.

DEFINING AND LOCATING PROBLEMS

Problem definition, the first step toward finding a solution or launching a research study, focuses on uncovering the nature and boundaries of a negative, or positive, situation or question. The first sign of a problem is usually a departure from some normal function, such as conflicts between or failures in attaining objectives. If a corporation's objective is a 12 percent return on investment and the current return is 6 percent, this discrepancy should be a warning flag. It is a symptom that something inside or outside the organization has blocked the attainment of the desired goal or that the goal is unrealistic. Decreasing sales, increasing expenses, or decreasing profits also signal problems. Conversely, when an organization experiences a dramatic rise in sales, or some other positive event, it may conduct marketing research to discover the reasons and maximize the opportunities stemming from them. In Figure 7.5, Nielsen promotes its ability to identify and solve problems through sales analysis.

To pin down the specific causes of the problem through research, marketers must define the problem and its scope in a way that requires probing beneath the superficial symptoms. The interaction between the marketing manager and the marketing researcher should yield a clear definition of the problem. Depending on their abilities, the manager and the researcher can apply various methods to shape this definition. Traditionally, problem formulation has been viewed as a subjective, creative process. Today, however, more objective and systematic approaches are utilized. For example, the delphi method for problem definition consists of a series of interviews with a panel of experts. With repeated interviews, the range of responses converges toward a "correct" definition of the problem.[4] This method introduces structure as well as objectivity into the process of problem definition. Researchers and decision makers should remain in the problem definition stage until they have determined precisely what they want from the research and how they will use it.

The research objective specifies what information is needed to solve the problem. Deciding how to refine a broad, indefinite problem into a clearly defined and researchable statement is a prerequisite for the next step in planning the research: developing the type of hypothesis that best fits the problem.

4. Raymond E. Taylor, "Using the Delphi Method to Define Marketing Problems," *Business*, October-December 1984, p. 17.

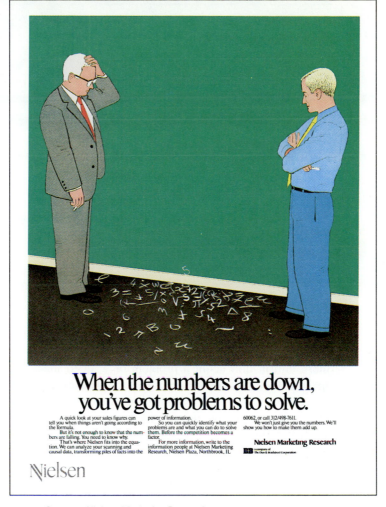

SOURCE: Courtesy Nielsen Marketing Research

DEVELOPING HYPOTHESES

The objective statement of a marketing research project should include hypothe drawn from both previous research and expected research findings. A **hypothesis** is an informed guess or assumption about a certain problem or set of circumstances. It is based on all the insight and knowledge available about the problem from previous research studies and other sources. As information is gathered, a researcher can test the hypothesis. For example, a consumer food products manufacturer such as H. J. Heinz might propose the hypothesis that children today have more influence on their families' buying decisions for ketchup and other grocery products. A marketing researcher would then gather data, perhaps through surveys of children and their parents, and draw conclusions as to whether the hypothesis is correct. Sometimes several hypotheses are developed during the actual study; the hypotheses that are accepted or rejected become the study's chief conclusions.

TABLE 7.2

Comparison of data-gathering approaches

PROJECT COMPONENT	EXPLORATORY STUDIES	DESCRIPTIVE OR CAUSAL STUDIES
PURPOSE	Provide general insights	Confirm insights Verify hypotheses
DATA SOURCES	Ill defined	Well defined
COLLECTION FORM	Open-end	Structured
SAMPLE	Small	Large
COLLECTION PROCEDURE	Flexible	Rigid
DATA ANALYSIS	Informal	Formal
RECOMMENDATIONS	Tentative	Conclusive

SOURCE: Adapted from A. Parasuraman, *Marketing Research*, © 1986 by Addison-Wesley Publishing Co. Reprinted by permission of Addison-Wesley Publishing Co., Reading, MA.

COLLECTING DATA

The kind of hypothesis being tested determines which approach will be used for gathering general data: exploratory, descriptive, or causal. When marketers need more information about a problem or want to make a tentative hypothesis more specific, they may conduct **exploratory studies**. For instance, they may review the information in the firm's databank or examine publicly available data. Questioning knowledgeable people inside and outside the organization may also yield new insights into the problem. An advantage of the exploratory approach is that it permits marketers to conduct ministudies with a very restricted database.

If marketers need to understand the characteristics of certain phenomena to solve a particular problem, **descriptive studies** can aid them. Such studies may range from general surveys of consumers' education, occupation, or age to specifics on how many consumers purchased Eagle Premiers last month or how many adults between the ages of 18 and 30 eat some form of oat bran at least three times a week. Some descriptive studies require statistical analysis and predictive tools. For example, a researcher trying to find out how many people will vote for a certain political candidate may have to survey registered voters to predict the results. Descriptive studies generally demand much prior knowledge and assume that the problem is clearly defined. The marketers' major task is to choose adequate methods for collecting and measuring data.

Hypotheses about causal relationships call for a more complex approach than a descriptive study. In **causal studies**, it is assumed that a particular variable X causes a variable Y. Marketers must plan the research so that the data collected prove or disprove that X causes Y. To do so, marketers must try to hold constant all variables except X and Y. For example, to find out whether new carpeting, miniblinds, and ceiling fans increase the number of rentals in an apartment complex, marketers need to keep all variables constant except the new furnishings and the rental rate. Table 7.2 compares the features of these types of research studies.

Marketing researchers have two types of data at their disposal. **Primary data** are observed and recorded or collected directly from respondents. This type of data

FIGURE 7.6
Approaches to collecting data

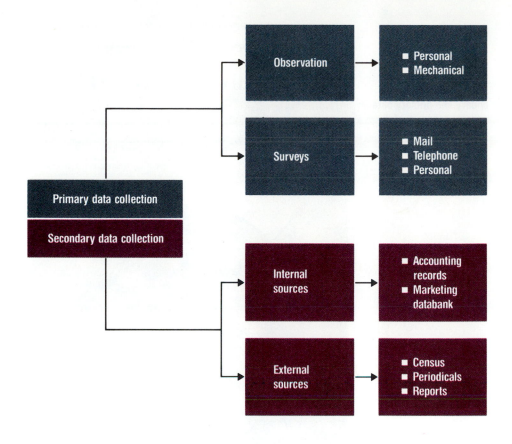

must be gathered by observing phenomena or surveying respondents. **Secondary data** are compiled inside or outside the organization for some purpose other than the current investigation. Secondary data include general reports supplied to an enterprise by various data services. Such reports might concern market share, retail inventory levels, and consumers' buying behavior. Figure 7.6 illustrates how primary and secondary sources differ. Commonly, secondary data are already available in private or public reports or have been collected and stored by the organization itself. In Figure 7.7, AT&T focuses on its database management services to improve companies' direct marketing programs. In the next section, we discuss the methods of gathering both secondary and primary data.

■ Secondary Data Collection

Marketers often begin the marketing research process by gathering secondary data. They may use available reports and other information from both internal and external sources to study a marketing problem.

Internal sources of secondary data can contribute tremendously to research. An organization's marketing databank may contain information about past marketing activities, such as sales records and research reports, which can be used to test hypotheses and pinpoint problems. An organization's accounting records are also an excellent source of data but, strangely enough, are often overlooked. The large volume of data an accounting department collects does not automatically flow to the marketing area. As a result, detailed information about costs, sales, customer ac-

SOURCE: AT&T American Transtech

counts, or profits by product category may not be part of the MIS. This condition develops particularly in organizations that do not store marketing information on a systematic basis.

Secondary data can also be gleaned from periodicals, government publications, and unpublished sources. Periodicals such as *Business Week, The Wall Street Journal, Sales and Marketing Management, American Demographics, Marketing Research,* and *Industrial Marketing* print general information that is helpful for defining problems and developing hypotheses. *Survey of Buying Power,* an annual supplement to *Sales and Marketing Management,* contains sales data for major industries on a county-by-county basis. Many marketers consult federal government publications such as the *Census of Business,* the *Census of Agriculture,* and the *Census of Population,* available from the Superintendent of Documents in Washington, D.C. Table 7.3 summarizes the major external sources of secondary data, excluding syndicated services.

Syndicated data services periodically collect general information, which they sell to clients. Arbitron, for example, supplies television stations and media buyers with estimates of the number of viewers at specific times. Selling Areas Marketing, Inc., (SAMI) furnishes monthly information that describes market shares for specific types of manufacturers. The A. C. Nielsen Company Retail Index provides data

TABLE 7.3
Guide to external sources of secondary data

TRADE JOURNALS	Virtually every industry or type of business has a trade journal. These journals give a feel for the industry—its size, degree of competition, range of companies involved, and problems. To find trade journals in the field of interest, check *Ulrich's*, a reference book that lists American and foreign periodicals by subject.
TRADE ASSOCIATIONS	Almost every industry, product category, and profession has its own association. Depending on the strength of each group, they often conduct research, publish journals, conduct training sessions, and hold conventions. A call or a letter to the association may yield information not available in published sources. To find out which associations serve which industries check the *Encyclopedia of Associations*.
INTERNATIONAL SOURCES	Periodical indexes, such as the *F&S Index International*, are particularly useful for overseas product or company information. More general sources include the *United Nations Statistical Yearbook* and the *International Labour Organization's Yearbook of Labour Statistics*.
GOVERNMENT	The federal government, through its various departments and agencies, collects, analyzes, and publishes statistics on practically everything. Government documents also have their own set of indexes: the *Monthly Catalog*. Other useful indexes for government-generated information are the *American Statistical Index* and the *Congressional Information Service*.
BOOKS IN PRINT (BIP)	BIP is a two-volume reference book found in most libraries. All books issued by U.S. publishers and currently in print are listed by subject, title, and author.
PERIODICAL INDEXES	The library's reference section contains indexes on virtually every discipline. The *Business Periodicals Index*, for example, indexes each article in all major business periodicals.
COMPUTERIZED LITERATURE-RETRIEVAL DATABASES	Literature-retrieval databases are periodical indexes stored in a computer. Books and dissertations are also included. Key words (such as the name of a subject) are used to search a database and generate references.

about products primarily sold through food stores and drugstores. This information includes total sales in a product category, sales of clients' own brands, and sales of important competing brands. The Market Research Corporation of America (MRCA) collects data through a national panel of consumers to provide information about purchases. MRCA maintains data on brands classified by age, race, sex, education, occupation, and family size.

Similar organizations operate at the local level. Market Search, a marketing research company in Indianapolis, for example, offers Indyindex. This monthly omnibus study for small Indianapolis businesses contains information gleaned from three hundred consumer telephone interviews about product preferences, prices, stores, and other marketing topics. Small businesses in Indianapolis use this research information to plan their marketing activities.[5]

Another type of secondary data, which is available for a fee, is demographic analysis. Companies that specialize in demographic databanks have special knowledge and sophisticated computer systems to work with the very complex U.S. Census databank. As a result, they are able to respond to specialized requests that the Census Bureau cannot or will not handle. Such information may be valuable in tracking demographic changes that have implications for consumer behavior.[6]

■ Primary Data Collection

The collection of primary data is a more lengthy and complex process than the collection of secondary data. The acquisition of primary data often requires an experimental approach to determine which variable or variables caused an event to occur.

Experimentation.   **Experimentation** involves maintaining certain variables constant so that the effects of the experimental variables may be measured. For instance, when the WordPerfect Corp. tests a change in its WordPerfect word processing computer program, all variables should be held constant except the change in the program. **Marketing experimentation** is a set of rules and procedures by which data gathering is organized to expedite analysis and interpretation.

In experimentation, an **independent variable** (a variable not influenced by or dependent on other variables) is manipulated and the resulting changes are measured in a **dependent variable** (a variable contingent on, or restricted to, one value or a set of values assumed by the independent variable). Figure 7.8 illustrates the relationship between these variables. For example, when Houghton Mifflin Company introduces a new edition of its *American Heritage Dictionary,* it may want to estimate the number of dictionaries that could be sold at various levels of advertising expenditure and prices. The dependent variable would be sales, and the independent variables would be advertising expenditures and price. Researchers would design the experiment so that other independent variables that might influence sales—such as distribution and variations of the product—would be controlled.

In designing experiments, marketing researchers must ensure that research techniques are both reliable and valid. A research technique has **reliability** if it produces almost identical results in successive repeated trials. But a reliable technique is not necessarily valid. To have **validity**, the method must measure what it is supposed to measure, not something else. A valid research method provides data

5. "Marketing Research Briefs," *Marketing News,* Jan. 21, 1983, p. 5.

6. Ronald L. Vaughn, "Demographic Data Banks: A New Management Resource," *Business Horizons,* November-December 1984, pp. 38–42.

FIGURE 7.8

Relationship between independent and dependent variables

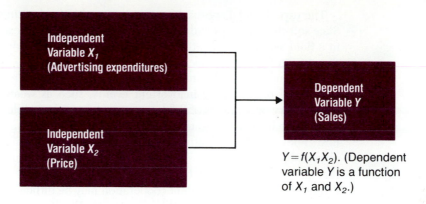

$Y = f(X_1 X_2)$. (Dependent variable Y is a function of X_1 and X_2.)

that can be used to test the hypothesis being investigated. For example, recent experiments on cold fusion by scientists at the University of Utah, Texas A & M University, and others lack both reliability and validity because the results of the experiments have not been repeated in successive trials and the scientists are not sure whether their experiments are measuring energy produced as a result of fusion or some other process.

One marketing research company, Information Resources, Inc., has brought a new dimension to experimental research by combining cable television, supermarket scanners, and computers. The company has placed its BehaviorScan microcomputers on televisions in thousands of households in major cities. The company can then track every commercial its panelists watch and every purchase they make in a supermarket or drugstore. The information provided by Information Resources helps marketers assess the effectiveness of their advertising by determining whether a viewer saw a particular advertisement and whether the advertisement led the viewer to buy the product.[7]

Experiments may be conducted in the laboratory or in the field; each research setting has advantages and disadvantages. In *laboratory settings*, participants or respondents are invited to a central location to react or respond to experimental stimuli. In such an isolated setting it is possible to control independent variables that might influence the outcome of an experiment. The features of laboratory settings might include a taste kitchen, video equipment, slide projectors, tape recorders, one-way mirrors, central telephone banks, and interview rooms. In an experiment to determine the influence of price (independent variable) on sales of a new canned soup (dependent variable), respondents would be invited to a laboratory—a room with table, chairs, and sample soups—before the soup was available in stores. The soup would be placed on a table with competitors' soups. Analysts would then question respondents about their reactions to the soup at various prices.

One problem with a laboratory setting is its isolation from the real world. It is simply not possible to duplicate all the conditions that affect choices in the marketplace. On the other hand, by controlling variables that cannot be controlled in the real world, laboratory experiments can focus on variables that marketers think may be significant for the success of a marketing strategy. Market Facts, Inc., a leading marketing research firm, reports that test market laboratories are being used more frequently today.[8]

7. Gary Levin, "IRI Says Data Can Now Link Ads to Sales," *Advertising Age,* Jan. 26, 1987, pp. 3, 74.

8. Based on a survey conducted by Market Facts, Inc., Apr. 28, 1983.

The experimental approach can also be used in *field settings*. A taste test of a new Slice soft-drink flavor conducted in a grocery store is one example of an experiment in a field setting. Field settings give the marketer an opportunity to obtain a more direct test of marketing decisions than laboratory settings.

There are several limitations to field experiments. Field experiments can be influenced or biased by inadvertent events, such as weather or major economic news. Carry-over effects of field experiments are impossible to avoid. What respondents have been asked to do in one time period will influence what they do in the next. For example, evaluating competing advertisements may influence attempts to obtain objective evaluations of new proposals for a firm's future advertising. The fact that previous advertising has been viewed influences respondents' evaluation of future advertising. Respondent cooperation may be difficult because respondents do not understand their role in the experiment. Finally, only a small number of variables can be controlled in field experiments. It is impossible, for example, to control competitors' advertising or their attempts to influence the outcome of the experiment. Tactics that competitors can use to thwart field efforts include couponing, reducing prices temporarily, and increasing advertising frequency.

Experimentation is used in marketing research to improve hypothesis testing. However, whether experiments are conducted in the laboratory or in the field, many assumptions must be made to limit the number of factors and isolate causes. Marketing decision makers must recognize that assumptions may diminish the reliability of the research findings. For example, viewing proposed advertisements on a videocassette recorder in a laboratory is different from watching the advertisements on television at home.

The gathering of primary data through experimentation may involve the use of sampling, survey methods, observation, or some combination of those techniques.

Sampling.   By systematically choosing a limited number of units, or a **sample**, to represent the characteristics of a total population, marketers can project the reactions of a total market or market segment. The objective of **sampling** in marketing research, therefore, is to select representative units from a total population. Sampling procedures are used in studying the likelihood of events based on assumptions about the future.

Since the time and the resources available for research are limited, it would be almost impossible to investigate all members of a population. A **population**, or "universe," comprises all elements, units, or individuals that are of interest to researchers for a specific study. For example, if a Gallup poll is designed to predict the results of a presidential election, all registered voters in the United States would constitute the population. A representative national sample of several thousand registered voters would be selected in the Gallup poll to project the probable voting outcome. The projection would be based on the assumption that no major political events would occur before the election.

Sampling techniques allow marketers to predict buying behavior fairly accurately on the basis of the responses from a representative portion of the population of interest. Figure 7.9 illustrates how one company provides sampling facilities in many metro markets in the United States. Sampling methods include random sampling, stratified sampling, area sampling, and quota sampling.

When marketers employ **random sampling**, all the units in a population have an equal chance of appearing in the sample. Random sampling is basic probability

FIGURE 7.9

Sampling U.S. metropolitan markets. Quality Controlled Services provides marketing research services in 21 metropolitan locations.

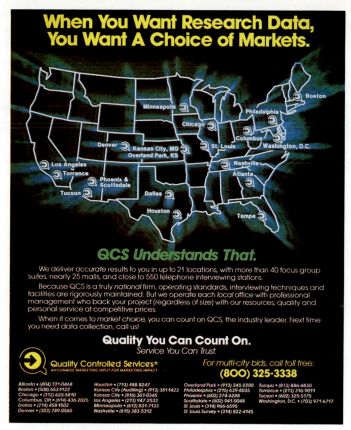

SOURCE: Quality Controlled Services

sampling. The various events that can occur have an equal or known chance of taking place. For example, a specific card in a regulation deck should have a 1/52 probability of being drawn at any one time. Similarly, if each student at a university or college has a unique identification number and these numbers are mixed up in a large basket, each student's number would have a known probability of being selected. Sample units are ordinarily chosen by selecting from a table of random numbers statistically generated so that each digit, zero through nine, will have an equal probability of occurring in each position in the sequence. The sequentially numbered elements of a population are sampled randomly by selecting the units whose numbers appear in the table of random numbers.

In **stratified sampling**, the population of interest is divided into groups according to a common characteristic or attribute, and then a probability sample is conducted within each group. The stratified sample may reduce some of the error that could occur in a simple random sample. By ensuring that each major group or segment of the population receives its proportionate share of sample units, investigators avoid including too many or too few sample units from each stratum. Usually, samples are stratified when researchers believe that there may be variations among different types of respondents. For example, many political opinion surveys are stratified by sex, race, and age.

Area sampling involves two stages: (1) selecting a probability sample of geographic areas, such as blocks, census tracts, or census enumeration districts, and (2) selecting units or individuals within the selected geographic areas for the sample. This approach is a variation of stratified sampling, with the geographic areas serving as the segments, or primary units, used in sampling. To select the units or individuals within the geographic areas, researchers may choose every nth house or unit, or random selection procedures may be used to pick out a given number of units or individuals from a total listing within the selected geographic areas. Area sampling may be used when a complete list of the population is not available.

Quota sampling differs from other forms of sampling in that it is judgmental; that is, the final choice of respondents is left to the interviewers. A study of consumers who wear eyeglasses, for example, may be conducted by interviewing any person who wears eyeglasses. In quota sampling, there are some controls—usually limited to two or three variables such as age, sex, and education—over the selection of respondents. The controls attempt to ensure that representative categories of respondents are interviewed.

Quota samples are unique because they are not probability samples; not everyone has an equal chance of being selected. Therefore, sampling error cannot be measured statistically. Quota samples are used most often in exploratory studies, when hypotheses are being developed. Often a small quota sample will not be projected to the total population, although the findings may provide valuable insights into a problem. Quota samples are useful when people with some unusual characteristic are found and questioned about the topic of interest. A probability sample used to study people allergic to cats would be highly inefficient.

Survey Methods. **Survey methods** include interviews by mail or telephone and personal interviews. Selection of a survey method depends on the nature of the problem, the data needed to test the hypothesis, and the resources, such as funding and personnel, that are available to the researcher. Table 7.4 summarizes and compares the advantages of the various methods. Researchers must know exactly what type of information is needed to test the hypothesis and what type of information can be obtained through interviewing. Table 7.5 lists the most frequently used consumer survey techniques. The data are based on a survey of large American consumer goods and services companies.

Gathering information through surveys is becoming more difficult because respondent rates are declining. There is also an indication that people with higher incomes and education are most likely to respond. Problems include difficulty in hiring qualified interviewers and respondents' reluctance to take part in surveys because of overly long questionnaires, dull topics, and time pressures.[9] Moreover, fear of crime makes respondents unwilling to trust interviewers. The use of "sugging"—sales techniques disguised as market surveys—has also contributed to decreased respondent cooperation.

In *mail surveys*, questionnaires are sent to respondents, who are encouraged to complete and return them. Mail surveys are used most often when the individuals chosen for questioning are spread over a wide area and funds for the survey are limited. A mail survey is the least expensive survey method as long as the response

9. Martha Farnsworth Riche, "Who Says Yes?" *American Demographics*, February 1987, p. 8; George Gallup, Jr., "Survey Research: Current Problems and Future Opportunities," *Journal of Consumer Marketing*, Winter 1988, pp. 27–29.

TABLE 7.4 *Comparison of the three basic survey methods*

	MAIL SURVEYS	TELEPHONE SURVEYS	PERSONAL INTERVIEW SURVEYS
ECONOMY	Potentially the lowest cost per interview if there is an adequate return rate; increased postage rates are raising costs	Avoids interviewers' travel expenses; less expensive than in-home interviews; most common survey method	In-home interviewing is the most expensive interviewing method; shopping mall, focus-group interviewing may lower costs
FLEXIBILITY	Inflexible; questionnaire must be short, easy for respondents to complete; no probing questions; may take more time to implement than other survey methods	Flexible because interviewers can ask probing questions, encourage respondents to answer questions; rapport may be gained, but observations are impossible	Most flexible method; respondents can react to visual materials, help fill out questionnaire; because observation is possible, demographic data are more accurate; in-depth probes are possible
INTERVIEWER BIAS	Interviewer bias eliminated; questionnaires can be returned anonymously	Some anonymity; may be hard to develop trust among respondents	Refusals may be decreased by interviewers' rapport-building efforts; interviewers' personal attributes may bias respondents
SAMPLING AND RESPONDENTS' COOPERATION	Obtaining a complete mailing list is difficult; nonresponse is a major disadvantage	Sample must be limited to respondents with telephones and listed numbers; busy signals, no answers, and nonresponse—including refusals—are problems	Not-at-homes are more difficult to deal with; focus-groups, shopping mall interviewing may overcome these problems

rate is high enough to produce reliable results. The main disadvantages of this method are the possibility of a low response rate or of misleading results, if respondents are significantly different from the population being sampled.

Researchers can boost mail survey response rates by offering respondents some incentive to return the questionnaire. When using mail survey techniques, incentives and follow-ups have been found to consistently increase response rates. But promises of anonymity, special appeals for cooperation, and questionnaire length have no apparent impact on the response rate. Other techniques for increasing the response rate, such as advance notification, personalization of survey materials, type of postage, corporate or university sponsorship, or foot-in-the-door techniques have had

TABLE 7.5

Changes in the frequency of use of survey research techniques

	1978	1983	1987	1987 vs. 1983
Central WATS	90%	91%	98%	+7
Shopping mall intercepts	89%	90%	86%	−4
Focus groups	87%	90%	98%	+8
Mail panel	53%	57%	67%	10
Custom mail	46%	33%	43%	+10
Purchase diary	46%	48%	37%	-11
Door-to-door	61%	47%	39%	−8
Trade surveys	33%	39%	40%	+1
Local telephone	67%	61%	°	°
Scanner panel	°	°	39%	°
Average number named	5.7	5.6	5.5	

° Not measured.

SOURCE: *Practices, Trends and Expectations for the Market Research Industry 1987*, Market Facts, Inc., Apr. 29, 1987, p. 23. Reprinted by permission.

mixed results, varying according to the population surveyed.[10] Although such techniques may help increase the response rates, they can introduce sample-composition bias, or nonresponse bias, which results when those responding to a survey differ in some important respect from those not responding to the survey. In other words, response-enhancing techniques may alienate some people in the sample and appeal to others, making the results nonrepresentative of the population of interest. Perhaps because of these problems and the others discussed earlier, firms surveyed in Table 7.5 spent less than 5 percent of their research funds for direct mail surveys.[11]

Premiums or incentives encouraging respondents to return questionnaires have been effective in developing panels of respondents who are regularly interviewed by mail. Mail panels, which are selected to represent a market or market segment, are especially useful for evaluating new products, providing general information about consumers, and providing records of consumers' purchases. As Table 7.5 indicates, 67 percent of the companies surveyed used consumer mail panels, but these panels represented a major budget share for less than 15 percent of the companies.[12] It is interesting that 37 percent of the sample used consumer purchase diaries. (These surveys are similar to mail panels, but consumers keep track of purchases only.) Consumer mail panels and consumer purchase diaries are much more widely used than custom mail surveys, but they do have shortcomings. Research indicates that the people who take the time to fill out a consumer diary have higher income and are more educated than the general population. If researchers include less educated consumers in the panel, they must risk poorer response rates.[13]

10. Jeffrey S. Conant, Denise T. Smart, and Bruce J. Walker, "Mail-Survey Facilitation Techniques: An Assessment and Proposal Regarding Reporting Practices" (working paper, Texas A&M University, 1990).

11. *Practices, Trends and Expectations for the Market Research Industry 1987*, Market Facts, Inc., April 29, 1987.

12. Ibid.

13. Riche, p. 8.

In *telephone surveys,* respondents' answers to a questionnaire are recorded by interviewers on the phone. A telephone survey has some advantages over a mail survey. The rate of response is higher because it takes less effort to answer the telephone and talk than to fill out a questionnaire and return it. If there are enough interviewers, telephone surveys can be conducted very quickly. Thus they can be used by political candidates or organizations seeking an immediate reaction to an event. In addition, this survey technique permits interviewers to gain rapport with respondents and ask probing questions. Moreover, the use of WATS (Wide Area Telecommunications Service) lines reduces the expense of long-distance telephone interviewing. According to a survey by the Council of American Survey Research Organizations (CASRO), telephone interviewing is the preferred survey method in more than 40 percent of the projects conducted by commercial survey research firms.[14] The data in Table 7.5 show that virtually all the surveyed firms used telephone interviewing.

Telephone interviews do have drawbacks. They are limited to oral communication; visual aids or observation cannot be included. Interpreters of results must make adjustments for subjects who are not at home or who do not have telephones. Many households are excluded from telephone directories by choice (unlisted numbers) or because the residents moved after the directory was published. If households with unlisted numbers are systematically excluded, the resulting sample will be somewhat older, more rural, more white, more educated, more retired, and more white-collar than the population of households with telephone service.[15]

These findings have serious implications for the use of telephone samples in conducting surveys. Some adjustment must be made for groups of respondents that may be undersampled because of a smaller-than-average incidence of telephone listings. Nondirectory telephone samples can overcome such bias. Various methods are available, including random-digit dialing (adding random numbers to the telephone prefix) and plus-one telephone sampling (adding one to the last digit of a number in the directory). These methods make it feasible to dial any working number, whether it is or is not listed in a directory.

Telephone surveys, like mail and personal interview surveys, are sometimes used to develop panels of respondents who can be interviewed repeatedly to measure changes in attitudes or behavior. Reliance on such panels is increasing.

Computer-assisted telephone interviewing permits an integration of questionnaire, data collection, and tabulations and provides data to aid decision makers in the shortest time possible. In computer-assisted telephone interviewing, the paper questionnaire is replaced by a computer monitor or video screen. Responses are entered on a terminal keyboard, or the interviewer can use a light pen (a pen-shaped flashlight) to record a response on a light-sensitive screen. On the most advanced devices, the interviewer merely points at the appropriate response on a touch-sensitive screen with his or her finger. Open-ended responses can be typed on the keyboard or recorded with paper and pencil.

Computer-assisted telephone interviewing saves time and facilitates monitoring the progress of interviews. Entry functions are largely eliminated; the computer determines which question to display on the screen, skipping irrelevant questions. Because data are available as soon as they are entered into the system, cumbersome

14. Diane K. Bowers, "Telephone Legislation," *Marketing Research,* March 1989, p. 47.

15. Patricia E. Moberg, "Biases in Unlisted Phone Numbers," *Journal of Advertising Research,* August-September 1982, p. 55.

hand computations are avoided and interim results can be quickly retrieved. With some systems, a microcomputer may be taken to off-site locations for use in data analysis. Some researchers say that computer-assisted telephone interviewing—including hardware, software, and operation costs—is less expensive than conventional paper and pencil methods.[16]

Marketing researchers have traditionally favored the *personal interview survey*, chiefly because of its flexibility. Various audiovisual aids—pictures, products, diagrams, or prerecorded advertising copy—can be incorporated into a personal interview. Rapport gained through direct interaction usually permits more in-depth interviewing, including probes, follow-up questions, or psychological tests. In addition, because personal interviews can be longer, they can yield more information. Finally, respondents can be selected more carefully, and reasons for nonresponse can be explored.

The nature of personal interviews has changed. In the past, most personal interviews, which were based on random sampling or prearranged appointments, were conducted in the respondent's home. Today, most personal interviews are conducted in shopping malls. *Shopping mall intercept interviews* involve interviewing a percentage of persons passing by certain "intercept" points in a mall. Although there are many variations of this technique, Table 7.5 indicates that shopping mall intercept interviewing is the third most popular survey technique, after WATS and focus-group interviewing. By 1987, not only did 86 percent of the major consumer goods and services companies use this technique, but almost half reported that shopping mall intercept interviewing was their major expenditure on survey research.[17]

Like any face-to-face interviewing method, mall intercept interviewing has many advantages. The interviewer is in a position to recognize and react to respondents' nonverbal indications of confusion. Respondents can be shown product prototypes, videotapes of commercials, and the like, and reactions can be sought. The mall environment lets the researcher deal with complex situations. For example, in taste tests, researchers know that all the respondents are reacting to the same product, which can be prepared and monitored from the mall test kitchen or some other facility. In addition, lower cost, greater control, and the ability to conduct tests requiring bulky equipment make shopping mall intercept interviews popular.

Research indicates that given a comparable sample of respondents, shopping mall intercept interviewing is a suitable substitute for telephone interviewing.[18] In addition, there seem to be no significant differences in the completeness of consumer responses between telephone interviewing and shopping mall intercept interviewing. In fact, for questions dealing with socially desirable behavior, shopping mall intercept respondents appear to be more honest about their past behavior.[19]

On-site computer interviewing, a variation of the mall intercept interview, consists of respondents completing a self-administered questionnaire displayed on a com-

16. Stephen M. Billig, "Go Slow, Be Wary When Considering Switch to Computer-Assisted Interviewing System," *Marketing News*, Nov. 26, 1982, sec. 2, p. 2.

17. *Practices, Trends and Expectations for the Market Research Industry 1987*, Market Facts, Inc., April 29, 1987.

18. Alan J. Bush and A. Parasuraman, "Mall Intercept Versus Telephone-Interviewing Environment," *Journal of Advertising Research*, April-May 1985, p. 42.

19. Alan J. Bush and Joseph F. Hair, Jr., "An Assessment of the Mall Intercept as a Data Collecting Method," *Journal of Marketing Research*, May 1985, p. 162.

puter monitor. MAX (Machine Answered eXamination), a microcomputer-based software package developed by POPULUS Inc., a Greenwich, Connecticut, research firm, conducts such interviews in shopping malls. After a brief lesson on how to operate MAX, respondents can proceed through the survey at their own pace. According to its developers, MAX provides not only faster and more accurate information, but also consistency, for each respondent is asked questions in the same way. MAX is flexible because it can ask different sets of relevant questions depending on the respondent's previous answers. In addition, respondents' answers are entered directly onto a computer disk and can be analyzed without someone having to code and key in the responses later, reducing the potential of information being incorrectly encoded. Its developers assert that "MAX is the interviewer we would all like to be. MAX is patient, nonjudgmental, remembering all that he is taught, and he keeps track of every answer."[20]

The object of a *focus-group interview* is to observe group interaction when members are exposed to an idea or concept. Often these interviews are conducted informally, without a structured questionnaire. Consumer attitudes, behavior, lifestyles, needs, and desires can be explored in a flexible and creative manner through focus-group interviews. Table 7.5 indicates that 98 percent of the firms surveyed used focus-group interviewing in 1987. Questions are open-ended and stimulate consumers to answer in their own words. Researchers can ask probing questions to clarify something they do not fully understand or something unexpected and interesting that may help explain consumer behavior. Cadillac used information obtained from focus groups to change its advertising so that the safety features of Cadillacs might be emphasized. The new advertisements pushed up Cadillac sales by 36 percent in test markets.[21] Marketing Update 7.2 describes the future of this marketing research technique.

Another research technique is the *in-home (door-to-door) interview*. As Table 7.5 indicates, 39 percent of the largest consumer companies use this technique. Because it may be desirable to eliminate group influence, the in-home interview offers a clear advantage when thoroughness of self-disclosure is important. In an in-depth interview of forty-five to ninety minutes, respondents can be probed to reveal their real motivations, feelings, behaviors, and aspirations. In-depth interviews permit the discovery of emotional "hot buttons" that provide psychological insights.[22]

Questionnaire Construction.   A carefully constructed questionnaire is essential to the success of any survey. Questions must be designed to elicit information that meets the study's data requirements. These questions must be clear, easy to understand, and directed toward a specific objective. Researchers need to define the objective before trying to develop a questionnaire because the objective determines the substance of the questions and the amount of detail. A common mistake in constructing questionnaires is to ask questions that interest the researchers but do not yield information useful in deciding whether to accept or reject a hypothesis. Finally, the most important rule in composing questions is to maintain impartiality.

20. Jeff Wiss, "Meet MAX: Computerized Survey Taker," *Marketing News*, May 22, 1989, p. 16.

21. James B. Treece and Wendy Zellner with Walecia Konrad, "Detroit Tries to Rev Up," *Business Week*, June 12, 1989, p. 82.

22. Hal Sokolow, "In-Depth Interviews Increasing in Importance," *Marketing News*, Sept. 13, 1985, p. 26.

The questions are usually of three kinds: open-end, dichotomous, and multiple choice.

OPEN-END QUESTION
What is your general opinion of the American Express Optima Card?

_____

_____

_____

DICHOTOMOUS QUESTION
Do you presently have an American Express Optima Card?

Yes _____
No _____

MULTIPLE-CHOICE QUESTION
What age group are you in?

Under 20 _____
20–29 _____
30–39 _____
40–49 _____
50–59 _____
60 and over _____

Researchers must be very careful about questions that a respondent might consider too personal or that might require him or her to admit activities that other people are likely to condemn. Questions of this type should be worded in such a way as to make them less offensive.

For testing special markets, where individuals (for instance, executives, scientists, and engineers) are likely to own or have access to a personal computer, questionnaires may be programmed on a computer disk and the disks delivered through the mail. This technique may cost less than a telephone interview and eliminate bias by simplifying flow patterns in answering questions. Respondents see less clutter on the screen than on a printed questionnaire; the novelty of the approach may also spark their interest and compel their attention.

Observation Methods.   In using **observation methods**, researchers record respondents' overt behavior, taking note of physical conditions and events. Direct contact with respondents is avoided; instead, their actions are examined and noted systematically. For example, researchers might use observation methods to answer the question, "How long does the average McDonald's restaurant customer have to wait in line before being served?"

Observation may also be combined with interviews. For example, during personal interviews, the condition of a respondent's home or other possessions may be observed and recorded, and demographic information such as race, approximate age, and sex can be confirmed by direct observation.

Data gathered through observation can sometimes be biased if the respondent is aware of the observation process. An observer can be placed in a natural market

FOCUS-GROUP INTERVIEWING IN THE 1990s

Focus-group interviews, which are generally informal group discussions about marketing ideas or concepts conducted by a marketer or marketing research firm, are used by most major organizations in developing marketing or business plans. In the 1980s, focus-group interviewing became one of the most widely practiced types of marketing research, expanding from the packaged goods industry into financial services, hard goods, and industrial applications.

However, the function of focus-group interviewing is expected to change in the 1990s. Traditionally, companies have relied on focus-group interviews to define the input going into quantitative studies, but the new trend is to conduct focus-group interviews after tabulating research results, to provide insight into why the results were achieved. The trend is also toward higher costs (the average today is $3,000 to $4,000 per group).

Other changes pertain to moderator guides and their reports. The moderator guides will be expected to involve clients in the development process. Their reports will concentrate on providing conclusions that interpret the findings and on making recommendations for action by the client. The reports will also contain fewer actual quotations from individual focus-group participants. The post–focus-group debriefing techniques are also being altered. The shift is toward disciplined debriefing that asks participants their reactions to the group session. Such debriefing can provide the link between concept development and application and serve as a rough check on validity and reliability.

Another new development in focus-group interviewing is the use of electronics to offer three-way capabilities. Computerized decision-making software can supplement research findings and consolidate opinions from three different audiences. For example, in health care research in a hospital setting, the three audiences would be past patients, physicians, and employees. The advantages of using electronics include easier scheduling of participating groups and more interaction among the three audiences.

SOURCES: Lynne Cunningham, "Electronic Focus Groups Offer 3-Way Capability," *Marketing News,* Jan. 8, 1990, pp. 22, 39; Thomas L. Greenbaum, "Focus Group Spurt Predicted for the '90s," *Marketing News,* Jan. 8, 1990, pp. 21, 22; and Nino DeNicola, "Debriefing Sessions: The Missing Link in Focus Groups," *Marketing News,* Jan. 8, 1990, pp. 20, 22.

environment, such as a grocery store, without biasing or influencing shoppers' actions. However, if the presence of a human observer is likely to bias the outcome or if human sensory abilities are inadequate, mechanical means may be used to record behavior. **Mechanical observation devices** include cameras, recorders, counting machines, and equipment to record physiological changes in individuals. For instance, a special camera can be used to record eye movements of respondents looking at an advertisement; the sequence of reading and the parts of the advertisement that receive greatest attention can be detected. Electric scanners in supermarkets are mechanical observation devices that offer an exciting opportunity for marketing research. Scanner technology can provide accurate data on sales and consumers' purchase patterns, and marketing researchers may buy such data from the supermarket.

Observation is straightforward and avoids a central problem of survey methods: motivating respondents to state their true feelings or opinions. However, observation tends to be descriptive. When it is the only method of data collection, it may not provide insights into causal relationships. Another drawback is that analyses based on observation are subject to the biases of the observer or the limitations of the mechanical device.

INTERPRETING RESEARCH FINDINGS

After collecting data to test their hypotheses, marketers interpret the research findings. Interpretation is easier if marketers carefully plan their data analysis methods early in the research process. They should also allow for continual evaluation of the data during the entire collection period. They can then gain valuable insight into areas that ought to be probed during the formal interpretation.

The first step in drawing conclusions from most research is displaying the data in table format. If marketers intend to apply the results to individual categories of the things or people being studied, cross tabulation may be quite useful, especially in tabulating joint occurrences. For example, using the two variables, gender and purchase rates of automobile tires, a cross tabulation could show how men and women differ in purchasing automobile tires.

After the data are tabulated, they must be analyzed. **Statistical interpretation** focuses on what is typical or what deviates from the average. It indicates how widely responses vary and how they are distributed in relation to the variable being measured. This interpretation is another facet of marketing research that relies on marketers' judgment or intuition. Moreover, when they interpret statistics, marketers must take into account estimates of expected error or deviation from the true values of the population. The analysis of data may lead researchers to accept or reject the hypothesis being studied. As shown in Figure 7.10, SPSS, a noted statistical analysis package producer for marketing research, provides data analysis and presentation graphics.

Data require careful interpretation by the marketer. If the results of a study are valid, the decision maker should take action; however, if it is discovered that a question has been incorrectly worded, the results should be ignored. For example, if a study by an electric utility company reveals that 50 percent of its customers believe that meter readers are "friendly," is that finding good, bad, or indifferent?

SOURCE: SPSS Inc.

Two important bench marks help interpret the result: how the 50 percent figure compares with that for competitors and how it compares with a previous time period. The point is that managers must understand the research results and relate the results to a context that permits effective decision making.[23]

REPORTING RESEARCH FINDINGS

The final step in the marketing research process is reporting the research findings. Before preparing the report, the marketer must take a clear, objective look at the findings to see how well the gathered facts answer the research question or support or negate the hypotheses posed in the beginning. In most cases, it is extremely doubtful that the study can provide everything needed to answer the research question. Thus in the report the researcher must point out the deficiencies and the reasons for them.

23. Michael J. Olivette, "Marketing Research in the Electric Utility Industry," *Marketing News*, Jan. 2, 1987, p. 13.

The report presenting the results is usually a formal, written report. Researchers must allow time for the writing task when they plan and schedule the project. Since the report is a means of communicating with the decision makers who will use the research findings, researchers need to determine beforehand how much detail and supporting data to include. They should keep in mind that corporate executives prefer reports that are short, clear, and simply expressed. Often researchers will give their summary and recommendations first, especially if decision makers do not have time to study how the results were obtained. A technical report allows its users to analyze data and interpret recommendations because it describes the research methods and procedures and the most important data gathered. Thus, researchers must recognize the needs and expectations of the report user and adapt to them.

When marketing decision makers have a firm grasp of research methods and procedures, they are better able to integrate reported findings and personal experience. If marketers can spot limitations in research from reading the report, then personal experience assumes additional importance in the decision-making process. Marketers who cannot understand basic statistical assumptions and data gathering procedures may misuse research findings. Consequently, report writers should be aware of the backgrounds and research abilities of those who will rely on the report in making decisions. Clear explanations presented in plain language make it easier for decision makers to apply the findings and diminish the chances of a report being misused or ignored. Talking with potential research users before writing a report can help researchers supply information that will indeed improve decision making.

The Importance of Ethical Marketing Research

Marketing research and systematic information gathering make successful marketing more likely. In fact, many companies, and even entire industries, have failed because of a lack of marketing research. The conventional wisdom about the evaluation and use of marketing research by marketing managers suggests that in the future managers will rely on marketing research to reduce uncertainty and to make better decisions than they could without such information.[24]

Clearly, marketing research and information systems are vital to marketing decision making. Because of this, it is essential that ethical standards be established and followed. Attempts to stamp out shoddy practices and establish generally acceptable procedures for conducting research are issues of great concern to marketing researchers. Other issues in marketing research relate to researcher honesty, manipulation of research techniques, data manipulation, invasion of privacy, and failure to disclose the purpose or sponsorship of a study in some situations. Too often respondents are unfairly manipulated and research clients are not told about flaws in data.

One common practice that hurts the image of marketing research is "sugging" ("selling under the guise of marketing research"). A leading marketing research association (ESOMAR) is attempting to get research companies and marketing research firms worldwide to adopt codes and policies prohibiting this practice.[25]

24. Hanjoon Lee, Frank Acits, and Ralph L. Day, "Evaluation and Use of Marketing Research by Decision Makers: A Behavioral Simulation," *Journal of Marketing Research,* May 1987, p. 187.

25. Lynn Colemar, "It's Selling Disguised as Research," *Marketing News,* Jan. 4, 1988, p. 1.

Because so many parties are involved in the marketing research process, developing shared ethical concern is difficult. The relationships among respondents who cooperate and share information, interviewing companies, marketing research agencies that manage projects, and organizations that use the data are interdependent and complex. Ethical conflict typically occurs because the parties involved in the marketing research process often have different objectives. For example, the organization that uses data tends to be result-oriented, and success is often based on performance rather than a set of standards. On the other hand, a data-gathering subcontractor is evaluated based on the ability to follow a specific set of standards or rules. The relationships among all participants in marketing research must be understood so that decision making becomes ethical. Without clear understanding and agreement, including mutual adoption of standards, ethical conflict will lead to mistrust and questionable research results.[26]

Marketing research is essential in planning and developing marketing strategies. Information about target markets provides vital input in planning the marketing mix and controlling marketing activities. It is no secret that companies can use information technology as a key to gaining an advantage over the competition.[27] In short, the marketing concept—the marketing philosophy of customer orientation—can be implemented better when adequate information about customers is available.

SUMMARY

To implement the marketing concept, marketers need information about the characteristics, needs, and wants of their target markets. Marketing research and information systems that furnish practical, unbiased information help firms avoid the assumptions and misunderstandings that could lead to poor marketing performance.

Marketing research is the systematic design, collection, interpretation, and reporting of information to help marketers solve specific marketing problems or take advantage of marketing opportunities. Marketing research is conducted on a special-project basis, with the research methods adapted to the problems being studied and to changes in the environment.

The marketing information system (MIS) is a framework for the day-to-day managing and structuring of information regularly gathered from sources both inside and outside an organization. The inputs into a marketing information system include the information sources inside and outside the firm considered useful for future decision making. Processing information involves classifying information and developing categories for meaningful storage and retrieval. Marketing decision makers then determine which information—the output—is useful for making decisions. Feedback enables those who are responsible for gathering internal and external data to adjust the information inputs systematically. Data brought into the organization through marketing research become part of its marketing databank, a file of data collected through both the MIS and marketing research projects.

26. O. C. Ferrell and Steven J. Skinner, "Ethical Behavior and Bureaucratic Structure in Marketing Research Organizations," *Journal of Marketing Research,* Feb. 1988, pp. 103–104.

27. Brandt Allen, "Make Information Services Pay Its Way," *Harvard Business Review,* January-February 1987, p. 57.

The increase in marketing research activities represents a transition from intuitive to scientific problem solving. Intuitive decisions are made on the basis of personal knowledge and past experience. Scientific decision making is an orderly, logical, and systematic approach. Minor, nonrecurring problems can be handled successfully by intuition. As the number of risks and alternative solutions increases, the use of research becomes more desirable and rewarding.

The five basic steps of planning marketing research are (1) defining and locating problems, (2) developing hypotheses, (3) collecting data, (4) interpreting research findings, and (5) reporting the findings.

Defining and locating the problem—the first step toward finding a solution or launching a research study—means uncovering the nature and boundaries of a negative, or positive, situation or question. A problem must be clearly defined for marketers to develop a hypothesis—an informed guess or assumption about that problem or set of circumstances—which is the second step in the research process.

To test the accuracy of hypotheses, researchers collect data—the third step in the research process. Researchers may use exploratory, descriptive, or causal studies. Secondary data are compiled inside or outside the organization for some purpose other than the current investigation. Secondary data may be collected from an organization's databank and other internal sources; from periodicals, government publications, and unpublished sources; and from syndicated data services, which collect general information and sell it to clients.

Primary data are observed and recorded or collected directly from respondents. Experimentation involves maintaining as constants those factors that are related to or may affect the variables under investigation so that the effects of the experimental variables may be measured. Marketing experimentation is a set of rules and procedures under which the task of data gathering is organized to expedite analysis and interpretation. In experimentation, an independent variable is manipulated and the resulting changes are measured in a dependent variable. Research techniques are reliable if they produce almost identical results in successive repeated trials; they are valid if they measure what they are supposed to measure and not something else. Experiments may take place in laboratory settings, which provide maximum control over influential factors, or in field settings, which are preferred when marketers want experimentation to take place in natural surroundings.

Other methods for collecting primary data include sampling, surveys, and observation. Sampling involves selecting representative units from a total population. In random sampling, all the units in a population have an equal chance of appearing in the sample. In stratified sampling, the population of interest is divided into groups according to a common characteristic or attribute, and then a probability sample is conducted within each group. Area sampling involves selecting a probability sample of geographic areas such as blocks, census tracts, or census enumeration districts and selecting units or individuals within the selected geographic areas for the sample. Quota sampling differs from other forms of sampling in that it is judgmental.

There are numerous survey methods, ranging from mail surveys, telephone surveys, computer-assisted telephone interviews, personal interview surveys, and shopping mall intercept interviews to on-site computer interviews, focus-group interviews, and in-home interviews. Questionnaires are instruments used to obtain information from respondents and to record observations; they should be unbiased and objective. Observation methods involve researchers recording respondents' overt behavior and taking note of physical conditions and events. Observation may be facilitated by mechanical observation devices.

To apply research findings to decision making, marketers must interpret and report their findings properly. Statistical interpretation is analysis that focuses on what is typical or what deviates from the average. After interpreting the research findings, the researchers must prepare a report of the findings that the decision makers can use and understand.

Marketing research and systematic information gathering increase the probability of successful marketing. In fact, marketing research is essential in planning and developing marketing strategies. Because of this, attempts to eliminate unethical marketing research practices and establish generally acceptable procedures for conducting research are important goals. However, because so many parties are involved in the marketing research process, shared ethical concern is difficult.

IMPORTANT TERMS

Marketing research	Dependent variable
Marketing information system (MIS)	Reliability
Marketing databank	Validity
Problem definition	Sample
Hypothesis	Sampling
Exploratory studies	Population
Descriptive studies	Random sampling
Causal studies	Stratified sampling
Primary data	Area sampling
Secondary data	Quota sampling
Syndicated data services	Survey methods
Experimentation	Observation methods
Marketing experimentation	Mechanical observation devices
Independent variable	Statistical interpretation

DISCUSSION AND REVIEW QUESTIONS

1. What is the MIS likely to include in a small organization? Do all organizations have a marketing databank?
2. What is the difference between marketing research and marketing information systems? In what ways do marketing research and the MIS overlap?
3. How do the benefits of decisions guided by marketing research compare with those of intuitive decision making? How do marketing decision makers know when it will be worthwhile to conduct research?
4. Give specific examples of situations in which intuitive decision making would probably be more appropriate than marketing research.
5. What is the difference between defining a research problem and developing a hypothesis?
6. What are the major limitations of using secondary data to solve marketing problems?
7. List some problems of conducting a laboratory experiment on respondents' reactions to the taste of different brands of beer. How would these problems differ from those of a field study of beer taste preferences?

8. In what situation would it be best to use random sampling? Quota sampling? Stratified or area sampling?

9. *Nonresponse* is the inability or refusal of some respondents to cooperate in a survey. What are some ways to decrease nonresponse in personal door-to-door surveys?

10. Make some suggestions for ways to encourage respondents to cooperate in mail surveys.

11. If a survey of all homes with listed telephone numbers is conducted, what sampling design should be used?

12. Give some examples of marketing problems that could be solved through information gained from observation.

■ CASES

7.1 How Marketing Research Helped Create a New "Cadillac Style"

When the 1980s began, Americans were able to choose from among 408 different automobile models; in 1990 there were 572 models available. The United States is the richest market for automobiles in the world, and every car maker wants to sell there. For every brand forced out of the U.S. market, there are two others to take its place. Consequently, Isuzu, Daihatsu, Mitsubishi, Hyundai, Geo, Saturn, and other brands have been introduced in the last ten years. With so many different models available, consumers have become simultaneously liberated, confused, and less brand loyal. A recent *Wall Street Journal* study found that 53 percent of car buyers tend to switch brands. Car makers are therefore having a harder time keeping customers, as well as getting customers to buy their brands in the first place. Other research suggests that car buyers ignore new models that lack a well-defined image. In the end, the most successful models will probably be those from car makers traditionally associated with quality and value. This is where marketing research becomes crucial. Automobile manufacturers must conduct marketing research in order to determine what car buyers need and want in a new car.

One company that is using marketing research to stay ahead of the competition is GM's Cadillac division. Cadillac, the best-selling domestic luxury car since 1948, has long been associated with high quality, luxury, and value. However, reaching the affluent car buyer has become harder for Cadillac because of competition from new models. Along with other well-established luxury brands—Lincoln's Town Car, Mercedes Benz, Volvo, and BMW—Cadillac suddenly found itself competing with Japanese luxury sedans like Honda's Acura, Nissan's Infiniti, and Toyota's Lexus.

Cadillac, along with luxury car makers in general, has found it increasingly difficult to reach potential customers. Marketing research indicated that luxury car makers were not effectively advertising to affluent consumers because traditional advertising did not reach the activities where these consumers spend most of their leisure time. Based on these research findings, Cadillac decided to alter its promotional activities. It recently signed to sponsor a series of Senior PGA Tour tournaments in the 1990s. Cadillac is also getting involved with other upscale lifestyle promotions such as yachting regattas, horse shows, and polo matches.

Lifestyle activities such as these had been a part of Cadillac advertising for many years. However, going into the 1990s, Cadillac felt the time had come to move toward a new concept of what "Cadillac style" meant. The problem was in deciding how to approach this new concept. Marketing research had already shown that consumers were less brand loyal than they had been in the past. And the recent introductions of Lexus and Infiniti meant that Cadillac *had* to choose the correct strategy for the 1990s.

Cadillac found the answer through marketing research. A *Wall Street Journal* national survey of potential car buyers indicated that 60 percent of those surveyed would buy anti-lock brakes in their next car, and 50 percent said they would buy a car with air bags. The same survey respondents, however, showed little interest in features such as turbo engines and electronic dashboards. Cadillac then conducted focus group interviews with potential buyers who already owned luxury imports and found that 50 percent would consider buying a redesigned Cadillac Eldorado or Seville. Past research of this type had only been able to find 10 percent of potential buyers who were willing to consider buying a Cadillac.

The fact that car buyers wanted more safety features posed a problem for Cadillac. The Big Three car makers had long held the belief that safety did not sell cars. However, Cadillac decided to ignore the theory and designed safer Eldorados and Sevilles for the 1992 model year. Cadillac immediately changed its advertising to emphasize the car's safety features, rather than its upscale image. Company officials felt that the well-established Cadillac image inherently would promote styling, luxury, and prestige. The new campaign, which used the theme "Building a safer automobile, Cadillac style," showed more of Cadillac's anti-lock brake and air-bag features and less upscale lifestyle images.

Cadillac is also designing its automobiles to satisfy its traditional Cadillac buyers: the age 50 and over market. Although the company had made smaller Eldorado, Seville, DeVille, and Fleetwood models in the mid-1980s, research suggested that luxury car buyers preferred the old "boulevard barges" with lavish interiors and massive size; so the company enlarged and restyled them in the 1988 and 1989 model years. The Fleetwood and DeVille sedans gained nine inches in length, and all Cadillacs got a more powerful V-8 engine in 1988. The company also reduced the car's defect rates by 40 percent over three years. To gain sales from younger import buyers, the company is attempting to use more distinctive styling in Cadillacs. Although it will be some time before Cadillac can determine the success of its redesigned automobiles, it will continue to conduct market research to determine the needs and wants of Cadillac buyers and to develop products and promotions accordingly.

SOURCES: Lesa Doll, "Prospecting Goes Further Upscale," *Advertising Age,* Jan. 22, 1990, pp. S10–S11; Paul Ingrassia and Gregory A. Patterson, "Is Buying a Car a Choice or a Chore?," *Wall Street Journal,* Oct. 24, 1989, p. B1; Raymond Serafin, "Caddy Goes for Golf," *Advertising Age,* Aug. 21, 1989, p. 16; Raymond Serafin and Patricia Strand, "Ads, Cadillac-Style," *Advertising Age,* Sept. 18, 1989, p. 84; Wendy Zellner, "The Boulevard Barge Is Cruising Again," *Business Week,* Feb. 5, 1990, pp. 52–53.

Questions for Discussion

1. How has marketing research helped Cadillac improve its promotional activities?
2. What kinds of risks are involved for Cadillac in redesigning the 1992 Eldorado and Seville and emphasizing safety features as suggested by focus group research?

7.2   Nielsen's People Meter

Traditionally, the survey methods used to collect data for marketing research have been mail, telephone, or personal interviews. However, A. C. Nielsen Company pioneered the use of a microwave computerized rating system—called a *people meter*—to measure national television audiences.

People meters transmit demographic information overnight on what television shows people are watching, the number of households that are watching the shows, and which family members are watching. The data are recorded automatically when household members press buttons on the meter. The people meters replace the old National Audience Composition (NAC) diaries used for the past thirty years to determine the viewing habits of consumers.

People meters were initially placed in two thousand homes in 1987. The device enables Nielsen monitors to record second-by-second viewing choices of up to eight household members, with the viewers using remote control keyboards to record their program selection. The people meter is the state of the art in electronic measuring equipment and underwent extensive testing and analysis before its introduction. According to Nielsen officials, the people meter determines national audience composition far more accurately than the old National Audience Composition (NAC) diary: it is also a much faster means of giving advertisers information about the television shows that their target market is watching, enabling them to reach that target market with their commercials. A study published by Roland Soong in a 1988 issue of the *Journal of Advertising Research* concludes that "the people meter sample is considerably more reliable than a diary sample with the same total number of households." The accuracy is increased because a computer records what show a person is viewing. Consequently, the system does not depend on a person's memory, as the diary did.

Despite its speed and accuracy in measuring audience composition, the people meter was initially criticized by the networks because its data showed a smaller number of network television viewers than did the NAC diary. The three major networks questioned the accuracy of the people meters. Indeed, in 1987, both ABC and CBS asked Nielsen to continue to use the NAC diary rather than the people meter for that year. During that period, the two networks also based their sales and programming decisions solely on the NAC. But ABC became so dissatisfied with "declining standards" that it canceled its contract with Nielsen early in the year. According to the network, the diary sample results were not as accurate because Nielsen had tied up most of it resources in the people meter. CBS also canceled its contract with Nielsen, and both CBS and ABC refused to buy the people meter data. CBS signed a contract with AGB, Nielsen's major competitor, to use its people meter instead. NBC agreed to use the Nielsen device but also questioned the meter's reliability.

Nielsen's and AGB's people meters have registered consistently lower ratings than the old diary system, leading to confusion and controversy throughout the industry. The networks were unhappy. After all, the higher the rating for a program, the more they could charge for commercial time during that program, whereas lower ratings meant significant losses of revenue. To protect themselves against such losses, stemming from people meter ratings, the networks raised prices for commercial time by 15 to 25 percent in 1987. Advertisers get "make-good" time, or free-advertisement time, from a network when the ratings for a show it sponsors fall below the guidelines for the original purchase contract. The result of this make-good time is higher price tags for advertisers.

However, after three years of meter use, the attitude of the networks has changed. The meter data enables the networks to spot viewing trends more quickly and respond with changes in programming schedules. People meters have made it easier and faster to show ratings and demographic shifts. They may force a change in the demographic groupings currently used for negotiations and guarantees. People meters have also improved audience definition; by simply pushing a designated button, users furnish personal information, such as age, sex, income, education and ethnic background. This information gives the networks more opportunity to market their product, as opposed to selling it. In the view of most advertising and network executives, the people meter has had limited impact so far. But as one network marketing vice president noted, the real advantages of the available data remain to be seen.

SOURCES: Brian Donlon, "TV Rating Rivals Tune in New Device," *USA Today,* Sept. 16, 1987, pp. 1B, 2B; Verne Gay, "Networks Zap Debut of Meters," *Advertising Age,* Sept. 7, 1987, pp. 1, 56; "People Meters to Be Sole Tool for '87 Nielsen TV Ratings," *Marketing News,* Jan. 30, 1987, p. 1; Roland Soong, "The Statistical Reliability of People Meter Ratings," *Journal of Advertising Research,* Feb.-March 1988, p. 56; and Wayne Walley, "Meters Set New TV Ground Rules," *Advertising Age,* Oct. 30, 1989, p. 12.

Questions for Discussion

1. What are the advantages and disadvantages of Nielsen's people meter compared with its old diary method?
2. Why do you think that Nielsen switched from the NAC diary to the people meter?
3. Does the people meter collect primary or secondary data? Why?

Stew Leonard's: The World's Largest Dairy Store

Stew Leonard's is the top-grossing, highest-volume food store in the world. Built on the philosophy that the customer is always right, Stew Leonard's offers food shoppers low prices, high product quality, excellent customer service, and a festive, Disney-like atmosphere. The Norwalk, Connecticut store draws 100,000 shoppers a week, some from as far away as Massachusetts, Rhode Island, Pennsylvania, and New York. Annual sales total $100 million.

Milkman and entrepreneur Stewart Leonard opened his store in 1969 after the state of Connecticut decided to route a highway through the small dairy he had inherited from his father. The original Stew Leonard's offered only eight products, but customers were attracted to the dairy store by the prices and Leonard's showmanship and marketing flair. Today, after twenty-six expansions, family-owned Stew Leonard's is a 106,000-square-foot complex built around a highly automated milk-processing operation. The store continues to present a narrow product mix—about 750 items, as compared to the 15,000 items conventional supermarkets stock. Nevertheless, Stew Leonard's sells in such volume that the store's per square foot sales of $2,700 recently earned the business a place in the Guinness Book of World Records.

Each year Stew Leonard's customers buy 10 million quarts of milk, 1 million pints of cream, 100 tons of cottage cheese, 2.9 million quarts of orange juice, and more than 500,000 pounds of butter. They also walk out with 1,040 tons of ground beef, 1,820 tons of Perdue poultry products, and 520 tons of fixings from the store's salad bar. According to the Food Marketing Institute, the bake shop that Stew Leonard's daughter, Beth, operates sells twenty times more baked goods than any other in-store bakery in the country—almost 3 million muffins, more than 500,000 pies, and 348 tons of freshly baked chocolate chip cookies annually. In addition, the store sells 2,000 pounds of pistachio nuts a week, which is 1 percent of the country's entire pistachio crop.

Customer Orientation

Stew Leonard's low prices—about 10 to 20 percent lower than prices at stores in a five-mile radius—are partly responsible for the store's popularity, but even more important is the store's responsiveness to customers. Indeed, the store opened in response to requests from Leonard's former milk route customers. Today, customer demand continues to dictate what products the store carries. Although Stew Leonard's may test-market as many as 10,000 different products in a year, an item must sell 1,000 units weekly to remain in inventory. Thus the store carries only the best-selling brands of such items as cereal, yogurt, and peanut butter. Stew Leonard's also emphasizes product quality. Because of its enormous sales volume, the store can buy by the truckload directly from producers, passing along the savings and freshness to customers. Stew Leonard's also has the leverage to order house brands made to its own specifications.

Stew Leonard's strong customer orientation is reflected in the two rules carved in a huge, three-ton granite boulder just outside the door. Rule 1 states that "the customer is always right." Rule 2 says, "If the customer is ever wrong, reread Rule 1." Customer service is the top priority at Stew Leonard's. To eliminate long check-out lines, the Leonards have equipped the store with twenty-five cash registers. Should any line back up to more than three customers, a store employee immediately passes out free ice cream or snacks to waiting customers. The Leonards also actively solicit ideas from their customers, both to keep up with trends and to improve service. About once a month, focus groups of customers are invited to critique the store's products and policies—and management listens (Stew Leonard's pays 10 customers $20 each in gift certificates to participate in the focus groups). For example, at the focus groups' suggestion, Stew Leonard's began to sell strawberries loose, instead of packaged. Originally the store's profit margin on strawberries decreased, but sales increased tenfold; the store was able to get a better deal from the supplier, and ultimately profits on strawberries were higher.

Stew Leonard's also acts promptly on the hundred-odd messages dropped into the store's suggestion box each day. When the Leonards followed one customer's suggestion that English muffins be displayed near bacon and eggs, muffin sales increased 50 percent. Another customer reported that he would have bought deli roast beef on special if the hard rolls had not been located clear across the store at the bakery. Leonard moved some rolls near the deli counter; sales of both rolls and deli roast beef doubled.

At Stew Leonard's nothing is too good for a customer. When a woman complained to Leonard the day after Thanksgiving that her turkey had been too dry, he immediately handed her a $20 turkey free of charge, knowing that her week-in, week-out business meant much more to the store than the price of a single turkey. Leonard also had high praise for the new courtesy booth employee who surprised a distraught customer with $50 in gift certificates after the customer was unable to find her missing sterling silver pen. Leonard's oft-repeated slogan gets the point across to all employees: "Satisfy the Customer; Teamwork gets it done; Excellence makes it better; Wow makes it fun!"

The "Wow!" is a reminder of Leonard's deeply held conviction that a food retailer must give customers a pleasant and memorable shopping experience if the store is to remain competitive. Hence Stew Leonard's is full of surprises reminiscent of Leonard's hero, Walt Disney. In the parking lot, for example, is "The Little Farm," a collection of one hundred live cows, goats, chickens, sheep, and geese. Inside the store, employees dressed as farm animals and cartoon characters roam the aisles, passing out balloons to children and telling shoppers about store specials. Installed above display cases along the store's single twisting aisle are larger-than-life musical robots, such as a big banjo-playing dog and a cow singing nursery rhymes with a farmer. Purchases totaling more than $100 set off electronic mooing at the cash registers.

Building Customer Loyalty

The Leonards also enhance the appeal of their products by bringing store functions out front, where customers can watch. The milk-processing plant (so highly automated that a tank truck's load of raw milk can be pasteurized and packaged in one day by just four employees) is enclosed in glass; customers see 150 half-gallon cartons of milk per minute moving along a conveyor belt. A plastic cow's head affixed to the front wall of the dairy plant moos when customers press a button. Butchers and fish cutters slice and package in full view of shoppers, and in the deli department an employee uses a special in-store demonstration oven to make pizza. Throughout the store, employees hand out samples of everything from gazpacho to cupcakes, in accordance with the Leonards' observation that sales quadruple when samples are available.

Because of all this, Stew Leonard's satisfied customers often take it on themselves to tell others about the store. The Leonards are fond of reminding their staff, "Lower the price; sell the best; word of mouth will do the rest." Several years ago a customer presented Leonard with a snapshot of herself standing in front of the Kremlin in Moscow, holding a Stew Leonard's plastic shopping bag. When Leonard posted the picture on the store's bulletin board, other customers began following suit. Today, an entire wall in the store is covered with more than seven thousand photos of customers at locations around the world—the Matterhorn, the Great Wall of China, the Egyptian pyramids, the North Pole, and the floor of the Pacific Ocean—each customer holding one of the 250,000 bags Stew Leonard's gives away each year. Such practices build customer loyalty, say the Leonards, and inspire customers to pass the word to friends.

Employee Motivation

Although Stew Leonard has had no formal management training (he studied dairy manufacturing at the University of Connecticut), numerous groups of Japanese and American executives have toured the store to observe his management style first-hand. In fact, many Japanese management policies parallel the techniques Leonard has developed instinctively. For example, at Stew Leonard's, the seven hundred employees, or "team members," regard themselves as one big family. The Leonards make a point of knowing each employee by name. Because the Leonards believe that productive employees motivate each other, they prefer to hire by referrals from the staff. As a result, about 55 percent of the employees have at least one other relative working in the store. Leonard's own family is heavily involved in the business: Leonard's wife Marianne, their four children, and several other relatives work there.

The Leonards recognize that only happy employees can produce satisfied customers. A nonunion operation, Stew Leonard's offers employee benefits on the scale of a large corporation. In addition, the Leonards encourage initiative by giving employees public recognition for their ideas. The Leonards look for "a good attitude" in potential employees and tell their team members, "If you're training the person under you to do a better job than you do, you're valuable to the company and will be promoted." About one hundred of the employees currently working at the store have graduated from Dale Carnegie courses conducted in-house. Outstanding employees also are rewarded with plaques, dinners, gift certificates, recognition in the company newsletter, and (for managers) profit sharing. On the store's walls are framed pictures of employees of the month and team members whose suggestions have saved the organization money. Leonard's own efforts earned him a Presidential Award for Entrepreneurial Achievement. He was also named Connecticut's Small Business Advocate of the Year by the U.S. Small Business Administration, and Stew Leonard's is featured in the book *A Passion for Excellence* as one of the best-run companies in America.

Until recently, Stew Leonard's was a single-store operation. However, after having developed all available space on the original site, the Leonards opened a second store in Danbury, Connecticut. The new Stew Leonard's—a two-story, 272,000-square foot facility on a 44-acre site—employs about four hundred persons and includes all the features of the Norwalk store, plus a garden center and parking space for eight hundred cars.

Questions for Discussion

1. Has Stew Leonard's adopted the philosophy of the marketing concept? Explain your answer.
2. In what ways does Stew Leonard's demonstrate a strong customer orientation?
3. What types of marketing research does Stew Leonard's use?
4. How does Stew Leonard's understanding of customer needs contribute to the firm's success?

SOURCES: Diane Feldman, "Quality Chitchat, Chickens, and Customer Service", *Management Review*, May 1989, pp. 8–9; Joanne Kaufman, "In the Moo: Shopping at Stew Leonard's," *Wall Street Journal*, Sept. 17, 1987, p. 26; Margaret Mahar, "Supermarketer," *Success!*, March 1986, pp. 50–53; Stew Leonard's Fact Sheet, B.L. Ochman Public Relations, New York; "Stew Leonard's Launches a New Invasion," *Progressive Grocer*, May 1986, p. 18; "Stew Leonard's In-Store Disneyland," *Incentive*, Jan. 1989, pp. 26, 30; "Supermarket Whiz Tells Bankers: Create Some Fun," *Marketing*, April 1989, p. 16.

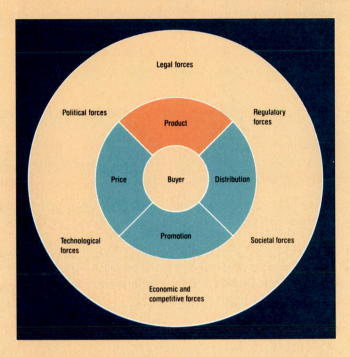

We are now prepared to analyze the decisions and activities associated with developing and maintaining effective marketing mixes. In Parts II through V we focus on the major components of the marketing mix: product, distribution, promotion, and price. Specifically, in Part II we explore the product ingredient of the marketing mix. Chapter 8 introduces basic concepts and relationships that must be understood if one is to make effective product decisions. Branding, packaging, and labeling are also discussed in this chapter. In Chapter 9 we analyze a variety of dimensions regarding product management, such as the ways that a firm can be organized to manage products, the development and positioning of products, product modification, and phasing out products. ◆

8 PRODUCT CONCEPTS

Objectives

To learn how marketers define products

To understand how to classify products

To become familiar with the concepts of product item, product line, and product mix and understand how they are connected

To understand the concept of product life cycle

To grasp the basic product identification concepts as they relate to branding, packaging, and labeling

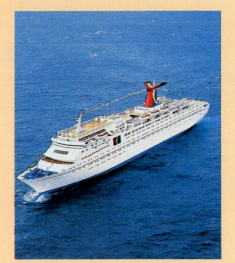

Using aggressive marketing and low prices, Carnival Cruise Lines has become the market leader in the cruise ship industry. Founded in 1972 by Ted Arison and currently headed by his son Micky, Carnival has no problem keeping its eight ocean liners filled with guests. The $5-billion-a-year cruise line industry is likely to keep growing at a fast pace: Only 4 or 5 percent of the 30 million Americans who can afford to take a cruise have actually done so.

To get Carnival where it is today, Arison changed the whole marketing strategy behind cruise ships. He made the ship itself the most important element of the cruise. Carnival therefore promotes its liners as "Fun Ships." Guests can enjoy three-, four-, or seven-day cruises; exotic ports of call; and all the food they can eat for about $395 to $2,395 (including airfare), some 20 percent less than on Carnival's competitors. Carnival ships offer casinos, gymnasiums, cocktail lounges, bingo, skeet shooting, shuffleboard, and Las Vegas–type shows.

Carnival also showers its guests with service—the ratio of guests to crew is two to one. Ship workers are ready to bring drink refills, turn down bed sheets, or lay out clothing. The ship's waiters and bus boys work long hours and receive short vacations but seem to be content; they remain with Carnival for an average of eight years. Carnival also shortened the duration of its cruises. Because of these activities, Carnival Cruise Lines began attracting younger and first-time customers.

Carnival works closely with travel agents, supplying them with a reservation system that allows cruises to be booked within minutes. It also sponsors a travel-agency-of-the-year competition and an incentive program that gives agents recommending Carnival cruises a chance for a $1,000 reward. ◆

Photo by Carnival Cruise Lines.

Based on information from "Carnival Shows Cruise Lines How to Hit High Seas," *U.S. News & World Report,* Aug. 29, 1988, p. 87; Eva Pomice, "Cruising to a Fortune Touting 'Love Boats' for the Masses," *U.S. News & World Report,* Aug. 1, 1988, pp. 43–44; Faye Rice, "How Carnival Stacks the Decks," *Fortune,* Jan. 16, 1989, pp. 108–110, 114, 116; and Paula Schnorbus, "Ain't We Got Fun!" *Marketing & Media Decisions,* March 1988, pp. 101–102, 104, 106.

The product is an important variable in the marketing mix. Products such as the vacation cruises offered by Carnival Cruise Lines are among a firm's most crucial and visible contacts with buyers. If a company's products do not meet its customers' desires and needs, the company will fail unless it makes adjustments. Developing a successful product, as Carnival has done, requires knowledge of fundamental marketing and product concepts.

In this chapter we first introduce and define the concepts that help clarify what a product is and how buyers view products. Next we examine the concepts of product mix and product line to help us understand product planning. Then we explore the stages of the product life cycle. Each life cycle stage generally requires a specific marketing strategy, operates within a certain competitive environment, and has its own sales and profit pattern. We conclude with a discussion of branding, packaging, labeling, and other characteristics that are a product's vital components.

What Is a Product?

A **product** is everything, both favorable and unfavorable, that one receives in an exchange. It is a complexity of tangible and intangible attributes, including functional, social, and psychological utilities or benefits.[1] A product can be an idea, a service, a good, or any combination of these three. This definition also covers supporting services that go with goods, such as installation, guarantees, product information, and promises of repair or maintenance. A **good** is a tangible physical entity, such as a box of Kellogg's Frosted Flakes or a Bic pen. A **service**, by contrast, is intangible; it is the result of the application of human and mechanical efforts to people or objects. Examples of services include Federal Express overnight delivery, medical examinations, and child day care. (Chapter 22 provides a detailed discussion of services marketing.) **Ideas** are concepts, philosophies, images, or issues. They provide the psychological stimulation that aids in solving problems or adjusting to the environment. For example, the World Wildlife Fund promotes endangered-wildlife conservation issues.

When buyers purchase a product, they are really buying the benefits and satisfaction they think the product will provide. A Mazda Miata sports car, for example, is purchased for excitement and fun, not just for transportation. Services, in particular, are purchased on the basis of promises of satisfaction. Promises, with the images and appearances of symbols, help consumers make judgments about tangible and intangible products.[2] Often, symbols and cues are used to make intangible products more tangible or real to the consumer. Merrill Lynch, for example, uses a bull to symbolize the firm's financial power and strength.

1. Part of this definition is adapted from James D. Scott, Martin R. Warshaw, and James R. Taylor, *Introduction to Marketing Management*, 5th ed. (Homewood, Ill.: Irwin, 1985), p. 215.

2. Theodore Levitt, "Marketing Intangible Products and Product Intangibles," *Harvard Business Review,* May-June 1981, pp. 94–102.

CLASSIFYING PRODUCTS

Products fall into one of two general categories. Products purchased to satisfy personal and family needs are **consumer products**. Those bought for use in a firm's operations or to make other products are **industrial products**. Consumers buy products to satisfy their personal wants, whereas industrial buyers seek to satisfy the goals of their organizations.

The same item can be both a consumer product and an industrial product. For example, when consumers purchase light bulbs for their homes, light bulbs are classified as consumer products. However, when a large corporation purchases light bulbs to provide lighting in a factory or office, the light bulbs are considered industrial products because they are used in the daily operations of the firm. Thus the buyer's intent—or the ultimate use of the product—determines whether an item is classified as a consumer or an industrial product.

Why do we need to know about product classifications? The main reason is that classes of products are aimed at particular target markets, and this affects distribution, promotion, and pricing decisions. Furthermore, the types of marketing activities and efforts needed differ among the classes of consumer or industrial products. In short, the entire marketing mix can be affected by how a product is classified. In this section we examine the characteristics of consumer and industrial products and explore the marketing activities associated with some of them.

■ Consumer Products

The most widely accepted approach to classifying consumer products relies on the common characteristics of consumer buying behavior. It divides products into four categories: convenience, shopping, specialty, and unsought products. However, not all buyers behave in the same way when purchasing a specific type of product. Thus a single product can fit into all four categories. To minimize this problem, marketers think in terms of how buyers *generally* behave when purchasing a specific item. In addition, they recognize that the "correct" classification can be determined only by considering a particular firm's intended target market. With these thoughts in mind, let us examine the four traditional categories of consumer products.

Convenience Products. **Convenience products** are relatively inexpensive, frequently purchased items for which buyers exert only minimal purchasing effort. They range from bread, soft drinks, and chewing gum to gasoline and newspapers. The buyer spends little time planning the purchase or comparing available brands or sellers. Even a buyer who prefers a specific brand will readily choose a substitute if the preferred brand is not conveniently available.

Classifying a product as a convenience product has several implications for a firm's marketing strategy. A convenience product is normally marketed through many retail outlets. Because sellers experience high inventory turnover, per-unit gross margins can be relatively low. Producers of convenience products such as Lay's potato chips and Crest toothpaste expect little promotional effort at the retail level and thus must provide it themselves in the form of advertising and sales promotion. Packaging is also an important element of the marketing mix for convenience products. The package may have to sell the product because many convenience items are available only on a self-service basis at the retail level.

FIGURE 8.1

Shopping product.
Vivitar cameras as well as most other brands of cameras are shopping products.

SOURCE: Client: Vivitar Corporation. Agency: Manhattan Communications.

Shopping Products.   **Shopping products** are items for which buyers are willing to expend considerable effort in planning and making the purchase. Buyers allocate much time for comparing stores and brands with respect to prices, product features, qualities, services, and perhaps warranties. Appliances, furniture, bicycles, stereos, and cameras (as shown in Figure 8.1) are examples of shopping products. These products are expected to last a fairly long time and thus are purchased less frequently than convenience items. Even though shopping products are more expensive than convenience products, few buyers of shopping products are particularly brand loyal. If they were, they would be unwilling to shop and compare among brands.

To market a shopping product effectively, a marketer considers several key issues. Shopping products require fewer retail outlets than convenience products. Because shopping products are purchased less frequently, inventory turnover is lower, and middlemen expect to receive higher gross margins. Although large sums of money may be required to advertise shopping products, an even larger percentage of resources is likely to be used for personal selling. Usually, the producer and the middlemen expect some cooperation from one another with respect to providing parts and repair services and performing promotional activities.

Specialty Products. **Specialty products** possess one or more unique characteristics, and a significant group of buyers is willing to expend considerable effort to obtain them. Buyers actually plan the purchase of a specialty product; they know exactly what they want and will not accept a substitute. An example of a specialty product is a Jaguar automobile or a painting by Andy Warhol. When searching for specialty products, buyers do not compare alternatives; they are concerned primarily with finding an outlet that has a preselected product available.

The fact that an item is a specialty product can affect a firm's marketing efforts several ways. Specialty products are often distributed through a limited number of retail outlets. Like shopping goods, they are purchased infrequently, causing lower inventory turnover and thus requiring relatively high gross margins.

Unsought Products. **Unsought products** are purchased when a sudden problem must be solved or when aggressive selling is used to obtain a sale that otherwise would not take place. In general, the consumer does not think of buying these products regularly. Emergency automobile repairs and cemetery plots are examples of unsought products. Life insurance and encyclopedias, in contrast, are examples of products that need aggressive personal selling. The salesperson tries to make consumers aware of benefits that can be derived from buying such products.

■ Industrial Products

Industrial products are usually purchased on the basis of an organization's goals and objectives. Generally, the functional aspects of the product are more important than the psychological rewards sometimes associated with consumer products. Industrial products can be classified into seven categories according to their characteristics and intended uses: raw materials, major equipment, accessory equipment, component parts, process materials, consumable supplies, and industrial services.[3]

Raw Materials. **Raw materials** are the basic materials that actually become part of a physical product. They include minerals, chemicals, agricultural products, and materials from forests and oceans. They are usually bought and sold according to grades and specifications, and in relatively large quantities.

Major Equipment. **Major equipment** includes large tools and machines used for production purposes, such as cranes and stamping machines. Normally, major equipment is expensive and intended to be used in a production process for a considerable length of time. Some major equipment is custom-made to perform specific functions for a particular organization, but other items are standardized and perform similar tasks for many types of firms. Because major equipment is so expensive, purchase decisions are often made by high-level management. Marketers of major equipment frequently must provide a variety of services, including installation, training, repair and maintenance assistance, and even aid in financing the purchase.

Accessory Equipment. **Accessory equipment** does not become a part of the final physical product but is used in production or office activities. Examples include typewriters, fractional-horsepower motors, calculators, and tools. Compared with

3. Robert W. Haas, *Industrial Marketing Management*, 3rd ed. (Boston: Kent Publishing, 1986), pp. 15–25.

major equipment, accessory items are usually much cheaper; purchased routinely, with less negotiation; and treated as expense items rather than capital items because they are not expected to last as long. Accessory products are standardized items that can be used in several aspects of a firm's operations. More outlets are required for distributing accessory equipment than for major equipment, but sellers do not have to provide the multitude of services expected of major equipment marketers.

Component Parts.   **Component parts** become a part of the physical product and are either finished items ready for assembly or products that need little processing before assembly. Although they become part of a larger product, component parts can often be easily identified and distinguished. Spark plugs, tires, clocks, and switches are all component parts of the automobile. Buyers purchase such items according to their own specifications or industry standards. They expect the parts to be of specified quality and delivered on time so that production is not slowed or stopped. Producers that are primarily assemblers, such as most lawn mower or computer manufacturers, depend heavily on the suppliers of component parts.

Process Materials.   **Process materials** are used directly in the production of other products. Unlike component parts, however, process materials are not readily identifiable. For example, Reichhold Chemicals, Inc., markets a treated fiber product: a phenolic-resin, sheet-molding compound, which is used in the production of aircraft flight deck instrument panels and cabin interiors. Although the material is not identifiable in the finished aircraft, it retards burning, smoke, and formation of toxic gas if molded components are subjected to fire or high temperatures. As with component parts, process materials are purchased according to industry standards or the purchaser's specifications.

Consumable Supplies.   **Consumable supplies** facilitate production and operations but do not become part of the finished product. Paper, pencils, oils, cleaning agents, and paints are in this category. Because such supplies are standardized items used in a variety of situations, they are purchased by many different types of organizations. Consumable supplies are commonly sold through numerous outlets and are purchased routinely. To ensure that supplies are available when needed, buyers often deal with more than one seller. Because these supplies can be divided into three subcategories—maintenance, repair, and operating (or overhaul) supplies—they are sometimes called **MRO items**.

Industrial Services.   **Industrial services** are the intangible products that many organizations use in their operations. They include financial, legal, marketing research, computer programming and operation, and janitorial services. Printing services for business, like those discussed in Figure 8.2, fall into the industrial services category. Purchasers must decide whether to provide their own services internally or obtain them outside the organization. This decision depends greatly on the costs associated with each alternative and how frequently the services are needed.

Product Line and Product Mix

Marketers must understand the relationships among all the products of their organization if they are to coordinate the marketing of the total group of products. The following concepts help describe the relationships among an organization's products. A **product item** is a specific version of a product that can be designated as a distinct offering among an organization's products, for example, Mead's Five Star two-subject spiral notebook. A **product line** includes a group of closely related product items that are considered a unit because of marketing, technical, or end-use considerations. All the spiral notebooks manufactured by Mead constitute one of its product lines. To come up with the optimum product line, marketers must understand buyers' goals. Figure 8.3 depicts Century Furniture's line of dining chairs. Specific product items in a product line usually reflect the desires of different target markets or the different needs of consumers.

A **product mix** is the composite, or total, group of products that an organization makes available to customers. For example, all the toothpastes, detergents, coffees, and other products that Procter & Gamble manufactures constitute its product mix. The **depth** of a product mix is measured by the number of different products offered in each product line. Marketing Update 8.1 describes Kellogg's efforts to add depth to its cereal product line. The **width** of the product mix is measured by the number of product lines a company offers. Figure 8.4 illustrates these concepts by showing the width of the product mix and the depth of each product line for

FIGURE 8.3
A product line.
This collection of products represents Century Furniture's line of dining chairs.

Look what we made for dinner.

If you'd like Queen Anne, Duncan Phyfe
or Jay Spectre at your table, they're available from Century Furniture.
Altogether, in fact, we offer 160 different styles of dining chairs and 65 impeccable finishes.
Including several faithful reproductions
from the collections of the Smithsonian Institution and British National Trust.
So why not call 1-800-852-5552 for more information,
or for the name of a store near you selling Century Furniture.
After all, nothing contributes more to a good dinner than the right company.

Century Furniture

SOURCE: Courtesy of Century Furniture

selected Procter & Gamble products. Procter & Gamble is known for using distinctive branding, packaging, and consumer advertising to promote individual items in its detergent product line. Tide, Bold, Gain, Dash, Cheer, and Oxydol—all Procter & Gamble detergents—share the same distribution channels and similar manufacturing facilities. Yet each is promoted as distinctive, and this claimed uniqueness adds depth to the product line.

PRODUCT LIFE CYCLES

Just as biological cycles progress through growth and decline, so do product life cycles. A new product is introduced into the marketplace; it grows; and when it loses appeal, it is terminated. Recall that our definition of a product focuses on tangible and intangible attributes. The total product might not be just a good, but also the ideas and services attached to it. Packaging, branding, and labeling techniques alter or help create products, so marketers can modify product life cycles. (Marketing strategies for different life cycle stages are discussed in Chapter 9.)

Laundry Detergents	Toothpastes	Bar Soaps	Deodorants	Shampoos	Coffees
Oxydol 1914	Gleem 1952	Ivory 1879	Secret 1956	Prell 1946	Folgers (vacuum packed) 1850
Ivory Snow 1930	Crest 1955	Kirk's 1885	Sure 1972	Head & Shoulders 1961	Instant Folgers (coffee crystals) 1963
Dreft 1933	Denquel 1980	Lava 1893		Pert Plus 1979	Instant High Point 1975
Tide 1946		Camay 1926		Ivory 1983	Folgers (decaffeinated) 1984
Cheer 1950		Zest 1952			Instant Folgers (decaffeinated) 1984
Dash 1954		Safeguard 1963			Folgers (Special Roast Flaked) 1986
Bold 1965		Coast 1974			Folgers (Gourmet Supreme) 1989
Gain 1966					
Era 1972					
Solo 1979					
Liquid Tide 1984					
Liquid Bold-3 1985					
Liquid Cheer 1986					
Liquid Lemon Dash 1987					
Tide with bleach 1988					
Liquid Dreft 1989					
Liquid Ivory Snow 1989					

Product line depth — Product mix width

FIGURE 8.4 *The concepts of width of product mix and product depth applied to selected Procter & Gamble products*

SOURCE: "Facts About Procter & Gamble," (Cincinnati: Public Affairs Division, Procter & Gamble, January 1990), pp. 4–6. Reprinted by permission of Procter & Gamble.

As Figure 8.5 shows, a **product life cycle** has four major stages: (1) introduction, (2) growth, (3) maturity, and (4) decline. As a product moves through its cycle, the strategies relating to competition, promotion, distribution, pricing, and market information must be periodically evaluated and possibly changed. Astute marketing managers use the life cycle concept to make sure that the introduction, alteration, and termination of a product are timed and executed properly. By understanding the typical life cycle pattern, marketers are better able to maintain profitable products and drop unprofitable ones.

■ **Introduction**

The **introduction stage** of the life cycle begins at a product's first appearance in the marketplace, when sales are zero and profits are negative. Profits are below zero because initial revenues are low and at the same time the company generally must cover large expenses for promotion and distribution. Notice in Figure 8.5 how sales should move upward from zero, and profits also should move upward from a position in which profits are negative due to high expenses.

Because of cost, very few product introductions represent major inventions. Developing and introducing a new product can mean an outlay of $20 million or more.

KELLOGG CO. ADDS DEPTH TO ITS CEREAL LINE

Kellogg Co., the 100-year-old cereal company based in Battle Creek, Michigan, was widely criticized when it did not diversify into markets other than cereals, while its major competitors, General Mills and Quaker Oats, ventured into other product categories. No one is questioning Kellogg's decision now. The company dominates the U.S. cereal market, having captured 41 percent of the dry cereal market. Kellogg's goal is a 50 percent market share.

To achieve its dominance of the cereal industry, Kellogg introduced a number of successful new cereals, such as Mueslix (a European-style granola mixture), Nutrific (a healthy combination of raisins, bran, barley, and almonds), and Pro Grain (a multigrain cereal coated with honey). Kellogg has also strongly supported its established brands: its world-famous Corn Flakes, Frosted Flakes, Rice Krispies, Fruit Loops, and Special K. None of these brands has lost a single market share point in more than six years. Kellogg has had success with line extensions as well.

Kellogg also benefited from a trend among adults that calls for healthy, tasty breakfast foods as opposed to the standard high-fat, high-cholesterol breakfasts of the past. Spotting this trend early, the company introduced more nutritious cereals—Mueslix, Nutrific, and Pro Grain—and even added fruit and nuts to some of its older brands, gaining a huge advantage over the competition. Cereal companies now are trying to position their products against Kellogg brands that have been going strong for years.

Moreover, Kellogg has increased its research and development spending to about $40 million a year. The company uses extensive marketing research, including psychographic research, to find out why consumers buy a specific brand of cereal. Kellogg executives also increased advertising budgets, doubling them in the last few years. A marketer at Kellogg boasted confidently, "We know more about the ready-to-eat-cereal market than anybody else." The stable management at Kellogg seems to know how to put that cereal knowledge to use. For example, Kellogg cereal packages are either white or honey-colored to evoke an image of health and purity.

SOURCES: Julie Liesse Erickson, "Cereal Makers Roll More Oats," *Advertising Age,* Mar. 6, 1989, p. 34; Rebecca Fannin, "Crunching the Competition," *Marketing & Media Decisions,* March 1988, pp. 70–75; and Wendy Zellner, "Kellogg Rides the Health Craze," *Business Week,* Apr. 14, 1989, pp. 28–31.

FIGURE 8.5

The four stages of the product life cycle

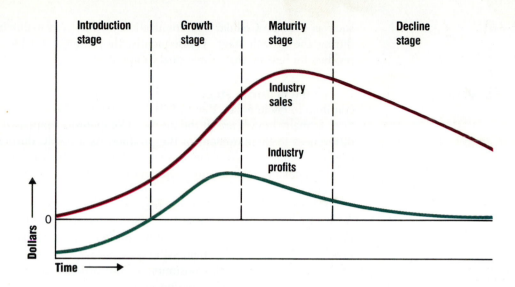

The failure rate for new products is quite high, ranging from 60 to 90 percent, depending on the industry and how product failure is defined. For example, in the food and beverage industry, 80 percent of all new products fail.[4] More typically, product introductions involve a new packaged convenience food, a new automobile model, or a new fashion in clothing rather than a major product innovation.

Potential buyers must be made aware of the new product's features, uses, and advantages. Two difficulties may arise at this point. Only a few sellers may have the resources, technological knowledge, and marketing know-how to launch the product successfully; and the initial product price may have to be high, to recoup expensive marketing research or development costs. Given these difficulties, it is not surprising that many products never get beyond the introduction stage

■ **Growth**

During the **growth stage**, sales rise rapidly and profits reach a peak and then start to decline (see Figure 8.5). The growth stage is critical to a product's survival because competitive reactions to the product's success during this period will affect the product's life expectancy. For example, California Cooler successfully marketed the first "wine cooler" but today competes against approximately fifty other brands. Profits decline late in the growth stage as more competitors enter the market, driving prices down and creating the need for heavy promotional expenses. At this point a typical marketing strategy encourages strong brand loyalty and competes with aggressive emulators of the product. During the growth stage, an organization tries to strengthen its market share and develop a competitive niche by emphasizing the product's benefits.

Aggressive promotional pricing, including price cuts, is typical during the growth stage. The cellular telephone industry in the United States is currently in the growth stage. Many competitors have entered the market. By adjusting their prices competitively, cellular telephone manufacturers such as Motorola and service providers

4. "New Product Failure: A Self-Fulfilling Prophecy?" *Marketing Communications*, April 1989, p. 27.

such as McCaw Cellular Communications are able to maintain their market lead during the growth stage. Consequently, they extend the life expectancy of their product far beyond that of marginal competitors.

■ Maturity

During the **maturity stage**, the sales curve peaks and starts to decline and profits continue to decline (see Figure 8.5). This stage is characterized by severe competition, as many brands are in the market. Competitors emphasize improvements and differences in their versions of the product. As a result, during the maturity stage weaker competitors are squeezed out or lose interest in the product. For example, some brands of videocassette recorders will perish as the VCR moves through the maturity stage.

During the maturity phase, the producers who remain in the market must make fresh promotional and distribution efforts; advertising and dealer-oriented promotions are typical during this stage of the product life cycle. The promoters must also take into account the fact that, as the product reaches maturity, buyers' knowledge of it attains a high level. Consumers of the product are no longer inexperienced generalists but instead are experienced specialists.

■ Decline

During the **decline stage**, sales fall rapidly (see Figure 8.5). New technology or a new social trend may cause product sales to take a sharp turn downward. When this happens, the marketer considers pruning items from the product line to eliminate those not earning a profit. At this time, too, the marketer may cut promotion efforts, eliminate marginal distributors, and, finally, plan to phase out the product.

Because most businesses have a product mix consisting of multiple products, a firm's destiny is rarely tied to one product. A composite of life cycle patterns is formed when various products in the mix are at different cycle stages. As one product is declining, other products are in the introduction, growth, or maturity stage. Marketers must deal with the dual problem of prolonging the life of existing products and introducing new products to meet organizational sales goals. For example, Kodak has prolonged the product life cycle of its 110mm cameras by adding built-in flashes, waterproof bodies, and other features. But Kodak has also continued to introduce new products, including the disposable 35mm Kodak Fling; Breeze, a new line of 35mm cameras; and Ektar, a new line of color films specifically for 35mm single-lens reflex cameras. In the next chapter you will learn more about the development of new products and how they can be managed in their various life cycle stages.

BRANDING

In addition to making decisions about actual products, marketers must make many decisions associated with branding, such as brands, brand names, brand marks, trademarks, and trade names. A **brand** is a name, term, design, symbol, or any other feature that identifies one seller's good or service as distinct from those of other sellers. A brand may identify one item, a family of items, or all items of that seller.[5] A

5. Peter D. Bennett, ed., *Dictionary of Marketing Terms* (Chicago: American Marketing Association, 1988), p. 18.

brand name is that part of a brand which can be spoken—including letters, words, and numbers—such as 7-Up. A brand name is often a product's only distinguishing characteristic. Without the brand name, a firm could not identify its products. To consumers, brand names are as fundamental as the product itself. Brand names simplify shopping, guarantee quality, and allow self-expression.[6]

The element of a brand that is not made up of words, but is often a symbol or design, is called a **brand mark**. One example is the red and white checkerboard square on Ralston Purina pet foods and Chex cereals. A **trademark** is a legal designation indicating that the owner has exclusive use of a brand or a part of a brand and that others are prohibited by law from using it. To protect a brand name or brand mark in the United States, an organization must register it as a trademark with the U.S. Patent Office. Finally, a **trade name** is the full and legal name of an organization, such as Ford Motor Company or Safeway Stores, Inc., rather than the name of a specific product.

■ Benefits of Branding

Branding provides benefits for both buyers and sellers. Brands help buyers identify specific products that they do and do not like, which in turn facilitates the purchase of items that satisfy their needs and reduces the time required to purchase the product. Without brands, product selection would be quite random because buyers could have no assurance that they were purchasing what they preferred. A brand also helps buyers evaluate the quality of products, especially when they are unable to judge a product's characteristics. That is, a brand may symbolize a certain quality level to a purchaser, and in turn the person lets that perception of quality represent the quality of the item. A brand helps to reduce a buyer's perceived risk of purchase. In addition, a brand may offer a psychological reward that comes from owning a brand that symbolizes status. Certain brands of watches (Rolex) and automobiles (Mercedes-Benz), for example, fall into this category.

Sellers benefit from branding because each company's brands identify its products, which makes repeat purchasing easier for consumers. Branding helps a firm introduce a new product that carries the name of one or more of its existing products because buyers are already familiar with the firm's existing brands. Branding also facilitates promotional efforts because the promotion of each branded product indirectly promotes all other products that are similarly branded.

Branding also helps sellers by fostering brand loyalty. To the extent that buyers become loyal to a specific brand, the company's market share for that product achieves a certain level of stability, allowing the firm to use its resources more efficiently. When a firm develops some degree of customer loyalty to a brand, it can charge a premium price for the product. For example, brand loyal buyers of Bayer aspirin are willing to pay two or three times more for Bayer than for a store brand of aspirin even though both have the same amount of pain-relieving agent. However, brand loyalty is declining, partly because of marketers' increased reliance on sales, coupons, and other short-term promotions, and partly because of the sometimes overwhelming array of similar new products from which consumers can choose. A *Wall Street Journal* survey found that 12 percent of consumers are not loyal to any brand, whereas 47 percent are brand loyal for one to five product types. Only 2 percent of the respondents were brand loyal for more than sixteen product types

6. James U. McNeal and Linda Zeren, "Brand Name Selection for Consumer Products," *MSU Business Topics,* Spring 1981, p. 35.

(see Figure 8.6).To stimulate loyalty to their brands, some marketers are stressing image advertising, mailing personalized catalogs and magazines to regular users, and creating membership clubs for brand users.[7]

■ Types of Brands

The two categories of brands are manufacturer and private distributor brands. **Manufacturer brands** are initiated by producers and ensure that producers are identified with their products at the point of purchase, for example, Green Giant, Sylvania Electric, and Apple Computer. A manufacturer brand usually requires a producer to become involved in distribution, promotion, and, to some extent, pricing decisions. Brand loyalty is created by promotion, quality control, and guarantees; it is a valuable asset to a manufacturer. The producer tries to stimulate demand for the product, which tends to encourage middlemen to make the product available

Private distributor brands (also called **private brands**, **store brands**, or **dealer brands**), are initiated and owned by resellers—wholesalers or retailers. The major characteristic of private brands is that the manufacturers are not identified on the products. Retailers and wholesalers use private distributor brands to develop more efficient promotion, to generate higher gross margins, and to improve store images. Private distributor brands give retailers or wholesalers freedom to purchase products of a specified quality at the lowest cost without disclosing the identity of the manufacturer. Wholesaler brands include IGA (Independent Grocers' Alliance) and Topmost (General Grocer). Familiar retailer brand names include Kenmore (Sears) and Penncraft (J.C. Penney). Many successful private brands are distributed nationally. Sears Kenmore washers, as shown in Figure 8.7, are as well known as most manufacturer brands. Sometimes retailers with successful distributor brands start manufacturing their own products to gain more control over product costs, quality, and design with the hope of increasing profits

Competition between manufacturer brands and private distributor brands (sometimes called "the battle of the brands") is intensifying in several major product categories, particularly, cheese, orange juice, sugar, and soft drinks. Private distributor brands now account for approximately 13 percent of all supermarket sales.[8] For manufacturers, developing multiple manufacturer brands and distribution systems has been an effective means of combating the increased competition from private brands. By developing a new brand name, a producer can adjust various elements of a marketing mix to appeal to a different target market. For example, Scott Paper has developed lower-priced brands of paper towels; it has tailored its new products to a target market that tends to purchase private brands..

Manufacturers find it hard to ignore the marketing opportunities that come from producing private distributor brands for resellers. If a manufacturer refuses to produce a private brand for a reseller, a competing manufacturer will. Moreover, the production of private distributor brands allows the manufacturer to use excess capacity during periods when its own brands are at nonpeak production. The ultimate decision whether to produce a private or a manufacturer brand depends on a company's resources, production capabilities, and goals.

7. Ronald Alsop, "Brand Loyalty Is Rarely Blind Loyalty; Rise in Coupons, Choices Blames for '80s Erosion," *Wall Street Journal*, Oct. 19, 1989, pp. B1, B6.

8. Judann Dagnoli, "New Study Blasts Private Labels," *Advertising Age*, June 19, 1989, p. 34.

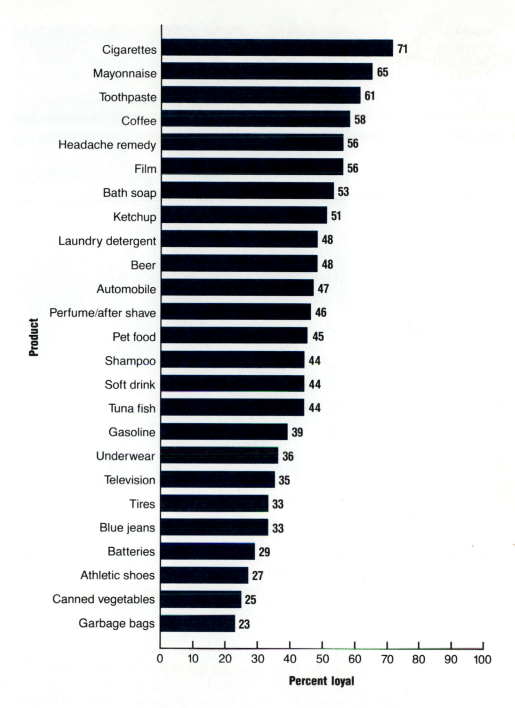

FIGURE 8.6
Percentage of users of selected products who are loyal to one brand

Product	Percent loyal
Cigarettes	71
Mayonnaise	65
Toothpaste	61
Coffee	58
Headache remedy	56
Film	56
Bath soap	53
Ketchup	51
Laundry detergent	48
Beer	48
Automobile	47
Perfume/after shave	46
Pet food	45
Shampoo	44
Soft drink	44
Tuna fish	44
Gasoline	39
Underwear	36
Television	35
Tires	33
Blue jeans	33
Batteries	29
Athletic shoes	27
Canned vegetables	25
Garbage bags	23

SOURCE: Data taken from the Centennial Survey, *Wall Street Journal,* Oct. 19, 1989, p. B1

FIGURE 8.7
Private distributor brand.
Sears' nationally known
Kenmore brand is a pri-
vate distributor brand.

SOURCE: Sears, Roebuck and Company

■ Selecting and Protecting a Brand

Marketers should consider a number of factors when they select a brand name. The name should be easy for customers (including foreign buyers, if the firm intends to market its products in other countries) to say, spell, and recall. Short, one-syllable names such as Cheer often satisfy this requirement. If possible, the brand name should suggest in a positive way the product's uses and special characteristics; negative or offensive references should be avoided. For example, a deodorant should be branded with a name that connotes freshness, dryness, or long-lasting protection, as do Ban, Dry Idea, and Ice Blue Secret. The name should indicate the product's major benefits. If a marketer intends to use a brand for a product line, it must be compatible with all products in the line. Finally, a brand should be designed so that it can be used and recognized in all of the various types of media. Finding the right brand name has become a challenging task because many obvious product names have already been used. In 1987, the U.S. Patent and Trademark Office registered 47,500 new trademarks, three times the number registered in 1980.[9]

9. Ronald Alsop, "It's Slim Pickings in Product Name Game," *Wall Street Journal*, Nov. 29, 1988, p. B1.

A marketer should also design a brand that can be protected easily through registration. Because of their designs, some brands can be legally infringed upon more easily than others. Although registration protects trademarks domestically for ten years and can be renewed indefinitely, a firm should develop a system for ensuring that its trademarks will be renewed as needed. To protect its exclusive rights to a brand, the company must make certain that the selected brand is not likely to be considered an infringement on any existing brand already registered with the U.S. Patent Office. This task may be complex because infringement is determined by the courts, which base their decisions on whether a brand causes consumers to be confused, mistaken, or deceived about the source of the product.[10] McDonald's is one company that aggressively protects its trademarks against infringement; it has brought charges against a number of companies with "Mc" names because it fears that the use of the "Mc" will give consumers the impression that these companies are associated with or owned by McDonald's.[11]

If possible, a marketer must guard against allowing a brand name to become a generic term used to refer to a general product category. Generic terms cannot be protected as exclusive brand names. For example, names such as aspirin, escalator, and shredded wheat—all brand names at one time—eventually were declared generic terms that refer to product classes; thus they no longer could be protected. To keep a brand name from becoming a generic term, the firm should spell the name with a capital letter and use it as an adjective to modify the name of the general product class, as in Kool-Aid Brand Soft Drink Mix.[12] Including the word *brand* just after the brand name is also helpful. An organization can deal with this problem directly by advertising that its brand is a trademark and should not be used generically. The firm can also indicate that the brand is trademarked with the symbol ®.

A U.S. firm that tries to protect a brand in a foreign country frequently encounters problems. In many foreign countries, brand registration is not possible; the first firm to use a brand in such a country has the rights to it. In some instances, a U.S. company actually has had to buy its own brand rights from a firm in a foreign country because the foreign firm was the first user in that country.

Marketers trying to protect their brands must also contend with brand counterfeiting. In the United States, for instance, one can purchase fake General Motors parts, Cartier watches, Jordache jeans, Vuitton handbags, Walt Disney character dolls, and a host of other products that are illegally marketed by manufacturers that do not own the brands. Many counterfeit products are manufactured overseas—in South Korea, Italy, or Taiwan, for example—but some are counterfeited in the United States. The International Anti-Counterfeiting Coalition estimates that roughly $60 billion in annual world trade involves counterfeit merchandise. The sale of this merchandise, obviously, reduces the brand owners' revenues from marketing their own legitimate products.

Brand counterfeiting is particularly harmful because the usually inferior counterfeit product undermines consumers' confidence in the brand and their loyalty to it. After unknowingly purchasing a counterfeit product, the buyer may blame the

---

10. George Miaoulis and Nancy D'Amato, "Consumer Confusion and Trademark Infringement," *Journal of Marketing*, April 1978, pp. 48–49.

11. Diane Schneidman, "Use of 'Mc' in Front of Travel Firms' Names Leads to Lawsuits," *Marketing News*, Nov. 20, 1987, p. 17.

12. "Trademark Stylesheet," U.S. Trademark Association, no. 1A.

legitimate manufacturer if the product is of low quality or—even worse—if its use results in damage or injury. Since the counterfeiting problem has grown so serious, many firms are taking legal action against counterfeiters. Others have adopted such measures as modifying the product or the packaging to make counterfeit items easier to detect; conducting public awareness campaigns; and monitoring distributors to ensure that they stock only legitimate brands.[13]

■ Branding Policies

Before it establishes branding policies, a firm must first decide whether to brand its products at all. If a company's product is homogeneous and similar to competitors' products, it may be difficult to brand. Raw materials, such as coal, sand, and farm produce, are hard to brand because of the homogeneity of such products and their physical characteristics.

Some marketers of traditionally branded products have embarked on a policy of not branding, often called generic branding. A **generic brand** indicates only the product category (such as aluminum foil) and displays federally required labeling but does not include the company name or other identifying terms. Supermarkets that sell generic brands often price them lower than their comparable private branded items. Purchasers of generic-brand grocery items tend to be concentrated in middle-income, large households that are price conscious and predisposed to select regularly low-priced alternatives, as opposed to temporarily lower-priced products.[14] Although at one time generic brands may have represented as much as 10 percent of all grocery sales, today generic brands account for less than 1 percent of all grocery sales.[15]

If a firm chooses to brand its products, it may opt for one or more of the following branding policies: individual, overall family, line family, and brand-extension branding. **Individual branding** is a policy of naming each product differently. As mentioned earlier, Procter & Gamble relies on an individual branding policy for its line of detergents, which includes Tide, Bold, Dash, Cheer, and Oxydol. A major advantage of individual branding is that if an organization introduces a poor product, the negative images associated with it do not contaminate the company's other products. An individual branding policy may also facilitate market segmentation when a firm wishes to enter many segments of the same market. Separate, unrelated names can be used, and each brand can be aimed at a specific segment.

In **overall family branding**, all of a firm's products are branded with the same name or at least part of the name, such as Kraft and Heinz. In some cases, a company's name is combined with other words to brand items. Arm & Hammer uses its name on all its products along with a generic description of the item, such as Arm & Hammer Heavy Duty Detergent, Arm & Hammer Pure Baking Soda, and Arm &

13. Ronald F. Bush, Peter H. Bloch, and Scott Dawson, "Remedies for Product Counterfeiting," *Business Horizons,* January-February 1989, pp. 59–65; Pete Engardio, with Todd Vogel and Dinah Lee, "Companies Are Knocking Off the Knockoff Outfits," *Business Week,* Sept. 26, 1988, pp. 86–88; and Michael Harvey, "A New Way to Combat Product Counterfeiting," *Business Horizons,* July-August 1988, pp. 19–28.

14. Martha R. McEnally and Jon M. Hawes, "The Market for Generic Brand Grocery Products: A Review and Extension," *Journal of Marketing,* Winter 1984, pp. 75–83.

15. Alan Miller, "Private Labels Gain Share in Non-Food and HBA Categories," *Private Label,* January/February 1990, pp. 86–88.

Hammer Carpet Deodorizer. Unlike individual branding, overall family branding means that the promotion of one item with the family brand promotes the firm's other products.

Sometimes an organization uses family branding only for products within a single line. This policy is called **line family branding**. Colgate-Palmolive Co., for example, produces a line of cleaning products that includes a cleanser, a powdered detergent, and a liquid cleaner, all under the name Ajax. Colgate also produces several brands of toothpaste, none of which carry the Ajax brand.

Brand-extension branding occurs when a firm uses one of its existing brand names as part of a brand for an improved or new product that is usually in the same product category as the existing brand. The makers of Arrid deodorant eventually extended the name Arrid to Arrid Extra-Dry and Arrid Double-X. There is one major difference between line family branding and brand-extension branding. With line family branding, all products in the line carry the same name, but with brand-extension branding, this is not the case. The producer of Arrid deodorant, for example, also makes other brands of deodorants. Line family branding and brand-extension branding are popular. Of the 10,558 new products introduced in 1988, 80 percent were brand or line extensions.[16]

An organization is not limited to a single branding policy. Instead, branding policy is influenced by the number of products and product lines the company produces, the characteristics of its target markets, the number and types of competing products available, and the size of its resources. Anheuser-Busch, Inc., for example, uses both individual and brand-extension branding. Most of the brands are individual brands; however, the Michelob Light brand is an extension of the Michelob brand.

■ Brand Licensing

A recent trend in branding strategies involves the licensing of trademarks. By means of a licensing agreement, a company may permit approved manufacturers to use its trademark on other products for a licensing fee. Royalties may be as low as 2 percent of wholesale revenues or better than 10 percent. The licensee is responsible for all manufacturing, selling, and advertising functions and bears the costs if the licensed product fails. Not long ago, only a few firms licensed their corporate trademarks but today licensing is a multibillion dollar business, and it is growing. Harley-Davidson, for example, has authorized the use of its name on non-motorcycle products such as cologne, wine coolers, gold rings, and shirts. McDonald's has licensed a line of children's sportswear, called McKids, to Sears.

The advantages of licensing range from extra revenues and low cost to free publicity, new images, and trademark protection. For example, Coca-Cola has licensed its trademark for use on glassware, radios, trucks, and clothing in the hope of protecting its trademark. Similarly, Winnebago Industries licensed a line of tents, air mattresses, and other camping gear to keep its name from becoming a generic term for "recreational vehicle." However, brand licensing is not without drawbacks. The major ones are a lack of manufacturing control, which could hurt the company's name, and bombarding consumers with too many unrelated products bearing the same name. Licensing arrangements can also fail because of poor timing, inappropriate distribution channels, or mismatching of product and name.

16. Bernice Kanner, "Growing Pains—and Gains; Brand Names Branch Out," *New York*, Mar. 13, 1989, pp. 22–23.

PACKAGING

Packaging involves the development of a container and a graphic design for a product. A package can be a vital part of a product, making it more versatile, safer, or easier to use. Like a brand name, a package can influence customers' attitudes toward a product and so affect their purchase decisions. For example, several producers of jellies, sauces, and ketchups have packaged their products in squeezable containers to make use and storage more convenient. Package characteristics help shape buyers' impressions of a product at the time of purchase or during use. In this section we examine the main functions of packaging and consider several major packaging decisions. We also analyze the role of the package in a marketing strategy.

■ Packaging Functions

Effective packaging means more than simply putting products in containers and covering them with wrappers. First of all, packaging materials serve the basic purpose of protecting the product and maintaining its functional form. Fluids such as milk, orange juice, and hair spray need packages that preserve and protect them; the packaging should prevent damage that could affect the product's usefulness and increase costs. Since product tampering has become a problem for marketers of many types of goods, several packaging techniques have been developed to counter this danger. Some packages are also designed to foil shoplifting.

Another function of packaging is to offer convenience for consumers. For example, small aseptic packages—individual-sized boxes or plastic bags that contain liquids and do not require refrigeration—strongly appeal to children and young adults with active lifestyles. The size or shape of a package may relate to the product's storage, convenience of use, or replacement rate. Small, single-serving cans of vegetables, for instance, may prevent waste and make storage easier. A third function of packaging is to promote a product by communicating its features, uses, benefits, and image. At times, a reusable package is developed to make the product more desirable. For example, the Cool Whip package doubles as a food-storage container.

■ Major Packaging Considerations

As they develop packages, marketers must take many factors into account. Obviously, one major consideration is cost. Although a variety of packaging materials, processes, and designs are available, some are rather expensive. In recent years, buyers have shown a willingness to pay more for improved packaging, but there are limits. Marketers should try to determine, through research, just how much customers are willing to pay for packages.

As already mentioned, developing tamper-resistant packaging is very important. Although no package is "tamper-proof," marketers can develop packages that are difficult to tamper with. At a minimum, all packaging must comply with the Food and Drug Administration's packaging regulations. However, packaging should also make any product tampering evident to resellers and consumers. Because new, safer packaging technologies are being explored, marketers should be aware of changes in packaging technology and legislation and be prepared to make modifications that will ensure consumer safety. One packaging innovation includes an inner pouch that displays the word "open" when air has entered the pouch after opening. Marketers also have an obligation to inform the public of the possibilities and risks of product tampering by educating consumers on how to recognize possible tampering and by placing warnings on packaging.[17] For example, nonprescription medications such as Advil are typically packaged in plastic containers with protective foil seals under child-proof caps; the container is then packaged in a cardboard box. Both the box and the container carry warnings stating, "If imprinted foil seal under cap is broken or missing when purchased, do not use." Although effective tamper-resistant packaging may be expensive to develop, when balanced against the costs of lost sales, loss of consumer confidence and company reputation, and potentially expensive product liability lawsuits, the costs of ensuring consumer safety are minimal.[18]

Marketers must also decide whether to package the product singly or in multiple units. Multiple packaging is likely to increase demand because it increases the amount of the product available at the point of consumption (in one's home, for example). However, multiple packaging does not work for infrequently used products because buyers do not like to tie up their dollars in an excess supply or store these products for a long time. Multiple packaging can, however, make products easier to handle and store (as in the case of six-packs used for soft drinks); it can also facilitate special price offers, such as a two-for-one sale. In addition, multiple packaging may increase consumer acceptance of a product by encouraging the buyer to try it several times. On the other hand, because they must buy several units, customers may hesitate to try the product at all.

Marketers should consider how much consistency is desirable among an organization's package designs. No consistency may be the best policy, especially if a firm's products are unrelated or aimed at vastly different target markets. To promote an overall company image, a firm may decide that all packages are to be similar or include one major element of the design. This approach is called **family packaging**. Sometimes it is used only for lines of products, as with Campbell soups, Weight Watchers' foods, and Planters nuts.

A package's promotional role is an important consideration. Through verbal and nonverbal symbols, the package can inform potential buyers about the product's content, features, uses, advantages, and hazards. A firm can create desirable images and associations by its choice of color, design, shape, and texture. Many cosmetics manufacturers, for example, design their packages to create impressions of richness, luxury, and exclusiveness. A package performs a promotional function when it is designed to be safer or more convenient to use, if such characteristics help stimulate demand.

To develop a package that has a definite promotional value, a designer must consider size, shape, texture, color, and graphics. Beyond the obvious limitation that the package must be large enough to hold the product, a package can be designed to appear taller or shorter. For instance, thin vertical lines make a package look taller; wide horizontal stripes make it look shorter. A marketer may want a package to appear taller because many people perceive something that is taller as being larger.

Colors on packages are often chosen to attract attention. People associate specific colors with certain feelings and experiences. Red, for example, is linked with fire, blood, danger, and anger; yellow suggests sunlight, caution, warmth, and vitality;

17. Fred W. Morgan, "Tampered Goods: Legal Developments and Marketing Guidelines," *Journal of Marketing*, April 1988, pp. 86–96.

18. Ibid.

blue can imply coldness, sky, water, and sadness.[19] When selecting packaging colors, marketers must decide whether a particular color will evoke positive or negative feelings when it is linked to a specific product. Rarely, for example, do processors package meat or bread in green materials because customers may associate green with mold. Marketers must also decide whether a specific target market will respond favorably or unfavorably to a particular color. Cosmetics for women are more likely to be sold in pastel packaging than are personal-care products for men. Packages designed to appeal to children often use primary colors and bold designs.

Packaging must also meet the needs of middlemen. Wholesalers and retailers consider whether a package facilitates transportation, storage, and handling. Resellers may refuse to carry certain products if their packages are cumbersome.

A final consideration is whether to develop packages that are environmentally responsible. A Cable News Network report on the growing garbage disposal problem in the United States stated that nearly 50 percent of all garbage consists of discarded plastic packaging, such as Styrofoam containers, plastic soft-drink bottles, carryout bags, and other packaging.[20] Plastic packaging material does not biodegrade, and paper requires the destruction of valuable forest lands. Consequently, a number of companies are exploring packaging alternatives; they are also recycling more materials. McDonald's is recycling its foam sandwich containers; Procter & Gamble markets Downy fabric softener in concentrated form, which requires less packaging than the ready-to-use version; H. J. Heinz is looking for alternatives to its plastic ketchup squeeze bottles. However, sales of concentrated Downy have been poor, and customers do not like Wendy's new paper plates and coffee cups; they prefer the old nondegradable foam ones. Other companies searching for alternatives to environmentally harmful packaging have experienced similar problems.[21] Thus marketers must carefully balance society's desires to preserve the environment against consumers' desires for convenience.

■ **Packaging and Marketing Strategy**

Packaging can be a major component of a marketing strategy. A unique cap or closure, a better box or wrapper, or a more convenient container may give a firm a competitive edge. As shown in Figure 8.8, Del Monte's Yogurt Cup, packaged in an air-tight, pop-top, single-serving container needs no refrigeration. Since it is targeted at kids, the package has been designed to go wherever they go. Manufacturers of beer, detergents, and most packaged foods spend a great deal of money to research consumers' reactions to packages. In the case of established brands, marketers should evaluate and change package designs to keep them looking stylish and up-to-date. For example, Quaker Oats Co. modified the packaging of its Instant Oatmeal line to emphasize the Quaker name by making its "Quaker man" symbol more predominant on the package. It also replaced stylized illustrations with appetizing photographs of the products and their ingredients. Kraft capitalized on the microwavability of its Cheez Whiz product by introducing new packaging that included portion-controlled plastic cups designed specifically for microwave ovens.[22]

19. James U. McNeal, *Consumer Behavior: An Integrative Approach* (Boston: Little, Brown, 1982), pp. 221–222.

20. "Not in My Backyard," CNN Special Report, Cable News Network, Dec. 19, 1988.

21. Alecia Swasy, "Ecology and Buyer Wants Don't Jibe," *Wall Street Journal,* Aug. 23, 1989, p. B1.

22. Howard Alport, "Does Your Packaging Need a Facelift?" *Marketing Communications,* March 1989, p. 38, 40.

FIGURE 8.8

Strategic packaging. Del Monte uses a single serving, air-tight, pop-top package that needs no refrigeration for its yogurt cup product.

SOURCE: Reprinted with permission of Del Monte Corporation

As package designs improve, it becomes harder for any one product to dominate because of packaging. However, marketers still attempt to gain a competitive edge through packaging. Skilled artists and package designers, who have experience in marketing research, test packaging to see what sells well, not just what is aesthetically appealing. Since the typical large store stocks fifteen thousand items or more, products that stand out are more likely to be bought.

LABELING

Labeling too is an important dimension related to packaging, for both promotional and informational reasons and for legal reasons. The Food and Drug Administration and the Consumer Product Safety Commission can require that products be labeled or marked with warnings, instructions, certifications, and manufacturer's identifications. Federal laws require disclosure of such data as textile identifications, potential hazards, and nutritional information. However, although consumers have responded favorably to the inclusion of this type of information on labels, evidence as to whether they actually use it has been mixed. Several studies indicate that consumers do not use nutritional information, whereas other studies indicate that the information is useful. Labels also can promote a manufacturer's other products or encourage proper use of products and therefore greater satisfaction with them.

Color and eye-catching graphics on labels overcome the jumble of words—known to designers as "mouse print"—that have been added to satisfy government regulations. Because so many similar products are available, an attention-getting device, or "silent salesperson," is needed to attract interest. As one of the most visible parts of a product, the label is an important element in the marketing mix.

OTHER PRODUCT-RELATED CHARACTERISTICS

When developing products, marketers make many decisions. Some of these decisions involve the physical characteristics of the product; others focus on less tangible supportive services that are very much a part of the total product.

■ Physical Characteristics of the Product

A crucial question that arises during product development is how much quality to build into the product. A major dimension of quality is durability. Higher quality often calls for better materials and more expensive processing, which increase production costs and, ultimately, the product's price. In determining the specific level of quality, a marketer must ascertain approximately what price the target market views as acceptable. In addition, a marketer usually tries to set a level for a specific product that is consistent with the firm's other products that carry a similar brand. Obviously, the quality of competing brands is a consideration.

A product's physical features require careful consideration by marketers and by those in research and development. Product development personnel at Gillette spent considerable resources dealing with the Sensor Razor's physical features (see Marketing Update 8.2). The prime basis for decisions about the physical features should be the needs and wants of the target market. If marketers do not know what physical features people in the target market want in a product, it is highly unlikely that the product will be satisfactory. Even a firm whose existing products have been designed to satisfy target market desires should continue to assess these desires periodically to determine whether they have changed enough to require alterations in the product.

■ Supportive Product-Related Services

All products, whether they are goods or not, possess intangible qualities. "When prospective customers can't experience the product in advance, they are asked to buy what are essentially promises—promises of satisfaction. Even tangible, testable, feelable, smellable products are, before they're bought, largely just promises."[23] Here we briefly discuss three product-related services: warranties, repairs and replacements, and credit. There are of course many other product-related services and product intangibles.

23. Theodore Levitt, "Marketing Intangible Products and Product Intangibles," *Harvard Business Review,* May-June 1981, p. 96.

DEVELOPMENT OF GILLETTE'S SENSOR RAZOR

If early sales figures are any indication, Gillette Company's high-tech razor, the Sensor, is a shaving sensation. Gillette has already invested 13 years, an estimated $200 million in research and development, and another $110 million on first-year television and print advertisement campaigns to launch the new product. Clearly, it's important that the $3.75 razor (a five-pack of cartridges costs about $3.79), or "shaving system," perform well to justify these high costs. Although some Gillette executives had been hesitant about making such a large investment (because its existing razors were already so profitable), so far Gillette's gamble seems warranted. After the Sensor's initial advertising blitz, Gillette's production wasn't even able to keep pace with retailers' demands as Sensors quickly disappeared off store shelves.

The Sensor is thought to be the most important product Gillette has ever introduced, as the company tries to regain the market share lost to disposable razors manufactured by Bic Corp. and other competitors. Gillette, which makes disposables as well, is the current market leader in North America and Europe with about 67 percent of the entire shaver market. But because the gross profit on shaving systems is much higher than it is on disposable razors, Gillette is eager to build an increased interest in the Sensor and establish market dominance for itself.

In 1977, a Gillette design engineer came up with the concept of a shaving cartridge housing blades that would float on springs and thus follow the contours of a man's face, allowing for an extremely comfortable and close shave. Years later, Gillette assembled a nine-member Sensor task force that worked on the razor seven days a week for 15 months.

The resulting product is an engineering and manufacturing marvel. The Sensor's cartridge contains two ultra-thin blades that are fused to a supporting space bar by micro-lasers. The blades "float" on springs made out of a resin called Noryl, a strong material that keeps its bounce over time. The design's complexity makes it difficult for competitors to copy the cartridge.

SOURCES: Alison Fahey, "Gillette Readies Sensor," *Advertising Age,* Sept. 18, 1989, pp. 1, 81; Alison Fahey, "Sensor Sensation," *Advertising Age,* Feb. 5, 1990, pp. 4, 49; Keith Hammonds, "Do High-Tech Razors Have the Edge?" *Business Week,* Jan. 22, 1990, p. 83; and Keith Hammonds, "How a $4 Razor Ends Up Costing $300 Million," *Business Week,* Jan. 29, 1990, pp. 62–63.

SOURCE: **Courtesy of Maytag Company**

The type of warranty a firm provides can be a critical issue for buyers, especially when expensive, technically complex goods such as appliances are involved. A **warranty** specifies what the producer will do if the product malfunctions. Maytag, for example, provides a money-back guarantee on its refrigerators (as shown in Figure 8.9). In recent years, government actions have required a warrantor to state more simply and specifically the terms and conditions under which the firm will take action. Because warranties must be more precise today, marketers are using them more vigorously as tools to give their brands a competitive advantage. In the automobile industry, for example, General Motors, Chrysler, and other car makers are increasingly using warranties as a competitive tool by providing longer periods of warranty protection and expanding the number of parts covered by warranties

Although it is more difficult to provide warranties or guarantees for services than for goods, some service marketers do guarantee customer satisfaction. An effective service guarantee should be unconditional, easy to understand and communicate, meaningful, easy to invoke, and easy and quick to collect on. The mail-order retailer

L. L. Bean, for instance, guarantees "100% satisfaction in every way." An L. L. Bean customer can return a product at any time, even years later, and get a replacement, a refund, or a credit for the returned good. To use another example, at lunch time, when customers are generally in a hurry, Bennigan's restaurants guarantee them fifteen-minute service—or a free meal. Such guarantees of satisfying the customer are beneficial because they force the service provider to focus on customers' definitions of good service. They also provide clear performance standards, generate feedback from customers on the quality of the service, and help build customer loyalty and sales.[24]

A marketer must also be concerned with establishing a system to provide replacement parts and repair services. This support service is especially important for expensive, complex industrial products that buyers expect to last a long time. Although the producer may furnish these services directly to buyers, it is more common for the producer to provide such services through regional service centers or middlemen. Regardless of how services are provided, it is important to customers that they be performed quickly and correctly.

Finally, a firm must sometimes provide credit services to customers. Even though credit services place a financial burden on an organization, they can yield several benefits. One of them is that a firm may acquire and maintain a stable market share. Many major oil companies, for example, have competed effectively against gasoline discounters by providing credit services. For marketers of relatively expensive items, offering credit services enables a larger number of people to buy the product, thus enlarging the market for the item. Another reason for offering credit services is to earn interest income from customers. The types of credit services offered depend on the characteristics of target market members, the firm's financial resources, the type of products sold, and the types of credit services that competitors offer.

SUMMARY

A product is everything, both favorable and unfavorable, that one receives in an exchange. It is a complex set of tangible and intangible attributes, including functional, social, and psychological utilities or benefits. A product can be an idea, a service, a good, or any combination of these three. When consumers purchase a product, they are buying the benefits and satisfaction that they think the product will provide.

Products can be classified on the basis of the buyer's intentions. Thus consumer products are those purchased to satisfy personal and family needs. Industrial products, on the other hand, are purchased for use in a firm's operations or to make other products. Consumer products can be subdivided into convenience, shopping, specialty, and unsought products. Industrial products can be divided into raw materials, major equipment, accessory equipment, component parts, process materials, consumable supplies, and industrial services.

24. Christopher W. L. Hart, "The Power of Unconditional Service Guarantees," *Harvard Business Review*, July-August 1988, pp. 54–62.

A product item is a specific version of a product that can be designated as a distinct offering among an organization's products. A product line is a group of closely related product items that are considered a unit because of marketing, technical, or end-use considerations. The composite, or total, group of products that an organization makes available to customers is called the product mix. The depth of a product mix is measured by the number of different products offered in each product line. The width of the product mix is measured by the number of product lines a company offers.

The product life cycle describes how product items in an industry move through (1) introduction, (2) growth, (3) maturity, and (4) decline. The life cycle concept is used to make sure that the introduction, alteration, and termination of a product are timed and executed properly. The sales curve is at zero at introduction, rises at an increasing rate during growth, peaks at maturity, and then declines. Profits peak toward the end of the growth stage of the product life cycle. The life expectancy of a product is based on buyers' wants, the availability of competing products, and other environmental conditions. Most businesses have a composite of life cycle patterns for various products. It is important to manage existing products and develop new ones to keep the overall sales performance at a desired level.

A brand is a name, term, design, symbol, or any other feature that identifies one seller's good or service as distinct from those of other sellers. A brand name is that part of a brand which can be spoken; the element that cannot be spoken is called a brand mark. A trademark is a legal designation indicating that the owner has exclusive use of a brand or a part of a brand and that others are prohibited by law from using it. A trade name is the legal name of an organization. Branding can benefit both marketers and customers. A manufacturer brand is initiated by a producer and makes it possible for producers to be identified with their products at the point of purchase. A private distributor brand is initiated and owned by a reseller. When selecting a brand, a marketer should choose one that is easy to say, spell, and recall and that alludes to the product's uses, benefits, or special characteristics. A generic brand indicates only the product category and does not include the company name or other identifying terms. Major branding policies are individual branding, overall family branding, line family branding, and brand-extension branding.

Packaging offers protection, economy, convenience, and promotion. When developing a package, marketers must consider packaging costs relative to the needs of target market members. There are other considerations as well: how to make packages tamper-resistant; whether to use multiple packaging and family packaging; how to design the package as an effective promotional tool; how best to accommodate middlemen; and whether to develop biodegradable packaging.

Labeling is an important aspect of packaging, for promotional, informational, and legal reasons. Various regulations and regulatory agencies can require that products be labeled or marked with warnings, instructions, certifications, and manufacturer's identifications.

When creating products, marketers must take into account other product-related considerations, such as physical characteristics and less tangible supportive services. Specific physical product characteristics that require attention are the level of quality, product features, textures, colors, and sizes. Supportive services that may be viewed as part of the total product include warranties, repairs and replacements, and credit services.

IMPORTANT TERMS

Product
Good
Service
Ideas
Consumer products
Industrial products
Convenience products
Shopping products
Specialty products
Unsought products
Raw materials
Major equipment
Accessory equipment
Component parts
Process materials
Consumable supplies
MRO items
Industrial services
Product item
Product line
Product mix
Depth (of product mix)

Width (of product mix)
Product life cycle
Introduction stage
Growth stage
Maturity stage
Decline stage
Brand
Brand name
Brand mark
Trademark
Trade name
Manufacturer brands
Private distributor brands
Generic brand
Individual branding
Overall family branding
Line family branding
Brand-extension branding
Family packaging
Labeling
Warranty

DISCUSSION AND REVIEW QUESTIONS

1. List the tangible and intangible attributes of a spiral notebook. Compare the benefits of the spiral notebook with those of an intangible product, such as life insurance.
2. A product has been referred to as a "psychological bundle of satisfaction." Is this a good definition of a product? Why or why not?
3. Is a roll of carpeting in a store a consumer product or an industrial product? Defend your answer.
4. How do convenience products and shopping products differ? What are the distinguishing characteristics of each type of product?
5. Would a stereo system that sells for $869 be a convenience, shopping, or specialty product?
6. In the category of industrial products, how do component parts differ from process materials?
7. How does an organization's product mix relate to its development of a product line? When should an enterprise add depth to its product lines rather than width to its product mix?
8. How do industry profits change as a product moves through the four stages of its life cycle?

9. What is the relationship between the concepts of product mix and product life cycle?
10. What is the difference between a brand and a brand name? Compare and contrast the terms *brand mark* and *trademark*.
11. How does branding benefit an organization?
12. What are the distinguishing characteristics of private distributor brands?
13. Given the competition between private distributor brands and manufacturer brands, should manufacturers be concerned about the popularity of private distributor brands? How should manufacturers fight back in the brand battle? At what point should a manufacturer make private brands?
14. The brand name Xerox is sometimes used generically to refer to photocopying machines. How can Xerox Corporation protect this brand name?
15. Identify and explain the four major branding policies and give examples of each. Can a firm use more than one policy at a time? Explain your answer.
16. Describe the functions that a package can perform. Which function is most important? Why?
17. Why is the determination of a product's quality level an important decision? What major factors affect this decision?

■ CASES

8.1 Kodak's Disposable Cameras

Eastman Kodak Co., one of the world's leading photographic companies, makes innovation a part of its everyday company strategy. Recently, Kodak introduced a line of single-use, or disposable, cameras. These cameras are very simple to operate: all one needs to do is aim and push a button. There are no adjustments for light level, exposure time, or focusing. After shooting all the exposures, the customer turns in the entire camera to the film processor. Depending on the model, these cameras retail from $8.35 for the Fling, to around $14 for the more specialized models. One model is a modified wide-angle camera; another can take pictures up to twelve feet underwater. They all use 35mm color film.

Very inexpensive to produce, these cameras are basically just a role of film in an encasement of plastic that has an elementary lens on the front and a minimum of internal parts. Kodak executives hope that the disposable cameras (Kodak prefers the name "single-use" cameras) become highly profitable.

The idea for the waterproof disposable camera emerged from a Kodak engineer's rafting trip that exposed his camera equipment to water damage. In this model, Weekend 35, the ultrasonically sealed plastic outer body protects the camera's internal parts and film from sand and dirt, as well as from water, snow, and rain. Since Kodak engineers originally designed the disposable prototype on a three-dimensional computer-aided system, they found it fairly easy to devise a waterproof disposable and perfect their new design on a computer terminal. They even contrived a special view finder suitable for use with a scuba mask.

The Stretch, Kodak's disposable panoramic camera, came into existence because of a consumer's frustration in attempting to photograph the Grand Canyon. Already having a lens that was capable of producing extra-wide photos, Kodak engineers built a camera around it.

Kodak management targets the cameras at several different groups. The first segment consists of children who are just learning about photography. The company views the disposables as ideal "starter" cameras: they are easy to use and the photographer is almost guaranteed an acceptable print. Youngsters might not be able to afford more expensive cameras, and their parents are spared the agony of thinking what a $300 model will look like after an enthusiastic child gets through with it.

Another target is the impulse buyer, who might spot the camera on the way out of a grocery store. The impulse buyer might want the disposable camera because it could be ready for special occasions, such as a spontaneous picnic or sporting event. According to Kodak marketers, serious or professional photographers might also be interested in owning a low-cost camera when a particular assignment might put the expensive equipment in jeopardy. Smaller disposable cameras are also easy to tote around. Still others who might opt for one of the disposable models are tourists or travelers who simply forget their cameras. However, forgetful individuals should beware: a disposable camera can cost twice as much as a roll of film.

SOURCES: "Kodak Develops Cameras for the Young and Forgetful," *Machine Design,* Apr. 7, 1988, p. 18; Leslie Helm, "Playing Leapfrog in Disposable Cameras," *Business Week,* May 1, 1989, p. 34; Francesca Lunzer Kritz, "Cameras for Forgetful Snapshooters," *U.S. News & World Report,* July 10, 1989, pp. 58–59; "New Products from Kodak," *New York Times,* Apr. 19, 1989, p. D4; Dan Richards, "Kodak's Wild Disposables are Wide and Wet; Fuji's is a Tele!" *Popular Photography,* July 1989, pp. 26, 85, 95.

Questions for Discussion

1. Does the addition of disposable cameras to Kodak's product mix add depth, width, or both of these dimensions to this product mix?
2. If Kodak's executives decided to use a common brand name for all three of its disposable cameras, what brand name would you propose? Explain.
3. To what degree, if any, does the sale of disposable cameras reduce or cut into the sales of Kodak's other cameras?

8.2 Disney Expands Its Product Mix

After the death of its founder, Walt Disney, in 1966, the Walt Disney Company seemed to lose its creative edge. As other studios diversified into television and video, Disney seemed content with its library of feature films and animated classics. The company was producing only three or four new movies a year, most of which bombed at the box office. Disney also pulled out of television after twenty-nine years of network programming. By the mid-1980s, Disney was dependent on theme parks and real estate development for about 75 percent of its revenues.

Today, however, Disney executives are intent on recapturing—and building on—the old Disney magic. Company executives say the Disney name, culture, movies, and library are the company's biggest resources, and Disney's plan is to simultaneously rejuvenate old assets and develop new ones. While continuing its traditional appeal to the family segment of the movie market, Disney, through its Touchstone Pictures division, is turning out films for adult audiences as well. The company is releasing both old and new programs for television syndication and testing new promotional and licensing projects. In addition, the Disney theme park has been exported. The Tokyo Disneyland is attracting millions of people a year, and a $2 billion Euro Disneyland is scheduled to open near Paris in 1992. Disney's overall strategy is to channel the company's revived creativity into improved theme parks, to use the parks to generate interest in Disney films, and to promote both parks and merchandise through Disney television shows.

Disney received its new lease on life a few years ago when threats of a corporate takeover prompted the company to replace its top executives. The new management moved quickly to tap the resources of the Disney television and film library. About two hundred Disney movies and cartoon packages are now available on videocassette, and other classic films, such as "Snow White," will now be released every five years instead of every seven. The studio plans to release one new animated movie for children every eighteen months and about a dozen adult films a year.

Disney is back on network television as well, with the return of the Disney Sunday Movie. The company also produces the comedy show *The Golden Girls*, along with two top-rated Saturday morning cartoon shows. Following the lead of other studios, Disney has moved into television syndication by marketing packages of feature movies, old cartoons, and *Wonderful World of Disney* programs. The company is syndicating *The Disney Afternoon,* a block of children's cartoons that will air from 3 to 5 P.M. New shows are also being produced for syndication. They include the popular game show *Win, Lose or Draw,* a business news program, and movie reviews by Gene Siskel and Roger Ebert. In an otherwise flat cable television market, the number of subscribers to the family-oriented Disney Channel has jumped dramatically—to four million. The channel now offers twenty-four-hour features and more original programming than any other pay service. Disney has even signed an agreement with the Chinese government to air a weekly television series starring Mickey Mouse and Donald Duck. The company may license the Chinese to produce Disney merchandise as well.

At home, too, marketing of Disney characters is receiving considerable emphasis. Recently, Mickey, Donald, and others visited hospital wards and marched in parades in a 120-city tour. Snow White and all seven dwarfs made a special appearance on the floor of the New York Stock Exchange to promote the celebration of Snow White's fiftieth birthday. Minnie Mouse now has a trendy new look and appears on clothing and watches and in a fashion doll line. Disney is also working with toy companies to develop new characters, such as Fluppy Dogs and Wuzzles, both of which will be sold in stores and featured in television shows. In addition, the company has opened nontourist retail outlets. Located primarily in shopping malls, Disney stores carry both licensed products and exclusive theme park merchandise.

Disney's revitalized market presence has been credited with increasing attendance at the Disney theme parks to more than fifty million people. In Florida, Disney has recently completed new hotels and a movie studio/tour attraction. Moreover, Disney is constructing a fifty-acre water park and adding $1.4 billion worth of new attractions to Walt Disney World. The company is also considering regional centers that would combine restaurants and shopping with evening entertainment.

Disney intends eventually to reduce the company's financial dependence on parks and hotels. The strategy is to triple the proportion of company profits from movies and television and to acquire such distribution outlets as movie theaters, television stations, and record companies. Recent business deals with Procter & Gamble Co., McDonald's Corp., Coca-Cola Co., Time Inc., M&M/Mars, and Sears, Roebuck and Co. will help increase Disney's profits and market presence still further.

SOURCES: Dudley Clendinen, "Disney's Mouse of Marketing," *New York Times,* Nov. 22, 1986, p. 41-L; Pamela Ellis-Simon, "Hi Ho, Hi Ho," *Marketing & Media Decisions,* September 1986, pp. 52–54; Andrea Gabor and Steve L. Hawkins, "Of Mice and Money in the Magic Kingdom," *U.S. News & World Report,* Dec. 22, 1986, pp. 44–46; Ronald Grover, "Disney's Magic," *Business Week,* Mar. 9, 1987, pp. 62–65; Scott Hume, "Sears Gains Exclusivity with Disney Contract," *Advertising Age,* Nov. 23, 1987, p. 63; Stephen Koepp, "Do You Believe in Magic?" *Time,* Apr. 25, 1988, pp. 66–76; Marcy Magiera, "Disney Tries Retailing," *Advertising Age,* June 1, 1987, p. 80; Myron Magnet, "Putting Magic Back in the Kingdom," *Fortune,* Jan. 5, 1987, p. 65; Raymond Roel, "Disney's Marketing Touch," *Direct Marketing,* January 1987, pp. 50–53; Stephen J. Sansweet, "Disney Co. Cartoons Are Going to China in Commercial Foray," *Wall Street Journal,* Oct. 23, 1986, p. 19; Susan Spillman, "Animation Draws on Its Storied Past," *USA Today,* Nov. 15, 1989, pp. 1B–2B; Wayne Walley, "Disney Enlists Time Inc., Mars to Honor Mickey," *Advertising Age,* June 6, 1988, pp. 3, 110; Wayne Walley, "P & G, Disney Link Videos, Products," *Advertising Age,* Jan. 18, 1988, p. 1; and Wayne Walley, "Roger Rabbit Makes Splash," *Advertising Age,* June 27, 1988, pp. 3, 110.

Questions for Discussion

1. Disney's product mix consists of many products. Does Disney have product lines? If so, what are they?
2. Disney labels many of its new movies for adults as Touchstone Productions. With a famous name like Disney, why does the firm not use the Disney name?
3. Do the products in the Disney product mix have product life cycles? Explain.

9 DEVELOPING AND MANAGING PRODUCTS

Objectives

To become aware of organizational alternatives for managing products

To understand the importance and role of product development in the marketing mix

To become aware of how existing products can be modified

To learn how product deletion can be used to improve product mixes

To gain insight into how businesses develop a product idea into a commercial product

To acquire knowledge about product positioning and the management of products during the various stages of the products' life cycles

Toy companies have introduced hundreds of dolls over the years, but there is only one Barbie. Ninety percent of all American girls between the ages of 3 and 11 own at least one and usually more. Other Mattel products have come and gone, but Barbie sales remain strong. In the toy industry, short-lived fads and complete failures are the norm. Thus, Mattel's successful management of Barbie, now over 30 years old, is a remarkable achievement.

Mattel has allowed Barbie to evolve along with the times—a difficult feat considering the amount of social change occurring since the doll's introduction in 1959. Barbie has become a model, a surgeon, an astronaut, and an aerobics instructor. However, Mattel has purposely not defined Barbie's personality so that she can be anyone a child wants her to be. She drives a Corvette and a Ferrari and manages to adorn herself with the latest styles.

Mattel employs nine fashion designers and a staff of hair stylists to keep Barbie in vogue. Mattel fashion experts patrol malls and amusement parks to spot the latest fashion trends. Mattel designs all of Barbie's clothes and electronically transfers the designs to factories in Malaysia. Largely because of Barbie and her glamorous tastes, Mattel is the fourth biggest producer of women's garments in the United States.

To keep consumer interest high, Mattel has introduced numerous nonclothing accessories, including Barbie houses, furniture, cars, luggage, wigs, and appliances. Mattel has even provided Barbie with a social system consisting of friend Midge and boyfriend Ken. Mattel's objective is to maintain high demand for Barbie by keeping her contemporary and by continuing to introduce Barbie-related products. ◆

Based on information in Patrick E. Cole, "Mattel Is Putting Its Dollhouse in Order," *Business Week,* Aug. 28, 1989, pp. 66–67; Barbara Kantrowitz, "Hot Date: Barbie and G.I. Joe," *Newsweek,* Feb. 20, 1989, p. 59; and Doug Stewart, "In the Cutthroat World of Toy Sales, Child's Play Is Serious Business," *Smithsonian,* December 1989, pp. 73–76, 78, 80–83.

To compete effectively and achieve its goals, an organization such as Mattel must be able to adjust its product mix in response to changes in buyers' preferences. A firm often has to modify existing products, introduce new products, or eliminate products that were successful perhaps only a few years ago. These adjustments and the way a firm is organized to make them are facets of product management.

This chapter first examines how businesses are organized to develop and manage products. Then we look at several ways to improve a product mix, including modifying the quality, function, or style of products; deleting weak products; and developing new products. The process of developing a new product from idea generation to commercialization is described in detail. We also examine product positioning—how marketers decide where a product should fit into the field of competing products and which benefits to emphasize. Finally, we consider issues and decisions associated with managing a product through the growth, maturity, and declining stages of its life cycle.

ORGANIZING TO MANAGE PRODUCTS

A company must often manage a complex set of products, markets, or both. Often, too, it finds that the traditional functional form of organization—in which managers specialize in business functions such as advertising, sales, and distribution—does not fit its needs. Consequently, management must find an organizational approach that accomplishes the tasks necessary to develop and manage products. Alternatives to functional organization include the product manager approach, the market manager approach, and the venture team approach.

A **product manager** is responsible for a product, a product line, or several distinct products that make up an interrelated group within a multiproduct organization. A **brand manager**, on the other hand, is responsible for a single brand. General Foods Corp., for example, has one brand manager for Maxim coffee and one for Maxwell House coffee. A product or brand manager operates cross-functionally to coordinate the activities, information, and strategies involved in marketing an assigned product. Product managers and brand managers plan marketing activities to achieve objectives by coordinating a mix of distribution, promotion (especially sales promotion and advertising), and price. They must consider packaging and branding decisions and work closely with personnel in research and development, engineering, and production. Marketing research helps product managers to understand consumers and find target markets. The product or brand manager approach to organization is used by many large, multiple-product companies in the consumer package goods business.

A **market manager** is responsible for managing the marketing activities that serve a particular group or class of customers. This organizational approach is particularly effective when a firm engages in different types of marketing activities to provide products to diverse customer groups. A company might have one market manager for industrial markets and another for consumer markets. These broad market categories might be broken down into more limited market responsibilities.

A **venture team** is designed to create entirely new products that may be aimed at new markets. Unlike a product or market manager, a venture team is responsible for all aspects of a product's development: research and development, production and engineering, finance and accounting, and marketing. Venture teams work outside established divisions to create inventive approaches to new products and markets. As a result of this flexibility, new products can be developed to take advantage of opportunities in highly segmented markets.

The members of a venture team come from different functional areas of an organization. When the commercial potential of a new product has been demonstrated, the members may return to their functional areas, or they may join a new or existing division to manage the product. The new product may be turned over to an existing division, a market manager, or a product manager. Innovative organizational forms such as venture teams are necessary for many companies, especially well-established firms operating primarily in mature markets. These companies must take a dual approach to marketing organization. They must accommodate the management of mature products and also encourage the development of new ones.[1]

MANAGING THE PRODUCT MIX

To provide products that satisfy target markets and achieve the organization's objectives, a marketer must develop, alter, and maintain an effective product mix (although seldom can the same product mix be effective for long). An organization's product mix may need several types of adjustments. Because customers' attitudes and product preferences change, their desire for a product may wane. People's fashion preferences obviously change quite often, but their attitudes and preferences for most products change over time.

In some cases a company needs to alter its product mix for competitive reasons. A marketer may have to delete a product from the mix because a competitor dominates the market for that product. Similarly, a firm may have to introduce a new product or modify an existing one to compete more effectively. A marketer may expand a firm's product mix to take advantage of excess marketing and production capacity.

Regardless of the reasons for altering a product mix, the product mix must be managed. In strategic market planning, many marketers rely on the portfolio approach for managing the product mix. The **product portfolio approach** tries to create specific marketing strategies to achieve a balanced mix of products that will bring maximum profits in the long run. The most time-consuming task in a portfolio analysis is collecting data about the products and their performance along selected dimensions. This requires hard data from the company's marketing information system (MIS)—for instance, on sales, profitability, market share, and industry growth. We examine product portfolio models in Chapter 19 in the discussion of strategic market planning. Here we consider three major ways to improve a product mix: modifying an existing product, deleting a product, and developing a new product.

1. Roger C. Bennet and Robert G. Cooper, "The Product Life Cycle Trap," *Business Horizons*, September-October 1984, pp. 7–16.

■ Modifying Existing Products

Product modification means changing one or more characteristics of a firm's product. It is most likely to be used in the maturity stage of the product life cycle, to give a firm's existing brand a competitive advantage. Altering a product mix this way entails less risk than developing a new product.

Under certain conditions, product modification can indeed improve a firm's product mix. First, the product must be modifiable. Second, existing customers must be able to perceive that a modification has been made (assuming that the modified item is still aimed at them). Third, the modification should make the product more consistent with customers' desires so that it provides greater satisfaction. There are three major ways to modify products: quality modifications, functional modifications, and style modifications.

Quality Modifications.   **Quality modifications** are changes that relate to a product's dependability and durability. Usually, they are executed by altering the materials or the production process. Reducing a product's quality may allow an organization to lower its price and direct the item at a larger target market.

By contrast, increasing the quality of a product may give a firm an advantage over competing brands. In fact, quality improvement has become a major tool for successfully competing with foreign marketers. Higher quality may enable a company to charge a higher price by creating customer loyalty and by lowering customer sensitivity to price. However, higher quality may require the use of more expensive components, less standardized production processes, and other manufacturing and management techniques that force a firm to charge higher prices.[2] Some firms, such as Caterpillar, are finding ways to both increase quality and reduce costs.

Functional Modifications.   Changes that affect a product's versatility, effectiveness, convenience, or safety are called **functional modifications**; they usually require that the product be redesigned. Typical product categories which have undergone considerable functional modifications include office and farm equipment, appliances and cleaning products. Procter & Gamble, as shown in Figure 9.1, modified Tide by adding bleach, which improved Tide's effectiveness. Functional modifications can make a product useful to more people, which enlarges its market. This type of change can place a product in a favorable competitive position by providing benefits competing items do not offer. Functional modifications can also help an organization achieve and maintain a progressive image. At times, too, functional modifications are made to reduce the possibility of product liability claims.

Style Modifications.   **Style modifications** change the sensory appeal of a product by altering its taste, texture, sound, smell, or visual characteristics. In making a purchase decision a buyer is swayed by how a product looks, smells, tastes, feels, or sounds. Thus a style modification may strongly affect purchases. For years automobile makers have relied on style modifications.

Through style modifications, a firm can differentiate its product from competing brands and thus gain a sizable market share. The major drawback in using style

---

2. Lynn W. Phillips, Dae R. Chang, and Robert D. Buzzell, "Product Quality, Cost Position and Business Performance: A Test of Some Key Hypotheses," *Journal of Marketing*, Spring 1983, pp. 26–43.

SOURCE: © The Procter & Gamble Company

modifications is that their value is determined subjectively. Although a firm may strive to improve the product's style, customers may actually find the modified product less appealing.

■ Deleting Products

Generally, a product cannot satisfy target market customers and contribute to the achievement of an organization's overall goals indefinitely. **Product deletion** is the process of eliminating a product that no longer satisfies a sufficient number of customers. A declining product reduces an organization's profitability and drains resources that could be used instead to modify other products or develop new ones. A marginal product may require shorter production runs, which can increase per-unit production costs. Finally, when a dying product completely loses favor with customers, the negative feelings may transfer to some of the company's other products.

Most organizations find it difficult to delete a product. It was probably a hard decision for Federal Express to drop ZapMail and admit that it was a failure. A decision to drop a product may be opposed by management and other employees who feel the product is necessary in the product mix. Salespeople who still have some loyal customers are especially upset when a product is dropped. Considerable

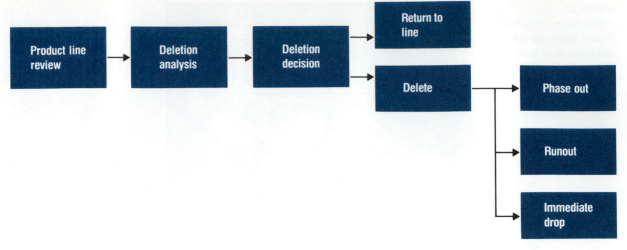

FIGURE 9.2 *Product deletion process*

SOURCE: Martin L. Bell, *Marketing: Concepts and Strategy,* 3rd ed., p. 267; copyright 1979, Houghton Mifflin Company; used by permission of Mrs. Martin L. Bell.

resources and effort are sometimes spent trying to change the product's marketing mix to improve its sales and thus avoid having to delete it.

Some organizations delete products only after they have become heavy financial burdens. A better approach is some form of systematic review in which each product is evaluated periodically to determine its impact on the overall effectiveness of the firm's product mix. Such a review should analyze a product's contribution to the firm's sales for a given period and include estimates of future sales, costs, and profits associated with the product. It should also gauge the value of making changes in the marketing strategy to improve the product's performance. A systematic review allows an organization to improve product performance and to ascertain when to delete products. Although many companies do systematically review their product mixes, a research study found that few companies have formal, written policies on the process of deleting products. The study also found that most companies based their decisions to delete weak products on poor sales and profit potential, low compatibility with the firms' business strategies, unfavorable market outlook, and historical declines in profitability.[3]

Basically, there are three ways of deleting a product: to phase it out, run it out, or drop it immediately (see Figure 9.2). A phaseout approach lets the product decline without a change in the marketing strategy. No attempt is made to give the product new life. A runout policy exploits any strengths left in the product. Intensifying marketing efforts in core markets or eliminating some marketing expenditures, such as advertising, may cause a sudden spurt of profits. This approach is commonly taken for technologically obsolete products, such as older models of computers and calculators. Often the price is reduced to get a sales spurt. The third alternative, dropping an unprofitable product immediately, is the best strategy when losses are too great to prolong the product's life.

3. Douglas M. Lambert and Jay U. Sterling, "Identifying and Eliminating Weak Products," *Business,* July-September 1988, pp. 3–10.

FIGURE 9.3

New product.
Feliners, a new product, is a diaper-like litter box liner.

SOURCE: Colgate Palmolive Company

Developing New Products

Developing and introducing new products is frequently expensive and risky. Thousands of new consumer products are introduced annually, and, as indicated in Chapter 8, anywhere from 60 to 90 percent of them fail. Lack of research is a leading cause of new-product failure. Other often-cited causes are technical problems in design or production and errors in timing the product's introduction. Although new-product development is risky, so is failure to introduce new products. For example, the makers of Timex watches gained a large share of the U.S. watch market through effective marketing strategies during the 1960s and early 1970s. By 1983, Timex's market share had slipped considerably, in part because Timex had failed to introduce new products. In recent times, however, Timex has introduced a number of new products and regained market share.

The term *new product* can have more than one meaning. A genuinely new product—like the VCR once was—offers innovative benefits. But products that are different and distinctly better are often viewed as new. The following items (listed in no particular order) are product innovations of the last thirty years: Post-It note pads, disposable lighters, birth-control pills, personal computers, felt-tip pens, seat belts, disposable razors, compact disc players, quartz watches, and contact lenses. Thus, a new product can be an innovative product that has never been sold by any organization, such as the diaper-like litter box liner advertised in Figure 9.3. It can also be a product that a given firm has not marketed previously, although similar

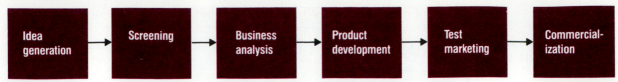

| Idea generation | → | Screening | → | Business analysis | → | Product development | → | Test marketing | → | Commercial-ization |

FIGURE 9.4 *Phases of new-product development*

products may have been available from other companies. The first company to introduce a VCR, for example, clearly was launching a new product. However, if Boeing introduced a VCR brand, this would also be viewed as a new product for Boeing because that organization has not previously marketed VCRs.

Before a product is introduced, it goes through the six phases of **new-product development** shown in Figure 9.4: (1) idea generation, (2) screening, (3) business analysis, (4) product development, (5) test marketing, and (6) commercialization. A product may be dropped, and many are, at any stage of development. In this section, we will look at the process through which products are developed, from the inception of an idea to a product offered for sale.

Idea Generation.   Businesses and other organizations seek product ideas that will help them achieve their objectives. This activity is **idea generation**. The fact that only a few ideas are good enough to be commercially successful underscores the difficulty of the task. Although some organizations get their ideas almost by chance, firms that are trying to effectively manage their product mixes usually develop systematic approaches for generating new product ideas. At the heart of innovation is a purposeful, focused effort to identify new ways to serve a market. Unexpected occurrences, incongruities, new needs, industry and market changes, and demographic changes all may indicate new opportunities.[4]

New product ideas can come from several sources. They may come from internal sources—marketing managers, researchers, sales personnel, engineers, or other organizational personnel. Brainstorming and incentives or rewards for good ideas are typical intrafirm devices for stimulating the development of ideas. For example, the idea for 3M Post-It adhesive-backed yellow notes came from an employee. As a church choir member, he used slips of paper for marking songs in his hymnal. Because the pieces of paper fell out, he suggested developing an adhesive-backed note.[5] Hewlett-Packard Co. keeps its labs open to engineers twenty-four hours a day to help generate ideas; it also encourages its researchers to devote 10 percent of company time to exploring their own ideas for new products.[6]

New product ideas may also arise from sources outside the firm—customers, competitors, advertising agencies, management consultants, and private research organizations. Johnson & Johnson, for example, acquired the technology for its new clear orthodontic braces through a joint venture with Saphikon, the developer of the

4. Peter F. Drucker, "The Discipline of Innovation," *Harvard Business Review,* May-June 1985, pp. 67–68.

5. Lawrence Ingrassia, "By Improving Scotch Paper, 3M Gets New Product Winner," *Wall Street Journal,* Mar. 31, 1983, p. 27.

6. Jonathan B. Levine, "Keeping New Ideas Kicking Around," *Business Week,* Innovation 1989 issue, p. 128.

technology behind the braces.[7] Sometimes, potential buyers of a product are questioned in depth to discover what attributes would appeal to them. Asking weekend fishermen what they wanted in a sonar fish finder led Techsonic Industries Inc. to develop its LCR (liquid crystal recorder) fish finder. Annual sales of the LCR reached $31 million within one year. The practice of asking customers what they want from its products has helped Techsonic maintain its leadership in the industry.[8]

Screening Ideas.   In the process of **screening ideas**, those with the greatest potential are selected for further review. During screening, product ideas are analyzed to determine whether they match the organization's objectives and resources. The company's overall ability to produce and market the product is also analyzed. Other aspects of an idea that should be weighed are the nature and wants of buyers and possible environmental changes. Compared with other phases, the largest number of new product ideas are rejected during the idea-screening phase.

At times a checklist of new-product requirements is used when making screening decisions. It encourages evaluators to be systematic and so reduces the chances of their overlooking some fact. If a critical factor on the checklist remains unclear, the type of formal research described in Chapter 7 may be needed. To screen ideas properly, it may be necessary to test product concepts: a product concept and its benefits can be described or shown to consumers. Several product concepts may be tested to discover which might appeal most to a particular target market.

Business Analysis.   During the **business analysis** stage, the product idea is evaluated to determine its potential contribution to the firm's sales, costs, and profits. In the course of a business analysis, evaluators ask a variety of questions: Does the product fit in with the organization's existing product mix? Is demand strong enough to justify entering the market and will the demand endure? What types of environmental and competitive changes can be expected, and how will these changes affect the product's future sales, costs, and profits? Are the organization's research, development, engineering, and production capabilities adequate? If new facilities must be constructed, how quickly can they be built and how much will they cost? Is the necessary financing for development and commercialization on hand or obtainable at terms consistent with a favorable return on investment?

In the business analysis stage, firms seek market information. The results of consumer polls, along with secondary data, supply the specifics needed for estimating potential sales, costs, and profits. At this point, a research budget should explore the financial objectives and related considerations for the new product.

Product Development.   **Product development** is the phase in which the organization finds out if it is technically feasible to produce the product and if it can be produced at costs low enough to make the final price reasonable. To test its acceptability, the idea or concept is converted into a prototype, or working model. The prototype should reveal tangible and intangible attributes associated with the product in consumers' minds. The product's design, mechanical features, and intangible

7. Joseph Weber, "Going Over the Lab Wall in Search of New Ideas," *Business Week,* Innovation 1989 issue, p. 132.

8. Joshua Hyatt, "Ask and You Shall Receive," *Inc.,* September 1989, pp. 90–101.

aspects must be linked to wants in the marketplace. Failure to determine how consumers feel about the product and how they would use it may lead to the product's failure. For example, Coca-Cola Company's Minute Maid division developed Minute Maid Squeeze-Fresh orange juice concentrate so that consumers could make one glass of juice at a time rather than mix and store a half gallon. In tests, however, the company discovered that consumers did not like Squeeze-Fresh because it was messy and they did not know how much concentrate to use to make one glass of juice.[9] Testing to determine how consumers view the product idea is therefore very important in the product development stage. As indicated in Marketing Update 9.1, Fisher-Price spends considerable time and money on research and development associated with its new products.

The development phase of a new product is frequently lengthy and expensive; thus a relatively small number of product ideas are put into development. If the product appears sufficiently successful during this stage to merit test-marketing, then during the latter part of the development stage marketers begin to make decisions regarding branding, packaging, labeling, pricing, and promotion for use in the test marketing stage.

Test Marketing. A limited introduction of a product in geographic areas chosen to represent the intended market is called **test marketing**. Its aim is to determine the reactions of probable buyers. For example, after McDonald's developed fried chicken products for its fast-food menu, it test-marketed the idea in some Texas McDonald's restaurants to find out how those customers felt about eating chicken at McDonald's.[10] (Marketing Update 9.2 details how McDonald's is test marketing pizza.) Test marketing is *not* an extension of the development stage; it is a sample launching of the entire marketing mix. Test marketing should be conducted only after the product has gone through development and after initial plans regarding the other marketing mix variables have been made.

Companies of all sizes use test marketing to lessen the risk of product failure. The dangers of introducing an untested product include undercutting already profitable products and, should the new product fail, loss of credibility with distributors and customers. Frito-Lay, for example, believed that it understood consumers' snack preferences well enough to introduce a new snack cracker called MaxSnax without first test marketing it. Even with strong advertising support, the product did not sell, and Frito-Lay was forced to eliminate the product from its snack line.[11]

Test marketing provides several benefits. It lets marketers expose a product in a natural marketing environment to gauge its sales performance. While the product is being marketed in a limited area, the company can strive to identify weaknesses in the product or in other parts of the marketing mix. A product weakness discovered after a nationwide introduction can be expensive to correct. Moreover, if consumers' early reactions are negative, marketers may not be able to convince consumers to try the product again. Thus making adjustments after test marketing can be crucial to the success of a new product. Test marketing also allows marketers to experiment

9. "Oops! Marketers Blunder Their Way Through the 'Herb Decade'," *Advertising Age*, Feb. 13, 1989, p. 66.

10. "Winging It at McDonald's," *USA Today*, Sept. 5, 1989, p. 1B.

11. "Oops! Marketers Blunder Their Way Through the 'Herb Decade'," *Advertising Age*, Feb. 13, 1989, p. 66.

FISHER-PRICE'S PRODUCT RESEARCH AND DEVELOPMENT

Fisher-Price, the East Aurora, New York division of Quaker Oats Co., takes toys very seriously: it runs a play laboratory to try to determine which new toys—their own and the competition's—will be the most popular with children. The play laboratory is part of an entire child research department at Fisher-Price where adults closely watch children at play. One-way mirrors hide researchers from the children, who frolic in a room filled with a large selection of toys. For Fisher-Price, the knowledge gained through this observation plays a major role in deciding which toys to place on the market.

The research and development personnel at Fisher-Price carefully examine how a child interacts with a toy, looking for a quality they term "play value." They see play value as the most important attribute of a new toy, as well as the most difficult to assess accurately.

Toy researchers make sure that toys can withstand rough handling. They analyze toys for potential hazards, such as hinges that might hurt small fingers or tiny parts that might pose a danger to very young children. Sometimes adult researchers are even called upon to chew on toys to see if any parts come loose. New toys face strenuous and extensive safety testing. Every piece of a new toy, in addition to the finished product, is scientifically abused to ensure that it will be safe in the hands of a child.

Executives at Fisher-Price know that it is the toys themselves that will ultimately spell success or failure for the company. Consequently, Fisher-Price dedicates a large part of its budget to research and development and a large chunk of its time to watching children play.

SOURCES: Doug Stewart, "In the Cutthroat World of Toy Sales, Child's Play Is Serious Business," *Smithsonian,* December 1989, pp. 73–76, 78, 80–83; Mary Lynne Vellinga, "Fisher-Price," Rochester, New York, *Democrat and Chronicle,* Apr. 4, 1988; and David J. Wallace, "Fisher-Price Toys with TV," *Advertising Age,* Feb. 13, 1989, p. S-8.

TABLE 9.1

*Popular test markets for
new products*

Akron, OH	Fort Wayne, IN	Portland, OR
Ann Arbor, MI	Grand Junction, CO	Providence, RI
Asheville, NC	Greensboro, NC	Raleigh, NC
Austin, TX	Hartford, CT	Richmond, VA
Bangor, ME	Huntsville, AL	Rockford, IL
Beaumont, TX	Jacksonville, FL	St. Louis, MO
Boise, ID	Kansas City, MO	Salem, NC
Buffalo, NY	Las Vegas, NV	Salt Lake City, UT
Cedar Rapids, IA	Little Rock, AK	San Francisco, CA
Charleston, WV	Lubbock, TX	Scranton, PA
Chicago, IL	Marion, IN	Sioux Falls, SD
Colorado Springs, CO	Melbourne, FL	Spokane, WA
Columbus, OH	Midland, TX	Springfield, IL
Dallas, TX	Mobile, AL	Syracuse, NY
Decatur, IL	Montgomery, AL	Tampa, FL
Detroit, MI	New Orleans, LA	Troy, NY
Durham, NC	Oklahoma City, OK	Washington, DC
Elkhart, IN	Orlando, FL	Wichita, KS
Evansville, IN	Philadelphia, PA	Yakima, WA
Fort Collins, CO	Pittsfield, MA	

SOURCE: "The Nation's Most Popular Test Markets," *Sales & Marketing Management,* March 1989, pp. 65–66. Reprinted by permission of Sales & Marketing Management. Copyright 1989.

with variations in advertising, price, and packaging in different test areas and to measure the extent of brand awareness, brand switching, and repeat purchases that result from alterations in the marketing mix.

The accuracy of test-marketing results often hinges on where the tests are conducted. Selection of appropriate test areas is very important. The validity of test market results depends heavily on selecting test sites that provide accurate representation of the intended target market. Table 9.1 lists some of the most popular test-market cities. The criteria used for choosing test cities depend on the product's characteristics, the target market's characteristics, and the firm's objectives and resources. Even though the selection criteria will vary from one company to another, the kind of questions that Table 9.2 presents can be helpful in assessing a potential test market.

Test marketing is not without risks, however. Not only is it expensive, but also a firm's competitors may try to interfere. A competitor may attempt to "jam" the test program by increasing advertising or promotions, lowering prices, and offering special incentives—all to combat the recognition and purchase of a new brand. Any such devices can invalidate test results. Sometimes, too, competitors copy the product in the testing stage and rush to introduce a similar product. It is therefore desirable to move quickly and commercialize as soon as possible after testing.

Because of these risks, many companies are using alternative methods to gauge consumer preferences. One such method is simulated test marketing. Typically,

TABLE 9.2

Questions to consider when choosing test markets

1. Is the area typical of planned distribution outlets?
2. Is the city relatively isolated from other cities?
3. What local media are available, and are they cooperative?
4. Does the area have a dominant television station? Does it have multiple newspapers, magazines, and radio stations?
5. Does the city contain a diversified cross section of ages, religions, and cultural/societal preferences?
6. Are the purchasing habits atypical?
7. Is the city's per capita income typical?
8. Does the city have a good record as a test city?
9. Would testing efforts be easily "jammed" by competitors?
10. Does the city have stable year-round sales?
11. Are retailers who will cooperate available?
12. Are research and audit services available?
13. Is the area free from unusual influences, such as one industry's dominance or heavy tourist traffic?

SOURCE: Adapted from "A Checklist for Selecting Test Markets," copyright 1982 *Sales & Marketing Management.* Reprinted by permission of Sales & Marketing Management. Copyright 1982.

consumers at shopping centers are asked to view an advertisement for a new product and given a free sample to take home. These consumers are subsequently interviewed over the phone and asked to rate the product. The major advantages of simulated test marketing are lower costs and tighter security, which reduces the flow of information to competitors and eliminates jamming. Scanner-based test marketing is another, more sophisticated version of the traditional test-marketing method.[12] Some marketing research firms, such as A. C. Nielsen Company, offer test-marketing services to help provide independent assessment of products.

Commercialization.   During the **commercialization** phase, plans for full-scale manufacturing and marketing must be refined and settled, and budgets for the project must be prepared. Early in the commercialization phase, marketing management analyzes the results of test-marketing to find out what changes in the marketing mix are needed before the product is introduced. For example, the results of test-marketing may tell the marketers to change one or more of the product's physical attributes, modify the distribution plans to include more retail outlets, alter promotional efforts, or change the product's price. However, as more and more changes are made based on test-marketing findings, the test-marketing projections may become less valid.

During this phase, the organization also has to gear up for production. Consequently, it may face sizable capital expenditures for plant and equipment and may need to hire additional personnel.

12. Eleanor Johnson Tracy, "Testing Time for Test Marketing," *Fortune,* Oct. 29, 1984, pp. 75–76.

TEST-MARKETING MCDONALD'S PIZZA

Eager to take a bigger bite out of the dinner market, McDonald's Corp. is trying to offer other items besides their traditional burgers, fries, and Chicken McNuggets. Executives of the franchise giant, which is based in Oak Brook, Illinois, think that pizza might bring in more afternoon and early evening traffic —the slowest sales period for McDonald's—as well as more revenues. Pizza is a $20-billion-a-year industry that keeps growing.

Several years ago, McDonald's experimented with mini pizza pies designed for individual meals but decided to terminate the "McPizzas" after they did not perform well in test-marketing. The new pizzas, called McDonald's Pizzas, are full-sized, fourteen-inch pizzas. Sold only after 4 P.M., the pizzas come in four varieties, with prices ranging from $6 to $10. Customers in test-market cities may choose from among cheese, sausage, pepperoni, or "deluxe" types. McDonald's will not sell pizza by the slice. The company is test-marketing the pizzas in and around Evansville, Indiana, and in some cities in Kentucky. Around Evansville, owners of local pizza parlors are concerned about the new competition.

Unlike the McPizzas, McDonald's new pizzas are made from fresh ingredients and baked to order. They can also be baked and served very fast. Since McDonald's customers get their Big Macs almost instantaneously, the company's management worried about the reaction to a long wait for a pizza. This problem was solved by developing a special superfast oven that bakes a pizza in five and a half minutes. A McDonald's spokesperson pointed out that the company wants to maintain its reputation for quick service and that a five- or six-minute wait is still extremely fast service for a pizza.

Test-marketing results for the new product have been favorable. However, McDonald's, true to its character of being very cautious when introducing new products, has no current plans to offer pizza in every one of its eight thousand outlets across the United States. It is taking a wait-and-see approach. Thus consumers in other parts of the country may not taste McDonald's pizza for a very long time—if ever. After all, McDonald's test-marketed its now popular salads for twelve years.

SOURCES: Stuart Elliott, "McDonald's Hopes McPizza Will Deliver," *USA Today,* Aug. 25, 1989, p. 1B; Richard Gibson, "McDonald's Fires Fast Pitch at Pizza Buffs," *Wall Street Journal,* Aug. 28, 1989, p. B4; and John Schwartz, "You Deserve a Pizza Today," *Newsweek,* Sept. 11, 1989, p. 46.

The product enters the market during the commercialization phase. When introducing a product, marketers often spend enormous sums of money for advertising, personal selling, and other types of promotion. These expenses, together with capital outlays, can make commercialization extremely costly; such expenditures may not be recovered for several years. For example, when Anheuser-Busch introduced Michelob Dry and the nonalcoholic O'Doul's beers, the company spent millions of dollars on advertising to communicate the new products' attributes.[13]

Commercialization is easier when customers accept the product rapidly. There is a better chance of this occurring if marketers can make them aware of a product's benefits. The following stages of the **product adoption process** are generally recognized as those that buyers go through in accepting a product:

1. *Awareness.*   The buyer becomes aware of the product.
2. *Interest.*   The buyer seeks information and is receptive to learning about the product.
3. *Evaluation.*   The buyer considers the product's benefits and determines whether to try it.
4. *Trial.*   The buyer examines, tests, or tries the product to determine its usefulness, relative to his or her needs.
5. *Adoption.*   The buyer purchases the product and can be expected to use it when the need for this general type of product arises again.[14]

This adoption model has several implications for the commercialization phase. First, the company must promote the product to create widespread awareness of its existence and its benefits. Samples or simulated trials should be arranged to help buyers make initial purchase decisions. At the same time, marketers should emphasize quality control and provide solid guarantees to reinforce buyer opinion during the evaluation stage. Finally, production and physical distribution must be linked to patterns of adoption and repeat purchases. (The product adoption process is also discussed in Chapter 14.)

Products are not usually launched nationwide overnight but are introduced through a process called a roll-out. Through a roll-out, a product is introduced in stages, starting in a set of geographic areas and gradually expanding into adjacent areas. Huggies Pull-Ups disposable training pants (see Figure 9.5) is a product that was rolled out. A note at the bottom of this advertisement states that the product is available in limited areas. It may take several years to market the product nationally. Sometimes the test cities are used as initial marketing areas, and the introduction becomes a natural extension of test-marketing. A product test-marketed in Sacramento, Denver, Dallas, St. Louis, and Atlanta, as the map in Figure 9.6 shows, could be introduced first in those cities. After the stage 1 introduction is complete, stage 2 could include market coverage of the states in which the test cities are located. In stage 3, marketing efforts could be extended into adjacent states. All remaining states would then be covered in stage 4. Gradual product introductions do not always occur state by state, however; other geographic combinations are used as well, such as groups of counties that overlap across state borders.

13. Ira Teinowitz, "A-B Goes to the Well and Comes Up Dry and . . ." *Advertising Age,* Mar. 20, 1989, pp. S-2, S-4.
14. Adapted from Everett M. Rogers, *Diffusion of Innovations* (New York: Macmillan, 1962), pp. 81–86.

SOURCE: Reprinted with permission of Kimberly-Clark Corporation

Gradual product introduction is popular for several reasons. It reduces the risks of introducing a new product. If the product fails, the firm will experience smaller losses if the item has been introduced in only a few geographic areas than if it has been marketed nationally. Furthermore, a company cannot introduce a product nationwide overnight because the system of wholesalers and retailers, necessary to distribute a product, cannot be established that quickly. The development of a distribution network may take considerable time. Keep in mind also that the number of units needed to satisfy the national demand for a successful product can be enormous, and a firm usually cannot produce the required quantities in a short time.

Despite the good reasons for introducing a product gradually, marketers realize that this approach creates some competitive problems. A gradual introduction allows competitors to observe what a firm is doing and to monitor results, just as the firm's own marketers are doing. If competitors see that the newly introduced product is successful, they may enter the same target market quickly with similar products. In addition, as a product is introduced region by region, competitors may expand their marketing efforts to offset promotion of the new product.

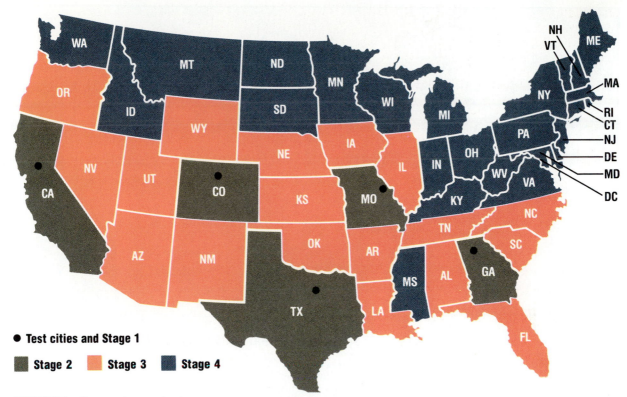

FIGURE 9.6 *Stages of expansion into a national market during commercialization*

SOURCE: Adapted from *Business: An Involvement Approach,* by Herbert G. Hicks, William M. Pride, and James D. Powell. Copyright © 1975 by McGraw-Hill. Used with permission of McGraw-Hill Book Company.

PRODUCT POSITIONING

The term **product positioning** refers to the decisions and activities intended to create and maintain a certain concept of the firm's product (relative to competitive brands) in customers' minds. When marketers introduce a product, they attempt to position it so that it seems to possess the characteristics the target market most desires. This projected image is crucial. *Product position* is the customers' concept of the product's attributes relative to their concept of competitive brands. Crest is positioned as a fluoride toothpaste that fights cavities and Close-Up is positioned as a whitening toothpaste that enhances the user's sex appeal.

Product positioning is a part of a natural progression when market segmentation is used. Segmentation lets the firm aim a given brand at a portion of the total market. Effective product positioning helps serve a specific market segment by creating an appropriate concept in the minds of customers in that market segment. Gillette Co.'s Dippity-Do hair gel product had been on the decline since its heyday in the 1960s, in part because women who used it then associated it with that era's popular bouffant hairstyles. Gillette therefore repositioned Dippity-Do for today's

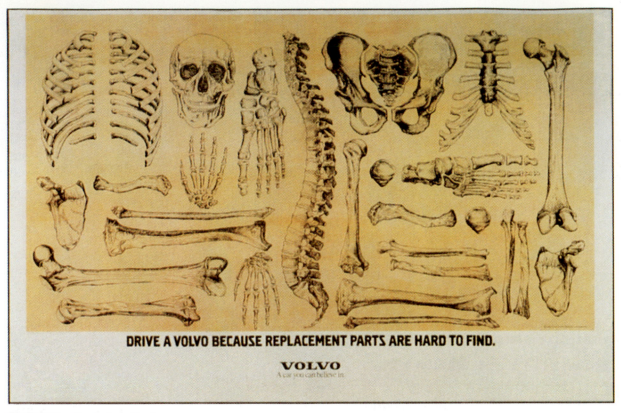

FIGURE 9.7 *Product positioning.*
Volvo has positioned itself to avoid competition by accenting its cars' safety characteristics for many years.

SOURCE: Courtesy of Volvo

hair styles by appealing to teen-agers who have no memories of the product's former use.[15]

A firm can position a product to compete head-on with another brand, as Pepsi has done against Coca-Cola, or to avoid competition, as 7-Up has done relative to other soft-drink producers. Head-to-head competition may be a marketer's positioning objective if the product's performance characteristics are at least equal to competitive brands and if the product is priced lower. Head-to-head positioning may be appropriate even when the price is higher if the product's performance characteristics are superior. Conversely, positioning to avoid competition may be best when the product's performance characteristics are not significantly different from competing brands. Moreover, positioning a brand to avoid competition may be appropriate when that brand has unique characteristics that are important to some buyers. Volvo, for example, has for years positioned itself away from competitors by focusing on the safety characteristics of its cars (see Figure 9.7). Competitors sometimes mention safety issues in their advertisements only temporarily.

15. Ronald Alsop, "Giving Fading Brands a Second Chance," *Wall Street Journal,* Jan. 24, 1989, p. B1.

Avoiding competition is critical when a firm introduces a brand into a market in which it already has one or more brands. Marketers usually want to avoid cannibalizing sales of their existing brands, unless the new brand generates substantially larger profits. When Coca-Cola reintroduced Tab, it attempted to position the cola so as to minimize the adverse effects on Diet Coke sales. Tab was positioned as the diet drink containing calcium—catering specifically to a female target market.

If a product has been planned properly, its attributes and brand image will give it the distinct appeal needed. Style, shape, construction, quality of work, and color help create the image and the appeal. If they can easily identify the benefits, then of course buyers are more likely to purchase the product. When the new product does not offer some preferred attributes, there is room for another new product or for repositioning an existing product.

MANAGING PRODUCTS AFTER COMMERCIALIZATION

Most new products start off slowly and seldom generate enough sales to produce profits immediately. As buyers learn about the new product, marketers should be alert for product weaknesses and make corrections quickly, to prevent its early demise. Marketing strategy should be designed to attract the segment that is most interested and has the fewest objections. If any of these factors need adjustment, this action, too, must be taken quickly to sustain demand. As the sales curve moves upward and the break-even point is reached, the growth stage begins.

■ **Marketing Strategy in the Growth Stage**

As sales increase, management must support the momentum by adjusting the marketing strategy. The goal is to establish the product's position and to fortify it by encouraging brand loyalty. As profits increase, the organization must brace itself for the entrance of aggressive competitors, who may make specialized appeals to selected market segments.

During the growth stage, product offerings may have to be expanded. To achieve greater penetration of an overall market, segmentation may have to be used more intensely. That would require developing product variations to satisfy the needs of people in several different market segments. Marketers should analyze the product position regarding competing products and correct weak or omitted attributes. Quality, functional, or style modifications may be required.

Gaps in the marketing channels should be filled during the growth period. Once a product has won acceptance, new distribution outlets may be easier to obtain. Sometimes marketers tend to move from an exclusive or selective exposure to a more intensive network of dealers to achieve greater market penetration. Marketers must also make sure that the physical distribution system is running efficiently and delivering supplies to distributors before their inventories are exhausted. Because competition increases during the growth period, service adjustments and prompt credit for defective products are important marketing tools.

Advertising expenditures may be lowered slightly from the high level of the introductory stage but are still quite substantial. As sales increase, promotion costs should drop as a percentage of total sales. A falling ratio between promotion expenditures and sales should contribute significantly to increased profits. The advertising messages should stress brand benefits. Coupons and samples may be used to increase market share.

After recovering development costs, a business may be able to lower prices. As sales volume increases, efficiencies in production can result in lower costs. These savings may be passed on to buyers. If demand remains strong and there are few competitive threats, prices tend to remain stable. If price cuts are feasible, they can improve price competition and discourage new competitors from entering the market. For example, when compact disc players were introduced in the early 1980s, they sported a $1,000 price tag. Primarily because of the price, the product was positioned as a "toy for audiophiles"—a very small market segment. To generate mass market demand, compact disc player manufacturers dropped their prices to around $200, and the cost of discs dropped from $22 to about $12. The price is now at a point where the margin is low but the turnover is high. Although only 13 percent of American homes have a compact disc player, compact discs now account for 40 percent of all U.S. music purchases.[16]

■ Marketing Strategy for Mature Products

Because many products are in the maturity stage of their life cycles, marketers must deal with these products and be prepared to improve the marketing mix constantly. During maturity, the competitive situation stabilizes and some of the weaker competitors drop out. It has been suggested that as a product matures, its customers become more experienced and specialized (especially for industrial products). As these customers gain knowledge, the benefits they seek may change as well. Thus new marketing strategies may be called for.[17]

Marketers may need to alter the product's quality or otherwise modify the product. A product may be rejuvenated through different packaging, new models, or style changes. Sales and market share may be maintained or strengthened by developing new uses for the product. In Figure 9.8, the maker of Hood Cottage Cheese is suggesting a new use for cottage cheese—as a hamburger topping.

During the maturity stage of the cycle, marketers actively encourage dealers to support the product. Dealers may be offered promotional assistance in lowering their inventory costs. In general, marketers go to great lengths to serve dealers and provide incentives for selling the manufacturer's brand, partly because private brands are a threat at this time. As we discuss in Chapter 8, private brands are both an opportunity and a threat to manufacturers, who may be able to sell their products through recognized private brand names as well as their own. However, private brands frequently undermine manufacturers' brands. Yet if manufacturers refuse to sell to private-brand dealers, competitors may take advantage of this opportunity.

To maintain market share during the maturity stage requires moderate and sometimes large advertising expenditures. Advertising messages focus on differentiating a brand from numerous competitors, and sales promotion efforts are aimed at both consumers and resellers.

A greater mixture of pricing strategies is used during the maturity stage. In some cases, strong price competition occurs and price wars may break out. On the other

16. Paul Farhi, "Compact Discs Turn Tables on Vinyl Record Sales," *Washington Post,* Mar. 1, 1989, pp. F1, F2.

17. F. Stewart DeBruicker and Gregory L. Summe, "Make Sure Your Customers Keep Coming Back," *Harvard Business Review,* January-February 1985, pp. 92–98.

FIGURE 9.8

Promoting new product uses.
The maker of Hood Cottage Cheese attempts to strengthen its market share by suggesting new uses for its product.

Beef Up Your Burger With Hood®

Break away from the boring burger by adding Hood Cottage Cheese on top. Garnish it with lettuce and tomato and you'll have a meal high in protein and calcium that your whole family will love. Just one more reason you can feel good about Hood.

Hood Cottage Cheese. Anything But Boring.

Hood Country Style

COTTAGE CHEESE

SOURCE: Courtesy of HP Hood Inc.

hand, firms may compete in other ways than through price. Marketers develop price flexibility to differentiate offerings in product lines. Markdowns and price incentives are more common, but prices may rise if distribution and production costs increase.

■ Marketing Strategy for Declining Products

As a product's sales curve turns downward, industry profits continue to fall. A business can justify maintaining a product as long as it contributes to profits or enhances the overall effectiveness of a product mix. In this stage, marketers must determine whether to eliminate the product or seek to reposition it in an attempt to extend its life. Usually, a declining product has lost its distinctiveness because similar competing products have been introduced. Competition engenders increased substitution and brand switching as buyers become insensitive to minor product differences. For these reasons, marketers do little to change a product's style, design, or other attributes during its decline. New technology, product substitutes, or environmental considerations may also indicate that the time has come to delete a product.

During a product's decline, outlets with strong sales volumes are maintained and unprofitable outlets are weeded out. An entire marketing channel may be eliminated if it does not contribute adequately to profits. Sometimes a new marketing channel, such as a factory outlet, will be used to liquidate remaining inventory of an obsolete product. As sales decline, the product becomes more obscure, but loyal buyers seek out dealers who carry it.

Advertising expenditures are at a minimum. Advertising of special offers may slow the rate of decline. Sales promotions, such as coupons and premiums, may temporarily regain buyers' attention. As the product continues to decline, the sales staff shifts its emphasis to more profitable products.

To have a product return a profit may be more important to a firm than to maintain a certain market share through repricing. To squeeze out all possible remaining profits, marketers may maintain the price despite declining sales and competitive pressures. Prices may even be increased as costs rise if a loyal core market still wants the product. In other situations, the price may be cut to reduce existing inventory so that the product can be deleted. Severe price reductions may be required if a new product is making an existing product obsolete.

Summary

Developing and managing products is critical to an organization's survival and growth. The various approaches available for organizing product management share common activities, functions, and decisions necessary to guide a product through its life cycle. A product manager is responsible for a product, a product line, or several distinct products that make up an interrelated group within a multiproduct organization. A brand manager is a product manager who is responsible for a single brand. Market managers are responsible for managing the marketing activities that serve a particular group or class of customers. A venture team is sometimes used to create entirely new products that may be aimed at new markets.

The product portfolio approach attempts to create specific marketing strategies to achieve a balanced product mix that will produce maximum long-run profits. To maximize the effectiveness of a product mix, an organization usually has to alter its mix through modification of existing products, deletion of a product, or new-product development. Product modification is changing one or more characteristics of a firm's product. This approach to altering a product mix can be effective when the product is modifiable, when customers can perceive the change, and when customers want the modification. Quality modifications are changes that relate to a product's dependability and durability. Changes that affect a product's versatility, effectiveness, convenience, or safety are called functional modifications. Style modifications change the sensory appeal of a product.

Product deletion is the process of eliminating a product that no longer satisfies a sufficient number of customers. Although a firm's personnel may oppose product deletion, weak products are unprofitable, consume too much time and effort, may require shorter production runs, and can create an unfavorable impression of the firm's other products. A product mix should be systematically reviewed to determine when to delete products. Products to be deleted can be phased out, run out, or dropped immediately.

A new product may be an innovation that has never been sold by any organization, or it can be a product that a given firm has not marketed previously, although similar products may have been available from other organizations. Before a product is introduced, it goes through the six phases of new-product development. In the idea generation phase, new product ideas may come from internal or external sources. In the process of screening ideas, those with the greatest potential are selected for further review. During the business analysis stage, the product idea is evaluated to determine its potential contribution to the firm's sales, costs, and profits. Product development is the stage in which the organization finds out if it is technically feasible to produce the product and if it can be produced at costs low enough so that the final price is reasonable. Test marketing is a limited introduction of a product in areas chosen to represent the intended market. The decision to enter the commercialization phase means that full-scale production of the product begins and a complete marketing strategy is developed. The process that buyers go through in accepting a product includes awareness, interest, evaluation, trial, and adoption.

Product positioning comprises the decisions and activities intended to create and maintain a certain concept of the firm's product (relative to competitive brands) in customers' minds. Product positioning is part of a natural progression when market segmentation is used. A firm can position a product to compete head-on with another brand or to avoid competition.

As a product moves through its life cycle, marketing strategies may require continual adaptation. In the growth stage, it is important to develop brand loyalty and a market position. In the maturity stage, a product may be modified or new market segments may be developed to rejuvenate its sales. A product that is declining may be maintained as long as it makes a contribution to profits or enhances the product mix. Marketers must determine whether to eliminate the declining product or try to reposition it to extend its life.

IMPORTANT TERMS

Product manager
Brand manager
Market manager
Venture team
Product portfolio approach
Product modification
Quality modifications
Functional modifications
Style modifications
Product deletion

New-product development
Idea generation
Screening ideas
Business analysis
Product development
Test marketing
Commercialization
Product adoption process
Product positioning

DISCUSSION AND REVIEW QUESTIONS

1. What organizational alternatives are available to a firm with two product lines having four product items in each line?
2. When is it more appropriate to use a product manager than a market manager? When might an alternative or combined approach be used?
3. What type of organization might use a venture team to develop new products? What are the advantages and disadvantages of such a team?

4. Do small companies that manufacture one or two products need to be concerned about developing and managing products? Why or why not?
5. Why is product development a cross-functional activity within an organization? That is, why must finance, engineering, manufacturing, and other functional areas be involved?
6. Develop information sources for new product ideas for the automobile industry.
7. Some firms believe that they can omit test marketing. What are some advantages and disadvantages of test marketing?
8. Under what conditions is product modification appropriate for changing a product mix? How does a quality modification differ from a functional modification? Can an organization make one modification without making the other?
9. Give several reasons why an organization might be unable to eliminate an unprofitable product.

■ CASES

9.1 Introduction of New Products at Hershey Foods Corp.

For years, Hershey's position at the top of the U.S. candy market was secure. Following the policy of founder Milton Hershey, the Pennsylvania chocolate maker let its high-quality products promote themselves. The company did not even advertise nationally until 1970. In the late 1960s, however, rival candy maker Mars, Inc. caught up with Hershey, surpassing Hershey's market share by as much as 14 percent at one point in the 1970s. To combat Mars' gains and to cushion itself against price fluctuations in the cocoa bean and sugar markets. Hershey began to diversify into noncandy product lines and to step up new-product introductions.

Hershey has since become the leader in the pasta industry, holding an 18 percent market share. Hershey sells five brands of pasta regionally in forty states; these brands include San Giorgio, Skinner, and American Beauty. Pasta sales account for nearly 10 percent of the company's revenues and 3 percent of profits.

Candy is, of course, Hershey's mainstay. Per capita consumption of candy and other snack foods is rising, despite Americans' current preoccupation with diet and fitness. Because Hershey's research shows that customers seldom buy the same candy bar twice in a row, the company keeps a broad range of products on the market by adapting existing candies and introducing new ones.

Many of Hershey's new products are aimed at candy customers over 18, who consume 55 percent of all candy sold and are prime targets for premium candy products. Hershey developed the Golden Almond and Golden Pecan lines, for example, from a premium box-candy product. These milk chocolate bars weigh 3.2 ounces, contain whole instead of chopped nuts, and sell for more than $1. Several years ago, Hershey introduced its Big Blocks, thicker and chewier versions of such favorites as Hershey Milk Chocolate and Hershey Almond. Two new smaller bars developed for adult tastes have also been selling well: Take Five, a chocolate-covered wafer and peanut cream bar, and Skor, a toffee bar with a chocolate coating.

Though ideas for new products at Hershey's come from many sources, they are usually channeled through the new product planning group, which is the liaison between research and marketing personnel. In many cases, Hershey's marketing division first identifies consumer needs; the new product planning group explores possibilities for filling those needs; and a third section, the product development group, designs prototypes for further testing. For example, when granola snacks became popular a few years ago, Hershey's product development group came up with New Trail granola bars to compete with products from the Quaker Oats Co. and General Mills, Inc. Some new-product prototypes originate in the Hershey kitchens as a part of food-preparation research. Still another team, the food science and technology group, conducts basic research into ingredient technology.

Hershey foresees continued growth in the chocolate and candy business and is satisfied with its present rate of diversification. Although cocoa beans (which sold for $2.60 a pound in 1977) are now below $1 per pound, Hershey has reduced its vulnerability to cocoa bean price swings through hedging, inventory, and pricing practices. Moreover, the company has recently made three major acquisitions. First it acquired the Dietrich Corp.—maker of Luden's cough drops, 5th Avenue candy bars, and Mellomints. Luden's holds 12 percent of the cough drop market, a category Mars investigated and declined to enter. Then Hershey paid RJR Nabisco $162 million for Nabisco Brands' candy and snack nut business in Canada, and it also bought the U.S. candy division of Britain's Cadbury-Schweppes P.L.C. The latter purchase brought in Peter-Paul Mounds, Almond Joy, York Peppermint Pattie, and the Cadbury candy line.

SOURCES: Kimberley Carpenter, "Candy May Be Dandy, but Confectioners Want a Sweeter Bottom Line," *Business Week*, Oct. 6, 1986, p. 66; Thomas N. Cochran, "Hershey Foods Corp.," *Barron's*, June 27, 1988, pp. 61–62; Judann Dagnoli, "Hershey Seeks Edge in Luden Buy," *Advertising Age*, Sept. 22, 1986, p. 113; Lynn Strongin Dodds, "Sweetening Up the Bottom Line," *Financial World*, Aug. 29, 1986, pp. 14–15; "Hershey and Advertising," *Hershey Foods Corp. Fact Sheet*; Steve Lawrence, "Bar Wars: Hershey Bites Mars," *Fortune*, July 8, 1985, pp. 52–54; Janet Novack, "The High-Profit Candy Habit," *Forbes*, June 29, 1987, p. 76; "R&D Profile: Hershey's," *Food Processing*, August 1986, pp. 21–22; and Philip E. Ross, "Hershey to Add Cadbury U.S. Candy," *New York Times*, July 23, 1988, p. 35L.

Questions for Discussion

1. Why has Hershey diversified into products with less chocolate or no chocolate?
2. Identify the departments in the Hershey organization and the roles they play in developing new products.
3. Unlike some of its competitors, Hershey generally has not diversified from treats or snack foods, except for pasta products. Assess Hershey's approach to product diversification.
4. Has Hershey's program of new-product introductions been effective?

9.2   Harley-Davidson's Product Management

Harley-Davidson Motor Co., headquartered in Milwaukee, has come roaring back to profitability after a decade of troubles. Strong competition from Japanese motorcycle manufacturers—Honda, Suzuki, Yamaha, and Kawasaki—caused Harley's market share for superheavyweight motorcycles (motorcycles with engine displacements greater than 850 cubic centimeters) to drop from 99.7 percent in 1972 to 23 percent in 1983. Harley simply could not compete with Japan's high-tech machines, low prices, and attractive designs. Harley executives were forced to re-evaluate their entire organization. Today Harley once again is the U.S. market share leader for superheavyweight motorcycles, largely because of its commitment to new product development and improved product quality.

Realizing the importance of product quality, Harley product managers understood that they had to turn to their customers for help. They began surveying customers to determine what was wanted in or on a motorcycle. Harley learned that bikers are very vocal about their likes and dislikes: motorcycle enthusiasts are eager to share their views on Harley products and how they can be improved.

Because of huge growth in the early 1970s, Harley was more interested in increasing production than in developing new products or improving product quality. The resulting motorcycles were inferior and outdated when compared with Japanese vehicles. When Harley sales figures plummeted, its executives knew that they had to undertake drastic modifications to ensure the company's survival. They increased the annual research and development budget from $2 million to $14 million.

Willie G. Davidson, Harley's vice president for styling and the grandson of one of the founders, began to attend biker rallies to gather ideas for potential product innovations. Seeing that many bikers liked to customize their motorcycles, he noted the most promising customer "developments" and suggested that Harley mimic these in the factory. In 1980, Harley engineers created a completely redesigned chassis and a new line of engines ranging from 883 to 1340 cc displacement. Davidson invented a new model, the Super Glide. Then Davidson introduced the Low Rider, the Wide Glide, and other successful models.

A senior vice president at Harley-Davidson views Davidson as an artistic genius. According to this executive, Davidson performed virtual miracles by simply manipulating decals and paint in the years before Harley-Davidson was able to bring new engines on-stream. Harley's survival may be due to the new models Davidson was able to create by cosmetically changing existing models. The Japanese motorcycle makers started copying Harley designs.

Customer complaints caused the company to introduce its quality-audit program. A few days before a new model, the Cafe Racer, was scheduled to come off the production line, an employee shocked a Harley executive with news of severe defects in the model. Deciding to make the Cafe Racer a new symbol of Harley-Davidson product quality, the CEO dispatched a team of engineers, service supervisors, and manufacturing managers to correct the problems. It cost the company about $100,000 to mend only a hundred of the Cafe Racers, but management believed that the investment in quality was worth it.

Harley improved the quality of its products by implementing three integrated programs: just-in-time manufacturing (called "materials-as-needed," or "MAN," at Harley), statistical operator control (SOC), and heavy reliance on employee involvement. The MAN system freed Harley from a bulky inventory and increased plant productivity. SOC gives assembly-line operators responsibility for the quality of individual parts. By consulting with line operators, Harley managers and engineers have been able to improve manufacturing processes and, consequently, improve motorcycles. None of these successful programs required large capital investments—Harley improved product quality by enhancing procedures.

Harley's product development strategies still continue to evolve as the company grows stronger. The company has even called its new power train the Evolution Engine. Clearly, Harley executives are determined to keep their customers happy and the product innovations rolling.

SOURCES: Vaughn Beals, "Harley-Davidson: An American Success Story," *Journal for Quality and Participation,* June 1988, pp. A19–A23; Vaughn Beals, "Operation Recovery," *Success,* February 1989, p. 16; "How Harley Beat Back the Japanese," *Fortune,* Sept. 25, 1989, pp. 155, 157, 162, 164; Tani Mayer, "Harley-Davidson Rides High," *Financial World,* Oct. 18, 1988, pp. 16, 18; Gary Miller, "Harley's Teerlink Thrives as Rank-and-File Kind of Guy," *Business Journal,* Milwaukee, Wisconsin, July 17, 1989, TRN 39:E9.

Questions for Discussion

1. Why did Harley's share of the superheavyweight motorcycle market drop so drastically between 1972 and 1983?
2. What sources did Harley use to generate new product ideas?
3. What steps has Harley taken to regain its competitiveness?

Procter & Gamble's Product Management

Procter & Gamble, the company founded in Cincinnati, Ohio by candlemaker William Procter and soapmaker James Gamble, has been described as the world's foremost marketer of packaged consumer goods. For more than 150 years, the founders' policy of selling quality products for premium prices has served the company well. Procter & Gamble, which employs 77,000 people, estimates that its products currently account for about 25 percent of all U.S. sales in the thirty-eight product categories in which the company competes. In thirty-three of those categories, Procter & Gamble products are among the top three brands; in nineteen categories, Procter & Gamble brands lead the market outright. Total sales exceed $21.4 billion annually.

In recent years, however, Procter & Gamble has suffered from maturing markets and intensified competition. A few years ago the company posted its first decline in annual earnings in almost four decades, after losing market share in its core businesses: disposable diapers, toothpaste, and detergents. Although performance in several product categories has improved since then, Procter & Gamble is still struggling to regain its former profitability. In the process, the company is experimenting with new ways of developing and marketing its products.

Traditionally, the longevity of Procter & Gamble brands has affected the company's success. In contrast to competing brands, many of which fade from the marketplace within twenty years, Procter & Gamble products often sell briskly for generations. Pampers diapers, for example, were launched in 1961; Crest toothpaste, in 1955; Tide laundry detergent, in 1946. Ivory soap, the brand that built Procter & Gamble's national reputation, has been in existence since 1879 (the product itself was actually introduced in 1878, as "Procter & Gamble's White Soap").

Brand Management at Procter & Gamble

In the past, the staying power of Procter & Gamble brands has rested largely on the company's system of brand management, a marketing approach Procter & Gamble pioneered almost sixty years ago. The brand management concept was originally proposed by Neil McElroy, a young Procter & Gamble advertising manager who was dissatisfied with sales of Camay, the bar soap Procter & Gamble introduced in 1926. What Camay (and every other Procter & Gamble product) needed, insisted McElroy, was the undivided attention of one person, with full responsibility for the marketing of the product. The "brand man" would be supported by an assistant and a marketing team, with additional help from a group monitoring product sales in the field. In other words, each Procter & Gamble brand would be managed as an individual business, in competition with other Procter & Gamble "businesses." By letting Procter & Gamble products compete with each other this way, McElroy believed that total sales would go up and the company would grow. McElroy eventually became chairman of the board.

Changing Market Conditions

Despite the system's effectiveness in the past, it eventually became outmoded—or at least inadequate in today's marketplace. For one thing, consumers have changed. Today, Procter & Gamble must sell its soaps, toothpastes, and diapers to not just a mass market of homemakers but to a heterogeneous mix of working couples, singles, male shoppers, and the elderly. These consumers are less likely to have similar tastes or to respond to the standardized national advertising Procter & Gamble used for so many years. Moreover, today's consumers are much less loyal to brands than their predecessors, preferring to shop by price—never Procter & Gamble's past point of emphasis—by buying less expensive products and taking advantage of coupons and other sales promotions. In some areas of the country, consumers favor regional brands. Southern coffee drinkers, for example, are as likely to buy a regional brand of coffee that offers strong taste or chicory flavor as they are to purchase Procter & Gamble's Folger's brand.

Also, the brand management system may have made it more difficult for Procter & Gamble to cope with the rapid proliferation of new products in today's market. Renowned for the thoroughness of its research, Procter & Gamble has always chosen to work years, if necessary, to ensure high product quality. In Procter & Gamble's former brand management system, brand managers' proposals were subject to approval by several layers of marketing hierarchy, and the company's research staff found it difficult even to gain a hearing for new products. In contrast, competitors have been getting new products to market quickly, leaving Procter & Gamble to catch up. For example, while Procter & Gamble was still testing reclosable tabs on its Pampers diapers, Kimberly-Clark was already gaining market share with its refastenable Huggies. In another case, Procter & Gamble was preoccupied with the development of Tartar Control Crest and responded only belatedly to Colgate's move into toothpaste gels and pump dispensers.

Other marketing problems have arisen from the growing independence of Procter & Gamble's wholesalers and retailers. In the past, few retailers had the technology to monitor accurately what their customers were buying; to know what to stock, they relied largely on manufacturers' market surveys. Thus Procter & Gamble, producer of numerous popular brands, could (and did) exercise great control over wholesalers and retailers. The company could restrict quantities of discounted brands, for example, or insist that stores carry all sizes of a product if they wanted any at all during special promotions. However, mergers in the food industry are now leading to a consolidation of power held by fewer wholesalers and retailers. Now that companies have sophisticated computer systems that can calculate product handling costs and update inventory instantaneously, large retailers no longer have to allot prominent brands shelf space.

Changes in Procter & Gamble's Product Management

Faced with today's complex marketing environment, therefore, Procter & Gamble has re-examined its traditional approach to brand management and product development. Procter & Gamble has now created more than fifty "business teams," or product development groups, that cut across departmental and divisional lines. When Procter & Gamble developed new Ultra Pampers, a business team was responsible for getting the product to market in half the time usually required.

Another business team came up with the drip-proof cap for Liquid Tide, Procter & Gamble's most popular new detergent brand in fifteen years. Still another team is credited with turning around Pringle's Potato Chips. Sales went up after the team developed new flavors, changed the product's double canister to a single container, and shifted the advertising focus from package to taste.

In some product groups, Procter & Gamble has placed related brands under a category brand manager, who decides where the company should place its resources for the group as a whole. Procter & Gamble's dishwashing liquids—Joy, Dawn, Ivory, and others—are now supervised by a category brand manager, who has reduced manufacturing and packaging costs by making the soaps' containers and formulations more alike. The company has also formed new-brand groups, which study possible extensions of existing brands. Although the brand manager still plays an important role, company insiders say the job has been expanded; the brand manager is becoming something of a general manager, visiting manufacturing plants, calculating costs, and performing other nonmarketing functions.

Another change for Procter & Gamble is its new approach to wholesalers and retailers. The company has clarified the wording of its contracts and has started offering extended credit and greater promotional flexibility. Procter & Gamble also is adjusting its pricing structure to allow retailers greater profit margins. Some products have been redesigned to cut distributors' handling costs. For example, the teardrop-shaped bottle originally used for Ivory shampoo has been replaced with a more square-shaped container that takes up less space and saves about 29 cents a case. Tide powdered detergent has been reformulated so that the same amount of detergent for the same number of washes now fits into a smaller box.

Procter & Gamble believes, however, that as in the past the most promising route to renewed profitability is new-product development. The company employs a research staff of six thousand and spends about $650 million annually researching new products and improving old ones. The company's soap and detergent businesses still account for about 25 percent of research expenditures. However, Procter & Gamble has been pushing into new areas as well, particularly in health care, where research has been supported by acquisitions. Procter & Gamble wants to expand into hair-care and skin-care products. In the area of ethical drugs, the company hopes to incorporate its prescription mouthwash, Peridex, into Scope or Crest (or sell it without a prescription) and may eventually market its drug Didronel as a treatment for osteoporosis.

Procter & Gamble also has great hopes for its new fat substitute, olestra. Olestra is said to look, act, and taste like a fat, without any of the calories of fat. Procter & Gamble says olestra may be useful in reducing cholesterol levels as well. If olestra becomes an established product, Procter & Gamble may not only include it in some of its own products but also license it to other firms.

Questions for Discussion

1. What was Procter & Gamble's original rationale for establishing a brand management approach for marketing its products?
2. Why has Procter & Gamble experienced difficulty competing in several core product categories?
3. To be more competitive, how has Procter & Gamble changed the manner in which it manages products?

SOURCES: Clark Ansberry, "P&G Posts $324 Million Quarterly Loss," *Wall Street Journal*, Aug. 11, 1987, p. 12; Brian Dumaine, "P&G Rewrites the Marketing Rules," *Fortune*, Nov. 6, 1989, pp. 35–36, 38, 40, 42, 46, 48; Laurie Freeman, "Extraordinary Means to Meet Basic Needs," *Advertising Age*, Aug. 20, 1987, p. 102; Laurie Freeman, "The House That Ivory Built," *Advertising Age*, Aug. 20, 1987, p. 4; Patricia Gallagher, "Artzt to Give Giant Broader World View," *USA Today*, Nov. 9, 1989, pp. 1B, 2B; Jennifer Pendleton, "Dealing with No. 1," *Advertising Age*, Aug. 20, 1987, pp. 122–123; Zachary Schiller, "The Marketing Revolution at Procter & Gamble," *Business Week*, July 25, 1988, pp. 72–73, 76; Zachary Schiller, "Procter & Gamble Goes on a Health Kick," *Business Week*, June 29, 1987, pp. 90–92; Julie Solomon and Carol Hymowitz, "Team Strategy," *Wall Street Journal*, Aug. 11, 1987, p. 1; Joseph Winski, "One Brand, One Manager," *Advertising Age*, Aug. 20, 1987, p. 86.

PART **III** **DISTRIBUTION DECISIONS**

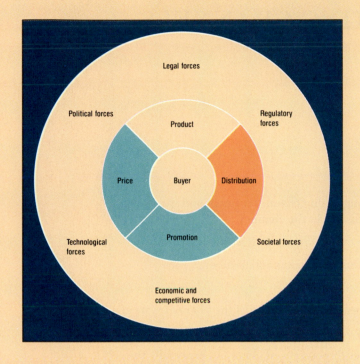

Providing customers with satisfying products is important but not enough for successful marketing strategies. These products must also be available in adequate quantities in accessible locations at the times when customers desire them. The chapters in Part III deal with the distribution of products and the marketing channels and institutions that provide the structure for making products available. In Chapter 10 we discuss the structure and functions of marketing channels and present an overview of institutions that make up these channels. In Chapter 11 we analyze the types of wholesalers and their functions. In Chapter 12 we focus on retailing and retailers. Specifically, we examine the types of retailers and their roles and functions in marketing channels. Finally, in Chapter 13 we analyze the decisions and activities associated with the physical distribution of products, such as order processing, materials handling, warehousing, inventory management, and transportation. ◆

10 MARKETING CHANNELS

Objectives

To understand the marketing channel concept and the types of marketing intermediaries in the channel

To discuss the justification of channel members

To examine the structure and function of the channel system

To explore the power dimensions of channels, especially the concepts of cooperation, conflict, and leadership

Change the World one diaper at a time.

Introducing biodegradable, chemical-free TenderCare™ disposable diapers.

Call 1·800·34·IM·DRY

Tender♥Care

Because babies should only be exposed to love.

A baby requires about ten thousand diaper changes over two or three years. Certainly, disposable diapers have made life for parents much more convenient. Convenience, however, sometimes has a high price: in today's "throw-away" society, landfills are rapidly filling up with plastics, such as those found in disposable diapers, and the plastics take up to five hundred years to fully decompose. Environmentalists and legislators are very concerned with the Environmental Protection Agency's prediction that one-third of the landfills in the United States will reach their capacities and shut down by 1995.

Product developers at Rocky Mountain Medical Corp., a division of RMed International Inc., think that they have a solution to the environmental problems caused by disposable diapers—biodegradable ones marketed under the name TenderCare. Rocky Mountain Medical officials claim that their diapers are more than 90 percent biodegradable, and the firm's researchers are experimenting to increase this percentage. According to an RMed spokesperson, TenderCare diapers decompose in two to five years. The plastic in TenderCare diapers has been mixed with corn starch, so that insects, bacteria, enzymes, and fungi will ingest the corn starch and break down the plastics in landfills.

Marketers at Rocky Mountain Medical are targeting their diapers at environmentally concerned parents who use regular disposables. Rocky Mountain Medical is distributing TenderCare diapers through health-food retail outlets and children's specialty stores. However, TenderCare diapers are primarily available through mail order. All these outlets are unconventional in that most disposable diapers are sold through grocery stores and discount houses. Marketers at Rocky Mountain Medical believe that their customers are so environmentally conscious that they will go to the extra trouble to buy TenderCare diapers through these unconventional outlets. ◆

Advertisement courtesy of RMED International Inc.

Based on information in Elizabeth G. Conlin, "Doing Double Time," *Inc.,* April 1989, p. 26; Barnaby J. Feder, "Fretting Over Demographics and Disposal," *New York Times,* Mar. 12, 1989, p. F15; Michael deCourcy Hinds, "Do Disposable Diapers Ever Go Away?" *New York Times,* Dec. 10, 1988, p. 33; and Annetta Miller, "A Pitched Battle for Baby's Bottom," *Newsweek,* Mar. 6, 1989, p. 44.

arketers of TenderCare diapers have decided to use unconventional retail outlets for distributing this product. Such distribution decisions are important and clearly will have an impact on the product's success. **Distribution** refers to activities that make products available to customers when and where they want to purchase them. Choosing which channels of distribution to use is a major decision in the development of marketing strategies.

This chapter focuses on the description and analysis of channels of distribution, or marketing channels. We first discuss the main types of channels and their structures and then explain the need for intermediaries as well as analyze the functions they perform. Next we outline several forms of channel integration. We explore how marketers determine the appropriate intensity of market coverage for a product and how they consider a number of factors when selecting suitable channels of distribution. Finally, after examining behavioral patterns within marketing channels, we look at several legal issues that affect channel management.

THE STRUCTURES AND TYPES OF MARKETING CHANNELS

A **channel of distribution** (sometimes called a **marketing channel**) is a group of individuals and organizations that direct the flow of products from producers to customers. Providing customer benefits should be the driving force behind all marketing channel activities. Buyers' needs and behavior are therefore important concerns of channel members.

Making products available benefits customers. Channels of distribution make products available at the right time, in the right place, and in the right quantity by providing such product-enhancing functions as transportation and storage. Although consumers do not see the distribution of a product, they value product availability that channels of distribution make possible.

Most, but not all, channels of distribution have marketing intermediaries. A **marketing intermediary**, or middleman, links producers to other middlemen or to ultimate users of the products. Marketing intermediaries perform the activities described in Table 10.1. There are two major types of intermediaries: merchants and functional middlemen (agents and brokers). **Merchants** take title to products and resell them, whereas **functional middlemen** do not take title.

Both retailers and wholesalers are intermediaries. Retailers purchase products for the purpose of reselling them to ultimate consumers. Merchant wholesalers resell products to other wholesalers and to retailers. Functional wholesalers, such as agents and brokers, expedite exchanges among producers and resellers and are compensated by fees or commissions. For purposes of discussion in this chapter, all wholesalers are considered merchant middlemen unless otherwise specified.

Channel members share certain significant characteristics. Each member has different responsibilities within the overall structure of the distribution system, but mutual profit and success can be attained only if channel members cooperate in delivering products to the market.

Although distribution decisions need not precede other marketing decisions, they do exercise a powerful influence on the rest of the marketing mix. Channel deci-

TABLE 10.1

Marketing channel activities that intermediaries perform

CATEGORY OF MARKETING ACTIVITIES	POSSIBLE ACTIVITIES REQUIRED
Marketing information	Analyze information such as sales data; perform or commission marketing research studies
Marketing management	Establish objectives; plan activities; manage and coordinate financing, personnel, and risk taking; evaluate and control channel activities
Facilitating exchange	Choose product assortments that match the needs of buyers
Promotion	Set promotional objectives, coordinate advertising, personal selling, sales promotion, publicity, and packaging
Price	Establish pricing policies and terms of sales
Physical distribution	Manage transportation, warehousing, materials handling, inventory control, and communication

sions are critical because they determine a product's market presence and buyers' accessibility to the product. The strategic significance of these decisions is further heightened by the fact that they entail long-term commitments. For example, it is much easier to change prices or packaging than distribution systems.

Because the marketing channel most appropriate for one product may be less suitable for another, many different distribution paths have been developed in most countries. The links in any channel, however, are the merchants (including producers) and agents who oversee the movement of products through that channel. Although there are many various marketing channels, they can be classified generally as channels for consumer products or channels for industrial products.

Channels for Consumer Products

Figure 10.1 illustrates several channels used in the distribution of consumer products. Besides the channels listed, a manufacturer may use sales branches or sales offices (discussed in Chapter 11).

Channel A describes the direct movement of goods from producer to consumers. Customers who harvest their own fruit from commercial orchards or buy cook ware from door-to-door salespeople are acquiring products through a direct channel. A producer that sells its goods directly from its factory to end users and ultimate consumers is using a direct marketing channel. Although this channel is the simplest, it is not necessarily the cheapest or the most efficient method of distribution.

Channel B, which moves goods from producer to retailers and then to consumers, is the frequent choice of large retailers, for they can buy in quantity from a manufacturer. Such retailers as J.C. Penney, K mart, and Sears, for example, sell clothing, stereos, and many other items that they have purchased directly from the producers. Automobiles are also commonly sold through this type of marketing channel.

A long-standing distribution channel, especially for consumer products, channel C takes goods from producer to wholesalers, then to retailers, and finally to consumers. It is a very practical option for a producer that sells to hundreds of thousands of consumers through thousands of retailers. A single producer finds it hard to do business directly with thousands of retailers. For example, consider the number of

FIGURE 10.1
Typical marketing channels for consumer products

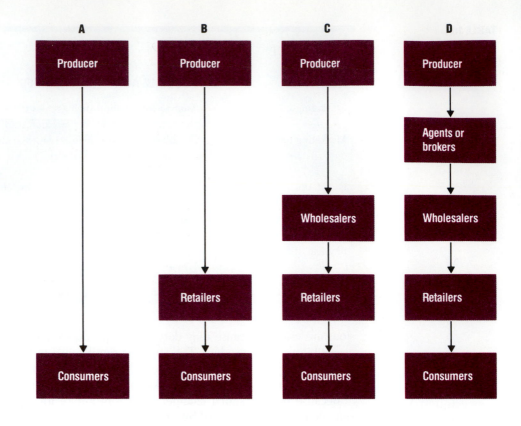

FIGURE 10.1
Typical marketing channels for consumer products

retailers that market Wrigley's chewing gum. It would be extremely difficult, if not impossible, for Wrigley's to deal directly with all the retailers that sell its brand of gum. Manufacturers of tobacco products, some home appliances, hardware, and many convenience goods sell their products to wholesalers, who then sell to retailers, who in turn do business with individual consumers.

Channel D—through which goods pass from producer to agents to wholesalers to retailers and only then to consumers—is frequently used for products intended for mass distribution, such as processed food. For example, to place its cracker line in specific retail outlets, a food processor may hire an agent (or a food broker) to sell the crackers to wholesalers. The wholesalers then sell the crackers to supermarkets, vending machine operators, and other retail outlets.

Contrary to popular opinion, a long channel may be the most efficient distribution channel for consumer goods. When several channel intermediaries are available to perform specialized functions, costs may be lower than if one channel member is responsible for all the functions.

■ Channels for Industrial Products

Figure 10.2 shows four of the most common channels for industrial products. As with consumer products, manufacturers of industrial products sometimes work with more than one level of wholesalers.

Channel E illustrates the direct channel for industrial products. In contrast to consumer goods, many industrial products—especially expensive equipment, such as steam generators, aircraft, and computers—are sold directly to the buyers. For example, Mitsubishi Aircraft International Corporation, a subsidiary of Mitsubishi Heavy Industries, Ltd., sells its Diamond I jets directly to corporate buyers. The

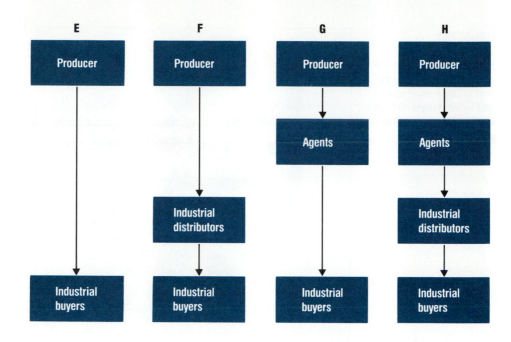

FIGURE 10.2
Typical marketing channels for industrial products

direct channel is most feasible for many manufacturers of industrial goods because they have fewer customers, and those customers are often clustered geographically. Buyers of complex industrial products also can receive technical assistance from the manufacturer more easily in a direct channel.

If a particular line of industrial products is aimed at a large number of customers, the manufacturer may use a marketing channel that includes industrial distributors, merchants who take title to products (channel F). Mitsubishi fork lifts and other construction products, for example, are sold through industrial distributors. Building materials, operating supplies, and air-conditioning equipment are frequently channeled through industrial distributors.

Channel G—producer to agents to industrial buyers—is often the choice when a manufacturer without a marketing department needs market information, when a company is too small to field its own sales force, or when a firm wants to introduce a new product or enter a new market without using its own salespeople. Thus a large soybean producer might sell its product to animal-food processors through an agent.

Channel H is a variation of channel G: goods move from producer to agents to industrial distributors and then to industrial buyers. A manufacturer without a sales force may rely on this channel if its industrial customers purchase products in small quantities or if they must be resupplied frequently and therefore need access to decentralized inventories. Japanese manufacturers of electronic components, for example, work through export agents that sell to industrial distributors serving small producers or dealers in the United States. Chapter 21 presents more information about marketing channels for industrial products.

■ **Multiple Marketing Channels**

To reach diverse target markets, a manufacturer may use several marketing channels simultaneously, with each channel involving a different group of intermediaries. For example, a manufacturer turns to multiple channels when the same product is directed to both consumers and industrial customers. When Del Monte Corp. markets ketchup for household use, the ketchup is sold to supermarkets through grocery

SOURCE: Used by permission of Kellogg Company

wholesalers or, in some cases, directly to the retailers, whereas ketchup going to restaurants or institutions follows a different distribution channel. In some instances, a producer may prefer **dual distribution**: the use of two or more marketing channels for distributing the same products to the same target market. Kellogg Co. sells its cereals (see Figure 10.3) direct to large retail grocery chains and to food wholesalers that, in turn, sell them to retailers. Dual distribution can cause dissatisfaction among wholesalers and smaller retailers.

JUSTIFICATIONS FOR INTERMEDIARIES

Even if producers and buyers are located in the same city, there are costs associated with exchanges. As Figure 10.4 shows, if five buyers purchase the products of five producers, twenty-five transactions are required. If one intermediary serves both producers and buyers, the number of transactions can be reduced to ten. Intermediaries become specialists in facilitating exchanges. They provide valuable assistance because of their access to, and control over, important resources for the proper functioning of the marketing channel.

Nevertheless, the press, consumers, public officials, and other marketers freely criticize intermediaries, especially wholesalers. Table 10.2 indicates that in a recent

FIGURE 10.4
Efficiency in ex-changes provided by an intermediary

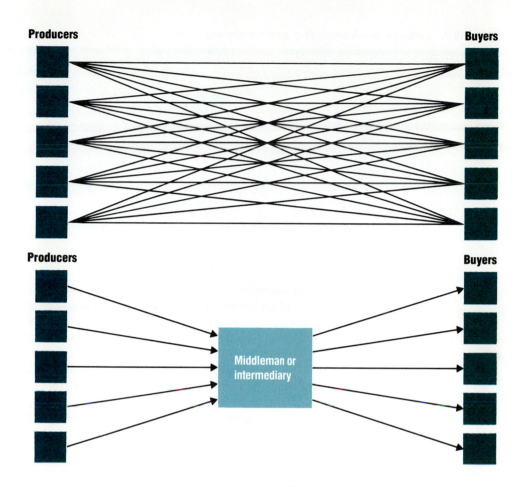

national survey of the general public 74 percent believed that "wholesalers frequently make high profits, which significantly increase prices that consumers pay." The critics accuse wholesalers of being inefficient and parasitic. Consumers often wish to make the distribution channel as short as possible, assuming that the fewer the intermediaries, the lower the price. Because suggestions to eliminate them come from both ends of the marketing channel, wholesalers must be careful to perform only those marketing activities that are truly desired. To survive, they must be more efficient and more service oriented than alternative marketing institutions.

Critics who suggest that eliminating wholesalers would lower prices for consumers do not recognize that this would not eliminate the need for the services wholesalers provide. Other institutions would have to perform those services, and consumers would still have to fund them. In addition, all producers would have to deal directly with retailers or consumers, meaning that every producer would have to keep voluminous records and hire enough personnel to deal with every customer. Even in a direct channel, consumers might end up paying a great deal more for products because prices would reflect the costs of inefficient producers' operations.

To illustrate the efficient service that wholesalers provide, assume that all wholesalers were eliminated. Because there are more than 1.3 million retail stores, a widely purchased consumer product—say candy—would require an extraordinary number of sales contacts, possibly more than a million, to maintain the current level

TABLE 10.2 *Consumer misunderstanding about wholesalers*

Statement: *Wholesalers frequently make high profits, which significantly increase prices that consumers pay.*

	TOTAL %	MALE %	FEMALE %
Strongly agree	35.5	33	38
Somewhat agree	38	40	36
Neither agree nor disagree	16	14	18
Somewhat disagree	8	9	7
Strongly disagree	2.5	4	1

SOURCE: O.C. Ferrell and William M. Pride, National multistage area probability sample of 2,045 households, 1985.

of product exposure. For example, Mars, Inc. would have to deliver its candy, purchase and service thousands of vending machines, establish warehouses all over the country, and maintain fleets of trucks. Selling and distribution costs for candy would skyrocket. Instead of a few contacts with food brokers, large retail organizations, and various merchant wholesalers, candy manufacturers would face thousands of expensive contacts with and shipments to smaller retailers. Such an operation would be highly inefficient, and its costs would be passed on to consumers. Candy bars would cost more, and they would be harder to find. Wholesalers are more efficient and less expensive not only for manufacturers but for consumers as well.

FUNCTIONS OF INTERMEDIARIES

Before we examine the functions of intermediaries in some detail, we should note that a distribution network helps overcome two major distribution problems. Consider a firm that manufactures jeans. The company specializes in the goods it can produce most efficiently, denim clothing. To make jeans the most economical way possible, the producer turns out a hundred thousand pairs of jeans each day. Few persons, however, want to buy a hundred thousand pairs of jeans. Thus the quantity of jeans that the company can produce efficiently is more than the average customer wants. We call this a *discrepancy in quantity*.

An **assortment** is a combination of products put together to provide benefits. A consumer creates and holds an assortment. The set of products made available to customers is an organization's assortment. Most consumers want a broad assortment of products. In addition to jeans, a consumer wants to buy shoes, food, a car, a stereo, soft drinks, and many other products. Yet our jeans manufacturer has a narrow assortment because it makes only jeans (and perhaps a few other denim clothes). There is a *discrepancy in assortment* because a consumer wants a broad assortment, but an individual manufacturer produces a narrow assortment.

Quantity and assortment discrepancies are resolved through the sorting activities of intermediaries in a marketing channel. **Sorting activities** are functions that allow channel members to divide roles and separate tasks. Sorting activities, as

FIGURE 10.5
Sorting activities conducted by intermediaries

Sorting out	Accumulation	Allocation	Assorting
Classifying heterogeneous supplies into homogeneous groups	Developing a bank or stock of homogeneous products to provide aggregate inventory	Breaking down homogeneous stocks (inventories) into smaller units	Combining products into collections or assortments that buyers want

Figure 10.5 shows, may be grouped into four main tasks: sorting out, accumulation, allocation, and assorting of products.[1]

Sorting Out

Sorting out, the first step in developing an assortment, is separating conglomerates of heterogeneous products into relatively uniform, homogeneous groups based on product characteristics such as size, shape, weight, or color. Sorting out is especially common in the marketing of agricultural products and other raw materials, which vary widely in size, grade, and quality and would be largely unusable in an undifferentiated mass. A tomato crop, for example, must be sorted into tomatoes suitable for canning, those for making tomato juice, and those for sale in retail food stores.

Sorting out for specific products follows a set of predetermined standards. The sorter must know how many classifications to use and the criteria for each classification and must usually provide for a group of miscellaneous leftovers as well. Certain product characteristics can be categorized more easily than others; appearance and size of agricultural products are more readily apparent than flavor or nutritional content, for instance. Because the overall quality of a crop or supply of raw material most likely will vary from year to year or from region to region, classifications must be somewhat flexible.

Changing consumer needs and new manufacturing techniques influence the sorting-out process. If sorting out results in manufactured goods with minor defects, these damaged or irregular products are often marketed at lower prices through factory outlet stores, which are growing in consumer popularity. Improved processing also permits the use of materials that might have been culled previously, such as the paper and aluminum now being recycled. In some industries, producers have stopped using natural materials because the manufacturing process demands the greater uniformity possible only with synthetic materials. Sorting out thus helps alleviate discrepancies in assortment by making relatively homogeneous products available for the next step, accumulation.

Accumulation

Accumulation is the development of a bank or inventory of homogeneous products that have similar production or demand requirements. Farmers who grow relatively small quantities of tomatoes, for example, transport their sorted tomatoes to central collection points, where tomatoes are accumulated in large lots for movement into the next level of the channel.

Combining many small groups of similar products into larger groups serves several purposes. Products move through subsequent marketing channels more eco-

1. Wroe Alderson, *Marketing Behavior and Executive Action* (Homewood, Ill.: Irwin, 1957), pp. 201–211.

nomically in large quantities because transportation rates are lower for bulk loads. In addition, accumulation gives buyers a steady supply of products in large volumes. If Del Monte had to frequently purchase small amounts of tomatoes from individual farmers, the company's tomato products would be produced much less efficiently. Instead, Del Monte buys bulk loads of tomatoes through brokers, thus maintaining a continuous supply of uniform-quality materials for processing. Accumulation lets producers continuously use up stocks and replenish them, thus minimizing losses from interruptions in the supply of materials.

For both buyer and seller, accumulation also alleviates some of the problems associated with price fluctuations and highly seasonal materials. Buyers may obtain large-volume purchases at lower prices because sellers are anxious to dispose of perishable goods; purchasing agents may accumulate stocks of materials in anticipation of price hikes. In other cases, sellers may receive higher prices because they enter into long-term supply contracts with producers or they agree to store accumulated materials until the producer is ready for them. Accumulation thus relieves discrepancies in quantity. It enables intermediaries to build up specialized inventories and allocate products according to customers' needs.

■ Allocation

Allocation is the breaking down of large homogeneous inventories into smaller lots. This process, which addresses discrepancies in quantity, enables wholesalers to buy efficiently in truckloads or carloads and then apportion products by cases to other channel members. A food wholesaler, for instance, serves as a depot, allocating products according to market demand. The wholesaler may divide a single truckload of Del Monte canned tomatoes among several retail food stores.

Because supply and demand are seldom in perfect balance, allocation is influenced by several factors (and can sometimes resemble rationing). At times price is the overriding consideration. The highest bidder, or perhaps the buyer placing the largest order, is allocated most of the stock. At other times an intermediary gives preference to customers whose loyalty has been established or to those whose businesses show the most growth potential. In still other cases, products are allocated through compromise and negotiation.

Depending on the product, allocation may begin with the manufacturer and continue through several levels of intermediaries, including retailers. Allocation ends when the ultimate user selects the desired quantity of a particular product from the assortment of products available.

■ Assorting

Assorting is the process of combining products into collections or assortments that buyers want to have available in one place. Assorting eliminates discrepancies in assortment by grouping products in ways that satisfy buyers. The same food wholesaler supplying supermarkets with Del Monte tomato products may also buy canned goods from competing food processors so that grocery stores can choose from a wide assortment of canned fruits and vegetables.

Buyers want an assortment of products at one location because of some task they want to perform or some problem they want solved. A buyer looking for a variety of products, all serving different purposes, requires a broad assortment from which to choose; a buyer with more precise needs or interests will seek out a narrower, and deeper, product assortment.

Assorting is especially important to retailers, and they strive to create assortments that match the demands of consumers who patronize their stores. Although no single customer is likely to buy one of everything in the store, a retailer must anticipate the probability of purchase and provide a satisfactory range of product choices. The risk involved is greater for some retailers than for others. For example, supermarkets purchase staple foods repeatedly, and these items can be stocked with little risk. But clothing retailers who misjudge consumer demand for "hot" fashion items can lose money if their assortments contain too few (or too many) of these products. Discrepancies in assortment reappear, in fact, when retailers fail to keep pace with shifts in consumer attitudes. New specialists—such as retail outlets for computer products—may even enter the market to provide assortments existing retailers do not offer.

CHANNEL INTEGRATION

Channel functions may be transferred among intermediaries and to producers and even customers. This section examines how channel members can either combine and control most activities or pass them on to another channel member. Remember, though, that the channel member cannot eliminate functions; unless buyers themselves perform the functions, they must pay for the labor and resources needed for the functions to be performed. The statement that "you can eliminate middlemen but you can't eliminate their functions" is an accepted principle of marketing.

Many marketing channels are determined by consensus. Producers and intermediaries coordinate their efforts for mutual benefit. Some marketing channels, however, are organized and controlled by a single leader, which can be a producer, a wholesaler, or a retailer, depending on the industry. The channel leader may establish channel policies and coordinate the development of the marketing mix. Sears, for example, is a channel leader for several of the many products it sells.

The various links or stages of the channel may be combined under the management of a channel leader either horizontally or vertically. Integration may stabilize supply, reduce costs, and increase coordination of channel members.

■ Vertical Channel Integration

Combining two or more stages of the channel under one management is **vertical channel integration**. One member of a marketing channel may purchase the operations of another member or simply perform the functions of the other member, eliminating the need for that intermediary as a separate entity. Total vertical integration encompasses all functions from production to ultimate buyer; it is exemplified by oil companies that own oil wells, pipelines, refineries, terminals, and service stations.

Whereas members of conventional channel systems work independently and seldom cooperate, participants in vertical channel integration coordinate their efforts to reach a desired target market. This more progressive approach to distribution enables channel members to regard other members as extensions of their own operations. At one end of an integrated channel, for example, a manufacturer might provide advertising and training assistance, and the retailer at the other end would buy the manufacturer's products in quantity and actively promote them.

In the past, integration has been successfully institutionalized in marketing channels called vertical marketing systems. A **vertical marketing system** (**VMS**) is a marketing channel in which a single channel member coordinates or manages channel activities to achieve efficient, low-cost distribution aimed at satisfying target market customers. Because efforts of individual channel members are combined in

FIGURE 10.6

Corporate vertical marketing system (VMS). By opening and operating its own production facilities and retail stores, The Limited has created a corporate VMS.

SOURCE: Courtesy of The Limited

a VMS, marketing activities can be coordinated for maximum effectiveness and economy, without duplication of services. Vertical marketing systems are also competitive, accounting for a growing share of retail sales in consumer goods.

Most vertical marketing systems today take one of three forms: corporate, administered, or contractual. The *corporate* VMS combines all stages of the marketing channel, from producers to consumers, under a single ownership. For example, The Limited (see Figure 10.6) established a corporate VMS operating corporate-owned production facilities and retail stores. Supermarket chains that own food processing plants and large retailers that purchase wholesaling and production facilities are other examples of corporate VMSs. Figure 10.7 contrasts a conventional marketing channel with a VMS, which consolidates marketing functions and institutions.

In an *administered* VMS, channel members are independent, but a high level of interorganizational management is achieved by informal coordination. Members of an administered VMS may agree, for example, to adopt uniform accounting and ordering procedures and to cooperate in promotional activities. Although individual channel members maintain their autonomy, as in conventional marketing channels, one channel member (such as the producer or a large retailer) dominates the administered VMS, so that distribution decisions take into account the system as a whole. Because of its size and power as a retailer, Wal-Mart exercises a strong influence over the independent manufacturers in its marketing channels, as do Kellogg Co. (cereal) and Magnavox (television and other electronic products).

Under a *contractual* VMS, the most popular type of vertical marketing system, interorganizational relationships are formalized through contracts. Channel members are linked by legal agreements that spell out each member's rights and obligations. For instance, franchise organizations such as McDonald's and Kentucky Fried Chicken are contractual VMSs. Other contractual VMSs include wholesaler-sponsored groups such as IGA (Independent Grocers' Alliance) stores, in which

FIGURE 10.7

Comparison of a conventional marketing channel and a vertical marketing system

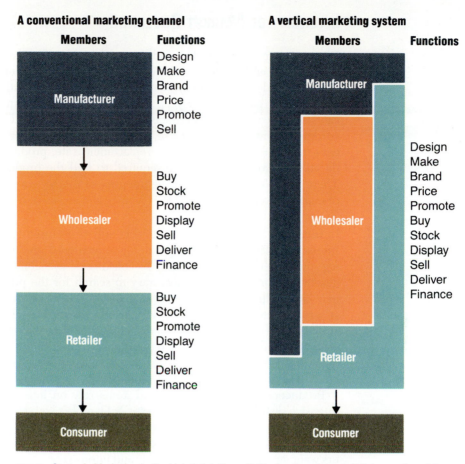

A conventional marketing channel

Members	Functions
Manufacturer	Design Make Brand Price Promote Sell
Wholesaler	Buy Stock Promote Display Sell Deliver Finance
Retailer	Buy Stock Promote Display Sell Deliver Finance
Consumer	

A vertical marketing system

Members	Functions
Manufacturer Wholesaler Retailer	Design Make Brand Price Promote Buy Stock Display Sell Deliver Finance
Consumer	

SOURCE: *Strategic Marketing*, by David J. Kollat, Roger D. Blackwell, and James F. Robeson. Copyright © 1972 by Holt, Rinehart and Winston, Inc. Reprinted by permission of Holt, Rinehart and Winston.

independent retailers band together under the contractual leadership of a wholesaler. Retailer-sponsored cooperatives, which own and operate their own wholesalers, are a third type of contractual VMS.

Horizontal Channel Integration

Combining institutions at the same level of operation under one management constitutes **horizontal channel integration**. An organization may integrate horizontally by merging with other organizations at the same level in a marketing channel level. For example, the owner of a dry cleaning firm might buy and combine several other existing dry cleaning establishments. Horizontal integration may enable a firm to generate sufficient sales revenue to integrate vertically as well.

Although horizontal integration permits efficiencies and economies of scale in purchasing, market research, advertising, and specialized personnel, it is not always the most effective method of improving distribution. Problems of "bigness" often follow, resulting in decreased flexibility, difficulties in coordination, and the need for additional marketing research and large-scale planning. Unless distribution functions for the various units can be performed more efficiently under unified management than under the previously separate managements, horizontal integration will not reduce costs or improve the competitive position of the integrating firm.

INTENSITY OF MARKET COVERAGE

Characteristics of the product and the target market determine the kind of coverage a product should get, that is, the number and kinds of outlets in which it is sold. To achieve the desired intensity of market coverage, distribution must correspond to the behavior patterns of buyers. Chapter 5 divides consumer products into three categories—convenience products, shopping products, and specialty products—according to how consumers make purchases. In considering products for purchase, consumers take into account the replacement rate, product adjustment (services), duration of consumption, time required to find the product, and similar factors.[2] These variables directly affect the intensity of market coverage. Three major levels of market coverage are intensive, selective, and exclusive distribution.

■ Intensive Distribution

In **intensive distribution**, all available outlets are used for distributing a product. Intensive distribution is appropriate for convenience products such as bread, chewing gum, beer, and newspapers. To consumers, availability means a store located nearby and minimum time necessary to search for the product at the store. Sales may have a direct relationship to availability. The successful sale of bread and milk at service stations or of gasoline at convenience grocery stores has shown that the availability of these products is more important than the nature of the outlet. Convenience products have a high replacement rate and require almost no service. To meet these demands, intensive distribution is necessary, and multiple channels may be used to sell through all possible outlets.

Producers of consumer packaged items rely on intensive distribution. In fact, intensive distribution is one of Procter & Gamble's key strengths. It is fairly easy for this company to formulate marketing strategies for many of its products (soaps, detergents, food and juice products, and personal-care products) because consumers want availability provided quickly and intensively.

■ Selective Distribution

In **selective distribution**, only some available outlets in an area are chosen to distribute a product. Selective distribution is appropriate for shopping products. Durable goods such as typewriters and stereos usually fall into this category. Such products are more expensive than convenience goods. Consumers are willing to spend greater searching time visiting several retail outlets to compare prices, designs, styles, and other features.

Selective distribution is desirable when a special effort—such as customer service from a channel member—is important. Shopping products require differentiation at the point of purchase. To motivate retailers to provide adequate presale service, selective distribution and company-owned stores are often used. Many industrial products are sold on a selective basis to maintain a certain degree of control over the distribution process. For example, agricultural herbicides are distributed on a selective basis because dealers must offer services to buyers, such as instructions about how to apply the herbicides safely or the option of having the dealer apply the herbicide. Evinrude outboard motors are sold by dealers on a selective basis.

■ Exclusive Distribution

In **exclusive distribution**, only one outlet is used in a relatively large geographic area. Exclusive distribution is suitable for products that are purchased rather infre-

2. Leo Aspinwall, "The Marketing Characteristics of Goods," in *Four Marketing Theories* (Boulder: University of Colorado Press, 1961), pp. 27–32.

FIGURE 10.8
Using exclusive distribution.
Rolls Royce, maker of Bentley automobiles, is a firm that uses exclusive distribution.

The Bentley Turbo R. The quintessential power trip.

quently, consumed over a long period of time, or require service or information to fit them to buyers' needs. Exclusive distribution is not appropiate for convenience products and many shopping products. It is used often as an incentive to sellers when only a limited market is available for products. For example, automobiles such as the Bentley (shown in Figure 10.8) are sold on an exclusive basis. A producer that uses exclusive distribution generally expects a dealer to be very cooperative with respect to carrying a complete inventory, sending personnel for sales and service training, participating in promotional programs, and providing excellent customer service.

SELECTION OF DISTRIBUTION CHANNELS

The process of selecting appropriate distribution channels for a product is often complex for a variety of reasons. Producers must choose specific intermediaries carefully, evaluating their sales and profit levels, performance records, other products carried, clientele, availability, and so forth. But producers must also examine other factors that influence distribution channel selection, including organizational objectives and resources, market characteristics, buyer behavior, product attributes, and environmental forces.

Organizational Objectives and Resources

A producer must consider what it is trying to accomplish in the marketplace and what resources can be brought to bear on the task. A company's objectives may be broad, such as higher profits, increased market share, and greater responsiveness to customers, or narrow, such as replacing an intermediary that has left the channel. The organization may possess sufficient financial and marketing clout to control its distribution channels—for example, by engaging in direct marketing or by operating its own trucking fleet. On the other hand, an organization may have no interest in performing distribution services or may be forced by lack of resources and experience to depend on middlemen.

The company must also evaluate the effectiveness of past distribution relationships and methods in light of its current goals. One firm might decide to maintain its basic channel structure but add members for increased coverage in new territories. Another company might alter its distribution channel so as to provide same-day delivery on all orders. When selecting distribution channels, organizational factors and objectives are important considerations.

Market Characteristics

Beyond the basic division between consumer markets and industrial markets, several market variables influence the design of distribution channels. Geography is one factor; in most cases, the greater the distance between the producer and its markets, the less expensive is distribution through intermediaries rather than through direct sales. A related consideration is market density. If customers tend to be clustered in several locations, the producer may be able to eliminate middlemen. Transportation, storage, communication, and negotiation are specific functions performed more efficiently in high-density markets. Market size—measured by the number of potential customers in a consumer or industrial market—is yet another variable. Direct sales may be effective if a producer has relatively few buyers for a product, but for larger markets the services of middlemen may be required.[3]

Buyer Behavior

Buyer behavior is a crucial consideration in selecting distribution channels. To be able to match intermediaries with customers, the producer must have specific, current information about customers who are buying the product and when and where they are buying it.[4] How customers buy is important as well. A manufacturer might find direct selling economically feasible for large-volume sales but inappropriate for small orders.

The producer must also understand how buyer specifications vary according to whether buyers perceive products as convenience, shopping, or specialty items (see Chapter 8). Customers for chewing gum, for example, are likely to buy the product frequently (even impulsively) from a variety of outlets. Buyers of home computers, however, carefully evaluate product features, dealers, prices, and postsale services. Buying patterns influence the selection of channels.

Buyers may be reached most effectively when producers are creative in opening up new distribution channels. The Hanes Company, manufacturer of L'eggs pantyhose, concluded that hosiery customers would be attracted to a product they could buy conveniently while grocery shopping. As a result of L'eggs' innovative strategy, supermarkets are now included in the distribution channels for several brands of women's hosiery.

3. Bert Rosenbloom, *Marketing Channels: A Management View* (Hinsdale, Ill.: Dryden, 1987), p. 160.

4. Ibid., p. 161.

■ Product Attributes

Another variable in the selection of distribution channels is the product itself. Because producers of complex industrial products must often provide technical services to buyers both before and after the sale, these products are usually shipped directly to buyers. Perishable or highly fashionable consumer products with short shelf lives are also marketed through short channels. In other cases, distribution patterns are influenced by the product's value; the lower the price per unit, the longer the distribution chain. Additional factors to consider are the weight, bulkiness, and relative ease of handling the products. Producers may find wholesalers and retailers reluctant to carry items that create storage or display problems.[5]

■ Environmental Forces

Finally, producers making decisions about distribution channels must consider forces in the total marketing environment—that is, such issues as competition, ecology, economic conditions, technology, society, and law. Technology, for example, has made possible electronic scanners, computerized inventory systems, telemarketing, and teleshopping devices, all of which are altering present distribution systems and making it harder for technologically unsophisticated firms to remain competitive. Changing family patterns and the emergence of important minority consumer groups are driving producers to seek new distribution methods for reaching market segments, and sometimes this search results in nontraditional approaches that increase competitive pressures. Interest rates, inflation, and other economic variables affect members of distribution channels at every level. Environmental forces are numerous and complex and must be taken into account if distribution efforts are to be appropriate, efficient, and effective.

BEHAVIOR OF CHANNEL MEMBERS

The marketing channel is a social system with its own conventions and behavior patterns. Each channel member performs a different role in the system and agrees (implicitly or explicitly) to accept certain rights, responsibilities, rewards, and sanctions for nonconformity. Moreover, each channel member expects certain things of every other channel member. Retailers, for instance, expect wholesalers to maintain adequate inventories and deliver goods on time. For their part, wholesalers expect retailers to honor payment agreements and keep them informed of inventory needs. In this section we discuss several issues related to channel member behavior, including cooperation, conflict, and leadership. Marketers need to understand these behavioral issues to make effective channel decisions.

■ Channel Cooperation

Channel cooperation is vital if each member is to gain something from other members.[6] Without cooperation, neither overall channel goals nor member goals can be realized. Policies must be developed that support all essential channel members; otherwise, failure of one link in the chain could destroy the channel.

There are several ways to improve channel cooperation. A marketing channel should consider itself a unified system, competing with other systems. This way, individual members will be less likely to take actions that would create disadvantages for other members. Similarly, channel members should agree to direct their

5. Ibid., pp. 254–255.

6. Wroe Alderson, *Dynamic Marketing Behavior* (Homewood, Ill.: Irwin, 1965), p. 239.

efforts toward a common target market so that channel roles can be structured for maximum marketing effectiveness, which in turn can help members achieve their individual objectives. It is crucial to define precisely the tasks that each member of the channel is to perform. This provides a basis for reviewing the intermediaries' performance and helps reduce conflicts because each channel member knows exactly what is expected of it.

■ Channel Conflict

Although all channel members work toward the same general goal—distributing products profitably and efficiently—members may sometimes disagree about the best methods for attaining this goal. Each channel member wants to maximize its own profits while maintaining as much autonomy as possible. However, if this self-interest creates misunderstanding about role expectations, the end result is frustration and conflict for the whole channel. For individual organizations to function together in a single social system, each channel member must clearly communicate and understand role expectations.

Because channel integration and coordination are achieved through role behavior, channel conflict often stems from perceived or real unmet role expectations. That is, members of the channel expect a given channel member to conduct itself in a certain way and to make a particular contribution to the total system. Wholesalers expect producers to monitor quality control and production scheduling, and they expect retailers to market products effectively. Producers and retailers expect wholesalers to provide coordination, functional services, and communication. But if members do not fulfill their roles—for example, if wholesalers or producers fail to deliver products on time or the producers' pricing policies cut into the margins of downstream channel members—conflict may ensue. As shown in Figure 10.9, the producer of TetraMin fish food is facing channel conflict because the pricing policies are resulting in low profit margins (and limited ability to compete) for retail pet stores. Marketing Update 10.1 tells how IBM deals with potential channel conflict.

Channel conflicts also arise when dealers overemphasize competing products or diversify into product lines traditionally handled by other, more specialized, intermediaries. In some cases, conflict develops because producers strive to increase efficiency by circumventing intermediaries, as is happening in marketing channels for microcomputer software. Many software-only stores are establishing direct relationships with software producers, bypassing wholesale distributors altogether. Some dishonest retailers are also pirating software or making unauthorized copies, thus cheating other channel members out of their due compensation. Consequently, suspicion and mistrust are heightening tensions in software marketing channels.[7]

A manufacturer embroiled in channel conflict may ship late (or not at all), withdraw financing, use promotion to build consumer brand loyalty, and operate or franchise its own retail outlet. To retaliate, a retailer may develop store brands, refuse to stock certain items, focus its buying power on one supplier or group of suppliers, and seek to strengthen its position in the marketing channel. Although there is no single method for resolving conflict, an atmosphere of cooperation can be re-established if two conditions are met. First, the role of each channel member must be specified. To minimize misunderstanding, all members must be able to expect unambiguous, agreed-on levels of performance from each other. Second, channel members must institute certain measures of channel coordination, which

7. Lanny J. Ryan, Gaye C. Dawson, and Thomas Galek, "New Distribution Channels for Microcomputer Software," *Business*, October-December 1985, pp. 21–22.

FIGURE 10.9
Channel conflict.
The pricing policies for TetraMin fish food are creating channel conflict among retailers.

K-MART *SELLS* THIS FOR $9.57

PETSHOPS *PAY* $8.69

TETRA SUGGESTS PETSHOPS SELL THIS FOR $13.99-14.99

ASK TETRA HOW YOU ARE SUPPOSED TO COMPETE WITH K-MART...

OR MAYBE YOU'RE NOT SUPPOSED TO COMPETE WITH THEM?

t.f.h.

THIS AD IS PAID FOR BY T.F.H. PUBLICATIONS. OUR LIVELIHOOD DEPENDS ON PETSHOPS, NOT K-MARTS!

SOURCE: Courtesy of T.F.H. Publications, Inc.

requires leadership and the benevolent exercise of control.[8] To prevent channel conflict, producers, or other channel members, may provide competing resellers with different brands, allocate markets among resellers, define direct sales policies to clarify potential conflict over large accounts, negotiate territorial issues between regional distributors, and provide recognition to certain resellers for the importance of their role in distributing to others. Hallmark, for example, distributes its Ambassador greeting-card line in discount stores and its name brand Hallmark line in upscale department stores, thus limiting the amount of competition among retailers carrying its products.[9]

■ **Channel Leadership**

The effectiveness of marketing channels hinges on channel leadership. Producers, retailers, or wholesalers may assume this leadership. To become a leader, a channel member must want to influence and direct overall channel performance. Furthermore, to attain desired objectives, the leader must possess **channel power**, which is

8. Adel I. El-Ansary, "Perspectives on Channel System Performance," in *Contemporary Issues in Marketing Channels,* ed. Robert F. Lusch and Paul H. Zinszer (Norman: University of Oklahoma Press, 1979), p. 50.

9. Kenneth G. Hardy and Allan J. Magrath, "Ten Ways for Manufacturers to Improve Distribution Management," *Business Horizons,* November-December 1988, p. 68.

COOPERATION IN IBM'S MARKETING CHANNELS

IBM, the world's fifth largest industrial corporation, is trying to recover from a period of slow growth. As part of the recovery process, IBM executives have restructured the company's complex distribution system. In the past, IBM has had problems when members of its direct sales force came into conflict with IBM independent distributors. To resolve these conflicts, IBM executives have instituted new policies that have brought about cooperation between these two groups.

Concerning the new policies, one IBM independent distributor has said that IBM "has never been more aggressive about working with, instead of working against, the third party channel." IBM's marketing officials have reshaped its "value-added channel"—distributors that receive preferable contractual terms and conditions in return for meeting a set of rigorous standards. IBM now manages the value-added distributors on an individual basis, offering different arrangements to each. The company's marketers determine individual distributor policy according to each distributor's market, the distributor's ability to sell products, and IBM salespeople's coverage in the distributor's territory. IBM marketers also award more favorable contracts to distributors whose software solutions to customer problems are compatible with IBM's computer hardware.

To encourage channel cooperation between distributors and direct salespeople, IBM has adopted a policy that requires direct-sales branch offices to pass on prospect leads to distributors. Moreover, IBM executives have installed a new accounts bonus program to reward ambitious distributors and have allowed distributors access to IBM computer demonstration centers.

Formerly, IBM used the titles "value-added reseller" to refer to distributors that sold mainly minicomputers and "value-added dealers" to refer to those that sold primarily microcomputers. Now the company calls these distributors "authorized industry remarketers." Under a new program, authorized industry remarketers receive special protection against price changes, an improved equipment return policy, and a better warranty system. IBM marketers are encouraging authorized industry remarketers and direct salespeople to call jointly on potential customers.

SOURCES: "Computers and Office Equipment," *Sales & Marketing Management,* June 1989, pp. 43–44; Joel Dreyfuss, "Reinventing IBM," *Fortune,* Aug. 14, 1989, pp. 31–35, 38; and Robert F. McCarthy, "IBM Muscles the Distribution Channel—Again," *Business Marketing,* August 1988, pp. 49–50, 52, 54, 56–57.

FIGURE 10.10
Determinants of channel leadership

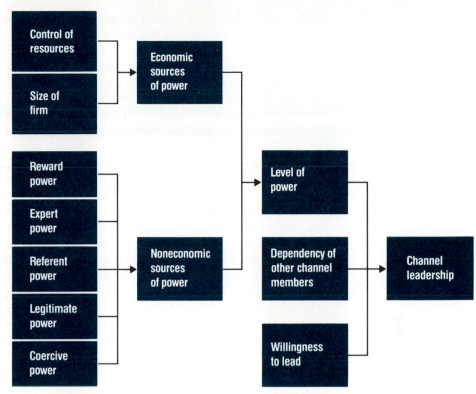

SOURCE: Reprinted by permission of Publishing Horizons, Inc., from *Marketing Channels and Strategies*, 2nd ed., by R. D. Michman and S. D. Sibley, 1980, p. 413.

the ability to influence another channel member's goal achievement. As Figure 10.10 shows, the channel leader derives power from seven sources, two of them economic and five noneconomic.

The five noneconomic powers—reward, expert, referent, legitimate, and coercive—are crucial for establishing leadership. A channel leader gains reward power by providing financial benefits. Expert power exists when other channel members believe that the leader provides special expertise required for the channel to function properly. Referent power emerges when other members strongly identify with and emulate the leader. Legitimate power is based on a superior-subordinate relationship. Coercive power is a function of the leader's ability to punish other channel members.[10]

In the United States, producers assume the leadership role in many marketing channels. A manufacturer—whose large-scale production efficiency demands increasing sales volume—may exercise power by giving channel members financing, business advice, ordering assistance, advertising, and support materials. For example, after Rubbermaid increased distribution for its products from sixty thousand to a hundred thousand outlets, it improved cooperative advertising plans and increased channel members' margins, both to motivate new channel members and to appease older channel members, which now had to compete with more outlets carrying

10. Ronald D. Michman and Stanley D. Sibley, *Marketing Channels and Strategies* (Columbus, Ohio: Grid Publishing, 1980), pp. 412–417.

Rubbermaid products.[11] Coercion causes dealer dissatisfaction that is stronger than any impact from rewards, so the use of coercive power can be a major cause of channel conflict.[12]

Retailers can also function as channel leaders, and with the rise of national chain stores and private-label merchandise they are increasingly doing so. Small retailers, too, may share in the leadership role when they command particular consumer respect and patronage in local or regional markets. Among large retailers, K mart, J.C. Penney, and Kroger base their channel leadership on wide public exposure to their products. These retailers control many brands and sometimes replace uncooperative producers. As the channel leader in the marketing of its private-label power tools, paints, tires, motor oil, batteries, and appliances, Sears exercises two types of power. First, its high-volume sales enable the company to offer profit reward to producers that supply the private-label goods; second, its marketing expertise means that many of the producers depend on Sears to perform all marketing activities.

Wholesalers assume channel leadership roles as well, although they were more powerful decades ago, when most manufacturers and retailers were small, underfinanced, and widely scattered. Today wholesaler leaders may form voluntary chains with several retailers, which they supply with bulk buying or management services or which market their own brands. In return, the retailers shift most of their purchasing to the wholesaler leader. The Independent Grocers' Alliance (IGA) is one of the best-known wholesaler leaders in the United States. IGA's power is based on the expert advertising, pricing, and purchasing knowledge it makes available to independent business owners. Other wholesaler leaders might also help retailers with store layouts, accounting, and inventory control.

LEGAL ISSUES IN CHANNEL MANAGEMENT

The multitude of federal, state, and local laws governing channel management are based on the general principle that the public is best served when competition and free trade are protected. Under the authority of such federal legislation as the Sherman Antitrust Act, the Clayton Act, the Federal Trade Commission Act, the Robinson-Patman Act, and the Celler-Kefauver Act, the courts and regulatory agencies determine under what circumstances channel management practices violate this underlying principle and must be restricted and when these practices may be permitted. Although channel managers are not expected to be legal experts, they should be aware that attempts to control distribution functions may have legal repercussions. The following practices are among those frequently subject to legal restraint.

■ **Dual Distribution**

A producer that distributes the same product through two or more different channel structures or sells the same or similar products through different channels under different brand names is engaging in dual distribution.[13] The courts do not consider this practice illegal when it promotes competition. For example, a manufacturer can

11. Hardy and Magrath, p. 68.

12. John F. Gaski and John R. Nevin, "The Differential Effects of Exercised and Unexercised Power Sources in a Marketing Channel," *Journal of Marketing Research,* July 1985, p. 139.

13. Bert Rosenbloom, *Marketing Channels: A Management View* (Hinsdale, Ill.: Dryden Press, 1987), p. 91.

legally open its own retail outlets where no other retailers are available to carry the manufacturer's products. But the courts view as a threat to competition a manufacturer who uses company-owned outlets to dominate or drive out of business independent retailers or distributors who handle its products. In such cases, dual distribution is a violation of the law. To avoid this interpretation, a producer should use a retail price that does not severely undercut the independent retailer's price.

■ Restricted Sales Territories

To tighten its control over the distribution of its products, a manufacturer may try to prohibit intermediaries from selling its products outside designated sales territories. The intermediaries themselves often favor this practice because it lets them avoid competition for the producer's brands within their own territories. Many companies have long followed the policy of restricting sales in this fashion. In recent years, the courts have adopted conflicting positions in regard to restricted sales territories. Although the courts have deemed restricted sales territories a restraint of trade among intermediaries handling the same brands (except for small or newly established companies), the courts have also held that exclusive territories can actually promote competition among dealers handling different brands. At present, the producer's intent in establishing restricted territories and the overall effect of doing so on the market must be evaluated for each case individually. Marketing Update 10.2 focuses on problems that arise when authorized intermediaries sell products to unauthorized intermediaries that, in turn, sell products in restricted sales territories.

■ Tying Contracts

When a supplier (usually a manufacturer or franchiser) furnishes a product to a channel member stipulating that the channel member must purchase other products as well, a **tying contract** exists.[14] Suppliers, for instance, may institute tying arrangements to move weaker products along with more popular items. To use another example, a franchiser may tie the purchase of equipment and supplies to the sale of franchises, justifying the policy as necessary for quality control and protection of the franchiser's reputation.

A related practice is full-line forcing. In this situation, a supplier requires that channel members purchase the supplier's entire line to obtain any of the products. Manufacturers sometimes use full-line forcing to ensure that intermediaries accept new products and that a suitable range of products is available to customers.

The courts accept tying contracts when the supplier alone can provide products of a certain quality, when the intermediary is free to carry competing products as well, and when a company has just entered the market. Most other tying contracts are considered illegal.

■ Exclusive Dealing

When a manufacturer forbids an intermediary to carry products of competing manufacturers, the arrangement is called **exclusive dealing**. A manufacturer receives considerable market protection in an exclusive dealing arrangement and may cut off shipments to an intermediary who violates such an agreement.

The legality of an exclusive dealing contract is generally determined by applying three tests. If the exclusive dealing blocks competitors from as much as 10 percent of the market, if the sales revenue involved is sizable, and if the manufacturer is much larger (and thus more intimidating) than the dealer, the arrangement is considered anticompetitive.[15] If, on the other hand, dealers and customers in a given

14. Ibid, p. 98.
15. Ibid., pp. 92–93.

BELL & HOWELL'S PROBLEMS WITH GRAY MARKETING

Gray marketing is the selling of trademarked goods through distribution channels that are not authorized by the trademark holder. Gray marketing occurs when a manufacturer-authorized channel member sells products to unauthorized members who, in turn, sell the products (often at lower prices) in markets already served by other authorized distributors. Products sold through a gray market are not counterfeit but are identical to those sold by authorized channel members. They are usually well-known brands that require very little promotion since their availability at a reduced price is all that is really needed to attract consumers. Watches, cameras, personal computers, designer clothes, perfumes, wines, batteries, appliances, and even automobiles are examples of products sold through gray markets.

One case of gray marketing involved Bell & Howell's Mamiya Co. (BHMC), which owns the U.S. exclusive distribution rights for the foreign-manufactured Mamiya cameras. Masel Supply Co. Corp. bought Mamiya cameras in a foreign market, imported them into the United States, and sold the cameras at lower prices than BHMC. With major retailers like K mart, J.C. Penney, and Montgomery Ward pursuing prestige items to bolster the image of their product lines, the demand for Mamiya cameras was high. Of course, consumers were drawn to the low prices of the gray-market cameras, so BHMC suffered from lost sales.

With BHMC financing product demonstrations, advertising, point-of-sale and post-sale services, and suffering lost sales, it decided to take action. BHMC filed suit against Masel seeking to prohibit Masel from importing and selling Mamiya cameras in the United States. A district court granted the injunction maintaining that the reputation of BHMC might be damaged by the Masel cameras that lacked warranties and various other quality control measures.

Currently, the U.S. courts are ruling on several gray market cases. There are also bills before Congress regarding the gray market issue. Some of the pending laws would restrict or outlaw gray marketing; others would allow gray marketers even more freedom.

SOURCES: Stephen Barlas, "Gray Marketing War Escalates," *Advertising Age,* Sept. 26, 1988, pp. 1, 2; Frank V. Cespedes, E. Raymond Corey, and V. Kasturi Rangan, "Gray Markets: Causes and Cures," *Harvard Business Review,* July-August 1988, pp. 75–82; Dale F. Duhan and Mary Jane Sheffet, "Gray Markets and the Legal Status of Parallel Importation," *Journal of Marketing,* July 1988, pp. 75–83; and Larry S. Lowe and Kevin McCrohan, "Gray Markets in the United States," *Journal of Consumer Marketing,* Winter 1988, pp. 45–51.

market have access to similar products or if the exclusive dealing contract strengthens an otherwise weak competitor, the arrangement is allowed

■ Refusal to Deal

For nearly seventy years, the courts have held that producers have the right to choose the channel members with whom they will do business (and the right not to choose others). Within existing distribution channels, however, suppliers may not refuse to deal with wholesalers or dealers just because these wholesalers or dealers had resisted policies that are anticompetitive or in restraint of trade. Suppliers are further prohibited from organizing some channel members in refusal-to-deal actions against other members who choose not to comply with illegal policies.[16]

SUMMARY

Distribution refers to activities that make products available to customers when and where they want to purchase them. A channel of distribution, or marketing channel, is a group of individuals and organizations that direct the flow of products from producers to customers. In most channels of distribution, producers and customers are linked by marketing intermediaries or middlemen, called merchants if they take title to products and functional middlemen if they do not take title. Channel structure reflects the division of responsibilities among members.

Channels of distribution are broadly classified as channels for consumer products or channels for industrial products. Within these two broad categories, different marketing channels are used for different products. Although some consumer goods move directly from producer to consumers, consumer product channels that include wholesalers and retailers are usually more economical and efficient. Industrial goods move directly from producer to end users more frequently than do consumer goods. Channels for industrial products may also include agents, industrial distributors, or both. Most producers have dual or multiple channels so that the distribution system can be adjusted for various target markets.

Although intermediaries can be eliminated, their functions are vital and cannot be dropped; these activities must be performed by someone in the marketing channel or passed on to customers. Because intermediaries serve both producers and buyers, they reduce the total number of transactions that would otherwise be needed to move products from producer to ultimate users. Intermediaries' specialized functions also help keep down costs.

An assortment is a combination of products assembled to provide benefits. Intermediaries perform sorting activities essential to the development of product assortments. Sorting activities allow channel members to divide roles and separate tasks. Through the basic tasks of sorting out, accumulating, allocating, and assorting products for buyers, intermediaries resolve discrepancies in quantity and assortment. The number and characteristics of intermediaries are determined by the assortments and by the expertise needed to perform distribution activities.

Integration of marketing channels brings various activities under the management of one channel member. Vertical integration combines two or more stages of the channel under one management. The vertical marketing system is managed centrally for the mutual benefit of all channel members. Vertical marketing systems

16. Ibid., pp. 96–97.

may be corporate, administered, or contractual. Horizontal integration combines institutions at the same level of channel operation under a single management.

A marketing channel is managed so that products receive appropriate market coverage. In choosing intensive distribution, producers strive to make a product available to all possible dealers. In selective distribution, dealers are screened to choose those most qualified for exposing a product properly. Exclusive distribution usually gives one dealer exclusive rights to sell a product in a large geographic area.

When selecting distribution channels for products, manufacturers evaluate potential channel members carefully. Producers also consider the organization's objectives and available resources; the location, density, and size of a market; buyers' behavior in the target market; characteristics of the product; and outside forces in the marketing environment.

A marketing channel is a social system in which individuals and organizations are linked by a common goal: the profitable and efficient distribution of goods and services. The positions or roles of channel members are associated with rights, responsibilities, and rewards, as well as sanctions for nonconformity. Channels function most efficiently when members cooperate, but when they deviate from their roles, channel conflict can arise. Effective marketing channels are usually a result of channel leadership.

Channel leaders can facilitate or hinder the attainment of other members' goals, and they derive this power from authority, coercion, rewards, referents, or expertise. Producers are in an excellent position to structure channel policy and to use technical expertise and consumer acceptance to influence other channel members. Retailers gain channel control through consumer confidence, wide product mixes, and intimate knowledge of consumers. Wholesalers become channel leaders when they have expertise that other channel members value and when they can coordinate functions to match supply with demand.

Federal, state, and local laws regulate channel management to protect competition and free trade. The courts may prohibit or permit a given practice depending on whether it violates this underlying principle. Various procompetitive legislation apply to distribution practices. The channel management practices frequently subject to legal restraint include dual distribution, restricted sales territories, tying contracts, exclusive dealing, and refusal to deal. When these practices strengthen weak competitors or increase competition among dealers, they may be permitted; in most other cases they are deemed illegal.

Important Terms

Distribution
Channel of distribution
Marketing intermediary
Merchants
Functional middlemen
Dual distribution
Assortment
Sorting activities
Sorting out
Accumulation
Allocation

Assorting
Vertical channel integration
Vertical marketing system (VMS)
Horizontal channel integration
Intensive distribution
Selective distribution
Exclusive distribution
Channel power
Tying contract
Exclusive dealing

DISCUSSION AND REVIEW QUESTIONS

1. Compare and contrast the four major types of marketing channels for consumer products. Through which type of channel is each of the following products most likely to be distributed: (a) new automobiles, (b) saltine crackers, (c) cut-your-own Christmas trees, (d) new textbooks, (e) sofas, (f) soft drinks?
2. "Shorter channels are usually a more direct means of distribution and therefore are more efficient." Comment on this statement.
3. Describe an industrial distributor. What types of products are marketed through industrial distributors?
4. Under what conditions is a producer most likely to use more than one marketing channel?
5. Why do consumers often blame intermediaries for distribution inefficiencies? List several of the reasons.
6. How do the major functions that intermediaries perform help resolve the discrepancies in assortment and quantity?
7. How does the number of intermediaries in the channel relate to the assortments retailers need?
8. Can one channel member perform all channel functions?
9. Identify and explain the major factors that influence decision makers' selection of marketing channels.
10. Name and describe firms that use (a) vertical integration and (b) horizontal integration in their marketing channels.
11. Explain the major characteristics of each of the three types of vertical marketing systems (VMSs).
12. Explain the differences among intensive, selective, and exclusive methods of distribution.
13. "Channel cooperation requires that members support the overall channel goals to achieve individual goals." Comment on this statement.
14. How do power bases within the channel influence the selection of the channel leader?
15. Under what conditions are tying contracts, exclusive dealing, and dual distribution judged illegal?

■ CASES

10.1   Marketing Channels for California Cooler

When California Cooler was introduced commercially in the early 1980s, the low-alcohol mixture of white wine and fruit juice was in a category by itself. Since then, as many as 150 cooler brands, both wine- and malt-based, have been jostling for a share of the cooler market, but California Cooler remains near the top, behind only Joseph E. Seagram and Sons' Seagram's Wine Coolers and E&J Gallo Winery's Bartles & Jaymes. Recently, California Cooler accounted for about 13.1 percent of the $1.6 billion cooler market; total sales of its citrus, orange, tropical fruit, and peach flavors were estimated at 9.1 million cases.

For the past several years, California Cooler has been owned by Brown-Forman Beverage Company, producer of such brands as Jack Daniel's Tennessee Whiskey and Southern Comfort. The product originated in the 1970s on a California beach, when Michael Crete stirred up chablis and citrus juice in plastic tubs as an alternative to cold beer for his volleyball-playing friends. The cooler was the hit of the party, and during the next few years Crete kept experimenting with the formula, taking note of rising consumer interest in nonalcoholic and low-alcohol beverages. Convinced that his cooler had market potential, Crete—then working as a beer and wine distributor—began to give his wine customers bottled samples. The customers asked for more, and by 1981 Crete decided to go into cooler production full-time.

Crete and a pal from high school, Stuart Bewley, each put up $5,000 to start the business. Operating first out of an abandoned migrant farm workers' camp and later from a vacant wine warehouse in Lodi, California, the two did everything themselves: mixing, bottling, capping, and labeling. Initially, they also handled distribution, supplying their accounts from the back of Bewley's 1953 pickup.

After five months, with the wine cooler sales totaling 700 cases, demand was beginning to exceed the fledgling company's modest production rate. Crete and Bewley hired one employee, paying him in stock, and decided to broaden their distribution network. Despite California Cooler's wine content, Crete and Bewley found beer wholesalers more receptive to the new product than wine distributors. For one thing, from the outset Crete and Bewley followed standard beer marketing practice by using foil-wrapped 12.7-ounce bottles (which resembled imported beers), 4-pack cartons, and 24-bottle cases. In addition, the cooler—clearly intended as a leisure-time beverage, not as a drink to be sipped with meals—was directed primarily at beer and soft-drink consumers, not at wine drinkers. Furthermore, the cooler sold better when chilled, and most wine distributors declined to work in the refrigerated cases ("cold boxes"), where beer wholesalers predominated.

Eventually, several Adolph Coors distributors agreed to carry California Cooler, and in 1982 sales zoomed to 80,000 cases. Distributors liked California Cooler because it could be warehoused and handled alongside beer and required only some rearranging of products in the cold boxes. Moreover, the new beverage, priced at less than $1 a bottle and seldom discounted, offered distributors healthy profits. Whereas most beer lines earned California distributors margins of 20 to 22 percent, California Cooler yielded returns closer to the 33 percent typical of wine products. California Cooler sold briskly and soon developed a following, even though at that point the product had been advertised only through in-store displays and by word of mouth.

The use of outside distribution enabled Crete and Bewley to move their wine cooler into mass markets that otherwise would have been out of reach. The California distributors who handled the cooler serviced various establishments, from family-owned liquor outlets to giant chain stores. After one year in outside distribution, California Cooler reached $1.4 million (180,000 gallons) in sales, and it was available throughout the state. The next year, after the company entered distribution in Texas and Arizona, sales were up to $26 million wholesale. Within two more years, California Cooler was being handled by a network of 500 beer wholesalers and being distributed in 49 states.

The success of California Cooler was noticed by the wine industry, where sales had become flat and no new product had been introduced for years. Competing wine coolers quickly appeared on the market, including Bartles & Jaymes, Sun Country (Canandaigua Wine Co.), and Seagram's Coolers. (Sales volume of all coolers jumped 1,900 percent within the first two years after the product was introduced.) Retailers finally accepted coolers as a permanent category, allocating the products more shelf space. At the same time, however, retailers became more selective about the brands they carried, sometimes limiting their stock to the top five or six coolers, plus one or two regional brands. The ensuing struggle for market share led producers to cut prices and to engage in heavy promotional spending.

After a time, certain weaknesses in California Cooler's wholesale network became evident, particularly in comparison with Gallo's powerful and aggresive distribution system. For example, although the beer distributors that carried California Cooler visited retailers frequently, their territories were smaller than those of wine distributors and often overlapped. A retailer might be contacted by a single Gallo distributor with one price, but by several beer wholesalers, each quoting different prices. In addition, California Cooler's competitors could field larger, more experienced sales forces. California Cooler's sales volume continued to increase, but the product's market share began to decline.

Today, although acknowledging the marketing strength of its competitors, Brown-Forman (which paid Crete and Bewley more than $55 million, plus a percentage of future sales for the ownership of California Cooler) insists that it has distribution muscle of its own. Brown-Forman recently reorganized and consolidated its sales territories for greater efficiency and strength in the distribution of its products, including California Cooler. Predicting continued growth in the cooler market, Brown-Forman executives plan to position California Cooler as a year-round beverage and will try to broaden the age segment targeted for the cooler. The company notes further that coolers now account for 25 percent of all wine products consumed in the United States and have entered foreign markets which are becoming increasingly important to the beverage business.

The number-one position in the wine cooler industry has changed three times in three years. With a new $30 million advertising and promotion campaign, a reformulation of the cooler ingredients, a redesigned package, and a new cherry-flavored product, Brown-Forman officials hope to regain and maintain the leading spot.

SOURCES: "Brown-Forman Aims to Bolster Presence in Wine Cooler Market," *Wall Street Journal,* June 11, 1987, p. 8B; Brown-Forman Inc., *1987 Annual Report,* pp. 8–10; "The Concoction That's Raising Spirits in the Wine Industry," *Business Week,* Oct. 8, 1984, p. 182; Harvey M. Lederman, "Cooler Success Freezes Out Most Competitors," *Advertising Age,* Oct. 6, 1986, p. S-1; Marcy Magiera, "A Cool Operator: California Cooler Gets Stylish As It Seeks to Ace Competitors," *Advertising Age,* May 16, 1988, pp. 3, 8; Paula Schnorbus, "Cool(ers) and the Gang," *Marketing & Media Decisions,* May 1987, pp. 127–128; Richard Street, "How They Became Kings of Coolers," *Nation's Business,* October 1985, p. 68; and Patricia Winters, "No Cooler on Beach," *Advertising Age,* Mar. 21, 1988, p. 80A.

Questions for Discussion

1. When establishing marketing channels for a product such as California Cooler, what important factors must be considered?
2. Why did Crete and Bewley select beer distributors to be part of the marketing channel for California Cooler?
3. Is California Cooler being distributed through intensive, selective, or exclusive distribution?

10.2 Channel Selection for Cincinnati Microwave's Escort and Passport Radar Detectors

For years motorists with a penchant for exceeding posted speed limits have been beating a mail-order path to the door of Cincinnati Microwave, maker of the Escort radar detector, a device that alerts speeding drivers to police radar signals. Though in recent years, their sales have declined when compared with the exponential sales figures of their early years, the executives at Cincinnati Microwave think they can regain their old momentum.

The Escort came into being when electrical engineers James Jaeger and Michael Valentine analyzed the workings of a radar detector Jaeger had just purchased and saw how the model could be improved. The two first offered their idea to Electrolert Inc., maker of the Fuzzbuster, the best-selling detector at that time. When Electrolert showed no interest, Valentine and Jaeger formed a partnership to build their own detectors. Working out of Jaeger's basement on money Valentine's father had lent them, the two entrepreneurs used sophisticated heterodyne technology to produce a detector with a microwave system to amplify and filter incoming signals, thereby increasing the detector's range and reducing false alarms.

To attract an upscale clientele, Jaeger and Valentine introduced the Escort at $245, a price almost twice that of competing models. They also decided to sell the product exclusively by mail. The fledgling company could not afford retail distribution, and direct marketing would minimize risk because the detectors could be manufactured as orders arrived and would not need to be shipped until customers' checks or credit card payments had cleared. In addition, mail-order distribution would enable Jaeger and Valentine to expand the company without tying up borrowed capital in extensive inventory.

Jaeger and Valentine published a toll-free telephone number in *Road & Track* and *Motor Trend* and took turns answering the phone. At first orders trickled in at a rate of 250 or so per month. By the end of the first year, Cincinnati Microwave had sold about 1,800 units. Then *Car & Driver* published results of comparison tests on radar detectors, calling the Escort the most reliable and sensitive model on the market. The magazine also exposed the fraudulent claims of a competing firm, whose entry was merely an Escort with a different exterior. Escort sales took off. Within six months Cincinnati Microwave was swamped with more than 1,400 orders every month; at one point the company was thirty-three weeks behind in filling orders.

After a year of rapid growth, Cincinnati Microwave regained control of operations by expanding production, computerizing many functions, and hiring more personnel. (During one period the company was adding ten to twenty new employees per week.) Four years after its founding, Cincinnati Microwave's revenues had risen from $2.1 million to $57.1 million. During the start-up period, Jaeger was in charge of production and Valentine handled marketing. After disagreements over strategy, however, Jaeger bought out Valentine and his father, took the company public, and began to delegate management functions to other executives.

Cincinnati Microwave expected the demand for radar detectors to level off after a few years, and increased competition from low-priced radar detectors, including some Japanese models, has hurt the company's sales immensely. Industry analysts think that Cincinnati Microwave made a huge mistake in not meeting competitors' prices on comparable radar detectors. Cincinnati Microwave's sales have also been hampered by the actions taken by some states to restrict the use of detectors.

Cincinnati Microwave's efforts to diversify into other product areas have not been successful. The company has discontinued its ventures into satellite television receivers and luggage. Cincinnati Microwave executives had great expectations from a product they named the Guardian Interlock. This device, an auto ignition interlock system designed to keep intoxicated drivers from starting their cars, never met anticipated sales predictions.

Currently, Cincinnati Microwave is entering the cellular telephone market in a joint marketing agreement with the telecommunications giant GTE. GTE Mobilnet will provide customers with cellular phone products and services, while Cincinnati Microwave will exclusively direct the advertising, selling, and distribution of the products. Executives from both companies think that cellular phones will appeal to the same customers who purchase high performance radar detectors—a group that Cincinnati Microwave is intimately familiar with. GTE Mobilnet will also furnish service support to cellular phones sold under the Cincinnati Microwave name (these phones will be manufactured by Motorola Inc. under a separate agreement).

Cincinnati Microwave's major strengths are its reputation for excellent customer service and a mailing list of two million names. By expanding its product mix, the company hopes to regain the success it once had. However, Cincinnati Microwave does not intend to abandon the radar detector industry. It has increased its investment in electronics research and development and plans to continue offering premium performance items while becoming more competitive as to price.

SOURCES: Warren Brown, "Radar Detector Maker Thrives Despite Attacks," *Washington Post,* June 1, 1986, p. F1; "Is Microwave's Future Calling with GTE Deal?" *Business Record* (Cincinnati, Ohio), Mar. 6, 1989; "Microwave Learning from Its Mistakes," *Cincinnati Enquirer,* Aug. 10, 1987, p. D6; "Microwave to Transfer Subsidiary's Product," *Cincinnati Business Courier,* Mar. 8, 1987, p. 9; Michele Morris, "Dollar Signs on a Radar Screen," *Financial World,* Aug. 22-Sept. 4, 1984, pp. 80–81; "New Market Detected," *Cincinnati Enquirer,* July 6, 1989; "Radar's Foe," *Barron's,* Dec. 23, 1985, pp. 35–36; Michael Rogers, "Speed Bumps Ahead for Cincinnati Microwave," *Fortune,* Apr. 28, 1986, p. 84; "Sales Drop Signals Problems for Cincinnati Microwave," *Cincinnati Enquirer,* Aug. 10, 1987, p. D1; Jolie B. Solomon, "Learning to Manage," *Wall Street Journal,* May 20, 1985, pp. 38C–40C; and Barry Stavro, "A License to Speed," *Forbes,* Sept. 10, 1984, p. 94.

Questions for Discussion

1. Why did Cincinnati Microwave initially select a direct distribution channel for its radar detectors?
2. What are the advantages and disadvantages of using a direct channel of distribution for products such as radar detectors?
3. If Cincinnati Microwave were to use a second marketing channel in addition to the direct channel, what channel would you recommend?

11 WHOLESALING

Objectives

To understand the nature of wholesaling in the marketing channel

To learn about wholesalers' activities

To understand how wholesalers are classified

To examine organizations that facilitate wholesaling

To explore changing patterns in wholesaling

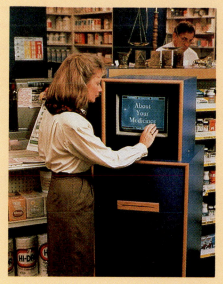

McKesson Corporation is the leading wholesale distributor of health care products in the United States. Though it also distributes beauty aids, general merchandise, specialty foods, bottled water, and office supplies, its primary line of business is drug wholesaling. Throughout its existence, McKesson has revolutionized the health care industry by providing health care retailers with distribution innovations, new avenues of customer support, and electronic information systems.

Decades ago, McKesson executives realized that because their firm offered the same physical products as its competitors, it needed to differentiate itself from other drug wholesalers by offering retailers more services and benefits than any other drug distributor. McKesson's Economost electronic order entry system assisted retailers in cutting costs. Giving retailers the capability to automatically order products using hand-held order-entry devices, McKesson reduced retailers' labor costs, product costs, and inventory holdings.

McKesson set out to assist in particular smaller retail drugstores that were competing with the larger health care chains. It organized these stores into purchasing cooperatives that could then receive volume discounts comparable to the ones given to giant chain operations. Using research gathered by its sales force, McKesson learned that the smaller stores wanted help with marketing research, shelf-management planning, centralized warehousing and storage, and cooperative advertising and joint marketing. McKesson assisted them in all these areas, thus establishing a loyal base of customers. Because of McKesson's efforts, the smaller drugstores were able to offer consumers reduced prices and better services—making them more profitable and stable enterprises. ◆

Photo courtesy Medical Strategies, Inc.

Based on information in Eric Clemons and Michael Row, "A Strategic Information System: McKesson Drug Company's Economost," *Planning Review,* September-October 1988, pp. 14–19; Meghan O'Leary, "Getting the Most Out of Buying at Cost," *CIO,* August 1989, pp. 86–88; and William L. Trombetta, "Channel Systems: An Idea Whose Time Has Come in Health Care Marketing," *Journal of Health Care Marketing,* September 1989, pp. 26–35.

I n this chapter we focus on wholesaling activities (such as those provided by McKesson) within a marketing channel. We view wholesaling as all exchanges among organizations and individuals in marketing channels, except transactions with ultimate consumers. First we examine the importance of wholesalers and their functions, noting the services they render to producers and retailers alike. Then we classify various types of wholesalers and facilitating organizations. Finally, we explore changing patterns in wholesaling.

The Nature and Importance of Wholesaling

Wholesaling comprises all transactions in which the purchaser intends to use the product for resale, for making other products, or for general business operations. It does not include exchanges with ultimate consumers. Wholesaling establishments are engaged primarily in selling products directly to industrial, reseller, government, and institutional users.

A **wholesaler** is an individual or organization engaged in facilitating and expediting exchanges that are primarily wholesale transactions. Only occasionally does a wholesaler engage in retail transactions, which are sales to ultimate consumers. There are more than 337,943 wholesaling establishments in the United States. Wholesale sales rose from $677 billion in 1977 to $1,526 billion in 1987, a 225 percent increase.[1]

The Activities of Wholesalers

More than 50 percent of all products are exchanged, or their exchange is negotiated, through wholesaling institutions. The North Pacific Lumber Co. of Portland, Oregon, for example, purchases lumber and other building supplies from mills and manufacturers and resells them to building supply home centers, hardware and lumber stores, professional builders and subcontractors, and other industrial firms.[2] Of course, it is important to remember that the distribution of all goods requires wholesaling activities, whether or not a wholesaling institution is involved. Table 11.1 lists the major activities wholesalers perform. The activities are not mutually exclusive; individual wholesalers may perform more or fewer activities than Table 11.1 shows. Wholesalers provide marketing activities for organizations above and below them in the marketing channel.

■ **Services for Producers**

Producers, above wholesalers in the marketing channel, have a distinct advantage when they use wholesalers. Wholesalers perform specialized accumulation and allocation functions for a number of products, thus allowing producers to concentrate on developing and manufacturing products that match consumers' wants.

1. *Statistical Abstract of the United States,* 1989, p. 761.

2. "Building Supply Home Centers' 1988 Wholesaler Giants," *Building Supply Home Centers,* September 1988, p. 58.

TABLE 11.1

Major wholesaling activities

ACTIVITY	DESCRIPTION
Wholesale management	Planning, organizing, staffing, and controlling wholesaling operations
Negotiating with suppliers	Serving as the purchasing agent for customers by negotiating supplies
Promotion	Providing a sales force, advertising, sales promotion, and publicity
Warehousing and product handling	Receiving, storing and stockkeeping, order processing, packaging, shipping outgoing orders, and materials handling
Transportation	Arranging and making local and long-distance shipments
Inventory control and data processing	Controlling physical inventory, bookkeeping, recording transactions, keeping records for financial analysis
Security	Safeguarding merchandise
Pricing	Developing prices and providing price quotations
Financing and budgeting	Extending credit, borrowing, making capital investments, and forecasting cash flow
Management and marketing assistance to clients	Supplying information about markets and products and providing advisory services to assist customers in their sales efforts

Wholesalers provide other services to producers as well. By selling a manufacturer's products to retailers and other customers and by initiating sales contacts with the manufacturer, wholesalers serve as an extension of the producer's sales force. Wholesalers also provide four forms of financial assistance. They often pay the costs of transporting goods; they reduce a producer's warehousing expenses and inventory investment by holding goods in inventory; they extend credit and assume the losses from buyers who turn out to be poor credit risks; and when they buy a producer's entire output and pay promptly or in cash, they are a source of working capital. In addition, wholesalers are conduits for information within the marketing channel, keeping manufacturers up-to-date on market developments and passing along the manufacturers' promotional plans to other middlemen in the channel.

Ideally, many producers would like more direct interaction with retailers. Wholesalers, however, usually have closer contact with retailers because of their strategic position in the marketing channel. Besides, even though a producer's own sales force is probably more effective in its selling efforts, the costs of maintaining a sales force and performing the activities normally done by wholesalers are usually higher than the benefits received from better selling. Wholesalers can also spread their costs over many more products than most producers, resulting in lower costs per product unit. For these reasons, many producers have chosen to control promotion and influence the pricing of products and shifted transportation, warehousing, and financing functions to wholesalers.

Wholesalers help their retailer customers select inventory. In industries where obtaining supplies is important, skilled buying is essential. A wholesaler who buys is a specialist in understanding market conditions and an expert at negotiating final purchases. For example, based on its understanding of local customer needs and market conditions, Lawrence R. McCoy & Co., a Massachusetts building-supply wholesaler, purchases inventory ahead of season so that it can provide its retail customers with the building supplies they want when they want them.[3] A retailer's buyer can thus avoid the responsibility of looking for and coordinating supply sources. Moreover, if the wholesaler makes purchases for several different buyers, expenses can be shared by all customers. Another advantage is that a manufacturer's salespersons can offer retailers only a few products at a time, but independent wholesalers have a wide range of products available.

By buying in large quantities and delivering to customers in smaller lots, a wholesaler can perform physical distribution activities—such as transportation, materials handling, inventory planning, communication, and warehousing—more efficiently and can provide more service than a producer or retailer would be able to do with its own physical distribution system. Furthermore, wholesalers can provide quick and frequent delivery even when demand fluctuates. They are experienced in providing fast delivery at low cost, which lets the producer and the wholesalers' customers avoid risks associated with holding large product inventories.

Because they carry products for many customers, wholesalers can maintain a wide product line at a relatively low cost. For example, a small Chrysler-Plymouth dealer in the Midwest discovered that it was cheaper to let wholesale suppliers provide automobile parts than to maintain a parts inventory at the dealership. Often wholesalers can perform storage and warehousing activities more efficiently, permitting retailers to concentrate on other marketing activities. When wholesalers provide storage and warehousing, they generally take on the ownership function as well, an arrangement that frees retailers' and producers' capital for other purposes. Marketing Update 11.1 deals with the variety of services that Super Valu provides to retailers.

CLASSIFYING WHOLESALERS

Many types of wholesalers meet the different needs of producers and retailers. In addition, new institutions and establishments develop in response to producers and retail organizations that want to take over wholesaling functions. Wholesalers adjust their activities as the contours of the marketing environment change.

Wholesalers are classified along several dimensions. Whether a wholesaler is owned by the producer influences how it is classified. Wholesalers are also grouped as to whether they take title to (actually own) the products they handle. The range of services provided is another criterion used for classification. Finally, wholesalers are classified according to the breadth and depth of their product lines. Using these dimensions, we discuss three general categories, or types, of wholesaling establishments: (1) merchant wholesalers, (2) agents and brokers, and (3) manufacturers' sales branches and offices.

3. Clarence Casson, "1988 Wholesaler Giants; Making All the Right Moves," *Building Supply Home Centers*, September 1988, p. 56.

SUPER VALU PROVIDES MANY SERVICES TO RETAILERS

Based in Elden Prairie, Minnesota, Super Valu Stores Inc. is the number two food wholesaling business in the United States (behind Fleming). Super Valu supplies grocery stores throughout the nation with food and non-food items from 18 distribution centers. In addition, Super Valu provides marketing assistance and design planning services to the stores it serves. The wholesaler monitors stores' performances and makes subsequent operating suggestions on how the stores might improve. Super Valu executives encourage retailers to modernize their facilities and may even make arrangement recommendations.

Super Valu spends about 50 percent, or over $243 million, of its total budget on its wholesale operations. Top Super Valu executives are firmly committed to reinvesting in their business. Much of Super Valu's wholesale budget currently is devoted to the expansion and modernization of warehouse facilities.

A computer innovation also has allowed Super Valu to more effectively monitor store orders and inventories—its electronic data interchange (EDI) system. EDI is a communications operation that uses electronic versions of such common business documents as purchase orders and invoices. By electronically communicating with retailers, Super Valu has cut down on ordering errors and provides much quicker service. In addition, the inventories of Super Valu's retailers have been reduced because they no longer have to overbuy to preserve sufficient stock levels. Super Valu executives are trying to convince their own suppliers to adopt EDI systems. They are pleased with the system's results and are eager to extend its applications.

As the general trend of consolidation in the grocery wholesale industry continues, it is likely that Super Valu will grow even larger. With its constant expansion and continued profitability, many Wall Street analysts consider Super Valu to be the best-managed company in its industry.

SOURCES: Torrey Byles, "Grocery Chain Says Invoices Key to Managing Inventory," *Journal of Commerce* Jan. 26, 1989, p. F9; Harlan S. Byrne, "Super Valu Stores Inc.," *Barron's,* Apr. 24, 1989, pp. 49–50; "Super Valu Stores Inc.," *City Business/Twin Cities* (Minneapolis, Minnesota), Feb. 8, 1988, p. G7; "Super Valu Stores Inc.," *Corporate Report* (Minneapolis, Minnesota), May 1, 1989, p. C4; and "Super Valu to Increase Capital Spending 25%," *Supermarket News,* Feb. 27, 1989, pp. 1, 40.

Merchant wholesalers are wholesalers that take title to goods and assume the risks associated with ownership. These independently owned businesses, which make up about two-thirds of all wholesale establishments, generally buy and resell products to industrial or retail customers. A producer is likely to use merchant wholesalers when selling directly to customers would be economically unfeasible. From the producer's point of view, merchant wholesalers are also valuable for providing market coverage, making sales contacts, storing inventory, handling orders, collecting market information, and furnishing customer support.[4] Some merchant wholesalers are even involved in packaging and developing private brands to help their retailer customers be competitive.

During the past thirty years, merchant wholesalers have expanded their share of the wholesale market, despite competition from other types of intermediaries. Now, they account for more than half (58 percent) of all wholesale revenues.[5] As a rule, merchant wholesalers for industrial products are better established and earn higher profits than consumer-goods merchant wholesalers; the latter normally deal in products of lower unit value and face more competition from other middlemen. Industrial-products wholesalers are also more likely to have selective distribution arrangements with manufacturers because of the technical nature of many industrial products.

Merchant wholesalers go by various names, including wholesaler, jobber, distributor, assembler, exporter, and importer.[6] They fall into one of two broad categories: full-service and limited-service. Figure 11.1 illustrates the different types of merchant wholesalers.

Full-Service Merchant Wholesalers.　　**Full-service wholesalers** are middlemen who offer the widest possible range of wholesaling functions. Their customers rely on them for product availability, suitable assortments, bulk-breaking (breaking large quantities into smaller ones), financial assistance, and technical advice and service.[7] Full-service wholesalers provide numerous marketing services to interested customers. Many large grocery wholesalers, for example, help retailers with store design, site selection, personnel training, financing, merchandising, advertising, coupon redemption, and scanning. Although full-service wholesalers often earn higher gross margins than other wholesalers, their operating expenses are also higher because they perform a wider range of functions. Full-service merchant wholesalers may handle either consumer products or industrial products and are categorized as general merchandise, limited-line, or specialty-line wholesalers.

General Merchandise Wholesalers.　　**General merchandise wholesalers** are middlemen who carry a wide product mix but offer limited depth within the product lines. They deal in such products as drugs, hardware, nonperishable foods, cosmetics, detergents, and tobacco. General merchandise wholesalers develop strong, mutually beneficial relationships with neighborhood grocery stores, hardware and appliance shops, and local department stores, which are their typical

4. Bert Rosenbloom, *Marketing Channels: A Management View* (Hinsdale, Ill.: Dryden Press, 1987), p. 63.

5. *Census of Wholesale Trade,* May 1985, p. 207.

6. Rosenbloom, p. 34.

7. Ibid., p. 63.

FIGURE 11.1
Types of merchant wholesalers

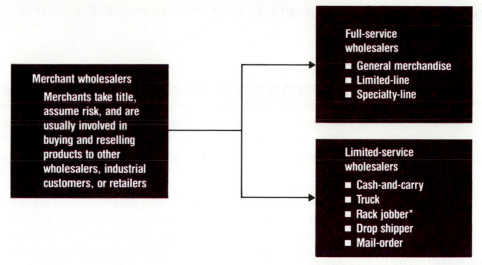

Merchant wholesalers

Merchants take title, assume risk, and are usually involved in buying and reselling products to other wholesalers, industrial customers, or retailers

Full-service wholesalers
- General merchandise
- Limited-line
- Specialty-line

Limited-service wholesalers
- Cash-and-carry
- Truck
- Rack jobber*
- Drop shipper
- Mail-order

*Rack jobbers, in many cases, provide such a large number of services that they can be classified as full-service, specialty-line wholesalers.

customers. The small retailers often obtain everything they need from these wholesalers. General merchandise wholesalers for industrial customers provide supplies and accessories and are sometimes called *industrial distributors* or *mill supply houses.*

Limited-Line Wholesalers. **Limited-line wholesalers** are wholesalers who carry only a few product lines, such as groceries, lighting fixtures, or oil-well drilling equipment, but offer an extensive assortment of products within those lines. They provide a range of services similar to those of full-service merchandise wholesalers. Limited-line wholesalers for industrial goods serve relatively large geographic areas and provide technical expertise; in consumer goods, they supply single- or limited-line retailers. Leading Edge Products, Inc., for example, is a limited-line wholesaler of computer equipment and supplies. The company markets printers, modems, screens, and its own private-label computer disks to the retailers who serve users of home and office computers.

Specialty-Line Wholesalers. Of all the wholesalers, **specialty-line wholesalers** are the middlemen who carry the narrowest range of products, usually a single product line or a few items within a product line. For example, wholesalers that carry shellfish, fruit, or other food delicacies are specialty-line wholesalers. (Marketing Update 11.2 discusses a successful specialty fruit wholesaler.) Specialty-line wholesalers understand the particular requirements of the ultimate buyers and offer customers detailed product knowledge and depth of choice. To provide sales assistance to retailers, specialty wholesalers may set up displays and arrange merchandise. In industrial markets, specialty wholesalers often are better able than manufacturers to give customers technical advice and service.

    Rack jobbers are specialty-line wholesalers who own and maintain their own display racks in supermarkets and drugstores. They specialize in nonfood

FRIEDA'S FINEST: SPECIALTY FRUIT WHOLESALER

Frieda's Finest, founded in 1962 by Frieda Caplan, is the leading wholesaler of exotic fruits and vegetables in the United States. Caplan, chief executive officer and chairman of the board of her company, specializes in selling unique foods and herbs in national and international markets. Dealing with such unusual items as purple potatoes, "burpless" cucumbers, babaco, tamarindos, taro root, and miniature coconuts, Caplan brought personality and many innovations to the produce wholesaling industry. In a male-dominated field, Frieda's Finest is the first wholesale produce firm to be founded, owned, and managed by a woman.

Caplan is personally responsible for transforming the Chinese gooseberry, which she renamed the kiwifruit, from a New Zealand commodity to a popular global product. She introduced spaghetti squash and alfalfa sprouts to the U.S. market; and in the early 1960s when other wholesalers dealt almost exclusively with canned mushrooms, Caplan sold retailers fresh ones—virtually being the first to bring fresh mushrooms to the American public.

Frieda's Finest offers many supporting services to both retailers and consumers. It helps stores by providing produce consulting services and advertising assistance in the form of in-store merchandising aids and camera-ready materials for newspaper advertisements. In addition, the company publishes a weekly "Hot Sheet" for produce managers that tells them which items are selling and mentions possible promotional opportunities. Frieda's Finest also provides consumers with a free newsletter (sent to anyone requesting it) and explanatory labels on the unusual foods that explain how they should be stored and prepared.

When compared to giant produce wholesalers like Dole and Chiquita, Frieda's Finest, with its annual revenues of only $20 million, is a small company. Ironically, after Caplan succeeds in turning an uncommon fruit like the kiwi into a popular item, the product ceases to be profitable for her because industry giants start marketing the product and (with their economies of scale) underpricing her goods. Thus, Caplan continues to search for unique fruits and vegetables to introduce to U.S. consumers.

SOURCES: Erik Larson, "Strange Fruits," *Inc.,* November 1989, pp. 80–82, 85, 88, 90; Maria La Ganga, "A Dozen Who Shaped the '80s," *Los Angeles Times,* January 1, 1990, Frieda's Finest/Produce Specialties, Inc. *News Release (Company Biography).*

TABLE 11.2 *Various services that limited-service merchant wholesalers provide*

	CASH-AND-CARRY	TRUCK	DROP SHIPPER[a]	MAIL ORDER
Physical possession of merchandise	Yes	Yes	No	Yes
Personal sales calls on customers	No	Yes	No	No
Information about market conditions	No	Some	Yes	Yes
Advice to customers	No	Some	Yes	No
Stocking and maintenance of merchandise in customers' stores	No	No	No	No
Credit to customers	No	Some	Yes	Some
Delivery of merchandise to customers	No	Yes	No	No

[a]Also called *desk jobber.*

items—particularly branded, widely advertised products sold on a self-serve basis —that the retailers themselves prefer not to order and stock because of risk or inconvenience. Health and beauty aids, toys, books, magazines, hardware, housewares, and stationery are typical products rack jobbers handle. The rack jobbers send out delivery persons to set up displays, mark merchandise, stock shelves, and keep billing and inventory records; retailers need only furnish the space. Most rack jobbers operate on consignment and take back unsold products.

Limited-Service Merchant Wholesalers.   **Limited-service wholesalers** provide only some marketing services and specialize in a few functions. Producers perform the remaining functions, or the functions are passed on to customers or other middlemen. Limited-service wholesalers take title to merchandise, but in many cases, they do not deliver merchandise, grant credit, provide marketing information, store inventory, or plan ahead for customers' future needs. Because they offer only restricted services, limited-service wholesalers are compensated with lower rates and thus earn smaller profit margins than full-service wholesalers.

Although certain types of limited-service wholesalers are few in number (and are not even categorized separately by the Census Bureau), they are important in the distribution of such products as specialty foods, perishable items, construction materials, and coal. In this section we discuss the specific functions of four typical limited-service wholesalers: cash and carry wholesalers, truck wholesalers, drop shippers, and mail-order wholesalers. (Table 11.2 is a summary of the services these wholesalers provide.)

Cash-and-Carry Wholesalers.   **Cash-and-carry wholesalers** are middlemen whose customers—usually small retailers and small industrial firms—will pay cash and furnish transportation. In some cases, full-service wholesalers set up cash-and-carry departments because they cannot otherwise supply small retailers profitably. Cash-and-carry middlemen usually handle a limited line of products with a high turnover rate—for instance, groceries, building materials, electrical supplies, or office supplies.

Metro Cash and Carry, for example, operates a huge wholesale grocery outlet in Hillside, Illinois. Metro caters to small grocery, gas station, and convenience store owners, who use the wholesaler as a source of stock for their own store shelves. To buy from Metro, customers must be business owners. They load products onto flat-bed carts, push them down aisles that are eleven feet long, and pay in cash or by check. The cash-only rule eliminates the need for a credit department, and transportation by customers eliminates the need for delivery persons and equipment.[8]

Cash-and-carry wholesaling developed after 1920, when independent retailers began experiencing competitive pressure from large chain stores. Today cash-and-carry wholesaling offers advantages to wholesaler and customers alike. The wholesaler has no expenditures for outside salespersons, marketing, research, promotion, credit, or delivery, and the customer benefits from lower prices and immediate access to products. Many small retailers whose accounts were refused by other wholesalers have survived because of cash-and-carry wholesalers.

Truck Wholesalers. **Truck wholesalers**, sometimes called truck jobbers or wagon jobbers, are middlemen who transport a limited line of products directly to customers for on-the-spot inspection and selection. These wholesalers are often small operators who own and drive their own trucks. Usually, truck wholesalers have regular routes and call on retailers and institutions to determine their needs.

Truck wholesalers play an important part in supplying small grocery stores with perishables, such as fruits and vegetables, which other wholesalers often choose not to carry. They may also sell meat, potato chips, supplies for service stations, and tobacco products. Although truck wholesalers perform selling, promotional, and transportation functions, they are generally classified as limited-service wholesalers because they do not extend credit. As a result of their low-volume sales and wide range of customer services, their operating costs are high.

Drop Shippers. **Drop shippers**, also known as desk jobbers, are intermediaries who take title to goods and negotiate sales but never take actual possession of products. They forward orders from retailers, industrial buyers, or other wholesalers to manufacturers and then arrange for carload shipments of items to be delivered directly from producers to customers. The drop shipper assumes responsibility for the products during the entire transaction, including the costs of any unsold goods.

Drop shippers are most commonly used in large-volume purchases of bulky goods, such as coal, coke, oil, chemicals, lumber, and building materials. Normally sold in carload quantities, these products are expensive to handle and ship relative to their unit value; extra loading and unloading is an added (and unnecessary) expense. One trend in this form of wholesaling is the use of more drop shipping from manufacturers to supermarkets. A drop shipment eliminates warehousing and deferred deliveries to the stores, and large supermarkets can sell entire truckloads of products rapidly enough to make drop shipping profitable.[9]

Because drop shippers incur no inventory costs and provide only minimal promotional assistance, they have low operating costs and can pass along some of the savings to their customers. In some cases, drop shippers do offer planning services, credit, and personal selling.

8. Eileen Norris, "Wholesaler Cashes in on Desire to Cut Costs," *Advertising Age,* Apr. 18, 1985, p. 32.

9. "Drop-Shipping Grows to Save Depot Costs," *Supermarket News,* Apr. 1, 1985, pp. 1, 17.

FIGURE 11.2
Types of agents and brokers

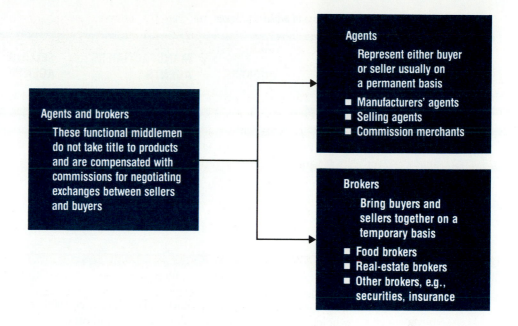

Agents and brokers

These functional middlemen do not take title to products and are compensated with commissions for negotiating exchanges between sellers and buyers

Agents

Represent either buyer or seller usually on a permanent basis

- Manufacturers' agents
- Selling agents
- Commission merchants

Brokers

Bring buyers and sellers together on a temporary basis

- Food brokers
- Real-estate brokers
- Other brokers, e.g., securities, insurance

Mail-Order Wholesalers. **Mail-order wholesalers** use catalogs instead of sales forces to sell products to retail, industrial, and institutional buyers. This is a convenient and effective method of selling small items to customers in remote areas. Mail order enables buyers to choose particular catalog items and then send in their orders and receive shipments through United Parcel Service, the U.S. Postal Service, or other carriers. Wholesalers can thus generate sales in locations that otherwise would be unprofitable to service.

Wholesale mail-order houses generally feature cosmetics, specialty foods, hardware, sporting goods, business and office supplies, and automotive parts. They usually require payment in cash or by credit card, and they give discounts for large orders. Mail-order wholesalers hold goods in inventory and offer some planning services but seldom provide assistance with promotional efforts.

■ **Agents and Brokers**

Agents and brokers (see Figure 11.2) negotiate purchases and expedite sales but do not take title to products. They are **functional middlemen**, intermediaries who perform a limited number of marketing activities in exchange for a commission, which is generally based on the product's selling price. **Agents** are middlemen who represent buyers or sellers on a permanent basis. **Brokers** are usually middlemen that either buyers or sellers employ temporarily. Together, agents and brokers account for 11.6 percent of the total sales volume of all wholesalers.[10]

Although agents and brokers perform even fewer functions than limited-service wholesalers, they are usually specialists in particular products or types of customers and can provide valuable sales expertise. They know their markets well and often form long-lasting associations with customers. Agents and brokers enable manufacturers to expand sales when resources are limited, to benefit from the services of a trained sales force, and to hold personal selling costs down. However, despite the

10. *Census of Wholesale Trade*, May 1985, p. 207.

TABLE 11.3 *Various services agents and brokers provide*

	BROKERS	MANUFACTURERS' AGENTS	SELLING AGENTS	COMMISSION MERCHANTS
Physical possession of merchandise	No	Some	No	Yes
Long-term relationship with buyers or sellers	No	Yes	Yes	Yes
Representation of competing product lines	Yes	No	No	Yes
Limited geographic territory	No	Yes	No	No
Credit to customers	No	No	Yes	Some
Delivery of merchandise to customers	No	Some	Yes	Yes

advantages they offer, agents and brokers face increased competition from merchant wholesalers, manufacturers' sales branches and offices, and direct sales efforts.

Here we look at three types of agents: manufacturers' agents, selling agents, and commission merchants. We also examine the brokers' role in bringing about exchanges between buyers and sellers. Table 11.3 summarizes these services.

Manufacturers' Agents.   **Manufacturers' agents**—who account for over half of all agent wholesalers—are independent middlemen who represent two or more sellers and usually offer customers complete product lines. They sell and take orders year-round, much like a manufacturer's sales office does. Restricted to a particular territory, a manufacturers' agent handles noncompeting and complementary products. The relationship between the agent and each manufacturer is governed by written agreements explicitly outlining territories, selling price, order handling, and terms of sale relating to delivery, service, and warranties. Manufacturers' agents are commonly used in the sale of apparel and accessories, machinery and equipment, iron, steel, furniture, automotive products, electrical goods, and certain food items.

Although most manufacturers' agents run small enterprises, their employees are professional, highly skilled salespersons. The agents' major advantages, in fact, are their wide range of contacts and strong customer relationships. These intermediaries help large producers minimize the costs of developing new sales territories and adjust sales strategies for different products in different locations. Agents are also useful to small producers that cannot afford outside sales forces of their own because the producers incur no costs until the agents have actually sold something. By concentrating on a limited number of products, agents can mount an aggressive sales effort that would be impossible with any other distribution method except producer-owned sales branches and offices. In addition, agents are able to spread operating expenses among noncompeting products and thus can offer each manufacturer lower prices for services rendered.

The chief disadvantage of using agents is the higher commission rate (usually 10 to 15 percent) they charge for new-product sales. When sales of a new product begin to build, total selling costs go up, and producers sometimes transfer the selling function to in-house sales representatives. For this reason, agents try to avoid depending on a single product line; most work for more than one manufacturer.

Manufacturers' agents have little or no control over producers' pricing and marketing policies. They do not extend credit, and they may not be able to provide technical advice. They do occasionally store and transport products, assist with planning, and provide promotional support. Some agents help retailers advertise and maintain a service organization. The more services offered, the higher the agent's commission.

Selling Agents.   **Selling agents** market either all of a specified product line or a manufacturer's entire output. They perform every wholesaling activity except taking title to products. Selling agents usually assume the sales function for several producers at a time and are often used in place of a marketing department. In contrast to other agent wholesalers, selling agents generally have no territorial limits and have complete authority over prices, promotion, and distribution. They play a key role in the advertising, marketing research, and credit policies of the sellers they represent, at times even advising on product development and packaging.

Selling agents, who account for about 1 percent of the wholesale trade, are used most often by small producers or by manufacturers who find it difficult to maintain a marketing department because of seasonal production or other factors. A producer having financial problems may also engage a selling agent. By so doing, the producer relinquishes some control of the business but may gain working capital by avoiding immediate marketing costs.

To avoid conflicts of interest, selling agents represent noncompeting product lines. The agents play an important part in the distribution of coal and textiles, and they also sometimes handle canned foods, household furnishings, clothing, lumber, and metal products. In these industries, competitive pressures increase the importance of marketing relative to production, and the selling agent is a source of essential marketing and financial expertise.

Commission Merchants.   **Commission merchants** are agents who receive goods on consignment from local sellers and negotiate sales in large central markets. Most often found in agricultural marketing, commission merchants take possession of truckload quantities of commodities, arrange for any necessary grading or storage, and transport the commodities to auction or markets where they are sold. When sales have been completed, an agent deducts a commission, plus the expense of making the sale, and then turns over the profits to the producer.

Sometimes called factor merchants, these agents may have broad powers regarding prices and terms of sale, and they specialize in obtaining the best price possible under market conditions. Commission merchants offer planning assistance and sometimes extend credit, but they do not usually provide promotional support. Because commission merchants deal in large volumes, their per unit costs are usually low. Their services are most useful to small producers who must get products to buyers but choose not to field a sales force or accompany the goods to market themselves. In addition to farm products, commission merchants may handle textiles, art, furniture, or seafood products.

Businesses—including farms—that use commission merchants have little control over pricing, although the seller can specify a minimum price. Generally, too, the seller is able to supervise the agent's actions through a check of the commodity prices published regularly in newspapers. Large producers, however, need to maintain closer contact with the market and therefore have limited need for commission merchants.

Brokers. Brokers seek out buyers or sellers and help negotiate exchanges. In other words, brokers' primary purpose is to bring buyers and sellers together. Thus brokers perform fewer functions than other intermediaries. They are not involved in financing or physical possession, have no authority to set prices, and assume almost no risks. Instead, they offer their customers specialized knowledge of a particular commodity and a network of established contacts.

Brokers are especially useful to sellers of certain types of products who market those products only occasionally. Sellers of used machines, seasonal food products, financial securities, and real estate may not know of potential buyers. A broker can furnish this information. The party who engages the broker's services—usually the seller—pays the broker's commission when the transaction is completed.

In the food industry—where brokers are most commonly found—**food brokers** are intermediaries who sell food and general merchandise items to retailer-owned and merchant wholesalers, grocery chains, industrial buyers, and food processors. Food brokers enable buyers and sellers to adjust to fluctuating market conditions; they also provide assistance in grading, negotiating, and inspecting foods (in some cases they store and deliver products). Because of the seasonal nature of food production, the association between food broker and producer is temporary. Many mutually beneficial broker-producer relationships, however, are resumed year after year. Because food brokers provide a range of services on a somewhat permanent basis and operate in specific geographic territories, they can more accurately be described as manufacturers' agents.

■ **Manufacturers' Sales Branches and Offices**

Sometimes called manufacturers' wholesalers, manufacturers' sales branches and offices resemble merchant wholesalers' operations. According to the *Census of Wholesale Trade*, these producer-owned middlemen account for about 9 percent of wholesale establishments and generate approximately one-third (31 percent) of all wholesale sales.[11]

Sales branches are manufacturer-owned middlemen selling products and providing support services to the manufacturer's sales force, especially in locations where large customers are concentrated and demand is high. They offer credit, deliver goods, give promotional assistance, and furnish other services. In many cases, they carry inventory (although this practice often duplicates the functions of other channel members and is now declining). Customers include retailers, industrial buyers, and other wholesalers. Branch operations are common in the electrical supplies (Westinghouse Electrical Corp.), plumbing (Crane Co. and American Standard), lumber, and automotive parts industries.

Sales offices are manufacturer-owned operations that provide services normally associated with agents. Like sales branches, they are located away from manufacturing plants, but unlike branches, they carry no inventory. A manufacturer's sales offices or branches may sell products that enhance the manufacturer's own product line. For example, Hiram Walker, Inc., a liquor producer, imports wine from Spain to increase the number of products that its sales offices can offer

11. *Census of Wholesale Trade*, May 1985, p. 207.

wholesalers. United States Tobacco Company imports Borkum Riff smoking tobacco from Sweden to add variety to its chewing tobacco and snuff lines.

Manufacturers may set up sales branches or sales offices so they can reach customers more effectively by performing wholesaling functions themselves. A manufacturer may also set up these branches or offices when needed specialized wholesaling services are not available through existing middlemen. In some situations, however, a manufacturer may bypass its wholesaling organization entirely—for example, if the producer decides to serve large retailer customers directly. One major distiller bottles private-label bourbon for California supermarkets and separates this operation completely from the company's sales office, which serves other retailers.

FACILITATING AGENCIES

The total marketing channel is more than a chain linking the producer, intermediary, and buyer. **Facilitating agencies**—transportation companies, insurance companies, advertising agencies, marketing research agencies, and financial institutions—may perform activities that enhance channel functions. Note, however, that any of the functions these facilitating agencies perform may be taken over by the regular marketing intermediaries in the marketing channel.

The basic difference between channel members and facilitating agencies is that channel members perform the negotiating functions (buying, selling, and transferring title), whereas facilitating agencies do not.[12] In other words, facilitating agencies assist in the operation of the channel but do not sell products. The channel manager may view the facilitating agency as a subcontractor to which various distribution tasks can be farmed out according to the principle of specialization and division of labor.[13] Channel members (producers, wholesalers, or retailers) may rely on facilitating agencies because they believe that these independent businesses will perform various activities more efficiently and more effectively than they themselves could. Facilitating agencies are functional specialists performing special tasks for channel members without getting involved in directing or controlling channel decisions. The following sections describe the ways in which facilitating agencies provide assistance in expediting the flow of products through marketing channels.

■ Public Warehouses

Public warehouses are storage facilities available for a fee. Producers, wholesalers, and retailers may rent space in a warehouse instead of constructing their own facilities or using a merchant wholesaler's storage services. Many warehouses also order, deliver, collect accounts, and maintain display rooms where potential buyers can inspect products.

To use goods as collateral for a loan, a channel member may place products in a bonded warehouse. If it is too impractical or expensive to physically transfer goods, the channel member may arrange for a public warehouser to verify that goods are in the member's own facilities and then issue receipts for lenders.[14] Under this

12. Rosenbloom, p. 61.

13. Ibid.

14. Ibid., p. 62.

arrangement, the channel member retains possession of the products but the warehouser has control. Many field public warehousers know where their clients can borrow working capital and are sometimes able to arrange low-cost loans.

Finance Companies

Wholesalers and retailers may be able to obtain financing by transferring ownership of products to a sales finance company, bank, or savings and loan association while retaining physical possession of the goods. Often called "floor planning," this form of financing enables wholesalers and retailers—especially automobile and appliance dealers—to offer a greater selection of products for customers and thus increase sales. When a product is sold, the dealer may have to pay off the loan immediately. The products financed through floor plans are usually well known, sell relatively easily, and present little risk.

Other financing functions are performed by factors—organizations that provide clients with working capital by buying their accounts receivable or by loaning money, using the accounts receivable as collateral. Most factors minimize their own risks by specializing in particular industries, the better to evaluate individual channel members within those industries. Factors usually lend money for a longer time than banks. They may help clients improve their credit and collection policies and may also provide management expertise.

Transportation Companies

Rail, truck, air, and other carriers are facilitating organizations that help manufacturers and retailers transport products. Each form of transportation has its own advantages. Railroads ship large volumes of bulky goods at low cost; in fact, a "unit train" is the cheapest form of overland transportation for ore, grain, or other commodities. Air transport is relatively expensive but often preferred for shipping high-value or perishable goods. Trucks, which usually carry short-haul, high-value goods, now carry more and more products because factories are moving closer to their markets. As a result of technological advances, pipelines now transport powdered solids and fluidized solid materials, as well as petroleum and natural gas.

Transportation companies sometimes take over the functions of other middlemen. Because of the ease and speed of using air transportation for certain types of products, air freight companies, such as those mentioned in Figure 11.3, can eliminate the need of maintaining large inventories and branch warehouses. In other cases, freight forwarders perform accumulation functions by combining less-than-full shipments into full loads and passing on the savings to customers—perhaps charging a carload rate rather than a less-than-carload rate.

Trade Shows and Trade Marts

Trade shows and trade marts enable manufacturers or wholesalers to exhibit products to potential buyers and thus help the selling and buying functions. **Trade shows** are industry exhibitions that offer both selling and nonselling benefits.[15] On the selling side, trade shows let vendors identify prospects; gain access to key decision makers; disseminate facts about their products, services, and personnel; and actually sell products and service current accounts through contacts at the show.[16] Trade shows also allow a firm to reach potential buyers who have not been approached through regular selling efforts. In fact, research indicates that most trade show visitors have not been contacted by a sales representative of any company

15. Thomas V. Bonoma, "Get More Out of Your Trade Shows," *Harvard Business Review,* January-February 1983, pp. 75–83.

16. Rosenbloom, p. 185.

FIGURE 11.3

Facilitating agencies.
Air express companies
such as DHL, Federal Express, and UPS facilitate
and sometimes perform
functions of marketing
channel members.

SOURCE: Courtesy of DHL

within the past year, and many are therefore willing to travel several hundred miles to attend trade shows to learn about new goods and services.[17] The nonselling benefits include opportunities to maintain the company image with competitors, customers, and the industry; gather information about competitors' products and prices; and identify potential channel members.[18] Trade shows have a positive influence on other important marketing variables, including maintaining or enhancing company morale, product testing, and product evaluation.

Trade shows can permit direct buyer-seller interaction and may eliminate the need for agents. Companies exhibit at trade shows because of the high concentration of prospective buyers for their products. Studies show that it takes, on the average, 5.1 sales calls to close an industrial sale but less than 1 sales call (0.8) to close a trade show lead. The explanation for the latter figure is that more than half of the customers who purchase a product based on information gained at a trade show order the product by mail or by phone after the show. When customers use these more impersonal methods to gather information, the need for major sales calls to provide such information is eliminated.[19]

17. "Trade Shows—Part 1; A Major Sales and Marketing Tool," *Small Business Report,* June 1988, pp. 34–39.

18. Rosenbloom, p. 185.

19. Richard K. Swandby and Jonathan M. Cox, "Trade Show Trends: Exhibiting Growth Paces Economic Strengths," *Business Marketing,* May 1985, p. 50.

Trade marts are relatively permanent facilities that firms can rent to exhibit products year-round. At these marts, such products as furniture, home decorating supplies, toys, clothing, and gift items are sold to wholesalers and retailers. In the United States, trade marts are located in several major cities, including New York, Chicago, Dallas, High Point (North Carolina), Atlanta, and Los Angeles. The Dallas Market Center, which includes the Dallas Trade Mart, the Home-furnishing Mart, the World Trade Center, the Decorative Center, Market Hall, InfoMart, and the Apparel Mart, is housed in six buildings designed specifically for the convenience of professional buyers.

CHANGING PATTERNS IN WHOLESALING

The nature of the wholesaling industry is changing. The distinction between wholesaling activities that any business can perform and the traditional wholesaling establishment is blurring. Changes in the nature of the marketing environment itself have transformed various aspects of the industry. For instance, they have brought about increasing reliance on computer technology to expedite the ordering, delivery, and handling of goods. The trend toward globalization of world markets has resulted in other changes, and astute wholesalers are responding to them. The two predominant shifts in wholesaling today are the consolidation of the wholesaling industry and the development of new types of retailers.

■ Wholesalers Consolidate Power

Like most major industries, the wholesale industry is experiencing a great number of mergers. In fact, some experts believe that the current wave of mergers will leave only 285,000 independent wholesalers, down from the 340,000 in existence now. Wholesaling firms are acquiring or merging with other firms primarily to achieve more efficiency in the face of declining profit margins. Consolidation also gives larger wholesalers more pricing power over producers. Some analysts have expressed concern that wholesalers' increased price clout will increase the number of single-source supply deals, which may reduce competition among wholesalers, as well as retailers and producers. Nevertheless, the trend toward consolidation of wholesaling firms appears to be continuing.[20]

One of the results of the current wave of consolidation in the wholesale industry is that more wholesalers are specializing. For example, McKesson Corp. once distributed chemicals, wines, and spirits but now focuses only on drugs. The new larger wholesalers can also afford to purchase and make use of more modern technology to physically manage inventories, provide computerized ordering services, and even help manage their retail customers' operations.[21]

■ New Types of Wholesalers

The trend toward larger retailers—superstores and the like (discussed in Chapter 12)—will offer opportunities to, as well as threaten, wholesaling establishments. Opportunities will develop from the expanded product lines of these mass merchandisers. A merchant wholesaler of groceries, for instance, may want to add other low-cost, high-volume products that are sold in superstores. On the other hand,

20. Joseph Weber, "Mom and Pop Move Out of Wholesaling," *Business Week,* Jan. 9, 1989, p. 91.

21. Ibid.

some limited-function merchant wholesalers may no longer have a role to play. For example, the volume of sales may eliminate the need for rack jobbers, who usually handle slow-moving products that are purchased in limited quantities. The future of independent wholesalers, agents, and brokers depends on their ability to delineate markets and furnish desired services.

Summary

Wholesaling includes all transactions in which the purchaser intends to use the product for resale, for making other products, or for general business operations. It does *not* include exchanges with the ultimate consumers. Wholesalers are individuals or organizations that facilitate and expedite primarily wholesale transactions.

More than half of all goods are exchanged through wholesalers, although the distribution of any product requires that someone must perform wholesaling activities, whether or not a wholesaling institution is involved. For producers, wholesalers perform specialized accumulation and allocation functions for a number of products, letting the producers concentrate on manufacturing the products. For retailers, wholesalers provide buying expertise, wide product lines, efficient distribution, and warehousing and storage services.

Various types of wholesalers serve different market segments. How a wholesaler is classified depends on whether the wholesaler is owned by a producer, whether it takes title to products, the range of services it provides, and the breadth and depth of its product lines. The three general categories of wholesalers are merchant wholesalers, agents and brokers, and manufacturers' sales branches and offices.

Merchant wholesalers are independently owned businesses that take title to goods and assume risk; they make up about two-thirds of all wholesale firms. They are either full-service wholesalers, offering the widest possible range of wholesaling functions, or limited-service wholesalers, providing only some marketing services and specializing in a few functions. Full-service merchant wholesalers include general-merchandise wholesalers, which offer a wide but relatively shallow product mix; limited-line wholesalers, which offer extensive assortments in a few product lines; and specialty-line wholesalers, which offer great depth in a single product line or in a few items within a line. Rack jobbers are specialty-line wholesalers that own and service display racks in supermarkets and drugstores. There are four types of limited-service merchant wholesalers. Cash-and-carry wholesalers sell to small businesses, require payment in cash, and do not deliver. Truck wholesalers sell a limited line of products from their own trucks directly to customers. Drop shippers own goods and negotiate sales but never take possession of products. Mail-order wholesalers sell to retail, industrial, and institutional buyers through direct-mail catalogs.

Agents and brokers, sometimes called functional middlemen, negotiate purchases and expedite sales but do not take title to products. They are usually specialists and provide valuable sales expertise. Agents represent buyers or sellers on a permanent basis. Manufacturers' agents offer customers the complete product lines of two or more sellers; selling agents market a complete product line or a producer's entire output and perform every wholesaling function except taking title to products; commission merchants receive goods on consignment from local sellers and negotiate sales in large central markets. Brokers, such as food brokers, negotiate exchanges between buyers and sellers on a temporary basis.

Manufacturers' sales branches and offices are vertically integrated units owned by manufacturers. Branches sell products and provide support services for the manufacturer's sales force in a given location. Sales offices carry no inventory and function much as agents do.

Facilitating agencies do not buy, sell, or take title but perform certain wholesaling functions. They include public warehouses, finance companies, transportation companies, and trade shows and trade marts. In some instances, these organizations eliminate the need for a wholesaling establishment.

The nature of the wholesaling industry is changing in response to changes in the marketing environment. The predominant changes are the increasing consolidation of the wholesaling industry and the growth of new types of wholesalers.

IMPORTANT TERMS

Wholesaling	Functional middlemen
Wholesaler	Agents
Merchant wholesalers	Brokers
Full-service wholesalers	Manufacturers' agents
General merchandise wholesalers	Selling agents
Limited-line wholesalers	Commission merchants
Specialty-line wholesalers	Food brokers
Rack jobbers	Sales branches
Limited-service wholesalers	Sales offices
Cash-and-carry wholesalers	Facilitating agencies
Truck wholesalers	Public warehouses
Drop shippers	Trade shows
Mail-order wholesalers	Trade marts

DISCUSSION AND REVIEW QUESTIONS

1. Is there a distinction between wholesalers and wholesaling? If so, what is it?
2. Would it be appropriate for a wholesaler to stock both interior wall paint and office supplies? Under what circumstances would this product mix be logical?
3. What services do wholesalers provide to producers and retailers?
4. Drop shippers take title to products but do not accept physical possession. Commission merchants take physical possession of products but do not accept title. Defend the logic of classifying drop shippers as wholesale merchants and commission merchants as agents.
5. What are the advantages of using agents to replace merchant wholesalers? What are the disadvantages?
6. What, if any, are the differences in the marketing functions that manufacturers' agents and selling agents perform?
7. Why are manufacturers' sales offices and branches classified as wholesalers? Which independent wholesalers are replaced by manufacturers' sales branches? Which independent wholesalers are replaced by manufacturers' sales offices?
8. "Public warehouses are really wholesale establishments." Please comment.
9. Discuss the role of facilitating organizations. Identify three facilitating organizations and explain how each type performs this role.

■ CASES

11.1 Anheuser-Busch and Its Wholesalers

St. Louis–based Anheuser-Busch, Inc., is the world's largest brewing company, with a market share that is increasing steadily. It currently produces one out of every three beers sold in the United States. Anheuser-Busch's brewery sales have recently neared $6.5 billion. Its products include Budweiser, Michelob, Michelob Light, Bud Light, Bud Dry, and Michelob Classic Dark.

In the United States and in Caribbean countries, Anheuser-Busch distributes beer through a network of about 1,000 independently owned wholesalers and 10 company-owned wholesale operations—a distribution system considered the strongest in the brewing industry. Anheuser-Busch's independent wholesalers employ about 30,000 people, more than 18,000 of whom work in direct beer marketing positions. (One Anheuser-Busch distributor is Frank Sinatra, who owns Somerset Distributing in California.) Company-owned distributorships employ about 1,600 people. Wholesalers handle volumes ranging from 870 barrels to 1.1 million barrels annually.

Anheuser-Busch's effective distribution system is bolstered by a variety of cooperative arrangements with wholesalers. For example, the company tries to ensure that its beers are sold to wholesalers FOB (free on board) from the "least cost" brewery. That is, the wholesaler must supply or pay for transportation from the brewery that can provide the product at the lowest shipping cost. But if a product must be shipped at a higher cost—perhaps because the nearest brewery does not produce a specific package—Anheuser-Busch compensates the wholesaler for the difference in cost. The company's traffic department also helps wholesalers arrange transportation. Some twenty years ago, Anheuser-Busch introduced its wholesaler equity program, and recently expanded it to give distributors exclusive territories where permitted by law. A wholesaler advisory panel, a cross section of wholesalers and top company managers, meets regularly to discuss and act on industry issues.

In addition, the ten distributorships in the company's wholesale operations division serve as a testing ground for programs that are made available to independent wholesalers. In one case, the company developed computer software to help wholesalers maximize retail shelf space. Anheuser-Busch wholesalers receive group discounts on computers, trucks, and insurance and can take company courses ranging from draught beer basics to dynamics of business readings. To build morale among wholesalers, Anheuser-Busch puts top executives in charge of its biggest-volume states (the company's president, August Busch III, handles California himself). Furthermore, every three years, the company throws a Las Vegas–style wholesalers' convention, with appearances by such celebrities as Bob Hope and Paul Newman.

Anheuser-Busch's most evident support for its distributors is its backing of special promotions: sporting events, college parties, rodeos, and festivals. The company may pay as much as half the cost of these events, in cooperation with local wholesalers. To improve sales of Michelob Light, for example, a local New York distributor decided to hold a Michelob Light Concentration Day. On that day, only Michelob Light was delivered to retailers. Tuxedo-clad representatives from the St. Louis headquarters rode on delivery trucks, accompanied by two Playboy Playmates. The distributorship sold 21,000 cases of Michelob Light in one day (it normally takes twenty days to sell that amount), and Anheuser-Busch is now staging Concentration Days in other cities.

The company has helped support everything from Chicago's Lithuanian festival to the Iron Man Triathlon in Hawaii. Just before Coors moved into the New York–New Jersey market, Anheuser-Busch supplied its wholesalers with a three-hundred-page "Coors Defense Plan," along with funding for promotional events that might have attracted Coors sponsorship. Coors was unable to reach an agreement with any major beer wholesalers and had to distribute through a soft-drink bottler instead.

For distributors, however, the price of such generous corporate support is unquestioned loyalty. Anheuser-Busch asks more of its wholesalers than any other brewer. Each year all distributors are requested to contribute ideas for local promotions—one for every brand. Furthermore, although the distributors are independent business owners, technically free to sell whatever they choose, Anheuser-Busch takes a dim view of wholesalers who decide to carry a competing product. When a Florida distributorship added Heineken and Amstel Light to its line, twenty-two Anheuser-Busch field managers swarmed in and rode the company's trucks for a week, and the distributor and his general manager were summoned to St. Louis for a meeting with top management.

Anheuser-Busch defends its policies, maintaining that the company will not allow "greedy" wholesalers to jeopardize market share. Although Anheuser-Busch has a lead over all other brewers, the company is taking no chances. It has enthusiastically entered and is actively pursuing its foreign markets, especially in Britain, where it is trying to establish an equally effective distribution system. Anheuser-Busch has launched several nonbeer beverages in recent years, including L.A. (a low-alcohol beer), Dewey Stevens (a low-calorie wine cooler aimed at women), and Zeltzer Seltzer (a flavored sparkling water). So far these products have not been marketed aggressively, and they may never be highly profitable. But with rival brewers entering these new markets, Anheuser-Busch wants to be able to supply its distributors with competing products. Along with its share of the market, say Anheuser-Busch executives, the company intends to maintain its share of wholesalers.

SOURCES: Anheuser-Busch Cos., Inc., *Annual Report, 1986;* Paul Hemp, "'King of Beers' in a Bitter Battle in Britain," *Wall Street Journal,* June 9, 1988, p. 26; Michael Oneal, "Anheuser-Busch: The Scandal May Be Small Beer After All," *Business Week,* May 11, 1987, pp. 72–73; and Patricia Sellers, "How Busch Wins in a Doggy Market," *Fortune,* June 22, 1987, pp. 99–100.

Questions for Discussion

1. Are Anheuser-Busch's wholesalers merchant wholesalers? Explain your answer. Are they full-service or limited-service wholesalers? Why?
2. Why does Anheuser-Busch give its wholesale distributors so much support?
3. Why has Anheuser-Busch introduced nonbeer products? Evaluate this practice.

11.2   Fleming Companies, Inc. Strives to Be Competitive

Fleming Companies, Inc., a food wholesaler based in Oklahoma City, services more than 5,200 food retailers in 37 states. It is now the industry leader in sales and is eager to retain this position. Fleming's annual $10.5 billion in sales makes it the largest food wholesaler in the United States, ahead of such staunch competitors as Minneapolis-based Super Valu Stores and Wetterau, located in Hazelwood, Missouri. As the wholesaling industry continues to consolidate and retailers demand more services from wholesalers, food wholesalers such as Fleming are forced to keep pace with these shifts.

Much of Fleming's growth in the past several years stems from its acquisition of other wholesale firms, a policy that has boosted its buying power, provided economies of scale, and allowed the company to spread fixed costs. With fewer than three hundred food wholesalers now remaining, Fleming is pursuing additional growth strategies to prepare for the day when acquisitions inevitably cease. Recently, Fleming acquired Malone & Hyde, a Memphis-based food wholesaler known for its innovative food distribution system. Fleming's CEO says that the firm will continue to acquire companies when there are mutual benefits for both Fleming and the company being bought.

Another of Fleming's growth strategies is to increase market share by offering a high degree of customer service. Fleming has long assisted its retail buyers with store planning and development, financial and insurance services, consumer services, printing, advertising, and other services—over one hundred services in all. Fleming was also one of the first wholesalers to electronically track the direct product profit of selected grocery items. Such information ultimately helps retailers determine which products are handled most economically. For years, too, Fleming has provided an extensive line of private labels, including IGA, Thriftway, and Piggly Wiggly, to give retailers a competitive tool against national brands. In addition, Fleming has established a Sales Training Institute to equip its sales and service representatives to meet retailers' needs more effectively. The institute covers such topics as electronic retail systems and retail counseling.

Fleming has always been a technological leader in the food wholesale industry. Soon, the company will introduce its computerized shelf tags in grocery stores. These tags provide the consumer with the price, size, and other information about a product and can be controlled by the retailer from a single control point, resulting in instantaneous price changes rather than the time-consuming manual method. Fleming is also experimenting with automatic ordering techniques that transfer inventory information directly from the check-out stand to a distribution center.

Through mechanization and computerization, Fleming plans to continue to improve its transportation, distribution, and warehouse systems. According to its top management, the company and the retailers already have unique market share positions in many of the leading cities throughout the United States. Fleming is striving to improve those market shares even more.

SOURCES: "Current Corporate Reports," *Barron's,* Feb. 13, 1989, p. 108; "Fleming Profit Declines 32%," *Supermarket News,* Feb. 13, 1989, p. 48; "Fleming Companies, Inc." *Wall Street Transcript,* Apr. 17, 1989, pp. 93,352–93,353, 93,359; and "Wholesaling," *Supermarket News,* Mar. 13, 1989, pp. 13–14, 16, 18, 20, 22–23.

Questions for Discussion

1. How would you classify Fleming as to the type of wholesaler?
2. In what ways is Fleming trying to gain an edge over its competitors?
3. What services is Fleming likely to be providing to producers?

12 RETAILING

Objectives

To understand the purpose and function of retailers in the marketing channel

To describe and distinguish major types of retailers

To understand nonstore retailing and franchising

To learn about strategic issues in retailing

The fourth largest retailer and the largest fashion-oriented store in the United States, J.C. Penney Co., experienced a long sales slump in the mid-1970s; it lasted until the early 1980s. Penney's management is turning the company around with a new strategy that emphasizes niche marketing, remodeling older, drab stores, and upgrading the retailer's image. The company wants consumers to associate J.C. Penney with stores such as Bloomingdale's and Macy's rather than K mart or Sears.

To begin the transformation, Penney's management eliminated the sporting goods, photography, and home electronics lines, as well as paint, hardware, and automotive supplies, from all stores. It has spent more than one billion dollars in store renovation and has allocated an additional one billion dollars for the early 1990s. Because J.C. Penney's catalog sales have been steadily growing, the company is enlarging its catalogs and expanding catalog services, such as twenty-four-hour order handling. At the same time, the company discontinued its Telaction subsidiary—an experimental home-shopping service. Finally, J.C. Penney moved its headquarters from Manhattan to Dallas and trimmed its headquarters staff.

J.C. Penney is trying to prove to consumers that its lower prices do not mean poor quality. The "new" J.C. Penney is designed to attract suburban, middle- to upper-middle-class shoppers (80 percent of J.C. Penney's stores are in malls) who appreciate a mixture of fashion and comfort in their apparel. Rather than pursue exclusive designer clothes, Penney executives have chosen to improve the company's more profitable private-label fashions while attracting popular national brands like Levi's and Bugle Boy jeans, Van Heusen, Joneswear, Maidenform, Henry Grethel, and others. Indeed, the company is now Levi's largest account. J.C. Penney is clearly a company that is trying new methods to make it more competitive and improve sales. ◆

Advertisement courtesy of J.C. Penney.

Based on information in Amy Dunkin and Brian Bremner, "The Newly Minted Penney: Where Fashion Rules," *Business Week*, Apr. 17, 1989, pp. 88–90; Thomas C. Hayes, "New Shine on a Tarnished Penney," *New York Times*, Apr. 23, 1989, p. F4; and Caroline E. Mayer, "Specialty Stores Get Special Push," *Washington Post*, Feb. 4, 1988, pp. E1, E3.

B y using effective marketing efforts, J.C. Penney is becoming successful again—repositioning itself as a major apparel retailer. Marketing methods that satisfy consumers serve well as the guiding philosophy of retailing. Retailers are an important link in the marketing channel because they are both marketers and customers for producers and wholesalers. They perform many marketing activities, such as buying, selling, grading, risk taking, and developing information about consumers' wants. Of all marketers, retailers are the most visible to ultimate consumers. They are in a strategic position to gain feedback from consumers and to relay ideas to producers and intermediaries in the marketing channel. Retailing is an extraordinarily dynamic area of marketing.

In this chapter we examine the nature of retailing and its importance in supplying consumers with goods and services. We discuss the major types of retail stores—department stores, mass merchandisers, and specialty retailers—and describe several forms of nonstore retailing, such as in-home retailing, telemarketing, automatic vending, and mail-order retailing. We also look at franchising, a retailing form that continues to grow in popularity. Finally, we present several strategic issues in retailing: location, product assortment, retail positioning, atmospherics, store image, scrambled merchandising, and the wheel of retailing.

THE NATURE OF RETAILING

Retailing includes all transactions in which the buyer intends to consume the product through personal, family, or household use. The buyers in retail transactions are ultimate consumers. A **retailer**, then, is an organization that purchases products for the purpose of reselling them to ultimate consumers. Although most retailers' sales are to consumers, nonretail transactions occasionally occur when retailers sell products to other businesses. Retailing activities usually take place in a store or in a service establishment, but exchanges through telephone selling, vending machines, and mail-order retailing occur outside stores.

It is fairly common knowledge that retailing is important to the national economy. There are approximately 1.33 million retailers operating in the United States.[1] This number has remained relatively constant for the past twenty years, but sales volume has increased more than fourfold, suggesting that the average size of stores has increased. Most personal income is spent in retail stores, and nearly one out of every seven persons employed in the United States works in a retail store.

By providing assortments of products that match consumers' wants, retailers create place, time, and possession utilities. *Place utility* is moving products from wholesalers or producers to a location where consumers want to buy them. *Time utility* involves the maintaining of specific business hours so that products are available when consumers want them. *Possession utility* means facilitating the transfer of ownership or use of a product to consumers.

In the case of services such as hair styling, dry cleaning, restaurants, and automotive repair, retailers themselves develop most of the product utilities. The services of such retailers provide aspects of form utility associated with the production process.

1. *Statistical Abstract of the United States, 1989,* p. 752.

Retailers of services usually have more direct contact with consumers and more opportunity to alter the product in the marketing mix.

The American retail markets are splintered, causing many retailers to create broad product offerings and target their products to many market segments. Consumers with different tastes, and with the ability and willingness to purchase, support a variety of retail establishments. In the following section we take a closer look at the major types of these establishments.

MAJOR TYPES OF RETAIL STORES

Retail stores seek to provide product mixes to match consumers' shopping preferences. These factors are important in classifying the stores according to three main types: department stores, mass merchandisers, and specialty retailers. However, there is generally much variation among stores of a particular type.

■ **Department Stores**

Department stores are large retail organizations employing at least twenty-five people and characterized by wide product mixes. To facilitate marketing efforts and internal management in these stores, related product lines are organized into separate departments, such as cosmetics, housewares, apparel, home furnishings, and appliances. Each department functions much as a self-contained business, and the buyers for individual departments are fairly autonomous.

Department stores are distinctly service oriented. Their total product includes credit, delivery, personal assistance, merchandise returns, and a pleasant atmosphere. Although some so-called department stores are actually large, departmentalized specialty stores, most department stores are shopping stores. That is, consumers compare price, quality, and service at one store with those at competing stores. Along with large discount stores, department stores are often considered the retailing leaders in a community and are found in most communities with populations of more than 25,000 people.

Typical department stores—Macy's, Marshall Field's, and Bloomingdale's (see Figure 12.1)—obtain a large proportion of their sales from apparel, accessories, and cosmetics. (Table 12.1 lists the top ten department store chains, ranked by sales volume.) Other products these stores carry include gift items, accessories, and luggage.

General merchandise department stores carry a larger number of product lines. To attract additional customers, many general merchandise department stores have recently added automotive, recreational, and sports equipment departments, as well as services such as insurance, hair care, travel advice, and income tax preparation. In some cases, space for these specialized services is leased out, with the proprietors managing their own operations and paying rent to the department stores.

Corporate chain department stores generate tremendous sales volume, which gives them considerable control over a wide range of the products they sell. J.C. Penney, Sears, and Montgomery Ward, for example, have many more store units and far greater sales volume than certain conventional department store units that usually operate regionally. Sears has been very successful in both integrating marketing activities and owning or controlling production. Consumers' loyalty and trusted private store brands make Sears extremely powerful in channel leadership

FIGURE 12.1

Department store. Bloomingdale's relies heavily on the sales of apparel, accessories, and cosmetics.

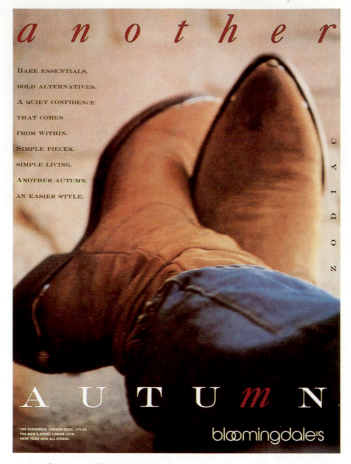

SOURCE: Courtesy of Bloomingdale's

and competitive status. Chain stores have high name recognition and advertise through many forms of media.

Although corporate chain department stores are relatively strong, many other types of department stores have encountered problems in recent years. Their overhead and operating expenses (about 35 percent of sales) are higher than those of most other retailers, partly because of the variety of services they offer. Besides, population growth is now centered in the suburbs; to stay close to their customers, many department stores have opened branch stores in outlying shopping centers and malls. Furthermore, department stores face competition from a growing number of specialty and discount retailers that cater to specific market segments.

In answer to these challenges, downtown department stores are often taking the lead in urban redevelopment projects designed to stimulate downtown business activity. Offering broad product assortments, the stores are working to attract not only tourists and downtown office workers, but also lower-income groups that live near central business districts. Suburban department stores are targeting market segments, trimming their overall product mixes, displaying merchandise in boutique settings, and sometimes expanding their budget-priced lines to ease the competitive

TABLE 12.1
*Top ten U.S. depart-
ment stores, ranked
by sales*

RANK	DEPARTMENT STORE	ANNUAL SALES (millions)
1	May Department Stores Co.	$11,525
2	R. H. Macy & Co., Inc.	3,902
3	Dillard	2,558
4	Nordstrom's	2,328
5	Mercantile	2,266
6	Carter Hawley Hale Stores, Inc.	1,567
7	Carson Pirie Scott	1,023
8	Strawbridge & Clothier	904
9	Neiman Marcus Group	781
10	Jacobson's	357

SOURCE: Reprinted by permission from *Chain Store Age Executive,* May 1989. Copyright Lebhar-Friedman, Inc., 425 Park Avenue, New York, N.Y. 10022.

pressure from specialty and discount stores. To attract and hold customers, some department stores are adding, rather than reducing, services. Macy's and Neiman Marcus, for example, offer personal shopping services to interested customers.[2]

Mass Merchandisers

Mass merchandisers are retailers that generally offer fewer customer services than department stores and emphasize lower prices, high turnover, and large sales volumes. They usually have a wider—and sometimes shallower—product mix than department stores. They are less likely than department stores to reorder sold-out sizes and styles. Mass merchandising operations are characterized by one-story, low-cost facilities; self-serve shopping; central check-out counters; and multiple purchases.[3] They appeal to large heterogeneous target markets, especially price-conscious consumers. With their relatively low operating costs, mass merchandisers project an image of efficiency and economy. These operations include discount stores, supermarkets, superstores, hypermarkets, warehouse/wholesale clubs, and warehouse and catalog showrooms.

Discount Stores. **Discount stores** are self-service, general merchandise outlets that regularly offer brand-name merchandise at low prices. Discounters accept lower margins than conventional retailers in exchange for high sales volume. To keep turnover high, they carry a wide but carefully selected assortment of products, from appliances to housewares and clothing. Major discount establishments also offer toys, automotive services, garden supplies, and sports equipment. Often a food supermarket is operated as a department within a discount store. Table 12.2 lists the top ten discount stores in the United States. Many of the discounters, such as Wal-Mart, are regional organizations. Most operate in large (fifty thousand to eighty thousand square feet) no-frills facilities, often in low-rent areas.

2. Leonard L. Berry and Larry G. Gresham, "Relationship Retailing: Transforming Customers into Clients," *Business Horizons,* November-December 1986, pp. 44–45.

3. J. Barry Mason and Morris L. Mayer, *Modern Retailing: Theory and Practice* (Plano, Texas: Business Publications, 1987), pp. 59–60.

TABLE 12.2
Top ten discount stores (ranked by retail sales)

RANK	CHAIN	ESTIMATED ANNUAL SALES (millions)
1	K mart Corporation	$27,299
2	Wal-Mart Stores, Inc.	20,649
3	Target Stores	6,300
4	Ames Department Stores	5,500
5	Bradlees	2,100
6	Meijer Thrifty Acres	2,100
7	Hills Department Stores	1,600
8	Marshall's, Inc.	1,600
9	Caldor	1,574
10	Rose's	1,439

SOURCE: "The Top 60 Companies in Sales," *Discount Merchandiser,* June 1989, pp. 44–45. Reprinted by permission.

Discount retailing developed on a large scale in the early 1950s, when postwar production began to catch up with consumer demand for appliances, home furnishings, and other hard goods. Discount stores in those days were often cash-only operations in warehouse districts, offering goods at savings of 20 to 30 percent over conventional retailers. Through the years, facing increased competition from department stores and other discount stores, discounters generally have improved store services, atmosphere, and location, raising prices and sometimes blurring the distinction between discount houses and department stores. Other discounters continue to focus on price alone. For example, Toys "R" Us, the nation's leading toy retailer, has long relied on a policy of using supermarket-style stores selling huge selections of toys at cut-rate prices.[4] Generally, however, many better-known discount houses have assumed the characteristics of department stores. As discounters upgrade their merchandise and facilities and provide more customer services, their risks and operating expenses increase. In recent years, rising costs have forced several discount chains to close because they could no longer price competitively.

Supermarkets.   **Supermarkets** are large, self-service stores that carry a complete line of food products, as well as some nonfood products, such as cosmetics and nonprescription drugs. A supermarket has minimum annual sales of $2 million, according to the Food Marketing Institute. Supermarkets are arranged in departments for maximum efficiency in stocking and handling products, but have central check-out facilities. They offer lower prices than smaller neighborhood grocery stores, and they usually provide free parking and may cash checks. They may be independently owned but more often are part of a chain operation. Table 12.3 lists the top ten supermarket chains.

Supermarkets, the first mass merchandisers, originated more than fifty years ago, when most food retailers were still small, limited-line organizations. Responding to

4. Amy Dunkin, with Keith H. Hammonds and Mark Maremont, "Now Toys 'R' Us Controls the Game Board," *Business Week,* Dec. 19, 1988, pp. 58–60.

TABLE 12.3

Top ten supermarket chains (ranked by sales volume)

RANK	COMPANY	ANNUAL SALES (millions)
1	Kroger Co.	$19,050
2	American Stores Co.	18,478
3	A & P, Inc.	10,068
4	Albertson's, Inc.	6,773
5	Winn-Dixie Stores, Inc.	4,800
6	Vons	3,917
7	Giant Food	2,987
8	Mott's	2,872
9	Nash Finch	2,097
10	Hannaforrd Bros.	1,261

SOURCE: Reprinted by permission from *Chain Store Age Executive,* May 1989. Copyright Lebhar-Friedman, Inc., 425 Park Avenue, New York, N.Y. 10022.

competitive pressures from chain food stores, certain independent food retailers began combining broad assortments of food products with low-price, self-service operations. Three factors made the high-volume experiment a success: the price-consciousness of Depression-era consumers; improved packaging and refrigeration technologies; and the widespread use of automobiles, which enabled the stores to attract many customers who formerly had patronized neighborhood stores. Within a few years, the supermarket became the dominant form of food retailing.

Today consumers make more than three-quarters of all their grocery purchases in the 37,000 supermarkets currently in operation. Even so, the supermarkets' total share of the food market is declining because consumers now have widely varying food preferences and buying habits, and in most communities they can choose from among a number of convenience stores, discount stores, and specialty food stores, as well as a wide variety of restaurants.

To remain competitive, some supermarkets are cutting back services, emphasizing low prices, and using promotion methods such as games or coupons. Other super-markets have converted to discount or warehouse retailing or both. Still other supermarkets have taken the opposite approach, dramatically expanding both services and product mixes. For example, at Gromer's Super Market in Elgin, Illinois, customers can use the post office, pay utility bills, buy lottery tickets, get documents notarized or photocopied, have film processed, pick up license plates and transfer auto titles, cash checks or use an ATM machine, rent rug-cleaning machines, and even get fingerprinted. The Superquinn supermarket chain in Ireland conducts regular focus group sessions with customers to find out what goods and services they want (and do not want).[5] About 60 percent of all supermarkets have service delis; many also offer floral departments, pharmacies, and photo-finishing services.[6]

Supermarkets are also trying to increase their efficiency and competitiveness with technological changes. Many supermarkets have replaced the cash registers at their check-out counters with electronic scanners, which identify and record purchases

5. "Service Equals Success in Supermarkets," *Marketing Communications,* April 1989, pp. 24–25, 31.

6. Ruth Hamel, "Food Fight," *American Demographics,* March 1989, pp. 36–39, 60.

via bar codes on each product. These detailed sales data let management maintain inventories on each item, identify buying patterns, and improve store and shelf layouts.[7] Regardless of the technology used, supermarkets must be operated efficiently because net profits after taxes are usually less than 1 percent of sales.

Superstores. **Superstores**—which originated in Europe but are fairly new to U.S. markets—are giant retail outlets that carry not only all food and nonfood products ordinarily found in supermarkets, but also many consumer products that are purchased routinely. In addition to a complete food line, superstores sell housewares, hardware, small appliances, clothing, personal-care products, garden products, and tires—in all, about four times as many items as supermarkets. Services available at superstores include laundry and dry cleaning, automotive repair, check cashing, bill paying, and snack bars.

Superstores combine features of discount houses and supermarkets. To cut handling and inventory costs, they use sophisticated operating techniques and often tall, visible shelving to display entire assortments of products. Most superstores have an area of about forty thousand square feet (compared with twenty thousand square feet in supermarkets), although some are as large as a hundred thousand square feet. Their sales volume is two to three times that of supermarkets, partly because they locate near good transportation networks that help generate the in-store traffic needed for profitability.

Consumers are most attracted to superstores by the lower prices and the one-stop shopping feature. Consequently, other food retailers, too, have started handling general merchandise because gross margin and net profit are higher on those items than on food items. Several supermarket chains, including Safeway and Kroger, have added supersized units or enlarged existing stores and product mixes. But superstores require large investments, stringent cost controls, appropriate facilities, and managers who can coordinate broad product assortments. Conventional supermarkets, hampered by economic uncertainty and lack of space for physical expansion, find it difficult to compete effectively with superstores.

Hypermarkets. **Hypermarkets** combine supermarket and discount store shopping into one location. Larger even than superstores, they measure an average of 225,000 square feet and offer 45,000 to 60,000 different types of products at low prices. They commonly allocate 40 to 50 percent of their selling space to grocery products and the remainder to general merchandise, including athletic shoes, designer jeans, and other apparel; refrigerators, televisions, and other appliances; housewares; cameras; toys; jewelry; hardware; and automotive supplies (see Figure 12.2).[8] Many lease space to noncompeting businesses such as banks, optical shops, and fast-food restaurants. Because they offer so many diverse products in one location, hypermarkets have been referred to as "malls without walls."[9] Wal-Mart and Cullum Cos. jointly operate several Hypermart USAs; other hypermarkets in the United States include Carrefour and Bigg's (a partnership between Euromarché and wholesaler Super Valu). All focus on low prices and vast selections of goods.

7. Mason and Mayer, p. 181.

8. David Rodgers, "Hypermarkets Need 'Something Special' to Succeed," *Supermarket Business,* May 1988, pp. 25–26, 158.

9. Priscilla Donegan, "Hypermarkets: Is America Ready?" *Progressive Grocer,* July 1988, pp. 21–34.

FIGURE 12.2

A hypermarket.
Wal-Mart's Hypermart USA, like other hyper- markets, makes an extensive variety of products available to customers through a vast retail facility.

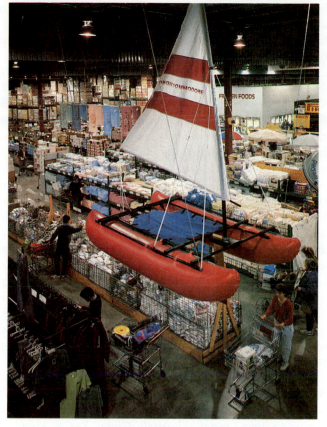

SOURCE: Sam's Wholesale Club, a Division of Wal-Mart Stores, Inc.

Although a popular retailing trend, hypermarkets are not new. The concept began in France after World War II. French-owned Carrefour successfully operates more than a hundred hypermarkets in France, Spain, and South America. The hypermar- ket concept was first introduced in the United States in the 1970s by the Oshawa Group and Fed Mart, but was abandoned largely because sales of general merchan- dise were slow, resulting in low overall margins for the stores, even though grocery products sold well. Analysts believe that today's hypermarkets face possible failure for the same reasons.[10] Nonetheless, Hypermart USA, Carrefour, and Bigg's all have plans to add new hypermarkets; Super Valu, K mart, Auchan (a French retailer), and other retailers also plan to develop their own hypermarkets.[11]

Warehouse/Wholesale Clubs. The **warehouse/wholesale club** is the newest form of mass merchandising—a large-scale, members-only selling operation that combines cash-and-carry wholesaling features with discount retailing. Small busi- ness owners account for about 60 percent of a typical warehouse club's sales. (Thus a warehouse/wholesale club could be viewed as a wholesaler.) For a nominal annual fee (usually about $25), small retailers may purchase products at wholesale prices for

10. Donegan, pp. 23–24.

11. Bill Saporito, "Retailers Fly into Hyperspace," *Fortune*, Oct. 24, 1988, pp. 148–152.

business use or for resale. Warehouse clubs also sell to ultimate consumers who are affiliated with government agencies, credit unions, schools, hospitals, and banks, but instead of paying a membership fee, individual consumers pay about 5 percent more on each item than do retailers.

Sometimes called buying clubs, warehouse clubs offer the same types of products as discount stores but in a limited range of sizes and styles. Whereas most discount stores carry forty thousand items, a warehouse club handles only four thousand to five thousand different products, usually acknowledged brand leaders.[12] But because their product lines are shallow and sales volumes high, warehouse clubs can offer a broad range of merchandise, including nonperishable foods, beverages, books, appliances, housewares, automotive parts, hardware, furniture, and sundries.

To keep their prices 20 to 40 percent lower than those of supermarkets and discount stores, warehouse clubs provide few services. They generally do not advertise, except through direct mail. Their facilities are often located in industrial parks and have concrete floors and aisles wide enough for fork lifts. Merchandise is stacked on pallets or displayed on pipe racks. All payments must be in cash, and customers must transport purchases themselves.

Still, warehouse clubs appeal to many price-conscious consumers and small retailers who may be unable to obtain wholesaling services from larger distributors. The sales volume of most warehouse clubs is four to five times that of a typical department store. With stock turning over at the average rate of eighteen times a year, warehouse clubs sell their goods before manufacturers' payment periods are up, virtually eliminating the need for capital.[13]

The warehouse club concept, which is expected to spread widely during the next few years, was pioneered in the United States in the late 1970s by Price Company, which has annual sales of $110 million per warehouse club.[14] Other warehouse club chains include Costco Wholesale Clubs, PACE Membership Warehouses, Sam's Wholesale Clubs (owned by Wal-Mart Stores), and BJ's Warehouse Club (owned by Zayre Corporation). As competition increases, the clubs may begin to offer more services. The Price Club, for example, tested an in-store pharmacy, optical department, and gas station in its San Diego store.[15]

Warehouse and Catalog Showrooms.   The **warehouse showroom** is a retail facility with five basic characteristics: (1) large, low-cost building, (2) use of warehouse materials handling technology, (3) use of vertical merchandise display space, (4) a large on-premises inventory, and (5) minimum services.

Although some superstores, hypermarkets, and discount supermarkets have used warehouse retailing, most of the best-known showrooms are operated by large furniture retailers. Wickes Furniture and Levitz Furniture Corporation brought sophisticated mass merchandising to the highly fragmented furniture industry. These high-volume, low-overhead operations stress less personnel and services. Lower costs are possible because some marketing functions have been shifted to consumers, who must transport, finance, and perhaps store merchandise. Most consumers carry away their purchases in the manufacturer's carton, although the stores will deliver for a fee.

12. Mason and Mayer, pp. 65-66.

13. Mason and Mayer, p. 66.

14. Andrew Kupfer, "The Final Word in No-Frills Shopping?" *Fortune,* Mar. 13, 1989, p. 30.

15. Jay L. Johnson, "Keeping Up with the Wholesale Clubs," *DM,* July 1987, p. 78.

In the **catalog showroom**, one item of each product is on display, often in a locked case, and remaining inventory is stored out of the buyer's reach. Using catalogs that have been mailed to their homes or are on counters in the store, customers order products by phone or in person. Clerks fill the orders from the warehouse area, and products are presented in the manufacturer's carton. In contrast to traditional catalog retailers, which offer no discounts and require that customers wait for delivery, catalog showrooms regularly sell below list price and often provide goods immediately.

Catalog showrooms usually sell jewelry, luggage, photographic equipment, toys, small appliances and housewares, sporting goods, and power tools. They advertise extensively and carry established brands and models that are not likely to be discontinued. Because catalog showrooms have higher product turnover, fewer losses through shoplifting, and lower labor costs than department stores, they are able to feature lower prices. They offer minimal services, however. Customers may have to stand in line to examine items or place orders. Still, such showrooms appear to be one of the fastest-growing areas of retailing, despite competition from discounters and wholesale clubs. Service Merchandise, Best Products, and Consumer Distributing are three of the largest catalog showroom retailers.

■ Specialty Retailers

In contrast to department stores and mass merchandisers, which offer broad product mixes, specialty retailers emphasize the narrowness and depth of their product lines. Despite their name, specialty retailers do not sell specialty items (except when the specialty goods complement the overall product mix). Instead, these retailers offer substantial assortments in a few product lines. In this section we examine two types of specialty stores: traditional specialty retailers and off-price retailers.

Traditional Specialty Retailers.   **Traditional specialty retailers** are stores carrying a narrow product mix with deep product lines. They are sometimes called limited-line retailers; if they carry unusual depth in one main product category, they may be referred to as single-line retailers.

Shopping goods such as apparel, jewelry, sporting goods, art supplies, fabrics, computers, and pet supplies are commonly sold through specialty retailers. For example, The Foot Locker, owned by Kinney Shoe Corp., specializes in a product mix of various types of athletic footwear. The Limited, Radio Shack, Hickory Farms, and The Gap (see Figure 12.3) are other retailers that offer limited product lines but great depth within those lines.

Although the number of chain specialty stores is increasing, most specialty stores are independently owned. Specialty stores occupy about two-thirds of the space in most shopping centers and malls and account for 40 to 50 percent of all general merchandise sales.[16] Florists, bakery shops, and bookstores are among the small, independent specialty retailers that appeal to local target markets, although these stores can, of course, be owned and managed by large corporations. Even if this kind of retailer adds a few supporting product lines, the store may still be classified as a specialty store.

Because they are usually small, specialty stores may have high costs in proportion to sales, and to satisfy customers they may have to carry some products with low turnover rates. On the other hand, these stores sometimes obtain lower prices from

16. Barry Berman and Joel Evans, *Retail Management: A Strategic Approach* (New York: Macmillan, 1986), p. 99.

SOURCE: Courtesy of The GAP

suppliers because they buy limited lines of merchandise in large quantities. Successful specialty stores understand their customer types and know what products to carry, thus reducing the risk of unsold merchandise. Marketing Update 12.1 discusses how Pier 1 has changed its product assortments and locations to better satisfy customers. Specialty stores usually offer better selections and more sales expertise than department stores, their main competitors. By capitalizing on fashion, service, personnel, atmosphere, and location, specialty retailers can position themselves strategically to attract customers in specific market segments. They may even become exclusive dealers in their markets for certain products. Through specialty stores, small business owners can provide unique services to match consumers' varied desires. For consumers dissatisfied with the impersonal nature of large retailers, the close, personal contact offered by a small specialty store can be a welcome change.

Off-Price Retailers.   **Off-price retailers** are stores that buy manufacturers' seconds, overruns, returns, and off-season production runs at below-wholesale prices for resale to consumers at deep discounts. Unlike true discount stores, which pay regular wholesale prices for their goods and usually carry second-line brand names, off-price retailers offer limited lines of national-brand and designer merchandise, usually clothing, shoes, or housewares. The number of off-price retailers has grown rapidly since the mid-1980s and now includes such major chains as T. J. Maxx and

PIER 1 IMPORTS CHANGES TO BE COMPETITIVE

Pier 1 Imports, Inc., which is based in Fort Worth, Texas, blossomed along with the flower children of the 1960s, selling incense, candles, beads, and other hippie paraphernalia. But Pier 1's reputation and sales figures dipped as the flower children matured into a status-minded generation of yuppies. Pier 1 made adjustments and now is focusing on several target markets. Pier 1 has more than 460 stores in 38 states and Canada, and the number is rising.

Pier 1 proudly calls itself the largest and fastest-growing specialty home furnishings and accessories store in North America. The "far-out" furnishings of past decades have been replaced by the casual trappings popular among today's young, college-educated professionals. According to a Pier 1 survey, these shoppers desire a home whose decor reflects their personalities and tastes. Pier 1 tries to provide them that opportunity. Pier 1 spent more than $1 million on marketing research to determine what its customers wanted from a store. It found that they craved convenient locations, fast check-outs, the opportunity to browse undisturbed, and product quality.

During the past several years, Pier 1 executives have closed sixty stores in what they consider bad locations, opened seventy stores in upscale areas, and refurbished 90 percent of the remaining stores. Realizing that the stores located in enclosed malls would never meet company sales expectations, Pier 1 management decided to close them. It will consider malls as possible sites only if they provide customers with easy access, so that customers will find it simple to load bulky merchandise.

Pier 1's nine buyers, who scan village markets, factories, and trade fairs, travel to more than sixty-five countries to purchase goods for the stores. Pier 1 has had manufacturing ties to many of these foreign countries for years, and these relationships help give the retailer clout in attempting to keep prices low. Buyers bring in chairs from Asia, pottery from Mexico, and loose cotton garments from India. All these goods are processed by one of Pier 1's computerized distribution centers.

The company's marketing officials have made a great effort to overhaul the advertising department as well, by replacing black-and-white newspaper advertisements with flashy color ones. Pier 1 management sees current advertising expenditures as a long-term investment.

SOURCES: James Dimeo, "Firm Hopes New Approach Will Succeed," *Dallas Times Herald,* Apr. 6, 1989, p. D4; "Inside Warehousing and Distribution," *Transportation & Distribution,* March 1988, pp. 61–62, 64; Stephen Madden, "Frequent Buyer," *Fortune,* Dec. 5, 1988, pp. 215–216; William Mehlman, "Pier 1 Imports, Inc.," *The Insider's Chronicle,* Mar. 7, 1988, p. 3; Kristen Moulton, "Faraway Lands, Ocean Passage and the Bottom Line," *Fort Worth (Texas) Star Telegram,* Jan. 3, 1989, p. G2; Ariane Sains, "Pier 1's Ship Has Finally Come In as Baby Boomers Mature," *Adweek's Marketing Week,* Jan. 9, 1989, pp. 43–44; and "Yuppies *Do* Have Feelings, Says Pier 1 Study," *Chain Store Age Executive,* May 1988, pp. 32, 36.

Marshall's. Marshall's, largest off-price retailer in the United States in terms of sales, has 317 stores and plans to open 200 more by 1994; T. J. Maxx has 328 stores and plans to open 45 more per year.[17]

Off-price stores charge 20 to 50 percent less than department stores for comparable merchandise but offer few customer services. They often feature community dressing rooms, central check-out counters, and no credit, returns, or exchanges. Off-price stores may or may not sell goods with original labels intact (Filene's Basement Stores do, Loehmann's outlets do not). They turn over their inventory nine to twelve times a year, three times as often as traditional specialty stores. They compete with department stores for the same customers: price-conscious members of suburban households who are knowledgeable about brand names.

To ensure a regular flow of merchandise into their stores, off-price retailers must establish long-term relationships with suppliers who can provide large quantities of goods at reduced prices. Manufacturers may approach the retailers with samples, discontinued products, or items that have not sold well; or the retailers may seek out producers, offering to pay cash for goods produced during the manufacturers' off-season. Although manufacturers benefit from such arrangements, they also risk alienating their specialty and department store customers.[18] Department stores tolerate off-price stores as long as they do not advertise brand names, limit their merchandise to lower-quality items, and are located away from the department stores. But when off-price retailers are able to obtain large stocks of in-season, top-quality merchandise—as many do—tension builds between department stores and manufacturers. In fact, some department stores, including Neiman Marcus and Woodward & Lothrop, are opening separate stores for selling their marked-down goods, in direct competition with the off-price retailers.[19]

Still, off-price retailing is expected to keep growing. In more and more communities, manufacturer-owned factory outlets and off-price stores have grouped together in off-price malls and shopping districts. Combined, these two forms of discount retailers now account for 13 percent of all retail sales.[20]

Nonstore Retailing and Direct Marketing

Nonstore retailing is the selling of goods or services outside the confines of a retail facility. This form of retailing accounts for an increasing percentage of sales and includes personal sales methods, such as in-home retailing and telemarketing, and nonpersonal sales methods, such as automatic vending and mail-order retailing (which includes catalog retailing).

Certain nonstore retailing methods are in the category of **direct marketing**: the use of nonpersonal media to introduce products to consumers, who then purchase the products by mail or telephone. In the case of telephone orders, salespersons may be required to complete the sales. Telemarketing and mail-order and catalog retail-

17. Judith Graham, "Marshall's, T. J. Maxx Duel over Off-Price Leadership," *Advertising Age,* June 26, 1989, p. 3.

18. Berman and Evans, p. 99.

19. Teri Agins, "Upscale Retailers Head to Enemy Turf," *Wall Street Journal,* Aug. 25, 1989, p. B1.

20. "Now It's Chic to Shop Cheap," *U.S. News & World Report,* Sept. 22, 1986, pp. 70–71.

ing are all examples of direct marketing, as are sales generated by coupons, direct mail, and toll-free 800 numbers.

In-Home Retailing

In-home retailing is selling via personal contacts with consumers in their own homes. Organizations such as Avon, Electrolux, and Fuller Brush Company send representatives to the homes of preselected prospects. Merchandise such as *World Book Encyclopedia,* Kirby vacuum cleaners, Amway products, and Mary Kay cosmetics are also sold to consumers in their homes.

Traditionally, in-home retailing relied on a random door-to-door approach. Some companies (such as World Book and Kirby, both divisions of Scott & Fetzer Co.) now use a more efficient approach. They first identify prospects by reaching them by phone or mail or intercepting them in shopping malls or at consumer trade fairs. These initial contacts are limited to a brief introduction and the setting of appointments. Several large retailers, such as J. C. Penney, offer in-home decorating services. Consumers find in-home selling of rugs, draperies, and home improvements helpful because these products must be coordinated with existing home interiors.

Some in-home selling, however, is still undertaken without information about sales prospects. Door-to-door selling without a prearranged appointment is a tiny proportion of total retail sales, probably less than 1 percent. Because it has so often been associated with unscrupulous and fraudulent techniques, door-to-door selling is illegal in some communities. Generally, this technique is regarded unfavorably because so many door-to-door salespersons are undertrained and poorly supervised. A big disadvantage of door-to-door selling is the large expenditure, effort, and time it demands. Sales commissions are usually 25 to 50 percent (or more) of the retail price; as a result, consumers often pay more than a product is worth. Door-to-door selling is used most often when a product is unsought—for instance, encyclopedias, which most consumers would not be likely to purchase in a store.

A variation of in-home retailing is the home demonstration or party plan, which such companies as Tupperware, Stanley Home Products, and Mary Kay Cosmetics use successfully. One consumer acts as host and invites a number of friends to view merchandise at his or her home, where a salesperson is on hand to demonstrate the products. The home demonstration is more efficient for the sales representative than contacting each prospect door-to-door, and the congenial atmosphere partly overcomes consumers' suspicions and encourages them to buy. Home demonstrations also meet the buyers' needs for convenience and personal service. Commissions and selling costs make this form of retailing expensive, however. Additionally, successful party-plan selling requires both a network of friends and neighbors who have the time to attend such social gatherings and a large number of effective salespersons. With so many household members now holding full-time jobs, both prospects and sales representatives are harder to recruit. The growth of interactive telephone-computer home shopping may also cut into party-plan sales.

Telemarketing

More and more organizations—IBM, Merrill Lynch, Allstate, Avis, Ford, Quaker Oats, Time, and American Express, to name a few—are using the telephone to strengthen the effectiveness of traditional marketing methods. **Telemarketing** is direct selling of goods and services by telephone based on either a cold canvass of the telephone directory or a prescreened list of prospective clients. (In some areas, certain telephone numbers are listed with an asterisk to indicate the people who consider sales solicitations a nuisance and do not want to be bothered.) Telemarketing can generate sales leads, improve customer service, speed up collection of past-due accounts, raise funds for nonprofit groups, and gather market data.[21]

In some cases, telemarketing uses advertising that encourages consumers to initiate a call or to request information about placing an order. This type of retailing is only a small part of total retail sales, but its use is growing. According to AT&T, U.S. companies spent $13.6 billion in one year on telemarketing phone calls and equipment (phones, lines, and computers). Telephone Marketing Resources estimates telephone sales of goods and services at $75 billion annually (the figure includes business-to-consumer sales and business-to-business sales).[22] Research indicates that telemarketing is most successful when combined with other marketing strategies, such as direct mail or advertising in newspapers, radio, and television.

■ Automatic Vending

Automatic vending makes use of machines and accounts for less than 2 percent of all retail sales. Approximately six million vending units generate about $21 billion in retail sales annually. Vending machine locations and the percentage of sales each generates are as follows:[23]

Plants and factories	38%
Public locations (e.g., stores)	26%
Offices	16%
Colleges and universities	6%
Government facilities	3%
Hospitals and nursing homes	3%
Primary and secondary schools	2%
Others	6%

Video game machines provide an entertainment service, and many banks now offer machines that dispense cash or offer other services, but these uses of vending machines are not reported in total vending sales volume.

Automatic vending is one of the most impersonal forms of retailing. Small, standardized, routinely purchased products (chewing gum, candy, newspapers, cigarettes, soft drinks, coffee) can be sold in machines because consumers usually buy them at the nearest available location. Machines in areas of heavy traffic provide efficient and continuous services to consumers. The elimination of sales personnel and the small amount of space necessary for vending machines give this retailing method some advantages over stores. The advantages are partly offset by the expense of the frequent servicing and repair needed.

■ Mail-Order Retailing

Mail-order retailing involves selling by description because buyers usually do not see the actual product until it arrives in the mail. Sellers contact buyers through direct mail, catalogs, television, radio, magazines, and newspapers. A wide assortment of products such as compact discs, books, and clothing is sold to consumers through the mail. Placing mail orders by telephone is increasingly common. The advantages of mail-order selling include efficiency and convenience. Mail-order houses, such as Lillian Vernon and L. L. Bean, can be located in remote, low-cost areas and forgo the expenses of store fixtures. Eliminating personal selling efforts

21. Kenneth C. Schneider, "Telemarketing as a Promotional Tool—Its Effects and Side Effects," *Journal of Consumer Marketing*, Winter 1985, pp. 29–39.

22. Joel Dreyfuss, "Reach Out and Sell Something," *Fortune*, November 26, 1984, pp. 127–128.

23. "V/T Census of the Industry Issue—1988," *Vending Times*, 1988, p. 49. Reprinted by permission.

FIGURE 12.4

Catalog retailing.
Spiegel, one of the oldest and largest catalog retailers, provides an extensive product mix to its customers.

Christmas Gifts.
Now Available At The Beach.

You may never have imagined doing your holiday shopping while the waves washed over the shoreline, but thanks to Spiegel its possible. Our 400 page Christmas Book features gift ideas from Ralph Lauren, Sony, Braun, Adrienne Vittadini, Gund and others. To receive your copy for only $3, simply call 1-800-345-4500 and ask for catalog 984.

Spiegel

SOURCE: Agency: McConnaughy Barocci Brown; Creative Director: Tom McConnaughy; Photographer: Howard Bjornson; Copywriter: Jim Schmidt; Client: Spiegel, Inc.

and store operations may result in tremendous savings that can be passed along to consumers in the form of lower prices. On the other hand, mail-order retailing is inflexible, provides limited service, and is more appropriate for specialty products than for convenience products.

When **catalog retailing** (a specific type of mail-order retailing) is used, customers receive their orders by mail (see Figure 12.4), or they may pick them up if the catalog retailer has stores, as do Montogomery Ward and Sears. Although in-store visits result in some catalog orders, most are placed by mail or telephone. General Foods created Thomas Garroway, Ltd., a mail-order service providing gourmet pasta, cheese, coffee, and similar items. Other packaged-goods manufacturers involved in catalog retailing include Hanes, Nestlé, Thomas J. Lipton, Sunkist, and Whitman Chocolates.[24] These catalog retailers are able to reach many two-income families who have more money and less time for special shopping. There are about six thousand catalogs in circulation, and catalog sales have been growing rapidly. Industry estimates place direct mail retail sales at $77 billion in 1988. Retail mail-order purchases amounted to $314 per person in 1988, up from $135 in 1981.[25]

24. Ronald Alsop, "Food Giants Take to Mails to Push Fancy Product Lines," *Wall Street Journal*, Feb. 28, 1985, p. 85.

25. "Mail Order Top 250+," *Direct Marketing*, July 1989, pp. 20–24.

FRANCHISING

Franchising is an arrangement whereby a supplier, or franchisor, grants a dealer, or franchisee, the right to sell products in exchange for some type of consideration. For example, the franchisor may receive some percentage of total sales in exchange for furnishing equipment, buildings, management know-how, and marketing assistance to the franchisee. The franchisee supplies labor and capital, operates the franchised business, and agrees to abide by the provisions of the franchise agreement. In the next section we look at the major types of retail franchises, the advantages and disadvantages of franchising, and trends in retailing.

■ Major Types of Retail Franchises

Retail franchise arrangements can generally be classified as one of three general types. In the first arrangement, a manufacturer authorizes a number of retail stores to sell a certain brand-name item. This franchise arrangement, one of the oldest, is common in the sales of passenger cars and trucks, farm equipment, shoes, paint, earth-moving equipment, and petroleum. About 90 percent of all gasoline is sold through franchised independent retail service stations, and franchised dealers handle virtually all sales of new cars and trucks. The second type of retail franchise occurs when a producer licenses distributors to sell a given product to retailers. This franchising arrangement is common in the soft-drink industry. Most national manufacturers of soft-drink syrups—Coca-Cola, Dr Pepper, Pepsi-Cola—franchise independent bottlers, which then serve retailers. In the third type of retail franchise, a franchisor supplies brand names, techniques, or other services, instead of a complete product. The franchisor may provide certain production and distribution services, but its primary role in the arrangement is the careful development and control of marketing strategies. This approach to franchising, which is the most typical today, is used by many organizations, including Holiday Inn, AAMCO, McDonald's, Dairy Queen, Avis, Hertz, Kentucky Fried Chicken, and H&R Block.

■ Advantages and Disadvantages of Franchising

Franchising offers several advantages to both the franchisee and the franchisor. It enables a franchisee to start a business with limited capital and to make use of the business experience of others. (The advertisement in Figure 12.5 focuses on some of the advantages provided by a Midas franchise). Moreover, an outlet with a nationally advertised name, such as Midas or Burger King, is often assured of customers as soon as it opens. If business problems arise, the franchisee can obtain guidance and advice from the franchisor at little or no cost. Franchised outlets are generally more successful than independently owned businesses: Only 5 to 8 percent of franchised retail businesses fail during the first two years of operation, whereas approximately 54 percent of independent retail businesses fail during that period.[26] The franchisee also receives materials to use in local advertising and can take part in national promotional campaigns sponsored by the franchisor.

The franchisor gains fast and selective distribution of its products through franchise arrangements without incurring the high cost of constructing and operating its own outlets. The franchisor therefore has more capital available to expand production and to use for advertising. At the same time, it can ensure, through the franchise agreement, that outlets are maintained and operated by its own standards. The franchisor also benefits from the fact that the franchisee, being a sole proprietor in

26. Al Urbanski, "The Franchise Option," *Sales & Marketing Management*, February 1988, pp. 28–33.

FIGURE 12.5
A franchise opportunity. Midas promotes the advantages and the availability of Midas franchises.

Golden opportunities are revealed every day.

Franchise opportunities from Midas come in lots of different guises. And just what's available on any given day may change tomorrow.

From time to time there are availabilities in America's urban areas. And there's always a wealth of opportunities in rural communities. Maybe there's a new Midas Muffler & Brake Shop already under construction that could have your name on it. Or, if you already own a repair shop, possibly you can convert it to Midas.

The opportunities are boundless, but they all lead to one result. As a Midas franchisee, you receive all the benefits of joining the industry leader.

Give us a call or write today; tell us where your interests lie. We'll provide you with more information about the possibilities today and in the future.

When it comes to opportunities for franchisees, nobody beats Midas.

1-800-327-0224

Richard C. Pope
National Director
Franchise Development
Midas International Corporation
225 N. Michigan Ave.
Chicago, IL 60601-7601

A Whitman Company

MiDAS®

SOURCE: Reprinted with permission of Midas International Corp., Chicago, ILL

most cases, is likely to be very highly motivated to succeed. The success of the franchise means more sales, which translate into higher royalties for the franchisor.

Despite their numerous advantages, franchise arrangements also have several drawbacks. The franchisor can dictate many aspects of the business: decor, the design of employees' uniforms, types of signs, and numerous details of business operations. In addition, franchisees must pay to use the franchisor's name, products, and assistance. Usually, there is a one-time franchise fee and continuing royalty and advertising fees, collected as a percentage of sales. Table 12.4 shows the one-time fees for the ten most expensive and the ten least expensive franchises. In addition, franchisees often must work very hard, putting in ten- and twelve-hour days, six days a week. In some cases, franchise agreements are not uniform: one franchisee may pay more than another for the same services. The franchisor also gives up a certain amount of control when entering into a franchise agreement. Consequently, individual establishments may not be operated in the exact way that the franchisor would operate them.

■ **Trends in Franchising**

Franchising has been used since the early 1900s, primarily for service stations and car dealerships. However, it has grown enormously since the mid-1960s. This growth has generally paralleled the expansion of the fast-food industry—the industry in which franchising is widely used. Of course, franchising is not limited to fast

TABLE 12.4 *The ten most expensive and the ten least expensive franchises*

10 MOST EXPENSIVE FRANCHISES		10 LEAST EXPENSIVE FRANCHISES	
Company	Start-up Cost and Franchise Fee	Company	Start-up Cost and Franchise Fee
1. Hampton Inn	$2.3 million	1. Packy the Shipper	$995
2. Quality Inns Intl.	$1.9 million	2. Novus Windshield Repair	$2,000
3. Econo Lodge	$1.8 million	3. Sunshine Polishing Systems	$2,675
4. Hardee's	$433,000	4. Coverall	$4,200
5. Roy Rogers	$396,000	5. Stork News	$5,000
6. McDonald's	$363,000	6. Chem-Dry	$9,000
7. Ponderosa Steakhouse	$342,000	7. Coustic Glo	$11,250
8. Jack-in-the-Box	$331,000	8. Jani-King	$13,500
9. Round Table Pizza	$322,000	9. Duraclean	$16,800
10. Super 8 Motels	$320,000	10. Video Data Services	$16,950

SOURCE: *USA Today,* Feb. 11, 1988, p. 8B. Copyright 1988 USA TODAY. Reprinted with permission.

foods. Franchise arrangements for health clubs, exterminators, hair salons, tax preparers, and travel agencies are widespread. The real estate industry has also experienced a rapid increase in franchising. Even professionals, such as dentists and lawyers, participate in franchise arrangements. In 1988, approximately $640 billion in sales at more than 509,000 franchised outlets accounted for about one-third of all retail sales in the United States.[27] The largest franchising sectors, ranked by sales, are automobile and truck dealers (52.4 percent), gasoline service stations (14.4 percent), restaurants (9.9 percent), and nonfood retailing (4.5 percent).[28]

Strategic Issues in Retailing

Consumers often have vague reasons for making a retail purchase. Whereas most industrial purchases are based on economic planning and necessity, consumer purchases often result from social influences and psychological factors. Because consumers shop for a variety of reasons—to search for specific items, to escape boredom, or to learn about something new—retailers must do more than simply fill space with merchandise; they must make desired products available, create stimulating environments for shopping, and develop marketing strategies that increase store patronage. In this section we discuss how store location, product assortment, retail positioning, atmospherics, store image, scrambled merchandising, and the wheel of retailing affect these retailing objectives.

27. Gail DeGeorge, "Fed-Up Franchisees: They're Mad as Hell And . . . ," *Business Week,* Nov. 13, 1989, p. 83; and "Franchising Gets an A+," *USA Today,* Oct. 26, 1988, p. 8B.

28. *Statistical Abstract of the U.S., 1989,* p. 760.

Location

Location, the least flexible of the strategic retailing issues, is one of the most important because location dictates the limited geographic trading area from which a store must draw its customers. Thus retailers consider a variety of factors when evaluating potential locations, including the location of the firm's target market within the trading area, the kinds of products being sold, the availability of public transportation, customer characteristics, and competitors' locations. The relative ease of movement to and from the site is important, including pedestrian and vehicular traffic, parking, and transportation. Most retailers prefer sites with high pedestrian traffic, although preliminary site investigations often include a pedestrian count to determine how many of the passers-by are truly prospective customers. Similarly, the nature of the area's vehicular traffic is analyzed. Certain retailers, such as service stations and convenience stores, depend on large numbers of driving customers but try to avoid overly congested locations. In addition, parking space must be adequate for projected demand, and transportation networks (major thoroughfares and public transit) must be able to accommodate customers and delivery vehicles.

Retailers also evaluate the characteristics of the site itself: the types of stores in the area; the size, shape, and visibility of the lot or building under consideration; and the rental, leasing, or ownership terms under which the building may be occupied. Retailers also look for compatibility with nearby retailers because stores that complement each other draw more customers for everyone. When making site location decisions, retailers must select from among several general types of locations: free-standing structures, traditional business districts, neighborhood shopping centers, community shopping centers, regional shopping centers, or nontraditional shopping centers.

Free-Standing Structures. Free-standing structures are buildings that are not connected to other buildings. An organization may build a structure or lease or buy one. A retailer, for example, may find that it is most successful when its stores are in free-standing structures close to a shopping mall but not in the mall. The use of free-standing structures allows retailers to physically position themselves away from or close to their competitors. It is not unusual for automobile dealers and fast-food restaurants to use free-standing structures and locate close to each other.

Traditional Business Districts. Traditional business districts consist of structures usually attached to one another and located in a central part of a town or city, for example, downtown. Often these structures are older. In some cities the traditional business districts are decaying and not viewed as viable locations for retailers. However, a number of towns and cities have taken steps to preserve or reinvigorate their traditional business districts, thus making them very attractive locations for certain types of retailers.

Neighborhood Shopping Centers. **Neighborhood shopping centers** usually consist of several small convenience and specialty stores such as small grocery stores, gas stations, and fast-food restaurants. They serve consumers who live less than ten minutes' driving time from the center. Many of these retailers consider their target markets to be consumers who live within a two- to three-mile radius of their stores. Because most purchases are based on convenience or personal contact, there is usually little coordination of selling efforts within a neighborhood shopping center. Generally, product mixes consist of essential products, and the depth of the product lines is limited. Convenience stores are most successful when they are closer to the consumer than, for example, supermarkets. A good strategy for neighborhood centers is to locate along travel patterns that allow the center to intercept the greatest number of potential consumers before they reach a regional shopping center.[29]

Community Shopping Centers.   **Community shopping centers** include one or two department stores and some specialty stores, as well as convenience stores. They serve a larger geographic area and draw consumers who are looking for shopping and specialty products that are not available in neighborhood shopping centers. Consumers drive longer distances to community shopping centers than to neighborhood shopping centers. The community shopping center is planned and coordinated to attract shoppers. Special events such as art exhibits, automobile shows, and sidewalk sales are used to stimulate traffic. The overall management of a community shopping center looks for tenants that complement the center's total assortment of products. Such centers have wide product mixes and deep product lines.

Regional Shopping Centers.   **Regional shopping centers** usually have the largest department stores, the widest product mixes, and the deepest product lines of all shopping centers. Many shopping malls are regional shopping centers, although some malls are community shopping centers. Regional shopping centers carry most products found in a downtown shopping district. With 150,000 or more consumers in their target market, regional shopping centers must have well-coordinated management and marketing activities. Figure 12.6 is an example of marketing efforts for a regional shopping center. Target markets may include "outshoppers"—customers who will forgo the convenience of hometown shopping and travel to out-of-town markets to purchase products.[30]

Because of the expense of leasing space in regional shopping centers, tenants are more likely to be national chains than small independent stores. These large centers usually advertise, have special events, furnish transportation to some consumer groups, and carefully select the mix of stores. When it is completed in 1992, Mall of America, near Minneapolis, will be one of the largest shopping malls in the world. It will contain eight hundred stores, including Nordstrom's and Bloomingdale's, and one hundred restaurants and nightclubs. The shopping center will feature Camp Snoopy, a theme park based on Charlie Brown's famous dog, as well as hotels, miniature golf courses, and water slides.[31]

Nontraditional Shopping Centers.   Two new types of discount malls or shopping centers are emerging that differ significantly from traditional shopping centers. The factory outlet mall features discount and factory outlet stores carrying traditional manufacturer brands, such as Van Heusen, Levi Strauss, Munsingwear, Healthtex, and Wrangler. Manufacturers own these stores and must make a special effort to avoid conflict with traditional retailers of their products. Manufacturers claim that

29. Franklin S. Houston and John Stanton, "Evaluating Retail Trade Areas for Convenience Stores," *Journal of Retailing,* Spring 1984, p. 135.

30. Jon M. Hawes and James R. Lumpkin, "Understanding the Outshopper," *Journal of the Academy of Marketing Science,* Fall 1984, pp. 200–217.

31. "The Minnesota Mallers," *U.S. News & World Report,* June 26, 1989, p. 12.

FIGURE 12.6

Promotion of a regional shopping center. Marketers of Southdale Mall, a regional shopping center located in Minneapolis, promote Southdale's expansion.

There's more than one way to change the face of fashion.

A new style of lipstick or blush can do a lot to change your look. But a whole new Southdale is going to change the very face of the city.

And it's happening right now. Over the course of the next year, we'll be expanding Dayton's and adding fifty new stores, parking decks, skylights, landscaping and a striking new style to the center.

All to give you an even greater variety of fashion to choose from. And a new look you'll fall in love with.

So come by Southdale and see what we're up to. Even during the construction, you'll find that we're still the best place in town to shop. Because no other center has so many of your favorite shops so close to home.

And that's the true beauty of Southdale.

SOUTHDALE. More Fashion In The Making.

SOURCE: Courtesy of Southdale Shopping Center

their stores are in noncompetitive locations, and indeed most factory outlet malls are located outside metropolitan areas. Not all factory outlets stock closeouts and irregulars, but most strive to avoid comparison with discount houses. The factory outlet mall attracts customers because of lower prices for quality and major brand names. The factory outlet mall operates in much the same way as the regional shopping center but probably draws traffic from a larger shopping radius. Promotional activity is at the heart of these new shopping centers. Craft shows, contests, and special events attract a great deal of traffic.

Another nontraditional shopping center is the miniwarehouse mall. These loosely planned centers sell space to retailers, who operate what are essentially retail stores out of warehouse bays. The developers of the miniwarehouse mall may also sell space to wholesalers or even to light manufacturers that maintain a retail facility in their warehouse bay. Some of these miniwarehouses are located in high-traffic areas and provide ample customer parking, as well as display windows that can be seen from the street. Home improvement materials, specialty foods, pet supplies, and garden and yard supplies are often sold in these malls. Unlike the traditional shopping center, the miniwarehouse mall usually does not have a coordinated promotional program and store mix. These nontraditional shopping centers come closest to a neighborhood or community shopping center.

FIGURE 12.7
Relationships between merchandise breadth and depth for a typical discount store, department store, and specialty store

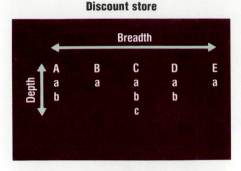

Discount store

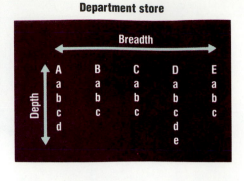

Department store

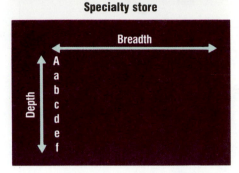

Specialty store

The capital letters represent the number of product lines, and the small letters depict the choices in any one product line. Thus it can be seen that discount stores are wide and shallow in merchandise assortment. Specialty stores, at the other extreme, have few product lines, but much more depth in the few they carry. The typical department store falls in between, having a broad assortment with many merchandise lines and medium depth in each line.

SOURCE: Robert F. Hartley, *Retailing: Challenge and Opportunity,* 3rd ed., p. 118. Copyright © 1984 by Houghton Mifflin Company. Used by permission.

■ Product Assortment

The product assortments that retailers develop vary considerably in breadth and depth. As discussed earlier, retail stores are often classified according to their product assortments. Conversely, a store's type affects the breadth and depth of the store's product offerings, as shown in Figure 12.7. Thus a specialty store has a single product line but considerable depth in that line. Godiva chocolate stores and Fannie May Candy Shops, for example, carry only one line of products but many items within that line. In contrast, discount stores may have a wide product mix (such as housewares, automotive services, apparel, and food). Department stores may have a wide product mix with different product line depths. Nevertheless, it is usually difficult to maintain a wide and deep product mix because of the inventories required. In addition, some producers prefer to distribute through retailers that offer less variety so that their products get more exposure and are less affected by the presence of competing brands.

Issues of product assortment are often a matter of what and how much to carry. When retailers decide what should be included in their product assortments, they consider the assortment's purpose, status, and completeness.[32] *Purpose* relates to how well an assortment satisfies consumers and at the same time furthers the retailer's goals. *Status* identifies by rank the relative importance of each product in an assortment: for example, motor oil might have low status in a store that sells convenience foods. *Completeness* means that an assortment includes the products necessary to satisfy a store's customers; the assortment is incomplete when some

32. C. Glenn Walters and Blaise J. Bergiel, *Marketing Channels,* 2nd ed. (Glenview, Ill.: Scott, Foresman, 1982), p. 205.

products are missing. An assortment of convenience foods must include milk to be complete because most consumers expect to be able to buy milk when purchasing other food products. New products are added to (and declining products are deleted from) an assortment when they meet (or fail to meet) the retailer's standards of purpose, status, and completeness.

The retailer also considers the quality of the products to be offered. The store may limit its assortments to expensive, high-quality goods for upper-income market segments; it may stock cheap, low-quality products for low-income buyers; or it may try to attract several market segments by offering a range of quality within its total product assortment.

How much to include in an assortment depends on the needs of the retailer's target market. A discount store's customers expect a wide and shallow product mix, whereas specialty-store shoppers prefer narrow and deep assortments. If a retailer can increase sales by increasing product variety, the assortment may be enlarged. If a broader product mix ties up too much floor space or creates storage problems, however, the retailer may stock only the products that generate the greatest sales. Other factors that affect product assortment decisions are the personnel, store image, inventory control methods, and the financial risks involved.

Retail Positioning

Because of the emergence of new types of stores (warehouse clubs, hypermarkets, and deep discounters) and the expansion of product offerings by traditional stores, competition among retailers is intense. Thus it is important for management to consider the retail organization's market positioning. **Retail positioning** involves identifying an unserved or underserved market niche, or segment, and serving the segment through a strategy that distinguishes the retailer from others in the minds of persons in that segment.[33]

There are several ways in which retailers position themselves. A retailer may position itself as a seller of high-quality, premium-priced products that provides many services. A store such as Neiman Marcus, which specializes in expensive high fashion clothing and jewelry, sophisticated electronics, and exclusive home furnishings, might be expected to provide wrapping and delivery, valet parking, personal shopping consultants, and fine-dining facilities. Nordstrom's, for example, emphasizes providing topnotch service, and even hires pianists to play in the main lobbies of its stores.[34] Another type of retail organization, such as Wal-Mart, may be positioned as a marketer of reasonable quality products at everyday low prices. As indicated at the beginning of this chapter, J.C. Penney has repositioned itself as one of the nation's largest apparel retailers. The Limited, profiled in Marketing Update 12.2, is positioned as a provider of trendy sportswear.

Atmospherics

Atmospherics is often used to help position a retailer. **Atmospherics** describes the physical elements in a store's design that appeal to consumers' emotions and encourage consumers to buy. Exterior and interior characteristics, layout, and displays all contribute to a store's atmosphere. Department stores, restaurants, hotels, service stations, and shops combine these elements in different ways to create specific atmospheres that may be perceived as warm, fresh, functional, or exciting.

33. George H. Lucas, Jr., and Larry G. Gresham, "How to Position for Retail Success," *Business,* April-June 1988, pp. 3–13.

34. Leslie Wayne, "Rewriting the Rules of Retailing," *New York Times,* Oct. 15, 1989, p. F6.

THE LIMITED ADJUSTS ITS RETAILING STRATEGY

After a period of almost exponential growth, The Limited Inc. is in a slump. The past few years have not been good to the retail clothing industry in general. Yet although its own sales figures have declined, The Limited, based in Columbus, Ohio, is still outguessing and outselling its competitors.

While other clothing store executives have adopted a "wait-and-see" strategy, The Limited is aggressively trying to attract more new customers and dazzle its regular shoppers. Although The Limited once targeted its fashion goods primarily toward teen-agers, it now caters to older, more affluent consumers. The company is building larger stores that carry children's clothing and menswear in addition to women's sportswear. The atmosphere of these new larger stores makes them appear sleek and stylish.

The Limited has already more than 3,500 stores in operation, and more are scheduled to open. The retailing company also owns other retailing chains, including Victoria's Secret (a lingerie chain), Lane Bryant, Limited Two (a children's fashion store), and the recently purchased Abercrombie & Fitch. The Limited's strategies seem to be paying off. The per-square-foot sales in its stores are about $60 higher than the industry average.

Aggressive retailing and marketing tactics have made The Limited one of the top clothing retailers in the world. A company executive once predicted that one company would dominate the industry—and that company would be The Limited. Management at The Limited is sure that the retailer will reach its goal of being a $2 billion company by the early 1990s. It responds quickly to fashion trends and even more quickly to marketing errors. As other retailers wait quietly for the fashion slump to end, The Limited is trying to activate a recovery.

SOURCES: Carol Hymowitz, "Limited Inc., on New Tack, Pulls Ahead of Retail Gang," *Wall Street Journal,* Feb. 24, 1989, pp. B1, B4; "The Limited's Approach," *Chain Store Age Executive,* December 1988, pp. 28, 30, 36; and Annette Tapert, "Happy Landings," *Working Woman,* September 1988, pp. 114–118.

Exterior atmospheric elements include the appearance of the storefront, display windows, store entrances, and degree of traffic congestion. Exterior atmospherics is particularly important to new customers, who tend to judge an unfamiliar store by its outside appearance and may not enter the store if they feel intimidated by the building or inconvenienced by the parking lot. Because consumers form general impressions of shopping centers and business districts, the businesses and neighborhoods surrounding a store will affect how buyers perceive the atmosphere of a store.

Interior atmospheric elements include aesthetic considerations such as lighting, wall and floor coverings, dressing facilities, and store fixtures. Interior sensory elements also contribute to atmosphere. Color, for example, can attract shoppers to a retail display. Many fast-food restaurants use bright colors such as red and yellow because these have been shown to make customers feel hungrier and eat faster, which increases turnover. Sound is another important sensory component of atmosphere and may consist of silence, soft music, or even noisiness. Scent may be relevant as well; within a store, the odor of perfume suggests an image different from that suggested by the smell of prepared food. A store's layout—arrangement of departments, width of aisles, grouping of products, and location of check-out areas—is yet another determinant of atmosphere. Closely related to store layout is the element of crowding. A crowded store may restrict exploratory shopping, impede mobility, and decrease shopping efficiency.

Once the exterior and interior characteristics and store layout have been determined, displays are added. Displays enhance the store's atmosphere and give customers information about products. When displays carry out a storewide theme, during the Christmas season, for instance, they attract customers' attention and generate sales. So do displays that present several related products in a group, or ensemble. Interior displays of products stacked or hanging neatly on racks create one kind of atmosphere; marked-down items grouped together on a sale table produce a different kind.

Retailers must determine the atmosphere the target market seeks and then adjust atmospheric variables to encourage the desired awareness and action in consumers. High-fashion boutiques generally strive for an atmosphere of luxury and novelty; discount department stores must not seem too exclusive and expensive. To appeal to multiple market segments, a retailer may create different atmospheres for different operations within the store; for example, the discount basement, the sports department, and the women's shoe department may each have a unique atmosphere.

■ Store Image

To attract customers, a retail store must project an image—a functional and psychological picture in the consumer's mind—that is acceptable to its target market. Although heavily dependent on atmospherics, a store's image is also shaped by its reputation for integrity, the number of services offered, location, merchandise assortments, pricing policies, promotional activities, and community involvement.

Characteristics of the target market—social class, lifestyle, income level, and past buying behavior—help form store image as well. How consumers perceive the store can be a major determinant of store patronage. Consumers from lower socioeconomic groups tend to patronize small, high-margin, high-service food stores and prefer small, friendly loan companies over large, impersonal banks, even though these companies charge high interest. Affluent consumers look for exclusive, high-quality establishments that offer prestige products and labels.

Retailers should be aware of the multiple factors that contribute to store image and recognize that perceptions of image vary. For example, one study found that consumers perceive Wal-Mart and K mart differently although the two sell almost the same products in stores that look quite similar, offer the same prices, and even have similar names. Researchers discovered that Wal-Mart shoppers spend more money at Wal-Mart and are more satisfied with the store than K mart shoppers are with K mart, in part because of differences in the retailers' images. For example, Wal-Mart employees wear vests; K mart employees do not. Wal-Mart purchases are bagged in paper sacks while K mart uses plastic bags. Wal-mart has wider aisles, recessed lighting, and carpeting in some departments. Even the retailers' logos affect consumers' perceptions: Wal-Mart's simple white and brown logo appears friendly and "less blatantly commercial," while K mart's red and turquoise blue logo conveys the impression that the stores have not changed much since the 1960s. These atmospheric elements give consumers the impression that Wal-Mart is more "upscale," warmer, and friendlier than K mart.[35]

■ Scrambled Merchandising

When retailers add unrelated products and product lines, particularly fast-moving items that can be sold in volume, to an existing product mix, they are practicing **scrambled merchandising**. For example, a convenience store might start selling lawn fertilizer. Retailers adopting this strategy hope to accomplish one or more of the following: (1) convert their stores into one-stop shopping centers, (2) generate more traffic, (3) realize higher profit margins, (4) increase impulse purchases.

However, in scrambling merchandise, retailers must deal with diverse marketing channels and thus may reduce their own buying, selling, and servicing expertise. The practice can also blur a store's image in consumers' minds, making it more difficult for a retailer to succeed in today's highly competitive, saturated markets. Finally, scrambled merchandising intensifies competition among traditionally distinct types of stores and forces suppliers to adjust distribution systems so that new channel members can be accommodated.

■ The Wheel of Retailing

As new types of retail businesses come into being, they strive to fill niches in the dynamic environment of retailing. One hypothesis regarding the evolution and development of new types of retail stores is the **wheel of retailing**. According to this theory, new retailers often enter the marketplace with low prices, margins, and status. The new competitors' low prices are usually the result of innovative cost-cutting procedures, and they soon attract imitators. Gradually, as these businesses attempt to broaden their customer base and increase sales, their operations and facilities become more elaborate and more expensive. They may move to more desirable locations, begin to carry higher-quality merchandise, or add customer services. Eventually, they emerge at the high end of the price/cost/service scales, competing with newer discount retailers following the same evolutionary process.[36]

For example, supermarkets have undergone many changes since their introduction in 1921. Initially, they provided limited services in exchange for lower food prices. However, over time they developed a variety of new services, including free coffee, gourmet food sections, and children's play areas. Now supermarkets are being challenged by superstores and hypermarkets, which offer more product choices than the original supermarkets and have undercut supermarket prices.

35. Francine Schwadel, "Little Touches Spur Wal-Mart's Rise; Shoppers React to Logo, Decor, Employee Vests," *Wall Street Journal*, Sept. 22, 1989, p. B1.

36. Stanley C. Hollander, "The Wheel of Retailing," *Journal of Marketing*, July 1960, p. 37.

FIGURE 12.8

The wheel of retailing, which explains the origin and evolution of new types of retail stores

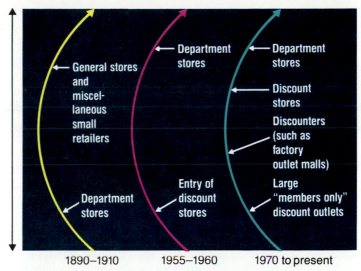

High prices and markups, many services, expensive surroundings

Low prices and markups, few services, austere surroundings

If the "wheel" is considered to be turning slowly in the direction of the arrow, then the department stores around 1900 and the discounters later can be viewed as coming on the scene at the low end of the wheel. As it turns slowly, they move with it, becoming higher-price operations, and at the same time leaving room for lower-price firms to gain entry at the low end of the wheel.

SOURCE: Adapted from Robert F. Hartley, *Retailing: Challenge and Opportunity*, 3rd ed., p. 42. Copyright 1984 by Houghton Mifflin Company. Used by permission.

Figure 12.8 illustrates the wheel of retailing for department stores and discount houses. Department stores such as Sears started out as high-volume, low-cost merchants competing with general stores and other small retailers; discount houses developed later, in response to the rising expenses of services in department stores. Many discount houses now appear to be following the wheel of retailing by offering more services, better locations, quality inventories, and, therefore, higher prices. Some discount houses are almost indistinguishable from department stores.

Like most hypotheses, the wheel of retailing may not fit every case. For example, it does not adequately explain the development of convenience stores, specialty stores, department store branches, and vending machine operations. Another major weakness of the theory is that it does not predict what retailing innovations will develop, or when. Still, the hypothesis works reasonably well in industrialized, expanding economies.

SUMMARY

Retailing includes all transactions in which the buyer intends to consume the product through personal, family, or household use. Retailers, which are organizations that sell products primarily to ultimate consumers, are important links in the marketing channel because they are customers for wholesalers and producers. Most retailing takes place inside stores or service establishments, but retail exchanges may also occur outside stores through telemarketing, vending machines, and mail-order catalogs. Retail institutions provide place, time, and possession utilities. In the case of services, retailers develop most of the product's form utility as well.

Retail stores are usually classified according to width of product mix and depth of product lines. The major types of retail stores are department stores, mass merchandisers, and specialty stores. Department stores are large retail organizations employing at least twenty-five people and characterized by wide product mixes in considerable depth for most product lines. Their product lines are organized into separate departments that function much as self-contained businesses do.

Mass merchandisers generally offer fewer customer services than department stores and emphasize lower prices, high turnover, and large sales volumes. This type of retailer includes discount stores (self-service, low-price general merchandise outlets), supermarkets (large, self-service food stores that also carry some nonfood products), superstores (giant retail outlets that carry all products found in supermarkets and most consumer products purchased on a routine basis), hypermarkets (one-stop combination supermarket and discount stores), warehouse/wholesale clubs (large-scale, members-only discount operations), and warehouse and catalog showrooms (low-cost operations characterized by warehouse methods of materials handling and display, large inventories, and minimum services).

Specialty retailers offer substantial assortments in a few product lines. They include traditional specialty retailers, which carry narrow product mixes with deep product lines, and off-price retailers, which sell brand-name manufacturers' seconds and production overruns to consumers at deep discounts.

Nonstore retailing is the selling of goods or services outside the confines of a retail facility. Direct marketing is the use of nonpersonal media to introduce products to consumers, who then purchase the products by mail or telephone. Forms of nonstore retailing include in-home retailing (selling via personal contacts with consumers in their own homes), telemarketing (direct selling of goods and services by telephone based either on a cold canvass of the telephone directory or on a prescreened list of prospective clients), automatic vending (selling through machines), and mail-order retailing (selling by description because buyers usually do not see the actual product until it arrives in the mail).

Franchising is an arrangement whereby a supplier grants a dealer the right to sell products in exchange for some type of consideration. Retail franchises are of three general types: a manufacturer may authorize a number of retail stores to sell a certain brand-name item; a producer may license distributors to sell a given product to retailers; or a franchisor may supply brand names, techniques, or other services instead of a complete product. Franchise arrangements have a number of advantages and disadvantages over traditional business forms, and their use is increasing.

To increase sales and store patronage, retailers must consider several strategic issues. Location determines the trading area from which a store must draw its customers and should be evaluated carefully. When evaluating potential sites, retailers take into account a variety of factors, including the location of the firm's target market within the trading area, the kinds of products being sold, the availability of public transportation, customer characteristics, and competitors' locations. Retailers can choose among several types of locations: free-standing structures, traditional business districts, neighborhood shopping centers, community shopping centers, regional shopping centers, or nontraditional shopping centers. The width, depth, and quality of the product assortment should be of the kind that can satisfy the retailer's target market customers.

Retail positioning involves identifying an unserved or underserved market niche, or segment, and serving the segment through a strategy that distinguishes the retailer from others in the minds of persons. Atmospherics comprises the physical elements of a store's design that can be adjusted to appeal to consumers' emotions and thus induce consumers to buy. Store image, which various consumers perceive differently, derives not only from atmosphere, but also from location, products offered, customer services, prices, promotion, and the store's overall reputation. Scrambled merchandising adds unrelated product lines to an existing product mix and is being used by a growing number of stores to generate sales.

The wheel of retailing hypothesis holds that new retail institutions start as low-status, low-margin, and low-price operators. As they develop, they increase service and prices and eventually become vulnerable to newer institutions, which enter the market and repeat the cycle. However, the wheel of retailing hypothesis may not apply in every case.

IMPORTANT TERMS

Retailing	Direct marketing
Retailer	In-home retailing
Department stores	Telemarketing
Mass merchandisers	Automatic vending
Discount stores	Mail-order retailing
Supermarkets	Catalog retailing
Superstores	Franchising
Hypermarkets	Neighborhood shopping centers
Warehouse/wholesale club	Community shopping centers
Warehouse showroom	Regional shopping centers
Catalog showroom	Retail positioning
Traditional specialty retailers	Atmospherics
Off-price retailers	Scrambled merchandising
Nonstore retailing	Wheel of retailing

DISCUSSION AND REVIEW QUESTIONS

1. What are the major differences between discount houses and department stores?
2. How does a superstore differ from a supermarket?
3. Should a warehouse/wholesale club be classified as a wholesaler or as a retailer?
4. In what ways are traditional specialty stores and off-price retailers similar? How do they differ?
5. Evaluate the following statement: "Direct marketing and nonstore retailing are about the same thing."
6. Why is door-to-door selling a form of retailing? Some consumers feel that direct mail-orders skip the retailer. Is this true?
7. If you were to open a retail business, would you prefer to open an independent store or to own a store under a franchise arrangement? Explain your preference.
8. What major issues should be considered when determining a retail site location?

9. Describe the three major types of shopping centers. Give examples of each type in your area.
10. How does atmosphere add value to products sold in a store? How important is atmospherics for convenience stores?
11. How should one determine the best retail store atmosphere?
12. Discuss the major factors that help determine a retail store's image.
13. Is it possible for a single retail store to have an overall image that appeals to sophisticated shoppers, extravagant ones, and bargain hunters? Why or why not?
14. In what ways does the use of scrambled merchandising affect a store's image?

■ CASES

12.1 Mrs. Fields Cookies Uses High Tech to Control Retail Outlets

To drum up customers for her fledgling cookie shop, entrepreneur Debbi Fields spent her first day in business giving away freshly baked chocolate chip cookies to pedestrians outside her small store in Palo Alto, California. The strategy worked; customers followed her into the shop, and by the end of the day she had made $75. Mrs. Fields Cookies now operates hundreds of retail outlets located across the United States. Today the company is experimenting with "combination" stores, which offer soups, sandwiches, and bagels, as well as cookies.

Compared with the huge success of its early years, however, Mrs. Fields Cookies has entered tough times—despite sophisticated technology, vigilant control of operations, and favorable employee morale throughout the company. Food industry experts think that Mrs. Fields oversaturated some markets and spread itself too thin in others. The cookie company has also been injured by rising rents and costs, which prompted it to close many stores. In addition, the cookie industry has become more competitive. The current fad for gourmet food and snacks has spawned about three thousand cookie companies in the United States, including Famous Amos Chocolate Chip Cookie Co., Blue Chip Cookies, Great American Chocolate Chip Cookie, and numerous regional and local firms. But Mrs. Fields Cookies is still the largest.

Using an innovative and sophisticated management information system, Mrs. Fields Cookies maintains direct control over its outlets and keeps its thousands of employees motivated and productive. Some analysts blame this strict control for the company's decline and believe that it continues to plague the firm. They claim that this management strategy cannot keep pace with the company's growth and cannot be effective in the future. Whatever the long-term consequences of strict control, it does help to fulfill the firm's commitment to product quality and customer service. Executives at Mrs. Fields are confident that their company will soon regain its earlier prosperity. They have a strong faith in their information processing system.

Designed by Randy Fields, Debbi's husband, the company's computer network provides a constant flow of information between every store manager and corporate headquarters at Park City, Utah. Each store has a Tandy personal computer hooked up to the IBM minicomputer at the Park City office, with a computer modem for transmitting daily store reports. This computer setup helps the company to achieve two objectives unusual for most cookie retailers. First, by automating (and thus speeding up) routine tasks, the system frees store managers from time-consuming paperwork and administrative chores. Second, because the interactive software encodes Debbi Fields' enthusiastic, people-first management style, the system projects her presence into each store and enables managers to duplicate the high quality standards and effective selling that first made her a success.

For example, at the start of every business day, using the Day Planner software, a store manager examines his or her store's performance for the three previous weeks and calculates how many customers will be needed and how many cookies must be sold that day to meet sales projections. The computer also helps the manager schedule that day's cookie baking to meet sales demand and yet have minimum leftovers. Although, if necessary, the manager could make these calculations personally, the computer saves valuable time. Then, throughout the day, the manager enters sales figures into the computer (the company is beginning to equip its stores with cash registers that transmit this information automatically to the computer). The computer, in turn, adjusts hourly projections and offers selling advice if customer count or total sales drop below predicted levels.

The computer assists with other managerial activities as well. It helps the manager determine how many employees to schedule for the upcoming two-week period, based on sales projections and mixing and baking times. With a special series of interview questions, it evaluates prospective employees and initiates the paperwork with the Park City office when the manager makes the final hiring decision. By asking the manager questions, the system also troubleshoots when equipment malfunctions, and it generates repair requests and alerts headquarters to pay the bill when repair services are required. In short, because the computer reorganizes and makes accessible the information that managers provide about their own operations, every store manager is equipped to make better day-to-day decisions.

Although the company does have area, district, and regional managers, the responsibility for monitoring the stores' daily reports and weekly inventory reports rests with just a few store controllers in Park City, who make sure that the reports tally with sales figures. In case of discrepancies, the controllers go, whenever possible, to the source of the problem. With store controllers tracking the routine figures, the company's executives are free to deal with the exceptions—the differences between expected outcome and actual outcome. They can concentrate on people, not numbers, just as Debbi Fields wants them to.

Moreover, as a result of the company's lean management structure, Debbi Fields maintains the personal contact with store managers that she believes is essential to product quality. Her managers also communicate with her electronically, through computer messages that she and her staff answer within forty-eight hours. For urgent matters, or whenever she wants managers to actually hear her voice, messages are sent and received by electronic PhoneMail. In the electronic sense, Debbi Fields is in all her stores at once.

Mrs. Fields Cookies began to automate its operations when its second store opened in 1978. The automation started with standard clerical chores and data entry, and the network has developed along with the company. Today Mrs. Fields Cookies spends about 0.5 percent of sales on data processing, buying only equipment that will pay for itself in two years or less. Two important principles keep the company's technology manageable. First, the firm maintains a single database so that all users have equal access and data have to be entered only once. Second, machines are delegated to perform any tasks that they are capable of performing. For example, the company plans to shift routine ordering functions to store computers. By comparing a store's weekly inventory report with projected sales, the computer should be able to determine the supplies needed, generate an order (with a copy on the screen for the manager to confirm or correct), match the invoice for supplies received with the original order, and issue a check to the supplier. Clerks then would be responsible for handling the exceptions.

SOURCES: "Blue Chip Cookies Puts Stock in Quality," *Chain Store Age Executive,* November 1987, pp. 190–191; Nancy Rivera Brooks, "To Entrepreneur, Success Tastes Sweet," *Los Angeles Times,* Sept. 4, 1986, sec. IV, p. 1; Buck Brown, "How the Cookie Crumbled at Mrs. Fields," *Wall Street Journal,* Jan. 26, 1989, p. B1; Mark Lewyn, "Executive Tales, Told by the Book," *USA Today,* Oct. 12, 1987, pp. 1–2B; "Mrs. Fields Automates the Way Cookie Sells," *Chain Store Age Executive,* April 1988, pp. 73–75; and Tom Richman, "Mrs. Fields' Secret Ingredient," *Inc.,* October 1987, pp. 65–67.

Questions for Discussion

1. Most entrepreneurs such as those at Mrs. Fields Cookies would have franchised the individual retail outlets instead of owning and managing them directly. How are the company's corporate-level managers able to manage hundreds of retail outlets effectively?
2. On what types of issues does the top management at Mrs. Fields focus?
3. How is the computer system used to aid in-store managers?

12.2   Jiffy Lube Expands Rapidly Through Franchises

To Jim Hindman, chief executive officer of Jiffy Lube International, Inc., the best marketing strategy is to be the market leader. In Hindman's view, by being number one in an industry, a firm automatically gains marketing advantages that its competitors have no chance of attaining. In less than ten years, Hindman transformed a seven-store company into a massive oil change franchise of more than 350 stores. For about $20, a customer receives new oil, a new oil filter, a chassis lubrication, fluids refills, an air filter inspection, a tire-inflation check, and a window wash—all in under ten minutes. Enough customers have thought this to be such a bargain that Jiffy Lube has been one of the fastest growing franchises in the lube and oil change business, which is now worth $10 billion a year. Today "quick-lube" operations control about 8 percent of the total motor oil market, with that share expected to exceed 30 percent within a few years.

Hindman in just four years, turned the nine-unit chain he had purchased from founder Ed Washburn into an operation comprising ninety-six centers. In the mid-80s, Jiffy Lube was well known on the East Coast and West Coast of the United States. Then Hindman decided to expand across the country. He could foresee substantial profits in the business and wanted to beat any potential competitors. By going deeply into debt, Hindman raised enough capital to expand his business very quickly, setting up Jiffy Lubes all over the United States. Hindman says that his view of expansion is like General George Patton's: he is going to take every inch of ground he can and then fight to hang on.

Hindman's notion that the best marketing approach is to be the industry leader seems to make sense. By being the first oil change store in the area, Jiffy Lube franchises often claimed the best locations. Developers want market leaders in their strip centers and shopping malls. Banks are more willing to lend money to market leaders because they are perceived as lower-risk borrowers, and banks also want to be associated with successful businesses. It is up to the competitors of market leaders to prove to consumers how they are different or better. In addition, market leaders do not have to compete on price as much. Customers will pay more for the "premium" services of the market leader.

Hindman is eager to maintain market share. He has assembled a sophisticated database and constantly reviews it to develop strategies to better satisfy Jiffy Lube customers. He discovered that working women are key visitors to Jiffy Lube. In response, Jiffy Lube marketing officials placed more women in their advertisements. Hindman's strategy also stresses television advertising: the company spends some $16 million a year on television commercials. In addition, Hindman emphasizes the importance of cleanliness (in facilities as well as employees) to his franchisees.

Jiffy Lube is facing some strong competition. There seems to be a general consumer shift away from do-it-yourself oil changes to quick-lube shops. Becoming more environmentally conscious, consumers will likely patronize quick-lube shops, where used motor oil can be easily and safely collected for recycling. Oil giants such as Quaker State, Pennzoil, and Valvoline have already entered the quick-lube market, and all have plans to expand their presence. Both Ford and General Motors have decided to open thousands of quick-lube centers at car dealerships. Major oil companies such as Shell, Exxon, and Mobil also plan to operate quick-lube outlets, both as stand-alone operations and as parts of traditional service stations. Given all this competition, it looks as though a major quick-lube industry shakeout may be imminent.

With his competitors bringing strength and capital to the fray, Hindman's strategy to capitalize on his position might prove ineffective. Besides, weighted down as he is with debt, Hindman might not have the financial flexibility to compete with other quick-lube operators.

SOURCES: Paul B. Brown, "Looking Out for Number One," *Inc.,* April 1989, pp. 165–166; Warren Brown, "Ford Entry into Field May Slow Jiffy Lube," *Washington Post,* Apr. 22, 1989, p. D12; "Jiffy Lube Can't Be Beat for Expert Service," *Nashua Telegraph* (Nashua, New Hampshire), Mar. 4, 1988, p. B8; and Michael Schroeder, "Quaker State Switches into a Quick-Change Artist," *Business Week,* Oct. 16, 1989, pp. 126–127.

Questions for Discussion

1. Why has Jiffy Lube been successful?
2. What are the advantages and disadvantages of Jiffy Lube's rapid expansion?
3. As the quick-lube segment of the oil change market becomes more competitive, what can Jiffy Lube do to stay competitive and remain the market leader?
4. Evaluate Hindman's decision to franchise Jiffy Lube units rather than operate them as company-owned units.

13

PHYSICAL DISTRIBUTION

Objectives

To understand how physical distribution activities are integrated into marketing channels and overall marketing strategies

To examine three important physical distribution objectives: customer service, total distribution costs, and cost trade-offs

To learn how efficient order processing facilitates product flow

To illustrate how materials handling is a part of physical distribution activities

To learn how warehousing facilitates the storage and movement functions in physical distribution

To understand how inventory management is conducted to develop and maintain adequate assortments of products for target markets

To gain insight into how transportation modes, which bridge the producer-customer gap, are selected and coordinated

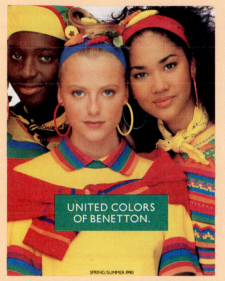

UNITED COLORS
OF BENETTON.

SPRING/SUMMER 1990

How important can eight people be to a multinational clothing manufacturer and retailer? To Benetton, the Italian sportswear company, the eight people who run the warehouse that handles the distribution of 50 million pieces of clothing a year are extremely important. These eight are responsible for processing 230,000 articles of clothing a day to serve 4,500 stores, of which 700 are located in the United States. Though sales in the garment industry have sagged recently, Benetton is still moving tremendous amounts of knit and cotton clothing. After their small clothing business expanded into an international fashion sensation, executives at Benetton realized that highly efficient physical distribution methods were a must.

Benetton has linked its sales agents, its factory, and its warehouse in an electronic loop. Suppose a student in San Francisco wants to buy a sweater identical to his older brother's Benetton sweater. He goes to a Benetton store and searches for it. He is disappointed when he finds that the sweater is not there. The salesperson assures him that the sweater will arrive in a month. The salesperson calls a Benetton sales agent, who places the sweater order on a personal computer. The information travels electronically to Italy, where a computer searches inventory data and finds that there are no more sweaters like the one requested. An order then automatically travels to a machine that cuts the material and immediately starts to knit the sweater. Workers put the finished sweater in a box with a bar-coded label and send it to the warehouse. In the warehouse, a computer commands a robot to retrieve the sweater and any other merchandise that needs to be transported to the same store. ◆

Photo courtesy of Benetton.

Based on information in Brian Dumaine, "How Managers Can Succeed Through Speed," *Fortune*, Feb. 13, 1989, p. 59; Martha Groves, "Retailer Benetton Hopes to Crack Soviet Market," *Los Angeles Times*, Jan. 7, 1989, sec. IV, pp. 2, 4; and Lena H. Sun, "Too Much, Too Fast? Benetton Sportswear Rethinks Strategy of Rapid Store Expansion," *Washington Post*, Oct. 11, 1988, pp. E1, E4.

Benetton's use of well-managed physical distribution activities, facilitated through the latest technologically advanced equipment, has helped it become a very large and highly successful retail leader. Physical distribution deals with the movement and handling of goods and the processing of orders, activities necessary to provide a level of service that will satisfy customers. Even though physical distribution is costly, it creates time and place utility, which maximizes the value of products by delivering them when and where they are wanted.

This chapter describes how marketing decisions are related to physical distribution. After considering basic physical distribution concepts, we outline the major objectives of physical distribution. We then examine each major distribution function: order processing, materials handling, warehousing, inventory management, and transportation. We close the chapter with a discussion of marketing strategy considerations in physical distribution. When reading this chapter, keep in mind how important customer service is to physical distribution and how physical distribution is related to marketing channels.

The Importance of Physical Distribution

Physical distribution is a set of activities—consisting of order processing, materials handling, warehousing, inventory management, and transportation—used in the movement of products from producers to consumers and end users. Planning an effective physical distribution system can be a significant decision in developing a marketing strategy. A company that has the right goods in the right place, at the right time, in the right quantity, and with the right support services is able to sell more than competitors who fail to accomplish these goals. Physical distribution is an important variable in a marketing strategy because it can decrease costs and increase customer satisfaction. In fact, speed of delivery, along with services and dependability, is often as important to buyers as cost.

Physical distribution deals with physical movement and inventory holding (storing and tracking inventory until it is needed) both within and among marketing channel members. Often one channel member will arrange the movement of goods for all channel members involved in exchanges. For example, a packing company ships fresh California cherries and strawberries (often by air) to remote markets on a routine basis. Frequently, buyers are found while the fruit is in transit.

The physical distribution system is often adjusted to meet the needs of a channel member. For example, a construction equipment dealer who keeps a low inventory of replacement parts requires the fastest and most dependable service when parts not in stock are needed. In this case, the distribution cost may be a minor consideration when compared with service, dependability, and timeliness.

Physical Distribution Objectives

For most companies, the main objective of physical distribution is to decrease costs while increasing service. In the real world, however, few distribution systems manage to achieve these goals in equal measure. The large inventories and rapid transportation essential to high levels of customer service drive up costs. On the other hand, reduced inventories and slower, cheaper transportation methods cause customer dissatisfaction. Physical distribution managers strive for a reasonable balance among service, costs, and resources. They determine what level of customer service is acceptable, yet realistic, develop a "system" outlook of figuring total distribution costs, and trade higher costs at one stage of distribution for savings in another. In this section we examine these three performance objectives more closely.

■ Customer Service

In varying degrees, all organizations attempt to satisfy customer needs and wants through a set of activities known collectively as customer service. Many companies claim that service to the customer is their top priority. Clearly, without customers, there would be no profit. Service may be as important in attracting customers and building sales as the cost or quality of the organization's products.

Customers require a variety of services. At the most basic level, they need fair prices, acceptable product quality, and dependable deliveries.[1] In the physical distribution area, availability, timeliness, and quality are the most important dimensions of customer service. These are the main factors that determine how satisfied customers are likely to be with a supplier's physical distribution activities.[2] Customers seeking a higher level of customer service may also want sizable inventories, efficient order processing, availability of emergency shipments, progress reports, post-sale services, prompt replacement of defective items, and warranties. Customers' inventory requirements influence the level of physical distribution service they expect. For example, customers that want to minimize inventory storage and shipping costs may require that suppliers assume the cost of maintaining inventory in the marketing channel, or the cost of premium transportation.[3] Because service needs vary from customer to customer, companies must analyze—and adapt to—customer preferences. Attention to customer needs and preferences is crucial to increasing sales and obtaining repeat sales. A company's failure to provide the desired level of service may mean the loss of customers.

Companies must also examine the service levels competitors offer and match those standards, at least when the costs of providing the services can be balanced by the sales generated. For example, companies may step up their efforts to identify the causes of customer complaints or institute corrective measures for billing and shipping errors. In extremely competitive businesses, such as the packaged food industry, firms may concentrate on product availability. To compete effectively, food processors may strive for inventory levels and order-processing speeds that are deemed unnecessary and too costly in other industries.[4]

Services are provided most effectively when service standards are developed and stated in terms that are specific, measurable, and appropriate for the product: for example, "98 percent of all orders filled within forty-eight hours." Standards should be communicated clearly to both customers and employees and rigorously enforced.

1. Carl M. Guelzo, *Introduction to Logistics Management* (Englewood Cliffs, N.J.: Prentice-Hall, 1986), p. 32.

2. John T. Mentzer, Roger Gomes, and Robert E. Krapfel, Jr., "Physical Distribution Service: A Fundamental Marketing Concept?" *Journal of the Academy of Marketing Science*, Winter 1989, p. 59.

3. Lloyd M. Rinehart, M. Bixby Cooper, and George D. Wagenheim, "Furthering the Integration of Marketing and Logistics Through Customer Service in the Channel," *Journal of the Academy of Marketing Science*, Winter 1989, p. 67.

4. Charles A. Taff, *Management of Physical Distribution and Transportation* (Homewood, Ill.: Irwin, 1984), p. 250.

In many cases, it is necessary to maintain a policy of minimum order sizes to ensure that transactions are profitable; that is, special service charges are added to orders smaller than a specified quantity. Many service policies also spell out delivery times and provisions for backordering, returning goods, and obtaining emergency shipments. The overall objective of any service policy should be to improve customer service just to the point beyond which increased sales would be negated by increased distribution costs.

■ Total Distribution Costs

Although physical distribution managers try to minimize the costs of each element in the system—order processing, materials handling, inventory, warehousing, and transportation—decreasing costs in one area often raises them in another. By using a total cost approach to physical distribution, managers can view the distribution system as a whole, not as a collection of unrelated activities. The emphasis shifts from lowering the separate costs of individual functions to minimizing the total cost of the entire distribution system.

The total cost approach calls for analyzing the costs of all possible distribution alternatives, even those considered too impractical or expensive. Total cost analyses weigh inventory levels against warehousing expenses, materials handling costs against various modes of transportation, and all distribution costs against customer service standards. The costs of potential sales losses from lower performance levels are also considered. In many cases, accounting procedures and statistical methods can be used to figure total costs. Where hundreds of combinations of distribution variables are possible, computer simulations may be helpful. In no case is a distribution system's lowest total cost the result of using a combination of the cheapest functions; instead, it is the lowest overall cost compatible with the company's stated service objectives.

■ Cost Trade-offs

A distribution system that attempts to provide a specific level of customer service for the lowest possible total cost must use cost trade-offs to resolve conflicts about resource allocations. That is, higher costs in one area of the distribution system must be offset by lower costs in another area if the total system is to remain cost effective.

Trade-offs are strategic decisions to combine (and recombine) resources for greatest cost effectiveness. When distribution managers regard the system as a network of interlocking functions, trade-offs become useful tools in a unified distribution strategy. Trade-offs are apparent in the American distribution strategy of Swedish furniture retailer IKEA, which sells large selections of stylish, ready-to-assemble furniture in several U.S. stores (see Case 13.1). To ensure that each store carries enough inventory to satisfy customers in the area, IKEA groups its American retail outlets into regions, each served by a separate distribution center. In addition, each IKEA store carries a five-week back stock of inventory. Thus IKEA has chosen to trade higher inventory warehousing costs for improved customer service.[5]

Now that we have discussed several of the physical distribution objectives that marketers may pursue, we are ready to take a closer look at specific physical distribution activities. For the remainder of the chapter, we focus on order processing, materials handling, warehousing, inventory management, and transportation.

5. Judith Graham, "IKEA Furnishing Its U.S. Identity," *Advertising Age*, Sept. 14, 1989, p. 79; and Jonathan Reynolds, "IKEA: A Competitive Company with Style," *Retail & Distribution Management (UK)*, May/June 1988, pp. 32–34.

ORDER PROCESSING

Order processing—the first stage in a physical distribution system—is the receipt and transmission of sales order information. Although management sometimes overlooks the importance of these activities, efficient order processing facilitates product flow. Computerized order processing, used by many firms, speeds the flow of information from customer to seller.[6] When carried out quickly and accurately, order processing contributes to customer satisfaction, repeat orders, and increased profits.

Generally, there are three main tasks in order processing: order entry, order handling, and order delivery.[7] Order entry begins when customers or salespersons place purchase orders by mail, telephone, or computer. In some companies, sales service representatives receive and enter orders personally and also handle complaints, prepare progress reports, and forward sales order information.[8]

The next task, order handling, involves several activities. Once an order has been entered, it is transmitted to the warehouse, where the availability of the product is verified, and to the credit department, where prices, terms, and the customer's credit rating are checked. If the credit department approves the purchase, the warehouse begins to fill the order. If the requested product is not in stock, a production order is sent to the factory or the customer is offered a substitute item.

When the order has been filled and packed for shipment, the warehouse schedules pickup with an appropriate carrier. If the customer is willing to pay for rush service, priority transportation is used. The customer is sent an invoice, inventory records are adjusted, and the order is delivered.

Order processing can be manual or electronic, depending on which method provides the greatest speed and accuracy within cost limits. Manual processing suffices for a small volume of orders and is more flexible in special situations; electronic processing is more practical for a large volume of orders and lets a company integrate order processing, production planning, inventory, accounting, and transportation planning into a total information system.[9] Wal-Mart and several hundred of its suppliers use electronic order-processing networks. Instead of sending paper purchase orders—which take five to ten days to reach their destination and then must be keyed into a supplier's system—Wal-Mart transmits purchase orders directly from its main data processing center to a participating vendor's computer.

MATERIALS HANDLING

Materials handling, or physical handling of products, is important in efficient warehouse operations, as well as in transportation from points of production to points of consumption. The characteristics of the product itself often determine how it will be handled. For example, bulk liquids and gases have unique characteristics that determine how they can be moved and stored.

---

6. Rinehart, Cooper, and Wagenheim, p. 67.

7. Guelzo, pp. 35–36.

8. Taff, p. 240.

9. Ibid., p. 244.

FIGURE 13.1
Materials handling.
Hardware Wholesalers,
Inc. (HWI) automates its
receiving procedures for
its 2900 independent
Hardware and Home
Center stores.

SOURCE: Hardware Wholesalers, Inc.

Materials handling procedures and techniques should increase the usable capacity of a warehouse, reduce the number of times a good is handled, and improve service to customers and increase their satisfaction with the product. Packaging, loading, movement, and labeling systems must be coordinated to maximize cost reduction and customer satisfaction (see Figure 13.1).

In Chapter 8 we note that the protective functions of packaging are important considerations in product development. Appropriate decisions about packaging materials and methods allow for the most efficient physical handling; most companies employ packaging consultants or specialists to accomplish this important task. Materials handling equipment is used in the design of handling systems. **Unit loading** is grouping one or more boxes on a pallet or skid; it permits movement of efficient loads by mechanical means, such as fork lifts, trucks, or conveyor systems. **Containerization** is the practice of consolidating many items into a single large container that is sealed at its point of origin and opened at its destination. The containers are usually eight feet wide, eight feet high, and ten, twenty, twenty-five, or forty feet long. They can be conveniently stacked and sorted as units at the point of loading; because individual items are not handled in transit, containerization greatly increases efficiency and security in shipping.

WAREHOUSING

Warehousing, the design and operation of facilities for storing and moving goods, is an important physical distribution function. Warehousing provides time utility by enabling firms to compensate for dissimilar production and consumption rates. That is, when mass production creates a greater stock of goods than can be sold immediately, companies may warehouse the surplus goods until customers are ready to buy. Warehousing also helps stabilize the prices and availability of seasonal items. Here we describe the basic functions of warehouses and the different types of warehouses available. We also examine the distribution center concept, a special warehouse operation designed so that goods can be moved rapidly.

■ Warehousing Functions

Warehousing is not limited simply to storage of goods. When warehouses receive goods by carloads or truckloads, they break down the shipments into smaller quantities for individual customers; when goods arrive in small lots, the warehouses assemble the lots into bulk loads that can be shipped out more economically.[10] Warehouses perform these basic distribution functions:

1. *Receiving goods.* The merchandise is accepted, and the warehouse assumes responsibility for it.
2. *Identifying goods.* The appropriate stockkeeping units are recorded, along with the quantity of each item received. The item may be marked with a physical code, tag, or other label, or it may be identified by an item code (a code on the carrier or container) or by physical properties.
3. *Sorting goods.* The merchandise is sorted for storage in appropriate areas.
4. *Dispatching goods to storage.* The merchandise is put away for later retrieval when necessary.
5. *Holding goods.* The merchandise is kept in storage and properly protected until needed.
6. *Recalling and picking goods.* Items customers have ordered are efficiently retrieved from storage and readied for the next step.
7. *Marshaling the shipment.* The items making up a single shipment are brought together and checked for completeness or explainable omissions. Order records are prepared or modified as necessary.
8. *Dispatching the shipment.* The consolidated order is packaged suitably and directed to the right transport vehicle. Necessary shipping and accounting documents are prepared.[11]

■ Types of Warehouses

A company's choice of warehouse facilities is an important strategic consideration. By using the right warehouse, a company may be able to reduce transportation and inventory costs or improve its service to customers; the wrong warehouse may drain company resources. Besides deciding how many facilities to operate and where to locate them, a company must determine which type of warehouse will be most appropriate. Warehouses fall into two general categories, private and public. In many cases, a combination of private and public facilities provides the most flexible approach to warehousing.

Private Warehouses. A **private warehouse** is operated by a company for shipping and storing its own products. Private warehouses are usually leased or purchased when a firm believes that its warehouse needs in given geographic markets are so substantial and so stable that it can make a long-term commitment to fixed facilities. They are also appropriate for firms that require special handling and storage features and want to control the design and operation of the warehouse.

10. Guelzo, p. 102.

11. Adapted from *Physical Distribution Systems* by John F. Magee. Copyright 1967 McGraw-Hill, Inc.

Some of the largest users of private warehouses are retail chain stores.[12] Retailers such as Sears, Radio Shack, and even Burger King find it economical to integrate the warehousing function with purchasing for and distribution to their retail outlets. When sales volumes are fairly stable, ownership and control of a private warehouse may provide benefits, such as property appreciation. Private warehouses, however, face fixed costs, such as insurance, taxes, maintenance, and debt expense. They also allow little flexibility when firms wish to move inventories to more strategic locations. Before tying up capital in a private warehouse or entering into a long-term lease, a company should consider its resources, the level of its expertise in warehouse management, and the role of the warehouse in its overall marketing strategy.

Public Warehouses.   **Public warehouses** rent storage space and related physical distribution facilities to other companies and sometimes provide distribution services such as receiving and unloading products, inspecting, reshipping, filling orders, financing, displaying products, and coordinating shipments. They are especially useful to firms with seasonal production or low-volume storage needs, companies with inventories that must be maintained in many locations, firms that are testing or entering new markets, and business operations that own private warehouses but occasionally require additional storage space. Public warehouses can also serve as collection points during product-recall programs. Whereas private warehouses have fixed costs, public warehouses' costs are variable (and often lower) because users rent space and purchase warehousing services only as needed.

In addition, many public warehouses furnish security for products that are being used as collateral for loans, a service that can be provided at either the warehouse or the site of the owner's inventory. A **field public warehouse** is a warehouse established by a public warehouse at the owner's inventory location. The warehouser becomes the custodian of the products and issues a receipt that can be used as collateral for a loan. Public warehouses can also provide **bonded storage**, a warehousing arrangement under which imported or taxable products are not released until the owners of the products have paid U.S. customs duties, taxes, or other fees. Bonded warehouses enable firms to defer tax payments on such items until the products are delivered to customers.

The Distribution Center.   A **distribution center** is a large, centralized warehouse that receives goods from factories and suppliers, regroups them into orders, and ships them to customers quickly, with the focus being on active movement of goods rather than passive storage.[13] Distribution centers are specially designed for the rapid flow of products. They are usually one-story buildings (to eliminate elevators) and have access to transportation networks, such as major highways or railway lines. Many distribution centers are highly automated, with computer-directed robots, fork lifts, and hoists collecting and moving products to loading docks. The new distribution center at Easton Aluminum is discussed in Marketing Update 13.1 Although some public warehouses offer such specialized services, most distribution centers are privately owned. They serve customers in regional markets and in some cases function as consolidation points for a company's branch warehouses.

12. James C. Johnson and Donald F. Wood, *Contemporary Physical Distribution & Logistics*, 2nd ed. (Tulsa, Okla.: PenWell Publishing Company, 1982), p. 356.

13. Guelzo, p. 102.

EASTON ALUMINUM'S DISTRIBUTION CENTER

A few years ago Easton Aluminum, Inc., a Van Nuys, California–based sporting goods company, began to suffer because of its success—the company was rapidly outgrowing its distribution system. Easton controls 95 percent of the $55-million-a-year aluminum baseball bat market; its aluminum arrows have dominated national and international archery competitions for fifty years; its Reflex ski poles are popular with top Nordic and Alpine skiers; and an increasing number of National Hockey League players are choosing Easton hockey sticks. Recently, to meet increased demand for its products, Easton designed and constructed a state-of-the-art distribution center on a ten-acre site in Salt Lake City.

The new distribution center receives Easton products from its manufacturing plants in the Orient and from its California and Salt Lake City plants in the United States. The center also distributes Mizuno products across North America, as Easton has the distribution rights to this Japanese sporting goods giant. Using computerized bar codes to track incoming and outgoing items, Easton claims that its data communications systems and its central computer produce highly accurate inventory records. Because of the special design of the 100,000-square-foot center, it has the storage capacity of a conventional 300,000-square-foot warehouse.

Easton officials claim that the distribution center has greatly improved customer service. Directed by remote radio computer devices, warehouse workers fill orders more quickly and more accurately, usually shipping out orders within twenty-four hours. The center has allowed Easton to solve staffing problems that were common at its former warehouses because the centralized system creates a more constant demand for the highly seasonal sporting products. Easton designed its system to accommodate future product demand increases, so it is likely that Easton will continue to reap the benefits of the new distribution center for years to come.

SOURCES: "Easton's $5 Million S.L. Plant the Hub of Global Sporting Goods Operation," *Deseret News* (Salt Lake City), Dec. 10, 1987, p. A8; Les Gould, "Building the Distribution Center of Their Dreams," *Modern Materials Handling,* July 1988, pp. 66–68; and Ronald Grover, "James Easton: Putting a 'Ping' in Baseball's Swing," *Business Week,* June 13, 1988, p. 57.

Distribution centers offer several benefits. Foremost among them is improved customer service. Distribution centers ensure product availability by maintaining full product lines. The speed of their operations cuts delivery time to a minimum. In addition, distribution centers reduce costs. Instead of having to make many smaller shipments to scattered warehouses and customers, factories can ship large quantities of goods directly to distribution centers at bulk-load rates, which lowers transportation costs; furthermore, rapid turnover of inventory lessens the need for warehouses and cuts storage costs. Some distribution centers also facilitate production by receiving and consolidating raw materials and providing final assembly for some products.

INVENTORY MANAGEMENT

Inventory management involves developing and maintaining adequate assortments of products to meet customers' needs. Because a firm's investment in inventory usually represents 30 to 50 percent of its total assets, inventory decisions have a significant impact on physical distribution costs and the level of customer service provided. When too few products are carried in inventory, the result is **stockouts**, or shortages of products, which cause brand switching, lower sales, and loss of customers. But when too many products (or too many slow-moving products) are carried, costs increase, as do the risks of product obsolescence, pilferage, and damage. The objective of inventory management, therefore, is to minimize inventory costs while maintaining an adequate supply of goods. Marketing Update 13.2 details how K mart is improving its inventory-handling methods.

There are three types of inventory costs. *Carrying costs* are holding costs; they include expenditures for storage space and materials handling, financing, insurance, taxes, and losses from spoilage of goods. *Replenishment costs* are related to the purchase of merchandise. The price of goods, handling charges, and expenses for order processing contribute to replenishment costs. *Stockout costs* include sales lost when demand for goods exceeds supply on hand and the clerical and processing expenses of backordering. All costs of obtaining and maintaining inventory must be controlled if profit goals are to be achieved.

Inventory managers deal with two issues of particular importance. They must know when to reorder and how much merchandise to order. The **reorder point** is the inventory level that signals that more inventory should be ordered. Three factors determine the reorder point: the anticipated time between the date an order is placed and the date the goods are received and made ready for resale to customers; the rate at which a product is sold or used up; and the quantity of **safety stock** on hand, or inventory needed to prevent stockouts. The optimum level of safety stock depends on the general demand and the standard of customer service to be provided. If a firm is to avoid shortages without tying up too much capital in inventory, some systematic method for determining reorder points is essential.

The inventory manager faces several trade-offs when reordering merchandise. Large safety stocks ensure product availability and thus improve the level of customer service; they also lower order-processing costs because orders are placed less frequently. Small safety stocks, on the other hand, cause frequent reorders and higher order-processing costs but reduce the overall cost of carrying inventory.

FIGURE 13.2

Effects of order size on an inventory system

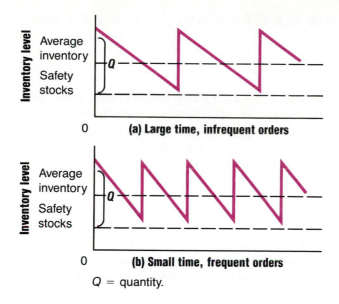

(a) Large time, infrequent orders

(b) Small time, frequent orders

Q = quantity.

(Figure 13.2 illustrates two order systems involving different order quantities but the same level of safety stocks. Figure 13.2(a) shows inventory levels for a given demand of infrequent orders; Figure 13.2(b) illustrates levels needed to fill frequent orders at the same demand.)

To quantify this trade-off between carrying costs and order-processing costs, a model for an **economic order quantity (EOQ)** has been developed (see Figure 13.3); it specifies the order size that minimizes the total cost of ordering and carrying inventory.[14] The fundamental relationships underlying the widely accepted EOQ model are the basis of many inventory control systems. Keep in mind, however, that the objective of minimum total inventory cost must be balanced against the customer service level necessary for maximum profits. Therefore, because increased costs of carrying inventory are usually associated with a higher level of customer service, the order quantity will often lie to the right of the optimal point in the figure, leading to a higher total cost for ordering and larger carrying inventory.

When management miscalculates reorder points or order quantities, inventory problems develop. Warning signs include an inventory that grows at a faster rate than sales, surplus or obsolete inventory, customer deliveries that are consistently late or lead times that are too long, inventory that represents a growing percentage of assets, and large inventory adjustments or write-offs.[15] However, there are several tools for improving inventory control. From a technical standpoint, an inventory system can be planned so that the number of products sold and the number of products in stock are determined at certain checkpoints. The control may be as

14. The EOQ formula for the optimal order quantity is EOQ = 2DR/I, where EOQ = optimum average order size, D = total demand, R = cost of processing an order, and I = cost of maintaining one unit of inventory per year. For a more complete description of EOQ methods and terminology, see Frank S. McLaughlin and Robert C. Pickardt, *Quantitative Techniques for Management Decisions* (Boston: Houghton Mifflin, 1978), pp. 104–119.

15. "Watch for These Red Flags," *Traffic Management,* January 1983, p. 8.

K MART STREAMLINES INVENTORY PROCESSING

It is estimated that 75 percent of all adult Americans shop at K mart at least once every three months. Since discount general merchandise retailers are very successful (with total sales of more than $21 billion), it follows that they need extremely efficient physical distribution methods to meet their requirements. K mart has one of the largest distribution networks in the United States. Its new automated distribution system allows distribution centers to move products to the 2,300 K mart locations faster and less expensively than before.

When redesigning their distribution system, K mart executives decided to reduce inventory at the stores and at the various regional distribution centers. The company experimented with a system called "automatic replenishment" for its small appliances. Automatic replenishment is a "sell one, send one" system. When a store sells a blender, a regional distribution center immediately ships another one to that store. The automatic replenishment system has worked so well for small appliances that K mart plans to set up the same system for large appliances, electronics, jewelry, and cameras. One K mart official remarked that automatic replenishment provides improved sales, gross margin, and inventory turnover.

Besides the automatic replenishment system, K mart has also installed a computer-assisted picking (CAP) system in its warehouses. The CAP system greatly speeds up the distribution process and reduces loader errors. K mart also saves money on labor as the CAP system has made many warehouse jobs obsolete.

K mart's distribution centers deliver information as well as products. A Kodak KAR-4000 computerized information system handles accounts payable and all correspondence to other K mart installations, as well as to outside vendors. K mart has also designed computerized packing and shipping systems that are used directly by employees on the warehouse floor. So far all of K mart's restructuring of its distribution system has saved the company money and speeded up the entire distribution process. K mart plans to automate its warehouses still further.

SOURCES: Steve Jacober, "K mart's New Directions for Hardgoods," *Discount Merchandising,* July 1988, pp. 18, 22, 24; Jay L. Johnson, "K mart's Automation Strategy," *Discount Merchandise,* June 1988, pp. 18, 20–21, 24; and "K mart Applies Automation to Information and Product Distribution," *IMC Journal,* January/February 1988, pp. 43–44.

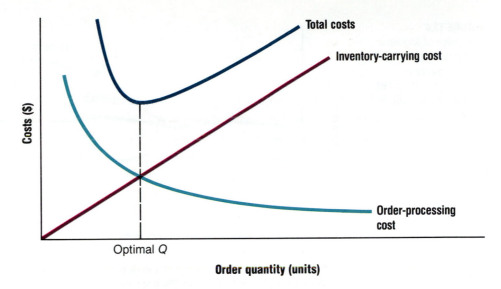

FIGURE 13.3
Economic order quantity (EOQ) model

simple as tearing off a code number from each product sold so that the correct sizes, colors, and models can be tabulated and reordered. A sizable amount of technologically advanced electronic equipment is available to aid in inventory management. In many larger stores, such as Wal-Mart and Toys "R" Us stores, check-out terminals connected to central computer systems instantaneously update inventory and sales records. For continuous, automatic updating of inventory records, some firms use pressure-sensitive circuits installed under ordinary industrial shelving to weigh inventory, convert the weight to units, and display any inventory changes on a video screen or computer printout.

Various techniques have also been used successfully to improve inventory management. The just-in-time concept, widely used in Japan as well as in some American companies, calls for companies to maintain low inventory levels and purchase products and materials in small quantities, just at the time they are needed for production. Ford Motor Company, for example, sometimes receives supply deliveries as often as every two hours.[16] Just-in-time inventory management depends on a high level of coordination between producers and suppliers, but the technique enables companies to eliminate waste and reduce inventory costs significantly. When Polaroid implemented just-in-time techniques as part of its zero base pricing program to reduce the overall cost of purchased materials, equipment, and services, it experienced cost reductions and avoidances averaging $20 million per year.[17]

Another inventory management technique, the 80/20 rule, holds that fast-moving products should generate a higher level of customer service than slow-moving products, on the theory that 20 percent of the items account for 80 percent of the sales. Thus an inventory manager attempts to keep an adequate supply of fast-selling items and a minimal supply of the slower-moving products.

16. David N. Burt, "Managing Suppliers Up to Speed," *Harvard Business Review,* July-August 1989, p. 128.

17. Ibid., p. 129.

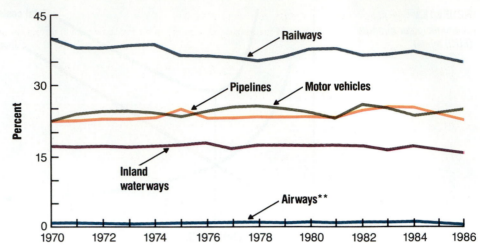

FIGURE 13.4
Ton-miles of domestic intercity freight traffic—percent distribution by type of transportation 1970 to 1987

*A ton-mile is the movement of 1 ton (2,000 pounds) of freight for the distance of 1 mile.
**Airways represent less than 1% intercity traffic.
SOURCE: *Statistical Abstract of the United States, 1989,* p. 589.

TRANSPORTATION

Transportation adds time and place utility to a product by moving it from where it is made to where it is purchased and used.[18] Because product availability and timely deliveries are so dependent on transportation functions, a firm's choice of transportation directly affects customer service. A firm may even build its distribution and marketing strategy around a unique transportation system if the on-time deliveries, which that system ensures, will give the firm a competitive edge. In this section we consider the principal modes of transportation, the criteria companies use to select one transportation mode over another, and several methods of coordinating transportation services.

■ **Transportation Modes**

As Figure 13.4 indicates, there are five major **transportation modes**, or methods of moving goods: railways, motor vehicles, inland waterways, airways, and pipelines. Each mode offers unique advantages; many companies have adopted physical handling procedures that facilitate the use of two or more modes in combination. Table 13.1 illustrates typical transportation modes for various products.

Railways. Railways carry heavy, bulky freight that must be shipped overland for long distances. Railways commonly haul minerals, sand, lumber, pulp, chemicals, and farm products, as well as low-value manufactured goods and an increasing number of automobiles. They are especially efficient for transporting full carloads, which require less handling—and can therefore be shipped at lower rates—than

18. Peter D. Bennett, ed., *Dictionary of Marketing Terms* (Chicago: American Marketing Association, 1988), p. 204.

TABLE 13.1 *Typical transportation modes for various products*

RAILWAYS	MOTOR VEHICLES	WATERWAYS	PIPELINES	AIRWAYS
Coal	Clothing	Petroleum	Oil	Flowers
Grain	Paper goods	Chemicals	Processed coal	Perishable food
Chemicals	Computers	Iron ore	Natural gas	Instruments
Lumber	Books	Bauxite	Water	Emergency parts
Automobiles	Fresh fruit	Grain		Overnight mail
Iron	Livestock			

less-than-carload quantities. Many companies locate their factories or warehouses near major rail lines or on spur lines for convenient loading and unloading.

Although railways haul more intercity freight than any other mode of transportation, accounting for more than one-third of all cargo ton-miles carried, their share of the transportation market has declined in recent years. High fixed costs, shortages of rail cars during peak periods, poor maintenance of tracks and equipment, and increased competition from other carriers, mainly trucks, have plagued railroad companies and diminished profits.

To improve customer service, railroads have turned to a variety of innovations. Several years ago, Railbox, a nationwide pool of 25,000 general-service boxcars, was formed; the boxcars belong to no single rail company and can be dispatched around the country wherever boxcars are in short supply. Rail yards are also speeding up the formation of outbound trains by using optical scanners to read coded labels on the sides of cars, which helps sort cars by destination. Other special services include unit trains, which carry a single commodity from point of origin to destination and bypass classification yards; run-through trains, which also run nonstop but carry more than one product; and minitrains, which run often and are therefore useful in just-in-time inventory systems.

Motor Vehicles.   Motor vehicles provide the most flexible schedules and routes of all major transportation modes because they can go almost anywhere. As indicated in Figure 13.5, Consolidated Freightways, for example, moves over 20 million pounds of freight daily, serving more than 50,000 cities in thirty-four states and eastern Canada. Trucks usually haul small shipments of high-value goods over short distances. Because trucks have a unique ability to move goods directly from factory or warehouse to customer, they are often used in conjunction with other forms of transport that cannot provide door-to-door deliveries.

The Interstate Commerce Commission (ICC) classifies motor vehicles (along with other transportation firms) as common, contract, private, or exempt carriers. Common carriers are legally obligated to serve all customers requesting their services, assuming that the carriers have the necessary equipment. Contract carriers function much the same as private transportation systems and haul freight only for

FIGURE 13.5

Motor vehicles. Consolidated Freightways promotes its capability to reach fifty thousand communities in thirty-four states and eastern Canada. It is promoting its commitment to service and customer satisfaction.

SOURCE: Consolidated Freightways, Inc., Corporate Advertising Campaign

customers that have written agreements with them. Private carriers are company-owned transport systems; although they are not economically regulated by the ICC, they are subject to safety regulations and prohibited from carrying other companies' products. Exempt carriers are freight haulers in any category who are carrying products exempted from regulation, such as unprocessed agricultural goods. As in many other industries, brokers bring together those wanting transport services and those providing them.

Although motor vehicles usually travel much faster than trains, they are somewhat more vulnerable to bad weather, and their services are more expensive. Trucks are also subject to the size and weight restrictions of the products they carry. In addition, motor carriers, especially common carriers, are sometimes criticized for high levels of loss and damage to freight and for delays from rehandling small shipments. In response, the trucking industry is turning to computerized tracking of shipments and developing new equipment to speed up loading and unloading.[19]

19. Guelzo, pp. 50–52.

Inland Waterways.   Water transportation is the cheapest method of shipping heavy, low-value, nonperishable goods such as ore, coal, grain, sand, and petroleum products. Water carriers offer considerable capacity. Tugboat-powered barges that travel along inland rivers, canals, and navigation systems can haul at least ten times the weight of one rail car, and deep-draft vessels operating within the Great Lakes–St. Lawrence Seaway system can carry up to 65,000 tons.[20]

However, many markets are accessible to water only with supplementary rail or truck transport. Furthermore, water transport is extremely slow and sometimes comes to a standstill during freezing weather. Companies that depend on water may ship their entire inventory during the summer and then store it for winter use. Droughts and floods also create difficulties for users of inland waterway transportation. Nevertheless, because water transportation is extremely fuel efficient, its volume is expected to double by the year 2000.[21]

Airways.   Air transportation is the fastest and most expensive form of shipping. It is used most often for perishable goods, for high value, low bulk items, and for products that must be delivered quickly over long distances, such as emergency shipments. The capacity of air transport is limited only by the capacity of individual aircraft. Medium-range jets can haul about 40,000 pounds of freight, and some new jet cargo planes equipped to carry containers can accommodate more than 200,000 pounds. Most air carriers transport a combination of passengers, freight, and mail.[22]

Although air transport accounts for less than 1 percent of total ton-miles carried, its importance as a mode of transportation is growing. Despite its expense, air transit can reduce warehousing and packaging costs and also losses from theft and damage, thus helping lower total costs. However, the truck transportation needed for pickup and final delivery adds to cost and transit time.

Pipelines.   Pipelines, the most automated transportation mode, usually belong to the shipper and carry the shipper's products. Most pipelines carry petroleum products or chemicals. For example, the Trans-Alaska Pipeline, owned and operated by a consortium of oil companies that includes Exxon, Mobil, and British Petroleum, transports crude oil from remote oil-drilling sites in central Alaska to shipping terminals on the coast for its owners. Slurry pipelines have been developed to carry pulverized coal, grain, or wood chips suspended in water. Even though pipelines have limited accessibility because of their fixed routes, pipeline use accounts for about one-fourth of all intercity ton-miles.

Pipelines move products slowly but continuously and at relatively low cost. They are a reliable mode of transportation and ensure low product damage and theft. However, their contents are subject to as much as 1 percent shrinkage, usually from evaporation, and products must be shipped in minimum quantities of 25,000 barrels for efficient pipeline operation.[23] They have also been a source of concern to environmentalists, who fear that installation and leaks could harm plants and animals.

20. Donald F. Wood and James C. Johnson, *Contemporary Transportation* (Tulsa, Okla.: Petroleum Publishing, 1980), pp. 290, 303.

21. Ibid., p. 289

22. Taff, p. 126.

23. Guelzo, p. 53.

TABLE 13.2 *Ranking of transportation modes by selection criteria, highest to lowest*

	COST	TRANSIT TIME	RELIABILITY	CAPABILITY	ACCESSIBILITY	SECURITY	TRACEABILITY
MOST	Air	Water	Pipeline	Water	Truck	Pipeline	Air
	Truck	Rail	Truck	Rail	Rail	Water	Truck
	Rail	Pipeline	Rail	Truck	Air	Rail	Rail
	Pipeline	Truck	Air	Air	Water	Air	Water
LEAST	Water	Air	Water	Pipeline	Pipeline	Truck	Pipeline

SOURCE: Certain of this information has been adapted from J. L. Heskett, Robert Ivie, and J. Nicholas Glaskowsky, *Business Logistics* (New York: Ronald Press, 1973). Used by permission.

Criteria for Selecting Transportation

Marketers select a transportation mode on the basis of costs, transit time (speed), reliability, capability, accessibility, security, and traceability.[24] Table 13.2 summarizes various cost and performance considerations that help determine the selection of transportation modes. It is important to remember that these relationships are approximations and that the choice of a transportation mode involves many trade-offs.

Costs. Marketers compare alternative modes of transportation to determine whether the benefits from a more expensive mode are worth the higher costs. Air freight carriers—for instance, UPS Next Day Air Services (depicted in Figure 13.6)—provide many benefits, such as high speed, reliability, security, and traceability, but at higher costs relative to other transportation modes. When speed is less important, marketers prefer lower costs. For example, bicycles are often shipped by rail because an unassembled bicycle can be shipped more than a thousand miles on a train for as little as $3.60. Bicycle wholesalers plan their purchases far enough in advance to be able to capitalize on this cost advantage.

Generally, marketers have been able to cut expenses and increase efficiency since transportation was deregulated in the late 1970s and early 1980s. Railroads, airlines, trucks, barges, and pipeline companies all have become more competitive and more responsive to customers' needs. Surveys reveal that in recent years transportation costs per hundredweight and as a percentage of sales have declined, now averaging $33.45 per hundredweight, or 7.5 percent of sales. This figure varies by industry, of course; electrical machinery, textiles, and instruments have transportation costs of only 3 or 4 percent of sales, whereas lumber products, chemicals, and food have transportation costs close to 15 percent of sales.

Transit Time. Transit time is the total time a carrier has possession of goods, including the time required for pickup and delivery, handling, and movement between the points of origin and destination. Closely related to transit time is frequency, or number of shipments per day. Transit time obviously affects a marketer's

24. John J. Coyle, Edward Bardi, and C. John Langley, Jr., *The Management of Business Logistics* (St. Paul, Minn.: West, 1988), pp. 327–329.

FIGURE 13.6 *Air express services.*
UPS promotes guaranteed delivery at a price that's up to half what other air express companies charge.

SOURCE: Courtesy of United Parcel Service of America, Inc.

ability to provide service, but there are some less obvious implications as well. A shipper can take advantage of transit time to process orders for goods enroute, a capability especially important to agricultural and raw materials shippers. Some railroads also let carloads already in transit be redirected, for maximum flexibility in selecting markets. For example, a carload of peaches may be shipped to a closer destination if the fruit is in danger of ripening too quickly.

Reliability.   The total reliability of a transportation mode is determined by the consistency of service provided. Marketers must be able to count on their carriers to deliver goods on time and in an acceptable condition. Along with transit time, reliability affects a marketer's inventory costs, including sales lost when merchandise is not available. Unreliable transportation necessitates higher inventory levels so that stockouts will be avoided. Reliable delivery service, on the other hand, enables customers to carry smaller inventories, at lower cost. To maintain desired levels of inventory, Wal-Mart ships more than 75 percent of its stock through its own distribution network, which includes sixteen distribution centers and a private fleet of trucks. Each Wal-Mart store receives a minimum of five shipments of merchandise per week, and the shipments arrive punctually better than 99 percent of the time.[25]

25. Wal-Mart Stores, Inc., *1989 Annual Report,* p. 11.

Capability.   Capability is the ability of a transportation mode to provide the appropriate equipment and conditions for moving specific kinds of goods. For example, many products must be shipped under controlled temperature and humidity. Other products, such as liquids or gases, require special equipment or facilities for shipment. In the railroad industry, a shipper with unusual transport needs can consult the *Official Railway Equipment Register*, which lists the various types of cars and equipment each railroad owns.

Accessibility.   A carrier's ability to move goods over a specific route or network (rail lines, waterways, or truck routes) is its accessibility. For example, marketers evaluating transportation modes for reaching Great Falls, Montana, would realistically consider rail lines, truck routes, and scheduled airline service but would eliminate water-borne carriers because Great Falls is inaccessible by water.

Some carriers differentiate themselves by serving areas their competitors do not. After deregulation, for instance, many large railroad companies sold off or abandoned unprofitable routes, making rail service inaccessible to shippers located on spur lines. Some shippers were forced to buy their own truck fleets just to get their products to market. In recent years, however, small, short-line railroad companies have started buying up track and creating networks of low-cost feeder lines to reach those underserved markets. Small shippers are regaining access to rail service, and the short-line companies are profiting.[26]

Security.   A transportation mode's security is measured by the physical condition of goods upon delivery. A firm does not incur costs directly when goods are lost or damaged because the common carrier is usually held liable. Nevertheless, poor service and lack of security indirectly lead to increased costs and lower profits for the firm because damaged or lost goods are not available for immediate sale or use.

Security problems vary considerably among transportation companies and geographic regions. In the Northeast, for example, truck hijacking is a rapidly growing crime. According to the Federal Bureau of Investigation (FBI), approximately 19,000 truck tractors and 47,000 trailers are listed as stolen each year. To combat the hijacking problem, The Federated Group, which operates a chain of electronics stores, implemented a two-way radio security system for all its trucks. The system allows Federated to track the location of each truck, its status, and its estimated time of arrival at the next location. In the event of a hijacking, the radio in each truck includes a hidden "panic button" that drivers can push to alert an operator at the company's communication headquarters, who then calls the police to give the location of the truck.[27] However, all transportation modes have security problems, and marketers must evaluate the relative risk of each mode.

Traceability.   Traceability is the relative ease with which a shipment can be located and transferred (or found if it is lost). Quick traceability is a convenience that some firms value highly. Shippers have learned that the tracing of shipments,

26. Gary Slutsker, "Working on the Railroads," *Forbes*, Mar. 24, 1986, p. 126.

27. "Federated Group Stymies Hijackers with Two-Way Radio," *Chain Store Age Executive*, November 1985, pp. 172, 175.

along with prompt invoicing and processing of claims, increases customer loyalty and improves a firm's image in the marketplace.[28] Federal Express, for example, relies on special computer systems to process and track the more than one million packages it receives each day for overnight delivery. At each stage of processing, from pickup to delivery, the location of every package is logged into the company's central computer in Memphis, Tennessee. If Federal Express is unable to track down a package within thirty minutes of a customer's query, the customer is charged nothing for the shipment.[29]

■ Coordinating Transportation Services

To take advantage of the benefits various types of carriers offer, and to compensate for their deficiencies, marketers often must combine and coordinate two or more modes of transportation. In recent years, **intermodal transportation**, as this integrated approach is sometimes called, has become easier because of new developments within the transportation industry.

Several kinds of intermodal shipping are available, all combining the flexibility of trucking with the low cost or speed of other forms of transport. Containerization, discussed earlier, facilitates intermodal transportation by consolidating shipments into sealed containers for transport by piggyback (shipping that combines truck trailers and railway flatcars), fishyback (truck trailers and water carriers), and birdyback (truck trailers and air carriers). As transportation costs increase, intermodal services gain popularity. Intermodal services have been estimated to cost 25 to 40 percent less than all-highway transport and account for about 12 to 16 percent of total freight transportation business.[30]

Specialized agencies, **freight forwarders**, provide other forms of transport coordination. These firms combine shipments from several organizations into efficient lot sizes. Small loads (less than five hundred pounds) are much more expensive to ship than full carloads or truckloads and frequently must be consolidated. The freight forwarder takes small loads from various shippers, buys transport space from carriers, and arranges for the goods to be delivered to their respective buyers. The freight forwarder's profits come from the margin between the higher, less-than-carload rates charged to each shipper and the lower carload rates the agency pays. Because large shipments require less handling, the use of a freight forwarder can speed transit time. Freight forwarders can also determine the most efficient carriers and routes and are useful for shipping goods to foreign markets.

One other transportation innovation is the development of **megacarriers**, which are freight transportation companies that provide several methods of shipment, such as rail, truck, and air service. CSX, for example, has trains, barges, container ships, trucks, and pipelines, which allows it to provide a multitude of transportation services (see Figure 13.7). Air carriers have increased their ground transportation services. As they have expanded the range of transportation alternatives, carriers have also put greater stress on customer service.

28. Thomas A. Foster and Joseph V. Barks, "Here Comes the Best," *Distribution*, September 1984, p. 25.

29. Federal Express Corporation, *Federal Express Corporation 1989 Annual Report;* and Brian Dumaine, "Turbulence Hits the Air Couriers," *Fortune,* July 21, 1986, pp. 101–102.

30. Allen R. Wastler, "Intermodal Leaders Ponder Riddle of Winning More Freight," *Traffic World,* June 19, 1989, pp. 14–15.

FIGURE 13.7 *Megacarrier.*
CSX is a megacarrier with the capability of providing transportation by trains, barges, container ships, trucks, and pipelines.

SOURCE: Courtesy of CSX Corporation

STRATEGIC ISSUES IN PHYSICAL DISTRIBUTION

The physical distribution functions discussed in this chapter—order processing, materials handling, warehousing, inventory management, and transportation—account for about half of all marketing costs. Moreover, these functions have a significant impact on customer service and satisfaction, which are of prime importance to marketers. Effective marketers accept considerable responsibility for the design and control of the physical distribution system. They work to ensure that the organization's overall marketing strategy is enhanced by physical distribution, with its dual objectives of decreasing costs while increasing customer service.

The strategic importance of physical distribution is evident in all elements of the marketing mix. Product design and packaging must allow for efficient stacking, storage, and transport; decisions to differentiate products by size, color, and style must take into account the additional demands that will be placed on warehousing and shipping facilities. Competitive pricing may depend on a firm's ability to provide reliable delivery or emergency shipments of replacement parts; a firm trying to lower its inventory costs may offer quantity discounts to encourage large purchases. Promotional campaigns must be coordinated with distribution functions so advertised products will be available to buyers; order-processing departments must be able to handle additional sales order information efficiently. Distribution planners must consider warehousing and transportation costs, which may influence—for example—the firm's policy on stockouts or its choice to centralize (or decentralize) its inventory.

No single distribution system is ideal for all situations, and any system must be evaluated continually and adapted as necessary. For instance, pressures to adjust service levels or reduce costs may lead to totally restructuring the marketing channel relationships; changes in transportation, warehousing, materials handling, and inventory may affect speed of delivery, reliability, and economy of service. Marketing strategists must consider customers' changing needs and preferences and recognize that changes in any one of the major distribution functions will affect all other functions. Consumer-oriented marketers analyze the characteristics of their target markets and then design distribution systems to provide products at acceptable costs.

Summary

Physical distribution is a set of activities that moves products from producers to consumers, or end users. These activities include order processing, materials handling, warehousing, inventory management, and transportation. An effective physical distribution system can be an important component of an overall marketing strategy because it can decrease costs and increase customer satisfaction. Physical distribution activities should be integrated with marketing channel decisions and should be adjusted to meet the unique needs of a channel member. For most firms, physical distribution accounts for about one-fifth of a product's retail price.

The main objective of physical distribution is to decrease costs while increasing customer service. To this end, physical distribution managers strive to balance service, distribution costs, and resources. Companies must adapt to customers' needs and preferences, offer service comparable to or better than their competitors, and develop and communicate desirable customer service policies. Costs of providing service are minimized most effectively through the total cost approach, which evaluates the costs of the system as a whole rather than as a collection of separate activities. Cost trade-offs must often be used to offset higher costs in one area of distribution with lower costs in another area.

Order processing, the first stage in a physical distribution system, is the receipt and transmission of sales order information. Order processing consists of three main tasks. Order entry is placing purchase orders from customers or salespersons by mail, telephone, or computer. Order handling involves checking customer credit, verifying product availability, and preparing products for shipping. Order delivery is provided by the carrier most suitable for a desired level of customer service. Order processing may be done manually or electronically, depending on which method gives the greatest speed and accuracy within cost limits.

Materials handling, or the physical handling of products, is an important element of physical distribution. Packaging, loading, and movement systems must be coordinated to take into account both cost reduction and customer requirements. Basic handling systems include unit loading on pallets or skids, movement by mechanical devices, and containerization.

Warehousing involves the design and operation of facilities for storing and moving goods. Private warehouses are owned and operated by a company for the purpose of distributing its own products. Public warehouses are business organizations that rent storage space and related physical distribution facilities to other firms. Public warehouses may furnish security for products that are being used as collateral for loans by establishing field warehouses. They may also provide bonded storage for companies wishing to defer tax payments on imported or taxable products. Distribution centers are large, centralized warehouses specially designed for the rapid movement of goods to customers. In many cases, a combination of private and public facilities is the most flexible approach to warehousing.

The objective of inventory management is to minimize inventory costs while maintaining a supply of goods adequate for customers' needs. All inventory costs—carrying, replenishment, and stockout costs—must be controlled if profit goals are to be met. To avoid stockouts without tying up too much capital in inventory, a firm must have a systematic method for determining a reorder point, the inventory level at which more inventory is ordered. The trade-offs between the costs of carrying larger average safety stocks and the costs of frequent orders can be quantified in the economic order quantity (EOQ) model. Inventory problems may take the form of surplus inventory, late deliveries, write-offs, and inventory that is too large in proportion to sales or assets. Methods for improving inventory management include systems for determining the number of products sold and in stock and management techniques such as just-in-time and the 80/20 rule.

Transportation adds time and place utility to a product by moving it from where it is made to where it is purchased and used. The five major modes of transporting goods in the United States are railways, motor vehicles, inland waterways, airways, and pipelines. Marketers evaluate transportation modes with respect to costs, transit time (speed), reliability, capability, accessibility, security, and traceability; final selection of a transportation mode involves many trade-offs. Intermodal transportation allows marketers to combine the advantages of two or more modes of transport; it is facilitated by containerization; freight forwarders, who coordinate transport by combining small shipments from several organizations into efficient lot sizes; and megacarriers, freight transportation companies that offer several methods of shipment.

Physical distribution affects every element of the marketing mix: product, price, promotion, and distribution. To give customers products at acceptable prices, marketers consider consumers' changing needs and any shifts within the major distribution functions. Then they adapt existing physical distribution systems for greater effectiveness. Physical distribution functions account for about half of all marketing costs and have a significant impact on customer satisfaction. Therefore, effective marketers are actively involved in the design and control of physical distribution systems.

IMPORTANT TERMS

Physical distribution
Order processing
Materials handling
Unit loading
Containerization
Warehousing
Private warehouse
Public warehouses
Field public warehouse
Bonded storage

Distribution center
Stockouts
Reorder point
Safety stock
Economic order quantity (EOQ)
Transportation
Transportation modes
Intermodal transportation
Freight forwarders
Megacarriers

DISCUSSION AND REVIEW QUESTIONS

1. Discuss the cost and service trade-offs in developing a physical distribution system.
2. What factors must physical distribution managers consider when developing a customer service mix?
3. Why should physical distribution managers develop service standards?
4. What is the advantage of using a total distribution cost approach?
5. What are the main tasks involved in order processing?
6. Discuss the advantages of using an electronic order-processing system. Which types of organizations are most likely to utilize electronic order processing?
7. How does a product's package affect materials handling procedures and techniques?
8. What is containerization? Discuss the major benefits of containerization.
9. Explain the major differences between private and public warehouses. What is a field public warehouse?
10. Under what circumstances should a firm use a private warehouse instead of a public one?
11. The focus of distribution centers is on active movement of goods. Discuss how distribution centers are designed for the rapid flow of products.
12. Describe the costs associated with inventory management.
13. Explain the trade-offs inventory managers face when reordering merchandise.
14. How can managers improve inventory control? Give specific examples of techniques.
15. Compare the five major transportation modes as to costs, transit time, reliability, capability, accessibility, security, and traceability.
16. What is transit time, and how does it affect physical distribution decisions?
17. Discuss the ways marketers can combine or coordinate two or more modes of transportation. What is the advantage of doing this?
18. Identify the types of containerized shipping available to physical distribution managers.
19. Discuss how the four elements of the marketing mix affect physical distribution strategy.

13.1 IKEA Uses High-Tech Physical Distribution

IKEA, one of Europe's largest furniture retailers, has invaded the U.S. market. A few years ago, the Swedish firm made its debut in this country with a two-story, six-acre store just outside Philadelphia. A year later, a second store opened near Washington, D.C., bringing IKEA's worldwide total to 85 stores in 19 countries. Now IKEA has stores in the Baltimore, Pittsburgh, New York City, and Los Angeles metropolitan areas.

The attractive Scandinavian styling and bright colors of IKEA's ready-to-assemble furniture and decorating accessories were an immediate success with American shoppers. Do-it-yourself furniture, however, is nothing new. British-based Conran introduced European design to American mass markets several years before IKEA arrived, and other firms that sell Scandinavian furniture, both assembled and knocked down, have been located within the United States since the 1960s. What sets IKEA apart, besides its low prices, is its transnational distribution system. Both benefits are possible partly because of IKEA's innovative flat-pack technology.

About 95 percent of IKEA's fourteen thousand product offerings are sold knocked down in flat boxes, which lowers prices by saving storage space and cutting shipping costs. IKEA's central warehouse in Amhult, Sweden, is staffed by just three people using computerized fork lifts and thirteen robots. Through a command from the keyboard operator, a fork lift glides down the aisles of the 200-yard-long building to locate the designated pallets and bring them to the robots. The robots then follow magnetic strips on the floor to deliver the pallets to the shipping dock. Once the products reach an IKEA store, they are held (still boxed) in a self-service warehouse adjoining the store's showrooms. After shoppers browse through the showrooms and examine IKEA's glossy catalog, they push supermarket-style carts into the self-service area, pull their boxed selections from bins and shelves, and proceed to the check-out line. The customers themselves transport most purchases home, although delivery service for such heavy items as sofas and cabinets is available for a fee.

IKEA is continually experimenting with ways to flat-pack more product per box. Whereas fully assembled bentwood chairs, for example, are usually shipped six to a pallet, IKEA engineers have figured out how to pack in twenty-eight chairs un-assembled. By farming out its in-house designs to the most efficient manufacturers and suppliers it can find, IKEA cuts costs even further. IKEA's "creative sourcing" might mean that a carpenter supplies wooden parts for tables; a shirt manufacturer, seat covers; and a third supplier, screws and bolts. On the average, IKEA's retail prices are up to 50 percent lower than those of its competitors.

Philadelphia shoppers took to the IKEA system quickly—so quickly in fact that at first the Pennsylvania store was almost overwhelmed. During the four-day grand opening, 130,000 shoppers made their way through the store's stylish room settings. Sales for the first three months totaled $8 million, up $2 million from initial projections. Since then, crowds have leveled off at about 30,000 people a week; the Virginia store draws about 15,000 people on a typical weekend.

But success has not been without problems. First, the U.S. stores are too small. Inadequate warehouse space and loading platforms have necessitated a night shift just to replenish the stock. Second, demand has routinely exceeded supply in some product categories. At one point, the Philadelphia store had a backlog of 15,000 requests for out-of-stock items. IKEA maintains two distribution centers in Canada to service its stores there, but most of the stock for the U.S. stores comes from the main warehouse in Sweden, spending six to eight weeks in transit before arriving at one of the company's huge distribution centers. The stockouts are troublesome, because many of IKEA's product designs are modular: If one piece is unavailable, sales of the other pieces are delayed. IKEA is also concerned about first-time shoppers who find an item out of stock and never return for a second visit. IKEA has responded by increasing its warehouse stock.

IKEA managers have alleviated many supply problems by building a multi-million-dollar distribution center in the Philadelphia area. The company also intends to use a greater number of domestic suppliers. At present Canadian manufacturers provide some of the products for the U.S. stores (as well as about 20 percent of the items in Canadian stores), and some of IKEA's sofas are now made in Knoxville, Tennessee. Another possibility for avoiding distribution delays is the purchase of a private shipping line. Although IKEA offers mail-order service in Europe (and, in fact, started out as a mail-order furniture company), the company has no current plans to establish a mail-order business in the United States, despite a deluge of requests from customers.

Instead, IKEA's long-range U.S. strategy calls for several new stores over the next few years, supported by five regional distribution and marketing systems. For now, IKEA is concentrating on setting up new stores on both coasts.

SOURCES: Janet Bamford, "Why Competitors Shop for Ideas at IKEA," *Business Week*, Oct. 9, 1989, p. 88; Eugene Carlson, "How a Major Swedish Retailer Chose a Beachhead in the U.S.," *Wall Street Journal*, Apr. 7, 1987, p. 37; Kimberley Carpenter, "Help Yourself," *Working Woman*, Aug. 1986, p. 56; Pat Corwin, "The Vikings Are Back—With Furniture," *Discount Merchandising*, April 1987, p. 52; Peter Fuhrman, "The Workers' Friend," *Forbes*, Mar. 21, 1988, pp. 124, 128; Judith Graham, "IKEA Furnishing Its U.S. Identity," *Advertising Age*, Sept. 18, 1989, p. 79; Bill Kelley, "The New Wave From Europe," *Sales & Marketing Management*, Nov. 1987, pp. 45–51; Mary Krienke, "IKEA = Simple Good Taste," *Stores*, Apr. 1986, p. 60; Kevin Maney, "Customers Flood USA IKEA Outlets," *USA Today*, Nov. 4, 1986, sec. B, p. 1; and Carolyn Pfaff, "IKEA: The Supermarket of Furniture Stores," *Adweek*, May 3, 1986, p. 26.

Questions for Discussion

1. What actions has IKEA taken to reduce its physical distribution problems?
2. Explain how IKEA's physical distribution system influences other parts of this organization's marketing strategies.
3. In the future, what types of physical distribution problems must IKEA resolve with respect to its U.S. stores?

13.2 Distribution of Holly Farms Pre-cooked Chicken

When it recently acquired former rival Holly Farms, Springdale, Arkansas–based Tyson Foods, Inc. became the largest producer and marketer of pre-cooked chicken products in the United States. Before buying Holly Farms, Tyson's chicken production was strained as it attempted to keep up with the demands of its booming food-service business and the public's increasing preference for chicken. However, in addition to gaining Holly Farms' pre-cooked chicken operation, Tyson has also inherited some of the same problems Holly Farms had with this type of product.

Over the last few years, as more health-conscious consumers sought diets lower in calories and cholesterol, the demand for chicken steadily rose. Because of this, and the growing demand for food that could be easily and quickly prepared at home, Holly Farms executives believed that their line of pre-cooked chicken products would be a great success. They did not anticipate the extensive distribution problems they would encounter. They also underestimated the high costs and waste involved with selling prepared foods.

The highest costs associated with pre-cooked chicken are distribution costs. One supermarket analyst refers to the distribution of fresh foods as a distribution "nightmare." He contends that there is no way that fresh food producers can adequately support their products at the retail level.

Perishable prepared foods are expensive to produce (labor costs are tremendous), relatively expensive for the consumers to buy, and subject to spoilage loss. The biggest problem with pre-cooked chicken is its short shelf life. Grocery retailers are accustomed to ordering food products long in advance, warehousing the products, and then placing them on shelves as shelf-space availability dictates. Grocers who did not make proper adjustments when handling Holly Farm products began to lose much of the chicken to spoilage because it was stored too long in warehouses. So even though consumers seemed to like the products, some supermarkets began to discontinue carrying them.

With some retail executives claiming that prepared foods account for 10 to 20 percent of total store sales, many grocers are eager to expand their pre-cooked food capabilities. Supermarkets now account for 22 percent of takeout food sales and several food analysts think that this percentage will keep growing. Other grocery experts disagree on the future of prepared foods. The chief executive officer of a New York supermarket chain has said flatly that prepared foods are not profitable. A vice president of the country's fourth largest chain has said that the profit return on pre-cooked food is questionable.

Holly Farms was trying to sell a popular consumer item that many supermarkets did not like. Also, since many supermarket chains are experimenting with their own versions of prepared chicken, some are not anxious to cooperate with Tyson in ironing out the distribution problems.

Tyson will need extensive interaction with retailers in order for its pre-cooked chicken line to be successful. Tyson may need to explore more advanced cooking technology that will enable its chicken products to have longer shelf lives. Tyson officials may have to rethink the entire distribution process set up by Holly Farms.

SOURCES: Judann Dagnoli, "Fresh Idea Remains Fraught with Problems," *Advertising Age,* May 8, 1989, pp. S-1, S-2; Diane Feldman, "Building a Better Bird," *Management Review,* May 1989, pp. 10–14; Bradley H. Gendell, "Cockfight," *Financial World,* July 11, 1989, pp. 26–27; "Holly Farms," *Arkansas Gazette* (Little Rock, Arkansas), Aug. 11, 1989, p. C2; and Kevin Kelly, "For Chicken Biggie Tyson, the Sky Could Be Falling," *Business Week,* Dec. 5, 1988, p. 32.

Questions for Discussion

1. Are the problems with the Holly Farms pre-cooked chicken products mainly distribution problems? Why or why not?
2. What types of issues should Tyson marketers consider in redesigning the distribution system for Holly Farms pre-cooked chicken products?
3. Should Tyson continue to produce the Holly Farms pre-cooked chicken products that are sold in supermarkets? Why or why not?

Channel Decisions for Texas Instruments' microLaser Printer*

Texas Instruments (TI), founded in the 1930s, employs 75,000 people worldwide, with major manufacturing sites in North America, South America, Europe, Asia, and Australia. TI serves a wide range of electronics markets and is divided into six major groups of specific applications. The Information Technology Group is comprised of Computer Systems, Industrial Automation, and Peripheral Products. The Peripheral Products Division (PPD), located in Temple, Texas, produces printers and portable computers and terminals. Because all phases of a new product introduction—including engineering, manufacturing, and marketing—are located together, the communication and coordination needed for a successful product launch exists.

The Laser Printer Market

The popularity of personal computers has prompted the growth of printers as a complementary product. There are several types of printers, including impact and laser printers. Impact printers utilize "pin printhead" technology, similar to that of a typewriter. In other words, the printhead makes a physical impact on the page being printed. Impact printers are generally less expensive than laser printers because they do not offer the print quality of laser technology. However, in markets where the ability to print multi-part forms is important, impact printers offer the best solution.

Today, non-impact printers, primarily lasers, are the fastest-growing segment of the entire printer industry. By 1992, over one million laser printers will be purchased in the United States alone. Laser technology has become popular because it offers excellent print quality, faster printing, quiet operation, and greater flexibility with graphics and styles of letters on a page. Laser printers are designed for environments where data/word processing, specialty publishing, and business communications are integral to daily operations.

Laser printers bring advanced technology to the market they serve. Never before have users been able to produce such high quality, professional documents. Users now manipulate technology previously available only in print shops. The emergence of desktop publishing makes it possible for companies to produce much of their own promotional items. University and college students are creating their own résumés and presentation materials using desktop publishing techniques.

The infiltration of such technology has brought the price of laser printers down dramatically. Now, laser printers require minimal user training and are considered a commodity in some markets.

---

* This case researched and written by Debbie M. Thorne, Texas A&M University

The Introduction of the microLaser Printer

In 1989, three new product introductions were to take place between July and November, including the microLaser laser printer. TI hoped that the microLaser would become the laser printer of choice in the world. When compared to leading competitors, the microLaser offers greater functionality in a smaller package. It was designed to fit easily on a desktop and perform numerous applications. The micro-Laser can handle many sizes of paper, envelopes, and transparencies and provides high quality printing for graphics, résumés, and presentation materials.

Current Distribution Strategy

The Laser Printer Marketing group has had high expectations for the microLaser. By virtue of its size, ease of use, and affordability, the microLaser has been positioned as a personal laser printer. It is small and relatively inexpensive. TI marketers hoped these attributes would encourage companies to purchase a microLaser for use with every personal computer they owned. A distribution strategy also had to be planned. Would TI continue its current distribution strategy or opt for a new one? TI had relied on distributors, original equipment manufacturers (OEMs), and value added resellers (VARs) to market its laser printers. OEMs would specify a high level of customization and remarket the printer under their own brand name, usually as a part of a system. The OEM might even request functional modifications to meet its customer needs. The printer was usually integrated with a computer and software to form a system that the OEM would sell as its own. A VAR was more likely to purchase the printer with the TI name on it and then integrate it with other brands of computers and software to form a system. Texas Instruments' authorized distributors, VARs, and OEMs usually sold into large volume accounts, such as governmental agencies, financial institutions and Fortune 1000 companies. In these situations, the purchase decision was often made by the companies' Management Information Systems department.

The industrial distribution strategy was focused on resellers and organizational buyers who were very familiar with the technical aspects of laser printers. Thus far, little attention had been given to retailers and less sophisticated end-users. Although the Texas Instruments name was recognized by many consumers, market research showed that little was known about TI laser printers. Most people either associated TI with its educational products, semiconductors, or for being forced out of the personal computer market. Perhaps these associations are reasons why retail distribution had not been pursued by the Peripheral Products Division. Additionally, from 1986 to 1989, Peripheral Products had no products suitable for the retail market.

Although TI's laser printers had never been marketed through computer retailers, several other complementary products had been in the past. In the late 1970s, when personal computers began to gain popularity, TI developed its own computer. The market was new and volatile. After a shakeout, IBM's personal computer emerged as the dominant player. In addition, TI had developed a computer not compatible with IBM. Software companies, printer manufacturers, and other computer-related firms supported IBM, not TI. This resulted in losses for TI and caused it to pull out of the retail environment. Since then, little attention has been paid to consumer markets and most distributing is done through industrial channels.

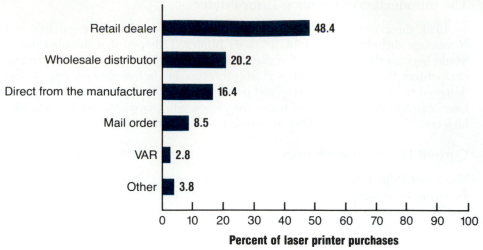

FIGURE 1   *Distribution channels used to purchase laser printers*

TI Explores New Distribution Channels

The development of the microLaser prompted PPD Marketing to explore new channels of distribution. Research revealed that 48 percent of laser printer purchases were made through retailers. Distributors and wholesalers accounted for an additional 20 percent of laser printer sales. Figure 1 depicts this graphically.

Texas Instruments mainly sold through the reseller market. However, data such as these proved that the market demanded new distribution channels. Retailers did sell to individual users and small business owners, but now larger corporations with decentralized buying were going to retail outlets for their purchases.

The facts seemed to indicate that PPD had no choice but to go into retail. But TI already had a less-than-desirable reputation with retailers, and it would be expensive to re-enter this channel. Perhaps it would be more profitable to stay with current channels and improve efficiency and relations within this established framework. After all, retailers were expected to be difficult to penetrate.

After much thought and analysis, TI executives decided to re-enter the retail market. The nature of the printer market and the increased popularity of laser printers demanded new distribution channels.

However, the move into retail was to be gradual. Support for retailers, including promotional campaigns, had to be designed, tested, and implemented. This channel demanded more support than the others and required that TI "pull" customers into the stores. Table 1 shows factors that are important to laser printer purchasers. Therefore, PPD Marketing had to find ways to reach end-users and purchasers to build name recognition and establish TI as a producer of high quality printers.

Questions for Discussion

1. Evaluate TI's decision to enter retail markets.
2. In what ways can TI build name recognition among end-users and purchasers?
3. How can TI gain support for its microLaser printer among retailers.

TABLE 1 *Factors influencing selection of laser printers (in rank order)*

FACTORS INFLUENCING USERS	FACTORS INFLUENCING COMPUTER RETAILERS
1. Quality, reliability and brand reputation	1. Service and support
2. Compatability with software	2. Price
3. Price	3. Variety of products the manufacturer offers
4. Ability to test before committing to purchase	4. Marketing and sales capabilities

SOURCES: "Desktop Publishing Drives a High-Tech Company," *Modern Office Technology*, May 1988, pp. 80, 85, 88; Peter H. Lewis, "Texas Instruments Gets Personal," *New York Times*, Nov. 5, 1989, p. A2; Whitney Lynn, "Selling Computer Products in Changing Channels," *Computer Reseller News*, Aug. 28, 1989, pp. 83–84; *Marketrends/1988: The State of the Printer Industry*, pp. 3–4; Rowland T. Moriarty and Thomas J. Kosnick, "High Tech Marketing: Concepts, Continuity, and Change," *Sloan Management Review*, Summer 1989, pp. 7–17; Personal interview with Bruce Foster (Channel Marketing Manager for Texas Instruments' Peripheral Products Division), Aug. 16, 1989; *Texas Instruments*, (a promotional booklet), 1988.

PART IV PROMOTION DECISIONS

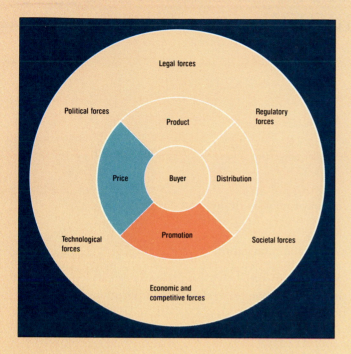

Part IV focuses on communication with target market members. A specific marketing mix cannot satisfy people in a particular target market unless they are aware of the product and where to find it. Some promotion decisions and activities relate to a specific marketing mix, whereas others, broader in scope, are geared to promoting the whole organization. Chapter 14 presents an overview of promotion. We describe the communication process and the major promotion methods that can be included in promotion mixes. In Chapter 15, we analyze the major steps required to develop an advertising campaign, and we explain what publicity is and how it can be used. Chapter 16 deals with the management of personal selling and the role it can play in a firm's promotion mix. This chapter also explores the general characteristics of sales promotion and sales promotion techniques. ◆

14

PROMOTION: AN OVERVIEW

Objectives

Objectives

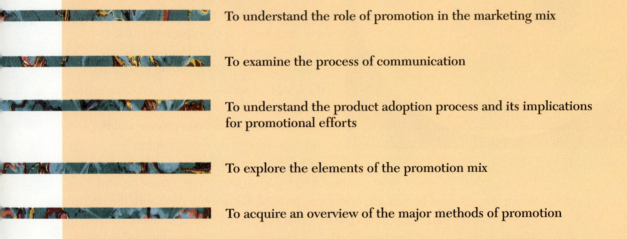

To understand the role of promotion in the marketing mix

To examine the process of communication

To understand the product adoption process and its implications for promotional efforts

To explore the elements of the promotion mix

To acquire an overview of the major methods of promotion

To explore factors that affect the choice of promotional methods

In 1984 the National Basketball Association (NBA), under the leadership of Commissioner David Stern, adopted an aggressive approach to promoting basketball. This new approach helped transform professional basketball from a lackluster money loser to the country's most prosperous professional sport in the 1990s.

In accomplishing this turnaround, Stern and other NBA executives and owners borrowed some of the marketing tricks and promotions commonly used by the Walt Disney Company. When the NBA expanded into Orlando, Florida, it sponsored a statewide contest to name the new team. Team mascots, colors, and players were paraded through the streets of Orlando long before the season started. When the Orlando Magic held its first home game in late 1989, the crowd was greeted with clouds of smoke, green lasers, dancers, and magicians. Such amusements have carried over into all games now. Despite a mediocre win-loss record, the Magic consistently draws more than fifteen thousand enthusiastic fans per game.

Promotions of this sort have succeeded for other NBA teams as well. In 1982, seventeen of the twenty-three NBA teams were losing money. Today the NBA is scoring big on all fronts. Gross revenues have climbed from $120 million in 1982 to $370 million in 1990, and average attendance has risen by 45 percent in the past five years. In addition, NBA Properties, the league's marketing and promotions arm, has seen souvenir sales jump 75 percent, to $525 million, after an aggressive direct catalog promotion. Perhaps the biggest coup of all is the NBA's recent television contract with NBC. Worth about $600 million, the four-year deal gives NBC the right to broadcast a minimum of twenty games a year. This contract alone provides some $5.6 million annually to each team. ◆

Photo by The Advertising Works.

Based on information in Anne M. Arrarte, "Sports Marketing: Poof! Magic Act Appears in Orlando," *Advertising Age,* Mar. 13, 1989, p. 88; Mark Bittman, "NBA Practices Full-Court Press in Marketing," *Advertising Age,* Oct. 31, 1985, pp. 26, 28, and "Sports Marketing: Hot NBA Takes Its Magic to New Courts," *Advertising Age,* Mar. 14, 1988, pp. S4, S6; Brian Moran, "NBA Caps Big Year in Marketing Push," *Advertising Age,* June 8, 1987, p. 83; Mark Robichaux, "New NBA Teams Shoot for Hoopla," *Wall Street Journal,* Dec. 12, 1989, p. B1; and Brenton Welling et al., "Basketball: Business is Booming," *Business Week (Industrial/Technology Edition),* Oct. 28, 1985, pp. 72–82.

Organizations use various promotional approaches to communicate with target markets, as the above example illustrates. This chapter looks at the general dimensions of promotion. First we define and examine the role of promotion. Next, to understand how promotion works, we analyze the meaning and process of communication, as well as the product adoption process. The remainder of the chapter discusses the major types of promotional methods and the factors that influence an organization's decision to use specific methods of promotion.

THE ROLE OF PROMOTION

People's attitudes toward promotion vary. Some hold that promotional activities, particularly advertising and personal selling, paint a distorted picture of reality because they provide only selected information to the customer. According to this view, the repetition of similar themes in promotion has brought about changes in social values, such as increased materialism.[1] It is viewed that promotional activities are unnecessary and wasteful and that promotion costs (especially advertising) are high—sometimes excessively so—resulting in higher prices. Still others take a positive view: that advertising messages often project wholesome values, such as affection, generosity, or patriotism,[2] or that advertising, as a powerful economic force, can free countries from poverty by communicating information.[3] Some observe that advertising of consumer products was a factor in the decline of communism and the move toward a free enterprise system in eastern Europe. However, none of these impressions is completely accurate.

The role of **promotion** is to communicate with individuals, groups, or organizations to directly or indirectly facilitate exchanges by informing and persuading one or more of the audiences to accept an organization's products. L. A. Gear, for example, recruited pop star Michael Jackson to communicate the benefits of its line of athletic shoes.[4] Rock Against Drugs (RAD), a nonprofit organization, employs popular rock musicians, such as Lou Reed, to communicate its antidrug messages to teen-agers and young adults. Like L. A. Gear and RAD, marketers try to communicate with selected audiences about their company and its goods, services, and ideas in order to facilitate exchanges. Marketing Update 14.1 describes how The Coca-Cola Company used and continues to use promotion to accept a new position for its "new" Coke product.

Marketers indirectly facilitate exchanges by focusing information about company activities and products on interest groups (such as environmental and consumer

1. Richard W. Pollay, "On the Value of Reflections on the Values in 'The Distorted Mirror,'" *Journal of Marketing,* July 1987, pp. 104–109.

2. Morris B. Holbrook, "Mirror, Mirror, on the Wall, What's Unfair in the Reflections on Advertising," *Journal of Marketing,* July 1987, pp. 95–103.

3. Richard N. Farmer, "Would You Want Your Granddaughter to Marry a Taiwanese Marketing Man?" *Journal of Marketing,* October 1987, pp. 111–116.

4. David Landis, "Michael Jackson Joins Sneakers Sales Pitch," *USA Today,* Sept. 14, 1989, p. 1B.

FIGURE 14.1
Information flows
into and out of an
organization.

groups), current and potential investors, regulatory agencies, and society in general. Some marketers use *cause-related marketing,* which links the purchase of their products to philanthropic efforts for a particular cause favored by their target market. Cause-related marketing often helps a marketer boost sales and generate good will through contributions to causes that members of its target markets want to support. For example, American Express used cause-related marketing to encourage its credit card holders to charge more often while helping to rebuild the Statue of Liberty. American Express pledged to donate a percentage of the amount of all purchases charged on its card to rebuilding the statue.[5] Similarly, Procter & Gamble has tied promotional efforts for some of its products with contributions to Special Olympics.

Viewed from this wider perspective, promotion can play a comprehensive communication role. Some promotional activities, such as publicity and public relations, can be directed toward helping a company justify its existence and maintain positive, healthy relationships between itself and various groups in the marketing environment. For example, PepsiCo sponsored the Texas Olympics, a series of athletic competitions for adults, children, and mentally and physically handicapped persons.

Although a company can direct a single type of communication—such as an advertisement—toward numerous audiences, marketers often design a communication precisely for a specific target market. A firm frequently communicates several different messages concurrently, each to a different group. For example, McDonald's Corp. may direct one communication toward customers for its Big Mac, a second message toward investors about the firm's stable growth, and a third communication toward society in general regarding the company's social awareness in supporting Ronald McDonald Houses, which provide support to families of children suffering from cancer.

To gain maximum benefit from promotional efforts, marketers must make every effort to properly plan, implement, coordinate, and control communications. Effective promotional activities are based on information from the marketing environment, often obtained from an organization's marketing information system (see Figure 14.1). How effectively marketers can use promotion to maintain positive relationships depends largely on the quantity and quality of information an organization takes in. For example, consumer research on zip-top plastic storage bags revealed that many customers were unsure whether the bags were properly sealed. Glad therefore developed a two-color seal for its bags—one side yellow, one side blue—which when effectively sealed appears as a green color. Because the basic role of promotion is to communicate, we should analyze what communication is and how the communication process works.

5. P. "Rajan" Varadarajan and Anil Menon, "Cause-Related Marketing: A Coalignment of Marketing Strategy and Corporate Philanthropy," *Journal of Marketing,* July 1988, pp. 58–74.

COCA-COLA REVAMPS COCA-COLA A SECOND TIME

In the face of declining market share, The Coca-Cola Company decided in 1985 to reformulate its flagship Coca-Cola brand to compete more directly with Pepsi, its sweeter archrival in the long-standing U.S. cola wars. The company had tested the new formula for years and was convinced that it was superior to the original formula as well as other cola competitors. Consumers, however, rejected the reformulated Coca-Cola and demanded the return of their original favorite. Thus, three months after the launch of Coke, the company reintroduced the original formula under the name Coca-Cola Classic; the reformulated version remained on the market under the name Coca-Cola, or "new" Coke.

After five years on the market, "new" Coke still failed to overtake Pepsi. In fact, at the end of the 1980s, "new" Coke fell off the top-ten soft-drink list and was called the "Edsel of the Eighties." The product reached its peak in 1985 with roughly 7.5 percent of the soft drink market. Market share eroded steadily from that point, down to about 1 percent of the market in the late 1980s. By contrast, Coca-Cola Classic and Pepsi each held 15.8 percent of the soft-drink market.

After reviewing the lackluster performance of the sweeter "new" Coke, the company decided in 1990 to reposition it under the name Coke II to compete head-on with Pepsi. The company hopes that with a new name, new look, and new promotion, Coke II can get past its rough start as an unwanted replacement for an American classic. The traditional red and white can was redesigned with splashes of blue—a Pepsi color. Although the formula of the product was not altered, advertising for Coke II will focus on "real cola taste."

Coca-Cola promises to heat up the cola wars with a very strong promotional campaign for Coke II. Traditional promotional vehicles—television and radio advertising, taste tests, and coupons will probably be used to convince skeptical consumers that Coke II tastes better than Pepsi. The success of Coke II's promotion campaign will probably determine whether consumers accept Coke II as a sweeter alternative to Coca-Cola Classic or view it as a Pepsi knockoff, with no clear brand identity.

SOURCES: Kate Fitzgerald, "Diet Coke Hits Recall Chart for First Time," *Advertising Age,* Feb. 2, 1990, p. 28; Michael J. McCarthy, "New Coke Gets New Name, New Can, New Chance," *Wall Street Journal,* March 7, 1990, pp. B1, B6; Thomas More, "He Put the Kick Back in Coke," *Fortune,* Oct. 26, 1987, pp. 46–56; Cable News Network (TV), March 7, 1990.

PROMOTION AND THE COMMUNICATION PROCESS

Communication can be viewed as the transmission of information. For communication to take place, however, both the sender and the receiver of the information must share some common ground. They must share a common understanding of the symbols used to transmit information, usually pictures or words. For instance, an individual transmitting the following message may believe he or she is communicating with you:

在工厂吾人製造化粧品，在商店吾人銷售希望。

However, communication has not taken place because few of you understand the intended message.[6] Thus we define **communication** as a sharing of meaning.[7] Implicit in this definition is the notion of transmission of information because sharing necessitates transmission.

As Figure 14.2 shows, communication begins with a source. A **source** is a person, group, or organization that has a meaning it intends and attempts to share with an audience. For example, a source could be a salesperson who wishes to communicate a sales message or an organization that wants to send a message to thousands of consumers through an advertisement. A **receiver** or audience is the individual, group, or organization that decodes a coded message. An audience is two or more receivers who decode a message. The intended receivers or audience of an advertisement for Motorola cellular telephones, for example, might be business persons who must frequently travel by car.

To transmit meaning, a source must convert the meaning into a series of signs that represent ideas or concepts. This is called the **coding process**, or *encoding*. When coding meaning into a message, a source must take into account certain characteristics of the receiver or audience. First, to share meaning, the source should use signs that are familiar to the receiver or audience. Marketers who understand this fact realize how important it is to know their target market and to make sure that an advertisement, for example, is written in language that the target market can understand. Thus when Du Pont advertised its Stainmaster carpeting, it did not mention the name of the chemical used to make the carpet resistant to spotting because it would have had little meaning to consumers seeing the advertisement. There have been some notable problems in translating English advertisements into Spanish for the U.S. Hispanic market segment. A beer advertisement with the tag line "Sueltate" was supposed to mean "Let go!" but actually invited Hispanics to "Get diarrhea!" And an airline advertisement intended to entice Hispanics to fly first class on leather seats invited them instead to fly naked.[8] Thus it is important that people understand the language used in promotion.

---

6. In case you do not read Chinese, this says, "In the factory we make cosmetics, and in the store we sell hope." Prepared by Chih Kang Wang.

7. Terence A. Shimp and M. Wayne Delozier, *Promotion Management and Marketing Communication* (Hinsdale, Ill.: Dryden Press, 1986), pp. 25–26.

8. Carlos E. Garcia, "Hispanic Market Is Accessible If Research Is Designed Correctly," *Marketing News*, Jan. 4, 1988, p. 46.

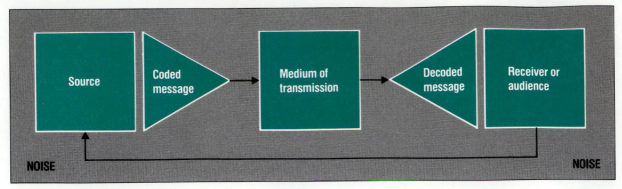

FIGURE 14.2 *The communication process*

Second, when coding a meaning, a source should try to use signs that the receiver or audience uses for referring to the concepts the source intends. Marketers should generally avoid signs that can have several meanings for an audience. For example, a national advertiser of soft drinks should avoid using the word *soda* as a general term for soft drinks. Although in some parts of the United States soda is taken to mean *soft drink,* in other regions it may connote bicarbonate of soda, an ice cream drink, or something that one mixes with Scotch whisky.

To share a coded meaning with the receiver or audience, a source must select and use a medium of transmission. A **medium of transmission** carries the coded message from the source to the receiver or audience. Transmission media include ink on paper, vibrations of air waves produced by vocal cords, chalk marks on a chalkboard, and electronically produced vibrations of air waves—in radio and television signals, for example.

When a source chooses an inappropriate medium of transmission, several problems may arise. A coded message may reach some receivers, but not the right ones. For example, suppose a community theater spends most of its advertising dollars on radio advertisements. If theatergoers depend mainly on newspapers for information about local drama, then the theater will not reach its intended target audience. Coded messages may also reach intended receivers in an incomplete form because the intensity of the transmission is weak. For example, radio signals can be received effectively only over a limited range that may vary depending on climatic conditions. Members of the target audience who live on the fringe of the broadcast area may receive a weak signal; others well within the broadcast area may also receive an incomplete message if they listen to their radios while driving or studying.

In the **decoding process**, signs are converted into concepts and ideas. Seldom does a receiver decode exactly the same meaning that a source coded. When the result of decoding is different from what was coded, **noise** exists. Noise has many sources and may affect any or all parts of the communication process. When a source selects a medium of transmission through which an audience does not expect to receive a message, noise is likely to occur. Noise sometimes arises within the medium of transmission itself. Radio static, faulty printing processes, and laryngitis are sources of noise. Interference on viewers' television sets during a commercial is noise and lessens the impact of the message. Noise also occurs when a source uses a sign that is unfamiliar to the receiver or that has a different meaning from the one the source intended. Noise also may originate in the receiver. As Chapter 4 dis-

FIGURE 14.3

Getting feedback.
With every complimentary tin of cookies shipped, the Radisson Hotel receives feedback that its message was understood.

SOURCE: Ad courtesy of Radisson Hotels International, Minneapolis, MN

cusses, a receiver may be unaware of a coded message because his or her perceptual processes block it out.

The receiver's response to a message is **feedback** to the source. The source usually expects and normally receives feedback, although it may not be immediate. During feedback, the receiver or audience is the source of a message that is directed toward the original source, which then becomes a receiver. Feedback is coded, sent through a medium of transmission, and is decoded by the receiver, the source of the original communication. It is logical, then, to think about communication as a circular process.

During face-to-face communication, such as a personal selling situation or product sampling, both verbal and nonverbal feedback can be immediate. Instant feedback lets communicators adjust their messages quickly to improve the effectiveness of their communication. For example, when a salesperson realizes through feedback that a customer does not understand a sales presentation, the salesperson adapts the presentation to make it more meaningful to the customer. In interpersonal communication, feedback occurs through talking, touching, smiling, nodding, eye movements, and other body movements and postures.

When mass communication such as advertising is used, feedback is often slow and difficult to recognize. If Disney World increased advertising to increase the number of visitors, it might be six to eighteen months before the firm could recognize the effects of the expanded advertising. Although it is harder to recognize, feedback does exist for mass communication. Figure 14.3 illustrates a unique program developed by the Radisson Hotel to obtain feedback on whether its message was received by its target market. Advertisers, for example, obtain feedback in the form of changes in sales volume or in consumers' attitudes and awareness levels. Thus after the state of Texas created its "Don't Mess With Texas" antilitter advertising campaign, using Texas musicians Willie Nelson, Stevie Ray Vaughan, and others, the state found that roadside littering declined by 60 percent over the course of the campaign.[9] This feedback—the decline in littering—made it clear that the advertising campaign was effective in communicating its antilitter message.

Each communication channel has a limit on the volume of information it can handle effectively. This limit, called **channel capacity**, is determined by the least efficient component of the communication process. To illustrate, think about communications that depend on vocal speech. An individual source can talk only so fast, and there is a limit to how much an individual receiver can take in aurally. Beyond that point, additional messages cannot be decoded; thus meaning cannot be shared. Although a radio announcer can read several hundred words a minute, a one-minute advertising message should not exceed 150 words because most announcers cannot articulate the words into understandable messages at a rate beyond 150 words per minute. This figure is the limit for both source and receiver, and marketers should keep this in mind when developing radio commercials. At times, a firm creates a television advertisement that contains several types of visual materials and several forms of audio messages, all transmitted to viewers at the same time. Such communication may not be totally effective because receivers cannot decode all the messages simultaneously.

Now that we have explored the basic communication process, we consider more specifically how promotion is used to influence individuals, groups, or organizations to accept or adopt a firm's products. Although we briefly touch upon the product adoption process in Chapter 9, we discuss it more fully in the following section to gain a better understanding of the conditions under which promotion occurs.

PROMOTION AND THE PRODUCT ADOPTION PROCESS

Marketers do not promote simply to inform, educate, and entertain; they communicate to facilitate satisfying exchanges. One long-run purpose of promotion is to influence and encourage buyers to accept or adopt goods, services, and ideas. At times, an advertisement may be informative or entertaining, yet it may fail to get the audience to purchase the product. For example, some ads for business computers seem to be weak in communicating benefits—they focus instead on getting customers to feel good about the product. The ultimate effectiveness of promotion is determined by the degree to which it affects product adoption among potential buyers or increases the frequency of current buyers' purchases.

To establish realistic expectations about what promotion can do, one should not view product adoption as a one-step process. Rarely can a single promotional activity cause an individual to buy a previously unfamiliar product. The acceptance of a product involves many steps. Although there are several ways to look at the **product**

9. Seth Kantor, "Engineer's Survey Helped Shape State's Ad Campaign Against Highway Littering," *Bryan-College Station Eagle,* Aug. 4, 1989, p. 2D.

Infiniti finally shows its cars

Nature scenes and different views of the car show up in the second part of Infiniti's campaign.

FIGURE 14.4 *Building awareness.*
Following teaser ads, Nissan aired commercials designed to inform and interest people in seeking more information about the Infiniti.

SOURCE: Nissan Motor Corporation, USA

adoption process, one common approach is to view it as consisting of five stages: awareness, interest, evaluation, trial, and adoption.[10]

In the awareness stage, individuals become aware that the product exists, but they have little information about it and are not concerned about getting more. When Nissan introduced its Infiniti automobile, for example, it used provocative teaser advertisements, which showed fields and oceans but not the car; the advertisements encouraged people to call a toll-free number for more information. As Figure 14.4 shows, later ads did show the Infiniti. Consumers enter the interest stage when they are motivated to get information about the product's features, uses, advantages, disadvantages, price, or location. During the evaluation stage, individuals consider whether the product will satisfy certain criteria that are crucial for meeting their specific needs. In the trial stage, they use or experience the product for the first time, possibly by purchasing a small quantity, by taking advantage of a free sample or demonstration, or by borrowing the product from someone. Supermarkets, for example, frequently offer special promotions to encourage consumers to taste products such as cheese, meat, snacks, or pizza. During this stage, potential adopters determine the usefulness of the product under the specific conditions for which they need it.

10. Adapted from Everett M. Rogers, *Diffusion of Innovations* (New York: Free Press, 1962), pp. 81–86, 98–102.

FIGURE 14.5

Effective promotion tools for reaching consumers in various stages of the product adoption process

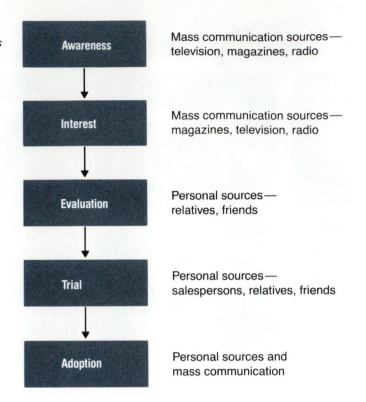

Awareness — Mass communication sources—television, magazines, radio

Interest — Mass communication sources—magazines, television, radio

Evaluation — Personal sources—relatives, friends

Trial — Personal sources—salespersons, relatives, friends

Adoption — Personal sources and mass communication

Individuals move into the adoption stage by choosing the specific product when they need a product of that general type. Do not assume, however, that because a person enters the adoption process she or he will eventually adopt the new product. Rejection may occur at any stage, including adoption. Both product adoption and product rejection can be temporary or permanent.

For the most part, people respond to different information sources at different stages of the adoption process. Figure 14.5 illustrates the most effective sources for each stage. Mass communication sources, such as television advertising, are often effective for moving large numbers of people into the awareness stage. Producers of consumer goods commonly use massive advertising campaigns when introducing new products. They do so to create product awareness as quickly as possible within a large portion of the target market.

Mass communications may also be effective for people in the interest stage who want to learn more about a product. During the evaluation stage, individuals often seek information, opinions, and reinforcement from personal sources—relatives, friends, and associates. In the trial stage, individuals depend on salespersons for information about how to use the product properly to get the most out of it. Marketers must use advertising carefully when consumers are in the trial stage. If advertisements greatly exaggerate the benefits of a product, the consumer may be disappointed when the product does not meet expectations.[11] It is best to avoid creating expectations that cannot be satisfied because rejection at this stage will

11. Lawrence J. Marks and Michael A. Kamins, "Product Sampling and Advertising Sequence, Belief Strength, Confidence and Attitudes," *Journal of Marketing Research,* August 1988, pp. 266–281.

FIGURE 14.6
Distribution of product adopter categories

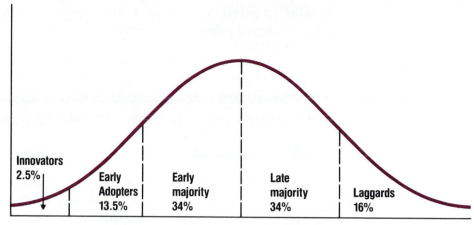

SOURCE: Reprinted with permission of The Free Press, a Division of Macmillan Inc., from *Diffusion of Innovations,* 3rd ed., by Everett H. Rogers. Copyright © 1962, 1971, 1983 by The Free Press.

prevent adoption. Friends and peers may also be important sources during the trial stage. By the time the adoption stage has been reached, both personal communication from sales personnel and mass communication through advertisements may be required. Even though the particular stage of the adoption process may influence the types of information sources consumers use, marketers must remember that other factors, such as the product's characteristics, price, uses, and the characteristics of customers, also affect the types of information sources that buyers desire.

Because people in different stages of the adoption process often require different types of information, marketers designing a promotional campaign must determine what stage of the adoption process a particular target audience is in before they can develop the message. Potential adopters in the interest stage will need different information than people who have already reached the trial stage.

When an organization introduces a new product, people do not all begin the adoption process at the same time, and they do not move through the process at the same speed. Of those people who eventually adopt the product, some enter the adoption process rather quickly, whereas others start considerably later. For most products, too, there is a group of nonadopters who never begin the process.

Depending on the length of time it takes them to adopt a new product, people can be divided into five major adopter categories: innovators, early adopters, early majority, late majority, and laggards.[12] Figure 14.6 illustrates each adopter category and the percentage of total adopters that it typically represents. **Innovators** are the first to adopt a new product. They enjoy trying new products and tend to be venturesome. **Early adopters** choose new products carefully and are viewed as "the people to check with" by persons in the remaining adopter categories. Persons in the **early majority** adopt just prior to the average person; they are deliberate and cautious in trying new products. **Late majority** people, who are quite skeptical of new products, eventually adopt new products because of economic necessity or social pressure. **Laggards**, the last to adopt a new product, are oriented toward the past. They are suspicious of new products, and when they finally adopt the innovation, it may already have been replaced by a newer product. When developing

12. Rogers, pp. 247–250.

promotional efforts, a marketer should bear in mind that persons in different adopter categories often need different forms of communication and different types of information.

To gain a better understanding of how promotion can move people closer to the acceptance of goods, services, and ideas, we turn to the major promotional methods available to an organization—the promotion mix.

THE PROMOTION MIX

Several types of promotional methods can be used to communicate with individuals, groups, and organizations. When an organization combines specific ingredients to promote a particular product, that combination constitutes the promotion mix for that product. The four possible ingredients of a **promotion mix** are advertising, personal selling, publicity, and sales promotion (see Figure 14.7). For some products, firms use all four ingredients; for other products, only two or three suffice. In this section we analyze the major ingredients of a promotion mix and the chief factors that influence an organization to include specific ingredients in the promotion mix for a specific product. In Chapters 15 and 16 we analyze the promotion mix in greater detail.

■ **Promotion-Mix Ingredients**

At this point we consider some general characteristics of advertising, personal selling, publicity, and sales promotion.

Advertising.   Advertising is a paid form of nonpersonal communication about an organization and its products that is transmitted to a target audience through a mass medium such as television, radio, newspapers, magazines, direct mail, mass transit vehicles, outdoor displays, or catalogs. Individuals and organizations use advertising to promote goods, services, ideas, issues, and people. Because it is highly flexible, advertising offers the options of reaching an extremely large target audience or focusing on a small, precisely defined segment of the population. For instance, McDonald's advertising focuses on a large audience of potential fast-food consumers, ranging from children to adults, whereas advertising for DeBeers' diamonds focuses on a much smaller and specialized target market.

Advertising offers several benefits. It can be an extremely cost-efficient promotional method because it can reach a vast number of people at a low cost per person. For example, the cost of a four-color, one-page advertisement in *Time* magazine is $120,130. Because the magazine reaches 4.6 million subscribers, the cost of reaching 1,000 subscribers is only $26.12. Advertising also lets the user repeat the message a number of times. Calvin Klein advertises many of its products (lingerie, cologne, clothes) on television, in magazines, and through outdoor advertising. In addition, advertising a product a certain way can add to its value. For example, Geo, which is sold and serviced by Chevrolet, is advertised as having more dealers than Honda, Toyota, and other Japanese companies combined. The visibility that an organization gains from advertising enhances the firm's public image.

Advertising also has several disadvantages. Even though the cost per person reached may be low, its absolute dollar outlay can be extremely high, especially for commercials during popular television shows. These high costs can limit, and sometimes prevent, the use of advertising in a promotion mix. Moreover, advertising

FIGURE 14.7
Possible ingredients for an organization's promotion mix

rarely provides rapid feedback. Measuring its effect on sales is difficult, and it ordinarily has less persuasive impact on customers than personal selling.

Personal Selling.   Personal selling involves informing customers and persuading them to purchase products through personal communication in an exchange situation. The phrase *purchase products* should be interpreted broadly to encompass the acceptance of ideas and issues. Telemarketing, which Chapter 12 describes as direct selling over the telephone, relies heavily on personal selling.

Personal selling has both advantages and limitations when compared with advertising. Advertising is general communication aimed at a relatively large target audience, whereas personal selling involves more specific communication aimed at one or several persons. Reaching one person through personal selling costs considerably more than it does through advertising, but personal selling efforts often have greater impact on customers. Personal selling also provides immediate feedback, which allows marketers to adjust their message to improve communication. It helps them determine and respond to customers' needs for information.

When a salesperson and customer meet face to face, they use several types of interpersonal communication. Obviously, the predominating communication form is language—both speech and writing. In addition, a salesperson and customer frequently use **kinesic communication**, or body language, by moving their heads, eyes, arms, hands, legs, or torsos. Winking, head nodding, hand gestures, and arm motions are forms of kinesic communication. A good salesperson can often evaluate a prospect's interest in a product or presentation by watching for eye contact and head nodding. **Proxemic communication**, a less obvious form of communication used in personal selling situations, occurs when either person varies the physical distance that separates the two people. When a customer backs away from a salesperson, for example, that individual may be saying that he or she is not interested in the product or may be expressing dislike for the salesperson. Touching, or **tactile communication**, can also be a form of communication, although it is not as popular in the United States as it is in many other countries. Handshaking is a common form of tactile communication in many countries.

Publicity.　　Publicity refers to nonpersonal communication in news story form about an organization or its products, or both, that is transmitted through a mass medium at no charge. Examples of publicity include magazine, newspaper, radio, and television news stories about new retail stores, new products, or personnel changes in an organization. Although both advertising and publicity are transmitted through mass communication, the sponsor does not pay the media costs for publicity and is not identified. Nevertheless, publicity should never be viewed as free communication. There are clear costs associated with preparing news releases and encouraging media personnel to broadcast or print them. A firm that uses publicity regularly must have employees to perform these activities or obtain the services of a public relations firm or an advertising agency. Either way, the firm bears the costs of the activities.

Publicity must be planned and implemented so that it is compatible with, and supportive of, other elements in the promotion mix. However, publicity cannot always be controlled to the extent that other elements of the promotion mix can be. For example, Domino's, the largest pizza-delivery company in the world, has received much negative publicity about the driving record of its delivery people. The company has experienced criticism about pressures from the company that all pizzas be delivered within thirty minutes, regardless of weather and driving conditions. Because of the heightened awareness of this issue, Domino's is minimizing its emphasis on the thirty-minute guarantee and focusing instead on product quality.

Sales Promotion.　　Sales promotion is an activity or material that acts as a direct inducement, offering added value, or incentive for the product, to resellers, salespersons, or consumers.[13] Examples of sales promotion include coupons (see Figure 14.8), bonuses, and contests used to enhance the sales of a product. Marketing Update 14.2 describes how some firms are using videos as sales promotion tools. The term *sales promotion* should not be confused with *promotion;* sales promotion is but a part of the more comprehensive area of promotion, encompassing efforts other than personal selling, advertising, and publicity. Currently, marketers spend about one and a half times as much on sales promotion as they do on advertising. Sales promotion appears to be growing in use more than advertising.

Marketers frequently rely on sales promotion to improve the effectiveness of other promotion mix ingredients, especially advertising and personal selling. For example, some firms allocate 25 percent of their annual promotion budget to trade shows in order to introduce new products, meet key industrial personnel, and identify likely prospects.[14]

Marketers design sales promotion to produce immediate, short-run sales increases. For example, over the years, Hardee's fast-food restaurants have successfully sold California Raisins figures with the purchase of their Cinnamon 'n Raisin Biscuits or other desserts. California Raisins characters made appearances in Hardee's restaurants, and radio stations held contests. These promotions have produced the largest single-month sales increase in Hardee's history (18 to 30 percent). Approximately fifteen million characters were sold during one four-week promo-

13. This definition is adapted from John F. Luick and William L. Ziegler, *Sales Promotion and Modern Merchandising* (New York: McGraw-Hill, 1968), p. 4.

14. Roger A. Kerin and William L. Cron, "Assessing Trade Show Functions and Performance: An Exploratory Study," *Journal of Marketing,* July 1987, pp. 87–94.

FIGURE 14.8
Example of a sales promotion.
LaChoy encourages sales through a cents-off coupon advertisement.

SOURCE: Courtesy of Beatrice/Hunt Wesson

tional period, and customer counts reached an all-time high.[15] Thus premiums can be extremely effective at generating short-term sales increases and supporting add-on purchases, such as a dessert item.

Generally, if a company employs advertising or personal selling, it either depends on them continuously or turns to them cyclically. However, a marketer's use of sales promotion tends to be irregular. Many products are seasonal. A company such as Toro may offer more sales promotions in July and August than in April or May—the peak selling season for tractors, lawn mowers, and other gardening equipment.

Now that we have discussed the basic components of an organization's promotion mix, we need to consider how that mix is created. We must examine what factors and conditions affect the selection of the promotional methods that a specific organization uses in its promotion mix for a particular product.

■ Selecting Promotion-Mix Ingredients

Marketers vary the composition of promotion mixes for many reasons. Although all four ingredients can be included in a promotion mix, frequently a marketer selects fewer than four. In addition, many firms that market multiple product lines use several promotion mixes simultaneously.

15. Russ Bowman, "Is Free Making a Comeback?" *Marketing & Media Decisions,* May 1988, p. 164.

USE OF VIDEO PROMOTIONS AND TIE-INS INCREASES

Many firms are discovering that offering free or discounted prerecorded video-cassettes with their products provides an incentive for customers to buy the products. Time Warner's *Sports Illustrated* magazine used eight different video promotions in 1989, ordering a minimum of 100,000 copies of each. Procter & Gamble has also used videotapes as incentives, offering a special edition of "Walt Disney Cartoon Classics" with the purchase of Tide laundry detergent and Ivory dishwashing liquid. In a new P&G offer, consumers can get a free NFL Films video, "Air of Excellence," when they purchase three of five toiletry products. P&G expects to give away 65,000 tapes. Yet another believer in videos as incentives is RJR Nabisco, which plans to offer an all-sports "follies" video produced by NFL Films.

Other video sales promotions involve tie-ins with film and home video releases. In a $15 million promotion, McDonald's Corp. teamed with the Walt Disney Company for the release of the animated film "The Little Mermaid" by offering a four-week Happy Meal promotion with a different Little Mermaid toy each week. Wendy's International mounted a similar campaign tied to the film "All Dogs Go to Heaven," offering one of six movie character figurines with the purchase of a Kids' Meal. The $15 million promotion was Wendy's most extensive movie tie-in to date. A previous promotion, tied to the film "Willow," cost Wendy's an estimated $5 million. Even the U.S. Postal Service has used video promotions. It offered a series of its commemorative stamps, depicting prehistoric dinosaurs, in a promotion teamed with MCA Home Video and the release of its animated movie "The Land Before Time." The postmaster general believes that the Postal Service should market its high-profit stamp collecting program more aggressively and join the many others using video tie-ins to boost product awareness and sales.

The increased use of videos as premium sales promotions has led to the development of companies that match programs with marketers and produce videos for product tie-ins. Thus in the $14 billion sales promotion industry, prerecorded videocassettes are serving as a valuable incentive to generate product sales.

SOURCES: Marcy Magiera, "Getting Animated: Big Mac, Wendy's Tie With Films," *Advertising Age,* Nov. 20, 1989, p. 39, Janet Meyers, "Stamp of Approval," *Advertising Age,* Aug. 14, 1989, p. 20; and Wayne Walley, "Videos Play Well as Premiums," *Advertising Age,* Aug. 14, 1989, p. 16.

An organization's promotion mix (or mixes) is not an unchanging part of the marketing mix. Marketers can and do change the composition of their promotion mixes. The specific promotion-mix ingredients employed and the intensity at which they are used depend on a variety of factors, including the organization's promotional resources, objectives, and policies; characteristics of the target market; characteristics of the product; and cost and availability of promotional methods.

Promotional Resources, Objectives, and Policies.   The quality of an organization's promotional resources affects the number and relative intensity of promotional methods that can be included in a promotion mix. If a company's promotional budget is extremely limited, the firm is likely to rely on personal selling because it is easier to measure a salesperson's contribution to sales than to measure the effect of advertising. A business must have a sizable promotional budget if it is to use regional or national advertising and sales promotion activities. Organizations with extensive promotional resources usually can include more ingredients in their promotion mixes. However, having more promotional dollars does not imply that they necessarily will use a greater number of promotional methods.

An organization's promotional objectives and policies also influence the types of promotion used. If a company's objective is to create mass awareness of a new convenience good, its promotion mix is likely to lean heavily toward advertising, sales promotion, and possibly publicity. If a company hopes to educate consumers about the features of durable goods, such as home appliances, its promotion mix may combine a moderate amount of advertising, possibly some sales promotion efforts designed to attract customers to retail stores, and a great deal of personal selling because this method is an excellent way to inform customers about these types of products. If a firm's objective is to produce immediate sales of consumer nondurables, the promotion mix will probably stress advertising and sales promotion efforts.

Characteristics of the Target Market.   The size, geographic distribution, and socioeconomic characteristics of an organization's target market also help dictate the ingredients to be included in a product's promotion mix. To some degree, market size determines the composition of the mix. If the size is quite limited, the promotion mix will probably emphasize personal selling, which can be quite effective for reaching small numbers of people. Organizations that sell to industrial markets and firms that market their products through only a few wholesalers frequently make personal selling the major component of their promotion mixes. When markets for a product consist of millions of customers, organizations use advertising and sales promotion because these methods can reach masses of people at a low cost per person. The Coca-Cola Company attempted to reach consumers through a nontraditional vehicle when it placed a commercial for diet Coke in the introduction of the home video version of the 1989 blockbuster, *Batman.* Warner Home Video, the distributor of *Batman,* believed that it would sell more than ten million copies of the videocassette, exposing millions of consumers to the diet Coke message at a low cost per person.[16]

The geographic distribution of a firm's customers can affect the combination of promotional methods used. Personal selling is more feasible if a company's customers are concentrated in a small area than if they are dispersed across a vast region.

16. Marcy Magiera, "Holy Batvideo! Christmas Already?" *Advertising Age,* Sept. 11, 1989, p. 6.

FIGURE 14.9

Using a combination of promotional methods. Because Hyatt and Avis customers are similar and pervasive in the United States, combining their sales promotion and advertising efforts makes sense.

SOURCE: Courtesy of Wizard Co.

When the company's customers are numerous and dispersed, advertising may be more practical. In Figure 14.9, Hyatt and Avis combine promotional efforts to reach a shared target market, which spans the United States.

The distribution of a target market's socioeconomic characteristics, such as age, income, or education, may dictate the types of promotional techniques that a marketer selects. For example, personal selling may be much more successful than print advertisements for communicating with less-educated people.

Characteristics of the Product.   Generally, promotion mixes for industrial products concentrate on personal selling. In promoting consumer goods, on the other hand, advertising plays a major role. Treat this generalization cautiously, however. Industrial goods producers do use some advertising to promote goods. Advertisements for computers, road building equipment, and aircraft are not altogether uncommon, and some sales promotion occasionally is used to promote industrial goods. Personal selling is used extensively for consumer durables, such as home appliances, automobiles, and houses, and consumer convenience items are promoted mainly through advertising and sales promotion. Publicity appears in promotion mixes for both industrial goods and consumer goods.

Marketers of highly seasonal products are often forced to emphasize advertising, and possibly sales promotion, because off-season sales will not support an extensive year-round sales force. Although many toy producers have sales forces to sell to resellers, a number of these companies depend to a large extent on advertising to promote their products.

The price of a product also influences the composition of the promotion mix. High-priced products call for more personal selling because consumers associate greater risk with the purchase of such products and usually want the advice of a salesperson. Few of us, for example, would be willing to purchase a refrigerator from a self-service establishment. For low-priced convenience items, marketers use advertising rather than personal selling at the retail level. The profit margins on many of these items are too low to justify the use of salespersons, and most customers do not need advice from sales personnel when buying such products.

A further consideration in creating an effective promotion mix is the stage of the product life cycle. During the introduction stage, a good deal of advertising may be necessary for both industrial and consumer products to make potential users aware of a new product. For many products, personal selling and sales promotion are helpful as well at this stage. In the case of consumer nondurables, the growth and maturity stages call for a heavy emphasis on advertising. Industrial products, on the other hand, often require a concentration of personal selling and some sales promotion efforts during these stages. In the decline stage, marketers usually decrease their promotional activities, especially advertising. Promotional efforts in the decline stage often center on personal selling and sales promotion efforts.

The intensity of market coverage is still another factor affecting the composition of the promotion mix. When a product is marketed through intensive distribution, the firm depends strongly on advertising and sales promotion. A number of convenience products, such as lotions, cereals, and coffee, are promoted through samples, coupons, and cash refunds. Where marketers have opted for selective distribution, marketing mixes vary considerably as to type and amount of promotional methods. Items handled through exclusive distribution frequently demand more personal selling and less advertising. Expensive watches, furs, and high-quality furniture are typical products promoted heavily through personal selling.

A product's use also affects the combination of promotional methods. Manufacturers of highly personal products, such as nonprescription contraceptives, feminine hygiene products, and hemorrhoid medications, count on advertising for promotion because many users do not like to talk with salespersons about such products.

Cost and Availability of Promotional Methods.   The costs of promotional methods are major factors to analyze when developing a promotion mix. National advertising and sales promotion efforts require large expenditures. For example, the average cost of producing a commercial in 1988 was $168,000.[17] However, if the efforts are effective in reaching extremely large numbers of people, the cost per individual reached may be quite small, possibly a few pennies per person. Not all forms of advertising are expensive, however. Many small, local businesses advertise their products through local newspapers, magazines, radio and television stations, and outdoor and transit signs.

Another consideration that marketers must explore when formulating a promotion mix is the availability of promotional techniques. Despite the tremendous number of media vehicles in the United States, a firm may find that no available advertising medium effectively reaches a certain market. For example, a stockbroker

17. Marcy E. Mullins, "USA Snapshots: TV Commercials Costs Rise," *USA Today,* Aug. 31, 1989, p. 1B.

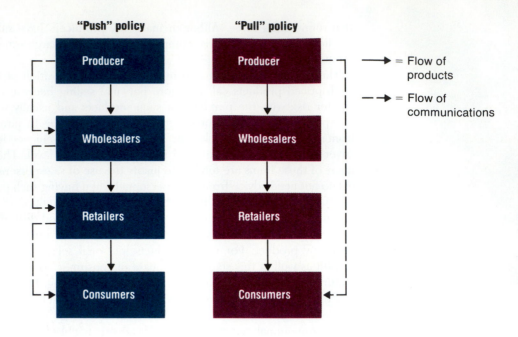

FIGURE 14.10
Comparison of push and pull promotional strategies

"Push" policy

"Pull" policy

Producer

Wholesalers

Retailers

Consumers

Producer

Wholesalers

Retailers

Consumers

→ = Flow of products

⇢ = Flow of communications

may discover that no advertising medium precisely targets investors and potential investors in the Boston Celtics basketball team. The problem of media availability becomes even more pronounced when marketers try to advertise in foreign countries. Some media, such as television, simply may not be available. The media that are available may not be open to certain types of advertisements. For example, in West Germany, advertisers are forbidden to make brand comparisons on television commercials. Other promotional methods have limitations as well. A firm may wish to increase the size of its sales force but be unable to find qualified personnel. In addition, some state laws prohibit the use of certain types of sales promotion activities, such as contests. Those techniques are thus "unavailable" in those locales.

Push Policy Versus Pull Policy

Another element that marketers should consider when they plan a promotion mix is whether to use a push policy or a pull policy. With a **push policy**, the producer promotes the product only to the next institution down the marketing channel. For instance, in a marketing channel with wholesalers and retailers, the producer promotes to the wholesaler because in this case the wholesaler is the channel member just below the producer (see Figure 14.10). Each channel member in turn promotes to the next channel member. A push policy normally stresses personal selling. Sometimes sales promotion and advertising are used in conjunction with personal selling to push the products down through the channel.

As Figure 14.10 shows, a firm using a **pull policy** promotes directly to consumers with the intention of developing a strong consumer demand for the products. It does so through advertising, sales promotion, and packaging that helps manufacturers build and maintain market share.[18] Because consumers are persuaded to seek

18. Alvin A. Achenbaum and F. Kent Mitchel, "Pulling Away from Push Marketing," *Harvard Business Review,* May-June 1987, p. 38.

the products in retail stores, retailers will in turn go to wholesalers or the producer to buy the products. The policy is thus intended to "pull" the goods down through the channel by creating demand at the consumer level.

Summary

The primary role of promotion is to communicate with individuals, groups, or organizations in the environment to directly or indirectly facilitate exchanges.

Communication is a sharing of meaning. The communication process involves several steps. First, the source translates the meaning into code, a process known as coding or encoding. The source should employ signs familiar to the receiver or audience and choose signs that the receiver or audience uses for referring to the concepts or ideas being promoted. The coded message is sent through a medium of transmission to the receiver or audience. The receiver or audience then decodes the message and usually supplies feedback to the source. When the decoded message differs from the encoded one, a condition called noise exists.

The long-run purpose of promotion is to influence and encourage customers to accept or adopt goods, services, and ideas. The product adoption process consists of five stages. In the awareness stage, individuals become aware of the product. People move into the interest stage when they seek more information about the product. In the evaluation stage, individuals decide whether the product will meet certain criteria that are crucial for satisfying their needs. During the trial stage, the consumer actually tries the product. In the adoption stage, the consumer decides to use the product on a regular basis. Rejection of the product may occur at any stage. The adopters can be divided into five major categories—innovators, early adopters, early majority, late majority, and laggards—according to the length of time it takes them to start using a new product.

The promotion mix for a product may include four major promotional methods: advertising, personal selling, publicity, and sales promotion. Advertising is a paid form of nonpersonal communication about an organization and its products that is transmitted to a target audience through a mass medium. Personal selling is a process of informing customers and persuading them to purchase products through personal communication in an exchange situation. Publicity is nonpersonal communication in news story form, regarding an organization, its products, or both, that is transmitted through a mass medium at no charge. Sales promotion is an activity or material that acts as a direct inducement, offering added value to or incentive for the product, to resellers, salespersons, or consumers.

There are several major determinants of what promotional methods to include in a promotion mix for a product: the organization's promotional resources, objectives, and policies; the characteristics of the target market; the characteristics of the product; and the cost and availability of promotional methods. Marketers must also consider whether to use a push policy or a pull policy. With a push policy, the producer promotes the product only to the next institution down the marketing channel. Normally, a push policy stresses personal selling. A firm that uses a pull policy promotes directly to consumers with the intention of developing a strong consumer demand for the products. Once consumers are persuaded to seek the products in retail stores, retailers in turn go to wholesalers or the producer to buy the products.

IMPORTANT TERMS

Promotion
Communication
Source
Receiver
Coding process
Medium of transmission
Decoding process
Noise
Feedback
Channel capacity
Product adoption process

Innovators
Early adopters
Early majority
Late majority
Laggards
Promotion mix
Kinesic communication
Proxemic communication
Tactile communication
Push policy
Pull policy

DISCUSSION AND REVIEW QUESTIONS

1. What is the major task of promotion? Do firms ever use promotion to accomplish this task and fail? If so, give several examples.
2. What is communication? Describe the communication process. Is it possible to communicate without using all the elements in the communication process? If so, which ones can be omitted?
3. Identify several causes of noise. How can a source reduce noise?
4. Describe the product adoption process. Under certain circumstances, is it possible for a person to omit one or more of the stages in adopting a new product? Explain your answer.
5. Describe a product that many persons are in the process of adopting. Have you begun the adoption process for this product? If so, what stage have you reached?
6. Identify and briefly describe the four major promotional methods that can be included in an organization's promotion mix. How does publicity differ from advertising?
7. What forms of interpersonal communication besides language can be used in personal selling?
8. How do market characteristics determine which promotional methods to include in a promotion mix? Assume that a company is planning to promote a cereal to both adults and children. Along what major dimensions would these two promotional efforts have to be different?
9. How can a product's characteristics affect the composition of its promotion mix?
10. Evaluate the following statement: "Appropriate advertising media are always available if a company can afford them."
11. Explain the difference between a pull policy and a push policy. Under what conditions should each policy be used?

14.1 Southwest Airlines Has Fun

Southwest Airlines, the eleventh largest airline in the United States, has been one of the most innovative promoters in the competitive airline industry in the 1980s. Chairman Herbert Kelleher has proven that a company can be run for both fun and profit. The key to Southwest's success has been the lowest operating costs in the industry, loyal employees, no-frills on-board service, low prices, and playful but effective promotion.

The focus of much of Southwest's promotion is Chairman Kelleher's zaniness and personal involvement with employees, passengers, and the general public. New employees watch "Southwest Shuffle," a rap-music video in which a number of employees, including Kelleher, rap out descriptions of their jobs and praise for the company. Kelleher often appears in television advertisements serving peanuts on his planes to illustrate Southwest's low-fare, no-frill service. He has also been known to board his planes dressed as the Easter bunny or a leprechaun. In a way, he is personally selling Southwest as a fun airline to both customers and Southwest employees. Everyone in the company is encouraged to get involved in entertaining and serving customers. On one recent Christmas flight, flight attendants dressed as reindeer, and the pilot sang Christmas carols. Kelleher knows many of his seven thousand employees by name, and they call him "Uncle Herb" or "Herbie."

One sales promotion event paired Southwest with Burger King in a two-for-one "buddy pass" airline ticket giveaway with the purchase of a Whopper, French fries, and Pepsi. Southwest viewed the promotion as a way to increase passenger traffic during the early months of the year, a traditionally slow period for all airlines. In another promotion, to herald the opening of Sea World in San Antonio, Kelleher had one of his 737 jets painted to look like a killer whale, one of Sea World's most popular attractions. Obviously, much publicity resulted from this event.

Southwest's style makes it an easy target for competitors' put-downs, but they are taken in stride. In one advertisement, Kelleher wore a paper bag on his head and offered such a bag to anyone embarrassed to fly on Southwest. If travelers choose Southwest, they can still get the bag for all the money they will save by flying Southwest.

Doing things differently is a source of pride at Southwest Airlines. It advertises no-frills service; its tickets resemble grocery store receipts; and travel agents cannot book travelers on its flights through computers, which saves the airline $25 million annually in booking fees. Despite its no-frills philosophy, the company's playful attitude and promotions have made it popular with travelers. The firm had $1 billion in revenues in 1989, and it hopes to achieve $2 billion by 1995. Even with rock-bottom fares, Southwest has been profitable because its costs average 30 percent below those of its competitors. Southwest has had sixteen straight years of profitability, a record that none of the larger airlines can match. Moreover, the Department of Transportation's monthly consumer report routinely ranks Southwest among the airlines lowest in complaints and highest in on-time flights. Southwest's on-time flight record can be attributed partly to a fifteen-minute turnaround time for planes versus an industry average of forty-five minutes.

Pending legislation in Congress has some analysts worried that Southwest could be squashed by the competition, but competition does not scare Kelleher. He has plans to diversify geographically, which would, he hopes, keep Southwest growing in revenue and profits. His plan is to double his fleet of airplanes to 170 by the late 1990s and to increase the frequency of flights on existing routes, as well as to open new routes in California and the Midwest. Promotion will be a key consideration in achieving these objectives.

SOURCES: Doug Carroll, "No-Frills Firm Flies Against the Ordinary," *USA Today,* Aug. 24, 1989, pp. 1B, 2B; Kevin Kelly, "Southwest Airlines: Flying High with 'Uncle Herb.'" *Business Week,* July 3, 1989, pp. 53–54; Dean Lampman, "Herb Kelleher, Chief of America West's Arch Rival, Keeps Lighter Side of Business in Mind," *Phoenix Business Journal,* May 2, 1988; and Stuart Manning, "Burger King, Southwest Airlines Offer 'Buddy Pass' Promo," *Dallas/Fort Worth Business Journal,* Dec. 5, 1988.

Questions for Discussion

1. What is the promotion mix at Southwest Airlines?
2. What role does Herbert Kelleher play in the promotion of Southwest Airlines?
3. What is the importance of publicity in Southwest Air's promotion mix?

14.2   Nissan Uses Promotion to Change Its Image

Nissan Motor Co., the American marketing subsidiary of the Japanese Nissan, has experienced declining sales and market share in recent years, due in large part to consumer confusion about Nissan's image. In 1958, Nissan began selling a compact car called the Bluebird in the United States. The Bluebirds were called Datsuns in Japan, and the name stuck in the United States, too. Thus, without much planning, the nameplate on the whole line of cars sold in the United States became Datsun over the next two decades. Many Americans associated the name Datsun with efficient and reliable cars, and the Datsun models 240Z and the later 280ZX sold well.

However, the Japan-based Nissan wanted to convey a uniform image around the world, and so in 1981, the company started marketing all its cars under the name Nissan. The Datsun nameplate disappeared with the introduction of the 1985 Maxima model. But many Americans continued to refer to the company's cars and trucks as Datsuns, and the name Nissan meant little to consumers. The confusion over the name may explain why Nissan experienced a decline in sales and market share of its automobiles and trucks in the United States during the late 1980s.

Another factor in Nissan's image problem was the company's change from mostly numbered models (210s, 510s, 280s) to more named ones (Stanzas, Maximas). Automobile analysts say that the confusion caused by this inconsistency led to fewer Nissan sales. At one point, Nissan had a one-hundred-day supply of unsold cars in showrooms and on loading docks, forty days above the industry average. By comparison, Toyota had only a twenty-day supply. As others in the automobile industry began promoting new models, Nissan was still flooded with older cars. New cars also piled up because Nissan had no "all-new" cars to sell. Every model was a carry-over from the previous model year with only slight modifications.

In an effort to confront the image problem, Nissan began a unique advertising campaign. The campaign was created to convince consumers that Nissan builds cars from a "people's point of view," with the driver in mind, and that Nissan cars are built with the help of "human engineering." The advertisements showed actors portraying Nissan designers discussing the ways people use their automobiles. The company attempted to establish itself by focusing on pride, sophistication, and the benefits that consumers want from an automobile or truck.

However, the commercials did not bring prospective buyers into Nissan showrooms. Instead sales fell by 40 percent, and many Nissan dealers were understandably critical of this effort. Nissan dropped the campaign soon after, and instead began a sales promotion campaign offering rebates of up to $1,000 on selected cars. The rebate program continued into the 1990 model year. Many experts believe that such sales promotions bring only short-run sales results and do not build a long-term brand image.

To solve its image and declining sales problems, Nissan reorganized its U.S. operations under eleven regional managers. It also introduced an aggressive owner-satisfaction program, called Owner 1, to make sure that owners were satisfied with purchases of new cars, as well as repairs of older cars.

In addition, Nissan sought to add "flash" to a complete line of new cars with distinctive and innovative designs. The promotions for five of the new cars stress sex, speed, and dreams. The campaign appeals to drivers' "fantasies" about their cars. The commercials feature cars outrunning jets, the admiration of attractive women and men, and trucks that make their owners feel free and fearless. In the glamour advertisement of the new campaign, a man dreams of a futuristic highway chase. While driving his $33,000 ZX Turbo, he outruns a black-helmeted motorcyclist, a black racing car, and a black fighter jet. However, the ad was criticized by automobile safety groups as irresponsible for promoting speeding. An advertisement for the 240SX features a woman fantasizing about driving her new car; her fantasy includes actor Ken Wahl from the popular television show *Wise Guy.*

Advertisements for Nissan's new Infiniti line of luxury cars (which compete with Mercedes-Benz, BMW, Jaguar, and Audi) are even more offbeat, showing images of waves, fields, or clouds, but never a car. However, Infiniti dealers have been overwhelmed with "tire-kickers," customers drawn in to check out the new line of cars. The Infiniti Q45 full-size four-door sedan has a base price of $38,000. Dealers have "contemplation rooms" for customers and use a decidedly soft-sell approach.

Nissan's revamped line-up and offbeat promotions are proving successful. Sales were up in 1990 after previous years of decline. Nissan is reestablishing itself and its reputation for making bold, exciting cars with distinctive and innovative designs. Promotion has played a key role in informing and persuading buyers to form a new image of Nissan cars.

SOURCES: James R. Healey, "Enthusiasm, Lines Welcome Nissan's Infiniti," *USA Today,* Nov. 8, 1989, p. 1B; David Landis, "Hot Models Recharge Sales, Image," *USA Today,* Sept. 13, 1989, pp. 1B, 2B; Michael Lev, "Nissan Tries To Build an Image Where There Was None," *Torrance Daily Breeze* (Torrance, Calif.), June 5, 1988; and Joseph B. White, "Nissan Motors Back to Basics: Sex, Speed," *Wall Street Journal,* Nov. 9, 1989, p. B6.

Questions for Discussion

1. What went wrong with Nissan's promotion in the 1980s?
2. What can Nissan do to improve its promotion in the 1990s?
3. Is "sex, speed, and dreams" a socially responsible message to use in automobile advertising?

15 ADVERTISING AND PUBLICITY

Objectives

To explore the uses of advertising

To become aware of the major steps involved in developing an advertising campaign

To find out who is responsible for developing advertising campaigns

To gain an understanding of publicity

To analyze how publicity can be used

Levi Strauss & Co., perceived as one of the best marketers in the apparel industry, spends an estimated $100 million annually advertising its 501 blue jeans and other clothing. In 1989, Levi's decided to replace its highly successful "501 Blues" advertising campaign, which helped double sales of button-fly 501 jeans and boosted Levi's to number one, with a 20 percent share in the $6.6 billion jeans market during the late 1980s.

Levi's introduced its $22 million "501 USA" campaign targeting the 16 to 24 age group. Each of the eight television commercials takes its title from the locale in which it was filmed: Boston, Chicago, Houston, and Hollywood, as well as Antelope Valley, California; Dubuque, Iowa; Lake Charles, Louisiana; and Cape Ann, Massachusetts. The advertisements highlight residents' loyalty to their communities; Levi's calls them "a big televised postcard from all across America." Levi's advertising agency, Foote, Cone & Belding, intended the advertisements to have the comfortable feel of an old pair of Levi's, be quite personal, and use unscripted, stream-of-consciousness dialogue, replacing the earlier "501 Blues" campaign's reliance on blues music.

Levi Strauss also advertises its Levi Dockers (a line of men's casual pants) and its 900 Series (a women's denim line) in an effort to convey the idea that Levi's is a brand for life. The Dockers advertisements seek to capitalize on brand loyalty among 25- to 49-year-old men who grew up with Levi's but want a nicer alternative to jeans. The company is advertising its 900 Series to boost its women's wear sales, a potentially lucrative segment that lags behind the jeans and menswear businesses. The campaign theme for the 900 Series is "Real life wears real jeans," and it is Levi's first appeal exclusively to women since 1983. By creatively using advertising, Levi's has been able to improve marketing activities that can increase market share. ◆

Advertisement courtesy of Levi Strauss and Company.

Based on information in Stuart Elliott, "Levi's Shelves 'Blues' for Red, White and Blue," *USA Today,* July 17, 1989, p. B1; "Everyone Knows His First Name," Levi Strauss & Co., P.O. Box 7215, San Francisco, CA 94120; Marcy Magiera, "Levi's Broadens Appeal," *Advertising Age,* July 17, 1989, pp. 1, 48; and Pat Sloan, "Lee, Wrangler Stay Out of Town," *Advertising Age,* July 17, 1989, p. 48.

This chapter explores the many dimensions of advertising and publicity. Initially, we focus on how advertising is used. Then we examine the major steps by which an advertising campaign is developed and describe who is responsible for developing such campaigns. As we analyze publicity, we compare its characteristics with those of advertising and explore the different forms it may take. Then we consider how publicity is used and what is required for an effective publicity program. Finally, we discuss negative publicity and some problems associated with the use of publicity.

THE NATURE OF ADVERTISING

Advertising permeates our daily lives. At times people view it positively; at other times they avoid it by taping television programs and then zapping over the commercials with the fast-forward button of their videocassette recorders. Some advertising informs, persuades, or entertains us; some of it bores, even insults, us. For example, consumer groups around the United States have been white washing billboards advertising tobacco products because they believe such advertisements encourage children to smoke.[1] Some of the most successful advertisements of the 1980s are highlighted in Marketing Update 15.1.

As mentioned in Chapter 14, **advertising** is a paid form of nonpersonal communication that is transmitted through mass media such as television, radio, newspapers, magazines, direct mail, mass transit vehicles, and outdoor displays. An organization can use advertising to reach a variety of audiences, ranging from small, precise groups, such as the stamp collectors of Idaho, to extremely large audiences, such as all the athletic shoe purchasers in the United States.

When people are asked to name major advertisers, most immediately mention business organizations. However, many types of organizations—including governments, churches, universities, civic groups, and charitable organizations—take advantage of advertising. In 1988, for example, the U.S. government was the thirty-sixth largest advertiser in the country, spending more than $295 million.[2] So even though we analyze advertising in the context of business organizations here, remember that much of what we say applies to all types of organizations.

Marketers sometimes give advertising more credit than it deserves. This attitude causes them to use advertising when they should not. For example, manufacturers of basic products such as sugar, flour, and salt often try to differentiate their products with minimal success. However, over the years, Morton's has tried to position its salt as different from the competition with the advertising slogan, "When it rains, it pours."

Under certain conditions, advertising can work effectively for an organization. The questions in Table 15.1 raise some general points that a marketer should consider when assessing the potential value of advertising as an ingredient in a product's promotion mix. The list is not all-inclusive. Numerous factors have a bearing on whether advertising should be used at all, and if so, to what extent.

1. "CBS This Morning," CBS (TV), April 11, 1990.
2. "100 Leading National Advertisers by Rank," *Advertising Age*, Sept. 27, 1989, p. 1.

ADVERTISING SUCCESSES OF THE 1980s

Looking back on the 1980s, it is easy to identify the successful products: Nintendo games, SPF sunscreens, Swatch watches, *USA Today*, athletic shoes, tartar control toothpastes, mini-vans, computers, microwave foods, and diet Coke. But what were the most successful advertisements of the 1980s?

Some of the most successful advertisements of the 1980s featured celebrity endorsers, creating very memorable and sometimes humorous commercials. Nike ran several popular advertising campaigns featuring celebrities including Michael Jordan and the "Bo's" (Jackson and Diddley). Michael J. Fox appeared in a series of humorous lifestyle ads for Pepsi, including one in which a photocopied can of Pepsi satisfies his thirst. And some marketers created their own celebrities, as Isuzu did with its infamous "liar" campaign starring Joe Isuzu, as well as Wendy's "Where's the Beef?" campaign featuring Clara Peller.

Other successful advertising campaigns featured animated characters rather than real celebrities. The California Raisins danced into American hearts while promoting raisins as a snack alternative. Animated Disney characters on a Pampers diaper came to life to the delight of the real baby in an ad. To promote Friskies kitten food, a cute kitten raced to the accompaniment of race-car sound effects to get to its food.

Apple Computers also excelled in the 1980s, airing particular commercials only once—for example, its "1984" spot during the Super Bowl of the same year. The spot dwelled on George Orwell's prediction that in 1984 people would be more like "lemmings," following and imitating, rather than innovative and individualistic like Apple. Sometimes the more sophisticated the message, such as Apple's, the more acclaim the commercial receives.

Social changes created the MTV era and another exemplary ad of the 1980s. "I want my MTV" was not only the tagline of MTV advertising but also became society's way of defining escapism and the youth movement. To be successful, advertising must stay in touch with societal trends and demands.

What advertisements will succeed in the 1990s? Stay tuned.

SOURCES: Joann Lipman, "Ads of the '80's: The Loved and the Losers," *Wall Street Journal,* Dec. 28, 1989, pp. B1, B4; Joann Lipman, "When It's Commerical Time, TV Viewers Prefer Cartoons to Celebrities Any Day," *Wall Street Journal,* February 16, 1990, pp. B1, B4; and Kathleen Deveny, "For Marketers, '80s Yielded Big Flops, Notable Success," *Wall Street Journal,* Nov. 28, 1989, p. B1.

TABLE 15.1   *Some issues to consider when deciding whether to use advertising*

1. **Does the product possess unique, important features?**

   Although homogeneous products such as cigarettes, gasoline, and beer have been advertised successfully, they usually require considerably more effort and expense than other products. On the other hand, products that are differentiated on physical rather than psychological dimensions are much easier to advertise. Even so, "being different" is rarely enough. The advertisability of product features is enhanced when buyers believe that those unique features are important and useful.

2. **Are "hidden qualities" important to buyers?**

   If by viewing, feeling, tasting, or smelling the product buyers can learn all there is to know about the product and its benefits, advertising will have less chance of increasing demand. Conversely, if not all product benefits are apparent to consumers on inspection and use of the product, advertising has more of a story to tell, and the probability that it can be profitably used increases. The "hidden quality" of vitamin C in oranges once helped explain why Sunkist oranges could be advertised effectively whereas the advertising of lettuce has been a failure.

3. **Is the general demand trend for the product favorable?**

   If the generic product category is experiencing a long-term decline, it is less likely that advertising can be used successfully for a particular brand within the category.

4. **Is the market potential for the product adequate?**

   Advertising can be effective only when there are sufficient actual or prospective users of the brand in the target market.

5. **Is the competitive environment favorable?**

   The size and marketing strength of competitors and their brand shares and loyalty will greatly affect the possible success of an advertising campaign. For example, a marketing effort to compete successfully against Kodak film, Morton salt, or Campbell soups would demand much more than simply advertising.

6. **Are general economic conditions favorable for marketing the product?**

   The effects of an advertising program and the sale of all products are influenced by the overall state of the economy and by specific business conditions. For example, it is much easier to advertise and sell luxury leisure products (stereos, sailboats, recreation vehicles) when disposable income is high.

7. **Is the organization able and willing to spend the money required to launch an advertising campaign?**

   As a general rule, if the organization is unable or unwilling to undertake an advertising expenditure that as a percentage of the total amount spent in the product category is at least equal to the market share it desires, advertising is less likely to be effective.

8. **Does the firm possess sufficient marketing expertise to market the product?**

   The successful marketing of any product involves a complex mixture of product and buyer research, product development, packaging, pricing, financial management, promotion, and distribution. Weakness in any area of marketing is an obstacle to the successful use of advertising.

SOURCE: Adapted from Charles H. Patti, "Evaluating the Role of Advertising," *Journal of Advertising,* Fall 1977, pp. 32–33. Used by permission.

FIGURE 15.1

Product advertisement for Acuvue contact lenses

SOURCE: Courtesy of Johnson & Johnson

THE USES OF ADVERTISING

Advertising can serve a variety of purposes. Individuals and organizations use it to promote products and organizations, to stimulate demand, to offset competitors' advertising, to make salespersons more effective, to increase the uses of a product, to remind and reinforce customers, and to reduce sales fluctuations.

■ **Promoting Products and Organizations**

Advertising is used to promote goods, services, ideas, images, issues, people, and indeed anything that the advertiser wants to publicize or foster. Depending on what is being promoted, advertising can be classified as institutional or product advertising. **Institutional advertising** promotes organizational images, ideas, or political issues. For example, some of Seagram's advertising promotes the idea that drinking and driving do not mix, in order to create and develop a socially responsible image.

Product advertising promotes goods and services. Business, government, and private nonbusiness organizations turn to it to promote the uses, features, images, and benefits of their products. When Johnson & Johnson introduced Acuvue disposable contact lenses, it used advertising to tout the benefits of disposable lenses. Some magazine advertisements for Acuvue lenses included a toll-free telephone number to call or postpaid card to send in to obtain more information about the uses and benefits of the new product (see Figure 15.1).

When a specific firm is the first to introduce an innovation, it tries to stimulate *primary demand*—demand for a product category rather than a specific brand of the product—through pioneer advertising. **Pioneer advertising** informs people about a product: what it is, what it does, how it can be used, and where it can be purchased. Because pioneer advertising is used in the introductory stage of the product life cycle when there are no competitive brands, it neither emphasizes the brand name nor compares brands. The first company to introduce the compact disc player, for instance, initially tried to stimulate primary demand by emphasizing the benefits of compact disc players in general rather than the benefits of its brand. Product advertising is also used sometimes to stimulate primary demand for an established product. Occasionally, an industry trade group, rather than a single firm, sponsors advertisements to stimulate primary demand. For example, to stimulate demand for dairy products, the National Dairy Board sponsors advertisements that promote their nutritional value (see Figure 15.2).

To build *selective demand,* or demand for a specific brand, an advertiser turns to competitive advertising. **Competitive advertising** points out a brand's uses, features, and advantages that benefit consumers but may not be available in competing

FIGURE 15.2
Stimulating primary demand.
The National Dairy Board stimulates primary demand for dairy products through the promotion of their nutritional value.

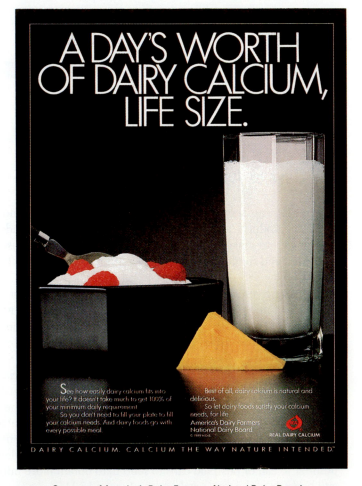

SOURCE: Courtesy of America's Dairy Farmers. National Dairy Board.

FIGURE 15.3

Using comparative advertising.
Tyco uses comparative advertising to illustrate its competitive advantage in similarly priced building sets.

SOURCE: Tyco Toys

brands. For example, Volvo heavily promotes the safety and crash-worthiness of Volvo automobiles in its advertising.

An increasingly popular form of competitive advertising is **comparative advertising**, in which two or more specified brands are compared on the basis of one or more product attributes. This type of advertising is prevalent among manufacturers of hamburgers, soft drinks, toothpastes, aspirin, tires, automobiles, and a multitude of other products. However, under the Trademark Law Revision Act of 1988, marketers using comparative advertising must not misrepresent the qualities or characteristics of the comparison product. For example, a commercial for Sorrell Ridge fruit preserves told viewers that the firm's preserves are made only from fruit and fruit juice, whereas competitor J. M. Smucker Co.'s preserves consist mostly of corn syrup and refined sugar but little fruit. Although Smucker did not file suit over the advertisements, its management worried that consumers might regard Smucker's preserves as less healthy, even though Smucker, too, has an all-fruit line of preserves—a fact the comparison made by Sorrell Ridge failed to mention.[3] Thus marketers must avoid misrepresenting either their own products or those of their competitors in advertising. Figure 15.3 provides a graphic depiction of the difference between similarly priced building blocks for children.

3. Jeffrey A. Trachtenberg, "Advertising: New Trademark Law to Increase Perils of Comparative Advertising," *Wall Street Journal*, June 1, 1989, p. B6.

■ Offsetting Competitors' Advertising

When marketers advertise to offset or lessen the effects of a competitor's promotional program, they are using **defensive advertising**. Although defensive advertising does not necessarily increase a company's sales or market share, it may prevent a loss in sales or market share. For example, when McDonald's test-marketed pizza in Evansville, Indiana, and Owensboro, Kentucky, Pizza Hut countered with defensive advertising to protect its market share and sales. The pizza maker advertised on both television and in newspapers in the two test cities, emphasizing that its product is made from scratch while McDonald's uses frozen dough.[4] Defensive advertising is used most often by firms in extremely competitive consumer product markets, such as the fast-food industry.

■ Making Salespersons More Effective

Business organizations that stress personal selling often use advertising to improve the effectiveness of sales personnel. Advertising created specifically to support personal selling activities tries to presell a product to buyers by informing them about its uses, features, and benefits and by encouraging them to contact local dealers or sales representatives. This form of advertising helps salespeople find good sales prospects. Advertising is often designed to support personal selling efforts for industrial products, insurance, and consumer durables, such as automobiles and major household appliances. For example, advertising may bring a prospective buyer to a showroom, but usually a salesperson plays a key role in closing the sale.

■ Increasing the Uses of a Product

The absolute demand for any product is limited because people in a market will consume only so much of it. Given both this limit on demand and competitive conditions, marketers can increase sales of a specific product in a defined geographic market only to a certain point. To improve sales beyond this point, they must either enlarge the geographic market and sell to more people or develop and promote a larger number of uses for the product. If a firm's advertising convinces buyers to use its products in more ways, then the sales of the products go up. For example, General Mills, the manufacturer of Cheerios cereal, used advertising to inform consumers that Cheerios contain oat bran, which has been found to help reduce cholesterol levels. The company is therefore attempting to position Cheerios as a part of a wholesome diet, as well as a popular children's cereal. When promoting new uses, an advertiser attempts to increase the demand for its own brand without driving up the demand for competing brands.

■ Reminding and Reinforcing Customers

Marketers sometimes employ **reminder advertising** to let consumers know that an established brand is still around and that it has certain uses, characteristics, and benefits. Procter & Gamble, for example, reminds consumers that its Crest toothpaste is still the best one for preventing cavities. **Reinforcement advertising**, on the other hand, tries to assure current users that they have made the right choice and tells them how to get the most satisfaction from the product. The aim of both reminder and reinforcement advertising is to prevent a loss in sales or market share. AT&T's advertising tells customers that its services are "the right choice."

■ Reducing Sales Fluctuations

The demand for many products varies from month to month because of such factors as climate, holidays, seasons, and customs. A business, however, cannot operate at peak efficiency when sales fluctuate rapidly. Changes in sales volume translate into

---

4. Scott Hume, "Pizza Hut Is Frosted; New Ad Takes Slap at McDonald's Test Product," *Advertising Age*, Sept. 18, 1989, p. 4.

FIGURE 15.4
General steps for developing and implementing an advertising campaign

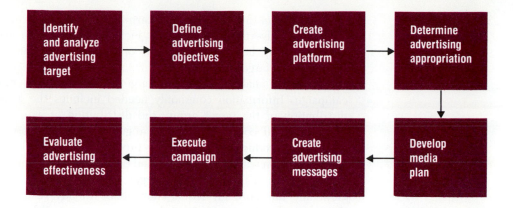

changes in the production or inventory, personnel, and financial resources required. To the extent that marketers can generate sales during slow periods, they can smooth out the fluctuations. When advertising reduces fluctuations, a manager can use the firm's resources more efficiently.

Advertising is often designed to stimulate sales during sales slumps. For example, advertisements promoting price reductions of lawn-care equipment or air conditioners can increase sales during fall and winter months. On occasion, a business advertises that customers will get better service by coming in on certain days rather than others. During peak sales periods, a marketer may refrain from advertising to prevent overstimulating sales to the point where the firm cannot handle all the demand. For example, coupons for the delivery of pizza are often valid only Monday through Thursday, not Friday through Sunday, which are the peak delivery times.

A firm's use of advertising depends on the firm's objectives, resources, and environmental forces. The degree to which advertising accomplishes the marketer's goals depends in large part on the advertising campaign.

DEVELOPING AN ADVERTISING CAMPAIGN

An **advertising campaign** involves designing a series of advertisements and placing them in various advertising media to reach a particular target market. As Figure 15.4 indicates, the major steps in creating an advertising campaign are (1) identifying and analyzing the advertising target, (2) defining the advertising objectives, (3) creating the advertising platform, (4) determining the advertising appropriation, (5) developing the media plan, (6) creating the advertising message, (7) executing the campaign, and (8) evaluating the effectiveness of the advertising. The number of steps and the exact order in which they are carried out may vary according to an organization's resources, the nature of its product, and the types of target markets or audiences to be reached. These general guidelines for developing an advertising campaign are appropriate for all types of organizations.

■ **Identifying and Analyzing the Advertising Target**

The **advertising target** is the group of people at which advertisements are aimed. For example, advertisements for Barbie cereal are directly targeted toward young girls who play with Barbie dolls, whereas the advertising target for Nintendo cereal is boys, and the target audience for Special K and Heartwise cereals is health-conscious adults. Identifying and analyzing the advertising target are critical processes;

CHAPTER 15   Advertising and Publicity   **469**

the information they yield helps determine the other steps in developing the campaign. The advertising target often includes everyone in a firm's target market. Marketers may, however, seize some opportunities to slant a campaign at only a portion of the target market.

Advertisers analyze advertising targets to establish an information base for a campaign. Information commonly needed includes the location and geographic distribution of the target group; the distribution of age, income, race, sex, and education; and consumer attitudes regarding the purchase and use of both the advertiser's products and competing products. The exact kinds of information that an organization will find useful depend on the type of product being advertised, the characteristics of the advertising target, and the type and amount of competition. Generally, the more advertisers know about the advertising target, the more likely they are to develop an effective advertising campaign. When the advertising target is not precisely identified and properly analyzed, the campaign may not succeed.

■ Defining the Advertising Objectives

The advertiser's next step is to consider what the firm hopes to accomplish with the campaign. Because advertising objectives guide campaign development, advertisers should define their objectives carefully to ensure that the campaign will achieve what they want. Advertising campaigns based on poorly defined objectives seldom succeed.

Advertising objectives should be stated clearly, precisely, and in measurable terms. Precision and measurability allow advertisers to evaluate advertising success: to judge, at the campaign's end, whether the objectives have been met, and if so, how well. To provide precision and measurability, advertising objectives should contain benchmarks—the current condition or position of the firm—and indicate how far and in what direction the advertiser wishes to move from these benchmarks. For example, the advertiser should state the current sales level (the benchmark) and the amount of sales increase that is sought through advertising. An advertising objective also should specify a time frame, so that advertisers know exactly how long they have to accomplish the objective. Thus an advertiser with average monthly sales of $450,000 (the bench mark) might set the following objective: "Our primary advertising objective is to increase average monthly sales from $450,000 to $540,000 within twelve months." This also tells the advertiser when evaluation of the campaign should begin.

If an advertiser defines objectives by sales, the objectives focus on raising absolute dollar sales, increasing sales by a certain percentage, or increasing the firm's market share. Frito-Lay, for example, increased product advertising for its Chee-Tos snack chips by 50 percent to counter a three-year decline in sales. The company said that the advertisements, which brought back the character Chester the Cheetah, boosted sales by 20 percent in the first months of the campaign.[5] However, even though an advertiser's long-run goal is to increase sales, not all campaigns are designed to produce immediate sales. Some campaigns are designed to increase product or brand awareness, make consumers' attitudes more favorable, or increase consumers' knowledge of a product's features. These objectives are stated in terms of communication. For example, when Apple Computer introduced home computers, its initial campaign did not focus on sales but on creating brand awareness and educating consumers about the features and uses of home computers. A specific

5. Laurie Freeman and Jennifer Lawrence, "Brand Building Gets New Life," *Advertising Age,* Sept. 4, 1989, p. 34.

FIGURE 15.5

Using research to develop an advertising platform.

Tylenol's use in hospitals versus ibuprofen brands illustrates that Tylenol is hospital approved—an effective advertising platform for Tylenol.

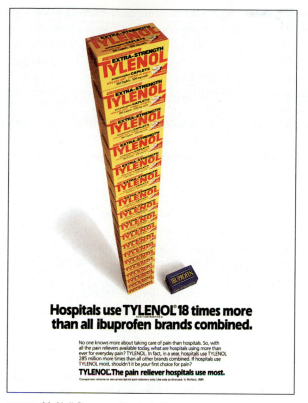

Hospitals use TYLENOL 18 times more than all ibuprofen brands combined.

No one knows more about taking care of pain than hospitals. So, with all the pain relievers available today, what are hospitals using more than ever for everyday pain? TYLENOL. In fact, in a year, hospitals use TYLENOL 285 million more times than all other brands combined. If hospitals use TYLENOL most, shouldn't it be your first choice for pain?

TYLENOL. The pain reliever hospitals use most.

SOURCE: McNeil Consumer Products Company

communication objective might be to increase product feature awareness from 0 to 40 percent in the target market by the end of six months.

■ Creating the Advertising Platform

Before launching a political campaign, party leaders develop a political platform, which states the major issues that will be the basis of the campaign. Like a political platform, an **advertising platform** consists of the basic issues or selling points that an advertiser wishes to include in the advertising campaign. A single advertisement in an advertising campaign may contain one or several issues in the platform. Although the platform sets forth the basic issues, it does not indicate how they should be presented.

A marketer's advertising platform should consist of issues that are important to consumers. One of the best ways to determine what those issues are is to survey consumers about what they consider most important in the selection and use of the product involved. For example, Procter & Gamble is testing refill packages for some of its cleaning products. The refill packages provide a unique benefit by not adding to the nation's solid-waste disposal problems.[6] Environmentally conscious consumers will consider this a positive selling feature. The selling features must not only be important to consumers; if possible, they should also be features that competitive products do not have.

Although research is the most effective method for determining the issues of an advertising platform, it is expensive. Figure 15.5 shows that Tylenol conducted

6. Laurie Freeman, "P&G to Unveil Refill Package," *Advertising Age,* Nov. 6, 1989, pp. 1, 69.

research on hospitals' use of pain relievers to develop a platform that helps give the product credibility among consumers. As a result, the advertising platform is most commonly based on the opinions of personnel within the firm and of individuals in the advertising agency, if an agency is used. This trial-and-error approach generally leads to some successes and some failures.

Because the advertising platform is a base on which to build the message, marketers should analyze this stage carefully. A campaign can be perfect as to the selection and analysis of its advertising target, the statement of its objectives, its media strategy, and the form of its message. But the campaign will still fail if the advertisements communicate information that consumers do not consider important when they select and use the product.

■ Determining the Advertising Appropriation

The **advertising appropriation** is the total amount of money that a marketer allocates for advertising for a specific time period. It is difficult to decide how much to spend on advertising for a specific period of time because there is no way to measure what the precise effects of spending a certain amount of money on advertising will be.

Many factors affect a firm's decision about how much to appropriate for advertising. The geographic size of the market and the distribution of buyers within the market have a great bearing on this decision. As Table 15.2 shows, both the type of product advertised and a firm's sales volume relative to competitors' sales volumes also play a part in determining what proportion of a firm's revenue is spent on advertising. Advertising appropriations for industrial products are usually quite small relative to the sales of the products, whereas consumer convenience items, such as soft drinks, soaps, and cosmetics, generally have large appropriations.

Of the many techniques used to determine the advertising appropriation, one of the most logical is the **objective and task approach**. Using this approach, marketers initially determine the objectives that a campaign is to achieve and then attempt to list the tasks required to accomplish them. The costs of the tasks are then calculated and added to arrive at the amount of the total appropriation. This approach has one main problem: marketers usually find it hard to estimate the level of effort needed to achieve certain objectives. A coffee marketer, for example, might find it extremely difficult to determine how much to increase national television advertising to raise a brand's market share from 8 to 12 percent. Because of this problem, advertisers do not widely use the objective and task approach.

In the more widely used **percent of sales approach**, marketers simply multiply a firm's past sales, plus a factor for planned sales growth or declines, by a standard percentage that is based on both what the firm traditionally spends on advertising and what the industry averages. This approach has one major flaw: it is based on the incorrect assumption that sales create advertising, rather than the reverse. Consequently, a marketer using the approach at a time of declining sales will reduce the amount spent on advertising. But such a reduction may further diminish sales. Though illogical, this technique has gained wide acceptance because it is easy to use and less disruptive competitively; it stabilizes a firm's market share within an industry. However, in times of declining sales, the fact remains that many firms do increase the percentage of their contribution to advertising in the hope of reversing the decline.

Another way to determine the advertising appropriation is the **competition-matching approach**. Marketers who follow this approach try to match their major

TABLE 15.2 *Sales volume and advertising expenditures for selected national advertisers (in millions of dollars)*

RANK	COMPANY	ADVERTISING EXPENDITURES	SALES MILLIONS	ADVERTISING EXPENDITURES AS PERCENT OF SALES
1	Phillip Morris	2058.2	31,742.0	6.5
2	Procter & Gamble Co.	1506.9	21,398.0	7.0
3	General Motors	1294.0	123,642.0	1.0
4	Sears, Roebuck & Co.	1045.2	50,251.0	2.1
5	RJR Nabisco	814.5	16,956.0	4.8
6	Grand Metropolitan PLC	773.9	10,681.0	7.2
7	Eastman Kodak	735.9	17,034.0	4.3
8	McDonald's Corp.	728.3	16,064.0	4.5
9	PepsiCo, Inc.	712.3	13,007.0	5.5
10	Kellogg Co.	683.1	4,349.0	15.7
11	Anheuser-Busch	634.5	9,705.0	6.5
12	K mart Corp.	632.0	27,301.0	2.3
13	Warner-Lambert Co.	609.2	3,908.0	15.6
14	Unilever NV	607.5	30,980.0	2.0
15	Nestle S.A.	573.8	27,051.0	2.1
16	Ford Motor Co.	569.8	92,446.0	0.6
17	AT&T	547.5	35,210.0	1.6
18	Chrysler Corp.	474.0	35,473.0	1.3
19	General Mills	470.1	5,621.0	8.4
20	Johnson & Johnson	468.8	9,000.0	5.2
21	Bristol-Myers Squibb	430.7	8,558.0	5.0
22	J.C. Penney Co.	426.6	14,833.0	2.9
23	Quaker Oats Co.	423.4	5,724.0	7.4
24	Ralston Purina Co.	421.0	5,876.0	7.2
25	Time Warner Co.	409.7	8,713.0	4.7

SOURCE: Adapted with permission from "100 Leading National Advertisers with U.S. Sales," *Advertising Age,* Sept. 27, 1989, pp. 24–122. Reprinted with permission from *Advertising Age,* September 27, 1989. Copyright Crain Communications Inc. All rights reserved.

competitors' appropriations in terms of absolute dollars or to allocate the same percentage of sales for advertising as their competitors do. Although a wise marketer should be aware of what competitors spend on advertising, this technique should not be used by itself because a firm's competitors probably have different advertising objectives and different resources available for advertising. Many companies and advertising agencies engage in quarterly competitive spending reviews, comparing competitors' dollar expenditures in print, radio, and television with their own spending levels. Competitive tracking of this nature occurs at both the national and regional levels.

At times, marketers use the **arbitrary approach**: a high-level executive in the firm states how much can be spent on advertising for a certain time period. The arbitrary approach often leads to underspending or overspending. Although hardly a scientific budgeting technique, it is expedient.

TABLE 15.3
Total advertising expenditures (in millions of dollars)

	1970	1975	1980	1985	1987 (est)
Newspapers	$ 5,704	$ 8,234	$14,794	$25,170	$28,541
Magazines	1,292	1,539	3,279	5,341	5,777
Television	3,596	5,263	11,366	20,738	24,388
Radio	1,308	1,980	3,777	6,490	7,242
Outdoor	234	335	600	945	1,068
Direct Mail	2,766	4,124	7,596	15,500	18,755
Business press	740	919	1,674	2,375	2,594
Miscellaneous	3,910	5,558	10,767	18,159	20,936
Total	$19,550	27,952	53,853	94,718	109,301

SOURCE: DDB Needham, *Worldwide Media Trends,* 1987 Edition. Reprinted by permission.

Establishing the advertising appropriation is critically important. If it is set too low, the campaign cannot achieve its full potential for stimulating demand. When too much money is appropriated for advertising, overspending results, and financial resources are wasted.

■ Developing the Media Plan

As Table 15.3 shows, advertisers spend tremendous amounts of money on advertising media. These amounts have grown rapidly during the past two decades. To derive the maximum results from media expenditures, a marketer must develop an effective media plan. A **media plan** sets forth the exact media vehicles to be used (specific magazines, television stations, newspapers, and so forth) and the dates and times that the advertisements will appear. The effectiveness of the plan determines how many people in the advertising target will be exposed to the message. It also determines, to some degree, the effects of the message on those individuals. Media planning is a complex task that requires thorough analysis of the advertising target.

To formulate a media plan, the planner selects the media for a campaign and draws up a time schedule for each medium. The media planner's primary goal is to reach the largest number of persons in the advertising target per dollar spent on media. In addition, a secondary goal is to achieve the appropriate message reach and frequency for the target audience while staying within the budget. *Reach* refers to the percentage of consumers in the advertising target actually exposed to a particular advertisement in a stated time period. *Frequency* is the number of times these targeted consumers were exposed to the advertisement.

Media planners begin with rather broad decisions; eventually, however, they must make very specific choices. A planner must first decide which kinds of media to use: radio, television, newspapers, magazines, direct mail, outdoor displays, mass transit vehicles, or a combination of two or more of these. After making the general media decision, the planner selects specific subclasses within each medium. Estee Lauder, for example, might advertise its Clinique cosmetic line in women's magazines, as well as during daytime, family, and late night television. Marketing Update 15.2 discusses media-planning decisions related to television advertising during the Super Bowl.

SUPER BOWL ADVERTISING: IS IT REALLY WORTH THE COST?

Since 1984, the world's biggest advertising showcase has also been one of the United States' most important sporting events. The Super Bowl is often used as a promotional vehicle for introducing new products, new advertisements, and new ideas. However, the rising costs of commercial air time, along with declining Super Bowl ratings, have made the Super Bowl a promotional medium only for deep-pocketed advertisers. Consequently, many advertisers are rethinking their Super Bowl promotion participation.

Super Bowl XXIV in 1990 set several records. Besides being the most lopsided game in Super Bowl history (the San Francisco 49ers defeated the Denver Broncos 55–10), the game had the lowest Super Bowl ratings in 21 years—an average of 39 percent of available households and 63 percent of those viewing at the time, or about 108.5 million people. Super Bowl XXIV also set a record for air-time costs. CBS charged $700,000 for each of the 56 30-second spots available during the game. However, CBS did not guarantee advertisers a certain number of viewers. As a result, IBM, Michelin, Volkswagen, Hyundai, and Dodge, and other former Super Bowl advertisers did not advertise during the game, citing low ratings and high costs.

Other major advertisers, however, stayed in the game. Master Lock spent its entire annual advertising budget on one 30-second spot that many picked as the best ad of the game. PepsiCo bought 3 minutes of air time, while Coca-Cola bought 2.5 minutes. In the ongoing cola wars, Pepsi's ads were judged to be more effective than Coke's. Budweiser bought 3.25 minutes of air time for its Bud Bowl II campaign, a rematch of Bud Bowl I from Super Bowl XXIII. Although the gimmick worked in 1989, the 1990 Bud Bowl ads were chosen as being among the game's worst ads.

Is Super Bowl advertising worth the cost? Many advertisers are starting to think not. However, those willing to pay the high prices while reaching fewer consumers suggest that the Super Bowl is still the best-watched program of the year. As one ad agency executive put it: "You realize it's a premium—but everyone is watching."

SOURCES: Ronald Blum, "Ratings Weren't Super," *(Memphis) Commercial Appeal,* Jan. 31, 1990, p. D3; "CBS Scores Early with Ad Sellout for Super Bowl," *Advertising Age,* Dec. 4, 1989, p. 3; Stuart Elliott, "Stars Help Top Ads Shine," *USA Today,* Jan. 29, 1990, p. 4B; Joanne Lipman, "Super Bowl Is Advertisers' Biggest Turf," *Wall Street Journal,* Jan. 8, 1990, pp. B1, B4.

Media planners take many factors into account as they devise a media plan. They analyze the location and demographic characteristics of people in the advertising target because the various media appeal to particular demographic groups in particular locations. For example, there are radio stations especially for teen-agers, magazines for men in the 18 to 34 age group, and television programs aimed at adults of both sexes. Media planners also should consider the sizes and types of audiences specific media reach. Several data services collect and periodically publish information about the circulations and audiences of various media.

The cost of media is an important but troublesome consideration. Planners try to obtain the best coverage possible for each dollar spent, yet there is no accurate way of comparing the cost and impact of a television commercial with the cost and impact of a newspaper advertisement.

The content of the message sometimes affects the choice of media. Print media can be used more effectively than broadcast media to present many issues or numerous details. The maker of Grey Poupon, a zesty brown mustard, developed recipes for using the product and presented them in advertisements that also invited readers to send away for a complete recipe book. Included in the print media buy were *Bon Appetit, The Cook's Magazine, Gourmet,* and *Food & Wine.* The print advertisements prompted an overwhelming response: ten thousand requests were processed in the first month. Use of the print medium allowed Grey Poupon to target a particular audience.[7] If an advertiser wants to promote beautiful colors, patterns, or textures, media that offer high-quality color reproduction—magazines or television—should be used instead of newspapers. For example, cosmetics can be effectively promoted in a full-color magazine advertisement, but the ad would be far less effective in black and white. Compare the black and white and color versions of the advertisement in Figure 15.6.

The information in Table 15.3 indicates that each medium is used quite differently than the others and that the pattern of media use has changed over the years. For example, the proportion of total media dollars spent on magazines has declined slowly but steadily since 1970. The media selected is determined by the characteristics, advantages, and disadvantages (such as the ones listed in Table 15.4) of the major mass media used for advertising.

Given the variety of vehicles within each medium, media planners must deal with a vast number of alternatives. The multitude of factors that affect media rates obviously add to the complexity of media planning. A **cost comparison indicator** lets an advertiser compare the costs of several vehicles within a specific medium (such as two newspapers) in relation to the number of persons reached by each vehicle. For example, the "milline rate" is the cost comparison indicator for newspapers; it shows the cost of exposing a million persons to a space equal to one agate line.[8]

■ Creating the Advertising Message

The basic content and form of an advertising message are a function of several factors. The product's features, uses, and benefits affect the content of the message. Characteristics of the people in the advertising target—their sex, age, education, race, income, occupation, and other attributes—influence both the content and

7. "Ad Mustard," *Inside Print,* January 1988, pp. 94, 96.

8. An agate line is one column wide and the height of the smallest type normally used in classified newspaper advertisements. There are fourteen agate lines in one column inch.

FIGURE 15.6 *Comparison of black and white and color advertisements.*
This example highlights the importance of selecting the right media for a message. This ad ran in *Vogue* magazine in full color.

SOURCE: Visage Beauté Cosmetics, Inc. P.O. Box 10928, B.H., CA 90213

form. When Procter & Gamble promotes its Crest toothpaste to children, the company emphasizes the importance of daily brushing and cavity control. When Crest is marketed to adults, tartar and plaque are discussed. To communicate effectively, an advertiser must use words, symbols, and illustrations that are meaningful, familiar, and attractive to the people who constitute the advertising target.

The objectives and platform of an advertising campaign also affect the content and form of its messages. For example, if a firm's advertising objectives involve large sales increases, the message demands hard-hitting, high-impact language and symbols. When campaign objectives aim at increasing brand awareness, the message may use much repetition of the brand name and words and illustrations associated with it. Thus, the advertising platform is the foundation on which campaign messages are built.

The choice of media obviously influences the content and form of the message. Effective outdoor displays and short broadcast spot announcements require concise, simple messages. Magazine and newspaper advertisements can include much detail and long explanations. Because several different kinds of media offer geographic selectivity, a precise message content can be tailored to a particular geographic

TABLE 15.4 *Characteristics, advantages, and disadvantages of major advertising media*

MEDIUM	TYPES	UNIT OF SALE	FACTORS AFFECTING RATES	COST COMPARISON INDICATOR	ADVANTAGES	DIS-ADVANTAGES
Newspaper	Morning Evening Sunday Sunday supplement Weekly Special	Agate lines Column inches Counted words Printed lines	Volume and frequency discounts Number of colors Position charges for preferred and guaranteed positions Circulation level	Milline rate = cost per agate line × 1,000,000 divided by circulation	Almost everyone reads a newspaper; purchased to be read; national geographic flexibility; short lead time; frequent publication; favorable for cooperative advertising; merchandising services	Not selective for socioeconomic groups; short life; limited reproduction capabilities; large advertising volume limits exposure to any one advertisement
Magazine	Consumer Farm Business	Pages Partial pages Column inches	Circulation level Cost of publishing Type of audience Volume discounts Frequency discounts Size of advertisement Position of advertisement (covers) Number of colors Regional issues	Cost per thousand (CPM) = cost per page × 1,000 divided by circulation	Socioeconomic selectivity; good reproduction; long life; prestige; geographic selectivity when regional issues are available; read in leisurely manner	High absolute dollar cost; long lead time

Medium	Forms	Units sold	Factors affecting rates	Cost basis	Advantages	Disadvantages
Direct mail	Letters, Catalogs, Price lists, Calendars, Brochures, Coupons, Circulars, Newsletters, Postcards, Booklets, Broadsides, Samplers	Not applicable	Cost of mailing lists, Postage, Production costs	Cost per contact	Little wasted circulation; highly selective; circulation controlled by advertiser; few distractions; personal; stimulates actions; use of novelty; relatively easy to measure performance; hidden from competitors	Expensive; no editorial matter to attract readers; considered junk mail by many; criticized as invasion of privacy
Radio	AM, FM	Programs: sole sponsor, co-sponsor, participative sponsor; Spots: 5, 10, 20, 30, 60 seconds	Time of day, Audience size, Length of spot or program, Volume and frequency discounts	Cost per thousand (CPM) = cost per minute × 1,000 divided by audience size	Highly mobile; low-cost broadcast medium; message can be quickly changed; can reach a large audience; geographic selectivity; socioeconomic selectivity	Provides only audio message; has lost prestige; short life of message; listeners' attention limited because of other activities while listening
Television	Network, Local, CATV	Programs: sole sponsor, co-sponsor, participative sponsor; Spots: 5, 10, 15, 30, 60 seconds	Time of day, Length of program, Length of spot, Volume and frequency discounts, Audience size	Cost per thousand (CPM) = cost per minute × 1,000 divided by audience size	Reaches large audience; low cost per exposure; uses audio and video; highly visible; high prestige; geographic and socioeconomic selectivity	High-dollar costs; highly perishable message; size of audience not guaranteed; amount of prime time limited
Inside transit	Buses, Subways	Full, half, and quarter showings are sold on a monthly basis	Number of riders, Multiple-month discounts, Production costs, Position	Cost per thousand riders	Low cost; "captive" audience; geographic selectivity	Does not reach many professional persons; does not secure quick results

TABLE 15.4 *(Continued)*

MEDIUM	TYPES	UNIT OF SALE	FACTORS AFFECTING RATES	COST COMPARISON INDICATOR	ADVANTAGES	DIS-ADVANTAGES
Outside transit	Buses Taxicabs	Full, half, and quarter showings; space also rented on per-unit basis	Number of advertisements Position Size	Cost per thousand exposures	Low cost; geographic selectivity; reaches broad, diverse audience	Lacks socio-economic selectivity; does not have high impact on readers
Outdoor	Papered posters Painted displays Spectaculars	Papered posters: sold on monthly basis in multiples called "showings" Painted displays and spectaculars: sold on per-unit basis	Length of time purchased Land rental Cost of production Intensity of traffic Frequency and continuity discounts Location	No standard indicator	Allows for repetition; low cost; message can be placed close to the point of sale; geographic selectivity; operable 24 hours a day	Message must be short and simple; no socio-economic selectivity; seldom attracts readers' full attention; criticized for being traffic hazard and blight on countryside

SOURCE: Some of the information in this table is from S. Watson Dunn and Arnold M. Barban, *Advertising: Its Role in Modern Marketing*, 6th ed. (Hinsdale, Ill.: Dryden Press, 1986); and Anthony F. McGann and J. Thomas Russell, *Advertising Media* (Homewood, Ill.: Irwin, 1981).

FIGURE 15.7

Geographic divisions for Sports Illustrated regional issues

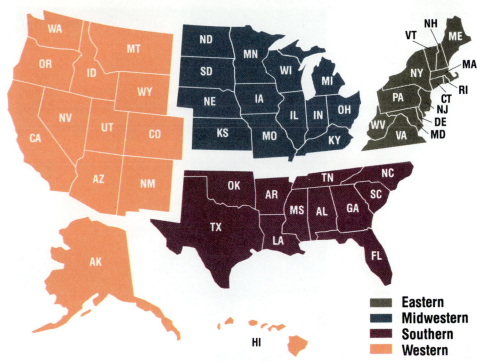

section of the advertising target. Some magazine publishers produce **regional issues**. For a particular issue, the advertisements and editorial content of copies appearing in one geographic area differ from those appearing in other areas. As Figure 15.7 shows, *Sports Illustrated* publishes four regional issues. A clothing manufacturer that advertises in *Sports Illustrated* might decide to use one message in the western region and another in the rest of the nation. A company may also choose to advertise in only a few regions. Such geographic selectivity lets a firm use the same message in different regions at different times.

The basic components of a print advertising message are shown in Figure 15.8. The messages for most advertisements depend on the use of copy and artwork. Let us examine these two elements in more detail.

Copy.   **Copy** is the verbal portion of an advertisement. It includes headlines, subheadlines, body copy, and the signature (see Figure 15.8). When preparing advertising copy, marketers attempt to move readers through a persuasive sequence called AIDA: attention, interest, desire, and action. Not all copy need be this extensive, however.

The headline is critical because often it is the only part of the copy that people read. It should attract readers' attention and create enough interest to make them want to read the body copy. The subheadline, if there is one, links the headline to the body copy. Sometimes it helps explain the headline.

Body copy for most advertisements consists of an introductory statement or paragraph, several explanatory paragraphs, and a closing paragraph. Some copywriters have adopted a pattern or set of guidelines to develop body copy systematically: (1) identify a specific desire or problem of consumers, (2) suggest the good or

FIGURE 15.8

Copy and artwork elements of printed ads. This ad clearly differentiates the basic elements of print advertising.

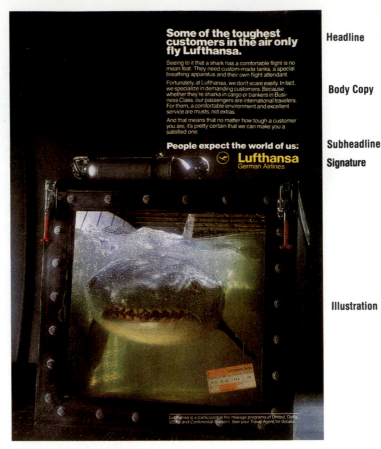

SOURCE: Lufthansa German Airlines

service as the best way to satisfy that desire or solve that problem, (3) state the advantages and benefits of the product, (4) indicate why the advertised product is the best for the buyer's particular situation, (5) substantiate the claims and advantages, and (6) ask the buyer for action.[9]

The signature identifies the sponsor of the advertisement. It may contain several elements, including the firm's trademark, logo, name, and address. The signature should be designed to be attractive, legible, distinctive, and easy to identify in a variety of sizes.

Because radio listeners often are not fully "tuned in" mentally, radio copy should be informal and conversational to attract listeners' attention, resulting in greater impact. The radio message is highly perishable. Thus radio copy should consist of short, familiar terms. Its length should not require a rate of speech exceeding approximately two and one-half words per second.

In television copy, the audio material must not overpower the visual material and vice versa. However, a television message should make optimal use of its visual portion. As Figure 15.9 illustrates, copy for a television commercial is initially

9. James E. Littlefield and C. A. Kirkpatrick, *Advertising Mass Communication in Marketing* (Boston: Houghton Mifflin, 1970), p. 178.

written in parallel script form. The video is described in the left column and the audio in the right column. When the parallel script is approved, the copywriter and artist combine the copy with the visual material through use of a **storyboard** (see Figure 15.10), which depicts a series of miniature television screens to show the sequence of major scenes in the commercial. Beneath each screen is a description of the audio portion that is to be used with the video message shown. Technical personnel use the storyboard as a blueprint when they produce the commercial.

Artwork.   **Artwork** consists of the illustration and layout of the advertisement (see Figure 15.8). Although **illustrations** are often photographs, they can also be drawings, graphs, charts, and tables. Illustrations are used to attract attention, to encourage the audience to read or listen to the copy, to communicate an idea quickly, or to communicate an idea that is difficult to put into words.[10] They are especially important because consumers tend to recall the visual portion of advertisements better than the verbal portions. Advertisers use a variety of illustration techniques, which are identified and described in Table 15.5.

The **layout** of an advertisement is the physical arrangement of the illustration, headline, subheadline, body copy, and signature. The arrangement of these parts in Figure 15.8 is only one possible layout. These same elements could be arranged in many ways. The final layout is the result of several stages of layout preparation. As it moves through these stages, the layout helps people involved in developing the advertising campaign exchange ideas. It also provides instructions for production personnel.

■ Executing the Campaign

The execution of an advertising campaign requires an extensive amount of planning and coordination. Regardless of whether an organization uses an advertising agency, many people and firms are involved in the execution of a campaign. Production companies, research organizations, media firms, printers, photoengravers, and commercial artists are just a few of the people and firms that contribute to a campaign.

Implementation requires detailed schedules to ensure that various phases of the work are done on time. Advertising management personnel must evaluate the quality of the work and take corrective action when necessary. In some instances, changes have to be made during the campaign so that it meets campaign objectives more effectively.

■ Evaluating the Effectiveness of the Advertising

There are a variety of ways to test the effectiveness of advertising. They include measuring achievement of advertising objectives; assessing the effectiveness of copy, illustrations, or layouts; and evaluating certain media.

Advertising can be evaluated before, during, and after the campaign. Evaluations performed before the campaign begins are called **pretests** and usually attempt to evaluate the effectiveness of one or more elements of the message. To pretest advertisements, marketers sometimes use a **consumer jury**, a number of persons who are actual or potential buyers of the advertised product. Jurors are asked to judge one or several dimensions of two or more advertisements. Such tests are based on the belief that consumers are more likely than advertising experts to know what will influence them.

10. S. Watson Dunn and Arnold M. Barban, *Advertising: Its Role in Modern Marketing*, 6th ed. (Hinsdale, Ill.: Dryden Press, 1986), p. 493.

```
                              Young & Rubicam
          200 RENAISSANCE CENTER, SUITE 1000, DETROIT, MICHIGAN 48243, (313) 446-860
          TJP44

          DATE:     8/31/89                    ORIG. COMM'L #:  FMCO-0308
          JOB #:    TB-26186                   NEW COMM'L #:  none
          TITLE:    BEWARE OF CAT              RECORD DATE:  8/29/89
          LENGTH:   :30 TV                     RECORD PLACE:
          CLIENT:   Lincoln-Mercury Div.       EDIT DATE/PLACE:
          PRODUCT:  Cougar XR7                 V/O TALENT:
          BY:       JP/sb/dg/clk               O/C TALENT:          .
          NUMBER:   Rev. #4                    MUSIC:
          MASTER:                              PRODUCER:  L. Rose


          VISUAL                                         AUDIO

          A pack of mongrel dogs spies     1|  VO:  Something wild is coming.  The
          an approaching Cougar XR7.        |
          They take up the chase.          2|  Cougar XR7.
                                            |
          The Cougar XR7 races around a    3|
          corner.  The dogs try in vain     |
          to follow.  The Cougar XR7       4|  It has speed-sensitive steering and
          stops.  The dogs stumble          |
          trying to stop.  The merry       5|  anti-lock brakes.
          chase continues.  Finally,        |
          the dogs chase the Cougar out    6|  But, most of all, it as a
          of the screen,.  We hear a        |
          load roar, and see the super:    7|  supercharged, 210-horsepower
                                            |
                                           8|  engine.
                                            |
                                           9|
                                            |
          BEWARE OF CAT                   10|  SFX:  ROARRRRRR!!!!!
                                            |
          The dogs retreat in fear        11|  SFX:  (DOGS YELPING IN REAR)
          across the screen.  A split-      |
          second later, the Cougar XR7    12|
          cruises triumphantly through      |
          frame.                          13|  VO:  It's becoming a cat-eat-dog
                                            |
                                          14|  world out there.
                                            |
                                          15|
                                            |
                                          16|  MUSIC:  "NOTHING MOVES YOU..."
                                            |
                                          17|
                                            |
                                          18|  VO:  Cougar.  All this, and the
                                            |
                                          19|  quality of a Mercury.
                                            |
          FMCO-0308                       20|
```

SOURCE: Reprinted with permission of Lincoln Mercury Division

To measure advertising effectiveness during a campaign, marketers usually take advantage of "inquiries." In the initial stages of a campaign, an advertiser may use several advertisements simultaneously, each containing a coupon or a form requesting information. The advertiser records the number of coupons that are returned from each type of advertisement. If an advertiser receives 78,528 coupons from advertisement A, 37,072 coupons from advertisement B, and 47,932 coupons from advertisement C, advertisement A is judged superior to advertisements B and C.

Evaluation of advertising effectiveness after the campaign is called a **posttest**. Advertising objectives often indicate what kind of posttest will be appropriate. If an advertiser sets objectives in terms of communication—product awareness, brand awareness, or attitude change—then the posttest should measure changes in one or more of these dimensions. Advertisers sometimes use consumer surveys or experiments to evaluate a campaign based on communication objectives. These methods are costly, however.

For campaign objectives that are stated in terms of sales, advertisers should determine the change in sales or market share that can be attributed to the campaign. Unfortunately, changes in sales or market share brought about by advertising cannot be measured precisely; many factors independent of advertisements affect a

FIGURE 15.10
Final storyboard.
This is the final story-
board for the Lincoln
Mercury Cougar XR7.

CLIENT:	LINCOLN MERCURY	LENGTH:	30 SECONDS
PRODUCT:	COUGAR XR7	COMM. NO.:	FMCO-0308
TITLE:	"BEWARE OF CAT"	DATE:	8/23/89

MAN: Nothing moves you.

ANNCR. V.O.: Something wild is coming.

The Cougar XR7.

It has speed-sensitive steering

(MUSIC)

(MUSIC)

and anti-lock brakes.

(MUSIC)

But, most of all,

it has a

supercharged,

210-horsepower

engine.

BEWARE OF CAT

(SFX: ROARRRRRR!!!!!)

(SFX: DOGS YELPING IN FEAR)

ANNCR. V.O.: It's becoming a cat-eat-dog world out there. (MUSIC: "NOTHING MOVES YOU . . .")

ANNCR. V.O.: Cougar. All this,

and the quality of a Mercury.

SOURCE: Reprinted with permission of Lincoln Mercury Division

firm's sales and market share. Competitive actions, government actions, and changes in economic conditions, consumer preferences, and weather are only a few factors that might enhance or diminish a company's sales or market share. However, by using data about past and current sales and advertising expenditures, an advertiser can make gross estimates of the effects of a campaign on sales or market share.

Because consumer surveys and experiments are so expensive, and because it is so difficult to determine the direct effects of advertising on sales, many advertisers evaluate print advertisements according to the degree to which consumers can remember them. The posttest methods based on memory include recognition and recall tests. Such tests are usually performed by research organizations through consumer surveys. If a **recognition test** is used, individual respondents are shown the actual advertisement and asked whether they recognize it. If they do, the interviewer asks additional questions to determine how much of the advertisement each respondent read. When recall is evaluated, the respondents are not shown the actual advertisement but instead are asked about what they have seen or heard recently.

Recall can be measured through either unaided recall or aided recall methods. In an **unaided recall test**, subjects are asked to identify advertisements that they have

TABLE 15.5 *Illustration techniques for advertisements*

ILLUSTRATION TECHNIQUE	DESCRIPTION
Product alone	Simplest method; advantageous when appearance is important, when identification is important, when trying to keep a brand name or package in the public eye, or when selling through mail order
Emphasis on special features	Shows and emphasizes special details or features as well as advantages; used when product is unique because of special features
Product in setting	Shows what can be done with product; people, surroundings, or environment hint at what product can do; often used in food advertisements
Product in use	Puts action into the advertisement; can remind readers of benefits gained from using product; must be careful not to make visual cliché; should not include anything in illustration that will divert attention from product; used to direct readers' eyes toward product
Product being tested	Uses test to dramatize product's uses and benefits versus competing products
Results of product's use	Emphasizes satisfaction from using product; can liven up dull product; useful when nothing new can be said
Dramatizing headline	Appeal of illustration dramatizes headline; can emphasize appeal but dangerous to use illustrations that do not correlate with headlines
Dramatizing situation	Presents problem situation or shows situation in which problem has been resolved
Comparison	Compares product with "something" established; the something must be positive and familiar to audience
Contrast	Shows difference between two products or two ideas or differences in effects between use and non-use; before-and-after format is a commonly used contrast technique
Diagrams, charts, and graphs	Used to communicate complex information quickly; may make presentations more interesting
Phantom effects	X-ray or internal view; can see inside product; helpful to explain concealed or internal mechanism
Symbolic	Symbols used to represent abstract ideas that are difficult to illustrate; effective if readers understand symbol; must be positive correlation between symbol and idea
Testimonials	Actually shows the testifier; should use famous person or someone to whom audience can relate

SOURCE: Dorothy Cohen, *Advertising* (New York: Wiley, 1972), pp. 458–464; and S. Watson Dunn and Arnold M. Barban, *Advertising: Its Role in Modern Marketing,* 6th ed. (Hinsdale, Ill.: Dryden Press, 1986), pp. 497–498.

seen recently but are not shown any clues to help them remember. A similar procedure is used with an **aided recall test**, except that subjects are shown a list of products, brands, company names, or trademarks to jog their memories. Several research organizations, including Daniel Starch and Gallup & Robinson, provide syndicated research services that test recognition and recall of advertisements.

The major justification for using recognition and recall methods is that people are more likely to buy a product if they can remember an advertisement about it than if they cannot. However, recalling an advertisement does not necessarily lead to buying the product or brand advertised. Research shows that the more "likable" an advertisement is, the more persuasive it will be with consumers. People who enjoy an advertisement are twice as likely to be convinced that the advertised brand is best. Of about 16 percent of those who liked an advertisement, a significant number increased their preference for the brand. Only a small percentage of those who were neutral about the advertisement felt more favorable toward the brand as a result of the advertisement.[11] The type of program in which the product is advertised can also affect consumers' feelings about the commercial and the product it promotes. Viewers judged commercials placed in happy programs as more effective and recalled them somewhat better.[12]

Researchers are also using a sophisticated technique called single-source data to help evaluate advertisements. With this technique, individuals' behaviors are tracked from television sets to the check-out counter. Monitors are placed in preselected homes, and microcomputers record when the television set is on and which station is being viewed. At the supermarket check-out, the individual in the sample household presents an identification card. The checker records the purchases by scanner, and the data are sent to the research facility. This technique is bringing more insight into people's buying patterns than ever before.

Who Develops the Advertising Campaign?

An advertising campaign may be handled by (1) an individual or a few persons within the firm, (2) an advertising department within the organization, or (3) an advertising agency.

In very small firms, one or two individuals are responsible for advertising (and many other activities as well). Usually these individuals depend heavily on personnel at local newspapers and broadcast stations for copywriting, artwork, and advice about scheduling media.

In certain types of large businesses—especially in larger retail organizations— advertising departments create and implement advertising campaigns. Depending on the size of the advertising program, an advertising department may consist of a few multiskilled persons or a sizable number of specialists, such as copywriters, artists, media buyers, and technical production coordinators. An advertising department sometimes obtains the services of independent research organizations and also hires free-lance specialists when they are needed for a particular project.

When an organization uses an advertising agency, such as Ogilvie & Mather or BBD&O, the firm and the agency usually develop the advertising campaign jointly. How much each party participates in the campaign's total development depends on the working relationship between the firm and the agency. Ordinarily, a firm relies on the agency for copywriting, artwork, technical production, and formulation of the media plan.

An advertising agency can assist a business in several ways. An agency, especially a larger one, supplies the firm with the services of highly skilled specialists—not only

11. Ronald Alsop, "TV Ads That Are Likeable Get Plus Ratings for Persuasiveness," *Wall Street Journal,* Feb. 20, 1986, p. 21.

12. Marvin E. Goldberg and Gerald J. Gorn, "Happy and Sad TV Programs: How They Affect Reactions to Commercials," *Journal of Consumer Research,* December 1987, pp. 387–403.

copywriters, artists, and production coordinators, but also media experts, researchers, and legal advisers. Agency personnel often have had broad experience in advertising and are usually more objective than a firm's employees about the organization's products.

Because an agency traditionally receives most of its compensation from a 15 percent commission on media purchases, a firm can obtain some agency services at a low or moderate cost. For example, if an agency contracts for $400,000 of television time for a firm, it receives a commission of $60,000 from the television station. Although the traditional compensation method for agencies is changing and now includes other factors, the media commission still offsets some costs of using an agency.

Now that we have explored advertising as a potential promotion-mix ingredient, let us consider a related ingredient, publicity.

PUBLICITY

As indicated in Chapter 14, **publicity** is communication in news story form, about an organization, its products, or both, that is transmitted through a mass medium at no charge. Publicity can be presented through a variety of vehicles, several of which we examine in this section.

Within an organization, publicity is sometimes viewed as part of public relations—a larger, more comprehensive communication function. **Public relations** is a broad set of communication activities used to create and maintain favorable relations between the organization and its publics: customers, employees, stockholders, government officials, and society in general. Publicity is the result of various public relations efforts. For example, when Wal-Mart decided to make a special effort to stock environmentally safe products and packaging, its public relations department sent out press releases to various newspapers, magazines, and television contacts, as well as to its suppliers. The result was publicity in the form of magazine articles, newspaper acknowledgments, and TV coverage.

■ **Publicity and Advertising Compared**

Although publicity and advertising both depend on mass media, they differ in several respects. Advertising messages tend to be informative or persuasive, whereas publicity is primarily informative. Advertisements are sometimes designed to have an immediate impact on sales; publicity messages are more subdued. Publicity releases do not identify sponsors; advertisements do. The sponsor pays for media time or space for advertising, but not for publicity. Communications through publicity are usually included as part of a program or a print story, but advertisements are normally separated from the broadcast programs or editorial portions of print media so that the audience or readers can easily recognize (or ignore) them. Publicity may have greater credibility than advertising among consumers because as a news story it may appear more objective. Finally, a firm can use advertising to repeat the same messages as many times as desired; publicity is generally not subject to repetition.

■ **Kinds of Publicity**

There are several types of publicity mechanisms. The most common is the **news release**, which is usually a single page of typewritten copy containing fewer than three hundred words. A news release, sometimes called a press release, also gives the firm's or agency's name, its address and phone number, and the contact person.

FIGURE 15.11

Example of a news release

NEWS RELEASE

Del Monte Foods, USA
P.O. Box 3575
San Francisco, CA 94119

FOR IMMEDIATE RELEASE

DMC 90-05
05/04/90

Contact: Dee Ann Campbell
(415) 442-5034

DEL MONTE FOODS TO ADD A
RECYCLING MESSAGE TO ALL GLASS AND CAN LABELS

SAN FRANCISCO -- Del Monte Foods today announced the addition of a
recycling message on a number of its products. Del Monte labels on cans produced this
year will carry the statement: *Contains Recycled Steel, Recycle Again.*

In addition, the company has produced an informative brochure for consumers which
discusses issues and provides information about the company's work in the area of solid
waste management.

"Del Monte Foods is committed to helping solve the problems associated with solid
waste management," said A. Ewan Macdonald, President and Chief Operating Officer.
"Approximately 25-30 percent of the raw steel going into cans produced and used by
Del Monte Foods facilities has already been recycled. By adding a recycle message to
our labels, we hope to increase the number of packages that are returned to recycling
centers."

- more -

SOURCE: Reprinted with permission of Del Monte Corporation

Automobile companies often use news releases to introduce new products. Figure 15.11 is an example of a news release. A **feature article** is a longer manuscript (up to three thousand words) that is usually prepared for a specific publication. A **captioned photograph** is a photograph with a brief description explaining the picture's content. Captioned photographs are especially effective for illustrating a new or improved product with highly visible features.

There are several other kinds of publicity. A **press conference** is a meeting called to announce major news events. Media personnel are invited to a press conference and are usually supplied with written materials and photographs. In addition, letters to the editor and editorials are sometimes prepared and sent to newspapers and magazines. However, newspaper editors frequently allocate space on their editorial pages to local writers and national columnists. Finally, films and tapes may be distributed to broadcast stations in the hope that they will be aired.

A marketer's choice of specific types of publicity depends on considerations that include the type of information being transmitted, the characteristics of the target audience, the receptivity of media personnel, the importance of the item to the public, and the amount of information that needs to be presented. Sometimes a marketer uses a single type of publicity in a promotion mix. In other cases, a marketer may use a variety of publicity mechanisms, with publicity being the primary ingredient in the promotion mix.

TABLE 15.6

Possible issues for publicity releases

Marketing developments	**Reports on current developments**
New products	Reports of experiments
New uses for old products	Reports on industry conditions
Research developments	Company progress reports
Changes of marketing personnel	Employment, production, and sales
Large orders received	statistics
Successful bids	Reports on new discoveries
Awards of contracts	Tax reports
Special events	Speeches by principals
Company policies	Analyses of economic conditions
New guarantees	Employment gains
Changes in credit terms	Financial statements
Changes in distribution policies	Organization appointments
Changes in service policies	Opening of new markets
Changes in prices	**Personalities—names are news**
News of general interest	Visits by famous persons
Annual election of officers	Accomplishments of individuals
Meetings of the board of directors	Winners of company contests
Anniversaries of the organization	Employees' and officers' advancements
Anniversaries of an invention	Interviews with company officials
Anniversaries of the senior officers	Company employees serving as judges
Holidays that can be tied to the	for contests
organization's activities	Interviews with employees
Annual banquets and picnics	**Slogans, symbols, endorsements**
Special weeks, such as Clean-up Week	Company's slogan—its history and
Founders' Day	development
Conferences and special meetings	A tie-in of company activities with
Open house to the community	slogan
Athletic events	Creation of a slogan
Awards of merit to employees	The company's trademark
Laying of cornerstone	The company's name plate
Opening of an exhibition	Product endorsements

SOURCE: Albert Wesley Frey, ed., *Marketing Handbook,* 2nd ed. (New York: Ronald Press), pp. 19–35. Copyright © 1965. Reprinted by permission of John Wiley & Sons, Inc.

■ Uses of Publicity

Publicity has a number of uses. It can make people aware of a firm's products, brands, or activities; help a company maintain a certain level of positive public visibility; and enhance a particular image, such as innovativeness or progressiveness. Companies also try to overcome negative images through publicity. Some firms seek publicity for a single purpose and others for several purposes. As Table 15.6 shows, publicity releases can tackle a multitude of specific issues.

■ Requirements of a Publicity Program

For maximum benefit, a firm should create and maintain a systematic, continuous publicity program. A single individual or department—within the organization or from its advertising agency or public relations firm—should be responsible for managing the program.

It is important to establish and maintain good working relationships with media personnel. Often personal contact with editors, reporters, and other news personnel is essential, for without their input a company may find it hard to design its publicity program so as to facilitate the work of media newspeople.

Media personnel reject a great deal of publicity material because it is poorly written or not newsworthy. To maintain an effective publicity program, a firm must strive to avoid these flaws. Guidelines and checklists can aid it in this task.

Finally, a firm has to evaluate its publicity efforts. Usually, the effectiveness of publicity is measured by the number of releases actually published or broadcast. To monitor print media and determine which releases are published and how often, an organization can hire a clipping service—a firm that clips and sends published news releases to client companies. To measure the effectiveness of television publicity, a firm can enclose a card with its publicity releases and request that the station record its name and the dates when the news item is broadcast, but station personnel do not always comply. Though some television and radio tracking services do exist, they are extremely costly.

■ Dealing with Unfavorable Publicity

Up to this point we have discussed publicity as a planned promotion-mix ingredient. However, companies may have to deal with unfavorable publicity regarding an unsafe product, an accident, the actions of a dishonest employee, or some other negative event. For example, when a United Airlines plane crashed in Sioux City, Iowa, killing half the passengers on board, the airline was faced with a negative situation. Such unfavorable publicity can be quick and dramatic. A single negative event that produces unfavorable publicity can wipe out a company's favorable image and destroy consumer attitudes that took years to build through promotional efforts. Moreover, the mass media today can disseminate information faster and to larger audiences than ever before, and bad news generally receives much attention in the media. Thus the negative publicity surrounding an unfavorable event now reaches more people.[13] By dealing effectively with a negative situation, an organization can minimize the damage from unfavorable publicity.

To protect an organization's image, it is important to avoid unfavorable publicity or at least to lessen its effects. First and foremost, the organization can directly reduce negative incidents and events through safety programs, inspections, and effective quality control procedures. But because firms obviously cannot eliminate all negative occurrences, they need to establish policies and procedures for the news coverage of such events. These policies should aim at reducing negative impact.

In most cases, organizations should expedite news coverage of negative events rather than try to discourage or block it. Facts are likely to be reported accurately, but if news coverage is discouraged, rumors and misinformation may be passed along. An unfavorable event can easily balloon into a scandal or a tragedy. It can even cause public panic.

Six Flags, a theme amusement park, established a set of policies and procedures to be used when a negative event occurs. The aim is to let news personnel enter the park quickly and to furnish them with as much information as possible. This approach not only tends to diminish the fallout from negative events, but also fosters a positive relationship with media personnel. Such a relationship is essential if news personnel are to cooperate with a company and broadcast favorable news stories about it.

13. Marc G. Weinberger and Jean B. Romeo, "The Impact of Negative Product News," *Business Horizons,* January-February 1989, p. 44.

■ Limitations in Using Publicity

Free media publicity is a double-edged sword: the financial advantage comes with several drawbacks. If company messages are to be published or broadcast, media personnel must judge them newsworthy. Consequently, messages must be timely, interesting, and accurate. Many communications simply do not qualify. It may take time and effort to convince media personnel of the news value of publicity releases.

Although marketers usually encourage media personnel to air a publicity release at a certain time, they control neither the content nor the timing of the communication. Media personnel alter the length and content of publicity releases to fit publishers' or broadcasters' requirements and may even delete the parts of the message that the firm deems most important. Furthermore, media personnel use publicity releases in time slots or positions that are most convenient for them; thus the messages often appear at times or in locations that may not reach the firm's target audiences. These limitations can be frustrating. Nevertheless, as you have seen in the earlier portions of this section, properly managed publicity offers an organization substantial benefits.

SUMMARY

Advertising is a paid form of nonpersonal communication that is transmitted to consumers through mass media, such as television, radio, newspapers, magazines, direct mail, mass transit vehicles, and outdoor displays. Both nonbusiness and business organizations use advertising.

Marketers use advertising in many ways. Institutional advertising promotes organizations' images and ideas, as well as political issues and candidates. Product advertising focuses on uses, features, images, and benefits of goods and services. To make people aware of a new or innovative product's existence, uses, and benefits, marketers rely on pioneer advertising in the introductory stage to stimulate primary demand for a general product category. They switch to competitive advertising to boost selective demand by promoting a particular brand's uses, features, and advantages.

Through advertising, a company can sometimes lessen the impact of a competitor's promotional program or make its own sales force more effective. To increase market penetration, an advertiser sometimes focuses a campaign on promoting a greater number of uses for the product. Some advertisements for an established product remind consumers that the product is still around and that it has certain characteristics and uses. Marketers may try to assure users of a particular brand that they are selecting the best brand. Marketers also use advertising to smooth out fluctuations in sales.

Although marketers may vary in how they develop advertising campaigns, they should follow a general pattern. First, they must identify and analyze the advertising target. Second, they should establish what they want the campaign to accomplish by defining the advertising objectives. The third step is creating the advertising platform, which contains the basic issues to be presented in the campaign. Fourth, advertisers must decide how much money to spend on the campaign; they arrive at this decision through the objective and task approach, the percent of sales approach, the competition-matching approach, or the arbitrary approach. Fifth, they must develop the media plan by selecting and scheduling the media to be used in the campaign. In the sixth stage, advertisers use copy and artwork to create the message.

In the seventh stage, the execution of an advertising campaign requires extensive planning and coordination. Finally, advertisers must devise one or more methods for evaluating the effectiveness of the advertisements.

Advertising campaigns can be developed by personnel within the firm or in conjunction with advertising agencies. When a campaign is created by the firm's personnel, it may be developed by only a few people, or it may be the product of an advertising department within the firm. The use of an advertising agency may be advantageous to a firm because an agency can provide highly skilled, objective specialists with broad experience in the advertising field at low to moderate costs to the firm.

Publicity is communication in news story form, regarding an organization, its products, or both, that is transmitted through a mass medium at no charge. Generally, publicity is part of the larger, more comprehensive communication function of public relations. Publicity is mainly informative and usually more subdued than advertising. There are many types of publicity, including news releases, feature articles, captioned photographs, press conferences, editorials, films, and tapes. Marketers can use one or more of these forms to achieve a variety of objectives. To have an effective publicity program, someone—either in the organization or in the firm's agency—must be responsible for creating and maintaining systematic and continuous publicity efforts.

An organization should avoid negative publicity by reducing the number of negative events that result in unfavorable publicity. To diminish the impact of unfavorable publicity, an organization should institute policies and procedures for dealing with news personnel when negative events do occur. Problems that organizations confront when seeking publicity include the reluctance of media personnel to print or air releases and a lack of control over the timing and content of messages.

IMPORTANT TERMS

Advertising
Institutional advertising
Product advertising
Pioneer advertising
Competitive advertising
Comparative advertising
Defensive advertising
Reminder advertising
Reinforcement advertising
Advertising campaign
Advertising target
Advertising platform
Advertising appropriation
Objective and task approach
Percent of sales approach
Competition-matching approach
Arbitrary approach
Media plan
Cost comparison indicator

Regional issues
Copy
Storyboard
Artwork
Illustrations
Layout
Pretests
Consumer jury
Posttest
Recognition test
Unaided recall test
Aided recall test
Publicity
Public relations
News release
Feature article
Captioned photograph
Press conference

DISCUSSION AND REVIEW QUESTIONS

1. What is the difference between institutional and product advertising?
2. When should advertising be used to stimulate primary demand? When should advertising be used to stimulate selective demand?
3. What are the major steps in creating an advertising campaign?
4. What is an advertising target? How does a marketer analyze the target audience after it has been identified?
5. Why is it necessary to define advertising objectives?
6. What is an advertising platform, and how is it used?
7. What factors affect the size of an advertising budget? What techniques are used to determine this budget?
8. Describe the steps required in developing a media plan.
9. What is the role of copy in an advertising message?
10. What role does an advertising agency play in developing an advertising campaign?
11. Discuss several ways to posttest the effectiveness of advertising.
12. What is publicity? How does it differ from advertising?
13. How do organizations use publicity? Give several examples of publicity releases that you observed recently in local media.
14. How should an organization handle negative publicity? Identify a recent example of a firm that received negative publicity. Did the firm deal with it effectively?
15. Explain the problems and limitations associated with using publicity. How can some of these limitations be minimized?

■ CASES

15.1   Dr Pepper Advertising

To the soda fountain customers of Morrison's Drug Store in Waco, Texas in the 1880s, the new drink tasted distinctly different. Charlie Alderton, a Morrison employee, invented the tasty soft drink made from 23 different flavors. He called it Dr Pepper, and the new drink caught on quickly among local residents. Today Dr Pepper is distributed worldwide with total annual sales of $220 million.

It is unlikely that Dr Pepper would have been so popular without some form of advertising. Dr Pepper has had a variety of advertising campaigns in its one-hundred-year history; the fact that some of its earlier advertising gimmicks (buttons, signs, and matchbook covers) are now valuable collectors' items is a measure of how successful these campaigns were. The Dr Pepper Company understands how important advertising is to its success and so continues to make it a top priority for increasing sales.

The company realizes that the key to its success is professional advertising that cuts through the clutter its competitors generate. Dr Pepper has to stand out on a national scale with competitive advertising to reach the people it wants with a message they will remember. In the 1950s, it was Frosty, a friendly St. Bernard dog, who attracted children to Dr Pepper; in the 1960s, adults were told about the friendly "Pepper-upper." In the 1970s, Dr Pepper became the "most original soft drink ever," and late in that decade, everyone was encouraged to "Be a Pepper" ("I'm a Pepper," "Wouldn't you like to be a Pepper, too?"). "Hold out for the out of the ordinary" continued into the 1980s. Finally Dr Pepper switched themes, from "Taste for originality" to "Just what the Dr ordered"; but the idea that it is fun to "Be a Pepper" did not change.

The previous advertising themes were aimed at only the 13-to-34-year-old target market, but now Dr Pepper seems to be addressing only two market segments—those who drink Dr Pepper and those who don't. Most television viewers have seen the heavy doses of advertisements reminding us that Dr Pepper is still alive and well and the reinforcement advertisements that say it is right to set ourselves apart from ordinary things and ordinary people by drinking Dr Pepper. This strengthens the notion that Dr Pepper is targeting a narrow market segment—defined not just by age but by an individualistic attitude. The cola giants, by contrast, use a mass appeal that defines the market in much broader terms.

An expanding range of products is being directed to health-conscious consumers. Diet products represent the leading sales growth of major brand lines, such as Dr Pepper, Pepsi, and Coke. The Diet Dr Pepper campaign told diet cola seekers to "throw your diet a curve" with diet Dr Pepper. The advertisements capitalized on the idea of searching for relationships through the "personal ads." One television spot showed a beautiful woman who wanted to spice up her life, with the copy from her personal advertisement rolling up the screen. Dr Pepper is, of course, the answer to her advertisement. To make certain the diet-soda spots were seen by the target market, they were run during shows the target market watched.

Dr Pepper simultaneously ran its regular Dr Pepper campaign on the same media, but with a slightly different message. The regular Dr Pepper commercials, with advertisements similar to the earlier "Be a Pepper" campaign, used popular music and upbeat people to catch the attention of the target market and convince them that Dr Pepper is indeed "just what the Dr ordered." These spots were more product oriented than earlier campaigns in an effort to get consumers to ask for Dr Pepper by name, instead of just whatever soft drink is on sale. The spots were aimed at both the 13-to-34-year-old core soft-drink market and consumers older than 35.

Although each campaign for Dr Pepper has featured new creative concepts, the basic platform has always remained the same. The advertisements continue to highlight the idea that Dr Pepper is different, bold, one of a kind. Pepper drinkers continue to be portrayed as being as unusual as the product they love. The key idea is that Pepper drinkers see themselves as normal; it is everyone else who is different. Thus Dr Pepper advertisements look at the world through the eyes of a Pepper drinker, who sees that world as backward, two-dimensional, and monotone.

SOURCES: Tom Bayer, "Aspartame, Ads Back Diet Dr Pepper," *Advertising Age,* Sept. 22, 1986, p. 12; Mike Duff, "Soft Drinks," *Supermarket Business,* Sept. 1989, pp. 217–222; *Clockdial* (Dr Pepper news magazine), January-February 1987; *Clockdial,* October-December 1986; *Clockdial,* Centennial Issue 1985; Jennifer Lawrence, "Dr Pepper Rx: Product Ads," *Advertising Age,* Apr. 20, 1987, pp. 3, 93; Barbara Lippert, "Cult Pepper Worship: Just What the Doctor Ordered," *Adweek,* Jan. 13, 1986, p. 21; and Candace Talmadge, "Dr Pepper Orders New Creative," *Adweek,* Apr. 20, 1987, pp. 1, 6.

Questions for Discussion

1. Based on the information in this case, assess whether Dr Pepper's advertising objectives were stated in terms of sales or communication.
2. What are the primary issues in Dr Pepper's advertising platform?
3. In general, do you believe that this campaign was successful?

15.2 The Energizer Bunny Marches On

"Nothing outlasts the Energizer. They keep going and going . . . ." To effectively communicate the message that its Energizer batteries last a long, long time, the Eveready Battery Co. introduced what has been called one of the most clever advertising campaigns in television history. The competitive product advertisements feature a stuffed pink battery-operated rabbit, called the Energizer bunny, or E.B. for short. It carries a drum, and hops through a parade of advertisement parodies. Although E.B. has appeared in earlier advertising campaigns for Energizer batteries, the new campaign has been surprisingly and amusingly successful.

In the series of television commercials, the Energizer bunny escapes from a real advertisement for Energizer batteries and marches through parodied commercials for fictional products such as flavored instant coffees, nasal spray, late-night albums by obscure artists, soap, snack chips, and Chateau Marmoset wine. After several seconds of seemingly real advertisement for instant coffee, for example, E.B. marches across the table banging his drum and knocks over the sugar bowl. In an advertisement for "Alarm!" soap, he appears in an already occupied shower wearing a yellow raincoat and hat, startling the shower's occupant. An advertisement for "Pigskins" pork rinds features former National Football League player Lyle Alzado. After following the real sixty-second battery commercial for several weeks, the fifteen-second parody spots now air alone, enhancing the surprise effect.

Chiat/Day/Mojo Inc., the campaign's creators, have paid attention to the tiniest details in the parodied commercials, even down to a "use only as directed" disclaimer for the fake nasal spray. The ads emphasize that "nothing outlasts the Energizer. They keep going and going and going . . . ." just like E.B. keeps going and going, even into other commercials. The campaign works because of the elements of surprise and humor. The long-lasting message is clearly evident, and the phony spots amuse consumers while standing out from the barrage of television advertising.

Emboldened by the success of the campaign, E.B. has begun marching through advertisements for real products, beginning with Purina Cat Chow. (Ralston Purina Co. is the corporate parent for both Eveready and Cat Chow.) In this commercial, E.B. dances along with a woman and her cat to the well-known "chow chow chow" step of the Purina Cat Chow campaign. There are also plans for E.B. to wander through commercials for Ralston's Chex cereals, Hostess Twinkies, and Wonder Bread. A company spokesperson says that most of Ralston Purina's consumer product divisions (cereal, pet food, and baking goods, as well as batteries) will be represented in future ads of the Energizer campaign. Because the ads do not make fun of specific products, Ralston Purina product managers probably will not object to their products being included in the campaign. Although combining two products in a television commercial is rare, combining two unrelated products is almost unheard of. In this case, however, the rarity appears to be successful, based on high advertising ratings and awards for excellent advertising.

An Eveready spokesperson indicated that it is too early to determine the effect of the campaign on sales, but the company has noted improvements in several key areas measured. Increasing consumer demand from the campaign has forced retailers to respond by moving Energizer battery displays to more prominent spaces in their stores. In fact, E.B. is so popular that an offer for a stuffed E.B. doll (for $14.95 and three proofs of purchase) drew ten thousand requests in two weeks—a response twenty times larger than a typical mail offer generates. The campaign also gained some extra publicity when an impostor E.B. made an appearance on the *Late Night with David Letterman Show*. Building on E.B.'s popularity with consumers, Eveready's $25 million to $30 million advertising campaign should help "energize" its battle against competitors in the battery market and increase its roughly 40 percent share of this $3 billion business.

SOURCES: Stuart Elliott, "He's Back: Energizer Bunny's Beat Goes On," *USA Today,* Dec. 6, 1989, p. 2B; Stuart Elliott, "Energizer Ads March to Different Drummer," *USA Today,* Oct. 24, 1989, p. 1B; Stuart Elliott and Sal Ruibal, "E.B. and Bo Led '89 Dream Team," *USA Today,* Dec. 28, 1989, p. 6B; Julie Liesse Erickson, "Energizer Bunny Will Plug Purina," *Advertising Age,* Dec. 4, 1989, pp. 1, 54; Julie Liesse Erickson, "Energizer Bunny Gets the Jump," *Advertising Age,* Oct. 23, 1989, p. 4; Bob Garfield, "Energizer's Parody Campaign Is One Bunny of a Concept," *Advertising Age,* Oct. 23, 1989, p. 120.

Questions for Discussion

1. Why are the Energizer battery advertisments so successful?
2. What is the advertising platform for the Energizer Bunny campaign?
3. What is the nature of publicity that Eveready gained with the Energizer Bunny campaign? Distinguish between the publicity and the advertising in this campaign.

16

PERSONAL SELLING AND SALES PROMOTION

Objectives

To understand the major purposes of personal selling

To learn the basic steps in the personal selling process

To identify the types of sales force personnel

To gain insight into sales management decisions and activities

To become aware of what sales promotion activities are and how they can be used

To become familiar with specific sales promotion methods used

Instead of napping or staring out windows, salespeople can spend time in airplanes, trains, and terminals more productively by using laptop computers. Sales force "automation" is growing in popularity as more and more companies are equipping their salespeople with portable and powerful computers. Newer, smaller, lighter, and more advanced laptop computers provide salespeople with immediate information about customers, inventory, and pricing. A better informed sales force is likely to be more confident and more credible to its customers.

Companies such as Compaq, Toshiba, Zenith, Mitsubishi, and NEC all offer laptop computers. Early laptop prototypes were relatively weak and had screens that were difficult to read. Realizing the potential of the laptop, however, computer firms aggressively sought and eventually succeeded in developing better technology. For several years, laptops have been the fastest growing segment of the personal computer industry.

Salespeople using laptop computers can check warehouse inventories and structure their sales pitches to promote an overstocked item or make special deals with customers. Salespeople can use spare travel time to update customer files or learn about new products. With facts easily accessible, salespeople can customize offers quickly and more efficiently. Laptop computers can also allow salespeople to spend more time actually conversing with customers and potential customers because routine data inputing can be accomplished at the salesperson's convenience.

Some laptops are now less bulky than the Sunday *New York Times* and can easily fit in a briefcase. Laptop batteries are now also capable of running a computer on a New York to Los Angeles flight. As technology continues to improve and prices continue to decrease, the majority of salespeople in the future may be using laptop computers. ◆

Photo by Schmid-Langsfield/The Image Bank

Based on information from Deidre A. Depke, Jonathan B. Levine, and Jim Bartimo, "Suddenly, the PC Juggernaut is Stuck in the Mud," *Business Week,* December 25, 1989, p. 45; "For Reps, the Future is in Their Laps," *Sales & Marketing Management,* April 1989, p. 89; Mark Ivey, "How Compaq Gets There Firstest With the Mostest," *Business Week,* June 26, 1989, pp. 146–147, 150; and Edward C. Baig, "Products of the Year," December 4, 1989, p. 164.

A s indicated in Chapter 14, personal selling and sales promotion are two possible ingredients in a promotion mix. Personal selling is the more widely used. Sometimes it is a company's sole promotional tool, although it is generally used in conjunction with other promotion-mix ingredients. Personal selling is becoming more professional and sophisticated, with sales personnel acting more as consultants and advisors. The use of laptop computers has better equipped the salesperson to satisfy customers. Laptop computers allow the salesperson to have easier access to inventory listings and prices, to spend more time interacting with customers, and to gain more credibility with clients. Sales promotion, too, is playing an increasingly important role in marketing strategies.

This chapter focuses on personal selling and sales promotion. We consider the purposes of personal selling, its basic steps, the types of salespersons, and how they are selected. We also discuss the major sales management decisions and activities, including setting objectives for the sales force and determining its size; recruiting, selecting, training, compensating, and motivating salespeople; managing sales territories; and controlling sales personnel. Then we examine several characteristics of sales promotion, the reasons for using sales promotion, and the sales promotion methods available for use in a promotion mix.

THE NATURE OF PERSONAL SELLING

Personal selling is a process of informing customers and persuading them to purchase products through personal communication in an exchange situation. For example, a salesperson describing the benefits of a Kenmore dryer to a customer in a Sears store is using personal selling. Personal selling gives marketers the greatest freedom to adjust a message to satisfy customers' information needs. In comparison with other promotion methods, personal selling is the most precise, enabling marketers to focus on the most promising sales prospects. Other promotion-mix ingredients are aimed at groups of people, some of whom may not be prospective customers. A major disadvantage of personal selling is its cost. Generally, it is the most expensive ingredient in the promotion mix. Personal selling costs are increasing faster than advertising costs.

Businesses spend more money on personal selling than on any other promotion-mix ingredient. Millions of people, including increasing numbers of women, earn their living through personal selling. A selling career offers high income, a great deal of freedom, a high level of training, and a high level of job satisfaction.[1] Unfortunately, consumers often view personal selling negatively. A study of how college marketing students perceived personal selling showed that approximately 25 percent of the survey group thought directly of door-to-door selling. In addition, 59 percent of all students surveyed had a negative impression of personal selling. Major corporations, professional sales associations, and academic institutions are making an effort to change the negative stereotypes of salespeople.[2]

1. Myron Gable and B. J. Reed, "The Current Status of Women in Professional Selling," *Journal of Personal Selling and Sales Management*, May 1987, pp. 33–39.

2. William A. Weeks and Darrel D. Muehing, "Students' Perceptions of Personal Selling," *Industrial Marketing Management*, May 1987, pp. 145–151.

Personal selling goals vary from one firm to another. However, they usually involve finding prospects, convincing prospects to buy, and keeping customers satisfied. Identifying potential buyers who are interested in an organization's products is critical. Because most potential buyers seek information before they make a purchase, salespersons must ascertain prospects' informational needs and then provide the relevant information. To do so, sales personnel must be well trained, both in regard to their products and in regard to the selling process in general.

Salespeople need to be aware of their competitors. They need to monitor new products being developed, and they should be aware of all competitors' sales activities in their sales territories. Salespeople must emphasize the advantages their products provide when their competitors' products do not offer that specific advantage.[3] Later in this chapter we discuss this issue in greater detail.

Few businesses survive solely on profits from one-sale customers. For long-run survival, most marketers depend on repeat sales. A company has to keep its customers satisfied to obtain repeat purchases. Besides, satisfied customers help attract new ones by telling potential customers about the organization and its products. Even though the whole organization is responsible for providing customer satisfaction, much of the burden falls on salespeople. The salesperson is almost always closer to customers than anyone else in the company and often provides buyers with information and service after the sale. Such contact not only gives salespeople an opportunity to generate additional sales, but also offers them a good vantage point for evaluating the strengths and weaknesses of the company's products and other marketing mix ingredients. Their observations are helpful in developing and maintaining a marketing mix that better satisfies both customers and the firm.

A salesperson may be involved with achieving one or more of the three general goals. In some organizations, there are persons whose sole job is to find prospects. This information is relayed to salespeople, who contact the prospects. After the sale, these same salespeople may do the follow-up work, or a third group of employees may have the job of maintaining customer satisfaction. In many smaller organizations, a single person handles all these functions. No matter how many groups are involved, several major sales tasks must be performed to achieve these general goals.

ELEMENTS OF THE PERSONAL SELLING PROCESS

The exact activities involved in the selling process vary among salespersons and differ for particular selling situations. No two salespersons use exactly the same selling methods. Nonetheless, many salespersons—either consciously or unconsciously—move through a general selling process as they sell products. This process consists of seven elements, or steps: prospecting and evaluating, preparing, approaching the customer, making the presentation, overcoming objections, closing, and following up.

■ **Prospecting and Evaluating**

Developing a list of potential customers is called **prospecting**. A salesperson seeks the names of prospects from the company's sales records, referrals, trade shows, newspaper announcements (of marriages, births, deaths, and so on), public records,

3. "Getting Ahead and Staying Ahead as the Competition Heats Up," *Agency Sales Magazine,* June 1987, pp. 38–42.

telephone directories, trade association directories, and many other sources. Sales personnel also use responses from advertisements that encourage interested persons to send in an information request form. Seminars and meetings may produce good leads. Seminars may be targeted at particular types of clients, such as attorneys, accountants, and specific business persons.

After developing the prospect list, a salesperson evaluates whether each prospect is able, willing, and authorized to buy the product. On the basis of this evaluation, some prospects may be deleted, and others are deemed acceptable and ranked according to their desirability or potential.

■ Preparing

Before contacting acceptable prospects, a salesperson should find and analyze information about each prospect's specific product needs, current use of brands, feelings about available brands, and personal characteristics. The most successful salespeople are thorough in their preparation. They prepare by identifying key decision makers, reviewing account histories and reports, contacting other clients for information, assessing credit histories and problems, preparing sales presentations, identifying product needs, and obtaining all relevant literature.[4] A salesperson with a lot of information about a prospect is better equipped to develop a presentation that precisely communicates with the prospect.

For example, Xerox developed an automated sales process to help salespersons prepare for complex sales situations after discovering that half its salespersons' time was taken up by sales-inhibiting activities, such as looking for forms and gathering information. Preparing an order required five to thirteen forms, and one-third of all orders were rejected because of mistakes on the forms. To overcome the problem, Xerox developed computer work stations to assist salespersons in shaping proposals, prospecting, and preparing, and to link salespersons throughout the company without a piece of paper having to be touched.[5]

■ Approaching the Customer

The **approach**—the manner in which a salesperson contacts a potential customer—is a critical step in the sales process. In more than 80 percent of initial sales calls, the purpose is to gather information about the buyer's needs and objectives. Creating a favorable impression and building rapport with the prospective client are also important tasks in the approach because the prospect's first impression of the salesperson is usually a lasting one, with long-run consequences. During the initial visit, the salesperson strives to develop a relationship rather than just push a product. The salesperson may have to call on a prospect several times before the product is considered.[6]

One type of approach is based on referrals. The salesperson approaches the prospect and explains that an acquaintance, an associate, or a relative had suggested the call. The salesperson who uses the cold canvass method calls on potential customers without their prior consent. Repeat contact is another common approach; when making the contact, the salesperson mentions a prior meeting. The exact type of approach depends on the salesperson's preferences, the product being sold, the firm's resources, and the characteristics of the prospect.

---

4. Thomas W. Leigh and Patrick F. McGraw, "Mapping the Procedural Knowledge of Industrial Sales Personnel: A Script-Theoretic Investigation," *Journal of Marketing*, January 1989, pp. 16–34.

5. Thayer C. Taylor, "Xerox: Who Says You Can't Be Big and Fast?" *Sales & Marketing Management*, November 1987, pp. 62–65.

6. Leigh and McGraw, pp. 16–34.

FIGURE 16.1

Enhancing the sales presentation. Panasonic Data Master allows a salesperson to show a product's applications, trends, and sales data.

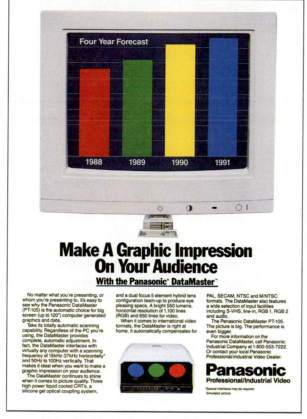

SOURCE: Matsushita Electric Corporation of America

■ Making the Presentation

During the sales presentation, the salesperson must attract and hold the prospect's attention to stimulate interest and stir up a desire for the product. The salesperson should have the prospect touch, hold, or actually use the product. If possible, the salesperson should demonstrate the product and get the prospect more involved with it to stimulate greater interest. Audiovisual materials may be used to enhance the presentation, as shown in Figure 16.1.

During the presentation, the salesperson must not only talk but listen. The sales presentation gives the salesperson the greatest opportunity to determine the prospect's specific needs by listening to questions and comments and observing responses. Even though the salesperson has planned the presentation in advance, she or he must be able to adjust the message to meet the prospect's information needs.

■ Overcoming Objections

An effective salesperson usually seeks out a prospect's objections in order to address them. If they are not apparent, the salesperson cannot deal with them, and they may keep the prospect from buying. One of the best ways to overcome a prospect's objections is to anticipate and counter them before the prospect has an opportunity to raise them. However, this approach can be risky because the salesperson may mention some objections that the prospect would not have raised. If possible, the salesperson should handle objections when they arise. They also can be dealt with at the end of the presentation.

■ Closing

Closing is the element in the selling process whereby the salesperson asks the prospect to buy the product or products. During the presentation, the salesperson may use a "trial close" by asking questions that assume the prospect will buy the product. For example, the salesperson might ask the potential customer about financial terms, desired colors or sizes, delivery arrangements, or the quantity to be purchased. The reactions to such questions usually indicate how close the prospect is to buying. A trial close allows prospects to indicate indirectly that they will buy the product without having to say those sometimes difficult words, "I'll take it."

A salesperson should try to close at several points during the presentation because the prospect may be ready to buy. One closing strategy involves asking the potential customer to take a tryout order. The sales representative should either guarantee a refund if the customer is not satisfied or make the order a free offer.[7] Often an attempt to close the sale will result in objections. Thus closing can be an important stimulus that uncovers hidden objections, which can then be addressed.

■ Following Up

After a successful closing, the salesperson must follow up the sale. In the follow-up stage, the salesperson should determine whether the order was delivered on time and installed properly, if installation was required. He or she should contact the customer to learn what problems or questions have arisen regarding the product. The follow-up stage can also be used to determine customers' future product needs.

TYPES OF SALESPERSONS

To develop a sales force, a marketing manager must decide what kind of salesperson will sell the firm's products most effectively. Most business organizations use several different kinds of sales personnel. Based on the functions they perform, salespersons can be classified into three groups: order getters, order takers, and support personnel. One salesperson can, and often does, perform all three functions.

■ Order Getters

To obtain orders, a salesperson must inform prospects and persuade them to buy the product. The **order getters**' job is to increase the firm's sales by selling to new customers and by increasing sales to present customers. This task sometimes is called creative selling. It requires that salespeople recognize potential buyers' needs and then give them the necessary information. Order-getting activities sometimes are divided into two categories: current customer sales and new-business sales.

Current Customer Sales. Sales personnel who concentrate on current customers call on people and organizations that have purchased products from the firm at least once. These salespeople seek more sales from existing customers by following up previous sales. Current customers can also be sources of leads for new prospects.

New-Business Sales. Business organizations depend on sales to new customers, at least to some degree. New-business sales personnel locate prospects and convert them to buyers. Salespersons in many industries help to generate new business, but industries that depend in large part on new-customer sales are real estate, insurance, appliances, heavy industrial machinery, and automobiles.

7. John Nemec, "Do You Have Grand Finales?" *American Salesman,* June 1987, pp. 3–6.

US Sprint, a long-distance telephone company, attempted to gain new business by encouraging potential customers to call and talk with sales representatives. The program tied in with the twenty-third Winter Olympics and offered a toll-free number that provided news about the Winter Olympics. The calls ran through Sprint's fiber-optic lines, allowing callers to sample the service. After receiving the Olympics information, callers were requested to stay on the line to talk with a Sprint sales representative. Customers who stayed on the line were probably pleased with the quality of Sprint service and had an interest in obtaining more information.[8]

■ Order Takers

Taking orders is a repetitive task that salespersons perform to perpetuate long-lasting, satisfying relationships with customers. **Order takers** seek repeat sales. One of their major objectives is to be absolutely certain that customers have sufficient product quantities where and when they are needed. Most order takers handle orders for standardized products that are purchased routinely and therefore do not require extensive sales efforts.[9] There are two groups of order takers: inside order takers and field order takers.

Inside Order Takers.   In many businesses, inside order takers, who work in sales offices, receive orders by mail and telephone. Certain producers, wholesalers, and even retailers have sales personnel who sell from within the firm rather than in the field. That does not mean that inside order takers never communicate with customers face to face. For example, salespersons in retail stores are classified as inside order takers.

Field Order Takers.   Salespersons who travel to customers are referred to as "outside," or "field," order takers. Often a customer and a field order taker develop an interdependent relationship. The buyer relies on the salesperson to take orders periodically (and sometimes to deliver them), and the salesperson counts on the buyer to purchase a certain quantity of products periodically. Use of laptop computers such as the one shown in Figure 16.2 can improve the field order taker's tracking of inventory and orders.

Field and inside order takers should not be thought of as passive functionaries who simply record orders in a machinelike manner. Order takers generate the bulk of many organizations' total sales.

■ Support Personnel

Support personnel facilitate the selling function but usually are not involved solely with making sales. They are engaged primarily in marketing industrial products. They locate prospects, educate customers, build goodwill, and provide service after the sale. Although there are many kinds of sales support personnel, the three most common are missionary, trade, and technical.

Missionary Salespersons.   **Missionary salespersons**, who are usually employed by manufacturers, assist the producer's customers in selling to their own customers. A missionary salesperson may call on retailers to inform and persuade them to buy the manufacturer's products. If the call is successful, the retailers purchase the

---

8. "Sprint in Hotline Promotion for Olympics," *Adweek's Marketing Week,* Feb. 1, 1988, p. 3.

9. William C. Moncrief, "Five Types of Industrial Sales Jobs," *Industrial Marketing Management,* 17 (1988), p. 164.

products from wholesalers, who are the producer's customers. Manufacturers of medical supplies and pharmaceutical products often use missionary salespersons to promote their products to physicians, hospitals, and retail druggists.

Trade Salespersons.   **Trade salespersons** are not strictly support personnel because they usually perform the order-taking function as well. However, they direct much of their efforts toward helping customers, especially retail stores, promote the product. They are likely to restock shelves, obtain more shelf space, set up displays, provide in-store demonstrations, and distribute samples to store customers. Food producers and processors commonly employ trade salespersons.

Technical Salespersons.   **Technical salespersons** give technical assistance to the organization's current customers. They advise customers on product characteristics and applications, system designs, and installation procedures. Because this job is often highly technical, the salesperson usually needs to have formal training in one of the physical sciences or in engineering. Technical sales personnel often sell technical industrial products, such as computers, heavy equipment, and steel.

When hiring sales personnel, marketers seldom restrict themselves to a single category because most firms require different types. Several factors dictate how many of each type of salesperson a particular company should have. A product's uses, characteristics, complexity, and price influence the kind of sales personnel used, as do the number of customers and their characteristics. The kinds of marketing channels and the intensity and type of advertising also have an impact on the selection of sales personnel.

MANAGEMENT OF THE SALES FORCE

The sales force is directly responsible for generating an organization's primary input: sales revenue. Without adequate sales revenue, a business cannot survive long. A firm's reputation is often determined by the ethical conduct of the sales force. On the other hand, the morale, and ultimately the success, of a firm's sales force is determined in large part by adequate compensation, room for advancement, adequate training, and management support, all key areas of sales management. When these elements are not satisfying to salespersons, they may leave for more satisfying jobs elsewhere. This problem of sales force turnover is the subject of Marketing Update 16.1. It is important to evaluate the input of salespeople because effective sales-force management determines a firm's success.

In this section we explore eight general areas of sales management: (1) establishing sales-force objectives, (2) determining sales-force size, (3) recruiting and selecting salespeople, (4) training sales personnel, (5) compensating salespeople, (6) motivating salespeople, (7) managing sales territories, and (8) controlling and evaluating sales-force performance.

■ Establishing Sales-Force Objectives

To manage a sales force effectively, a sales manager must develop sales objectives. Sales objectives tell salespersons what they are expected to accomplish during a specified time period. They give the sales force direction and purpose and serve as performance standards for the evaluation and control of sales personnel. For example in Figure 16.3 the manufacturer of software, Intel, is encouraging salespeople to suggest an additional piece of software—just as McDonald's suggests fries and soft drinks. A sales-force objective for Intel would be to generate 5 percent additional units in sales through suggestion selling. As with all types of objectives, sales objectives should be stated in precise, measurable terms and should specify the time period and the geographic areas involved.

Sales objectives are usually developed for both the total sales force and each salesperson. Objectives for the entire force are normally stated in terms of sales volume, market share, or profit. Volume objectives refer to a quantity of dollars or sales units. For example, the objective for an electric drill producer's sales force might be to sell $10 million worth of drills annually or 600,000 drills annually. When sales goals are stated in terms of market share, they usually call for an increase in the proportion of the firm's sales relative to the total number of products sold by all businesses in that particular industry. When sales objectives are based on profit, they are generally stated in terms of dollar amounts or return on investment.

Sales objectives, or quotas, for individual salespersons are commonly stated in terms of dollar or unit sales volume. Other bases used for individual sales objectives include average order size, average number of calls per time period, and the ratio of orders to calls.

MANAGING SALES-FORCE TURNOVER

Sales-force turnover—the replacement of employees who leave a company—is an area of increasing concern for companies that rely on personal selling. Turnover across all sales positions more than tripled from 1983 to 1988, from an average of 7.6 percent to 27 percent. Turnover costs the average company nearly $250,000 a year in time spent in recruiting and training replacements and in the loss of potential business.

A survey of 500 sales representatives and managers in the United States and Canada found that the top three reasons salespeople cite for leaving their jobs are inadequate compensation, lack of advancement opportunities, and personality conflicts. A natural conflict often exists between salespeople, who are generally motivated by self-achievement, and managers, who are motivated by power and who often make less money than those they manage. About one-third of the survey respondents indicated better management support would improve their jobs. Although a majority of the respondents were highly satisfied with both the quality of the goods or services they sold and their companies' reputations, they were least satisfied with the things that management used to help salespeople prepare for and perform their jobs: sales tools, sales incentives, and sales training programs.

Sales force managers can reduce turnover by promoting greater job satisfaction and stronger company loyalty. Conducting surveys to determine how salespeople feel about their jobs may indicate that different reward systems are needed. High performers tend to respond to pay satisfaction; low performers generally leave when they are no longer satisfied with their jobs.

Another suggestion for reducing turnover is using an open-door style of management, including weekly sessions with salespeople to spot potential problems. Other suggestions include keeping issues in perspective (e.g., compensation versus other work-related issues), conducting periodic audits to determine causes of job dissatisfaction, establishing recruiting standards for prospective employees, and re-evaluating training programs so that salespeople have essential product knowledge and sales skills.

SOURCES: Lynn G. Coleman, "Sales Force Turnover Has Managers Wondering Why," *Marketing News,* Dec. 4, 1989, pp. 6, 21; George H. Lucas, Jr., A. Parasuraman, Robert A. Davis, and Ben M. Enis, "An Empirical Study of Salesforce Turnover," *Journal of Marketing,* July 1987, pp. 34–59; Lester L. Tobias, "Is Salesperson Turnover Bashing Your Bottom Line?" *Business Marketing,* June 1986, pp. 78–82; George H. Lucas, Jr., Emin Babakus, and Thomas N. Ingram, "An Empirical Test of the Job Satisfaction-Turnover Relationship: Assessing the Role of Job Performance for Retail Managers," *Journal of the Academy of Marketing Science,* 1990, forthcoming.

FIGURE 16.3

Establishing objectives. Intel promotes suggestion selling of software to assist salespeople in meeting their sales goals.

SOURCE: Courtesy of Intel Corporation

■ Determining Sales-Force Size

Deciding how many salespersons to use is important because it influences the company's ability to generate sales and profits. Moreover, the size of the sales force affects the compensation methods used, salespersons' morale, and overall sales-force management. Sales-force size must be adjusted from time to time because a firm's marketing plans change, as do markets and forces in the marketing environment. One danger is to cut back the size of the sales force to increase profits. The sales organization could lose its strength and resiliency, preventing it from rebounding when growth rebounds or better market conditions prevail. The organization that loses capacity from cutbacks may not have the energy to accelerate.[10]

There are several analytical methods for determining the optimal size of the sales force; however, a detailed discussion of these methods is beyond the scope of this text. Although marketing managers may use one or several analytical methods, they normally temper their decisions with a good deal of subjective judgment.

10. A. J. Magrath, "Are You Overdoing 'Lean and Mean'?" *Sales & Marketing Management,* January 1988, pp. 46–53.

Recruiting and Selecting Salespeople

To create and maintain an effective sales force, a sales manager must recruit the right type of salespeople. **Recruiting** is a process by which the sales manager develops a list of applicants for sales positions. The cost of hiring, training, and retaining a salesperson is soaring; currently, costs can reach $100,000 or more.[11]

To ensure that the recruiting process results in a pool of qualified salespersons from which to hire, a sales manager should establish a set of required qualifications before beginning to recruit. Although for years marketers have attempted to enumerate a set of traits that characterize effective salespeople, there is currently no such set of generally accepted characteristics. Therefore a sales manager must develop a set tailored to the sales tasks in a particular company. Two activities can help establish this set of requirements. The sales manager should prepare a job description that lists the specific tasks salespersons are to perform. The manager also should analyze the characteristics of the firm's successful salespersons, as well as those of ineffective sales personnel. From the job description and the analysis of traits, the sales manager should be able to develop a set of specific requirements and be aware of potential weaknesses that could lead to failure.

A sales manager generally recruits applicants from several sources: departments within the firm, other firms, employment agencies, educational institutions, respondents to advertisements, and individuals recommended by current employees. The specific sources a sales manager uses depend on the type of salesperson required and the manager's experiences with particular sources.

The process of hiring a sales force varies tremendously from one company to another. One technique used to determine whether potential candidates will be good salespeople is an assessment center. Assessment centers are intense training environments that place candidates in realistic problem settings in which they must give priorities to their activities, make decisions, and act on their decisions. Candidates are judged by experienced managers or trained observers. Assessment centers have proven valuable in selecting good salespeople.[12]

Sales management should design a selection procedure that satisfies the company's specific needs. The process should include enough steps to yield the information needed for making accurate selection decisions. However, because each step incurs a certain expense, there should be no more steps than necessary. The stages of the selection process should be sequenced so that the more expensive steps, such as physical examination, are near the end. Fewer people will then move through the higher-cost stages.

Recruitment should not be sporadic; it should be a continuous activity aimed at reaching the best applicants. The selection process should systematically and effectively match applicants' characteristics and needs with the requirements of specific selling tasks. Finally, the selection process should ensure that new sales personnel are available where and when they are needed.

Recruitment and selection of salespeople are not one-time decisions. The market and marketing environment change, as do an organization's objectives, resources, and marketing strategies. Maintaining the proper mix of salespeople thus requires the firm's sales management's continued decision making.

11. Coleman, pp. 6, 21.

12. Patrick C. Fleenor, "Selling and Sales Management in Action: Assessment Center Selection of Sales Representatives," *Journal of Personal Selling & Sales Management,* May 1987, pp. 57–59.

THE **TOYOTA** TOUCH

ATOYOT

THE ONLY PRESSURE IN A SHOWROOM SHOULD BE IN THE TIRES.

Nobody wants to be pressured into anything. Especially anything as important as buying a car or truck. Toyota understands that a relaxed shopping environment leads to a productive shopping experience. And a productive shopping experience is what every car manufacturer should strive for. That's the thinking behind The Toyota Touch. A philosophy based on the simple notion of common courtesy. Our goal is to make the only pressure you feel in a Toyota showroom that of a good, firm handshake.

TOYOTA QUALITY
WHO COULD ASK FOR ANYTHING MORE!

SOURCE: Courtesy of Toyota Motor Sales U.S.A., Inc.

■ Training Sales Personnel

Many organizations have formal training programs; others depend on informal on-the-job training. Some systematic training programs are quite extensive; others are rather short and rudimentary. Regardless of whether the training program is complex or simple, its developers must consider what to teach, who to train, and how to train them. In Figure 16.4, Toyota communicates that its sales force provides minimal pressure in dealing with potential customers.

A sales training program can concentrate on the company, on products, or on selling methods. Training programs often cover all three areas. Training for experienced company salespersons usually emphasizes product information, although salespeople also must be informed about new selling techniques and any changes in company plans, policies, and procedures.

Training programs can be aimed at newly hired salespeople, at experienced salespersons, or both. Ordinarily, new sales personnel require comprehensive training, whereas experienced personnel need both refresher courses about established products and training that gives them new-product information. Training programs can be directed at the entire sales force or at one segment of it.

Sales training may be done in the field, at educational institutions, in company facilities, or in several of these locations. Some firms train new employees before assigning them to a specific sales position. Other businesses, however, put them into the field immediately and provide formal training only after the new salespersons have gained a little experience. Training programs for new personnel can be as short as several days or as long as three years; some are even longer. Sales training for experienced personnel is often scheduled during a period when sales activities are not too demanding. Because training of experienced salespeople is usually a recurring effort, a firm's sales management must determine the frequency, sequencing, and duration of these activities.

Sales managers, as well as other salespeople, often engage in sales training—whether daily on the job or periodically in sales meetings. Salespeople sometimes receive training from technical specialists within their own organizations. In addition, a number of individuals and organizations sell special sales training programs. Appropriate materials for sales training programs range from films, texts, manuals, and cases to programmed learning devices and audio- and videocassettes. As for teaching methods, lectures, demonstrations, simulation exercises, and on-the-job training can all be effective. The choice of methods and materials for a particular sales training program depends on the type and number of trainees, the program's content and complexity, its length and location, the size of the training budget, the number of teachers, and the teachers' preferences.

■ Compensating Salespeople

To develop and maintain a highly productive sales force, a business must formulate and administer a compensation plan that attracts, motivates, and retains the most effective individuals. The plan should give sales management the desired level of control and provide sales personnel with an acceptable level of freedom, income, and incentive. It should also be flexible, equitable, easy to administer, and easy to understand. Good compensation programs facilitate and encourage proper treatment of customers.

Even though these requirements appear to be logical and easily satisfied, it is actually quite difficult to incorporate them all into a simple program. Some of them will be satisfied, and others will not. Studies evaluating the impact of financial incentives on sales performance indicate five general responses. For money-sensitive individuals, an increase in incentives will usually increase their sales efforts, and a decrease in financial rewards will diminish their efforts. Unresponsive salespeople will sell at the same level regardless of the incentive. Leisure-sensitive salespeople tend to work less when the incentive system is implemented. Income satisfiers normally adjust their performance to match their income goal. Understanding potential reactions and analyzing the personalities of the sales force can help management evaluate whether an incentive program might work.[13] Therefore, in formulating a compensation plan, sales management must strive for a proper balance of freedom, income, and incentives.

The developer of a compensation program must determine the general level of compensation required and the most desirable method of calculating it. In analyzing

13. Rene Y. Darmon, "The Impact of Incentive Compensation on the Salesperson's Work Habits: An Economic Model," *Journal of Personal Selling & Sales Management,* May 1987, pp. 21–32.

the required compensation level, sales management must ascertain a salesperson's value to the company on the basis of the tasks and responsibilities associated with the sales position. The sales manager may consider a number of factors, including salaries of other types of personnel in the firm, competitors' compensation plans, costs of sales-force turnover, and the size of nonsalary selling expenses.

Sales compensation programs usually reimburse salespersons for their selling expenses, provide a certain number of fringe benefits, and deliver the required compensation level. To do that, a firm may use one or more of three basic compensation methods: straight salary, straight commission, or a combination of salary and commission. In a **straight salary compensation plan**, salespeople are paid a specified amount per time period. This sum remains the same until they receive a pay increase or decrease. In a **straight commission compensation plan**, salespeople's compensation is determined solely by the amount of their sales for a given time period. A commission may be based on a single percentage of sales or on a sliding scale involving several sales levels and percentage rates. In a **combination compensation plan**, salespeople are paid a fixed salary and a commission based on sales volume. Some combination programs require a salesperson to exceed a certain sales level before earning a commission; others offer commissions for any level of sales.

Traditionally, department stores have paid salespeople straight salaries, but combination compensation plans are becoming popular. R. H. Macy & Co., for example, is offering commissions (averaging 6 to 8 percent) to a large segment of its sales force. The practice has made its salespeople more attentive to a customer's presence and needs; it has also attracted older, more experienced salespeople, who tend to be in short supply.[14]

Table 16.1 lists the major characteristics of each sales-force compensation method. Notice that the combination method is most popular. When selecting a compensation method, sales management weighs the advantages and disadvantages shown in Table 16.1.

Proper administration of the sales-force compensation program is crucial for developing high morale and productivity among sales personnel. A good salesperson is very marketable in today's work place, and successful sales managers switch industries on a regular basis. Basic knowledge and skills related to sales management are in demand, and sometimes new insights can be gained from different work experiences. For example, Charles of the Ritz Group, Ltd., hired a sales and promotion manager for its skin sun-care product line away from Joseph E. Seagram & Sons, Inc., a leading distilled spirits company.[15] To maintain an effective compensation program and retain productive employees, sales management should periodically review and evaluate the plan and make necessary adjustments.

■ **Motivating Salespeople**

A sales manager should develop a systematic approach for motivating salespersons to be productive. Motivating should not be viewed as a sporadic activity reserved for periods of sales decline. Effective sales-force motivation is achieved through an organized set of activities performed continuously by the company's sales manage-

14. Aimee Stern, "Commissions Catch on at Department Stores," *Adweek's Marketing Week,* Feb. 1, 1988, p. 5.

15. Martin Everett, "Would It Pay You to Switch Industries?" *Sales & Marketing Management,* January 1988, pp. 32–36.

TABLE 16.1 *Characteristics of sales-force compensation methods*

COMPENSATION METHOD	FREQUENCY OF USE (%)[a]	WHEN ESPECIALLY USEFUL	ADVANTAGES	DISADVANTAGES
Straight salary	17.4	Compensating new salespersons; firm moves into new sales territories that require developmental work; salespersons need to perform many nonselling activities	Gives salesperson maximum amount of security; gives sales manager large amount of control over salespersons; easy to administer; yields more predictable selling expenses	Provides no incentive; necessitates closer supervision of salespersons' activities; during sales declines, selling expenses remain at same level
Straight commission	6.5	Highly aggressive selling is required; nonselling tasks are minimized; company cannot closely control sales-force activities	Provides maximum amount of incentive; by increasing commission rate, sales managers can encourage salespersons to sell certain items; selling expenses relate directly to sales resources	Salespersons have little financial security; sales manager has minimum control over sales force; may cause salespeople to give inadequate service to smaller accounts; selling costs less predictable
Combination	76.1	Sales territories have relatively similar sales potentials; firm wishes to provide incentive but still control sales-force activities	Provides certain level of financial security; provides some incentive; selling expenses fluctuate with sales revenue	Selling expenses less predictable; may be difficult to administer

[a]The figures are computed from "Alternative Sales Compensation and Incentive Plans," *Sales & Marketing Management,* Feb. 17, 1986, p. 57. *Note:* The percentage for Combination includes compensation methods that involved any combination of salary, commission, or bonus.

SOURCE: Based on the *Harvard Business Review* article "How to Pay Your Sales Force" by John P. Steinbrink (July/August 1978).

ment. For example, scheduled sales meetings can motivate salespeople. Periodic sales meetings have four main functions: recognizing and reinforcing performing salespeople, sharing sales techniques that are working, focusing employees' efforts on matching the corporate goals and evaluating their progress toward achieving these goals, and teaching the sales staff about new products and services.[16]

16. Terese Hudson, "Holding Meetings Sharpens Employees' Sales Skills," *Savings Institutions,* July 1987, pp. 109–111.

Although financial compensation is important, a motivational program must also satisfy nonfinancial needs. Sales personnel, like other people, join organizations to satisfy personal needs and achieve personal goals. Sales managers must become aware of their personnel's motives and goals and then attempt to create an organizational climate that lets sales personnel satisfy their personal needs.

A sales manager can use a variety of positive motivational incentives other than financial compensation. For example, enjoyable working conditions, power and authority, job security, and an opportunity to excel are effective motivators. Salespeople can be motivated by their company's efforts to make their job more productive and efficient. For example, Honeywell Information Systems developed a computerized sales support system that has increased sales productivity by 31 percent and reduced sales-force turnover by 40 percent within a year. This system can track leads and provide customer profiles and competitor data.[17]

Sales contests and other incentive programs can also be effective motivators. Sales contests can motivate salespersons to focus on increasing sales or new accounts, promote special items, achieve greater volume per sales call, cover territories better, and increase activity in new geographic areas.[18] Some companies have found such incentive programs to be powerful motivating tools that marketing managers can use to achieve corporate goals. (In Figure 16.5, Nikon promotes a variety of cameras as potential salesperson incentives.) Properly designed, an incentive program can pay for itself many times over. However, for an incentive system to succeed, the marketing objectives must be accepted by participants and prove effective in the marketplace. Some organizations also use negative motivational measures: financial penalties, demotions, even terminations.

■ Managing Sales Territories

The effectiveness of a sales force that must travel to its customers is influenced, to some degree, by sales management's decisions regarding sales territories. Sales managers deciding on territories must consider size, shape, routing, and scheduling.

Creating Sales Territories. Several factors enter into the design of the size and shape of sales territories. First, sales managers must construct the territories so that sales potentials can be measured. Thus sales territories often consist of several geographic units for which market data are obtainable, such as census tracts, cities, counties, or states. Sales managers usually try to create territories that have similar sales potentials or that require about the same amount of work. If territories have equal sales potentials, they will almost always be unequal in geographic size. The salespersons who get the larger territories will have to work longer and harder to generate a certain sales volume. Conversely, if sales territories that require equal amounts of work are created, sales potentials for those territories will often vary. If sales personnel are partially or fully compensated through commissions, they will have unequal income potentials. Many sales managers try to balance territorial workloads and earning potentials by using differential commission rates. Although a sales manager seeks equity when developing and maintaining sales territories, some inequities will always prevail.

17. Dan Woog, "Taking Sales High Tech," *High Tech Marketing*, May 1987, pp. 17–22.

18. Sandra Hile Hart, William C. Moncrief, and A. Parasuraman, "An Empirical Investigation of Salespeople's Performance, Effort and Selling Method During a Sales Contest," *Journal of the Academy of Marketing Science*, Winter 1989, pp. 29–39.

SOURCE: Courtesy of Nikon/The Bettmann Archive

A territory's size and shape should also be designed to help the sales force provide the best possible customer coverage and to minimize selling costs. Territory size and shape should take into account the density and distribution of customers.

Routing and Scheduling Salespeople.   The geographic size and shape of a sales territory are the most important factors affecting routing and scheduling of sales calls. Next are the number and distribution of customers within the territory, followed by the frequency and duration of sales calls. The person in charge of routing and scheduling must consider the sequence in which customers are called on, the specific roads or transportation schedules to be used, the number of calls to be made in a given period, and what time of day the calls will occur. In some firms, salespeople plan their own routes and schedules with little or no assistance from the sales manager; in other organizations, the sales manager draws up the routes and schedules. No matter who plans the routing and scheduling, the major goals should be to minimize salespersons' nonselling time (the time spent traveling and waiting) and maximize their selling time. The planners should try to achieve these goals in a way that holds a salesperson's travel and lodging costs to a minimum.

Controlling and Evaluating Sales-Force Performance

To control and evaluate sales-force activities properly, sales management needs information. A sales manager cannot observe the field sales force daily and so relies on call reports, customer feedback, and invoices. Call reports identify the customers called on and present detailed information about interaction with those clients. Traveling sales personnel often must file work schedules indicating where they plan to be during specific future time periods.

The dimensions used to measure a salesperson's performance are determined largely by sales objectives. These objectives are normally set by the sales manager. If an individual's sales objective is stated in terms of sales volume, then that person should be evaluated on the basis of sales volume generated. Even though a salesperson may be assigned a major objective, he or she is ordinarily expected to achieve several related objectives as well. Thus salespeople are often judged along several dimensions. Sales managers evaluate many performance indicators, including average number of calls per day, average sales per customer, actual sales relative to sales potential, number of new-customer orders, average cost per call, and average gross profit per customer.

To evaluate a salesperson, a sales manager may compare one or more of these dimensions with a predetermined performance standard. However, sales management commonly compares one salesperson's performance with the performance of other employees operating under similar selling conditions or compares current performance with past performance. Sometimes management judges factors that have less direct bearing on sales performance, such as personal appearance, knowledge of the product, and competitors.

After evaluating salespeople, sales managers must take any needed corrective action because it is their job to improve the performance of the sales force. They may have to adjust performance standards, provide additional sales training, or try other motivational methods. Corrective action may demand comprehensive changes in the sales force.

Many industries, especially technical ones, are monitoring their sales forces and increasing productivity through the use of laptop (portable) computers. In part, the increasing use of computers in technical sales is a response to customers' greater technical sophistication. Product information—especially information on price, specifications, and availability of products—helps salespeople to be more valuable. Some companies that have provided their sales forces with laptops expect a 15 to 20 percent increase in their sales.[19]

THE NATURE OF SALES PROMOTION

As defined earlier, **sales promotion** is an activity or material (or both) that acts as a direct inducement, offering added value or incentive for the product, to resellers, salespersons, or consumers.[20] It encompasses all promotional activities and materials other than personal selling, advertising, and publicity. In competitive markets, where products are very similar, sales promotion provides additional inducements

19. Robert Martinott, "The Traveling Salesman Goes High Tech," *Chemical Week,* June 10, 1987, pp. 22–24.

20. John F. Luick and William L. Ziegler, *Sales Promotion and Modern Merchandising* (New York: McGraw-Hill, 1968); and Don E. Schultz and William A. Robinson, *Sales Promotion Management* (Chicago: Crain Books, 1982).

that encourage purchases. For example, Stanley Works, which manufactures hand tools, ran a sales promotion called "Secret to Security," in which customers who purchased $15 worth of Stanley products received a $35 Stanley remote lamp-timer system for free.[21] Sales promotions such as this one are designed to generate short-term sales and good will toward the promoter.

Sales promotion has grown dramatically in the last ten years, largely because of the focus of American business on short-term profits and value and the perceived need for promotional strategies that produce short-term sales boosts.[22] The most significant change in promotion expenditures in recent years has been the transfer of funds usually earmarked for advertising to sales promotion. Companies now spend 40 percent of their combined advertising and sales promotion budgets on advertising and 60 percent on sales promotion.[23] Fundamental changes in marketing, which have led to a greater emphasis on sales promotion, mean that advertising agencies have had to increase their participation in sales promotion to maintain revenues.[24]

An organization often uses sales promotion activities in concert with other promotional efforts to facilitate personal selling, advertising, or both. Sales promotion efforts are not always secondary to other promotion-mix ingredients. Companies sometimes use advertising and personal selling to support sales promotion activities. For example, marketers frequently use advertising to promote contests, free samples, and premiums. Manufacturers' sales personnel occasionally administer sales contests for wholesale or retail salespersons. The most effective sales promotion efforts are highly interrelated with other promotional activities. Decisions regarding sales promotion therefore often affect advertising and personal selling decisions, and vice versa.

SALES PROMOTION OPPORTUNITIES AND LIMITATIONS

Sales promotion can increase sales by providing an extra incentive to purchase. There are many opportunities to motivate consumers, resellers, and salespeople to take a desired action. Some kinds of sales promotion are designed specifically to stimulate resellers' demand and effectiveness; some are directed at increasing consumer demand; and others focus on both resellers and consumers. Regardless of the purpose, marketers need to ensure that the sales promotion objectives are consistent with the organization's overall objectives, as well as its marketing and promotion objectives.

Although sales promotion can support a brand image, excessive price-reduction sales promotion, such as coupons, can affect brand image. Firms therefore must decide between short-term sales increases and the long-run need for a desired reputation and brand image.[25] As already noted, sales promotion now exceeds adver-

21. Ken Fitzgerald, "Ad Support Builds for Tools," *Advertising Age,* Aug. 28, 1989, p. 20.

22. Thomas McCann, "Promotions Will Gain More Clout in the '90s," *Marketing News,* Nov. 6, 1989, pp. 4, 24.

23. Scott Hume, "Premiums & Promotions: After Buying Binge, What?" *Advertising Age,* Sept. 12, 1988, pp. S1–S5.

24. Laurie Petersen, "Agencies See Gold in Promo Field," *Adweek,* Oct. 23, 1989, pp. 1, 76.

25. W. E. Phillips and Bill Robinson, "Continued Sales (Price) Promotion Destroys Brands: Yes; No," *Marketing News,* Jan. 16, 1989, pp. 4, 8.

tising in total expenditures, but in the future brand advertising may become more important relative to sales promotion. Some firms that shifted from brand advertising to sales promotion have lost market share.

For example, Minute Maid orange juice (owned by Coca-Cola Foods) experienced its most dramatic sales declines after shifting the majority of advertising spending to sales promotion while one of its major competitors, Tropicana, continued to focus on brand advertising. Minute Maid's advertising budget was reduced by approximately 40 percent from 1984 to 1988. Consequently, Minute Maid's share of the fruit beverage category dropped from 12.4 percent to 9.5 percent. To counter Minute Maid's decline in market share, Coca-Cola introduced a $30 million advertising campaign for Minute Maid in 1989 to provide a sustained brand image for Minute Maid orange juice. Similarly, when General Foods boosted the advertising budget for its Maxwell House coffee by 50 percent, Maxwell House gained a 30 percent share of the coffee market.[26] These examples do not mean that advertising always works better than sales promotion. There are trade-offs between these two forms of promotion, and the marketing manager must determine the right balance to achieve maximum promotional effectiveness.

SALES PROMOTION METHODS

Most sales promotion methods can be grouped into the categories of consumer sales promotion and trade sales promotion. **Consumer sales promotion techniques** encourage or stimulate consumers to patronize a specific retail store or to try a particular product. **Trade sales promotion methods** stimulate wholesalers and retailers to carry a producer's products and to market these products aggressively.

Marketers consider a number of factors before deciding which sales promotion methods to use. They must take into account both product characteristics (size, weight, costs, durability, uses, features, and hazards) and target market characteristics (age, sex, income, location, density, usage rate, and shopping patterns). How the product is distributed and the number and types of resellers may determine the type of method used. The competitive and legal environment may also influence the choice.

In this section we look closely at several consumer and trade sales promotion methods to learn what they entail and what goals they can help marketers achieve.

■ **Consumer Sales Promotion Methods**

Consumer sales promotion by manufacturers and resellers amounts to approximately $4 billion annually, divided between mail-in offers and direct incentives, including coupon plans.[27] In this section we discuss coupons, demonstrations, frequent user incentives, point-of-purchase displays, free samples, money refunds, premiums, cents-off offers, and consumer contests and sweepstakes.

Coupons.   **Coupons** are used to stimulate consumers to try a new or established product, to increase sales volume quickly, to attract repeat purchasers, or to introduce new package sizes or features. Coupons usually reduce the purchase price of an item. For example, the NutraSweet Company offered a coupon for a free

26. Laurie Freeman and Jennifer Lawrence, "Brand Building Gets New Life," *Advertising Age,* Sept. 4, 1989, pp. 3, 34.

27. "Consumer Incentives," *Incentive,* May 1988, pp. 48–59.

FIGURE 16.6
A coupon for a new product

trial-size package or 60 cents off the price of other packages of its new Sugar Delight sweetener (see Figure 16.6). The savings may be deducted from the purchase price or offered as cash. For best results, coupons should be easy to recognize and state the offer clearly. The nature of the product (seasonality, maturity, frequency of purchase, and the like) is the prime consideration in setting up a coupon promotion.

More than two thousand manufacturers distribute coupons, which are used by approximately 80 percent of all households. One study found that pride and satisfaction from obtaining savings through the use of coupons and price consciousness were the most important determinants of coupon use.[28] Coupons are distributed through free-standing inserts (FSIs), print advertising, direct mail, and in stores. Historically, FSIs have been the dominant vehicle for coupons.[29] When deciding on the proper vehicle for their coupons, marketers should consider strategies and objectives, redemption rates, availability, circulation, and exclusivity. The whole coupon distribution and redemption area has become very competitive. To draw

28. Emin Babakus, Peter Tat, and William Cunningham, "Coupon Redemption: A Motivational Perspective," *Journal of Consumer Marketing,* Spring 1988, p. 40.

29. Donna Campanella, "Sales Promotion: Couponmania," *Marketing and Media Decisions,* June 1987, pp. 118–122.

customers to their stores, grocers may double and sometimes even triple the value of the coupons they bring in. But because the practice of doubling and tripling coupons is expensive, many of these retailers have asked manufacturers to reduce the face value of the coupons they offer.[30]

There are several advantages to using coupons. Print advertisements with coupons are often more effective than nonpromotional advertising for generating brand awareness. Generally, the larger the coupon's cash offer, the better the recognition generated. Another advantage is that coupons are a good way to reward present users of the product, win back former users, and encourage purchases in larger quantities. Coupons also let manufacturers determine whether the coupons reached the intended target market because they get the coupons back.

Coupons also have drawbacks. Fraud and misredemption are possible, and the redemption period can be quite lengthy. The approximate redemption rate is 3.6 percent, with 10 to 15 percent of the coupons accepted being misredemptions. In addition, some experts believe that coupons are losing their value because so many manufacturers are offering them, and consumers have therefore learned not to buy without some incentive, whether it be a coupon, a rebate, or a refund. There has been a general decline in brand loyalty among heavy coupon users. On the other hand, many consumers only redeem coupons for products they normally buy. Studies have shown that about 75 percent of coupons are redeemed by people who already use the brand on the coupon. So, as an incentive to try and to continue to use a new brand or product, coupons have questionable success. Another problem with coupons is that stores often do not have enough of the coupon item in stock. This situation can generate ill will toward both the store and the product.[31]

Although the use of coupons as a sales promotion technique is expected to grow in the next few years, a concern among marketers about their effectiveness could well diminish their appeal. However, coupons will probably remain a major sales promotion component for stimulating trial of new products. Coupons will also be used to increase the frequency of purchase for established products that show sluggish sales. On the other hand, successful established products may be reducing their profits if 75 percent of the coupons are redeemed by brand-loyal customers.[32]

Demonstrations.   **Demonstrations** are excellent attention getters. Manufacturers often use them temporarily either to encourage trial use and purchase of the product or to actually show how the product works. Because labor costs can be extremely high, demonstrations are not used widely. They can, however, be highly effective for promoting certain types of products, such as appliances, cosmetics, and cleaning supplies. Cosmetics marketers such as Clinique (owned by Estee Lauder), for example, sometimes offer potential customers "makeovers" to demonstrate their products' benefits and proper application.

Frequent User Incentives.   Many firms develop incentive programs to reward individual consumers who engage in repeat (frequent) purchases. For example, most major airlines offer a frequent flyer program through which customers who have flown a specified number of miles are rewarded with free tickets for additional

30. Alison Fahey, "Coupon War Fallout," *Advertising Age*, Sept. 4, 1989, p. 2.

31. Campanella, pp. 118–122.

32. Ibid.

FIGURE 16.7

Example of a user incentive.
TWA promotes its Frequent Flight Bonus Program to encourage repeat business.

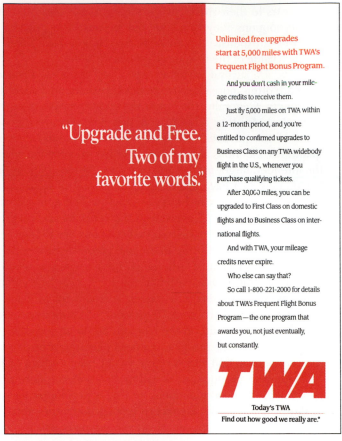

Unlimited free upgrades start at 5,000 miles with TWA's Frequent Flight Bonus Program.

"Upgrade and Free. Two of my favorite words."

And you don't cash in your mileage credits to receive them.

Just fly 5,000 miles on TWA within a 12-month period, and you're entitled to confirmed upgrades to Business Class on any TWA widebody flight in the U.S., whenever you purchase qualifying tickets.

After 30,000 miles, you can be upgraded to First Class on domestic flights and to Business Class on international flights.

And with TWA, your mileage credits never expire.

Who else can say that?

So call 1-800-221-2000 for details about TWA's Frequent Flight Bonus Program—the one program that awards you, not just eventually, but constantly.

TWA

Today's TWA
Find out how good we really are.®

SOURCE: Courtesy of Trans World Airlines

travel (see Figure 16.7). Thus frequent user incentives help foster customer loyalty to a specific company or group of cooperating companies that provide extra incentives for patronage. Frequent user incentives have also been used by service businesses, such as auto rental agencies, hotels, and credit card companies, as well as by marketers of consumer goods. Procter & Gamble, for example, launched the GiftLink Shoppers Reward program, in conjunction with Ralston Purina, Kraft, Campbell Soup, and Ocean Spray, to reward brand loyal customers for their regular support. Consumers enrolled in the program earn "points" each time they purchase a brand listed in the program. They can redeem these points for merchandise—for instance, Samsonite luggage or Black & Decker small appliances.[33]

An older frequent user incentive is trading stamps. **Trading stamps** are dispensed in proportion to the amount of a consumer's purchase and can be accumulated and redeemed for goods. Retailers use trading stamps to attract consumers to specific stores. Stamps are attractive to consumers as long as they do not drive up the price of goods. They are effective for many types of retailers. Trading stamps were very popular in the 1960s, but their use as a sales promotion method declined

33. Michael J. McCarthy, "Rewarding 'Frequent Buyer' for Loyalty," *Wall Street Journal*, June 21, 1989, p. B1.

dramatically in the 1970s. However, Sperry & Hutchinson (marketer of S&H Green Stamps) and Quality Stamps, Inc., are testing different forms of trading stamps, such as electronic stamps and trading seals, in an effort to revive their use.[34]

Point-of-Purchase Displays.　　**Point-of-purchase (P-O-P) materials** include such items as outside signs, window displays, counter pieces, display racks, and self-service cartons. Innovations in P-O-P displays include sniff-teasers, which give off a product's aroma in the store as consumers walk within a radius of four feet, and computerized interactive displays, which ask a series of multiple-choice questions and then release information on a screen to help consumers make a product decision.[35] These items, which are often supplied by producers, attract attention, inform customers, and encourage retailers to carry particular products. A retailer is likely to use point-of-purchase materials if they are attractive, informative, well constructed, and in harmony with the store. With 66 percent of all purchases resulting from in-store decisions, P-O-P materials can help sustain incremental sales if a brand's essential components—brand name, positioning, and visual image—are the basis of the P-O-P display.[36]

A survey of retail store managers indicated that almost 90 percent believed that P-O-P materials sell products. The retailers surveyed also said that P-O-P is essential for product introductions. Different forms of display material are carried by different types of retailers. Convenience stores, for example, favor window banners and "shelf talkers" (on-the-shelf displays or signs), whereas chain drugstores prefer floor stands and devices that provide samples.[37]

Free Samples.　　Marketers use **free samples** for several reasons: to stimulate trial of a product, to increase sales volume in the early stages of a product's life cycle, or to obtain desirable distribution. The sampling program should be planned as a total event, not merely a giveaway.[38] Sampling is the most expensive of all sales promotion methods because production and distribution through such channels as mail delivery, door-to-door delivery, in-store distribution, and on-package distribution entail very high costs. In designing a free sample, marketers should consider certain factors, such as the seasonality of the product, the characteristics of the market, and prior advertising. Free samples are not appropriate for mature products and slow-turnover products.

Money Refunds.　　With **money refunds**, consumers submit proof of purchase and are mailed a specific amount of money. Usually, manufacturers demand multiple purchases of the product before a consumer can qualify for a refund. For example, Panasonic marketed a line of VHS tapes that featured a $1 rebate per tape, for up to twelve purchases. A customer had to send in a proof of purchase from inside each tape package and the sales receipt. This method, used primarily to

34. Lynn G. Coleman, "Electronic Trading Stamps Successful in Test Market," *Marketing News,* June 19, 1987, p. 2.

35. Joe Agnew, "P-O-P Displays Are Becoming a Matter of Consumer Convenience," *Marketing News,* Oct. 9, 1987, p. 14.

36. Ibid., p. 16.

37. Alison Fahey, "Study Shows Retailers Rely on P-O-P," *Advertising Age,* Nov. 27, 1989, p. 83.

38. "Sampling Accelerates Adoption of New Products," *Marketing News,* Sept. 11, 1987, p. 21.

promote trial use of a product, is relatively low in cost. Nevertheless, because money refunds sometimes generate a low response rate, they have limited impact on sales.

One of the problems with money refunds or rebates is that many people perceive the redemption process as too complicated. Consumers also have negative perceptions of manufacturers' reasons for offering rebates. They may believe that these are new, untested products or products that haven't sold well. If these perceptions are not changed, rebate offers may degrade the image and desirability of the product being promoted. If the promotion objective in the rebate offer is to increase sales, then an effort should be made to simplify the redemption process and proof-of-purchase requirements.[39]

Premiums.   **Premiums** are items offered free or at minimum cost as a bonus for purchasing a product. They can attract competitors' customers, introduce different sizes of established products, add variety to other promotional efforts, and stimulate loyalty. Inventiveness is necessary, however; if an offer is to stand out and achieve a significant number of redemptions, the premium must be matched to both the target audience and the brand's image.[40] To be effective, premiums must be easily recognizable and desirable. For example, to spur sales in the off-season, Northwest Airlines and Pan American Airlines offered $200 to $1,000 in cash to first-class and business-class international travelers.[41] Premiums usually are distributed through retail outlets or the mail, but they may also be placed on or in packages.

Cents-off Offers.   When a **cents-off offer** is used, buyers receive a certain amount off the regular price shown on the label or package. Similar to coupons, this method can be a strong incentive for trying the product; it can stimulate product sales, yield short-lived sales increases, and promote products in off-seasons. It is an easy method to control and is used frequently for specific purposes. However, if used on an ongoing basis, it reduces the price to customers who would buy at the regular price, and frequent use of cents-off offers may cheapen a product's image. In addition, the method often requires special handling by retailers.

Consumer Contests and Sweepstakes.   In **consumer contests**, individuals compete for prizes based on their analytical or creative skill. This method generates traffic at the retail level. Marriott Corp. and Hertz Corp. cosponsored a scratch-card contest with a golf theme to boost sales during the slow winter travel season. Contestants received game cards upon check-in at a Marriott hotel or a Hertz rental counter and scratched off spots to see if they had won prizes such as cars, vacations, or golf clubs.[42] However, marketers should exercise care in setting up a contest. Problems or errors may anger consumers or result in lawsuits, as illustrated by the incident described in Marketing Update 16.2. Contestants are usually more involved in consumer contests than they are in sweepstakes, which we discuss next, even though the total participation may be lower. Contests may be used in conjunction with other sales promotion methods, such as coupons.

39. Peter Tat, William A. Cunningham, and Emin Babakus, "Consumer Perceptions of Rebates," *Journal of Advertising Research,* August-September 1988, p. 48.

40. Gerrie Anthea, "Sales Promotion: Putting Up the Premium," *Marketing* (U.K.), Apr. 16, 1987.

41. Jennifer Lawrence, "Airlines Give Rebates a Spin," *Advertising Age,* Oct. 30, 1989, p. 58.

42. Steven W. Colford, "Marriott Sets Largest Promo," *Advertising Age,* Oct. 2, 1989, p. 58.

KRAFT'S SALES CONTEST GOES AWRY

Although consumer contests are often effective sales promotion techniques for established products, this method of generating traffic at the retail level can sometimes go awry, as in the case of Kraft's "Ready to Roll" contest.

Kraft's "Ready to Roll" contest appeared in advertisements in Sunday editions of Chicago and Houston newspapers. The advertisements included a game piece that consumers who wished to participate in the game had to match to game pieces found in specially marked packages of Kraft Singles cheese slices. Contest prizes included one $17,000 Dodge Caravan, 100 bicycles, 500 skateboards, and 8,000 packages of cheese. The odds of winning the van were projected at one in 15,160,000.

Unfortunately, because of a printing error, most of the game pieces matched, and thus nearly everyone who played the game won a prize. After receiving dozens of calls from would-be winners, Kraft executives realized that an error had been made and declared the contest null and void. To appease disappointed and angry consumers who believed they had won, Kraft proposed an alternate compensation plan, agreed to by Illinois law enforcement officials and the Texas attorney general's Consumer Protection Division. Under the plan, Kraft offered cash awards to consumers who mailed in their winning game pieces according to the announced rules and by the deadlines. Kraft awarded nearly 10,000 "winners" of the Caravan $250 each. "Winners" of other prizes received cash as follows—$50 to bike winners, $25 to skateboard winners, and $5 to cheese winners. In addition, each of the 21,000 valid entries was entered in a random drawing for four Caravans, 400 bicycles, 2,000 skateboards, and 32,000 packages of cheese.

Estimates of the costs to Kraft for the botched contest were between $2.8 million and $4 million in cash and $1 million for prizes and administrative costs, including pulling unpurchased cheese packages off supermarket shelves. Experts say Kraft probably cannot recoup its $4 million goodwill gesture from any insurance policy, but a company spokesperson indicated that the mostly positive response from consumers has been very reassuring in terms of future sales.

SOURCES: James Cox, "Everyone's a Winner—Except Kraft," *USA Today,* June 14, 1989, p. 1; Harris Collingwood, "Kraft Is the Big Loser in This Contest," *Business Week,* June 26, 1989, p. 70; Julie Erickson and Ira Teinowitz, "Not Really 'Ready to Roll'," *Advertising Age,* June 19, 1989, pp. 1, 74; Richard Gibson, "Now If Only This Would Happen Over at Publishers Clearing House," *Wall Street Journal,* June 14, 1989, p. B1; "Kraft Cancels Contest," *Marketing News,* July 3, 1989, p. 21; "Kraft Offers to Pay Cash to 'Winners' of Contest," *Wall Street Journal,* June 16, 1989, p. A2; and "Kraft Snafu Could Cost $4 Million," *Advertising Age,* July 10, 1989, p. 53.

The entrants in a **consumer sweepstakes** submit their names for inclusion in a drawing for prizes. Sweepstakes are used to stimulate sales and, as with contests, are sometimes teamed with other sales promotion methods. Sweepstakes are used more often than consumer contests, and they tend to attract a greater number of participants. The cost of a sweepstakes is considerably less than the cost of a contest.[43] Successful sweepstakes can generate widespread interest and short-term increases in sales or market share. However, sweepstakes are prohibited in some states.

■ Trade Sales Promotion Methods

Producers use sales promotion methods to encourage resellers, especially retailers, to carry their products and promote them effectively. The methods include buy-back allowances, buying allowances, counts and recounts, free merchandise, merchandise allowances, cooperative advertising, dealer listings, premium or push money, sales contests, and dealer loaders.

Buy-Back Allowances. A **buy-back allowance** is a certain sum of money given to a purchaser for each unit bought after an initial deal is over. This method is a secondary incentive in which the total amount of money that resellers can receive is proportional to their purchases during an initial trade deal, such as a coupon offer. Buy-back allowances foster cooperation during an initial sales promotion effort and stimulate repurchase afterward. The main drawback of this method is its expense.

Buying Allowances. A **buying allowance** is a temporary price reduction to resellers for purchasing specified quantities of a product. A soap producer, for example, might give retailers $1 for each case of soap purchased. Such offers may be an incentive to handle a new product, achieve a temporary price reduction, or stimulate the purchase of an item in larger than normal quantities. The buying allowance, which takes the form of money, yields profits to resellers and is simple and straightforward to use. There are no restrictions on how resellers use the money, which increases the method's effectiveness.

Counts and Recounts. The **count and recount** promotion method is based on the payment of a specific amount of money for each product unit moved from a reseller's warehouse in a given time period. Units of a product are counted at the start of the promotion and again at the end to determine how many have moved from the warehouse. This method can reduce retail stockouts by moving inventory out of warehouses and can also clear distribution channels of obsolete products or packages and reduce warehouse inventories. The count and recount method might benefit a producer by decreasing resellers' inventories, making resellers more likely to place new orders. However, this method is often difficult to administer and may not appeal to resellers who have small warehouses.

Free Merchandise. **Free merchandise** is sometimes offered to resellers who purchase a stated quantity of the same or different products. Occasionally, free merchandise is used as payment for allowances provided through other sales promotion methods. To avoid handling and bookkeeping problems, the giving of free merchandise usually is accomplished by reducing the invoice.

43. Eileen Norris, "Everyone Will Grab at a Chance to Win," *Advertising Age*, Aug. 22, 1983, p. M10.

Merchandise Allowances. A **merchandise allowance** is a manufacturer's agreement to pay resellers certain amounts of money for providing special promotional efforts, such as advertising or displays. This method is best suited to high-volume, high-profit, easily handled products. One major problem with using merchandise allowances is that some retailers perform their activities at a minimally acceptable level simply to obtain the allowances. Before paying retailers, manufacturers usually verify their performance. Manufacturers hope that the retailers' additional promotional efforts will yield substantial sales increases.

Cooperative Advertising. **Cooperative advertising** is an arrangement whereby a manufacturer agrees to pay a certain amount of a retailer's media costs for advertising the manufacturer's products. The amount allowed is usually based on the quantities purchased. Before payment is made, a retailer must show proof that advertisements did appear. These payments give retailers additional funds for advertising. They can, however, put a severe burden on the producer's advertising budget. Some retailers exploit cooperative advertising programs by crowding too many products into one advertisement. Surprisingly, though, not all available cooperative advertising dollars are used. Some retailers cannot afford to advertise; others can afford it but do not want to advertise. Still others actually do advertising that qualifies for an allowance but are not willing to undertake the paperwork required for reimbursement from producers.[44]

Dealer Listings. A **dealer listing** is an advertisement that promotes a product and identifies the names of participating retailers who sell the product. Dealer listings can influence retailers to carry the product, build traffic at the retail level, and encourage consumers to buy the product at participating dealers.

Premium or Push Money. **Premium** or **push money** is used to push a line of goods by providing additional compensation to salespeople. This promotion method is appropriate when personal selling is an important part of the marketing effort; it is not effective for promoting products that are sold through self-service. Although this method often helps a manufacturer obtain commitment from the sales force, often it can be very expensive.

Sales Contests. A **sales contest** is designed to motivate distributors, retailers, and sales personnel by recognizing outstanding achievements. The Colt Car Co., importer of Japanese-made Mitsubishi cars into the United Kingdom, designed a sales contest that offered dealers an incentive trip for two to Barbados if they improved their sales figures by 10 to 12 percent. Approximately 50 percent of the dealers met this sales goal and won the trip.[45] To be effective, this method must be equitable for all salespersons involved. One advantage to the method is that it can achieve participation at all levels of distribution. However, the results are temporary, and prizes are usually expensive.

44. Ed Crimmins, "A Co-op Myth: It Is a Tragedy That Stores Don't Spend All Their Accruals," *Sales & Marketing Management,* Feb. 7, 1983, pp. 72–73.

45. Gillian Upton, "Sales Promotion: Getting Results Barbados Style," *Marketing (U.K.),* Apr. 16, 1987, pp. 37–40.

Dealer Loaders. A **dealer loader** is a gift to a retailer who purchases a specified quantity of merchandise. Often dealer loaders are used to obtain special display efforts from retailers by offering essential display parts as premiums. For example, a manufacturer might design a display that includes a sterling silver tray as a major component and give the tray to the retailer. Marketers use dealer loaders to obtain new distributors and push larger quantities of goods.

Summary

Personal selling is the process of informing customers and persuading them to purchase products through personal communication in an exchange situation. The three general purposes of personal selling are finding prospects, convincing them to buy, and keeping customers satisfied.

Many salespersons—either consciously or unconsciously—move through a general selling process as they sell products. In prospecting, the salesperson develops a list of potential customers. Before contacting acceptable prospects, the salesperson prepares by finding and analyzing information about the prospects and their needs. The approach is the manner in which a salesperson contacts a potential customer. During the sales presentation, the salesperson must attract and hold the prospect's attention to stimulate interest and desire for the product. If possible, the salesperson should handle objections when they arise. Closing is the stage in the selling process when the salesperson asks the prospect to buy the product or products. After a successful closing, the salesperson must follow up the sale.

In developing a sales force, marketing managers must consider which types of salespersons will sell the firm's products most effectively. The three classifications of salespersons are order getters, order takers, and support personnel. Order getters inform both current customers and new prospects and persuade them to buy. Order takers seek repeat sales and fall into two categories: inside order takers and field order takers. Sales support personnel facilitate the selling function, but their duties usually extend beyond making sales. The three types of support personnel are missionary, trade, and technical salespersons.

The effectiveness of sales-force management is an important determinant of a firm's success because the sales force is directly responsible for generating an organization's sales revenue. The major decision areas and activities on which sales managers must focus are establishing sales-force objectives, determining sales-force size, recruiting and selecting salespeople, training sales personnel, compensating salespeople, motivating salespeople, managing sales territories, and controlling and evaluating the sales force.

Sales objectives should be stated in precise, measurable terms and specify the time period and the geographic areas involved. The size of the sales force must be adjusted from time to time because a firm's marketing plans change, as do markets and forces in the marketing environment.

Recruiting and selecting salespeople involves attracting and choosing the right type of salesperson to maintain an effective sales force. When developing a training program, managers must consider a variety of dimensions, such as who should be trained, what should be taught, and how the training should occur. Compensation of salespeople involves formulating and administrating a compensation plan that attracts, motivates, and holds the right types of salespeople for the firm. Motivation of salespeople should allow the firm to attain high productivity. Managing sales territories, another aspect of sales-force management, focuses on such factors as size, shape, routing, and scheduling. To control and evaluate sales-force performance, the sales manager must use information obtained through salespersons' call reports, customer feedback, and invoices.

Sales promotion is an activity or material (or both) that acts as a direct inducement, offering added value or incentive for the product, to resellers, salespersons, or consumers. Marketers use sales promotion to identify and attract new customers, to introduce a new product, and to increase reseller inventories. Sales promotion techniques fall into two general categories: consumer and trade. Consumer sales promotion methods encourage consumers to trade at specific stores or to try a specific product. These methods include coupons, demonstrations, frequent user incentives, free samples, money refunds, premiums, cents-off offers, and consumer sweepstakes and contests. Trade sales promotion techniques stimulate resellers to handle a manufacturer's products and market these products aggressively. These techniques include buy-back allowances, buying allowances, counts and recounts, free merchandise, merchandise allowances, cooperative advertising, dealer listings, premium or push money, sales contests, and dealer loaders.

IMPORTANT TERMS

Personal selling
Prospecting
Approach
Closing
Order getters
Order takers
Support personnel
Missionary salespersons
Trade salespersons
Technical salespersons
Recruiting
Straight salary compensation plan
Straight commission
    compensation plan
Combination compensation plan
Sales promotion
Consumer sales promotion
    techniques
Trade sales promotion
    methods
Coupons

Demonstrations
Trading stamps
Point-of-purchase
    (P-O-P) materials
Free samples
Money refunds
Premiums
Cents-off offer
Consumer contests
Consumer sweepstakes
Buy-back allowance
Buying allowance
Count and recount
Free merchandise
Merchandise allowance
Cooperative advertising
Dealer listing
Premium or push money
Sales contest
Dealer loader

Discussion and Review Questions

1. What is personal selling? How does personal selling differ from other types of promotional activities?
2. What are the primary purposes of personal selling?
3. Identify the elements of the personal selling process. Must a salesperson include all these elements when selling a product to a customer? Why or why not?
4. How does a salesperson find and evaluate prospects? Do you consider any of these methods questionable ethically?
5. Are order getters more aggressive or creative than order takers? Why or why not?
6. Identify several characteristics of effective sales objectives.
7. How should a sales manager establish criteria for selecting sales personnel? What are the general characteristics of a good salesperson?
8. What major issues or questions should be considered when developing a training program for the sales force?
9. Explain the major advantages and disadvantages of the three basic methods of compensating salespersons. In general, which method do you most prefer? Why?
10. What major factors should be taken into account when designing the size and shape of a sales territory?
11. How does a sales manager—who cannot be with each salesperson in the field on a daily basis—control the performance of sales personnel?
12. What is sales promotion? Why is it used?
13. For each of the following, identify and describe three techniques and give several examples: (a) consumer sales promotion methods and (b) trade sales promotion methods.
14. What types of sales promotion methods have you observed recently?

■ Cases

16.1 Fuller Brush

In 1906, Alfred Fuller went door to door selling the household brushes he made in his basement. Before long, he had an army of Fuller Brush people knocking on doors all over the country. Fuller salespeople are masters of personal selling. The Fuller selling technique involved nonstop talking and free samples. Alfred Fuller believed that if a salesperson could get inside a potential customer's door, a sale could be completed. He also felt that a belief in one's own ability to succeed was important in closing a sale. Today, the Fuller Brush Company, now owned by the Sara Lee Corporation, has become a leader in door-to-door sales and one of the most highly regarded manufacturers of household supplies in the country. Fuller Brush derives 50 percent of its income from sales in Mexico, where it employs 70,000 salespeople.

There are now about 13,000 Fuller Brush sales representatives in the United States (ranging in age from 17 to 85), down from 30,000 in the late 1960s. As the numbers have dwindled so too has the profile changed. Today's "Fuller Brush man" is likely to be a woman—80 percent of Fuller's sales force are now women. Ninety percent of the company's sales force is part time, but more people are making Fuller Brush a full-time job due to increased sales incentives, including such prizes as sailboats, televisions, and computers.

Although Fuller representatives still sell door to door, they usually call ahead to set up a time and date for making their sales presentation. A list of regular Fuller Brush customers in their region is given to each new salesperson, as well as mailing lists bought from Bloomingdale's and other department stores from which a potential client base can be built. Representatives generally do not sell over the telephone to new clients. Instead, the first call is spent telling the customer about the Fuller Brush Company. Crime-induced fear of strangers has decreased the effectiveness of the cold sales call in most areas.

Sales training for Fuller representatives has improved over the years. They usually maintain a low-key sales approach. Most favor a soft-sell approach because of the high quality of Fuller Brush products. Company representatives try to visit customers twice a month. Many salespeople leave catalogs so that the customers will have a full opportunity to decide what they want to purchase.

Fuller has cut its prices since 1984 and often discounts the prices of popular products to regular customers. The company has expanded its product line to include kitchen utensils and gardening tools, in addition to the traditional grooming products, brushes, and cleaning products. Despite the expansion of the product line—50 new products are introduced each year—Fuller does not advertise nationally. The company believes that advertising is unnecessary because customers already know about its products; however, commissions to salespeople have been increased to boost sales. Also, salespeople who successfully recruit a friend as a new representative in the sales force may receive up to 10 percent of the new recruit's sales.

Fuller is suffering from a problem common to other door-to-door marketing companies: a shrinking customer base. Almost 60 percent of all women today work outside the home, so it is often difficult for a Fuller representative to catch customers at home. To overcome this problem, Fuller distributed its first nationwide mail-order catalog in 1987. The company's '88 catalog won a Gold Award from the American Catalog Awards, Housewares Division. The catalog conveys the message of high quality products and personalized service.

Despite the shortcomings of personal selling door to door, well over half of Fuller's revenues still come from home sales. The company hopes that its mail-order catalog will boost sales even higher by introducing its products to a wider clientele.

SOURCES: "Brushing Up at Fuller," *Newsweek*, Sept. 7, 1987, p. 44; Teresa Burney, "Brushing Up a Reputation," *St. Petersburg (FL) Times*, Aug. 14, 1988; Gerald Carson, "The Fuller Brush Man," *American Heritage*, Aug.-Sept. 1986, pp. 26–31; "Fuller Brush Man Uses Soft Sell, Humor to Boost Sales," *Marketing News*, Jan. 18, 1988, p. 3; "Gold Award: Fuller Brush Has an Old-Fashioned Flair for Salesmanship," *Catalog Age*, Sept. 1989, pp. 87, 89; Kerry Hannon, "A Foot in the Door," *Forbes*, Oct. 20, 1986, pp. 134–136; Pamela J. Podger, "Fuller Brush: It's Sprucing Up Its Image," *Middlesex News*, Oct. 2, 1988; Harvey Shore, "Brush Strokes: The Life and Thought of Alfred C. Fuller (1885-1973)," *Business Quarterly*, Spring 1986, pp. 16–17.

Questions for Discussion

1. Why has Fuller Brush been so successful in door-to-door personal selling?
2. Discuss changes in the marketing environment that may impact the company's success in the 1990s.

16.2 Wilkinson Sword USA Develops Its Own Sales Force

In November 1984, Wilkinson Sword USA, the U.S. subsidiary of London-based Wilkinson Sword Ltd., consisted of only two persons: Norman Prolux, president, and Ronald Mineo, vice president of sales. For the previous thirty years, the company had relied on the sales forces of other companies to sell its line of razors and blades. The company decided that it needed to develop its own sales force to gain better control over its selling activities. According to vice president Mineo, with independent salespersons the company was not able to achieve the focus its product lines required to compete efficiently. All its competitors had their own sales forces. Once the decision had been made to establish an independent sales force, company president Prolux pointed out, "No longer will our products be sixteenth in line in the manufacturers' rep's bag." In less than two years, the firm grew to nearly a hundred employees, including thirty-four salespeople, through a careful recruitment and selection process.

Before recruiting and hiring the first new salesperson, Wilkinson developed marketing and sales strategy. Next, the company analyzed its existing and potential accounts. The account analysis identified twenty-five key accounts that would be assigned to two key account managers working out of Wilkinson's Atlanta headquarters. Another four hundred primary and secondary accounts would be divided among field salespeople and sales managers.

However, designing Wilkinson's sales force was easy compared to finding just the right people to fill the sales positions. The New York area was especially difficult to staff because the company had to find two truly exceptional salespeople who could be trusted with its multi-million dollar territories in the area. The fact that Prolux and Mineo had to function as salespeople themselves to maintain the business while attempting to recruit and hire permanent salespersons further complicated the process. Furthermore, Wilkinson set high standards for its sales force: it wanted salespeople with five years of experience in the better health and beauty aids companies. Its new hires included salespeople with experience at Procter & Gamble, Colgate, and Gillette.

Hiring experienced salespeople can be a costly proposition. Mineo estimates that the twenty-four salespeople hired during the first year cost the company $0.5 million in recruiting, training, salaries, bonuses, and related costs. In some cases, Wilkinson paid as much as $15,000 to an employment agency to lure one person. To ensure that it was offering competitive salaries, Wilkinson surveyed other firms in the field. Its strategy was to offer a compensation package at least as good as the competition and, in some cases, as much as 10 percent better.

In January 1985, Wilkinson began interviewing candidates for its new sales force. The first seven were hired by early February; and by the beginning of April, eight more had been hired. By mid-September, the company had hired twenty-four salespersons. Thus it took the firm nine months to find qualified and compatible salespersons. Plans were then approved to hire the last ten salespeople to complete the initial sales force.

The new Wilkinson sales force seemed to work out quite well from the beginning. Wilkinson Sword was acquired by Swedish Match in 1987, and the company's future looks positive. The company has begun hiring retail merchandisers to support its sales efforts by reducing out-of-stocks, building incremental facings and displays, and monitoring pricing.

SOURCES: Rayna Skolink, "The Birth of a Sales Force," *Sales & Marketing Management,* March 10, 1986, pp. 42–44; Jules Arbose, "Swedish Match Again Strikes Out in New Directions," *International Management* (U.K.) Oct. 1987, pp. 87–90; Gay Jervey, "Gillette, Wilkinson Heat Up Disposable Duel," *Advertising Age,* June 10, 1985, p. 12.

Questions for Discussion

1. What can Wilkinson expect to gain from having its own sales force?
2. Evaluate Wilkinson's approach to developing a sales force.

McDonald's Promotion

Ever since Ray Kroc founded the first McDonald's restaurant in April 1955, the number-one fast-food chain has inundated the world with strategic promotional campaigns and slick advertising. The sheer breadth of McDonald's advertising is astounding. While reading the morning newspaper, you may see an advertisement for an Egg McMuffin. In early afternoon you hear a radio commercial for a specially priced Quarter Pounder after 4 P.M.; in the evening you see a television commercial for a new Happy Meal premium guaranteed to tempt even the most discriminating children.

To understand the importance of McDonald's advertising, it helps to look back to the birth of McDonald's in the mid-1950s. After World War II, automobiles became a firm fixture in American lives. Suburban growth was on the upswing, spirits were high, and people became more concerned with time, or the lack of it. Patience seemed to have become a lost virtue. Some carhop hamburger establishments had developed reputations as teen hangouts. But at the local McDonald's, customers pulled up, got out of their cars and walked up to the window to order hamburgers, fries, and milkshakes. The service was always fast, and a McDonald's hamburger in Pittsburgh tasted the same as one in Peoria.

McDonald's Franchise Network

Ray Kroc instilled in McDonald's a strong commitment to standards of excellence best expressed in the firm's QSC&V creed—quality, service, cleanliness, and value. But perhaps most importantly, as it expanded, McDonald's developed a strong network of franchises. Especially in the beginning, the McDonald's franchisee was a small business person, an entrepreneur, who embraced Ray Kroc's philosophies. Kroc only sold single-unit franchises which, at the time, cost $950 and 1.9 percent of revenue. As franchises succeeded, so did McDonald's. To many, McDonald's hamburgers and French fries represented the standard by which future fast food companies were judged—companies such as Burger King, Wendy's, and Hardee's.

To ensure the success of its franchises and further its growth, McDonald's developed one of the most finely tuned advertising and promotional machines in the country. It has used only four different "umbrella" campaigns since 1979, ensuring that the advertising messages it communicated to consumers were consistent. The advertisements' effectiveness is highlighted in the fact that McDonald's has regularly ranked among the ten best-recalled advertisers in *Advertising Age's* AdWatch monthly surveys since the surveys were begun in 1982. In 1989, McDonald's spent approximately $1.1 billion in advertising and promotion. With nearly 11,000 restaurants and total sales of $17.5 billion, that figure represents approximately 6.3 percent of sales (see Figure 1). In fact, McDonald's is the most heavily advertised single brand in the U.S.

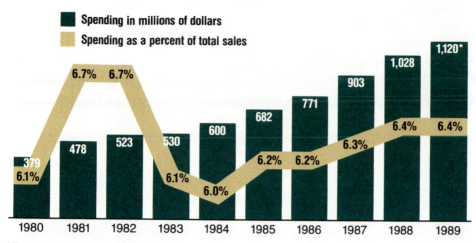

FIGURE 1 *McDonald's increasing promotion budget*

■ **Spending in millions of dollars**
▨ **Spending as a percent of total sales**

*Estimated by *Advertising Age*

SOURCE: Reprinted with permission from *Advertising Age,* January 1, 1990, Copyright Crain Communications, Inc. All rights reserved.

Market Segmentation

One secret ingredient in McDonald's promotion strategy is its ability to divide the fast-food market into specific segments and advertise directly and effectively to that segment. Target markets for McDonald's advertising include children, "tweens" (early teenagers), adults, blacks, and Hispanics. Within each of these categories there may be subcategories. A message targeted at adults, for example, may tell of a new product or promotion or remind consumers of an existing product. In addition, an adult-targeted message may tell parents about the current Happy Meal premium available, a tactic known by McDonald's as Adult Support of Youth.

McDonald's carefully schedules its broadcast commercials for specific times of the day (dayparts) and in programs that have the highest viewership (ratings) among their target audiences. For example, commercials promoting Happy Meals to children will be run in top-rated Saturday morning and after-school programming.

Breakdowns on ethnic viewership provided by radio and television stations allow McDonald's to target specific advertisements to those segments. To ensure that these advertisements are effective, McDonald's employs national black and Hispanic consumer advertising agencies as well as a national agency to handle network advertising and 56 local advertising agencies to support regional and local store marketing.

Fast-Food Promotion Trends

McDonald's has established a number of trends in fast-food promotion that have changed the way the industry does business. In 1981, the company introduced a contest promotion, the "Build a Big Mac" game card, to promote its Big Mac sandwich. Game cards are now a regularly used promotion technique by McDonald's and its competitors. Many McDonald's restaurants offer afternoon bingo games, with

McDonald's food and stuffed animals as prizes. Hungry bingo players, mostly senior citizens, have boosted sales before and after the scheduled games. McDonald's has also successfully introduced new products such as chicken McNuggets, popularizing finger foods in the fast-food industry, and the McChicken sandwich. McDonald's is now the second largest seller of chicken in the U.S., and number-one Kentucky Fried Chicken is facing a declining market share.

Competition from fast-food competitors Burger King, Hardee's, and Wendy's comes most frequently in the form of discounting. Tactically, McDonald's has responded with the Menu Song Contest, Scrabble, Happy Birthday Big Mac, Monopoly, and French Fry coupon promotions. Approximately 20 percent of the meal transactions in a single year involve some kind of discount.

One promotional tactic McDonald's uses to support sales growth, without discounting or expanding its menu to extremes, is successful limited-time products. Products such as Cheddar Melt and McRib are examples of limited-time products introduced to generate traffic without discounting. The company believes that such limited-time offerings encourage consumers to visit their local McDonald's more often to enjoy a new limited-time product, and such offerings allow uncompromised pricing integrity. Nevertheless, discount offers, such as 99-cent Big Macs or 49-cent hamburgers, are still very strong and pervasive competitive tools for McDonald's.

New products provide the greatest promise to break out of the discounting mode. McDonald's is experimenting with packaged celery and carrot sticks, cinnamon rolls, Western Omelet McMuffins, breakfast burritos, and pizza. Intense competition is causing relentless pursuit of each consumer's fast-food dollars. McDonald's is faced with a saturated market, changing consumer eating habits, and a short supply of teenagers to work behind its counters.

Public Relations

If McDonald's has a tagline or corporate image it would like to convey, it would be one of caring or giving back to its local communities. In 1984, the company built an Olympic swimming stadium in Los Angeles and became aggressively involved in national athletic sponsorships. After founder Ray Kroc died in 1984, the company created Ronald McDonald Children's Charities in his memory. Across the United States, Ronald McDonald Houses provide low-cost housing to families of young cancer patients. McDonald's support and concentration on public relations can also be seen on Little League fields, in fund-raising efforts, and in many schools across the country.

Ronald McDonald is perhaps the best known spokesperson in the world. With the Hamburglar, Grimace, and an occasional Birdie the Early Bird at his side, Ronald makes McDonald's come alive to children. The clown character talks of things children understand. McDonald's targets children at an early age, hoping the premiums, toys, coloring books, personal appearances by Ronald and company, and so on will foster children's loyalty to McDonald's. Stories abound of parents who have to drive an extra couple of blocks to avoid driving by McDonald's and setting their children off with cries of "I want a Happy Meal" or to play on the playground equipment.

The Future

McDonald's is highly concerned about where its growth may come from next. McDonald's sales are not showing the steady growth they did several years ago. In fact, on an inflation-adjusted basis, sales are flat. Price discounting by McDonald's and its competitors may be one factor behind the flattening sales. The competition is coming not only from hamburger chains but also from Pizza Hut (two for the price of one offers), Kentucky Fried Chicken (a bucket with fixin's for $9.95), and Taco Bell (which offers 59-cent tacos and burritos).

McDonald's is also fighting to maintain its image of quality and cleanliness. A survey by Consumer Network research group showed McDonald's receiving a 5.6 rating on a scale of 10 in overall customer satisfaction. McDonald's does not confirm such ratings, but recent television commercials have focused on cleanliness and service. One spot aired in 1989 replayed a 1970s commercial, "Grab a Bucket and Mop," showing McDonald's pride and teamwork. A labor shortage is contributing to McDonald's problems; a part of McDonald's advertising budget is now directed toward hiring new employees. The two main target markets are senior citizens and working mothers.

How will McDonald's endure into the twenty-first century? Probably the same way it has through the past three decades. The company will continue to rely on its effective promotion skills while learning to adapt those skills to new markets, such as Eastern Europe. Two McDonald's restaurants recently opened in Moscow; twenty more are planned for the Russian capital.

Questions for Discussion

1. Evaluate McDonald's approach to promotion. Contrast this with other familiar fast food restaurants (e.g., Wendy's, Burger King, Hardees, etc.).
2. What are the risks associated with the use of sales promotion?
3. What is the value to McDonald's of becoming so heavily involved in public relations activities?

SOURCES: Scott Hume, "McDonald's Fred Turner: Making All the Right Moves," *Advertising Age*, Jan. 1, 1990, pp. 6, 17; Scott Hume, "Fast-food Chains Do Menu Shuffle," *Advertising Age*, Aug. 14, 1989, p. 4; James Cox, "A Crack in the Golden Arches?" *USA Today*, July 27, 1989, p. 3B; Richard Gibson and Robert Johnson, "Big Mac, Cooling Off, Loses Its Sizzle," *Wall Street Journal*, Sept. 29, 1989, p. B1; John Iams and Julie Skur Hill, "Big Mac Ad Bites into Soviet TV," *Advertising Age*, January 15, 1990, p. 12; Robert Johnson, "McDonald's Combines A Dead Man's Advice with Lively Strategy," *Wall Street Journal*, Dec. 18, 1987, pp. 1, 13; Dennis Miemiec, "McDonald's Patrons Flip over Bingo," *Detroit Free Press*, January 12, 1989, p. F10; Penny Moser, "The McDonald's Mystique," *Fortune*, July 4, 1988, pp. 112–116.

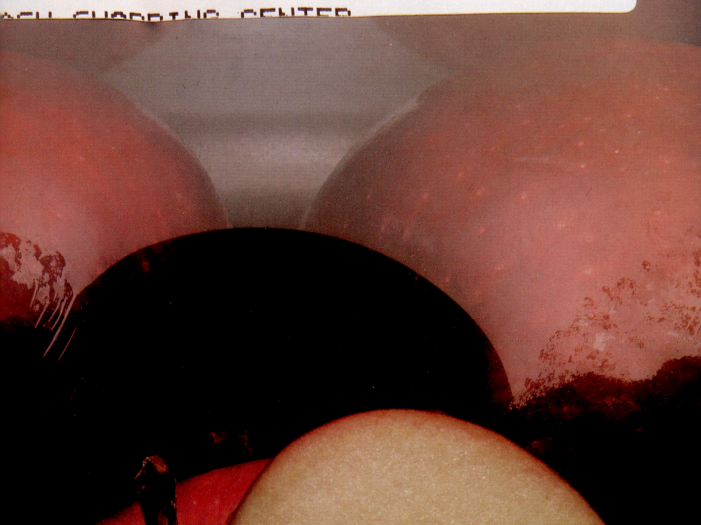

APPLES RED DEL 4 PACK

NET WT. lbs

TOTAL PRICE $

1.79

Price/lb. $

DEC 13   3005

DATE

30304 201796

Publix

PUBLIX SUPER MKTS., INC.
LAKELAND, FLA. 33802

V PRICING DECISIONS

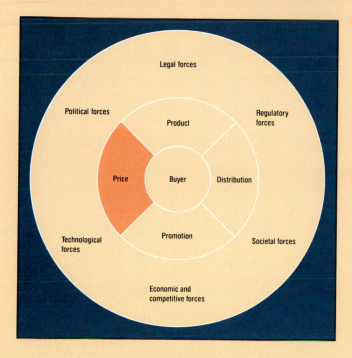

If an organization is to provide a satisfying marketing mix, the price must be acceptable to target market members. Pricing decisions can have numerous effects on other parts of the marketing mix. For example, a product's price can influence how customers perceive it, what types of marketing institutions are used in distributing the product, and how the product is promoted. In Chapter 17, we discuss the importance of price and look at some of the characteristics of price and nonprice competition. Then we examine the major factors that affect marketers' pricing decisions. Eight major stages used by marketers in establishing prices are discussed in Chapter 18. ◆

17 PRICING CONCEPTS

Objectives

To understand the nature and importance of price

To become aware of the characteristics of price and nonprice competition

To examine various pricing objectives

To explore key factors that may influence marketers' pricing decisions

To consider issues affecting the pricing of products for industrial markets

Status symbols are expensive by nature—sleek European sports cars, eighteen-karat gold watches, and ostrich-skin briefcases are all very costly. Though smaller and less expensive, fancy fountain pens have become a common sight in the hands of influential businesspeople. The pens carry hefty price tags and are much more difficult to maintain than ballpoints, porous point pens, or roller-ball pens. However, recent sales figures indicate that the once semi-obsolete fountain pen is making a comeback as the writing instrument of choice for status-minded individuals.

Of the premium-priced fountain pens, Montblanc pens are probably the most prestigious. Named after the highest mountain in Europe, German-made Montblanc fountain pens cost from about $150 to $7,400 (for a solid gold one). The most popular model costs about $475. Prestige pricing has worked well for Montblanc, placing the pen in the same category as Rolex watches, Porsche sunglasses, BMW automobiles, and Gucci luggage. Former president Ronald Reagan, British prime minister Margaret Thatcher, and fictional super-spy James Bond all use Montblanc pens.

Parker also makes high-priced "power" pens, bringing back its Duofold model that was popular during the 1920s. The Duofold comes in a blue and maroon marbled finish and sells for about $250. Waterman and S.T. Dupont also sell fine fountain pens. The Waterman Le Man series comes in seven sizes and the pens are priced at around $225. Dupont pens have a distinctive Chinese lacquer finish and are priced from $295 to $400 (for the gold-flecked models). ◆

Photo by Michael Grecco/Stock, Boston.

Based on information in Michelle Hill, "Writing in Rarefied Air," *Bridgewater Courier-News* (Bridgewater, N.J.), June 25, 1989, pp. G1, G2; Allen Norwood, "Pen Offers Status—At Only $295," *Charlotte Observer,* (Charlotte, N.C.), Nov. 20, 1988, pp. 1C, 3C; and Sharon Schlegel, "Fountain Pens Ink New Success as Status Symbols," *Chicago Sun-Times,* Mar. 26, 1989.

These companies are using price, along with other elements, to distinguish their pens from competitive brands and to give them an exclusive, upscale image. As in the case of these firms, pricing is a crucial element in most organizations' marketing mixes. In this chapter we focus first on the nature of price and its importance to marketers. Then we consider some of the characteristics of price and nonprice competition. Next we explore the various types of pricing objectives that marketers may establish, and we examine in some detail the numerous factors that can influence pricing decisions. Finally, we discuss selected issues related to the pricing of products for industrial markets.

THE NATURE OF PRICE

To a buyer, **price** is the value placed on what is exchanged. Something of value —usually buying power—is exchanged for satisfaction or utility. As described in Chapter 2, buying power depends on a buyer's income, credit, and wealth. It is a mistake to believe that price is always money paid or some other financial consideration. In fact, trading of products—**barter**—is the oldest form of exchange. Money may or may not be involved.

Buyers' interest in price stems from their expectations about the usefulness of a product or the satisfaction they may derive from it. Because buyers have limited resources, they must allocate their buying power so that they can obtain the most desired products. Buyers must decide whether the utility gained in an exchange is worth the buying power sacrificed. Almost anything of value—ideas, services, rights, and goods—can be assessed by a price because in our society the financial price is the measurement of value commonly used in exchanges. Thus a painting by Picasso may be valued, or priced, at $2 million. Financial price, then, quantifies value. It is the basis of most market exchanges.

■ Terms Used to Describe Price

Price is expressed in different terms for different exchanges. For instance, automobile insurance companies charge a *premium* for protection from the cost of injuries or repairs stemming from an automobile accident. An officer who stops you for speeding writes a ticket that requires you to pay a *fine*. If a lawyer defends you, a *fee* is charged, and if you use a railway or taxi, a *fare* is charged. A *toll* is charged for the use of bridges or turnpikes. *Rent* is paid for the use of equipment or an apartment. A *commission* is remitted to an agent for the sale of real estate. *Dues* are paid for membership in a club or group. A *deposit* is made to hold or lay away merchandise. A *tip* helps pay waitresses or waiters for their services. *Interest* is charged for the loan that you obtain, and *taxes* are paid for government services. The value of many products is called *price*. Although price may be expressed in a variety of ways, it is important to remember that the purpose of this concept is to quantify and express the value of the items in a market exchange.

■ The Importance of Price to Marketers

As pointed out in Chapter 9, developing a product may be a lengthy process. It takes time to plan promotion and to communicate benefits. Distribution usually requires a long-term commitment to dealers who will handle the product. Often price is the only thing a marketer can change quickly to respond to changes in demand or to the actions of competitors. Bear in mind, however, that under certain circumstances the price variable may be relatively inflexible.

Price is also a key element in the marketing mix because it relates directly to the generation of total revenue. The following equation is an important one for the entire organization:

$$\text{Profits} = \text{Total Revenues} - \text{Total Costs}$$

or

$$\text{Profits} = (\text{Prices} \times \text{Quantities Sold}) - \text{Total Costs}$$

Prices affect an organization's profits, which are its lifeblood for long-term survival. Price affects the profit equation in several ways. It directly influences the equation because it is a major component. It has an indirect impact because it can be a major determinant of the quantities sold. Even more indirectly, price influences total costs through its impact on quantities sold.

Because price has a psychological impact on customers, marketers can use it symbolically. By raising a price, they can emphasize the quality of a product and try to increase the status associated with its ownership. By lowering a price, they can emphasize a bargain and attract customers who go out of their way—spending extra time and effort—to save a small amount. Price can have a strong effect on sales.

Price and Nonprice Competition

A product offering can compete on a price or nonprice basis. The choice will affect not only pricing decisions and activities, but also those associated with other marketing mix decision variables.

■ Price Competition

When **price competition** is used, a marketer emphasizes price as an issue and matches or beats the prices of competitors. As discussed in Marketing Update 17.1, Bic engages in price competition by pricing its perfume at $5.00 and emphasizing price in its advertisements. To compete effectively on a price basis, a firm should be the low-cost producer of the product. If all firms producing goods in an industry charge the same price, the firm with the lowest costs is the most profitable. Firms that stress low price as a key element in the marketing mix tend to produce standardized products. A seller using price competition may change prices frequently or at least must be willing and able to do so. Whenever competitors change their prices, the seller must respond quickly and aggressively. As shown in Figure 17.1, the U.S. Postal Service and United Parcel Service engage in direct price competition in their pricing of overnight air express services.

Price competition gives a marketer flexibility. Prices can be altered to account for changes in the firm's costs or in demand for the product. If competitors try to gain market share by cutting prices, an organization competing on a price basis can react quickly to such efforts. However, a major drawback of price competition is that competitors, too, have the flexibility to adjust their prices. Thus they can quickly match or beat an organization's price cuts. A price war may result, as has occurred in the fast-food industry. When the Taco Bell and Wendy's chains reduced the price of many of their menu items to less than $1, other fast-food chains were forced to lower prices or offer specials to remain competitive. McDonald's is offering

BIC PERFUME ENGAGES IN PRICE COMPETITION

The Milford, Connecticut–based Bic Corp., known for its disposable lighters, shavers, and pens, has entered the perfume business. By diversifying, Bic is attempting to subsidize its profitable core products. With more individuals becoming health-conscious and fewer and fewer people smoking, Bic executives realize that future sales of Bic lighters—Bic's largest and most profitable line—will probably drop sharply. Furthermore, Bic's shavers are facing increasing competition from companies such as Gillette and a host of foreign challengers; and, though Bic still controls 50 percent of the pen market, Gillette's Paper Mate, Write Brothers, and Flair pens are making gains. The growing popularity of Mitsubishi Pencil Co.'s metal-point roller pens, currently holding a ten percent market share, has also weakened Bic's market position.

Bic's French parent company, Société Bic (which owns 61 percent of Bic), introduced a fragrance line in Europe in 1988, hoping to capitalize on the $3 billion retail perfume market. Later that year, Bic launched the perfumes in the United States. Though some analysts think that Bic will certainly fail in an industry where a glamorous image is so important, Bic hopes to attract consumers with low prices.

Imported from France, Bic's four fragrances—Parfum Bic Jour, Parfum Bic Nuit, Parfum Bic for men, and Parfum Bic Sport—sell for about five dollars for a quarter-ounce bottle. Bic packages the perfumes in unbreakable glass spray bottles with a specially developed atomizer that delivers about a third less perfume than other pumps, providing about 300 sprays per bottle. Bic hopes the fragrances will attract men and women between the ages of 18 and 40 because of their portability and fun image, as well as their low prices. Société Bic, the actual manufacturer of the products, has focused on improving the production process while maintaining quality to increase sales volume and keep prices low.

Bic supported the introduction of its perfumes into the United States with a $20 million advertising and promotions budget that stressed the product's price. The fragrances have been popular in Europe, and Bic executives hope that the perfumes—sold at locations next to their lighters, shavers, and pens—will also become the first successful mass-marketed fragrances in the United States.

SOURCES: "Bic Begins Campaign for New Perfume Line," *New York Times,* Mar. 20, 1989, p. D9; "Bic Counts on a New Age for Spray Perfume," *New York Times,* Oct. 17, 1988, p. 28; "France's Bic Bets U.S. Customers Will Go for Perfume on the Cheap," *Wall Street Journal,* Jan. 12, 1989, p. B4; Resa W. King, "Will $4 Perfume Do the Trick for Bic?" *Business Week,* June 20, 1988, pp. 89, 92.

FIGURE 17.1 *Price competition.*
Overnight air express organizations compete on the basis of price.

coupons, and many other fast-food restaurants offer 99 cent sandwiches.[1] Furthermore, if a user of price competition is forced to raise prices, competing firms that are not under the same pressures may decide not to raise their prices.

■ Nonprice Competition

Nonprice competition occurs when a seller elects not to focus on price and instead emphasizes distinctive product features, service, product quality, promotion, packaging, or other factors to distinguish its product from competing brands. Thus nonprice competition is based on factors other than price. Nonprice competition gives an organization the opportunity to increase its brand's unit sales through means other than changing the brand's price. As shown in Figure 17.2, John Deere, for instance, does not compete on a price basis but instead offers a money-back trial period for its lawn mowers. One major advantage of nonprice competition is that a firm can build customer loyalty toward its brand. If customers prefer a brand because of nonprice issues, they may not be easily lured away by competing firms and brands. Customers whose primary attraction to a store is based on nonprice factors are less likely to leave their regular store for a lower competitive price. Price

---

1. Udayan Gupta and Jeffrey A. Tannenbaum, "Casualties in the Fast-Food Price Wars," *Wall Street Journal*, Oct. 23, 1989, p. B1.

FIGURE 17.2

Nonprice competition.
For its lawn mowers,
John Deere uses non-
price competition by pro-
moting issues other than
price.

THE JOHN DEERE PROMISE.
NO UNHAPPY RETURNS.

What you see in front of you is our new 1989 walk-behind. It comes with a durable easy-starting engine, a 5-speed shift-on-the-go transmission and an easy on/off rear bagger.

It also comes with something else, our John Deere Promise: "Test drive it for a full month. If you don't agree it's the best mower you've ever used, you can bring it

back for a full refund." That's some offer. But then, it's some mower. To locate your nearest participating dealer, call 1-800-544-2122.

NOTHING RUNS LIKE A DEERE®

SOURCE: Deere and Company

is not the most durable factor from the standpoint of maintaining customer loyalty.[2] But when price is the primary reason that customers buy a particular brand, the competition can attract such customers through price cuts.

Nonprice competition is workable under the right conditions. A company must be able to distinguish its brand through unique product features, higher quality, customer service, promotion, packaging, and the like. Buyers not only must be able to perceive these distinguishing characteristics but must also view them as desirable. The distinguishing features that set a particular brand apart from its competitors should be difficult, if not impossible, for competitors to imitate. Finally, the organization must extensively promote the distinguishing characteristics of the brand to establish its superiority and to set it apart from competitors in the minds of buyers.

Foreign firms put less emphasis on price than do their U.S. counterparts. They look for a competitive edge by concentrating on promotion, research and development, marketing research, and marketing channel considerations. In a study of pricing strategy, five foreign firms stated specifically that they emphasize research

2. Michael J. O'Connor, "What Is the Logic of a Price War?" Arthur Andersen & Company, *International Trends in Retailing*, Spring 1986.

and development and technological superiority; competition based on price was seldom a major marketing consideration.[3]

A marketer attempting to compete on a nonprice basis is still not able to simply ignore competitors' prices, however. The organization must be aware of competitors' prices and will probably price its brand near or slightly above competing brands. As an example, Sony sells television sets in a highly competitive market and charges higher prices for its sets; but it is successful nonetheless. Sony's emphasis on high product quality both distinguishes it from its competitors and allows it to set higher prices. Therefore, price still remains a crucial marketing mix component in situations that call for nonprice competition.

PRICING OBJECTIVES

Pricing objectives are overall goals that describe what the firm wants to achieve through its pricing efforts. Because pricing objectives influence decisions in most functional areas—including finance, accounting, and production—the objectives must be consistent with the organization's overall mission and purpose. Since deregulation, banks have become more interested in pricing. As competition intensified, bank executives realized that their products had to be priced to meet not only short-term profit goals, but also long-term strategic objectives.[4] Because of the many areas involved, a marketer often uses multiple pricing objectives. In this section we look at a few of the typical pricing objectives that companies might set for themselves.

■ Survival

A fundamental pricing objective is survival. Most organizations will tolerate difficulties such as short-run losses and internal upheaval if they are necessary for survival. Because price is a flexible and convenient variable to adjust, it is sometimes used to increase sales volume to levels that match the organization's expenses.

■ Profit

Although businesses may claim that their objective is to maximize profits for their owners, the objective of profit maximization is rarely operational because its achievement is difficult to measure. Because of this difficulty, profit objectives tend to be set at levels that the owners and top-level decision makers view as satisfactory. Specific profit objectives may be stated in terms of actual dollar amounts or in terms of percentage change relative to the profits of a previous period.

■ Return on Investment

Pricing to attain a specified rate of return on the company's investment is a profit-related pricing objective. Most pricing objectives based on return on investment (ROI) are achieved by trial and error because not all cost and revenue data needed to project the return on investment are available when prices are set. General Motors, for example, uses ROI pricing objectives.

The objective of return on investment may be used less as managers and marketers in diversified companies stress the creation of shareholder value. When share-

3. Saeed Samier, "Pricing in Marketing Strategies of U.S. and Foreign-Based Companies," *Journal of Business Research,* 1987, pp. 15–23.

4. Robert P. Ford, "Pricing Operating Services," *Bankers Magazine,* May-June 1987.

holder value is used as a performance objective, strategies—including those involving price—are evaluated on the basis of the impact they will have on the value investors perceive in the firm.[5]

Market Share

Market share, which is a product's sales in relation to total industry sales, can be an appropriate pricing objective. Many firms establish pricing objectives to maintain or increase market share. For example, Volkswagen AG cut prices on its 1990 model Jettas, Golfs, Cabriolets, and Vanagons by 5 to 14 percent, and introduced two new models—the Corrado and Passat—at lower than expected prices to boost its share of the U.S. automobile market from its present 1.3 percent.[6]

Maintaining or increasing market share need not depend on growth in industry sales. Remember that an organization can increase its market share even though sales for the total industry are decreasing. On the other hand, an organization's sales volume may, in fact, increase while its market share within the industry decreases, assuming that the overall market is growing.

Cash Flow

Some organizations set prices to recover cash as fast as possible. Financial managers are understandably interested in quickly recovering capital spent to develop products. This objective may have the support of the marketing manager who anticipates a short product life cycle.

Although it may be acceptable in some situations, the use of cash flow and recovery as an objective oversimplifies the value of price in contributing to profits. A disadvantage of this pricing objective could be high prices, which might allow competitors with lower prices to gain a large share of the market.

Status Quo

In some cases, an organization may be in a favorable position and, desiring nothing more, may set an objective of status quo. Status quo objectives can focus on several dimensions—maintaining a certain market share, meeting (but not beating) competitors' prices, achieving price stability, or maintaining a favorable public image. A status quo pricing objective can reduce a firm's risks by helping stabilize demand for its products. The use of status quo pricing objectives sometimes minimizes pricing as a competitive tool, leading to a climate of nonprice competition in an industry.

Product Quality

A company might have the objective of product quality leadership in the industry. For example, AM International, an industrial marketer of graphics equipment and supplies, has said that one of its organizational objectives is to be ranked within two years as one of the top two firms in its industry in terms of product quality and customer satisfaction.[7] This goal normally dictates a high price to cover the high product quality and, in some instances, the high cost of research and development. Cross pens, shown in Figure 17.3, are premium-priced to cover high production costs and to help maintain its high quality image.

5. George S. Day and Liam Fahey, "Valuing Market Strategies," *Journal of Marketing*, July 1988, pp. 45–57.

6. David Landis, "It's Cutting Prices to Win Lost Ground," *USA Today*, Oct. 4, 1989, pp. 1B, 2B.

7. *AM International 1989 Annual Report*, p. 5.

FIGURE 17.3

Product quality pricing objective.
Cross pens carry a high price to cover high production costs and to help maintain a high quality image.

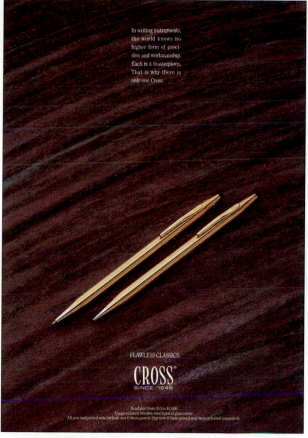

SOURCE: Courtesy A.T. Cross Co.

FACTORS AFFECTING PRICING DECISIONS

Pricing decisions can be complex because of the number of details that must be considered. Frequently there is considerable uncertainty about the reactions to price on the part of buyers, channel members, competitors, and others. Price is also an important consideration in marketing planning, market analysis, and sales forecasting. It is a major issue when assessing a brand's position relative to competing brands. Most factors that affect pricing decisions can be grouped into one of the eight categories shown in Figure 17.4. In this section we explore how each of these eight groups of factors enters into price decision making.

■ **Organizational and Marketing Objectives**

Marketers should set prices that are consistent with the organization's goals and mission. For example, a retailer trying to position itself as value oriented may wish to set prices that are quite reasonable relative to product quality. In this case, a marketer would not want to set premium prices on products but would strive to price products in line with this overall organizational goal.

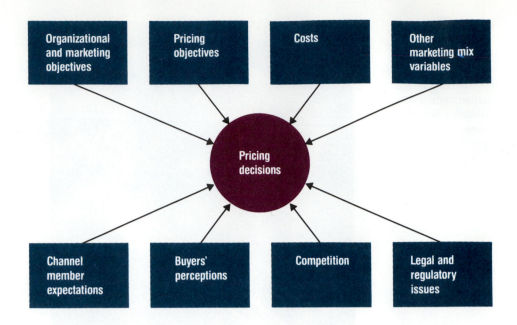

FIGURE 17.4
Factors that affect pricing decisions

- Organizational and marketing objectives
- Pricing objectives
- Costs
- Other marketing mix variables

Pricing decisions

- Channel member expectations
- Buyers' perceptions
- Competition
- Legal and regulatory issues

The firm's marketing objectives must also be considered. Decision makers should make pricing decisions that are compatible with the organization's marketing objectives. Say, for instance, that one of a producer's marketing objectives is a 12 percent increase in unit sales by the end of the next year. Assuming that buyers are price sensitive, increasing the price or setting a price above the average market price would not be in line with the firm's sales objective. For example, Polaroid Corp. chose to focus on price when developing the marketing strategy for its Impulse instant camera. The Impulse complements the Spectra camera, a much-higher-priced product in the category. Although the Spectra has been quite successful, Polaroid executives believed that there was a need for new products at a low cost. Polaroid has chosen price as the key variable in its advertising campaign for the Impulse camera.[8]

■ Types of Pricing Objectives

The type of pricing objectives a marketer uses obviously will have considerable bearing on the determination of prices. An objective of a certain target return on investment requires that prices be set at a level that will generate a sales volume high enough to yield the specified target. A market share pricing objective usually causes a firm to price a product below competing brands of similar quality to attract competitors' customers to the company's brand. This type of pricing can lead to lower profits. A marketer sometimes uses temporary price reductions in the hope of gaining market share. A cash flow pricing objective may cause an organization to set a relatively high price, which can place the product at a competitive disadvantage. On the other hand, a cash flow pricing objective sometimes results in a long, sustained low price. However, this type of objective is more likely to be addressed by using temporary price reductions, such as sales, rebates, and special discounts.

8. "Polaroid to Introduce New Instant Camera," *Adweek's Marketing Week,* Jan. 11, 1988, p. 3.

■ Costs

Obviously, costs must be an issue when establishing price. A firm may temporarily sell products below cost to match competition, to generate cash flow, or even to increase market share, but in the long run it cannot survive by selling its products below cost. Even when a firm has a high-volume business, it cannot survive if each item is sold slightly below what it costs. A marketer should be careful to analyze all costs so that they can be included in the total cost associated with a product.

Besides considering the costs associated with a particular product, marketers must also take into account the costs that the product shares with others in the product line. Products often share some costs, particularly the costs of research and development, production, and distribution. Services are especially subject to cost sharing. For example, the costs of a bank building are spread over the costs of all services the bank offers.[9] Most marketers view a product's cost as a minimum, or floor, below which the product cannot be priced. We discuss cost analysis in more detail in the next chapter and in Chapter 20.

■ Other Marketing Mix Variables

All marketing mix variables are highly interrelated. Pricing decisions can influence decisions and activities associated with product, distribution, and promotion variables. A product's price frequently affects the demand for the item. A high price, for instance, may result in low unit sales, which in turn may lead to higher production costs per unit. Conversely, lower per-unit production costs may result from a low price. For many products, buyers associate better product quality with a high price and poorer product quality with a low price. This perceived price-quality relationship influences customers' overall image of products or brands. The price sometimes determines the degree of status associated with ownership of the product.

Pricing decisions influence the number of competing brands in a product category. When a firm introduces a product, sets a relatively high price, and achieves high unit sales, competitors may be attracted to this product category. If a firm uses a low price, the low profit margin may be unattractive to potential competition.

The price of a product is linked to several dimensions of its distribution. Premium-priced products often are marketed through selective or exclusive distribution; lower-priced products in the same product category may be sold through intensive distribution. For example, Cross pens are distributed through selective distribution and Bic pens through intensive distribution. The manner in which a product is stored and transported may also be associated with its price. When a producer is developing the price of a product, the profit margins of marketing channel members such as wholesalers and retailers must be considered. Channel members must be adequately compensated for the functions they perform. Inadequately compensated channel members will withdraw from a marketing channel.

The way a product is promoted can be affected by its price. Bargain prices are often included in advertisements, whereas premium prices are less likely to appear in advertising messages. The issue of a premium price is sometimes included in advertisements for upscale items, such as luxury cars or fine jewelry. Higher-priced products are more likely to require personal selling efforts than lower-priced ones. A customer may purchase an inexpensive watch in a self-service environment but hesitate to buy an expensive watch in the same store, if it is available there.

9. Joseph P. Guiltinan, "The Price-Bundling of Services: A Normative Framework," *Journal of Marketing*, April 1987, pp. 74–85.

The price structure can affect a salesperson's relationship with customers. A complex pricing structure takes longer to explain to customers, is more likely to confuse the buyer, and may cause misunderstandings that result in long-term customer dissatisfaction. For example, the pricing structures of many airlines are complex and frequently confuse ticket sales agents and travelers alike.

■ Channel Member Expectations

When making price decisions, a producer must consider what distribution channel members (such as wholesalers and retailers) expect. A channel member certainly expects to receive a profit for the functions it performs. The amount of profit expected depends on what the intermediary could make if it were handling a competing product instead. Also, the amount of time and the resources required to carry the product influence intermediaries' expectations.

Channel members often expect producers to provide discounts for large orders and quick payment. (Discounts are discussed later in this chapter.) At times, resellers expect producers to provide several support activities, such as sales training, service training, repair advisory service, cooperative advertising, sales promotions, and perhaps a program for returning unsold merchandise to the producer. These support activities clearly have costs associated with them, and a producer must consider these costs when determining prices. Failure to price the product so that the producer can provide some of these support activities may cause resellers to view the product less favorably.

■ Buyers' Perceptions

One important question that marketers should assess when making price decisions is "How important is the price to people in the target market?" The importance of price is not absolute; it can vary from market segment to market segment and from person to person. Members of one market segment may be more sensitive to price than members in a different target market. Moreover, the importance of price will vary across different product categories. Price may be a more important factor in the purchase of gasoline than in the purchase of a pair of jeans because buyers may be more sensitive to the price of gasoline than to the price of jeans.

For numerous products, buyers have a range of acceptable prices. This range can be fairly narrow in some product categories but wider in others. A marketer should become aware of the acceptable range of prices in the relevant product category. (This issue and related ones are discussed in more detail in Chapter 18.)

Consumers' perceptions of price may also be influenced by all products in a firm's product line. The perception of price depends on a product's actual price, plus the consumer's reference price—that is, the consumer's expectation of price. Exposure to a range of prices in a product line affects the consumer's expectations and perceptions of acceptable prices.[10]

Buyers' perceptions of a product relative to competing products may allow or encourage a firm to set a price that differs significantly from the prices of competing products. If the product is deemed superior to most of the competition, a premium price may be feasible. Strong brand loyalty sometimes provides the opportunity to charge a premium price. Schwinn, for instance, has developed strong customer loyalty for its high-quality bicycles (see Figure 17.5). Thus, it is able to charge premium prices for its products. On the other hand, if buyers view the product

10. Susan M. Petroshius and Kent B. Monroe, "Effect of Product-Line Pricing Characteristics on Product Evaluations," *Journal of Consumer Research,* March 1988, pp. 511–519.

FIGURE 17.5

Pricing according to buyers' perceptions. Schwinn is able to charge premium prices for its products because it has developed strong customer loyalty for its high-quality bicycles.

Remember your first Schwinn?

Schwinn. It was the name everyone wanted on their bike. You were proud if you owned one, envious if you didn't. Quite simply, it was the best there was.

Well, if you loved one then, you oughta see one now! Introducing the 1989 Schwinn bicycles—a whole new line of All-Terrain and Lightweight bicycles. Everything from contemporary sport models all the way to high performance racers. With lighter, more ergonomic frames. And smoother, easier shifting and braking than you've ever known before.

Along with the new technology comes the quality that's been synonymous with Schwinn for over 90 years. Backed by the service of the Schwinn dealer, and the "No-Time-Limit" warranty* for which Schwinn is famous.

So, drop in at your Authorized Schwinn Dealer today (see the Yellow Pages under bicycles) and get a look at the all-new Schwinn bikes for 1989. They're even better than you remember!

SCHWINN CYCLING AND FITNESS

If you loved one then, you oughta see one now!

*See your Authorized Schwinn Dealer for details.

SOURCE: Courtesy Schwinn Bicycle Company

unfavorably (assuming that they are not extremely negative), a lower price may be required to generate sales. There is a considerable body of research on the relationship between price and consumers' perceptions of quality. Consumers use price as an indicator of quality when brands are unfamiliar, and the perceived risk of making unsatisfactory choices is high. They also rely on price if there is little information available and judging a product's attributes is difficult.[11]

■ Competition

A marketer needs to know competitors' prices so that the firm can adjust its own prices accordingly. This does not mean that a company will necessarily match competitors' prices; it may set its price above or below theirs. However, matching competitors' fares is an important strategy for survival in the airline industry.[12] As indicated in Marketing Update 17.2, US Sprint monitors competitors' prices in an attempt to price its services approximately 10 percent below competitive services.

11. Valerie A. Zeithaml, "Consumer Perceptions of Price, Quality and Value: A Means-End Model and Synthesis of Evidence," *Journal of Marketing,* July 1988, pp. 2–22.

12. Andrew T. Chalk and John A. Steiber, "Managing the Airlines in the 1990's," *Journal of Business Strategy,* Winter 1987, pp. 87–91.

US SPRINT FACES STRONG PRICE COMPETITION

US Sprint Communications Co., based in Kansas City, Missouri, has come from a constantly declining market share and near bankruptcy to become a viable and growing telecommunications company. Before Sprint's recovery, its executives were having constant problems with high operating and equipment costs and an inefficient billing system. Though American Telephone & Telegraph (AT&T) and MCI Communications Corp. control 68 percent and 12 percent, respectively, of the long-distance telephone market, which is worth $50 billion a year, Sprint officials are proud of the 8 percent market share they hold. They are prouder still of the gains that they are making. The CEO of Sprint has indicated that Sprint's goal is to rise above the competition to become the best telecommunications company in the world.

With a new billing system and a superefficient fiber-optic telecommunications network, Sprint executives believe that they are ready to battle the telecommunications giants. Sprint's telephone and data communications "switched services" provide the company with less expensive means of channeling calls and data than the conventional methods used by AT&T and MCI.

Besides a more aggressive marketing campaign and a larger advertising budget, Sprint executives are using pricing to wrest customers away from AT&T. Sprint officials have set their prices at about 10 percent below those of AT&T. With prices at that level, Sprint can keep taking away business from AT&T without antagonizing the giant into a price war that Sprint would likely lose. Sprint's strategy seems to be working effectively.

Sprint officials also want to increase their international presence. Because AT&T's international pricing is regulated, Sprint can set considerably lower prices. As a result, Sprint's share of the international market is expanding.

SOURCES: Bob Brown, "AT&T Losing Ground to MCI, US Sprint," *Network World,* Sept. 20, 1988, pp. 9–10; Paul R. Strauss, "Ready to Switch? Dial Up Services Faring Better Against Leased Lines," *Data Communications,* December 1988, pp. 56, 58; and William C. Symonds, "People Aren't Laughing at US Sprint Anymore," *Business Week,* July 31, 1989, pp. 82–83, 86.

SOURCE: American Isuzu Motors, Inc.

When adjusting prices, a marketer must assess how competitors will respond. Will competitors change their prices (some, in fact, may not), and if so, will they raise or lower them? For example, is it likely that the maker of the $35,000 Range Rover will change its price based on the pricing of the Isuzu Trooper shown in Figure 17.6? In Chapter 2 we describe several types of competitive market structures. The structure that characterizes the industry to which a firm belongs affects the flexibility of price setting.

When an organization operates as a monopoly and is unregulated, it can set whatever prices the market will bear. However, the company may avoid pricing the product at the highest possible level for fear of inviting government regulation or because it wants to penetrate a market by using a lower price. If the monopoly is regulated, it normally has less pricing flexibility; the regulatory body lets it set prices that generate a reasonable, but not excessive, return. A government-owned monopoly may price products below cost to make them accessible to people who otherwise could not afford them. Transit systems, for example, are sometimes operated this way. However, government-owned monopolies sometimes charge higher prices to control demand. In states with state-owned liquor stores, the price of liquor tends to be higher than in states where liquor stores are not owned by a government body.

In an oligopoly there are only a few sellers and there are high barriers to competitive entry. The automotive, mainframe-computer, and steel industries exemplify oligopolies. A firm in such industries can raise its price, hoping that its competitors will do the same. When an organization cuts its price to gain a competitive edge, other firms are likely to follow suit. Thus very little is gained through price cuts in an oligopolistic market structure.

A market structure characterized by monopolistic competition means numerous sellers with differentiated product offerings. The products are differentiated by physical characteristics, features, quality, and brand images. The distinguishing characteristics of its product may allow a company to set a different price than its competitors. However, firms engaged in a monopolistic competitive market structure are likely to practice nonprice competition, discussed earlier in this chapter.

Under conditions of perfect competition, there are many sellers. Buyers view all sellers' products as the same. All firms sell their products at the going market price, and buyers will not pay more than that. This type of market structure, then, gives a marketer no flexibility in setting prices.

■ Legal and Regulatory Issues

At times government action sways marketers' pricing decisions. To curb inflation, the federal government may invoke price controls, "freeze" prices at certain levels, or determine the rates at which prices can be increased. In some states, regulatory agencies set prices on such products as insurance, dairy goods, and electricity.

Many regulations and laws affect pricing decisions and activities. The Sherman Antitrust Act prohibits conspiracies to control prices, and in interpretating the act, courts have ruled that price fixing among firms in an industry is illegal. Not only must marketers refrain from fixing prices; they must also develop independent pricing policies and set prices in ways that do not even suggest collusion. Both the Federal Trade Commission Act and the Wheeler-Lea Act prohibit deceptive pricing. In establishing prices, marketers must not deceive customers.

The Robinson-Patman Act has had a strong impact on pricing decisions. For various reasons, marketers may wish to sell the same type of product at different prices. Provisions in the Robinson-Patman Act, as well as those in the Clayton Act, limit the use of such price differentials. If price differentials tend to lessen or injure competition, they are considered discriminatory and are forbidden. However, not all price differentials are discriminatory. Marketers can use them for a product if any one of the following conditions is satisfied:

1. The price differentials do not injure or lessen competition.
2. The price differentials result from differences in the costs of selling to various customers.
3. The customers are not competitors.
4. The price differentials arise because the firm has had to cut its price to a particular buyer to meet competitors' prices.

Until 1975, manufacturers of consumer goods could set and enforce minimum retail prices for their products in some states. Now the Consumer Goods Pricing Act prohibits the use of price maintenance agreements among producers and resellers involved in interstate commerce.

Retailers and wholesalers in states that have effective unfair trade practices acts are limited in their use of pricing as a competitive tool. Because such acts place a "floor" under prices that retailers and wholesalers can regularly charge, marketers who compete on the basis of price must be aware of legal constraints on their competitors' pricing policies.

PRICING FOR INDUSTRIAL MARKETS

As previously mentioned, industrial markets consist of individuals and organizations that purchase products for resale, for use in their own operations, or for producing other products. Establishing prices for this category of buyers is sometimes different from setting prices for consumers. Industrial marketers have experienced much change because of economic uncertainty, sporadic supply shortages, and an increasing interest in service. Differences in the size of purchases, geographic factors, and transportation considerations require sellers to adjust prices. In this section, we discuss several issues unique to the pricing of industrial products, including discounts, geographic pricing, transfer pricing, and price discrimination.

■ Price Discounting

Producers commonly provide intermediaries with discounts off list prices. Although there are many types of discounts, they usually fall into one of five categories: trade, quantity, cash, seasonal discounts, and allowances.

Trade Discounts. A reduction off the list price given by a producer to a middleman for performing certain functions is called a **trade**, or **functional**, **discount**. A trade discount is usually stated in terms of a percentage or series of percentages off the list price. Middlemen are given trade discounts as compensation for performing various functions, such as selling, transporting, storing, final processing, and perhaps providing credit services. Although certain trade discounts are often a standard practice within an industry, discounts do vary considerably among industries.

Quantity Discounts. Deductions from list price that reflect the economies of purchasing in large quantities are called **quantity discounts**. Price quantity discounts are used to pass cost savings, gained through economies of scale, to the buyer. Cost savings usually occur in four areas. First, fewer but larger orders reduce per-unit selling costs. Second, fixed costs, such as billing and sales contracts, remain the same—or even go down. Third, there are lower costs for raw materials because quantity discounts are often available to the seller. Fourth, longer production runs mean no increases in holding costs.[13] Finally, a large purchase may shift some of the storage, finance, and risk-taking functions to the buyer. Thus quantity discounts usually reflect legitimate reductions in costs.

Quantity discounts can be either cumulative or noncumulative. **Cumulative discounts** are quantity discounts aggregated over a stated period of time. Purchases of $10,000 in a three-month period, for example, might entitle the buyer to a 5 percent, or $500, rebate. Such discounts are supposed to reflect economies in selling and encourage the buyer to purchase from one seller. **Noncumulative discounts** are one-time reductions in prices based on the number of units purchased, the dollar value of the order, or the product mix purchased. Like cumulative discounts, these discounts should reflect some economies in selling or trade functions.

Cash Discounts. A **cash discount**, or price reduction, is given to a buyer for prompt payment or cash payment. Accounts receivable are an expense and a collection problem for many organizations. A policy to encourage prompt payment is a popular practice and sometimes a major concern in setting prices.

---

13. James B. Wilcox, Roy D. Howell, Paul Kuzdrall, and Robert Britney, "Price Quantity Discounts: Some Implications for Buyers and Sellers," *Journal of Marketing*, July 1987, pp. 60–61.

Discounts are based on cash payments or cash paid within a stated time. For example, "2/10 net 30" means that a 2 percent discount will be allowed if the account is paid within 10 days. However, if the buyer does not make payment within the 10-day period, the entire balance is due within 30 days without a discount. If the account is not paid within 30 days, interest may be charged.

Seasonal Discounts.   A price reduction to buyers who purchase goods or services out of season is a **seasonal discount**. These discounts let the seller maintain steadier production during the year. For example, automobile rental agencies offer seasonal discounts in winter and early spring to encourage firms to use automobiles during the slow months of the automobile rental business.

Allowances.   Another type of reduction from the list price is an **allowance**—a concession in price to achieve a desired goal. Trade-in allowances, for example, are price reductions granted for turning in a used item when purchasing a new one. Allowances help give the buyer the ability to make the new purchase. This type of discount is popular in the aircraft industry. Another example is promotional allowances, which are price reductions granted to dealers for participating in advertising and sales support programs intended to increase sales of a particular item.

■ Geographic Pricing

Geographic pricing involves reductions for transportation costs or other costs associated with the physical distance between the buyer and the seller. Prices may be quoted as being F.O.B. (free-on-board) factory or destination. An **F.O.B. factory** price indicates the price of the merchandise at the factory, before it is loaded onto the carrier vehicle, and thus excludes transportation costs. The buyer must pay for shipping. An **F.O.B. destination** price means that the producer absorbs the costs of shipping the merchandise to the customer. This policy may be used to attract distant customers. Although F.O.B. pricing is an easy way to price products, it is sometimes difficult for marketers to administer, especially when a firm has a wide product mix or when customers are dispersed widely. Because customers will want to know about the most economical method of shipping, the seller must keep abreast of shipping rates.

To avoid the problems involved in charging different prices to each customer, **uniform geographic pricing**, sometimes called postage-stamp pricing, may be used. The same price is charged to all customers regardless of geographic location, and the price is based on average shipping costs for all customers. Gasoline, paper products, and office equipment are often priced on a uniform basis.

Zone prices are regional prices that take advantage of a uniform pricing system; prices are adjusted for major geographic zones as the transportation costs increase. For example, a Florida manufacturer's prices may be higher for buyers on the Pacific Coast and in Canada than for buyers in Georgia.

Base-point pricing is a geographic pricing policy that includes the price at the factory, plus freight charges from the base point nearest the buyer. This approach to pricing has virtually been abandoned because its legal status has been questioned. The policy resulted in all buyers paying freight charges from one location, say Detroit or Pittsburgh, regardless of where the product was manufactured.

When the seller absorbs all or part of the actual freight costs, **freight absorption pricing** is being used. The seller might choose this method because it wishes to do business with a particular customer or to get more business; more business will cause the average cost to fall and counterbalance the extra freight cost. This strategy is used to improve market penetration and to retain a hold in an increasingly competitive market.

■ Transfer Pricing

When one unit in a company sells a product to another unit, **transfer pricing** occurs. The price is determined by one of the following methods:

Actual full cost: calculated by dividing all fixed and variable expenses for a period into the number of units produced

Standard full cost: calculated on what it would cost to produce the goods at full plant capacity

Cost plus investment: calculated as full cost, plus the cost of a portion of the selling unit's assets used for internal needs

Market-based cost: calculated at the market price less a small discount to reflect the lack of sales effort and other expenses

The choice of a method of transfer pricing depends on the company's management strategy and the nature of the units' interaction. The company might initially choose to determine price by the actual full cost method. But later price changes could result in a market-based method or another method that the management of the company decides is best for its changed business situation.[14]

An organization must also ensure that transfer pricing is fair to all units that must purchase its goods or services. For example, Bellcore, the centralized research organization that supports the seven regional telephone companies formed from the breakup of AT&T, found that the prices charged by its secretarial, word processing, graphics, and technical publications divisions for the services they provided were too high. As a result, engineers and researchers had to take time away from their duties to type documents and prepare presentation materials to reduce their own costs. Upon investigation, Bellcore discovered that the four service divisions were themselves paying more than their share for overhead and rent expenses. Bellcore revised its methods of allocating overhead and rent. Lower overhead and rental charges coupled with improved efficiency in the four service divisions, allowed them to reduce their costs by 31 percent, enabling them to charge more reasonable prices for their services provided to other divisions.[15]

■ Price Discrimination

A policy of **price discrimination** results in different prices being charged to give a group of buyers a competitive advantage. For example, a producer of a standard sporting goods product reported the following retail pricing variation among major accounts for an item wholesaling for $100: warehouse clubs, $120; discount houses, $150 to $160; middle-income department stores, $200 to $210; and upscale department stores and specialty stores, $225.[16]

Price differentiation becomes discriminatory, and illegal, when a seller gives one reseller or industrial buyer an advantage over competitors by providing products at a price lower than other similar customers can obtain. As mentioned earlier, price differentials are legal when they can be justified on the basis of cost savings, when they are used to meet competition in good faith, or when they do not damage

14. Robert G. Eccles, "Control with Fairness in Transfer Pricing," *Harvard Business Review*, November–December 1983, pp. 149–161.

15. Edward J. Kovac and Henry P. Troy, "Getting Transfer Prices Right: What Bellcore Did," *Harvard Business Review*, September–October 1989, pp. 148–154.

16. Isadore Barmash, "Trying to Sell Without Sales," *New York Times*, May 3, 1987, p. E1.

TABLE 17.1
Principal forms of price discrimination

BASES OF DISCRIMINATION	EXAMPLES
Buyers' incomes	Income-based sliding scale for doctors' fees
Buyers' earning power	Royalties paid for use of patented machines and processes
Buyers' age and sex	Children's haircuts, lower admission charges for individuals in uniform, senior citizen rates
Buyers' location	Zone prices, in-state versus out-of-state tuition, lower export prices (dumping)
Buyers' status	Lower prices to new customers, quantity discounts to big buyers
Use of product	Railroad rates, public utility rates
Qualities of products	Relatively higher prices for deluxe models
Labels on products	Lower prices of unbranded products
Sizes of products	Relatively lower prices for larger sizes (the "giant economy" size)
Peak and off-peak services	Lower prices for off-peak services, excursion rates in transportation, off-season rates at resorts, holiday and evening telephone rates

competition. Thus, if customers are not in competition with each other, different prices may be charged legally.

Price differentiation is a form of market segmentation that companies use to provide a marketing mix that satisfies different segments. Because different market segments perceive the value of a particular product differently, depending on the product's importance and value to the industrial buyer, marketers may charge different prices to different market segments. Price discrimination can also be used to modify demand patterns, support sales of other products, help move obsolete goods or excessive inventories, fill excess production capacity, and respond to competitors' activities in particular markets.[17] Table 17.1 shows the principal forms of price discrimination. For price discrimination to work, several conditions are necessary: (1) the market must be segmentable; (2) the cost of segmenting should not exceed the extra revenue from price discrimination; (3) the practice should not breed customer ill will; (4) competition should not be able to steal the segment that is charged the higher price; and (5) the practice should not violate any applicable laws.

SUMMARY

Price is the value placed on what is exchanged. The buyer exchanges buying power —which depends on the buyer's income, credit, and wealth—for satisfaction or utility. Price is not always money paid; barter, the trading of products, is the oldest form of exchange. Price is a key element in the marketing mix because it relates

17. Michael H. Morris, "Separate Prices as a Marketing Tool," *Industrial Marketing Management*, 16, 1987, pp. 79–86.

directly to the generation of total revenue. The profit factor can be determined mathematically by multiplying price by quantity sold to get total revenues, and then subtracting total costs. Price is the only variable in the marketing mix that can be adjusted quickly and easily to respond to changes in the external environment.

A product offering can compete on either a price or a nonprice basis. Price competition emphasizes price as the product differential. Prices fluctuate frequently, and price competition among sellers is aggressive. Nonprice competition emphasizes product differentiation through distinctive features, services, product quality, or other factors. Establishing brand loyalty by using nonprice competition works best when the product can be physically differentiated and the customer can recognize these distinguishing characteristics.

Pricing objectives are overall goals that describe the role of price in a firm's long-range plans. The most fundamental pricing objective is the organization's survival. Price can be easily adjusted to increase sales volume or to combat competition so that the organization can stay alive. Profit objectives, which are usually stated in terms of sales dollar volume or percentage change, are normally set at a satisfactory level rather than at a level designed for profit maximization. A sales growth objective focuses on increasing the profit base by increasing sales volume. Pricing for return on investment (ROI) has a specified profit as its objective. A pricing objective to maintain or increase market share implies that market position is linked to success. Other types of pricing objectives include cash flow and recovery, status quo, and product quality.

A group of eight factors enters into price decision making: organizational and marketing objectives, pricing objectives, costs, other marketing mix variables, channel member expectations, buyers' perceptions, competition, and legal and regulatory issues. When setting prices, marketers should make decisions consistent with the organization's goals and mission. Pricing objectives heavily influence price-setting decisions. Most marketers view a product's cost as the floor below which a product cannot be priced. Due to the interrelation of the marketing mix variables, price can affect product, promotion, and distribution decisions. The revenue that channel members expect for the functions they perform must also be considered when making price decisions.

Buyers' perceptions of price vary. Some consumer segments are sensitive to price, but others may not be; thus before determining price, a marketer needs to be aware of its importance to the target market. Knowledge of the prices charged for competing brands is essential for the firm so that it can adjust its prices relative to those of competitors. Government regulations and legislation influence pricing decisions. Congress has enacted several laws to enhance perfect competition in the marketplace. Moreover, the government has the power to invoke price controls to curb inflation.

Unlike consumers, industrial buyers purchase products to use them in their own operations or for producing other products. When adjusting prices, industrial sellers take into consideration the size of the purchase, geographic factors, and transportation requirements. Producers commonly provide discounts off list prices to intermediaries. The categories of discounts include trade, quantity, cash, and seasonal discounts, and allowances. A trade discount is a price reduction for performing such functions as storing, transporting, final processing, or providing credit services. If a middleman purchases in large enough quantities, the producer gives a quantity discount, which can be either cumulative or noncumulative. A cash discount is a price reduction for prompt payment or payment in cash. Buyers who purchase goods or services out of season may be granted a seasonal discount. A final type of reduction from the list price is an allowance, such as a trade-in allowance.

Geographic pricing involves reductions for transportation costs or other costs associated with the physical distance between the buyer and the seller. A price quoted as F.O.B. factory means that the buyer pays for shipping from the factory; an F.O.B. destination price means that the producer pays for shipping. This is the easiest way to price products, but it can be difficult for marketers to administer. When the seller charges a fixed average cost for transportation, the practice is known as uniform geographic pricing. Zone prices take advantage of a uniform pricing system adjusted for major geographic zones as the transportation costs increase. Base-point pricing resembles zone pricing; prices are adjusted for shipping expenses incurred by the seller from the base point nearest the buyer. A seller who absorbs all or part of the freight costs is using freight absorption pricing.

When a price discrimination policy is adopted, different prices are charged to give a group of buyers a competitive advantage. Price differentials are legal only when they can be justified on the basis of cost savings, when they meet competition in good faith, or when they do not attempt to damage competition.

IMPORTANT TERMS

Price	Allowance
Barter	Geographic pricing
Price competition	F.O.B. factory
Nonprice competition	F.O.B. destination
Pricing objectives	Uniform geographic pricing
Trade, or functional, discount	Zone prices
Quantity discounts	Base-point pricing
Cumulative discounts	Freight absorption pricing
Noncumulative discounts	Transfer pricing
Cash discount	Price discrimination
Seasonal discount	

DISCUSSION AND REVIEW QUESTIONS

1. Why are pricing decisions so important to an organization?
2. Compare and contrast price and nonprice competition. Describe the conditions under which each form works best.
3. How does a pricing objective of sales growth and expansion differ from an objective to increase market share?
4. Why is it crucial that marketing objectives and pricing objectives be considered when making pricing decisions?
5. In what ways do other marketing mix variables affect pricing decisions?
6. What types of expectations may channel members have about producers' prices, and how do these expectations affect pricing decisions?
7. How do legal and regulatory forces influence pricing decisions?
8. Compare and contrast a trade discount and a quantity discount.
9. What is the reason for using the term F.O.B.?
10. What is the difference between a price discount and price discrimination?

17.1 Pricing of Al Dente Pasta

In 1981, Monique Deschaine started making gourmet pasta in a friend's restaurant in Ann Arbor, Michigan, after the restaurant closed for the night. She laid her pasta out to dry on the restaurant tables and had to rush to finish before the restaurant opened the next day at 10 A.M. By 1988, her business, Al Dente, Inc., was a small growing company with annual sales of more than $200,000. Al Dente pasta had also achieved a national reputation through references in several national magazines, including *Atlantic Monthly* and *The Gourmet Retailer.*

Deschaine started her pasta business by making all the pasta herself, about seven pounds at a time, on one small machine. She promoted her pasta through in-store demonstrations of specific recipes. Her hard work paid off, and today she leaves the pasta making to four full-time employees in her own shop, though she supervises them closely. With a state-of-the-art pasta machine, Al Dente can now press a hundred pounds of linguine and spaghetti at a time, although the product is still hand-rolled and hand-sheeted. Each day the company makes about five hundred pounds of pasta, which is distributed in Chicago, Detroit, and on both coasts.

Deschaine insists on making Al Dente pasta with the freshest ingredients: 100 percent semolina flour moistened with hand-cracked eggs fresh from a nearby farm. Ingredients for differently flavored pastas—egg, tomato, spinach, herb, and unusual flavors such as spicy sesame, blue corn, walnut, three-pepper, and wild mushroom—are mixed right into the dough. Deschaine uses no salt, preservatives, or artificial additives. She refuses to compromise on quality: "Making perfect pasta is a painstaking step-by-step process. We pride ourselves on doing each step well, so that Al Dente pasta looks, cooks, and tastes right." The term *al dente* literally means "to the tooth" and refers to perfectly made and cooked pasta.

The market Deschaine faces is very competitive. When pricing her pasta, she found competitors' costs and the actual cost of doing business to be the key determining factors. The competitors' price determined the upper limit that could be charged for a gourmet pasta. At the same time, she had a minimum price that she had to earn to stay in business. Her pasta is distributed both through brokers and through specialty food distributors. The brokers arrange for sales directly between Deschaine and retailers for 10 to 15 percent of the sales price; they do not warehouse any Al Dente pasta. Specialty food distributors warehouse the pasta and sell it to department, specialty, and gift stores, as well as to independent grocers and some grocery chains. Specialty food distributors buy the pasta from Deschaine and then mark up sales to retailers by 25 percent. Retailers in turn are given a suggested retail price list, which recommends a 33 to 50 percent markup, resulting in a selling price from $2.99 to $3.49 per twelve-ounce bag.

Deschaine has found that her profit margin of $1.50 per bag is slim. She offers free display racks for all retailers (at a cost to her of $30) and pays for all shipping of the pasta by common carrier. In addition, she grants distributors a 10 percent discount for trade shows. A new distributor may be offered a 10 percent discount to secure the relationship.

Although standard mass market pasta from Prince can cost less than $1 (per twelve- to sixteen-ounce bag), Deschaine's primary competition comes from gourmet producers, such as Gaston Dupre, Pastamania, and Contadina (see Table 17.A). The market is stable in its pricing, with competitors striving for a psychological

TABLE 17.A
Size and cost of selected brands of gourmet pasta

MANUFACTURER	OUNCE	COST	COST PER OUNCE (cents)
Gaston Dupre	8	$1.99	24.9
Pastamania	12	$2.39	19.9
Contadina	9	$2.29	25.4
Al Dente	12	$2.99	24.9

pricing advantage by offering smaller packaging in comparison to Al Dente's twelve-ounce package.

Al Dente will not reduce quality to increase profitability. When trying to increase profits, Deschaine either looks for a less expensive bag manufacturer or lower-cost labels or—most importantly—a rise in sales volume, which results in greater economies of scale. Outsiders may think that a small business has extraordinary flexibility in its pricing. That usually is not the case, as many new entrants painfully find out each year.

SOURCES: Karen Grassmuck, "Pasta Point of No Return," *Ann Arbor News,* Jan. 17, 1988; Al Dente press releases 1987, 1988; telephone interview (quoted by permission) with Monique Deschaine, Mar. 21, 1988, and Apr. 7, 1988.

Questions for Discussion

1. How has Al Dente been able to sell pasta at approximately three times the price of such common supermarket brands as Prince?
2. What are the advantages of using psychological pricing in selling gourmet pasta? How have the specified competitors addressed this issue?
3. What would the advantages and disadvantages be for Al Dente if it lowered its selling price?

17.2   The Coke and Pepsi Price War

Coca-Cola Company and PepsiCo, Inc. have fought for soft-drink supremacy on supermarket shelves, in vending machines, at soda fountains, and in the media. In the $43 billion retail soft-drink market, both firms want to be the clear market leader. A one percentage point shift in the $16 billion food store soft-drink market amounts to $160 million in sales. In the scramble for consumer dollars, a price war broke out between the two companies as each slashed prices to attract consumers.

At a store in Tempe, Arizona, traffic jams developed in the parking lot and checkout lines stretched to the meat department as shoppers hauled away cases of Coke priced at 59 cents per six-pack. The store was selling Coca-Cola at the rate of 2,900 cases a day. At another Tempe store, six-packs of Pepsi priced at 79 cents were selling almost as quickly.

Though grocery prices recently have increased overall, soft-drink prices have declined sharply. In the past, the price war generally intensified around holidays and in the summer but now battles are fought daily. In food stores, where the price war is primarily centered, 90 percent of the soft drinks sold have been on sale. Sometimes, by featuring their own price specials to draw consumers, retailers play the two companies against each other, pressuring them to continue to either lower prices more, offer lower prices for longer periods of time, or both.

The numbers change constantly but current figures indicate that Coca-Cola leads the industry overall and Pepsi leads in the supermarket category. Pepsi has held the position as supermarket leader since the disastrous introduction of New Coke. Both companies are eager to become the choice of the average person—who drinks over 42 gallons of soft drinks a year. According to Pepsi's statistics, 50 percent of the individuals who consume soft drinks are not completely loyal to either Pepsi or Coke.

Pepsi's own internal bottling division accounts for 40 percent of the Pepsi sold in the United States. Coca-Cola owns 49 percent of its primary bottler, Coca-Cola Enterprises. Both companies sell soft-drink concentrate to their bottlers. It is the bottlers who actually combine the syrup with carbonated water and sell it to grocers. In the midst of the cola price war, Pepsi and Coca-Cola bottlers are on the front line. The cola war is especially heated (that is, the price-slashing is particularly heavy) in Los Angeles, Phoenix, and several Texas cities where respective company-owned bottlers compete directly with each other.

When the soft-drink giants wage price wars, the producers of brands such as Dr Pepper, Royal Crown Cola, and 7 Up suffer the most. Because 75 percent of the soda market belongs to Coca-Cola and Pepsi, smaller competitors must continuously try to underprice them. When Coca-Cola and Pepsi lower prices, earnings at the smaller firms decrease rapidly.

Some marketers think that the extended price war between Pepsi and Coke has damaged the brand image of both. The price war has also affected brand loyalty as consumers seek bargains rather than a particular soft drink. The price war may last indefinitely since it is unlikely that one company will raise prices if the other does not. Consumers, accustomed to paying low prices, might reject higher prices altogether and look to other brands to satisfy their thirsts.

SOURCES: Mike Duff, "Soft Drinks," *Supermarket Business,* Sept. 1989, pp. 217–222; Kevin Hanley, "Couponing for Customers," *Target Marketing,* Nov. 1986, pp. 13–14; Karen Hoggan, "Head to Head," *Marketing,* June 22, 1989, pp. 20–21; Warren Kornblum, "More Than the Price Has to Be Right," *Retail Control,* Oct. 1987, pp. 7–16; Betsy Morris, "Coke and Pepsi: Cola War Marches On," *Wall Street Journal,* June 3, 1987, p. 33; Stephen W. Quickel, "Coke vs. Pepsi: A 100 Years War," *Business Month,* Jan. 1989, pp. 10–11; Patricia Winters, "Coke's Game Plan," *Advertising Age,* Nov. 7, 1988, p. 4; and Patricia Winters, "Jackson, Houston Hard Acts to Follow," *Advertising Age,* Sept. 11, 1989, pp. S13, S14.

Questions for Discussion

1. What type of pricing objectives is Coca-Cola and Pepsi most likely to have? Explain.
2. Does a price war help to build brand loyalty? Why or why not? If brand loyalty were stronger among cola drinkers, would a price war be advisable? Explain.
3. What major factors are most likely to influence which company will win an extended price war?

18 SETTING PRICES

Objectives

To understand eight major stages of the process used to establish prices

To explore issues connected with selecting pricing objectives

To grasp the importance of identifying the target market's evaluation of price

To gain insight into demand curves and the price elasticity of demand

To examine the relationships among demand, costs, and profits

To learn about analyzing competitive prices

To understand the different types of pricing policies

To scrutinize the major kinds of pricing methods

Businesses are experiencing a general fax frenzy. Customers are faxing orders to restaurants, architects are faxing tentative plans to their offices, and free-lance artists are faxing designs everywhere. More than 1.4 million fax machines are sold annually, and this figure is expected to grow. Just a few years ago, there were only seven fax manufacturers; now, there are twenty-five that offer sixty brands to American customers. The industry sales leaders are Sharp and Murata—both achieving market leader positions by producing relatively inexpensive machines that appeal to small- and medium-sized businesses.

The purchase of fax machines actually saves money for smaller companies by reducing the need for express mail service and messengers. Business analysts expect sales of fax machines to increase dramatically in the future as more and more individuals start working out of their own homes. These workers will most likely be attracted to basic "low-end" machines, usually costing less than $1,500.

Xerox created the first commercial fax machine in 1970, but it was Sharp and Murata that produced the earliest no-frills models. With a continually growing list of competitors in the low-priced part of the market, both Sharp and Murata are investing heavily in research and development to solidify their positions as industry leaders. South Korean fax machine manufacturers, such as Samsung and Daewoo, might pose a challenge to established companies. Analysts expect these Korean firms to drive the price of fax machines down to about $300. ◆

Advertisement courtesy of Sharp Corp.

Based on information in Jeffrey H. Epstein, "The Future in Fax," *Direct Marketing*, March 1989, pp. 28, 30; Sherli Evans, "Fax: Looking Fine in '89," *Industry Week*, May 15, 1989, pp. BC3–BC4, BC6–BC7; Frederick H. Katayama, "Who's Fueling the Fax Frenzy," *Fortune*, Oct. 23, 1989, pp. 151–152, 156.

I n the fax machine market, demand is strong and the number of producers is increasing. These conditions require that fax machine marketers give frequent consideration to setting and altering prices. Setting prices of products such as fax machines requires careful analysis of numerous issues. In this chapter we examine eight stages of a process that marketers can use when setting prices.

Figure 18.1 illustrates these eight stages. Stage 1 is the development of a pricing objective that is congruent with the organization's overall objectives and its marketing objectives. In stage 2, both the target market's evaluation of price and its ability to buy must be assessed. Then, in stage 3, marketers should examine the nature and price elasticity of demand. Stage 4, which consists of analyzing demand, cost, and profit relationships, is necessary for estimating the economic feasibility of alternative prices. Evaluation of competitors' prices, which constitutes stage 5, helps determine the role of price in the marketing strategy. Stage 6 is the selection of a pricing policy, or the guidelines for using price in the marketing mix. Stage 7 involves choosing a method for calculating the price charged to customers. Stage 8, the determining of the final price, depends on environmental forces and marketers' understanding and use of a systematic approach to establishing prices. These stages are not rigid steps that all marketers must follow but rather guidelines that provide a logical sequence for establishing prices. In some situations, additional stages may need to be included in the price-setting process; in others, certain stages may not be necessary.

SELECTION OF PRICING OBJECTIVES

In Chapter 17 you learned about the various types of pricing objectives. Selecting pricing objectives is an important task because pricing objectives form the basis for decisions about other stages of pricing. Thus pricing objectives must be explicitly stated. The statement of pricing objectives should include the time period during which the objectives are to be accomplished.

FIGURE 18.1

Stages for establishing prices

Marketers must be certain that the pricing objectives they set are consistent with the organization's overall objectives and marketing objectives. Inconsistent objectives cause internal conflicts and confusion and can prevent the organization from achieving its overall goals. Furthermore, pricing objectives inconsistent with organizational and marketing objectives may cause marketers to make poor decisions during the other stages in the price-setting process.

Organizations normally have multiple pricing objectives, some short-term and others long-term. For example, the pricing objective of gaining market share is normally short-term because it often requires the firm to price its product quite low relative to competitors' prices. An organization should have one or more pricing objectives for each product. For the same product aimed at different market segments, marketers sometimes choose different pricing objectives. A marketer typically alters pricing objectives over time.

ASSESSING THE TARGET MARKET'S EVALUATION OF PRICE AND ITS ABILITY TO BUY

Although we generally assume that price is a significant issue for buyers, the importance of price depends on the type of product, the type of target market, and the purchase situation. For example, in general, buyers are probably more sensitive to gasoline prices than to luggage prices. With respect to the type of target market, the price of an airline ticket is much more important to a tourist than to a business traveler. The purchase situation also affects the buyer's view of price. Most movie goers would never pay, in other situations, the prices paid for soft drinks, popcorn, and candy at movie concession stands. By assessing the target market's evaluation of price, a marketer is in a better position to know how much emphasis to place on price. Information about the target market's price evaluation may also help a marketer determine how far above the competition a firm can set its prices.

As we point out in Chapter 4, the people who make up a market must have the ability to buy a product. Buyers must need a product, be willing to use their buying power, and have the authority (by law or social custom) to buy. Their ability to buy, as does their evaluation of price, has direct consequences for marketers. The ability to purchase involves such resources as money, credit, wealth, and other products that could be traded in an exchange. Understanding customers' buying power and knowing how important a product is to them in comparison with other products helps marketers correctly assess the target market's evaluation of price.

DETERMINING DEMAND

Determining the demand for a product is the responsibility of marketing managers, who are aided in this task by marketing researchers and forecasters. Marketing research and forecasting techniques yield estimates of sales potential or the quantity of a product that could be sold during a specific period. (Chapter 4 describes such techniques as surveys, time series analyses, correlation methods, and market tests.) These estimates are helpful in establishing the relationship between a product's price and the quantity demanded.

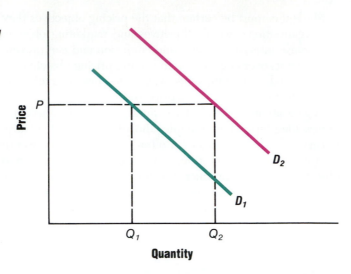

The Demand Curve

For most products, the quantity demanded goes up as the price goes down, and as the price goes up, the quantity demanded goes down. Thus there is an inverse relationship between price and quantity demanded. As long as the marketing environment and buyers' needs, ability (purchasing power), willingness, and authority to buy remain stable, this fundamental inverse relationship will continue.

Figure 18.2 illustrates the effect of one variable—price—on the quantity demanded. The classic **demand curve** (D1) is a graph of the quantity of products expected to be sold at various prices, if other factors remain constant.[1] It illustrates that as price falls the quantity demanded usually rises. Demand depends on other factors in the marketing mix, including product quality, promotion, and distribution. An improvement in any of these factors may cause a shift to, say, demand curve D2. In such a case, an increased quantity (Q2) will be sold at the same price (P).

There are many types of demand and not all conform to the classic demand curve shown in Figure 18.2. Prestige products, such as selected perfumes and jewelry, seem to sell better at high prices than at low ones. For example, the jewelry shown in Figure 18.3 is known to be expensive and thus has a prestigious image. These products are desirable partly because their expense makes buyers feel elite. If the price fell drastically and many people owned them, they would lose some of their appeal.

The demand curve in Figure 18.4 shows the relationship between price and quantity for prestige products. Demand is greater, not less, at higher prices. For a certain price range—from P1 to P2—the quantity demanded (Q1) goes up to Q2. After a point, however, raising the price backfires. If the price of a product goes too high, the quantity demanded goes down. The figure shows that if the price is raised from P2 to P3, quantity demanded goes back down from Q2 to Q1.

Demand Fluctuations

Changes in buyers' needs, variations in the effectiveness of other marketing mix variables, the presence of substitutes, and dynamic environmental factors can influence demand. Restaurants and utility companies experience large fluctuations in

1. Reprinted from *Dictionary of Marketing Terms,* Peter D. Bennett, Ed., 1988, p. 54, published by the American Marketing Association. Used by permission.

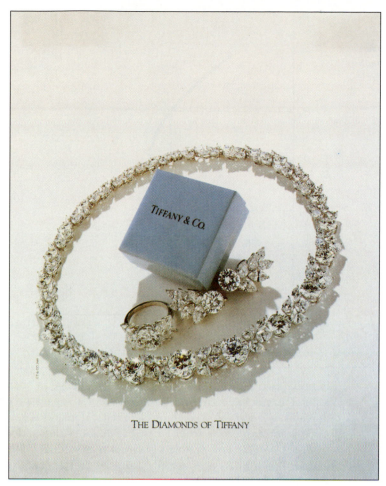

THE DIAMONDS OF TIFFANY

SOURCE: © Tiffany & Co., 1989

demand daily. Toy manufacturers, fireworks suppliers, and air-conditioning and heating contractors also face demand fluctuations because of the seasonal nature of these items. The demand for fax machines, single-serving low-calorie meals, and fur coats have changed significantly over the last few years. In some cases, demand fluctuations are predictable. It is no surprise to restaurants and utility company managers that demand fluctuates. However, changes in demand for other products may be less predictable and this leads to problems for some companies. Although demand can fluctuate unpredictably, some firms have been able to anticipate changes in demand by correlating demand for a specific product to demand for the total industry or to some other economic variable. If a brand maintains a fairly constant market share, its sales can be estimated as a percentage of industry sales.

Gauging Price Elasticity of Demand

Up to this point, we have been discussing how marketers identify the target market's evaluation of price and its ability to purchase and how they examine demand to learn whether price is related inversely or directly to quantity. The next stage in the process is to gauge price elasticity of demand. **Price elasticity of demand** provides a measure of the sensitivity of demand to changes in price. It is formally defined as the percentage change in quantity demanded relative to a given percentage change

FIGURE 18.4

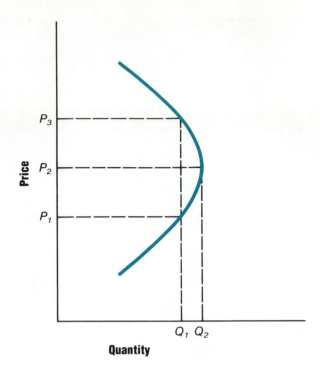

in price[2] (see Figure 18.5). The percentage change in quantity demanded caused by a percentage change in price is much greater for elastic demand than for inelastic demand. For a product such as electricity, demand is relatively inelastic. When its price is increased, say from P1 to P2, quantity demanded goes down only a little, from Q1 to Q2. For products such as recreational vehicles, demand is relatively elastic. When price rises sharply, from P1 to P2, quantity demanded goes down a great deal, from Q1 to Q2.

If marketers can determine price elasticity of demand, then setting a price is much easier. By analyzing total revenues as prices change, marketers can determine whether a product is price elastic. Total revenue is price times quantity; thus 10,000 rolls of wallpaper sold in one year at a price of $10 per roll equals $100,000 of total revenue. If demand is *elastic*, a change in price causes an opposite change in total revenue—an increase in price will decrease total revenue, and a decrease in price will increase total revenue. An *inelastic* demand results in a change in the same direction in total revenue—an increase in price will increase total revenue, and a decrease in price will decrease total revenue. The following formula determines the price elasticity of demand:

$$\text{Price Elasticity of Demand} = \frac{\% \text{ Change in Quantity Demanded}}{\% \text{ Change in Price}}$$

For example, if demand falls by 8 percent when a seller raises the price by 2 percent, the price elasticity of demand is −4 (the negative sign indicating the inverse relationship between price and demand). If demand falls by 2 percent when price is increased by 4 percent, then elasticity is −$^1/_2$. The less elastic the demand, the more beneficial it is for the seller to raise the price. Products without readily available

2. Bennett, p. 150.

FIGURE 18.5
Elasticity of demand

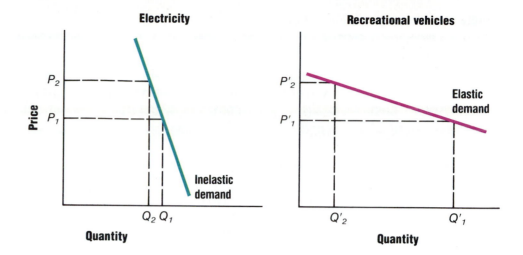

substitutes and for which consumers have strong needs (for example, electricity, appendectomies) usually have inelastic demand.

Marketers cannot base prices solely on elasticity considerations. They must also examine the costs associated with different volumes and see what happens to profits.

ANALYSIS OF DEMAND, COST, AND PROFIT RELATIONSHIPS

Having examined the role of demand in setting prices and the various costs and their relationships, we can now explore the relationships among demand, cost, and profit. To stay in business, a company has to set prices that cover all its costs. There are two approaches to understanding demand, cost, and profit relationships: marginal analysis and breakeven analysis.

■ **Marginal Analysis**

Marginal analysis is the examination of what happens to a firm's costs and revenues when production (or sales volume) is changed by one unit. Both production costs and revenues must be evaluated. To determine the costs of production, it is necessary to distinguish among several types of costs. **Fixed costs** do not vary with changes in the number of units produced or sold. The cost of renting a factory does not change because production increases from one shift to two shifts a day or because twice as much wallpaper is sold. Rent may go up, but not because the factory has doubled production or revenue. **Average fixed cost** is the fixed cost per unit produced and is calculated by dividing fixed costs by the number of units produced.

Variable costs vary directly with changes in the number of units produced or sold. The wages for a second shift and the cost of twice as much paper are extra costs that occur when production is doubled. Variable costs are usually constant per unit; that is, twice as many workers and twice as much material produces twice as many rolls of wallpaper. **Average variable cost**, the variable cost per unit produced, is calculated by dividing the variable costs by the number of units produced.

Total cost is the sum of average fixed costs and average variable costs times the quantity produced. The **average total cost** is the sum of the average fixed cost and

TABLE 18.1 *Costs and their relationships*

1 QUANTITY	2 FIXED COST	3 AVERAGE FIXED COST (2) ÷ (1)	4 AVERAGE VARIABLE COST	5 AVERAGE TOTAL COST (3) + (4)	6 TOTAL COST (5) × (1)	7 MARGINAL COST
1	$40	$40.00	$20.00	$60.00	$ 60	$10
2	40	20.00	15.00	35.00	70	5
3	40	13.33	11.67	25.00	75	15
4	40	10.00	12.50	22.50	90	20
5	40	8.00	14.00	22.00	110	30
6	40	6.67	16.67	23.33	140	40
7	40	5.71	20.00	25.71	180	

the average variable cost. **Marginal cost (MC)** is the extra cost a firm incurs when it produces one more unit of a product. Table 18.1 illustrates various costs and their relationships. Notice that the average fixed cost declines as the output increases. The average variable cost follows a U shape, as does the average total cost. Because the average total cost continues to fall after the average variable cost begins to rise, its lowest point is at a higher level of output than that of the average variable cost. The average total cost is lowest at 5 units at a cost of $22, whereas the average variable cost is lowest at 3 units at a cost of $11.67. As shown in Figure 18.6, marginal cost equals average total cost at the latter's lowest level, between 5 and 6 units of production. In Table 18.1 this occurs between 5 and 6 units of production. Average total cost decreases as long as the marginal cost is less than the average total cost, and it increases when marginal cost rises above average total cost.

Marginal revenue (MR) is the change in total revenue that occurs when a firm sells an additional unit of a product. Figure 18.7 depicts marginal revenue and a demand curve. Most firms in the United States face downward-sloping demand curves for their products. In other words, they must lower their prices to sell additional units. This situation means that each additional product sold provides the firm with less revenue than the previous unit sold. MR then becomes less than average revenue, as Figure 18.7 shows. Eventually, MR reaches zero and the sale of additional units merely hurts the firm.

However, before the firm can determine if a unit makes a profit, it must know its cost, as well as its revenue, because profit equals revenue minus cost. If MR is a unit's addition to revenue and MC is a unit's addition to cost, then MR minus MC tells us whether the unit is profitable or not. Table 18.2 illustrates the relationships between price, quantity sold, total revenue, marginal revenue, marginal cost, and total cost. It indicates where maximum profits are possible at various combinations of price and cost.

Profit is maximized where MC = MR (see Table 18.2). In this table MC = MR at four units. The best price is $33.75 and the profit is $45. Up to this point, the additional revenue generated from an extra unit of sale exceeds the additional total cost. Beyond this point, the additional cost of another unit sold exceeds the additional revenue generated, and profits decrease. If the price was based on minimum

FIGURE 18.6

FIGURE 18.6
Typical marginal cost and average cost relationships

average total cost—$22 (Table 18.1)—it would result in less profit: only $40 (Table 18.2) for five units at a price of $30 versus $45 for four units at a price of $33.75.

Graphically combining Figures 18.6 and 18.7 into Figure 18.8 shows that any unit for which MR exceeds MC adds to a firm's profits, and any unit for which MC exceeds MR subtracts from a firm's profits. The firm should produce at the point where MR equals MC because this is the most profitable level of production.

This discussion of marginal analysis may give the false impression that pricing can be highly precise. If revenue (demand) and cost (supply) remained constant, then prices could be set for maximum profits. In practice, however, cost and revenue change frequently. The competitive tactics of other firms or government action can quickly undermine a company's expectations of revenue. Thus marginal analysis is only a model from which to work. It offers little help in pricing new products before costs and revenues are established. On the other hand, in setting prices of existing products, especially in competitive situations, most marketers can benefit by understanding the relationship between marginal cost and marginal revenue.

Breakeven Analysis

The point at which the costs of producing a product equal the revenue made from selling the product is the **breakeven point**. If a wallpaper manufacturer has total annual costs of $100,000 and the same year it sells $100,000 worth of wallpaper, then the company has broken even.

FIGURE 18.7
Typical marginal revenue and average revenue relationships

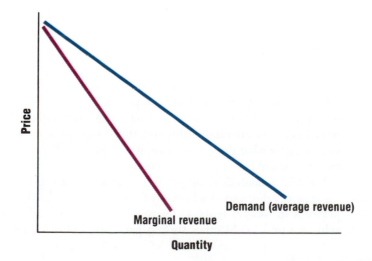

TABLE 18.2 *Marginal analysis: method of obtaining maximum profit-producing price*

1	2	3	4	5	6	7
PRICE	QUANTITY SOLD	TOTAL REVENUE (1) × (2)	MARGINAL REVENUE	MARGINAL COST	TOTAL COST	PROFIT (3) − (6)
$57.00	1	$ 57	$57	$—	$ 60	−$ 3
55.00	2	110	53	10	70	40
40.00	3	120	10	5	75	45
33.75[a]	**4**	**135**	**15**	**15**	**90**	**45**
30.00	5	150	15	20	110	40
27.00	6	162	12	30	140	22
25.00	7	175	13	40	180	−5

[a] Boldface indicates best price-profit combination.

Figure 18.9 illustrates the relationships of costs, revenue, profits, and losses involved in determining the breakeven point. Knowing the number of units necessary to break even is important in setting the price. If a product priced at $100 per unit has an average variable cost of $60 per unit, then the contribution to fixed costs is $40. If total fixed costs are $120,000, here is the way to determine the breakeven point in units:

$$\text{Breakeven Point} = \frac{\text{Fixed Costs}}{\text{Per Unit Contribution to Fixed Costs}}$$

$$= \frac{\text{Fixed Costs}}{\text{Price} - \text{Variable Costs}}$$

$$= \frac{\$120,000}{\$40}$$

$$= 3,000 \text{ Units}$$

To calculate the breakeven point in terms of dollar sales volume, multiply the breakeven point in units by the price per unit. In the preceding example, the breakeven point in terms of dollar sales volume is 3,000 (units) times $100, or $300,000.

To use breakeven analysis effectively, a marketer should determine the breakeven point for each of several alternative prices. This determination allows the marketer to compare the effects on total revenue, total costs, and the breakeven point for each price under consideration. Although this comparative analysis may not tell the marketer exactly what price to charge, it will identify highly undesirable price alternatives that should definitely be avoided.

Breakeven analysis is simple and straightforward. It does assume, however, that the quantity demanded is basically fixed (inelastic) and that the major task in setting prices is to recover costs. It focuses more on how to break even than on how to achieve a pricing objective, such as percentage of market share or return on invest-

FIGURE 18.8
Combining the marginal
cost and marginal reve-
nue concepts for optimal
profit

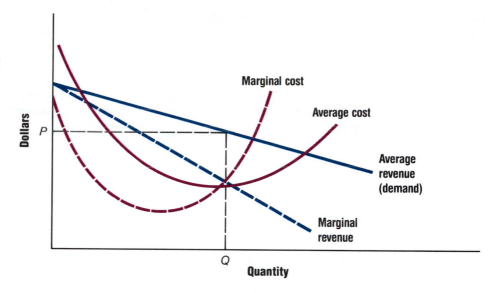

ment. Nonetheless, marketing managers can use this concept to determine whether a product will achieve at least a breakeven volume. In other words, it is easier to answer the question "Will we sell at least the minimum volume necessary to break even?" than the question "What volume of sales will we expect to sell?"

EVALUATION OF COMPETITORS' PRICES

In most cases, marketers are in a better position to establish prices when they know the prices charged for competing brands. Learning competitors' prices may be a regular function of marketing research. Some grocery and department stores, for example, have full-time comparative shoppers who systematically collect data on prices. Companies may also purchase price lists, sometimes weekly, from syndicated marketing research services.

Finding out what prices competitors are charging is not always easy, especially in producer and reseller markets. Competitors' price lists are often closely guarded. Even if a marketer has access to price lists, they may not reflect the actual prices at which competitive products are sold because those prices may be established through negotiation.

Knowing the prices of competing brands can be very important for a marketer. Competitors' prices and the marketing mix variables that they emphasize partly determine how important price will be to customers. Marketers in an industry in which nonprice competition prevails need competitive price information to ensure that their organization's prices are the same as its competitors' prices. In some instances, an organization's prices are designed to be slightly above competitors' prices to give its products an exclusive image. Alternatively, another company may use price as a competitive tool and attempt to price its product below those of competitors. Toys "R" Us, for example, has acquired a large market share through aggressive competitive prices.

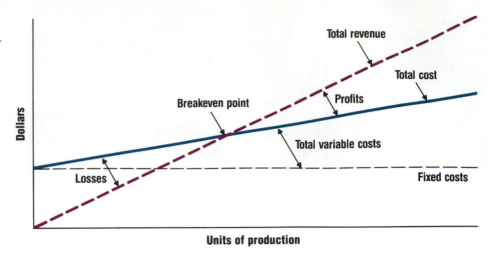

FIGURE 18.9
Determining the break-even point

SELECTION OF A PRICING POLICY

A **pricing policy** is a guiding philosophy or course of action designed to influence and determine pricing decisions. Pricing policies set guidelines for achieving pricing objectives. They are an important component of an overall marketing strategy. Generally, pricing policies should answer this recurring question: How will price be used as a variable in the marketing mix? This question may relate to (1) introduction of new products, (2) competitive situations, (3) government pricing regulations, (4) economic conditions, or (5) implementation of pricing objectives. Pricing policies help marketers solve the practical problems of establishing prices. Let us examine the most common pricing policies.

<table>
<tr><td>■ **Pioneer**
Pricing Policies</td><td>Pioneer pricing—setting the base price for a new product—is a necessary part of formulating a marketing strategy. The base price is easily adjusted (in the absence of government price controls), and its establishment is one of the most fundamental decisions in the marketing mix. The base price can be set high to recover development costs quickly or to provide a reference point for developing discount prices to different market segments.</td></tr>
</table>

When marketers set base prices, they also consider how quickly competitors will enter the market, whether they will mount a strong campaign on entry, and what effect their entry will have on the development of primary demand. If competitors will enter quickly, with considerable marketing force, and with limited effect on the primary demand, then a firm may adopt a base price that will discourage their entry.

Price Skimming. **Price skimming** is charging the highest possible price that buyers who most desire the product will pay. This pioneer approach provides the most flexible introductory base price. Demand tends to be inelastic in the introductory stage of the product life cycle.

Price skimming can provide several benefits, especially when a product is in the introductory stage of its life cycle. A skimming policy can generate much-needed initial cash flows to help offset sizable developmental costs. When introducing a new model of camera, Polaroid initially uses a skimming price to defray large research and development costs. Price skimming protects the marketer from prob-

SOURCE: Courtesy Hyundai Motor America

lems that arise when the price is set too low to cover costs. When a firm introduces a product, its production capacity may be limited. A skimming price can help keep demand consistent with a firm's production capabilities. The use of a skimming price may attract competition into an industry because the high price makes that type of business appear to be quite lucrative.

Penetration Price. A **penetration price** is a price below the prices of competing brands and is designed to penetrate a market and produce a larger unit sales volume. When introducing a product, a marketer sometimes uses a penetration price to gain a large market share quickly. As shown in Figure 18.10, Hyundai is using penetration pricing for its Excel. This approach places the marketer in a less flexible position than price skimming because it is more difficult to raise a penetration price than to lower or discount a skimming price. It is not unusual for a firm to use a penetration price after having skimmed the market with a higher price.

Penetration pricing can be especially beneficial when marketers suspect that competitors could enter the market easily. First, if the penetration price lets one marketer gain a large market share quickly, competitors might be discouraged from entering the market. Second, entering the market may be less attractive to competitors when a penetration price is used because the lower per-unit price results in lower per-unit profit; this may cause competitors to view the market as not being especially lucrative. Mazda, for instance, used penetration pricing when it introduced the MX-5 Miata to gain market share quickly and to discourage competitors from entering that market segment (see Marketing Update 18.1).

A penetration price is particularly appropriate when demand is highly elastic. Highly elastic demand means that target market members would purchase the product if it was priced at the penetration level but few would buy the item if it was priced higher. A marketer should consider using a penetration price when a lower price would result in longer production runs, increasing production significantly and reducing the firm's per-unit production costs.

■ Psychological Pricing

Psychological pricing encourages purchases based on emotional rather than rational responses. It is used most often at the retail level. Psychological pricing has limited use for industrial products.

Odd-Even Pricing.   Through **odd-even pricing**—that is, ending the price with certain numbers—marketers try to influence buyers' perceptions of the price or the product. Odd pricing assumes that more of a product will be sold at $99.95 than at $100. Supposedly, customers will think, or at least tell friends, that the product is a bargain—not $100, mind you, but $99, plus a few insignificant pennies. Also, customers are supposed to think that the store could have charged $100 but instead cut the price to the last cent, to $99.95. Some claim, too, that certain types of customers are more attracted by odd prices than by even ones. However, there are no substantial research findings that support the notion that odd prices produce greater sales. Nonetheless, even prices are far more unusual today than odd prices.

Even prices are used to give a product an exclusive or upscale image. An even price supposedly will influence a customer to view the product as being a high-quality, premium brand. A shirt maker, for example, may print on a premium shirt package a suggested retail price of $32 instead of $31.95; the even price of the shirt is used to enhance its upscale image.

Customary Pricing.   In **customary pricing**, certain goods are priced primarily on the basis of tradition. Recent economic uncertainties have made most prices fluctuate fairly widely, but the classic example of the customary, or traditional, price is the candy bar. For scores of years, the price of a candy bar was 5 cents. A new candy bar would have had to be something very special to sell for more than a nickel. This price was so sacred that rather than change it manufacturers increased or decreased the size of the candy bar itself as chocolate prices fluctuated. Now, of course, the nickel candy bar has disappeared, probably forever. Yet most candy bars still sell at a consistent but obviously higher price. Thus customary pricing remains the standard for this market.

Prestige Pricing.   In **prestige pricing**, prices are set at an artificially high level to provide prestige or a quality image. Pharmacists report that some consumers complain if a prescription does not cost enough. Apparently, some consumers associate a drug's price with its potency. Consumers may also associate the quality of beer with its price. The beer industry caters to this perception, as evidenced by its jargon: popular (meaning inexpensive), premium (meaning higher-priced), and super premium (meaning expensive).[3]

3. Trish Hall, "Miller Seeks to Regain Niche as Envy of Beer Industry," *Wall Street Journal,* Dec. 3, 1986, p. 6.

PRICING OF THE MAZDA MX-5 MIATA

Mazda is anxious to overhaul its image: it no longer wants to be known as the lower-priced Japanese alternative to Honda and Toyota. As part of its image alteration, Mazda has introduced the Mazda MX-5 Miata. Mazda engineers designed the Miata along the lines of the classic British two-seat automobiles of the 1960s. Mazda's new Miata does resemble earlier Triumphs and Austin-Healeys, but the Miata does not require as much maintenance. Car magazines in the United States have praised the Miata—*Road & Track* has named the Miata one of the five best cars in the world. They only rated Ferrari's Testarossa better. The car magazines tout the Miata as a solid, fun-to-drive car, but register amazement at the sticker price. At a reasonable manufacturer-suggested retail price of under $14,000, Mazda has made high-performance cars affordable.

A research and development specialist at Mazda concluded that there was a great demand for a "cheap" two-seat sports car. So from the beginning, Mazda designers and engineers considered cost as important as performance and styling. According to Mazda's product program manager, the Miata is a much simpler car than either the Mazda 323 or 626. For example, the Miata uses a 120-horsepower, 1.6-liter four-cylinder engine instead of Mazda's expensive rotary engine.

To keep consumer costs down, the Miata lacks many of the sophisticated gadgets that sports cars today are noted for. Options on the Miata are limited and the car is available in only a few colors. Mazda has limited production of the Miata to 20,000 the first year and 40,000 every year after that. The simple design and great performance of the Miata have caught the public's attention, but the low sticker price has made the car an automotive sensation. In Charlotte, North Carolina, car dealerships sold out Miatas on the first day they were available. People were actually paying *more* than the sticker price to get one. The relative scarcity of the car has helped Miata sales. As one automobile analyst stated, the scarcity "raises the mystique of the cars."

SOURCES: Larry Armstrong, "Mazda Rolls Out a Poor Man's Maserati," *Business Week,* June 26, 1989, p. 66; Ken Gross, "Back to the Future," *Automotive Industries,* April 1989, pp. 92–94; and Kathy Barks Hoffman, "Sporty Miata Zips to Fast Start," *USA Today,* July 11, 1989, p. B1.

FIGURE 18.11
Prestige pricing.
Miele uses pricing to po-
sition its dishwasher as a
prestige product.

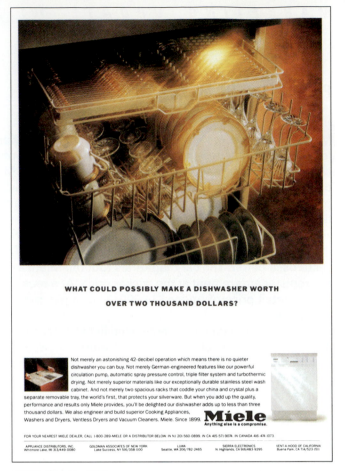

WHAT COULD POSSIBLY MAKE A DISHWASHER WORTH

OVER TWO THOUSAND DOLLARS?

Not merely an astonishing 42-decibel operation which means there is no quieter dishwasher you can buy. Not merely German-engineered features like our powerful circulation pump, automatic spray pressure control, triple filter system and turbothermic drying. Not merely superior materials like our exceptionally durable stainless steel wash cabinet. And not merely two spacious racks that coddle your china and crystal plus a separate removable tray, the world's first, that protects your silverware. But when you add up the quality, performance and results only Miele provides, you'll be delighted our dishwasher adds up to less than three thousand dollars. We also engineer and build superior Cooking Appliances, Washers and Dryers, Ventless Dryers and Vacuum Cleaners. Miele. Since 1899.

Miele
Anything else is a compromise.

FOR YOUR NEAREST MIELE DEALER, CALL 1-800-289-MIELE OR A DISTRIBUTOR BELOW. IN NJ 201-560-0899. IN CA 415-571-9074. IN CANADA 416-474-1073.

| APPLIANCE DISTRIBUTORS, INC. Whitmore Lake, MI 313/449-0080 | GOLDMAN ASSOCIATES OF NEW YORK Lake Success, NY 516/358-1100 | LUWA Seattle, WA 206/782-2465 | SIERRA ELECTRONICS N. Highlands, CA 916/483-9295 | VENT-A-HOOD OF CALIFORNIA Buena Park, CA 714/523-1511 |

SOURCE: Courtesy Miele

Prestige pricing is used especially when buyers associate a higher price with higher quality. Typical product categories in which selected products are prestige priced include perfumes, automobiles, liquor, jewelry, and appliances (see Figure 18.11). If producers that use prestige pricing lowered their prices dramatically, it would be inconsistent with the perceived images of such products.

Price Lining.   When an organization sets a limited number of prices for selected groups or lines of merchandise, it is using **price lining**. A retailer may have various styles and brands of similar quality men's shirts that sell for $15. Another line of higher quality shirts may sell for $22. Price lining simplifies consumers' decision making by holding constant one key variable in the final selection of style and brand within a line. In product line pricing, the company should look at the prices of the overall product line to ensure that the price of the new model lies within the range of existing prices for that line. Failure to consider the impact of the new model's price relative to the existing product line may change buyers' perceptions of all the models in the line.[4]

4. Kent B. Monroe, "Effect of Product Line Pricing Characteristics on Product Evaluation," *Journal of Consumer Research*, March 1987, p. 518.

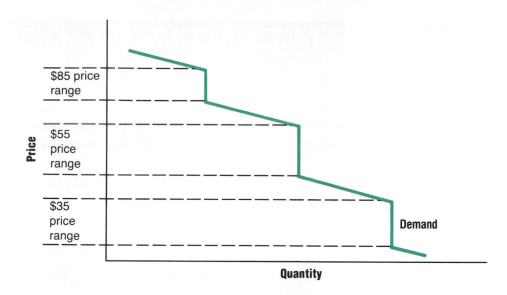

FIGURE 18.12
Price lining

The basic assumption in price lining is that the demand is inelastic for various groups or sets of products. If the prices are attractive, customers will concentrate their purchases without responding to slight changes in price. Thus a women's dress shop that carries dresses priced at $85, $55, and $35 might not attract many more sales with a drop to, say, $83, $53, and $33. The "space" between the prices of $55 and $35, however, can stir changes in consumer response. With price lining, the demand curve looks like a series of steps, as shown in Figure 18.12.

■ Professional Pricing

Professional pricing is used by persons who have great skill or experience in a particular field or activity. Some professionals who provide such products as medical services feel that their fees (prices) should not relate directly to the time and involvement in specific cases; rather, a standard fee is charged regardless of the problems involved in performing the job. Some doctors' and lawyers' fees are prime examples: $35 for a checkup, $400 for an appendectomy, and $199 for a divorce. Other professionals set prices in other ways.

The concept of professional pricing carries with it the idea that professionals have an "ethical" responsibility not to overcharge unknowing customers. In some situations, a seller can charge customers a high price and continue to sell many units of the product. Medicine offers several examples. If a diabetic requires one insulin treatment per day to survive, the individual will buy that treatment whether its price is $1 or $10. In fact, the patient surely would purchase the treatment even if the price went higher. In these situations sellers could charge exorbitant fees. Drug companies claim that despite their positions of strength in this regard, they charge "ethical" prices rather than what the market will bear. In 1989 Burroughs-Wellcome Co. reduced the price of its AIDS-treatment drug AZT by 20 percent partly in response to pressure from AIDS patients and activists. However, some feel that the $6,400 annual price tag of AZT treatments is still far too high.[5]

■ Promotional Pricing

Price is an ingredient in the marketing mix, and it often is coordinated with promotion. The two variables sometimes are so interrelated that the pricing policy is

5. Marylin Chase, "Burroughs-Wellcome Cuts Price of AZT Under Pressure from AIDS Activists," *Wall Street Journal*, Sept. 19, 1989, p. A3.

FIGURE 18.13
Special-event pricing.
Valentine's Day as well
as other special days
provide opportunities for
special-event pricing.

SOURCE: Courtesy of Service Merchandise

promotion oriented. Examples of promotional pricing include price leaders, special-event pricing, superficial discounting, and experience curve pricing.

Price Leaders.   Sometimes a firm prices a few products below the usual markup, near cost, or below cost, which results in prices known as **price leaders**. This type of pricing is used most often in supermarkets and department stores to attract consumers by giving them special low prices on a few items. Management hopes that sales of regularly priced merchandise will more than offset the reduced revenues from the price leaders.

Special-Event Pricing.   To increase sales volume, many organizations coordinate price with advertising or sales promotion for seasonal or special situations. **Special-event pricing** involves advertised sales or price cutting that is linked to a holiday, season, or event. As shown in Figure 18.13, Service Merchandise uses Valentine's Day as a basis for special-event pricing of selected jewelry items. If the pricing objective is survival, then special sales events may be designed to generate the necessary operating capital. Special-event pricing also entails coordination of production, scheduling, storage, and physical distribution. Whenever there is a sales lag, special-event pricing is an alternative that marketers should consider.

Superficial Discounting.   **Superficial discounting**, sometimes called "was-is pricing" is fictitious comparative pricing, for example, "Was $259, is $199." The Federal Trade Commission and the Better Business Bureau discourage these deceptive markdowns. Legitimate discounts are not questioned but when a pricing policy gives only the illusion of a discount, it is unethical and in some states illegal.

As an example of superficial discounting, consider one retailer that sells 93 percent of its power tools on sale with discounts ranging from 10 to 40 percent. The retailer's frequent special events or sales mean that the tools are sold at sale prices most of the year. To combat such superficial discounting, Canada requires retailers to post a base price for at least six months before discounting a product.

■ **Experience Curve Pricing**

In **experience curve pricing**, a company fixes a low price that high-cost competitors cannot match and thus expands its market share. This practice is possible when a firm gains cumulative production experience and is able to reduce its manufacturing costs at a predictable rate through improved methods, materials, skills, and machinery. Texas Instruments used this strategy in marketing its calculators. The experience curve depicts the inverse relationship between production costs per unit and cumulative production quantity. To take advantage of the experience curve, a company must gain a dominant market share early in a product's life cycle. An early market share lead, with the greater cumulative production experience that it implies, will place a company further down the experience curve than its competitors. To avoid antitrust problems, companies must objectively examine the competitive structure of the market before and after implementing the experience curve strategy. The strategy should not be anticompetitive, and the company must have specific and accurate data that will be unshakable in a court of law. Under the proper conditions—a high probability of success, suitable precaution, and sound legal counsel—the method is perfectly acceptable as a primary policy.[6]

DEVELOPMENT OF A PRICING METHOD

After selecting a pricing policy, a marketer must choose a **pricing method**, a mechanical procedure for setting prices on a regular basis. The pricing method structures the calculation of the actual price. The nature of a product, its sales volume, or the amount of product the organization carries will determine how prices are calculated. For example, a procedure for pricing the thousands of products in a supermarket must be simpler and more direct than that for calculating the price of a new earth-moving machine manufactured by Caterpillar. In this section we examine three types of market-oriented pricing methods: cost-oriented, demand-oriented, and competition-oriented pricing.

■ **Cost-Oriented Pricing**

In **cost-oriented pricing**, a dollar amount or percentage is added to the cost of a product. The method thus involves calculations of desired margins or profit margins. Cost-oriented pricing methods do not necessarily take into account the economic aspects of supply and demand, nor do they necessarily relate to a specific pricing

6. Alan R. Beckenstein and H. Landis Gabel, "Experience Curve Pricing Strategy: The Next Target of Antitrust?" *Business Horizons,* September-October 1982, pp. 71–77.

policy or ensure the attainment of pricing objectives. They are, however, simple and easy to implement. Two common cost-oriented pricing methods are cost-plus and markup pricing.

Cost-Plus Pricing. In **cost-plus pricing**, the seller's costs are determined (usually during a project or after a project is completed), and then a specified dollar amount or percentage of the cost is added to the seller's cost to set the price. When production costs are difficult to predict or production takes a long time, cost-plus pricing is appropriate. Custom-made equipment and commercial construction projects are often priced by this method. The government frequently uses such cost-oriented pricing in granting defense contracts. One pitfall for the buyer is that the seller may increase costs to establish a larger profit base. Furthermore, some costs, such as overhead, may be difficult to determine.

In periods of rapid inflation, cost-plus pricing is popular, especially when the producer must use raw materials that are fluctuating in price. For industries in which cost-plus pricing is common and sellers have similar costs, price competition may not be especially intense.

Markup Pricing. A common pricing method among retailers is **markup pricing**. In markup pricing, a product's price is derived by adding a predetermined percentage of the cost, called *markup*, to the cost of the product. Although the percentage markup in a retail store varies from one category of goods to another (35 percent of cost for hardware items and 100 percent of cost for greeting cards, for example), the same percentage often is used to determine the price on items within a single product category, and the same or similar percentage markup may be standardized across an industry at the retail level. Using a rigid percentage markup for a specific product category reduces pricing to a routine task that can be performed quickly.

Markup can be stated as a percentage of the cost or as a percentage of the selling price. The following example illustrates how percentage markups are determined and points out the differences in the two methods. Assume that a retailer purchases a can of tuna at 45 cents, adds 15 cents to the cost, and then prices the tuna at 60 cents. Here are the figures:

$$\text{Markup as a Percentage of Cost} = \frac{\text{Markup}}{\text{Cost}}$$

$$\text{Markup as a Percentage of Selling Price} = \frac{\text{Markup}}{\text{Selling Price}}$$

$$= \frac{15}{60}$$

$$= 25.0\%$$

Obviously, when discussing a percentage markup, it is important to know whether the markup is based on cost or selling price.

Markups normally reflect expectations about operating costs, risks, and stock turnovers. Wholesalers and manufacturers often suggest standard retail markups that are considered profitable. An average percentage markup on cost may be as high as 100 percent or more for jewelry or as low as 20 percent for the textbook you are reading. To the extent that retailers use similar markups for the same product category, price competition is reduced. In addition, using rigid markups is convenient—the major reason that retailers, who face numerous pricing decisions, favor this method.

Demand-Oriented Pricing

Rather than basing the price of a product on its cost, marketers sometimes use a pricing method based on the level of demand for the product: **demand-oriented pricing**. This method results in a high price when demand for the product is strong and a low price when demand is weak. Most long-distance telephone companies, such as MCI, Sprint, and AT&T, use demand-oriented pricing. To use this method, a marketer must be able to estimate the amounts of a product that consumers will demand at different prices. The marketer then chooses the price that generates the highest total revenue. Obviously, the effectiveness of this method depends on the marketer's ability to estimate demand accurately. As reported in Marketing Update 18.2, Sonesta International Hotels employs demand-oriented pricing by using a computer-based yield management approach.

A marketer may favor a demand-oriented pricing method called **price differentiation** when the firm wants to use more than one price in the marketing of a specific product. Price differentiation can be based on such considerations as type of customer, type of distribution channel used, or the time of the purchase. Here are several examples. A twelve-ounce canned soft drink costs less from a supermarket than from a vending machine. Florida hotel accommodations are more expensive in the winter than in the summer. A home owner pays more for air conditioner filters than does an apartment complex owner, who purchases the same size filters in greater quantity. Christmas tree ornaments are usually cheaper on December 26 than on December 16. As shown in Figure 18.14, Marriott Suites charges $119 per night during the week and $69 on weekends.

For price differentiation to work properly, the marketer must be able to segment a market on the basis of different strengths of demand and then keep the segments separate enough so that segment members who buy at lower prices cannot then sell to buyers in segments that are charged a higher price. This isolation could be accomplished, for example, by selling to geographically separated segments.

Price differentiation is often facilitated in international marketing by the geographic distance between markets. For example, Matsushita Electric Co. sells cordless Panasonic telephones in Japan at eight times what cordless telephones of slightly lower quality sell for in the United States. When a Japanese trading company reimported the U.S. cordless phones and sold them for $80 instead of the Japanese model, which cost $657, consumers lined up to buy the cheaper telephone. To combat the reimportation, Matsushita bought up all the unsold made-for-export Panasonic telephones it could find to eliminate the wide price differential. (The major difference between the telephones was that the U.S. telephone had a range of forty meters and the Japanese telephone had a range of fifty meters, which is surprising, because the average Japanese home is much smaller than the average U.S. home.) For years, U.S. manufacturers have accused the Japanese of subsidizing foreign trade wars with high profits from their relatively closed home market.[7]

Price differentiation can also be based on employment in a public service position. For example, USAIR, Inc., as well as most other airlines, permits 50 percent

7. "Frantic Cheap Phone Buy-Up Reveals a Lot About Japanese Marketing," *Ann Arbor News* (Ann Arbor, Mich.), Feb. 14, 1988, p. C9.

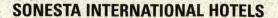

SONESTA INTERNATIONAL HOTELS

For years, officials of Cambridge, Massachusetts–based Sonesta International Hotels have sought the most effective ways to market and manage their hotels. In semi-annual conventions, Sonesta management listens to suggestions from suppliers and customers on how its hotel services and facilities can be improved. At these meetings, Sonesta hotel managers learn about new concepts in hotel operations and discuss possible changes in procedures, sometimes implementing customer recommendations. With an earnest dedication to professionalism and efficiency, Sonesta management is committed to improving customer relations, hotel services, and general procedures for doing business.

To better control room inventory and to set prices that help to maximize revenues, Sonesta uses an artificial-intelligence-based yield management system. Advances in computer technology have allowed Sonesta managers to update prices daily so that they can match hotel room fares with the market demands of each day. Hotel yield management is based on correlating previous customer behavior patterns with current room demands and forecasts of future occupancy. Sonesta managers use yield management to make constant adjustments in prices so that the most profitable balance between room supply and demand can be achieved.

The hotel industry usually groups guests into two segments: business and leisure. Each segment has its own distinct price-elasticity and time-sensitivity characteristics. Business room bookings tend to be made immediately before a trip; leisure travelers usually book rooms well in advance. Price does not seem to be a major consideration for traveling business people, but it is a primary factor when pleasure travelers are securing reservations. Sonesta's yield management approach considers these and other important elements to determine what the price will be of a room on a particular date. If the demand for rooms changes for that date, the room prices will change.

SOURCES: "Improving the Profit Yield When Products are 'Perishable,'" *Industrial Marketing Digest,* Second Quarter 1989, pp. 131–136; Walter J. Relihan III, "The Yield-Management Approach to Hotel-Room Pricing," *The Cornell Hotel and Restaurant Administration Quarterly,* May 1989, pp. 40–45; and Rayna Skolnik, "Sonesta Tells Customers, 'We Hear You,'" *Sales & Marketing Management,* Nov. 11, 1985.

FIGURE 18.14
Price differentiation.
Due to variation in demand, the price of a Marriott Suite is $119 per night during the week and $69 on weekends.

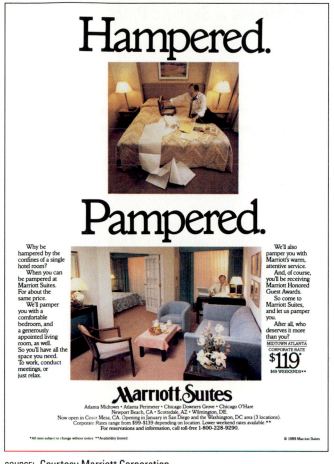

SOURCE: Courtesy Marriott Corporation

off each regular one-way or round-trip fare for all U.S. military personnel on active duty, leave, furlough, or a pass.

Compared with cost-oriented pricing, demand-oriented pricing places a firm in a better position to reach higher profit levels, assuming that buyers value the product at levels sufficiently above the product's cost. To use demand-oriented pricing, however, a marketer must be able to estimate demand at different price levels, which is often difficult to do accurately.

Competition-Oriented Pricing

In using **competition-oriented pricing**, an organization considers costs and revenue secondary to competitors' prices. The importance of this method increases if competing products are almost homogeneous and the organization is serving markets in which price is the key variable of the marketing strategy. A firm that uses competition-oriented pricing may choose to be below competitors' prices, above competitors' prices, or at the same level. The price of this textbook that the bookstore paid to the publishing company was determined using competition-oriented pricing. Competition-oriented pricing should help attain a pricing objective to increase sales or market share. Competition-oriented pricing methods may be combined with cost approaches to arrive at price levels necessary for a profit.

DETERMINING A SPECIFIC PRICE

Pricing policies and methods should direct and structure the selection of a final price. If they are to do so, it is important for marketers to establish pricing objectives, to know something about the target market, and to determine demand, price elasticity, costs, and competitive factors. In addition to those economic factors, the manner in which pricing is used in the marketing mix will affect the final price.

Although we suggest a systematic approach to pricing, in practice prices often are finalized after only limited planning, or they may be set without planning, just by trial and error. Then marketers determine whether revenue, minus costs, yields a profit. This approach to pricing is not recommended because it makes it difficult to discover pricing errors. If prices are based on both unrealistic pricing methods and unrealistic sales forecasts, a firm may resort to price gimmickry to sell its products. This approach should be avoided because it can become permanent. The domestic car industry is a current example of how pricing incentives, such as cash rebates and discount financing, can become an essential and permanent part of pricing.[8]

In the absence of government price control, pricing remains a flexible and convenient way to adjust the marketing mix. In most situations, prices can be adjusted quickly—in a matter of minutes or over a few days. This flexibility and freedom do not characterize the other components of the marketing mix. Because so many complex issues are involved in establishing the right price, pricing is indeed as much an art as a science.

SUMMARY

The eight stages in the process of establishing prices are these: (1) selecting pricing objectives; (2) assessing the target market's evaluation of price and its ability to purchase; (3) determining demand; (4) analyzing demand, cost, and profit relationships; (5) analyzing competitors' prices; (6) selecting a pricing policy; (7) developing a pricing method; and (8) determining a specific price.

The first stage, setting pricing objectives, is critical because pricing objectives form a foundation on which the decisions of subsequent stages are based. Organizations may use numerous pricing objectives: short-term and long-term ones, and different ones for different products and market segments.

The second stage in establishing prices is an assessment of the target market's evaluation of price and its ability to purchase. This stage tells a marketer how much emphasis to place on price and may help the marketer determine how far above the competition the firm can set its prices. Understanding customers' buying power and knowing how important a product is to the customers in comparison with other products helps marketers correctly assess the target market's evaluation of price.

In the third stage, the organization must determine the demand for its product. The classic demand curve is a graph of the quantity of products expected to be sold at various prices, if other factors are held constant. It illustrates that, as price falls, the quantity demanded usually increases. However, for prestige products, there is a direct positive relationship between price and quantity demanded: demand in-

8. Ray Hellstern, "A Pricing Strategy for the U.S. Steel Producer," *Akron Business and Economic Review,* Spring 1987, p. 53.

creases as price increases. Next, price elasticity of demand—the percentage change in quantity demanded relative to a given percentage change in price—must be determined. If demand is elastic, a change in price causes an opposite change in total revenue. Inelastic demand results in parallel change in total revenue when a product's price is changed.

Analysis of demand, cost, and profit relationships—the fourth stage of the process—can be accomplished through marginal analysis or breakeven analysis. Marginal analysis is the examination of what happens to a firm's costs and revenues when production (or sales volume) is changed by one unit. Marginal analysis combines the demand curve with a firm's costs to develop an optimum price for maximum profit. Fixed costs do not vary with changes in the number of units produced or sold; average fixed cost is the fixed cost per unit produced. Variable costs vary directly with changes in the number of units produced or sold. Average variable cost is the variable cost per unit produced. Average total cost is the sum of average fixed cost and average variable cost times the quantity produced. The optimum price is the point at which marginal cost (the cost associated with producing one more unit of the product) equals marginal revenue (the change in total revenue that occurs when one additional unit of the product is sold). Marginal analysis is only a model; it offers little help in pricing new products before costs and revenues are established.

Breakeven analysis—determining the number of units necessary to break even—is important in setting the price. The point at which the costs of production equal the revenue made from selling the product is the breakeven point. To use breakeven analysis effectively, a marketer should determine the breakeven point for each of several alternative prices. This determination makes it possible to compare the effects on total revenue, total costs, and the breakeven point for each price under consideration. However, this approach assumes that the quantity demanded is basically fixed and that the major task is to set prices to recover costs.

A marketer needs to be aware of the prices charged for competing brands. This allows a firm to keep its prices the same as competitors' prices when nonprice competition is used. If a company uses price as a competitive tool, it can price its brand below competing brands.

A pricing policy is a guiding philosophy or course of action designed to influence and determine pricing decisions. Pricing policies help marketers solve the practical problems of establishing prices. Two types of pioneer pricing policies are price skimming and penetration pricing. With price skimming, an organization charges the highest price that buyers who most desire the product will pay. A penetration price is a lower price designed to penetrate the market and produce a larger unit sales volume. Psychological pricing, another pricing policy, encourages purchases that are based on emotional rather than rational responses. It includes odd-even pricing, customary pricing, prestige pricing, and price lining. A third pricing policy, professional pricing, is used by people who have great skill or experience in a particular field. Promotional pricing, in which price is coordinated with promotion, is another type of pricing policy. Price leaders, special-event pricing, and superficial discounting are examples of promotional pricing. Experience curve pricing fixes a low price that high-cost competitors cannot match. Experience curve pricing is possible when experience reduces manufacturing costs at a predictable rate.

A pricing method is a mechanical procedure for assigning prices to specific products on a regular basis. Three types of pricing methods are cost-oriented, demand-oriented, and competition-oriented pricing. In using cost-oriented pricing, a firm determines price by adding a dollar amount or percentage to the cost of the product. Two common cost-oriented pricing methods are cost-plus and markup pricing. Demand-oriented pricing is based on the level of demand for the product. To use this method, a marketer must be able to estimate the amounts of a product that buyers will demand at different prices. Demand-oriented pricing results in a high price when demand for a product is strong and a low price when demand is weak. In the case of competition-oriented pricing, costs and revenues are secondary to competitors' prices. Competition-oriented pricing and cost approaches may be combined to arrive at price levels necessary for a profit.

IMPORTANT TERMS

Demand curve	Customary pricing
Price elasticity of demand	Prestige pricing
Fixed costs	Price lining
Average fixed cost	Professional pricing
Variable costs	Price leaders
Average variable cost	Special-event pricing
Total cost	Superficial discounting
Average total cost	Experience curve pricing
Marginal cost (MC)	Pricing method
Marginal revenue (MR)	Cost-oriented pricing
Breakeven point	Cost-plus pricing
Pricing policy	Markup pricing
Price skimming	Demand-oriented pricing
Penetration price	Price differentiation
Psychological pricing	Competition-oriented pricing
Odd-even pricing	

DISCUSSION AND REVIEW QUESTIONS

1. Identify the eight stages that make up the process of establishing prices.
2. Why do most demand curves demonstrate an inverse relationship between price and quantity?
3. List the characteristics of products that have inelastic demand. Give several examples of such products.
4. Explain why optimum profits should occur when marginal cost equals marginal revenue.
5. The Chambers Company has just gathered estimates for doing a breakeven analysis for a new product. Variable costs are $7 a unit. The additional plant will cost $48,000. The new product will be charged $18,000 a year for its share of general overhead. Advertising expenditures will be $80,000, and $55,000 will be spent on distribution. If the product sells for $12, what is the breakeven point in units? What is the breakeven point in dollar sales volume?
6. Why should a marketer be aware of competitors' prices?
7. For what type of products would a pioneer price-skimming policy be most appropriate? For what type of products would penetration pricing be more effective?

8. Why do consumers associate price with quality? When should prestige pricing be used?
9. Are price leaders a realistic approach to pricing?
10. What are the benefits of cost-oriented pricing?
11. Under what conditions is cost-plus pricing most appropriate?
12. If a retailer purchases a can of soup for 24 cents and sells it for 36 cents, what is the percentage markup on selling price?

■ CASES

18.1   Dr. Denton A. Cooley's Cut-Rate Heart Surgery

Dr. Denton A. Cooley, the renowned heart specialist who pioneered American heart transplants and implanted the first artificial heart in a human, has brought "every-day low prices" to heart bypass surgery. Surgeons perform coronary artery bypass surgery to treat angina, a severe chest pain that occurs when the heart muscle is deprived of oxygenated blood. Bypass surgery is Dr. Cooley's specialty. He is an expert at replacing older, clogged arteries with new ones. As the population of the United States ages overall, bypass surgery is likely to become more common. Dr. Cooley's pricing strategy makes this sophisticated surgery more affordable and may also prove to be an effective marketing tool in an area that is relatively new to marketing.

Dr. Cooley's marketing approach is to create a high-volume, low-cost business. Dr. Cooley charges a flat rate for a standard bypass—about $15,000. This rate is 40 percent less than the national average for similar surgery. If Dr. Cooley is successful with his flat-fee surgery, surgeons using other surgical procedures may adopt this approach. The medical field may adopt its own version of a price war.

It usually takes a surgeon six hours to perform the triple-bypass operation that Dr. Cooley performs in two hours, thanks to his expert team of five surgeons. He works five days a week, often 12 hours at a time with only small breaks. Because Dr. Cooley and his team perform thirty-five to forty operations each day, some physicians have criticized his approach, calling it "assembly line" surgery. Dr. Cooley has responded by remarking, "If it's an assembly line, it's a Rolls-Royce line."

Because 30 percent of Dr. Cooley's income comes from the work his team performs, he is looking for ways to increase volume. Dr. Cooley offers a "bundled" service that allows patients or their insurance companies to pay for everything—services, supplies, and specialists—with one fee. This more practical billing procedure makes Dr. Cooley's operations even more attractive to patients and insurance companies. A study by the Inspector General's office, the overseer of U.S. health agencies, has concluded that Medicare could reduce its $1.5 billion-a-year bill for heart surgery by 13 percent if Medicare patients were operated on by Dr. Cooley and his team. The 13 percent savings includes the costs of transporting the patients to Houston and housing them there.

Dr. Cooley is marketing his reputation as well as low prices. In thirty years of practice, he has performed over 80,000 heart operations, more than any other doctor in the world. Almost 90 percent of his bypass patients live at least five years, and 74 percent live over ten years. Dr. Cooley is constantly seeking and experimenting with new technology in his battle with heart disease, the number-one killer in the United States today. The battle is strenuous, but the rewards—in patient lives and in the $9.7 million a year he earns—are exceptional.

SOURCES: Kathy A. Fackelmann, "Shopping for Bypass Discounts," *Perspectives,* Sept. 21, 1987, pp. 1–4; Mark Ivey, "Will Denton Cooley Make Medical History Again?" *Business Week,* Mar. 27, 1989, pp. 56, 58; and Carol Stevens, "Is This the Beginning of DRGs for Doctors?" *Medical Economics,* Jan. 16, 1989, pp. 27–28, 33–34, 36.

Questions for Discussion

1. Is the flat-fee approach effective for pricing major medical services such as open-heart surgery? Explain.
2. Is Dr. Cooley using demand-oriented, cost-oriented, or competition-oriented pricing methods? Explain.
3. Evaluate the price elasticity of demand for open heart surgery.

18.2   Toys "R" Us Competes Through Price

Toys "R" Us is leading the U.S. toy market with its chain of over 400 warehouse-style toy supermarkets spread across the nation. It has long been an innovator, in both its pricing policies and its toy supermarket design. Toys "R" Us brings customers into the store by discounting such baby-care products as strollers and disposable diapers below cost. The strategy is that once parents are in the store, they will spend the money they saved on the discounted baby goods on toys.

Toys "R" Us stores are usually located along commercial highways, well away from shopping malls, to keep down costs and prevent customers from being distracted by other toy merchants. Isolation from shopping malls also means that customers will load up their shopping carts because they do not have to lug their purchases through crowded malls.

The first Toys "R" Us store was opened in 1957 as the Children's Supermarket (with the "r's" printed backward to encourage name recognition) and offered name-brand toys and baby goods below normal retail price. Today, it still offers name-brand toys at 20 to 50 percent below retail price. Each store has a full stock of thousands of different toys and baby goods tracked by a computer system that almost eliminates stockouts. Managers don't place orders for toys, the toys just arrive on time, thus averting the Toys "R" Us definition of a major disaster—not having a certain toy on display and ready to sell.

Toys "R" Us sets its price for a particular item based on how much it projects customers will pay for it. The company then determines the price at which it is willing to purchase the toy from the manufacturer and negotiates fiercely with the manufacturers to get the toy at that price. The company has a definite advantage in negotiations because it buys in such large volume. Toy manufacturers also treat Toys "R" Us well because the company is often a testing ground for new toys. Price is so important to the Toys "R" Us strategy that even when demand for a toy is high and supplies are short, the company will not raise its price on the toy to make a quick profit.

Market share is Toys "R" Us' main pricing objective; and for now it is the number-one toy store in the United States. The company says it is willing to cut prices to retain its leading position. Other toy stores are scrambling to meet the competition for Toys "R" Us; those that do not change their strategies wind up out of the toy market altogether. Many stores, such as K mart, expand their toy lines only for the six-week Christmas season and bring customers in with sales. Although Toys "R" Us never holds sales, it maintains its huge selection and discount prices year-round. Customers who found good buys at Toys "R" Us at Christmas will also shop there for children's birthdays and other special days, when other retail stores have a limited selection. Even new parents who drop in to Toys "R" Us for discounted baby products tend to return to buy toys. The company also sells sporting-goods "toys," such as footballs and bicycles, suitable for older teens, young adults, and family members of almost any age.

Some competitors have adopted the Toys "R" Us supermarket approach and have tried to meet Toys "R" Us prices throughout the year. Other stores are trying nonprice competition, by offering educational and baby-sitting services. However, Toys "R" Us intends to rely on its nonprice attributes of convenience, selection, and inventory, as well as price competition, to hold its position.

Toys "R" Us has expanded internationally to Britain, Germany, Canada, Japan, and other parts of Asia with over 80 stores. The company has plans for many other stores overseas to take advantage of the world toy market, which is nearly double that of the U.S. toy market. Additionally, it opened Kids "R" Us in the United States, a chain of children's clothing stores similar to the toy stores.

Toys "R" Us has customer loyalty behind it. Customers know that they can find *the* toy that a child wants, at the best price, at Toys "R" Us. And if the child does not like the toy, the purchaser may return it for a full refund with no questions asked.

SOURCES: Robert J. Cole, "Toys 'R' Us to Open Stores in Japan Within Two Years," *New York Times,* Sept. 27, 1989, pp. D1, D6; Dan Dorfman, "Toys 'R' Us: Mattel Play?" *USA Today,* June 28, 1987, p. 2B; Trish Hall, "Finding Gold in Overalls and Bibs," *New York Times,* Dec. 25, 1988, p. F1, F10; Mark Maremont, Dori Jones Yang, and Amy Dunkin, "Toys 'R' Us Goes Overseas—and Finds that Toys 'R' Them, Too," *Business Week,* Jan. 26, 1987, pp. 71–72; David Owen, "Where Toys Come From," *Atlantic Monthly,* Oct. 1986, pp. 64–78; Jesus Sanchez, "Toymakers Make a Play for Market," *USA Today,* Feb. 10, 1987, pp. 1B–2B.

Questions for Discussion

1. What are Toys "R" Us' major pricing objectives?
2. Assess Toys "R" Us' practice of not raising the prices of products that are scarce and in high demand.
3. A major disadvantage of using price competition is that competitors can match prices. Evaluate this potential for Toys "R" Us.

Sears' Everyday Low Prices

With sales and profits sagging and competitors like J.C. Penney, K mart, and Wal-Mart thriving, the top executives at Chicago-based Sears, Roebuck & Co. felt an urgent need to restructure their organization. The world's largest retailer was rapidly losing ground to newer, leaner, more vital companies. Once the mainstay of U.S. retailing, Sears was now losing customers to discount stores, specialty retailers, and trendier competitors. Sears market share dropped 33 percent in the 1980s—and its market share is continuing to decline.

When Sears adopted everyday low prices, in essence it also adopted the "if you can't beat them, join them" philosophy. Wal-Mart, Toys "R" Us, and Circuit City—three of the most successful retailers over the last decade—all have everyday low pricing. Everyday low pricing cuts labor and advertising costs, and it is more convenient for shoppers who do not have to be on the constant surveillance for sales. Some retailing executives think that everyday low prices result in more uniform selling patterns, avoiding the roller-coaster demands associated with promotional cycles.

With its administrative and selling expenses among the highest in retailing, Sears officials decided to take drastic actions and adopt an "everyday low prices" strategy. Sears closed its 824 stores for 42 hours to reprice the approximately 50,000 items in each store. Sears complemented its price reductions with an enormous media blitz: Sears aired over 2,000 television and radio spots and ran 900 newspaper advertisements in one three-week period. Some industry sources estimated that Sears spent about $100 million to promote its new pricing strategy methods. Sears directors knew the strategy was risky because consumers accustomed to periodic sales might be confused by the sudden change and might not respond positively. They also realized that their new low prices might incite "price wars" from discounters.

Sears, which had actually pioneered the concept of a "sale," made perhaps its most radical change in its 100-year history when it adopted everyday low pricing. Sears' traditional weekly sales promotions were expensive for the company to run. Sears officials wanted to cut selling costs so they decided to terminate the labor intensive, heavily promoted weekly sales.

Initially, Sears' turn to "everyday low prices" seemed to work brilliantly as sales and customer traffic increased and a majority of randomly surveyed consumers indicated that they were more likely to shop at Sears than before. After a couple of months, however, sales slowed.

Sears executives claimed that they reduced prices by as much as half on 75 percent of the stores' inventory. Recently, however, the attorney general offices of several states have filed suit against Sears. For example, the New York Attorney General, after an 18-month investigation, claimed that Sears' prices had remained "largely unchanged" despite the everyday-low-price rhetoric. The suit asserts that Sears' new prices do not offer consumers significant savings. Sears could face devastating consequences if the New York state court finds it guilty of deceptive advertising. Many consumers might never "trust" Sears again.

Sears top management strongly denies any wrongdoing and has filed a motion to expedite the New York trial. A high-ranking officer of Sears' merchandising group notes that the company's gross profit has decreased since Sears switched to everyday low pricing and offers this as proof that the company has indeed lowered prices.

The New York Attorney General's office is not convinced and is seeking an injunction that would prohibit Sears from continuing their everyday low price advertising. The suit also attempts to secure unspecified restitution for consumers and a penalty for Sears' violation of a 1986 agreement with the Attorney General's office regarding low-price advertisements.

Sears' revised marketing tactic will de-emphasize pricing and accentuate the company's traditional strengths of reliability and quality merchandise, and its now broader selection of brand name products. Sears executives have decided to stress value and savings instead of low prices.

Despite these serious allegations, everyday low pricing did not invigorate sales at Sears for a number of other reasons. First, consumers are being bombarded with everyday low price advertisements so the concept has lost much of its novelty and effectiveness. Second, because Sears is structured differently from a discounter like K mart, everyday low prices for Sears are not as productive. K marts are low overhead, free-standing stores—customers can be seen browsing through the store with shopping carts. Sears stores are usually in malls, and shoppers go to Sears to buy specific items. Third, the market for durable goods is down in the United States, and Sears relies heavily on these products. Fourth, an everyday-low-price strategy requires extra efficient operations to preserve profit margins. Operations at Sears have been less than efficient in several key areas.

Questions for Discussion

1. In what other ways could Sears use pricing as a competitive tool?
2. Does the pricing strategy have to be the same across all of Sears' departments within a store? Explain.
3. How should Sears cope with the legal problems associated with its everyday-low-prices strategy?
4. Should Sears continue with its everyday-low-prices strategy? Why or why not?

SOURCES: Isadore Barmash, "Big Crowds Greet the New Sears," *The New York Times*, March 2, 1989, pp. D1, D6; Amy Dunkin, "Little Prices are Looking Good to Big Retailers," *Business Week*, July 3, 1989, pp. 42, 44; James E. Ellis and Brian Bremner, "Will the Big Markdown Get the Big Store Moving Again?" *Business Week*, March 13, 1989, pp. 110–114; Kate Fitzgerald, "Can Sears Pull it Off?" *Advertising Age*, November 7, 1988, pp. 2, 74; Kate Fitzgerald, "Sears Breaks Biggest Blitz," *Advertising Age*, February 27, 1989, pp. 2, 75; Kate Fitzgerald, "Sears' Plan on the Ropes," *Advertising Age*, January 8, 1990, pp. 1, 42; Paul Glastris, "A Season of Hope for Sears," *U.S. News & World Report*, December 11, 1989, pp. 52–53; B.H. Lawrence, "Sears' Discounting Gamble," *Washington Post*, March 26, 1989, pp. H1, H6, H7; Francine Schwadel, "Sears Calls it 'Low Prices,' New York Calls it Misleading," *The Wall Street Journal*, December 22, 1989, pp. B1, B4; and Lena H. Sun, "Sears Sets New Sales Strategy: Lower Prices," *Washington Post*, March 1, 1989, pp. F1, F5.

PART **VI** **MARKETING MANAGEMENT**

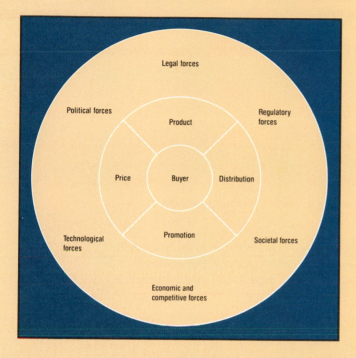

We have divided marketing into several sets of variables and have discussed the decisions and activities associated with each variable. By now, you should understand (1) how to analyze marketing opportunities, and (2) the components of the marketing mix. It is time to put all these components together in a discussion of marketing management issues. In Chapter 19 we discuss strategic market planning, focusing on the planning process, the setting of marketing objectives, the assessment of opportunities and resources, and specific product/market matching approaches to strategic market planning. Chapter 20 deals with other marketing management issues, including organization, implementation, and control. It explores approaches to organizing a marketing unit, issues regarding strategy implementation, and techniques for controlling marketing strategies. ◆

19 STRATEGIC MARKET PLANNING

Objectives

To understand the strategic market planning process

To explore and examine three major tools to assist in strategic market planning: product-portfolio analysis, the market attractiveness–business position model, and Profit Impact on Marketing Strategy (PIMS)

To evaluate strategic market planning and relate it to the development of functional marketing strategies and activities

To gain an overview of the marketing plan

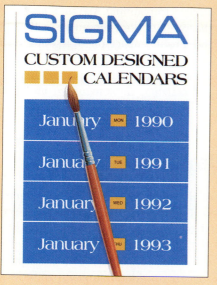

Sigma Marketing Concepts is a publisher of high-quality, creatively designed promotional calendars, which are sold directly to businesses for use as marketing tools. From 1985 to 1987, Sigma's sales volume grew rapidly. To ensure continued growth, Sigma reviewed its recent performance and organizational changes; from these findings, it developed long-range strategic market plans and made several changes in its marketing strategy.

Sigma's management first sold the printing and production portion of its business so that it could focus exclusively on marketing custom-designed desk pad calendar products. Sigma and the buyer of the production plant entered into a long-term contract under which the buyer would handle all of Sigma's calendar production, using the same plant and staff that had handled production for the past twenty years. This transaction freed Sigma from the daily problems of production and plant management and allowed it to concentrate all its resources and efforts on creating and marketing new calendar products.

The company developed a revised marketing strategy that focused on a new target market and improved promotion and distribution of its product line. It also expanded the product line to include wall planners, pocket planners, and diaries. Each product was designed to allow Sigma to maintain its differential advantage of offering high advertising flexibility and creativity. The target market was revised to focus on large, service-customer contact companies. After choosing prospects, Sigma initially contacted key marketing executives by phone and then sent them direct mail packages containing samples. This was followed by a call to answer questions and to encourage/close orders.

The new marketing strategy appears to be very successful. The company has added to its list of satisfied customers, such prime accounts as Federal Express Corp., Nabisco Brands, Inc., Fidelity Investments, and Jacob Suchard Brach Candies. Sigma Marketing Concepts continues to monitor and evaluate its internal and external environments. The company's founder, Don Sapit, believes that this practice contributes to Sigma's current level of success. ◆

Photo courtesy of Sigma Marketing Concepts.

Based on interviews with Donald Sapit, Renee Mudd, and Warren Eldridge, Sigma Marketing Concepts, 1987.

This chapter looks closely at one portion of strategic marketing: planning. We start with an overview of the strategic market planning process, including the development of organizational goals and corporate strategy. We also examine organizational opportunities and resources as they relate to planning. We then look at some tools used in strategic market planning: the product-portfolio analysis, the market attractiveness–business position model, and Profit Impact on Marketing Strategy (PIMS). Next we examine competitive strategies for marketing and close with a look at marketing planning and the development of a marketing plan. Other aspects of the marketing management process—organizing, implementing, and controlling—are covered in Chapter 20.

STRATEGIC MARKET PLANNING DEFINED

A **strategic market plan** is an outline of the methods and resources required to achieve an organization's goals within a specific target market. It takes into account not only marketing, but also all functional aspects of a business unit that must be coordinated. These functional aspects include production, finance, and personnel. Environmental issues are an important consideration as well. The concept of the strategic business unit is used to define areas for consideration in a specific strategic market plan. Each **strategic business unit (SBU)** is a division, product line, or other profit center within the parent company. Borden's strategic business units, for example, consist of dairy products, snacks, pasta, niche grocery products such as RealLemon juice and Cremora coffee cream, and other units such as glue and paints. Each sells a distinct set of products to an identifiable group of customers, and each competes with a well-defined set of competitors. Each SBU's revenues, costs, investments, and strategic plans can be separated and evaluated from those of the parent company. SBUs operate in a variety of markets, which have differing growth rates, opportunities, degrees of competition, and profit-making potential. In Figure 19.1, Toshiba promotes one of its strategic business units, its Computer Systems Division. Strategic planners therefore must recognize the different performance capabilities of each SBU and carefully allocate scarce resources among these divisions.

The process of **strategic market planning** yields a marketing strategy that is the framework for a marketing plan. A **marketing plan** includes the framework and entire set of activities to be performed; it is the written document or blueprint for implementing and controlling an organization's marketing activities. Thus a strategic market plan is *not* the same as a marketing plan; it is a plan of *all* aspects of an organization's strategy in the marketplace. A marketing plan, in contrast, deals primarily with implementing the market strategy as it relates to target markets and the marketing mix.[1]

Figure 19.2 shows the components of strategic market planning. The process is based on the establishment of an organization's overall goals, and it must stay within the bounds of the organization's opportunities and resources. When the firm has determined its overall goals and identified its resources, it can then assess its oppor-

---

1. Derek F. Abell and John S. Hammond, *Strategic Market Planning* (Englewood Cliffs, N.J.: Prentice-Hall, 1979), p. 10.

FIGURE 19.1 *Toshiba promotes one of its strategic business units.*
Other Toshiba SBUs include industrial equipment and high-tech electronics used in ship construction.

SOURCE: Toshiba America Information Systems, Inc.

tunities and develop a corporate strategy. Marketing objectives must be designed so that their achievement will contribute to the corporate strategy and so that they can be accomplished through efficient use of the firm's resources.

To achieve its marketing objectives, an organization must develop a marketing strategy, or a set of marketing strategies, as shown in Figure 19.2. The set of marketing strategies that are implemented and used at the same time is referred to as the organization's **marketing program**. Through the process of strategic market planning, an organization can develop marketing strategies that, when properly implemented and controlled, will contribute to the achievement of its marketing objectives and its overall goals. As we have mentioned before, to formulate a marketing strategy, the marketer identifies and analyzes the target market and develops a marketing mix to satisfy individuals in that market. Marketing strategy is best formulated when it reflects the overall direction of the organization and is coordinated with all the firm's functional areas.

As indicated in Figure 19.2, the strategic market planning process is based on an analysis of the environment, by which it is very much affected. Environmental forces can place constraints on an organization and possibly influence its overall goals; they also affect the amount and type of resources that a firm can acquire. However, these forces can create favorable opportunities as well—opportunities that can be translated into overall organizational goals and marketing objectives. For example, when oil prices declined during the second half of the 1980s, consumers

FIGURE 19.2
Components of strategic market planning

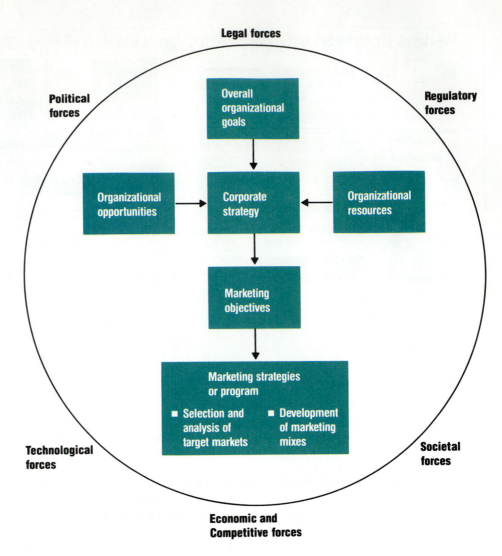

once again turned to large "gas-guzzling" automobiles. This situation created an opportunity for manufacturers of large cars, such as Cadillac, Oldsmobile (General Motors divisions) and Lincoln (a division of Ford).

Marketers differ in their viewpoints concerning the effect of environmental variables on marketing planning and strategy. Some take a deterministic perspective, believing that firms must react to external conditions and tailor their strategies and organizational structures to deal with these conditions. According to others, however, companies can influence their environments by choosing what markets to compete in. Furthermore, they can change the structures of their industries, engaging in activities such as mergers and acquisitions, demand creation, or technological innovation.[2]

2. P. Rajan Varadarajan, Terry Clark, and William Pride, "Determining Your Company's Destiny," working paper, Texas A&M University, 1990.

Regardless of which viewpoint is adopted, environmental variables play a part in the creation of a marketing strategy. When environmental variables affect an organization's overall goals, resources, opportunities, or marketing objectives, they also affect its marketing strategies, which are based on these factors. Environmental forces more directly influence the development of a marketing strategy through their impact on consumers' needs and desires. In addition, these forces have a bearing on marketing mix decisions. For instance, competition strongly influences marketing mix decisions. The organization must diagnose the marketing mix activities it performs, taking into account competitors' marketing mix decisions, and develop some competitive advantage to support a strategy. Thus as Honda and Toyota entered the luxury automobile market with the Accura and Lexus models, European car makers BMW, Mercedes, and Jaguar had to change their marketing strategies to maintain their market shares. They did so by lowering prices to compete with the new Japanese models.

In the next sections we discuss the major components of the strategic market planning process: organizational goals, organizational opportunities and resources, and corporate strategy, as well as the tools that aid in strategic market planning and some competitive marketing strategies.

ORGANIZATIONAL GOALS

A firm's organizational goals should be derived from its *mission,* the broad tasks that the organization wants to accomplish. IBM, for example, has stated that its mission is helping businesspeople make decisions. A company's mission and overall organizational goals should guide all its planning efforts. Its goals should specify the ends or results that are sought. For example, a firm in serious financial trouble may be concerned solely with short-run results needed for staying in business. There usually is an airline or major retailer being forced by cash shortages to take drastic action to stay in business. On the other hand, some companies have more optimistic goals. Often manufacturers such as General Motors have goals that relate to return on investment. A successful company, however, may want to sacrifice the current year's profits for the long run and at the same time pursue other goals, such as increasing market share.

ORGANIZATIONAL OPPORTUNITIES AND RESOURCES

There are three major considerations in assessing opportunities and resources: evaluating market opportunities, environmental scanning (discussed in Chapter 2), and understanding the firm's capabilities.

■ **Market Opportunities**

A **market opportunity** arises when the right combination of circumstances occurs at the right time to allow an organization to take action toward reaching a target market. An opportunity provides a favorable chance or opening for the firm to generate sales from identifiable markets. For example, in reaction to the over-

FIGURE 19.3

Responding to marketing opportunities. When research highlighted the potential benefits of oat bran, Kellogg responded to this opportunity by creating its new Common Sense™ Oat Bran cereal.

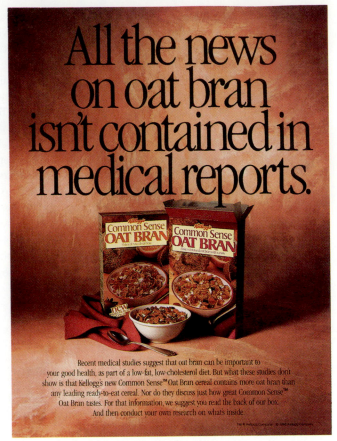

All the news on oat bran isn't contained in medical reports.

Recent medical studies suggest that oat bran can be important to your good health, as part of a low-fat, low-cholesterol diet. But what these studies don't show is that Kellogg's new Common Sense™ Oat Bran cereal contains more oat bran than any leading ready-to-eat cereal. Nor do they discuss just how great Common Sense™ Oat Bran tastes. For that information, we suggest you read the back of our box. And then conduct your own research on what's inside.

whelming growth in cereals and other foods containing oat bran (which some researchers believe helps lower cholesterol levels), the Quaker Oats Company developed an advertising campaign to remind consumers that Quaker oatmeal products have always contained oat bran. The commercials, which featured actor Wilford Brimley, told consumers that eating oatmeal is "the right thing to do," and helped boost sales of Quaker oatmeal dramatically.[3] Increasing concerns about cancer and heart disease gave Quaker a market opportunity to reach consumers who are especially health conscious by touting the health benefits of its oatmeal. Kellogg also took advantage of the popularity of oat bran by creating its Common Sense™ Oat Bran cereal (see Figure 19.3). Interestingly, in 1990, a study published in a leading medical journal questioned the effect of oat bran on lowering cholesterol. The conclusion was that avoiding high cholesterol animal products was what really lowered cholesterol. Therefore, some of the oat bran mystique vanished overnight. The term *strategic window* has been used to describe what are often temporary periods of optimum fit between the key requirements of a market and the particular capabilities of a firm competing in that market.[4]

3. Zachary Schiller, with Russell Mitchell, Wendy Zellner, Lois Therrien, Andrea Rothman, and Walecia Konrad, "The Great American Health Pitch," *Business Week,* Oct. 9, 1989, p. 116.

4. Derek F. Abell, "Strategic Windows," *Journal of Marketing,* July 1978, p. 21.

The attractiveness of market opportunities is determined by market factors, such as size and growth rate, as well as competitive, financial, economic, technological, social, legal, and political factors.[5] Because each industry and product are somewhat different, the factors that determine attractiveness tend to vary.

Market requirements relate to customers' needs or desired benefits. Market requirements are satisfied by components of the marketing mix that provide buyers with these benefits. Of course, buyers' perceptions of what requirements fulfill their needs and provide the desired benefits determine the success of any marketing effort. Marketers must devise strategies to outperform competitors by finding out what product attributes buyers use to select products. An attribute must be important and differentiating if it is to be useful in strategy development. When marketers fail to understand buyers' perceptions and market requirements, the result may be failure. First Nationwide Financial Corp., for example, assumed that working-class consumers would want to take care of their banking needs while shopping for discount products. It opened 170 minibank branches in K mart stores in 12 states. But K mart shoppers were not interested or were reluctant to handle their banking needs outside of traditional banking channels, and First Nationwide was forced to close all the K mart branches.[6]

■ Environmental Scanning

In Chapter 2 we define environmental scanning as the process of collecting information about the marketing environment because such knowledge helps marketers identify opportunities and assists in planning. Some companies have derived substantial benefits from establishing an "environmental scanning (or monitoring) unit" within the strategic planning group or including line management in teams or committees to conduct environmental analysis. This approach engages management in the process of environmental forecasting and enhances the likelihood of successfully integrating forecasting efforts into strategic market planning.[7] Results of forecasting research show that even simple quantitative forecasting techniques outperform the unstructured intuitive assessments of experts.[8]

Environmental scanning to detect changes in the environment is extremely important if a firm is to avoid crisis management. An environmental change can suddenly alter a firm's opportunities or resources. Reformulated, more effective strategies may then be needed to guide marketing efforts. For example, after Congress passed legislation requiring that 10 percent of all cars sold in the United States in the late 1990s run on "clean" fuels such as methanol and ethanol, American car makers had to reformulate their strategies to provide for the development and marketing of automobiles that will cost more and will run on higher-priced fuels.[9] Because automobile manufacturers have engaged in environmental scanning and were aware that such legislation might indeed be enacted because of social and political concerns, most had already begun developing plans for cars powered by

---

5. Abell and Hammond, p. 213.

6. Ken Wells, "Bank Checks Out of K mart, Realizing That Interest at Stores Was Too Low," *Wall Street Journal*, Feb. 13, 1989, p. B3.

7. Liam Fahey, William K. King, and Vodake K. Naraganan, "Environmental Scanning and Forecasting in Strategic Planning—The State of the Art," *Long Range Planning*, February 1981, p. 38.

8. David M. Georgaff and Robert G. Mundick, "Managers' Guide to Forecasting," *Harvard Business Review*, January-February 1986, p. 120.

9. "The Bumpy Road to 'Clean Fuels,'" *U.S. News & World Report*, June 26, 1989, pp. 10–11.

FIGURE 19.4

Federal Express promotes its capabilities and resources. Federal Express flies to more countries overseas than any of its competitors. Its experience in shipping internationally also gives it a competitive advantage.

clean fuel. Ford Motor Company, for example, is already testing a car that can run on methanol, ethanol, gasoline, or any combination of those fuels.[10] Environmental scanning should identify new developments and determine the nature and rate of change. As illustrated in Marketing Update 19.1, environmental scanning has highlighted several changing trends beneficial to domestic beer marketers.

■ **Capabilities and Resources**

A firm's capabilities relate to distinctive competencies that it has developed to do something well and efficiently. A company is likely to enjoy a differential advantage in an area where its competencies outmatch those of its potential competition.[11] In Figure 19.4, Federal Express promotes their widespread international presence. Often a company may possess manufacturing or technical skills that are valuable in areas outside of its traditional industry. For example, BASF, known for its manufacture and development of audio- and videotapes, produced a new type of lightweight plastic that has uses in other industries.

Today marketing planners are especially concerned with resource constraints. Shortages in energy and other scarce economic resources often limit strategic planning

10. Ibid.

11. Philip Kotler, "Strategic Planning and the Marketing Process," *Business,* May-June 1980, pp. 6–7.

A BOOST FOR DOMESTIC BEER

In 1989, for the first time in 20 years, U.S. beer imports declined while sales of domestic beers increased. Although U.S. beer drinkers have become more concerned with value and their waistlines and less concerned with status in recent years, most of the import sales decline stems from the strategic actions by domestic beer marketers, which have introduced a variety of new brands and packaging to lure import-drinking customers home.

With the introduction of the premium brands Miller Genuine Draft, Coors Extra Gold, Michelob Dry, and Bud Dry, American brewers began to recapture market share. After only four years on the market, Miller Genuine Draft became one of the top ten brands sold in 1989—a feat virtually unheard of for a brand that had spent such a limited time on the market.

In addition, the introduction of packaging innovations such as the Coors "Party-Ball" and long-neck bottles helped boost domestic sales. Corona Extra, a Mexican import, had long been the only long-necked brand sold in the U.S. American brewers not only adopted long-neck packaging, but also began selling long-necks in twelve-packs—a design more traditionally used for canned beer.

When a weaker U.S. dollar in 1990 contributed to a 4 to 5 percent increase in import prices, some domestic brewers began discounting their premium beers, possibly affecting their price/quality image. In addition, recent campaigns against drunk driving have resulted in a decline in beer consumption in bars and restaurants. Because about two-thirds of import brands are consumed in these places, they have lost a disproportionate amount of sales relative to domestic brands that are mostly consumed at home. Thus, social and legal changes in the marketing environment have given domestic brands a strategic advantage.

SOURCES: Marj Charlier, "Beer Imports' Brisk Growth Is Bottled Up by Soft Dollar, Stiffer U.S. Competition," *Wall Street Journal,* Feb. 2, 1990, pp. B1, B6; Theodore Gage, "Import Brands Find Squeeze Is Tighter," *Advertising Age,* July 27, 1981, p. S49; Kevin T. Higgins, "Beer Importers Upbeat About Future Despite Warning Signs," *Marketing News,* Oct. 25, 1985, pp. 1, 9; Eileen Norris, "Import Uses Novel in Growing Beer Niche," *Advertising Age,* Jan. 31, 1985, p. 5.

options. On the other hand, planning to avoid shortages can backfire. Many electric utilities decided to build nuclear power plants in the 1970s, to compensate for an expected shortfall of fossil fuels, only to find the political, social, and technological problems of nuclear power almost impossible to overcome. Moreover, an adequate supply of fossil fuels still exists to power traditional plants that generate electricity. But as the public grows more concerned about pollution and the so-called greenhouse effect—the increased warming of the earth caused by pollution—nuclear power plants may once again become a plausible alternative.

CORPORATE STRATEGY

Corporate strategy determines the means for utilizing resources in the areas of production, finance, research and development, personnel, and marketing to reach the organization's goals. A corporate strategy determines not only the scope of the business but also its resource deployment, competitive advantages, and overall coordination of production, finance, marketing, and other functional areas. The term *corporate* in this context does not apply only to corporations; corporate strategy is used by all organizations, from the smallest sole proprietorship to the largest multinational corporation.

Corporate strategy planners are concerned with issues such as diversification, competition, differentiation, interrelationships among business units, and environmental issues. They attempt to match the resources of the organization with the opportunities and risks in the environment. For example, McDonald's, as part of its corporate strategy to give back to the local community, strongly supports youth sports and amateur athletics (see Figure 19.5). Corporate strategy planners are also concerned with defining the scope and role of the strategic business units of the firm so that they are coordinated to reach the ends desired.

TOOLS FOR STRATEGIC MARKET PLANNING

A number of tools have been proposed to aid marketing managers in their planning efforts. Based on ideas used in the management of financial portfolios, several models that classify an organization's product portfolio have been proposed. These models allow strategic business units or products to be classified and visually displayed according to the attractiveness of various markets and the business's relative market share within those markets. Three of these tools—the Boston Consulting Group (BCG) product-portfolio analysis, the market attractiveness–business position model, and the Profit Impact on Marketing Strategy (PIMS)—are discussed next.

■ **The Boston Consulting Group (BCG) Product-Portfolio Analysis**

Just as financial investors have different investments with varying risks and rates of return, firms have a portfolio of products characterized by different market growth rates and relative market shares. **Product-portfolio analysis**, the Boston Consulting Group approach, is based on the philosophy that a product's market growth rate and its relative market share are important considerations in determining its marketing strategy. All the firm's products should be integrated into a single, overall matrix

FIGURE 19.5
Matching resources with environmental opportunities. McDonald's supports youth and amateur sports as a part of their corporate strategy. This is a socially responsible activity to improve opportunities for children in amateur sports—one of its target markets.

SOURCE: © 1986 McDonald's Corporation, used with permission.

and evaluated to determine appropriate strategies for individual SBUs and the overall portfolio strategies. However, a balanced product-portfolio matrix is the end result of a number of actions—not just the result of the analysis alone. Portfolio models can be created on the basis of present and projected market growth rate and proposed market share strategies (build share, maintain share, harvest share, or divest business). Managers can use these models to determine and classify each product's expected future cash contributions and future cash requirements.

Generally, managers who use a portfolio model must examine the competitive position of a product (or product line) and the opportunities for improving that product's contribution to profitability and cash flow.[12] The BCG analytical approach is more of a diagnostic tool than a guide for making strategy prescriptions.

Figure 19.6, which is based on work by the BCG, enables the marketing manager to classify a firm's products into four basic types: stars, cash cows, dogs, and problem

12. Joseph P. Guiltinan and Gordon W. Paul, *Marketing Management: Strategies and Programs* (New York: McGraw-Hill, 1982), p. 31.

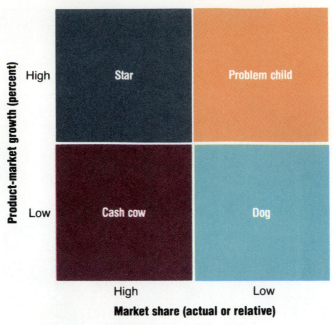

FIGURE 19.6
Illustrative growth-share matrix developed by the Boston Consulting Group

SOURCE: *Perspectives,* No. 66, "The Product Portfolio." Reprinted by permission from The Boston Consulting Group, Inc., Boston, MA. © copyright 1970.

children.[13] Stars are products with a dominant share of the market and good prospects for growth. However, they use more cash than they generate to finance growth, add capacity, and increase market share. Cash cows have a dominant share of the market but low prospects for growth; typically, they generate more cash than is required to maintain market share. Dogs have a subordinate share of the market and low prospects for growth; these products are often found in mature markets. Problem children, sometimes called "question marks," have a small share of a growing market and generally require a large amount of cash to build share.

The growth-share matrix in Figure 19.6 can be expanded to show a firm's whole portfolio by providing for each product (1) its dollar sales volume, illustrated by the size of a circle on the matrix; (2) its market share relative to competition, represented by the horizontal position of the product on the matrix, and (3) the growth rate of the market, indicated by the position of the product in the vertical direction. Figure 19.7 suggests marketing strategies appropriate for cash cows, stars, dogs, and problem children.

The long-term health of an organization depends on having some products that generate cash (and provide acceptable profits) and others that use cash to support growth. Among the indicators of overall health are the size and vulnerability of the cash cows, the prospects for the stars, if any, and the number of problem children and dogs. Particular attention must be paid to those products with large cash appetites. Unless the company has an abundant cash flow, it cannot afford to sponsor many such products at one time. If resources, including debt capacity, are spread

13. George S. Day, "Diagnosing the Product Portfolio," *Journal of Marketing,* April 1977, pp. 30–31.

FIGURE 19.7

Characteristics and strategies for the four basic product types in the growth-share matrix

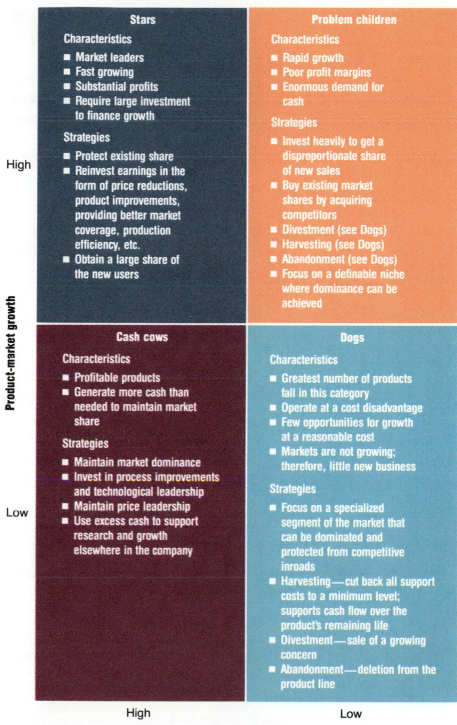

Product-market growth

High

Stars

Characteristics
- Market leaders
- Fast growing
- Substantial profits
- Require large investment to finance growth

Strategies
- Protect existing share
- Reinvest earnings in the form of price reductions, product improvements, providing better market coverage, production efficiency, etc.
- Obtain a large share of the new users

Problem children

Characteristics
- Rapid growth
- Poor profit margins
- Enormous demand for cash

Strategies
- Invest heavily to get a disproportionate share of new sales
- Buy existing market shares by acquiring competitors
- Divestment (see Dogs)
- Harvesting (see Dogs)
- Abandonment (see Dogs)
- Focus on a definable niche where dominance can be achieved

Low

Cash cows

Characteristics
- Profitable products
- Generate more cash than needed to maintain market share

Strategies
- Maintain market dominance
- Invest in process improvements and technological leadership
- Maintain price leadership
- Use excess cash to support research and growth elsewhere in the company

Dogs

Characteristics
- Greatest number of products fall in this category
- Operate at a cost disadvantage
- Few opportunities for growth at a reasonable cost
- Markets are not growing; therefore, little new business

Strategies
- Focus on a specialized segment of the market that can be dominated and protected from competitive inroads
- Harvesting—cut back all support costs to a minimum level; supports cash flow over the product's remaining life
- Divestment—sale of a growing concern
- Abandonment—deletion from the product line

High   **Low**

Market share

SOURCE: Concepts in this figure adapted from George S. Day, "Diagnosing the Product Portfolio," *Journal of Marketing,* April 1977, pp. 30-31.

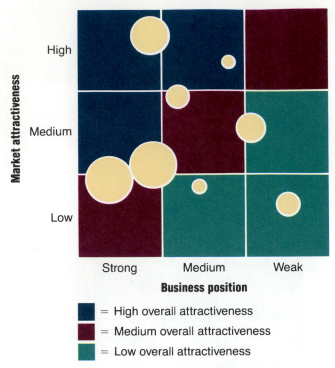

FIGURE 19.8
Market attractiveness–business position matrix

Market attractiveness

High

Medium

Low

Strong Medium Weak

Business position

■ = High overall attractiveness

■ = Medium overall attractiveness

■ = Low overall attractiveness

The area of each circle represents the relative dollar sales on the matrix.

SOURCE: Adapted from Derek F. Abell and John S. Hammond, *Strategic Market Planning: Problems and Analytical Approaches,* © 1979, p. 213. Reprinted by permission of Prentice-Hall, Inc., Englewood Cliffs, N.J.

too thin, the company will end up with too many marginal products and will be unable to finance promising new product entries or acquisitions in the future.

Market Attractiveness– Business Position Model

The **market attractiveness–business position model**, illustrated in Figure 19.8, is another two-dimensional matrix. However, rather than using single measures to define the vertical and horizontal dimensions of the matrix, the model employs multiple measurements and observations. The vertical dimension, *market attractiveness,* includes all strengths and resources that relate to the market, such as seasonality, economies of scale, competitive intensity, industry sales, and the overall cost and feasibility of entering the market. The horizontal axis, *business position,* is a composite of factors such as sales, relative market share, research and development, price competitiveness, product quality, and market knowledge as they relate to the product in building market share. A slight variation of this matrix is called General Electric's Strategic Business Planning Grid because General Electric is credited with extending the product-portfolio planning tool to examine market attractiveness and business strength.

The best situation is for a firm to have a strong business position in an attractive market. The upper left area in Figure 19.8 represents the opportunity for an invest/ grow strategy, but the matrix does not indicate how to implement this strategy. The purpose of the model is to serve as a diagnostic tool to highlight SBUs that have an opportunity to grow or that should be divested or approached selectively. SBUs that occupy the invest/grow position can lose their position through faulty marketing strategies.

Decisions on allocating resources to SBUs of medium overall attractiveness should be arrived at on a basis relative to other SBUs that are either more or less attractive. The lower right area of the matrix is a low-growth harvest/divest area. Harvesting is a gradual withdrawal of marketing resources on the assumption that sales will decline at a slow rate but profits will still be significant at a lower sales volume. Harvesting and divesting may be appropriate strategies for SBUs characterized by low overall attractiveness.

■ Profit Impact on Marketing Strategy (PIMS)

The Strategic Planning Institute (SPI) developed a databank of information on three thousand strategic business units of two hundred different firms during the period 1970–1983 for the **Profit Impact on Marketing Strategy (PIMS)** research program.[14] The sample is somewhat biased because it is composed primarily of large, profitable manufacturing firms marketing mature products, and service firms and distribution companies are underrepresented. However, 19 percent of the sample is composed of international businesses.[15] The member organizations of the institute provide confidential information on successes, failures, and marginal products. Figure 19.9 shows a PIMS data form. The data are analyzed to provide members with information about how similar organizations have performed under a given set of circumstances and about the factors that contribute to success or failure in given market conditions.

The unit of observation in PIMS is the SBU. Table 19.1 shows the types of information provided on each business in the PIMS database. The PIMS database includes both diagnostic and prescriptive information to assist in analyzing marketing performance and formulating marketing strategies. The analysis focuses on options, problems, resources, and opportunities.

The PIMS project has identified more than thirty factors that affect the performance of firms. These factors can be grouped into three sets of variables: (1) those relating to the structure of the marketplace in which the firm competes; (2) those that describe the firm's competitive position within that market; and (3) those that relate to the strategy chosen by the firm.[16] These factors may interact, as well as directly affect performance and profitability. Some of the main findings of the PIMS project are discussed briefly below.

Strong Market Position. Market position refers to the relative market share that a firm holds in relation to its competition. Firms that have a large share of a market tend to be the most profitable. However, it should be noted that market share does not necessarily create profitability. It is the result of business strategies such as the marketing of high-quality products, or the provision of good service.

High-Quality Products. Organizations that offer higher-quality products tend to be more profitable than their competitors. They are able to demand higher prices

14. Robert Jacobson, "Distinguishing Among Competing Theories of the Market Share Effect," *Journal of Marketing*, October 1988, pp. 68–80.

15. George S. Day, *Analysis for Strategic Market Decisions* (St. Paul, Minn.: West, 1986), pp. 117–118.

16. Robert D. Buzzell and Bradley T. Gale, *The PIMS Principles: Linking Strategy to Performance* (New York: Free Press, 1987).

FIGURE 19.9
Sample page from PIMS data forms

103: "LIFE CYCLE" STAGE OF PRODUCT CATEGORY

How would you describe the stage of development of the types of products or services sold by this business during the last three years? *(Check one)*

. . . Introductory Stage: Primary demand for product just starting to grow; products or services still unfamiliar to many potential users ☐ 1

. . . Growth Stage: Demand growing at 10% or more annually in real terms; technology or competitive structure still changing ☐ 2

. . . Maturity Stage: Products or services familiar to vast majority of prospective users; technology and competitive structure reasonably stable ☐ 3

. . . Decline Stage: Products viewed as commodities; weaker competitors beginning to exit ☐ 4

104: What was this business's first year of commercial sales? *(Check one)*

Prior to 1930	1930-1949	1950-1954	1955-1959	1960-1964	1965-1969	1970-1974	1975-
☐ 0	☐ 1	☐ 2	☐ 3	☐ 4	☐ 5	☐ 6	☐ 7

105: At the time this business first entered the market, was it . . . *(Check one)*

. . . One of the pioneers in first developing such products or services? ☐ 1

. . . An early follower of the pioneer(s) in a still growing, dynamic market? ☐ 2

. . . A later entrant into a more established market situation? ☐ 3

106-107: PATENTS AND TRADE SECRETS

Does this business benefit *to a significant degree* from patents, trade secrets, or other proprietary methods of production or operation . . .

106: Pertaining to products or services? NO ☐ 0 YES ☐ 1

107: Pertaining to processes? NO ☐ 0 YES ☐ 1

108: STANDARDIZATION OF PRODUCTS OR SERVICES

Are the products or services of this business . . . *(Check one)*

. . . More or less standardized for all customers? ☐ 0

. . . Designed or produced to order for individual customers? ☐ 1

109: FREQUENCY OF PRODUCT CHANGES

Is it typical practice for the business and its major competitors to change all or part of the line of products or services offered . . . *(Check one)*

. . . Annually (for example, annual model changes)? ☐ 1

. . . Seasonally? ☐ 2

. . . Periodically, but at intervals longer than one year? ☐ 3

. . . No regular, periodic pattern of change? ☐ 4

110: TECHNOLOGICAL CHANGE

Have there been *major* technological changes in the products offered by the business or its major competitors, or in methods of production, during the last 8 years? *(If in doubt about whether a change was "major," answer NO.)* NO ☐ 0 YES ☐ 1

SOURCE: PIMS Data Form reproduced by permission of the Strategic Planning Institute [PIMS program], Cambridge, Mass., 1979.

for those products. Moreover, high-quality offerings instill customer loyalty, foster repeat purchases, insulate firms from price wars, and help build market share. In Figure 19.10, Coca-Cola promotes its ongoing commitment to quality. It appears impossible for firms to overcome inferior offerings with high levels of marketing expenditures. Advertising is no substitute for product quality.

Lower Costs. Firms achieve lower costs through economies of scale, ability to bargain with suppliers, or backward integration. Low costs heighten profitability levels.

Investment and Capital Intensity. The higher the required investment to compete in an industry, the more pressure there is on a firm to fully use its production capacity. Moreover, these factors tend to have a negative impact on profitability.

TABLE 19.1 *Types of information provided on each business in the PIMS database*

Characteristics of the business environment Long-run growth rate of the market Short-run growth rate of the market Rate of inflation of selling price levels Number and size of customers Purchase frequency and magnitude	**Structure of the production process** Capital intensity (degree of automation, etc.) Degree of vertical integration Capacity utilization Productivity of capital equipment Productivity of people Inventory levels
Competitive position of the business Share of the served market Share relative to largest competitors Product quality relative to competitors Prices relative to competitors Pay scales relative to competitors Marketing efforts relative to competitors Pattern of market segmentation Rate of new product introductions	**Discretionary budget allocations** Research and development budgets Advertising and promotion budgets Sales force expenditures **Strategic moves** Patterns of change in the controllable elements above **Operating results** Profitability results Cash flow results Growth results

SOURCE: Reproduced by permission of the Strategic Planning Institute (PIMS program), Cambridge, Mass.

■ **Significance of Strategic Market Planning Approaches**

The approaches presented here provide an overview of the most popular analytical methods used in strategic market planning. However, the Boston Consulting Group's portfolio analysis, the market attractiveness–business position model, and the Profit Impact on Marketing Strategy research program are used not only to diagnose problem areas or to recognize opportunities, but also to facilitate the allocation of resources among business units. They are not intended to serve as formulas for success or prescriptive guides, which lay out cut-and-dried strategic action plans.[17] These approaches are supplements to, not substitutes for, the marketing manager's own judgment. The real test of each approach, or any integrated approach, is how well it helps management diagnose the firm's strengths and weaknesses and prescribe strategic actions for maintaining or improving performance. The emphasis should be on making sound decisions with the aid of these analytical tools.[18]

Another word of caution regarding the use of portfolio approaches is necessary. The classification of SBUs into a specific portfolio position hinges on four factors: (1) the operational definition of the matrix dimensions; (2) the rules used to divide a dimension into high and low categories; (3) the weighting of the variables used in

17. Day, Analysis for *Strategic Market Decisions*, p. 10.

18. David W. Cravens, "Strategic Marketing's New Challenge," *Business Horizons*, March-April 1983, p. 19.

FIGURE 19.10
A commitment to quality.
Coca-Cola offers a high-quality product and remains the number-one-selling soft drink.

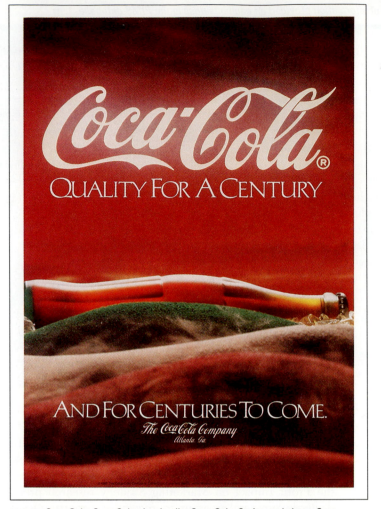

composite dimensions, if composite dimensions are used; and (4) the specific model used.[19] In other words, changes in any of these four factors may well result in a different classification for a single SBU.

The key to understanding the tools for strategic market planning described in this chapter is recognition that strategic market planning takes into account all aspects of a firm's strategy in the marketplace. Most of this book is about functional decisions and strategies of marketing as a part of business. This chapter focuses on the recognition that all functional strategies, including marketing, production, and finance, must be coordinated to reach organizational goals. Results of a survey sponsored by the *Harvard Business Review* of top industrial firms indicate that portfolio

19. Yoram Wind, Vijay Majahan, and Donald J. Swire, "An Empirical Comparison of Standardized Portfolio Models," *Journal of Marketing*, Spring 1983, pp. 89–99.

FIGURE 19.11
Competitive strategies

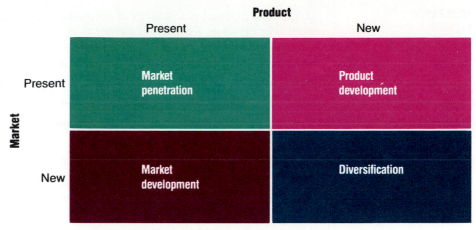

SOURCE: H.I. Ansoff, *Corporate Strategy,* McGraw-Hill, 1965, p. 109. Used by permission of the author.

planning and other depersonalized planning techniques help managers strengthen their planning process and solve the problems of managing diversified industrial companies. However, the results also indicate that analytical techniques alone do not result in success. Management must blend these analyses with managerial judgment to deal with the reality of the existing situation.

There are other tools that aid strategic market planning besides those examined here. For example, for many years marketing planners have used the product life cycle concept, discussed in Chapters 8 and 9. Many firms have their own approaches to planning that incorporate, to varying degrees, some of the approaches discussed here. All strategic planning approaches have some similarity in that several of the components of strategic market planning outlined in Figure 19.2 (especially market/product relationships) are related to a plan of action for reaching objectives.

DEVELOPING COMPETITIVE STRATEGIES FOR MARKETING

After analyzing business operations and business performance, the next step in strategic market planning is to determine future business directions and develop marketing strategies. A business may choose one or more competitive strategies, including intense growth, diversified growth, and integrated growth. Figure 19.11 shows these competitive strategies on a product-market matrix. This matrix can help in determining growth that can be implemented through marketing strategies.

■ **Intense Growth**

Intense growth can take place when current products and current markets have the potential for increasing sales. There are three main strategies for intense growth: market penetration, market development, and product development.

Market penetration is a strategy of increasing sales in current markets with current products. Wendy's, for example, cut prices on many of its menu items to 99 cents in an effort to enlarge its market share in the increasingly competitive fast-food industry.

Market development is a strategy of increasing sales of current products in new markets. For example, a European aircraft manufacturer was able to enter the U.S. market by offering Eastern Airlines financing that Boeing could not match.

Product development is a strategy of increasing sales by improving present products or developing new products for current markets. Tandem Computers, Inc., for example, has marketed specialty computers for commercial use for several years but only recently developed its first mainframe computer—the NonStop Cyclone—to compete head-on with IBM in Tandem's market.[20]

■ Diversified Growth

Diversified growth occurs when new products are developed to be sold in new markets. Firms have become increasingly diversified since the 1960s. Diversification offers some advantages over single-business firms because it allows firms to spread their risk across a number of markets. More importantly, it allows firms to make better and wider use of their management, technical, and financial resources. For example, marketing expertise can be used across businesses, and they may also share advertising themes, distribution channels, warehouse facilities, or even sales forces.[21] The three forms of diversification are horizontal, concentric, and conglomerate.

Horizontal diversification results when new products that are not technologically related to current products are introduced to current markets. Sony Corp., for example, has diversified from an electronics giant to a filmmaker through its purchase of Columbia Pictures. The purchase gave Sony a library of 2,700 movies, including *Ghostbusters 2* and *When Harry Met Sally*, as well as 23,000 television episodes, which it may use to help establish its new line of 8mm VCRs.[22]

In *concentric diversification,* the marketing and technology of new products are related to current products, but the new ones are introduced into new markets. For instance, Dow Chemical is diversifying into agricultural chemicals and pharmaceuticals through joint ventures with corporations in those industries.[23]

Conglomerate diversification occurs when new products are unrelated to current technology, products, or markets and are introduced to markets new to the firm. For example, Bass P.L.C., a British brewer, acquired the American Holiday Inn hotel chain.

■ Integrated Growth

Integrated growth can occur in the same industry that the firm is in and in three possible directions: forward, backward, and horizontally. A company growing through forward integration takes ownership or increased control of its distribution system. For example, a shoe manufacturer might start selling its products through wholly owned retail outlets. In backward integration, a firm takes ownership or

---

20. Jonathan B. Levine, "This Cyclone Is Out to Rain on IBM's Parade," *Business Week,* Oct. 23, 1989, p. 114.

21. Roger A. Kerin, Vijay Majahan, and P. Rajan Varadarajan, *Contemporary Perspectives on Strategic Marketing Planning* (Boston: Allyn & Bacon, 1990).

22. Ronald Grover, "When Columbia Met Sony . . . A Love Story," *Business Week,* Oct. 9, 1989, pp. 44–45.

23. David Woodruff, "Has Dow Chemical Found the Right Formula?" *Business Week,* Aug. 7, 1989, pp. 62, 64.

increased control of its supply systems. A newspaper company that buys a paper mill is integrating backward. Horizontal integration occurs when a firm takes ownership or control of some of its competitors. For example, Polly Peck International P.L.C., a British fruit grower and distributor, purchased Del Monte's fresh fruit division.[24]

MARKETING PLANNING

As we noted at the start, this chapter deals with the planning aspect of marketing management. In this section we describe how the strategic plan is implemented. **Marketing planning** is a systematic process that involves assessing marketing opportunities and resources, determining marketing objectives, and developing a plan for implementation and control. The objective of marketing planning is the creation of a marketing plan.

Figure 19.12 illustrates the **marketing planning cycle**. Note that marketing planning is a circular process. As the dotted feedback lines in the figure indicate, planning is not unidirectional. Feedback is used to coordinate and synchronize all stages of the planning cycle.

The duration of marketing plans varies. Plans that cover a period of one year or less are called **short-range plans**. **Medium-range plans** usually encompass two to five years. Marketing plans that extend beyond five years are generally viewed as **long-range plans**. These plans can sometimes cover a period as long as twenty years. Marketing managers may have short-, medium-, and long-range plans all at the same time. Long-range plans are relatively rare. However, as the marketing environment continues to change and business decisions become more complex, profitability and survival will depend more and more on the development of long-range plans.[25]

The extent to which marketing managers develop and use plans also varies. Although planning provides numerous benefits, some managers do not use formal marketing plans because they spend almost all their time dealing with daily problems, many of which would be eliminated by adequate planning. However, planning is becoming more important to marketing managers, who realize that planning is necessary to develop, coordinate, and control marketing activities effectively and efficiently. When formulating a marketing plan, a new enterprise or a firm with a new product does not have current performance to evaluate or an existing plan to revise. Therefore, its marketing planning centers on analyzing available resources and options to assess opportunities. Managers can then develop marketing objectives and a strategy. In addition, many firms recognize the need to include information systems in their plans so that they can have continuous feedback and keep their marketing activities oriented toward objectives. (Information systems are discussed in Chapter 7.) One research study, which examined 207 different companies, found that those that have maintained or increased their planning departments during the

24. Mark Maremont, with Judith H. Dobrzynski, "Meet Asil Nadir, the Billion-Dollar Fruit King," *Business Week*, Sept. 18, 1989, p. 32.

25. Ronald D. Michman, "Linking Futuristics with Marketing Planning, Forecasting, and Strategy," *Journal of Consumer Marketing*, Summer 1984, pp. 17, 23.

FIGURE 19.12
The marketing planning cycle

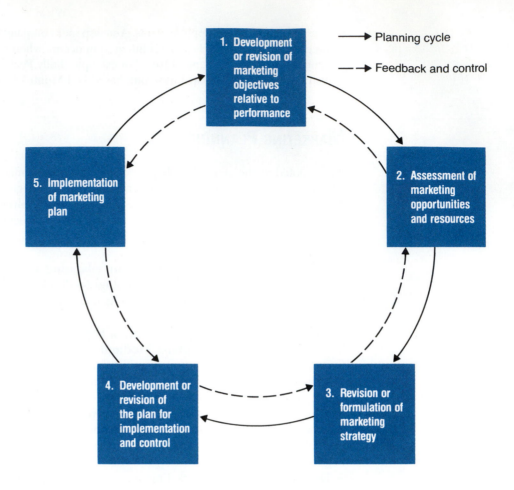

past five years and increased their allocation of resources to planning activities out-performed those whose planning departments have become smaller.[26]

To illustrate the marketing planning process, consider the decisions that went into the planning of the introduction of *USA Today,* a national newspaper. Table 19.2 lists several of the more important marketing decisions. Of course, to reach the objective, a detailed course of action was communicated throughout the organization. In short, specific marketing plans should do the following:

1. Specify expected results so that the organization can anticipate what its situation will be at the end of the current planning period
2. Identify the resources needed to carry out the planned activities so that a budget can be developed
3. Describe in sufficient detail the activities that are to take place so that responsibilities for implementation can be assigned
4. Provide for the monitoring of activities and results so control can be exerted[27]

26. Vasudevan Ramanujam and N. Venkatraman, "Planning and Performance: A New Look at an Old Question," *Business Horizons,* May-June 1987, pp. 19–25.

27. David J. Luck, O. C. Ferrell, and George Lucas, *Marketing Strategy and Plans,* 3rd ed. (Englewood Cliffs, N.J.: Prentice-Hall, 1989), p. 328.

TABLE 19.2

*Planning for the intro-
duction of a national
newspaper:* USA Today

Objective: Achieve 1 million in circulation by reaching an upscale market, primarily of males who hold professional and managerial positions and who made at least one trip of 200 miles or more within the last year.

Opportunity: Paper tends to be a second newspaper purchase for readers. *USA Today* is not in competition directly with local papers, and it is not positioned against other national newspapers/magazines.

Market: Circulation within a 200-mile radius of 15 major markets, representing 54% of the U.S. population, including such cities as Chicago, Houston, New York, Los Angeles, and Denver.

Product: Superior graphic quality; appeal to the TV generation through short stories, a color weather map, and other contemporary features.

Price: Competitive.

Promotion: Pedestal-like vending machines with attention-grabbing design and a higher position than competitors to differentiate the paper and bring it closer to eye level. Outdoor advertising and some print advertising promotes the paper.

Distribution: Newsstand, vending machines in high-traffic locations, and direct mail.

Implementation and control: Personnel with experience in the newspaper business who can assist in developing a systematic approach for implementing the marketing strategy and design as well as an information system to monitor and control the results.

SOURCE: Kevin Higgins, "*USA Today* Nears Million Reader Mark," *Marketing News,* Apr. 15, 1983, pp. 1, 5. Reprinted by permission of the American Marketing Association.

Obviously, the marketing plan needs to be carefully written to attain these objectives. In the final section of this chapter, we will take a closer look at the marketing plan itself.

THE MARKETING PLAN

As mentioned earlier, the marketing plan is the written document or blueprint governing all of a firm's marketing activities, including the implementation and control of those activities. A marketing plan serves a number of purposes:

1. It offers a "road map" for implementing the firm's strategies and achieving its objectives.
2. It assists in management control and monitoring of implementation of strategy.
3. It informs new participants in the plan of their role and function.
4. It specifies how resources are to be allocated.
5. It stimulates thinking and makes better use of resources.
6. It assigns responsibilities, tasks, and timing.
7. It makes participants aware of problems, opportunities, and threats.[28]

28. William A. Cohen, *The Practice of Marketing Management: Analysis, Planning, and Implementation* (New York: Macmillan, 1988), pp. 44–46.

TABLE 19.3

A marketing plan

I. **Executive Summary**

II. **Situation Analysis**
   A. Description of markets, current marketing strategies
   B. Description of measures of performance

III. **Opportunities and Threats**
   A. Greatest challenges or threats to future marketing activities
   B. Opportunity analysis

IV. **Environment**
   A. Legal, political, and regulatory factors
   B. Social and cultural factors
   C. Economic factors
   D. Competitive factors
   E. Technological factors

V. **Company Resources**
   A. Financial resources
   B. Human resources
   C. Experience and expertise

VI. **Marketing Objectives**

VII. **Marketing Strategies**
   A. Target market
   B. Marketing mix

VIII. **Financial Projections and Budgets**
   A. Delineation of costs
   B. Estimates of sales and revenues
   C. Expected return on investment for implementing the marketing plan

IX. **Controls and Evaluation**
   A. Measures of performance
   B. Monitoring and evaluating performance

A firm should have a plan for each marketing strategy it develops. Because such plans must be changed as forces in the firm and in the environment change, marketing planning is a continuous process.

Organizations use many different formats when devising marketing plans. Plans may be written for strategic business units, product lines, individual products or brands, or specific markets. Most plans share some common ground, however, by including an executive summary, opportunity and threat analysis, a description of environmental forces, an inventory of company resources, a description of marketing objectives, an outline of the marketing strategy, financial projections and budgets, and benchmarks or controls for monitoring and evaluating the action taken (see Table 19.3). In the following sections we consider the major parts of a typical marketing plan, as well as the purpose that each part serves.

■ Executive Summary

The executive summary is a synopsis (often only one or two pages long) outlining the main thrust of the entire report. It includes an introduction, the major aspects of the marketing plan, and a statement about the costs of implementing the plan. Such a summary helps executives who need to know what information the plan contains but are not involved in approving or making decisions related to the plan and can pass up the details.

■ Situation Analysis

The situation analysis provides an appraisal of the difference between the firm's current performance and past stated objectives. It includes a summary of data that relate to the creation of the current marketing situation. This information is obtained from both the firm's external and internal environment, usually through its marketing information system. Depending on the situation, details on the composition of target market segments, marketing objectives, current marketing strategies, market trends, sales history, and profitability may be included.

■ Opportunity and Threat Analysis

In the analysis of opportunities and threats, a detailed examination of opportunities or threats present in the firm's operating environment is provided. It examines opportunities and threats with regard to specific target markets along with their size and growth potential. Possible market opportunities may be described in this section. It develops an ordering of priorities for action in light of the unit's internal capabilities for dealing with the circumstances.

■ Environmental Analysis

The environmental section of the marketing plan describes the current state of the marketing environment, including the legal, political, regulatory, technological, competitive, social, and economic forces, as well as ethical considerations. It also makes predictions about future directions of those forces.

For example, Panasonic surveyed its marketing environment and discovered that many consumers who own VCRs do not know how to program or operate their units for anything but the simpler functions. They therefore developed a user-friendly VCR to appeal to the majority of consumers who would seem to prefer a simpler product (see Figure 19.13).

As mentioned earlier, environmental forces can hamper an organization in achieving its objectives. The section also describes the possible impact of these forces on the implementation of the marketing plan. Most marketing plans include extensive analyses of competitive, legal, and regulatory forces, perhaps even creating separate sections for these influential forces of the marketing environment. It is important to note here that, because the forces of the marketing environment are dynamic, marketing plans should be reviewed and possibly modified periodically to adjust to change.

■ Company Resources

A firm's human and financial resources, as well as its experiences and expertise, are major considerations in developing a marketing plan. Thus the marketing plan should delineate the human, financial, and physical resources available for implementing the plan, as well as describe resource constraints that may affect implementation. It should also describe any distinctive competencies that may give the firm an edge in the marketplace. The plan should take into account strengths and weaknesses that may influence the firm's ability to implement a selected marketing strategy.

FIGURE 19.13
*Analyzing environmental
needs.*
Because of consumer
confusion in operating
VCRs, Panasonic devel-
oped an "easier" on-
screen programming
feature.

SOURCE: Matsushita Electric Corporation of America

■ Marketing Objectives

This section describes the objectives underlying the plan. A **marketing objective** is a statement of what is to be accomplished through marketing activities. It specifies the results expected from marketing efforts. A marketing objective should be expressed in clear, simple terms so that all marketing personnel understand exactly what they are trying to achieve. It should be written in such a way that its accomplishment can be measured accurately. If a company has an objective of increasing its market share by 12 percent, the firm should be able to measure changes in its market share accurately. A marketing objective should also indicate the time frame for accomplishing the objective. For example, a firm that sets an objective of introducing three new products should state the time period in which this is to be done.

Objectives may be stated in terms of degree of product introduction or innovation, sales volume, profitability per unit, or gains in market share. They must also be consistent with the firm's overall organizational goals.

■ Marketing Strategies

This section provides a broad overview of the plan for achieving the marketing objectives, and ultimately, the organizational goals. Marketing strategy focuses on defining a target market and developing a marketing mix to gain long-run competi-

FIGURE 19.14
Developing strategies that meet consumers' perceptions.
Celebrity endorsers enhance the American Express card's image as a privilege and an achievement of success.

Neil Simon. Cardmember since 1974.

Membership Has Its Privileges.

Don't leave home without it.
Call 1-800-THE CARD to apply.

SOURCE: Courtesy of American Express

tive and consumer advantages. There is a degree of overlap between corporate strategy and marketing strategy. Marketing strategy is unique in that it has the responsibility to assess buyer needs and the firm's potential for gaining competitive advantage, both of which ultimately must guide the corporate mission.[29] In other words, marketing strategy guides the firm's direction in relationships between customers and competitors. Marketing Update 19.2 profiles Bruno's, a chain of grocery stores, which has developed a customer-oriented marketing strategy. The bottom line is that a marketing strategy must be consistent with consumer needs, perceptions, and beliefs. American Express shows highly successful individuals as card members, fulfilling consumers' perceptions that to be a member is a privilege (see Figure 19.14). Thus this section should describe the firm's intended target market and how product, promotion, distribution, and price will be used to satisfy the needs of the members of the target market.

29. Yoram Wind and Thomas S. Robertson, "Marketing Strategy: New Directions for Theory and Research," *Journal of Marketing,* Spring 1983, p. 12.

BRUNO'S DEVELOPS A CONSUMER-ORIENTED MARKETING STRATEGY

When Vincent Bruno, a native-born Sicilian, opened his first store on a Birmingham, Alabama corner in 1932, his strategy was to offer quality groceries at low prices, cash-only. Much of that same philosophy guides Bruno's strategy today. Although other grocery chains in the competitive Southeast, such as Food Lion, Kroger, and Albertson's, are better known, none are doing as well as Bruno's. Bruno's sales have been growing at a rate of over 20 percent for more than 15 years, compared to only 2 percent in the grocery business in general.

Bruno's targets local customers for a specific store, and then develops the right product mix, promotion, prices, and store location to be successful. Stores range from the 40,000-square-foot Food Worlds, which have a stripped-down look and sell food still stacked in manufacturer's cartons, to the top-of-the-line 59,000-square-foot Bruno's Food and Pharmacy stores, which cater to upscale customers. Each of these stores has a full-service in-store bank and a huge variety of gourmet items.

A creative family management team enables Bruno's to do without the layers of middle management that slow decision making in larger chains. All of Bruno's buying is done by a committee of family members that typically buys in massive quantities for one year at a time. This strategy of "forward buying" guarantees volume discounts which are then passed on to customers. Goods are delivered to Bruno's two highly computerized warehouses where they are inventoried, priced, and put onto Bruno's own fleet of trucks for overnight delivery to the stores. Shelves are then stocked at night to minimize the inconvenience to customers. Forward buying, low overhead, and effective management all help reduce costs and allow Bruno's to focus on its customers' needs.

Bruno's plans include further expansion and the successful operation of American Fare—a 260,000-square-foot hypermarket outside Stone Mountain, Georgia, operated in a joint venture with K mart. The company recently acquired Piggly Wiggly's south Georgia operations, which it plans to use to expand into northern Georgia and Florida. Based on Bruno's past success, its current strategic market plans will likely be successful.

SOURCES: Jay L. Johnson, "American Fare Opens in Atlanta," *Discount Merchandiser*, Feb. 1989, pp. 28, 30; Jay L. Johnson, "K mart's Hypermarket: American Fare," *Discount Merchandiser*, Mar. 1989, pp. 32–40; Stephen Kindel, "Rebel Sell," *Financial World*, Jan. 9, 1990, pp. 22–24.

Financial Projections and Budgets

The financial projections and budgets section outlines the returns expected through implementation of the plan. The costs incurred will be weighed against expected revenues. A budget must be prepared to allocate resources to accomplish marketing objectives. It should contain estimates of the costs of implementing the plan, including the costs of advertising, sales force training and compensation, development of distribution channels, and marketing research.

Controls and Evaluation

This section details how the results of the plan will be measured. For example, results of an advertising campaign designed to increase market share may be measured in terms of increases in sales volume or improved brand recognition and acceptance by consumers. Next, a schedule for comparing the results achieved with the objectives set forth in the marketing plan is developed. Finally, guidelines may be offered outlining who is responsible for monitoring the program and taking remedial action.

SUMMARY

A strategic market plan is an outline of the methods and resources required to achieve the organization's goals within a specific target market; it takes into account all functional areas of a business unit that must be coordinated. A strategic business unit (SBU) is a division, product line, or other profit center within the parent company and is used to define areas for consideration in a specific strategic market plan. The process of strategic market planning yields a marketing strategy that is the framework for a marketing plan. A marketing plan includes the framework and entire set of activities to be performed; it is the written document or blueprint for implementing and controlling an organization's marketing activities.

Through the process of strategic market planning, an organization can develop marketing strategies that, when properly implemented and controlled, will contribute to achieving the organization's overall goals. The set of marketing strategies that are implemented and used at the same time is referred to as the organization's marketing program. Environmental forces are important in the strategic market planning process and very much affect it. These forces imply opportunities and threats that influence an organization's overall goals.

A firm's organizational goals should be derived from its mission, the broad tasks the organization wants to achieve. These goals should guide planning efforts.

There are three major considerations in assessing opportunities and resources: evaluation of market opportunities, monitoring of environmental forces, and understanding the firm's capabilities. A market opportunity, or strategic window, opens when the right combination of circumstances occurs at the right time, and an organization can take action toward a target market. An opportunity offers a favorable chance for the company to generate sales from markets. Market requirements relate to the customers' needs or desired benefits. The market requirements are satisfied by components of the marketing mix that provide buyers with these benefits. Environmental scanning is a search for information about events and relationships in a company's outside environment; such information aids marketers in planning. A firm's capabilities relate to distinctive competencies that it has developed to do something well and efficiently. A company is likely to enjoy a differential advantage in an area where its competencies outmatch those of its potential competition.

Corporate strategy determines the means for utilizing resources in the areas of production, finance, research and development, personnel, and marketing to reach the organization's goals.

A number of tools have been developed to aid marketing managers in their planning efforts, including the Boston Consulting Group (BCG) product-portfolio analysis, the market attractiveness–business position model, and Profit Impact on Marketing Strategy (PIMS). The BCG approach is based on the philosophy that a product's market growth rate and its market share are key factors influencing marketing strategy. All the firm's products are integrated into a single, overall matrix and evaluated to determine appropriate strategies for individual SBUs and the overall portfolio strategies.

The market attractiveness–business position model is a two-dimensional matrix. The market attractiveness dimension includes all the sources of strength and resources that relate to the market; competition, industry sales, and the cost of competing are among the sources. The business position axis measures sales, relative market share, research and development, and other factors that relate to building a market share for a product.

The Profit Impact on Marketing Strategy (PIMS) research program has developed a databank of confidential information on the successes, failures, and marginal products of more than three thousand strategic business units of the two hundred members of the Strategic Planning Institute. The unit of observation in PIMS is an SBU. The results of PIMS include diagnostic and prescriptive information to assist in analyzing marketing performance and formulating marketing strategies. The analysis focuses on options, problems, resources, and opportunities.

These tools for strategic market planning are used only to diagnose problem areas or recognize opportunities. They are supplements to, not substitutes for, the marketing manager's own judgment. The real test of each approach, or any integrated approach, is how well it helps management diagnose the firm's strengths and weaknesses and prescribe strategic actions for maintaining or improving performance.

Competitive strategies that can be implemented through marketing include intense growth, diversified growth, and integrated growth. Intense growth includes market penetration, market development, or product development. Diversified growth includes horizontal, concentric, and conglomerate diversification. Integrated growth includes forward, backward, and horizontal integration.

Marketing planning is a systematic process that involves assessing opportunities and resources, determining marketing objectives, developing a marketing strategy, and developing plans for implementation and control. Short-range marketing plans cover one year or less; medium-range plans usually encompass two to five years; plans that last for more than five years are long-range.

A marketing plan is the written document or blueprint for implementing and controlling an organization's marketing activities. A well-written plan clearly specifies when, how, and who is to perform marketing activities. Typical marketing plans include an executive summary, situation analysis, opportunity and threat analysis, a description of the impact of the marketing environment forces, a summary of company resources, marketing objectives, marketing strategies, financial projections and budgets, and prescriptions for controlling and evaluating the results of the marketing plan.

IMPORTANT TERMS

Strategic market plan
Strategic business unit (SBU)
Strategic market planning
Marketing plan
Marketing program
Market opportunity
Market requirements
Corporate strategy
Product-portfolio analysis
Market attractiveness–business
   position model

Profit Impact on Marketing
   Strategy (PIMS)
Intense growth
Diversified growth
Integrated growth
Marketing planning
Marketing planning cycle
Short-range plans
Medium-range plans
Long-range plans
Marketing objective

DISCUSSION AND REVIEW QUESTIONS

1. Why should an organization develop a marketing strategy? What is the difference between strategic market planning and the strategy itself?
2. Identify the major components of strategic market planning, and explain how they are interrelated.
3. In what ways do environmental forces affect strategic market planning? Give specific examples.
4. What are some of the issues that must be considered in analyzing a firm's opportunities and resources? How do these issues affect marketing objectives and market strategy?
5. Why is market opportunity analysis necessary? What are the determinants of market opportunity?
6. In relation to resource constraints, how can environmental scanning affect a firm's long-term strategic market planning? Consider product costs and benefits affected by the environment.
7. What are the major considerations in developing the product-portfolio grid? Define and explain the four basic types of products suggested by the Boston Consulting Group.
8. When should marketers consider using PIMS for strategic market planning?
9. Why do you think more firms are diversifying? Give some examples of diversified firms.
10. What benefits do marketing managers gain from planning? Is planning necessary for long-run survival? Why or why not?
11. How should an organization establish marketing objectives?

19.1 Back Yard Burgers

Back Yard Burgers, Inc. (BYB) is a twelve-unit franchise operation founded in 1988 by Lattie Michael in Cleveland, Mississippi. BYB is positioned in the double drive-through, carry-out-only segment of the fast-food restaurant industry. It bases its marketing strategy on providing customers "value for the dollar." While menu items are reasonably priced—a basic hamburger costs $1.49 and gourmet burgers are $1.99—each offers "something extra," that prepared-in-your-own-back-yard taste. All hamburgers are made by hand and charbroiled over an open-flame grill. Customers also receive value and quality from the extra amount of the quality Iowa ground chuck used in every Back Yard Burger—most chains use four ounces for their highest priced burger, but BYB serves a full five ounces in each one. BYBs also offer a unique variety, from the basic Back Yard Burger to the gourmet-style mushroom, Mexicali, Italian, Hawaiian burgers, the charbroiled chicken sandwich, and other different selections.

When BYB developed a market plan, it first had to assess opportunities in the highly competitive fast-food industry. The market growth rate and the relative market share that the company could attain were important considerations in determining its marketing strategy. The firm noted that, according to the National Restaurant Association, fast food is the fastest growing segment of the restaurant industry, with national sales estimates of $65.1 billion in 1989, an increase of $7.9 billion in two years. In addition, sales of food consumed off the premises account for 50 percent of the overall food sales by the major fast-food chains. The high rate of growth and the growing trend of drive-through facilities led Lattie Michael to conclude that there was an excellent opportunity for a double drive-through, carry-out-only gourmet hamburger restaurant.

Purchases of food prepared outside the home have risen with the increase in two-income families. Joe Weiss, Memphis BYB franchise holder and corporate staffer, said, "This is the way the American public is going. They want to get their food and go home and eat with their family, even if they don't cook it at home." BYB therefore targets this group with quality products and fast service.

BYB attracts franchisees with a low investment for setup and operating costs and a high expected rate of return on investment. The franchise fee is $16,000, and there are ongoing royalty fees. All BYB franchise operations use a prefabricated modular unit with double drive-throughs and a walk-up window in front. The franchisee's costs for the building range from $175,000 to $320,000. Franchisees may purchase land or rent space for the building. If customer traffic patterns in a particular location prove to be unprofitable, the whole building can be moved to another site. Franchisees can purchase rights to an entire territory or to one location. There are franchises in San Diego, Jacksonville, Florida; Asheville, North Carolina; Memphis and Knoxville, Tennessee; and several in Mississippi. Michael, the founder, who is also director of franchise operations, has received an average of ten inquiries a week from potential franchisees and expects to have more than fifty units opened by the end of the company's second business year. He hopes eventually to take the chain nationwide and even worldwide.

Michael stresses quality, service, and courtesy in the BYB operation. Each store is designed so that the manager is always in the center of the operations and can monitor what is going on at all times. The food preparation is very labor-intensive; each restaurant grinds and makes its own patties from fresh 100 percent beef chuck every day. Shakes are made from hand-dipped ice cream, and lemonade is made from freshly squeezed lemons. A computer is used to track how many seconds a customer spends at the drive-through, with a goal of 45 seconds per car. An alarm sounds after 60 seconds to alert employees that the goal is not being met.

Back Yard Burgers developed this market plan and its marketing strategies after analyzing a market opportunity, monitoring the environment, and assessing the capabilities and resources of Back Yard Burgers. Thus far the marketing strategy appears to be successful in the existing markets. Long-run success, however, will depend on BYB management's understanding of customer needs, monitoring of competition, and a willingness to adapt to a changing environment.

SOURCES: "BY Burgers 'with That Backyard Taste,'" *Okaloosa Business News*, February 1989, p. 5; "BY Burgers Plans Expansion in Fast-Food Field," *Knoxville News-Sentinel*, June 7, 1989, p. W2; Laura Campbell, "New Outlet of Burgers Is Different," *Commercial Appeal*, Dec. 3, 1989, pp. C1–C2; information packet furnished by Lattie Michael, Director of Franchise Operations, Back Yard Burgers, Inc., 1989; and Paul McAfee, "Back Yard Burger Opens Soon," *Farragut Press Enterprise*, July 4, 1989, p. 5B.

Questions for Discussion

1. In a very competitive fast-food market, what differentiates the Back Yard Burger marketing strategy?
2. What are the strengths and weaknesses of the Back Yard Burger strategy?
3. Ten years from now, will Back Yard Burger be able to successfully compete against McDonald's, Burger King, and other proven market leaders?

19.2 Paramount Pictures

Although the products marketed by Hollywood studios differ from those of other companies, like any other business, they too are vulnerable to threats and open to opportunities. They must develop marketing strategies and implement them if they are to produce the blockbuster movies and hit television shows that consumers want to see. Paramount Pictures Corporation is one studio that has developed successful marketing strategies.

Business is good for Paramount today, with movie blockbusters such as *Indiana Jones and the Last Crusade* and hit television shows, "Cheers," "Dear John," "The Arsenio Hall Show," and "Star Trek: The Next Generation." But things were not always so glamorous for the studio division of Paramount Communications Inc. (formerly Gulf + Western). In early 1986, Paramount had a dismal 1.5 percent share of the market, down from a 1984 high of 19.1 percent. In addition, the management team that had led the studio to glory with the films *Flashdance, An Officer and a Gentleman,* and *Raiders of the Lost Ark* had left for positions with 20th Century-Fox or the Walt Disney Company. With the exception of one huge hit, *Beverly Hills Cop,* Paramount was also owner of a large collection of movie flops.

Then, Frank Mancuso, a twenty-seven-year Paramount veteran, assumed the post of chairman of the company. Mancuso hired the industry's best production and marketing executives and began a strategy of establishing long-term relationships between the studio and major film producers and stars. This strategy proved to be the answer to Paramount's film production woes.

Shortly after Mancuso assumed the chairmanship of Paramount, the company began turning out one hit after another—often from ideas turned down by other film studios. One such idea was a script about young naval air cadets, which Paramount produced at a cost of more than $17.5 million under the name *Top Gun*. *Top Gun* went on to become the top-grossing hit of 1986 with revenues of $270 million. *Crocodile Dundee* in 1986 and *Beverly Hills Cop II, Fatal Attraction,* and *The Untouchables* in 1987 were other Paramount success stories. By the end of 1987, Paramount had captured the number-one position in the market two years in a row and a 20 percent share of the U.S. market.

The secret to Paramount's success lies partly in the whimsical entertainment tastes of American consumers. However, a great deal of its success can be attributed to its strategy of nurturing successful long-term relationships and projects. Paramount has carefully milked one of its oldest TV cash cows, "Star Trek," with video releases of the original episodes, five feature films, and the current number-one syndicated program on television—"Star Trek: The Next Generation." Long-term relationships with other cash cows and stars, such as actor/comedians Eddie Murphy and Arsenio Hall and major directors Steven Spielberg and George Lucas, have also contributed to the studio's current string of hits.

Nurturing such long-term relationships are the only means of securing success through the development of sequels and television spinoffs. The success of movie "franchises" such as the *Indiana Jones* trilogy, the five *Star Trek* movies, and seven Eddie Murphy pictures bear out the importance of securing these long-term contracts. Within the industry, Paramount's exclusive contract with Eddie Murphy is considered to be the best of them all. Murphy's seven movies with Paramount have a combined income of more than $1 billion, not counting the additional revenue generated through television, video cassettes, and cable TV.

The success of these long-term relationships has allowed Paramount to be aggressive in marketing and media usage. Paramount's landmark deal with Pepsi, which placed a Pepsi promotional spot on the *Top Gun* video release, was the first of its kind. The joint Paramount/Pepsi promotion of the *Top Gun* video made the movie the most heavily promoted title in history. The video sold an estimated 3 million units. As a result of this and other promotions, Paramount became known as the master of publicity and word-of-mouth promotion.

However, Paramount's product-line style of movie-making strategy is not without risks. Paramount runs the risk of staking its future on past successes, and even on a single superstar, Eddie Murphy. Some of its franchises are already mature, such as the *Star Trek* movies because of the aging of the principal actors. Other franchises have finished: *Indiana Jones and the Last Crusade* was the last of the highly successful trilogy featuring Harrison Ford.

Thus, despite its successful long-term relationships and successful franchises, Paramount must constantly look for new franchises and hot new stars. Paramount is currently exploring the possibility of doing a series of movies based on its *Star Trek: The Next Generation* television series. It also recently signed Arsenio Hall to an exclusive, long-term television and film contract. In addition, Paramount is looking overseas for new ideas and stars. One project under development is a remake of the French film, *Trop Belle Pour Toi (Too Beautiful for You)*. The firm's European production operation will produce two to four films annually, boosting the studio's film output to nineteen or twenty from its current average of fourteen.

Thus, Paramount Picture's strategy is to milk its cash cows, while constantly looking for and developing its stars. As one company executive said, "We won't just sit back and make *Beverly Hills Cop III, IV, and V* and call it a day."

SOURCES: Ronald Grover, "Fat Times for Studios, Fatter Times for Stars," *Business Week*, July 24, 1989, p. 48; Laura Landro, "It's a Record Race for Movie Makers," *Wall Street Journal*, Nov. 3, 1989, p. B2; Laura Landro, "Paramount Plans Movie Unit in London to Tap Growing International Market," *Wall Street Journal*, Jan. 12, 1990, p. B4; Laura Landro, "Paramount's Marketers Try for a 'New' Eddie Murphy," *Wall Street Journal*, July 7, 1988, p. E25; Laura Landro, "Sequels and Stars Help Top Movie Studios Avoid Major Risks," *Wall Street Journal*, June 6, 1989, pp. A1, A18; Marcy Magiera, "Paramount Axes DMB&B as Studios Watch Costs," *Advertising Age*, Jan. 15, 1990, p. 4; Joe Mandese, "Hollywood's Top Gun," *Marketing & Media Decisions*, Mar. 1988, pp. 109, 112, 114; Paramount Communications, Inc. (formerly Gulf + Western) *Annual Report*, 1988.

Questions for Discussion

1. What is the role of strategic market planning at Paramount Pictures?
2. Relate the product portfolio matrix scheme to the analysis of products (movies) at Paramount Pictures.

20 IMPLEMENTING STRATEGIES AND MEASURING PERFORMANCE

Objectives

To understand how the marketing unit fits into a firm's organizational structure

To become familiar with the ways of organizing a marketing unit

To examine several issues relating to the implementation of marketing strategies

To understand the control processes used in managing marketing strategies

To learn how cost and sales analyses can be used to evaluate the performance of marketing strategies

To become aware of the major components of a marketing audit

The first Home Depot, a do-it-yourself home repair warehouse store, opened in Atlanta in 1979. Today, there are more than one hundred Home Depot outlets with sales exceeding $3 billion. Although most do-it-yourself warehouse stores offer deep discounts with minimal service, Home Depot offers low prices and unusually helpful customer service. The company aims to demystify the mechanics of home repairs and improvements for do-it-yourselfers. The company is successful because of hands-on management that carefully implements its market plan and controls operations. Home Depot's organization is based on expert buying, innovative merchandising, efficient inventory control, and motivated salespeople.

Each Home Depot stocks 25,000 items, versus 10,000 carried by a typical home center. To determine what products consumers want, Home Depot conducts extensive market research. It adds and deletes products to match demand on the basis of this research and computerized sales tracking records. The company introduced an advanced inventory control system, which allows inventory to turn six times a year rather than its earlier four and a half times. As a result, it has a smaller inventory and needs less working capital to finance it.

Home Depot's salespeople give the firm an edge over its competitors. Ninety percent of its employees are full-time and earn higher-than-average salaries with full benefits; most of its competitors are staffed with part-time minimum-wage earners. Salespeople are given detailed product information and hands-on training so that they can assist do-it-yourselfers in purchasing and using all items needed for a project. Home Depot's hands-on management of its outlets includes regular store visits and training classes for all new and potential store managers, emphasizing the company philosophy of low prices and quality service. ◆

Photo courtesy of Home Depot.

Based on information in Home Depot, *1987 Annual Report;* Bill Saporito, "The Fix Is In at Home Depot," *Fortune,* Feb. 29, 1988, pp. 73–74, 79; and Home Depot, Third Quarter Report, Oct. 29, 1989.

$\boxed{T}$ his chapter focuses first on the marketing unit's position in the organization and the ways the unit itself can be organized. Then we examine several issues regarding the implementation of marketing strategies. Next we consider the basic components of the process of control and discuss the use of cost and sales analyses to evaluate the effectiveness of marketing strategies and measure the firm's performance. Finally, we describe a marketing audit.

ORGANIZING MARKETING ACTIVITIES

The structure and relationships of a marketing unit, including lines of authority and responsibility that connect and coordinate individuals, strongly affect marketing activities. This section first looks at the place of marketing within an organization and examines the major alternatives available for organizing a marketing unit. Then it shows how marketing activities can be structured to fit into an organization so as to contribute to the accomplishment of overall objectives.

■ Centralization Versus Decentralization

The organizational structure that a company uses to connect and coordinate various activities affects its success. Basic decisions relate to how various participants in the company will work together to make important decisions, as well as to coordinate, implement, and control activities. Top managers create corporate strategies and coordinate lower levels. A **centralized organization** is one in which the top-level managers delegate very little authority to lower levels of the organization. In a **decentralized organization**, decision making authority is delegated as far down the chain of command as possible. The decision to centralize or decentralize the organization directly affects marketing in the organization.

In a centralized organization, major marketing decisions originate with top management and are transmitted to lower levels of management. A decentralized structure gives marketing managers more opportunity for making key strategic decisions. IBM has adopted a decentralized management structure so that its marketing managers have a chance to customize strategies for customers. On the other hand, Hewlett-Packard Co. and 3M have become more centralized by consolidating functions or eliminating divisional managers.[1] Although decentralizing may foster innovation and a greater responsiveness to customers, a decentralized company may be inefficient or appear to have a blurred marketing strategy when dealing with larger customers. A centralized organization avoids confusion among the marketing staff, vagueness in marketing strategy, and autonomous decision makers who are out of control. Of course, overly centralized companies often become dependent on top management and respond too slowly to be able to solve problems or seize new opportunities. Obviously, finding the right degree of centralization for a particular company is a difficult balancing act.

■ The Place of Marketing in an Organization

Because the marketing environment is so dynamic, the position of the marketing unit within the organization has risen during the past twenty-five years. Firms that truly adopt the marketing concept develop a distinct organizational culture—a culture based on a shared set of beliefs that make the customer's needs the pivotal

1. Larry Reibstein, "IBM's Plan to Decentralize May Set a Trend—But Imitation Has a Price," *Wall Street Journal*, Feb. 19, 1988, p. 17.

FIGURE 20.1

Meeting customer needs and desires.

Panasonic developed Prism Television monitors to meet consumer needs and desires for a high-quality picture and excellent sound in large screen televisions.

Panasonic Improved Definition Technology. A picture that's more than just lifelike, it's bigger than life.

Non-Interlaced Double Scanning. Line and Frame Interpolation with Motion Detection. That's what engineers see when they look at the new Prism IDTV. What you'll see when you look at this new Prism Projection TV is a 51-inch (diagonal) picture that's clearer and more detailed than an ordinary TV.

That's because this Prism TV has a built-in computer that's more powerful than a standard Personal Computer.* Sixty times each second the internal computer evaluates and enhances the picture you're seeing. Making scan lines, flicker and video noise practically invisible.

And to make sure the experience of owning a Prism Television is as impressive as its technology, we created the Prism Club. Its privileges include priority in-home service and toll-free information hot lines.

New Prism IDTV—even if you're not an engineer you can see why its technology is so impressive. ■

*Based on memory capacity comparisons. TV picture simulated.

PRISM IDTV TECHNOLOGY. IT TAKES AN ENGINEER TO EXPLAIN IT. IT TAKES AN INSTANT TO APPRECIATE IT.

PRISM
Panasonic®
just slightly ahead of our time.®

SOURCE: Matsushita Electric Corporation of America

point of a firm's decisions about strategy and operations.[2] Instead of developing products in a vacuum and then trying to convince consumers to make purchases, companies using the marketing concept begin with an orientation toward their customers' needs and desires. As shown in Figure 20.1, Panasonic meets consumers' needs for a clear, high-quality wide screen monitor by providing the Prism line, with its high-resolution picture and "Dome Sound System." If the marketing concept serves as a guiding philosophy, the marketing unit will be closely coordinated with other functional areas, such as production, finance, and personnel.

Marketing must interact with other functional departments in a number of key areas. It needs to work with manufacturing in determining the volume and variety of the company's products. Those in charge of production rely on marketers for accurate sales forecasts. Research and development departments depend heavily on information gathered by marketers about product features and benefits desired by consumers. Decisions made by the physical distribution department hinge on information about the urgency of delivery schedules and cost/service tradeoffs.[3] For example, at Honda Motor Co., Ltd., all departments have worked together for a

2. Rohit Despande and Frederick E. Webster, Jr., "Organizational Culture and Marketing: Defining the Research Agenda," *Journal of Marketing*, January 1989, pp. 3–15.

3. Michael D. Hutt and Thomas W. Speth, "The Marketing Strategy Center: Diagnosing the Industrial Marketer's Interdisciplinary Role," *Journal of Marketing*, Fall 1984, pp. 16–53.

FIGURE 20.2
*Organizational chart of
a marketing-oriented
firm*

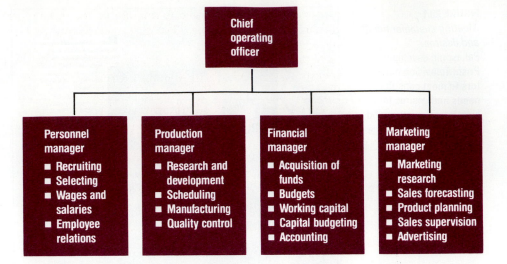

long time, whereas at Chrysler Corp., the manufacturing group was not even on the product design committee until 1981. With rapid market segmentation forcing automobile companies to design cars even faster than in the past, coordination among engineering, production, marketing, and finance is essential.[4]

A **marketing-oriented organization** concentrates on discovering what buyers want and providing it in a way that lets it achieve its objectives. Such a company has an organizational culture that effectively and efficiently produces a sustainable competitive advantage. It focuses on customer analysis, competitor analysis, and the integration of the firm's resources to provide customer value and satisfaction, as well as long-term profits.[5] As Figure 20.2 shows, the marketing manager's position is at the same level as those of the financial, production, and personnel managers. Thus the marketing manager takes part in top-level decision making. Note, too, that the marketing manager is responsible for a variety of activities. Some of them—sales forecasting and supervision and product planning—would be under the jurisdiction of other functional managers in production- or sales-oriented firms.

Both the links between marketing and other functional areas (such as production, finance, and personnel) and the importance of marketing to management evolve from the firm's basic orientation. Marketing encompasses the greatest number of business functions and occupies an important position when a firm is marketing oriented; it has a limited role when the firm views the role of marketing as simply selling products that the company makes. However, a marketing orientation is not achieved simply by redrawing the organizational chart; management must also adopt and use the marketing orientation as a management philosophy.

■ Major Alternatives for Organizing the Marketing Unit

How effectively a firm's marketing management can plan and implement marketing strategies depends on how the marketing unit is organized. Effective organizational planning can give the firm a competitive advantage. The organizational structure of a marketing department establishes the authority relationships among marketing

---

4. John Bussy, "Manufacturers Strive to Slice Time Needed to Develop Products," *Wall Street Journal,* Feb. 23, 1988, p. 18.

5. John C. Narver and Stanley F. Slater, "Creating a Market-Oriented Business," *The Channel of Communications,* Summer 1989, pp. 5–8.

personnel and specifies who is responsible for making certain decisions and performing particular activities. This internal structure provides the vehicle for directing marketing activities.

In organizing a marketing unit, managers divide the work into specific activities and delegate responsibility and authority for those activities to persons in various positions within the unit. These positions include, for example, the sales manager, the research manager, and the advertising manager.

No single approach to organizing a marketing unit works equally well in all businesses. A marketing unit can be organized according to (1) functions, (2) products, (3) regions, or (4) types of customers. The best approach or approaches depend on the number and diversity of the firm's products, the characteristics and needs of the people in the target market, and many other factors.

Firms often use some combination of organization by functions, products, regions, or customer types. Product features may dictate that the marketing unit be structured by products, whereas customers' characteristics require that it be organized by geographic region or by types of customers. IBM has organized by product types (mainframe and midsize computers, personal computers, and so on), but many financial institutions organize by customers because personal banking needs differ from commercial ones. By using more than one type of organization, a flexible marketing unit can develop and implement marketing plans to match customers' needs precisely. To develop organizational plans that give a firm a competitive advantage, four issues should be considered:

1. Which jobs or levels of jobs need to be added, deleted, or modified? For example, if new products are important to the success of the firm, marketers with strong product development skills should be added to the organization.
2. How should reporting relationships be structured to create a competitive advantage? This question is discussed further in the following descriptions of organizational structure.
3. Who should be assigned the primary responsibility for accomplishing work? Identifying primary responsibility explicitly is critical for effective performance appraisal and reward systems.
4. Should any committees or task forces be organized?[6]

Organizing by Functions. Some marketing departments are organized by general marketing functions, such as marketing research, product development, distribution, sales, advertising, and customer relations. The personnel who direct these functions report directly to the top-level marketing executive. This structure is fairly common because it works well for some businesses with centralized marketing operations, such as Ford and General Motors. In more decentralized firms, such as grocery store chains, functional organization can raise severe coordination problems. The functional approach may, however, suit a large centralized company whose products and customers are neither numerous nor diverse.

Organizing by Products. An organization that produces and markets diverse products may find the functional approach inadequate. The decisions and problems related to a single marketing function for one product may be quite different from those related to the same marketing function for another product. As a result,

6. Dave Ulrich, "Strategic Human Resources Planning: Why and How?" *Human Resources Planning,* 10, No. 1, 1987, pp. 25–57.

businesses that produce diverse products sometimes organize their marketing units according to product groups. Organizing by product groups gives a firm the flexibility to develop special marketing mixes for different products.

The product management system, which was introduced by Procter & Gamble, operates in about 85 percent of firms in the consumer packaged goods industry. In this structure, the product manager oversees all activities related to his or her assigned product. He or she develops product plans, sees that they are implemented, monitors the results, and takes corrective action as necessary. The product manager is also responsible for acting as a liaison between the firm and its marketing environment, transmitting essential information about the environment to the firm.[7] The product manager may also draw on the resources of specialized staff in the company.

Organizing by Regions.   A large company that markets products nationally (or internationally) may organize its marketing activities by geographic regions. Managers of marketing functions for each region report to their regional marketing manager; all the regional marketing managers report directly to the executive marketing manager. At Frito-Lay (a subsidiary of PepsiCo), for example, four regional marketing vice presidents who have responsibility for marketing efforts in their regions report to the senior vice president for marketing at the company's Dallas headquarters. Frito-Lay adopted this regional structure to put more senior management personnel into the field, to get closer to customers, and to enable the company to respond more quickly and efficiently to regional competitors.[8] This form of organization is especially effective for a firm whose customers' characteristics and needs vary greatly from one region to another.

A firm with marketing managers for each separate region has a complete marketing staff at its headquarters to provide assistance and guidance to regional marketing managers. Pizza Hut (another PepsiCo subsidiary) maintains a full marketing department in Wichita, Kansas, with regional offices having a regional marketing manager and regional marketing supervisors. However, not all firms organized by regions maintain a full marketing staff at their home offices. Firms that try to penetrate the national market intensively sometimes divide regions into subregions.

Organizing by Types of Customers.   Sometimes the marketing unit is organized according to types of customers. This form of internal organization works well for a firm that has several groups of customers whose needs and problems differ significantly. For example, Bic Corp. may sell pens to large retail stores, wholesalers, and institutions. Retailers may want more rapid delivery of small shipments and more personal selling by the producer than do either wholesalers or institutional buyers. Because the marketing decisions and activities required for these two groups of customers differ considerably, the company may find it efficient to organize its marketing unit by types of customers.

In an organization with a marketing department broken down by customer group, the marketing manager for each group reports to the top-level marketing executive and directs most marketing activities for that group. A marketing manager directs all activities needed to market products to a specific customer group.

7. Steven Lysonski, "A Boundary Theory Investigation of the Product Manager's Role", *Journal of Marketing*, Winter 1985, pp. 26–40.

8. Jennifer Lawrence, "Frito Reorganizes," *Advertising Age*, June 26, 1989, p. 4.

IMPLEMENTING MARKETING ACTIVITIES

The planning and organizing functions provide purpose, direction, and structure for marketing activities. However, until marketing managers implement the marketing plan, exchanges cannot occur. In fact, organizers of marketing activities can become overly concerned with planning strategy while neglecting implementation. According to former executives of the Pillsbury Company, upper management was so preoccupied with numbers and procedures that the business suffered because of the time spent developing plans. Each year, separate units spent the summer and fall revising a new five-year plan. Obviously, implementation of plans is important to the success of any organization.[9] Proper implementation of a marketing plan depends on internal marketing to employees, the motivation of personnel who perform marketing activities, effective communication within the marketing organization, and the coordination of marketing activities. In Figure 20.3, Aerospatiale promotes its team-work philosophy in business with other countries and internally.

■ **Internal Marketing**

Marketing activities cannot be effectively implemented without the cooperation of employees. Employees are the essential ingredient in increasing productivity, providing customer service, and beating the competition. Thus, in addition to marketing activities targeted at external customers, firms use internal marketing to attract, motivate, and retain qualified internal customers (employees) by designing internal products (jobs) that satisfy employees' wants and needs.[10] **Internal marketing** refers to the managerial actions necessary to make all members of the marketing organization understand and accept their respective roles in implementing the marketing strategy. This means that everyone, from the president of the company down to the hourly workers on the shop floor, must understand the role they play in carrying out their jobs and implementing the marketing strategy. Everyone must do his or her part to ensure that customers are satisfied. All personnel within the firm, both marketers and those who perform other functions, must recognize the tenet of customer orientation and service that underlies the marketing concept. Customer orientation is fostered by training and education and by keeping the lines of communication open throughout the firm.

Like external marketing activities, internal marketing may involve market segmentation, product development, research, distribution, and even public relations and sales promotion.[11] For example, an organization may sponsor sales contests to encourage sales personnel to boost their selling efforts. Some companies, including Chaparral Steel of Midlothian, Texas, and United Technologies, encourage employees to work for their companies' industrial customers for a period of time, often while continuing to receive their regular salaries. This helps the employees (and ultimately the company) to understand better the customer's needs and problems, allows them to learn valuable new skills, and heightens their enthusiasm for their regular jobs. The ultimate result is more satisfied employees and improved customer relations.

9. Richard Gibson and Robert Johnson, "Why Pillsbury's Chief from the 70's Is Again Taking Firm's Helm," *Wall Street Journal,* Mar. 1, 1988, p. 25.

10. James H. Donnelly, Jr., Leonard L. Berry, and Thomas O. Thompson, *Marketing Financial Services* (Homewood, Ill.: Dow Jones-Irwin, 1985), pp. 229–245.

11. Sybil F. Stershic, "Internal Marketing Campaign Reinforces Service Goals," *Marketing News,* July 31, 1989, p. 11.

SOURCE: Courtesy of Aerospatiale

Motivating Marketing Personnel

An important element in implementing the marketing plan, and in internal marketing, is motivating marketing personnel to perform effectively. People work to satisfy physical, psychological, and social needs. To motivate marketing personnel, managers must discover their employees' needs and then develop motivational methods that help employees satisfy those needs. It is crucial that the plan to motivate employees be fair, ethical, and well understood by employees. Additionally, rewards to employees must be tied to organizational goals. In general, to improve employee motivation, companies need to find out what workers think, how they feel, and what they want. Some of this information can be attained from an employee attitude survey. A firm can motivate its workers by directly linking pay with performance, informing workers how their performance affects department and corporate results, following through with appropriate compensation, promoting or implementing a flexible benefits program, and adopting a participative management approach.[12]

Consider the following example. Suppose a salesperson can sell product A or B to a particular customer, but not both products. Product A sells for $200,000 and contributes $20,000 to the company's profit margin. Product B sells for $60,000 and has a contribution margin of $40,000. If the salesperson receives a commission of 3

12. David C. Jones, "Motivation the Catalyst in Profit Formula," *National Underwriter*, July 13, 1987, pp. 10, 13.

percent of sales, he or she would obviously prefer to sell product A, even though the sale of product B contributes more to the company's profits. If the salesperson's commission was based on contribution margin instead of sales and the firm's goal was to maximize profits, both the firm and the salesperson would benefit more from the sale of product B.[13] By tying rewards to organizational goals, the company encourages behavior that meets organizational goals.

Besides tying rewards to organizational goals, managers must use different motivational tools to motivate individuals, based on an individual's value system. For example, some employees value recognition more than a slight pay increase. Managers can reward employees with money, plus additional fringe benefits, prestige or recognition, or even nonfinancial rewards such as job autonomy, skill variety, task significance, and increased feedback. A survey of Fortune 1000 companies found that "the majority of organizations feel that they get more for their money through non-cash awards, if given in addition to a basic compensation plan."[14]

■ Communicating Within the Marketing Unit

With good communication, marketing managers can motivate personnel and coordinate their efforts. Marketing managers must be able to communicate with the firm's high-level management to ensure that marketing activities are consistent with the company's overall goals. Communication with top-level executives keeps marketing managers aware of the company's overall plans and achievements. It also guides what the marketing unit is to do and how its activities are to be integrated with those of other departments—such as finance, production, or personnel—with whose management the marketing manager must also communicate to coordinate marketing efforts. For example, marketing personnel must work with the production staff to help design products that customers want. To direct marketing activities, marketing managers must communicate with marketing personnel at the operations level, such as sales and advertising personnel, researchers, wholesalers, retailers, and package designers.

To facilitate communication, marketing managers should establish an information system within the marketing unit. The marketing information system (discussed in Chapter 7) should allow for easy communication among marketing managers, sales managers, and sales personnel. Marketers need an information system to support a variety of activities, such as planning, budgeting, sales analyses, performance evaluations, and the preparation of reports. An information system should also expedite communications with other departments in the organization and minimize destructive competition among departments for organizational resources.

■ Coordinating Marketing Activities

Because of job specialization and differences related to marketing activities, marketing managers must synchronize individuals' actions to achieve marketing objectives. In addition, they must work closely with managers in research and development, production, finance, accounting, and personnel to see that marketing activities mesh with other functions of the firm. Marketing managers must coordinate the activities of marketing staff within the firm and integrate those activities with the marketing efforts of external organizations—advertising agencies, resellers (wholesalers and retailers), researchers, and shippers, among others. In Figure 20.4, Ford promotes its quality commitment in a magazine ad. Coordinated efforts make this message

13. The example is adapted from Edward B. Deakin and Michael W. Maher, *Cost Accounting*, 2nd ed. (Homewood, Ill.: Irwin, 1987), pp. 838–839.

14. Jerry McAdams, "Rewarding Sales and Marketing Performance," *Management Review*, April 1987, p. 36.

FIGURE 20.4
*Ford's slogan is
promoted in many media.*
The Ford message is fa-
miliar because it is
spread through the mass
media in a coordinated
way.

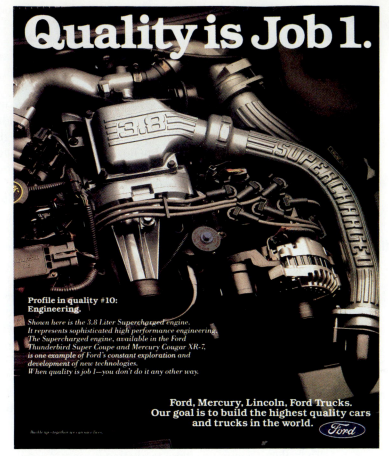

SOURCE: Courtesy of Ford Motor Company

evident to customers in TV commercials and other media. Marketing managers can improve coordination by using internal marketing activities to make each employee aware of how his or her job relates to others and how his or her actions contribute to the achievement of marketing plans.

CONTROLLING MARKETING ACTIVITIES

To achieve marketing objectives as well as general organizational objectives, marketing managers must effectively control marketing efforts. The **marketing control process** consists of establishing performance standards, evaluating actual performance by comparing it with established standards, and reducing the differences between desired and actual performance. Dunkin' Donuts, for example, has developed a program to control consistency throughout its franchises. Dunkin' Donuts controls the quality of operations in its franchised units by having franchisees attend Dunkin' Donuts University. Owners and managers of Dunkin' Donuts are required to pass a six-week training course, covering everything from customer relations and marketing to production, including a test of making 140 dozen doughnuts in 8 hours. As

FIGURE 20.5
*The marketing control
process*

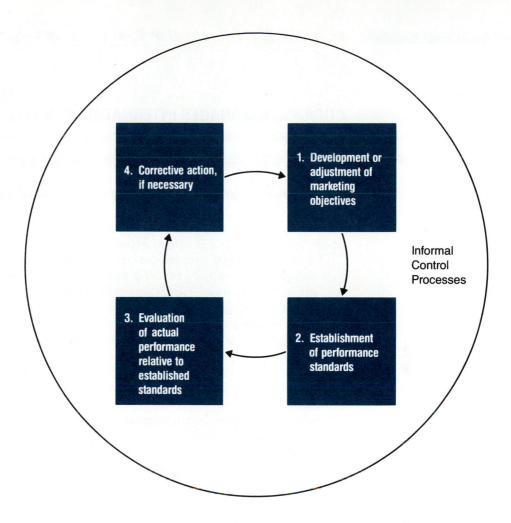

part of the test, an instructor randomly selects 6 of the 1,680 doughnuts made to ascertain that they weigh 12 to 13 ounces and measure $7^3/4$ inches when stacked. The Dunkin' Donuts University was opened to guarantee uniformity in all aspects of the business operations throughout the 1,700 franchise units.[15] The Coca-Cola Company's efforts to implement and control its marketing strategy are discussed in Marketing Update 20.1.

Although the control function is a fundamental management activity, it has received little attention in marketing. There are both formal and informal control systems in organizations. The formal marketing control process, as mentioned before, involves performance standards, evaluation of actual performance, and corrective action to remedy shortfalls (see Figure 20.5). The informal control process, however, involves self-control, social or group control, and cultural control through acceptance of a firm's value system. Which type of control system dominates depends on the environmental context of the firm.[16] We discuss these steps in the control process and consider the major problems they involve.

15. "Higher Education in Doughnuts," *Ann Arbor News*, Mar. 9, 1988, p. B7.

16. Bernard J. Jaworski, "Toward a Theory of Marketing Control: Environmental Context, Control Types, and Consequences," *Journal of Marketing*, July 1988, pp. 23–39.

COCA-COLA MANAGES INTERNATIONAL BOTTLERS

Coca-Cola may seem as American as apple pie, but the Coca-Cola name is one of the most recognized brands in the world. The company sells roughly 47 percent of all the soft drinks consumed globally, more than twice as much as PepsiCo, its nearest rival. In 1989, 80 percent of Coke's operating earnings came from foreign markets, up from 50 percent in 1985. Amazing as it may seem, more Coca-Cola is sold in Japan each year than in the United States.

Coke's international success did not happen overnight. When most American companies were only thinking about global marketing strategies, Coke was implementing them. First, Coke carefully guided and set standards for its overseas bottling partners. To maintain control of its overseas bottlers, Coke generally invested in them, spending more than $1 billion in joint bottling ventures worldwide in the 1980s. If bottlers fail to perform as expected, Coke reviews their contracts and takes corrective action, sometimes resulting in ownership of its own bottling plants. When French bottler Pernod Richard S.A. disagreed with Coke over how to revive slow soft-drink sales in France, the company took control to solve the problem.

The second part of Coke's international strategy consists of aggressive advertising, packaging, and marketing to foreign consumers. Sometimes being "The Real Thing" isn't enough to ensure success. In many countries, such as Indonesia, Coke attempted to change consumer tastes by incorporating native tastes into the Coca-Cola formula. Thus, by selling strawberry, pineapple, and banana-flavored soft drinks, Indonesians became accustomed to carbonated beverages.

By aggressively marketing to foreign consumers, Coke created markets with a high probability of success. It is this high probability of success that allows Coke to be firm but fair with its bottlers. At times, Coke's international bottlers may feel pressure to achieve Coke's high standards. However, the dominance of the Coca-Cola brand in most foreign markets all but guarantees success for Coke and its bottlers. Until its competitors move to adopt global marketing strategies, Coca-Cola will remain not just "The Real Thing" but "The Only Thing" in many foreign markets.

SOURCES: "How Coke Markets to the World," *Journal of Business Strategy,* Sept.-Oct. 1988, pp. 4–7; Michael J. McCarthy, "The Real Thing: As a Global Marketer, Coke Excels by Being Tough and Consistent," *Wall Street Journal,* Dec. 19, 1989, pp. A1, A6; Robert McGough, "No More Mr. Nice Guy," *Financial World,* July 25, 1989, pp. 30–34.

■ Establishing Performance Standards

Planning and controlling are closely linked because plans include statements about what is to be accomplished. For purposes of control, these statements function as performance standards. A **performance standard** is an expected level of performance against which actual performance can be compared. Examples of performance standards might be the reduction of customers' complaints by 20 percent, a monthly sales quota of $150,000, or a 10 percent increase per month in new customer accounts. Performance standards are also given in the form of budget accounts; that is, marketers are expected to achieve a certain objective without spending more than a given amount of resources. As stated earlier, performance standards should be tied to organizational goals. Performance standards can relate to product quality.

■ Evaluating Actual Performance

To compare actual performance with performance standards, marketing managers must know what marketers within the company are doing and have information about the activities of external organizations that provide the firm with marketing assistance. (We discuss specific methods for assessing actual performance later in this chapter.) Information is required about the activities of marketing personnel at the operations level and at various marketing management levels. Most businesses obtain marketing assistance from one or more external individuals or organizations, such as advertising agencies, middlemen, marketing research firms, and consultants. To maximize benefits from external sources, a firm's marketing control process must monitor their activities. Although it may be difficult to obtain the necessary information, it is impossible to measure actual performance without it.

Records of actual performance are compared with performance standards to determine whether and how much of a discrepancy exists. For example, a salesperson's actual sales are compared with her or his sales quota. If there is a significant negative discrepancy, the marketing manager takes corrective action.

■ Taking Corrective Action

Marketing managers have several options for reducing a discrepancy between established performance standards and actual performance. They can take steps to improve actual performance, can reduce or totally change the performance standard, or do both. Changes in actual performance may require the marketing manager to use better methods of motivating marketing personnel or find more effective techniques for coordinating marketing efforts.

Sometimes performance standards are unrealistic when they are written. In other cases, changes in the marketing environment make them unrealistic. For example, a company's annual sales goal may become unrealistic if several aggressive competitors enter the firm's market. In fact, changes in the marketing environment may force managers to change their marketing strategy completely. Publisher Harcourt Brace Jovanovich was forced to alter its marketing strategy after its efforts to repel a hostile takeover left it heavily in debt, as described in Marketing Update 20.2.

■ Requirements for an Effective Control Process

A marketing manager should consider several requirements in creating and maintaining effective control processes.[17] Effective control hinges on the quantity and quality of information available to the marketing manager and the speed at which it is received. The control process should be designed so that the flow of information is rapid enough to allow the marketing manager to quickly detect differences between actual and planned levels of performance. A single control procedure is not

17. See Theo Haimann, William G. Scott, and Patrick E. Connor, *Management,* 5th ed. (Boston: Houghton Mifflin, 1985), pp. 478–492.

suitable for all types of marketing activities, and internal and environmental changes affect an organization's activities. Therefore, control procedures should be flexible enough to adjust to both varied activities and changes in the organization's situation. For the control process to be usable, its costs must be low relative to the costs that would arise if controls were lacking. Finally, the control process should be designed so that both managers and subordinates can understand it.

■ Problems in Controlling Marketing Activities

When marketing managers attempt to control marketing activities, they frequently run into several problems. Often the information required to control marketing activities is unavailable or is only available at a high cost. Even though marketing controls should be flexible enough to allow for environmental changes, the frequency, intensity, and unpredictability of such changes may hamper effective control. In addition, the time lag between marketing activities and their effects limits a marketing manager's ability to measure the effectiveness of marketing activities.

Consider the problems of demand fluctuation in the video game industry. By failing to control the number of video game products offered, Nintendo (which controls 70 percent of the U.S. market), Atari (16 percent of the U.S. market), and Sega (10 percent of the U.S. market) glutted the market with so many video game titles that consumers were confused and disappointed with the numerous look-alike products. Companies are avoiding past mistakes by carefully analyzing the success of video games and deleting older games that are no longer profitable. For example, Nintendo withdrew eighteen of its thirty-six games to make room for new-product introductions. This careful analysis and control of product offerings has helped home video games make a comeback from being a spectacular but short-lived fad of the early 1980s.[18]

Because marketing and other business activities overlap, marketing managers cannot determine the precise cost of marketing activities. Without an accurate measure of marketing costs, it is difficult to know if the effects of marketing activities are worth their expense. Finally, marketing control may be difficult because it is very hard to develop exact performance standards for marketing personnel.

METHODS OF EVALUATING PERFORMANCE

There are specific methods for assessing and improving the effectiveness of a marketing strategy. A marketer should state in the marketing plan what a marketing strategy is supposed to accomplish. These statements should set forth performance standards, which usually are stated in terms of profits, sales, or costs. Actual performance must be measured in similar terms so that comparisons are possible. This section describes sales analysis and cost analysis, two general ways of evaluating the actual performance of marketing strategies.

■ Sales Analysis

Sales analysis uses sales figures to evaluate a firm's current performance. It is probably the most common method of evaluation because sales data partially reflect the target market's reactions to a marketing mix and often are readily available, at least in aggregate form.

18. Jeffrey A. Tannenbaum, "Video Games Revive—and Makers Hope This Time the Fad Will Last," *Wall Street Journal*, Mar. 8, 1988, p. 35.

HARCOURT BRACE JOVANOVICH

Harcourt Brace Jovanovich, Inc. (HBJ), the nation's largest educational, scientific, and medical publisher, has also been the second largest operator of theme parks, including Sea World and Cypress Gardens, and one of the nation's 100 largest insurance companies. However, after successfully repelling a hostile takeover attempt in 1987, the company was left with $2.9 billion in debt. The company therefore had to develop and implement new strategies and carefully monitor the resulting performance.

HBJ management decided the company should focus exclusively on its extensive publishing and insurance operations. To do this and reduce debt, the company sold its theme parks and related real estate, which had generated 22 percent of HBJ's total revenue in 1988. Although the sale significantly reduced debt and positioned the company for excellent growth, HBJ experienced larger than expected losses in its publishing business in 1989 due to high marketing costs and book returns. The company was forced to lay off employees in its publishing division to cut costs. Moreover, the high interest costs of maintaining nearly $3 billion in debt were ballooning. The company reported a net loss of more than $53 million in 1988.

However, the outlook for HBJ is positive in the elementary and high school textbook-publishing segment because of increasing enrollment and the variety of instructional materials HBJ markets. Other marketing opportunities for HBJ include publication of bar review and accounting accreditation courses, job training materials, office and school graphic equipment and supplies, and videotape and videodisc instructional materials. The company has consolidated its insurance operations in Michigan and Nebraska with those in Florida in order to further cut costs.

After selling some minor operations, refinancing debt, consolidating some operations to reduce costs and eliminate duplicate jobs, and finally, selling its theme parks and real estate, Harcourt Brace Jovanovich's performance will hopefully return to par. Its management will, of course, continue to carefully monitor the company's performance and take additional corrective actions as necessary.

SOURCES: Harcourt Brace Jovanovich, *Annual Report,* 1988; Michael J. McCarthy, "Harcourt to Sell Its Theme Parks and Other Land," *Wall Street Journal,* June 21, 1989, p. A6; Jay McCormick, "HBJ Plans to Sell Its Theme Parks, Real Estate," *USA Today,* June 21, 1989, p. 3B; Susan G. Strother, "HBJ Faces Questions at Meeting," *Orlando Sentinel,* May 19, 1989, pp. B1, B6; Susan G. Strother, "Shareholders of HBJ Get Upbeat Report," *Orlando Sentinel,* May 20, 1989, pp. C1, C6.

FIGURE 20.6
Evaluating performance through sales data. Godiva will use sales data from this holiday season to forecast holiday sales for future years.

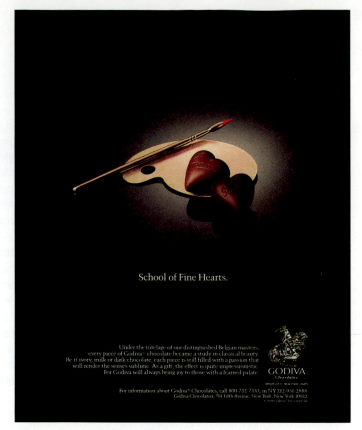

School of Fine Hearts.

Under the tutelage of our distinguished Belgian masters, every piece of Godiva® chocolate became a study in classical beauty. Be it ivory, milk or dark chocolate, each piece is still filled with a passion that will render the senses sublime. As a gift, the effect is quite impressionistic. For Godiva will always bring joy to those with a learned palate.

For information about Godiva® Chocolates, call 800-732-7333, in NY 212-951-2888. Godiva Chocolatier, 701 Fifth Avenue, New York, New York 10022

GODIVA
Chocolatier

SOURCE: Godiva Chocolatier

Marketers use current sales data to monitor the impact of current marketing efforts. For example, Godiva (Figure 20.6) attempts to measure the sales of its chocolates during selected holiday seasons. However, that information alone is not enough. To provide useful analyses, current sales data must be compared with forecasted sales, industry sales, specific competitors' sales, or the costs incurred to achieve the sales volume. For example, knowing that a variety store attained a $600,000 sales volume this year does not tell management whether its marketing strategy has been successful. However, if managers know that expected sales were $550,000, then they are in a better position to determine the effectiveness of the firm's marketing efforts. In addition, if they know that the marketing costs needed to achieve the $600,000 volume were 12 percent less than budgeted, they are in an even better position to analyze their marketing strategy precisely.

Types of Sales Measurements. Although sales may be measured in several ways, the basic unit of measurement is the sales transaction. A sales transaction results in a customer order for a specified quantity of an organization's product sold under specified terms by a particular salesperson or sales group on a certain date. Many organizations record these bits of information about their transactions. With such a record, a company can analyze sales in terms of dollar volume or market share.

Firms frequently use dollar volume sales analysis because the dollar is a common denominator of sales, costs, and profits. However, price increases and decreases affect total sales figures. For example, if a company increased its prices by 10 percent this year and its sales volume is 10 percent greater than last year, it has not experienced any increase in unit sales. A marketing manager who uses dollar volume analysis should factor out the effects of price changes.

A firm's market share is the firm's sales of a product stated as a percentage of industry sales of that product. For example, Coca-Cola at one time sold 40 percent of all the cola sold annually in the United States and thus had a market share of 40 percent. Market share analysis lets a company compare its marketing strategy with competitors' strategies. The primary reason for using market share analysis is to estimate whether sales changes have resulted from the firm's marketing strategy or from uncontrollable environmental forces. When a company's sales volume declines but its share of the market stays the same, the marketer can assume that industry sales declined (because of some uncontrollable factors) and that this decline was reflected in the firm's sales. However, if a company experiences a decline in both sales and market share, it should consider the possibility that its marketing strategy is not effective.

Even though market share analysis can be helpful in evaluating the performance of a marketing strategy, the user must interpret results cautiously. When attributing a sales decline to uncontrollable factors, a marketer must keep in mind that such factors do not affect all firms in the industry equally. Not all firms in an industry have the same objectives, and some change objectives from one year to the next. Changes in the objectives of one company can affect the market shares of one or all companies in that industry. For example, if a competitor significantly increases promotional efforts or drastically reduces prices to increase market share, then a company could lose market share despite a well-designed marketing strategy. Within an industry, the entrance of new firms or the demise of established ones also affects a specific firm's market share, and market share analysts should attempt to account for these effects. Kentucky Fried Chicken, for example, probably re-evaluated its marketing strategies when McDonald's introduced its own fried chicken product.

Bases for Sales Analysis.   Whether it is based on sales volume or market share, sales analysis can be performed on aggregate sales figures or on disaggregated data. Aggregate sales analysis provides an overview of current sales. Although helpful, aggregate sales analysis is often insufficient because it does not bring to light sales variations within the aggregate. It is not uncommon for a marketer to find that a large proportion of aggregate sales comes from a small number of products, geographic areas, or customers. (This is sometimes called the "iceberg principle" because only a small part of an iceberg is visible above the water.) To find such disparities, total sales figures usually are broken down by geographic unit, salesperson, product, customer type, or a combination of these categories.

In sales analysis by geographic unit, sales data can be classified by city, county, district, state, country, or any other geographic designation for which a marketer collects sales information. Actual sales in a geographic unit can be compared with sales in a similar geographic unit, with last year's sales, or with an estimated market potential for the area. For example, if a firm finds that 18 percent of its sales are coming from an area that represents only 8 percent of the potential sales for the product, then it can be assumed that the marketing strategy is successful in that geographic unit.

Because of the cost associated with hiring and maintaining a sales force, businesses commonly analyze sales by salesperson to determine the contribution each salesperson makes. Performance standards for each salesperson are often set in terms of sales quotas for a given time period. Evaluation of actual performance is accomplished by comparing a salesperson's current sales to a pre-established quota or some other standard, such as the previous period's sales. If actual sales meet or exceed the standard and the sales representative has not incurred costs above those budgeted, that person's efforts are acceptable.

Sales analysis is often performed according to product group or specific product item. Marketers break down their aggregate sales figures by product to determine the proportion that each contributed to total sales. Columbia Pictures, for example, might break down its total sales figures by box office figures for each film produced. A firm usually sets a sales volume objective—and sometimes a market share objective—for each product item or product group, and sales analysis by product is the only way to measure such objectives. A marketer can compare the breakdown of current sales by product with those of previous years. In addition, within industries for which sales data by product are available, a firm's sales by product type can be compared with industry averages. To gain an accurate picture of where sales of specific products are occurring, marketers sometimes combine sales analysis by product with sales analysis by geographic area or salesperson.

Analyses based on customers are usually broken down by types of customers. Customers can be classified by the way they use a firm's products, their distribution level (producer, wholesaler, retailer), their size, the size of orders, or other characteristics. Sales analysis by customer type lets a firm ascertain whether its marketing resources are allocated in a way that achieves the greatest productivity. For example, sales analysis by type of customer may reveal that 60 percent of the sales force is serving a group that makes only 15 percent of total sales.

A considerable amount of information is needed for sales analyses, especially if disaggregated analyses are desired. The marketer must develop an operational system for collecting sales information; obviously, the effectiveness of the system for collecting sales information largely determines a company's ability to develop useful sales analyses.

■ Marketing Cost Analysis

Although sales analysis is critical for evaluating the effectiveness of a marketing strategy, it gives only part of the picture. A marketing strategy that successfully generates sales may also be extremely costly. To get a complete picture, a firm must know the marketing costs associated with using a given strategy to achieve a certain sales level. **Marketing cost analysis** breaks down and classifies costs to determine which are associated with specific marketing activities. By comparing costs of previous marketing activities with results generated, a marketer can better allocate the firm's marketing resources in the future. Marketing cost analysis lets a company evaluate the effectiveness of an ongoing or recent marketing strategy by comparing sales achieved and costs incurred. By pinpointing exactly where a company is experiencing high costs, this form of analysis can help isolate profitable or unprofitable customer segments, products, or geographic areas.

For example, the market share of Komatsu Ltd., a Japanese construction equipment manufacturer, was declining in the United States as a result of increasing prices because of the high yen value. Komatsu thus developed an equal joint venture with Dresser Industries, making it the second largest company in this industry. The joint venture with Dresser allowed Komatsu to shift a large amount of its final assembly to the United States, to Dresser plants that had been running at 50 percent capacity. By using Dresser's unused capacity and existing U.S. plants, Ko-

FIGURE 20.7
Marketing costs generate sales.
Hiring celebrities to promote a product is usually effective, though often costly.

Your average Joe would be sitting here with a Diet Coke.

NEW DIET PEPSI
The Taste That Beats Diet Coke.

Diet Pepsi is a trademark of PepsiCo, Inc. Diet Coke is a registered trademark of the Coca-Cola Company. NutraSweet and the NutraSweet symbol are registered trademarks of The NutraSweet Company for its brand of sweetening ingredient.

SOURCE: Pepsi-Cola Company, Division of PepsiCo Inc.

matsu avoided the start-up costs of new construction and gained an immediate manufacturing presence in the United States.[19] This cost-control tactic should enable Komatsu to use price more effectively as a marketing variable to compete with number one Caterpillar Tractor Co.

In some organizations, personnel in other functional areas—such as production or accounting—see marketers as primarily concerned with generating sales, regardless of the costs incurred. By conducting cost analyses, marketers can undercut this criticism and put themselves in a better position to demonstrate how marketing activities contribute to generating profits. Even though hiring a spokesperson such as Joe Montana (see Figure 20.7) is costly, sales goals cannot be reached without large expenditures for promotion in the soft drink industry. Cost analysis should show if promotion costs are effective in increasing sales.

Determining Marketing Costs. The task of determining marketing costs is often complex and difficult. Simply ascertaining the costs associated with marketing a product is rarely adequate. Marketers must usually determine the marketing costs of serving specific geographic areas, market segments, or even specific customers.

A first step in determining the costs is to examine accounting records. Most accounting systems classify costs into **natural accounts**—such as rent, salaries,

19. Kevin Kelly and Neil Gross, "A Weakened Komatsu Tries to Come Back Swinging," *Business Week*, Feb. 22, 1988, p. 48.

office supplies, and utilities—which are based on how the money was actually spent. Unfortunately, many natural accounts do not help explain what marketing functions were performed through the expenditure of those funds. It does little good, for example, to know that $80,000 is spent for rent each year. The analyst has no way of knowing whether the money is spent for the rental of production, storage, or sales facilities. Therefore, marketing cost analysis usually requires that some of the costs in natural accounts be reclassified into **marketing function accounts**, which indicate the function performed through the expenditure of funds. Common marketing function accounts are transportation, storage, order processing, selling, advertising, sales promotion, marketing research, and customer credit.

Natural accounts can be reclassified into marketing function accounts as shown in the simplified example in Table 20.1. Note that a few natural accounts, such as advertising, can be reclassified easily into functional accounts because they do not have to be split across several accounts. For most of the natural accounts, however, marketers must develop criteria for assigning them to the various functional accounts. For example, the number of square feet of floor space used was the criterion for dividing the rental costs in Table 20.1 into functional accounts. In some instances, a specific marketing cost is incurred to perform several functions. A packaging cost, for example, could be considered a production function, a distribution function, a promotional function, or all three. The marketing cost analyst must reclassify such costs across multiple functions.

Three broad categories are used in marketing cost analysis: direct costs, traceable common costs, and nontraceable common costs. **Direct costs** are directly attributable to the performance of marketing functions. For example, sales force salaries might be allocated to the cost of selling a specific product item, selling in a specific geographic area, or selling to a particular customer. **Traceable common costs** can be allocated indirectly, using one or several criteria, to the functions that they support. For example, if the firm spends $80,000 annually to rent space for production, storage, and selling, the rental costs of storage could be determined on the basis of cost per square foot used for storage. **Nontraceable common costs** cannot be assigned according to any logical criteria and thus are assignable only on an arbitrary basis. Interest, taxes, and the salaries of top management are nontraceable common costs.

The manner of dealing with these three categories of costs depends on whether the analyst uses a full cost or a direct cost approach. When a **full cost approach** is used, cost analysis includes direct costs, traceable common costs, and nontraceable common costs. Proponents of this approach claim that if an accurate profit picture is desired, all costs must be included in the analysis. However, opponents point out that full costing does not yield actual costs because nontraceable common costs are determined by arbitrary criteria. With different criteria, the full-costing approach yields different results. A cost-conscious operating unit can be discouraged if numerous costs are assigned to it arbitrarily. To eliminate such problems, the **direct cost approach**, which includes direct costs and traceable common costs but not nontraceable common costs, is used. Opponents say that this approach is not accurate because it omits one cost category.

Methods of Marketing Cost Analysis. Marketers can use several methods to analyze costs. The methods vary in their precision. This section examines three cost analysis methods—analysis of natural accounts; analysis of functional accounts; and cost analysis by product, geographic area, or customer.

TABLE 20.1 *Reclassification of natural accounts into functional accounts*

PROFIT AND LOSS STATEMENT

		FUNCTIONAL ACCOUNTS					
		ADVERTISING	PERSONAL SELLING	TRANSPORTATION	STORAGE	MARKETING RESEARCH	NON-MARKETING
Sales	$250,000						
Cost of goods sold	45,000						
Gross profit	205,000						
Expenses (natural accounts)							
Rent	$ 14,000		$ 7,000		$6,000		$ 1,000
Salaries	72,000	$12,000	32,000	$7,000		$1,000	20,000
Supplies	4,000	1,500	1,000			1,000	500
Advertising	16,000	16,000					
Freight	4,000			2,000			2,000
Taxes	2,000				200		1,800
Insurance	1,000				600		400
Interest	3,000						3,000
Bad debts	6,000						6,000
Total	$ 122,000	$ 29,500	$ 40,000	$ 9,000	$ 6,800	$ 2,000	$ 34,700
Net profit	$ 83,000						

Marketers sometimes can determine marketing costs by performing an analysis of natural accounts. The precision of this method depends on how detailed the firm's accounts are. For example, if accounting records contain separate accounts for production wages, sales-force wages, and executive salaries, the analysis can be more precise than if all wages and salaries are lumped into a single account. An analysis of natural accounts is more meaningful, and thus more useful, when current cost data can be compared with those of previous periods or with average cost figures for the entire industry. Cost analysis of natural accounts frequently treats costs as percentages of sales. The periodic use of cost-to-sales ratios lets a marketer ascertain cost fluctuations quickly.

As indicated earlier, the analysis of natural accounts may not shed much light on the cost of marketing activities. In such cases, natural accounts must be reclassified into marketing function accounts for analysis. Whether certain natural accounts are reclassified into functional accounts and what criteria are used to reclassify them will depend to some degree on whether the analyst is using direct costing or full costing. After natural accounts have been reclassified into functional accounts, the cost of each function is determined by summing the costs in each functional account. Once the costs of these marketing functions have been determined, the analyst is ready to compare the resulting figures with budgeted costs, sales analysis data, cost data from earlier operating periods, or perhaps average industry cost figures, if these are available.

Although marketers ordinarily get a more detailed picture of marketing costs by analyzing functional accounts than by analyzing natural accounts, some firms need an even more precise cost analysis. The need is especially great if the firms sell several types of products, sell in multiple geographic areas, or sell to a wide variety of customers. Activities vary in marketing different products in specific geographic locations to certain customer groups. Therefore the costs of these activities also vary. By analyzing the functional costs of specific product groups, geographic areas, or customer groups, a marketer can find out which of these marketing entities are the most cost effective to serve. In Table 20.2, the functional costs derived in Table 20.1 are allocated to specific product categories.

A similar type of analysis could be performed for geographic areas or for specific customer groups. The criteria used to allocate the functional accounts must be developed so as to yield results that are as accurate as possible. Use of faulty criteria is likely to yield inaccurate cost estimates that in turn lead to less effective control of marketing strategies. Marketers determine the marketing costs for various product categories, geographic areas, or customer groups and then compare them to sales. This analysis lets them evaluate the effectiveness of the firm's marketing strategy or strategies.

THE MARKETING AUDIT

A **marketing audit** is a systematic examination of the marketing group's objectives, strategies, organization, and performance. Its primary purpose is to identify weaknesses in ongoing marketing operations and plan the necessary improvements to correct these weaknesses. The marketing audit does not concern itself with the firm's marketing position because that is the purpose of the firm's marketing plan.

TABLE 20.2 *Functional accounts divided into product group costs*

FUNCTIONAL ACCOUNTS		PRODUCT GROUPS		
		A	B	C
Advertising	$29,500	$14,000	$ 8,000	$ 7,500
Personal selling	40,000	18,000	10,000	12,000
Transportation	9,000	5,000	2,000	2,000
Storage	6,800	1,800	2,000	3,000
Marketing research	2,000		1,000	1,000
Total	**$87,300**	**$38,800**	**$23,000**	**$25,500**

Rather, the marketing audit evaluates how effectively the marketing organization performed its assigned functions.[20]

Like an accounting or financial audit, a marketing audit should be conducted regularly instead of just when performance control mechanisms show that the system is out of control. The marketing audit is not a control process to be used only during a crisis, although a business in trouble may use it to isolate problems and generate solutions.

A marketing audit may be specific and focus on one or a few marketing activities, or it may be comprehensive and encompass all of a company's marketing activities. Table 20.3 lists many possible dimensions of a marketing audit. An audit might deal with only a few of these areas, or it might include them all. Its scope depends on the costs involved, the target markets served, the structure of the marketing mix, and environmental conditions. The results of the audit can be used to reallocate marketing effort and to re-examine marketing opportunities. For example, Russell Athletics determined that durability was important to consumers and therefore warranted its High Cotton sweats for five years (see Figure 20.8).

The marketing audit should aid evaluation by doing the following:

1. Describing current activities and results related to sales, costs, prices, profits, and other performance feedback
2. Gathering information about customers, competition, and environmental developments that may affect the marketing strategy
3. Exploring opportunities and alternatives for improving the marketing strategy
4. Providing an overall database to be used in evaluating the attainment of organizational goals and marketing objectives

Marketing audits can be performed internally or externally. An internal auditor may be a top-level marketing executive, a companywide auditing committee, or a manager from another office or of another function. Although it is more expensive, an audit by outside consultants is usually more effective because external auditors have more objectivity, more time for the audit, and greater experience.

20. William A. Band, "A Marketing Audit Provides an Opportunity for Improvement," *Sales & Marketing Management in Canada*, March 1984, pp. 24–26.

TABLE 20.3 *Dimensions of a marketing audit*

Part I. The Marketing Environment Audit

Macroenvironment

A. Economic-demographic
1. What does the company expect in the way of inflation, material shortages, unemployment, and credit availability in the short run, intermediate run, and long run?
2. What effect will forecasted trends in the size, age distribution, and regional distribution of population have on the business?

B. Technological
1. What major changes are occurring in product technology? In process technology?
2. What are the major generic substitutes that might replace this product?

C. Political-legal
1. What laws are being proposed that may affect marketing strategy and tactics?
2. What federal, state, and local agency actions should be watched? What is happening with pollution control, equal employment opportunity, product safety, advertising, price control, etc., that is relevant to marketing planning?

D. Cultural
1. What attitude is the public taking toward business and the types of products produced by the company?
2. What changes in consumer lifestyles and values have a bearing on the company's target markets and marketing methods?

E. Ecological
1. Will the cost and availability of natural resources directly affect the company?
2. Are there public concerns about the company's role in pollution and conservation? If so, what is the company's reaction?

Task Environment

A. Markets
1. What is happening to market size, growth, geographical distribution, and profits?
2. What are the major market segments and their expected rates of growth? Which are high opportunity and low opportunity segments?

B. Customers
1. How do current customers and prospects rate the company and its competitors on reputation, product quality, service, sales force, and price?
2. How do different classes of customers make their buying decisions?
3. What evolving needs and satisfactions are the buyers in this market seeking?

C. Competitors
1. Who are the major competitors? What are the objectives and strategy of each major competitor? What are their strengths and weaknesses? What are the sizes and trends in market shares?
2. What trends can be foreseen in future competition and substitutes for this product?

D. Distribution and dealers
1. What are the main trade channels bringing products to customers?
2. What are the efficiency levels and growth potentials of the different trade channels?

E. Suppliers
1. What is the outlook for the availability of key resources used in production?
2. What trends are occurring among suppliers in their patterns of selling?

F. Facilitators and marketing firms
1. What is the outlook for the cost and availability of transportation services?
2. What is the outlook for the cost and availability of warehousing facilities?
3. What is the outlook for the cost and availability of financial resources?
4. How effectively is the advertising agency performing? What trends are occurring in advertising agency services?

G. Publics
1. Where are the opportunity areas or problems for the company?
2. How effectively is the company dealing with publics?

Part II. Marketing Strategy Audit

A. Business mission
1. Is the business mission clearly focused with marketing terms and is it attainable?

TABLE 20.3 *Dimensions of a marketing audit (continued)*

B. Marketing objectives and goals

1. Are the corporate objectives clearly stated? Do they lead logically to the marketing objectives?
2. Are the marketing objectives stated clearly enough to guide marketing planning and subsequent performance measurement?
3. Are the marketing objectives appropriate, given the company's competitive position, resources, and opportunities? Is the appropriate strategic objective to build, hold, harvest, or terminate this business?

C. Strategy

1. What is the core marketing strategy for achieving the objectives? Is it sound?
2. Are the resources budgeted to accomplish the marketing objectives inadequate, adequate, or excessive?
3. Are the marketing resources allocated optimally to prime market segments, territories, and products?
4. Are the marketing resources allocated optimally to the major elements of the marketing mix, i.e., product quality, service, sales force, advertising, promotion, and distribution?

Part III. Marketing Organization Audit

A. Formal structure

1. Is there a high-level marketing officer with adequate authority and responsibility over those company activities that affect customer satisfaction?
2. Are the marketing responsibilities optimally structured along functional, product, end user, and territorial lines?

B. Functional efficiency

1. Are there good communication and working relations between marketing and sales?
2. Is the product-management system working effectively? Are the product managers able to plan profits or only sales volume?
3. Are there any groups in marketing that need more training, motivation, supervision, or evaluation?

C. Interface efficiency

1. Are there any problems between marketing and manufacturing, R&D, purchasing, finance, accounting, and legal that need attention?

Part IV. Marketing Systems Audit

A. Marketing information system

1. Is the marketing intelligence system producing accurate, sufficient, and timely information about developments in the marketplace?
2. Is marketing research being adequately used by company decision makers?

B. Marketing-planning system

1. Is the marketing-planning system well conceived and effective?
2. Is sales forecasting and market-potential measurement soundly carried out?
3. Are sales quotas set on a proper basis?

C. Marketing control system

1. Are the control procedures (monthly, quarterly, etc.) adequate to ensure that the annual-plan objectives are being achieved?
2. Is provision made to analyze periodically the profitability of different products, markets, territories, and channels of distribution?
3. Is provision made to examine and validate periodicially various marketing costs?

D. New-product development system

1. Is the company well organized to gather, generate, and screen new product ideas?
2. Does the company do adequate concept research and business analysis before investing heavily in a new idea?
3. Does the company carry out adequate product and market testing before launching a new product?

Part V. Marketing-Productivity Audit

A. Profitability analysis

1. What is the profitability of the company's different products, served markets, territories, and channels of distribution?
2. Should the company enter, expand, contract, or withdraw from any business segments, and what would be the short- and long-run profit consequences?

B. Cost-effective analysis

1. Do any marketing activities seem to have excessive costs? Are these costs valid? Can cost-reducing steps be taken?

TABLE 20.3 *Dimensions of a marketing audit (continued)*

Part VI. Marketing Function Audits

A. Products

1. What are the product line objectives? Are these objectives sound? Is the current product line meeting these objectives?
2. Are there particular products that should be phased out?
3. Are there new products that are worth adding?
4. Are any products able to benefit from quality, feature, or style improvements?

B. Price

1. What are the pricing objectives, policies, strategies, and procedures? Are prices set on sound cost, demand, and competitive criteria?
2. Do the customers see the company's prices as being in or out of line with the perceived value of its products?
3. Does the company use price promotions effectively?

C. Distribution

1. What are the distribution objectives and strategies?
2. Is there adequate market coverage and service?
3. How effective are the following channel members: distributors, manufacturers' reps, brokers, agents, etc.?
4. Should the company consider changing its distribution channels?

D. Advertising, sales promotion, and publicity

1. What are the organization's advertising objectives? Are they sound?
2. Is the right amount being spent on advertising? How is the budget determined?
3. Are the ad themes and copy effective? What do customers and the public think about the advertising?
4. Are the advertising media well chosen?
5. Is the internal advertising staff adequate?
6. Is the sales promotion budget adequate? Is there effective and sufficient use of sales promotion tools, such as samples, coupons, displays, and sales contests?
7. Is the publicity budget adequate? Is the public relations staff competent and creative?

E. Sales force

1. What are the organization's sales-force objectives?
2. Is the sales force large enough to accomplish the company's objectives?
3. Is the sales force organized along the proper principle(s) of specialization (territory, market, product)? Are there enough (or too many) sales managers to guide the field sales reps?
4. Does the sales compensation level and structure provide adequate incentive and reward?
5. Does the sales force show high morale, ability, and effort?
6. Are the procedures adequate for setting quotas and evaluating performance?
7. How does the company's sales force compare to the sales forces of competitors?

SOURCE: Philip Kotler, *Marketing Management: Analysis, Planning, and Control,* 6th ed. © 1988, pp. 748–751. Adapted by permission of Prentice-Hall, Inc., Englewood Cliffs, N.J.

There is no single set of procedures for all marketing audits. However, firms should adhere to several general guidelines. Audits are often based on a series of questionnaires that are administered to the firm's personnel. These questionnaires should be developed carefully to ensure that the audit focuses on the right issues. Auditors should develop and follow a step-by-step plan to guarantee that the audit is systematic. When interviewing company personnel, the auditors should strive to talk with a diverse group of people from many parts of the company. The auditor should become familiar with the product line, meet with headquarters staff, visit field organizations, interview customers, interview competitors, and analyze information for a report on the marketing environment.[21]

21. Ely S. Lurin, "Audit Determines the Weak Link in Marketing Chain," *Marketing News,* Sept. 12, 1986, pp. 35–37.

FIGURE 20.8

Using the results of a marketing audit.
A marketing audit showed that consumers want their sweats to last; therefore, Russell Athletics warrants their High Cottons for five years.

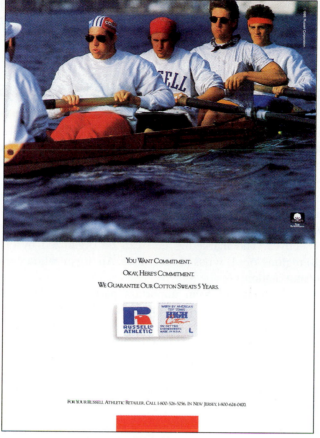

YOU WANT COMMITMENT.
OKAY, HERE'S COMMITMENT.
WE GUARANTEE OUR COTTON SWEATS 5 YEARS.

FOR YOUR RUSSELL ATHLETIC RETAILER, CALL 1-800-526-5256. IN NEW JERSEY, 1-800-624-0470.

SOURCE: Courtesy of Russell Athletic

To achieve adequate support, the auditors normally focus first on the firm's top management and then move down through the organizational hierarchy. The auditor looks for different points of view within various departments of the organization or a mismatch between the customers' and the company's perception of the product as signs of trouble in an organization.[22] The results of the audit should be reported in a comprehensive written document, which should include recommendations that will increase marketing productivity and determine the company's general direction.

The marketing audit lets an organization change tactics or alter day-to-day activities as problems arise. For example, marketing auditors often wonder whether a change in budgeted sales activity is caused by general market conditions or is due to a change in the firm's market share.

Although the concept of auditing implies an official examination of marketing activities, many organizations audit their marketing activities informally. Any attempt to verify operating results and to compare them with standards can be considered an auditing activity. Many smaller firms probably would not use the word *audit*, but they do perform auditing activities.

Several problems may arise in an audit of marketing activities. Marketing audits can be expensive in time and money. Selecting the auditors may be difficult because

22. Ibid.

objective, qualified personnel may not be available. Marketing audits can also be extremely disruptive because employees sometimes fear comprehensive evaluations, especially by outsiders.

SUMMARY

The organization of marketing activities involves the development of an internal structure for the marketing unit. The internal structure is the key to directing marketing activities. A centralized organization is one in which the top-level managers delegate very little authority to lower levels of the firm. In a decentralized organization, decision-making authority is delegated as far down the chain of command as possible. In a marketing-oriented organization, the focus is on finding out what buyers want and providing it in a way that lets the organization achieve its objectives. The marketing unit can be organized by (1) functions, (2) products, (3) regions, or (4) types of customers. An organization may use only one approach or a combination.

Implementation is an important part of the marketing management process. Proper implementation of a marketing plan depends on internal marketing to employees, the motivation of personnel who perform marketing activities, effective communication within the marketing organization, and the coordination of marketing activities. Internal marketing refers to the managerial actions necessary to make all members of the marketing organization understand and accept their respective roles in implementing the marketing strategy. To attract, motivate, and retain qualified internal customers (employees), firms employ internal marketing by designing internal products (jobs) that satisfy employees' wants and needs. Marketing managers must also motivate marketing personnel. A company's communication system must allow the marketing manager to communicate with high-level management, with managers of other functional areas in the firm, and with personnel involved in marketing activities both inside and outside the organization. Finally, marketing managers must coordinate the activities of marketing personnel and integrate these activities with those in other areas of the company and with the marketing efforts of personnel in external organizations.

The marketing control process consists of establishing performance standards, evaluating actual performance by comparing it with established standards, and reducing the difference between desired and actual performance. Performance standards, which are established in the planning process, are expected levels of performance with which actual performance can be compared. In evaluating actual performance, marketing managers must know what marketers within the firm are doing and must have information about the activities of external organizations that provide the firm with marketing assistance. Then actual performance is compared with performance standards. Marketers must determine whether a discrepancy exists and, if so, whether it requires corrective action, such as changing the performance standards or improving actual performance.

To maintain effective marketing control, an organization needs to develop a comprehensive control process that evaluates its marketing operations at a given time. The control of marketing activities is not a simple task. Problems encountered include environmental changes, time lags between marketing activities and their effects, and difficulty in determining the costs of marketing activities. In addition to these, it may be hard to develop performance standards.

Control of marketing strategy can be achieved through sales and cost analyses. For the purpose of analysis, sales are usually measured in terms of either dollar volume or market share. For a sales analysis to be effective, it must compare current sales performance with forecasted company sales, industry sales, specific competitors' sales, or the costs incurred to generate the current sales volume. A sales analysis can be performed on the firm's total sales, or the total sales can be disaggregated and analyzed by product, geographic area, or customer group.

Marketing cost analysis involves an examination of accounting records and, frequently, a reclassification of natural accounts into marketing function accounts. Such an analysis is often difficult because there may be no logical, clear-cut way to allocate natural accounts into functional accounts. The analyst may choose either direct costing or full costing. Cost analysis can focus on (1) an aggregate cost analysis of natural accounts or functional accounts or (2) an analysis of functional accounts for products, geographic areas, or customer groups.

To control marketing strategies, it is sometimes necessary to audit marketing activities. A marketing audit is a systematic examination of the marketing group's objectives, strategies, organization, and performance. A marketing audit attempts to identify what a marketing unit is doing, to evaluate the effectiveness of these activities, and to recommend future marketing activities.

IMPORTANT TERMS

Centralized organization
Decentralized organization
Marketing-oriented organization
Internal marketing
Marketing control process
Performance standard
Sales analysis
Marketing cost analysis

Natural accounts
Marketing function accounts
Direct costs
Traceable common costs
Nontraceable common costs
Full cost approach
Direct cost approach
Marketing audit

DISCUSSION AND REVIEW QUESTIONS

1. What determines the place of marketing within an organization? Which type of organization is best suited to the marketing concept? Why?
2. What factors can be used to organize the internal aspects of a marketing unit? Discuss the benefits of each type of organization.
3. Why might an organization use multiple bases for organizing its marketing unit?
4. What is internal marketing? Why is it important in implementing marketing strategies?
5. Why is motivation of marketing personnel important in implementing marketing plans?
6. How does communication help in implementing marketing plans?
7. What are the major steps of the marketing control process?

8. List and discuss the five requirements for an effective control process.
9. Discuss the major problems in controlling marketing activities.
10. What is a sales analysis? What makes it an effective control tool?
11. Identify and describe three cost analysis methods. Compare and contrast direct costing and full costing.
12. How is the marketing audit used to control marketing program performance?

■ CASES

20.1   IBM Struggles to Maintain Leadership in the Computer Industry

International Business Machines, or "Big Blue," has been a leader in the computer industry since the 1960s. Several of its products, including the System/370 mainframe computers and the IBM PC line of personal computers, set standards followed by many computer makers. However, despite its reputation for providing high-quality computers and strong service to its customers, the company has experienced declining sales, profits, and market share in recent years.

Recognizing that IBM's performance was not up to par, Chairman John Akers reorganized IBM early in 1988 to make it more responsive to customers' needs and more competitive in a stagnating computer market. The reorganization effort was intended to boost sales, speed up new-product development time, remove excessive corporate layers, and improve products and service to customers. It was also expected to improve coordination among the firm's various divisions and improve morale. IBM combined its personal computer and typewriter divisions because customers of those products have similar needs. It also merged its mainframe division with the less profitable midsize computer division. The organization was decentralized somewhat, giving decision-making responsibilities to six major product and marketing divisions to help reduce the bureaucracy that had slowed down new-product development and dissatisfied customers. To avoid laying off employees, IBM asked 15,000 employees, mostly in management, to retire early, and allowed another 25,000 positions to remain vacant. It retrained and moved thousands of other employees to new positions within the company. Although these efforts helped improve the company's performance somewhat, IBM faced two more years of slow growth, in part because of increasing competition in its mainframe and personal computer markets.

Analysts believe that IBM's problems stem from having too many employees, high overhead, and too great a reliance on its cash cow, mainframe computers. Mainframe computer sales contribute 50 percent to the company's revenues and 65 percent to its profits. The multi-million dollar mainframes also link the company to its largest, most profitable customers and influence all their computer and software purchases. But the IBM-dominated mainframe computer market is maturing; growth has been slowing and competition is fierce. Amdahl Corp. and Hitachi Data Systems, which market IBM-compatible machines, and Digital Equipment Corp. have been stealing market share with computers that are more powerful and less expensive than IBM's System/370 workhorse. Moreover, more powerful minicomputers and personal computers can now tackle some jobs that only mainframes could handle before. As a result, sales of mainframes in general are flat, with growth slowing down to 3 or 4 percent a year.

IBM also faces problems in other segments of the computer market. Sales of midrange computers, including the AS/400 minicomputer, have been soft. As with mainframes, the slow sales of midrange computers can be attributed to increasingly powerful personal computers and workstations which can handle more complex applications that once required a minicomputer or mainframe. IBM also lacks products in two growth segments of the computer industry. IBM has no products in the Japanese-dominated laptop-computer market, which is growing at 40 percent annually. In the workstation market, which is growing at 30 percent annually, IBM has few products and commands only a 2 percent share.

IBM is also suffering because of numerous product delays. For example, it delayed deliveries of its Model 3090–S central mainframe processors by a few months because of quality problems in the processors' logic microchips. And, in January 1990, it announced that it had indefinitely postponed the introduction of a long-awaited mainframe disk drive, which was to have been introduced late in 1989, because of technical problems.

Everything is not all bad for IBM, however. It continues to lease System/370 and AS/400 equipment at competitive rates that competitors find hard to match. Leasing, however, accounts for only 4 percent of IBM's revenues. Analysts also praise the company's recent investments in software companies, the use of faster chips in its PCs, and plans to introduce another mainframe disk drive in 1990. In the personal computer market, IBM is recovering somewhat from a slow period with the help of new products such as the PS/2 systems that run on OS/2 software. In 1989, these and other IBM PCs accounted for 30 percent of dealer sales, up slightly from the previous year.

To correct IBM's current poor performance several steps have been taken. IBM is discounting prices on many products by up to 40 percent. However, the price discounting has turned customers' focus to price instead of IBM's traditionally strong service. The price competition in the mainframe market is especially harmful to IBM because the profits from that division are used to subsidize low prices in other, more competitive markets and to help fund vital product development. In an industry in which equipment can become obsolete in a matter of a few years, continued product and technology development is critical to computer manufacturers' survival.

Moreover, IBM announced in January 1990 that it would mount yet another restructuring to cut costs. Company executives say they will make the company more competitive by slashing costs by $1 billion, and by eliminating 10,000 jobs, again through early retirements and attrition rather than layoffs. The company took a $2.3 billion pretax charge against earnings, 4th quarter 1989, to cover severance pay, consolidations, and other expenses associated with reorganizing. After restructuring, Akers vows that IBM will show "modest growth" in revenues in 1990, for the first time since 1985.

Despite Akers' positive forecast, analysts continue to predict gloom for Big Blue. They point out that IBM has repeatedly forecasted turnarounds that have yet to materialize. Critics blame John Akers for IBM's dismal performance in the last few years, particularly for the manufacturing problems, product delays, and managerial decisions that have blemished IBM's reputation and its earnings. They urge IBM to cut costs even further and eliminate another 30,000 jobs to reach Akers' goal of operating margins of 18 percent. Many believe that IBM's longstanding policy of no layoffs has been preserved at the expense of shareholder value and that IBM's board of directors are reluctant to criticize executives or enact tough cost-cutting measures. They also accuse IBM of clinging to its old line of mainframe computers at the expense of developing technologically sophisticated new products that could help boost the company's revenue and image. One analyst said, "Times have changed. But I'm not sure IBM adapted to those changes fast enough for themselves or their shareholders."

Thus, even after two restructurings and drastic cost-cutting measures, IBM managers must continue to monitor the marketing environment as well as the company's performance. Further changes in the company's corporate and marketing strategies may be necessary to make the company more profitable by developing and marketing products that satisfy consumers.

SOURCES: Paul B. Carroll, "Big Blues: Hurt by a Pricing War, IBM Plans a Writeoff and Cut of 10,000 Jobs," *Wall Street Journal,* Dec. 6, 1989, pp. A1, A8; John Hillkirk, "As IBM Falters, Shareholders and Critics Take Aim at Akers," *USA Today,* Dec. 6, 1989, p. 10B; Geoff Lewis, with Anne R. Field, John J. Keller, and John W. Verity, "Big Changes at Big Blue," *Business Week,* Feb. 15, 1988, pp. 92–98; Larry Reibstein, "IBM's Plan to Decentralize May Set a Trend—But Imitation Has a Price," *Wall Street Journal,* Feb. 19, 1988, p. 17; John W. Verity, "A Slimmer IBM May Still Be Overweight," *Business Week,* Dec. 18, 1989, pp. 107–108; and John W. Verity, "What's Ailing IBM? More Than This Year's Earnings," *Business Week,* Oct. 16, 1989, pp. 75–86.

Questions for Discussion

1. Why is IBM's performance so disappointing?
2. Are organization or implementation important considerations in turning IBM around?

20.2   Ford Merkur: The Edsel of the '80s

In 1957, Ford introduced the Edsel to fill a gap between its low-end and high-end car lines. Although Ford saw the move as a good positioning tactic, the consumer saw the Edsel as too much like other available cars. As a result, Ford lost $350 million on the Edsel and eventually stopped producing it.

Almost 30 years later in 1985, Ford introduced the Merkur, a $28,000 luxury sedan built by Ford of Europe in West Germany. The Merkur, a top-selling model in Germany, was the company's first new car franchise in the United States since the Edsel. However, much to the dismay of Ford, the Merkur would fare no better than its predecessor. In a surprising repeat of history, Ford discontinued imports of the Merkur in 1989, only four years after the luxury car's debut.

The Merkur (pronounced mare-COOR) was originally intended to entice young, affluent buyers who did not like the Lincoln Town Car image to visit Lincoln-Mercury dealerships. The Town Car was a barge-like flagship of the Lincoln-Mercury division which had a strong appeal to older consumers. The first Merkur, the XR4Ti, did not sell well in part because American buyers did not like the car's unusual double-wing rear spoiler. In May 1987, Ford began importing the Scorpio sedan from West Germany to sell next to a redesigned XR4Ti in Lincoln-Mercury showrooms. Ford officials expected the two Merkurs to sell about 15,000 cars per year. In 1988, Ford reached that goal as Merkur sales climbed to 15,261 cars.

However, it was all downhill from there. Less than a year after the Merkur's 1985 launch, the West German mark rose sharply against the dollar, causing Merkur prices to rise. In addition, both the Scorpio and the XR4Ti suffered from poor quality. Ford promised Merkur owners that it would fix for free a variety of problems, including malfunctioning air conditioners, engine stalling, and general electrical problems. By the third quarter of 1988, Ford had most of the problems solved and Merkur satisfaction ratings were on the rise.

But the improvements came too late. In the fall of 1988, Ford stopped importing the XR4Ti because of the slow sales. Sales of the Scorpio also plummeted. Total Merkur sales for the first nine months of 1989 dropped 46 percent from the previous year to only 6,320 cars. In September of 1989 alone, the 670 Merkur dealers nationwide managed to sell only 93 Scorpios. As a result, Ford cancelled plans to outfit the Scorpio with air bags; and in October of 1989, it stopped importing the Merkur altogether.

The Scorpio continues to be sold in Europe where company officials call it a "success." But European Scorpio sales have been slipping since it won the European Car of the Year title in 1986. In 1988, Ford had sold 86,185 Scorpios in Europe, down 6 percent from 1987. Moreover, as of October 1989, Ford had sold only 67,405 Scorpios in Europe.

Why did the Merkur fail in the U.S.? Although Ford and its advertising agency, Young and Rubicam, claimed not to know what went wrong, the most likely answer seems to be the lack of a sound marketing strategy. Like the Edsel, the Merkur was introduced to satisfy Ford's marketing needs rather than the needs of the consumer. As a result, the Merkur was brought into the U.S. market with few changes in marketing style.

For example, many felt that the Merkur suffered from an image problem because it was a European import selling side by side with domestic models. As a result, many dealers considered the Merkur an outsider that they did not feel obligated to support. Others believed that the name, XR4Ti, and the styling did not convey prestige. Still others cite the ineffectiveness of the $13 million advertising campaign Ford used to introduce the Merkur as a cause of its failure. Many import car buyers want taut suspension, quick steering, quick acceleration, and high quality in a neat roomy package. They were comparing the Merkur to BMWs, Volvos, and Audis.

Although Ford spent about $50 million to convert the Merkur to U.S. safety and emission standards, it overlooked other items in the design that were essential to U.S. consumers of luxury automobiles. As a result, many import buyers felt that the car was overpriced. In 1989, the Merkur Scorpio listed for nearly as much as a Lincoln Continental.

The death of the Merkur wasn't nearly as costly to Ford as was the demise of the Edsel because Merkur was a relatively low-budget project with limited sales goals. Still, Ford's "Edsel of the '80s" came at a time when the company's golden image was showing signs of strain.

SOURCES: "Detroit's New Goal: Putting Yuppies in the Driver's Seat," *Business Week, (Industrial/Technology Edition),* September 3, 1984, pp. 46, 50; Rebecca Fannin, "Who Killed Merkur?" *Marketing and Media Decisions,* January 1989, pp. 66–69; William J. Hampton, "Detroit's Big Gamble," *Business Week (Industrial/Technology Edition),* January 13, 1986, pp. 30–31; Jesse Snyder, "U.S. Drawing More Foreign Car Entries," *Advertising Age,* July 8, 1985, pp. 3, 63; Joseph B. White, "Ford Ends Imports of Merkur in an '80s Echo of Edsel," *Wall Street Journal,* October 20, 1989, pp. B1, B6.

Questions for Discussion

1. Why did the Merkur fail?
2. Did Ford effectively implement the Merkur marketing strategy?

Texas Air's Marketing Strategy

In 1987, Texas Air (a Houston-based holding company that owned Continental Airlines and New York Air) bought Eastern Airlines and the financially troubled People Express (which also owned Frontier Airlines). Texas Air merged Continental, New York Air, and People Express into one full-service, low-fare airline under the Continental banner, making Continental the third largest airline in the United States. Eastern Airlines remained an independent carrier, with most of its flights limited to east of the Mississippi River. After making these acquisitions, Texas Air controlled the country's largest airline system, carrying 20 percent of the nation's airline passengers.

Texas Air strived to give its customers what they wanted: the best possible service at the best possible price. The airline was and is committed to this low-price, high-value service, and follows a cost-conscious, consumer-oriented philosophy to maintain it. Texas Air claims that it follows this philosophy in the air and on the ground with friendly personnel, efficient baggage handling, convenient schedules and routes, tasty in-flight snacks and meals, and modern equipment.

Cutting Costs

Even before deregulation of the airline industry, Texas Air was a pioneer in cutting costs and setting low fares. Because Texas Air's costs were the lowest in the U.S. airline industry, the company thought it could make a profit even on its reduced fares. Although maintaining the lowest price possible was a primary objective of Texas Air, the company's managers realized that low costs and fares alone could not ensure success. As a result, Texas Air consolidated and improved its reservation services and set up a better frequent-flier program. However, when these improved services failed to attract enough passengers, Texas Air turned to massive discounting—a form of price competition—to fill its empty seats. As a result, an all-out fare war erupted in the airline industry.

The result of this heightened competition was a further decline in Texas Air's market share and a $466 million loss in 1987. Other airlines pressured the company to raise its fares and give up its position as the industry's price leader. When Texas Air did raise its fares—an increase of 12 to 18 percent in 1988—it sent mixed signals to airline passengers and the airline industry, which did not coincide with Texas Air's commitment to low cost and high quality.

Improving Customer Satisfaction

Although Texas Air claimed to offer the best service at the best value, the company's passenger satisfaction ratings did not bear out that claim. During the fare wars, the company had a tremendous increase in passenger complaints, including late departures, canceled flights, lost baggage, and dirty planes. In February 1988, Continental Airlines had the highest passenger complaint rate among all air carriers. At the same time, the U.S. Department of Transportation evaluated fourteen major airlines for on-time arrivals: Eastern ranked eleventh and Continental ranked thirteenth.

After increasing coach fares in the spring of 1988, both Continental and Eastern announced that they would reduce their discount fares. In response, all major airlines matched the reductions. Despite these pricing skirmishes with its competitors, Texas Air was still losing market share and passenger complaints continued to rise. In April 1988, the Federal Aviation Administration imposed a $823,000 fine against Eastern for safety-related violations. Only fourteen months earlier, Eastern had been fined $9.5 million for similar safety violations. In addition, the Department of Transportation announced an investigation of Texas Air to determine if the company was "fit, willing, and able" to carry commercial air traffic. Though the investigation concluded that Texas Air was financially fit and safe to fly, Continental and Eastern both continued to rank at the bottom for on-time arrivals and passenger satisfaction.

Then, in 1989, the bottom fell out, and Texas Air suffered its worst year ever. *Fortune* ranked the company last in its annual survey of America's most admired transportation corporations. Texas Air's performance for fiscal year 1988 was the worst in aviation history: Continental lost $315 million and Eastern lost $345 million, but Texas Air in total lost over $718 million. Then, in March 1989, Eastern's 8,500 machinists went on strike, demanding $150 million in wage and work-rule concessions. In a show of sympathy, 3,400 Eastern pilots and flight attendants also walked out. The result was a sudden drop in revenue and market share that forced Eastern Airlines to file for Chapter 11 bankruptcy protection. However, Eastern kept flying by hiring machinists, pilots, and other personnel outside of the union. The result was a much smaller airline servicing only a portion of its pre-strike schedules and routes.

Restructuring

By November of 1989, Eastern's planes were still flying less-than-half full. In addition, the entire airline industry began facing increasing fuel costs. Despite these difficulties, Eastern made deeper fare cuts in order to attract passengers. Although the lower fares did bring in some new passengers, Eastern's loading factor was expected to remain below 60 percent well into early 1990. In order to break even, Eastern needed a loading factor well into the 70 percent range. Still under bankruptcy protection, Eastern lost over $800 million in 1989, beating its 1988 record loss. Some of Eastern's creditors estimated that the company was losing over $2 million a day. Under pressure from creditors, Texas Air chairman Frank Lorenzo was forced to restructure the company.

Lorenzo's goal was either to sell Eastern Airlines or to use the protection of bankruptcy to reorganize and resume operations with lower costs and no unionized labor. As a part of the restructuring, Texas Air sold its Eastern shuttle (a service from Washington D.C. to New York) to Donald Trump, who renamed it the Trump Shuttle. In addition, Eastern sold its South American routes to Pan American Airlines. By the end of 1989, a smaller nonunion Eastern was trying to emerge from Chapter 11. Although the reorganization effort yielded $850 million in cash flow by the fall of 1989, the cash hungry Texas Air was still a long way from rebuilding into a profitable enterprise.

In an effort to lure back passengers with memories of the $125 million in unhonored pre-strike tickets, Eastern began discounting fares in the spring of 1990 up to 45 percent below the industry's least expensive fares. However, the image of Eastern remained tarnished with questionable reliability and the oldest planes of any airline in the industry. At the same time, Continental proposed a 4 percent increase on all domestic and international fares to help offset a 43 percent increase in fuel costs for the fourth quarter of 1989.

Since that time, Continental has returned to operating profitability. Through a combination of eliminating money-losing flights and building up more lucrative routes (like the South Pacific), Continental raised its 1989 operating profits to about $170 million after losing $69 million in 1988. However, the company remains loaded with debt and still suffers from a tarnished image. Recent efforts to combat Continental's woes include a joint venture with Scandinavian Airline Systems, a widely respected international airline. The combination of Texas Air and SAS's international routes gives Continental the critical international link it needs. In addition, Continental began sending its employees to "charm school" in order to improve service. The result of these combined efforts was a 12 percent increase in passenger loadings going into late 1989.

Unfortunately, conditions at Eastern are not quite as cheerful. Although Eastern's pilots and flight attendants ended their eight-and-a-half month sympathy strike in late November 1989, the machinists were still off the job one year after walking off their jobs. And, although Lorenzo agreed to pay off all of Eastern's creditors by April of 1990 as part of the Chapter 11 restructuring, doubting creditors were studying three options: liquidating the airline, selling it, or forcing a merger with Continental. The least appealing of these options to Lorenzo was the proposed merger—a forced merger could expose Continental to the bankruptcy process.

Through all of the turmoil, Eastern expected to be out of bankruptcy reorganization by June 30, 1990. In one of the last phases of the restructuring, Eastern agreed to pay its unsecured creditors 50 cents on each dollar owed, or a total of $490 million. After reorganization, Eastern will still be a fairly large airline, but much smaller than its pre-strike size. Before the strike, Eastern operated over 250 planes. Now, it will operate around 160 planes.

With Continental and Eastern headed in seemingly opposite directions, the future of the Texas Air Corporation remains in question. Many investors are dumping stock in both Continental and Eastern, forcing their respective stock prices to record low levels. Many investors and industry analysts blame Texas Air chairman Frank Lorenzo for the company's problems. They cite his erratic marketing style, lack of a consistent strategy, and his tendency to ignore advice as major determinants of Texas Air's problems. Others, however, blame the industry as a whole for most of the company's troubles.

Still, Texas Air employees seem to feel that the company has a fighting chance for survival. There is more talk of employee cooperation and rapport than before the troubles began. Many employees say that management is more interested in raising morale and gathering opinions than they used to be. However, though things may be slowly improving for Texas Air, it is not out of the woods yet. Only time will tell if the company has the ability to meet its challenges effectively in search of long-term profitability and survival.

Questions for Discussion

1. What strategies did Eastern and Continental pursue? What was Texas Air's strategy? Did the corporate and business unit strategies seem to fit together? Why or why not?

2. Is it possible to have low fares and still maintain or increase passenger satisfaction ratings? Which is more important to an airline's survival: low fares or high passenger satisfaction? Why?

3. If you were a creditor of Eastern Airlines, which of three options (liquidating, selling, or merging) would you be most in favor of and why? What if you were a shareholder?

SOURCE: Based on information from Francis C. Brown III, "Texas Air Decision to Lift Fares Ensures Success of Some Boosts Planned by Others," *Wall Street Journal,* Sept. 14, 1987, p. 26; Doug Carroll, "Eastern Trims Its Wings: A Year Later, Its Future is Still Cloudy," *USA Today,* Mar. 5, 1990, pp. 1B–2B; Doug Carroll, "Texas Air Reports Record Loss," *USA Today,* Feb. 7, 1990, pp. 1B, 3B; Bob Davis et al., "U.S. Sets Investigation of Texas Air Over Safety, Financing Practices," *Wall Street Journal,* Apr. 14, 1988, p. 3H; Jo Ellen Davis et al., "Continental: Full Planes May Not Mean Full Coffers," *Business Week,* Mar. 16, 1987, p. 37; "Do Airlines Put Money Where Your Mouth Is?" *Wall Street Journal,* Apr. 7, 1988, p. 27; Thomas G. Donlan, "Why People's Woes Won't Aid Its Rivals," *Barron's,* June 30, 1986, p. 28; James E. Ellis et al., "Can United Afford Texas Air's Low Fares?" *Business Week,* Feb. 16, 1987, p. 34; Chuck Hawkins and James E. Ellis, "Has Lorenzo Fired the First Salvo in a Fare War?" *Business Week,* Sept. 14, 1987, pp. 37–38; James R. Healey, "Texas Air: Fare's Fair," *USA Today,* Mar. 2, 1987, p. 1B; Josef Hebert, "FAA Fines Eastern, Plans New Probe," *Detroit Free Press,* Apr. 14, 1988, p. 16A; Mark Ivey and Gail DeGeorge, "Lorenzo May Land A Little Short of the Runway," *Business Week,* Feb. 5, 1990, pp. 46–48; Bridget O'Brian, "Eastern Pilots, Attendants End 264–Day Strike," *Wall Street Journal,* Nov. 24, 1989, p. A3; James Ott, "Texas Air Agrees to Acquire People Express for $297 Million," *Aviation Week & Space Technology,* Sept. 22, 1986, pp. 30–32; Jana Pewitt, "Jobs up in Air for Eastern Pilots," *USA Today,* Nov. 24, 1989, p. 2B; David Poulson, "Air-Fare Wars Bombarding the Trenches," *USA Today,* Feb. 6, 1987, p. 1B; Cecilia Preble, "People Express, New York Air Merging Under Continental Umbrella," *Aviation Week & Space Technology,* Jan. 19, 1987, pp. 32–33; Dana Ragen, "Reaching New Heights," *Continental,* Feb. 1987, pp. 10–13; Mike Sheridan, "Continental Says It Won't Match Rivals by Hiking Fares," *Houston Chronicle,* Sept. 1, 1987, pp. 1C, 7C; Candace Talmadge, "Dogfight Near for Air Giants?" *Adweek,* Feb. 23, 1987, pp. 1,6; Candace Talmadge, "Texas Air Throws Discount Fares into Disarray," *Adweek,* Sept. 7, 1987, p. 6; "Lorenzo Turns to Terra Firma," *Business Week,* Sept. 7, 1987, p. 34; Texas Air Corporation, *1988 Annual Report,* Aug. 1, 1989; Paulette Thomas, "Airlines Cutting Discount Fares in Some Areas," *Wall Street Journal,* Apr. 6, 1988, p. 23; Paulette Thomas, "Texas Air's Operating Woes Intensify as Units Face Growing Liquidity Crunch, *Wall Street Journal,* Apr. 7, 1988, p. 14; Paulette Thomas et al., "Airline Backfire: Texas Air Triggered Investigation of Itself With Shuttle Gambit," *Wall Street Journal,* Apr. 15, 1988, pp. 1, 16; and Paulette Thomas and Jonathan Dahl, "Continental Air Triggers Increases in Fares Used by Business Travelers," *Wall Street Journal,* Mar. 4, 1988, p. 23.

VII SELECTED APPLICATIONS

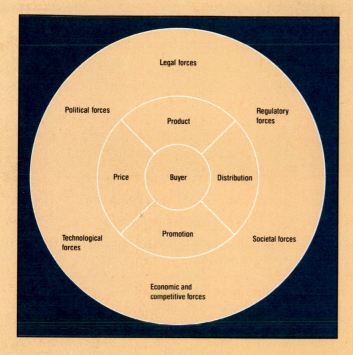

The remaining chapters in this book discuss and highlight strategic applications in industrial, services, and international marketing. We emphasize the features and issues that are unique to each of these selected areas of marketing. We also focus on aspects that impact formulating and implementing marketing strategies. Chapter 21 analyzes the development of industrial marketing strategy and discusses the decisions and activities that characterize industrial marketing. Chapter 22 explores selected aspects of services and nonbusiness marketing strategies. Chapter 23 focuses on international marketing and on the development and implementation of marketing strategies for foreign markets. ◆

21 INDUSTRIAL MARKETING

Objectives

To understand some unique characteristics of industrial marketing

To learn how to select and analyze industrial target markets

To find out how industrial marketing mix components differ from the components in consumer product marketing mixes

The taste of Tyson starts from scratch.

Tyson

The story of Tyson Foods, the leading U.S. poultry producer, is a perfect case of an industrial marketing success. Tyson's secret is the leadership of Don Tyson, the company's 59-year-old chief executive officer. Since he took control of the company in 1967, Tyson has emphasized aggressive growth through acquisitions and the necessity of always looking toward the future.

Because more Americans are eating out, Tyson decided to focus his company's marketing efforts on restaurants, hospitals, hotels, schools, and other organizational markets. The effort paid off in 1980 when Tyson became McDonald's sole supplier of Chicken McNuggets (a Don Tyson creation). In 1982 Tyson acquired a company called Mexican Original. Today, the company is posting record sales as a major supplier to Taco Bell. As a result of this company focus, Tyson Foods now commands 77 percent of the organizational food-service market for poultry.

Despite this success, Tyson Foods came to the point of diminishing returns in 1988. Don Tyson, however, saw yet another opportunity in the market, and in 1989, after a long-running, lawsuit-plagued battle, Tyson Foods acquired the Holly Farms Corporation of Memphis, Tennessee. Because Holly Farms was one of the largest poultry suppliers to retailers, Tyson saw the merger as the perfect strategic move. The combined companies gave Tyson a 20 percent share of the *total* poultry market-more than twice that of its nearest rival, ConAgra.

Moving into the 1990s, Tyson's latest goal is to double the size of his $4 billion company by 1995. Part of the strategic plan includes extending the Tyson label to poultry products overseas and pork products in the United States. Don Tyson is excited about the company's future; and with all of Tyson's past successes, no one doubts his ability to make it happen. ◆

Advertisement courtesy of Tyson Foods, Inc.

Based on information from Dick Anderson, "Don Tyson Rules the Roost," *Southpoint,* Dec. 1989, pp. 16–20; Steve Bergsman, "Its Own Corner in the Supermarket," *Global Trade,* July 1989, pp. 30, 32; Bradley H. Gendell, "Cockfight," *Financial World,* July 11, 1989, pp. 26–27; Kevin Kelly, "For Chicken Biggie Tyson, the Sky Could Be Falling," *Business Week (Industrial/Technology Edition),* Dec. 5, 1988, p. 32.

S ome of the problems that industrial marketers experience resemble those of consumer product marketers, and industrial marketers, too, rely on basic marketing concepts and decisions. However, they apply those concepts and decisions in different ways, which take into account the nature of industrial markets and products.

Industrial marketing is a set of activities directed toward facilitating and expediting exchanges involving industrial products and customers in industrial markets. As mentioned in Chapter 6, an industrial product differs from a consumer product in that it is purchased to be used directly or indirectly to produce other products or to be used in the operations of an organization. Chapter 6 also classifies industrial products into seven categories: raw materials, major equipment, accessory equipment, component parts, process materials, consumable supplies, and industrial services. As Chapter 4 explains, an organizational or industrial market consists of individuals or groups who purchase a specific kind of product for one of three purposes: resale, direct use in producing other products, or use in general daily operations. Industrial markets consist of numerous types of customers, including commercial producers, governments, and institutions.

Aside from product and market differences, industrial marketing is unique for these reasons: (1) the buyer's decision-making process, (2) characteristics of the product market, and (3) the nature of environmental influences.[1] These differences influence the development and implementation of industrial marketing strategies.

This chapter focuses on dimensions unique to developing marketing strategies for industrial products. First, we examine the selection and analysis of industrial target markets. Then we discuss the distinctive features of industrial marketing mixes.

SELECTION AND ANALYSIS OF INDUSTRIAL TARGET MARKETS

Marketing research is becoming more important in industrial marketing, especially in selecting and analyzing target markets. Most of the marketing research techniques that we discuss in Chapter 7 can be applied to industrial marketing. In this section we focus on important and unique approaches to selecting and analyzing industrial target markets.

Industrial marketers have easy access to a considerable amount of information about potential customers, for much of this information appears in government and industry publications. However, comparable data about ultimate consumers are not available. Even though industrial marketers may use different procedures to isolate and analyze target markets, most follow a similar pattern: (1) determining who potential customers are and how many there are, (2) locating where they are, and (3) estimating their purchase potential.[2]

1. Edward F. Fern and James R. Brown, "The Industrial/Consumer Marketing Dichotomy: A Case of Insufficient Justification," *Journal of Marketing,* Spring 1984, pp. 168–177.

2. Robert W. Haas, *Industrial Marketing Management* (New York: Petrocelli Charter, 1976), pp. 37–48.

FIGURE 21.1
Utilizing SIC codes.
SIC codes allow Tennessee's Resource Valley to provide businesses with specific location assessment data by industry.

SOURCE: Courtesy of Tennessee's Resource Valley

■ Determining Who Potential Customers Are and How Many There Are

Much information about industrial customers is based on the **Standard Industrial Classification (SIC) system**, which the federal government developed to classify selected economic characteristics of industrial, commercial, financial, and service organizations. Figure 21.1 shows how Tennessee's Resource Valley utilizes SIC codes to provide specific information to businesses. Table 21.1 shows how the SIC system can be used to categorize products. Various types of business activities are separated into lettered divisions, and each division is divided into numbered, two-digit major groups. For example, major group 22 includes all firms that manufacture textile mill products. Each major group is divided into three-digit-coded subgroups, and each subgroup is separated into detailed industry categories that are coded with four-digit numbers. In the most recent SIC Manual, there are 83 major groups, 596 subgroups, and 1005 detailed industry categories.[3] To categorize manufacturers in more detail, the *Census of Manufacturers* further subdivides manufacturers (Division D) into five- and seven-digit-coded groups. The fifth digit denotes the product class, and the sixth and seventh digits designate the specific product.

Much data are available for each SIC category through various government publications, such as *Census of Business*, *Census of Manufacturers*, and *County Business*

3. *1987 Standard Industrial Classification Manual* (U.S. Office of Management and Budget, Washington, D.C.).

TABLE 21.1

Example of product classi-fication in the Standard Industrial Classification system

LEVEL	SIC CODE	DESCRIPTION
Division	D	Manufacturing
Major group	22	Textile mill products
Industry subgroup	225	Knitting mills
Detailed industry	2251	Women's full-length and knee-length hosiery
Product category	22513	Women's finished seamless hosiery
Product item	2251311	Misses' finished knee-length socks

SOURCES: *1987 Standard Industrial Classification Manual,* U.S. Office of Management and Budget; and *Census of Manufacturers 1982,* U.S. Bureau of the Census.

Patterns. Table 21.2 shows types of information that can be obtained through government sources. Some data are available by state, county, and metropolitan area. Industrial market data also appear in such nongovernment sources as Dun & Bradstreet's *Market Identifiers, Sales & Marketing Management's Survey of Industrial Purchasing Power,* and other trade publications.

The SIC system is a ready-made tool that allows industrial marketers to divide industrial firms into market segments based mainly on the types of products manufactured or handled. Although the SIC system is a vehicle for segmentation, it must be used in conjunction with other types of data to enable a specific industrial marketer to determine exactly which customers it can reach and how many of them.

Input-output analysis works well in conjunction with the SIC system. This type of analysis is based on the assumption that the output or sales of one industry are the input or purchases of other industries. **Input-output data** tell what types of industries purchase the products of a particular industry. A major source of national input-output data is the *Survey of Current Business,* published by the Office of Business Economics, U.S. Department of Commerce. It presents input-output data for eighty-three industries in matrix form.

After learning which industries purchase the major portion of an industry's output, the next step is to find the SIC numbers for those industries. Because firms are grouped differently in the input-output tables and the SIC system, ascertaining SIC numbers can be difficult. However, the Office of Business Economics does provide some limited conversion tables with the input-output data. These tables can assist industrial marketers in assigning SIC numbers to the industry categories used in the input-output analysis. For example, the motor vehicle and equipment industry, an industry that buys significant quantities of paint and related products, can be converted into SIC categories 3711 and 3715.

Having determined the SIC numbers of the industries that buy the firm's output, an industrial marketer is in a position to ascertain the number of firms that are potential buyers nationally, by state, and by county. Government publications such as the *Census of Business,* the *Census of Manufacturers,* and *County Business Patterns* report the number of establishments within SIC classifications, along with other types of data, such as those shown in Table 21.2. For manufacturing industries, *Sales & Marketing Management's Survey of Industrial Purchasing Power* contains state and county SIC information about the number and size of plants and shipment sizes. Unlike most government sources, this survey is updated annually.

TABLE 21.2

Types of government information available about industrial markets (based on SIC categories)

Value of industry shipments
Number of establishments
Number of employees
Exports as a percentage of shipments
Imports as a percentage of apparent consumption
Compound annual average rate of growth
Major producing areas

■ Locating Industrial Customers

At this point, an industrial marketer knows what types of industries purchase the kinds of products her or his firm produces, as well as the number of establishments in those industries and certain other information. However, that marketer still has to find out the names and addresses of potential customers. Du Pont, in Figure 21.2, utilizes a reply ad to encourage potential customers to send directly for information about its Tysul brand chemicals, providing Du Pont with viable sales leads.

One approach to identifying and locating potential customers is to use state or commercial industrial directories, such as *Standard & Poor's Register* and Dun & Bradstreet's *Middle Market Directory* or *Million Dollar Directory*. These sources contain such information about a firm as its name, SIC number, address, phone number, and annual sales. By referring to one or more of these sources, an industrial marketer can isolate industrial customers that have SIC numbers, determine their locations, and thus develop lists of potential customers by city, county, and state.

A second approach, more expedient but also more expensive, is to use a commercial data company. Dun & Bradstreet, for example, can provide a list of firms that fall into a particular four-digit SIC group. For each company on the list, Dun & Bradstreet gives the name, location, sales volume, number of employees, type of products handled, names of chief executives, and other information.

Either approach can effectively identify and locate a group of potential industrial customers. However, an industrial marketer probably cannot pursue all firms on the list. Because some companies have a greater purchase potential than others, the marketer must determine which segment or segments to pursue.

In industrial marketing, situation-specific variables may be more relevant in segmenting markets than are general customer characteristics. Industrial customers concentrate on benefits sought; therefore, understanding end use of the product is more important than the psychology of decisions or socioeconomic characteristics. Segmenting by benefits rather than customer characteristics can provide insight into the structure of the market and opportunities for new customers.[4]

■ Estimating Purchase Potential

To estimate the purchase potential of industrial customers or groups of customers, an industrial marketer must find a relationship between the size of potential customers' purchases and a variable available in SIC data, such as the number of employees. For example, a paint manufacturer might attempt to determine the average number of gallons purchased by a specific type of potential industrial customer

4. Peter Doyle and John Saunders, "Market Segmentation and Positioning in Specialized Industrial Markets," *Journal of Marketing*, Spring 1985, p. 25.

FIGURE 21.2 *Locating industrial customers.*
Du Pont locates potential customers for its Tysul brand wastewater hydrogen peroxide by advertising its benefits and providing an information request form.

SOURCE: Du Pont Company

relative to the number of persons employed. If the industrial marketer has no previous experience in this market segment, it will probably be necessary to survey a random sample of potential customers to establish a relationship between purchase sizes and numbers of persons employed. Once this relationship has been established, it can be applied to potential customer segments to estimate their purchases. After deriving these estimates, the industrial marketer selects the customers to be included in the target market.

Despite their usefulness in isolating and analyzing industrial target markets, SIC data pose several problems for users. First, a few industries do not have specific SIC designations. Second, because a transfer of products from one establishment to another is counted as a part of total shipments, double counting may occur when products are shipped between two establishments within the same firm. Third, because the Census Bureau is prohibited from publishing data that would identify a specific business organization, some data—such as value of total shipments—may be understated. Finally, because SIC data are provided by government agencies, there is usually a significant lag between the time the data are collected and when that information becomes available.

CHARACTERISTICS OF INDUSTRIAL MARKETING MIXES

After selecting and analyzing a target market, an industrial marketer must create a marketing mix that will satisfy the customers in that target market. In many respects, the general concepts and methods involved in developing an industrial marketing mix are similar to those used in consumer product marketing. Here we focus on the features of industrial marketing mixes that differ from the marketing mixes for consumer products. We examine each of the four components in an industrial marketing mix: product, distribution, promotion, and price.

■ Product

1. Service

After selecting a target market, the industrial marketer has to decide how to compete. Production-oriented managers fail to understand the need to develop a distinct appeal for their product to give it a competitive advantage. Positioning the product (discussed in Chapter 9) is necessary to successfully serve a market, whether consumer or industrial.[5]

Compared with consumer marketing mixes, the product ingredients of industrial marketing mixes often include a greater emphasis on services, both before and after sales. Services, including on-time delivery, quality control, custom design, and a nationwide parts distribution system, may be important components of the product. Coca-Cola, USA focuses on its product offering and service for industrial markets (see Figure 21.3).

2. Technical advice

3. Competition from buyer

4. functional characteristics

Before making a sale, industrial marketers provide potential customers with technical advice regarding product specifications, installation, and application. Many industrial marketers depend heavily on long-term customer relationships that perpetuate sizable repeat purchases. Therefore industrial marketers also make a considerable effort to provide services after the sale. John Deere, long the leading manufacturer of heavy farming equipment, is striving to maintain its long-term relationships with American farmers through innovation and service, as described in Marketing Update 21.1. Because industrial customers must have products available when needed, on-time delivery is another service included in the product component of many industrial marketing mixes. An industrial marketer unable to provide on-time delivery cannot expect the marketing mix to satisfy industrial customers. Availability of parts must also be included in the product mixes of many industrial marketers because a lack of parts can result in costly production delays. The industrial marketer who includes availability of parts within the product component has a competitive advantage over a marketer who fails to offer this service. Furthermore, customers whose average purchases are large often desire credit; thus some industrial marketers include credit services in their product mixes.

When planning and developing an industrial product mix, an industrial marketer of component parts and semifinished products must realize that a customer may decide to make the items instead of buying them. In some cases, then, industrial marketers compete not only with each other, but with their own potential customers as well.

Frequently, industrial products must conform to standard technical specifications that industrial customers want. Thus industrial marketers often concentrate on functional product features rather than on marketing considerations. This fact has important implications for industrial salespeople. Rather than concentrate just on

5. Doyle and Saunders, p. 25.

FIGURE 21.3

Product in industrial marketing.
Coca-Cola USA promotes its product offerings and service to industrial customers. The number of brands, marketing, and operational support are key components of its marketing strategy.

SOURCE: Coca Cola, Coca Cola classic, diet Coca Cola, Sprite, and cherry Coca Cola are registered trademarks of The Coca Cola Company. Permission for reproduction of materials granted by the company.

selling activities, they must assume the role of consultants, seeking to solve their customers' problems and influencing the writing of specifications.[6]

Because industrial products are rarely sold through self-service, the major consideration in package design is protection. There is less emphasis on the package as a promotional device. Marketing Update 21.2 describes the International Paper Co., which markets paper goods and packaging for other businesses.

Research on industrial customer complaints indicates that industrial buyers usually complain when they encounter problems with product quality or delivery time. On the other hand, consumers' complaints pertain to other problems, such as customer service and pricing. This type of buyer feedback allows industrial marketers to gauge marketing performance. It is important that industrial marketers respond to valid complaints because the success of most industrial products depends on repeat purchases. Because buyer complaints serve a useful purpose, many industrial firms facilitate this feedback by providing customer service departments.[7]

6. Erin Anderson and Anne T. Coughlan, "International Market Entry and Expansion via Independent or Integrated Channels of Distribution," *Journal of Marketing,* January 1987, pp. 71–82.

7. Hiram C. Barksdale, Jr., Terry E. Powell, and Ernestine Hargrove, "Complaint Voicing by Industrial Buyers," *Industrial Marketing Management,* May 1984, pp. 93–99.

JOHN DEERE FACES TOUGH CHALLENGE

For more than twenty-five years, the number-one tractor on U.S. farms has been the familiar, green John Deere. However, a recession in the farming industry during the 1980s not only hurt farmers but the makers of farm equipment as well. This trend caused a 70 percent plunge in unit sales of Deere's most important machines. In response, Deere trimmed its payroll, invested in new product research, and revamped its factories.

The farm crisis began to abate in the early 1990s, and Deere seemed poised to take off again. However, while Deere was overhauling its operations, other equipment manufacturers were gearing up to go after the same market. The JI Case unit of Tenneco, Inc., formed from what was left of International Harvester, became a powerful number two in the industry. In addition, the Ford Motor Company started selling a full line of farm equipment. Deere therefore found itself in a fierce three-way fight for the business of the nation's 2.2 million farmers.

Along with the increased competition came changes in farm equipment itself. While Deere remained number one in market share and sales, the Case name had become synonymous with the latest technology. Case created the quiet cab and moved the exhaust pipe to the side to give farmers a clear view through the windshield, popular innovations that Deere did not have at the time. However, Deere had an innovation of its own. Deere had long been known for its traveling employees—factory workers who travelled country roads to visit farmers. On many of these trips, farmers told the workers that they disliked combines with side-mounted cabs because of their unbalanced feel. Deere responded by developing a 1989 model combine with a center-mounted cab.

The 1989 sales for the big three manufacturers were $4.1 billion for Deere, $2.9 billion for Case, and $2.3 billion for Ford. These figures represent sales of only 9,111 units, of which 40 percent were sold by Deere. It is no wonder that the latest Deere combine with air conditioning, a quiet pressurized cab, AM/FM stereo, and a "buddy seat" sells for over $100,000. In the future, Deere plans to emphasize innovation, service, and the availability of replacement parts.

SOURCES: John Deere Corporation, *Annual Report,* 1988; "Planting Deep and Wide at John Deere," *Forbes,* Mar. 14, 1983, pp. 119–123; Robert L. Rose, "Deere Faces Challenge Just When Farmers Are Shopping Again," *Wall Street Journal,* Feb. 8, 1990, pp. A1, A6.

If an industrial marketer is in a mature market, growth can come from attracting market share from another industrial marketer, or a firm can look at new applications or uses for its products. Wescon Products of Wichita, Kansas, is a maker of hand trucks and other handling devices, mainly for heavy industrial customers. In recent years, prospects for sales growth have been quite limited because heavy manufacturing has been on the decline in the United States. To compensate, the company developed a Gadabout, a stylish hand truck that is useful in offices, and thereby made further growth in its hand truck business possible.[8]

■ Distribution

The distribution ingredient in industrial marketing mixes differs from that of consumer products with respect to the types of channels used; the kinds of intermediaries available; and the transportation, storage, and inventory policies. Nonetheless, the primary objective of the physical distribution of industrial products is to ensure that the right products are available when and where needed.

As discussed in Chapter 10, distribution channels tend to be shorter for industrial products than for consumer products (refer back to Figure 10.2, which shows four commonly used industrial distribution channels). Although **direct distribution channels**, in which products are sold directly from producers to users, are not used frequently in the distribution of consumer products, they are the most widely used for industrial products. More than half of all industrial products are sold through direct channels. Industrial buyers like to communicate directly with producers, especially when expensive or technically complex products are involved. For this reason, industrial buyers prefer to purchase expensive and highly complex mainframe computers directly from IBM, Cray, and other mainframe producers. In these circumstances, an industrial customer wants the technical assistance and personal assurances that only a producer can provide.

A second industrial distribution channel involves an industrial distributor to facilitate exchanges between the producer and customer (channel F in Figure 10.2). An **industrial distributor** is an independent business organization that takes title to products and carries inventories. Thus industrial distributors are merchant wholesalers; they assume possession and ownership of goods, as well as the risks associated with ownership. Figure 21.4 describes how Canon provides color laser copying. Although an 800 number is provided, service and sales are provided through a dealer network. Industrial distributors usually sell standardized items, such as maintenance supplies, production tools, and small operating equipment. Some industrial distributors carry a wide variety of product lines; others specialize in one or a small number of lines. Industrial distributors can be most effectively used when a product has broad market appeal, is easily stocked and serviced, is sold in small quantities, and is needed rapidly to avoid high losses (as is a part for an assembly line machine).[9]

Industrial distributors offer sellers several advantages. They can perform the needed selling activities in local markets at relatively low cost to a manufacturer. They can reduce a producer's financial burden by providing their customers with credit services. And because industrial distributors usually maintain close relationships with their customers, they are aware of local needs and can pass on market information to producers. By holding adequate inventories in their local markets, industrial distributors reduce the producers' capital requirements.

8. "Consider: Industrial Marketers Entering the Consumer Zone," *Marketing News,* Aug. 30, 1985, p. 1.

9. James D. Hlavacek and Tommy J. McCuistion, "Industrial Distributors: When, Who, and How?" *Harvard Business Review,* March-April 1983, p. 97.

INTERNATIONAL PAPER CO. INVESTS IN THE 1990s

International Paper Co. (IP) has claimed that most Americans cannot go through a day without using at least one of its products; and that claim may not be far off. Today, the company is the world's leading industrial marketer of bleached board, a material used in milk and juice cartons. Nevertheless, the company has embarked on a multibillion dollar capital improvements and acquisition spree to gain new opportunities.

CEO and chairman John Georges imposed strict cost-cutting measures, cutting one-third of the corporate staff. He sold marginal operations and spent $7 billion to modernize IP's aging paper mills. The modernization effort gave IP an opportunity to convert some paper mills from newsprint and brown liner-board, a packaging material, to the faster-growing, higher-margin market for white paper used in offices and schools. IP also acquired new technologies from its acquisitions of Hammermill, a marketer of fine writing papers; Masonite Corp., a manufacturer of composite wood products; and Ilford Group, a producer of photographic materials. The purchase of Aussedat Rey, France's second-largest paper company, which holds 10 percent of the European market for copy paper, will give IP a stronger foothold in Europe.

Despite its new focus on white paper, IP has not neglected its cash cow: packaging materials used by companies such as Tropicana, Procter & Gamble, and Minute Maid. Its new Classicpack box already commands 20 percent of the packaging market in the poultry industry. IP's AnvilBox has helped Sunnyside Nurseries, which markets flowers to supermarkets and florists, to improve distribution. IP designed the AnvilBox not only to protect delicate flowers through the rigors of handling, storage, and travel, without collapsing, but also to facilitate more efficient use of pallet and trailer space, thus reducing Sunnyside's costs.

IP's modernization and growth strategy boosted its earnings from 3 percent to 12 percent in late 1988. The company is currently exploring opportunities brought about by its recent acquisitions, such as the possibility of marketing a four-color copier (including the paper, of course), based on technology obtained from its purchase of Ilford.

SOURCES: "Flower Marketer Scores Knockout in Boxing Match," *Transportation & Distribution,* Feb. 1988, pp. 50–51; Suzanne Loeffelholz, "Putting It on Paper," *Financial World,* July 25, 1989, pp. 26–29; and Joy Palmer, "No Lumbering Giant: International Paper Races to New Peaks in Earnings," *Barron's,* Jan. 2, 1989, pp. 13, 25–26.

FIGURE 21.4 *Industrial distribution.*
While Canon provides promotional support, color copiers are purchased through dealers and retailers.

SOURCE: By permission of Canon USA, Inc.

There are, though, several disadvantages to using industrial distributors. Industrial distributors may be difficult to control because they are independent firms. Because they often stock competing brands, an industrial seller cannot depend on them to sell a specific brand aggressively. Furthermore, industrial distributors maintain inventories, for which they incur numerous expenses; consequently, they are less likely to handle bulky items or items that are slow sellers relative to profit margin, need specialized facilities, or require extraordinary selling efforts. In some cases, industrial distributors lack the technical knowledge necessary to sell and service certain industrial items.

In the third industrial distribution channel (Channel G in Figure 10.2), a manufacturers' agent is employed. As described in Chapter 10, a manufacturers' agent or representative is an independent business person who sells complementary products of several producers in assigned territories and is compensated through commissions. Unlike an industrial distributor, a manufacturers' agent does not acquire title to the products and usually does not take possession. Acting as a salesperson on behalf of the producers, a manufacturers' agent has no latitude, or very little, in negotiating prices or sales terms.

Using manufacturers' agents can benefit an industrial marketer. These agents usually possess considerable technical and market information and have an established set of customers. For an industrial seller with highly seasonal demand, a manufacturers' agent can be an asset because the seller does not have to support a year-round sales force. That manufacturers' agents are paid on a commission basis also may be an economical alternative for a firm that has highly limited resources and cannot afford a full-time sales force.

Certainly, the use of manufacturers' agents is not problem-free. Even though straight commissions may be cheaper for an industrial seller, the seller may have little control over manufacturers' agents. Because of the compensation method, manufacturers' agents generally want to concentrate on their larger accounts. They are often reluctant to spend adequate time following up sales, to put forth special selling efforts, or to provide sellers with market information when such activities reduce the amount of productive selling time. Because they rarely maintain inventories, manufacturers' agents have a limited ability to quickly provide customers with parts or repair services.

The fourth industrial distribution channel (Channel H in Figure 10.2) has both a manufacturers' agent and an industrial distributor between the producer and the industrial customer. This channel may be appropriate when the industrial marketer wishes to cover a large geographic area but maintains no sales force because of highly seasonal demand or because the firm cannot afford a sales force. This type of channel can also be useful for an industrial marketer that wants to enter a new geographic market without expanding the firm's existing sales force.

So far, our discussion has implied that all channels are equally available and that an industrial producer can select the most desirable option. However, in a number of cases, only one or perhaps two channels are available for the distribution of certain types of products. An important issue in channel selection is the manner in which particular products are normally purchased. If customers ordinarily buy certain types of products directly from producers, it is unlikely that channels with intermediaries will be effective. Other dimensions that should be considered are the product's cost and physical characteristics, the costs of using various channels, the amount of technical assistance customers need, and the size of product and parts inventory needed in local markets.

Physical distribution decisions regarding transportation, storage, and inventory control are especially important for industrial marketers. Some raw materials and other industrial products may require special handling; for example, toxic chemicals used in the manufacture of some products must be shipped, stored, and disposed of properly to ensure that they do not harm people or the environment. In addition, the continuity of most industrial buyer-seller relationships depends on the seller's having the right products available when and where the customer needs them. This requirement is so important that industrial marketers must sometimes make a considerable investment in order-processing systems, materials-handling equipment, warehousing facilities, and inventory control systems. Archer Daniels Midland Company processes agricultural commodities from their purchase to finished product. Most of its processed products are sold to industrial markets (Figure 21.5).

Many industrial purchasers are moving away from traditional marketing exchange relationships, where the buyer buys primarily on price from multiple suppliers, to more tightly knit, relational exchanges, which are long-lasting agreements between manufacturers and suppliers that are less price driven.[10] Just-in-time inventory management systems are providing the rationale underlying these new types of relationships. In order to reduce inventory costs and to eliminate waste, buyers

10. Gary L. Frazier, Robert E. Spekman, and Charles R. O'Neal, "Just-In-Time Exchange Relationships in Industrial Markets," *Journal of Marketing*, October 1988, pp. 52–67.

FIGURE 21.5

Archer Daniels Midland Company is an industrial distributor.

This company must carefully control its purchase of grains and production of vegetable oils, flours, sweeteners, and soy proteins for industrial markets.

OUR JOB BEGINS WHERE HIS LEAVES OFF.

At the Archer Daniels Midland Company, we buy, transport, process and sell the agricultural abundance of America. We are the bridge between the farmer and an increasingly hungry world.

As such, we play a major role in bringing America's grain and oilseed crops to market in a virtually endless number of forms. We make vegetable oils, flours,

sweeteners and soy proteins. We process corn, wheat, soybeans, peanuts, sunflowers, flax, barley, sugarcane and rice.

Take the hard work of millions of farmers like this one. Add the hard work of thousands of ADM people. The sum is a single-minded, systematic approach to using America's abundance to help feed a hungry world.

ADM
ARCHER DANIELS MIDLAND COMPANY

SOURCE: Archer Daniels Midland Company

purchase new stock just before it is needed in the manufacturing process. In order for this system to be effective, they must share a great deal of information with their suppliers since these relationships are collaborative.

■ Promotion

The combination of promotional efforts used in industrial marketing mixes generally differs greatly from those for consumer products, especially convenience goods. The differences are evident in the emphasis on various promotion-mix ingredients and the activities performed in connection with each promotion-mix ingredient.

For several reasons, most industrial marketers rely on personal selling to a much greater extent than do consumer product marketers (except, perhaps, marketers of consumer durables). Because an industrial seller often has fewer customers, personal contact with each customer is more feasible. Some industrial products have technical features that are too numerous or too complex to explain through nonpersonal forms of promotion. Moreover, industrial purchases are frequently high in dollar value and must be suited to the job and available where and when needed; thus industrial buyers want reinforcement and personal assurances from industrial sales personnel. Because industrial marketers depend on repeat purchases, sales personnel must follow up sales to make certain that customers know how to use the purchased items effectively, as well as to ensure that the products work properly.

Salespeople need to perform the role of educators, showing buyers clearly how the product fits their needs. When purchase of a product is critical to the future profitability of the industrial buyer, buying decision makers gather extensive amounts of information about all alternative products. To deal with such buyers successfully, the seller must have an extremely well-trained sales force that is knowledgeable not only about its own company's products, but also about competitors' offerings. Besides, if sales representatives offer thorough and reliable information, they can reduce the industrial buyer's uncertainty, as well as differentiate their firm's product from the competition. Finally, the gathering of information lengthens the decision-making process. Thus it is important for salespeople to be patient; not to pressure their clients as they make important, new, and complex decisions; and to continue providing information to their prospects throughout the entire process.[11]

As Table 21.3 illustrates, the average cost of an industrial sales call varies from industry to industry. Selling costs are comprised of salaries, commissions, bonuses, and travel and entertainment expenses. The average cost of an industrial call is $229.70.[12] Keep in mind, though, that some industrial sales are very large. A Boeing salesperson, for instance, closed a sale with Delta Airlines for commercial aircraft worth $3 billion.[13] But on the average, only 350 aircraft are sold each year, resulting in sales of $105 billion. Generally, aircraft salespeople work the hardest three to five years before a sale is made.[14]

Because of the escalating costs of advertising and personal selling, telemarketing, the creative use of the telephone to enhance the salesperson's function, is on the upswing. Some of the activities in telemarketing include toll-free 800 phone lines and data-terminal-assisted personal sales work stations that take orders, check stock and order status, and provide shipping and billing information.

Although not all industrial salespeople perform the same sales activities, they can generally be grouped into the following categories, as described in Chapter 16: technical, missionary, and trade or inside order takers. An inside order taker could effectively use telemarketing. Regardless of how sales personnel are classified, industrial selling activities differ from consumer sales efforts. Because industrial sellers are frequently asked for technical advice about product specifications and uses, they often need technical backgrounds and are more likely to have them than consumer sales personnel. Compared with typical buyer-seller relationships in consumer product sales, the interdependence that develops between industrial buyers and sellers is likely to be stronger; sellers count on buyers to purchase their particular products and buyers rely on sellers to provide information, products, and related services when and where needed. Although industrial salespeople do market their products aggressively, they almost never use hard-sell tactics because of their role as technical consultants and the interdependence between buyers and sellers.

Advertising is emphasized less in industrial sales than in consumer transactions. Some of the reasons given earlier for the importance of personal selling in industrial promotion mixes explain why. However, advertising often supplements personal selling efforts. Because the cost of an industrial sales call is high and continues to rise, advertisements that allow sales personnel to perform more efficiently and effec-

11. Daniel H. McQuiston, "Novelty, Complexity, and Importance as Causal Determinants of Industrial Buyer Behavior," *Journal of Marketing,* April 1989, pp. 66–79.

12. Laboratory of Advertising Performance (LAP) Report 8052.3. McGraw-Hill Research.

13. Steve Sulerno, "The Close of the New Salesmanship," *PSA,* April 1985, p. 63.

14. "Aircraft Industry Emerging from Engineering Dominance," *Marketing News,* Aug. 2, 1985, p. 7.

TABLE 21.3 *The average cost of an industrial sales call among selected industries*

SIC#	INDUSTRY	NUMBER OF INDUSTRIAL COMPANIES REPORTING	AVERAGE DAILY NUMBER OF SALES CALLS PER SALESPERSON	AVERAGE COST OF INDUSTRIAL SALES CALL	AVERAGE DAILY SALES CALL COSTS[a] PER SALESPERSON
26	Paper and allied products	12	3.3	$263.70	$ 870.21
27	Printing and publishing	18	3.2	$148.60	$ 475.52
28	Chemicals and allied products	41	4.0	$155.20	$ 620.80
29	Petroleum and coal products	12	5.3	$ 99.10	$ 525.23
30	Rubber and miscellaneous plastics products	37	4.4	$129.30	$ 568.92
32	Stone, clay and glass products	18	4.3	$169.70	$ 729.71
33	Primary metal industries	15	3.9	$363.90	$ 1,419.21
34	Fabricated metal products	113	3.9	$186.10	$ 725.79
35	Machinery, except electrical	275	3.5	$257.30	$ 900.55
3573	Electronic computing equipment (computer hardware)	17	4.2	$452.60	$ 1,900.92
36	Electrical and electronic equipment	137	3.5	$238.40	$ 834.40
37	Transportation equipment	41	2.9	$255.90	$ 742.11
38	Instruments and related products	73	3.9	$209.50	$ 817.05
39	Miscellaneous manufacturing industries	16	3.8	$130.90	$ 497.42
50	Wholesale trade–durable goods	29	5.1	$139.80	$ 712.98
73	Business services	30	2.8	$227.20	$ 636.16

[a]This cost is determined by multiplying the average daily number of calls per salesperson by the average cost per sales call for each industry.

SOURCE: Laboratory of Advertising Performance (LAP), Report #8052.3, McGraw-Hill Research, 1221 Avenue of the Americas, New York, N.Y. 10020. Reprinted by permission.

tively are worthwhile for industrial marketers. Advertising can make industrial customers aware of new products and brands; inform buyers about general product features, representatives, and organizations; and isolate promising prospects by providing inquiry forms or the addresses and phone numbers of company representatives. To ensure that appropriate information is sent to a respondent, it is crucial that the inquiry be specific as to the type of information desired, the name of the company and respondent, the company's SIC number, and the size of the organization.

Because the demand for most industrial products is derived demand, marketers can sometimes stimulate demand for their products by stimulating consumer demand. Thus an industrial marketer occasionally sponsors an advertisement promoting the products sold by the marketer's customers.

When selecting advertising media, industrial marketers primarily choose such print media as trade publications and direct mail; they seldom use broadcast media. Trade publications and direct mail reach precise groups of industrial customers and avoid wasted circulation. In addition, they are best suited for advertising messages that present numerous details and complex product information (which are frequently the types of messages that industrial advertisers wish to get across).

Compared with consumer product advertisements, industrial advertisements are usually less persuasive and more likely to contain a large amount of copy and numerous details. In Figure 21.6, copy is expanded to explain product features and the benefits of AirFlo produce racks that are sold to supermarkets. In contrast, marketers that advertise to reach ultimate consumers sometimes avoid extensive advertising copy because consumers are reluctant to read it. Industrial advertisers, however, believe that industrial purchasers with any interest in their products will search for information and read long messages.

Sales promotion activities, too, can play a significant role in industrial promotion mixes. They encompass such efforts as catalogs, trade shows, and trade sales promotion methods that include merchandise allowances, buy-back allowances, displays, sales contests, and other methods discussed in Chapter 16. Industrial marketers go to great lengths and considerable expense to provide catalogs that describe their products to customers. Customers refer to various sellers' catalogs to determine specifications, terms of sale, delivery times, and other information about products. Catalogs thus help buyers decide which suppliers to contact.

Trade shows can be effective vehicles for making many customer contacts in a short time. One study found that firms allocate 25 percent of their annual promotion budgets to trade shows to communicate with their current and potential customers, promote their corporate image, introduce new products, meet key account executives, develop mailing lists, identify sales prospects, and find out what their competitors are doing. Although trade shows take second place to personal selling, they rank above print advertising in influencing industrial purchases, particularly at the need recognition and vendor evaluation stages of the industrial buying process.[15]

Many firms that participate in trade shows lack specific objectives for what they hope to accomplish by such participation. Firms with the most successful trade show programs have written objectives for the tasks they wish to achieve, and they carefully select the type of show in which to take part so that the attendees match the firm's target market.[16]

15. Roger A. Kerin and William L. Cron, "Assessing Trade Show Functions and Performance; An Exploratory Study," *Journal of Marketing*, July 1987, pp. 87–94.

16. Ibid.

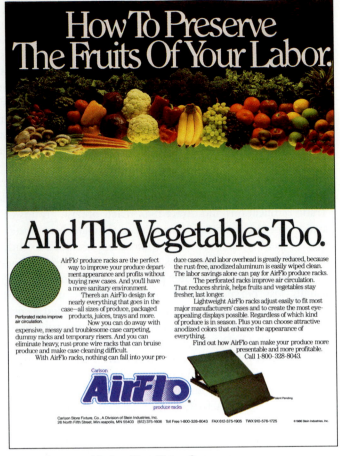

SOURCE: Courtesy of Carlson Store Fixture Company

How industrial marketers use publicity in their promotion mixes may not be much different from the way that marketers of consumer products use it.

■ **Price**

Compared with consumer product marketers, industrial marketers face many more price constraints from legal and economic forces. As indicated in Chapter 2, the Robinson-Patman Act significantly influences producers' and wholesalers' pricing practices by regulating price differentials and the use of discounts. When the federal government invokes price controls, ordinarily the effect is to regulate industrial marketers' prices directly and to a greater extent than consumer product prices. With respect to economic forces, an individual industrial firm's demand is often highly elastic, requiring the firm to approximate competitors' prices. This condition often results in nonprice competition and a considerable amount of price stability.

Today's route to sustainable competitive advantage lies in offering customers something that the competition does not offer—something that helps them increase their productivity and profitability. Firms achieve high market share not by offering low prices, but by offering their customers superior value and product quality.[17]

17. John C. Narver and Stanley F. Slater, "Creating a Market-Oriented Business," *The Channel of Communications,* Summer 1989, pp. 5–8.

Customers are willing to pay higher prices for quality products.[18] Companies such as Caterpillar Tractor Co., Hewlett-Packard Co., and 3M have shown that a value-based strategy can win a commanding lead over competition. Such firms emphasize the highest-quality products at slightly higher prices.

Although there are a variety of ways for determining prices of industrial products, the three most common are administered pricing, bid pricing, and negotiated pricing. With **administered pricing**, the seller determines the price (or series of prices) for a product, and the customer pays that specified price. Marketers who use this approach may employ a one-price policy in which all buyers pay the same price, or they may set a series of prices that are determined by one or more discounts. In some cases, list prices are posted on a price sheet or in a catalog. The list price is a beginning point from which trade, quantity, and cash discounts are deducted. Thus the actual (net) price an industrial customer pays is the list price less the discount(s). When a list price is used, an industrial marketer sometimes specifies the price in terms of list price times a multiplier. For example, the price of an item might be quoted as "list price × .78," which means the seller is discounting the item so that the buyer can purchase the product at 78 percent of the list price. Simply changing the multiplier lets the seller revise prices without having to issue new catalogs or price sheets.

With **bid pricing**, prices are determined through sealed or open bids. When a buyer uses sealed bids, select sellers are notified that they are to submit their bids by a certain date. Normally, the lowest bidder is awarded the contract, providing the buyer believes the firm is able to supply the specified products when and where needed. In an open bidding approach, several but not all sellers are asked to submit bids. In contrast to sealed bidding, the amounts of the bids are made public. Finally, an industrial purchaser sometimes uses negotiated bids. Under this arrangement, the customer seeks bids from a number of sellers and screens the bids. Then the customer negotiates the price and terms of sale with the most favorable bidders, until a final transaction is consummated or until negotiations are terminated with all sellers.

Sometimes a buyer will be seeking either component parts to be used in production for several years or custom-built equipment to be purchased currently and through future contracts. In such instances, an industrial seller may submit an initial, less profitable bid to win "follow-on" (subsequent) contracts. The seller that wins the initial contract is often substantially favored in the competition for follow-on contracts. In such a bidding situation, an industrial marketer must determine how low the initial bid should be, the probability of winning a follow-on contract, and the combination of bid prices on both the initial and the follow-on contract that will yield an acceptable profit.[19]

For certain types of industrial markets, a seller's pricing component may have to allow for **negotiated pricing**. That is, even when there are stated list prices and discount structures, negotiations may determine the actual price an industrial customer pays. Negotiated pricing can benefit seller and buyer because price negotiations frequently lead to discussions of product specifications, applications, and perhaps product substitutions. Such negotiations may give the seller an opportunity

---

18. Robert Jacobson and David A. Aaker, "The Strategic Role of Product Quality," *Journal of Marketing*, October 1987, pp. 31–44.

19. Douglas G. Brooks, "Bidding for the Sake of Follow-On Contracts," *Journal of Marketing*, January 1978, p. 35.

to provide the customer with technical assistance and perhaps sell a product that better fits the customer's requirements; the final product choice might also be more profitable for the seller. The buyer benefits by gaining more information about the array of products and terms of sale available and may acquire a more suitable product at a lower price.

Some industrial marketers sell in markets in which only one of these general pricing approaches prevails. Such marketers can simplify the price components of their marketing mixes. However, a number of industrial marketers sell to a wide variety of industrial customers and must maintain considerable flexibility in pricing.

Summary

Industrial marketing is a set of activities directed at facilitating and expediting exchanges involving industrial products and customers in industrial markets.

Industrial marketers have a considerable amount of information available to them for use in planning their marketing strategies. Much of this information is based on the Standard Industrial Classification (SIC) system, which categorizes businesses into major industry groups, industry subgroups, and detailed industry categories. The SIC system provides industrial marketers with information needed to identify market segments. It can best be used for this purpose in conjunction with other information, such as input-output data. After identifying target industries, the marketer can locate potential customers by using state or commercial industrial directories or by employing a commercial data company. The marketer then must estimate the potential purchases of industrial customers by finding a relationship between a potential customer's purchases and a variable available in published sources.

Like marketers of consumer products, an industrial marketer must develop a marketing mix that satisfies the needs of customers in the industrial target market. The product component frequently emphasizes services because they are often of primary interest to industrial customers. The marketer must also consider that the customer may elect to make the product rather than buy it. Industrial products must meet certain standard specifications that industrial users want.

The distribution of industrial products differs from that of consumer products in the types of channels used; the kinds of intermediaries available; and transportation, storage, and inventory policies. A direct distribution channel is common in industrial marketing. Also used are channels containing manufacturers' agents, industrial distributors, or both agents and distributors. Channels are chosen on the basis of availability, the typical mode of purchase for a product, and several other variables.

Personal selling is a primary ingredient of the promotional component in industrial marketing mixes. Sales personnel often act as technical advisers both before and after a sale. Advertising sometimes is used to supplement personal selling efforts. Industrial marketers generally use print advertisements containing more information but less persuasive content than consumer advertisements. Other promotional activities include catalogs and trade shows.

The price component for industrial marketing mixes is influenced by legal and economic forces to a greater extent than it is for consumer marketing mixes. Pricing may be affected by competitors' prices, as well as by the type of customer who buys the product.

IMPORTANT TERMS

Industrial marketing
Standard Industrial Classification
   (SIC) system
Input-output data
Direct distribution channels

Industrial distributor
Administered pricing
Bid pricing
Negotiated pricing

DISCUSSION AND REVIEW QUESTIONS

1. How do industrial products differ from consumer products?
2. What function does the SIC system help industrial marketers perform?
3. List some sources that an industrial marketer can use to determine the names and addresses of potential customers.
4. How do industrial marketing mixes differ from those of consumer products?
5. What are the major advantages and disadvantages of using industrial distributors?
6. Why do industrial marketers rely on personal selling more than consumer products marketers?
7. Why would an industrial marketer spend resources on advertising aimed at stimulating consumer demand?
8. Compare three methods for determining the price of industrial products.

■ CASES

21.1 Mack Truck Company

The Mack Truck Company builds and services trucks for worldwide businesses ranging from logging to construction companies. The company is unique as a manufacturer of trucks in that it makes its own power train components, diesel engines, transmissions, and rear axle carriers. Mack's strength lies in its understanding of industrial customers' needs and providing products and prices that positively influence purchase decisions. Other strengths include the company's reputation for quality, service, innovative design, engineering, and manufacturing. However, Mack's two greatest problems are a declining truck market and union difficulties.

To remain profitable despite an overall decline in truck sales, Mack has reduced costs and improved price competitiveness by closing plants, laying off employees, particularly from its corporate staff, upgrading its engine and transmission plant, and constructing an $80 million high technology, non-union plant in South Carolina. In addition, it has established a computer network for its distribution system. Perhaps one of Mack's most effective activities has been a partnership with Renault to market a new line of Class 8 lighter-weight trucks. The new line has been extremely successful.

South Carolina was so anxious to secure industrial growth that it offered Mack a $16.9 million package of tax breaks and special incentives to build its non-union plant in Winnsboro, South Carolina. Many existing plants could not compete with new opportunities such as the one in South Carolina for several reasons: union wages, aging equipment, and no tax incentives. Fearing loss of jobs because of the new plant, the United Auto Workers union has made concessions to keep other Mack plants open and jobs secure. In several Pennsylvania plants, six-year contracts, 10 percent wage cuts, and no-strike clauses were the result of negotiations between the UAW and Mack.

Mack's target markets are independent truckers who typically select large, powerful, and well-equipped trucks, and fleet customers who have specific customized needs. Its marketing strategy is to target these segments of the truck market by catering to their specific price, product, and distribution needs. For Mack, this means that many different variations of trucks are made for specific customers. One of Mack's largest, most visible fleet customers is the United Parcel Service, which has been a Mack customer for nearly 30 years. Mack manufactures UPS trucks according to specific modifications and specifications provided by UPS.

Mack has a far-reaching U.S. network of company-owned branches, independent distributors, and service dealers. Its field organization helps the company understand customer needs and fulfill presale expectations through service after the sale. The company is focusing on the future, with commitments such as a product council consisting of key distributors who join the corporate engineering staff to determine future market needs.

SOURCES: Julie Candler, "Mack Trucks' Turnaround," *Nation's Business,* Nov. 1988, pp. 60–61; Christopher S. Eklund, "The UAW Takes on Mack—and Its Own Members," *Business Week,* Mar. 23, 1987, p. 116H; Greg Myers, "Bidding Wars," *Business and Economics Review,* Jan/Feb/March 1987, pp. 8–14; and Robert Wrubel, "Putting the Hammer Down," *Financial World,* Oct. 20, 1987, pp. 25–29.

Questions for Discussion

1. What is Mack Truck's marketing strategy?
2. How is Mack dealing with competition?

21.2   Navistar International: A Born-Again Industrial Marketer

Navistar International Corporation, formerly known as International Harvester Company, is the country's largest manufacturer of medium- and heavy-duty trucks. After more than seventy years of producing trucks, Navistar leads Ford Motor Company, General Motors Corp., Isuzu Motors Ltd., and other truck manufacturers in sales of class 6, 7, and 8 vehicles with a 27.5 percent share of the market.

Before its transformation from International Harvester to Navistar several years ago, the venerable company was teetering on the edge of bankruptcy. Despite record sales of $8.4 billion in 1979, the next four years were the worst in the company's long history; recession, aging physical plants, bloated corporate costs, and a bitter strike caused losses totaling $2.9 billion. The company was forced to sell off its agricultural and construction equipment divisions, retaining only its profitable business in trucks, engines, and spare parts. In all, the troubled company dismissed more than eighty thousand of its employees and closed forty-two plants worldwide.

After a long series of restructuring and refinancing moves, Navistar returned to profitability until the fourth quarter of 1989, when it reported its first quarterly loss in three years, as heavy truck sales decreased 31 percent. Reduced demand and higher component costs accounted for much of the loss. Navistar expected to report a loss in the first quarter of 1990 as well, due to slow sales and price discounting.

According to Navistar executives, the company will focus on three dependable market segments, which account for 75 percent of its business. These are "private, traditional" customers, truckload fleets, and school buses. The private, traditional market is defined as trucks operating in support of the user's primary business, where the primary business is not trucking. Navistar will put less emphasis on sales to specialty carriers and construction markets. However, it will continue to participate in some other markets where it plays a smaller part. In the distribution industry, the company will rely on products from Nissan Diesel Co. Ltd. of Japan rather than develop similar products of its own.

Navistar intends to use the "customer-driven" marketing approach the company took in its earlier, more prosperous days. According to some industry observers, Navistar has become noticeably more attuned to the market, perhaps because the company had to work so closely with dealers, customers, and suppliers to resolve its financial problems. Communication between company executives and dealers has improved. Advisory committees meet regularly to discuss objectives, advertising, financing, and new business. To keep abreast of the market, Navistar also instituted programs to pinpoint emerging trends in the trucking industry and to apprise its manufacturing and engineering divisions of the customer needs that its salespeople have identified.

Despite the emphasis on service, price remains an important factor in truck sales, which have fallen off for all truck companies in recent years. Deregulation has forced many transportation companies to make more efficient use of existing equipment rather than purchase new equipment. The decline in heavy industries has also reduced the demand for freight haulers, and they, in turn, have less cash available for new vehicles. Some Navistar heavy-truck dealers have had to cut prices by as much as 40 percent, just to stay competitive. However, the dealers point out that the price cutting is industrywide, and they maintain that service will ultimately build customer loyalty.

To reduce truck inventories, Navistar cut production in the last quarter of 1989 to 338 trucks a day, down from a production record of 438 trucks a day in the second quarter of 1989. Truck assembly was suspended for seven days in Springfield, Ohio, and for twelve days in Chatham, Ontario.

Navistar intends to acquire companies related to the corporation's core businesses. If all goes according to plan, as much as half of Navistar's sales and earnings will come from businesses other than trucks and engines, giving the company some protection from cyclical fluctuations in the trucking industry.

SOURCES: Kathleen Deveny, "Can the Man Who Saved Navistar Run It, Too?" *Business Week,* Mar. 9, 1987, p. 88; Bill Kelley, "Navistar Starts on the Road Back," *Sales & Marketing Management,* July 1986, pp. 49–51; Michael Lelyveld, "Navistar International to Place More Emphasis on Key Markets," *Journal of Commerce,* Sept. 29, 1987; Michael S. Lelyveld, "Navistar May Supply the Engines for Nissan's Mid-Sized Trucks," *Journal of Commerce,* June 5, 1987, p. 1A; Scott McMurray, "Navistar Posts Loss For the First Time in Three Years," *Wall Street Journal,* Dec. 8, 1989, p. B4; Thomas Moore, "Old-Line Industry Shapes Up," *Fortune,* Apr. 27, 1987, p. 32; Brian S. Moskol, "It's Either Trucks or Bust," *Industry Week,* May 12, 1986, pp. 73–74; Barry Stavro, "A Surfeit of Equity," *Forbes,* Dec. 29, 1986, p. 62.

Questions for Discussion

1. Describe how customers for a Navistar freight hauler are different from Ford Probe automobile buyers?
2. Evaluate Navistar's strategy to cut prices to maintain market share. What are the implications if competitors continue lowering their prices?
3. Evaluate Navistar's complete marketing mix. How has their focus changed since the days when they were known as International Harvester?

22

SERVICES MARKETING

Objectives

To understand the nature and characteristics of services

To classify services

To understand the development of strategies for services

To explore the concept of marketing services in nonbusiness situations

To understand the development of service strategies in nonbusiness organizations

To describe methods for controlling nonbusiness service activities

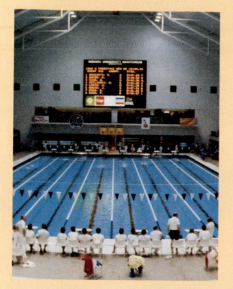

To ensure future growth, the city of Indianapolis, Indiana, has adopted a marketing strategy to position itself as the amateur sports capital of the United States. The city already had a foundation for this position as the home of the Indianapolis 500, the world's biggest professional automobile race (and the largest attendance of any sport), and the home-away-from-home for the Hoosier (Indiana University) basketball team.

Since 1974, Indianapolis has built a dozen sports facilities at a cumulative cost of $142 million. The opportunity to host its first major amateur athletic event—the National Sports Festival—boosted the city's image and gave it the confidence to host future sporting events. In 1987, Indianapolis won the bid to host the Tenth Pan-American Games, the second largest multisport event in the world. The direct economic impact on Indianapolis from the Games was an estimated $125 million spent in restaurants, hotels, shopping centers, and other Indianapolis businesses.

Indianapolis has used a vigorous marketing strategy to promote itself as the amateur sports capital of the United States. These activities have greatly benefited the people of Indianapolis, both financially and in recognition and esteem in the eyes of the sporting world. Sports, which began as a municipal development tool, has fueled tremendous growth in Indianapolis. Visitors streaming into the city for sporting events generally like what they see—a clean, courteous, and comparatively crime-free city. Residents are taking a greater pride in their city than ever before. City officials now hope to host the Olympics at some future date. Indianapolis is currently scheduled to host a Final Four College Basketball tournament in the nineties, and the outlook for the city's position as an amateur sports capital looks excellent. ◆

Photo by Rick Baughn, Office of Learning Technologies, Indiana University-Purdue University at Indianapolis

Based on information in Richard Edel, "Onetime 'Hick Town' Becomes International Star," *Advertising Age*, Apr. 20, 1987, pp. S7, S10, S12; William Giese, "Hospitable Hoosiers Roll Out the Hype," *USA Today*, July 27, 1987, pp. 1A, 2A; Richard Kerin, "Marketing Indianapolis Sports and Statistics to Numb the Mind," *Sales & Marketing Management*, May 1987, pp. 45–47; Brian Smith, "On the Waterfront," *USAir Magazine*, Nov. 1989, pp. 96–99.

This chapter presents concepts that apply specifically to the marketing of services. Services marketing involves marketing in not-for-profit organizations such as education, health care, charities, and government, as well as for-profit areas such as finance, personal services, and professional services.

The chapter first focuses on the growing importance of service industries in our economy. Second, it addresses the unique characteristics of services and the problems they present to marketers. Third, it presents various classification schemes that can help service marketers develop marketing strategies. In addition, we discuss a variety of marketing mix considerations. Finally, we define nonbusiness marketing and examine the development of nonbusiness marketing strategies and the control of nonbusiness marketing activities.

THE NATURE AND CHARACTERISTICS OF SERVICES

As we mention in Chapter 8, all products—goods, services, or ideas—possess a certain amount of intangibility. A service is an intangible product involving a deed, a performance, or an effort that cannot be physically possessed.[1] We should note that few products can be classified as a pure good or a pure service. Consider, for example, an automobile. When consumers purchase a car, they take ownership of a physical item that provides transportation, but the warranty associated with the purchase is a service. When consumers rent a car, they purchase a transportation service that is provided through temporary use of an automobile. Most products, such as automobiles and automobile rentals, contain both tangible and intangible components. One component, however, will dominate, and it is this dominant component that leads to the classification of goods, services, and ideas.

Figure 22.1 illustrates the tangibility concept by placing a variety of products on a continuum of tangibility and intangibility. Tangible-dominant products are typically classified as goods, and intangible-dominant products are typically considered services. Thus, as defined in Chapter 8, services are intangible-dominant products that are the result of the application of human and mechanical efforts to people or objects.

■ **Growth and Importance of Services**

The increasing importance of services in the U.S. economy has led many people to call the United States the world's first service economy. The service industries—encompassing trade, communications, transportation, food and lodging, financial and medical services, education, government, and technical services—account for about 60 percent of the national income and three-fourths of the nonfarm jobs in the United States. In generating 44 million new jobs in the past thirty years, these industries have absorbed most of the influx of women and minorities into the work force and fueled every recent economic recovery.[2]

One major catalyst of the growth in consumer services has been the general economic prosperity of the United States, which has led to an increase in financial services, travel, entertainment, and personal care. Lifestyle changes have similarly encouraged expansion of the service sector. In the past forty years, the number of

1. Leonard L. Berry, "Services Marketing Is Different," *Business Horizons,* May-June 1980, pp. 24–29.

2. James L. Heskett, "Lessons in the Service Sector," *Harvard Business Review,* March-April 1987, p. 118.

Goods (tangible) — Bananas · Jewelry · Compact disc player · Automobiles/maintenance · Fast food restaurants · Airlines · Financial services · Tanning salons · Telephone services · Education — **Services (intangible)**

FIGURE 22.1 *A continuum of product tangibility and intangibility*

women in the work force has more than doubled. With approximately 68 percent of the women between the ages of 18 and 34 now working, the need for child care, domestic services, and other time-saving services has increased. Consumers want to avoid tasks such as meal preparation, house cleaning, home maintenance, and tax preparation; consequently, franchise operations, such as Subway Sandwiches, Merry Maid, Chemlawn, and H & R Block, have experienced rapid growth. Furthermore, Americans have become more fitness and recreation oriented, and so the demand for fitness and recreational facilities has escalated. In terms of demographics, the U.S. population is growing older, and this change has promoted tremendous expansion of health-care services. Finally, the number and complexity of goods needing servicing have spurred demand for repair services.

Not only have consumer services grown in our economy; business services have prospered as well. Business or industrial services include repairs and maintenance, consulting, installation, equipment leasing, marketing research, advertising, temporary office personnel, and janitorial services. Expenditures for business and industrial services have risen even faster than expenditures for consumer services. This growth has been attributed to the increasingly complex, specialized, and competitive business environment. Large retailers, such as Sears, are successfully incorporating additional services into their retail stores. Providing additional services at one location is an excellent way to satisfy and keep customers who need and want more and more services. Sears operates its traditional department stores but in addition offers optical services, financial services, automotive services, and so on. If customers enter a store for one service, they will be more likely to eventually shop at the store again or try another service that the retailer provides.[3]

■ Characteristics of Services

The problems of service marketing are not the same as those of goods marketing. To understand these unique problems, it is first necessary to understand the distinguishing characteristics of services. Services have four basic characteristics: (1) intangibility, (2) inseparability of production and consumption, (3) perishability, and (4) heterogeneity.[4] Table 22.1 summarizes these characteristics and the marketing problems they entail.

Intangibility stems from the fact that services are performances. They cannot be seen, touched, tasted, or smelled, nor can they be possessed. Intangibility also relates to the difficulty that consumers may have understanding service offerings.[5]

3. David Pottruck, "Building Company Loyalty and Retention Through Direct Marketing," *Journal of Services Marketing,* Fall 1987, p. 56.

4. Valarie A. Zeithaml, A. Parasuraman, and Leonard L. Berry, "Problems and Strategies in Services Marketing," *Journal of Marketing,* Spring 1985, pp. 33–46.

5. John E. G. Bateson, "Why We Need Service Marketing," in *Conceptual and Theoretical Developments in Marketing,* ed. O. C. Ferrell, S. W. Brown, and C. W. Lamb, Jr. (Chicago: American Marketing Association, 1979), pp. 131–146.

TABLE 22.1
Service characteristics and marketing problems

UNIQUE SERVICE FEATURES	RESULTING MARKETING PROBLEMS
Intangibility	Cannot be stored
	Cannot be protected through patents
	Cannot be readily displayed or communicated
	Prices are difficult to set
Inseparability	Consumer is involved in production
	Other consumers are involved in production
	Centralized mass production is difficult
Perishability	Services cannnot be inventoried
Heterogeneity	Standardization and quality are difficult to control

SOURCE: Valarie A. Zeithaml, A. Parasuraman, Leonard L. Berry, "Problems and Strategies in Services Marketing," *Journal of Marketing,* Spring 1985, pp. 33–46. Used by permission of the American Marketing Association.

Services have a few tangible attributes, called **search qualities**, that can be viewed prior to purchase. When consumers cannot view a product in advance and examine its properties, they may not understand exactly what is being offered. Even when consumers do gain sufficient knowledge about service offerings, they may not be able to evaluate the possible alternatives. On the other hand, services are rich in experience and credence qualities. **Experience qualities** are those qualities that can be assessed only after purchase and consumption (satisfaction, courtesy, and the like). **Credence qualities** are those qualities that cannot be assessed even after purchase and consumption.[6] An appendix operation is an example of a service high in credence qualities. How many consumers are knowledgeable enough to assess the quality of an appendectomy, even after it has been performed? In summary, it is difficult to go into a store, examine a service, purchase it, and take it home with you.

Related to intangibility is **inseparability** of production and consumption. Services are normally produced at the same time they are consumed. A medical examination is an example of simultaneous production and consumption. In fact, the doctor cannot possibly perform the service without the patient's presence, and the consumer is actually involved in the production process. With other services, such as air travel, many consumers are simultaneously involved in production. Because of high consumer involvement in most services, standardization and control are difficult to maintain.

Because production and consumption are simultaneous, services are also characterized by **perishability**. In other words, unused capacity in one time period cannot be stockpiled or inventoried for future time periods. Consider the airlines' seating-capacity dilemma. Each carrier maintains a sophisticated reservations system to juggle ticket prices and ensure maximum revenues for every flight. On a single day, Delta Air Lines, Inc., may use its computer to make 79,000 fare changes, and American Airlines, Inc., 106,000 fare changes, thus assuring these airlines maximum use of seats available on each flight.[7] This attempt to maximize profit on each flight

6. Valarie A. Zeithaml, "How Consumer Evaluation Processes Differ Between Goods and Services," in *Marketing of Services,* ed. James H. Donnelly and William R. George (Chicago: American Marketing Association, 1981), pp. 186–190.

7. Kenneth Labich, "Winners in the Air Wars," *Fortune,* May 11, 1987, p. 68.

has led to overbooking, which means that airlines may sell tickets for more seats than are available to compensate for "no-shows"—people who have made reservations but may not actually take that particular flight. The airlines' dilemma illustrates how service perishability presents problems very different from the supply and demand problems encountered in the marketing of goods.[8] Unoccupied seats on an airline flight cannot be stored for use on another flight that is booked to capacity.

Finally, because most services are labor-intensive, they are susceptible to **heterogeneity**. People typically perform services, and people do not always perform consistently. There may be variation from one service to another within the same organization or variation in the service that a single individual provides from day to day and from customer to customer. Thus standardization and quality are extremely difficult to control. But this fact may also lead to customizing services to meet consumers' specific needs. Because of these factors, service marketers often face a dilemma: how does one provide efficient, standardized service at some acceptable level of quality while simultaneously treating each customer as a unique person? Giving "good service" is a major concern of all service organizations, and it is often translated into more personalized service.[9]

CLASSIFICATION OF SERVICES

Services are a very diverse group of products, and an organization may provide more than one kind. Examples of services include car rentals, repairs, health care, barber shops, health spas, tanning salons, amusement parks, day care, domestic services, legal counsel, banking, insurance, air travel, education, business consulting, dry cleaning, and accounting. Nevertheless, services can be meaningfully analyzed by using a five-category classification scheme: (1) type of market, (2) degree of labor-intensiveness, (3) degree of customer contact, (4) skill of service provider, and (5) goal of the service provider. Table 22.2 summarizes this scheme.

Services can be viewed in terms of the market or type of customer they serve—consumer or industrial. The implications of this distinction are very similar to those for all products and therefore are not discussed here. In Figure 22.2, Blue Cross and Blue Shield markets its health-care insurance to businesses as opposed to direct consumer marketing (see p. 707).

A second way to classify services is by degree of labor-intensiveness. Many services, such as repairs, education, and hair care, rely heavily on human labor. Other services, such as telecommunications, health spas, and public transportation, are more equipment-intensive. The mutual fund industry relies on computer technologies to facilitate handling daily transactions. Use of computer technologies has enabled mutual fund companies to improve service and expand offerings. For example, Fidelity Investments has $80 billion in assets, more than two million customers, and twenty-four-hour service. Customers can call anytime to check fund prices or move money between funds. The firm logs an average of 1,700 calls a night between

8. Leonard L. Berry, Valarie A. Zeithaml, and A. Parasuraman, "Responding to Demand Fluctuations: Key Challenge for Service Businesses," in *AMA Educators Proceedings,* ed. Russell Belk et al. (Chicago: American Marketing Association, 1984), pp. 231–234.

9. Carol F. Surprenant and Michael R. Solomon, "Predictability and Personalization in the Service Encounter," *Journal of Marketing,* April 1987, p. 86.

TABLE 22.2
Classification of services

CATEGORY	EXAMPLES
TYPE OF MARKET	
Consumer	Repairs, child care, legal counsel
Industrial	Consulting, janitorial services, installation
DEGREE OF LABOR INTENSIVENESS	
Labor-based	Repairs, education, haircuts
Equipment-based	Telecommunications, health spas, public transportation
DEGREE OF CUSTOMER CONTACT	
High contact	Health care, hotels, air travel
Low contact	Repairs, dry cleaning, postal service
SKILL OF THE SERVICE PROVIDER	
Professional	Legal counsel, health care, accounting services
Nonprofessional	Domestic services, dry cleaning, public transportation
GOAL OF THE SERVICE PROVIDER	
Profit	Financial services, insurance, health care
Nonprofit	Health care, education, government

midnight and 4 A.M.[10] For many mutual fund customers, the service they receive is just as important as the performance of their funds.

Labor (people-based) services are more susceptible to heterogeneity than are most equipment-based services. Marketers of people-based services must recognize that service providers are often viewed as the service itself. Therefore, strategies relating to selecting, training, motivating, and controlling employees are very important.

The third way services can be classified is by customer contact. High-contact services include health care, hotels, real estate agencies, and restaurants; low-contact services include repairs, movie theaters, dry cleaning, and spectator sports.[11] Note that high-contact services generally involve actions that are directed toward individuals. Because these services are directed at people, the consumer must be present during production. Although it is sometimes possible for the service provider to go to the consumer, high-contact services typically require that the consumer go to the production facility. Thus the physical appearance of the facility may be a major component of the consumer's overall evaluation of the service. Because the consumer must be present during production of a high-contact service, the process of production may be just as important as its final outcome.

Low-contact service, in contrast, commonly involves actions directed at things. Consequently, the consumer is usually not required to be present during service delivery. The consumer's presence, however, may be required to initiate or terminate the service. A dry cleaner, for example, must provide and maintain dry-cleaning

10. "The People's Choice: Mutual Funds," *Business Week*, Feb. 24, 1986, p. 56.

11. Christopher H. Lovelock, "Classifying Services to Gain Strategic Marketing Insights," *Journal of Marketing*, Summer 1983, p. 15.

FIGURE 22.2 *Promoting services to industrial consumers.*
Although Blue Cross and Blue Shield markets its health-care services directly to consumers, this ad focuses on industrial consumers—businesses.

SOURCE: Blue Cross and Blue Shield Association

equipment and a facility to house the equipment. Although they must be present to initiate the provision of the service, consumers need not be present during the cleaning process. The appearance of the production facilities and the interpersonal skills of actual service providers are thus not as critical in low-contact services as they are in high-contact services.[12]

Skill of the service provider is a fourth way to classify services. Professional services tend to be more complex and more highly regulated than nonprofessional services. In the case of legal counsel, for example, consumers often do not know what the actual service will involve or how much it will cost until the service is completed because the final product is very situation-specific. Additionally, attorneys are regulated both by law and by professional associations.

Finally, services can be classified according to the goal of the service provider— profit or nonprofit. The second half of this chapter examines nonbusiness marketing. Most nonbusiness organizations provide services rather than goods.

12. Christopher H. Lovelock, *Services Marketing* (Englewood Cliffs, N.J.: Prentice-Hall, 1984), pp. 49–64.

DEVELOPING MARKETING STRATEGIES FOR SERVICES

Before we discuss the development of a marketing mix for service firms, we need to reiterate a major point: the marketing concept is equally applicable to goods, services, and ideas. The marketing of services, like the marketing of goods, requires the identification of a viable target market segment, the development of a service concept that addresses the consumer's needs within that segment, the creation and implementation of an operating strategy that will adequately support the service concept, and the design of a service delivery system that will support the chosen operating strategy.[13]

Table 22.3 illustrates the approaches that marketers of services can take to achieve consumer satisfaction. A basic requirement of any marketing strategy, however, is a development phase, which includes defining target markets and finalizing a marketing mix. The following seven precepts need to be considered when developing a service marketing strategy:

1. Make sure that marketing occurs at all levels, from the marketing department to the point where the service is provided.
2. Allow flexibility in providing the service—when there is direct interaction with the customers, customize the service to their wants and needs.
3. Hire and maintain high-quality personnel and market your organization or service to them; often it is the people in a service organization who differentiate one organization from another.
4. Consider marketing to existing customers to increase their use of the service or create loyalty to the service provider.
5. Quickly resolve any problems in providing the service, to avoid damaging your firm's reputation for quality.
6. Think high technology to provide improved services at a lower cost. Continually evaluate how to customize the service to each consumer's unique needs.
7. Brand your service to distinguish it from that of the competition. For example, instead of simply seeking a moving truck, a customer would seek a rental from U-Haul because of U-Haul's name recognition.[14]

In the following sections we discuss the marketing mix requirements for finalizing a services marketing strategy.

■ Product

Goods can be defined in terms of their physical attributes, but services cannot because they are intangible. As we point out earlier in the chapter, it is often difficult for consumers to understand service offerings and to evaluate possible service alternatives. To overcome this problem, five hospitals in the Tampa Bay area used the cartoon character Snuffy Smith in a promotional campaign to help senior citizens understand the complicated paperwork associated with obtaining free or low-cost medical services. The sixty-second commercials covered such topics as how to fill out insurance forms and how to get quicker check-in at the hospital. The

13. Heskett, pp. 118–126.

14. Leonard L. Berry, "Big Ideas in Services Marketing," *Journal of Services Marketing*, Fall 1987, pp. 5–9.

TABLE 22.3 *Examples of approaches to consumer satisfaction for marketers of services*

SERVICE INDUSTRY	OUTCOME SOUGHT BY BUYER	TECHNICAL POSSIBILITIES	STRATEGIC POSSIBILITIES
Higher education	Educational attainment	Help professors to be effective teachers; offer tutoring	Admit better prepared students (or, for a fee, give them better preparation before entry)
Hospitals	Health	Instruct patients in how to manage their current problems and prevent others	Market preventive medicine services (weight loss, stress reduction, etc.)
Banks	Prosperity	Offer money management courses; provide management assistance to small businesses	Market and financial expertise, probably by industry specialization
Plumbing repairs	Free-flowing pipes	Provide consumers with instructions and supplies to prevent further clogs	Diversify (e.g., point-of-use water-purification systems)

SOURCE: Adapted from Betsy D. Gelb, "How Marketers of Intangibles Can Raise the Odds for Consumer Satisfaction," *Journal of Services Marketing,* Summer 1987, p. 15.

campaign was highly successful and resulted in thousands of calls to the toll-free number provided in the advertisement.[15]

There may also be tangibles (such as facilities, employees, or communications) associated with a service. These tangible elements help form a part of the product and are often the only aspects of a service that can be viewed prior to purchase. Consequently, marketers must pay close attention to associated tangibles and make sure that they are consistent with the selected image of the service product.[16] For example, because consumers perceive bus terminals as plagued by crime and therefore hesitate to use bus services for long-distance travel, Greyhound Lines, Inc., spent $30 million to update its terminals and open new ones. The company also installed a computer system to reduce the time consumers spend waiting for tickets.[17] Improving the physical appearance of Greyhound terminals and reducing the time required to provide some services are tangible cues that consumers can use to judge Greyhound's services. Figure 22.3 relates AT&T's speed of service directly to the speed of a Porsche 911 luxury sports car.

15. "Seniors Learn About Healthcare from Cartoon Character," *Services Marketing Newsletter,* Winter 1987, p. 2.

16. G. Lynn Shostack, "Breaking Free from Product Marketing," *Journal of Marketing,* April 1977, pp. 73–80.

17. Kevin Kelly, "Greyhound Is Bringing Travelers Down to Earth Again," *Business Week,* June 19, 1989, pp. 52–53.

FIGURE 22.3

Providing speed of service.

To reinforce in consumers' minds and provide a tangible cue about the speed of service, AT&T equates its ability to connect long-distance calls with the time it takes a Porsche 911 to go from 0 to 60.

Both come with a service guarantee. One won't get stuck in traffic.

A Porsche 911 Carrera can do 0 to 60 in 6.1 seconds. But not during rush hour.

The AT&T Worldwide Intelligent Network can connect most long distance calls in under 6 seconds, twenty-four hours a day, 365 days a year. AT&T has a special signaling system that actually scouts ahead for clear message paths before each call is routed. Only AT&T gives you the most reliable service available, and a service guarantee.

That means, no matter where you call from, you're assured of AT&T's low prices, uncompromising sound quality, immediate credit for misdialed calls, efficient operators, and the ability to call anywhere in the world.

When you're on the road, you want a service guarantee, so make sure you hear "Thank you for using AT&T." Then your calls won't get stuck in traffic.

We're here to help. For assistance, call 1 800 222-0300.

AT&T
The right choice.

© 1989 AT&T

SOURCE: © 1989 AT&T

The service product is often equated with the service provider; for example, the teller or the beautician becomes the service a bank or a beauty parlor provides. Because consumers tend to view services in terms of the service personnel and because personnel are inconsistent in their behavior, it is imperative that marketers effectively select, train, motivate, and control contact people. Service marketers are selling long-term relationships as well as performance.

After testing many variables, the Strategic Planning Institute (SPI) developed an extensive database on the impact of various business strategies on profits. The institute found that "relative perceived product quality" is the single most important factor in determining long-term profitability. In fact, because there are generally no objective measures to evaluate the quality of professional services (medical examination, legal services, and so forth), the customer is actually purchasing confidence in the service provider.[18] The strength or weakness of the service provided often affects consumers' perceptions of product quality. Of the companies in the SPI database,

18. Sak Onkvisit and John J. Shaw, "Service Marketing: Image, Branding, and Competition," *Business Horizons,* January-February 1989, p. 16.

businesses that rate low on service lose market share at the rate of 2 percent a year and average a 1 percent return on sales. Companies that score high on service gain market share at the rate of 6 percent a year, average a 12 percent return on sales, and charge a significantly higher price.[19] These data indicate that firms having service-dominant products must score high on service quality.

Because services are performances rather than tangible goods, the concept of service quality is difficult to grasp. However, price, quality, and value are important considerations of consumer choice and buying behavior for both goods and services.[20] It should be noted that it is not objective quality that matters, but the consumer's subjective perceptions. Instead of quality meaning conformance to a set of specifications—which frequently determine levels of product quality—service quality is defined by customers.[21] Moreover, quality is frequently determined in a comparison context. In the case of services, quality is determined by contrasting what the consumer expected a service to be with her or his actual service experience.[22] Marketing Update 22.1 describes how AT&T dealt with a quality problem in its long-distance telephone service.

Service providers and service consumers may have quite different views of what constitutes service quality. Consumers frequently enter service exchanges with a set of predetermined expectations. Whether a consumer's actual experiences exceed, match, or fall below these expectations will have a great effect on future relationships between the consumer and the service provider. To improve service quality, a service provider must adjust its own behavior to be consistent with consumers' expectations or reeducate consumers so that their expectations will parallel the service levels that can be achieved.[23] A study of doctor-patient relationships proposed that when professional service exceeds client expectations a true person-to-person bonding relationship develops. However, the research also revealed that what doctors viewed as being quality service was not necessarily what patients perceived as quality service. Although interaction with the physician was the primary determinant of the overall service evaluation, patients made judgments about the entire service experience, including factors such as the appearance and behavior of receptionists, nurses, and lab technicians; the way the office was decorated; and even the sign outside the building.[24]

Other product concepts discussed in Chapters 8 and 9 are also relevant here. Management must make decisions regarding the product mix, positioning, branding, and new-product development of services. It can make better decisions if it analyzes the organization's service products as to complexity and variability. Complexity is determined by the number of steps required to perform the service. Variability reflects the amount of diversity allowed in each step of service provision. In a highly

19. Tom Peters, "More Expensive, But Worth It," *U.S. News & World Report,* Feb. 3, 1986, p. 54.

20. Valarie A. Zeithaml, "Consumer Perceptions of Price, Quality, and Value: A Means-End Model and Synthesis of Evidence," *Journal of Marketing,* July 1988, pp. 2–22.

21. Leonard L. Berry, "8 Keys to Top Service at Financial Institutions," *American Banker,* August 1987.

22. A. Parasuraman, Valarie A. Zeithaml, and Leonard L. Berry, "SERVQUAL: A Multiple-Item Scale for Measuring Consumer Perceptions of Service Quality," *Journal of Retailing,* Spring 1988, pp. 12–40.

23. Stephen W. Brown and Teresa A. Swartz, "A Gap Analysis of Professional Service Quality," *Journal of Marketing,* April 1989, pp. 92–98.

24. Ibid.

AT&T FACES DISRUPTION OF ITS
LONG-DISTANCE TELEPHONE SERVICE

On January 15, 1990, American Telephone and Telegraph Co. (AT&T), the nation's largest long-distance telephone service provider, faced a crisis as millions of Americans across the nation inexplicably got busy signals when dialing outside their local calling area. The nine-hour disruption of service, the first ever to affect AT&T's entire nationwide network, was frustrating to both customers and AT&T, which has long promoted its reputation for quality and reliable service.

Especially frustrating to AT&T executives was the fact that experts could not quickly pinpoint the cause of the service disruption; they could only stand by helplessly while AT&T customers complained and threatened to take their business elsewhere. Engineers eventually traced the shutdown to a defective switch that sent out trouble messages to other switches across the country. When the switch recovered, it sent out a burst of backed-up calls, overwhelming another switch. This started a chain reaction that caused other AT&T switches to block calls. It was nearly midnight before engineers identified the problem and sent software to the switches that would stop the problem and break the cycle.

Fortunately, the incident occurred on Martin Luther King Day, a national holiday honored by many businesses. The volume of calls on that day was therefore less than the eighty million calls AT&T handles on a regular weekday. Nonetheless, the shutdown affected normal long-distance calls and toll-free 800 lines. Among the companies hurt by it were telemarketers and airline reservation systems.

AT&T not only lost revenues from the disruption, but it also lost credibility with customers who believed in its promoted reputation for quality, reliability, and high technology. AT&T's largest competitors, MCI and Sprint, quickly took advantage of the situation. They launched an avalanche of advertising, promoting the reliability of their own services, and made sales calls on regular AT&T long-distance customers, hoping to get new business after the disaster. To make amends to its customers, AT&T offered one day of free long-distance calls to consumers who were inconvenienced by the disruption of service.

SOURCES: Peter Coy, with Mark Lewyn, "The Day That Every Phone Seemed Off the Hook," *Business Week,* Jan. 29, 1990, pp. 39–40; Andrea Gabor, "A Busy Signal Heard Round the World," *U.S. News & World Report,* Jan. 29, 1990, p. 46; John J. Keller, Mary Lu Carnevale, and Julie Amparano Lopez, "Glitch Imperils AT&T's Marketing Edge," *Wall Street Journal,* Jan. 17, 1990, pp. B1, B2; and John J. Keller, "Software Bug Closes AT&T's Network, Cutting Phone Service for Millions in U.S.," *Wall Street Journal,* Jan. 16, 1990, p. A3.

FIGURE 22.4

Complexity/variability grid for medical services

SOURCE: Adapted from Lynn Shostack, 1985 American Marketing Association Faculty Consortium on Services Marketing, Texas A&M University, July 7–11. Reprinted by permission of the American Marketing Association.

variable service, every step in performing the service may be unique, whereas in cases of low variability, every performance of the service is standardized.[25] For example, services provided by physicians are both complex and variable. Patient treatment may involve many steps, and the doctor has considerable discretion in shaping the treatment for each individual patient.

An examination of the complete service delivery process, including the number of steps and the number of decisions, enables marketers to plot their service products on a complexity/variability grid, such as the one in Figure 22.4. The position of a service on the grid has implications for its positioning in the market. Furthermore, any alterations in the service delivery process that shift the position of the service on the complexity/variability grid have an impact on the positioning of the service in the marketplace. Table 22.4 details the effects of such changes. When structuring the service delivery system, marketers should explicitly consider the firm's marketing goals and target market.

■ **Promotion**

As intangible-dominant products, services are not easily promoted. The intangible is difficult to depict in advertising, whether the medium is print, television, or radio. Service advertising should thus emphasize tangible cues that will help consumers understand and evaluate the service. The cues may be the physical facilities in which the service is performed or some relevant tangible object that symbolizes the service itself.[26] For example, restaurants may stress their physical facilities—clean, elegant, casual, and so on—to provide cues as to the quality or nature of the service. Insurance firms, such as Allstate Insurance Co. and Travelers Co., use objects as symbols to help consumers understand their services. Outstretched hands ("You're in good hands with Allstate") symbolize security, and the "Travelers Umbrella" suggests the

25. G. Lynn Shostack, "Service Positioning Through Structural Change," *Journal of Marketing,* January 1987, pp. 34–43.

26. William R. George and Leonard L. Berry, "Guidelines for the Advertising of Services," *Business Horizons,* July-August 1981, pp. 52–56.

DOWNSHIFTING COMPLEXITY/VARIABILITY	UPSHIFTING COMPLEXITY/ VARIABILITY
Standardizes the service	Increases costs
Requires strict operating controls	Indicates higher-margin/lower-volume strategy
Generally widens potential market	Personalizes the service
Lowers costs	Generally narrows potential market
Indicates lower-margin/higher-volume strategy	Makes quality more difficult to control
Can alienate existing markets	

SOURCE: Adapted from G. Lynn Shostack, 1985 American Marketing Association Faculty Consortium on Services Marketing, Texas A&M University, July 7–11, 1985.

protection Travelers' insurance plans provide. In Figure 22.5, Dreyfus shows that its fund management will provide more opportunities in retirement than traditional retirement plans. Service providers may also focus on the characteristics they believe customers want from their services in advertising. AT&T emphasizes the reliability of its long-distance telephone services, while its competitor Sprint focuses on the quality of sound in its advertisements.[27]

In order to be successful, firms must not only maximize the difference between the value of the service to the customer and the cost of providing it; they must also design the service with employees in mind. Contact personnel are critical to the perception of quality service. They must be provided with sufficient tools and knowledge to furnish the type of service that the customer desires. Because service industries are information-driven, they can substitute knowledgeable, highly trained personnel for the capital assets used in more product-oriented businesses.[28]

Thus employees in a service organization are an important secondary audience for service advertising. We have seen that variability in service quality, which arises from the labor-intensive nature of many services, is a problem for service marketers and that consumers often associate the service with the service provider. Advertising can have a positive effect on customer contact personnel. It can shape employees' perceptions of the company, their jobs, and how management expects them to perform. It can be a tool for motivating, educating, and communicating with employees.[29]

Personal selling is potentially powerful in services because this form of promotion lets consumers and salespeople interact. When consumers enter into a service transaction, they must, as a general rule, interact with service firm employees. Customer contact personnel can be trained to use this opportunity to reduce customer uncertainty, give reassurance, reduce dissonance, and promote the reputation of the

27. Mark Lewyn, "AT&T, MCI, Sprint Battle for Business," *USA Today,* July 18, 1989, pp. 1B, 2B.

28. Heskett, pp. 118–125.

29. George and Berry, pp. 55–70.

FIGURE 22.5 *Promoting services.*
By providing savings plans and other money management ideas, Dreyfus symbolizes security to consumers by attempting to show that they will have more options than traditional retirement plans offer.

SOURCE: Dreyfus Service Corporation

organization.[30] Once again, this emphasizes the importance of properly managing contact personnel.

Although consumer-service firms have the opportunity to interact with actual customers and those potential customers who contact them, they have little opportunity to go out into the field and solicit business from all potential consumers. The very large number of potential customers and the high cost per sales call rule out such efforts. On the other hand, marketers of industrial services, like the marketers of industrial goods, are dealing with a much more limited target market and may find personal selling the most effective way of reaching customers.

Sales promotions, such as contests, are feasible for service firms, but other types of promotions are more difficult to implement. How do you display a service? How do you give a free sample without giving away the whole service? A complementary visit to a health club or a free skiing lesson could possibly be considered a free sample to entice a consumer into purchasing a membership or taking lessons. Some

30. William R. George and J. Patrick Kelly, "The Promotion and Selling of Services," *Business,* July-September 1983, pp. 14–20.

banks have sponsored contests with prizes such as mortgages that the winner does not have to repay or credit cards for which the winner does not have to pay the balance for a year. Although the role of publicity and the implementation of a publicity campaign do not differ significantly in the goods and service sectors, service marketers appear to rely on publicity much more than goods marketers do.[31]

Consumers tend to value word-of-mouth communications more than company-sponsored communications. This preference is probably true for all products but especially for services because they are experiential in nature. For this reason, service firms should attempt to stimulate word-of-mouth communications.[32] They can do so by encouraging consumers to tell their friends about satisfactory performance. Many firms, for instance, prominently display signs urging customers to tell their friends if they like the service and to tell the firm if they do not. Some service providers, such as hair stylists, give their regular customers discounts or free services for encouraging friends to come in for a haircut. Word of mouth can be simulated through communications messages that feature a testimonial—for example, television advertisements showing consumers who vouch for the benefits of a service a particular firm offers.

One final note should be made in regard to service promotion. The promotional activities of most professional service providers, such as doctors, lawyers, and CPAs, are severely limited. Until recently, all these professionals were prohibited by law from advertising. Although these restrictions have now been lifted, there are still many obstacles to be overcome. Not used to seeing professionals advertise, consumers may reject advertisements for those who do. Furthermore, professionals are not familiar with advertising and consequently do not always develop advertisements appropriate for their services. Increasingly, lawyers are being forced to consider advertising because many potential clients do not know that they need legal services, there is an oversupply of lawyers, and there are more franchised law firms in shopping centers, causing a distinct change in the competition. Consumers want more information about legal services, and lawyers have a very poor public image.[33] On the other hand, physicians are more skeptical of the impact of advertising on their image and business. Many physicians are attempting to expand their customer base by promoting extended office hours, making house calls, consulting by telephone, and opening more offices.[34] Despite the trend toward professional services advertising, the professions themselves exert pressure on their members not to advertise or promote because such activities are still viewed as highly unprofessional.

■ **Price**

Price plays both an economic and a psychological role in the service sector, just as it does with physical goods. However, the psychological role of price in respect to services is magnified somewhat because consumers must rely on price as the sole indicator of service quality when other quality indicators are absent. In its economic

31. John M. Rathmell, *Marketing in the Services Sector* (Cambridge, Mass.: Winthrop, 1974), p. 100.

32. George and Kelly, pp. 14–20; George and Berry, pp. 55–70.

33. Doris C. Van Doren and Louise W. Smith, "Marketing in the Restructured Professional Services Field," *Journal of Services Marketing,* Summer 1987, pp. 69–70.

34. Joyce Jensen and Steve Larson, "Nation's Physicians Adding Healthcare Services, Marketing Their Practices to Attract New Patients," *Modern Healthcare,* July 16, 1987, pp. 49–50.

role, price determines revenue and influences profits. Knowing the real costs of each service provided is vital to sound pricing decisions.[35]

Services may also be bundled together and then sold for a single price. Service bundling is a practical strategy because in many types of services there is a high ratio of fixed to variable costs and high cost sharing among service offerings. Moreover, the demand for certain services is often interdependent. For example, BankAmerica Corp. offers a package of banking services—checking and savings accounts and credit lines that become active when customers overdraw their other accounts—called Alpha, which the bank promotes as one-stop shopping for its customers. Linking these services together helped BankAmerica reverse a decline in its deposits.[36] Price bundling may help service marketers cross-sell to their current customers, or acquire new customers. The policy of price leaders also may be used by discounting the price of one service product when the customer purchases another service at full price.[37]

As noted in Table 22.1, service intangibility may complicate the setting of prices. When pricing physical goods, management can look to the cost of production (direct and indirect materials, direct and indirect labor, and overhead) as an indicator of price. It is often difficult, however, to determine the cost of service provision and thus identify a minimum price. Price competition is severe in many service areas characterized by standardization. Usually price is not a key variable when marketing is first implemented in an organization. Once market segmentation and specialized services are directed to specific markets, specialized prices are set. Next comes comparative pricing as the service becomes fairly standardized. Price competition is quite common in legal services related to divorce and bankruptcy, in long-distance phone service, and in airline transportation.[38]

Many services, especially professional services, are situation-specific. Thus neither the service firm nor the consumer knows the extent of the service prior to production and consumption. Once again, because cost is not known beforehand, price is difficult to set. Despite the difficulties in determining cost, many service firms use cost-plus pricing. Others set prices according to the competition or market demand.

Pricing of services can also help smooth fluctuations in demand. Given the perishability of service products, this is an important function. A higher price may be used to deter or offset demand during peak periods, and a lower price may be used to stimulate demand during slack periods. For example, Domino's Pizza, the second largest pizza chain in the United States, may offer two pizzas for the price of one to minimize sales declines during slow sales months.[39] Airlines rely heavily on price to help smooth their demand, as do many other operations, such as bars and entertainment clubs, movie theaters, resorts, and hotels.

35. James B. Ayers, "Lessons from Industry for Healthcare," *Administrative Radiology,* July 1987, p. 53.

36. Charles McCoy, "Combat Banking: A Slashing Pursuit of Retail Trade Brings BankAmerica Back," *Wall Street Journal,* Oct. 2, 1989, pp. A1, A4.

37. Joseph P. Guiltinan, "The Price Bundling of Services: A Normative Framework," *Journal of Marketing,* April 1987, p. 74.

38. Stephen W. Brown, "New Patterns Are Emerging in Service Marketing Sector," *Marketing News,* June 7, 1985, p. 2.

39. Raymond Serafin, "Domino's Pizza Takes 'Fresh' Angle," *Advertising Age,* Feb. 29, 1988, p. 34.

FIGURE 22.6

Distributing services. The U.S. Postal Service provides commemorative stamps to increase revenue. Because of their widespread distribution, limited-run stamps such as this one generate interest among collectors.

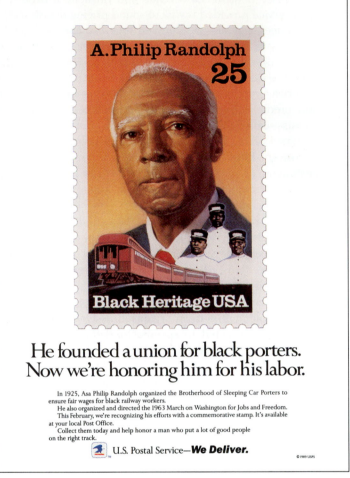

SOURCE: © 1989, USPS, Reprinted with permission

■ **Distribution**

In the service context, distribution is making services available to prospective users. Marketing intermediaries are the entities between the actual service provider and the consumer that make the service more available and more convenient to use.[40] In Figure 22.6, the Postal Service strives to make consumers aware of its commemorative stamp supporting America's Black Heritage. Because of the widespread distribution of stamps through post offices and other outlets, the government has been able to create limited-run special edition stamps, which are in turn collected and raise revenue nationally. The distribution of services is very closely related to product development. Indirect distribution of services may be made possible by a tangible representation or a facilitating good, for example, a bank credit card.[41]

40. James H. Donnelly, Jr., "Marketing Intermediaries in Channels of Distribution for Services," *Journal of Marketing,* January 1976, pp. 55–70.

41. Ibid.

Almost by definition, service industries are limited to direct channels of distribution. Many services are produced and consumed simultaneously; in high-contact services in particular, service providers and consumers cannot be separated. In low-contact services, however, service providers may be separated from customers by intermediaries. Dry cleaners, for example, generally maintain strategically located retail stores as drop-off centers, and these stores may be independent or corporate owned. Consumers go to the retail store to initiate and terminate service, but the actual service may be performed at a different location. The separation is possible because the service is directed toward the consumer's physical possessions, and the consumer is not required to be present during delivery.

Other service industries are developing unique ways to distribute their services. To make it more convenient for consumers to obtain their services airlines, car rental companies, and hotels have long been using intermediaries: travel agencies. In financial services marketing, the two most important strategic concerns are the application of technology and the use of electronic product delivery channels—such as automatic teller machines (ATMs) and electronic funds transfer systems—to provide customers with financial services in a more widespread and convenient manner.[42] Consumers no longer must go to their bank for routine transactions; they can now receive service from the closest ATM. Bank credit cards have enabled banks to extend their credit services to consumers over widely dispersed geographic areas through a nationwide network of intermediaries, namely, the retail merchants who assist consumers in applying for and using the cards.

■ Strategic Considerations

In developing marketing strategies, the marketer must first understand what benefits the customer wants, how the marketer is perceived relative to the competition, and what services consumers buy.[43] In other words, the marketer must develop the right service for the right people at the right price and at the right place. The marketer must remember to communicate with consumers so that they are aware of the need-satisfying services available to them.

One of the unique challenges service marketers face is matching supply and demand. We have seen that price can be used to help smooth demand for a service. There are other ways, too, that marketers can alter the marketing mix to deal with the problem of fluctuating demand. Through price incentives, advertising, and other promotional efforts, marketers can remind consumers of busy times and encourage them to come for service during slack periods. Additionally, the product itself can be altered to cope with fluctuating demand. Restaurants, for example, may change their menus, vary their lighting and decor, open or close the bar, and add or delete entertainment. A ski resort may install an alpine slide to attract customers during the summer. Finally, distribution can be modified to reflect changes in demand. Theaters have traditionally offered matinees during the weekend, when demand is greater, and some libraries have mobile units that travel to different locations during slack periods.[44]

42. Nigel A. L. Brooks, "Strategic Issues for Financial Services Marketing," *Journal of Services Marketing,* Summer 1987, p. 65.

43. Yoram Wind, "Financial Services: Increasing Your Marketing Productivity and Profitability," *Journal of Services Marketing,* Fall 1987, p. 8.

44. Lovelock, *Services Marketing,* pp. 279–289.

MARKETING STRATEGIES	NONMARKETING STRATEGIES
Use different pricing	Hire extra help/lay off employees
Alter product	Work employees overtime/part-time
Change distribution	Cross-train employees
Use promotional efforts	Use employees to perform nonvital tasks during slack times
	Subcontract work/seek subcontract work
	Slow the pace of work
	Turn away business

Before understanding such strategies, service marketers must first grasp the pattern and determinants of demand. Does the level of demand follow a cycle? What are the causes of this cycle? Are the changes random?[45] The need to answer such questions is best illustrated through an example. An attempt to use price decreases to shift demand for public transportation to off-peak periods would most likely fail because of the cause of the cyclical demand for public transportation: employment hours. Employees have little control over working hours and are therefore unable to take advantage of pricing incentives.

Table 22.5 summarizes ways service firms may deal with the problem of fluctuating demand. Note that the strategies fall into two categories: marketing and nonmarketing strategies. Nonmarketing strategies essentially involve internal, employee-related actions.[46] They may be the only available alternatives when fluctuations in demand are random. For example, a strike or natural disaster, such as the 1989 San Francisco earthquake, may cause fluctuations in consumer demand for public transportation.

NONBUSINESS MARKETING

Remember that earlier we broadly defined marketing as a set of individual and organizational activities aimed at facilitating and expediting satisfying exchanges in a dynamic environment through the creation, distribution, promotion, and pricing of goods, services, and ideas. Most of the previously discussed concepts and approaches to managing marketing activities also apply to nonbusiness situations. Of special relevance is the material offered in the first half of this chapter because many nonbusiness organizations provide services.

Nonbusiness marketing includes marketing activities conducted by individuals and organizations to achieve some goal other than ordinary business goals of profit, market share, or return on investment. Nonbusiness marketing can be divided into

45. Ibid.

46. Leonard L. Berry, Valarie A. Zeithaml, and A. Parasuraman, "Responding to Demand Fluctuations: Key Challenge for Service Businesses," in *AMA Educators Proceedings,* ed. Russell Belk et al. (Chicago: American Marketing Association, 1984), pp. 231–234.

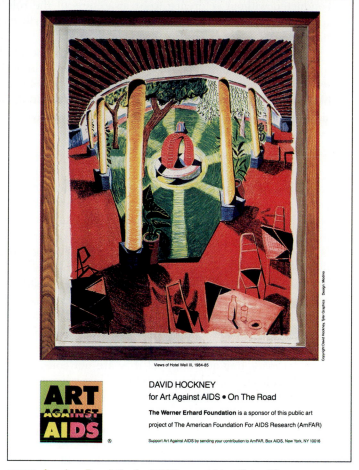

Views of Hotel Well III, 1984-85

DAVID HOCKNEY
for Art Against AIDS • On The Road

The Werner Erhard Foundation is a sponsor of this public art
project of The American Foundation For AIDS Research (AmFAR)

Support Art Against AIDS by sending your contribution to AmFAR, Box AIDS, New York, NY 10016

SOURCE: American Foundation for AIDS Research/Livet Richard Co.

two categories: nonprofit-organization marketing and social marketing. Nonprofit-organization marketing is the application of marketing concepts and techniques to organizations such as hospitals and colleges. Social marketing is the development of programs designed to influence the acceptability of social ideas, such as contributing to a foundation for AIDS research or getting people to recycle more newspapers, plastics, and aluminum.[47] Art Against Aids is a fund raising association to support AIDS research (see Figure 22.7).

As discussed in Chapter 1, an exchange situation exists when individuals, groups, or organizations possess something that they are willing to give up in an exchange. In nonbusiness marketing, the objects of the exchange may not be specified in financial terms. Usually, such exchanges are facilitated through **negotiation** (mutual discussion or communication of terms and methods) and **persuasion** (convincing and prevailing upon by argument). Often negotiation and persuasion are

47. J. Whyte, "Organization, Person and Idea Marketing as Exchange," *Quarterly Review of Marketing* (U.K.), January 1985, pp. 25–30.

conducted without reference to or awareness of the role that marketing plays in transactions. We are concerned with nonbusiness performance of marketing activities, whether the exchange is consummated or not.

In the rest of this chapter, we first examine the concept of nonbusiness marketing to determine how it differs from marketing activities in business organizations. Next we explore the overall objectives of nonbusiness organizations, their marketing objectives, and the development of their marketing strategies. We close the discussion by illustrating how an audit of marketing activities can promote marketing awareness in a nonbusiness organization.

■ Why Is Nonbusiness Marketing Different?

Traditionally and mistakenly, people have not thought of nonbusiness exchange activities as marketing. But consider the following example. The University of Minnesota developed a comprehensive marketing program to fill the stands at women's basketball games. An essential feature of the plan was awareness-building advertisements to encourage people to attend the games. Promotions have helped Minnesota boost average attendance at women's basketball games to about one thousand, but more than just advertising will be necessary to realize the goal of five thousand fans per game. The creator of the program hopes to develop a marketing campaign that can be applied generically to women's sports across the nation.[48]

Many nonbusiness organizations strive for effective marketing activities. Charitable organizations and supporters of social causes are major nonbusiness marketers in this country. Political parties, unions, religious sects, and fraternal organizations also perform marketing activities, yet they are not considered businesses. Whereas the chief beneficiary of a business enterprise is whoever owns or holds stock in it, in theory the only beneficiaries of a nonbusiness organization are its clients, its members, or the public at large. Marketing Update 22.2 describes how some not-for-profit organizations are using marketing activities to help achieve their objectives.

Nonbusinesses have a greater opportunity for creativity than most business organizations, but trustees or board members of nonbusinesses are likely to have trouble judging performance when services can be provided only by trained professionals. It is harder for administrators to evaluate the performance of doctors, professors, or social workers than it is for sales managers to evaluate the performance of salespersons in a for-profit organization.

Another way in which nonbusiness marketing differs from for-profit marketing is that nonbusiness is sometimes quite controversial. Nonbusiness organizations such as Greenpeace, the National Rifle Association, and the National Organization for Women spend lavishly on lobbying efforts to persuade Congress, the White House, and even the courts to support their interests, in part because acceptance of their aims by all of society is not always guaranteed. However, marketing as a field of study does not attempt to state what an organization's goals should be or to debate the issue of nonbusiness versus business goals. Marketing only attempts to provide a body of knowledge and concepts to help further an organization's goals. Individuals must decide whether they approve or disapprove of a particular organization's goal orientation. Most marketers would agree that profit and consumer satisfaction are appropriate goals for business enterprises, but there probably would be considerable disagreement about the goals of a controversial nonbusiness organization.

48. Kevin T. Higgins, "Gopher the Goal: Minnesota Marketers Donate Services, Media to Aid Women's Sports Program," *Marketing News,* Feb. 14, 1986, p. 1.

NOT-FOR-PROFIT ORGANIZATIONS USE MARKETING TO PROMOTE THEIR GOALS

To be heard over other nonbusiness advertising, reach the general public, and meet its goals, a nonbusiness organization must create a sense of uniqueness about itself, its message, and its mission. Marketing activities help not-for-profit organizations focus on their missions, determine specific needs, and decide who can help in the achievement of their goals. A well-planned and implemented marketing strategy can help accomplish these goals.

For example, United Way of America, which has 2,300 local units, developed a marketing strategy to unite the local units and created a message that represented the units as one group. A volunteer group of experts helped launch a national television ad campaign in which each commercial related a story of human need and how United Way helped fill that need. Other tools used by United Way included home videos, films, and a slide show. The success of the organization's marketing efforts led it to publish a how-to book for other charities, entitled *Competitive Marketing*.

Other marketing-shy organizations have experimented with programs under the label of "communications," saying that marketing is in reality basic communications techniques: research and evaluating results. The American Red Cross, for example, raised $300,000 using cause-related marketing techniques in conjunction with MasterCard International Inc. MasterCard made a small donation for each purchase during a specific time period.

Public budget cuts and soaring operating costs have led many zoos to try imaginative promotions and liaisons with corporate partners. For example, Washington National Zoo supporters host champagne breakfasts in the reptile house. The North Carolina Zoo ran a television ad featuring a punk couple on a motorcycle roaring past a child with the narration, "If this is the only wildlife your kids have seen lately, maybe it's time for a trip to the zoo." Kellogg Co. enclosed free zoo passes in each box of some cereal brands to boost zoo visits, a promotion termed "a win-win situation" by Kellogg. Such marketing efforts seem to be working. More than 112 million people visited North American zoos and aquariums in 1989, more than the combined attendance at professional football, basketball, and baseball games.

SOURCES: Michael Allen, "Let's Hope Pythons Don't Enjoy a Sip of Veuve Clicquot," *Wall Street Journal,* Feb. 12, 1990, pp. A1, A4; Jill Andresky, "Scrooged," *Financial World,* Apr. 4, 1989, pp. 114–116; Karen Schwartz, "Nonprofits' Bottom-Line: They Mix Lofty Goals and Gutsy Survival Strategies," *Marketing News,* Feb. 13, 1989, pp. 1–2; and Kathleen Vyn, "Nonprofits Learn How-To's of Marketing," *Marketing News,* Aug. 14, 1989, pp. 1–2.

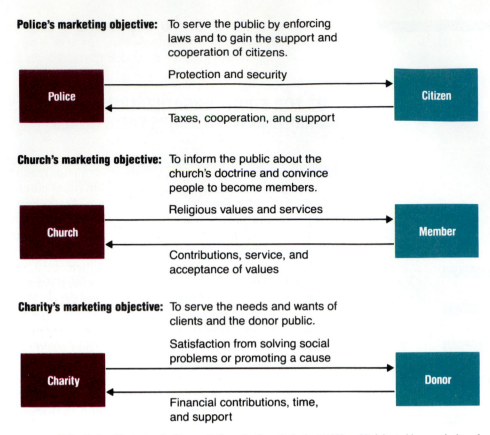

FIGURE 22.8
Examples of marketing objectives for different types of exchanges

Police's marketing objective: To serve the public by enforcing laws and to gain the support and cooperation of citizens.

Police → Protection and security → Citizen

Police ← Taxes, cooperation, and support ← Citizen

Church's marketing objective: To inform the public about the church's doctrine and convince people to become members.

Church → Religious values and services → Member

Church ← Contributions, service, and acceptance of values ← Member

Charity's marketing objective: To serve the needs and wants of clients and the donor public.

Charity → Satisfaction from solving social problems or promoting a cause → Donor

Charity ← Financial contributions, time, and support ← Donor

SOURCE: Philip Kotler, *Marketing for Nonprofit Organizations,* 2nd ed., © 1982, p. 38. Adapted by permission of Prentice-Hall, Inc., Englewood Cliffs, N.J.

■ Nonbusiness Marketing Objectives

The basic aim of nonbusiness organizations is to obtain a desired response from a target market. The response could be a change in values, a financial contribution, the donation of services, or some other type of exchange. Nonbusiness marketing objectives are shaped by the nature of the exchange and the goals of the organization. For example, the Easter Seal telethon has raised more than $200 million since its inception in 1972; the telethon is the charity's largest annual fund-raising event. Telethons have three specific marketing objectives: (1) to raise funds to support programs, (2) to plead a case in behalf of disabled people, and (3) to inform the public about the organization's programs and services. Tactically, telethons have received support by presenting quality programs and services; generating extensive grassroots support; portraying disabled people in a positive and dignified way; developing national, regional, and local support; and providing quality entertainment.[49] Figure 22.8 illustrates how the exchanges and the purpose of the organization can influence marketing objectives. (These objectives are used as examples and may or may not apply to specific organizations.)

Nonbusiness marketing objectives should state the rationale for an organization's existence. An organization that defines its marketing objective as providing a prod-

49. John Garrison, "Telethons—The Positive Story," *Fund Raising Management,* November 1987, pp. 48–52.

uct can be left without a purpose if the product becomes obsolete. However, serving and adapting to the perceived needs and wants of a target public, or market, enhances an organization's chance to survive and achieve its goals.

■ Developing Nonbusiness Marketing Strategies

Nonbusiness organizations must also develop marketing strategies by defining and analyzing a target market and creating and maintaining a marketing mix that appeals to that market.

Target Markets.   We must revise the concept of target markets slightly to apply it to nonbusiness organizations. Whereas a business is supposed to have target groups that are potential purchasers of its product, a nonbusiness organization may attempt to serve many diverse groups. In Figure 22.9, Hofstra University is promoting excellence to potential and current students, financial supporters, and the general public. For our purposes, a **target public** is broadly defined as a collective of individuals who have an interest in or concern about an organization, a product, or a social cause. The terms *target market* and *target public* are difficult to distinguish for many nonbusiness organizations. The target public of the Partnership for a Drug Free America is parents, adults, and concerned teen-agers. However, the target market for the organization's advertisements is potential and current drug users. When an organization is concerned about changing values or obtaining a response from the public, it views the public as a market.[50]

In nonbusiness organizations, direct consumers of the product are called **client publics** and indirect consumers are called **general publics**.[51] For example, the client public for a university is its student body, and its general public includes parents, alumni, and trustees. The client public usually receives most of the attention when an organization develops a marketing strategy. The techniques and approaches to segmenting and defining target markets discussed in Chapter 4 apply also to nonbusiness target markets.

Developing a Marketing Mix.   A marketing mix strategy limits alternatives and directs marketing activities toward achieving organizational goals. The strategy should outline or develop a blueprint for making decisions about product, distribution, promotion, and price. These decision variables should be blended to serve the target market.

In tackling the product variable, nonbusiness organizations deal more often with ideas and services than with goods. Problems may evolve when an organization fails to define what is being provided. What product does the Peace Corps provide? Its services include vocational training, health services, nutritional assistance, and community development. It also markets the ideas of international cooperation and the implementation of U.S. foreign policy. The Peace Corps product is more difficult to define than the average business product. As indicated in the first part of this chapter, services are intangible and therefore need special marketing efforts. The marketing of ideas and concepts is likewise more abstract than the marketing of tangibles, and it requires much effort to present benefits.

50. Philip Kotler, *Marketing for Nonprofit Organizations* (Englewood Cliffs, N.J.: Prentice-Hall, 1982), p. 37.
51. Ibid.

FIGURE 22.9
Nonbusiness markets.
Hofstra University
serves many groups:
students, the community
at large through employ-
ment and student devel-
opment, and philan-
thropists who may be
looking for worthwhile
organizations to support.

SOURCE: Courtesy of Hofstra University

Because most nonbusiness products are ideas and services, distribution decisions relate to how these ideas and services will be made available to clients. If the product is an idea, selecting the right media (the promotional strategy) to communicate the idea will facilitate distribution. The availability of services is closely related to product decisions. By nature, services consist of assistance, convenience, and availability. Availability is part of the total service. For example, making a product such as health services available calls for knowledge of such retailing concepts as site location analysis.

Developing a channel of distribution to coordinate and facilitate the flow of nonbusiness products to clients is a necessary task, but in a nonbusiness setting the traditional concept of the marketing channel may need to be reviewed. The independent wholesalers available to a business enterprise do not exist in most nonbusiness situations. Instead, a very short channel—nonbusiness organization to client—is prevalent because production and consumption of ideas and services are often simultaneous.

Making promotional decisions may be the first sign that nonbusiness organizations are performing marketing activities. Nonbusiness organizations use advertising and publicity to communicate with clients and the public. Direct mail remains the primary means of fund raising for social services such as those provided by the Red Cross and Special Olympics. In addition to direct mail, the Special Olympics uses telephone solicitation and television advertising.[52] Personal selling is also used by many nonbusiness organizations, although it may be called something else. Churches and charities rely on personal selling when they send volunteers to recruit new members or request donations. The U.S. Army uses personal selling when its recruiting officers attempt to convince men and women to enlist. Special events to obtain funds, communicate ideas, or provide services are sales promotion activities. Contests, entertainment, and prizes offered to attract donations resemble the sales promotion activities of business enterprises. Amnesty International, for example, has held worldwide concert tours, featuring artists such as Sting and Phil Collins, to raise funds and increase public awareness of political prisoners around the world.

The number of advertising agencies that are donating their time for public service announcements (PSAs) is increasing, and the quality of print PSAs is improving notably. Nonprofit groups are becoming increasingly interested in the impact of advertising on their organizations, and they realize that second-rate PSAs can cause a credibility loss.[53]

Although product and promotion techniques might require only slight modification when applied to nonbusiness organizations, pricing is generally quite different and the decision making more complex. The different pricing concepts that the nonbusiness organization faces include pricing in user and donor markets. There are two types of monetary pricing: *fixed* and *variable*. Membership fees, such as the amount paid to become a friend of the Brookfield Zoo, represent a fixed approach to pricing, whereas zoo fund-raising activities that lead to a donation represent a variable pricing structure.[54]

The broadest definition of price (valuation) must be used to develop nonbusiness marketing strategies. Financial price, an exact dollar value, may or may not be charged for a nonbusiness product. Economists recognize the giving up of alternatives as a cost. **Opportunity cost** is the value of the benefit that is given up by selecting one alternative rather than another. This traditional economic view of price means that if a nonbusiness organization can convince someone to donate time to a cause or to change his or her behavior, then the alternatives given up are a cost to (or a price paid by) the individual. Volunteers who answer phones for a university counseling service or suicide hotline, for example, give up the time they could have spent studying or doing other things, and the income they might have earned from working at a business organization.

For other nonbusiness organizations, financial price is an important part of the marketing mix. Nonbusiness organizations today are raising money by increasing the prices of their services or starting to charge for services if they have not done so before. They are using marketing research to determine what kinds of products people will pay for.[55] Pricing strategies of nonbusiness organizations often stress public and client welfare over equalization of costs and revenues. If additional funds are needed to cover costs, then donations, contributions, or grants may be solicited.

52. Eileen Norris, "Direct Marketing: Charities Step Up Solicitations," *Advertising Age,* July 27, 1987, pp. S4, S6.

53. Meryl Davids, "Doing Well by Doing Good," *Public Relations Journal,* July 1987, pp. 17–21.

54. Leyland F. Pitt and Russell Abratt, "Pricing in Non-Profit Organizations—A Framework and Conceptual Overview," *Quarterly Review of Marketing* (U.K.), Spring-Summer 1987, pp. 13–15.

55. Kelly Walker, "Not-for-Profit Profits," *Forbes,* September 10, 1984, p. 165.

1. **Product mix offerings**
   A. Types of product or services
   B. Number of organizations offering the product or service
2. **Financial resources**
   A. Types of fundings used
      1. Local grants
      2. State grants
      3. Federal grants
      4. Foundations
      5. Public solicitation
      6. Fees charged
   B. Number using each type of funding
   C. Number using combinations of funding sources
3. **Size**
   A. Budget (cash flows)

   B. Number of employees
      1. By organization
      2. Total industrywide
   C. Number of volunteers
      1. By organization
      2. Total industrywide
   D. Number of customers serviced
      1. By type of service
      2. By organization
      3. Total industrywide
4. **Facilities**
   A. Number and type
      1. By organization
      2. Total industrywide
   B. Location
      1. By address
      2. By zip code
      3. By census tract

SOURCE: Adapted from Philip D. Cooper and George E. McIlvain, "Factors Influencing Marketing's Ability to Assist Non-Profit Organizations," *Evolving Marketing Thought for 1980, Proceedings of the Southern Marketing Association,* John H. Summey and Ronald D. Taylor, eds. (Nov. 19–22, 1980), p. 315. Used by permission.

■ Controlling Nonbusiness Marketing Activities

To control marketing activities in nonbusiness organizations, managers use information obtained in the marketing audit to make sure that goals are achieved. Table 22.6 lists several helpful summary statistics. It should be obvious that the data in Table 22.6 are useful for both planning and control. Control is designed to identify what activities have occurred in conformity with the marketing strategy and to take corrective action where any deviations are found. The purpose of control is not only to point out errors and mistakes but to revise organizational goals and marketing objectives as necessary. In Figure 22.10, one way to measure the impact of the advertisement is to audit the number of books ordered through the 800 number for the Singapore Tourism Council.

Because of federal and state spending cuts, the need to encourage public support or donations is increasingly important. Many potential contributors decide which charities to support based on the amount of money actually used in charitable programs. Charities are more aggressively examining their own performance and effectiveness. For example, the Salvation Army contributes to the needy 86 cents out of every dollar it receives; its employees are basically volunteers who work for almost nothing. Charities are making internal changes to increase their effectiveness, and many are hiring professional managers to help with strategic planning in developing short-term and long-range goals.

To control nonbusiness marketing activities, managers must make a proper inventory of activities performed and prepare to adjust or correct deviations from standards. Knowing where and how to look for deviations and knowing what types of deviations to expect are especially important in nonbusiness situations. Because

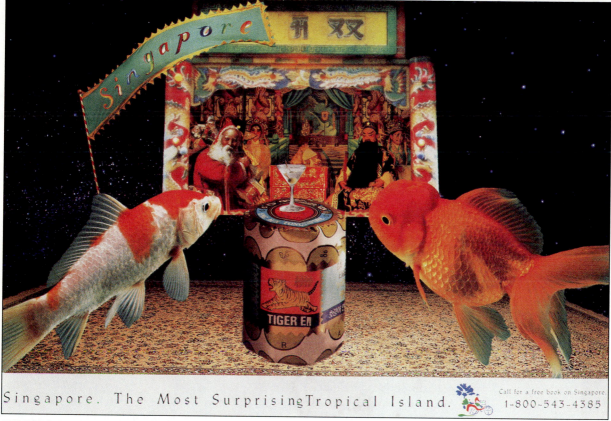

FIGURE 22.10 *Measuring the impact of advertising.*
The Singapore Tourism Council can measure the success of this advertisement by reviewing the number of calls on the 800-number and books shipped in response.

SOURCE: Client: Singapore Tourist Promotion Board; Agency: Baley Group

nonbusiness marketing activities may not be perceived as marketing, managers must clearly define what activity is being examined and how it should function.

It may be difficult to control nonbusiness marketing activities because it is often hard to determine whether goals are being achieved. A mental health center that wants to inform community members of its services may not be able to find out whether it is communicating with persons who need assistance. Surveying to discover the percentage of the population that is aware of a mental health program can show whether the awareness objective has been achieved, but it fails to indicate what percentage of the persons with mental health problems has been assisted. The detection and correction of deviations from standards is certainly a major purpose of control, but standards must support the organization's overall goals. Managers can refine goals by examining the results that are being achieved and analyzing the ramifications of those results.

Techniques for controlling overall marketing performance must be compatible with the nature of an organization's operations. Obviously, it is necessary to control the marketing budget in most nonbusiness organizations, but budgetary control is not tied to profit and loss standards; responsible management of funds is the objective. Central control responsibility can facilitate orderly, efficient administration and planning. For example, Illinois Wesleyan University evaluates graduating students' progress to control and improve the quality of the educational product. The audit phase relies on questionnaires sent to students and their employers after graduation. The employer completes a questionnaire to indicate the student's progress; the student completes a questionnaire to indicate what additional concepts or skills were needed to perform duties. In addition, a number of faculty members interview certain employers and students to obtain information for control purposes. Results of the audit are used to develop corrective action if university standards have not been met. Corrective action might include an evaluation of the deficiency and a revision of the curriculum.

SUMMARY

Services are intangible-dominant products that cannot be physically possessed—the result of applying human or mechanical efforts to people or objects. They are a growing part of the U.S. economy. Services have four distinguishing characteristics: intangibility, inseparability of production and consumption, perishability, and heterogeneity. Because services include a diverse group of industries, classification schemes are used to help marketers analyze their products and develop the most appropriate marketing mix. Services can be viewed as to type of market, degree of labor intensiveness, degree of customer contact, skill of the service provider, and goal of the service provider.

When developing a marketing mix for services, several aspects deserve special consideration. Regarding product, service offerings are often difficult for consumers to understand and evaluate. The tangibles associated with a service may be the only visible aspect of the service, and marketers must manage these scarce tangibles with care. Because services are often viewed in terms of the providers, service firms must carefully select, train, motivate, and control employees. Service marketers are selling long-term relationships as well as performance.

Promoting services is problematic because of their intangibility. Advertising should stress the tangibles associated with the service or use some relevant tangible object. Customer contact personnel should be considered an important secondary audience for advertising. Personal selling is very powerful in service firms because customers must interact with personnel; some forms of sales promotion, however, such as displays and free samples, are difficult to implement. The final component of the promotion mix, publicity, is vital to many service firms. Because customers value word-of-mouth communications, messages should attempt to stimulate or simulate word of mouth. Many professional service providers, however, are severely restricted in their use of promotional activities.

Price plays three major roles in service firms. It plays a psychological role by indicating quality and an economic role by determining revenues. Price is also a way to help smooth fluctuations in demand.

Service distribution channels are typically direct because of simultaneous production and consumption. However, innovative approaches such as drop-off centers, intermediaries, and electronic distribution are being developed.

Fluctuating demand is a major problem for most service firms. Marketing strategies (product, price, promotion, and distribution), as well as nonmarketing strategies (primarily internal, employee-based actions), can be used to deal with the problem. Before attempting to undertake any such strategies, however, service marketers must understand the patterns and determinants of demand.

Nonbusiness marketing includes marketing activities conducted by individuals and organizations to achieve goals other than normal business goals. Nonbusiness marketing uses most concepts and approaches applied to business situations.

The chief beneficiary of a business enterprise is whoever owns or holds stock in the business, but the beneficiary of a nonbusiness enterprise should be its clients, its members, or its public at large. The goals of a nonbusiness organization reflect its unique philosophy or mission. Some nonbusiness organizations have very controversial goals, but many organizations exist to further generally accepted social causes.

The marketing objective of nonbusiness organizations is to obtain a desired response from a target market. Developing a nonbusiness marketing strategy consists of defining and analyzing a target market and creating and maintaining a marketing mix. In nonbusiness marketing, the product is usually an idea or service. Distribution is not involved as much with the movement of goods as with the communication of ideas and the delivery of services, which results in a very short marketing channel. Promotion is very important in nonbusiness marketing; personal selling, sales promotion, advertising, and publicity are all used to communicate ideas and inform people about services. Price is more difficult to define in nonbusiness marketing because of opportunity costs and the difficulty of quantifying the values exchanged.

It is important to control nonbusiness marketing strategies. Control is designed to identify what activities have occurred in conformity with marketing strategy and to take corrective actions where deviations are found. The standards against which performance is measured must support the nonbusiness organization's overall goals.

IMPORTANT TERMS

Intangibility	Nonbusiness marketing
Search qualities	Negotiation
Experience qualities	Persuasion
Credence qualities	Target public
Inseparability	Client publics
Perishability	General publics
Heterogeneity	Opportunity cost

DISCUSSION AND REVIEW QUESTIONS

1. Identify and discuss the distinguishing characteristics of services. What problems do these characteristics present to marketers?
2. What is the significance of "tangibles" in service industries?
3. Analyze a house cleaning service in terms of the five classification schemes, and discuss the implications for marketing mix development.
4. How do search, experience, and credence qualities affect the way consumers view and evaluate services?
5. Discuss the role of promotion in services marketing.

6. Analyze the demand for dry cleaning, and discuss ways to cope with fluctuating demand.
7. Compare and contrast the controversial aspects of nonbusiness versus business marketing.
8. Relate the concepts of product, distribution, promotion, and price to a marketing strategy aimed at preventing drug abuse.
9. What are the differences among clients, publics, and consumers? What is the difference between a target public and a target market?
10. What is the function of control in a nonbusiness marketing strategy?
11. Discuss the development of a marketing strategy for a university. What marketing decisions should be made in developing this strategy?

■ CASES

22.1   Holiday Corporation Looks to "Promus" of Brighter Future

In August of 1989, the Holiday Corporation announced the sale of its entire Holiday Inn hotel chain to Bass PLC of London, a British brewing and hospitality company. This move followed a 1987 deal in which Holiday sold its international Holiday Inns to Bass. The deal, finalized in February of 1990, had an estimated price tag of $2.25 billion.

The sale to Bass included all the Holiday Inns worldwide, Crowne Plaza Hotels, Holiday Inn University at Olive Branch, Mississippi, the Holidex reservation system, the Priority Club frequent guest program, the Holiday Inn headquarters building in Memphis, Tennessee, and several other companies around the world. One condition of the sale was that Holiday drop its association with the ownership and management of the Holiday Inn hotel chain. The Holiday Corporation therefore assumed a new name, The Promus Companies. However, the new company retained the senior management team of the Holiday Corporation.

The sale made Bass the largest hotel company in the world in number of rooms (a title formerly held by Holiday), and second only to Best Western in the number of hotels. After the sale, Promus was left with four remaining businesses—Embassy Suites, Inc., Hampton Inns, Inc., Homewood Suites Equity Development Corp., and Harrah's hotels and casinos. After the sale, Promus became the world's thirteenth largest hotel company in number of rooms, and fourteenth in number of hotels.

With the Holiday Inn hotels gone, Promus can now concentrate on high quality service rather than on being the world's largest hotel company. Holiday has long been known for providing unmatched service to its customers. On average, Holiday's guest ratings are 18 percent higher than those of other hotel chains. Better service stimulates strong customer demand, which in turn leads to higher occupancy rates.

Promus' five-year strategic plan includes a very aggressive expansion program within all four of its businesses—Embassy Suites, Hampton Inns, Homewood Suites, and Harrah's. However, now that the excessive real estate holdings have been sold along with Holiday Inn, the strategy specifically excludes the ownership of real estate assets. In this way, Promus can focus on being a developer, manager, and franchiser of hotels without the hassles of owning the real estate.

Each of Promus' retained businesses operates in a separate and distinct market. Hampton competes in the limited-service, upper-economy market against hotels such as LaQuinta, Days Inn, and Comfort Inn. Embassy Suites is positioned in the lower upscale segment against Crowne Plaza (now owned by Bass PLC), Hilton, Sheraton, and Ramada. Homewood Suites, a recent addition to the Promus family, is targeted at the extended-stay traveler who lodges for at least five nights. Homewood's only significant competition is Marriott's Residence Inns.

While a great deal of Promus' business is in the hotel sector, a large part of its future business lies in the gaming industry. Harrah's, the world's premier casino/hotel company, is the only company with properties in each of the five major U.S. gaming markets—Atlantic City, New Jersey, and Las Vegas, Reno, Lake Tahoe, and Laughlin, Nevada. Harrah's competitors include Caesar's Palace, Circus Circus, Trump Palace, and the MGM Grand. Developments are underway that should help Harrah's achieve above average growth for the next five years. Each of the five Harrah's hotels and casinos has plans to expand the number of rooms, the size of the casinos, and the number of restaurants.

SOURCES: Tom Graves, "Leisure and Hospitality Sizable Part of U.S. Economy," *Industry Surveys,* Mar. 10, 1988, pp. L34–L35; Holiday Corporation, *Annual Report,* 1988; Laura Koss, "Holiday Inns Sold to Bass," *Business Travel News,* Sept. 5, 1989, p. 4; and Susan A. Thorp, "Promus Faces Office Squeeze," *(Memphis) Commercial Appeal,* Jan. 31, 1990, pp. B4, B8.

Questions for Discussion

1. What marketing problems did Holiday Corporation have before the sale of Holiday Inns to Bass PLC of London?
2. What marketing segmentation issues exist in positioning Embassy Suites, Hampton Inns, Homewood Suites, and Harrah's hotels and casinos?
3. Discuss the merits of being the number-one hotel in the world in number of rooms (Bass) versus the fourteenth largest hotel company in number of rooms (Promus). How will these relative size positions affect service quality?

22.2   Don't Mess with Texas!

In the first half of the 1980s, Texas taxpayers were paying $24 million a year for picking up litter along Texas roads and highways. Previous anti-litter programs and promotional campaigns were unsuccessful in persuading Texans to "pitch in" instead of "pitching out" litter onto the roadside. A tight state budget in the middle of the decade forced the Texas Department of Highways and Public Transportation to take drastic action to reduce the amount of money spent to eliminate the trash problem.

In 1985, research by the Institute for Applied Research found that the primary Texas litterer was male, 18 to 34 years old, and more blue-collar than professional. Texas-based advertising agency Gurasich, Spence, Darilek and McClure (GSD&M), known for its innovative ideas, was asked to create a marketing campaign to reach this client public (whom the state labeled "Bubba") in an effort to reduce the state's expenditures for litter cleanup. Their tough goal: reduce litter 25 percent by August 31, 1986.

The agency realized that anti-litter slogans that would stop people from other states dead in their tracks would not slow down a Texan: They had to talk bold and tough to get Bubba's attention. "Don't Mess with Texas," the campaign theme it developed, would appeal to Texans' state pride, nationalism, and ego. Texans in general are quite proud of their state and their frontier heritage; Bubba in particular would probably sit up and listen to such an appeal.

When the campaign television and radio spots were planned, the agency chose Bubba's favorite stars to voice the message. In one commercial, Texas guitarist Stevie Ray Vaughan played the state's theme song, "The Eyes of Texas," seated before a giant Texas flag. Other commercials featured popular Texas musicians the Fabulous Thunderbirds, Johnny Dee and the Rocket 88s, Joe Ely, and Willie Nelson playing or singing anti-litter ditties. Musician Johnny Rodriguez sang the message in Spanish to reach the state's large Hispanic population. Texas sports heroes such as Ed "Too Tall" Jones, Randy White, and Mike Scott set an example by picking up roadside litter in some spots. Both paid advertisements and public service announcements were used to get the "Don't Mess with Texas" message across. To increase the impact, more advertisements were run during the spring and summer months, when littering seemed to hit its peak. Some of the spots were so popular that radio listeners and television viewers called the stations and requested that they be run more often!

Other forms of promotion carried the message too. Bumper stickers, litter bags, and decals with the "Don't Mess with Texas" message were distributed free for the asking. The message also appeared on highway road signs. Texas businesses, civic groups, and individuals sponsored the message on T-shirts, coffee cups, key chains, store windows, company trucks, billboards, and even grocery sacks. The state also held "The Great Texas Trash-Off" to encourage Texans to kick the littering habit for one day; 16,000 volunteers picked up trash along roadsides. The trash-off is now an annual event.

The state has spent nearly $2 million on the campaign since it began in 1985. In 1986, the state asked the Institute for Applied Research to again survey the amount of litter on Texas roadsides. The researchers found that roadside litter had been reduced by 29 percent in less than one year! Deliberate littering dropped by 41 percent, and accidental littering (things blowing out the back of pickup trucks, car windows, and so on) dropped 18 percent. The Institute, which has conducted similar litter surveys across the nation, cited the 29 percent one-year drop in roadside litter as the largest one-year reduction in litter it has *ever* measured. An awareness survey conducted during the same time found that 60 percent of Texans were familiar with the "Don't Mess with Texas" message. A follow-up study conducted in 1989 found that overall littering on Texas highways had declined 60 percent since the campaign began; state highway cleanup crews have reported that they are collecting less trash and making their rounds faster than ever before.

The "Don't Mess with Texas" approach was incredibly effective in achieving its objective: to get young, blue-collar Texas men to stop throwing trash on the highway. The agency carefully defined its target and spoke directly to that target in words and gestures that group used every day. The slogan also made Texans feel better about their state and gave them a new rallying cry, perhaps one day to replace "Remember the Alamo."

Texas has no plans to abandon the successful campaign in the near future; in fact, the campaign has been greatly expanded. New spots are being created to appeal to a wider target public, not just Bubba. Some of the advertisements also address litter on Texas beaches, rivers, and lakes. All the spots feature popular Texans, and cartoon figures have been added as well, all telling the state that "messin' with Texas is a big drag . . . it's mighty reckless to mess with Texas." Texas is the only state that relies entirely on a commercial advertising campaign to reduce roadside litter.

SOURCES: "Campaign Gets 'Bubba's' to Quit Messin'," *Marketing News,* June 19, 1987, p. 16; "Don't Mess with Texas: A Phenomenal Success," Gurasich, Spence, Darilek and McClure, Austin Texas, 1987; "How to Talk Trash to Texans . . . Plus, the Antidote for Boring Advertising," Gurasich, Spence, Darilek and McClure, Austin Texas, 1987; Seth Kantor, "Engineer's Survey Helped Shape State's Ad Campaign Against Highway Littering," *(Bryan-College Station, TX) Eagle,* August 4, 1989, p. 2D; Michael McCullar, "Trash on Roads Down 29% After Ads," *Austin American-Statesman,* Sept. 22, 1986, pp. A1, A8; press release issued by the State Department of Highways and Public Transportation, Sept. 22, 1986; and a telephone conversation with Nick Turnham, public affairs officer, Brazos County, Texas Department of Highways and Public Transportation, Bryan, Texas, June 25, 1987.

Questions for Discussion

1. How well did the state of Texas define and target its client publics?
2. How does this campaign differ from that usually expected of a for-profit business?
3. Do you see any potential problems with the continuation of the campaign?

23 INTERNATIONAL MARKETING

Objectives

To define the nature of international marketing

To understand the importance of international marketing intelligence

To recognize the impact of environmental forces on international marketing efforts

To become aware of regional trade alliances and markets

To examine the potential of marketing mix standardization among nations

To describe adaptation of the international marketing mix when standardization is impossible

To look at ways of becoming involved in international marketing activities

Texas-based Granada Corporation helps ranchers around the world improve the quality of their cattle through its embryo transfers (in which cattle embryos from superior animals are implanted in surrogate cows), semen collection, and artificial insemination services. It is also one of the few firms conducting research in cloning and gene-transfer technologies. In addition to domestic marketing activities, Granada has to adjust its marketing activities when it provides its services outside the United States.

Granada uses marketing and advertising programs to make American and foreign ranchers aware of its services. Much of its marketing effort focuses on educating ranchers about embryo transfer technology and its benefits. Its marketing expertise enables it to bypass overseas sales agents and go directly to ranchers. Sometimes the ranchers approach Granada first.

Most of the foreign customers who are interested in the high-technology service offered by Granada can afford it and therefore can arrange to pay in American dollars. Many ranchers arrange payment through letters of credit at an American bank. Thus Granada is somewhat insulated against fluctuating exchange rates and the economic woes of other nations, particularly Mexico. The company does have to worry about customs regulations regarding the transfer of technology and the sale of services across international boundaries. In addition, some foreign governments have tried to obtain the technology for themselves. As with all companies engaged in international trade, Granada must be very careful to obey all laws and regulations and yet ensure that it receives all payment that it deserves for its services. That can be especially difficult when dealing with farmers and ranchers in struggling countries. ◆

Photo courtesy of Granada BioSciences Inc.

Based on information in Marj Charlier, "New Breed of Ranchers Is Cloning Cows," *Wall Street Journal*, Feb. 22, 1989, p. B4; O. C. Ferrell, "Rules of the Exporting Road," *Texas Business Prospects International*, August 1986, pp. 56, 58; Michele Kay, "A Willing Texas," *Texas Business Prospects International*, August 1986, pp. 54, 56; and Gary Taylor, "Granada Embryo Transfer Co.," *Texas Business Prospects International*, August 1986, p. 60.

International marketing is marketing activities performed across national boundaries.[1] The worldwide marketing operations of Granada Corporation's embryo transfer service provides a good example of how the management of international marketing activities requires an understanding of marketing variables and a grasp of the environmental complexities of foreign countries. In many cases, serving a foreign target market requires more than minor adjustments of marketing strategies.

This chapter looks closely at the unique features of international marketing and at the marketing mix adjustments businesses make when they cross national boundaries. We begin by examining American firms' levels of commitment to and degree of involvement in international marketing. Then we consider the importance of international marketing intelligence when a firm is moving beyond its domestic market. Next we focus on the need to understand various environmental forces in international markets and discuss several regional alliances and markets. We also analyze marketing mix standardization and adaptation. At the close of the chapter, we describe a number of ways of getting involved in international marketing.

INVOLVEMENT IN INTERNATIONAL MARKETING

Before international marketing could achieve its current level of importance, enterprises with the necessary resources had to develop an interest in expanding their businesses beyond national boundaries. Once interested, marketers engage in international marketing activities at several levels of involvement. Regardless of the level of involvement, however, they must choose either to customize their marketing strategies for different regions of the world or to standardize their marketing strategies for the entire world.

■ Multinational Involvement

The level of involvement in international marketing covers a wide spectrum, as shown in Figure 23.1. Casual or accidental exporting is the lowest level of commitment. For example, the products of a small medical-supplies manufacturer might occasionally be purchased by hospitals or clinics in nearby countries; its products might also be purchased by other countries through an export agent. Active exporting concentrates on selling activities to gain foreign market acceptance of existing products. Full-scale international marketing involvement means that top management recognizes the importance of developing international marketing strategies to achieve the firm's goals. Globalization of markets requires total commitment to international marketing; it embodies the view that the world is a single market.

■ Globalization Versus Customization of Marketing Strategies

Only full-scale international marketing involvement and globalization of markets represent a full integration of international marketing into strategic market planning. Traditional full-scale international marketing involvement is based on products customized according to cultural, regional, and national differences. In full-scale international marketing, marketing strategies are developed to serve specific target markets. From a practical standpoint, this means that to standardize the marketing

---

1. Vern Terpstra, *International Marketing*, 4th ed. (Hinsdale, Ill.: Dryden Press, 1987), p. 4.

Casual or accidental exporting	Active exporting	Full-scale international marketing involvement	Globalization of markets
Occasional, unsolicited foreign orders are received. There is no real commitment to international marketing.	This is an attempt to create sales without significant changes in the firm's products and overall operations. An active effort to find foreign markets for existing products is most typical.	Markets across national boundaries are a consideration in the marketing strategy. International marketing activities are seen as a part of overall planning.	Companies try to operate as if the world were one large market, ignoring regional and national differences.

National or domestic orientation ⟵——————————————⟶ Global orientation

FIGURE 23.1 *Levels of involvement in international marketing*

mix, the strategy needs to group countries by social, cultural, technological, political, and economic similarities.

In contrast, **globalization** involves developing marketing strategies as though the entire world (or regions of it) were a single entity; a globalized firm markets standardized products in the same way everywhere.[2] For many years, organizations have attempted to globalize the marketing mix as much as possible by employing standardized products, promotion campaigns, prices, and distribution channels for all markets. The economic and competitive payoffs for globalized marketing strategies are certainly great. Brand name, product characteristics, packaging, and labeling are among the easiest marketing mix variables to standardize; media allocation, retail outlets, and price may be more difficult. In the end, the degree of similarity among the various environmental and market conditions determines the feasibility of globalization.

Some companies have moved from customizing or standardizing products for a particular region of the world to offering globally standardized products that are advanced, functional, reliable, and low priced.[3] Nike, for example, provides a standardized product worldwide (see Figure 23.2). As we stated earlier, a firm committed to globalization develops marketing strategies as if the entire world (or major regions of it) were a single entity. Examples of globalized products are electrical equipment, western American clothing, movies, soft drinks, rock music, cosmetics, and toothpaste. Sony televisions, Levi jeans, and American cigarette brands seem to make year-to-year gains in the world market. Even McDonald's, Pizza Hut, and Kentucky Fried Chicken restaurants seem to be widely accepted in markets throughout the world. Attempts are now being made to globalize industrial products, such as computers, robots, and carbon filters, and professional engineering products, such as earth-moving equipment and communications equipment. But the

2. Theodore Levitt, "The Globalization of Markets," *Harvard Business Review,* May-June 1983, p. 92.

3. Ibid.

FIGURE 23.2 *Example of globalization.* Nike offers globally standardized products.

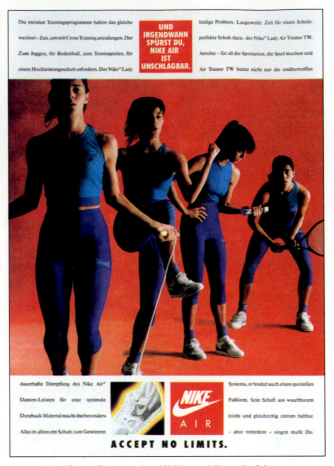

SOURCE: Pete Stone, Photographer; Weiden and Kennedy, Ad agency

question remains whether promotion, pricing, and distribution of these products can also be standardized.

Debate about the feasibility of globalized marketing strategies has continued since the birth of the idea in the 1960s. Surprisingly, questions about standardized advertising policies are the leading concern. However, it should be remembered that there are degrees of both customization and globalization. Neither strategy is implemented in its pure form.[4] The debate will doubtless continue about which products, if any, can be fully globalized. Some firms, such as Black & Decker and Coca-Cola, have adopted globalized marketing strategies. For some products—such as soft drinks—a global marketing strategy, including advertising, seems to work well, but for others—such as beer—strategies must accommodate local, regional, and national differences.[5]

4. Subhash C. Jain, "Standardization of International Marketing Strategy: Some Research Hypotheses," *Journal of Marketing,* January 1989, pp. 70–79.

5. "Global Brands Need Local Ad Flavor," *Advertising Age,* Sept. 3, 1984, p. 26.

INTERNATIONAL MARKETING INTELLIGENCE

Despite the debate over globalization of markets, most American firms perceive international markets as differing in some ways from domestic markets. Analyses of international markets and possible marketing efforts can be based on many dimensions. Table 23.1 lists the types of information that international marketers need.

Gathering secondary data (see Table 23.2) should be the first step in analyzing a foreign market. Sources of information include U.S. government publications, financial service firms, international organizations such as the United Nations, foreign governments, and international trade organizations. American firms seeking to market their products in the Soviet Union, for example, can obtain information about Soviet markets and regulations from the U.S. Department of Commerce, the USSR Chamber of Commerce and Industry, the Soviet trade organization Amtorg, and numerous other organizations. Depending on the source, however, secondary data can be misleading. The reliability, validity, and comparability of data from some countries are often problematic.

To overcome these shortcomings, marketers may need primary data to understand consumers' buying behavior in the country under investigation. Marketers may have to adjust techniques of collecting primary data for foreign markets. Attitudes toward privacy, unwillingness to be interviewed, language differences, and low literacy rates can be serious research obstacles. In a bicultural country such as Canada, a national questionnaire that uses identical questions is impossible because of the cultural and language differences. In many areas of Africa, where the literacy rate is low, self-administered questionnaires would never work.

Primary research should uncover significant cultural characteristics before a product is launched so that the marketing strategy is appropriate for the target market. It may be necessary to investigate basic patterns of social behavior, values, and attitudes to plan a final marketing strategy. Overall, the cost of obtaining such information may be higher than the cost of domestic research; the reasons include the large number of foreign markets to be investigated, the distance between the marketer and the foreign market, unfamiliar cultural and marketing practices, language differences, and the scarcity or unreliability of published statistics.[6]

After analyzing secondary and primary data, marketers should plan a marketing strategy. Finally, after market entry, review and control will result in decisions to withdraw from the foreign market, to continue to expand operations, or to consider additional foreign markets.

ENVIRONMENTAL FORCES IN INTERNATIONAL MARKETS

A detailed analysis of the environment is essential before a company enters a foreign market. If a marketing strategy is to be effective across national borders, the complexities of all the environments involved must be understood. In this section we see how differences in the cultural, social, economic, political and legal, and technological forces of the marketing environment in other countries affect marketing activities.

6. Vern Terpstra, "Critical Mass and International Marketing Strategy," *Journal of the Academy of Marketing Science,* Summer 1983, pp. 269–282.

TABLE 23.1   *Information needed for international marketing analyses*

PRELIMINARY SCREENING

Demographic/Physical Environment
Population size, growth, density
Urban and rural distribution
Climate and weather variations
Shipping distance
Product-significant demographics
Physical distribution and
  communication network
Natural resources

Political Environment
System of government
Political stability and continuity
Ideological orientation
Government involvement in
  business
Government involvement in
  communications
Attitudes toward foreign business
  (trade restrictions, tariffs,
  nontariff barriers, bilateral trade
  agreements)
National economic and
  developmental priorities

Economic Environment
Overall level of development
Economic growth: GNP,
  industrial sector
Role of foreign trade in the
  economy
Currency, inflation rate,
  availability, controls, stability
  of exchange rate
Balance of payments
Per capita income and distribution
Disposable income and expenditure
  patterns

Social/Cultural Environment
Literacy rate, educational level
Existence of middle class
Similarities and differences in
  relation to home market
Language and other cultural
  considerations

ANALYSIS OF INDUSTRY MARKET POTENTIAL

Market Access
Limitations on trade: tariff levels,
  quotas
Documentation and import
  regulations
Local standards, practices, and
  other nontariff barriers
Patents and trademarks
Preferential treaties
Legal considerations: investment,
  taxation, repatriation,
  employment, code of laws

Product Potential
Customer needs and desires
Local production, imports,
  consumption
Exposure to and acceptance
  of product
Availability of linking products
Industry-specific key indicators
  of demand
Attitudes toward products of
  foreign origin
Competitive offerings
Availability of intermediaries
Regional and local transportation
  facilities
Availability of manpower
Conditions for local manufacture

ANALYSIS OF COMPANY SALES POTENTIAL

Sales Volume Forecasting
Size and concentration of
  customer segments
Projected consumption
  statistics
Competitive pressures
Expectations of local
  distributors/agents

Landed Cost
Costing method for exports
Domestic distribution costs
International freight insurance
Cost of product modification

Cost of Internal Distribution
Tariffs and duties
Value-added tax
Local packaging and assembly
Margins/commission allowed
  for the trade
Local distribution and
  inventory costs
Promotional expenditures

Other Determinants of Profitability
Going price levels
Competitive strengths and
  weaknesses
Credit practices
Current and projected
  exchange rates

SOURCE: Adapted from S. Tamer Cavusgil, "Guidelines for Export Market Research," *Business Horizons,* November-December 1985, pp. 30–31. Used by permission.

TABLE 23.2 *Sources of secondary information for international marketing*

TYPE OF INFORMATION	U.S. DEPARTMENT OF COMMERCE SOURCES	OTHER SOURCES
Foreign market information	Business America Foreign economic trends Overseas business reports International economic indicators	Business International Dun & Bradstreet International Chase World Information Corp. Stanford Research Institute International Trade Reporter Accounting firms Foreign trade organizations
Export market research	Country market sectoral surveys Global market surveys International market research	Market research firms Advertising agencies Publishing companies Trade associations Library of Congress section tracking
International statistics	Export statistics profile Customer service statistics	Predicasts U.S. foreign trade reports Foreign brokerage houses United Nations International Monetary Fund OECD, EEC, GATT
Overseas representatives	Customized export mailing list World traders data reports Agent/distributor service	Banks International Chambers of Commerce Consulting firms Direct telephone contact
Sales leads	Trade opportunities program Strategic and industrial product sales group Major export projects program Export information reference room	Banks International Chambers of Commerce Consulting firms State development agencies
Reference data on foreign markets	World traders data reports	Banks International Chambers of Commerce Consulting firms State development agencies Corporate information databases

SOURCES: S. Tamer Cavusgil, "Guidelines for Export Market Research," *Business Horizons,* November-December 1985, p. 32; and Leonard M. Fuld, "How to Gather Foreign Intelligence Without Leaving Home," *Market News,* Jan. 4, 1988, pp. 24, 47. Data used by permission.

■ Cultural Forces

In Chapter 4 we define culture as the concepts, values, and tangible items, such as tools, buildings, and foods, that make up a particular society. Culture is passed on from one generation to another; in a way, it is the blueprint for acceptable behavior in a given society. When products are introduced into one nation from another, acceptance is far more likely if there are similarities between the two cultures.

The connotations associated with body motions, greetings, colors, numbers, shapes, sizes, and symbols vary considerably across cultures (Table 23.3 gives a few

TABLE 23.3 *Sampling of cultural variations*

COUNTRY/ REGION	BODY MOTIONS	GREETINGS	COLORS	NUMBERS	SHAPES, SIZES, SYMBOLS
Japan	Pointing to one's own chest with a forefinger indicates one wants a bath. A forefinger to the nose indicates "me."	Bowing is the traditional form of greeting.	Positive colors are in muted shades. Combinations of black, dark gray, and white have negative overtones.	Positive numbers are 1, 3, 5, 8. Negative numbers are 4, 9.	Pine, bamboo, or plum patterns are positive. Cultural shapes such as Buddha-shaped jars should be avoided.
India	Kissing is considered offensive and not seen on television, in movies, or in public places.	The palms of the hands touch and the head is nodded for greeting. It is considered rude to touch or shake hands with a woman.	Positive colors are bold colors such as green, red, yellow, or orange. Negative colors are black and white if they appear in relation to weddings.	To create brand awareness, numbers are often used as a brand name.	Animals such as parrots, elephants, tigers, or cheetahs are often used as brand names or on packaging. Sexually explicit symbols are avoided.
Europe	Raising only the index finger signifies a person wants two items. When counting on one's fingers, "one" is often indicated by thumb, "two" by thumb and forefinger.	It is acceptable to send flowers in thanks for a dinner invitation, but not roses (for sweethearts) or chrysanthemums (for funerals).	Generally, white and blue are considered positive. Black often has negative overtones.	The numbers 3 or 7 are usually positive. 13 is a negative number.	Circles are symbols of perfection. Hearts are considered favorably at Christmas time.
Latin America	General arm gestures are used for emphasis.	The traditional greeting is a hearty embrace and a friendly slap on the back.	Popular colors are generally bright or bold yellow, red, blue, or green.	Generally, 7 is a positive number. Negative numbers are 13, 14.	Religious symbols should be respected. Avoid national symbols such as flag colors.
Middle East	The raised eyebrow facial expression indicates "yes."	The word "no" must be mentioned three times before it is accepted.	Positive colors are brown, black, dark blues, and reds. Pink, violets, and yellows are not favored.	Positive numbers are 3, 5, 7, 9; 13, 15 are negative.	Round or square shapes are acceptable. Symbols of six-pointed star, raised thumb, or Koranic sayings are avoided.

SOURCE: James C. Simmons, "A Matter of Interpretation," *American Way,* April 1983, pp. 106–111; and "Adapting Export Packaging to Cultural Differences," *Business America,* Dec. 3, 1979, pp. 3–7.

examples). For multinational marketers, these cultural differences have implications that pertain to product development, personal selling, advertising, packaging, and pricing. For example, the illustration of feet is regarded as despicable in Thailand. An international marketer also must know a country's customs regarding male-female social interaction. In Italy it is unacceptable for a salesman to call on someone's wife if the husband is not home. In Thailand certain Listerine television commercials that portrayed boy-girl romantic relationships were unacceptable.

Product adoption and use are also influenced by consumers' perceptions of other countries. When consumers are generally unfamiliar with products from another country, their perceptions of the country itself affect their attitude toward and adoption of the product. If a country has a reputation for producing quality products, and therefore has a positive image in consumer's minds, marketers from that country will want to make the country of origin well known. Conversely, marketers may want to dissociate themselves from a particular country. Because American cars have not been viewed by the world as being quality products, Chrysler, for example, may want to advertise in Japan that Colt is "not another American compact."[7]

Culture may also affect marketing negotiations and decision-making behavior on the part of marketers, industrial buyers, and other executives. Research has shown that when marketers use a problem-solving approach—that is, gain information about a particular client's needs and tailor products or services to meet those needs—it leads to increased customer satisfaction in marketing negotiations in France, Germany, the United Kingdom, and the United States. However, the attractiveness of the salesperson and his or her similarity to the customer increase the levels of satisfaction only for Americans. Furthermore, marketing negotiations proceed differently in the various cultures, and the role and status of the seller are more important in both the United Kingdom and France.[8]

Social Forces

Marketing activities are primarily social in purpose; therefore they are structured by the institutions of family, religion, education, health, and recreation. For example, in Greece, where sunbathing is a commonplace form of recreation, U.S. products such as Johnson & Johnson Baby Sunblock have a large target market (see Figure 23.3). In every nation, these social institutions can be identified. By finding major deviations in institutions among countries, marketers can gain insights into the adaptation of a marketing strategy. Although football is a popular sport in the United States and a major opportunity for many television advertisers, soccer is the most popular television sport in Europe. Yet fan violence has caused major advertisers in the United Kingdom to have second thoughts about supporting such events with millions of advertising dollars.[9] The role of children in the family and a society's overall view of children also influence marketing activities. For example, the use of cute, cereal-loving children in advertising for Kellogg's is illegal in France. In the Nether-

7. C. Min Han, "Country Image: Halo or Summary Construct?" *Journal of Marketing Research*, May 1989, pp. 222–229.

8. Nigel G. G. Campbell, John L. Graham, Alain Jolibert, and Hans Gunther Meissner, "Marketing Negotiations in France, Germany, the United Kingdom, and the United States," *Journal of Marketing*, April 1988, pp. 49–62.

9. Brian Oliver, "U.K. Soccer Advertising in Trouble," *Advertising Age,* July 8, 1985, p. 36.

lands, children are banned from confectionery advertisements, and candy makers are required to place a little toothbrush symbol at the end of each confectionery spot.[10]

■ Economic Forces

Economic differences dictate many of the adjustments that must be made in marketing abroad. The most prominent adjustments are caused by differences in standards of living, availability of credit, discretionary buying power, income distribution, national resources, and conditions that affect transportation.

In terms of the value of all products produced by a nation, the United States has the largest gross national product in the world, $3,640 billion. **Gross national product (GNP)** is an overall measure of a nation's economic standing in terms of the value of all products produced by that nation for a given period of time. However, it does not take into account the concept of GNP in relation to population (GNP per capita). The United States has a GNP per capita of $15,380. The aggregate GNP of a very small country may be low. Austria's, for instance, is $67.2 billion, but the GNP per capita, a measure of the standard of living, is $8,892. The Soviet Union has one of the highest GNPs in the world ($1,998 billion) but only a $7,268 GNP per capita.[11] This figure means that the average Soviet citizen has less discretionary income than do citizens in countries with higher GNPs per capita. Knowledge about per capita income, aggregate GNP, credit, and the distribution of income provides general insights into market potential.

Opportunities for international marketers are not limited to countries with the highest incomes. Some nations are progressing at a markedly faster rate than they were a few years ago, and these countries—especially in Latin America, Africa, Eastern Europe, and the Middle East—have great market potential for specific products. However, marketers must understand the political and legal environment before they can convert buying power into actual demand for specific products.

■ Political and Legal Forces

A country's political system, national laws, regulatory bodies, national pressure groups, and courts all have great impact on international marketing. A government's policies toward public and private enterprise, consumers, and foreign firms influence marketing across national boundaries. For example, the Japanese have established many barriers to imports into their country. Even though they are reducing the tariffs on thousands of items, many nontariff barriers still make it difficult for American companies to export their products to Japan.[12] Just a few years ago, companies exporting electronic equipment to Japan had to wait for the Japanese government to inspect each item. A government's attitude toward cooperation with importers has a direct impact on the economic feasibility of exporting to that country.

Differences in political and government ethical standards are illustrated by what the Mexicans call *la mordida,* "the bite." The use of payoffs and bribes is deeply entrenched in many governments. Because U.S. trade and corporate policy, as well as U.S. law, prohibits direct involvement in payoffs and bribes, American companies

---

10. Laurel Wentz, "Local Laws Keep International Marketers Hopping," *Advertising Age,* July 11, 1985, p. 20.

11. *Statistical Abstract of the United States,* 1988, p. 805.

12. Lee Smith, "Japan Wants to Make Friends," *Fortune,* Sept. 2, 1985, p. 84.

FIGURE 23.3
The social aspects of international marketing. Widespread societal acceptance of sunbathing makes a product like baby sunscreen marketable in Greece.

SOURCE: Courtesy of Johnson & Johnson

may have a hard time competing with foreign firms that engage in this practice. Some U.S. businesses that refuse to make payoffs are forced to hire local consultants, public relations firms, or advertising agencies—which results in indirect payoffs. The ultimate decision about whether to give small tips or gifts where they are customary must be based on a company's code of ethics. However, it is illegal for U.S. firms to attempt to make large payments or bribes to influence policy decisions of foreign governments under the Foreign Corrupt Practices Act of 1977. The act also subjects all publicly held U.S. corporations to demanding internal control and record-keeping requirements related to their overseas operations. Corporations that fail to meet the requirements may face civil or criminal prosecution of corporate officers, directors, employees, agents, or stockholders.[13]

■ Technological Forces

Much of the marketing technology used in North America and other industrialized regions of the world may be ill suited for developing countries. For example, advertising on television or through direct mail campaigns may be difficult in countries

13. Jyotic N. Prasad and C. P. Rao, "Foreign Payoffs and International Business Ethics Revisited," in *Marketing Comes of Age*, ed. David M. Klein and Allen E. Smith (Southern Marketing Association, 1984), pp. 260–264.

that lack up-to-date broadcast and postal services. Nonetheless, many countries —particularly China, South Korea, Mexico, and the Soviet Union—want to engage in international trade, often through partnerships with American and Japanese firms, so that they can gain valuable industrial and agricultural technology. But the export of technology that has strategic importance to the United States may require the approval of the U.S. Department of Defense. For example, the Soviet Union wanted to buy General Electric jet engines for its airlines. When GE applied for the license to export the jet engines to the Soviet Union, its request was denied. Yet GE was licensed to sell these same engines to Israel for use on jet fighters.

REGIONAL TRADE ALLIANCES AND MARKETS

Although some firms are beginning to view the world as one huge marketplace, various regional trade alliances and specific markets may create difficulties or opportunities for companies engaging in international marketing. This section examines several regional trade alliances and changing markets, including the United States and Canada trade pact, the *maquiladora* industries of Mexico, the 1992 unification of Europe, the Pacific Rim markets, and changing conditions in eastern Europe and the Soviet Union.

■ **United States and Canada Trade Pact**

In 1989 the United States and Canada signed the Free Trade Agreement (FTA), which essentially merged the American and Canadian markets and formed the largest free-trade zone in the world. The agreement calls for the elimination of most tariffs and other trade restrictions over a ten-year period so that goods and services can flow more easily each way across the U.S.–Canadian border. Trade between the United States and Canada already totals more than $160 billion annually, and the FTA will make trade and investment across the border even "more profitable, less cumbersome, and more secure."[14] In Figure 23.4, CNGT promotes its efficient transportation system for goods between Canada and the United States.

Although passage of the trade pact was controversial and required lengthy negotiations, most experts believe that it will enable firms in both countries to compete more successfully against Asian and European rivals. When all the provisions are in effect in the year 2000, the treaty will enlarge Canada's markets ten times, and the United States will have unrestricted access to a market the size of California. Canadians are expected to ship more minerals, livestock, and forest products to the United States; American investments in Canada and sales of paper goods are likely to increase. Some experts estimate that the gross national products of the two countries could rise by 1 to 5 percent, as keener competition spurs companies on both sides to greater efficiency and productivity.[15] The tariff reductions mandated

14. Albert G. Holzinger, "A New Era in Trade," *Nation's Business,* September 1989, p. 67.

15. Gordon Bock, "Big Hug from Uncle Sam," *Time,* Oct. 19, 1987, p. 50; Madelaine Drohan, "A Critical Concern," *Maclean's,* Jan. 4, 1988, pp. 42–43; Mushtaq Luqmani and Zahir A. Quraeshi, "The U.S.– Canada Free Trade Pact: Issues and Perspectives," *Developments in Marketing Science,* Vol. XII, Academy of Marketing Science Proceedings, 1989, pp. 113–115; Edith Terry, Bill Javerski, Steven Dryden, and John Pearson, "A Free-Trade Milestone," *Business Week,* Oct. 19, 1987, pp. 52–53; "The Trade Pact Benefits Both Sides," *Business Week,* Oct. 19, 1987, p. 154.

FIGURE 23.4 *The Canada–U.S. partnership.*
CNGT acknowledges the importance of free trade between Canada and the United States.

SOURCE: Courtesy of Canadian National/Grand Trunk Western Railways

by the FTA will especially benefit smaller American and Canadian firms because it will allow them to create more efficient economies of scale for the unified market and to earn higher profit margins.[16]

■ **United States and Mexico Trade: The *Maquiladora* Industries**

Although trade relations between the United States and Mexico are not as formalized as those with Canada, the relationship has been flourishing in recent years. In 1990, a Mexico–United States free trade agreement similar to the Canadian FTA was proposed. The Border Industrialization Plan of 1965 established the *maquiladora* system between the United States and Mexico. Under this system, U.S. firms establish labor-intensive assembly plants, called *maquilas*, in Mexico. A U.S. firm may lease a Mexican-owned *maquila*, subcontract production through a *maquila*, or assume part ownership of a *maquila*. The U.S. company supplies the *maquila* with components for assembly, processing, or repair, and the Mexican plant returns the finished products to the United States for further processing or shipment to customers. The company pays a U.S. tariff only on the value added to the product in

16. Holzinger, pp. 67–69.

Mexico. Although the original plan established a relationship between Mexico and U.S. companies, some Japanese, Korean, and European companies are also using *maquiladora* plants.[17]

The system has many benefits for U.S. firms and for the Mexican economy. Mexico has one of the lowest labor-cost rates in the world. Furthermore, in recent years, the value of the peso has fallen dramatically relative to the value of the American dollar, making investment in Mexican plants more profitable. Finally, because of Mexico's proximity to the United States, it is less expensive to transport goods and components to and from Mexico than to and from other nations. Mexico derives benefits from the *maquiladora* system because the arrangement increases economic development by facilitating foreign exchange and providing employment. In 1987 there were 1,200 *maquilas* employing 310,000 Mexican workers, up from 620 plants employing 120,000 workers in 1980.[18]

■ Europe 1992

Just as the Free Trade Agreement between the United States and Canada removed barriers to trade between those two nations, the unification of Europe in 1992 will permit virtually free trade among the twelve member nations of the European Community (EC). Although Germany, France, Italy, the United Kingdom, Spain, the Netherlands, Belgium, Denmark, Greece, Portugal, Ireland, and Luxembourg currently exist as separate markets, in 1992 they will merge into the largest single market in the world, with more than 320 million consumers. The unification will allow marketers to develop one standardized product for all twelve nations instead of customizing products to satisfy the regulations and restrictions of each country.[19]

Although the twelve nations of the EC will essentially function as one large market and consumers in the EC are likely to become more homogeneous in their needs and wants, marketers must be aware that cultural and social differences among the twelve member nations may require modifications in the marketing mix for consumers in each nation. Some researchers believe that after 1992 it will be possible to segment the European Community into six markets on the basis of cultural, geographic, demographic, and economic variables. The six markets would be (1) the United Kingdom and Ireland; (2) central and northern France, southern Belgium, central Germany, and Luxembourg; (3) Spain and Portugal; (4) southern Germany, northern Italy, and southeastern France; (5) Greece and southern Italy; and (6) Denmark, northern Germany, the Netherlands, and northern Belgium.[20] Differences in taste and preferences among these markets are significant for international marketers. For example, the British prefer front-loading washing machines while the French prefer top-loading machines. Consumers in Spain eat far more poultry products than Germans do.[21] Preference differences may exist even within

17. Thomas V. Greer, "The Maquiladora Program: Nature and Current Status," *Developments in Marketing Science,* Vol XII, Academy of Marketing Science Proceedings, 1989, pp. 108–111.

18. Greer, pp. 108–111; and Benito E. Flores, "Mexico's Maquiladora Industries: An Overview and Perspectives," *Texas A&M Business Forum,* Fall 1987, pp. 27–32.

19. John Hillkirk, "It Could Be Trade Boom or Bust," *USA Today,* Jan. 12, 1989, p. 4B.

20. Sandra Vandermerwe and Marc-André L'Huillier, "Euro-Consumers in 1992," *Business Horizons,* January-February 1989, pp. 34–40.

21. Eric G. Friberg, "1992: Moves Europeans Are Making," *Harvard Business Review,* May-June 1989, p. 89.

the same country, depending on the geographic region. Thus international marketing intelligence efforts are likely to remain very important in determining European consumers' needs and developing marketing mixes that satisfy those needs.

■ Pacific Rim Nations

Companies of the Pacific Rim nations—Japan, China, South Korea, Taiwan, Singapore, Hong Kong, the Philippines, Malaysia, Indonesia, Australia, and Indochina —have become increasingly competitive and sophisticated in their marketing efforts in the last three decades. The Japanese in particular have made tremendous inroads into world consumer markets for automobiles, motorcycles, watches, cameras, and audio and video equipment. Products from Sony, Sanyo, Toyota, Mitsubishi, Canon, Suzuki, and others are sold all over the world and have set standards of quality by which other products are often judged. Managers from other nations study and imitate Japan's highly efficient management and manufacturing techniques. However, Japan's marketing muscle has not escaped criticism. The United States and Europe rely on Japan's informal trade restraints on its exports of cars, textiles, steel, and audio and video consumer products. The United States has also been critical of Japan's reluctance to accept imports from other nations.

South Korea has become very successful in world markets with familiar brand names such as Samsung, Daewoo, and Hyundai. But even before those companies became household words, their products achieved strong success under American company labels such as GE, GTE, RCA, and J. C. Penney. Korean companies are now taking market share away from Japanese companies in the world markets for videocassette recorders, color televisions, and computers, despite the fact that the Korean market for these products is limited. In Canada, the Hyundai Excel overtook Japan's Honda in just eighteen months.[22] With Europe and Japan blocking entry to some of their markets, Korean firms have decided to go head to head with Japanese and American manufacturers for a piece of the U.S. market.

Because of its drive toward modernization, the People's Republic of China was thought to have great market potential and opportunities for joint venture projects. However, limited consumer demand and political instability dimmed those prospects. In particular, a 1989 student prodemocracy uprising in Beijing reversed several years of business progress in China. Given the political instability, many foreign companies reduced their presence in China or left altogether; other firms became more cautious in their relations with China.[23]

Less visible Pacific Rim regions, such as Singapore, Taiwan, and Hong Kong, are major manufacturing and financial centers of the Pacific Rim. Singapore also has large world markets for pharmaceutical and rubber goods. Hong Kong, however, faces an uncertain future after it moves from British control to control by the People's Republic of China in 1997. Taiwan may have the most promising future of all the Pacific Rim nations. It has a strong local economy and has lowered many import barriers, sending imports up by 42 percent, to nearly $50 billion in 1988. Taiwan is beginning to privatize state-run banks and is also opening its markets to foreign firms. Some analysts believe that it may replace Hong Kong as a regional

22. Leslie Helm, with Laxmi Nakarmi, Jang Jung Soo, William J. Holstein, and Edith Terry, "The Koreans Are Coming," *Business Week,* Dec. 25, 1985, pp. 46–52.

23. Dori Jones Yang and Dinah Lee, with William J. Holstein and Maria Shao, "China: The Great Backward Leap," *Business Week,* June 19, 1989, pp. 28–32.

financial power center when Hong Kong reverts to Chinese control.[24] Firms from Thailand and Malaysia are also blossoming, carving out niches in the world markets for a variety of products, from toys to automobile parts.[25]

■ Changing Relations with Eastern Europe and the Soviet Union

The Soviet Union and other Eastern European nations (Poland, Hungary, East Germany, Yugoslavia, Czechoslovakia, Rumania, and Bulgaria), following a policy of *perestroika,* are experiencing great political and economic changes. The Communist Party's centrally planned economies are being replaced by democratic institutions in most of these countries. In fact, changes in the Eastern European countries have been the fastest breaking developments in international marketing. These seven countries are very different in terms of technology, infrastructure, foreign investment laws, and speed of change.[26] As a result, they are becoming increasingly market oriented.

Soviet leader Mikhail Gorbachev has implemented widespread measures to improve the economic environment of the Soviet Union, measures aimed primarily at making his nation more responsive to the forces of supply and demand. For instance, government-owned businesses have been granted more autonomy to make marketing decisions.[27] Other economic reform plans include replacing the Soviet Union's system of state-owned enterprises and farms with independent businesses leased or owned by workers, shareholders, cooperatives, and joint ventures; overhauling the system of centrally determined prices; and setting free-market prices for many products.

The reformers of the Soviet, Polish, and Hungarian economies want to reduce trade restrictions on imports and offer incentives to encourage exports to and investment in their countries.[28] For example, General Motors agreed to a $150 million joint venture in Hungary in 1990. In addition, General Motors reached an agreement with East Germany to build 150,000 Opels a year in a government-owned factory.[29] Because of these economic and political reforms, productivity in Eastern Europe and the Soviet Union is expected to increase as workers are given more incentives and control, raising the possibility that Eastern Europe will become an economic powerhouse rivaling the United States and Japan. There is also speculation that some of the Eastern European nations will ultimately join the European Community, allowing freer trade across all European borders.[30] In free elections, East Germany voted to reunify with West Germany. As Germany becomes one, unified country, its impact on the European Community will be great.

Because of the changing economic conditions in Eastern Europe and the Soviet Union, there are many marketing opportunities in these countries for American,

24. Dori Jones Yang, with Dirk Bennett and Bill Javerski, "The Other China Is Starting to Soar," *Business Week,* Nov. 6, 1989, pp. 60–62.

25. Louis Kraar, "Asia's Rising Export Powers," *Fortune,* Special Pacific Rim 1989 issue, pp. 43–50.

26. "East Bloc Business," *USA Today,* March 19, 1990, p. 6B.

27. Richard L. Kirkland, "Russia: Where Gorbanomics Is Leading," *Fortune,* Sept. 28, 1987, pp. 82–84; and Misha G. Knight, "The Russian Bear Turns Bullish on Trade," *Business Marketing,* April 1987, pp. 83–84.

28. Peter Gumbel, "Soviet Reformers Urge Bold Push to Liberalize Faltering Economy," *Wall Street Journal,* Oct. 27, 1989, p. A9.

29. "VW, GM Plan East German Ventures," *Chicago Tribune,* March 13, 1990, Sec. 3, p. 1.

30. John Templeman, Thane Peterson, Gail E. Schares, and Jonathan Kapstein, "The Shape of Europe to Come," *Business Week*, Nov. 27, 1989, pp. 60–64.

Western European, and Asian firms. Some American firms, including Monsanto, Combustion Engineering, McDonald's, and Pizza Hut, are marketing products in the Soviet Union, either through joint ventures with Soviet firms or through direct ownership.[31] Siemens, Federal Express, Procter & Gamble, and Occidental Petroleum are also among the many companies considering doing business in Eastern Europe. The countries of Eastern Europe are building new hotels and improving telephone, airline, and ground transportation services to facilitate international trade, as well as for the benefit of their citizens.[32] Marketing Update 23.1 highlights the activities taken by some firms in response to the fall of the Berlin Wall in 1989. However, because of the swift and uncontrolled nature of the changes taking place in Eastern Europe and the Soviet Union, firms considering marketing their products in these countries must carefully monitor events and proceed cautiously.

STRATEGIC ADAPTATION OF MARKETING MIXES

Once a U.S. firm determines foreign market potentials and understands the foreign environment, it develops and adapts its marketing mix. Creating and maintaining the marketing mix is the final step in developing the international marketing strategy. Only if foreign marketing opportunities justify the risk will a company go to the expense of adapting the marketing mix. Of course, in some situations new products are developed for a specific country. In these cases, there is no existing marketing mix and no extra expense to consider in serving the foreign target market.

■ **Product and Promotion**

As Figure 23.5 shows, there are five possible strategies for adapting product and promotion across national boundaries: (1) keep product and promotion the same worldwide, (2) adapt promotion only, (3) adapt product only, (4) adapt both product and promotion, and (5) invent new products.[33]

Keep Product and Promotion the Same Worldwide. This strategy attempts to use in the foreign country the product and promotion developed for the U.S. market, an approach that seems desirable wherever possible because it eliminates the expenses of marketing research and product redevelopment. PepsiCo and Coca-Cola use this approach in marketing their soft drinks. Although both translate promotional messages into the language of a particular country, they market the same product and promotion messages around the world. Despite certain inherent risks that stem from cultural differences in interpretation, exporting advertising copy does provide the efficiency of international standardization, or globalization. Global advertising embraces the same concept as global marketing, discussed earlier in this chapter. An advertiser can save hundreds of thousands of dollars by running the same advertisement worldwide.

31. Kirkland, pp. 82–84; and Knight, pp. 83–84.

32. Kevin Maney, "Eager East's Welcome Mat Is a Bit Shabby," *USA Today*, Oct. 23, 1989, pp. 1B, 2B; and Peter Gumbel,"Corporate America Flocking to Moscow," *Wall Street Journal*, Oct. 24, 1989, p. A18.

33. Warren J. Keegan, *Global Marketing Management*, 4th ed. (Englewood Cliffs, N.J.: Prentice-Hall, 1989), pp. 378–382.

AS THE BERLIN WALL CRUMBLES, MARKETING OPPORTUNITIES EMERGE

For nearly thirty years, the concrete Berlin Wall loomed as both a physical barrier and a symbol of the political, social, and economic differences between democratic West Germany and communist East Germany. It had been erected in August 1961 to stop a massive westward flow of refugees. With the overthrow of communist regimes throughout Eastern Europe in 1989, the wall became just a physical barrier between East and West Germans. While residents and souvenir seekers chiseled away at the wall itself, the symbolic implications of the fall of the wall resulted in new marketing opportunities.

Less than a month after the dramatic decision was made to open the wall, PepsiCo, AT&T, and Quintessence, which makes Jovan fragrances, filmed commercials at the site. The three American companies designed their commercials first to make an emotional appeal and second to stimulate product sales. The Quintessence commercial depicts the reunion of a family split by the wall. An East German grandfather, laden with gifts, drops a teddy bear while crossing through a newly opened gate in the wall. It is returned by a guard, and a "peace on earth" message flashes on the screen followed by a list of Quintessence products. Pepsi's advertisement shows a child giving a border guard a rose with Handel's "Hallelujah" Chorus playing in the background. The AT&T advertisements focus on communication between family and friends previously separated by the wall.

The rapidly changing political climate in Europe has opened more than just the Berlin Wall for entrepreneurs willing to invest in ventures. Although such investments can be risky and the obstacles to trade are many, some Americans are overcoming the obstacles and reaching trade agreements. For example, Imported Cars Inc. of Middletown, Connecticut, joined an auto parts venture after recognizing an opportunity to sell auto parts in Eastern Europe. A trade newsletter publisher is exploring the feasibility of publishing a newsletter about trade with Eastern Europeans. One entrepreneur compared the opportunities in Eastern Europe to the Gold Rush days of America. Although there is a chance to strike it rich, many companies may find only fool's gold.

SOURCES: "A Batch of Really Off-the-Wall Ads," *U.S. News & World Report,* Dec. 18, 1989, pp. 11–12; "Colas Toast Crumbling of Berlin Wall," *Adweek,* Dec. 11, 1989, p. 61; Marc Fisher, "East Germany to Tear Down Berlin Wall," *Commercial Appeal,* Jan. 3, 1990, pp. A1, A10; and Thomas R. King, "Berlin Wall Lands Role in 3 U.S. Spots," *Wall Street Journal,* Dec. 5, 1989, p. B6.

FIGURE 23.5
*International product
and promotion strategies*

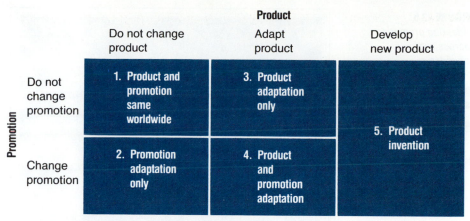

SOURCE: Adapted from Warren J. Keegan, *Global Marketing Management,* 4th ed., Englewood Cliffs, N.J.: Prentice-Hall, 1989, pp. 378–382. Used by permission.

Adapt Promotion Only.   This strategy leaves the product basically unchanged but modifies its promotion. For example, Panasonic provides similar products throughout the world but modifies ad copy to directly communicate product features (see Figure 23.6). This approach may be necessary because of language, legal, or cultural differences associated with the advertising copy. When Polaroid introduced its SX-70 camera in Europe, for example, it used the same television commercials and print advertisements, featuring "well-known" celebrities, that it used in the United States. However, because the celebrities were not well known in Europe, the commercials were not effective, and sales of the SX-70 were low initially. Only when Polaroid adapted its promotion to appeal to regional needs and tastes did the SX-70 begin to achieve success.[34] Promotional adaptation is a low-cost modification compared with the costs of redeveloping engineering and production and physically changing products.

Generally, the strategy of adapting only promotion infuses advertising with the culture of people who will be exposed to it. Often promotion combines thinking globally and acting locally. At company headquarters, a basic global marketing strategy is developed, but promotion is modified to fit each market's needs.

Adapt Product Only.   The basic assumption in modifying a product without changing its promotion is that the product will serve the same function under different conditions of use. Soap and detergent manufacturers have adapted their products to local water conditions and washing equipment without changing their promotions. Household appliances also have been altered to use different types of electricity.

A product may have to be adjusted for legal reasons. Japan, for example, has some of the most stringent automobile emission requirements in the world. American automobiles that fail emission standards cannot be marketed in Japan. Sometimes, products must be adjusted to overcome social and cultural obstacles. Jell-O introduced a powdered gelatin mix that failed in England because the English were used

34. Kamran Kashani, "Beware the Pitfalls of Global Marketing," *Harvard Business Review,* September-October 1989, pp. 93–94.

FIGURE 23.6

Adapting promotion across national boundaries.
Panasonic adapts the promotion of its portable stereo.

Der wird überall
angemacht.

Sogar aus 10 m Entfernung.

Mit dem RX-DS30 können Sie sich auch auf Distanz bestens unterhalten. Ein leichter Druck
auf die IR-Fernbedienung, und schon spielt er, was Sie wollen: Cassetten, CD's oder Radio.
Und zwar mit 2 x 25 Watt. Dabei sorgt das variable Extra-Bass-System für klare, satte Bässe.
Feinheiten wie die leichtgängigen Tipptasten, der sanfte Cassettenauswurf und das schöne
Design entgehen Ihnen natürlich ab einer gewissen Entfernung. Deswegen sollten Sie den
RX-DS30 ruhig mal aus nächster Nähe anmachen: bei Ihrem Fachhändler. **Panasonic**

DIE WELT SIEHT AUF PANASONIC.

SOURCE: Matsushita Electric Industrial Company, Ltd.

to buying gelatin in jelled form. Resistance to a product is frequently based on attitudes and ignorance about the nature of new technology. It is often easier to change the product than to overcome technological biases.

Adapt Both Product and Promotion. When a product serves a new function or is used differently in a foreign market, then both the product and its promotion need to be altered. For example, when Procter & Gamble marketed its Cheer laundry detergent in Japan, it promoted the product as being effective in all temperatures, just as it does in the United States. Most Japanese, however, wash clothes in cold water and therefore do not care about all-temperature washing. Moreover, the Japanese often add a lot of fabric softener to the wash, and Cheer did not produce many suds under those conditions. Procter & Gamble thus reformulated Cheer so that it would not be affected by the addition of fabric softeners and changed the promotion to emphasize "superior" cleaning in cold water. Cheer then became one of Procter & Gamble's most successful products in Japan.[35] Adaptation of both product and promotion is the most expensive strategy discussed thus far, but it should be considered if the foreign market appears large enough.

35. Allecia Swasy, "After Early Stumbles, P&G Is Making Inroads Overseas," *Wall Street Journal,* Feb. 6, 1989, p. B1.

FIGURE 23.7
Strategies for international distribution and pricing

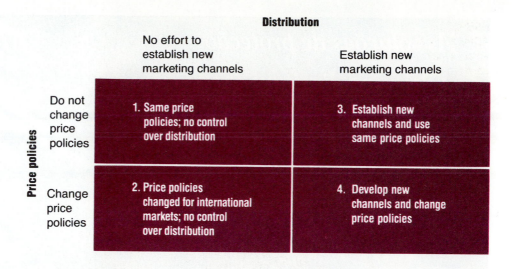

Distribution

	No effort to establish new marketing channels	Establish new marketing channels
Do not change price policies	1. Same price policies; no control over distribution	3. Establish new channels and use same price policies
Change price policies	2. Price policies changed for international markets; no control over distribution	4. Develop new channels and change price policies

Price policies

Invent New Products.   This strategy is selected when existing products cannot meet the needs of a foreign market. General Motors developed an all-purpose, jeeplike motor vehicle that can be assembled in underdeveloped nations by mechanics with no special training. The vehicle is designed to operate under varied conditions; it has standardized parts and is inexpensive. Colgate-Palmolive Co. developed an inexpensive, all-plastic, hand-powered washing machine that has the tumbling action of a modern automatic machine. The product, marketed in underdeveloped countries, was invented for households that have no electricity. Strategies that involve the invention of products are often the most costly, but the payoff can be great.

■ Distribution and Pricing

Decisions about the distribution system and pricing policies are important in developing an international marketing mix. Figure 23.7 illustrates different approaches to these decisions.

Distribution.   A firm can sell its product to an intermediary that is willing to buy from existing market channels in the United States, or it can develop new international marketing channels. Obviously, a service company, such as Citicorp, needs to develop its own distribution systems to market its products (see Figure 23.8). However, many products, such as toothpaste, are distributed through intermediaries and brokers. The firm must consider distribution both between countries and within the foreign country.

In determining distribution alternatives, the existence of retailers and wholesalers that can perform marketing functions between and within nations is one major factor. If a foreign country has a segmented retail structure consisting primarily of one-person shops or street vendors, it may be difficult to develop new marketing channels for products such as packaged goods and prepared foods. Quite often in Third World countries, certain channels of distribution are characterized by ethnodomination. *Ethnodomination* occurs when an ethnic group occupies a majority position within a marketing channel. Indians, for example, own approximately 90 percent of the cotton gins in Uganda; the Hausa tribe in Nigeria dominates the trade in kola nuts, cattle, and housing; and Chinese merchants dominate the rice

FIGURE 23.8 *International distribution.*
A services-oriented company, such as Citicorp, must develop its own distribution channels to ensure adequate control of its marketing processes.

SOURCE: Citibank, N.A., a subsidiary of Citicorp

economy in Thailand. Marketers must be sensitive to ethnodomination and recognize that the ethnic groups operate in subcultures unique in social and economic organization.[36]

If the product being sold across national boundaries requires service and information, then control of the distribution process is desirable. Caterpillar, for example, sells more than half its construction and earth-moving equipment in foreign countries. Because it must provide services and replacement parts, Caterpillar has established its own dealers in foreign markets. Regional sales offices and technical experts are also available to support local dealers. A manufacturer of paintbrushes, on the other hand, would be more concerned about agents, wholesalers, or other manufacturers that would facilitate the product's exposure in a foreign market. Control over the distribution process would not be so important for that product because services and replacement parts are not needed.

36. Douglass G. Norvell and Robert Morey, "Ethnodomination in the Channels of Distribution of Third World Nations," *Journal of the Academy of Marketing Science,* Summer 1983, pp. 204–235.

Research suggests that international firms use independently owned marketing channels when they market in countries perceived to be highly dissimilar to their home markets. However, when they market complex products, they develop vertically integrated marketing channels to gain control of distribution. To manage the distribution process from manufacture to customer contact requires an expert sales force that must be trained to specifically sell the firm's products. Moreover, when products are unique or highly differentiated from those of current competitors, international firms also tend to design and establish vertically integrated channels.[37]

It is crucial to realize that a nation's political instability can jeopardize the distribution of goods. For example, when the United States invaded Panama in late 1989, the Panama Canal was closed for several days, delaying shipments of goods through the canal. Similarly, during the political unrest in China, military activity and fighting made it difficult to move goods into and out of certain areas. Thus we want to stress again the importance of monitoring the environment when engaging in international marketing. Companies that market products in unstable nations may need to develop alternate plans to allow for sudden unrest or hostility and ensure that the distribution of their products is not jeopardized.

Pricing.   The domestic and foreign prices of products are usually different. For example, the prices charged for Walt Disney videos in Spain may differ from U.S. prices for Walt Disney videos. The increased costs of transportation, supplies, taxes, tariffs, and other expenses necessary to adjust a firm's operations to international marketing can raise prices. A key decision is whether the basic pricing policy will change (as discussed in Chapter 16). If it is a firm's policy not to allocate fixed costs to foreign sales, then lower foreign prices could result.

American pharmaceutical manufacturers have been accused of selling their products in foreign markets at low prices (without allocating research and development costs) while charging American customers high prices that include all research and development expenses. The sale of U.S. products in foreign markets—or vice versa—at lower prices (when all costs have not been allocated or when surplus products are sold) is called **dumping**. Dumping is illegal in many countries if it damages domestic firms and workers.

A cost-plus approach to international pricing is probably the most common method used because of the compounding number of costs necessary to move products from the United States to a foreign country. Of course, as our discussion of pricing policies in Chapter 16 points out, understanding consumer demand and the competitive environment is a necessary step in selecting a price.

The price charged in other countries is also a function of foreign currency exchange rates. Fluctuations in the international monetary market can change the prices charged across national boundaries on a daily basis. There has been a trend toward greater fluctuation (or float) in world money markets. For example, a sudden variation in the exchange rate, which occurs when a nation devalues its currency, can have wide-ranging effects on consumer prices.

37. Erin Anderson and Anne T. Coughlan, "International Market Entry and Expansion via Independent or Integrated Channels of Distribution," *Journal of Marketing,* January 1987, pp. 71–82.

DEVELOPING ORGANIZATIONAL STRUCTURES FOR INTERNATIONAL MARKETING

The level of commitment to international marketing is a major variable in deciding what kind of involvement is appropriate. A firm's options range from occasional exporting to expanding overall operations (production and marketing) into other countries. In this section we examine exporting, licensing, joint ventures, trading companies, direct ownership, and other approaches to international involvement.

■ Exporting

Exporting is the lowest level of commitment to international marketing and the most flexible approach. A firm may find an exporting intermediary that can perform most marketing functions associated with selling to other countries. This approach entails minimum effort and cost. Modifications in packaging, labeling, style, or color may be the major expenses in adapting a product. There is limited risk in using export agents and merchants because there is no direct investment in the foreign country.

Export agents bring together buyers and sellers from different countries; they collect a commission for arranging sales. Export houses and export merchants purchase products from different companies and then sell them to foreign countries. They are specialists at understanding customers' needs in foreign countries.

Foreign buyers from companies and governments provide a direct method of exporting and eliminate the need for an intermediary. Foreign buyers encourage international exchange by contacting domestic firms about their needs and the opportunities available in exporting. Domestic firms that want to export with a minimum of effort and investment seek out foreign importers and buyers.

■ Licensing

When potential markets are found across national boundaries—and when production, technical assistance, or marketing know-how is required—**licensing** is an alternative to direct investment. The licensee (the owner of the foreign operation) pays commissions or royalties on sales or supplies used in manufacturing. An initial down payment or fee may be charged when the licensing agreement is signed. Exchanges of management techniques or technical assistance are primary reasons for licensing agreements. Yoplait yogurt is a French yogurt that is licensed for production in the United States; the Yoplait brand tries to maintain a French image. Marketing Update 23.2 profiles another yogurt marketer, TCBY, which uses licensing arrangements in its overseas operations.

Licensing is an attractive alternative to direct investment when the political stability of a foreign country is in doubt or when resources are unavailable for direct investment. Licensing is especially advantageous for small manufacturers wanting to launch a well-known brand internationally. For example, all Spalding sporting products are licensed worldwide. The Questor Corporation owns the Spalding name but produces no goods itself. Pierre Cardin has issued five hundred licenses and Yves St. Laurent two hundred to make their products.[38] Lowenbrau has used licensing agreements, including one with Miller in the United States, to increase sales worldwide without committing capital to build breweries.

38. John A. Quelch, "How to Build a Product Licensing Program," *Harvard Business Review*, May-June 1985, pp. 186–187.

TCBY USES LICENSING FOR INTERNATIONAL EXPANSION

Frank D. Hickingbotham opened the first TCBY (The Country's Best Yogurt) store in Little Rock, Arkansas in 1981. By 1989 the company had 1,175 stores selling frozen yogurt in 49 states, Canada, the Bahamas, Singapore, Taiwan, and Malaysia. The 28 Canadian stores have been the most successful of all the international operations, and the company hopes eventually to have 100 stores there. With total sales of more than $210 million, TCBY's net income was up 52 percent over 1987, to almost $20 million. TCBY is more than six times bigger than its largest, yogurt-only competitor, but the market is filling quickly with competitors hoping for a piece of the frozen yogurt sales pie. The company hopes to increase its presence in international markets as a safeguard against the eventual erosion of TCBY's market share in the United States by competitive organizations.

TCBY has expanded internationally through licensing arrangements. The company tries to find a master licensee who is financially able to open all potential stores or has the expertise needed to subfranchise in a particular area. It prefers that qualified buyers approach it rather than actively seeking franchisees. Because of high duties and heavy restrictions on milk products, TCBY has not yet entered the European market, but that may change if the company determines that there is enough interest.

Foreign TCBY stores are built to look as much as possible like their American counterparts, with brightly colored formica tables and counters, fresh greenery, and clean, well-lit seating. Building materials are obtained locally if possible, but if necessary, are shipped from the United States to ensure uniformity. One concession made in Asian countries, however, is lowering counters by six inches so that customers have a better view of available yogurt toppings. Toppings, flavors, and product availability vary across international markets, but traditional vanilla and chocolate flavors fare well in all countries. Whether franchises are opened in the domestic market or the foreign one, TCBY expects to continue its successful formula of good timing, good taste, and good management.

SOURCES: Jerry Huston, "TCBY aims to remain atop field," *Commercial Appeal,* Dec. 10, 1989, pp. C1, C2; TCBY Enterprises, Inc., Annual Report, 1988; TCBY Enterprises, Inc., Equities Research Basic Report, March 10, 1989.

Joint Ventures

In international marketing, a **joint venture** is a partnership between a domestic firm and a foreign firm or government. Joint ventures are especially popular in industries that call for large investments, such as natural resources extraction or automobile manufacturing. Control of the joint venture can be split equally, or one party may control decision making. Joint ventures are often a political necessity because of nationalism and governmental restrictions on foreign ownership. They also provide legitimacy in the eyes of the host country's citizens. Local partners have firsthand knowledge of the economic and sociopolitical environment, access to distribution networks, or privileged access to local resources (raw material, labor management, contacts, and so on). Moreover, entrepreneurs in many less-developed countries actively seek associations with a foreign partner as a ready means of implementing their own corporate strategy.[39]

Joint ventures are assuming greater global importance because of cost advantages and the number of inexperienced firms entering foreign markets. They may be the result of a trade-off between a firm's desire for completely unambiguous control of an enterprise and its quest for additional resources. They may occur when internal development or acquisition is not feasible or unavailable or when the risks and constraints leave no other alternative. As project sizes increase in the face of global competition and firms attempt to spread the huge costs of technological innovation, there is increased impetus to form joint ventures.[40] Several European truck makers are considering mergers and joint ventures with other European firms to consolidate their power after the unification of Europe in 1992 and the deregulation of the European trucking industry in 1993. Volvo and Renault have developed a partnership, and Britain's Leyland and the Netherlands' DAF have already joined forces.[41]

Increasingly, once a joint venture succeeds, nationalism spurs a trend toward expropriating or purchasing foreign shares of the enterprise. On the other hand, a joint venture may be the only available means for entering a foreign market. For example, American construction firms bidding for business in Saudi Arabia have found that joint ventures with Arab construction companies gain local support among the handful of people who make the contracting decisions.

Strategic alliances, the newest form of international business structure, are partnerships formed to create competitive advantage on a worldwide basis. They are very similar to joint ventures. The number of strategic alliances is growing at an estimated rate of about 20 percent per year.[42] In fact, in some industries, such as automobiles and computers, strategic alliances are becoming the predominate means of competing. International competition is so fierce and the costs of competing on a global basis so high that few firms have the individual resources to go it alone. Thus individual firms that lack all the internal resources essential for international success may seek to collaborate with other companies.[43]

---

39. Andrew Kupfer, "How to Be a Global Manager," *Fortune,* Mar. 14, 1988, pp. 52–58.

40. Kathryn Rudie Harrigan, "Joint Ventures and Competitive Advantage," *Strategic Management Journal,* May 1988, pp. 141–158.

41. A. Dunlap Smith, "Europe's Truckmakers Face Survival of the Biggest," *Business Week,* Nov. 6, 1989, p. 68.

42. "More Companies Prefer Liaisons to Marriage," *Wall Street Journal,* Apr. 12, 1988, p. 35.

43. Thomas Gross and John Neuman, "Strategic Alliances Vital in Global Marketing," *Marketing News,* June 1989, pp. 1–2.

The partners forming international strategic alliances often retain their distinct identities, and each brings a distinctive competence to the union. However, the firms share common long-term goals. What distinguishes international strategic alliances from other business structures is that member firms in the alliance may have been traditional rivals competing for market share in the same product class.[44] An example of such an alliance is the New United Motor Manufacturing, Inc. (NUMMI), formed by Toyota and General Motors to make Chevrolet Novas and Toyota Tercels. This alliance united the quality engineering of Japanese cars to the marketing expertise and market access of General Motors.

Trading Companies

A **trading company** provides a link between buyers and sellers in different countries. A trading company, as its name implies, is not involved in manufacturing or owning assets related to manufacturing. It buys in one country at the lowest price consistent with quality and sells to buyers in another country. An important function of trading companies is taking title to products and undertaking all the activities necessary to move the products from the domestic country to a foreign country. For example, large grain-trading companies operating out of home offices in both the United States and overseas control a major portion of the world's trade in basic food commodities. These trading companies sell agricultural commodities that are homogeneous and can be stored and moved rapidly in response to market conditions.

Trading companies reduce risk for companies interested in getting involved in international marketing. A trading company will assist producers with information about products that meet quality and price expectations in domestic or international markets. Additional services a trading company may provide include consulting, marketing research, advertising, insurance, product research and design, legal assistance, warehousing, and foreign exchange.

In 1982 the Export Trading Company Act was passed to facilitate the efficient operation of trading companies in the United States. Besides allowing banks to invest in trading companies, the Export Trading Act created a new certification procedure that enables companies to apply for limited protection from antitrust laws when conducting export operations. The program has been less successful than the government had hoped, however. As of 1987, only eighty-two export trading companies had been created under provisions of the act. They generated $554 million in sales. This sales level falls far short of that envisioned by the creators of the program.[45] The best known U.S. trading company is Sears World Trade, which specializes in consumer goods, light industrial items, and processed foods. A trading company acts like a wholesaler, taking on much of the responsibility of finding markets while facilitating all marketing aspects of a transaction.

Direct Ownership

Once a company makes a long-term commitment to marketing in a foreign nation that has a promising political and economic environment, **direct ownership** of a foreign subsidiary or division is a possibility. Although most discussions of foreign investment concern only manufacturing equipment or personnel, the expenses of

44. Margaret H. Cunningham, "Marketing's New Frontier: International Strategic Alliances," working paper, Queens University (Ontario), 1990.

45. John E. Stiner, "The Future of the Export Trading Company Act," *Business America,* Oct. 12, 1987, pp. 3–9.

FIGURE 23.9

Example of a multinational enterprise.
Opel is the product of General Motors' direct ownership of a foreign subsidiary.

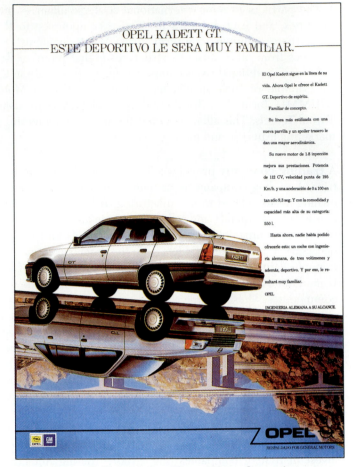

SOURCE: Reprinted with permission of General Motors Corporation

developing a separate foreign distribution system can be tremendous. The opening of retail stores in Europe, Canada, or Mexico can require a large financial investment in facilities, research, and management.

The term **multinational enterprise** refers to firms that have operations or subsidiaries located in many countries. Often the parent firm is based in one country, and it cultivates production, management, and marketing activities in other countries. The firm's subsidiaries may be quite autonomous in order to respond to the needs of individual international markets. Firms such as General Motors, Du Pont, Citicorp, and ITT are multinational companies with worldwide operations (see Figure 23.9). Table 23.4 lists the twenty largest multinationals. Look at the contribution of foreign profit as a percentage of total profit to see how important international involvement can be. Many of these firms could not operate at an acceptable profit without their foreign subsidiaries.

A wholly owned foreign subsidiary may be allowed to operate independently of the parent company so that its management can have more freedom to adjust to the local environment. Cooperative arrangements are developed to assist in marketing

TABLE 23.4
*The Twenty Largest U.S.
Multinationals*

1988 RANK	COMPANY	FOREIGN REVENUE (MILLIONS)	TOTAL REVENUE (MILLIONS)	FOREIGN REVENUE AS PERCENT OF TOTAL
1	Exxon	$ 48,192	67,292	71.6%
2	Ford Motor	41,842	92,446	45.3
3	IBM	34,361	59,681	57.6
4	Mobil	33,039	49,237	67.1
5	General Motors	29,128	120,338	24.2
6	Citicorp	16,451	32,024	51.4
7	Texaco	16,325	33,544	48.7
8	E.I. du Pont de Nemours	12,896	32,917	39.2
9	ITT	10,419	24,239	43.0
10	Dow Chemical	9,185	16,682	55.1
11	Procter & Gamble	7,294	19,336	37.7
12	Eastman Kodak	7,010	17,034	41.2
13	Chase Manhattan	6,080	12,365	49.2
14	Xerox	5,739	16,441	34.9
15	Digital Equipment	5,665	11,475	49.4
16	United Technologies	5,279	18,518	28.5
17	Chevron	5,264	25,196	20.9
18	Philip Morris	5,258	25,920	20.3
19	Hewlett-Packard	5,068	9,831	51.6
20	American International Group	4,979	13,613	36.6

SOURCE: Excerpted by permission of *Forbes* magazine, July 24, 1989. © Forbes Inc. 1989.

efforts, production, and management. A wholly owned foreign subsidiary may export products to the home nation. Some American automobile manufacturers, for example, import cars built by their foreign subsidiaries. A foreign subsidiary offers important tax, tariff, and other operating advantages. One of the greatest advantages is the cross-cultural approach. A subsidiary usually operates under foreign management, so that it can develop a local identity. The greatest danger in such an arrangement comes from political uncertainty: a firm may lose its foreign investment.

SUMMARY

Marketing activities performed across national boundaries are usually significantly different from domestic marketing activities. International marketers must have a profound awareness of the foreign environment. The marketing strategy ordinarily is adjusted to meet the needs and desires of foreign markets.

The level of involvement in international marketing can range from casual exporting to globalization of markets. Although most firms adjust their marketing mixes for differences in target markets, some firms are able to standardize their marketing efforts worldwide. Traditional full-scale international marketing involvement is based on products customized according to cultural, regional, and national differences. Globalization, however, involves developing marketing strategies as if the entire world (or regions of it) were a single entity; a globalized firm markets standardized products in the same way everywhere.

Marketers must rely on international marketing intelligence to understand the complexities of the international marketing environment before they can formulate a marketing mix. Therefore, they collect and analyze secondary data and primary data about international markets.

Environmental aspects of special importance include cultural, social, economic, political, and legal forces. Cultural aspects of the environment that are most important to international marketers include customs, concepts, values, attitudes, morals, and knowledge. Marketing activities are primarily social in purpose; therefore they are structured by the institutions of family, religion, education, health, and recreation. The most prominent economic forces that affect international marketing are those that can be measured by income and resources. Credit, buying power, and income distribution are aggregate measures of market potential. Political and legal forces include the political system, national laws, regulatory bodies, national pressure groups, and courts. Foreign policies of all nations involved in trade determine how marketing can be conducted. The level of technology helps define economic development within a nation and indicates the existence of methods to facilitate marketing.

Various regional trade alliances and specific markets are creating difficulties and opportunities for firms, including the United States and Canada trade pact, the *maquiladora* industries of Mexico, the unification of Europe in 1992, the Pacific Rim markets, and changing conditions in Eastern Europe and the Soviet Union.

After a country's environment has been analyzed, marketers must develop a marketing mix and decide whether to adapt product or promotion. There are five possible strategies for adapting product and promotion across national boundaries: (1) keep product and promotion the same worldwide, (2) adapt promotion only, (3) adapt product only, (4) adapt both product and promotion, and (5) invent new products. Foreign distribution channels are nearly always different from domestic ones. The allocation of costs, transportation considerations, or the costs of doing business in foreign nations will affect pricing.

There are several ways of getting involved in international marketing. Exporting is the easiest and most flexible method. Licensing is an alternative to direct investment; it may be necessitated by political and economic conditions. Joint ventures and strategic alliances are often appropriate when outside resources are needed, when there are governmental restrictions on foreign ownership, or when changes in global markets encourage competitive consolidation. Trading companies are experts at buying products in the domestic market and selling to foreign markets, thereby taking most of the risk in international involvement. Direct ownership of foreign divisions or subsidiaries is the strongest commitment to international marketing and involves the greatest risk. When a company has operations or subsidiaries located in many countries, it is termed a multinational enterprise.

Important Terms

International marketing
Globalization
Gross national product (GNP)
Dumping
Licensing

Joint venture
Strategic alliances
Trading company
Direct ownership
Multinational enterprise

Discussion and Review Questions

1. How does international marketing differ from domestic marketing?
2. What must marketers consider before deciding whether to become involved in international marketing?
3. Why are the largest industrial corporations in the United States so committed to international marketing?
4. Why was so much of this chapter devoted to an analysis of the international marketing environment?
5. A manufacturer recently exported peanut butter with a green label to a nation in the Far East. The product failed because it was associated with jungle sickness. How could this mistake have been avoided?
6. Relate the concept of reference groups (Chapter 4) to international marketing.
7. How do religious systems influence marketing activities in foreign countries?
8. Which is more important to international marketers, a country's aggregate GNP or its GNP per capita? Why?
9. If you were asked to provide a small tip (or bribe) to have a document approved in a foreign nation where this practice was customary, what would you do?
10. In marketing dog food to Latin America, what aspects of the marketing mix need to be altered?
11. What should marketers consider as they decide whether to license or to enter into a joint venture in a foreign nation?
12. Discuss the impact of strategic alliances on marketing strategies.

■ Cases

23.1 Porsche AG

Founded in 1930 by Dr. Ferdinand Porsche, the company known today as Porsche AG began as a research and development firm. The original company accepted contracts from individuals and firms to design new automobiles, airplanes, and ships. The company built prototypes of each design and thoroughly tested them. If the firm that commissioned the work approved the design, the product was then produced by one of the large manufacturing companies in Germany. After World War II, the Porsche family experienced a period of hardship, disappointment, and personal tragedy. Porsche's son, Dr. Ferry Porsche, began a company to manufacture family-designed sports cars in 1948. Despite depressed economic conditions, the company persevered and prospered. By 1973, Porsche AG had built and sold some 200,000 Porsche automobiles, gaining world recognition for its cars and their promise of "driving in its purest form."

Porsche today is organized into three divisions located in three suburbs of Stuttgart: the factory, in Zuffenhausen; testing, engineering, and design, in Weissach; and marketing, in Ludwigsburg. The Porsche Research and Development Center has produced the 959 race car, an aircraft engine, the TAG motor, and designs for ambulances, mobile surgery units, gliders, fire engines, and fork-lift trucks. The company holds more than two thousand patents, and innovations developed by Porsche are in several manufacturers' car models.

The popularity of Porsche cars stems from their reputation for outstanding performance. Not only are the cars produced in a painstaking fashion, but Porsche AG also takes maintenance and repair very seriously. Porsche mechanics receive five days of classroom instruction each year at the Porsche marketing center in Ludwigsburg, more training than any other car company provides. Until 1984, U.S. Porsche mechanics also flew to Germany for training, but now they receive instruction at Porsche training centers at home. In its advertising, the company encourages customers to rely only on Porsche experts for their cars' repair and maintenance of their cars to prevent the customers from having unsatisfactory experiences with unqualified mechanics. This action further differentiates Porsche automobiles from the competition.

Despite Porsche's reputation for excellence, the company has fallen on hard times. It was forced to raise prices on cars sold in the U.S. because of changes in the dollar-market exchange rate. Because of the price increases, a weakening U.S. dollar, and lower-priced Japanese imitations, sales in the United States dropped significantly in 1988. Roughly 60 percent of all Porsches are sold in the United States. Production in 1988 dropped from the record levels in 1986–1987 (more than fifty thousand cars). This overdependence on the U.S. market caused the firm to implement an austerity program. The program includes lowering production output, reducing costs (lower dividends and fewer employees), revamping all three model lines, and pulling out of the lower end of the luxury car market. The company is also trying to enter new markets, including Spain and Japan, to boost sales and increase profits.

Porsche is successful in markets where the social climate favors people who want to demonstrate their success and the economic climate is conducive to the entrepreneur. Porsche management believes that its customers have high personal goals and a drive to achieve, do not like to compromise, and give their best efforts every time. Although not averse to risk, they prepare thoroughly for new ventures. Porsche customers are goers and doers, but not showoffs. To succeed, Porsche AG must exhibit some of its customers' traits. Customers must be able to identify with the firm, to see in the company the same characteristics they see in themselves.

Questions for Discussion

1. Evaluate international marketing opportunities for Porsche AG. What are the company's strengths and weaknesses?
2. What obstacles must Porsche overcome to be successful selling Porsche automobiles in the United States?
3. What is the role of diversification in the Porsche AG corporate strategy?

SOURCES: Joseph M. Callahan and Lance A. Ealey, "Porsche's Schutz Reveals U.S. Marketing Plans," *Industries,* March 1985, p. 50; Gred V. Guterl, John Dornberg, and Kevin Sullivan, "Three to Get Ready," *Business Month,* March 1988, pp. 42–50; "It Shortens the Path," *Christophorous,* August 1984; Maria Kielmas, "Stalled Porsche: But Is There a U-Turn in Its Future?" *Barron's,* June 27, 1988, pp. 14–15, 37; Ron Lewald, "Porsche's U.S. Backfire," *International Management,* April 1988, pp. 42–45; Richard Morais, "What Price Excellence?" *Forbes,* Nov. 17, 1986, p. 234; *Plan Your Success,* 2nd ed. (Stuttgart: *Dr. Ing. h.c. Ferry Porsche,* 1985), pp. 1, 3; *Dr. Ing. h.c. Ferry Porsche* and John Bentley, *We at Porsche* (Garden City, N.Y.: Doubleday, 1976), p. 263; "Porsche," *Ward's Auto World,* January 1985, pp. 52–53; *Porsche Brochure for Distribution,* Stuttgart: *Dr. Ing. h.c. F. Porsche AG,* 1984; John A. Russell, "Porsche Puts High Value on Its People, Schutz Says," *Automotive News,* Aug. 4, 1986, p. 64; Gail Schares and Mark Maremont, "Jaguar and Porsche Try to Pull Out of the Slow Lane," *Business Week,* Dec. 12, 1988, pp. 84–85; Peter Schutz and Jack Cook, "Porsche and Nichemanship," *Harvard Business Review,* March-April 1986, pp. 98–106; and Jesse Snyder, "Porsche Looks for New Brand to Sell in U.S.," *Automotive News,* Dec. 15, 1986, p. 1.

23.2 Parker Pen's Globalization Strategy

When Parker Pen Company decided to launch a global marketing strategy several years ago, some observers were puzzled. Although Parker's name was well-known, the Wisconsin-based company brought limited resources to the task. Annual sales of Parker writing instruments had never exceeded $225 million, and the company had never budgeted more than $20 million a year for advertising. Still, Parker's high-quality products were sold in 154 countries, and its marketing executives were eager to design and implement a global strategy for Parker Pen. In their view, cultural and competitive similarities would be more important than differences, meaning that the same product could be sold the same way in many different markets, and with much lower marketing costs. They believed, in short, that Parker Pen would provide a classic test of global marketing theory.

Parker's then president, James Peterson, also believed that global marketing would be crucial to the survival of the faltering company. The company's weaknesses had been obscured for years by strong overseas sales and a weak U.S. dollar. At home, not only were competitors introducing mass-marketed, disposable pens, but even as Parker attempted to guard its reputation for quality, the company was losing its share of the domestic expensive-pen market to A. T. Cross Company and Sheaffer Eaton. Furthermore, Parker's manufacturing process was inefficient. New-product development had been neglected; and advertising worldwide, which had been left to local marketers, was handled by more than forty different agencies. Profits were plunging, and most of the profits were generated by Manpower Temporary Services, a subsidiary of Parker Pen.

Peterson's first move was to streamline Parker's operations by cutting the payroll by half, reducing the product line from 500 different writing instruments to 100, and spending $20 million to upgrade Parker's manufacturing facilities. Then Peterson and his marketing team embarked on a two-pronged program with far-reaching consequences. They began production of cheap pens that could compete in the under-$3 market, and they standardized everything associated with Parker products under a "global umbrella." From then on, all packaging and point-of-sale display materials would use the same striking black motif. The advertising budget would be centralized, and one advertising agency would handle accounts worldwide. A single theme—"Make your mark with a Parker"—would be used for all products and in all markets, and advertisements would feature the same graphics, photography, and typefaces; only the languages of the copy would vary. In addition, advertising would spotlight Parker's new, inexpensive products instead of the quality pens that were the company's trademark.

These two decisions—to produce cheap pens and to use a uniform marketing strategy for all Parker products—were eventually considered major blunders by many inside Parker Pen. Long-time Parker Pen employees objected that the lower-quality pens ran counter to Parker's carefully nurtured status image. Parker's European managers argued that advertising should take into account the differences among markets.

However, Parker's new management insisted that the company's future lay in high-tech, high-volume production of cheap pens for a global market, and implementation of the new strategy proceeded. At first, sales of the new roller-ball pen and other writing instruments increased. Then, just as demand was picking up, the automated production line began to shut down—repeatedly. Parker employees were forced to return to the assembly lines to take over for the malfunctioning systems. The defect rate soared, and before the problems were resolved, the marketing division set aside strategies and forecasts and sold whatever products were available.

A few months later, the global advertising campaign was launched. In accordance with the "one product, one market" policy, advertisements for different markets had identical layout, illustrations, and text; only the languages in which they were written were different. Because the theme was so general, the advertisements appealed to no one in particular, especially not to those buyers who viewed writing instruments as status symbols. Resentment against the global marketing strategy mounted within the company, and when the failure of the advertising campaign could no longer be ignored, Peterson resigned, followed by his hand-picked marketing executives. The pen business suffered a $500,000 loss and was purchased in 1986 by a group of Parker's international managers and a British venture capital company.

Now based in Newhaven, England, Parker Pen Ltd. is a profitable company, with 1988 pretax profits of $38 million. Although the reorganized firm uses the now-functioning Wisconsin plant and owes some of its success to the greater operating efficiency the former management brought about, the new owners have instituted several policies of their own. Parker's inexpensive pens receive less emphasis in advertising, and plans to produce disposable pens were dropped. The company is working to restore its reputation for quality and reliability. It intends to add perceived value, rather than volume, to its products. In addition, except for the marketing of the company's Duofold Centennial model, a $312 18-carat goldnib fountain pen targeted to a tiny market segment, global advertising has been abandoned.

SOURCES: Leigh Bruce, "Parker Pen's Script for Recovery," *International Management*, Dec. 1986, p. 43; Kevin Cote, "Parker Pen Finds Black Ink," *Advertising Age*, July 13, 1987, p. 49; Lori Kesler, "Marketing to the Affluent: Parker Rebuilds a Quality Image," *Advertising Age*, Mar. 21, 1988, p. S12; John Marcom, Jr., "Pennmanship With a Flourish," *Forbes*, Apr. 3, 1989, pp. 152, 154; David O'Reilly, "The Write Approach," *Marketing*, May 21, 1987, pp. 22–23; and Joseph M. Winski and Laurel Wentz, "Parker Pen: What Went Wrong?," *Advertising Age*, June 2, 1986, p. 1.

Questions for Discussion

1. Are some products more susceptible to successful marketing through a global marketing approach than others? Explain your answer.
2. Specifically, are writing instruments among the products that can be effectively marketed through global marketing? Why or why not?
3. Evaluate Parker Pen's decision to compete in the under-$3 market.

Federal Express Expands Services Internationally

Frederick W. Smith founded Federal Express Corp. in 1973 with part of an $8 million inheritance. At the time, the U.S. Postal Service and United Parcel Service (UPS) were the only means for delivering letters and packages, and they often took several days or more to get packages to their destinations. While a student at Yale in 1965, Smith wrote a paper proposing an independent overnight-delivery service. Although he got a C on the paper, he did not lose sight of his vision. Smith recognized that in today's high-tech world, time is money, and he believed that many businesses would be willing to pay more to get letters, documents, and packages delivered overnight. He was right.

Federal Express began shipping packages overnight from Memphis, Tennessee, on April 17, 1973. On that first night of operations, the company handled six packages, one of which was a birthday present sent by F.W. Smith himself. Today Federal Express has more than $5 billion in revenues and handles more than half of all the overnight package and document transactions within the United States. According to the company, Federal Express does not just transport packages anywhere in the United States and to much of the rest of the world; it moves *information* for both consumers and industrial customers.

Federal Express offers a valuable service to businesspeople who need letters, documents, and packages delivered overnight. When a customer needs a package shipped, Federal Express sends a courier to pick up the package and take it to a Federal Express office, from where it is trucked to the nearest airport. The package is usually flown to the company's Memphis superhub for sorting and then flown to the airport nearest its destination. The package is then trucked to another Federal Express office, where a courier picks it up and hand delivers it to the correct recipient. All this takes place overnight: many packages are delivered before 10:30 A.M. the next day. Couriers use handheld computers to keep track of packages. Federal Express confirms that more than 98 percent of its deliveries are made on time.

Federal Express has tens of thousands of drop boxes in the United States, and 1,500 service centers and airport facilities around the world. It owns a fleet of over 350 airplanes and 29,000 trucks and vans for handling delivery. The company even has its own weather forecasting service, ensuring that most of its flights arrive within fifteen minutes of schedule. Most packages are sorted at the Memphis superhub (in the middle of the night), but other packages and documents are trucked directly to their destination whenever convenient. For international deliveries to the United Kingdom, West Germany, Spain, and one hundred other countries, Federal Express uses a combination of direct services and independent contractors.

Promotion, Pricing, and Competition

As with other services, promotion of Federal Express' delivery service is difficult because of its intangible nature. Federal Express promotes its service, convenience, efficiency, price, and customer service. Its ongoing campaign, "When it absolutely,

FIGURE 1

Market shares of domestic air-cargo shipments, 1988

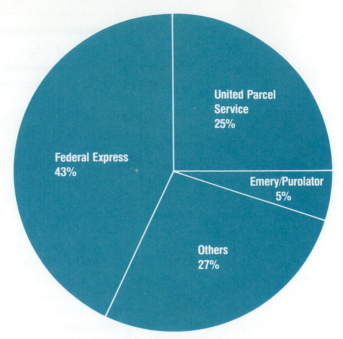

United Parcel Service 25%

Federal Express 43%

Emery/Purolator 5%

Others 27%

SOURCE: Copyright, Oct. 2, 1989, *U.S. News & World Report.*

positively, has to be there overnight," appealed to businesspeople and was one of the most successful slogans in the service industry. When Federal Express began opening service centers all over the United States, it promoted each one with a huge grand opening celebration, complete with direct mail invitations, radio remotes, and door prizes. It reinforced this promotion with excellent customer relations. In a 1985 campaign to highlight the company's international service, Federal Express used point-of-sale materials and gave a World Atlas to each new customer making an international shipment. The international campaign boosted international volume in the service centers 46 percent.

Because Federal Express depends on its employees to promote its service, the company hires the best people it can and offers them the best training and compensation possible. As a result, Federal Express employees are loyal and have very high levels of service and efficiency.

Federal Express charges $15 for delivery of its Overnight Letter packages before 10:30 the next morning. Prices vary for larger packages and international shipments. Customers can save $3 by dropping packages off at a Federal Express office instead of having a courier pick it up. They can save more money by using the company's new Standard Overnight Service, which offers next-day afternoon delivery at a cost of $11.25 ($8.25 if dropped off) for letter packages. Although the U.S. Postal Service currently charges $8.75 for its Express Mail delivery service and the United Parcel Service charges $8.50 for its overnight letter delivery, Federal Express believes it offers customers more service and efficiency for its price.

Despite offering a vital service and having motivated employees and successful promotions, Federal Express faces a maturing market for its services. Figures 1 and 2 indicate that competition is squeezing the company's profits. The company that created the overnight delivery service now faces intense competition from the U.S. Postal Service, United Parcel Service, and electronic mail (facsimile machines and

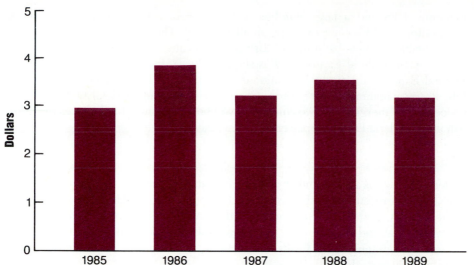

SOURCE: Federal Express Corp. *1989 Annual Report*. Federal Express Corp. 2005 Corporate Avenue, Memphis, Tennessee 38132.

FIGURE 2
Federal Express net income per share, in dollars from continuing operations, year's end May 31

computer links). Many companies that once sent important documents overnight via Federal Express now fax those documents or send them via computer modem. Federal Express's own experiment in electronic mail service, ZapMail, was abandoned after only three years because it was never profitable. Some experts believe that Federal Express could lose as much as 30 percent of its letter business to electronic mail. Moreover, the intense competition among air express companies has cut Federal's operating profit to 8.2 percent in 1989.

Expanding International Operations

Dropping ZapMail allowed Federal Express to focus on expanding its overseas operations, the most rapidly growing area of the overnight market. Because of the globalization of the economy, businesses need to be able to communicate quickly with employees around the world, with partners in other nations, and with other businesses. Thus Federal Express began international operations in 1975 with shipments to and from the United States' biggest trading partner, Canada. In 1984, Federal Express bought Gelco International, enabling it to start operations in Europe and the Far East. Federal Express was also named the official air express carrier for the 1988 Olympic Games in Seoul, a designation that the company used in promotions. In 1990, the company offered service to one hundred countries.

Federal Express's most important strategic move into international markets to date was its 1988 purchase of Tiger International Inc., the owner of the Flying Tiger Line air freight service, for $880 million. The purchase gave Federal Express valuable routes, airport facilities, and expertise in European and Asian markets which it had been struggling to enter. Such valuable assets would have taken Federal Express years to develop on its own. The purchase also gave Federal valuable landing slots in Sydney, Singapore, Bangkok, Hong Kong, Seoul, Paris, Brussels, and Tokyo.

The purchase of Tiger has created some problems for Federal Express. The purchase left the company with a debt of $2.1 billion. It also thrust the company into the heavy-freight distribution market, which is more cyclical and capital intensive than small-package distribution. In addition, many of Tiger's key customers, including UPS and a large number of freight forwarders, are Federal Express competitors, and they are unhappy about the deal. The new Federal Express may lose valuable business from freight forwarders because they will be shut out of the market when Federal Express begins shipping heavy freight door to door. Finally, Federal Express inherited 6,500 union employees from Tiger, which it must weave into its own nonunion work force. Chairman, president, and CEO Fred Smith concedes that merging the two companies will be a challenge, but believes the effort will make Federal Express a powerful global delivery service.

The Future

Federal Express is also counting on the current trend of just-in-time inventory to help boost its revenues. With its sophisticated computer tracking system and overnight delivery, Federal actually manages the inventories of some customers at its Memphis, Oakland (California), and Newark hubs. IBM, for example, employs Federal to warehouse parts for its workstations, enabling it to cut its delivery costs and close 120 parts depots.

In an effort to retain its leading market share, Federal Express has entered UPS's traditional turf: loading-dock deliveries. The company has expanded its two-day ground delivery service of heavy packages and plans to add still more trucks and vans. If necessary, Smith says the company will cut its prices to compete with UPS, Airborne Express, DHL, and other air express companies. Federal Express also plans to shift its emphasis from letters to packages, which generate higher profits.

Federal Express continues to try to improve its services through more sophisticated computers and customer relations and further overseas expansion. The company has been highly successful because it recognized a need—overnight delivery of important letters and packages—and it filled that need. There is no doubt Fred Smith's C paper has become an indispensable part of the world of business.

Questions for Discussion

1. Federal Express is an international firm that provides a service for industrial customers. How does the Federal Express marketing strategy permit effective competition with other overnight delivery companies?
2. What challenges does Federal Express face in maintaining a 50 percent share of the overnight delivery market?

SOURCES: 1989 Federal Express Corp. *Annual Report*; Greg Clarkin, "Overnight Delivery; Consolidation Looms, Fax Threatens," *Adweek's Marketing Week*, Sept. 12, 1988, p. F.P. 75; Dean Foust, with Jonathan Kapstein, Pia Farrell, Peter Finch, and Chris Power, "Mr. Smith Goes Global," *Business Week*, Feb. 13, 1989, pp. 66–72; Dean Foust, with Resa W. King, "Why Federal Express Has Overnight Anxiety," *Business Week*, Nov. 9, 1987, pp. 62, 66; "The History," fact sheet provided by Federal Express, 1988; Larry Reibstein, "Federal Express Faces Challenges to Its Grip on Overnight Delivery," *Wall Street Journal*, Jan. 8, 1988, pp. 1, 8; "The Rise and Fall of ZapMail: A Postmortem," case prepared by George Lucas, Memphis State University, 1988; Glenn Ruffenach, "Federal Express Earnings Plunge 79% But Firm, Some Others See Turnaround," *Wall Street Journal*, March 20, 1990, p. A3; Carl Williams, "The Challenge of Retail Marketing at Federal Express," *Journal of Services Marketing*, Summer 1987, pp. 25–38; Clemens P. Work, "The Flying-Package Trade Takes off," *U.S. News & World Report*, Oct. 2, 1989, pp. 47, 50.

A CAREERS IN MARKETING

SOME GENERAL ISSUES

As we note in Chapter 1, between one-fourth and one-third of the civilian work force in the United States is employed in marketing-related jobs. Although there obviously are a multitude of diverse career opportunities in the field, the number of positions in its different areas varies. For example, millions of workers are employed in many facets of sales, but relatively few people work in public relations and marketing research.

Many nonbusiness organizations now recognize that they do, in fact, perform marketing activities. For that reason, marketing positions are increasing in government agencies, hospitals, charitable and religious groups, educational institutions, and similar organizations.

Even though financial reward is not the sole criterion for selecting a career, it is only practical to consider how much you might earn in a marketing job. Table A.1 illustrates top ten salary positions for middle managers in marketing. Note that all these careers relate directly to marketing. A national sales manager may earn $60,000 to $100,000 or an even higher salary. Brand managers make $35,000 to $60,000. A media manager could earn $30,000 to $55,000. Generally, entry-level marketing personnel earn more than their counterparts in economics and liberal arts but not as much as people who enter accounting, chemistry, or engineering positions. Starting salaries for marketing graduates averaged $20,844, according to the 1988 College Placement Council Salary Survey. Marketers who advance to higher-level positions often earn high salaries, and a significant proportion of corporate executives held marketing jobs before attaining top-level positions.

Another important issue is whether you can enjoy the work associated with a particular career. Because you will spend almost 40 percent of your waking hours on the job, you should not allow such factors as economic conditions or status to override your personal goals as you select a lifelong career. Too often, people do not weigh these factors realistically. You should give considerable thought to your choice of a career, and you should adopt a well-planned, systematic approach to finding a position that meets your personal and career objectives.

TABLE A.1
Top salary ranges for middle managers in marketing

POSITION	SALARY RANGE
National sales manager	$60,000– $100,000
Corporate strategic market planner	$55,000– 75,000
International sales	50,000– 75,000
Advertising account supervisor	40,000– 70,000
Distribution manager	40,000– 60,000
Sales promotion manager	40,000– 55,000
Product/brand manager	35,000– 60,000
Purchasing manager	35,000– 55,000
Media manager	30,000– 55,000
Retail manager	25,000– 45,000

After determining your objectives, you should identify the organizations that are likely to offer desirable opportunities. Learn as much as possible about these organizations before setting up employment interviews; job recruiters are impressed with applicants who have done their homework.

When making initial contact with potential employers by mail, enclose a brief, clearly written letter of introduction. After an initial interview, you should send a brief letter of thanks to the interviewer. The job of getting the right job is important, and you owe it to yourself to take this process seriously.

THE RÉSUMÉ

The résumé is one of the keys to being considered for a good job. Because it states your qualifications, experiences, education, and career goals, the résumé is a chance for a potential employer to assess your compatibility with the job requirements. For the employer's and individual's benefit, the résumé should be accurate and current.

To be effective, the résumé can be targeted toward a specific position, as Figure A.1 shows. This document is only one example of an acceptable résumé. The job target section is specific and leads directly to the applicant's qualifications for the job. Capabilities show what the applicant can do and that the person has an understanding of the job's requirements. Skills and strengths should be highlighted as to how they relate to the specific job. The achievement section indicates success at accomplishing tasks or goals within the job market and at school. The work experience section includes educational background, which adds credibility to the résumé but is not the major area of focus; the applicant's ability to function successfully in a specific job is the major emphasis.

Common suggestions for improving résumés include deleting useless information, improving organization, using professional printing and typing, listing duties (not accomplishments), maintaining grammatical perfection, and avoiding an overly elaborate or fancy format.[1] One of the biggest problems in résumés, according to a

1. T. Jackson, "Writing the Targeted Resume," *Business Week's Guide to Careers,* Spring 1983, pp. 26–27.

FIGURE A.I
A résumé targeted
toward a specific
position

```
                          LORRAINE MILLER
                          2212 WEST WILLOW
                           (416) 862-9169


EDUCATION:  B.A. Arizona State University  1987  Marketing

POSITION DESIRED:  PRODUCT MANAGER WITH AN INTERNATIONAL FIRM PROVIDING FUTURE
                   CAREER DEVELOPMENT AT THE EXECUTIVE LEVEL.

QUALIFICATIONS:

  * communicates well with individuals to achieve a common goal

  * handles tasks efficiently and in a timely manner

  * knowledge of advertising, sales, management, marketing research, packaging, pricing,
    distribution, and warehousing

  * coordinates many activities at one time

  * receives and carries out assigned tasks or directives

  * writes complete status or research reports

EXPERIENCES:

  * Assistant Editor of college paper

  * Treasurer of the American Marketing Association (student chapter)

  * Internship with 3-Cs Advertising, Berkeley, CA

  * Student Assistantship with Dr. Steve Green, Professor of Marketing, Arizona State University

  * Achieved 3.6 average on a 4.0 scale throughout college

WORK RECORD:

1984 – Present          Blythe and Co., Inc.
                          * Junior Advertising Account Executive

1982 – Present          Assistantship with Dr. Steve Green
                          * Research Assistant

1980 – 1982             The Men
                          * Retail sales and consumer relations

1976 – 1980             Tannenbaum Trees, Inc.
                          * Laborer
```

survey of personnel experts, is distortions and lies; 36 percent of the experts thought that this was a major problem.[2] People lie most often about previous salaries and tasks performed in former jobs.

TYPES OF MARKETING CAREERS

In considering marketing as a career, the first step is to evaluate broad categories of career opportunities in the areas of marketing research, sales, public relations, industrial buying, distribution management, product management, advertising, retail management, and direct marketing. Keep in mind that the categories described here are not all-inclusive and that each encompasses hundreds of marketing jobs.

2. Burke Marketing Research for Robert Hall Inc. Reported in *USA Today,* Oct. 2, 1987, p. B–1.

■ Marketing Research

Clearly, marketing research and information systems are vital aspects of marketing decision making. Marketing researchers spend more than $1 billion each year surveying Americans to determine their habits, preferences, and aspirations.[3] The information about buyers and environmental forces that research and information systems provide improves a marketer's ability to understand the dynamics of the marketplace and make effective decisions.

Marketing researchers gather and analyze data relating to specific problems. Marketing research firms are usually employed by a client organization, which could be a provider of goods or services, a nonbusiness organization, the government, a research consulting firm, or an advertising agency. The activities performed include concept testing, product testing, package testing, advertising testing, test-market research, and new-product research.

A researcher may be involved in one or several stages of research, depending on the size of the project, the organization of the research unit, and the researcher's experience. Marketing research trainees in large organizations usually perform a considerable amount of clerical work, such as compiling secondary data from a firm's accounting and sales records and periodicals, government publications, syndicated data services, and unpublished sources. A junior analyst may edit and code questionnaires or tabulate survey results. Trainees also may participate in primary data gathering by learning to conduct mail and telephone surveys, conducting personal interviews, and using observational methods of primary data collection. As a marketing researcher gains experience, the researcher may become involved in defining problems and developing hypotheses; designing research procedures; and analyzing, interpreting, and reporting findings. Exceptional personnel may assume responsibility for entire research projects.

Although most employers consider a bachelor's degree sufficient qualification for a marketing research trainee, many specialized positions require a graduate degree in business administration, statistics, or other related fields. Today, trainees are more likely to have a marketing or statistics degree than a liberal arts degree. Also, trainees who are capable of immediate productivity and more complex tasks are more desirable.[4] Courses in statistics, data processing, psychology, sociology, communications, economics, and English composition are valuable preparations for a career in marketing research.

The U.S. Bureau of Labor Statistics indicates that marketing research provides abundant employment opportunity, especially for applicants with graduate training in marketing research, statistics, economics, and the social sciences. Generally, the value of information gathered by marketing information and research systems will become more important as competition increases, thus expanding the opportunities for prospective marketing research personnel.

The three major career paths in marketing research are with independent marketing research agencies/data suppliers, advertising agency marketing research departments, and marketing research departments in businesses. In a company in which marketing research plays a key role, the researcher is often a member of the marketing strategy team. Surveying or interviewing consumers is the heart of the marketing research firm's activities. A statistician selects the sample to be surveyed, analysts design the questionnaire and synthesize the gathered data into a final

3. Judith George, "Market Researcher," *Business Week Careers,* October 1987, p. 10.

4. Marcia Fleschner, "Evolution of Research Takes the Profession to New Heights," *Collegiate Edition Marketing News,* March 1986, p. 1.

report, data processors tabulate the data, and the research director controls and coordinates all these activities so that each project is computed to the client's satisfaction (i.e., consumer and industrial product manufacturers).[5] In marketing research agencies, a researcher deals with many clients, products, and problems. Advertising agencies use research as an ingredient in developing and refining campaigns for existing or potentially new clients.[6]

Salaries in marketing research depend on the type, size, and location of the firm as well as the nature of the positions. Generally, starting salaries are somewhat higher and promotions somewhat slower than in other occupations requiring similar training. Typical starting salaries are $21,000 to $25,000 per year. Salaries range from $14,000 to $18,000 for a junior analyst, $35,000 or more for a senior analyst, and research directors often earn salaries of more than $60,000. In addition, the role of marketing in overall corporate planning is becoming more important as companies seek marketing information for strategic planning purposes. Marketing research directors are reporting to higher levels of management than ever before, and the number of corporate vice presidents who receive marketing research as regular input in decision making has doubled in recent years.

■ Sales

Millions of people earn a living through personal selling. Chapter 13 defines personal selling as a process of informing customers and persuading them to purchase products through personal communication in an exchange situation. Although this definition describes the general nature of many sales positions, individual selling jobs vary enormously with respect to the type of businesses and products involved, the educational background and skills required, and the specific activities sales personnel perform. Because the work is so varied, sales occupations offer numerous career opportunities for people with a wide range of qualifications, interests, and goals. A sales career offers the greatest potential compensation. The following two sections describe what is involved in wholesale and manufacturer sales.

Wholesale Sales   Wholesalers perform activities to expedite transactions in which purchases are intended for resale or to be used to make other products. Wholesalers thus provide services to both retailers and producers. They can help match producers' products to retailers' needs and can provide accumulation and allocation services that save producers time, money, and resources. Some activities associated with wholesaling include planning and negotiating transactions; assisting customers with sales, advertising, sales promotion, and publicity; handling transportation and storage activities; providing customers with inventory control and data processing assistance; establishing prices; and giving customers technical, management, and merchandising assistance.

The background wholesale personnel need depends on the nature of the product handled. A drug wholesaler, for example, needs extensive technical training and product knowledge and may have a degree in chemistry, biology, or pharmacology. A wholesaler of standard office supplies, on the other hand, may find it more important to be familiar with various brands, suppliers, and prices than to have technical knowledge about the products. A new wholesale representative may begin a career as a sales trainee or hold a nonselling job that provides experience with inventory,

---

5. Judith George, "Market Researcher," *Business Week Careers,* October 1987, p. 10.

6. "What It's Like to Work in Marketing Research Depends on Where You Work—Supplier, Ad Agency, Manufacturer," *Collegiate Edition Marketing News,* December 1985, pp. 1 and 3.

prices, discounts, and the firm's customers. A college graduate usually enters the sales force directly out of school. Competent salespersons also transfer from manufacturer and retail sales positions.

The number of wholesale sales positions is expected to grow about as fast as the average for all occupations. Earnings for wholesale personnel vary widely because commissions often make up a large proportion of their incomes.

Manufacturer Sales   Manufacturer sales personnel sell a firm's products to wholesalers, retailers, and industrial buyers; they thus perform many of the same activities wholesale salespersons handle. As is the case with wholesaling, the educational requirements for manufacturer sales depend largely on the type and complexity of the products and markets. Manufacturers of nontechnical products usually hire college graduates who have a liberal arts or business degree and give them training and information about the firm's products, prices, and customers. Manufacturers of highly technical products generally prefer applicants who have degrees in fields associated with the particular industry and market involved.

More and more sophisticated marketing skills are being utilized in industrial sales. Industrial marketing originally followed the commodity approach to complete a sale, whereby the right product is in the right place at the right time and for the right price. Today industrial sales use the same marketing concepts and strategies as do marketers selling to consumers.

Employment opportunities in manufacturer sales are expected to experience average growth. Manufacturer sales personnel are well compensated and earn above-average salaries. Most are paid a combination of salaries and commissions, and the highest salaries are paid by manufacturers of electrical equipment, food products, and rubber goods. Commissions vary according to the salesperson's efforts, abilities, and sales territory and the type of products sold.

■ Public Relations

Public relations encompasses a broad set of communication activities designed to create and maintain favorable relations between the organization and its publics—customers, employees, stockholders, government officials, and society in general. Public relations specialists help clients both create the image, issue, or message they wish to present and communicate it to the appropriate audience. According to the Public Relations Society of America, 120,000 persons work in public relations in the United States. Half the billings found in the 4,000 public relations agencies and firms come from Chicago and New York. The highest starting salaries can also be found there. Expect the average starting salary to be $15,000 or less but salaries can increase rapidly.[7] Communication is basic to all public relations programs. To communicate effectively, public relations practitioners first must gather data about the firm's client publics to assess their needs, identify problems, formulate recommendations, implement new plans, and evaluate current activities.

Public relations personnel disseminate large amounts of information to the organization's client publics. Written communication is the most versatile tool of public relations, and good writing ability is essential. Public relations practitioners must be adept at writing for a variety of media and audiences. It is not unusual for a person in public relations to prepare reports, news releases, speeches, broadcast

7. Jan Greenberg "Inside Public Relations," *Business Week Careers,* February 1988, pp. 46–48.

scripts, technical manuals, employee publications, shareholder reports, and other communications aimed at both organizational personnel and external groups. In addition, a public relations practitioner needs a thorough knowledge of the production techniques used in preparing various communications.

Public relations personnel also establish distribution channels for the organization's publicity. They must have a thorough understanding of the various media, their areas of specialization, the characteristics of their target audiences, and their policies regarding publicity. Anyone who hopes to succeed in public relations must develop close working relationships with numerous media personnel to enlist their interest in disseminating an organization's communications.

A college education combined with writing or media-related experience is the best preparation for a career in public relations. Most beginners have a college degree in journalism, communications, or public relations, but some employers prefer a business background. Courses in journalism, business administration, marketing, creative writing, psychology, sociology, political science, economics, advertising, English, and public speaking are recommended. Some employers require applicants to present a portfolio of published articles, television or radio programs, slide presentations, and other work samples. Other agencies are requiring written tests that include activities such as writing sample press releases. Manufacturing firms, public utilities, transportation and insurance companies, and trade and professional associations are the largest employers of public relations personnel. In addition, sizable numbers of public relations personnel work for health-related organizations, government agencies, educational institutions, museums, and religious and service groups.

Although some larger companies provide extensive formal training for new personnel, most new public relations employees learn on the job. Beginners usually perform routine tasks such as maintaining files about company activities and searching secondary data sources for information that can be used in publicity materials. More experienced employees write press releases, speeches, and articles and help plan public relations campaigns.

Employment opportunities in public relations are expected to increase faster than the average for all occupations through the 1990s. One caveat is in order, however: Competition for beginning jobs is keen. The prospects are best for applicants who have solid academic preparation and some media experience. Areas that are projected to offer the most opportunity are in public relations agencies in the areas of product publicity, mergers and acquisitions, and financial and investor relations.[8] Abilities that differentiate candidates such as a basic understanding of computers are becoming increasingly important.

■ Industrial Buying

Industrial buyers, or purchasing agents, are responsible for maintaining an adequate supply of the goods and services that an organization needs for operations. In general, industrial buyers purchase all items needed for direct use in producing other products and for use in the day-to-day operations. Industrial buyers in large firms often specialize in purchasing a single, specific class of products, for example, all petroleum-based lubricants. In smaller organizations, buyers may be responsible for purchasing many different categories of items, including such goods as raw materials, component parts, office supplies, and operating services.

8. Jan Greenberg, "Inside Public Relations," *Business Week Careers*, February 1988, p. 47.

An industrial buyer's main job is selecting suppliers who offer the best quality, service, and price. When the products to be purchased are standardized, buyers may compare suppliers by examining catalogs and trade journals, making purchases by description. Buyers who purchase highly homogeneous products often meet with salespeople to examine samples and observe demonstrations. Sometimes, buyers must inspect the actual product before purchasing; in other cases, they invite suppliers to bid on large orders. Buyers who purchase specialized equipment often deal directly with manufacturers to obtain specially designed items made to specifications. After choosing a supplier and placing an order, an industrial buyer usually must trace the shipment to ensure on-time delivery. Finally, the buyer sometimes is responsible for receiving and inspecting an order and authorizing payment to the shipper.

Training requirements for a career in industrial buying relate to the needs of the firm and the types of products purchased. A manufacturer of heavy machinery may prefer an applicant who has a background in engineering; a service company, on the other hand, may recruit liberal arts majors. Although it is not generally required, a college degree is becoming increasingly important for buyers who wish to advance to management positions. Entry-level positions are in the $18,000 to $23,000 range.

Employment prospects for industrial buyers are expected to increase faster than average through the 1990s. Opportunities will be excellent for individuals with a master's degree in business administration or a bachelor's degree in engineering, science, or business administration. In addition, companies that manufacture heavy equipment, computer equipment, and communications equipment will need buyers with technical backgrounds.

Distribution Management

A distribution (or traffic) manager arranges for the transportation of goods within firms and through marketing channels. Transportation is an essential distribution activity that permits a firm to create time and place utility for its products. It is the distribution manager's job to analyze various transportation modes and select the combination that minimizes cost and transit time while providing acceptable levels of reliability, capability, accessibility, and security.

To accomplish this task, a distribution manager performs many activities. First, the individual must choose one or a combination of transportation modes from the five major modes available: railways, motor vehicles, inland waterways, pipelines, and airways. Then the distribution manager must select the specific routes the goods will travel and the particular carriers to be used, weighing such factors as freight classifications and regulations, freight charges, time schedules, shipment sizes, and loss and damage ratios. In addition, this person may be responsible for preparing shipping documents, tracing shipments, handling loss and damage claims, keeping records of freight rates, and monitoring changes in government regulations and transportation technology.

Distribution management employs relatively few people and is expected to grow about as fast as the average for all occupations in the near future. Manufacturing firms are the largest employers of distribution managers, although some traffic managers work for wholesalers, retail stores, and consulting firms. Salaries of experienced distribution managers vary but generally are much higher than the average for all nonsupervisory personnel.

Entry-level positions for distribution management are in the $20,000 to $25,000 per year salary range. Starting jobs are diverse, varying from inventory control, traffic scheduling, operations management, or distribution management. Inventory management is an area of great opportunity because many U.S. firms see inventory costs as high relative to foreign competition, especially that from the Japanese. Just-in-time inventory systems are designed by inventory control specialists to work with the bare minimum of inventory.[9]

Most employers prefer graduates of technical programs or seek people who have completed courses in transportation, logistics, distribution management, economics, statistics, computer science, management, marketing, and commercial law. A successful distribution manager must be adept at handling technical data and be able to interpret and communicate highly technical information.

■ Product Management

The product manager occupies a staff position and is responsible for the success or failure of a product line. Product managers coordinate most of the marketing activities required to market a product; however, because they hold a staff position, they have relatively little actual authority over marketing personnel. Even so, they take on a large amount of responsibility and typically are paid quite well relative to other marketing employees. Being a product manager can be rewarding both financially and psychologically, but it can also be frustrating because of the disparity between responsibility and authority.

A product manager should have a general knowledge of advertising, transportation modes, inventory control, selling and sales management, sales promotion, marketing research, packaging, pricing, and warehousing. The individual must be knowledgeable enough to communicate effectively with personnel in these functional areas and to make suggestions and help assess alternatives when major decisions are being made.

Product managers usually need college training in an area of business administration. A master's degree is helpful, although a person usually does not become a product manager directly out of school. Frequently, several years of selling and sales management are prerequisites for a product management position, which often is a major step in the career path of top-level marketing executives. The average salary for an experienced product manager is $35,000 to $60,000.

■ Advertising

Advertising pervades our daily lives. As we detail in Chapter 14, business and nonbusiness organizations use advertising in many ways and for many reasons. Advertising clearly needs individuals with diverse skills to fill a variety of jobs. Creative imagination, artistic talent, and expertise in expression and persuasion are important for copywriters, artists, and account executives. Sales and managerial ability are vital to the success of advertising managers, media buyers, and production managers. Research directors must have a solid understanding of research techniques and human behavior.

Advertising professionals disagree on the most beneficial educational background for a career in advertising. Most employers prefer college graduates. Some employers seek individuals with degrees in advertising, journalism, or business; others prefer graduates with broad liberal arts backgrounds. Still other employers rank relevant work experience above educational background.

9. Nicholas Basta, "Inventory and Distribution," *Business Week's Guide to Careers,* Spring–Summer 1985, p. 23.

"Advertisers look for generalists," says Kate Preston, a staff executive of the American Association of Advertising Agencies, "thus there are just as many economics or general liberal arts majors as M.B.A.s." Common entry-level positions in an advertising agency are found in the traffic department, account service (account coordinator), or in the media department (media assistant). Starting salaries in these positions are often quite low but to gain experience in the advertising industry, employees must work their way up in the system. The entry-level salaries of media assistants and account coordinators are often $15,000 or less.[10]

A variety of organizations employ advertising personnel. Although advertising agencies are perhaps the most visible and glamorous of employers, many manufacturing firms, retail stores, banks, utility companies, and professional and trade associations maintain advertising departments. Advertising jobs also can be found with television and radio stations, newspapers, and magazines. Other businesses that employ advertising personnel include printers, art studios, letter shops, and package-design firms. Specific advertising jobs include advertising manager, account executive, research director, copywriter, media specialist, and production manager.

Employment opportunities for advertising personnel are expected to decrease in the early nineties as agency acquisitions and mergers continue. General economic conditions, however, strongly influence the size of advertising budgets and, hence, employment opportunities.

■ Retail Management

More than 20 million people in the United States work in the retail industry.[11] Although a career in retailing may begin in sales, there is more to retailing than simply selling. Many retail personnel occupy management positions. Besides managing the sales force, they focus on selecting and ordering merchandise, promotional activities, inventory control, customer credit operations, accounting, personnel, and store security.

How retail stores are organized varies. In many large department stores, retail management personnel rarely get involved with actually selling to customers; these duties are performed by retail salespeople. However, other types of retail organizations may require management personnel to perform selling activities from time to time.

Large retail stores offer a variety of management positions besides those at the very top, including assistant buyers, buyers, department managers, section managers, store managers, division managers, regional managers, and vice president of merchandising. The following list describes the general duties of four of these positions; the precise nature of these duties varies from one retail organization to another.

A section manager coordinates inventory and promotions and interacts with buyers, salespeople, and ultimate consumers. The manager performs merchandising, labor relations, and managerial activities and can rarely expect to get away with as little as a forty-hour work week.

The buyer's task is more focused. In this fast-paced occupation, there is much travel, pressure, and need to be open-minded with respect to new and potentially successful items.

10. Vincent Daddiego, "Making It In Advertising," *Business Week Careers*, February 1988, p. 42.

11. Eleanor May, *Future Trends in Retailing* (Cambridge, Mass.: Marketing Science Institute, 1987), p. 1.

The regional manager coordinates the activities of several stores within a given area. Sales, promotions, and procedures in general are monitored and supported.

The vice president of merchandising has a broad scope of managerial responsibility and reports to the president at the top of the organization.

Traditionally, retail managers began their careers as salesclerks. Today, many large retailers hire college-educated people, put them through management training programs, and then place them directly into management positions. They frequently hire people with backgrounds in liberal arts or business administration. Sales and retailing are the greatest employment opportunities for marketing students.

Retail management positions can be exciting and challenging. Competent, ambitious individuals often assume a great deal of responsibility very quickly and advance rapidly. However, compensation programs for entry-level positions (management trainees) have historically been below average. This situation is changing rapidly with major specialty, department, and discount stores offering entry salaries in the $20,000 to $25,000 range. In addition, a retail manager's job is physically demanding and sometimes entails long working hours. Nonetheless, positions in retail management often provide numerous opportunities to excel and advance.

■ Direct Marketing

One of the most dynamic areas in marketing is direct marketing, in which the seller uses one or more direct media (telephone, mail, print, or television) to solicit a response. For example, Shell Oil uses its credit card billings (direct mail) to sell a variety of consumer products.

The telephone is a major vehicle for selling many consumer products, such as magazines. Telemarketing is direct selling to customers using a variety of technological improvements in telephone services; it is an estimated $91 billion a year industry creating jobs in sales, marketing strategy, and marketing technology. According to the American Telemarketing Association (Glenview, Illinois), $73 billion of the industry's sales come from business-to-business marketing, not from selling to consumers at home. In addition, the telemarketing industry has been growing an average of 30 percent per year. Starting salaries in telemarketing are $19,000 to $26,000.[12]

The use of direct mail catalogs appeals to market segments such as working women or people who find going to retail stores difficult or inconvenient. Newspapers and magazines offer great opportunity, especially in special market segments. *Golf Digest*, for example, is obviously a good medium for selling golfing equipment. Cable television provides many new opportunities for selling directly to consumers. Interactive cable will offer a new method to expand direct marketing by developing timely exchange opportunities for consumers.

The volume of goods distributed through direct marketing is a strong indicator of opportunity for careers in this growing area. H. B. Crandall, president of Crandall Associates, New York, stated that job candidates with experience could "write their own ticket." He continued, "People with five years' experience are getting phenomenal salary offers. People with one year's experience are getting offers unheard of in any other marketing field."[13]

12. Nicholas Basta, "Telemarketing," *Business Week's Guide to Careers*, Dec. 1985, p. 27.

13. Kevin Higgins, "Economic Recovery Puts Marketers in Catbird Seat," *Marketing News*, Oct. 14, 1983, pp. 1, 8.

The most important asset in direct marketing is experience. Employers often look to other industries to locate experienced professionals. In a choice between an M.B.A. or an individual with a direct marketing background, the experienced individual would be hired.[14] This preference means that if you can get an entry-level position in direct marketing, you will have a real advantage in developing a career.

Jobs in direct marketing include buyers, such as department store buyers, who select goods for catalog, telephone, or direct mail sales. Catalog managers develop marketing strategies for each new catalog that goes into the mail. Research/mail-list management involves developing lists of products that will sell in direct marketing and lists of names that will respond to a direct mail effort. Order fulfillment managers direct the shipment of products once they are sold. Nearly all nonprofit organizations have fund-raising managers who use direct marketing to obtain financial support.[15]

The executive vice president of the advertising agency Young & Rubicam, Inc. in New York stated that direct marketing will have to be used "not as a tactic, but as a strategic tool."[16] Direct marketing's effectiveness is enhanced by periodic analysis of advertising and communications at all phases of contact with the consumer. Direct marketing involves all aspects of the marketing decision. It is becoming a more professional career area that provides great opportunity.

14. Ibid.

15. Nicholas Basta, "Direct Marketing," *Business Week Careers*, March 1986, p. 52.

16. "Wonderman Urges: Replace Marketing War Muskets with the Authentic Weapon—Direct Marketing," *Marketing News*, July 8, 1983, pp. 1, 12.

B FINANCIAL ANALYSIS IN MARKETING

Our discussion in this book focused more on fundamental concepts and decisions in marketing than on financial details. However, marketers must understand the basic components of selected financial analyses if they are to explain and defend their decisions. In fact, they must be familiar with certain financial analyses if they are to reach good decisions in the first place. We therefore examine three areas of financial analyses: cost-profit aspects of the income statement, selected performance ratios, and price calculations.[1] To control and evaluate marketing activities, marketers must understand the income statement and what it says about the operations of their organization. They also need to be acquainted with performance ratios, which compare current operating results with past results and with results in the industry at large. In the last part of the appendix, we discuss price calculations as the basis of price adjustments. Marketers are likely to use all these areas of financial analysis at various times to support their decisions and to make necessary adjustments in their operations.

THE INCOME STATEMENT

The income, or operating, statement presents the financial results of an organization's operations over a period of time. The statement summarizes revenues earned and expenses incurred by a profit center, whether it is a department, brand, product line, division, or entire firm. The income statement presents the firm's net profit or net loss for a month, quarter, or year.

Table B.1 is a simplified income statement for a retail store. The owners of the store, Rose Costa and Nick Schultz, see that net sales of $250,000 are decreased by the cost of goods sold and by other business expenses to yield a net income of $83,000. Of course, these figures are only highlights of the complete income statement, which appears in Table B.2.

---

1. We gratefully acknowledge the assistance of Jim L. Grimm, Professor of Marketing, Illinois State University, in writing this appendix.

STONEHAM AUTO SUPPLIES INCOME STATEMENT FOR THE YEAR ENDED DECEMBER 31, 1990

Net Sales	$250,000
Cost of Goods Sold	45,000
Gross Margin	$205,000
Expenses	122,000
Net Income	$ 83,000

The income statement can be used in several ways to improve the management of a business. First, it enables an owner or manager to compare actual results with budgets for various parts of the statement. For example, Rose and Nick see that the total amount of merchandise sold (gross sales) is $260,000. Customers returned merchandise or received allowances (price reductions) totaling $10,000. Suppose the budgeted amount was only $9,000. By checking the ticket for sales returns and allowances, the owners can determine why these events occurred and whether the $10,000 figure could be lowered by adjusting the marketing mix.

After subtracting returns and allowances from gross sales, Rose and Nick can determine net sales from the statement. They are pleased with this figure because it is higher than their sales target of $240,000. Net sales is the amount the firm has available to pay its expenses.

A major expense for most companies that sell goods (as opposed to services) is the cost of goods sold. For Stoneham Auto Supplies, it amounts to 18 percent of net sales. Other expenses are treated in various ways by different companies. In our example, they are broken down into standard categories of selling expenses, administrative expenses, and general expenses.

The income statement shows that the cost of goods Stoneham Auto Supplies sold during fiscal year 1990 was $45,000. This figure was derived in the following way. First, the statement shows that merchandise in the amount of $51,000 was purchased during the year. In paying the invoices associated with these inventory additions, purchase (cash) discounts of $4,000 were earned, resulting in net purchases of $47,000. Special requests for selected merchandise throughout the year resulted in $2,000 of freight charges, which increased the net cost of delivered purchases to $49,000. Adding this amount to the beginning inventory of $48,000, the cost of goods available for sale during 1990 was $97,000. However, the records indicate that the value of inventory at the end of the year was $52,000. Because this amount was not sold, the cost of goods that were sold during the year was $45,000.

Rose and Nick observe that the total value of their inventory increased by 8.3 percent during the year:

$$\frac{\$52,000 - \$48,000}{\$48,000} = \frac{\$4,000}{\$48,000} = \frac{1}{12} = .0825 \text{ or } 8.3\%$$

Further analysis is needed to determine whether this increase is desirable or undesirable. (Note that the income statement provides no details concerning the composition of the inventory held on December 31; other records supply this information.)

STONEHAM AUTO SUPPLIES INCOME STATEMENT FOR THE YEAR ENDED DECEMBER 31, 1990

Gross Sales			$260,000
Less: Sales returns and allowances			10,000
Net Sales			$250,000
Cost of Goods Sold			
Inventory, January 1, 1990 (at cost)		$48,000	
Purchases	$51,000		
Less: Purchase discounts	4,000		
Net purchases	$47,000		
Plus: Freight-in	2,000		
Net cost of delivered purchases		$49,000	
Cost of goods available for sale		$97,000	
Less: Inventory, December 31, 1990 (at cost)		52,000	
Cost of goods sold			$ 45,000
Gross Margin			$205,000
Expenses			
Selling expenses			
Sales salaries and commissions	$32,000		
Advertising	16,000		
Sales promotions	3,000		
Delivery	2,000		
Total selling expenses		$53,000	
Administrative expenses			
Administrative salaries	$20,000		
Office salaries	20,000		
Office supplies	2,000		
Miscellaneous	1,000		
Total administrative expenses		$43,000	
General expenses			
Rent	$14,000		
Utilities	7,000		
Bad debts	1,000		
Miscellaneous (local taxes, insurance, interest, depreciation)	4,000		
Total general expenses		$26,000	
Total expenses			$122,000
Net Income			$ 83,000

If Nick and Rose determine that inventory on December 31 is excessive, they can implement appropriate marketing action.

Gross margin is the difference between net sales and cost of goods sold. Gross margin reflects the markup on products and is the amount available to pay all other expenses and provide a return to the owners. Stoneham Auto Supplies had a gross margin of $205,000:

Net Sales	$250,000
Cost of Goods Sold	− 45,000
Gross Margin	$205,000

Stoneham's expenses (other than cost of goods sold) during 1990 totaled $122,000. Observe that $53,000, or slightly more than 43 percent of the total, constituted direct selling expenses:

$$\frac{\$53,000 \text{ selling expenses}}{\$122,000 \text{ total expenses}} = .434 \text{ or } 43\%$$

The business employs three salespersons (one full-time) and pays competitive wages for the area. All selling expenses are similar to dollar amounts for fiscal year 1989, but Nick and Rose wonder whether more advertising is necessary because inventory increased by more than 8 percent during the year.

The administrative and general expenses are also essential for operating the business. A comparison of these expenses with trade statistics for similar businesses indicate that the figures are in line with industry amounts.

Net income, or net profit, is the amount of gross margin remaining after deducting expenses. Stoneham Auto Supplies earned a net profit of $83,000 for the fiscal year ending December 31, 1990. Note that net income on this statement is figured before payment of state and federal income taxes.

Income statements for intermediaries and for businesses that provide services follow the same general format as that shown for Stoneham Auto Supplies in Table B.2. The income statement for a manufacturer, however, is somewhat different in that the "purchases" portion is replaced by "cost of goods manufactured." Table B.3 shows the entire Cost of Goods Sold section for a manufacturer, including cost of goods manufactured. In other respects, income statements for retailers and manufacturers are similar.

■ Selected Performance Ratios

Rose and Nick's assessment of how well their business did during fiscal year 1990 can be improved through selective use of analytical ratios. These ratios enable a manager to compare the results for the current year with data from previous years and industry statistics. Unfortunately, comparisons of the current income statement with income statements and industry statistics from other years are not very meaningful because factors such as inflation are not accounted for when comparing dollar amounts. More meaningful comparisons can be made by converting these figures to a percentage of net sales, as this section shows.

The first analytical ratios we discuss, the operating ratios, are based on the net sales figure from the income statement.

■ Operating Ratios

Operating ratios express items on the income, or operating, statement as percentages of net sales. The first step is to convert the income statement into percentages of net sales, as illustrated in Table B.4.

STONEHAM AUTO SUPPLIES INCOME STATEMENT FOR THE YEAR ENDED DECEMBER 31, 1990

Cost of Goods Sold

Finished goods inventory, January 1, 1990			$ 50,000
Cost of goods manufactured			
Work-in-process inventory, January 1, 1990		$ 20,000	
Raw materials inventory, January 1, 1990	$ 40,000		
Net cost of delivered purchases	240,000		
Cost of goods available for use	$280,000		
Less: Raw materials inventory December 31, 1990	42,000		
Cost of goods placed in production		$238,000	
Direct labor		$ 32,200	
Manufacturing overhead			
Indirect labor	$ 12,000		
Supervisory salaries	10,000		
Operating supplies	6,000		
Depreciation	12,000		
Utilities	10,000		
Total manufacturing overhead		$ 50,000	
Total manufacturing costs		$320,000	
Total work-in-process		$340,000	
Less: Work-in process inventory, December 31, 1990		22,000	

Cost of goods manufactured	$318,000
	$368,000
Cost of goods available for sale	
Less: Finished goods inventory, December 31, 1990	48,000
Cost of Goods Sold	**$320,000**

STONEHAM AUTO SUPPLIES INCOME STATEMENT AS A PERCENTAGE OF NET SALES FOR THE YEAR ENDED DECEMBER 31, 1990

			Percentage of net sales
Gross Sales			103.8%
Less: Sales returns and allowances			3.8
Net Sales			100.0%
Cost of Goods Sold			
Inventory, January 1, 1990 (at cost)		19.2%	
Purchases	20.4%		
Less: Purchase discounts	1.6		
Net purchases	18.8%		
Plus: Freight-in	.8		
Net cost of delivered purchases		19.6	
Cost of goods available for sale		38.8%	
Less: Inventory, December 31, 1990 (at cost)		20.8	
Cost of goods sold			18.0
Gross Margin			82.0%
Expenses			
Selling expenses			
Sales salaries and commissions	12.8%		
Advertising	6.4		
Sales promotions	1.2		
Delivery	0.8		
Total selling expenses		21.2%	
Administrative expenses			
Administrative salaries	8.0%		
Office salaries	8.0		
Office supplies	0.8		
Miscellaneous	0.4		
Total administrative expenses		17.2%	
General expenses			
Rent	5.6%		
Utilities	2.8		
Bad debts	0.4		
Miscellaneous	1.6		
Total general expenses		10.4%	
Total expenses			48.8
Net Income			33.2%

After making this conversion, the manager looks at several key operating ratios: two profitability ratios (the gross margin ratio and the net income ratio) and the operating expense ratio.

For Stoneham Auto Supplies, these ratios are determined as follows (see Tables B.2 and B.4 for supporting data):

$$\text{Gross margin ratio} = \frac{\text{gross margin}}{\text{net sales}} = \frac{\$205,000}{\$250,000} = 82\%$$

$$\text{Net income ratio} = \frac{\text{net income}}{\text{net sales}} = \frac{\$83,000}{\$250,000} = 33.2\%$$

$$\text{Operating expense ratio} = \frac{\text{total expense}}{\text{net sales}} = \frac{\$122,000}{\$250,000} = 48.8\%$$

The gross margin ratio indicates the percentage of each sales dollar available to cover operating expenses and achieve profit objectives. The net income ratio indicates the percentage of each sales dollar that is classified as earnings (profit) before payment of income taxes. The operating expense ratio indicates the percentage of each dollar needed to cover operating expenses.

If Nick and Rose feel that the operating expense ratio is higher than historical data and industry standards, they can analyze each operating expense ratio in Table B.4 to determine which expenses are too high and can then take corrective action.

After reviewing several key operating ratios, in fact, managers will probably want to analyze all the items on the income statement. For instance, by doing so, Nick and Rose can determine whether the 8 percent increase in inventory was necessary.

■ Inventory Turnover

The inventory turnover rate, or stockturn rate, is an analytical ratio that can be used to answer the question, "Is the inventory level appropriate for this business?" The inventory turnover rate indicates the number of times that an inventory is sold (turns over) during one year. To be useful, this figure is then compared with historical turnover rates and industry rates.

The inventory turnover rate can be computed on cost as follows:

$$\text{Inventory turnover} = \frac{\text{cost of goods sold}}{\text{average inventory at cost}}$$

Rose and Nick would calculate the turnover rate from Table B.2 as follows:

$$\frac{\text{Cost of goods sold}}{\text{Average inventory at cost}} = \frac{\$45,000}{\$50,000} = 0.9 \text{ time}$$

They find that inventory turnover is less than once per year (0.9 time). Industry averages for competitive firms are 2.8 times. This figure convinces Rose and Nick that their investment in inventory is too large and that they need to reduce their inventory.

■ Return on Investment

Return on investment (ROI) is a ratio that indicates management's efficiency in generating sales and profits from the total amount invested in the firm. For example, for Stoneham Auto Supplies the ROI is 41.5 percent, which compares well with competing businesses.

We use figures from two different financial statements to arrive at ROI. The income statement, already discussed, gives us net income. The balance sheet, which states the firm's assets and liabilities at a given point in time, provides the figure for total assets (or investment) in the firm.

The basic formula for ROI is

$$\text{ROI} = \frac{\text{net income}}{\text{total investment}}$$

For Stoneham Auto Supplies, net income for fiscal year 1990 is $83,000 (see Table B.2). If total investment (taken from the balance sheet for December 31, 1990) is $200,000, then

$$\text{ROI} = \frac{\$83,000}{\$200,000} = 0.415 \text{ or } 41.5\%$$

The ROI formula can be expanded to isolate the impact of capital turnover and the operating income ratio separately. Capital turnover is a measure of net sales per dollar of investment; the ratio is figured by dividing net sales by total investment. For Stoneham Auto Supplies,

$$\text{Capital turnover} = \frac{\text{net sales}}{\text{total investment}}$$

$$= \frac{\$250,000}{\$200,000} = 1.25$$

ROI is equal to capital turnover times the net income ratio. The expanded formula for Stoneham Auto Supplies is

$$\text{ROI} = (\text{capital turnover}) \times (\text{net income ratio})$$

or

$$\text{ROI} = \frac{\text{net sales}}{\text{total investment}} \times \frac{\text{net income}}{\text{net sales}}$$

$$= \frac{\$250,000}{\$200,000} \times \frac{\$83,000}{\$250,000}$$

$$= (1.25)(33.2\%) = 41.5\%$$

Price Calculations

An important step in setting prices is selecting a pricing method, as indicated in Chapter 18. The systematic use of markups, markdowns, and various conversion formulas helps in calculating the selling price and evaluating the effects of various prices. The following sections will provide more detailed information about price calculations.

■ **Markups**

As indicated in the text, markup is the difference between the selling price and the cost of the item. That is, selling price equals cost plus markup. The markup must cover cost and contribute to profit; thus markup is similar to gross margin on the income statement.

Markup can be calculated on either cost or selling price as follows:

$$\text{Markup as percentage of cost} = \frac{\text{amount added to cost}}{\text{cost}} = \frac{\text{dollar markup}}{\text{cost}} \cdot$$

$$\text{Markup as percentage of selling price} = \frac{\text{amount added to cost}}{\text{selling price}} = \frac{\text{dollar markup}}{\text{selling price}}$$

Retailers tend to calculate the markup percentage on selling price.

Examples of Markup

To review the use of these markup formulas, assume that an item costs $10 and the markup is $5.

$$\text{Selling price} = \text{cost} + \text{markup}$$

$$\$15 = \$10 + \$5$$

Thus

$$\text{Markup percentage on cost} = \frac{\$5}{\$10} = 50\%$$

$$\text{Markup percentage on selling price} = \frac{\$5}{\$15} = 33\ 1/3\%$$

It is necessary to know the base (cost or selling price) to use markup pricing effectively. Markup percentage on cost will always exceed markup percentage on price, given the same dollar markup, so long as selling price exceeds cost.

On occasion, we may need to convert markup on cost to markup on selling price, or vice versa. The conversion formulas are

$$\text{Markup percentage on selling price} = \frac{\text{markup percentage on cost}}{100\% + \text{markup percentage on cost}}$$

$$\text{Markup percentage on cost} = \frac{\text{markup percentage on selling price}}{100\% - \text{markup percentage on selling price}}$$

For example, if the markup percentage on cost is 33 1/3 percent, then the markup percentage on selling price is

$$\frac{33\ 1/3\%}{100\% + 33\ 1/3\%} = \frac{33\ 1/3\%}{133\ 1/3\%} = 25\%$$

If the markup percentage on selling price is 40 percent, then the corresponding percentage on cost would be as follows:

$$\frac{40\%}{100\% - 40\%} = \frac{40\%}{60\%} = 66\ 2/3\%$$

Finally, we can show how to determine selling price if we know the cost of the item and the markup percentage on selling price. Assume that an item costs $36 and the usual markup percentage on selling price is 40 percent. Remember that selling price equals markup plus cost. Thus if

$$100\% = 40\% \text{ of selling price} + \text{cost}$$

then

$$60\% \text{ of selling price} = \text{cost}$$

In our example, cost equals $36. Then

$$0.6X = \$36$$

$$X = \frac{\$36}{0.6}$$

$$\text{Selling price} = \$60$$

Alternatively, the markup percentage could be converted to a cost basis as follows:

$$\frac{40\%}{100\% - 40\%} = 66\ 2/3\%$$

Then the computed selling price would be as follows:

$$\text{Selling price} = 66\ 2/3\%\ (\text{cost}) + \text{cost}$$

$$= 66\ 2/3\%\ (\$36) + \$36$$

$$= \$24 + \$36$$

$$= \$60$$

By remembering the basic formula—selling price equals cost plus markup—you will find these calculations straightforward.

■ Markdowns

Markdowns are price reductions a retailer makes on merchandise. Markdowns may be useful on items that are damaged, priced too high, or selected for a special sales event. The income statement does not express markdowns directly because the change in price is made before the sale takes place. Therefore separate records of markdowns would be needed to evaluate the performance of various buyers and departments.

The markdown ratio (percentage) is calculated as follows:

$$\text{Markdown percentage} = \frac{\text{dollar markdowns}}{\text{net sales in dollars}}$$

In analyzing their inventory, Nick and Rose discover three special automobile jacks that have gone unsold for several months. They decide to reduce the price of each item from $25 to $20. Subsequently, these items are sold. The markdown percentage for these three items is

$$\text{Markdown percentage} = \frac{3\ (\$5)}{3\ (\$20)} = \frac{\$15}{\$60} = 25\%$$

Net sales, however, include all units of this product sold during the period, not just those marked down. If ten of these items have already been sold at $25 each, in addition to the three items sold at $20, then the overall markdown percentage would be

$$\text{Markdown percentage} = \frac{3\ (\$5)}{10\ (\$25) + 3\ (\$20)}$$

$$= \frac{\$15}{\$250 + \$60} = \frac{\$15}{\$310} = 4.8\%$$

Sales allowances also are a reduction in price. Thus the markdown percentages should also include any sales allowances. It would be computed as follows:

$$\text{Markdown percentage} = \frac{\text{dollar markdowns} + \text{dollar allowances}}{\text{net sales in dollars}}$$

DISCUSSION AND REVIEW QUESTIONS

1. How does a manufacturer's income statement differ from a retailer's income statement?

2. Use the following information to answer questions a through c:

   Company TEA
   Fiscal year ended June 30, 1991

Net Sales	$500,000
Cost of Goods Sold	300,000
Net Income	50,000
Average Inventory at Cost	100,000
Total Assets (total investment)	200,000

   a. What is the inventory turnover rate for TEA Company? From what sources will the marketing manager determine the significance of the inventory turnover rate?

   b. What is the capital turnover ratio for fiscal year 1991? What is the net income ratio? What is the return on investment (ROI)?

   c. How many dollars of sales did each dollar of investment produce for TEA Company in fiscal year 1991?

3. Product A has a markup percentage on cost of 40 percent. What is the markup percentage on selling price?

4. Product B has a markup percentage on selling price of 30 percent. What is the markup percentage on cost?

5. Product C has a cost of $60 and a usual markup percentage of 25 percent on selling price. What price should be placed on this item?

6. Apex Appliance Company sells twenty units of product Q for $100 each and ten units for $80 each. What is the markdown percentage for product Q?

Glossary

A

Accessory equipment Equipment used in production or office activities; does not become a part of the final physical product.

Accumulation A process through which an inventory of homogeneous products that have similar production or demand requirements is developed.

Administered pricing A process in which the seller sets a price for a product, and the customer pays that specified price.

Advertising A paid form of nonpersonal communication about an organization and/or its products that is transmitted to a target audience through a mass medium.

Advertising appropriation The total amount of money that a marketer allocates for advertising for a specific time period.

Advertising platform The basic issues or selling points that an advertiser wishes to include in the advertising campaign.

Advertising target The group of people at whom advertisements are aimed.

Agent A marketing intermediary who receives a commission or fee for expediting exchanges; represents either buyers or sellers on a permanent basis.

Aided recall test A posttest method of evaluating the effectiveness of advertising in which subjects are asked to identify advertisements they have seen recently; they are shown a list of products, brands, company names, or trademarks to jog their memory.

Allocation The breaking down of large homogeneous inventories into smaller lots.

Allowance Concession in price to achieve a desired goal; for example, industrial equipment manufacturers give trade-in allowances on used industrial equipment to enable customers to purchase new equipment.

Approach The manner in which a salesperson contacts a potential customer.

Arbitrary approach A method for determining the advertising appropriation in which a high-level executive in the firm states how much can be spent on advertising for a certain time period.

Area sampling A variation of stratified sampling, with the geographic areas serving as the segments, or primary units, used in random sampling.

Artwork The illustration in an advertisement and the layout of the components of an advertisement.

Assessment center An intense training center at which sales candidates are put into realistic, problematic settings where they must prioritize activities, make decisions, and act on their decisions to determine whether each candidate will make a good salesperson.

Assorting Combining products into collections, or assortments, that buyers want to have available at one place.

Assortment A combination of similar or complementary products put together to provide benefits to a specific market.

Atmospherics The conscious designing of a store's space to create emotional effects that enhance the probability that consumers will buy.

Attitude The knowledge and positive or negative feelings about an object.

Attitude scale A measurement instrument that usually consists of a series of adjectives, phrases, or sentences about an object; subjects are asked to indicate the intensity of their feelings toward the object by reacting to the statements in a certain way. It can be used to measure consumer attitudes.

Automatic vending Nonstore, nonpersonal retailing; includes coin-operated, self-service machines.

Average cost Total costs divided by the quantity produced.

Average fixed cost The fixed cost per unit produced; it is calculated by dividing the fixed costs by the number of units produced.

Average revenue Total revenue divided by the quantity produced.

Average total cost The sum of the average fixed cost and the average variable cost.

Average variable cost The variable cost per unit produced; it is calculated by dividing the variable cost by the number of units produced.

B

Barter The trading of products.

Base-point pricing A geographic pricing policy that includes the price at the factory, plus freight charges from the base point nearest the buyer.

Benefit segmentation The division of a market according to the various benefits that customers want from the product.

Better Business Bureau A local, nongovernmental regulatory group supported by local businesses that aids in settling problems between specific business firms and consumers.

Bid pricing A determination of prices through sealed bids or open bids.

Bonded storage A storage service provided by many public warehouses, whereby the goods are not released until U.S. customs duties, federal or state taxes, or other fees are paid.

Brand A name, term, symbol, design, or combination of these that identifies a seller's products and differentiates them from competitors' products.

Brand-extension branding A type of branding in which a firm uses one of its existing brand names as part of a brand for an improved or new product that is usually in the same product category as the existing brand.

Brand manager A type of product manager responsible for a single brand.

Brand mark The element of a brand, such as a symbol or design, that cannot be spoken.

Brand name The part of a brand that can be spoken—including letters, words, and numbers.

Breakdown approach A general approach for measuring company sales potential based on a general economic forecast—or other aggregate data—and the market sales potential derived from it; company sales potential is based on the general economic forecast and the estimated market sales potential.

Breakeven point The point at which the costs of producing a product equal the revenue made from selling the product.

Broker A functional middleman who performs fewer functions than other intermediaries; the primary function is to bring buyers and sellers together for a fee.

Buildup approach A general approach to measuring company sales potential in which the analyst initially estimates how much the average purchaser of a product will buy in a specified time period and then multiplies that amount by the number of potential buyers; estimates are generally calculated by individual geographic areas.

Business analysis An analysis providing a tentative sketch of a product's compatibility in the marketplace, including its probable profitability.

Buy-back allowance A certain sum of money given to a purchaser for each unit bought after an initial deal is over.

Buying allowance A temporary price reduction to resellers for purchasing specified quantities of a product.

Buying behavior The decision processes and acts of people involved in buying and using products.

Buying center The group of people within an organization who are involved in making organizational purchase decisions; these people take part in the purchase decision process as users, influencers, buyers, deciders, and gatekeepers.

Buying power Resources such as money, goods, and services that can be traded in an exchange situation.

Buying power index A weighted index consisting of population, effective buying income, and retail sales data. The higher the index number, the greater the buying power.

C

Captioned photograph A photograph with a brief description that explains the picture's content.

Cash-and-carry wholesaler A limited service wholesaler that sells to customers who will pay cash and furnish transportation or pay extra to have products delivered.

Cash discount A price reduction to the buyer for prompt payment or cash payment.

Catalog retailing A type of mail-order retailing in which selling may be handled by telephone or in-store visits and products are delivered by mail or picked up by the customers.

Catalog showrooms A form of warehouse showroom in which consumers shop from a mailed catalog and buy at a warehouse where all products are stored out of buyers' reach. Products are provided in the manufacturer's carton.

Causal study Research planned to prove or disprove that x causes y or that x does not cause y.

Centralized organization An organization in which the top-level managers delegate very little authority to lower levels of the organization.

Cents-off offer A sales promotion device for established products whereby buyers receive a certain amount off the regular price shown on the label or package.

Channel capacity The limit on the volume of information that a communication channel can handle effectively.

Channel conflict Friction between marketing channel members, often resulting from role deviance or malfunction; absence of an expected mode of conduct that contributes to the channel as a system.

Channel cooperation A helping relationship among channel members that enhances the welfare and survival of all necessary channel members.

Channel of distribution *See* marketing channel.

Channel leadership The guidance that a channel member with one or more sources of power gives to other channel members to help achieve channel objectives.

Channel power The ability of one channel member to influence another channel member's goal achievement.

Clayton Act Passed in 1914, this act prohibits specific

practices, such as price discrimination, exclusive dealer arrangements, and stock acquisitions, whose effect may substantially lessen competition and tend to create a monopoly.

Client public The direct consumers of the product of a nonbusiness organization; for example, the client public of a university is its student body.

Closing The element in the selling process in which the salesperson asks the prospect to buy the product.

Code of ethics Formalized statement of what a company expects of its employees with regard to ethical behavior.

Coding process The process by which a meaning is placed into a series of signs that represent ideas; also called encoding.

Cognitive dissonance Dissatisfaction that may occur shortly after the purchase of a product, when the buyer questions whether he or she should have purchased the product at all or would have been better off purchasing another brand that was evaluated very favorably.

Combination compensation plan A plan by which salespeople are paid a fixed salary and a commission based on sales volume.

Commercialization A phase of new-product development in which plans for full-scale manufacturing and marketing must be refined and settled and budgets for the product must be prepared.

Commission merchant An agent often used in agricultural marketing who usually exercises physical control over products, negotiates sales, and is given broad powers regarding prices and terms of sale.

Communication A sharing of meaning through the transmission of information.

Community shopping center Shopping center that includes one or two department stores and some specialty stores, as well as convenience stores; serves several neighborhoods and draws consumers who are not able to find desired products in neighborhood shopping centers.

Company sales forecast The amount of a product that a firm actually expects to sell during a specific period at a specified level of company marketing activities.

Comparative advertising Advertising that compares two or more identified brands in the same general product class; the comparison is made in terms of one or more specific product characteristics.

Competition Generally viewed by a business as those firms that market products similar to, or substitutable for, its products in the same target market.

Competition-matching approach A method of ascertaining the advertising appropriation in which an advertiser tries to match a major competitor's appropriations in terms of absolute dollars or in terms of using the same percentage of sales for advertising.

Competition-oriented pricing A pricing method in which an organization considers costs and revenue secondary to competitors' prices.

Competitive advertising Advertising that points out a brand's uses, features, and advantages that benefit consumers but may not be available in competing brands.

Competitive structure The model used to describe the number of firms that control the supply of a product and how it affects the strength of competition; factors include number of competitors, ease of entry into the market, the nature of the product, and knowledge of the market.

Component part A finished item ready for assembly or a product that needs little processing before assembly and that becomes a part of the physical product.

Comprehensive spending patterns The percentages of family income allotted to annual expenditures for general classes of goods and services.

Concentration strategy A market segmentation strategy in which an organization directs its marketing efforts toward a single market segment through one marketing mix.

Conflict of interest Results from marketers' taking advantage of situations for their own selfish interests rather than for the long-run interest of the business.

Consumable supplies Items that facilitate an organization's production and operations, but do not become part of the finished product.

Consumer buying behavior The buying behavior of ultimate consumers—people who purchase products for personal or household use and not for business purposes.

Consumer buying decision process The five-stage decision process consumers use in making purchases.

Consumer contest A sales promotion device for established products based on the analytical or creative skill of contestants.

Consumer Goods Pricing Act Federal legislation that prohibits the use of price maintenance agreements among producers and resellers involved in interstate commerce.

Consumer jury A panel used to pretest advertisements; it consists of a number of persons who are actual or potential buyers of the product to be advertised.

Consumer market Purchasers and/or individuals in their households who intend to consume or benefit from the purchased products and who do not buy products for the main purpose of making a profit.

Consumer movement A social movement through which people attempt to defend and exercise their rights as buyers.

Consumer movement forces The major forces in the consumer movement are consumer organizations, consumer laws, consumer education, and independent consumer advocates. The three major areas stressed are product safety, disclosure of information, and protection of the environment.

Consumer product Product purchased for ultimate satisfaction of personal and family needs.

Consumer Product Safety Commission A federal agency created to protect consumers by setting product standards, testing products, investigating product complaints, banning products, and monitoring injuries through the National Electronic Surveillance System.

Consumer protection legislation Laws enacted to protect consumers' safety, to enhance the amount of information available, and to warn of deceptive marketing techniques.

Consumer sales promotion method A sales promotion method that encourages or stimulates customers to patronize a specific retail store or to try and/or purchase a particular product.

Consumer spending patterns Information indicating the relative proportions of annual family expenditures or the actual amount of money that is spent on certain types of goods or services.

Consumer sweepstakes A sales promotion device for established products in which entrants submit their names for inclusion in a drawing for prizes.

Containerization The practice of consolidating many items into one container that is sealed at the point of origin and opened at the destination.

Convenience products Relatively inexpensive, frequently purchased items for which buyers want to exert only minimal effort.

Cooperative advertising An arrangement in which a manufacturer agrees to pay a certain amount of a retailer's media costs for advertising the manufacturer's products.

Copy The verbal portion of advertisements; includes headlines, subheadlines, body copy, and signature.

Corporate strategy The strategy that determines the means for utilizing resources in the areas of production, finance, research and development, personnel, and marketing to reach the organization's goals.

Correlation methods Methods used to develop sales forecasts as the forecasters attempt to find a relationship between past sales and one or more variables, such as population, per capita income, or gross national product.

Cost comparison indicator Allows an advertiser to compare the costs of several vehicles within a specific medium relative to the number of persons reached by each vehicle.

Cost-oriented pricing A pricing policy in which a firm determines price by adding a dollar amount or percentage to the cost of a product.

Cost-plus pricing A form of cost-oriented pricing in which first the seller's costs are determined and then a specified dollar amount or percentage of the cost is added to the seller's cost to set the price.

Count and recount A sales promotion method based on the payment of a specific amount of money for each product unit moved from a reseller's warehouse in a given period of time.

Coupon A new-product sales promotion technique used to stimulate trial of a new or improved product, to increase sales volume quickly, to attract repeat purchasers, or to introduce new package sizes or features.

Credence qualities Qualities of services that cannot be assessed even after purchase and consumption; for example, few consumers are knowledgeable enough to assess the quality of an appendix operation, even after it has been performed.

Culture Everything in our surroundings that is made by human beings, consisting of tangible items as well as intangible concepts and values.

Cumulative discount Quantity discount that is aggregated over a stated period of time.

Customary pricing A type of psychological pricing in which certain goods are priced primarily on the basis of tradition.

Customer forecasting survey The technique of asking customers what types and quantities of products they intend to buy during a specific period so as to predict the sales level for that period.

Customer orientation An approach to marketing in which a marketer tries to provide a marketing mix that satisfies the needs of buyers in the target market.

Cycle analysis A method of predicting sales by analyzing sales figures for a period of three to five years to ascertain whether sales fluctuate in a consistent, periodic manner.

D

Dealer listing An advertisement that promotes a product and identifies the names of participating retailers that sell the product.

Dealer loader A gift, often part of a display, that is given to a retailer for the purchase of a specified quantity of merchandise.

Decentralized organization An organization in which decision-making authority is delegated as far down the chain of command as possible.

Decline stage The stage in a product's life cycle in which sales fall rapidly and profits decrease.

Decoding process The stage in the communication process in which signs are converted into concepts and ideas.

Defensive advertising Advertising used to offset or lessen the effects of a competitor's promotional program.

Demand curve A line showing the relationship between price and quantity demanded.

Demand-oriented pricing A pricing policy based on the level of demand for the product—resulting in a higher price when demand for the product is strong and a lower price when demand is weak.

Demand schedule The relationship, usually inverse, between price and quantity demanded; classically, a line sloping downward to the right, showing that as price falls, quantity demanded will increase.

Demographic factors Personal characteristics such as age, sex, race, nationality, income, family, life cycle stage, and occupation; also called socioeconomic factors.

Demonstration A sales promotion method manufacturers use temporarily to encourage trial use and purchase of the product or to show how the product works.

Department store A type of retail store having a wide product mix; organized into separate departments to facilitate marketing efforts and international management.

Dependent variable A variable contingent on, or restricted to, one or a set of values assumed by the independent variable.

Depression A stage of the business cycle during which unemployment is extremely high, wages are very low, total disposable income is at a minimum, and consumers lack confidence in the economy.

Depth (of product mix) The average number of different products offered to buyers in a firm's product line.

Depth interview Personal interview with an open, informal atmosphere; this interview may take several hours. It is used to study motives.

Derived demand A characteristic of industrial demand that arises because industrial demand derives from the consumer demand.

Descriptive study A type of study undertaken when marketers see that knowledge of the characteristics of certain phenomena is needed to solve a problem; may require statistical analysis and predictive tools.

Direct cost approach An approach to determining marketing costs in which cost analysis includes direct costs and traceable common costs but does not include nontraceable common costs.

Direct costs Costs directly attributable to the performance of marketing functions.

Direct distribution channels Distribution channels in which products are sold directly from producer to ultimate users.

Direct marketing The use of nonpersonal media to introduce products by mail or telephone.

Direct ownership A long-run commitment to marketing in a foreign nation in which a subsidiary or division is owned by a foreign country through purchase.

Discount store A self-service, general merchandise store positioned as having low prices.

Discretionary income Disposable income that is available for spending and saving after an individual has purchased the basic necessities of food, clothing, and shelter.

Disposable income After-tax income.

Distribution The activities that make products available to customers when and where they want to purchase them.

Distribution center A large, centralized warehouse that receives goods from factories and suppliers, regroups the goods into orders, and ships the orders to customers quickly, with the focus on active movement of goods rather than passive storage.

Distribution variable The marketing mix variable in which marketing management attempts to make products available in the quantities desired, with adequate service, to a target market and to keep the total inventory, transportation, communication, storage, and materials handling costs as low as possible.

Diversified growth A type of growth that occurs in three forms, depending on the technology of the new products and the nature of the new markets the firm enters; the three forms are horizontal, concentric, and conglomerate.

Drop shipper A limited service wholesaler that takes title to products and negotiates sales but never physically handles products.

Dual distribution A channel practice whereby a producer distributes the same product through two or more different channels.

Dumping The sale of products in foreign markets at lower prices than those charged in the domestic market (when all costs are not allocated or when surplus products are sold).

E

Early adopters Individuals who choose new products carefully and are viewed by persons in the early majority, late majority, and laggard categories as being "the people to check with."

Early majority Individuals who adopt a new product just prior to the average person; they are deliberate and cautious in trying new products.

Economic forces Forces that determine the strength of a firm's competitive atmosphere and affect the impact of marketing activities because they determine the size and strength of demand for products.

Economic institutions An environmental force in international markets made up of producers, wholesalers, retailers, buyers, and other organizations that produce, distribute, and purchase products.

Economic order quantity (EOQ) The order size that minimizes the total cost of ordering and carrying inventory.

Effective buying income Similar to disposable income; it includes salaries, wages, dividends, interest, profits, and rents, less federal, state, and local taxes.

Encoding *See* Coding process.

Environmental monitoring The process of seeking information about events and relationships in a company's environment to assist marketers in identifying opportunities and in planning.

Environmental scanning The collecting of information about the forces in the marketing environment.

Equalized workload method A method of determining sales-force size in which the number of customers multiplied by the number of sales calls per year required to serve these customers effectively is divided by the average number of calls each salesperson makes annually.

Ethical pricing A form of professional pricing in which the demand for the product is inelastic and the seller is a professional who has a responsibility not to overcharge the client.

Exchange Participation by two or more individuals, groups, or organizations, with each party possessing something of value that the other party desires. Each must be willing to give up its "something of value" to get "something of value" held by the other, and all parties must be willing to communicate with each other.

Exclusive dealing A situation in which a manufacturer forbids an intermediary to carry products of competing manufacturers.

Exclusive distribution A type of market coverage in which only one outlet is used in a geographic area.

Executive judgment A sales forecasting method based on the intuition of one or more executives.

Experience curve pricing A pricing approach in which a company fixes a low price that high-cost competitors cannot match and thus expands its market share; this approach is possible when a firm gains cumulative production experience and is able to reduce its manufacturing costs to a predictable rate through improved methods, materials, skills, and machinery.

Experience qualities Qualities of services that can be assessed only after purchase and consumption (taste, satisfaction, courtesy, and the like).

Experimentation Research in which the factors that are related to or may affect the variables under investigation are maintained as constants so that the effects of the experimental variables may be measured.

Expert forecasting survey Preparation of the sales forecast by experts, such as economists, management consultants, advertising executives, college professors, or other persons outside the firm.

Exploratory studies A type of research conducted when more information is needed about a problem and the tentative hypothesis needs to be made more specific; it permits marketers to conduct ministudies with a very restricted database.

Extensive decision making The considerable time and effort a buyer spends seeking alternative products, searching for information about them, and then evaluating them to determine which one will be most satisfying.

External search The process of seeking information from sources other than one's memory.

F

Facilitating agency An organization that performs activities helpful in performing channel functions but does not buy, sell, or transfer title to the product; it can be a transportation company, an insurance company, an advertising agency, a marketing research agency, or a financial institution.

Family packaging A policy in an organization that all packages are to be similar or are to include one major element of the design.

Feature article A form of publicity that is up to three thousand words long and is usually prepared for a specific publication.

Federal Trade Commission A governmental group, consisting of five commissions, established to prevent the free enterprise system from being stifled or fettered by monopoly or anticompetitive practices; it provides direct protection to consumers from unfair or deceptive trade practices.

Federal Trade Commission Act (1914) Established the Federal Trade Commission and currently regulates the greatest number of marketing practices.

Feedback The receiver's response to a decoded message.

Field public warehouse A warehouse established by a public warehouse at the owner's inventory location; the warehouser becomes the custodian of the products and issues a receipt that can be used as collateral for a loan.

Fixed cost The cost that does not vary with changes in the number of units produced or sold.

F.O.B. (free-on-board) destination Part of a price quotation, used to indicate who must pay shipping charges. F.O.B. destination price means that the producer absorbs the costs of shipping the merchandise to the customer.

F.O.B. (free-on-board) factory Part of a price quotation; used to indicate who must pay shipping charges. F.O.B. factory price indicates the price of the merchandise at the factory, before it is loaded onto the carrier vehicle; the buyer must pay for shipping.

Food broker An intermediary that sells food and other grocery products to retailer-owned and merchant wholesalers, grocery chains, industrial buyers, and food processors. Both buyers and sellers use food brokers to cope with fluctuating market conditions.

Franchising An arrangement in which a supplier (franchisor) grants a dealer (franchisee) the right to sell products in exchange for some type of consideration.

Free merchandise A sales promotion method aimed at retailers whereby free merchandise is offered to resellers that purchase a stated quantity of product.

Free samples A new-product sales promotion technique that marketers use to stimulate trial of a product, to increase sales volume in early stages of the product's life cycle, or to obtain desirable distribution.

Freight absorption pricing Pricing for a particular customer or geographical area whereby the seller absorbs all or part of the actual freight costs.

Freight forwarders Businesses that consolidate shipments from several organizations into efficient lot sizes, which increases transit time and sometimes lowers shipping costs.

Full-cost approach An approach to determining marketing costs in which cost analysis includes direct costs, traceable common costs, and nontraceable common costs.

Full-service wholesaler A marketing intermediary that provides most services that can be performed by wholesalers.

Functional discount *See* trade discount.

Functional middleman A marketing intermediary that does not take title to products but usually receives a fee for expediting exchanges.

Functional modification A change that affects a product's versatility, effectiveness, convenience, or safety, usually requiring the redesigning of one or more parts of the product.

Functional wholesaler A marketing intermediary that expedites exchanges among producers and resellers and is compensated by fees or commissions.

G

General merchandise wholesaler Full-service merchant wholesaler that carries a very wide product mix.

General public The indirect consumers of the product of a nonbusiness organization; for instance, the general public of a university includes alumni, trustees, parents of students, and other groups.

Generic brand A brand that indicates only the product category (such as *aluminum foil*), not the company name and other identifying terms.

Geographic pricing A form of pricing that involves reductions for transportation costs or other costs associated with the physical distance between the buyer and the seller.

Globalization of markets The development of marketing strategies as if the entire world (or regions of it) were a single entity; products are marketed the same way everywhere.

Good A tangible item.

Government markets Markets made up of federal, state, county, and local governments, spending billions of dollars annually for goods and services to support their internal operations and to provide such products as defense, energy, and education.

Gross National Product (GNP) An overall measure of a nation's economic standing in terms of the value of all products produced by that nation for a given period of time.

Group interview A method of uncovering people's motives relating to some issue, such as product usage, with an interviewer generating discussion on one or several topics among the six to twelve people in the group.

Growth state The product life cycle stage in which sales rise rapidly; profits reach a peak and then start to decline.

H

Heterogeneity A condition resulting from the fact that people typically perform services; there may be variation from one service provider to another or variation in the service provided by a single individual from day to day and from customer to customer.

Heterogeneous market A market made up of individuals with diverse product needs for products in a specific product class.

Horizontal channel integration The combining of institutions at the same level of operation under one management.

Hypothesis A guess or assumption about a certain problem or set of circumstances; reasonable supposition that may be right or wrong.

I

Idea A concept, image, or issue.

Idea generation The search by businesses and other organizations for product ideas that help them achieve their objectives.

Illustrations Photographs, drawings, graphs, charts, and tables, used to encourage an audience to read or watch an advertisement.

Implicit bargaining A method of employee motivation that recognizes the various needs of different employees and is based on the theory that there is no one best way to motivate individuals.

Impulse buying An unplanned buying behavior that involves a powerful, persistent urge to buy something immediately.

Income The amount of money received through wages, rents, investments, pensions, and subsidy payments for a given period.

Incremental productivity method A plan by which a marketer should continue to increase the sales force as long as the additional sales increases are greater than the additional selling costs that arise from employing more salespeople.

Independent variable A variable free from the influence of, or not dependent on, other variables.

Individual branding A branding policy in which each product is named differently.

Industrial buying behavior *See* Organizational buying behavior.

Industrial distributor An independent business organization that takes title to industrial products and carries inventories.

Industrial market A market consisting of individuals, groups, or organizations that purchase specific kinds of products for resale, for direct use in producing other products, or for use in day-to-day operations; also called organizational market.

Industrial marketing A set of activities directed toward facilitating and expediting exchanges involving industrial markets and industrial products.

Industrial product A product purchased to be used directly or indirectly to produce other products or to be used in the operations of an organization.

Industrial service An intangible product that an organization uses in its operations, such as a financial product or a legal service.

Inelastic demand A type of demand in which a price increase or decrease will not significantly affect the quantity demanded.

Inflation A condition in which price levels increase faster than incomes, causing a decline in buying power.

Information inputs The sensations we receive through our sense organs.

In-home retailing A type of nonstore retailing that involves personal selling in consumers' homes.

Innovators The first consumers to adopt a new product; they enjoy trying new products and tend to be venturesome, rash, and daring.

Input-output data A type of information, sometimes used in conjunction with the SIC system, that is based on the assumption that the output or sales of one industry are the input or purchases of other industries.

Inseparability A condition in which the consumer frequently is directly involved in the production process because services normally are produced at the same time that they are consumed.

Institutional advertising A form of advertising promoting organizational images, ideas, and political issues.

Institutional market A market that consists of organizations seeking to achieve goals other than such normal business goals as profit, market share, or return on investment.

Intangibility A characteristic of services: because services are performances, they cannot be seen, touched, tasted, or smelled, nor can they be possessed.

Integrated growth The type of growth that a firm can have within its industry; three possible growth directions include forward, backward, and horizontal.

Intense growth The type of growth that can occur when current products and current markets have the potential for increasing sales.

Intensive distribution A form of market coverage in which all available outlets are used for distributing a product.

Intermodal transportation Combining and coordinating two or more modes of transportation.

Internal search An aspect of an information search where buyers first search their memory for information about products that might solve their problem.

International marketing Marketing activities performed across national boundaries.

Introduction stage The stage in a product's life cycle beginning at a product's first appearance in the marketplace, when sales are zero and profits are negative.

J

Job enrichment A method of employee motivation that gives employees a sense of autonomy and control over their work, with employees being encouraged to set their own goals.

Joint demand A characteristic of industrial demand that occurs when two or more items are used in combination to produce a product.

Joint venture A partnership between a domestic firm and foreign firms and/or governments.

K

Kinesic communication Commonly known as body language, this type of interpersonal communication occurs in face-to-face selling situations when the salesperson and customers move their heads, eyes, arms, hands, legs, and torsos.

L

Labeling An important dimension of packaging for promotional, informational, and legal reasons; regulated by numerous federal and state laws.

Laggards The last consumers to adopt a new product; they are oriented toward the past and suspicious of new products.

Late majority People who are quite skeptical of new

products; they eventually adopt new products because of economic necessity or social pressure.

Layout The physical arrangement of the illustration, headline, subheadline, body copy, and signature of an advertisement.

Learning A change in an individual's behavior that arises from prior behavior in similar situations.

Legal forces Forces that arise from the legislation and interpretation of laws; these laws, enacted by government units, restrain and control marketing decisions and activities.

Level of involvement The intensity of interest that one has for a particular product in a particular buying decision.

Licensing (international) An arrangement in international marketing in which the license pays commissions or royalties on sales or supplies used in manufacturing.

Limited decision making The type of consumer decision making used for products that are purchased occasionally and when a buyer needs to acquire information about an unfamiliar brand in a familiar product category.

Limited-line wholesaler Full-service merchant wholesaler that carries only a few product lines.

Limited service wholesaler A marketing intermediary that provides only some marketing services and specializes in a few functions.

Line family branding A branding policy in which an organization uses family branding only for products within a line, not for all its products.

Long-range plan A plan that covers more than five years.

M

Mail-order retailing A type of nonpersonal, nonstore retailing that uses direct mail advertising and catalogs and is typified by selling by description. The buyer usually does not see the actual product until it is delivered.

Mail-order wholesaler An organization that sells through direct mail by sending catalogs to retail, industrial, and institutional customers.

Mail surveys Questionnaires sent to respondents, who are encouraged to complete and return them.

Major equipment A category of industrial products that includes large tools and machines used for production purposes.

Manufacturer brand A brand initiated by a producer; makes it possible for a producer to be identified with its product at the point of purchase.

Manufacturers' agent An independent business person who sells complementary products of several producers in assigned territories and is compensated through commissions.

Marginal cost The cost associated with producing one more unit of a product.

Marginal revenue (MR) The change in total revenue that occurs after an additional unit of a product is sold.

Market An aggregate of people who, as individuals or as organizations, have needs for products in a product class and who have the ability, willingness, and authority to purchase such products.

Market attractiveness/business position model A two-dimensional matrix designed to serve as a diagnostic tool to highlight SBUs that have an opportunity to grow or that should be divested.

Market density The number of potential customers within a unit of land area, such as a square mile.

Marketing Individual and organizational activities that facilitate and expedite satisfying exchange relationships in a dynamic environment through the creation, distribution, promotion, and pricing of goods, services, and ideas.

Marketing audit A systematic examination of the objectives, strategies, organization, and performance of a firm's marketing unit.

Marketing audit report A written summary produced after the marketing audit has been conducted; it includes recommendations that will increase marketing productivity and develops a recommendation as to the business' general direction.

Marketing channel A group of interrelated intermediaries who direct products to customers; also called channel of distribution.

Marketing concept A managerial philosophy that an organization should try to satisfy customers' needs through a coordinated set of activities that at the same time allows the organization to achieve its goals.

Marketing control process A process that consists of establishing performance standards, evaluating actual performance by comparing it with established standards, and reducing the differences between desired and actual performance.

Marketing cost analysis A method for helping to control marketing strategies whereby various costs are broken down and classified to determine which costs are associated with specific marketing activities.

Marketing databank A file of data collected through both the marketing information system and marketing research projects.

Marketing environment The environment that surrounds both the buyer and the marketing mix; it consists of political, legal, regulatory, societal, consumer movement, economic, and technological forces. Environmental variables affect a marketer's ability to facilitate and expedite exchanges.

Marketing ethics Moral evaluation of decisions based on accepted principles of behavior that result in an action being judged right or wrong.

Marketing experimentation A set of rules and procedures under which the task of data gathering is organized to expedite analysis and interpretation.

Marketing function account Classification of costs that indicates which function was performed through the expenditure of funds.

Marketing information system (MIS) A system that establishes a framework for the day-to-day managing and structuring of information gathered regularly from sources both inside and outside an organization.

Marketing intelligence All the data gathered as a basis for marketing decisions.

Marketing intermediary A member of a marketing channel, usually a merchant or an agent, acting to direct products to buyers.

Marketing management A process of planning, organizing, implementing, and controlling marketing activities to facilitate and expedite exchanges effectively and efficiently.

Marketing mix Consists of four major variables: product, price, distribution, and promotion.

Marketing objective A statement of what is to be accomplished through marketing activities.

Marketing-oriented organization An organization that attempts to determine what target market members want and then tries to produce it.

Marketing plan The written document or blueprint for implementing and controlling an organization's marketing activities related to a particular marketing strategy.

Marketing planning A systematic process that involves assessing marketing opportunities and resources, determining market objectives, and developing a plan for implementation and control.

Marketing program A set of marketing strategies that are implemented and used at the same time.

Marketing research The part of marketing intelligence that involves specific inquiries into problems and marketing activities to discover new information so as to guide marketing decisions.

Marketing strategy A plan for selecting and analyzing a target market and creating and maintaining a marketing mix.

Market manager A person responsible for the marketing activities that are necessary to serve a particular group or class of customers.

Market opportunity An opportunity that arises when the right combination of circumstances occurs at the right time to allow an organization to take action toward generating sales from a target market.

Market planning cycle The five-step cycle that involves developing or revising marketing objectives relative to performance, assessing marketing opportunities and resources, formulating marketing strategy, developing the plan for implementation and control, and implementing the marketing plan.

Market requirement Related to customers' needs or desired benefits, the market requirement is satisfied by components of the marketing mix that provide benefits to buyers.

Market sales potential The amount of a product that specific customer groups would purchase within a specified period at a specific level of industrywide marketing activity.

Market segment A group of individuals, groups, or organizations sharing one or more similar characteristics that make them have relatively similar product needs.

Market segmentation The process of dividing a total market into groups of people with relatively similar product needs, for the purpose of designing a marketing mix (or mixes) that more precisely matches the needs of individuals in a selected segment (or segments).

Market share A firm's sales in relation to total industry sales, expressed as a decimal or percentage.

Market test A stage of new-product development that involves making a product available to buyers in one or more test areas and measuring purchases and consumer responses to promotion, price, and distribution efforts.

Markup A percentage of the cost or price of a product added to the cost.

Markup pricing A pricing method where the price is derived by adding a predetermined percentage of the cost to the cost of the product.

Mass merchandiser A retail operation that tends to offer fewer customer services than department stores and to focus its attention on lower prices, high turnover, and large sales volume; the category includes supermarkets and discount houses.

Materials handling Physical handling of products.

Maturity stage A stage in the product life cycle in which the sales curve peaks and starts to decline as profits continue to decline.

Mechanical observation devices Cameras, recorders, counting machines, and equipment to record movement, behavior, or physiological changes in individuals.

Media plan A plan that sets forth the exact media vehicles to be used for advertisements and the dates and times that the advertisements are to appear.

Medium of transmission That which carries the coded message from the source to the receiver or audience; examples include ink on paper and vibrations of air waves produced by vocal cords.

Medium-range plans Plans that usually encompass two to five years.

Megacarrier A freight transportation company that provides many methods of shipment, such as rail, truck, and air service.

Merchandise allowance A sales promotion method aimed at retailers; it consists of a manufacturer's agreement to pay resellers certain amounts of money for providing special promotional efforts, such as setting up and maintaining a display.

Merchant A marketing intermediary who takes title to merchandise and resells it for a profit.

Merchant wholesaler A marketing intermediary who takes title to products, assumes risk, and is generally involved in buying and reselling products.

Missionary salesperson A support salesperson, usually employed by a manufacturer, who assists the producer's customers in selling to their own customers.

Modified-rebuy purchase A type of industrial purchase in which a new-task purchase is changed the second or third time, or the requirements associated with a straight-rebuy purchase are modified.

Money refund A new-product sales promotion technique in which the producer mails a consumer a specific amount of money when proof of purchase is established.

Monopolistic competition A market structure in which a firm has many potential competitors; to compete, the firm tries to develop a differential marketing strategy to establish its own market share.

Monopoly A market structure existing when a firm produces a product that has no close substitutes and/or when a single seller may erect barriers to potential competitors.

Motive An internal energizing force that directs a person's behavior toward his or her goals.

MRO items An alternative term for supplies: supplies can be divided into Maintenance, Repair, and Operating (or overhaul) items.

Multinational enterprise A firm that has operations or subsidiaries in several countries.

Multisegment strategy A market segmentation strategy in which an organization directs its marketing efforts at two or more segments by developing a marketing mix for each selected segment.

Multivariable segmentation Market division achieved by using more than one characteristic to divide the total market; this approach provides more information about the individuals in each segment than does single-variable segmentation.

N

National Advertising Review Board A self-regulatory unit created by the Council of Better Business Bureaus and three advertising trade organizations; it screens national advertisements to check for honesty and processes complaints about deceptive advertisements.

Natural account Classification of costs based on what the money is actually spent for; typically a part of a regular accounting system.

Negotiated pricing A determination of price through bargaining even when there are stated list prices and discount structures.

Negotiation Mutual discussion or communication of the terms and methods of an exchange.

Neighborhood shopping center A shopping center that usually consists of several small convenience and specialty stores and serves consumers who live less than ten minutes' driving time from the center.

New product Any product that a given firm has not marketed previously.

New-produce development A process consisting of six phases: idea generation, screening, business analysis, product development, test-marketing, and commercialization.

News release A form of publicity that is usually a single page of typewritten copy containing fewer than three hundred words.

New-task purchase A type of industrial purchase in which an organization is making an initial purchase of an item to be used to perform a new job or to solve a new problem.

Noise A condition in the communication process existing when the decoded message is different from what was coded.

Nonbusiness marketing Marketing activities conducted by individuals and organizations to achieve some goal other than ordinary business goals such as profit, market share, or return on investment.

Noncumulative discount A one-time price reduction based on the number of units purchased, the size of the order, or the product combination purchased.

Nonprice competition A policy in which a seller elects not to focus on price and instead emphasizes distinctive product features, service, product quality, promotion, packaging, or other factors to distinguish its product from competing brands.

Nonprofit organization marketing The application of marketing concepts and techniques to such nonprofit groups as hospitals and colleges.

Nonstore retailing A type of retailing where consumers purchase products without visiting a store.

Nontraceable common costs Costs that cannot be assigned to any specific function according to any logical criteria and thus are assignable only on an arbitrary basis.

O

Objective and task approach An approach to determining the advertising appropriation: marketers first determine the objectives that a campaign is to achieve, and then ascertain the tasks required to accomplish those objectives; the costs of all tasks are added to ascertain the total appropriation.

Observation method A research method where researchers record the overt behavior of subjects, noting physical conditions and events. Direct contact with subjects is avoided; instead, their actions are examined and noted systematically.

Odd-even pricing A type of psychological pricing that assumes that more of a product will be sold at $99.99 than at $100.00, indicating that an odd price is more appealing than an even price to customers.

Off-price retailer A store that buys manufacturers' seconds, overruns, returns, and off-season merchandise for resale to consumers at deep discounts.

Oligopoly A competitive structure existing when a few sellers control the supply of a large proportion of a product; each seller must consider the actions of other sellers to changes in marketing activities.

Open bids Prices submitted by several, but not all, sellers; the amounts of these bids are not made public.

Opportunity cost The value of the benefit that is given up by selecting one alternative rather than another.

Order getter A type of salesperson who increases the firm's sales by selling to new customers and by increasing sales to present customers.

Order processing The receipt and transmission of sales order information in the physical distribution process.

Order taker A type of salesperson who primarily seeks repeat sales.

Organizational buying behavior The purchase behavior of producers, government units, institutions, and resellers; also called industrial buying behavior.

Organizational market Individuals or groups who purchase a specific kind of product for one of three purposes: resale, direct use in producing other products, or use in general daily operations; also called industrial market.

Overall family branding A policy of branding all of a firm's products with the same name or at least a part of the name.

P

Patronage motives Motives that influence where a person purchases products on a regular basis.

Penetration price A lower price designed to penetrate the market and thus quickly produce a larger unit sales volume.

Percent of sales approach A method for establishing the advertising appropriation whereby marketers simply multiply a firm's past sales, forecasted sales, or a combination of the two by a standard percentage based on both what the firm traditionally has spent on advertising and what the industry averages.

Perception The process by which an individual selects, organizes, and interprets information inputs to create a meaningful picture of the world.

Perfect competition Ideal competitive structure that would entail a large number of sellers, none of which could significantly influence price or supply.

Performance standard An expected level of performance against which actual performance can be compared.

Perishability A condition where, because of simultaneous production and consumption, unused capacity to produce services in one time period cannot be stockpiled or inventoried for future time periods.

Personal interview survey A face-to-face interview that allows more in-depth interviewing, probing, follow-up questions, or psychological tests.

Personality An internal structure in which experience and behavior are related in an orderly way.

Personal selling A process of informing customers and persuading them to purchase products through personal communication in an exchange situation.

Personal factors Factors influencing the consumer buying decision process that are unique to particular individuals.

Persuasion The activity of convincing or prevailing upon an individual or organization to bring about an exchange.

Physical distribution An integrated set of activities that deal with managing the movement of products within firms and through marketing channels.

PIMS (Profit Impact on Marketing Strategy) A Strategic Planning Institute (SPI) research program which provides reports on the products of SPI member firms; these reports assist the member firms in analyzing marketing performance and formulating marketing strategies.

Pioneer advertising A type of advertising that informs persons about what a product is, what it does, how it can be used, and where it can be purchased.

Point-of-purchase materials A sales promotion method that uses such items as outside signs, window displays, and display racks to attract attention, to inform customers, and to encourage retailers to carry particular products.

Political and legal institutions Public agencies, laws, courts, legislatures, and government bureaus.

Political forces Forces that strongly influence the economic and political stability of our country not only through decisions that affect domestic matters but through their authority to negotiate trade agreements and to determine foreign policy.

Population All elements, units, or individuals that are of interest to researchers for a specific study.

Posttest An evaluation of advertising effectiveness after the campaign.

Premiums Items that are offered free or at a minimum cost as a bonus for purchasing.

Press conference A meeting used to announce major news events.

Prestige pricing Setting prices at a high level to facilitate a prestige or quality image.

Pretest Evaluation of an advertisement before it is actually used.

Price The value placed on what is exchanged.

Price competition A policy whereby a marketer emphasizes price as an issue and matches or beats the prices of competitors also emphasizing low prices.

Price differentiation A demand-oriented pricing method whereby a firm uses more than one price in the marketing of a specific product; differentiation of prices can be based on several dimensions, such as type of customers, type of distribution used, or the time of the purchase.

Price discrimination A policy of charging some buyers lower prices than other buyers, which gives those paying less a competitive advantage,

Price elasticity of demand A measure of the sensitivity of demand to changes in price.

Price leaders Products sold at less than cost to increase sales of regular merchandise.

Price lining A form of psychological pricing in which an organization sets a limited number of prices for selected lines of products.

Price skimming A pricing policy whereby an organization charges the highest possible price that buyers who most desire the product will pay.

Price variable A critical marketing mix variable in which marketing management is concerned with establishing a value for what is exchanged.

Pricing method A mechanical procedure for setting prices on a regular basis.

Pricing objectives Overall goals that describe the role of price in an organization's long-range plans.

Pricing policy A guiding philosophy or course of action designed to influence and determine pricing decisions.

Primary data Information observed and recorded or collected directly from subjects.

Private brand See private distributor brand.

Private distributor brand A brand that is initiated and owned by a reseller; also called private brand.

Private warehouse A storage facility operated by an organization for the purpose of distributing its own products.

Problem definition The first step in the research process toward finding a solution or launching a research study; the researcher thinks about the best ways to discover the nature and boundaries of a problem or opportunity.

Process materials Materials used directly in the production of other products; unlike component parts, they are not readily identifiable.

Procompetitive legislation Laws enacted to preserve competition.

Producer market A market consisting of individuals and business organizations that purchase products for the purpose of making a profit by using them to produce other products or by using them in their operations.

Product Everything (both favorable and unfavorable) that one receives in an exchange; it is a complexity of tangible and intangible attributes, including functional, social, and psychological utilities or benefits. A product may be a good, a service, or an idea.

Product adoption process The five-stage process of buyer acceptance of a product: awareness, interest, evaluation, trial, and adoption.

Product advertising Advertising that promotes goods and services.

Product assortment A collection of a variety of different products.

Product deletion The elimination of some products that no longer satisfy target market customers or contribute to achievement of an organization's overall goals.

Product development A stage in creating new products that moves the product from concept to test phase and also involves the development of the other elements of the marketing mix (promotion, distribution, and price).

Product differentiation The use of promotional efforts to differentiate a company's products from its competitors' products, with the hope of establishing the superiority and preferability of its products relative to competing brands.

Production orientation The viewpoint that increasing the efficiency of production is the primary means of increasing an organization's profits.

Production-oriented organization A firm that concentrates on either improving production efficiency or producing high-quality, technically improved products; it has little regard for customers' desires.

Product item A specific version of a product that can be designated as a unique offering among an organization's products.

Product life cycle The course of product development, consisting of several stages: introduction, growth, maturity, and decline. As a product moves through these stages, the strategies relating to competition, pricing, promotion, distribution, and market information must be evaluated and possibly changed.

Product line A group of closely related products that are considered a unit because of marketing, technical, or end-use considerations.

Product manager A person who holds a staff position in a multiproduct company and is responsible for a product, a product line, or several distinct products that are considered an interrelated group.

Product mix The composite of products that an organization makes available to consumers.

Product mix depth See depth (of product mix).

Product mix width *See* width (of product mix).

Product modification The changing of one or more of a product's characteristics.

Product-portfolio analysis (BCG approach) A strategic planning approach based on the philosophy that a product's market growth rate and its relative market share are important considerations in determining its marketing strategy.

Product-portfolio approach An approach to managing the product mix that attempts to create specific marketing strategies to achieve a balanced mix of products that will produce maximum long-run profits.

Product positioning The decisions and activities that are directed toward trying to create and maintain the firm's intended product concept in customers' minds.

Product-specific spending patterns The dollar amounts families spend for specific products within a general product class.

Product variable That aspect of the marketing mix dealing with researching consumers' product wants and planning the product to achieve the desired product characteristics.

Professional pricing Pricing used by persons who have great skill or experience in a particular field or activity, indicating that a price should not relate directly to the time and involvement in a specific case; rather, a standard fee is charged regardless of the problems involved in performing the job.

Professional services Complex and frequently regulated services that usually require the provider to be highly skilled; for example, accounting or legal services.

Projective technique A test in which subjects are asked to perform specific tasks for particular purposes while in fact they are being evaluated for other purposes; assumes that subjects will unconsciously "project" their motives as they perform the tasks.

Promotion The communication with individuals, groups, or organizations to directly or indirectly facilitate exchanges by influencing audience members to accept an organization's products.

Promotion mix The specific combination of promotional methods that an organization uses for a particular product.

Promotion variable A major marketing mix component used to facilitate exchanges by informing an individual or one or more groups of people about an organization and its products.

Prospecting Developing a list of potential customers for personal selling purposes.

Prosperity A stage of the business cycle characterized by a combination of low unemployment and relatively high aggregate income, which causes buying power to be high (assuming a low inflation rate).

Proxemic communication A subtle form of interpersonal communication used in face-to-face interactions when either party varies the physical distance that separates them.

Psychological factors Factors that operate within individuals to partially determine their general behavior and thus influence their behavior as buyers.

Psychological pricing A pricing method designed to encourage purchases that are based on emotional reactions rather than rational responses.

Publicity Nonpersonal communication in news story form, regarding an organization and/or its products, that is transmitted through a mass medium at no charge.

Public relations A broad set of communication activities used to create and maintain favorable relations between the organization and its publics, such as customers, employees, stockholders, government officials, and society in general.

Public warehouses Business organizations that provide rented storage facilities and related physical distribution facilities.

Pull policy Promotion of a product directly to consumers with the intention of developing strong consumer demand.

Purchasing power A buyer's income, credit, and wealth available for purchasing products.

Push money An incentive program designed to push a line of goods by providing salespeople with additional compensation.

Push policy The promotion of a product only to the next institution down the marketing channel.

Q

Quality modification A change that relates to a product's dependability and durability and is generally executed by alterations in the materials or production process used.

Quality of life The enjoyment of daily living, enhanced by leisure time, clean air and water, an unlittered earth, conservation of wildlife and natural resources, and security from radiation and poisonous substances.

Quantity discounts Deductions from list price that reflect the economies of purchasing in large quantities.

Quota sampling Nonprobability sampling in which the final choice of respondents is left to the interviewers.

R

Rack jobbers Middlemen (also called service merchandisers) similar to truck wholesalers but providing the extra service of cleaning and filling a display rack.

Random factor analysis A method of predicting sales whereby an attempt is made to attribute erratic sales variations to random, nonrecurrent events, such as a regional power failure or a natural disaster.

Random sampling A type of sampling in which all the units in a population have an equal chance of appearing in the sample; probability sampling.

Raw materials Basic materials that become part of a physical product; obtained from mines, farms, forests, oceans, and recycled solid wastes.

Real-estate brokers Brokers who, for a fee or commission, bring buyers and sellers together to exchange real estate.

Receiver The individual, group, or organization that decodes a coded message.

Recession A stage in the business cycle during which unemployment rises and total buying power declines, stifling both consumers' and businesspeople's propensity to spend.

Reciprocity A practice unique to industrial sales in which two organizations agree to buy from each other.

Recognition test A posttest method of evaluating the effectiveness of advertising; individual respondents are shown the actual advertisement and asked whether they recognize it.

Recovery A stage of the business cycle during which the economy moves from recession toward prosperity.

Recruiting A process by which the sales manager develops a list of applicants for sales positions.

Reference group A group with which an individual identifies so much that he or she takes on many of the values, attitudes, or behaviors of group members.

Regional issues Versions of a magazine that differ across geographic regions and in which a publisher can vary the advertisements and editorial content.

Regional shopping center A type of shopping center that usually has the largest department stores, the widest product mix, and the deepest product lines of all shopping centers in an area; usually there are at least 150,000 customers in the target area.

Regulatory forces Forces arising from regulatory units at all levels of government; these units create and enforce numerous regulations that affect marketing decisions.

Reinforcement advertising An advertisement attempting to assure current users that they have made the right choice and telling them how to get the most satisfaction from the product.

Reliability A condition existing when a sample is representative of the population; it also exists when repeated use of an instrument produces almost identical results.

Reminder advertising Advertising used to remind consumers that an established brand is still around and that it has certain uses, characteristics, and benefits.

Reorder point The inventory level that signals that more inventory should be ordered.

Reseller market A market consisting of intermediaries, such as wholesalers and retailers, that buy finished goods and resell them for the purpose of making a profit.

Retailer An intermediary that purchases products for the purpose of reselling them to ultimate consumers.

Retailer coupon A sales promotion method used by retailers when price is a primary motivation for consumers' purchasing behavior; usually takes the form of a "cents-off" coupon that is distributed through advertisements and is redeemable only at a specific store.

Retailing Activities required for exchanges in which ultimate consumers are the buyers.

Robinson-Patman Act A law directly influencing pricing and promotions policies; the law prohibits price differentials and promotional allowances that are discriminatory.

Role A set of actions and activities that a person in a particular position is supposed to perform, based on the expectations of both the individual and the persons around the individual.

Routine response behavior The type of decision making used by a consumer when buying frequently purchased, low-cost items that require very little search and decision effort.

S

Safety stock The inventory needed to prevent a stockout (running out of a product).

Sales analysis A process for controlling marketing strategies whereby sales figures are used to evaluate performance.

Sales branches Similar to merchant wholesalers in their operations; may offer credit, delivery, give promotional assistance, and furnish other services.

Sales contest A sales promotion method used to motivate distributors, retailers, and sales personnel through the recognition of outstanding achievements.

Sales-force forecasting survey Estimation by members of a firm's sales force of the anticipated sales in their territories for a specified period.

Sales forecast The amount of a product that a company expects to sell during a specific period at a specified level of marketing activities.

Sales office Provides service normally associated with agents; owned and controlled by the producer.

Sales orientation A focus on increasing an organization's sales as the major way to increase profits.

Sales-oriented organization An organization acting on its belief that personal selling and advertising are the primary tools used to generate profits and that most products—regardless of consumers' needs—can be sold if the right quantity and quality of personal selling and advertising are used.

Sales potential The maximum percentage of market potential that an individual firm within an industry can expect to obtain for a specific product.

Sales promotion An activity and/or material that acts as a direct inducement to resellers, salespersons, or consumers; it offers added value or incentive to buy or sell the product.

Sample A limited number of units that are believed to be representative of the total population under study for marketing research purposes.

Sampling Selecting representative units from a total population.

Scientific decision making An approach that involves systematically seeking facts and then applying decision-making methods other than trial and error or generalization from experience.

Scrambled merchandising The addition of unrelated products and product lines to an existing product mix, particularly fast-moving items that can be sold in large volume.

Screening ideas A stage in the product development process in which the ideas that do not match organizational objectives are rejected and those with the greatest potential are selected for further development.

Sealed bids Prices submitted to a buyer, to be opened and made public at a specified time.

Search qualities Tangible attributes of services that can be viewed prior to purchase.

Seasonal analysis A method of predicting sales whereby an analyst studies daily, weekly, or monthly sales figures to evaluate the degree to which seasonal factors, such as climate and holiday activities, influence a firm's sales.

Seasonal discounts A price reduction that sellers give to buyers who purchase goods or services out of season; these discounts allow the seller to maintain steadier production during the year.

Secondary data Information compiled inside or outside the organization for some purpose other than the current investigations.

Segmentation variable A dimension or characteristic of individuals, groups, or organizations that is used to divide a total market into segments.

Selective distortion The changing or twisting of currently received information that occurs when a person receives information inconsistent with his or her feelings or beliefs.

Selective distribution A form of market coverage in which only some available outlets in an area are chosen to distribute a product.

Selective exposure Selection of some inputs to be exposed to our awareness while many others are ignored because of the inability to be conscious of all inputs at one time.

Selective retention The phenomenon of remembering information inputs that support personal feelings and beliefs and forgetting inputs that do not.

Self-concept One's own perception of oneself.

Selling agents Intermediaries who market all of a specified product line or the entire output of a manufacturer; they have control over the manufacturer's marketing effort and may be used in place of a marketing department.

Service An intangible that results from applying human and mechanical efforts to people or objects.

Service heterogeneity See heterogeneity.

Service inseparability See inseparability.

Service intangibility See intangibility.

Service perishability See perishability.

Sherman Antitrust Act Legislation passed in 1890 to prevent businesses from restraining trade and monopolizing markets.

Shopping product An item for which buyers are willing to put forth considerable effort in planning and making the purchase.

Short-range plans Plans that cover a period of one year or less.

Single-variable segmentation The simplest form of segmentation, achieved by using only one characteristic to divide—or segment—the market.

Situational factors The set of circumstances or conditions that exist when a consumer is making a purchase decision.

Social class An open aggregate of people with similar social ranking.

Social factors The forces that other people exert on one's buying behavior.

Social institutions An environmental force in international markets, including the family, education, religion, health, and recreational systems.

Social marketing Marketing that involves the development of programs designed to influence the acceptability of social ideas or causes.

Social responsibility An approach to marketing decisions that takes into account how these decisions may affect society as a whole and various groups and individuals within society.

Societal forces Forces that pressure marketers to provide high living standards and enjoyable lifestyles through socially responsible decisions and activities; the structure and dynamics of individuals and groups and the issues of concern to them.

Socioeconomic factors See demographic factors.

Sorting activities The way channel members divide roles and separate tasks, including the roles of sorting out, accumulating, allocating, and assorting products.

Sorting out The first step in developing an assortment; involves breaking down conglomerates of heterogeneous supplies into relatively homogeneous groups.

Source A person, group, or organization that has a meaning that it intends and attempts to share with a receiver or an audience.

Special-event pricing Advertised sales or price cutting to increase revenue or lower costs.

Specialty-line wholesaler A merchant wholesaler that carries a very limited variety of products designed to meet customers' specialized requirements.

Specialty product An item that possesses one or more unique characteristics that a significant group of buyers is willing to expend considerable purchasing efforts to obtain.

Specialty retail A type of store that carries a narrow product mix with deep product lines.

Standard Industrial Classification (SIC) System A system developed by the federal government for classifying industrial organizations, based on what the firm primarily produces; also classifies selected economic characteristics of commercial, financial, and service organizations; uses code numbers to classify firms in different industries.

Statistical interpretation An analysis that focuses on what is typical or what deviates from the average; indicates how widely respondents vary and how they are distributed in relation to the variable being measured.

Stockout A condition that exists when a firm runs out of a product.

Storyboard A blueprint used by technical personnel to produce a television commercial; combines the copy with the visual material to show the sequence of major scenes in the commercial.

Straight commission compensation plan A plan according to which a salesperson's compensation is determined solely by the amount of his or her sales for a given time period.

Straight-rebuy purchase A type of industrial purchase in which a buyer purchases the same products routinely under approximately the same terms of sale.

Straight salary compensation plan A plan according to which salespeople are paid a specified amount per time period.

Strategic business unit (SBU) A division, product line, or other profit center within a parent company that sells a distinct set of products and/or services to an identifiable group of customers and competes against a well-defined set of competitors.

Strategic marketing planning A process through which an organization can develop marketing strategies that, when properly implemented and controlled, will contribute to achieving the organization's overall goals.

Strategic market plan A comprehensive plan that takes into account not only marketing but all other functional areas of a business unit that must be coordinated, such as production, finance, and personnel, as well as concern about the environment.

Strategy The key decision or plan of action required to reach an objective or set of objectives.

Stratified sampling A type of sampling in which units in a population are divided into groups according to a common characteristic or attribute; then a probability sample is conducted within each group.

Style modification Modification directed at changing the sensory appeal of a product by altering its taste, texture, sound, smell, or visual characteristics.

Subculture A division of a culture based on geographic regions or human characteristics, such as age or ethnic background.

Superficial discounting A deceptive markdown sometimes called "was-is pricing" (the firm never intended to sell at the higher price); this is fictitious comparative pricing.

Supermarket A large, self-service store that carries broad and complete lines of food products, and perhaps some nonfood products.

Superstore A giant store that carries all food and non-food products found in supermarkets, as well as most products purchased on a routine basis; sales are much greater than at discount stores or supermarkets.

Supplies See consumable supplies.

Support personnel Members of the sales staff who facilitate the selling function but usually are not involved only with making sales.

Survey methods Interviews conducted by mail, telephone, or in person to obtain factual information from or about those being interviewed, or to find out their opinions and values.

Symbolic pricing A type of psychological pricing in which prices are set at an artificially high level to provide prestige or a quality image.

Syndicated data services External sources of information that a marketer uses to study a marketing problem. Examples include American Research Bureau (ARB), Selling Areas Marketing, Inc. (SAMI), the A.C. Nielsen Company Retail Index, the Market Research Corporation of America (MRCA); they collect general information that is sold to subscribing clients.

T

Tactile communication Interpersonal communication through touching.

Target market A group of people for whom a firm creates and maintains a marketing mix.

Target public A group of people who have an interest in or a concern about an organization, a product, or a social cause.

Technical salesperson A support salesperson who directs efforts toward the organization's current customers by providing technical assistance in system design, product application, product characteristics, or installation.

Technological forces Forces that influence marketing decisions and activities because they affect people's lifestyles and standards of living, influence their desire for products and their reaction to marketing mixes, and have a direct impact on maintaining a marketing mix by influencing all its variables.

Technology The knowledge of how to accomplish tasks and goals.

Technology assessment A procedure by means of which managers try to foresee the effects of new products and processes on the firm's operation, on other business organizations, and on society in general.

Telemarketing A form of personal selling where highly trained account executives do everything over the telephone that face-to-face salespeople do.

Telephone retailing A type of nonstore retailing based on a cold canvass of the telephone directory or a screening of prospective clients before calling.

Telephone surveys The soliciting of respondents' answers to a questionnaire over the telephone, with the answers being written down by the interviewer.

Test marketing A limited introduction of a product in areas chosen to represent the intended market to determine probable buyers' reactions to various parts of a marketing mix.

Time series analysis A technique in which the forecaster, using the firm's historical sales data, tries to discover patterns in the firm's sales volume over time.

Total costs The sum of fixed costs and variable costs.

Total market approach An approach in which an organization designs a single marketing mix and directs it at an entire market for a specific product category; also called undifferentiated approach.

Total revenue The price times quantity.

Traceable common costs Costs that can be allocated indirectly, using one or several criteria, to the functions that they support.

Trade (or functional) discount A reduction off the list price a producer gives to a middleman for performing certain functions.

Trademark A legal designation indicating that the owner has exclusive use of a brand or part of a brand and that others are prohibited by law from using it.

Trade mart A relatively permanent facility that firms can rent to exhibit products year-round.

Trade name The legal name of an organization, rather than the name of a specific product.

Trade salesperson A type of salesperson not strictly classified as support personnel because he or she performs the order-taking function as well.

Trade sales promotion method A category of sales promotion techniques that stimulate wholesalers and retailers to carry a producer's products and to market these products aggressively.

Trade show A show whose purpose is to let manufacturers or wholesalers exhibit products to potential buyers; therefore assists in the selling and buying functions; commonly held annually at a specified location.

Trading company A company that provides a link between buyers and sellers in different countries; it takes title to products and provides all the activities necessary to move the product from the domestic country to a market in a foreign country.

Trading stamps A sales promotion method used by retailers to attract consumers to specific stores and to increase sales of specific items by giving extra stamps to purchasers of those items.

Traditional specialty retailer A store that carries a narrow product mix with deep product lines.

Transfer pricing The type of pricing used when one unit in a company sells a product to another unit; the price is determined by one of the following methods: actual full cost, standard full cost, cost plus investment, or market-based cost.

Transit time The total time that a carrier has possession of the goods.

Transportation Moving a product from where it is made to where it is purchased and used, and thus adding time and place utility to the product.

Transportation modes Railways, motor vehicles, waterways, pipelines, and airways used to move goods from one location to another.

Trend analysis An analysis that focuses on aggregate sales data, such as company's annual sales figures, over a period of many years to determine whether annual sales are generally rising, falling, or staying about the same.

Truck wholesaler A wholesaler that provides transportation and delivery of products directly to customers for inspection and selection.

Tying contract An agreement in which a supplier agrees to sell certain products to a dealer if the dealer consents to buy other products the supplier sells.

U

Unaided recall test A posttest method of evaluating the effectiveness of advertising; subjects are asked to identify advertisements that they have seen or heard recently but are not shown any clues to stimulate their memories.

Undifferentiated approach An approach in which an organization designs a single marketing mix and directs it at an entire market for a specific product category; same as total market approach.

Unfair trade practices acts State laws, enacted in

more than half the states, that prohibit wholesalers and retailers from selling products below their costs or below their costs plus a certain percentage of markup.

Uniform geographic pricing A type of pricing, sometimes called "postage-stamp price," that results in fixed average transportation; used to avoid the problems involved in charging different prices to each customer.

Unit loading Grouping one or more boxes on a pallet or skid.

Unsought products Products purchased because of a sudden need that must be solved (e.g., emergency automobile repairs) or when aggressive selling is used to obtain a sale that otherwise would not take place (e.g., encyclopedias).

V

Validity A condition that exists when an instrument does measure what it is supposed to measure.

Variable cost A cost that varies directly with changes in the number of units produced or sold.

Vending *See* automatic vending.

Venture team An organizational unit established to create entirely new products that may be aimed at new markets.

Vertical channel integration The combining of two or more stages of a marketing channel under one management.

Vertical marketing system A marketing channel in which channel activities are coordinated or managed by a single channel member to achieve efficient, low-cost distribution aimed at satisfying target market customers.

W

Warehouse showroom A type of retail store with high volume and low overhead; lower costs are effected by shifting some marketing functions to consumers, who must transport, finance, and perhaps even store merchandise.

Warehouse/wholesale club A large-scale, members-only establishment that combines features of cash-and-carry wholesaling with discount retailing.

Warehousing Designing and operating facilities for storing and moving goods.

Warranty Document that specifies what the producer will do if the product malfunctions.

Wealth The accumulation of past income, natural resources, and financial resources.

Wheeler-Lea Act Makes unfair and deceptive acts or practices unlawful, regardless of whether they injure competition.

Wheel of retailing A hypothesis that holds that new types of retailers usually enter the market as low-status, low-margin, low-price operators but eventually evolve into high-cost, high-price merchants.

Wholesaler An intermediary that buys from a producer or another intermediary and sells to another reseller; performs such marketing activities as transportation, storage, and information gathering necessary to expedite exchanges.

Wholesaling All marketing transactions in which purchases are intended for resale or are used in making other products.

Width (of product mix) The number of product lines a company offers.

Willingness to spend A disposition toward expected satisfaction from a product; influenced by the ability to buy, as well as numerous psychological and social forces.

Z

Zone prices Regional prices that vary for major geographic zones, as the transportation costs differ.

Name Index

Davidson, Willie G., 298
Davis, Bob, 673n
Davis, Jo Ellen, 673n
Davis, Robert A., 508n
Dawn dishwashing liquid, 302
Dawson, Gaye C., 80n, 324n
Dawson, Scott, 256n
Day, George S., 548n, 612n, 613(illus.), 615n
Day, Ralph L., 224n
Daylight-Saving Time Coalition, 33
Day Planner software, 395
Days Inn motels, 733
DDB Needham, 474(table)
Deakin, Edward B., 645n
Dear John, 633
DeBruicker, F. Stewart, 292n
de Cordoba, Jose, 137n
Dee, Johnny, 734
Deere and Company (John Deere), 545, 546(illus.)
DeGeorge, Gail, 382n, 673n
Del Monte Corporation, 28, 260, 261(illus.) 311, 316, 621
Delozier, M. Wayne, 439n
Delta Air Lines, Inc., 70, 110, 120, 704
DeNicola, Nino, 221
Denver Broncos, 475
Department of Justice, 36
Department of Transportation, 457, 671
Depke, Deidre A., 499
Deschaine, Monique, 563
Despande, Rohit, 639
Deveny, Kathleen, 463n, 699n
Dewey Stevens wine cooler, 360
Dewkist Plants, Inc., 42
DHL (air express service), 355, 774
Diamond I jets (Mitsubishi), 310
Diddley, Bo, 463
Diet caffeine-free Coke, 125
Diet Coke, 125, 291
Diet Dr Pepper, 495
Dietrich Corporation, 297
Diet Rite Cola, 19
Digital Equipment Corporation (DEC), 666, 765(table)
Dillard, 367(table)
Dimeo, James, 375n
Dimmler, Eleni, 45n
Dippity-Do hair gel, 289
Disney, Walt, 269
Disney Company. *See* Walt Disney Company, The
Disney World, 441
Dixon, Carol, 200n
Dobrzynski, Judith H., 621n
Dodds, Lynn Strongin, 297n
Dodge Caravan, 525
Dodge Division (Chrysler Corp.), 475
Dole, 346
Doll, Lesa, 229n
"Dome Sound System" (Panasonic), 639
Dominguez, Luis V., 112n

Domino's Pizza Inc., 71(illus.), 126–127, 448, 717
Donaton, Scott, 197n
Donegan, Priscilla, 197n, 370n, 371n
Donlan, Thomas G., 673n
Donlon, Brian, 231n
Donnelly, James H., 704n
Donnelly, James H., Jr., 643n, 718n
Donohue, F. Charles, 42
"Don't Mess with Texas," 734
Dorfman, Dan, 595n
Dornberg, John, 769n
Dow, Charles H., 64
Dow Chemical Company, The, 620, 765 (table)
Dow Jones & Co., Inc., 64
Dow Jones Information Services, 65
Downy fabric softener, 88, 260
DowVision, 65
Doyle, Mona, 163n
Doyle, Peter, 681n, 683
Dresser Industries, 654
Dreyfus Funds, 714, 715(table)
Dreyfuss, Joel, 326n, 378n
Drohan, Madelaine, 748n
Dr Pepper, 117, 565
Dr Pepper Company, 117, 380, 494–495
Drucker, Peter F., 280n
Dryden, Steven, 748n
Dry Idea deodorant, 254
Duff, Mike, 495n, 565n
Dugas, Christine, 137n
Duhan, Dale F., 330n
Dumaine, Brian, 107n, 303n, 399n, 419n
Dunham, Andrea, 198n
Dunkin, Amy, 363n, 368n, 595n, 597n
Dunkin' Donuts franchises, 646–647
Dunkin' Donuts University, 646–647
Dunn, S. Watson, 483n
Duofold Centennial pens, 770
du Pont de Nemours & Company, Inc., E.I., 89, 90, 439, 682(illus.), 764, 765(table)
Duraclean franchise, 382(table)

Ealey, Lance A., 769n
Eastern Airlines, Inc., 670–673
Eastern shuttle, 671
Easter Seal telethon, 724
Eastman Kodak, Inc., 107, 250, 268–269, 473, 765(table)
Easton, James, 407n
Easton Aluminum, Inc., 406, 407
Ebbers, Al, 139n
Eberhard Faber Inc., 193–194
Ebert, Roger, 270
EC. *See* European Community
Eccles, Robert G., 559n
Econo Lodge franchise, 382(table)
Economost electronic order entry system, 339
Edel, Richard, 701n
EDI (Electronic Data Exchange of Super Valu), 343

Edsel automobiles, 668, 669
Egghead Discount Software, 7
Egg McMuffin, 534
E.I du Pont de Nemours & Company. *See* du Pont
Eklund, Christopher S., 698n
El-Ansary, Adel I., 325n
Eldridge, Warren, 601n
Electrolert Inc., 336
Electrolux, 377
Elliott, Stuart, 67n, 99n, 286n, 461n, 475n, 497n
Ellis, James E., 597n, 673n
Ellis-Simon, Pamela, 271n
Ely, Joe, 734
Embassy Suites, Inc., 732
Energizer Bunny (E.B.), 496–497
Engardio, Pete, 256n
Engel, James F., 140n
Enis, Ben M., 508n
Environmental Protection Agency (EPA), 40(table), 307
EPA. *See* Environmental Protection Agency
Epstein, Jeffrey H., 567n
Erickson, Julie Liesse, 20n, 27n, 171n, 248n, 497n, 525n
Escher, M.C., 150(illus.)
Escort radar detectors, 336
Euro Disneyland, 270
Euromarche, 370
European Community (EC), 750–751
Evans, Joel, 373n, 376n
Evans, Sherli, 567n
Eveready Battery Company, 496–497
Everett, Martin, 513n
Export Trading Company Act (1982), 763
Express Mail (USPS), 545(illus.), 772
Exxon Corporation, 96–99, 397, 415, 765(illus.)
Exxon Valdez, 46, 96–99, 156

Faber, Kaspar, 193
Faber-Castell Corporation, A.W., 193–194
Fabulous Thunderbirds, 168, 734
Fackelmann, Kathy A., 594n
Fahey, Alison, 263n, 521n, 523n
Fahey, Liam, 548n, 607n
Famous Amos Chocolate Chip Cookie Company, The, 394
Fancy Feast cat food, 147
Fannie May Candy Shops, Inc., 386
Fannin, Rebecca, 248n, 669n
Farhi, Paul, 292n
Farmer, Richard N., 436n
Farney, Dennis, 65n
Farrell, Pia, 774n
Fatal Attraction, 634
FBI (Federal Bureau of Investigation), 418
FCC. *See* Federal Communications Commission
FDA. *See* Food and Drug Administration
Featherspring International foot supports, 41

RCA, 195
RC Cola, 19
Reader's Digest Association, Inc., 13, 13(illus.)
Reagan, Ronald, 39, 541
RealLemon juice, 602
Red Cross, American, 723, 727
Reed, B.J., 500n
Reeves, William G., 42n
Reflex ski poles, 407
Reibstein, Larry, 638n, 668n, 774n
Reichhold Chemicals, Inc., 244
Reidenbach, R. Eric, 68n, 81n
Reilly, Patrick, 40n, 65n
Relihan III, Walter J., 588n
Renault, Inc., 762
Rest, James R., 70n
Reynolds, Jonathan, 402n
Rice, Faye, 239n
Richards, Dan, 269n
Riche, Martha Farnsworth, 214n, 216n
Richman, Tom, 396n
Ricoh Mirai camera, 10
Rinehart, Lloyd M., 401n, 403n
RISC (reduced instruction set computing), 194
Ritz crackers, 28
R.J. Reynolds Industries, Inc. See RJR Nabisco, Inc.
RJR Nabisco, Inc., 17, 28–29, 67, 95, 199, 297, 450, 473
RMed International Inc., 307
Road & Track magazine, 336, 581
Robert Hall Inc., A3n
Robertson, Thomas S., 148n, 627n
Robeson, James F., 319(illus.)
Robichaux, Mark, 121n, 435n
Robin, Donald P., 68n, 81n
Robinson, Bill, 518n
Robinson, William A., 517n
Robinson-Patman Act (1936), 37, 60, 79, 328, 556, 694
Rock Against Drugs (RAD), 436
Rocky Mountain Medical Corporation, 307
Rodgers, David, 370n
Roel, Raymond, 271n
Rogers, Everett M., 287n, 443n, 445(fig.), 445n
Rogers, Michael, 337n
Rolex watches, 251, 541
Rolls Royce, 321
Romeo, Jean B., 491n
Ronald McDonald, 536
Ronald McDonald Houses, 437, 536
Ronald McDonald's Children's Charities, 536
Roosevelt, Franklin D., 95
Rose, Robert L., 685n
Rosenbloom, Bert, 322n, 323n, 328n, 329n, 344n, 353n, 354n, 355n
Rose's, 368(table)
Ross, Philip E., 297n
Rothman, Andrea, 606n
Rothman, Matt, 137n

Round Table Pizza franchise, 382(table)
Row, Michael, 339n
Royal Crown Cola Company, 19, 565
Roy Rogers franchise, 382(table)
Rubbermaid Incorporated, 327, 328
Ruffenach, Glenn, 774n
Ruibal, Sal, 497n
Russell, John A., 769n
Russell Athletic, 663(illus.)
Russell Corporation, The, 82, 84(illus.)
Ryan, Lanny J., 80n, 324n

Saatchi and Saatchi Ltd, 91(illus.)
Safeway Stores, Inc., 120, 251
Sains, Ariane, 375n
St. Louis Post-Dispatch, 134–135
St. Louis Sun, 134–135
Salem cigarettes, 28
Sales & Marketing Management, 208, 284(table), 285(table)
Sales & Marketing Management 1989 Survey of Buying Power, 51(table)
Samier, Saeed, 547n
Samsung, 567, 751
Sam's Wholesale Club, 371 and (illus.), 372
Sanchez, Jesus, 595n
San Francisco 49ers, 475
San Giorgio pasta, 296
Sansweet, Stephen J., 271n
Sanyo, 751
Saphikon, 280
Sapit, Donald, 601n
Saporito, Bill, 29n, 371n, 637n
Sara Lee Corporation, 69, 87, 530
SAS. See Scandinavian Airline Systems
Saturn automobiles, 228
Saunders, John, 681n, 683n
Scandinavian Airline Systems (SAS), 672
Schares, Gail E., 752n, 769n
Scheslinger, Jacob, 75n
Schiller, Zachary, 303n, 606n
Schlegel, Sharon, 541n
Schlossberg, Howard, 137n
Schmidt, Jim, 379(illus.)
Schmitt, Richard B., 99n
Schneider, Kenneth C., 378n
Schneidman, Diane, 255n
Schnorbus, Paula, 239n, 335n
Schroeder, Michael, 397n
Schultz, Don E., 517n
Schuster, Camille P., 96n
Schutz, Peter, 769n
Schwadel, Francine, 7n, 390n, 597n
Schwartz, John, 286n
Schwartz, Karen, 723n
Schwinn Bicycle Company, 552, 553(illus.)
Scorpio automobiles, 668–669
Scotch tape, 189
Scott & Fetzer Company, 377
Scott, Daryle V., 101, 101n
Scott, James D., 240n
Scott, Mike, 734
Scott, William G., 649n
Scott Paper Company, 252

Seagram and Sons, Inc., Joseph E., 130, 333–334, 513
Sears, Roebuck and Company, 270, 309, 328, 363, 365, 379, 406, 473, 596–597, 703
Sea World theme park, 457, 651
Secret deodorant, 111
Sega video games, 650
Sellers, Patricia, 110n, 146n, 360n
Selling Areas Marketing, Inc. (SAMI), 208
Seminoles T-shirts, 139
Sensor razor (Gillette), 263
Serafin, Raymond, 64n, 160n, 229n, 717n
Service Merchandise, 584(illus.)
7-UP, 251, 565
Shao, Maria, 173n, 751n
Sharp Calculators, 144
Sharp Electronics Corporation, 567
Shaw, Jim, 181n
Shaw, John J., 710n
Sheaffer Eaton, 769
Shearson Lehman Hutton, Inc., 88
Sheffet, Mary Jane, 330n
Shell Oil Company, 88, 397
Sheraton hotels, 733
Sheridan, Mike, 673n
Sherman Antitrust Act (1890), 35, 60, 328, 556
Sherrid, Pamela, 31n
Sheth, Jagdish N., 140n
Shimp, Terence A., 439n
Shore, Harvey, 531n
Shostack, G. Lynn, 709n, 714(table)
Shostack, Lynn, 713(illus.)
Shurtuff Envelopes, 188(illus.)
Shurtuff Mills Inc., 188(illus.)
Sibley, Stanley D., 327n and (illus.)
Siemens, 753
Sigma Marketing Concepts, 601
Simmons, James C., 744(table)
Simon, Herbert, 57n
Simplot Company, J.R., 17, 26–27
Sinatra, Frank, 359
Singapore Tourism Council, 728, 729(illus.)
Singapore Tourist Promotion Board, 729(illus.)
Siskel, Gene, 270
Six Flags amusement parks, 491
Skinner, Steven J., 225n
Skinner pasta, 296
Skolnik, Rayna, 533n, 588n
SKOR toffee bars, 296
Slater, Stanley F., 640n, 694n
Slice soft drink, 212
Sloan, Pat, 461n
Slovak, Julianne, 21
Slutsker, Gary, 418n
Smart, Denise T., 216n
Smart, Tim, 90n
Smith, A. Dunlap, 762n
Smith, Allen E., 747n
Smith, Brian, 701n
Smith, Frederick W., 771, 774
Smith, Lee, 746n

Subject Index